The Career of Philosophy

Volume I

FROM THE MIDDLE AGES
TO THE ENLIGHTENMENT

The Career of

PHILOSOPHY

Volume I

From the Middle Ages

to the Enlightenment

BY JOHN HERMAN RANDALL, JR.

FREDERICK J. E. WOODBRIDGE PROFESSOR
OF PHILOSOPHY, COLUMBIA UNIVERSITY

COLUMBIA UNIVERSITY PRESS

NEW YORK AND LONDON

COPYRIGHT © 1962 COLUMBIA UNIVERSITY PRESS

Fourth printing and Columbia Paperback Edition 1970

STANDARD BOOK NUMBER: 231-08677-6

PRINTED IN THE UNITED STATES OF AMERICA

For MERCEDES

Wie das Gestirn,
Ohne Hast, aber ohne Rast

Foreword

THERE MAY SEEM little excuse for writing still another history of modern philosophizing on the present scale. The late nineteenth century saw two distinguished examples, Windelband's *Geschichte der Neueren Philosophie* (1878), never translated into English; and Høffding's, translated in 1900 as *The History of Modern Philosophy*. Both are in two long volumes; and both are unified histories, not a series of monographs, like Kuno Fischer's monumental project. Høffding, as a Dane, could preserve a balance between the German tradition, on the one hand, and the British and French on the other. And Windelband's is distinguished by its endeavor to view philosophy as intimately connected with the general intellectual and scientific currents of modern culture. It is hoped that the present attempt may display something of these two virtues. Our own century has seen comparable histories brought out in France, in Italy, and in Germany. But nothing on a like scale has appeared in English since 1900.

Yet with the history of philosophy above all it is true that each new generation will view the past in the novel light of its own intellectual problems, and its own emphases and importances. There seems room for the attempt to write a history of modern philosophy from a perspective of American philosophizing in midcentury, and not from the perspective of late nineteenth-century philosophical idealism. On a much shorter scale, in the last few years several volumes have done this job brilliantly. But they disregard all that has been discovered in the last generation about the continuity between medieval and modern philosophizing; they fail to embody the results of several decades of research on that least known period in the history of Western philosophy, the transition from the thirteenth to the seventeenth centuries, when modern philosophy is conventionally supposed to have "begun."

Ever since the early studies of Gilson on Descartes, I have been impressed by the essential continuity between medieval and modern philosophy. The conviction has grown that seventeenth-century philosophy, in Descartes, Spinoza, and Hobbes, to say nothing of Leibniz, can be understood only as the bringing to bear of some one of the medieval philosophical traditions on the interpretation and generalization of the basic ideas of the new science of nature. Hence there is needed a knowledge of those medieval philosophies of science. There is needed a knowledge of what happened to them during the Renaissance. There is needed a knowledge of how that science had itself emerged gradually since the twelfth century, not as a mere discovery of facts but as a body of ideas organized in terms of certain controlling assumptions. There is needed a knowledge of just what its intellectual challenges were, from Galileo through the shifting currents of seventeenth-century science to its stabilization in Newton.

Hence Book One starts with the three great medieval philosophies of knowledge. Book Two tells of the coming of humanistic values and the new science, dipping back into the Middle Ages where necessary and relevant. Book Three, "The Assimilation of Science," tells of the first interpretations and generalizations of the new science, in the seventeenth-century philosophical systems with which modern philosophy "began." Book Four, "The Order of Nature," treats the reactions to Newtonian science in the eighteenth century, carrying the story through the British and the French Enlightenments. It is hoped a further volume will begin with Leibniz and the building of the German tradition, and will pursue the story through classic German philosophizing, and through the nineteenth-century reactions to natural science and to industrial society, to the present-day movements, from Wittgenstein to Heidegger. It will attempt to exhibit these contemporary critical philosophies of experience as all parts of a philosophical enterprise common to our own times.

From this sketch it will be apparent that modern philosophy is here seen as primarily the response to challenging new scientific ideas—to Galileo, Newton, Darwin, Einstein, Freud, Franz Boas, and the like. During the modern period, it has been chiefly science that has driven men to the searching thought that is philosophy. This is true even of those philosophers who have tried to escape from science, like the romantic idealists and the present-day existentialists; they are heavily colored by what they are trying to emancipate themselves from.

But this fruitful encounter with science has to be seen against the background of the successive waves of liberation from the constriction of medieval institutions—the stages of individualistic protest, which color most social and political thought, even in the seventeenth century, and in the Enlightenment become as important a stimulus to philosophic thinking as science itself. Economic and group conflicts generate and limit intellectual problems, and likewise limit the answers that will be given. But the content of the philosophic answers themselves comes largely from reflection on the problems posed by science, and is expressed in terms derived from such reflection. For its understanding, modern philosophy thus demands, as a kind of backdrop, a knowledge of the cultural and social developments and issues against which it has been carried on. But the immediate source of its technical problems, above all of its central "problem of knowledge," has been the working out of the successive stages of scientific thought, both on the methodological and the substantive sides.

One feature of this history is the large number of extensive quotations from the writings of the philosophers themselves. This seems preferable to paraphrases that are bound to be translations of the thinker's ideas into the technical language of the historian's own philosophy. Much of the philosophic analysis itself is effected through juxtaposing different and often conflicting passages from the thinker being examined, thus suggesting an immanent criticism. The quotations are rather more extensive for those figures that are less well known; some familiarity is assumed with the important texts of the major classics of philosophy. It will be observed no attempt is made to refrain from responsible criticism of the assumptions of the men analyzed.

The study of the history of philosophy has seemed fascinating ever since as a sophomore my philosophical and historical imagination was stirred by Dean Frederick J. E. Woodbridge, at Columbia.

Though his historical writings were regrettably slender, Wood-bridge was a great teacher, and his influence on his students has been profound. It would be a satisfaction to think that this study, though it includes much material unfamiliar to Woodbridge, and doubtless many specific analyses he would have disagreed with, still illustrates his general approach, and sets out from his philo-sophical orientation. Indebtedness should also be acknowledged to John Dewey's conception of the philosophical enterprise; in these pages Woodbridge's approach has been extended in the direction of Dewey's cultural concerns. But Woodbridge and Dewey al-ways seemed to share essentially the same conception of the func-tion of philosophy and the same general orientation, though in somewhat different languages.

Those who have taught me through the written word have been innumerable; through the spoken word, too numerous to indicate. But I cannot omit the much that has been learned from seminars given jointly with fellow-inquirers, Horace L. Friess, James Gutmann, Stuart Hampshire, George L. Kline, Paul O. Kristeller, John E. Smith, and Philip P. Wiener. I have profited especially from the extensive knowledge of the German tradition of Horace L. Friess and James Gutmann, from the knowledge of the scientific tradition of Ernest Nagel, and from the general his-torical knowledge of H. S. Thayer and James J. Walsh. Perhaps most stimulating of all have been the suggestions of Herbert W. Schneider, never consulted without my receiving illumination. Nor should there fail of mention the initial encouragement of John J. Coss, and of his successors as chairman of the Department of Philosophy at Columbia, Herbert W. Schneider, Irwin Edman, James Gutmann, and Robert D. Cumming, who have created condi-tions that foster productive scholarship in the members of the De-partment. Last but in the fore, acknowledgment is due to those many students over the years, whose challenges and insights make teaching the best way of learning. Deep gratitude is due to the con-sideration of the Columbia University Press, with special thanks to Joan McQuary, who labored valiantly to bring some consistency into these pages.

A word is in order about the title. When first hitting tenta-tively upon "The Career of Philosophy in Modern Times," I had in mind to suggest all the manifold intellectual and cultural currents that impinge upon a career; and that I would emphasize more strongly than ever. But unfortunately, further analysis of the theory of history brought the conclusion that there are two different kinds of temporal entities, "histories" and "careers"; and I have committed myself to the proposition that philosophy is the kind of thing that enjoys a history but not a career. To be sure, I could escape this seeming contradiction by the time-honored philosophical device of making a distinction. "Philosophy" in general has had no career; but "modern philosophy" has been sufficiently integrated by its persistent and recurrent problems in a single culture to be said to have enjoyed a unified "career" from its outset in the thirteenth century. Much in the following pages would substantiate such a claim, and that much is highly significant. But it is far simpler to admit that in using "career" in the title the term is being employed in its popular sense, without making any technical distinction.

J. H. R., Jr.

Columbia University
February 1, 1962

Contents

Contents

BOOK THREE

THE ASSIMILATION OF SCIENCE

BOOK FOUR

THE ORDER OF NATURE

xiv   Contents

BOOK ONE

The Heritage of Modern Thought

I

The Cultural and Social Functions
of Philosophy

IT IS CUSTOMARY to begin any study of the history of philosophy by defining philosophy itself. Like most customs, this is both extremely convenient and exceedingly foolish. It is convenient, for by confining the selection of materials to one's own philosophical problems, it is easy to make the entire course of history lead up to one's own solutions, and thus be freed of responsibility for considering what may well be more important ideas. It is foolish, for no really satisfactory definition of what men are agreed to call philosophy has ever been offered, beyond the literal one of "love of wisdom." And were we to take refuge in this ancient device, we should but multiply our troubles: for what in this world of ours is wisdom? There is at least no serious doubt but that certain men have been philosophers: Hegel, for instance, has been so acclaimed, and so has John Dewey. But was John Dewey wise? Did he even love wisdom? To raise such questions is to precipitate another fight.

It is safer to admit that philosophy is like poetry or religion: every definition is the expression of a particular and limited perspective upon a domain as broad as human life itself. Like searchlights directed into the night, the familiar definitions do indeed throw much into relief, but they leave far more in outer darkness than they illuminate. There is no question here, then, of imparting a new one at this point. Rather, this whole volume will be gently insinuating what philosophy is by pointing to what she has been and has done. For it is only fair to serve warning that it is written from a definite conception of the nature and function of philosophic thought. That conception has grown out of an examination of the philosophers themselves, of the problems and ideas that have seemed to them important. It has taken form as those problems and ideas when pressed revealed why they were important, why they drove subtle minds to searching thought. To the incurious many, philosophy has always seemed a seductive deceiver: promising all things, she has delivered not even truth. What she can give, and that in full abundance, she manifests not in her tempting words but in her living deeds. The words may only paint a poet's vision; if they be no better founded, at least they are no worse. The deeds are mighty, and they leave enduring trace. A philosophic idea, like the words in which it is clothed, when held up by itself and contemplated with too great reiteration, soon seems but a chain of meaningless sounds. How well the academic life has made that clear! But observe it at work in its natural environment: there is laid bare the secret of its long career. Viewed as an imaginative vision, an ultimate expression of the judgments and aspirations of human nature, a great philosophy may touch our mind with its clarified perfection, its architectonic beauty, without stirring our heart or compelling our will. But when we grasp the climate of opinion out of which that organic structure of ideas arose, when we sense the great social and intellectual conflicts that drove men to construct it, when we see it performing in the world of men that function for which it was created, then we no longer wonder at its appeal and power.

And so, in ignorance of her deeds, it is idle to analyze philosophy's character. It is far wiser to tell the story of her life. She belongs to the oldest profession in the world: she exists to give men pleasure, and to satisfy their imperious needs. When young and blooming, she was a favorite of the rich but cultivated and discriminating Greeks, who kept her in idleness for the sheer delight of her conversation. She had not even to lift a finger; and it was rumored the gods themselves loved her and her alone. But as she grew older, her charms faded, she waxed more austere, and took to giving sound advice on every occasion. And when the Romans burst into her garden, with their American moralism and fear of idleness, they led her off and set her to work as the handmaiden of Morality. She has been a working-girl ever since. Most of her life she has spent in serving Theology; but she had really quite an easy time of it, especially toward the end, when her mistress was too decrepit to watch over her goings-on. From this servitude she was rescued by a handsome young admirer who loved to hear the tales of her ancient glory; but she was soon enslaved again by Science, who set her to work clearing fields and putting up fences. Science found her invaluable in private, but was apt to cut her dead in public. She has just put in a century working for the faith of our grandmothers; but the old lady died at last, bequeathing her effects to the brazen young Neo-Orthodoxy, who will have nothing to do with her. At present she is entertaining proposals from the rich but ailing old Capitalism, and from the up-and-coming heirs of Marx and Lenin, earning her board and keep in the meantime by doing some cleaning up for the physicists, and angling hopefully for an invitation to set up housekeeping in UNESCO. For all the hard work she has done, she is scarcely an honest woman; and notoriously she can bake no bread. For centuries she has been a campfollower: you will find her always where the fighting has been fiercest, wherever men have been torn loose from their familiar domestic ties, when their wives have been left behind, or have run away, or are just grown too wrinkled and old. She consorts with men, comforts men, tells them what they want to hear; and with the wisdom of her incredible experience she teaches them how to win. No wonder countless soldiers in the strife of ideas have thought her the one woman in the world, *das Ewig-Weibliche*, and have sworn to her undying allegiance. But *mutabilis semper femina;* she turns up in some other camp with a new set of finery. She is indispensable, but quite without conscience.

In some such fashion the function of philosophic thought is to be conceived, as the eternal but everchanging handmaiden of men's ideas and ideals, appearing always with the fighters, for new and old alike, indefatigably setting their baggage and their weapons in order; trying to organize the materials of human experience into some tidier and reasonably coherent arrangement, fitting opposed or irrelevant beliefs together into some not too chaotic scheme, adjusting warring values to give some direction to life without excluding too much; forging new weapons out of the shattered remnants of the old; always leading men on to fresh ground, to the unsuspected implications of their ideas; and pausing, now and again, to point to tantalizing glimpses of something calm and serene above the tumult.

The main features of human experience remain universal: birth, growing up, making a living, getting on with one's fellows—the urge of sex, the desire to understand—failure, frustration, sickness and death. And this universal pattern does run through all those really great philosophies which, though they start as battle-cries in some human struggle, have yet raised themselves some little way above the conflict to a more comprehensive view of life. But the particular ways in which these recurrent experiences are regulated and met, the particular beliefs in terms of which they have been interpreted and rationalized, form a bewildering variety. Especially, those conflicts between ideas which lead men to the searching thought that is philosophy, that impingement of novel experience upon traditional beliefs and values which impels men to construct their systems, the emergence of new ideas irrelevant to or logically incompatible with the old, which yet have somehow to be adjusted to them, and worked into the accustomed pattern of living and thinking—these conflicts are in each case historically unique.

If philosophic problems be defined as those questions in which philosophers have been interested—or, what amounts to the same thing, as those problems which have generated a philosophic response and given birth to philosophers; if they be seen to emerge whenever the strife of ideas and experience forces men back to fundamental assumptions in any field: then such problems have varied from age to age, and are to be understood only as expressions of the basic conflicts within a culture that drive men to thorough-going criticism. As a social and cultural enterprise, philosophy is the expression in thought of cultural change itself: it is the intellectual phase or moment of the process by which conflicts within a civilization are analyzed and clarified, resolved and composed. This distinctive social and historical function of philosophical thinking is the reason why Western civilization, with its never-ending succession of tensions and conflicts, exhibits so rich a record of philosophic thought, and why our present task of organizing our industrial and scientific culture so sorely needs philosophic reflection, and offers so golden an opportunity for philosophic achievement. A civilization that has grown stable and static may have inherited "a philosophy," but it produces no philosophic thought. That comes only with conflicts. And the problems so generated in our own civilization have been as different as, how to save one's soul, how to make Aristotle a good Catholic, how to understand scientific method, how to be a poet in an age of science, how to remain a Christian with a college degree, how to be a liberty-loving democrat with a five-year plan, how to confine the passions of nationalism within one world.

In this sense, the aims of philosophic thinking are never the same. The problems of one age are ultimately irrelevant to those of another. What have we in common with the intellectual difficulties of our grandfathers' generation, now so incredibly remote? What bond is there between the aims and problems of an Athenian poet, like Plato; a Roman senator, like Cicero; a medieval monk, like Thomas Aquinas; a seventeenth-century scientific pioneer, like Descartes; a German professor, like Kant; and an American publicist—supply the name yourself. But though these varied problems be irrelevant, the fact that problems must be faced does not vary. And the facing of problems, whatever their specific content, illustrates a recurrent pattern. The history of human thought, and the history of philosophical ideas in particular, exhibits with unusual clarity the general structure of social and cultural change. This fact made a tremendous impression on Hegel, and led him to base his comprehensive philosophy upon it. He and his Marxian followers have called it the "dialectic of history." And whether the structure of cultural conflict and change be properly called "dialectical" or not—the answer seems to be "no"—it remains true that it is impossible to gain any real insight into the history of philosophical ideas without being led to formulate a philosophy of cultural and social change.

The philosophical problems of one age, like the cultural conflicts out of which they take their rise, are irrelevant to those of another. But the pattern illustrated by each conflict and solution remains pretty much the same; and it is a pattern we can be fairly sure our own conflicts will follow. To discover that pattern in example after example is one of the fruits of studying philosophy historically. Moreover, the great philosophies, those that have seen beyond their special problems of adjustment and partisan loyalty, though they speak in different languages, seem to an attentive ear to be speaking of the same universal structure of experience. And this recurrent refrain comes not only from the fact that they once spoke a common tongue, which was Greek, and along with much that is colloquial and in the latest fashion have preserved archaisms that point to a common source. Greek and modern alike have seen the same world, and each in his own dialect is trying to express the same permanences of man's experience of that world. The significant message in each case is unique, it is pertinent to the particular problems that called it forth. But though the languages differ, and the scenes to which they are appropriate are varied, there are similarities of linguistic structure and of background that run through them all.

Where attention has not been so closely focused on immediate conflicts as to obscure all further vision, a discerning eye can perceive certain persistent distinctions, certain recurrent types of logical antithesis—the one and the many, permanence and change, the real and the ideal, reason and experience, form and matter, structure and process. And whatever the starting-point in a particular fight, wherever these distinctions have been used honestly and without bias to interpret all the facts, men have approached a common metaphysics, a common conception of what is, and how it is to be understood. These great antitheses, first put into words by the Greeks, and slowly elaborated by subsequent generations, have often been regarded as problems, matters to be settled once and for all if man have the wit. But they form rather a set of tools, of concepts and ideas to be employed in rendering man's changing experience intelligible, an intellectual instrument of criticism in meeting cultural conflicts. They are not so much problems to be solved, as distinctions to be used, used in the good fight and the enduring quest. The enemy, the fight, the quest, are ever new; but fighting is not, nor are the weapons by which men can conquer.

Face to face with the tangled web of history, men have been sorely puzzled by these twin facts of persistence and change, of continuity and novelty. Each new generation is convinced that it is standing at the turning point in human affairs. All men hitherto have been living in a dream world of their own devising; we first of all have glimpsed the truth. To us alone of mortals nature has at last revealed her face. And on our shoulders lies the shaping of the future, the burden of fighting for the truth against intrenched greed and privilege wrapped in the cloak of ignorance and superstition. And it is indeed so: upon our actions rests the course of future events. Surely each day some daring soul finds that nature has first revealed her facts to him; surely ignorance and superstition have not yet been vanquished; surely greed and privilege as never before are blocking the path to peace and justice and security.

Yet when we turn to look upon the past, what strikes us most even in the midst of the greatest revolutions is the continuity of human beliefs and habits. The mountainous waves men were so sure would overwhelm them seem but ripples and eddies of the steady current of change. The fires and thunders were crises in words and symbols; the real revolutions had been preparing for generations, and took further generations to make themselves fully felt. Men die much as they were born, with but new words for old certainties halting upon their lips. The greatest changes of all come not as the thief in the night, but as the oak-tree from the acorn. The most radical of thinkers is soaked in tradition; he spends a lifetime bending ancient ideas to a slightly different use, and his followers soon revert to the familiar pattern while still mumbling the novel terms. And it is so: men can work only upon what they have inherited. Fresh experience and novel problems they must understand with the instruments they have learned from those who came before them. New ideas they must grasp in the concepts they already know, for they have no others; new habits they must work slowly into the accustomed pattern of their lives.

Half a century ago the balance was loaded in favor of continuity. The great name of Darwin was invoked to cover an eager search into slow growths and steady evolutions. Today fashion has shifted to the side of novelty and sharp mutations; from Bergson to Marx we have been taught to spell "evolution" with an "R." And for the partisans of each insight the claims of their rivals have presented a problem: in the light of certain vision, mere facts stand no chance. But in truth the joint presence of continuity and novelty in human history need present no problem. Men are always facing novel problems and fresh experience as a result of what they have done and discovered. But they must face them with institutions, habits, and ideas they have taken over from the past. What they have already learned from experience they bring to the challenge of fresh experience. If they are successful, they have learned more and created anew.

History is thus a continual readaptation of old materials, in the light of changing needs and problems. It can always be asked, why were these materials and these instruments selected? why were these particular combinations chosen, this novel architecture employed? For history is a construction made by men, not by God or by metaphysical forces. Whatever pattern or patterns we may find there illustrated, are not the causes of the facts that have brought them into being, they are resultants. They are not principles of explanation: it is they that need to be explained. History is made by men, by groups of men living in a natural environment, partly intractable and inescapably there, partly lending itself to human efforts at its reconstruction. Those efforts are always particular and piecemeal. But they have consequences; and those consequences, even when not intended or even envisaged, are as inescapably there as any other parts of man's environment. Men do something in their need, and then find they have to do something else. In solving one problem they find they have created others. In learning how to grow more grain and better wool, they find they have undermined a whole culture, and have to create a new science, a new ethics, and a new theology. In a different jargon, we can say that changes in the instruments of production demand ultimately the creation of new ideologies—because they have changed the character of man's experience. The architects are men; and there is much in the structures they build that is the product of what Aristotle called chance. But the purposes for which they are built, the needs they are to serve, the materials that are employed and the tools that are used, are not due to chance, though they are equally beyond human control. History is a human achievement; like everything human, one within natural limits, but nevertheless an achievement.

If this be true of all human activities, it is especially true of ideas, of philosophy. Their history is both cumulative and original. Ideas seized upon because they meet the needs generated by one type of experience, have a structure and implications of their own. That structure can be followed out by men who have the interest or motive. But men are always far more concerned to use ideas than to understand them; and when other elements of their culture, only remotely related to those ideas, have developed so far as to generate another type of experience, men feel the need of new ideas. So out of the ruins of previous structures they set out to build a new one.

Intellectually, while there has been a genuine continuity of materials in our own civilization, there has been no orderly progress, no simple fixed line of development moving through time. There has been rather a series of successive lootings. No great philosophy has ever been refuted: it has been discarded as irrelevant to another type of experience. The system of Aristotle was not refuted by the Hellenistic schools that succeeded it; the need for salvation, for a way of deliverance, grew more pressing than the desire to understand. The imposing medieval Christian or Jewish syntheses were never refuted by the scientific humanitarianisms to which men turned; men came to feel other values more important than the goods they had secured. And if our scientific philosophies are destined to be superseded by other and more dogmatic views of nature and society, it will not be because they have been disproved, but because they have been made irrelevant by our intense need of social direction and military security, even at the sacrifice of the searching mind and the critical temper.

The history of philosophic thought in the West has thus been a series of episodes. The Greeks built an intelligible world: they invented the ideas and concepts, they made the distinctions, in terms of which they could create an ordered intellectual life. Since then there have been successive attempts to use Greek thought to interpret a novel and alien experience. The Oriental peoples employed it to rationalize a religious theocracy, the Christians, to rationalize the Hebrew-Oriental religious tradition, the Schoolmen, to organize medieval society and culture, the moderns, to understand and make rationally consistent a scientific method that has persisted in remaining unintelligible. Each episode involved a misunderstanding of Greek thought, and each a striking-off of original ideas. The consequence has been a piling up of confusion, yet at the same time of an extraordinarily rich and fertile mass of ideas. The Trinity, for example, started as the assertion of the intelligibility of the world and the power of reason: it grew into a mystery and a flaming faith. Modern science started as the rational vision of the secret of the universe: it has culminated in a wholly non-rational method of transforming the world. At times, the dead weight of the material transmitted has been too much for fresh creation. Problems themselves have been inherited and not generated by living experience.

Only too often this has been the curse of "modern philosophy." In such a case, only knowledge of the past when they were alive can free us of their corpses. To take the classic instance for philosophy, to understand why the very fact of the existence of knowledge became in the eighteenth century an insoluble problem, frees us from the need of finding it a problem today.

Modern Philosophy and Modern Culture

WHATEVER its proper nature or its conscious aspiration, whatever ultimate insights it may have won or whatever sure truths it may have come to enshrine, the first and clearest function of philosophic thought in the long history of our Western civilization has been to express and illuminate the process of cultural change. Conflict, struggle, and the compelling need for readaptation and reconstruction have been the factors that generated our philosophical inquiry. This has been doubly true of that segment of our past we rather arbitrarily cut off and designate as "modern." During the entire "modern" period, whenever we conceive it to have begun, intellectual energy has been devoted to justifying and assimilating a set of facts and ideas that seemed irrelevant and unintelligible in terms of the generally accepted beliefs. So true is this that if we look beyond chronology for some defining characteristic by which to mark off "modern philosophy," we cannot do better than choose the fundamental conflict between two types of knowledge, one of ancient repute and one in process of being born. Despite its infinite ramifications in every party battle, in every practical problem of adjustment, the central problem of modern philosophy, the focus to which all other problems have ultimately led, has been the "problem of knowledge."

Now knowledge will always present a number of particular problems so long as men learn new ideas and forge new tools of thought. But these problems will normally be either psychological, concerned with the origin and growth of knowledge, or logical, dealing with its structure and tests. The fact of knowledge in general presents a central metaphysical or "epistemological" problem only when two conflicting types of knowledge are struggling for men's allegiance. And this has been the case ever since Aristotelian science entered in the twelfth century to compete with the tradition of Christian religious and moral truth. It has persisted until the acceptance in present-day philosophies of an enlarged and deepened science and scientific method as the single type of human knowledge. For those who welcome such a solution wholeheartedly, the characteristic problem of modern philosophy has indeed ended, and "modern philosophy" itself is over. But with the rise on every hand of dogmatic social gospels that can hardly appeal to science for their foundation, and of sophisticated versions of a special religious "truth," it seems likely that "modern philosophy" will come to a new birth. Faith and reason are not yet at one.

As a result of their persistent variance, "modern" philosophic thought displays profound intellectual analysis, but little wisdom. It has been committed in advance to what was bound to be at best an ingenious solution, a solution men might gratefully accept, but which they could not really believe. The great philosophies of modern times remain as splendid monuments to the significant battles that have made us what we are. We cannot understand ourselves or our own tools and weapons without a knowledge of what those thinkers did. But they had no time to build from the goods at hand any really satisfying conception of the Good Life; they were too busy exploring the method, or quarreling over whether man is free to do so or not. And so we miss in them the human wisdom shared by all the philosophies of Greece, even those of the Hellenistic Age, and of the Middle Ages at their best. The moderns constructed critical methods galore, but they had little vision. And so though their systems remain indispensable historical exhibits, they fail to touch the heart of man. Even the visions to which modern philosophy could rise came at the beginning; and the greatest of all, that of Spinoza, has seemed a belated survival from an earlier time. Though Spinoza saw with modern eyes, he did not gaze upon the object of the modern search. And ironically enough, that enduring vision which best expresses the whole modern temper, Bacon's dream of the power that science was to give to man, came to one who failed to recognize science when he saw it, and so scarcely belongs to the "modern" philosophers at all.

This character of Western thought, its essential function of compromise and assimilation, is rooted in the very nature of Western civilization itself. Unlike the other great civilizations of the past and of the Orient, the European world has never reached a stage of stable equilibrium. It has always been "dynamic," "progressive"; it has always found itself in an "age of transition." The dominant factor making for this perpetual flux, the steady increase in scope and range of its economic activities, had already appeared with the twelfth-century revival of agriculture, trade, and town life; thereafter it continued at an accelerated rate. Whatever changes this steady increase in material production may have precipitated, it has itself known no sharp break. And thus there has been created a type of social experience fundamental in modern times, an experience quite unlike that of the ancient world. Men have lived always in an expanding society, in a world outgrowing its older forms and trying to escape them. Greek thought was born with Plato in an atmosphere of defeat: it sought primarily consolation, at first in knowledge, and then frankly in salvation. Modern philosophy, save for brief interludes when the rapidity of change left men bewildered, has never sought consolation. It has led rather in intellectual revolt, reconstruction, assimilation and readjustment. The impingement of new conditions and new ideas has been an old story. Westerners have always felt their world disintegrating and their problems insoluble. To their leaders this has been the breath of freedom, the challenge to invent new harmonies and new syntheses. The fight may be deadly, but the goal is sure. There have always been those who saw only a collapse of civilization. But it is the rebels who have built our world.

Intellectually, all the problems of medieval and modern philosophy have arisen from the conflict of new experience and new knowledge with traditional thought and attitudes. And the first great clash, generating the characteristic problems of modern thought, came in the early thirteenth century with the impact of Aristotle upon the Augustinian tradition. For just as basic to Western culture as its dynamic character has been the fact that all its materials came from without. To understand its own expanding experience it had for centuries to go to school to alien masters. There was the ancient world with all its riches from Athenian thought to Roman law. For the greater part of its intellectual history the West has been engaged in learning from the Mediterranean past. Only in the last two centuries has it really begun to generate its ideas out of its own experience; before then it had to refashion the tools of alien minds to the needs of its own eager life. The consequences for Western thought have been momentous. From the very beginning its philosophers have had to learn, not from their own experience, but from the experience of others. It is no wonder they have piled perplexity upon confusion, no wonder the structures they built have never seemed just right.

Had the varied and complex culture in which the ancient world eventuated been preserved entire, as in Byzantium, there might have been a civilization on a high level, like the Byzantine, but without great conflicts and hence without fresh thought. Had western Europeans plundered it at one fell swoop, like the Arabs, there might have been a brief burst of power and achievement, and then an Arab stagnation. But cut off as they were from the East and its riches, they had to build up their own material life slowly and painfully, and to rediscover piecemeal what Greeks and Romans had done, as they themselves advanced to the point where they could begin to appreciate. The very slowness of their assimilation of ancient culture kept their own in a state of perpetual ferment; no laboriously won set of ideas had time to crystallize before they were driven to deal with another.

Slowly and in successive stages the Westerners wrought the achievements of the ancient world into the pattern of their own life. They did not assimilate the varied elements in the order in which their predecessors had invented them; their culture has been far from a recapitulation of the one they robbed. The order of learning depended rather on the growth of their own powers of understanding and appreciation, and that in turn upon the level of economic development they had achieved. Their first acquaintance was naturally with the ideas nearest to them. The one great institution they directly inherited, the Church, had enshrined in Augustinian Christianity the Neoplatonic philosophy and scheme of values in which the ancient world had ended its days. When once curiosity had been aroused and could be sustained by European experience, it was here the first tentative explorations were made. Augustinian

Platonism was the first philosophy of medieval Europe; it suited well the monasteries where it was cultivated. The second store of booty was stolen from the richer Moslems, Aristotelian science; it found a congenial habitat in the medieval universities. These two were united in the thirteenth-century synthesis, the first great reconciliation and "solution" of the European mind. But that structure, however imposing, endured but a generation. The synthesis of Aristotle and Platonism soon advanced on new paths of its own, and the late Middle Ages are the story of its independent development under the impetus of further economic and social growth. European towns, first in Italy, then in the North, had by this time created a life not unlike that of the ancient city state; those who found it good welcomed the secular humanism of ancient literature, expressive of so similar an experience. And finally the rising tide of commerce and craftsmanship turned men to the mathematical and mechanical science of the Alexandrians. Thus in succession, with many a mixture and cross-current, Europe had mastered the four great bodies of ideas she was to learn from her schooling—Platonism, Aristotelianism, humanism, and mathematical physics.

All four are blended and fused in the philosophical structures of the seventeenth century, and bent to express the confident hopes of a world just emancipated from medieval forms. Those seventeenth-century syntheses made the last full use of the ancient materials. For Europe had now perfected an intellectual instrument that was to carry its thought beyond anything the Greeks had achieved. Thereafter "science" was to pursue an independent development, to become itself the chief intellectual force of innovation. Hand in hand with the maturing economic developments, it was to pose the most difficult problems and to suggest the most promising solutions. In the eighteenth century Europe first came of intellectual age. Since then its perplexities have come, not from the attempt to learn the lessons of others, but from the need to understand and face the consequences of its own ideas.

Hence since the twelfth century there has been a fundamental continuity in the type of philosophical problem which our expanding society has raised. Ever lurking close in the background, and coming to the fore in time of greatest stress, has been the problem of reconstructing social institutions as their older forms have been outgrown. The twelfth and thirteenth centuries were a kind of apprentice period for the organization of medieval society on the basis of Greek thought and Roman law and political ideals. For a brief interlude there was achieved a social and cultural synthesis, the structure that still haunts us as "the Middle Ages," the idea of social unity, of a functional society. It was never embodied in practice, and it remained an ideal for but a generation or two; it was always precarious and unstable. Then the growing forces of commerce made that social synthesis, with its institutions and ideals, increasingly inadequate, and provoked an individualistic reaction, a demand for the cardinal freedom to build up the modern world. All subsequent medieval and modern thought has thus been colored by the necessity of vindicating an ever-growing individualism against the collectivism inherited from the early Middle Ages. All the great intellectual and philosophic movements since then—the rebellion of the Thomistic combination of individualism and collectivism against the earlier Platonic realism, the struggle of nominalism against Thomism, the Renaissance, the Reformation, the rationalism of science, the Enlightenment, Romanticism, nineteenth-century liberalism and humanitarianism—these have all been successive waves of individualism in conduct, in religion, and in thought. And now that machine technology has built up a new social structure within the ruins of the old, a structure quite irrelevant to the whole ideology of freedom and individuality, we have to buck the whole current of our long intellectual tradition to retrace our steps and recover a new form of collectivism adequate to our industrial age. This history explains why the task is so hard, why it often seems easier to try to wipe out that past completely, instead of remolding it to our needs —as if men could eradicate the very roots of their being!

The moral problems of medieval and modern philosophy have likewise been essentially those of conciliating diverse values. The task was first to harmonize Christian ethics with those of Greek humanism, and then to adjust the fusion of both to the values of a scientific and industrial world—an adjustment that is peculiarly our own problem of moral reconstruction. Western Europe started in its professed ideals, though never in fact, with a dualistic view of life as something to be saved from; that was the lesson set for it by Augustinian Christianity. Such a view was the natural expression of the decaying Hellenistic world in which it was formed. It was imposed from without on the barbarian Western peoples as an integral part of the only civilization they could know. But it was totally alien to their own experience. They were not decaying, they possessed an immense exuberance and vitality; they were already thirsting for power and prosperity, in love with the world and the flesh, and willing to go to the devil to get them—as they have. It was but natural that such men should be attracted by Greek thought and by the Roman philosophy of Power; though it was also natural that they should fail to understand Greek thought as an aesthetic vision of intelligibility, and should turn it into an instrument of power—Plato into a moral romanticism, and Aristotle into an amoral technology. But that Europeans should have tried to be Christians— that passes all human comprehension. It is as incredible as that modern Americans should be able to convince themselves they ought to follow the teachings of Jesus, and sometimes even do so— which though quite a different thing is an equal miracle. No wonder Western civilization has always found its real ideals at variance with its professed Christian dualism. Its history is one long record of revolt of men devoted to pleasure, prosperity, and power against even lip-service to Christian ethics. Their dualistic way of life has been swamped by successive waves of ethical naturalism: the Aristotelian ethic of Thomas, the humanism of the Renaissance, the this-worldly asceticism of the Puritans, the rational naturalism of the eighteenth century, the irrational naturalism of the romantic movement, and finally the scientific and industrial naturalism of today. And we still wonder why "Christianity has never been tried"!

And against this background of conflicting social forms and human values, philosophers have had to face their problems of intellectual conciliation, the adjustment of traditional beliefs to new "knowledge." First Neoplatonic and Augustinian Christianity had to be harmonized with Aristotelian science; and in that problem of fitting the contents of Faith to the results of Reason was born the characteristic dualism of modern thought, between a transcendental but familiar realm of moral and religious truth, and an accessible but strange realm of scientific knowledge. It was first solved, for the thirteenth century, by Thomas and Duns Scotus, who for that reason if for no other deserve the title of the first "modern philosophers." Ever since philosophers have been adjusters!

The problem grew still more acute when that medieval synthesis of Platonism and Aristotelianism was confronted in the seventeenth century by mathematical physics: the whole Greco-Christian tradition had somehow to be harmonized with "natural science." The eighteenth-century thinkers tried it, and failed; it was solved for Newtonian science by Kant and his successors. And when the development of a new type of science in the late nineteenth century made that solution impossible, the Christian world had already been abandoned by all thoughtful Christians.

More technically, the intellectual problem of modern philosophy arose as the adjustment of Greek thought, as embodied in the three great scholastic traditions, to the mathematical physics that was the glory of the seventeenth century—of the Greek conception of science as a series of implications deduced from first principles to the new conception of the world as a congeries of particles of matter in motion. Descartes began the attempt; Spinoza and Leibniz alone came near a solution, and hence are today the only living philosophers of the seventeenth century. This central problem of knowledge was solved for Newtonian science by Kant. And now that Newtonian science is dead, and science has become an experimental manipulation of hypotheses and postulate systems, philosophers are trying to adjust this new science of ours to the various forms of nineteenth-century Kantian synthesis.

Thus the course of modern philosophy is intelligible, if at all, only against the background of the scholastic materials with which it started, as successively modified by the ideas of science and the forces of industrial society. The rationalism of the medieval Augustinians and Thomists determined the nature, the method, the logic, and the ideal of science until the criticisms of Hume and Kant in the eighteenth century; it was reborn in Hegel, and is flourishing today in our many forms of logical realism. The empiricism of the English Franciscans at Oxford, of Ockham and his followers, has descended in a direct line through Hobbes, Locke, Hume, and the Mills, to the modern scientific empiricists of Cambridge and Vienna. These traditional schemes have been modified with each fresh use to which they have been put; but in the record of modern philosophy the persistence of traditional concepts and assumptions is as clear as the facing of ever-fresh problems and materials.

How then is "modern philosophy" to be delimited? What criterion of selection is to be employed? The history of philosophy, in truth, since German professors captured it and made it the handmaiden of academic advancement, has been a rigid tradition. Philosophy began with Thales, it falls neatly into Ancient, Medieval, and Modern, and it culminates in the men now writing for your favorite philosophical journal, God forgive them their sins! This German model was brought back across the sea, along with beer steins and Schwarzwald clocks, by the sentimental American students of the late nineteenth century. It contains a fixed set of figures; they are indeed important, but the list is far too narrow. It leaves out some of the greatest names, men like Galileo and Newton, Marx and Darwin, without whose ideas there would have been no philosophical thought at all. And it leaves out practically all the history, all those great realms of ideas in which the philosophers have worked, all the social and intellectual conflicts that drove them to philosophy.

In this tradition, Kant is the central figure. All who came before him are *Vorkantianer*, all who came after are basking in his glory. "Modern philosophy" began with Descartes because he raised the problem Kant finally settled for Newtonian science. There is usually an introduction dealing with the Renaissance, commencing with those Greeks who initiated it at the fall of Constantinople; and since he was a German, Nicholas of Cusa often heads the list.

In sober fact, any starting-point for modern philosophy must be arbitrarily chosen. Both its materials and its problems invite one to an endless quest. The materials with which modern thinkers worked go back to ancient Greece, though even when the classics themselves were read, they were usually understood in their medieval formulations. Whether one emphasizes the underlying economic development, the drive for individualism, the appearance of humanistic values, or the reckoning with physical science, there is no stopping point short of the thirteenth century. It has been only our ignorance of the intellectual life of the later Middle Ages that has obscured the fundamental continuity between medieval and so-called modern times. And on the other hand not till the eighteenth century did Europe really advance beyond Greek thought to something fundamentally new. Albert and Thomas, or Newton and Locke, might with equal validity claim to be the first of the moderns. What is clear is that the central themes of modern philosophy have been the grappling with science and with individualistic values. But science and a humanistic ethic were both rooted in the medieval past, and so were the ideas in terms of which they were understood. With full awareness, then, of its arbitrary character, we can do no better than abide in general by the familiar meaning of "modern." But we shall find ourselves constantly driven back to that medieval heritage at every turn.

3

The Three Medieval Philosophical Traditions

OUT OF THE eager medieval appropriation of the thought of the ancient world, three great philosophical traditions emerged as an integral part of the European heritage, three great bodies of ideas lying ready at hand for the interpretation and understanding of whatever new intellectual materials might be won. All through the tumultuous Renaissance and the single-minded Reformation they continued to form the substance of the teaching of the official seats of learning, the universities. And though those disdainful and adventurous scholars explored all the continents of Greek and Roman thought, and brought back from their expeditions much rich booty, when they finally settled down to rebuild their world in terms of science, it was to these medieval traditions that they turned for tools. They might reject in impatience the content of medieval learning; they could not but employ its forms. The medieval vision of the world gave place to one more austere if more exalted; but men had still no words or language to express the new save those that had served to formulate the old. Since modern thought grew out of the long search for a fruitful intellectual method, and since the first great problems of the science that crowned that effort concerned its very structure and validity, these were the interests that determined what men drew upon. In examining the materials of the medieval heritage, we shall therefore focus attention, as did the pioneers of the first age of science, upon the theories of knowledge there waiting to be used. Each of the three major philosophical traditions had its own conception of the nature and structure of science, of the proper object of the mind and the way to attain it; each had a theory of method and of logic of its own.

I

Oldest in medieval thought, though last to be elaborated in the ancient world, was the Augustinian philosophy. It was the Christian form of Neoplatonism, that rational tradition to which St. Augustine had turned to still his intellectual doubts. In Hellenistic times the followers of Plato had maintained his faith in reason in the midst of a despairing world; with great care and painful analysis they had elaborated his vision of knowledge, though with little attention to his shrewd judgment of its natural conditions. To St. Augustine, seeking above all things certainty of vision, the Neoplatonic doctrine promised a sure foundation for the mind. With great subtlety he adjusted it to his theory of salvation, wherein with equal certainty the will was firmly grounded in God's irresistible grace. But what was so clear to his own living experience has rarely come to other men with equal force: the Augustinian theory of knowledge and the Augustinian theory of grace have seldom appealed with deep conviction to the same men. Those seeking above all salvation have felt the power of the latter, especially if they have sought it outside the Church. It was the very breath of life to the Reformers and to their many late medieval predecessors; but they were blind to the Augustinian vision of Truth. The thinkers of the early Middle Ages, however, felt no such need of salvation: that came as a natural operation of the unquestioned Church. What they were groping for was rather knowledge; and in the writings of Augustine they found it, simple, clear and certain as God himself. And so his Neoplatonic vision of Truth and Being became one of the great strains of medieval thought. This vision of truth, not his vision of grace, is what is meant by the "Augustinian tradition," which dominated the early Middle Ages, was reborn in the seventeenth century as mathematical rationalism, has persisted in some form during the whole modern period, and is flourishing today more vigorously than ever. It is one of the greatest scientific philosophies in Western thought. Ironically enough, it first came to the West formulated in terms of theological symbols—proof, if need be, that theological language can express a profoundly human and scientific philosophy. It is also a vision of unsurpassed beauty, with no trace of the harsh dualism of the Augustinian doctrine of moral salvation.

It was the chief vehicle by which the Middle Ages received the aesthetic quality of Greek and Platonic thought.

The Augustinian intellectual vision, like all Platonism, is at once a theory of knowledge and a theory of being, of how we know and of what is to be known. For thought is the measure of being, and what the mind beholds is alone truly real. The proper object of knowledge is the soul and God. Man is a rational being, and his natural end is to know the highest Truth, that *sapientia* or wisdom which is the Logos or Word of God himself. And man can know the Truth; Augustine's first step is to refute the scepticism in which he had wandered so long. Man has certain knowledge, for even when he doubts, he cannot doubt that he is doubting. "*Si enim fallor, sum.*" That is, thought indubitably exists, and there exists a thinker; and in knowing that he is a thinker man has at least one certain truth. The realm of Truth is thus to be approached by turning within the soul, within oneself. And so Augustine undertakes an acute and subtle analysis of this fact of knowledge as it exists within the soul. He brings remarkable psychological penetration to bear on establishing his distinctive version of the Platonic theory of knowledge. His method had momentous influence, for it was the form in which the great Platonic philosophy was transmitted to the Middle Ages and the seventeenth century.

The most certain thing about man is that he is a thinker, a rational soul using a mortal and earthly body, an *animus*. The highest part of this soul, and hence of man, is *mens*, mind, which contains both discursive reason, *ratio* or *dianoia*, and *intelligentia* or *intellectus*, *Nous*, direct intellectual vision. By careful self-examination we find three levels of knowledge in the soul: sense; the inner sense that perceives both sensations and itself; and reason, which knows sense, the inner sense, and itself, and judges sensations, proclaiming, "there is a man, there is a horse." Reason has *scientia*, understanding of temporal things. All such knowledge depends upon sensations. But sensations, though they cannot occur without the action of corporeal things on the bodily sense organ, are not the imprint of things on a passive mind. Augustine has a much subtler conception of experience than the mechanical view of the atomists, or the logical and biological view of Aristotle. Mind is not passive but active, even in sensation, which is an action of the mind in response to a passion of the body, an act of attention directed toward a bodily change, something internal to mind and not received from without. We perceive only bodily things, but perception itself is not bodily: though stimulated by the body, it is essentially an action of the mind on itself, and within itself.

All the more then is the mind active when we turn from sensible to rational knowledge: the mind draws its ideas not from without but from within. Take the clearest case in which ideas are presumed to be conveyed to the mind from outside, teaching. Does the teacher really teach ideas to his pupil? Think how rarely the ideas the pupil gets are those intended by the teacher! And even when communication is successful, the pupil really learns, not from the teacher without, but from the "teacher within." What, for example, is a *sarabella*? The teacher explains, it is a kind of turban. But that is an explanation only if the pupil already knows what a turban is, and knows the words and terms in which the kind is expressed. No, the teacher can never teach any idea which is not already present, at least in its elements, in the pupil's mind. We can never learn from without: knowledge is rather "like remembering." Such is Augustine's version of the slave-boy of the *Meno*. Signs and suggestions from without, in the teacher's words or in things, call forth ideas from within the mind, from the truth somehow there.

But the truth is not there full-fledged before the suggestion: teachers are of some use after all. They would not be if they taught only their own ideas: they must make us see a common truth. Augustine rejects the notion of "innate ideas," of the literal reminiscence of the Platonists. Knowledge is rather a remembering without any previous learning. The Platonists' theory breaks down in face of the fact that there is no "remembering" of sensible things. We must have experience. Nor is truth something produced by the mind itself; how could a temporal and changing mind produce eternal truth? Knowledge is not an invention, it is a discovery, a finding: of a truth common to teacher and pupil, to all rational minds. It is a learning from an Intelligible Teacher within the soul, a kind of "memory of the present."

The human *intellectus* or reason is the highest level to be found in man. There is but one thing higher in the universe, this Truth or Master within, this Intelligible World or Realm of Ideas, of eternal and immutable Truth, which is the *Sapientia*, the Word, the Logos that is God himself. And so Augustine identifies the Christian God with the realm of ideas, the realm of *Nous*, of the Platonic tradition. God is that Truth which is the origin of all truth. Since mathematics and the relations of figures and numbers form the clearest illustration of truth, God is the realm of logical and mathematical subsistence. But just as for the Platonists, mathematics is ultimately important for Augustine as the certain road to the relations of perfections, of the ends of things. Thus the highest conception of Greek science, the idea of a Logos, a rational structure or substance, is identified with the God of Christianity. In such fashion Augustine effected a complete harmony between religion and science, between the aspiration of the saint and the knowledge of the thinker, for the Platonic science of the ancient world, just as Albert and Thomas did for the Aristotelian science of the thirteenth century, and Spinoza for that of the seventeenth—by identifying their objects. Though often tried, such identification has never been really successful again. This was the form in which was handed down the old Greek notion, that that which is most clearly understood and most intelligible is *theios*, Divine. God is that which science most completely knows, not that which eludes science.

Naturally Augustine had no need of proving the existence of God: for God is that rational structure in the universe which alone makes proof possible. Every time man proves anything, as that two and two are four, he is inevitably illustrating God's existence: for God is the structure of all proof. It is this structure, this intelligible order, that is divine, that is God. It is necessary only to analyze any truth whatsoever to find the way to Him who is its intelligible source.

Human reason is changing and fallible; the Divine Reason or Truth is unchanging and eternal. It is the common possession of all men, it is ever there, the standard of all human truth. At times Augustine uses words which suggest that man's intellect beholds the divine Truth and Wisdom directly, participates in it, the Divine Mind, and is therefore eternal. This occurs especially when he is employing Platonic arguments for the immortality of *Nous*. But more often the God that is Truth is the Source of human truths, the *Arche* or Principle of the Intelligible Realm, the ground of all intelligibility; in this conception he is following the hierarchical notion of the Neoplatonists, in which the Source of Truth is one step above the realm of truths in which the human mind participates. God is not the light of the intelligible realm, but the Sun that is the source of that light, the Sun in whose light we see light. God is the Teacher in the soul, and human truths are the image of the Truth that is God, the seal, the imprint, the signature in man's mind. Knowledge is a Divine Illumination; God, in shedding light upon the soul, is not the object seen but the agent making us see its own image, causing the "seminal reasons" there planted to sprout. God is a logical structure, itself transcendent, working in us, in much the fashion as in the more humanistic and individualistic philosophy of Thomas it is the human Active Intellect, a part of the individual soul, that makes us know.[1]

Augustine himself is not always clear: he prefers to employ metaphors—God, the Divine Wisdom, is one step higher than the truths the intellect perceives, which are but its immediate reflection. But whether the wisdom in the soul is God, the Logos itself, or is immediately dependent on him, God is still inescapably there, the basic fact in all knowing. The Divine Illumination of the human intellect, like the influence of Divine Grace on the human will, is the immediate working of God in the soul. Without God thus working, no knowledge or righteousness is possible for man. In thus emphasizing the omnipotence of God in both knowing and acting, Augustine is trying to preserve a parallel between his theory of truth and his theory of grace. But they differ in that this illumina-

[1] The functions of the Divine Illuminator in Augustine and of the Active Intellect in Thomas differ, however, because of their different conceptions of the soul and of experience, and the different problems the two men are facing in connection with knowledge. The Thomistic Active Intellect "abstracts" intelligible forms from the sense images or phantasmata by which they are brought into the soul from the outside world; it abstracts concepts or universals from particulars, and actualizes them in the mind. But there is no need for the Augustinian Divine Illumination to "abstract" anything, for ideas are already in the soul, and are there as universals, not as imbedded in particulars. It does not actualize ideas; its function is to make us see their truth, their certainty. Augustine is offering a theory of truth and judgment, not a theory of the formation of concepts—a theory of logic, not of psychology. What we see in the Divine Light is the truth of our ideas, not their content; from it we gain a standard of judgment, not a source of information. And though men find it by turning within, that standard comes from without —not from the rationality of man, but from the intelligibility of the universe of truth. The mind needs the Divine Light to judge what ideas are true, as the will needs the divine Grace to choose what is good.

tion is natural, and bestowed on all men alike, while grace is supernatural and is reserved for the elect. And in the end the God who
so freely gives illumination to all has little in common with the God
who so thriftily and economically bestows grace.

This body of ideas, the divine illumination, the Reason in the
soul directly accessible to human reason, the logical realism, the
turning for knowledge not to the world but within, was the source
of all the mystical doctrines of the Middle Ages, and proved ultimately the successful rival of Aristotelian science. It was also the
source of all modern exact science, which emerged in the Middle
Ages in extremely close dependence upon the Augustinian philosophy, which found in the seventeenth century its first great interpretation in Cartesianism, a philosophy almost purely Augustinian in
character, and reached its most successful synthesis, in Spinoza,
through insistence on the essential parts of Augustinian thought.

Moreover, Augustine's insistence that we must begin with self-
examination, with the structure of knowledge and its implications
as we find it in consciousness, became, when Descartes turned to it,
the starting-point of the main current of modern philosophy; which
ever since has started where Augustine started, with the fact of
knowledge, not where Aristotle started, with the world of things—
which has sought always to get from ideas to things, not from things
to ideas. In science we call it the use of hypothesis, and reckon it
our chief glory; in philosophy we call it the "critical philosophy,"
or "idealism." And the whole great stream of modern philosophy,
from Descartes through Kant and the Germans down to Russell
and Whitehead, Brunschvicg and Meyerson, Cassirer and Husserl,
appears as a further elaboration of this Augustinian method. Augustine might well claim to be the "first modern philosopher." His
thought indeed forms the great tradition, extended, criticized, reconstructed, but never overthrown by rivals. It is the tradition in
which even our philosophies of experience have their roots. For
just that element in Dewey which an Aristotelian finds most un-
congenial goes back ultimately to St. Augustine.

This Augustinian theory of the nature and object of knowledge
had a long and varied history during the Middle Ages. What appear
in Augustine himself as suggestions and metaphors were systematized
and reduced to a precise doctrine by the Schoolmen of the thirteenth

century. But by that time an awakened interest in nature and the discovery of the imposing body of Aristotelian science, which did not limit its object to God and the soul, had already raised the fundamental problem which every form of Platonism has had to face, and which emerged with redoubled intensity when the Augustinian theory was applied to physics in the seventeenth century: what is the relation between the science of eternal truths—in modern times it had become definitely mathematics—and the natural world and our knowledge of it? The great Augustinians of the thirteenth century were forced to come to terms with Aristotle's theory of experience; their theory of knowledge has become a subtle blend between the divine illumination of eternal truth and the Aristotelian theory of abstraction from sense-materials. Sense indeed furnished the content of knowledge, but rational illumination enables us to judge its validity.

St. Bonaventura formulated this combination of Platonic apriorism and Aristotelian empiricism in the form in which it was to endure in the European heritage. A knowledge of natural objects comes ultimately from sense experience. The sensible species of things are conveyed to the soul's perceptive power in phantasmata or sense images. Then the possible intellect, by virtue of the power conferred upon it by the active intellect, receives and judges the intelligible forms abstracted from these phantasmata. But their relations, or first principles, are judged not by their origin, but in the light of the eternal truths within. The terms of these relations, the "species" comprised in principles, are abstracted from sense; but we judge their validity by the innate light of the divine reason with its standard of eternal truth. It is this power of judging which is innate and apriori; its content, the principles of things, is gained by exercising this power on sensible forms. God's reasons, or eternal truths, working in our intellect, form the standard by which we judge; they act in the intellect without our directly perceiving them. They are not objects of knowledge, not known themselves, but they are the indispensable apriori means of knowing the truth of principles. Knowledge is a product of these divine rules with which the mind is conjoined and the sensible species on which they operate, God's eternal reasons in us judging sense. The psychology is empirical and Aristotelian, but the theory of logic and truth remains Platonic and Augustinian.

II

The second great medieval theory of knowledge was the Aristotelian view as finally made acceptable in the imposing thought of Thomas Aquinas. It is not a vision of divine truth, but a sober statement of how men know the world which is their natural home. It too is a theory of what is known as well as of how we know, of being in the measure that man can know it. For man is a rational animal, and the world is a world that can be understood by reason. But it does not pretend, like the Platonists, to identify thought and being: thought is the measure of being only as being is intelligible to a rational animal. As rational, man can understand the universe; but as animal, he is limited to that aspect of the universe which such an animal can experience. As Thomas puts it, *quidquid recipitur recipitur per modum recipientis*, whatever is known is known in the manner in which man can know it. And knowledge itself is to be understood in the light of a detailed analysis and description of that manner. But Thomas regards as identical with this first principle the second: *Cognitum est in cognoscente per modum cognoscentis*—what is known in that manner is truly known.

This fundamental principle of all knowledge thus points in two directions. On the one hand, man can know of the world only that which he can learn from experience with it; he is limited by the extent of his rational observation. In Aristotle as in Thomas this was a protest against the Platonism which proudly boasted of a direct and internal vision of truth. But in Aristotle this was a statement of fact, not a limitation of knowledge; for Aristotle believed there was nothing in the world which could not enter into man's experience. Thomas, however, was a Christian, convinced by faith that he was living in the universe of Augustine; and there was much in that universe which no rational animal could possibly experience. Thomas's adoption of empiricism, therefore, set grave limits to human knowledge; and it created for him the problem of adjusting faith to reason, of fitting what had been revealed to Christian souls to what a rational animal could learn from experience.

But on the other hand the world *is* intelligible to a rational animal, and experience is the means whereby the intelligible aspect of things is conveyed to the mind. Whatever exists has a form or essence, that whereby it can be understood. Whatever occurs has a set of causes whereby that occurrence can be rationally grasped. Whatever can be experienced has certain principles in terms of which human thought can find it intelligible. The forms, the causes, the principles of things are made accessible through experience and man's reflection on it. To find those principles is the object of human knowledge, to advance from observed facts to the reasons why. And it can be done; for though knowledge must come from experience, it comes from a rational experience with an intelligible world. What experience conveys can be put into language and expressed in words and propositions and demonstrations; and though man cannot say all that the world is, what he can say is truly said. The world has the power of being understood, and man's understanding is the operation of that power, the expression of the world's intelligibility. In the act of knowing, the power of the mind to understand and the power of the world to be understood receive a single fulfillment: human knowledge becomes one with what the world really is. The mind itself becomes the intelligible structure of things.

The details of this construing of the fact of knowledge varied in the different Aristotelian schools of the Middle Ages; all made a systematic elaboration of suggestions and statements not so neatly or precisely ordered in Aristotle himself. But the scheme of Thomas can serve as sufficient illustration. Man is a rational animal, the complete union of body and soul. The soul is the form of the body, that which makes it what it is; but it is not to be identified with man himself. As the soul is the principle in terms of which the actions of the complete man are to be understood, so the body is the instrument which performs those actions. The body is therefore the indispensable instrument of all human functioning. In knowing, therefore, it must be the whole man that knows, not the soul alone. The only human knowledge depends on materials furnished by the bodily senses. The Augustinian philosophy is suited to pure intelligences, to angels, but not to men, whose minds can perceive ideas not directly and immediately, but only as embedded in sense-images. To know anything immaterial—to know God, for example—man must start from the facts of experience, from sense-facts; and he can continue only so far as is necessary to understand those facts and no further. God is not to be reached through the soul alone, as the Augustinians held, but by rational inference from sense-experience. And where God or any other immaterial being produces no effects in experience—what his essence is—he cannot be known.

The human soul is a set of powers and activities; those concerned with knowledge are sense and intellect, or mind. Sense is the power of receiving the sensible forms or qualities of objects. A wall, for example, has the power of being seen as white, and the eye has the power of seeing it as white. In the act of perceiving, the whiteness of the wall becomes actual in the eye: the eye itself receives that whiteness. But the eye does not receive the matter of the wall, the bricks, but only the sensible form or "species" of whiteness. Sense, therefore, can be defined as the power of becoming all the sensible forms or qualities of things. What sets that power in operation, what actualizes it, is the motion of the medium working upon the sense organ.

Now the rational soul, mind or *intellectus*, is to be conceived as nearly as possible on the analogy of sense. The intellect is the power of becoming the intelligible forms of all things without their matter; it is a kind of "place" where universals are actualized, where the understandable aspects of things are understood. The activity of the intellect is to realize the intelligibility inherent in the world. What sets that power in operation? what makes us know, as light makes us see? Now just as there is an intellect that becomes all things, Aristotle had said, so there must be in the soul a power that makes all things; and this power is impassive and apart, and is deathless and eternal. Centuries of puzzling over what Aristotle might have meant, and what in the light of religious hopes he must have meant, eventuated in Thomas's verdict: there is a passive intellect in the soul where ideas are realized, and there is an active intellect differing from all the other powers that constitute the soul, in that it needs no bodily instrument, but is wholly immaterial, that is the agent in bringing knowledge to pass.

How then do we know particular things? According to Thomas, by a process involving several successive stages of actualization. The motion of the transmitting medium imprints phantasmata upon the sense-organs. A phantasm is an image or likeness of a particular object, and is itself a particular material thing, with a sensible species or form of its own—the particular quality of brownness of this table, for example. These sensible species or forms are actualized in the sense-organ, collected in the central "common sense," and preserved in the "imagination," a kind of storehouse of sense-images, as particulars, as forms embedded in the images or likenesses of particular objects—of this table as brown, hard, smooth, etc. But these forms are still only potentially intelligible. To become really understood, to become objects of knowledge and not merely of sense, the universal which was potentially in the object, and has been conveyed by the sensible forms into the mind as in a kind of vehicle, must be abstracted from these particular sensible species or qualities. It must be made actually intelligible. This is the "abstractive" function of the active intellect, which is twofold: First, to actualize the intelligible species existing potentially in the sensible species, and secondly, to separate it from them. That is, the active intellect, a power of the human mind, considers sensible species in the stored up phantasms, illuminates them so that the intelligible species is thrown into relief, and then actualizes it as a universal in the possible, potential, or passive intellect, that power of the mind that can become the intelligible aspect of things. The active intellect works on the brownness, hardness, and smoothness in the image or phantasm, and makes us recognize a "table," a universal, or meaning. For to know that this thing is a table is quite different from knowing that it is brown: it is to know its essence, and not merely its accidents. The first is the function of intellect, the second of sense. Yet meaning is never known without sense experience of that which has a meaning; to know what things are we must first have observed them.

The mind knows itself in the same way, by abstracting from sense: it first knows its objects, then arrives at its own operations, and finally at its own nature. And immaterial substances above itself in the scale of being it knows only by likewise reflecting on sense materials, and only so far as sense-materials permit it to go.

This is a theory of the function of the individual knower, not, like the Augustinian treatment of knowledge, a theory of the intelligibility of the world. It is a theory of how meanings are discovered, how concepts are generated, not of how the truth of ideas is judged and tested—a theory of psychology, not of logic. Knowledge is conceived in humanistic and individualistic terms, not in terms of the structure of the universe.

Yet the object of knowledge is that intelligible structure, and we know truly only when we can say not merely that things are as they are but why they are so. We know, that is, in terms of the causes or principles that in the nature of things make them what they are. True science is rational demonstration from self-evident principles, on the model of geometry. Every subject-matter that lends itself to human knowledge contains such principles in terms of which it can be understood. They are learned, like everything else, from experience. Many sensations often repeated make a memory, and many memories make a rational experience, an experience in which the universal principle implicit in particular instances becomes plain and manifest. Science is the realization in thought and the expression in words of the intelligible structure inherent in a subject-matter: it is possessed when we can say why things of a certain sort have to be as they are and act as they do.

If all knowledge is thus of universals, of the principles and definitions and kinds of things—if we know things in terms of the patterns into which they naturally fall, of the knowable structure in which we find them embedded—how is it possible to know particular objects, to know the things that fall into those graspable kinds and patterns? Strictly speaking, says Thomas, we cannot: not directly at least. We can only feel or sense individual things, and then recognize their kind. The knowledge that there are particulars comes from a complicated process of reflection, in which the mind turns back upon itself and ultimately realizes there must have been something to set it in motion. That is, universals or meanings are the object of knowledge, while perceptions and sensations are reached only by an analysis of that knowledge. We have images, but we know universals or meanings, the structure in which they are caught up.

This is not a representative theory of knowledge, like later forms of empiricism: it does not maintain that we know ideas representing objects. It is not a form of presentational realism, of realistic empiricism, like the view of Ockham and Hobbes, that we know particular objects directly. What we know is not particulars, but their meaning or pattern; but that pattern does not "represent" particulars, it is what makes them what they are—it is what is intelligible in their nature, their form or essence, which experience conveys without distortion to the mind. And this Thomistic view thus rests upon the basic presupposition which seventeenth-century science was to shatter, that things have an intelligible aspect, and that experience is a logical process through which those intelligible aspects are realized in the mind.

III

The third great medieval theory of knowledge was that of the *via moderna* which sprang from the critical thought of William of Ockham—the theory of the "terminists" who dominated the fourteenth- and fifteenth-century schools. Like that of Thomas, it too purported to be a version of the Aristotelian view of knowledge and of logic; and in the materials it drew upon, the Aristotelian principles it elaborated, and the hostility it shared toward the Platonic realism of the Augustinians, it could well claim a foundation in the logic of Aristotle. It too derived all knowledge from experience, and it too saw its culmination in science as the expression in demonstrative form of why things are as they are. Yet this second medieval version of Aristotelian empiricism had one point in common with the Augustinian theory: like that other, it started with the fact of knowledge and its structure, not with the world. It was a theory of man's experience, not of the universe as experienced. And ultimately in modern thought it flowed together with the Augustinian theory of man's inner experience of reason to form our "critical" philosophies of experience.

For Ockham's philosophy was essentially a theory of knowledge, of its nature and structure. Starting from the Aristotelian logic as an analysis of the way knowledge is formulated and expressed in discourse, as a matter of the right use of language and terms, Ockham accentuated the differences between thought and being already present in germ in the Thomistic view. The way in which man knows the world is not the way in which the world naturally exists: for knowledge is the expression of universals, while in nature only particular and individual things are found. An analysis of knowledge, therefore, is not at the same time an analysis of the world as known: what discourse expresses in language is not the intelligible structure of things, but is rather knowledge itself. Knowledge to be sure is knowledge: we do know the individual substances of which the world is made up. But the intelligible structure expressed in our science and demonstration is the structure of knowledge and not of the world. The world needs no such structure to be what it is; it is man who needs it in his mind to know the world. Concepts, universals, meanings, principles, are "intentions" of the mind, and not of the essence of things; they are instruments used by the mind in knowing, but they are not themselves the ultimate objects of knowledge, the implicit pattern of things. They are signs in the mind signifying what things are; they stand for things, and as so standing can be used and manipulated. They are made, *ficta*, in the mind itself, by the action of things upon it, by experience; and as such they are natural signs, as smoke is the sign of fire or a groan the sign of pain. But there is no call to impute to the world itself these instruments of knowing it generates in human minds. The world is what it is without being known. Thought is not the measure of being: it is the interpretation of human experience.

Thomas and Ockham, in repeating the familiar Aristotelian phrases, seem often to be using the selfsame words; but what they are saying is very different. For Thomas, it is the structure of things itself which is actualized in knowledge and expressed in discourse. In the act of knowing the knowable aspect of things and the power of the mind to know receive a common fulfillment: the mind becomes itself the very pattern of what is. Knowledge is equally the fullest expression of the mind's power to know and the world's power to be known: the world, which exists as potentially intelligible, becomes what it can most fully be only when it is understood. For Ockham, this fundamental relation of *identity* between knower and what is known, between knowledge and the knowable aspect of the world, has been replaced by a quite different relation: that of *suppositio*, of standing for or signifying. Knowledge is not the realization of the world's intelligibility, it is a sign which stands for the objects in the world.

That intimate and complementary relation between man and world, between intelligent animal and intelligible environment, which is essential in the Aristotelianism of Thomas, has been completely ruptured in the Aristotelianism of Ockham. The fact of knowledge no longer has implications for the nature of the world that sustains it; its only implications are for man and his manner of knowing the world, whatever be its nature. It is no accident that one of the first outcomes of this Ockhamite theory of knowledge and experience was to initiate a critical attack upon Aristotle's theory of nature itself. The structure of nature is no longer to be construed in terms of the structure of knowledge, as a potentiality for what is there actual. It is to be described as what it is simply observed to be. And so the basic ideas of physics as they were to be elaborated in the seventeenth century make their first appearance among the Ockhamite empiricists of the fourteenth century. Once freed from the necessity of finding nature at every turn intelligible, the Ockhamites could construct an intelligible theory of how nature works. But equally with their successors three centuries later, they could give no intelligible account of their power to do so. The history of the Ockhamites in the fourteenth century and of the empiricists in the seventeenth follows the same pattern: both could elaborate the structure of knowledge and create a natural science, but both were led to a destructive and sceptical attack upon the very possibility of the existence of knowledge itself.

The Augustinian theory of knowledge demands a mathematical realm in which to function; it is the overwhelming fact of mathematics in our science that has kept it alive. The Aristotelianism of Thomas demands a world which is the seat of intelligibility; wellnigh swamped by the purely mechanical view of early modern science, it is just recovering in our electrical world. The Ockhamite theory makes no demands save that there be a world to generate knowledge; and therefore it has persisted in each of the successive worlds our science has described. Being a theory of knowledge and not of nature, it has been adapted to the physics of Aristotle, of Newton, and of Einstein alike. But being a theory of experience rather than of what is experienced, it has always proceeded from an initial realism as to the cause of experience to an experience that has forgotten its cause. Its fate has been, in the fourteenth century, in the eighteenth, and in the twentieth, to fall into a subjectivism from which only the most strenuous efforts have been able to extricate it. That history is an important part of modern thought.

Its first initiators, like Ockham or Hobbes, have escaped the paradoxes toward which their successors have uniformly advanced. For Ockham demonstrative science must be rigidly deductive, like geometry. But science is essentially an affair of discourse, of propositions which are made up of terms. The terms stand for mental "intentions" or concepts, and the propositions thus signify a coupling of concepts. A proposition is true when both subject and predicate stand for the same thing, so that truth is a property of discourse or language when it expresses an identity of signification. But verbal propositions are themselves the expression of prior mental propositions; for words are signs chosen arbitrarily to stand for concepts, and a verbal proposition is true if it leads to the formation of a true mental coupling of concepts.

A concept is a passion of the soul, a mental quality or existence, which is itself the natural sign of the real thing or things for which it stands. Every real thing exists as something particular and individual. Concepts or universals are nothing but intentions of the mind formed by the intellect to express the essence of things and serve as signs for them. Such "natural universals" are natural signs which can be predicated of many things, signs in the same way that smoke is the natural sign of fire, a groan, of pain, or laughter, of internal joy. Such natural signs are the primary material of knowledge; words or terms are artificial signs invented to stand for them in discourse, for that for which the mental intentions generated by things stand naturally.

The object of science, therefore, is not things themselves as immediately known, but concepts standing for things, expressed in terms instituted to stand for what those concepts signify. It is propositions and not things which form the subject-matter of science, for only propositions can be said to be truly understood. Even our knowledge of mental propositions is strictly speaking of concepts and their relations rather than of real things. Science can be said to be about individual things only in the sense that it is for individual things that the terms of our propositions stand. More properly, science is not about individual things, but about universals that stand for individuals (*de universalibus pro individuis*).

Such is the character of demonstrative or certain knowledge. It is the coupling together of signs which stand for the same things.

But our knowledge of those signs themselves, and of the individual things for which they stand, must all come from sense experience. For real things, anything that exists, whether body or mental state or term, being particular and individual, can be known only by direct observation, not by reasoning. Such direct knowledge of particulars, physical, mental, or logical, whether gained by sense or by intellect, Ockham calls "intuitive"; by it alone we know existent things and their qualities—that this table is brown, for example. Only from such intuitive knowledge of sense do we obtain a knowledge of real existence. For only by intuitive knowledge do we give assent to contingent propositions about existent things, that a thing is when it is, and that it is not when it is not. This real or intuitive knowledge is particular, not universal; it deals with observable facts, not with universals or reasons why.

Since only particulars exist, only particular things can be causes; causes are observable facts producing other facts, not universal principles. They are intuitively known, by immediate observation: if they are present, the effect follows, if absent, it does not. The Aristotelian principle that whatever is moved must be moved by something else, is neither self-evident nor deduced from self-evident axioms, and can therefore not be used as a principle of demonstration. We can be certain of causes only when we intuitively observe them. "That any created thing is determinately an efficient cause cannot be demonstrated or proved, but is manifest only from experience, if in its presence the effect follows, and in its absence it does not."

How, then, do we derive from this intuitive knowledge of particular things the concepts and universals which stand as their signs in our reasoned knowledge? Every particular thing is so constituted as to move the intellect to receive it confusedly or distinctly. If Socrates is thus known so confusedly as to be indistinguishable from Plato, he causes the intellect to receive the concept "man"; if he is known distinctly as Socrates, he is received as that individual. If the intellect has been moved in both ways, we can then say, this Socrates is a man. Such knowledge of concepts is immediate and direct: there is no need to assume the presence of any "form" or "species," sensible or intelligible. Nothing is required besides the intellect and the thing known itself.

Universals are commonly said to be "abstracted" from particulars, and knowledge of them is called "abstractive." How are universals, that is, concepts that can stand for many individuals, really formed? They are caused naturally by things without any activity of the intellect or will; hence there is no need to assume any "active intellect." First the intellect has an intuitive knowledge of the particulars; there then follows naturally a second act of the intellect, distinct from the former, which produces the universal. Such a universal concept is therefore something made by the intellect resembling those objects which it first knew intuitively, a kind of "image," copy (*similitudo*), or construct (*fictio*). It is true, Ockham admits on closer analysis, that for such abstractive knowledge something is needed besides the intellect and its object, something left in the image-making power by intuitive sense knowledge, else in the absence of the thing perceived there would be no image. But that thing that remains is not so much a "species" as a tendency or *habitus*, a tendency to imagine the object formerly sensed; it is therefore properly speaking not a new thing, but an act of the intellect. Such an act can serve as a copy of the perceived thing, it can signify and stand for it, it can be the subject or predicate of a proposition, as well as any supposed "construct." If we will, what is left as a deposit from experience can be called a quality actually existing in the mind as an individual thing, serving by its nature as a sign of things without. But whether these universal concepts be taken as "constructs," or as acts of the mind itself, or as particular psychical existences, the important thing is their function of signifying or standing for external objects. In any event they are signs, to which corresponds a similar reality in things themselves; they are not like chimeras, pure figments of the mind: they are natural signs, not arbitrary, like words. It is these signs which are known directly by the intellect in reasoning, and used as the terms of all its propositions; in whatever manner they are naturally generated, their function is to be used as the instruments of knowledge. As signs, they are known intuitively, like all individual things; in its psychological functioning there is no difference between intuitive and abstractive knowledge.

Since Ockham is most insistent that universals are natural signs existing in the mind alone, and that everything existing in nature is wholly individual, it is a little difficult to determine what these signs that stand for "many individuals" in nature are really signs of. If everything that exists is a pure particular, and all intelligible structure is in the mind as an instrument of knowledge, and not in the world of things at all, why should the one sign "man" serve for Socrates and Plato rather than for Socrates and a line? Ockham denies that all such groupings are arbitrary: universal concepts are not chosen at will, they are "natural" signs, else would there be no species and genera by nature. From the sole fact that Plato is a different individual (*solo numero*) from Socrates, and that by his nature Plato is "very like" (*simillimus*) Socrates, the term "man" can be predicated of both; nor is there other cause to be sought than that Socrates is Socrates and Plato is Plato and each is a man. A universal does express or explain the essence or nature of a substance. For the truth of discourse it need not be assumed that Socrates and Plato agree *in* any third thing or things (*in aliquo*), but only that they agree *because* of certain things (*aliquibus*), that is, of what they themselves are (*se ipsis*). If it be said they agree in being "men," that can only mean that "man" is a common term that can be predicated of both of them (by a *suppositio simplex*); it certainly cannot mean that they agree in some common thing, "humanity," which they possess (by a *suppositio personalis*).

This looks suspiciously as though Ockham, like so many empiricists, had mistaken things expressed for mere terms of expression, reducing them to the latter; and it is clear that like his successors he is forced to admit that in denying all universal character to things he did not mean there are no "real kinds" or "similarities" in Nature. And yet—"Genus [or Kind] is not something common to many things because of some identity in them, but because of a certain community of the sign, by which the same sign is common to the many things it designates" (*Expositio aurea*, Praedicab. de Genere). In the end he puts the similarity in the sign, not in things! Such are the straits to which one is pushed who maintains that though knowledge is "of" universals, only pure particulars exist. But Ockham himself escaped this paradox of giving intelligible expression to a world with no intelligible structure, as he escaped the allied empiricist problem of subjectivism—which he categorically rejected—through his doctrine of natural signs. The mental concepts and logical terms which are the immediate objects of knowledge and discourse are signs of real things, and real kinds of things: they are the instruments which the mind uses in knowing the world.

Ockham's theory is a form of presentational realism: In knowing, a passive mind directly perceives particular real objects, their properties and relations. There is no need of any "active intellect" to abstract nonexistent "forms" and "species." A universal is generated naturally in the mind by direct contact with objects without any activity of the mind itself. This complete passivity of the mind, this spectator theory of knowledge, has persisted as the fundamental assumption of the empiricist tradition; together with those of a structureless world of pure particulars, and of the contents of the mind itself as the immediate object of knowledge, it has formed the major British tradition. These presuppositions are combined in Ockham with an elaborate theory of science as the manipulation of terms or signs in discourse.

This is the Ockhamite position to which the English thinkers, Hobbes, Locke, and Newton, turned to interpret seventeenth-century science. For it, the object of science is to define and analyze terms, which stand for individual things causally related. Its method is to observe by sense particular things causing other things, and then to define one's terms in such a way that the same consequences will follow logically from an analysis of the terms as follow in experience from the things for which those terms stand. The task of the scientist is to construct a rigorous postulate system that can represent or serve as the sign of the observed course of natural events. Science is a demonstrative system; but it must correspond to the observations of sense. The Ockhamite position thus combines a realistic view of sense knowledge with a representative theory of science. In this discrepancy lie the seeds of scepticism, which speedily developed in the fourteenth-century Schools, and again in the eighteenth-century when it was applied once more.

The Coming of Humanism and Science

I: THE REVOLUTION IN VALUES

THE REORIENTATION OF THE INTELLECTUAL TRADITIONS TOWARD NEW ENDS

I

Humanistic Values and the Philosophic Traditions

THE FORMAL BREAK with "medieval thought" has traditionally been assigned to the Humanists, on their own recognizances; and in truth, though every generation since the twelfth century had seen its own group of "*moderni*," it was the Humanists who, looking back once more at the treasures of the ancient world, first discovered that the intervening period had been a *medium aevum*. That break, if break there has to be in the living web of human ideas, might with equal justice be attributed to those earlier "moderns" of the fourteenth century, the Ockhamites, who so acutely punctured the nice adjustment of faith and reason, of Christian theology and Aristotelian science, which Thomas and Scotus had built up, and which still passes with most men as the content of "medieval thought"; and laid the foundation in idea and achievement for a mathematical and experimental science. Or it might be credited to the Augustinian mystics of the early fourteenth century, who revolted against the barren and godless science of the schools, called men back to a personal religious experience, prepared the Protestant consciousness of modern times, and by their criticism of scientific knowledge initiated the long current of philosophical idealism and transcendentalism. Which of these movements one chooses depends upon how one takes his "medieval thought," and what one finds to be "modern." All played their part in the break-up of medieval institutions; each is intelligible only against the common background of economic expansion and reconstruction; and each worked with inherited materials, and even in expressing its new insights remained in fundamental continuity with tradition. If the Ockhamites seem now to us closer to the "modernism" of seventeenth- and eighteenth-century science, we must not forget that the Humanist movement arose in conscious opposition to their scientific interests, and that the Augustinian revival which in turn dominated the sixteenth century was definitely hostile to both.

I

Since Burckhardt, it has been the fashion to regard the essence of the Renaissance as "the rediscovery of the world and of the natural man." But this seems far too simple a rendering of the complexities of the compromises, cross-currents, and reactions of the intellectual life of the fifteenth and sixteenth centuries, even in Italy. The humanistic values, the emphasis on the dignity and worth of human nature, did indeed receive powerful expression from some of the Italians; but so had they likewise in the humanism of thirteenth-century Thomas. And surely the new Augustinism of the sixteenth century is the nadir of human self-esteem, a valley of total depravity between two peaks of rational animality. As for the world, where the later scholasticism had served a scientific and increasingly naturalistic vision, both Humanists and Augustinians turned from nature and its knowledge to concentrate narrowly upon man and his destiny. The one value these diverse currents all share is an increasing individualism, an increasing impatience with the older forms of social organization—the natural reflex of the outgrowing of all the now inadequate institutions of a simpler economy. But even here, of individualism such as the eighteenth century was to know, of laissez faire, there is not a trace. Men still needed the aid of their fellows even in their rebellion; and most of all they needed the aid of the newly sovereign state.

Nevertheless it remains true that what novelty is expressed in the intellectual movements of the fifteenth century is a novelty of feelings and values rather than of systematic thought. For all their personalistic and anti-institutional emphasis, the mystics went back in their philosophy to the Augustinism of the earlier Middle Ages, before the corrupting Aristotelian naturalism had made its appearance. And though the humanists turned from the otherworldliness and asceticism of the medieval Christian ethic, they did not desert the main outlines of the medieval world-view. The great intellectual revolution in western Europe had come much earlier, in the thirteenth century, with the introduction and assimilation of Aristotelian science; and the development of that science in the fourteenth century represented far more of a break with the earlier Christian philosophy than anything put forward during the humanistic Renaissance. The two scientific schools of the later Middle Ages, the Ockhamites and the Averroists, had both not only achieved a naturalistic, rationalistic, and genuinely scientific temper; they had already begun that steady progress in critical procedure and indeed in knowledge of nature which, kept alive during the domination of other interests, came into its own by the end of the sixteenth century. The movement we know as "the Renaissance" was indeed a rejection of this scientific interest for other concerns, practical, artistic, and at bottom religious. For most men this rejection was realized in life and action rather than in theory, and carried to its highest point by statesmen, artists, or engineers, not by systematic thinkers. When it finally achieved conscious philosophical expression, it was to religious philosophies going back to the Hellenistic Age that it turned—philosophies that endeavored to combat the rising secularism with older forms of Christianity, less corrupted by the scientific and naturalistic spirit, and more accommodating to individualistic values. What it objected to in the organized Aristotelian learning of the universities was not its synthesis with religious values, and certainly not any otherworldliness and asceticism; it was in the interests rather of a purer and deeper religious life that the Humanists on both sides of the Alps opposed Aristotle. In mystics like Eckhart, Tauler, Suso, and Gerson, this return to the religious and imaginative world of the earlier Augustinian tradition is clear enough; but though dressed up with more conscious scholarship, and though broader and more universal in its horizons, the Neoplatonism of the Florentine Academy or the "philosophy of Christ" of an Erasmus or a Lefèvre d'Étaples is a similar revulsion from scientific thought to the religious imagination.

The crime of Aristotle and the Schoolmen was at bottom that they had served to organize the institutions of a society and culture from which men were struggling to emancipate themselves. They and their science belonged to the *ancien régime*. From Petrarch and Boccaccio on to the Collège Royale, the humanistic movement was a revolt against the vested interests, the complacency and the academic conservatism of the professional intellectuals. Where the Aristotelian tradition remained definitely allied with the older ecclesiastical institutions and culture, Aristotle was doomed. But where, as in northern Italy, it had itself come to express the new culture of a commercial society, it was able easily to assimilate the individualistic values of an age of rapid reconstruction. And it is no accident that while the Church-controlled science of the North drove all those who felt the new currents into open rebellion against science itself, the anticlerical science of the Italian universities could progress steadily in self-criticism to the achievement of a Galileo.

As an educational revolt in the interests of an emerging type of culture against a too neatly organized intellectual life, Humanism naturally had to effect a "renaissance of learning": that is, the Humanists had to stop studying the traditional textbooks and to begin to read something else. When they abandoned the curriculum that had prevailed since the thirteenth century, Peter Lombard and the medieval commentators on the Bible and on Aristotle, they had the whole of ancient literature at their disposal. Dissatisfied with what their predecessors had made out of this material, they went to school to the ancients again for a fresh start. And since the essence of the medieval treatment had been dialectic, the logical elaboration of ancient wisdom, they turned for their method to the other two instrumental sciences of the trivium, grammar and rhetoric. Where the Schoolmen had sought truth in the rational consideration of an author's propositions, the humanists sought it in the careful elucidation of an authority's meaning; where the Schoolmen defended its validity by argument against searching objections, the Humanists sought to persuade men to accept it by the skillful use of words. That is, they were scholars rather than scientists, and poets rather than philosophers. And these grammarians introduced an authoritarianism the Middle Ages had never known: the authority of a text took precedence over the authority of reason. When applied to the Bible and the Church Fathers, the Protestant reliance on the Word of God in Holy Writ was the inevitable result. The Church, following Augustine, had found the Word of God to be the Master within, Reason itself. Methodologically, the Humanists represented less the discovery of new texts than a new way of reading texts long possessed: the grammarian replaced the dialectician.

II

Different men turned to different parts of ancient literature. Naturally it was the Latin writings that were most accessible; there in Cicero, Seneca, and the poets was the record of a prosperous urban society much like the one they had just created. There was the experience of a people to whom science meant little, and the Schoolmen's "truths of God" nothing at all—a people whose culture was the *studium humanitatis ac litterarum*, the cultivation of great men and of effective pleading. What more natural than to oppose such a congenial culture to the one they were trying to escape? From the Romans the only philosophy to be learned was an unsystematic and anthropocentric Stoicism, a practical wisdom that enhanced the dignity of human nature and its power to endure. With every man schooled on Roman literature, it is not surprising that throughout the Renaissance and well into the eighteenth century there runs a strong current of Stoic ethics, so appropriate to the turmoils of that time, cropping out again and again in men who profess quite different theoretical views—and an even more widespread Stoic temper of mind. Cicero and Seneca formed a large part of the content of Humanistic education; and believe it or not, in those days men seem actually to have taken seriously what they studied in school. This temper appears in figures as diverse as Pomponazzi and Spinoza, Descartes and Hume; it was especially strong in the early Italian Humanists, like Salutati (d. 1406), Bruni (1369–1444), and the first Humanist pope, Pius II (d. 1464, Aeneas Sylvius Piccolomini), and in those northern Humanists like Erasmus who remained grammarians rather than philosophers. There was little turning to the Stoic metaphysics; only Justus Lipsius (1547–1606), a Belgian scholar who founded a school of Stoics with considerable influence on men like Arminius and Grotius, adhered to the Stoic system as a whole. The greatest inspiration of Stoicism, to legal theory and jurisprudence, came indirectly through Roman law.

Epicurean hedonism also made an appeal to the less religious minds, though as a total philosophy it too had to wait until the seventeenth century to find an advocate in Gassendi. Lorenzo Valla (1407–1457), an ironical and critical spirit, a true anticlerical, though he died as secretary to the pope, defended hedonism in *De voluptate*

(1431) against the Stoa, as the only two philosophies worthy of consideration by a Humanist. The rights of nature must prevail; man cannot help seeking pleasure. Indeed, what is Christianity itself but a sublimated form of hedonism?

Who could call beatitude by a better name than pleasure? . . . Whence it is not virtue (the Stoic *honestas*) but pleasure that is to be sought after for its own sake, as well by those who wish to rejoice in this life as in that to come.[1]

Between the Garden and the Church there is no hostility; with the cloister there is open war, "for the life of Christ is not guarded in the monk's hood alone." The prostitute is better than the nun; she makes men happy while the nun lives in shameful and futile celibacy. In *De professione religiosorum* this hard-headed and daring critic denied all value to asceticism and holiness.

III

For those who demanded a more intellectual philosophy, there were the Greeks, and above all Plato, the natural refuge of those fleeing Aristotle and science. With his poetic, imaginative, and religious interests, so closely akin to their own; with his intellectual affinity to the philosophic core of the Christian tradition, which they were trying to recover from its scholastic accretions and defend against science and a naturalistic secularism, Plato made an irresistible appeal to the grammarians and artists of the Renaissance. It is customary, indeed, to view the whole humanistic movement as philosophically a turning from Aristotle to Platonism. It is true that among the gifted literary and artistic circle in Florence there was unbounded enthusiasm for Plato. It is also true that Platonism was the most imposing alternative to the Aristotelian schools, the one best adapted to a religious revival, and best combining the imaginative values of religion with the values of a humane life. It had already been thoroughly Christianized in the familiar Augustinian tradition; and St. Augustine dominates the various currents of religious revival and reform, from the mystics and Cusanus onward. It was natural for grammarians to go behind him to his intellectual sources in Neoplatonism.

But not only does this view overlook the strong undercurrent of

[1] Valla, *De voluptate*, Lib. III, cap. 9.

Latin Stoicism, permeating Renaissance Platonism itself; it must not be forgotten that Aristotle continued to inspire the vigorous intellectual life of the Italian universities. The new humanistic tendencies appeared as early in that living Aristotelianism as in the Florentine Academy; and they were there allied with and not opposed to the already flourishing scientific movement. Indeed, that mathematical and mechanical development which by the end of the sixteenth century produced Galileo owes very little to the Platonic revival, but received powerful stimulus from the critical Aristotelianism of Padua. And while there is little in a Platonist like Pico not to be found in Philo of Alexandria, the naturalistic humanism initiated by Pomponazzi and culminating in Zabarella is a genuinely original philosophy, the sanest and most critical of all the philosophical expressions of the Renaissance. In truth, what Humanism brought was not any new philosophy, but new values which, when incorporated into each of the major philosophical traditions, altered their emphases and gave them a characteristic Renaissance stamp.

The commercial cities of northern Italy had long enjoyed and taught in their universities a thoroughly secular and anticlerical philosophy. By the fifteenth century that nice blend of Aristotelian science and Christian faith which Thomas and Duns Scotus had constructed had retreated into the monastic orders. In the universities of Padua, Bologna, and Pavia there reigned an Aristotelianism that made little attempt to accommodate itself to theology. Unlike Paris, where the Faculty of Theology crowned the Sorbonne, at Padua there was only a Faculty of Medicine besides that of Arts; and Aristotle was there taught as a preparation, not for an ecclesiastical career, but for the study of medicine, with a consequent emphasis on his scientific methodology and his natural history. The teachers normally held medical degrees themselves; they applied Aristotle to medical problems, and they interpreted him in the light of the medical writers of the Greek and Arabic traditions. Like most of the other Schoolmen from Thomas down, they regarded Averroes as the chief guide and commentator. But unlike Thomas and the theologians they had little motive to disagree with him on those points where that naturalistic pantheist followed Aristotle or his Hellenistic commentators rather than the true faith. This version of Aristotle without benefit of clergy is hence known as Latin Averroism. It had accompanied the introduction of Aristotle in the thirteenth century, making originally a great appeal to the arts faculty struggling against the theologians at Paris. When Siger de Brabant, its spokesman, was condemned by the bishop in 1270 and 1277, and refuted by the more accommodating modernism of Thomas, it took refuge at Padua. From the days of Marsilio of Padua, John of Jandun, and Pietro d'Abano (d. 1315), the latter a physician and professor of medicine and natural philosophy at Padua itself, this Averroistic interpretation of Aristotle prevailed in the Italian universities. After Padua became Venetian territory in 1405, the lords of that leading anticlerical state jealously protected these Averroists against inquisition and Jesuits alike, and Padua became the Italian center of science, anticlericalism, and rationalism in thought.

Averroes himself, a physician and judge rather than theologian, had applied a rigid legal method to interpreting the works of Aristotle. But struggling with Arabic texts, and relying on the Neoplatonic Hellenistic commentators, he found much cosmic mysticism and pantheism in his philosopher. Creation is eternal, by emanations; there is no creation in time, and hence no first man, no Adam and Eve, no Fall. Matter is eternal, and so is that mysterious Intellect of which Aristotle speaks. It is deathless and unremitting, the Intelligence of the lowest sphere, common to all men and particularizing itself in their individual souls, as light illuminates their bodies. These human intellects live on after death only as moments in the single intellect of mankind. Hence there is no personal immortality, no heaven or hell, and no last judgment.

These views, whether Aristotelian or no, are obviously not Christian; and the earliest Latin Averroists frankly admitted that the conclusions of reason, philosophy, and Aristotle are not the conclusions of faith. Faith is true, but Aristotle is more interesting, held Siger, taking an irrationalist or agnostic position. But Jandun, recognizing no authority save reason in agreement with experience, and meaning thereby Averroes' Aristotle, maintained all these characteristic Averroistic doctrines as an open rationalist, mocked at faith, and called Thomas a compromising theologian. His writings are satirical and ironical in the Voltairean sense. The fifteenth-century Paduans maintained on such matters a less defiant and more Christian Averroism. As the Church was thoroughly tamed in Padua, and no menace, they were not enough concerned with Christianity to be violently anticlerical. But the supremacy of natural reason, the denial of creation and immortality, with their theological consequences, and the unity of the intellect were taught in the universities and, we are told, accepted by most Venetian gentlemen. Such a philosophy expressed just that stage of scepticism towards the religious system, just that stage of antisupernaturalism rather than of positive naturalism and humanism, reached by the northern Italian cities in the fourteenth century—a rational defense of the attitude so well expressed in Boccaccio, and so horrifying to Petrarch.

This was a naturalistic and scientific, rather than a humanistic philosophy; its conception of human nature emphasized man's dependence on the world rather than his freedom and glory. And the unity of the intellect is a collective and impersonal conception, with little scope for the individualistic and subjectivistic values the Humanists prized. It is small wonder that from Petrarch down the Humanists felt in strong opposition to this reigning philosophy, and that their own intellectual defenses and rationalizations were developed in contrast to it. As against its Aristotle, they turned to Plato; as against its anticlericalism, they turned to a free and modernizing religious gospel; as against its scientific interest, they turned to human nature; and above all, as against its collectivism they turned to the dignity and worth of the human personality. The personal immortality of the soul became the banner under which men fought for individualism. And so "spiritual" Florence set out on a crusade against naturalistic Venice. But it was not against medieval asceticism and otherworldliness in defense of a "discovery of the world and man" that their philosophy was aimed; it was against a scientific rationalism in the name of a more personal interpretation of the world. And the answer of Padua was not to abandon its naturalism, but to introduce into it those individualistic values it had lacked. Thus the two great rivals in early sixteenth-century Italy are a scientific and an imaginative and religious humanism, with the former more widespread and rapidly increasing in strength.

I V

The Florentine Academy indeed retained a strong strain of asceticism in its modernistic defense of religion; Pico's end as a follower of Savonarola is symbolic. But Ficino had seen that mere preaching against the irreligious Averroists was not enough.

We need a philosophic religion which the philosophers will hear with pleasure, and which will perhaps persuade them. With a few changes, the Platonists would be Christians.[2]

And so he turned to "that pious philosophy" which had come down through the ancient civilizations until it was finally consummated at Athens by the divine Plato. In thus appealing from Aristotle to the Platonic tradition, the Florentines were taking no unprecedented step. They merely sought—and found—a new version of the medieval Augustinian philosophy, that older Platonism in terms of which Christian theology had originally been formulated. They penetrated beyond the medieval additions to the intellectual core of the Christian tradition; it is not surprising they found their Plato essentially at one with revealed religion. But now for the first time men began to turn to the dialogues themselves. Doctrines derived therefrom had already served first as the rationalization of an other-worldly religion; then, as the inspiration of a mathematical science of nature, as they were again to serve as its interpretation. But now, men's interests had shifted to man the artist, man the lover of the beauties and glories of this world. So though what they found was still primarily the religious, Neoplatonic Plato—Plotinus rather than the dialogues as we understand them, and Augustine rather than Plotinus, even when they read Plato's own words—they were now in a position to appreciate something of the humanistic, artistic, and imaginative side of Plato. Intellectually they were indeed left with a theological Neoplatonism, with the Christian world-view minus its Oriental values, its dualism and need for magic—with a single Truth, Platonic in philosophy, Christian in theology, and humanistic in values. And yet the Renaissance did manage to make its Platonism an artistic way of life, a this-worldly religion of the imagination—attractive in contour, and wistfully reminiscent of another world, like the Platonism of Botticelli's pencil, and like it also thin and disembodied, and ever trembling on the verge of the Christian mystery. With wider horizons, it grew eclectic and universal, embraced the love of perfection wherever it might be discerned, and identified it with the essence of Christian faith.

After Chrysoloras had finally taught a few Italians to read Greek,

[2] Ficino, *Theologia platonica de immortalitate animorum* (1482; ed. used, Paris, 1559), Proemium.

his master Pletho introduced them to the ideas of Plato. Georgius Gemistos Plethon (1355–1450) was a Greek from Constantinople who hated the whole Orthodox tradition with its Aristotelian scholasticism. He dallied for a while with the Moslems in Adrianople, and tried to erect Platonism into a new and definitely anti-Christian philosophy, a return to the universal theism of the Hellenistic world. In 1438 he came on a mission to the Council of Ferrara and Florence, called to reunite the Eastern and Western Churches. But strengthening the Church was furthest from his intention. He improved the opportunity instead by lecturing on Plato's superiority to Aristotle; in 1440 he wrote a pamphlet against the latter, *De platonicae et aristotelicae philosophiae differentiis.* His great success led Cosimo to found a Platonic Academy for the humanistic circle; Florence soon became the center of Italian Platonism and humanism, a philosophical rival to scientific Padua. It was the metaphysics and theology of Aristotle Pletho opposed; he specifically excepts the physics. Following Proclus, he tried to revive the pagan gods of Greece in the guise of the Platonic ideas, turned into natural forces and deified. Aristotle's naturalism, his feeling for fact and downright common sense, he found repugnant; he wanted instead to soar up into the realm of ideas to gain a unified imaginative vision of the world. His is a sentimental protest against Aristotle's God as cold and aloof, against all barren logic in the interest of a mythical neoplatonic theosophy. As to the rational meaning of Plato's Ideas, that was to him a "most difficult and obscure question" not necessary to solve, for he felt rather than understood their importance.

His companion at the council of Florence was Basilius Bessarion (1403–1472), a Platonist of very different stamp. Essentially a conciliator, he actually managed to effect a brief church union; he became cardinal and almost pope. Though a pupil of Pletho, he had no grudge against the Church or Aristotle; indeed he counseled moderation and respectful argument against the Stagirite. For him, Plato, Aristotle, and Christianity were all really the same, if one but understood them aright; and what they were was Platonism.

V

When Cosimo founded the Academy in 1459, he established as its head the first Italian disciple of the new Platonism, Marsilio

Ficino (1433–1499). Ficino was not a reformer but essentially a scholar and recluse. Though he possessed little originality, he was an able translator and commentator; from his pioneer Latin versions of the Platonic dialogues (1483) and Plotinus (1492) the Renaissance derived its knowledge of Platonism. The Academy was a free gathering rather than a formal organization; it met in the gardens of the Villa Medici at Fiesole, and in the nearby Badia. Under Medici patronage and attendance it flourished, especially during the rule of Lorenzo. Plato's birthday was at this time November 7; the devoted admirers celebrated it as a true Italian *festa*.

Ficino's own neoplatonic mind saw symbols everywhere, and felt all ideas at once—Platonism, Christianity, the Jewish mysteries, Islam are at bottom all the same. Jesus and Socrates taught the same gospel and died the same death—they are really the same man. His first writing, *De voluptate* (1457), showed how Plato and Aristotle are agreed in a common Neoplatonism. His chief effort, *Theologia platonica de immortalitate animorum* (1482), bent all the resources of his Platonism to defending this universal religion against the Paduans. He naturally makes no distinction between the dialogues and the Neoplatonists: in the workshop of Plotinus, Porphyry, Jamblichus and Proclus the gold of the Platonic philosophy was first purified in the fire of the keenest criticism. Indeed, Plotinus is to Plato as Christ is to the Father.

Ficino's general scheme of realms of being is quite traditional: there are five main steps stretching up to the One. At the bottom is passive matter without quality, pure multiplicity and quantity. Above it stands the active principle of Quality, inhering in matter but itself indivisible. Then comes "soul," movable in its action though immutable in its essence. Angelic intelligences are wholly immutable, but many; over them stands the absolute One itself. Traditional also is Ficino's Augustinian theory of knowledge, stripped of the Aristotelian psychology with which the Middle Ages had provided it, and buttressed from the *Meno* and the *Phaedo*. All knowledge is from innate formulae in the mind, which, stimulated by sense objects, recall the divine ideas. Not by abstraction from particulars—for how could a mere heap generate a single simple concept?—but by divine illumination:

The mind cannot make the true definitions of essences out of the accidental images of things, but it constructs them out of reasons infused by the origin of all things.

All knowledge comes from God acting within the soul.

More original is the Renaissance coloring Ficino gives his thought. This divine illumination is clearest in the aesthetic insight of the artist.

Every mind loves the round form the first time it beholds it, without knowing the reason for this judgment. Every mind cherishes a certain appropriateness and proportion in the human body, or harmony in numbers and tones. It calls a certain bearing and posture beautiful and worthy, it prizes the light of wisdom and the intuition of truth. Now if each mind always and everywhere makes these assumptions, and approves them, without knowing why—it can only be because here it is acting by force of a necessary and thoroughly natural instinct.[3]

God, working through this innate sense of harmony and proportion, reveals his infinite and immortal ideas, and thus makes the soul immortal. Humanistic also is the insistence that the soul's union with the body is no fall from a higher estate, but rather the indispensable means of knowing the beauty and the multiplicity of particular forms—"Am farbigem Abglanz haben wir das Leben." The very incompleteness of individual things is their appropriate manifestation of the divine nature.

Nothing in the world is misshapen or to be despised.[4]

Most characteristic of all is man's estate in Ficino's universe. The soul of man contains in itself an infinite number of determinations; this adaequation to infinity is the surest proof of its immortality. For how could that which discovers, defines, and measures infinity fail itself to be infinite? The soul is like the center of a circle, a self-living point.

She bears within herself the images of the divine essences, on which she depends, as the grounds and models of the lower things which she has in a certain manner created. She is the middle of all and possesses the powers of all. She enters into everything, without losing a part of herself, since she is the true connection of things, when she addresses herself to another. So may she rightly be called the Center of nature, the middle

[3] *Theologia platonica*, Lib. XI, cap. 5.   [4] *De christiana religione*, cap. 18.

of the universe, the chain of the world, the countenance of all and the bond and fetter of all things.[5]

This mediating position is the soul's fortune and greatness.

For she is immutable and mutable. She agrees in the one with higher things, in the other with lower. If she agrees with both, she desires both. Wherefore by a certain natural instinct she ascends to higher things and descends to lower. And when she ascends, she does not forsake the lower, and when she descends she does not leave the higher. For if she forsook either, she would fall into the other extreme, nor would she be the true link between both worlds.[6]

This is not only the dignity and glory of man, it is his cosmic function.

Thus that heavenly ray shed upon the lower world returns through the soul of man once more to the higher regions, when the images of ideas, dissipated in matter, are collected in the imagination, purified in the reason, and finally escape their particularity in universals. Thus the soul of man restores the decay of the universe, since by her action the world, once spiritual and now made corporeal, is ever purified and daily made more spiritual.[7]

With such an exalted conception of human power, Ficino breaks with the Augustine he follows elsewhere as religious authority, over human freedom; like Cusanus he abandons the doctrine of election. Grace comes from within, it is a free decision in the soul; for the soul is self-moving and not bound by the divine decrees. And he also joins the Greeks in generous recognition of all sincere religious aspiration.

Divine providence does not permit there to be at any time any region of the world entirely deprived of religion, although it permits in various places and times various rites of worship to be observed. Perhaps indeed this kind of variety by God's will provides a certain admirable ornament in the universe. For it is indeed more important that the highest king be honored, than that he be honored in this way or in that.[8]

Like Pico and indeed all the Italian Platonists, Ficino concentrates his religious thought in the Platonic doctrine of Love or Eros. Eros

[5] *Theologia platonica*, Lib. III, cap. 2.
[6] *Theologia platonica*, Lib. III, cap. 2.
[7] *Theologia platonica*, Lib. XVI, cap. 3.
[8] *De christiana religione*, cap. 4.

is the aspiration of will in which theology and psychology meet, the active and dynamic mean between divine and earthly. The *Symposium* forms the core of this Platonic religion. In transmitting his commentary on that dialogue together with *De christiana religione*, Ficino wrote:

I send to you the love I promised. I send also the religion, that you may know my love is religious and my religion a religion of love.[9]

This Eros differs from the Christian *caritas* in being a striving, an aspiration, a never-satisfied desire, not the *amor sui* of Thomas, the pure and disinterested love of the Franciscans. It is a human passion, not a divine goal. Yet Ficino does not follow Plato in making it wholly an upward yearning toward mere ideals that cannot reciprocate. With Augustine and the Christian mystics, it is a mutual love between a personal God and man—the divine grace itself.

It is the characteristic of all divine spirits that when they contemplate the higher they do not cease to gaze upon the lower and to care for it. This is also the peculiarity of our soul, that it takes upon itself the care and fostering not only of its own body but also of the bodies of all earthly things and of the earth itself.[10]

And thus it is love which binds the world together, and binds man into a single human unity of body and soul.

For soul is never forced elsewhere, but by love it merges itself in the body, and by love it emerges from the body.[11]

This theme of a love not of the flesh fleshly, but of all spiritual beauty, which yet is human in its passionate desire and yearning, and human also in its starting point, was the most popular message of the Platonists; and in many a garden and castello the *Symposium* was prolonged far into the night. Cardinal Bembo, Castiglione his Plato, and Leo the Hebrew, in his *Dialoghi d'Amore*, have all left inimitable portrayals of a love still too Christian for the full-bodied Plato, yet far too human for Bernard or the Victorines—a love at once the love of the flesh in its beauty, and the intellectual love of God.

[9] *Epistolae* (Venice, 1494), Lib. I, col. 632.
[10] Cited in Ernst Cassirer, *Individuum und Kosmos in der Philosophie der Renaissance* (1927), p. 140.
[11] *Theologia platonica*, Lib. XVI, cap. 7.

VI

If Ficino was the crabbed scholar pouring over his books of mystic lore the better to express a new joy in beauty and human aspiration after the perfect, Giovanni Pico della Mirandola (1463–1494), youthful, gorgeous, wildly rich and incredibly noble of birth, was the very incarnation of this Platonic beauty and love. Possessed of "all tongues"—he knew Hebrew and Arabic besides Greek, and read widely in them all—what did it matter that all his ideas were known in ancient Alexandria? Surely never before had any one been so suffused with a sense of the power of man! At twenty-four he posted 900 theses at Rome, drawn from his wide learning, and challenged the world to confute them, promising to pay the expenses of any scholar who would come to dispute with him. Alas, the Church forbade this noble gesture, and excommunicated him. Crushed in spirit, he did not survive long; at the last Savonarola captured him, and he was buried in the Dominican habit—a fitting symbol of what the Reformation was to do to the Renaissance.

For Pico, Plato, Aristotle, Jesus, the Cabbala, in fact everybody, really meant the same thing. There is one true religion with differing symbols. Beginning with an allegorical interpretation of Moses, he worked all his life on a great *Concordia Platonis et Aristotelis* which he left unfinished.

For there is no question natural or divine, in which Aristotle and Plato do not agree in sense and substance, although their words may seem to differ.[12]

I seem to recognize two things in Plato, a Homeric power of eloquence, and a sense entirely the same as Aristotle's, so that if you consider the words, there is nothing more opposed, but if the matter, nothing more in accord.[13]

More clearly even than Ficino, Pico expressed the Renaissance sense of human power in his *Oration on the Dignity of Man*, prepared as introduction to his 900 theses. Not only is man the microcosm, the mean binding earth and heaven together; he is the master and lord of his own destiny, a free and self-created spirit. For with things,

[12] *Opera* (Basel, 1601 ed.), I, 83.   [13] *Opera*, I, 368.

their operations follow their being; but with man, what he is follows from what he does.

Then the Supreme Maker decreed that unto Man, on whom he could bestow naught singular, should belong in common whatsoever had been given to his other creatures. Therefore he took man, made in his own individual image, and having placed him in the center of the world, spake to him thus: "Neither a fixed abode, nor a form in thine own likeness, nor any gift peculiar to thyself alone, have we given thee, Adam, in order that what abode, what likeness, what gifts thou shalt choose, may be thine to have and to possess. The nature allotted to all other creatures, within laws appointed by ourselves, restrains them. Thou, restrained by no narrow bonds, according to thy own free will, in whose power I have placed thee, shalt define thy nature for thyself. I have set thee midmost the world, that hence thou mightest the more conveniently survey whatsoever is in the world. Nor have we made thee either heavenly or earthly, mortal or immortal, to the end that thou, being, as it were, thy own free maker and moulder, shouldst fashion thyself in what form may like thee best. Thou shalt have power to decline unto the lower or brute creatures. Thou shalt have power to be reborn unto the higher, or divine, according to the sentence of thy intellect." Thus to Man, at his birth, the Father gave seeds of all variety and germs of every form of life.[14]

Pico's most influential work was his great attack *In Astrologiam*. Though astrology was intimately bound up with the Cabbala and the other lore he admired, his sense of human power was too strong to submit man's destinies to the stars. There is no astrology in Plato and Aristotle, nor are there any occult qualities and forces in the stars beyond what can be observed. Nature moves by "its own principles," motion and heat. Places, the various signs and houses of the stars, have no influence.

Aside from the common influence of motion and light no peculiar force resides in the heavens.[15]

Astrology is no *vera causa*. The stars are not even signs, for "the heavens cannot be the sign of a thing of which they are not the cause." (IV, xii) Pico's chief objection is moral, founded on human freedom: as microcosm, man is above the influence of the stars.

[14] Eng. tr. in J. A. Symonds, *The Revival of Learning* (1877), p. 35.
[15] *In Astrologiam*, Lib. III, cap. v.

There is nothing great on earth beside man, nothing great in man beside the mind and soul; if you ascend therefrom, you transcend the heavens, if you incline to the body and regard the heavens, you behold yourself as a fly and something less than a fly.[16]

Matter cannot rule spirit; man's destiny depends on himself, *sors animae filia*.

VII

From Florence this Platonism was carried far and wide. Johann Reuchlin (1455–1522) brought it to Heidelberg and South Germany; he was a friend of Pico, and wrote extensively on the Cabbalistic art. Mutianus Rufus (1471–1526) gathered a band of Humanists about him at Erfurt and preached the gospel of the universal religion. Wherever the Florentine influence was felt, there sprang up Neoplatonic enthusiasts, viewing the world as a chain of realms of being stretching up to God, and the soul as a microcosm, to be illuminated by symbol on symbol. There appeared discourses on immortality and love, imaginative and uncritical. There was preached the idea of a universal religion, humanistic in its values, Platonic in its thought: there is one God, who has revealed himself to man wheresoever is to be found a teacher of a humanistic, common-sense morality. It was the spirit of Plutarch, the spirit of Alexandria. The common man needs different symbols, the one God has many names, Jupiter, Apollo, Moses, Christ. They all designate the same divine reality, they all taught the same universal and natural moral law. Pinturicchio has well portrayed this religion—on the walls of the Borgia apartments! These men did not oppose Aristotle's physics, for they were not interested. They were artists, not scientists. Obliterate all intellectual distinctions in one common, sympathetic and imaginative wave of religious feeling. Such a program was the very antithesis of the logical clarity of the schoolmen—and of the Padua Aristotelians. It is a recurrent attitude, whenever intellectual interests are pushed into the background by imaginative or moral feeling.

[16] *Ibid.*, Lib. III, cap. xxvii.

2

The Rediscovery of the Hellenic Aristotle

THE FLORENTINE CIRCLE and most of the humanists beyond the Alps were not academic scholars, but men whose Platonistic enthusiasm crowned other interests, literary, artistic, or professional. The organized intellectual life of the universities remained loyal to the Aristotelian tradition. In most countries the fifteenth century saw the teaching and refinement of the earlier philosophies, Scotism, Ockhamism, and Thomism, with little basically new. But in northern Italy, at Padua, Bologna, and Pavia, and to a lesser extent at Siena, Pisa, and the brilliant new university of Ferrara, Aristotelianism was still a living and growing body of ideas. What Paris had been in the thirteenth century, and Oxford and Paris together in the fourteenth, Padua became in the fifteenth: the center in which ideas from all Europe were combined into an organized and cumulative body of knowledge. A succession of great teachers, Paul of Venice (d. 1429), Cajetan of Thiene (d. 1465), and Nicoletto Vernia (d. 1499), carried that knowledge to the point where in the next century it could find fruitful marriage with the new interest in the mathematical sciences. In the Italian schools alone the emerging science of nature did not mean a sharp break with reigning theological interests. To them it came rather as the natural outcome of a sustained and cooperative criticism of Aristotelian ideas. If in the sixteenth century the more

The substance of this chapter, in somewhat expanded form, was printed in *The Renaissance Philosophy of Man*, ed. E. Cassirer, P. O. Kristeller, and J. H. Randall, Jr. (1948), as the Introduction to an Eng. tr. of Pomponazzi's *De Immortalitate Animae*. It was reprinted in J. H. Randall, Jr., *The School of Padua and the Emergence of Modern Science*: Series *Saggi e Testi* of Il Centro per la Storia della Tradizione Aristotelica nel Veneto of the University of Padua and the Columbia University Seminar on the Renaissance, No. I (Padua, 1961), with some additions and the Latin texts.

original minds were finally led to a formal break with the Padua teaching, we must not forget that even Galileo occupied a chair there from 1592 to 1610, and that he remained in method and philosophy if not in physics a typical Padua Aristotelian.

That Italian Aristotelianism was thus able to lead the European schools in the fifteenth and sixteenth centuries is due to several circumstances, not the least of which is the settled commercial prosperity the Italian cities had now achieved. Fundamental also was the close alliance between the study of Aristotle and the study of medicine, which led to strong emphasis on the physical writings and on methodological questions; a physician's Aristotle is bound to differ from a theologian's. And the liberty of teaching and speculation guaranteed by Venice since 1405 attracted the best minds from all over Italy, especially the philosophical southerners. Padua remained till the days of Galileo the leading scientific school of Europe, the stronghold of the Aristotelian qualitative physics, and the trainer even of those who were to break with it.

I

To the story of he development of natural science in this Padua school we shall return later. But scientific Padua felt also the effects of the same humanistic impluse and the same revival of learning that were inspiring Florence in the second half of the Quattrocento. To the challenge of Ficino it responded by proving that Aristotle as well as Plato spoke Greek; and to his attack on their traditional Averroism, with its fatalism and its strange conception of human nature that minimized all that was personal and individual, the Paduans replied, not by accepting his Platonic religious modernism, but by reorganizing their own naturalistic and scientific thought around a more individualistic conception of man and his destiny. To the Florentine Platonic humanism they opposed an Aristotelian humanism close to the naturalism of Aristotle himself and fitting in well with their dominant scientific interests. Not until Spinoza and the eighteenth-century Newtonians is there another figure who manages to effect so "modern" a blend between humanism and scientific naturalism as Pomponazzi and Zabarella; Spinoza, indeed, can well be understood as a mathematically minded Averroist.

In 1497 the Faculty of Arts at Padua petitioned the Senate of

Venice for a new chair for the teaching of Aristotle in Greek. The Senate acceded, and Leonicus Thomaeus, who knew Greek from his native Epirus, was installed as the first to expound the Stagirite in his own tongue. This event marks not only the end of several decades of effort to rediscover Aristotle himself; it marks also the end of the older literal-minded Averroism. Vernia and Nifo, its last defenders, had already, with better texts, and under pressure from the Humanist bishop of Padua, abandoned the crudities of Averroes' view of man's nature. Thereafter not even Achillini was prepared to defend the literal unity of the intellect; and Averroism thenceforth meant primarily a vision of knowledge and a freedom from theological compromise.

Bruni had begun a fresh translation of Aristotle; Bessarion had done the *Metaphysics*. The Paduans used in part the new version of the Venetian antischolastic Ermolao Barbaro, but chiefly that of Argyropolus, a Byzantine who taught at Padua before joining the Medici circle. The orthodox Averroists had emphasized the logical side of Aristotle, using the traditional Latin terms and distinctions from which the master's own functional meaning had evaporated. These abstract nouns reinforced the Platonizing tendencies of the Averroistic commentaries to make independent existences out of the substantives of discourse. Verbs were turned into nouns, and operations into substances. The result can best be described as a very Neoplatonic or dialectical naturalism. The first effect of Humanism in Padua was to send men directly to the Greek text and the ancient commentators. The group of innovating "Alexandrists" who appear at the end of the century derive their name from Alexander of Aphrodisias, the best of the Greek commentators on Aristotle, whom they cited and studied. But the Averroists had likewise cited Alexander; his views they found discussed in the Commentator himself. The significant difference is not that another commentator is followed, but that we find a group of Aristotelians thinking and talking in Greek, with a sense of the Greek words and distinctions, and considering not isolated texts, but the whole course and spirit of the argument. We suddenly discover a functional Aristotle as the setting for the Aristotelian logical distinctions; we find the operations of things given more importance than the statement of their essences. We find real Hellenists, real Aristotelian naturalists. And we find strong humanistic interests: whereas before the *Physica* had been the center of study, now it is the *De Anima* and the interpretation of human nature that awaken controversy. Portius, an "Alexandrist," tells us how when he began to lecture on the *Meteors*, he was interrupted by his students with loud cries of, "We want the Soul!" Like the Platonists, the Paduans began discussing God, freedom, and immortality in relation to the individual soul; but unlike them, they arrived through Aristotle at naturalistic conclusions.

I I

Though the older Averroists had been more concerned with the world than with man, they had maintained an essentially impersonal and pantheistic view of human nature. Man is a composite of animal body and "cogitative soul"; he is an individual substance with a matter and a form of his own. His body is a mixture of the four elements; his proper form, the "cogitative soul," is a power of the senses or imagination—that is, it is a bodily function, a material form, which comes into being with the body and suffers corruption with it. But man could not know without an additional rational soul, which by becoming the forms of all things understands them. In order to assimilate the forms of things without their matter, this passive or "possible" intellect must be, as Aristotle said, "apart and impassive and unmixed." It cannot therefore be the form or entelechy of any particular body, joined to and subject to its matter; it is not united to the body save in conferring upon it the function of knowing. It is a perfect and eternal substance, the lowest in that hierarchy of "intelligences" which inform the heavenly spheres. United to men, not in its being but in its operation of intellection, this possible intellect uses the human body as art uses an instrument or a workman a knife. In this operation of intellection, it combines with man's power of receiving images, or "cogitative soul," to form the speculative or theoretical intellect by which a man actually knows.

The rational soul is thus like a sailor coming into a ship already constituted, and giving to man his outstanding operation, which is to contemplate and understand, just as a sailor steering a ship gives it the operation of navigation.[1]

[1] Zabarella, *De rebus naturalibus libri 30* (Venice, 1590), Lib. 27, *De mente humana*, cap. 3.

Being immaterial and eternal and apart from all matter, the possible intellect

is not multiplied in accordance with the number of men, but is only one in number in the whole human species; it is the lowest of the intelligences, to which is assigned the whole human species as its own proper "sphere," and that species is thus like one of the heavenly orbs. When any man dies, this intellect does not perish, but remains the same in number in those that are left.[2]

This single intellect of mankind thus enjoys an impersonal immortality; but individuals and their cogitative souls suffer dissolution and death. Men perish; only in the function of knowing do they partake of the eternal. Or rather, knowing is not a personal function at all; it is Truth which knows itself now in this man, now in another. For though this single human intellect is independent in existence, it cannot know truth save as it employs the sensitive powers of this or that human body.

The motives for this view are in part dialectical, like the arguments advanced for it; they aim at achieving consistency in the Aristotelian concepts, rather than at taking account of the facts of experience. Aristotle had said that intellect is "apart" from matter and independent of it, a deathless and eternal activity. He had also made clear that whatever is eternal, independent of matter and not individuated by it, can be only one in number in a single species. Moreover, if each body had its own intellect, then those intellects would depend on the body for their separate existence and die with it. They would be themselves parts of the body or bodily powers; as particular and material they could never know universals or indivisibles or abstract things, but could receive only particulars. They would thus be indistinguishable from sense. Nor could intellect be multiplied and individuated miraculously by an act of creation, as the faithful (and the Thomists) held, thus escaping these natural consequences. As Vernia puts it,

The moderns receive such an impossibility because they have been accustomed to hear it from childhood. For custom is second nature.[3]

[2] *Ibid.*, cap. 10.
[3] Vernia, *Contra Averrois opinionem de unitate intellectus* (Venice, 1505; dated 1492), fol. 7r.

But though these arguments are technical and dialectical, the motives behind them are fundamentally Platonic. The mind that knows Truth must be itself a member of a Platonic realm of Truth, itself an Idea, eternal and nonexistent, unchanging and impersonal, and not bound by the limitations of a particular body.

The possible intellect is a form capable of existing without matter. For it has an operation which does not depend on the body; neither therefore does its being. And if it does not in fact operate without sense phantasms, nevertheless it is capable of so doing.[4]

For there is no mean between the abstract and the material. Every form is thus either derived from the power of matter, and subject to generation and corruption, or else eternal in past and future, and separated from matter in its being.[5]

There must indeed be one realm of Truth common to all men. How could pupil learn from teacher were there two truths in two intellects? And such an eternal Truth always actualized *is* what we mean by intellect. Truth must ever be kept alive in some mind, and to be humanly accessible, in a human mind.

The speculative intellect is born and dies in this or that individual; in the human species as a whole it is eternal. There is always some thought being imagined in the imagination of someone, and consequently intelligible species and intellection being received in the possible intellect. In this way are first principles eternal, and the arts and sciences. And thus the possible intellect never ceases, absolutely speaking, from knowing,[6]

as it would if it depended on any particular individual.

Under the criticism of the Florentines, this Platonic emphasis grew stronger. Plato, Aristotle, and Averroes agree in everything but words, says Vernia. Philosophy is always perfect somewhere, in some human mind.

The intellect is always in act with respect to some individual of whatever species. And if not in this northern quarter in which we are, it will be so in the southern habitable part. The being of the world is never

---

[4] Achillini, *Opera Omnia* (Venice, 1508), *De intelligentiis,* Quod. III, Dubium i.

[5] Nifo, *De intellectu libri 6* (Venice, 1554; dated 1492), Lib. II, par. 15.

[6] Cajetan of Thiene, *Super libros De Anima* (Venice, 1514), Lib. III, Text. 5, Quest. 2.

wholly without some such individual being. Hence universals are the same with all men; whence comes the knowledge of all that is known.[7]

And the later Averroists, like Zimara, came more and more to identify this unity of the intellect with the unity of the rational principles in all men.

There is discernible here also a strong social sense of the unity of all men in the knowledge of the Truth. Knowledge is not a fragmentary individual possession, it belongs to all mankind, which forms, as it were, taken as a whole, a single Man. Men are essentially communistic in knowing—a psychological position that accords well with the theory of popular sovereignty advanced in the *Defensor Pacis* of the two early Averroists, John of Jandun and Marsilio of Padua. In a word, for the Averroists mind or intellect is not so much a personal activity as a realm. As befitted their impersonal interest in nature, their sense of the intelligibility of the world was far stronger than their sense of the individual intelligence of the knower.

Alexander Achillini, who taught a vigorous and independent Averroism both at Padua and from 1508 to 1512 at Bologna, tried to find a place for human individuality within this framework. Man is a true substance, made single and individual by his cogitative soul in conjunction with the possible intellect. Differences in intellectual power come from the body, rather than the intellect, from the senses and the bodily spirits, from the greater efforts of different cogitative souls.

And thinking is in our own power, not only because the intellect is our form, but also because the operation of the senses which thinking follows is in our power.[8]

But Padua had already found a better defense for humanistic values in the thought of Achillini's lifelong antagonist, Pomponazzi.

This Averroistic view of man was vigorously maintained by Nicoletto Vernia, holder of the first chair in philosophy from 1468 to 1499, "so that almost all Italy was converted to the error."[9] Vernia became involved in a quarrel with the Scotist theologians, who had little intellectual standing at Padua; and the Bishop finally got him and his pupil Nifo to cover their views with a transparent

[7] Vernia, *De unitate intellectus,* Opinio Averrois.
[8] Achillini, *De intelligentiis,* Quod. III, Dub. ii.
[9] A. Riccoboni, *De gymnasio patavino* (Padua, 1598), VI, cap. x, fol. 134.

veil of submission. But writing of the last decade of the century, Contarini could say:

> When I was in Padua, in that most celebrated university of all Italy the name and authority of Averroes the Commentator were most esteemed; and all agreed to the positions of this author, and took them as a kind of oracle. Most famous with all was his position on the unity of the intellect, so that he who thought otherwise was considered worthy of the name neither of peripatetic nor philosopher.[10]

Contarini goes on to say that he too was convinced that Aristotle believed in a single immortal intellect. Unable to accept such a view, and like all the Paduans holding that Thomas' theory of special creation violated the principles of natural reason, he judged "the opinion of Alexander of Aphrodisias preferable to all others." Confronted by a choice between an impersonal immortality of the soul and a personal mortality, like many Paduans of that day he sided with human individuality and joined the *sectatores Alexandri*. For Alexander had figured in all the Averroistic discussions from Siger and Jaundun on as the foil to Averroes. He was the Aristotelian with a naturalistic and biological interpretation of the human mind; against him Averroes had insisted on the immaterial and abstract and therefore immortal nature of the operation of knowing, and hence of "intellect" as such. In the Commentator men found that Alexander believed

> that intellect is multiplied with the multiplication of individuals of the human species; and that it is subject to generation and corruption like other natural forms through the most noble mixture of primary qualities and the dissolution of that mixture.[11]

Generated naturally from the elements, it is inseparable from matter, and though the highest power of the soul, has a bodily instrument like sense.

What kept the Paduans from accepting this view was not its naturalism and denial of personal immortality: that they had long welcomed, and the Thomists they regarded as mere compromising theologians. What they missed in it was rather that Platonic vision of Truth they deeply felt and thought they found in Aristotle him-

[10] Cardinal G. Contarini, *Opera* (Paris, 1571), p. 179.
[11] Paul of Venice, *Summa Naturalium* (Venice, 1476; ed. Venice, 1503, as *Summa philosophiae naturalis*), Lib. V, *De Anima*, sec. II, cap. 37.

self. For in the act of knowing man seemed to them to lift himself above the limitations of an animal body and to see with a transparency and clarity no merely biological creature has a right to possess. The Paduans were not merely anticlericals, they believed in a rational science; and until some way could be found to reconcile the rational vision of truth with its biological conditions, they persisted in their Platonism. Intellect could not be mere matter. It is significant that the atomism of Lucretius was always held at Padua to be crudely unscientific. So long as there seemed to be no mean between the purely material and the abstract reason, they insisted that human nature participates in the latter.

When the actual text of Alexander was made known and read, it was found that he did provide such a mean. He was no mere materialist, as Averroes had charged: he made a place for reason.

Alexander maintained that the intellective soul is a form constituting matter, and derived from the power of matter; yet it is not "organic," for it is not localized in any organ of the human body.[12]

Alexander held it to belong to the things that are generated; but with some part of itself it agrees with things eternal, namely, in understanding and willing; which comes from its being a mean between the eternal and the non-eternal, and the first of material forms.[13]

III

The man who solved this dilemma of the Paduan theory of human nature was Pietro Pomponazzi of Mantua (1462–1525). Called "the last scholastic and the first enlightener," he did indeed partake of the nature of both: of the latter in his fiery zeal against the theologians, his scorn for all comfortable and compromising modernism in religion, and his sober vision of the natural destiny of man; of the former in his refusal to leave the bounds of the Aristotelian tradition, in his meticulous use of the medieval method of refutation, and in his painstaking attention to the reasons by which a position was defended. But as the Renaissance mean between the two, he shared the spirit of his age: its concentration on man and his destiny, its

[12] Zabarella, *Commentarii in 3 Aristotelis libros De Anima* (Frankfurt, 1606), Lib. III, Text. 6, col. 743.
[13] Luigi Ferri, *La psicologia di P. Pomponazzi secondo un manoscritto della Biblioteca Angelica di Roma* (Rome, 1877), containing selections from an unpublished commentary on the *De Anima*, Lib. III, Text. 8, p. 156.

view of human nature as the link between heaven and earth, its reverence for the authority of the ancients—for him, Aristotle— and despite all theory its Stoic temper of mind. Like his great Platonic rival Ficino he sought to examine man's destiny in independence of all dogma; but whereas the Florentine vindicated the dignity of the individual soul by elevating it in freedom above Nature, the Paduan made the soul a natural inhabitant of an orderly universe. Within his close-knit argument there burns a vision of man, more akin to the insight of that other Florentine, Machiavelli, than to the sentimental piety of the Academy—and to that of the lens-grinder of Amsterdam. Nor is Pomponazzi merely the realist as against aspiration, the man who came closer to the biological Aristotle than any save his own follower Zabarella. To our way of thinking, though he stripped both Thomism and Averroism of their accretions of Platonism, he was a better Platonist than Ficino or Mirandola: for he knew that Platonism is vision and not metaphysics, and that vision he respected and fought for.

Pomponazzi did not start as an Averroist; he was brought up by his teachers as a Thomist, and he early distinguished himself against the pupils of Vernia. Indeed, he remained a good Thomist, within the free spirit of Padua, until he left for Ferrara in 1509 when the wars closed the university. The Padua system provided every professor with an antagonist or *concurrens* of different views who lectured at the same hours. Pomponazzi taught first against the Averroist Nifo; after Bembo secured him Vernia's chair on the latter's death in 1499, his *concurrens* was Fracanziano. Achillini removed to Padua in 1506, a bitter rival; and both went to Bologna together. All these opponents of Pomponazzi were Averroists; two, pupils of Vernia; and the disputes with Fracanziano in particular seem to have shaken his Thomism. They were over the relation of the intelligences to the heavenly spheres, a question fundamental to human nature, since the intellect was an "intelligence" and mankind a "sphere." They convinced him that a *forma informans et dans esse*, that is, a true substantial form, cannot be separable from its matter. Too proud to admit defeat, and still too much of a Thomist to become a narrow Averroistic partisan, he left for Bologna to reconstruct his thought. There in 1516 appeared his short but epoch-making essay, *De immortalitate animae.*

Pomponazzi was thus a Thomist half-converted to Averroism. He consistently uses Thomas against the unity of Averroes' position, and Averroes against the separability and immortality of Thomas'. The naturalism and, he would have said, the Aristotelianism of each he employs against the Platonism of the other. It is significant of the cooperative character of the Padua school that he advances hardly a new argument, but merely collects and marshals with great skill the arguments elaborated for generations. He may have found the inspiration for his intermediary position in Alexander, and he certainly puts it in Alexander's mouth; but in neither his commentaries nor his less formal treatises does he follow Alexander in detail, or any of the Greeks. Averroes, Thomas, Jandun, and the Latins in general are his chief supports. And yet out of this traditional material comes a position of striking originality and power: that a natural bodily function, a *forma materialis*, can behold rational truth. Pomponazzi may have derived his interpretation of Aristotle from Thomas de Vio, Cardinal Gaetano, a Dominican teaching at Padua with him, who published a commentary on the *De Anima* in 1509, maintaining that Aristotle taught the mortality of the soul. But his problem, and its solution, are his own.

For it is the problem of man's nature, his operations and their conditions, and their unity in a single being.

Man's nature is not simple but multiple, not certain but twofold, a mean between mortal and immortal. This is clear if we inspect his essential operations, from which we gather his essence. His vegetative and sensitive functions, which cannot be exercised without bodily instruments, point to mortality. His thinking and willing, operations which are exercised without bodily instrument, and argue separability and immateriality, and hence immortality, number him among things immortal . . . The ancients spoke well who placed him between the eternal and the temporal, as neither purely eternal nor purely temporal, since he participates in both natures, and existing between them has the power to assume which he will.[14]

How are these two natures combined in man? Pomponazzi contemptuously brushes aside the Averroistic answer.

Not only is it false in itself, it is unintelligible and monstrous, and entirely alien to Aristotle; nay, I think that Aristotle never even thought

[14] Pomponazzi, *De immortalitate animae* (1516), cap. I.

of such nonsense, let alone believed it, though almost everyone takes it as his opinion. (cap. IV)

Thomas' despised refutation is conclusive. It is madness to say that Socrates is Plato, or that it is not Socrates himself who knows.

Socrates is distinguished from Plato, as this man from that man; but he is this man only through the intellect. Hence the intellect of Socrates is different from the intellect of Plato. For if the intellect of both were one, both would have the same being and operations; but what can be thought of more foolish? (cap. V)

Nor does the Platonic view, that man is a soul using a body, a combination of mover and moved, serve better to account for the individual unity experience reveals; this position Thomas has abundantly refuted also. For it soul and body have no more unity than oxen and a cart.

If the essence by which I feel were different from that by which I think, how could it be that I who feel am the same as I who think? For we could then say that two men joined together had a mutual cognition, which is ridiculous. (cap. VI)

But the view of Thomas himself, though true in faith, seems contrary to Aristotle and to natural reason. Thomas is right in taking the intellect as the true form and entelechy of the human body, as its natural functioning. He is wrong in making it separable from matter, and capable of continued existence after death. Pomponazzi goes on to give a thoroughly naturalistic and functional interpretation of Aristotle. In all its operations the intellect needs the body and the corporeal sense images it furnishes.

Aristotle says, It is necessary for the knower always to have before him some image; and by experience we know that we always need images, as each observes in himself, and as an injury to the organs demonstrates. . . . Hence Aristotle says, If then knowing is either imagination, or never takes place without imagination, intellect can never be separated. (cap. VIII)

The answer to his problem which Pomponazzi thinks agrees with Aristotle and natural reason, is that the soul is essentially and truly mortal, relatively (*secundum quid*) and improperly speaking immortal. He bases this position on an analysis of the operations of the soul, particularly those connected with the function of knowing, and on their conditions. All knowing, both sensitive and intellectual, is a function of the same soul; and it is true that in some fashion all knowing abstracts from matter. But there are three modes of separation from matter, corresponding to three modes of cognition in the universe. There is the total separation from matter by which the intelligences know; there is the lowest separation by which the sensitive powers know, needing a body both as their subject and as their object, and limited to particulars. But there is a third and intermediary kind of separation—here Pomponazzi diverges from Averroes—in which the body is needed as object but not as subject. And this mean is the human intellect.

The sensitive soul is *simpliciter* the act of an organic physical body, for it needs the body as subject, since it performs its office only in an organ, and as object. But the mean, which is the human intellect, is in none of its operations either totally freed from the body or totally immersed in it; hence it does not need the body as subject, but does as object. (cap. IX)

Hence on the one hand the soul is a material form, a bodily function, generated by the parents and not by special creation:

The human soul, the supreme and most perfect of material forms, is truly a form beginning with and ceasing to be with the body, nor can it in any way operate or exist without the body; (cap. IX)

on the other hand,

since it is a mean between the absolutely abstract and the immersed in matter, in a certain manner it participates in immortality, as its essential operation shows. For it does not depend on the body as subject, in which it agrees with the intelligences and differs from the beasts; but needs the body as object, in which it agrees with the beasts, and is mortal. . . . To need an organ as subject is to be received in the body in a manner both quantitative and bodily, with extension, as we say all the organic powers receive and perform their functions, like the eye in seeing and the ear in hearing. . . . Whence we say the intellect does not need the body as subject in its knowing, not because knowing in no wise takes place in the body, since if the intellect is in the body it cannot be that its immanent operation should not also be in it in some fashion. For where the subject is, there must its accident be. But knowing is said not to be in an organ and in the body, since it is not in it in a quantitative and bodily manner. Wherefore intellect can reflect on itself, reason, and grasp universals; which organic and extended powers cannot do at all. This all comes from the essence of intellect, since as intellect it does not depend on matter or quantity. (cap. IX)

In a word, while knowing requires material conditions, and is thus the activity of a human body, it does not function materially, but rises above the limitations of those conditions to grasp universals and truth.

The human intellect indeed cannot know unless in matter there exist sensible quantities and qualities; for it cannot operate without existing, and it cannot exist without the required conditions; but it does not follow that it knows by means of those conditions. It is the same with sense. For the visual power does not see unless the eye is warm; but it does not see by means of warmth or any other real quality, but by visible species. (cap. X)

Knowing needs a body, but it does not take place in any localized part of the body; it would then be "organic," and limited by its organ. Knowing takes place in the body as a whole.

Hence just as intellect is in the whole body, so is knowing. And thus Alexander did well to make the whole body the instrument of intellect, since intellect comprehends all its powers, and not any determinate part . . . But although the whole body is thus the instrument of intellect as though it were its subject, it is not truly the subject, since knowing is not received therein in a bodily manner. (cap. X)

Although Pomponazzi follows the whole Greek tradition in deriving the nature of the soul from an analysis of its function of knowing, he examines also and refutes all the extraneous moral and pragmatic arguments for immortality. To know the soul is mortal is in fact a great gain, for it makes possible at last a human morality, a chief end for man as man in which the humanistic values are aimed at. And since the Averroists had also denied personal immortality, Pompo-nazzi seems in his restrained tones to be delivering to that age, so eager to find a way of living based on the nature of man himself, the wisdom of the long Padua tradition: the community of mankind in knowledge and truth.

The whole human race can be compared to one single man. But in one human individual there are multiple and divers members, ordered to divers offices or divers proximate ends, yet all are directed to a single end . . . The universal human race is like a body composed of different members, with different offices but ordered to the common utility of the human race. Each gives to the other, and receives from him to whom he gives, and all have reciprocal works. Nor can all be of equal perfec-tion, but to some are given gifts more perfect, to some less perfect . . .

All men in pursuing this common end should communicate in three intellects: the theoretical, the practical, and the productive. For no man of mature and due age fails to possess something of these three intellects, as there is no member which does not participate in blood and natural heat . . . The end of the human race in general is to participate in these three intellects, by which men communicate with each other and live; and one is useful or necessary to another, as all the members in a man communicate in vital spirits, and have mutual operations together. And from this end no man can be absolved.

As to the practical intellect, which is proper to man, every man should possess it perfectly. For that the human race be rightly preserved every man must be morally virtuous, and so far as possible shun vice . . . With the other intellects it is not necessary, nor is it possible. Nor does it agree with the human race; for the world would not endure if every one were theoretical; nor would man himself, since it is impossible for one kind of man, like the philosophical, to be sufficient unto itself . . . Whence the general end of the human race is to participate relatively in the theoretical and productive, but perfectly in the practical . . . Thus not everyone has the final end which suits the part: it is enough that he have the common human end. Whence if man is mortal, every man can have the end which suits man universally; what suits the most perfect part, not every man can, nor is it fitting . . . Happiness does not consist in the theoretical power of demonstration, as suitable for the whole human race, but as suiting its principal part. And though the other parts cannot arrive at such happiness, still are they not entirely deprived of all happiness, since they can have something of the theoretical and something of the productive, and the practical perfectly. Which power can make almost everyone blessed. For farmer or artisan, poor or rich, if he live morally, can be called happy, and truly so called, and can depart contented with his lot.

And since such speculation does not seem able to make man happy, as it is weak and obscure, I say that although it be so in relation to eternal things, and to that of the intelligences, still among mortal things nothing can be found more excellent, as Plato says in the *Timaeus*. Nor should a mortal desire immortal happiness, since the immortal does not suit the mortal, just as immortal wrath does not suit mortal man. Whence we suppose that to each thing a proportionate end is assigned. For if man is temperate, he does not desire the impossible, nor is it fitting: for to have such happiness is proper to the gods, who do not depend on matter and on change. The opposite prevails with the human race, which is a mean between the mortal and the immortal.

And if it be added that since man knows he will soon be lost, and that he can be taken off in many ways, he will have more misery than happiness; I say that it belongs to an illiberal man not to wish to restore what he has freely accepted. He will give thanks to God and nature, and will always be prepared to die, nor will he fear death, since fear of the inevitable is vain; and he will see nothing evil in death. And if it be inferred, that the condition of man is far worse than that of any brute; surely in my opinion this is not said philosophically, since the works of beasts, though they bring content to their kind, do not content the intellect. Who would prefer to be a stone or a stag of long life, rather than a man of however low degree? . . . The wise man would much prefer to be in extreme necessity and in the greatest tribulation, rather than to be a fool, ignorant, and vicious under the opposite conditions. (cap. XIV)

And for the rewards and punishments of the hereafter Pomponazzi has only scorn.

No evil remains in essence unpunished, nor any good unrewarded in essence. For reward and punishment have two meanings: one is essential and inseparable, the other accidental and separable. The essential reward of virtue is virtue itself, which makes man happy. For human nature can possess nothing greater than virtue itself, since it alone makes man secure and removed from all perturbation. All things work together for him who loves the good; fearing nothing, hoping for nothing, but in prosperity and adversity ever the same, as is said in the *Ethics*. But it is the opposite with vice. For the punishment of the vicious is vice itself, than which nothing can be more miserable, nothing more unhappy . . .

Accidental reward or punishment are those that can be separated, like gold or any penalty. And not all good is rewarded thus, and not all evil punished. Nor is this unfitting, since they are accidental. There are two things to be known: first, that accidental reward is far more imperfect than essential reward, for gold is more imperfect than virtue. And accidental punishment is far less evil than essential punishment; for accidental punishment is the punishment of a penalty, essential, that of guilt: but the punishment of guilt is far worse than the punishment of a penalty. Secondly, when good is accidentally rewarded, essential good seems to be diminished, and not to remain in perfection. For example, if anyone acts virtuously without hope of reward, and another with hope of reward, the act of the second is not considered as virtuous as that of the first. Whence he is rewarded more essentially who is not rewarded accidentally. Likewise he who acts viciously and is punished accidentally seems to be punished less than he who is not punished accidentally; for the punishment of guilt is greater and worse than the punishment of penalty, and when the punishment of penalty is added to guilt, it diminishes the guilt. Whence he who is not punished accidentally is punished more essentially than he who is punished accidentally . . . Whence those who claim that the soul is mortal seem better to save the grounds of virtue than those who claim it to be immortal. For the hope of reward and the fear of punishment seem to import a certain servility which is contrary to the grounds of virtue. (cap. XIV)

Although Pomponazzi concluded his essay with the formal contention that the immortality of the soul is a "neutral problem," like that of the eternity of the world, and that neither its affirmation nor its denial can be proved by natural reason, an uproar broke out among the clergy. They persuaded the Patriarch and the Doge to burn the book and proclaim him a heretic; a copy was sent to his patron, Cardinal Bembo, to be condemned in Rome. But Bembo found no heresy in it, and Leo X, who loved a good fight, encouraged both sides in the controversy. In 1517 Pomponazzi answered his various detractors in an *Apology*, and in 1519 wrote a *Defensorium* against the voluminous and labored defense of Thomas by Nifo. The *Apology* is a more detailed and better book than the first: stung by the attacks, Pomponazzi replies with passion to the monks and priests, and with searching analysis to the criticisms of his old fellow-student and Thomist Contarini. Immortality is no longer a neutral problem: it is wholly contrary to natural principles. He is prepared to die for its truth as an article of faith; but he will not teach that it can be demonstrated by reason.

A philosopher cannot do this; especially if he be a teacher, for in so teaching he would be teaching falsehood, he would be an unfaithful master, his deception could be easily detected, and he would be acting contrary to the profession of philosophy.[15]

Natural theology is indeed so weak and ridiculous that it brings Christianity itself into disrepute: like so many rationalists since, Pomponazzi defends the letter of orthodoxy against the liberals and Platonists. Only with the resurrection of the body, with supernatural grace and redemption, is immortality consistently conceivable. Indeed, were the soul by nature immortal, how would grace be a merit? With great clarity he works out the logic of immortality—all founded, of course, on the abrogation of natural knowledge. The plea from ignorance receives short shrift.

Contarini, however, pushed him to a more exact analysis of the soul's functioning, and an interpretation of all the doubtful Aris-

[15] *Apologia*, Lib. III, cap. 3.

totelian passages. At first he had maintained that intellect does not need the body as subject; Contarini forced more radical views. In the *Apology* intellect has become extended, like other forms, but is still indivisible; finally, in *De nutritione* (1521), he admits divisibility also. Intellect is indissolubly united to the body in its existence; it is in its functioning that it rises above the body, acts independently, and receives universals. Thus a mortal soul can know immortal truths: it is in the act of knowing, not in its substantial character, that it is "separable and impassive and unmixed"—an interpretation thoroughly Aristotelian in spirit. Only for Contarini's question, Why then has the intellect no localized organ? did Pomponazzi have no answer; it remained for Zabarella to make the "imagination" the organ of intellect.

IV

Pomponazzi did not confine his naturalism to psychology. He saw in nature an orderly uniformity of law that admitted no miracles, no demons or angels, not even any direct divine intervention. In *De naturalium effectuum admirandorum causis* (1520) he sought to explain all miraculous cures and events through purely natural causes, through natural powers not ordinarily experienced, and through the constant and regular influence of the heavens. Against Pico's denial of astrology as incompatible with human freedom, he tried to make an orderly and rational science of the stars, opposed to all superstition—the naturalist's answer to the humanist.

All prophecy, whether vaticination, or divination, or excess, or speaking with tongues, or the invention of arts and sciences, in a word, all the effects observed in this lower world, whatever they be, have a natural cause.[16]

The recorded miracles of religion are not events contrary to the natural order, they are merely unaccustomed and rare. The very conception of an immaterial spirit precludes any particular operation.

In vain do we assume daemons; for it is ridiculous and foolish to forsake what is observable, and what can be proved by natural reason, to seek what is unobservable, and cannot be proved with any verisimilitude.[17]

[16] *Apologia*, Lib. II, cap. 7.   [17] *De causis*, cap. 1; (ed. 1567, p. 20).

No effect is produced upon us by God immediately, but only through the means of his ministers. For God orders and disposes everything in an orderly and smooth manner, and imposes an eternal law on things which it is impossible to transgress. (cap. 10)

Pomponazzi goes on to give a naturalistic account of the origin and development of religions themselves.

Those men who are not philosophers, and who indeed are like beasts, cannot understand how God and the heavens and nature operate. Therefore angels and daemons were introduced for the sake of the vulgar, although those who introduced them knew they could not possibly exist. For in the old testament many things are alleged which cannot be understood literally. They have a mystic sense, and were said because of the ignorant vulgar, which cannot understand anything not bodily. For the language of religions, as Averroes said, is like the language of poets: poets make fables which though literally impossible, yet embrace the truth of the intellect. For they make their stories that we may come into truth, and instruct the rude vulgar, to lead them to good and withdraw them from evil, as children are led by the hope of reward and the fear of punishment. By these corporeals they are led to the knowledge of incorporeals, as we lead infants from liquid food to food more solid. (cap. 10)

Religions are born and die like all things human; for their renewing striking signs are needed among men, and therefore powers are placed in nature whose exercise is rarely called for.

Since a change of religion is the greatest of all changes, and it is difficult to pass from the familiar to what is most unfamiliar, for the new religion to succeed there is need that strange and surprising things be done. Whence on the advent of a new religion men making "miracles" are produced by the heavenly bodies, and are rightly believed to be sons of God . . . It is with religions as with other things subject to generation and corruption: we observe that they and their miracles are weak at first, then they increase, come to a climax, then decline, until they return to nothing. Whence now too in our own faith all things are growing frigid, and miracles are ceasing, except those counterfeit and stimulated, for it too seems to be near its end. (cap. 12)

In *De Fato, libero arbitrio, et de praedestinatione* (1520) Pomponazzi, starting from a treatise of Alexander's, made his choice between human freedom and natural law. After a detailed survey of the attempts to reconcile freedom and providence, he concludes that none has succeeded: it is either fate and providence, or free will, but not both. No view is satisfactory; the Stoics had the most consistent answer. And thus the Paduans ended by opposing a Stoic determinism to the freedom of the Florentines. Pomponazzi's whole view of natural law is in fact more Stoic than scientific in the seventeenth-century sense: it is the universe as a whole acting through "the heavens" that determines particular events, rather than some determinate sequence. And Alexandrianism can well be called a Stoic Aristotelianism.

V

Fifty years later the Padua school reached its pinnacle in Giacomo Zabarella (1532–1589). Heir of both the Alexandrians and the Averroists, and with encyclopedic interests that embraced the entire range of scientific studies, he was able in *De rebus naturalibus* (1590) to discuss each of the problems elaborated by the Paduans for over three hundred years, and with incomparable clarity and lucidity to sum up their collective wisdom in fresh contact with Aristotle's own words. The scholastic temper remaining in Pomponazzi has disappeared. With an exact knowledge of the Aristotelian text—he had a number of Greek codices—he combines a simplicity, a naturalness, and a directness of thought that bring him as close to the elusive Aristotelian spirit as any confessed follower has ever managed to come. Indeed, Aristotle's thought has been made so transparently his own that it seems unjust to call him a follower: it is Aristotle himself, speaking in the Latin of Padua—not the syllogistic Aristotle with a category for every emergency, but the Aristotle who insists on the primacy of subject-matter, of fact, of experience. It is the Aristotelian language used to express, not what the ancient Greek thought, but the truth itself. Zabarella is best known and most original in his logical writings, in which he completed the methodological advances of his predecessors and made them ready for Galileo: to this achievement we must return. But he summed up also the best wisdom of the Humanists about human nature, about its natural destiny and its high estate, combining a sober recognition of its finite conditions with that lingering odor of immortality which is the characteristic stamp of all humanism.

On the soul Zabarella stands much closer to Pomponazzi than to the Averroists: the Mantuan came nearer to Aristotle, he judged, than any other, though he left some questions unresolved. Zabarella is clear and explicit on all points—clearer than Aristotle's statements, though always close to his spirit. And he is both more humanistic and more naturalistic than Pomponazzi: the human soul does more itself, is less dependent on cosmic agencies, but it has ceased to be a "mean" and become frankly a bodily function. No more lucid analysis has ever been made of how reason can be a natural life of the body.

The soul is the principle of the animate body, both as form and as effective of its operations.

Form is duplex: one kind informs matter, and gives specific being and constitutes a thing as a difference added to genus; the other is form which does not give being, but supervenes upon the thing already constituted and possessing specific being, as something nobler, and gives only operation . . . The figure of a ship is called its "informing act," the sailor its "assisting act." . . . The question is, whether the rational soul is the form of man, as the figure of a ship is the form of a ship, or whether it is in man as the sailor is in the ship.[18]

To this question there can be but one answer:

The body is not the act of the soul, but the soul is the act of the body; it is not body, but something belonging to body, namely its act and perfection, whence the soul cannot exist without the body, since a perfection cannot exist without that of which it is the perfection . . . He who does not see that Aristotle plainly says that every soul is an informing form, is blind.[19]

The rational soul is thus clearly a bodily function, derived by natural generation from the power of matter; it is divisible and extended with the extension of the body.

Yet Aristotle rightly holds that in a sense the mind is "unmixed" with matter.

Our intellect can be called mixed or unmixed with the body in two ways: first, in its being (*secundum suum esse*), and secondly, in its operation (*secundum suum operari*), that is, as first act of the body, or in respect and relation to the second act . . . The first "unmixed" Aristotle never attributes to the intellect, but rather a contrary mixture, so that both Averroes and Saint Thomas are wrong.[20]

[18] Zabarella, *De rebus naturalibus; De mente humana*, cap. 2.
[19] *Commentarii in De Anima* (Frankfurt, 1606), Lib. II, col. 342.
[20] *Commentarii in De Anima*, Lib. III, Texts 6, 4.

Nor can anyone infer from the fact that the intellect in receiving uses no organ, that it is a form not joined to the body and not giving the body its being; it since is one thing to consider the intellect in its being, and another in its operation. For in its being it is a form of the body and truly informs matter, but in its operation it is more elevated above matter than the other parts of the soul, and in the reception of species does not use any part of the body as recipient,[21]

—though it can never operate without the simultaneous aid of the body in sense images.

The nature of the soul is admirable indeed, and raised above the conditions of the body, especially the intellective soul: for it is the form of man, by which man is man, and yet so sublime, and so incommensurate with the body, that it can receive intelligible species, without the body's receiving them. By its operation man is said to operate and know, for it is the form by which man is man, and therefore for it to operate is nothing else than for man to operate and know.[22]

Zabarella agreed that this is the human or possible intellect which though mortal in its being can behold immortal truth.

But besides the human mind, which is called possible, Aristotle thought there was necessary another active mind, without which there could be no thinking in man . . . What is this active intellect? Is it some part of our soul, or not, and what is its nature, and what is its function in our thinking? [23]

It does not abstract universals from particulars, as Thomas and Pomponazzi believed; that is the function of the human passive intellect, and nothing else intervenes actively in the process of knowing. The possible intellect can judge as well as receive, it can separate the universal from the particular; and Thomas was right in putting both an active and a passive power in the human mind. He was wrong in not seeing that before this abstraction can take place, the sense images have to be illuminated and made distinct; and this illumination and distinction is the work of the active intellect. As light illuminates colors and makes it possible for sense to receive and judge them, so the active intellect illuminates all our sense images and throws into relief their rational structure. It acts on the images, not on the human mind. It is a perfection and form joined to the images, and constituting with them one single object, like illuminated color;

[21] *De mente humana*, cap. 13.   [22] *De Anima*, III, Text. 6.
[23] *De rebus naturalibus*, Lib. 29: *De mente agente*, cap. 1.

it is that object, not the active intellect, which acts on the human mind.

The office of abstracting does not belong to the active intellect, but to the passive intellect; but abstraction necessarily presupposes the operation of the active intellect, which illuminates the images and makes clear and conspicuous all the natures and quiddities in them.[24]

This intellectual light functions, not by being itself intelligent, but by being intelligible; though as the actualization of the intelligible it is intellect, it does not function in human thinking as intellect, but as the intelligible structure of man's experience. Thus to Aristotle's question, What makes us know? Zabarella answers, It is Truth itself, the rational structure of the universe, joined to the images in our experience as their intelligible form. "The active intellect acts as intelligible and in the manner of an object"—not as a separate intelligible object in itself, but as the reason of the intelligibility of all other things. And it is this rational structure which is alone immortal and eternal, for it is God himself functioning as the world's intelligibility—God or Nature, one is tempted to add, in view of the striking resemblance between this thoroughly naturalized Averroism and the position of Spinoza.

In his view of the world, as distinguished from human nature, Zabarella like the other sixteenth-century Paduans followed the Averroistic interpretation of Aristotle, with its emphasis upon the heavens and their power through motion and light to induce the warmth that brings into being all earthly things—an emphasis not forgotten by the pupil of the Paduans, Telesio. The universe is eternal: matter, a quantitatively indeterminate power of receiving all forms, and motion are eternal. Although there was vigorous discussion of the mathematical innovations of the Ockhamite physicists, and their factual and experimental criticisms of Aristotle were accepted, the sixteenth-century Paduans on the whole continued a defense of the Aristotelian qualitative physics. The humanistic spirit, in fact, brought a new reverence for the authority of Aristotle, aided by the transparent fiction of the double truth, which identified Aristotle with the principles of natural reason.

This is clear in the last of the Padua Aristotelians, Cesare Cremonini (1550–1631). An outstanding anticlerical and religious ration-

[24] *De mente agente*, cap. 8.

alist, who led the successful fight against a Jesuit school at Padua, he was saved from the Inquisition only by the Venetian authorities. He maintained the Averroistic denial of creation, the immortality of the soul, and the personality and providence of God; God is only a final cause, the heavens are the efficient cause, and their being, properties, and laws are independent of God. Cremonini was at the same time the most vigorous and acute opponent of his friend and colleague Galileo, in the name of the Aristotelian physics and astronomy. In his many commentaries, written too late to find a publisher in the seventeenth century, the idea of a qualitative and logical physics really comes to grips with the triumphant new quantitative and mathematical physics of Galileo.

The rigorous Aristotelian doctrines of the Paduans enjoyed no vogue outside Italy; elsewhere the theologians dominated the schools. But their moral and religious rationalism, their critique of the ecclesiastical complex of ideas, had wide influence in France, and was the chief force in forming the thought of the *libertins* whom only the triumph of Cartesian rationalism was able to check for a generation, and who came into their own in the eighteenth century in alliance with a more novel and fashionable kind of science. Symbolic is the figure of Vanini, who combined Averroism with the new pantheistic nature philosophy of Cardano and Telesio, and, far from the protection of Padua, was burned at Toulouse in 1619.

3

Humanism North of the Alps: The Philosophy of Christ and the Augustinian Sceptics

I

THOUGH THE NORTHERN Humanists were dependent for both inspiration and ideas on the Italians, and though many of them, like Reuchlin and Colet, were in direct contact with the Florentine group, they brought those ideas into a significantly different situation and developed them in an atmosphere in which the currents of nationalistic divergence from the south were already felt. These differences, rooted in the more rapidly expanding economy of the northern lands, had come to center about the proper way to effect the necessary reconstruction of Christian institutions and traditions. In their diverging attitude toward the religious problem the northern Humanists already foreshadowed the solution which more resolute if less enlightened men were to give. The northerners took their religion more seriously and more literal-mindedly than the less dissatisfied Italians; they were both more attached to what they conceived to be its essence, and less willing to accept with a tolerant smile the accretions that had clustered about it. Hence the same grammarian's urge that led the Italians to seek enrichment in the pagan classics, in Plato and in Aristotle, led the Germans and French to concentrate on the Bible and the Church Fathers. Where the Italians were modernists, complacently accepting their inherited rites and practices provided they be allowed to interpret them with understanding imagination, the Germans were religious liberals and radicals, with genuine faith in the one thing needful and the resolve to share that faith with all men.

The Italians, profiting by their religion, did not need to break with it. Their humanists and naturalists could understand and enjoy

it; for the intellectual upper class, belief faded, but feeling and attachment remained. The northerners kept far more of the older
literal-minded belief and passionate faith: they remained more medieval in temper, more anxious to effect a real fusion between religion
and the new interests. And thus it was they who in their working
compromise created a genuinely new and vital type of religion;
while the Italians, with little support in popular feeling, soon gave
way before the constricting Counter Reformation and the deaden-
ing hand of Trent.

The German Renaissance passed speedily through its brief flowering into the Reformation; its intellectual expression took the form
of new theologies rather than new philosophies, new programs for
action rather than new ways of understanding. Its rejection of Aristotle was much more complete than the Italians': it had no basis
whatever for understanding the naturalism of the Paduan movement.
At the outset it was indeed allied with the new interest in astronomy:
Peurbach, leading astronomer of the fifteenth century, was the first
to lecture at Vienna on Virgil and Horace; Regiomontanus translated the Almagest from Greek at Rome under Bessarion's direction,
and returned to lead the Nuremberg Humanist circle. And from
Cusanus to Kepler there was a flourishing current of anti-Aristotelian
nature philosophy in Germany. But when the Germans turned to
Platonism to escape the science of the schools, it was not to the
artistic and worldly Platonism of Florence, but to the medieval and
religious Platonism of their own mystic and Augustinian tradition,
a Platonism that tended to concentrate on the soul and God, and
dismissed the world as of little consequence. In this Augustinian
tradition there were no easy steps from sense experience up to the
vision of the divine: for it the gulf between mere reason and faith
was wide and deep. The dominance of Augustine in both its philosophy and its theology is indeed the characteristic intellectual trait of
the northern Renaissance. But it was not the Platonic rationalism
of Augustine, which the Middle Ages had discovered and which was
again to inspire the seventeenth century: it was his scepticism of
human reason and science in the light of the divine wisdom. Whether
with the Reformers men passed at once from the soul to God, and
found that wisdom in his revelation, or with the Humanists tarried
in the examination of the soul itself, and found there a natural human

wisdom, they had but pity for the weakness and scorn for the presumption of mere science. The most original of the humanistic philosophies of the north, the so-called scepticism of Montaigne and his French followers, is a thoroughly humanized Augustinian scepticism.

This dominance of an antiscientific Augustinism is clear in the earliest German Humanists. Rudolf Agricola (1442–1485), Rudolf von Langen, and Alexander Hegius, rector of the mystic school at Deventer, were pupils of Thomas à Kempis before they were touched by the Italian learning. Johann Reuchlin (1455–1522) brought the Florentine Platonism to German soil; there he accentuated its hostility not only to scholasticism but to all rational knowledge. Reason (*ratio*) and the syllogism, indeed all discursive thought, can arrive only at practically useful opinion, never at genuine science. For that there is needed the divine illumination of the *mens*. "Knowledge of supernatural beliefs depends on mind, not on reason." Such illumination had been accorded the wise teachers of old, the Jews and Pythagoras; by the cabbalistic art we can recover it for our day. And so Reuchlin bent his great philological gifts in many tongues to the elucidation of a negative theology and a mystic gnosis.

As the ecclesiastical situation grew more tense, the Humanists concentrated more and more on discovering the authoritative Christian tradition in its original texts, the Bible and the Fathers. Biblical critics and reformers of churchly abuses, they desired to make of Christianity a purer and simpler gospel for this world. The hierarchies and realms of being of the Italian Platonists meant little to them; what men like Mutianus Rufus or Erasmus took over from the Florentines was rather their idea of a universal and simple religion. But they did not seek this "essence of Christianity" in the strange lore of other religions; they turned directly to the careful examination of the literature of Christianity itself.

II

Jacques Lefèvre d'Étaples (Jacobus Faber, 1455–1536), leader of the French Humanists, applied the grammarian's method to the Scriptures, and emerged with the message of Jesus and the Protestantism of Paul. Returned from a visit to the Italian teachers in 1492, where he had met Ficino, Pico, and Ermolao Barbaro, he first set himself to expounding and editing the Greek Aristotle in Barbaro's very Christian interpretation; the "restored" Aristotle in France was thus by no means the naturalistic scientist of Padua. He edited Cusanus' works, in 1514, attracted by that synthesis of Greek and Christian ideas, and by its mathematical suggestions. But he turned more and more to biblical study as far superior to concern with human doctrines. In 1521 Guillaume Briçonnet, Bishop of Meaux, called him to head a circle of Humanists and theologians who were to produce the first translation of the Bible into French. The intimate and personal religion of St. Paul became the center of his thought: he commented on the Pauline epistles in typical Reformation fashion. Many of the younger men who worked with him became Huguenot leaders; protected by Margaret of Navarre, he died peacefully without breaking with the church.

Lefèvre disclaims any intellectual aid save the Bible itself:

The Bible contains all things which pass beyond, I do not say the gates of our intelligence, but those of all created intelligence not united by essence to Divinity.[1]

But he speaks the language of Augustinian wisdom:

Rational knowledge aids us to discover divine vestiges; but intellectual knowledge alone elevates us to the contemplation of the invisible and incomprehensible light.[2]

Human intelligences which have not received the divine light are able to produce nothing not more harmful than profitable, and are incapable of furnishing to souls a life-giving nurture . . . If human intelligences imagine themselves to have something of power, that is pure presumption on their part; what they give birth to is barren, heavy, obscure, and contains rather a poison than a food wholesome and conforming to the soul's needs.[3]

Paul himself is only the instrument of the divine wisdom acting in him; the grace of the divine light is necessary to make human intelligence fruitful.

Since it is within the soul that this grace operates, and since the

---

[1] *Correspondance des réformateurs*, ed. A. L. Herminjard, I, 92.
[2] A. Renaudet, *Préréforme et humanisme à Paris 1494–1517* (1916), p. 599.
[3] Herminjard, I, 4–5.

end of life is to cultivate the spirit in conformity with Scripture, the practice of this simple Pauline religion leads to a typical Augustinian inwardness, a concern with the inner self and its careful analysis. More philosophical in his interests and less concentrated on this narrow personal mysticism of Paul, Lefèvre's pupil, Bovillus (Bouillé, 1470–1553) employed the Platonism of Cusanus to place this inward self-criticism in a cosmic setting. The macrocosm is to be read in the mirror of the microcosm; there is true wisdom to be sought, the wisdom that is reflective self-knowledge, in which man recognizes at once his union with the divine and the peculiar individuality of his own spirit. Man's greatness lies in this power to achieve a reduplication of himself, to become a *"homohomo,"* to live in the divine and to see himself as so living. The Augustinian inwardness of these early French humanists culminates in the less mystical self-portraiture of Montaigne.

III

Inspired less by the personal religion of Paul and more by the ethical teachings of the Gospels and the pagan classics was Dutch Desiderius Erasmus (1467–1536), twelve years his junior, but equally valiant in bringing the methods of the grammarian to the discovery and defense of the "essence of Christianity." Greatest of all the Humanists as a personality and a literary influence, though scarcely more of a philosophical thinker than Lefèvre, Erasmus is the very epitome of the strength and the weakness of humanism as an active force in the affairs of men. He sharpened the twin weapons of the Humanist, the grammarian's criticism and the rhetorician's persuasion, to their most consummate perfection. As grammarian he edited the Latin fathers, Jerome, Hilary, Ambrose, and Augustine, crowning this work with a critical edition of the Greek New Testament. His intellectual inspiration was Roman rather than Greek, Cicero and the Fathers, not the speculations of Plato and Aristotle; and among the Fathers it was not the philosophical and mystical Augustine but the literary and urbane Jerome that was his favorite. He typifies the fatal indifference and hostility of the whole Humanist movement to the speculative or scientific imagination. From his student days he lumped together the logic-chopping of the Schoolmen and the fruitful developments of the mathematicians; any concern with science or with nature was a subject for ridicule and a distraction from the humane wisdom of life. With Cicero and Petrarch he judged the secrets of nature to be hidden beyond human powers, and not worth the fruitless search.

Through his friend and teacher John Colet he absorbed from the Florentine Platonists not their metaphysics but their practical program, a universal and tolerant ethical religion; stripped of its intellectuality and directed solely to conduct, this served as his one general guiding idea through all his subtle but mordant attacks on the religious institutionalism about him. His own grammarian's contribution was to reveal that simple moral teaching as the true lesson of the gospels and the genuine "philosophy of Christ," to bring the authority of Scripture to bear against the medieval corruption of biblical Christianity. He prided himself on being the Christianizer of the Renaissance and the humanizer of Christianity:

I brought it about that humanism, which among the Italians and especially among the Romans savored of nothing but pure paganism, began nobly to celebrate Christ.[4]

He saw in Jesus not a mystic redeemer but an enlightened moral teacher, and in the "philosophy of Christ" not a gospel of supernatural salvation but a call to a personal life of love, sympathy and forbearance.

The true way to worship the saints is to imitate their virtues, and they care more for this than for a hundred candles. Truly the yoke of Christ would be sweet and his burden light, if petty human institutions added nothing to what he himself imposed. He commanded us nothing save love one for another, and there is nothing so bitter that charity does not soften and sweeten it. Everything according to nature is easily borne, and nothing accords better with the nature of man than the philosophy of Christ, of which almost the sole end is to give back to fallen nature its innocence and integrity . . . Would that men were content to let Christ rule by the laws of the gospel and that they would no longer seek to strengthen their obscurant tyranny by human decrees.[5]

Disregarding the philosophical speculations for which he cared nothing in his search for the kernel of humane moral teaching, he easily found this simple humanitarian and undogmatic "philosophy

---

[4] Erasmus to Maldonato, March 30, 1527. In Preserved Smith, *Erasmus* (1923), p. 358.
[5] *Greek Testament,* ed. Erasmus, note to Matthew XI:30.

of Christ" in the Sermon on the Mount and in the counsel of Plato
and the Stoics alike; all shared equally in divine inspiration. Of the
Greeks he held,

Their philosophy lies rather in the affections than in syllogisms; it is a
life more than a debate, an inspiration rather than a discipline; a transformation rather than a reasoning. What else, pray, is the philosophy
of Christ? [6]

Like the Florentines, he wanted the Church to drop its elaborate
theology and sacraments to become a rational aid to the natural
moral life of men. But he was less willing to allow external rites and
ceremonies to remain as symbols, for he had not the imaginative
vision to see their human function; and against the essence of the
monastic ideal as well as its perversions he was far more bitter.

The world was put into a deeper slumber by ceremonies than it could
have been by mandrake; monks, or rather pseudo-monks reigned in the
consciences of men, for they had bound them on purpose in inextricable
knots. [7]

But he has the same exalted conception of human dignity and worth,
of man's power and freedom; without, to be sure, the philosophical
acumen to give it systematic grounding like the Platonists. Hence
when he was persuaded to defend human freedom and autonomy
against Luther, in his *Diatribe de libero arbitrio* (1524), his most
pretentious philosophical writing reveals his want of theoretical
power.

Erasmus had at first welcomed Luther's reforming attempts. But
Luther's full-bodied reaffirmation of the need for supernatural redemption was opposed to everything he stood for; and of the German's deep religious experience of the omnipotence of divine grace
he had not a trace himself.

By free will we mean that power of the human will by which man is
able to apply himself to those things which lead to his eternal salvation,
or turn aside from them.

Only if man has such a power can the gospel teaching possess
validity. Against that fact all the opposing passages in Paul must fall
away. Human freedom does not conflict with God's omnipotence,

[6] *Paraclesis*, in *Opera omnia* (Leyden, 1703), V, 141.
[7] Erasmus to Maldonato, in Preserved Smith, p. 359.

because the will of man and the will of God are cooperating powers: grace is the principal cause, human freedom the secondary cause. Luther's reply in *De servo arbitrio* was crushing, and led to Erasmus' final break with the reformer; despite Erasmus' desire for mediation, between the gospel of Luther and the philosophy of Christ there could be no reconciliation.

But if Erasmus was weak at the dialectic he disclaimed, in the art of rhetoric he had no equal between Lucian and Voltaire. Master of irony and innuendo, he flashed his rapier against all the enemies of the humanistic ideal, and in defense of a tolerant, humane, and cosmopolitan culture. These generous qualities have endeared him to all who hope that sweetness and light may prevail over the irrationalities of traditions outgrown and the eternal folly of mankind, that a passionate liberality of mind may be able to usher in a better day without the barbarism of new faiths and fanaticisms in bitter combat with the old. It was indeed tragic that he and his civilized Humanists had to give way before Luther and Calvin and Loyola, that they could not build gradually within the old Church a new culture and a new religion. It is easy to see in Erasmus the liberal caught between cold interest and burning faith, the liberal whose exposure of superstitious abuses and cruel dogmatism was used, not to banish intolerance and bitterness from the world, but to usher in new folly and new dogmas. But in truth Erasmus was of those liberals whose energies are exhausted in being liberal, without ever coming to grips with what has to be done. He looked backward rather than toward the new age; his program was that of a witty, charming, and mediating conservative. He lived too soon to ally himself with the scientific naturalism to which the future belonged. In excluding science from the world he was trying to build, he did not see that without scientific knowledge the liberal attitude is a slender reed, even as without that spirit science is a dangerous weapon. In the absence of that sure support, all his battles against the past made but for the substitution of new fanaticisms for old. Humanism, rejected as a guide to life by the priests of the old and the prophets of the new alike, slumbered on as an academic tradition until the scientific vision of the Enlightenment called it once more into the thick of the fight.

IV

German humanism was snuffed out by the deep convictions of the Reformation; in France it lived on under the protection of the sovereign secular state. Its stronghold was in the Collège Royale, founded by François I to offset the scholastic Sorbonne; there Ramus long waged war against Aristotle and science. As the struggle of Catholics and Huguenots grew sharper, to many the best way out seemed to lie in a purely secular culture; and amongst these *libertins*, supporters of the *Politiques* and the supremacy of the state, the Padua anticlericalism found fertile soil. To others the universal rational religion of the Florentines seemed more promising: Guillaume Postel proposed it in *De orbis terrae concordia* (1542). In such natural religion a real unity could be found which neither the sectarian Protestants nor the equally fanatical Catholics of Trent could furnish. Postel defended Platonism against the Paduans, rational religion against the freethinkers. And Jean Bodin (1530–1596), greatest French theorist of absolute monarchy on a purely secular basis, sought religious support for the Bourbon cause in the simple universal rational religion of the humanists. His *Colloquium heptaplomeres* demands tolerance for all confessions, as alike relatively true, in so far as they embody the religion of reason and nature of which they are all offspring: the unity of God, his moral worship, and belief in freedom, immortality, and future judgment. Only atheism and sedition should be suppressed by the state. Others in those troublous times found salvation in Stoicism, with Guillaume du Vair; the French Stoicism of the sixteenth and early seventeenth centuries was spiritualistic rather than naturalistic like that of the Paduans, and emphasized the autonomy of the human soul.

From its beginnings in the circle at Meaux, French Humanism had been far more distrustful of reason than the Italians or Erasmus; it had sought wisdom in the wellsprings of the inner life and in the careful analysis of the complexities of the human soul. As the bitterness of the wars of "religion" increased, this Augustinian opposition between man's thinking about the world and his inward experience of himself was accentuated; men unwilling to enter the partisan strife were thrown back upon the integrity of their own souls. But now disillusionment had been added as to the possibility of finding any universal truths about God even in the self; the one sure knowledge that needed no imposition on others was a knowledge of man himself. Scepticism as to all disturbing dogmas and creeds with their bloody fruits, and a Socratic self-knowledge leading to a Stoic acceptance and endurance, seemed the only way to inner peace while the storms were raging. The self-protecting arguments of the ancient sceptics found a welcome in the France of the three Henris; they seemed the best way to free a human morality based on man himself from any entanglement with theological speculations. In the greatest of these French Humanists, Montaigne, the exploration of human nature bore fruit not only in an utterly independent and autonomous practical wisdom of life; it rose above the resigned acceptance of the limitations of man's powers to a fascinated rejoicing in his infinite diversity. Montaigne can claim great credit for initiating that study of human nature which was to play so large a part in philosophic method for the next two centuries.

French scepticism may thus be regarded as a humanization of the widely current Augustinian temper of mind. Like all the Renaissance Augustinism, it was a protest against Aristotelian natural science, against starting with the world rather than with the human soul. True wisdom, a knowledge of the soul and God, is sharply opposed to the science of the temporal relations of the soul to the things of the world, with all the reinforcements that Sextus Empiricus can bring. But for it the study of the self is no mere prelude to the true theology. For its protest is just as strong against all superrational doctrines: wisdom is now confined to the soul alone, and God is wholly identified with the Nature that appears in the soul as Human Nature. This wisdom that is essentially self-knowledge, as against scientific and theological speculation exposed to all the traditional sceptical arguments, is the thread running through the wandering *Essays* of Michel de Montaigne (1533–1592). The Augustinian distinction between *Science* and *Sagesse* is fundamental in his endless application of the Augustinian method of self-examination. *Sagesse* is a knowledge of one's own nature, of a nature not accessible through the science and learning of men, but directly present in the soul to the discerning observer. It is a natural rather than a divine illumination, a natural grace bestowed on reason, conferring the power of self-discipline in the natural virtues, and a standard for rational discipline in the civic virtues of common living.

V

Montaigne was a magistrate of Bordeaux who retired into his castle and his well-stocked library to live amongst religious tumults as a contemporary of Plutarch. Why is there all this bitter conflict over creeds and theologies? Why this fight between seven sacraments and two? Why not admit we don't know, and that it would make no difference if we did; then we could stop killing each other. Montaigne stood for a tolerance based on scepticism as to any knowledge extending beyond man's own complex nature, any natural science, any theological doctrine, any social relation based on mere custom; and an intolerance of human pride of intellect and "presumption." For the world, it is best to follow the custom of the country and not to bother one's neighbors. One thing is certain, that natural *sagesse* which comes from rational insight into one's own nature: it leads to humility, the simple virtues, and a modest rational enjoyment of the goods nature has bestowed.

In his retirement Montaigne set out to record his opinions, qualities and moods for his friends. But the public reception of the *Essays* of 1580 led him to turn what had started as mere self-expression into a deliberate method. In portraying himself, he is really portraying Man; for "every man has in himself the whole form of human nature." [8] Indeed, he comes to set his self-study up in opposition to all other philosophy: "This is my metaphysic, this is my physic." [9] Presumption is our natural and original malady. We refuse to recognize the actual conditions of our being. We believe the world was made for us. Vacillation and irresolution is the most common and visible defect of our nature. We are chameleons with an infinite diversity. What imaginable custom is there that some do not follow, to the horror of the rest? And our ignorance is universal. Honest ignorance is bad enough, learned ignorance is worse, and the ignorance of those who presume to teach others worst of all. Even the Academics who deny that truth is attainable are presumptuous; best of all are the Pyrrhonic sceptics who are still seeking.

In his *Apologie de Raymond Sebonde*—a natural theologian whose

[8] Book III, ch. 12.   [9] III, 13.

work he had edited at his father's instigation—Montaigne marshals in fairly systematic form the sceptical arguments showing that this ignorance is inherent in the limitations of human nature. The natural theology founded on final causes collapses under his questioning. And what becomes of pantheism if the universe be really infinite? What can we hope to know of such a world? And the moral universe is equally infinite: Montaigne never tires of multiplying the variety of human customs. All values are relative and depend on the valuer:

We call value in things, not what they have, but what we bring to them.[10]

What kind of goodness is it which yesterday was respected and approved, tomorrow is no longer; which becomes a crime when we cross a river? what kind of truth, which is bounded by these mountains and is a lie beyond them? (II, 12)

Respect for laws does not come from their being just, but from their being laws; this alone is the mystic ground of their authority; they have no other. (II, 12)

Yet this very moral relativism frees man from dependence on any of the arbitrary conventions forced on him from without, and throws him back on himself, on his own nature. If the bounds of knowledge spring from the nature of man, it is nature within him that appears as the law-giver. If it is we who in our judgment assign all values, then values spring from our own being. And scepticism thus serves to introduce us to the true wisdom that is within our souls, that natural wisdom which in our theories and our customs we have so overlaid with sophistry and argument.

I love such as laws and religions do not make, but merely authorize; such as can subsist without their aid; born in us with their own roots, by the sowing of the universal reason, imprinted on every man whose nature is not destroyed. (III, 12)

What is this "nature" on which the relativity of all knowledge throws us back? Not a world to be described by science, for it is not in man's power to know the least part of the universe. It is the natural limits and conditions which man finds within himself. There is the only sure guide, the only human wisdom. And "divine wisdom

[10] Montaigne, *Essays*, I, ch. 40.

and human wisdom have no other distinction than that the former is eternal." (II, 12) For whatever the relation between God and nature, their voice within the soul is one. Nature is a proud and pitiless order, whose course is not to be altered; yet she is also a compassionate and gentle guide, the bestower of all good gifts. Pitiless she is if man rebels against the conditions she imposes; if he submits, she is the source of all his good. She can even teach man to die nobly—Montaigne has only scorn for the presumption that has invented the idea of immortality.

Leave this world—so speaks Allmother Nature to us—as you have entered it. The same step which you have taken without suffering or fear from death to life, take from life back to death. Your death is a member of the universe, a member in the life of all . . . Shall I interrupt this harmonious chain of things for you? It is a condition of your creation, a part of yourself. You flee in it only from yourself. (I, 19)

This natural wisdom teaches that while there is no single *summum bonum*, there are many goods, some freely bestowed, some to be striven after. Health, beauty, wisdom, and wealth, one must take as they are granted. But by *sagesse* the natural inclinations may be developed and directed, and in this harmonious development the soul can find its natural end in virtue and happiness. If we allow this natural wisdom to guide the reason, then we shall make the most of what we have; if we try artificially to dispense with it, to proceed by reason alone, we shall fall into the difficulties of all such human presumption. For reason guided by nature, by an appreciation of the natural conditions of human action and belief, is what wisdom is.

VI

If Montaigne is too large and too personal a figure to fit neatly into any facile classification, and if the suggestions of a philosophic position that can be found in his *Essays* are overshadowed by the fascination of the realistic portrait of man that emerges from his rambling pages, his friend and disciple Pierre Charron (1541–1603) sharpened his tentative distinctions and judgments into a more systematic philosophy and brought them back into the main stream of typically Augustinian scepticism as the preparation for true wisdom. Charron was a lawyer who despite his genial exterior had a strong strain of religious pessimism that led him to the priesthood;

as a teacher in Bordeaux he came under the influence of the older man. In 1593 he published a Catholic apologetic, his *Trois verités;* installed as canon in Candom, he issued in 1601 his true views in *De la sagesse.* He had learned from his teacher to accommodate himself to popular prejudice and custom.

The saying that everyone practices play acting holds in the truest sense of the wise man, who is always a different man within from what he shows himself without.[11]

When therefore his work brought theological attacks, and earned him the epithet of "brutal atheist," he willingly modified his radical attitude. Nevertheless he was stricken dead two years later on a visit to Paris.

His book is directed to the discovery of the true wisdom, to be found in the soul alone, without benefit of worldly opinions, of science, or of religious support. The start must be from a thorough examination of oneself: "The true science and the true study of man is man." When man has discovered the weakness and impotence of all his eager searching for truth, he realizes that to live well is to follow nature. With much reliance on the Stoic Seneca, Charron goes on to explain how this is to be done. Man is full of vanity, weakness, inconstancy, and misery. He differs from the animals only in degree; his one superiority, the mind, is the source of evils and crimes that no animal would commit. We know nothing; only our will is in our power. If we allow wisdom to guide it, we can master our passions; but to hear wisdom's voice we must be freed from all dogmatic prejudices to enjoy a universal and full liberty of mind. That is the true *preud'homie.*

The spring of this *preud'homie* is the law of nature, that is to say, the universal equity and reason, which shines and illuminates within each of us. It acts in accordance with God: for this natural light is a beam and ray of divinity, an emanation and dependence of the eternal and divine law. It acts also in accordance with itself, for it acts in accordance with what is noblest and richest in itself.[12]

Much more clearly than Montaigne Charron declares the independence of this wisdom from all religious dogma; in the marriage of piety and morality, the latter goes first and does not rest on the

---

[11] Charron, *De la sagesse,* II, ch. ii.   [12] *De la sagesse,* II, ch. iii, par. 4.

former, else were it a mere slave of the law under the whip of hope and fear.

I want man to be good without heaven or hell; to me these words are horrible and abominable: Were I not a Christian, did I not fear God and damnation, I would do that. O miserable coward, what merit do you deserve for what you do? You are not wicked, because you dare not be, and fear a beating. I want you to dare, but not to have the will, even though you are sure you will never be punished. You are good so that you may be paid and given great thanks. I want you to be good though no one ever know of it, I want you to be good because nature and reason, that is, God himself, want it; the general order and policing of the world, of which you are a part, requires it so; because you cannot consent to be otherwise, without going against yourself, your being, your good, your end, let come what will. I want also piety and religion, not to make, cause, or engender the *preud'homie* already born in you and with you, planted there by nature; but to approve it, authorize it, and crown it.[13]

The scepticism to which both Montaigne and Charron appeal as an instrument of self-knowledge and the road to wisdom had already been formally stated in more negative fashion and to different ends. Agrippa von Nettesheim (1486–1535), the German Neoplatonic magician and nature enthusiast, had turned at the close of a restless and tumultuous life to the peace of the ancient doubters. His *De incertitudine et vanitate scientiarum* (1527) marshals the sceptic's weapons against the alchemy and astrology and magic he had sought as well as against the schools, and castigates the clergy and the Church; all human life is worthless in the light of the lost paradise of certain mystic knowledge for which Agrippa still hoped. In France, Bonaventure des Périers had written a Lucianesque *Cymbalum Mundi* (1537) mocking the miracles and gospels. Omer Talon's *Academia* (1548) attacked especially the "philosophy of the pagans and the gentiles" in Aristotle, "the father of atheists and fanatics," in the true interest of Christian piety. In the year after that in which Montaigne's *Essays* appeared, 1581, Francisco Sanchez, Professor of Medicine at Montpellier and later at Toulouse, and in close touch with the Italian physicians, published a treatise on *The Very Noble and First Universal Science, That Nothing Is Known* (*Quod nihil scitur*). Sanchez's scepticism is directed primarily against the logical

[13] *De la sagesse*, II, ch. v, par. 29.

science of the Schoolmen in the interest not of a wisdom human or divine, but of a more empirical science. His spirit is close to that of the Italian empiricists:

We must not turn to men and their writings, which is to abandon nature, but above all we must put ourselves by experience in contact with things.

Sanchez employs the sceptic analysis against the scholastic textbooks he had to lecture on as professor: they are a mere play of words and definitions. True science is a perfect knowledge of the thing itself; but things are infinite in number, and so bound together in a system of changing internal relations that no one can be known without knowing the whole. Thus if the self be truly a microcosm, it too is unknowable: Sanchez's analysis does not stop with the certainty of self-knowledge. All knowledge, though it be imperfect, comes from sense images: since of the self we have not even these, of its nature we can arrive at no determinate conclusion. Perfect knowledge of things is limited to him who has created them. In comparison with this ideal, man must recognize that he knows nothing. He can gain, however, a modest knowledge by turning to observation, experiment, and critical judgment; and Sanchez's scepticism as to absolute knowledge sends him to the relative knowledge of the observer of nature. He added nothing to its method or practice, however; and as cardinal example of man's ignorance he took the magnet, with which experimental inquiry was to begin.

This French scepticism persisted well into the seventeenth century until the tide of Cartesian rationalism overwhelmed it. As late as 1671 François de la Mothe le Vayer (1588–1672) defended Sextus Empiricus, whose works were translated by his pupil Samuel Sorbière. But the main stream entered into the Augustinian framework, where Malebranche used it once more as the prelude to a Platonic rationalism, and Pascal as the approach to the human wisdom of Christian faith.

4

The Philosophical Significance of
the Reformation

I

THE REFORMATION was even less of an intellectual and philosophical movement than the humanistic Renaissance: its leaders detested natural reason, and turned for their inspiration not to ancient philosophies but to the theologies of the early Church. Nor was the central problem of religious salvation the problem that was to provoke modern thought. For the already stirring tides of scientific inquiry the Reformers had only hostility and contempt. They did not even possess that conception of a free and self-directing human personality which, for all their intellectual weakness in defending it, binds the Humanists to the later world. The one modern value they shared with Humanism, the individualistic protest against medieval institutions, was a very restricted and corporate individualism. And yet what the Reformers stood for, the principles to which they appealed and the changes they effected, had a profound influence on all subsequent philosophical thinking, so that without their labors it is inconceivable that European culture could have pursued the course it did. That all these consequences were indirect and wholly unintended is a cardinal illustration of the irrationality of human history.

The Reformation at its outset was not primarily an intellectual, moral or even religious movement; for a generation its confusion meant a distinctly lower level in all these respects. It started at bottom as an anticlerical revolt, as a pioneer enterprise in "trustbusting," in breaking the monopoly of the medieval Church. It was a product, that is, of the same forces that led to the Renaissance: the economic expansion that made all earlier institutions seem tight and constricting, the incipient capitalism that was to progress so rapidly in the north, the rising nationalisms that could not live within the circle of a united Christendom. And its outcome was much the same: a this-worldly ascetic morality of Puritanism, and a reaffirmation of traditional beliefs. Like the Humanists, the Reformers introduced certain characteristically modern judgments of life; but like them also, they reverted intellectually to world-views that antedated the Aristotelian naturalism of the later Middle Ages.

The Reformers stood for individualism, and they broke the power of the medieval ecclesiastical organization, where the Humanists had not; for they did not deny the need for supernatural salvation, but found a mechanism for it outside the Church. They stood for a moral ideal for this world, and they buttressed it with a religious sanction, where the Humanists had not. They succeeded, that is, in destroying the sacramental authority of the Church, and her traditional otherworldly asceticism. In the light of these deeds, it is not surprising that modern philosophy and modern thought should have flourished so largely on Protestant soil, and that even science, which started either under the Church's auspices, or among the anticlericals, but not in the Augustinian tradition to which the Protestants appealed, should have come to its own in northern Europe. In particular, the criticism of the ends of life—modern ethical thought— has been a prerogative of the Protestant cultures. The individualistic ethics thus built up over several centuries is in fact the greatest handicap Protestantism bears today. The Romantic idealism of the nineteenth century was almost wholly Protestant; it can with much truth appeal to Luther and his forbears as its founders. More naturalistic philosophies have since the eighteenth century been normally rather the product of a fading Catholicism.

The Protestants in their Augustinism made the personal life and experience primary, the test of all else: witness the "empiricism" of the British, and the richer *Geistesleben* of the Germans. They remained faithful to the Augustinism that had broken with the classic tradition of contemplation and theoria. For them too, *Im Anfang war die That*, not the Logos. Their attitude was at bottom not intellectual but moral; they sought primarily the means of acting, not of knowing. This enduring characteristic of German thought reached its most elaborate expression in Kant's foundation of pure or scientific reason on practical or moral reason. And the main stream of

British thought has been an appeal to experience as a test of ideas to be used in action, as an instrument for criticising political opponents.

II

It was no accident that the break with the Church was carried on in the name of the author of the *Confessions*, even as had been all the reforming and critical movements since the days of Wyclif and Hus. Nor is it surprising that those who had the courage of revolt should have appealed to the particular Augustine they did. That many-sided personality had managed to give consummate expression to most of the diverse needs to which the human spirit is a victim. Man's moral weakness he felt intensely, and the blessed salvation that comes when God sends his saving grace to strengthen the will. Man's intellectual feebleness and doubt he had bitterly experienced, and the sure certainty that comes from the divine illumination of the rational Master within. And man's individual impotence he knew, till he found the comfort and support of a great divinely instituted body of brothers in Christ. Augustine was an empiricist who tested everything in the fire of his own burning experience. He was a rationalist with a Platonic vision of truth all naked and alone. And he was an institutionalist who fully realized the human craving for social authority. To few has it been given to feel all these needs with the equal intensity of the African religious genius. Men have normally come to Augustine, as come they must, in search of one or another of the ways of salvation he bountifully offers. Since he made no attempt to fit them together in one comprehensive and neatly articulated scheme, but held them bound only in his living experience, it has been possible to select from his riches that vehicle of salvation that would satisfy one's own craving.

Augustine is the great Doctor of the organized Church, and as such Catholics have never been willing to give him up. He is also the great master and inspiration of the Christian Platonism of the Middle Ages, of that rational illumination which is divine wisdom and truth; as such we have found the Humanists appealing to him against the barren man-made learning of the Schools. And we have seen him using the dialectic of scepticism to send men to themselves and the natural wisdom there to be found.

No one of these Augustines was the Augustine of the Reformers. Against the Catholic they were in full revolt, although they poured over his writings to justify their own conception of the invisible Church. For his rational Platonism they cared surprisingly little, though it was deeply imbedded in the medieval mystical tradition on which Luther in particular drew so heavily. And though they agreed with his sceptical contempt for mere human reason, they had little stomach for a natural wisdom which ended, in Montaigne, in the counsel to give obedience to the established Church. Their Augustine was the struggling sinner who lay crushed under the burden of man's estate, the sinner to whom came the intense personal experience of a saving grace without human mediation. Theirs is the Augustine of total depravity and irresistible grace, the Augustine who was driven in combat with the humanism of Pelagius to press man down to utter abnegation before the all-controlling will of the Almighty. Redemption belongs not to man, nor any human institution: redemption is God's alone.

III

The course of history records many a great edifice of ideas erected to organize and express and validate an integrated culture; it also records the struggles by which that architecture was wrecked. There has been a kind of alternation between the use of reason to criticize traditional experience, and experience to criticize a crystallized reason. At bottom the Reformers had to resort to the profundities of individual experience because reason belonged to their antagonists. The Greeks had been able to appeal to reason and nature in criticizing their social traditions, for those traditions were confessedly rooted in the immemorial experience of the group. But the great Schoolmen had already followed the Greeks; they had built up the harmonized theory of medieval society by an application of those very rational tests. In Thomas, both lay society and its capstone in the Church were thoroughly grounded in the law of nature and reason. The Reformers needed therefore another test, the appeal to man's living experience. Just so, when men felt the inadequacy of eighteenth-century rationalism, critical and revolutionary enough in its day, experience was the only criterion by which the Romanticists could judge it wanting.

And this seems the ultimate reason for the intellectual failure of the Humanist movement. Their critical weapon was the appeal to natural reason, not to experience. But the defenders of what they were attacking were far abler masters of that instrument than they. The whole band of Humanists could produce no philosophy of reason to compare with the skilled work of the great minds of the Counter Reformation, of a Suarez or a Bellarmin. And at best the appeal to reason could produce merely a clarification and reorganization from within, as happened in the Gallican church in the seventeenth century, not a radically new orientation. Only when united with a critical empiricism, and buttressed by the rationally organized material of a wider scientific experience, could reason become a radical instrument in the Enlightenment.

And so the Protestants appealed once more to experience in protest against existing social and intellectual systems, in the interest of new social and moral values which had come to be widely felt. Since the scientists appealed rather to reason—the reason of mathematics —at the beginning they appealed very largely on Catholic soil, in Italy and France. But the resulting philosophies of experience that emerged when the fighting zeal of Protestantism had loosened were Protestant and not Catholic; and they were social and moral in their ultimate orientation, not scientific.

Hence though the religious inspiration of the Reformers lay in the Augustinism of the fourteenth- and fifteenth-century mystics, and stretched behind them to Bonaventura and Dionysios, to the Neoplatonic philosophy of the ancient world, the effect of their critical efforts was to make that Augustinian tradition much more individual and subjective, to root it once more in the intense personal experience whence it had originally grown. And the whole Protestant emphasis on the awful destiny of the individual soul, as related directly to the universe with no social or institutional intermediaries—the whole stripping away of the ecclesiastical side of Augustine—was to make experience for the first time not the common and objective pathway by which every man might reach the world, but something private and individual. As science built on the public and open experience of the Aristotelians, so the moral philosophies of Protestantism built on this new private and personal experience. The German tradition was thus fixed as an Augustinian position suffused with *Innerlichkeit*, and the British as an Ock-hamism made relativistic and subjective. And when science entered to remake the intellectual world, both were forced still further in-ward: with no remaining locus in the mechanistic world, they took up a permanent abode in individual experience, bringing all values with them into the soul. Thus the Augustinian inwardness of the Protestants combined with the Augustinian scepticism of the French Humanists to prepare the ground for that dualism between the world and human experience which Cartesian mechanics was to consummate and Newton endorse.

I V

Why did the Reformation succeed where the Renaissance failed? If we look beyond this inner dialectic of ideas, it is clear that it suc-ceeded because it was more medieval in spirit, more willing to compromise: it gave a new solution, embodying new values, to what remained essentially a medieval problem, the problem of super-natural salvation. Because it was a compromise, the Reformation solution was bound to be unstable, containing within itself the seeds of further transformation. Catholicism crystallized at Trent because it refused to make any compromise with new conditions; it lost that power to assimilate novel elements which had contributed so much to the greatness of its long career—lost it at least till the present generation. Its subsequent history is primarily political, not intel-lectual; its leaders in modern times have been statesmen, not philoso-phers, even when they have been statesmen of ideas. The only alternative, in Catholic lands, to the full system of the Church, has been a complete break—the familiar anticlericalism with its derived atheism. In contrast, Protestantism during the modern period has been able to grow, to assimilate new elements, to adapt itself to changing conditions—at least until our generation; though often its adaptation has meant more of a discarding than an embracing, and between its periodic revivals it has shrunk into very narrow com-pass.

The one exception to the intellectual crystallization of Catholi-cism at Trent was the Gallican Church. By the Concordat of Bo-logna, in 1516, she had won pretty complete political and economic autonomy, the root demands of the Protestant revolt. Hence as a national institution she could not only crush the Huguenots; she was able in the seventeenth century to assimilate Cartesianism, and to produce the Oratory and Malebranche, Fénélon and Bossuet, to say nothing of Pascal. Cartesianism did for France what Protestantism did for Germany and Britain: it broke ecclesiastical authority and enthroned the private judgment of reason. It kept France intellectually with northern, not Latin Europe; it withstood the worst shock of the Counter Reformation. The rational and Augustinian Catholicism of the seventeenth century soon collapsed, the Gallican Church was conquered by the Jesuits and Ultramontanism. But it had done its work; the eighteenth century did not succumb, but was driven to open revolt.

V

If we examine in more detail the two major forms of Protestantism, we find each embedded in a set of ideas which provoked further independent developments quite incidental to the purposes of their founders. Intellectually both were in intention, however, conservative, fundamentalist, Augustinian reactions against the modernizing papacy and Curia in Italy. They were a protest against both the humanism of the Renaissance, and the rationalism and naturalism of the scholastics, against, that is, the sufficiency of moral philosophy and of scientific thought.

Luther's chief intellectual inspiration, aside from the gospels and Paul, came from the fourteenth-century German mystics, especially the *Theologia Germanica*, of which he drank deeply. But for their speculative Platonism he cared nothing; religion for him was not a matter of knowledge or doctrine but a passionate emotional experience, the direct awareness of God's forgiving love in Christ. What concerned him was the fact of salvation itself and the Christian life it made possible as a present reality. He felt little intellectual need to explain either man's estate or the blessed peace that came when faith in God's mercy brought release from His condemnation and wrath. He was not a philosopher, hardly even a theologian; he was a religious genius who used his own living experience as the touchstone by which to separate what was divine from what was mere human invention in the Christian tradition. He is consequently at his best when he allows that experience freest reign, as in *The*

Liberty of a Christian Man, and speaks with the authority of what he has felt within himself; he is at his worst when in controversy he tries to force the doctrines of others to express what he has himself lived through. This appeal to the inner experience, this personal mysticism, has always been the core of the Lutheran tradition, to which it has returned again and again when its lack of independent intellectual content has entangled it too deeply with other strange philosophies.

Luther had been brought up in the terminist school that prevailed in the German universities of his day; he studied Gabriel Biel, Pierre d'Ailly, and Ockham, and he knew the Scotists, before turning to Augustine and the mystics. This scholastic education both disgusted him with the subtleties of the "sophists," and by its scepticism of rational theology confirmed his own experience of the impotence of all human works, even those of reason, to find God. He came to despise not only the Schoolmen, but all philosophy and science, and even reason itself, so soon as it presumes to raise itself above the concerns of the practical life. The scholastic Aristotle is the defense of the Papists; the Greek Aristotle of the Humanists is a mere naturalist who denies the immortality of the soul. His ethics is the worst enemy of grace, his dialectic cannot even reach a knowledge of nature. His friend Melanchthon's enthusiasm Luther could never share: "Aristotle is to theology as darkness to light." At its best, reason is stone blind in all things pertaining to salvation; at its worst, Luther's language knows no bounds.

We know that reason is the Devil's harlot, and can do nothing but slander and harm all that God does and says. If outside of Christ you wish by your own thoughts to know your relation to God, you will break your neck. Thunder strikes him who examines. It is Satan's wisdom to tell what God is, and by doing so he will draw you into the abyss. Therefore keep to revelation and do not try to understand.[1]

Luther did not hesitate to accept the theory of a double truth:

The Sorbonne has set up the most pernicious doctrine, that what is worked out as true in philosophy must obtain as truth in theology also.[2]

When he tried to justify this irrationalism, he fell back on the prevailing Scotist and Ockhamite voluntarism:

[1] Luther, cited in Preserved Smith, *Age of the Reformation* (1920), p. 625.
[2] *Ibid.*

God is inscrutable and unknowable will. Of God's will there is no cause nor reason, to prescribe it rule and measure, since there is nothing equal or superior to it, but it is itself the rule of all things. If there were for it any rule or measure or cause or reason, it could not be the will of God. Not because he ought to will thus is that right which he wills; on the contrary, because he wills thus is that right which he wills.[3]

Because of this radical contingency in creation, there is a basic irrationality in the universe which makes any rational natural science impossible. It is no wonder Luther dismissed the Copernican theory as a mere idle novelty, quite useless even if it did not contradict the Bible. No faulty scientific hypothesis could lead to God. And the one universal law implanted in men, the moral law of which philosophy speaks, is given only as a schoolmaster to lead us to Christ and the Gospel.

Even Luther's high predestinarianism is not a philosophical determinism like Augustine's; nor is it worked out with harsh consistency from God's omnipotence, like Calvin's. It starts rather from the human situation; Luther knew in his own experience that the whole process of salvation, from the initial gift of faith, must come from God. His answer to Erasmus, *De servo arbitrio* (1525), admits an indeterminism and human freedom in temporal things.

Man is divided into two kingdoms. In one he acts by his own will and counsel, without the precepts and mandates of God, namely in the things inferior to him. In the other he is not left to his own counsel, but he acts and is led by the will and counsel of God without will of his own.[4]

It is only to salvation or damnation that man is predestined; and God's choice depends upon his inscrutable will. This purely religious determinism could not become, like Calvin's, the basis of a fixed order of nature: for Luther's gaze was wholly concentrated on man.

VI

It fell to the lot of Philipp Melanchthon (1497–1560) to erect the Lutheran gospel into a philosophical system. Melanchthon came to Wittenberg as a young teacher of Greek, full of plans for a new edition of Aristotle and a humanistic reform of education. He was a

---

[3] Luther, *De servo arbitrio*.   [4] Luther, *De servo arbitrio*.

grandnephew of Reuchlin, trained on Agricola's rhetorical dialectic, and a great admirer of the Erasmian ideals. The force of Luther's personality swept him into the evangelical movement; but he could not long forget his scholarly and intellectual interests, and since he had never had Luther's intense experience, he gradually brought back into the body of Lutheran teaching he proceeded to formulate much of the intellectual system of the Schoolmen and much of the ethical spirit of the Humanists. As *praeceptor Germaniae* he organized Protestant education along humanistic lines; he reinstated the idea of natural law, which Luther had opposed to the Gospel; he set natural theology once more beside revealed theology; and he crowned the educational ladder with a systematic philosophy. But it was not the Platonism of the Renaissance nor any of its Augustinian variants that he employed to consolidate the intellectual life of Lutheranism; it was Aristotle as the Humanists understood him, with a strong Stoic and Ciceronian admixture in ethics. And for a century and a half the Protestant universities in the Germanies were given over to a sterile Aristotelian scholasticism that shut them off from all contact with the currents of modern philosophy or the rising tide of natural science.

Melanchthon published a long series of textbooks in which he arranged this Aristotelian system with neatness and precision. "There is need of philosophy not only for method," he said, "but the theologian must take many things from physics." [5]

A kind of philosophy must be chosen which has the least sophistry and keeps a just method: such is the teaching of Aristotle . . . We cannot dispense with the monuments of Aristotle. I plainly feel that great confusion of doctrine will follow, if Aristotle is neglected, who is the one and only constructor of method; although he who takes Aristotle as his principal guide and seeks a simple and unsophistical doctrine can also take something now and then from other authors.[6]

And so Aristotle furnishes the framework on which ancient learning, especially that of Cicero and Galen, is organized. In dialectics Melanchthon follows the terminists, with an admixture of the Humanist rhetoric of Agricola. In physics he follows Aristotle closely, with strong emphasis on a natural theology of final causes. The

[5] Melanchthon, *Rede über die Philosophie.*
[6] *Corpus Reformatorum,* XI, 282; XIII, 656.

Copernican theory he calls "an evil and godless opinion" to be put down by the authorities. In psychology he uses Holy Writ to decide the dubious passages of the *De Anima;* but as a Humanist he finds the will free, and God not responsible for sin, and in Ethics the natural law of the Stoics coincides with the Gospel teachings.

The many schoolmasters who built on Melanchthon in the fifteenth and sixteenth centuries added a metaphysics to make a well-rounded theological Aristotelianism with few traces of originality or philosophic interest. In controversy with the reformed theologians, who showed a preference for the Calvinistic logic of Ramus, they borrowed from Suarez and the other Jesuit Thomists, and from Zabarella and the Padua Aristotelians. This Protestant scholasticism combined with the economic destruction of the religious wars to delay for two centuries any independent development of German thought. It lasted till the Pietistic movement at the close of the seventeenth century returned to the mystical core of the Lutheran tradition; and in its dissolution it paved the way for the scientific Aufklärung as well as for Romanticism. Its presence helps to explain why Cartesian science, when it came to Germany, found scholasticism still a living force; why Leibniz had to come to terms with the ideas of Aristotle, whereas in England with scholasticism dead Newton had nothing to deter him from complete allegiance to the new science; and why in consequence Leibniz was saved from the one-sided blunders of the Newtonians.

VII

The Reformed faith had no heritage of mysticism, like the Lutherans, and no Melanchthon to reintroduce a conflicting scholasticism. The background of both Zwingli and Calvin was not medieval but humanistic; intellectually both were primarily scholars and grammarians. Zwingli indeed before he came under Luther's influence was close to the universal ethical religion of the Humanists. Trained in the humanistic center of Basel, a friend of Erasmus and his circle, a close student of the ancients, the fathers, and the Italian and German moderns who were reviving their spirit, and as parish priest plunged into the midst of the Swiss political struggles, he began to work for an ethical reform of the Church long before he heard of Luther. More systematic and intellectual in his interest, he lacked Luther's profound religious experience and sense of sin; he accepted the latter's doctrine of salvation, with its emphasis on the sole power of the divine grace, partly as the best defense for a break with Catholic authority, and partly because he was convinced he found it in the Bible. What Luther had felt in his own inner struggles coincided, moreover, with the conception of God Zwingli had worked out from Cicero and Seneca, from the Florentine Platonists, especially Pico, and above all from Augustine's voluntaristic Platonism. God is the sole activity, the only cause, the only will in the universe. And to provide a theoretical foundation for Luther's empirical doctrine of salvation, Zwingli pushed to the limit this view of the all-controlling cosmic power and will of God. A knowledge of God in his own nature precedes the knowledge of God in Christ.

In his *De Providentia* Zwingli strips the Augustinian conception of God of its Platonic rationalism and interprets it in the spirit of the more radical Scotist voluntarists; it is significant that his Basel theological teacher had been a Scotist. God is absolute good, absolute intelligence, absolute power; these qualities manifested in all finite things constitute his providence, the perpetual and immutable rule and administration of the universe.

Since being and existence are prior to living and operating, and are their foundation, it follows that whatever lives or operates lives and operates from that and in that from which and in which it is and exists. . . . Since the infinite is one and single, there can be nothing outside it.

Every event is caught up in this universal order of providence; the laws of nature are but its constant expression. The will of man and his salvation are hence not unique events, but an integral part of God's cosmic providence; revelation and salvation are to be found everywhere, and their perfection in Christ is the climax of a long preparation. Hence Christianity is not essentially new, but merely the most complete revelation of God's beneficent providence; the enlightened Hebrews and Greeks received much of the divine truth. Man is the bond between earth and heaven; when united in the living faith in Christ, and in his active imitation, men fully realize their mediating function.

Where Augustine had shrunk from developing the full consequences of taking God as the only will, because he would not make God responsible for evil, Zwingli had no such compunctions; nor did he have Augustine's Neoplatonic conception of evil as non-being to help him out. God's providence decrees not only the fall of Adam, but all sin and unrighteousness; without sin there would have been no incarnation and no redemption, and the world's goal could not have been attained. Zwingli follows the Scotist theodicy that God's will is subject to no moral law, but rather itself the foundation of all good and evil. With the Humanists Zwingli extended the circle of the elect beyond Christianity; but the cause of election is inscrutable, and in it human merit plays no part.

VIII

Calvin, the systematizer and codifier of the Reformed faith, was likewise trained in humanistic learning; but he took from it, and from his legal studies, not the philosophical interests of Zwingli, but the rigid grammarian's method of seeking the letter of his texts. Like the Jesuits of the Catholic Reformation, he succeeded in integrating the formal discipline of the humanistic training with his intense religious impulse, but only at the expense of stripping both of every vestige of philosophical concern. Gone are the conflicts in Zwingli between Platonic universalism and Pauline redemption. There is left the Augustinian doctrine of salvation purified of all Platonic metaphysics, and developed with cruel logic and appalling consistency. And yet through Calvin's harsh pages there shines a sense of reality and vivid personal feeling that is missing in the more philosophical Zwingli. His vision of God's omnipotence breathes a selfless devotion to that great Will which is in itself the standard of all Right, a passionate acceptance of the ways of the universe as man's only good, and a celebration of that universe despite all personal desire—the supreme expression of that religious feeling that rejoices in the very impotence of man before the order of things as they are. And in his defense of double predestination, of the elect to salvation and the reprobate to damnation, there is a true insight: for omniscience the end justifies the means, but the petty ends of man, who cannot know how nature will dispose of his acts, and how they will emerge from the interplay of things, cannot be foreseen with such clarity.

This high predestinarianism of Zwingli, Calvin, and their Reformed followers carries on the thought of those Scotists who had likewise sought to make Augustine consistent by abandoning his Platonic metaphysics. Wyclif and Hus, drawing directly from Scotus, had already anticipated the vision of cosmic determinism. These Scotists developed the same omnipotence of the divine will, the same rigidly determined order in things without rational basis. Nature has a fixed and immutable structure, but this structure as a whole is arbitrary: there is no discoverable reason why it is not different, it is not in any intelligible sense teleological, it must be accepted as the will of God. The universe and its structure is a fact, an order to be discovered, not to be rationally deduced, describable but not explicable. Once discovered, natural events are to be explained in terms of it; its constancy makes prediction possible. This is a theological expression of empiricism, like the ethical consequence that good is good because God has so willed it; and once the authority of Revelation in Scripture broke down, men began to seek that order and that good in their experience of nature, without further question why it should be as it is.

Thus when the Calvinistic authoritarianism was dissolved, there proved to be a great congeniality of spirit between this Scotist voluntarism and the new mechanical science. Again and again scientists came out of the Calvinistic background with a sense of the sheer order of natural events, the inscrutable will of nature whose decrees were to be discovered and accepted as facts. It was no accident that Cartesian science was welcomed by the Jansenists and by Puritan England, and that its chief seat in the late seventeenth century was at the University of Leyden in Calvinistic Holland. And the first application of the scientific critique to the religious tradition, the religion of reason founded on a natural ethics, arose where this science impinged on Calvinism, in Holland and England. The law of God, in perfect conformity to which man finds his salvation and his chief end, became identical with the law of nature.

IX

Yet for all the importance these ideas came to have, they were but accidental and indirect results of the Reformation and the intellectual form given its two major currents. Like the religious toleration that also finally eventuated in Protestant lands, they were certainly the last things in the world the Reformers themselves intended. As distinguished from the novel values they introduced, the main outlines of their thought remained wholly within the medieval world. The chief changes the Reformers consciously introduced brought a new emphasis upon a medieval problem, and offered a new solution to it. They wanted first a simplification of the body of Christian belief and a concentration upon the doctrine of salvation as central; secondly, an individualistic emphasis on salvation as a personal rather than a corporate matter, as a direct and immediate relation between the soul and God; and thirdly, the sloughing off of the whole medieval sacramental system with its priestly hierarchy. The Protestants had no sacraments at all, in the Catholic sense; no vehicles of grace, *ex opere operato*, but simply signs of the Word, testimonies of God's love for man. But these changes left untouched the medieval world within which both Catholics and Protestants felt the need of salvation, the whole Christian drama of human destiny—the corruption of man's nature, God's wrath, the epic of the fall and of redemption through Christ's sacrifice—though for them redemption became mystical rather than magical. They were left, in a word, with the whole scheme of Augustinian Christianity, minus its Platonism and its doctrine of the Church. The intellectual effort of the Reformers was thus toward a concentration, a subtraction of ideas, toward an abandonment of most of the elements the Middle Ages has assimilated from Greek thought.

And yet the chief influence of the Reformation, before the inevitable theological disintegration and reconstruction set in, was not intellectual but moral. Into the Christian epic the Reformers incorporated a novel, this-worldly, individualistic, natural, and human way of life. The most revolutionary consequence of their change in the medieval scheme of salvation was to divorce the pattern of moral values from that scheme, to make ethics something human and independent. The Reformers made salvation a purely religious problem, not dependent upon human conduct at all: salvation must precede conduct, it must come from faith, not works. Luther's mysticism led him to make religion non-moral, a matter of inner experience: the Christian is already saved when he realizes God has forgiven him, has reinstated him in his favor or grace; justification is a change in God's attitude, not a transformation in human nature. Such divine forgiveness or salvation is free; the Christian is already saved, and hence freed from all fear on that score. Just because he does not have to do anything further to win salvation, he is free to follow the God he knows and trusts for God's sake rather than his own self-interest. In the *Liberty of a Christian Man* Luther penned one of the noblest of all expressions of the ideal of an unselfish moral life, of disinterested love and service to one's fellow man. For the Christian, all natural goods are means to this end; and thus not only is the nerve of monasticism cut, but with release from concern for salvation the whole humanistic ideal is installed. Even Luther himself could not remain true to this profound confidence in human nature; but his conception of moral liberty and autonomy entered into the tradition to flower again, when fertilized by Enlightenment naturalism, in Kant. The Catholic, Luther felt, could never do a genuinely good deed, for no deed is good that is done for hope of a reward.

Calvin achieved in a different way the same divorce of the moral life from the religious problem. Starting from God's decrees, he insisted that election is foreordained, that salvation has been long decided for every soul, godliness and holiness are quite beyond man's power. But the elect are predestined to holiness as well; they will glorify God for his sake, not their own; they will seek and follow his laws without hope of gain. For them Christian liberty is the freedom from all earthly restraint to practice perfect conformity with the Word—a word which, when men ceased to look for it in Holy Writ alone, became the natural moral law of the seventeenth and eighteenth century.

Thus both Lutheranism and Calvinism made for a disinterested moral life, freed from all religious hopes or fears; and in Protestantism this moral experience tended to become the basis of all faith in God himself. That is, by severing moral ideals and moral experience from the religious scheme, by giving them an independent foundation, Protestantism left the way open to assimilate any pattern of values that might seem good in the light of man's actual social experience. This helps to explain why it has been so characteristic of Protestantism to be the Volksreligion of a rapidly changing society, to be so responsive to the novel demands of the shifting social experience of the modern world; and why conversely the Protestant can change his intellectual beliefs completely without fundamentally affecting his independent code of values—a circumstance so incomprehensible to the Catholic.

The outcome of a scheme of salvation built on a medieval need was thus to open the way to a thoroughly modern ethic. This meant at first the assimilation of a pattern of life natural to a commercial society, the dignity of labor, the simple joy in the practice of one's calling; and under the sterner discipline of the Puritans, the devotion to the virtues of thrift, industry, sober self-direction, and a this-worldly asceticism—virtues accentuated where Calvinism came to express the ideals of the rising business class. Much has been made of the recent discovery that the ethic of Puritanism lent itself admirably to the aims of a capitalistic and acquisitive society busily engaged in accumulating its resources. Yet when with the rise of industrialism social experience changed from an economy of thrift and scarcity to an economy of consumption, Protestant ethic shifted easily from its initial this-worldly asceticism to an ethic of pleasure and enjoyment and humanitarianism, to become the familiar ideals of the country club and the Rotary Club; and with the socially sensitive, who feel the experience of very different classes in our society, it seems able with equal ease to emerge with a thoroughgoing collectivistic scheme of values. It is this very responsiveness of Protestantism to the values actually felt in the experience of widely different societies and classes that is the chief hope that it can rid itself of the agricultural and commercial individualism that still so largely dominates it in America and come to express the more collectivistic values of industrial society.

In fact, the essence of Protestant ethics seems to be not any particular scheme of values, least of all the Puritan ideal of the seventeenth century, but rather its responsiveness to any situation. Today Protestants vary from the John Birch Society to Christian socialism; and there seems little to prevent them in America, should they ever come to feel deeply the communistic ideal, from combining it with their Protestantism—as some of them did during the 1930's.

The chief effect of the Reformation morally—and since the ideas of Protestantism remained medieval, and the intellectual basis of modern thought was laid later, and by science, its moral consequences were of greatest import—the chief effect of the Reformation was to give religious consecration, not, as the interpretation in fashion today would have it, to the ethics of the business class—that was but temporary—but to any scheme of secular ethics. Protestants were freed from bondage to the medieval pattern of values, maintained with magnificent devotion by the Catholic Church, to embrace any scheme that appealed to them. In its complete acceptance of the world, the flesh, and the devil, Protestantism has tended to become merely an emotional force in support of the reigning variety of social ideals, offering no opposition to any ideal deeply felt, but at the same time little independent guidance or wisdom. This fact has become both a peril and a promise—the peril of the unloveliest kind of worldliness, the most degraded form of "humanism," into which American popular religion has sunk, a complacent expression of the crudest aspects of American life—and a promise of the freedom to develop an intelligent faith in the best values attainable in an industrial and scientific civilization.

5

The Heritage of Political Ideas from the Sixteenth Century: Secular and National Sovereignty and the Rise of Liberalism

I

DURING that intermediary period between the medieval and the modern world we call the "Renaissance," the major political change occurring in western Europe was the rise of absolute territorial monarchy, "sovereign" as against, first, any super-national religious power from without—specifically, as against the papacy and its claim to spiritual, and indirectly to temporal jurisdiction throughout Christendom; and "sovereign" as against secondly, any feudal or religious power within its domain. This period saw the emergence of the "great state," as we may distinguish the sixteenth-century social revolution from that in which later the industrial revolution produced the "great society." To those who supported such national monarchies, they seemed the only alternative to the *Kleinpolitik* of the warring states and principalities in Italy, kept in turmoil by the conflicting interests of the Renaissance despots and their supporters, and above all of the papacy; to the disastrous dynastic quarrels of Lancaster and York in England, in which the older feudal nobility almost committed suicide; to the wars of religious ideology following the Lutheran and Reformed breaks from the Catholic Church in the Germanies; and to the religious wars between the Huguenots, the Catholic *Ligue*, and the *Politiques* that accompanied the dying out of the House of Valois in France and the coming to the throne of the Huguenot Henri of Navarre.

Looking back in the light of what came afterwards, we can say that the need of strong central government was felt and supported in the interests of the commercial middle classes. But the new great states granted at least some sort of *de facto* toleration to minority religious groups. The Peace of Augsburg in 1555 established international toleration in Germany on the basis of *cuius regio eius religio*, in 1598 France issued her Edict of Nantes, and England under Elizabeth allowed fair scope to law-abiding Catholics and considerable freedom to Calvinists. Hence Protestant groups, Calvinists in particular, suported the new national states in the struggles, and in Scotland, Holland, and England managed to take over for a time the government themselves. This religious support was of great importance, for it was these same religious minorities that spearheaded the next major political conflict, the effort to set constitutional limits to the newly won absolute power of the secular government. The liberties that in the seventeenth century emerged in Holland and in England, under what the English call the Whig tradition, were, as Figgis puts it, the result of the struggle of religious organizations to survive. They were equally the result of the struggle of the commercial middle classes for law and order, and for control over taxation. Partly because the "fundamental law" of the French monarchy forbade the king to impose new taxes without the consent of representative bodies, the French middle class did not come to the support of the Huguenots when toleration stopped with the revocation of the Edict of Nantes in 1685. France had to win her liberties the hard way, in a different intellectual climate.

In these struggles, the absolute territorial state needed two theoretical defenses, one against the feudal lords, the other against the Church and clergy, both at home and in Rome. It needed theories criticizing feudal law, and theories criticizing canon law. These two needs generated two sets of political ideas. As against the authority of feudal custom or common law, there was worked out the theory of the absolute sovereignty of the territorial monarch. As against the divine right of the Church to exert spiritual authority, there was elaborated the theory of the divine right of kings. The first theory, since it was opposing a secular authority, could employ a secular argument. It relied upon the Roman civil law, already revived during the Middle Ages at twelfth-century Bologna, as the instrument for bringing some order out of feudal society. In England Roman law entered into the "equity" of the King's Bench, and merged with the older tradition. The second political theory, since it was opposing a spiritual authority—after Luther and Calvin it became several spiritual authorities—had to turn to a religious theory stated in theological terms. These supports of divine right monarchy are hence not particularly philosophical in character, though they often achieve generality, within acceptance of Christian presuppositions. The most familiar such theory, the patriarchal scheme of Sir Robert Filmer, refuted by Locke in his first *Treatise on Civil Government* (1689), is already a secularized version: it tries to prove that absolute rule is the most "natural" form of government, using Scripture only as the best source for information on primitive society and the early development of political institutions. The earlier forms rely much more heavily on scriptural authority.

The theory of divine right monarchy was thus a defense of secular as against spiritual power, of the rights of the great state as against the pope and the clergy—rights as zealously defended in Catholic France as in Protestant England. In 1516 François I managed, by the Concordat of Bologna, to win the root demands of the emerging great state, the freedom of the French or Gallican Church to control its own appointments and fiscal arrangements under the king; by this agreement the Church was able to retain its lands. In the Germanies and in England, the same rights were won not by agreement but by revolt from the Church; the Protestant German princes and the new capitalistic landlord adventurers in England made hay on the rich lands of the former monastic establishments. In its social and economic function, besides establishing a power strong enough to guarantee *de facto* religious toleration, the theory of the divine right of kings has thus aptly been called the first apologetic of bigger and better business. The theory was advanced by the Roman civilian lawyers; by the Protestant Reformers: Wyclif out-Erastianed Erastus, and called for confiscation of church lands, Luther put his faith in princes, and stamped on his Church the doctrine of passive obedience to the powers that be; by the Bourbon apologists in France, the supporters of the Huguenot Henri of Navarre and the Salic law during the religious wars, notably by William Barclay, who took on both the Catholic Bellarmin and the Calvinist Buchanan in his *De regno et regali potestate adversus Buchananum, Brutum* [pseudonymous author of the *Vindiciae contra Tyrannos*], *Boucherium et reliquos monarchomachos* (1600) and *De potestate papae* (1609); and by the later Bossuet under Louis XIV, as well as by James I. Significantly, the successful and unchallenged Spanish monarchy of the Habsburgs and the popular Tudor monarchy needed no theory of divine right, and produced little significant political philosophy in their support.

The theory of the divine right of kings—of the absolute and secular great state—was opposed in these conflicts by the supporters of an independent and superior spiritual power and religious authority. Here Catholic and Calvinistic theories tended to coincide, for both Churches maintained the medieval doctrine of the "two kingdoms" and of an independent spiritual power. For the Calvinists, the political outcome where they were in a minority was rather accidental; for Calvin himself, where he was in power, in Geneva, or hoped to be, as in France, held strongly to the traditional teaching of passive obedience, and to the supremacy and ruling authority of the Presbyterian elders over the civil magistrates. The later strong Calvinistic defense of religious liberties was wholly unintended.

Both Calvinists and papalist Jesuits opposed the absolute monarchy in the name of medieval natural rights founded on natural law, of the social contract, and of an emerging constitutionally limited government. Here figure the great Spanish Jesuits. Juan de Mariana (*De rege et regis institutione*, 1599) became notorious for defending the tyrannicide even of a legitimate heretical monarch, and publicly justified the assassination of Henri III of France. Thomas Aquinas and the tradition going back to John of Salisbury had always defended the murder of a usurper, and would thus have condoned the killing of those who to Catholics were both usurpers, William of Orange and Queen Elizabeth. Francisco Suarez (*Tractatus de legibus ac Deo legislatore*, 1612; and his systematic writings on jurisprudence) with Mariana and Mola develops a secular theory of limited government that relies on the medieval tradition of a community with moral rights under the law of nature prior to the establishment of civil society; they thus foreshadow John Locke.

Here belong also the Protestant "*monarchomachi*," or opponents of secular absolutism: Calvin himself with his high estimate of the spiritual power; the French Huguenots, chief theorists of whom were François Hotman, who in *Franco-Gallia* (1573) demonstrated as a constitutional historian that France had never been an absolute monarchy, and "Brutus" (probably Hubert Languet), the author of the *Vindiciae contra tyrannos* (1579), the ablest political theory produced by the Huguenots during the French religious wars, and a work of genuine political philosophy; the Scottish Presbyterians John Knox and George Buchanan (*De jure regni apud Scotos*, 1579), written for his pupil the young James VI, later James I of England, whom it did not amuse; and the English Puritans.

It is manifestly impossible to oppose a secular, rational argument to a religious authority claiming a basis in supernatural revelation. A religious argument is clearly needed. Hence all the sixteenth- and seventeenth-century defenses of secular government and absolutism were theological and not philosophical, like all the attacks upon the position. Lutherans, Anglicans, the seventeenth-century Gallican Church, under attack, all emphasized the supremacy of the secular power, the king, with whose fortunes their own were so closely linked. They stood for political absolutism and secularism. But since even before Luther nailed up his theses, certain more philosophical minds had attempted to defend the needed strong central government of secular absolutism by rational argument. This rational defense of secular as against spiritual power was worked out by a few men who realized the dangers of meeting fire with fire, of opposing to spiritual claims those of a rival and secular spiritual authority, the State—the dangers of deifying the National State itself. These men were trying to get a rational, not a theological defense of the emerging great state. They were the naturalistic and secular thinkers of the Renaissance.

In Italy the secularizing tendencies had already gone farthest. Here emerged Machiavelli, the republican idealist and politician, who in his *Discorsi* on the first ten books of Livy sets the strength and wealth of the middle-class city-state like Florence or early Rome over against the people. But he was so single-mindedly insistent on secularism and on the national unity of Italy that he was willing to sacrifice his republicanism to it, in *Il Principe* (1513), that masterpiece of political craftsmanship and amoral concern with securing ends regardless of moral cost. In France Bodin, in his *Six livres de la république* (1576), supporter of the *Politiques* before Paris proved worth a mass, produced what is next to Machiavelli's the outstanding work of political philosophy of the sixteenth century, in a secular defense of the strong centralized government of the nascent Bourbon monarchy.

These rationalists were secularists and naturalists, but they lived and wrote before the new "science" had appeared upon the scene. It remained for Hobbes to be the first to bend the new science of Galileo to a rational theory of the commonwealth. Thereafter, till Vico, Montesquieu, and the Romantic philosophers appeared to urge an historical method for the science of society, the demonstrative methods of the physical sciences were the model for all political philosophers.

Despite the protests of religious groups in the name of earlier medieval theories of society, the great state carried everything before it, and won its battle for secularism and the subordination of all spiritual power, even in Catholic lands like France and Spain. The second great political theory of modern times, constitutionalism, emerged when the alliance between religious minorities, especially the Calvinists, and the new commercial classes was cemented. The religious groups still wanted exemption from secular political control, or "Erastianism": they were led to demand toleration and full rights of citizenship. The emerging commercial classes, and in England the new capitalistic landlords, had grown strong enough to demand autonomy against their earlier protector and patron, the sovereign king. On a major scale this occurred in the rebellion of the northern Netherlands in the sixteenth century against the Spanish monarchy, and in the seventeenth-century struggles in England that eventuated in the settlement of 1689 and the triumph of Whig principles.

Political constitutionalism thus grew up under a religious and theological ideology, worked out in the sixteenth-century battles for secularism. Both the Jesuits, opposed to the Catholic monarchies that were too nationalistic, and the Calvinists alike maintained the medieval notion of an independent spiritual power with indefeasible rights that should exercise indirect "spiritual" authority over the secular state. Where the latter got the chance, in the English Commonwealth, and in New England, they proceeded to set up Calvin's own brand of theocracy, beckoning from Geneva. The Jesuits in particular kept alive the medieval notion of a representative assembly of the moral community of the nation: except when they were in power, in Paraguay, and in France and Spain on occasion after the 1648 settlement brought them influence, they maintained in theory constitutional polity against absolutism.

In the eighteenth century, this "spiritual power" was identified with the newly discovered and divine Order of Nature, and won the support of the new science for its "natural law." Hence the Enlightenment doctrine of natural rights derived equally from the ancient Stoic and medieval religious "law of nature" and the new Newtonian one. Together they were made the basis of the eighteenth-century revolutionary movements.

Now, the divine right absolute monarchy of the seventeenth century, with its policy of mercantilism and of intelligent regulation in economic life, is obviously far closer in theory and in major practice to the modern collectivistic welfare state, than its great rival, the Whig and Liberal state founded on constitutional rights supported by an independent and spiritual power, that flourished during the eighteenth century, and until the new intellectual currents of German Romanticism began to be felt, in the nineteenth century, and has endured as a strong tradition in English-speaking lands down to the present. Today, in our present conventional division of the world between "totalitarian" political institutions and the liberal constitutionalism of the "free world," we can still discern the political ideas of the defenders of divine right monarchy in conflict with those of the constitutionalists of the seventeenth century. At present, the main supports of liberal constitutionalism, in the institutional sense, against all the pressures stemming from a centralized economic direction, remain the Calvinistic heritage in America, and the Catholic heritage in Europe.

In the sixteenth and seventeenth centuries the forces making for the great state were strong and powerful, as are those magnifying centralized political power today. But something is still to be said for the notion of an independent "spiritual power," embodied in institutions strong enough to maintain themselves as platforms for independent criticism of the political powers that be. Traditionally, these institutions have been the churches; the long difficulties have come from a monopoly of spiritual power in a single institution. They have performed this essential political function of criticism. It might be well were the universities to proceed to exercise a similar function of independent criticism, and not send all their luminaries to support the great state in Washington or Whitehall.

In any event, it is impossible to understand the political philosophizing that runs as a bright thread through modern thinking unless it is seen as reconstructions of these ideas worked out in the conflicts of the earlier transitional age. Just as the philosophical systems of the seventeenth century remain unintelligible without the background of the three great medieval theories of science on which they drew, so are the political philosophies of the seventeenth and eighteenth centuries unintelligible except as readaptations of the theories worked out in the emancipating political movements of the sixteenth. Here there will be treated briefly Machiavelli, and Bodin, as the forerunners of Hobbes and Spinoza; the *Vindiciae*, with a look at Mariana and Suarez; and the Dutch constitutionalists and rationalists, Althusius and Grotius.

II

Niccolò Machiavelli (1469–1527) was primarily a disgruntled but reflective administrator and diplomatist, hardly a political philosopher at all. Bodin takes him to task for not adding any "philosophy" to his historical analyses and practical maxims, meaning some framework of general principles. Yet Machiavelli expresses so clearly that aspect of the emerging system of European politics, already fully advanced among the Italian city-states, that sets it off most clearly from medieval political theorizing, that he has always seemed the first spokesman of the new secular state, independent of all restraint of ecclesiastical law or the law of nature, steering its precarious course only by a calculation of expediency and relative power—that sovereign political unit—in western Europe it had become the national state—whose sole guide was "reasons of state," *ragioni di stato*. Machiavelli accepted the aims of the power politics he found in his Italian world; he set forth the methods and techniques by which they had been carried on since the days of the Greeks. His astute intelligence—of the fox rather than the lion—considered everything but the imponderables. Since one of the imponderables he vastly underestimated was religion, and since for two centuries religion was to furnish the occasion for most political and international disputes, his professional skill was destined to meet many setbacks when others tried to employ it against self-taught but remarkably effective amateurs who sought power not for itself but for their further ends. When the rest of Europe had finally reached the stage of secularization gained by the Quattrocento Italy in which he grew up, new currents were astir: the people, whom Machiavelli despised, saying, "Most men are bad," were on the point of asserting their "badness" on a demonic scale that swept everything before it. Public opinion had become an irresistible power, "fraternity" or nationalism proved an explosive force which power politics could not quite control. And men in national groups sought "liberty," which perhaps they did not quite understand, but which Machiavelli understood still less. One element saves Machiavelli's reputation as a prophet: his passionate Italian patriotism, which endeared him to the *Risorgimento*, and to Italians driven to desperation at being pushed around nationally, as when they were compelled to embrace Mussolini's Fascism. Meanwhile, the rulers and administrators of Europe practiced his precepts for their own ends, often taking the trouble, like Frederick the Great, to write books refuting him while they were doing it.

The sole claim Machiavelli can make to being a political philosopher is that his craftsman's techniques were rooted in a conception of human nature as constant and determinable. In this, he foreshadowed the theorists from Hobbes onward who derived their political axioms from human nature and its needs, and made the analysis of that human nature the source of their systems—the devotees of the new science of politics who began in the seventeenth century to combat resort to the so-called "law of nature" as the source of political axioms.

Born the son of a lawyer, Machiavelli entered the service of the Republican government of Florence in 1494, the year the Medici were expelled. From 1498 to 1512 he served as secretary to the Chancellery, an important policy-making official in the foreign office. In 1500 he had the opportunity on a mission to study Cesare Borgia at first hand. From 1503 to 1506 he was trying to substitute a citizens' militia for mercenary troops. The latter year he was sent as ambassador to Julius II; in 1507, as envoy to Emperor Maximilian at Bolzano.

In 1512 the Medici returned, and Machiavelli's active career was over. Deprived of his office, put into prison and tortured the next year, he was banished from political life to his farm, where he devoted himself to writing up the fruits of his experience. In 1513, in disgrace, he completed his *Il Principe*, recommending his talents and experience to the new master of Florence, Lorenzo, in his dedication: "It is not possible to make a better gift than to offer you the opportunity of understanding in the shortest time all that I have learned in many years with so many troubles and dangers." Digesting his accumulated experience into a little volume, he ends: "If your magnificence from the summit of your greatness will some time turn your eyes to these lower regions, you will see how unmeritedly I suffer the great and continued malignity of fortune."

Meanwhile he had started his *Discorsi* on the first ten books of Livy. This was not finished until 1520, and was then dedicated to two men of intelligence without wide political influence:

I send you a gift, which if it answers ill the obligations I owe you, is at any rate the greatest which Niccolò Machiavelli has it in his power to offer. For in it I have expressed what I have learned or observed for myself, during a long experience and constant study of human affairs.

The *Discorsi* express Machiavelli's admiration for the Roman republic in particular, and for republican government in general, under which he had won his own success. In the *Principe* he says of it, "I will leave out all discussion of republics, inasmuch as in another place I have written of them at length."

Which was the true Machiavelli, the republican idealist of the *Discorsi*, or the tool and instrument of princes of the *Principe?* The answer is, obviously both: Machiavelli was no simple figure. Yet he himself felt no great difference between the two works: in both he is the "moralizing" hard-boiled reporter commenting on his long experience observing the game of politics. And as Villari, his biographer, points out, anyone familiar with the *Discorsi* and knowing the specific purpose for which the *Principe* was written, could have foretold nearly everything in the *Principe*. Both books alike reveal Machiavelli's distinctive qualities: the objective reporting of rascalities, the ruling out of moral inhibitions as irrelevant to politics, the belief that political success depends on force and craft, the disillusioned view of human nature. Machiavelli is the seasoned Washington reporter who has put behind him his early liberal impulses as out of place in his job. And like a first-class reporter, what he tells is indispensable but not the last word. What is missing in the *Principe*, as hardly likely to interest Lorenzo, is his enthusiasm for popular government under the conditions of the Roman Republic, but hardly applicable to Renaissance Italy, corrupted by the chicaneries of the Church. Perhaps Machiavelli's last illusion remained the conviction that without the Church things would have been better—like the Communist still convinced that life could be rosy, once capitalism has been eliminated. In retirement Machiavelli wrote also on *The Art of War* (1520), *Le istorie Fiorentine* (1520–1527), a cynical comedy, *Mandragola*, a scurrilous novel, *Belphegor*, in addition to his acute diplomatic dispatches and his letters.

Machiavelli starts from the constancy of human nature. Arguing it is safer for the ruler to be feared than to be loved, he writes:

Because it is to be asserted in general of men that they are ungrateful, fickle, false, cowards, covetous and as long as you succeed they are yours entirely; they will offer you their blood, property, life and children, as is said above, when the need is far distant, but when it approaches they turn against you.[1]

The same judgment is expressed in the *Discorsi:*

Since the desires of men are insatiable, nature prompting them to desire all things and fortune permitting them to enjoy but few, there results a constant discontent in their minds, and a loathing of what they possess.[2]

The common people have but little gratitude or political sense; for their own good they must be kept constantly deceived.

A people, deceived by a false show of advantage, will often labor for its own destruction . . . and unless it be convinced by some one whom it trusts that the course on which it is bent is injudicious, . . . will bring danger to the state. And should it happen, as is sometimes the case, that, having been deceived before . . . there is none in whom the people trust, their ruin is inevitable.[3]

Confronted with a people he has enslaved, a prince

will find a very few of them desiring freedom that they may obtain power, but all the rest, whose number is countless, only desiring it that they may live securely. For in all republics, whatever the form of their government, barely forty or fifty citizens have any place in the direction

---

[1] *Il Principe,* ch. xvii. Tr. W. K. Marriott, Everyman ed.
[2] *Discorsi,* Book II, Preface.   [3] *Discorsi,* Book I, ch. xvi.

of affairs, who, from their number being so small, can easily be reckoned with, either by making away with them, or by allowing them such a share of honors as, looking to their position, may reasonably content them. All those others whose sole aim it is to live safely, are well contented where the prince enacts such laws and ordinances as provide for the general security, while they establish his own authority; and when he does this, and the people see that nothing induces him to violate these laws, they soon begin to live happily and without anxiety. Of this we have an example in the kingdom of France, which enjoys perfect security from this cause alone, that its kings are bound to compliance with an infinity of laws upon which the well-being of the whole people depends. (Book I, ch. xvi)

And Machiavelli could judge thus three years after Luther nailed up his theses and for two centuries made "living safely" far from the popular goal! As he himself points out, "There is nothing more terrible than an uncontrolled and headless mob; on the other hand there is nothing more feeble." But the people are no worse than most rulers: "I maintain that this infirmity with which historians tax the multitude may with equal reason be charged against any individual man, but most of all against princes."

In treating political techniques in their own terms Machiavelli is doing what Aristotle did in those naturalistic parts of his *Politics* where he is advising tyrants how to maintain their power. The Italian practices he describes are paralleled in Commines' memoirs setting forth the way in which Louis XI built the French state. And the great Leonardo was likewise notoriously indifferent as to what master he sold his genius to. In all this, Machiavelli is hardly the detached, "scientific" observer and generalizer. He was devoted to the acquiring and maintaining of political power, and he sweepingly condemns rulers who allow their states to grow weak. His empiricism is that of common sense and shrewd practical foresight; his method is not "historical," as was Bodin's, for instance, for he is precluded from any historical sense of development by his conviction that human nature remains always and everywhere the same. For him history is not the basis of a generalization, it illustrates a conclusion already held.

Besides the ancient Roman republicans, Machiavelli admires French institutions, and he approves the Swiss, whose civic virtues grow out of their private morality. The Germans, too, still maintain the ancient Roman virtues. In fact, Machiavelli is one of the original preachers of "moral man and immoral society."

The Christian virtues themselves Machiavelli condemns for their unworldliness, and contrasts Christianity to its disfavor with the more virile religions of ancient times:

> Our religion places the supreme happiness in humility, lowliness, and a contempt for worldly objects, whilst the other, on the contrary, places the supreme good in grandeur of soul, strength of body, and all such other qualities as render men formidable. . . . These principles seem to me to have made men feeble, and caused them to become an easy prey to evil-minded men, who can control them more securely, seeing that the great body of men, for the sake of gaining Paradise, are more disposed to endure injuries than to avenge them. (Book II, ch. ii)

Religion is the opium of the people. In Machiavelli as in Marx this is scarcely an objective and disinterested judgment. Nor was his appraisal of the far from unworldly Italian Church:

> Through the ill example of the Roman court, the country has lost all religious feeling and devoutness. . . . To the Church therefore and to the priests we Italians owe this great debt, that through them we have become wicked and irreligious. And a still greater debt we owe them for what is the immediate cause of our ruin—that by the Church our country is kept divided. For no country was ever united or prosperous that did not yield obedience to some one prince or commonwealth, as has been the case with France or Spain. (Book I, ch. xii)

There is irony in Machiavelli's anticlericalism and anti-Christian feeling. For he is really agreeing with the Augustinian theory of government as necessary after the Fall because of the corruption of man's nature: only civil authority can keep original sin in check. What is Machiavelli doing but crossing the t's and dotting the i's on this most orthodox Christian political theory?

Machiavelli sums up his creed:

> I am persuaded that the world, remaining continually the same, has in it a constant quantity of good and evil; but this good and evil shift about from one country to another.

At the moment, the good predominates in the French, in the Turks, in the kingdom of the Soldan and the states of Germany. In Italy, evil now has the upper hand.

At the end of the *Principe*, Machiavelli's disillusionment asks whether the game is worth the candle. Is it not best to let things take their course, since Fortuna governs all?

> There are those who maintain it is unnecessary to labor much in affairs, but let chance govern them. . . . Sometimes, pondering all this, I am in some degree inclined to their opinion. Nevertheless . . . I hold it to be true that Fortune is the arbiter of one half of our actions, but she still leaves us to direct the other half or perhaps a little less.[4]

Whether he intended to put it there or not, it is possible to pull a political philosophy out of Machiavelli's writings. Human nature is essentially egoistic and selfish; it is profoundly aggressive and acquisitive. Security is possible only through strong government and the force of laws. When furnished with a systematic doctrine of human nature, this side of Machiavelli became the political philosophy of Hobbes.

Conflict is normal; in a healthy society interests are held in equilibrium. The rivalry of patricians and plebeians in Rome was the secret of Roman strength: it made Rome a strong, warlike, conquering people. So he approves Polybius' counsel of a mixed constitution.

Again, everything depends on the lawgiver and the way his laws mold the national character. Only law holds selfish men together: moral obligations are derived from law and government. This view also Hobbes systematized. The ruler himself is outside morality, as its source. The emphasis on the will of God as the sole standard of right and wrong in Scotist and Ockhamite theology has been naturalized into the will of the prince. Machiavelli never upheld Hobbes's political absolutism; side by side with his admiration for the strong ruler—like Cesare Borgia—went his admiration for a free, self-governing people. The strong despot, he thinks, is needed to found the state, and to reform it when it has been corrupted. His power will then "wither away" into legal self-government. This hope has likewise been expressed more recently. Like Aristotle, he holds, the prince is most successful who approaches most closely the just legal ruler. The nobility, on the other hand, are basically opposed in interest both to the ruler and to the middle class: they must be extirpated, as the experience of the Italian city-states had shown. And Machiavelli has a passionate hatred of mercenary sol-

[4] *Principe*, ch. xxv.

diers and *condottieri;* they joined the papacy as the twin ruiners of Italy.

Above all, national patriotism overrides every other duty:

For where the very safety of the country depends upon the resolution to be taken, no considerations of justice or injustice, humanity or cruelty, nor of glory or of shame, should be allowed to prevail. But putting all other considerations aside, the only question should be, What course will save the life and liberty of the country? [5]

National unification and a strong Italy under an absolute monarch— this was the end for which any means that would secure the power that would bring it about were justified. Behind the façade of the shrewd old cynical diplomat burned the spirit of the religious fanatic—the spirit Luther was to unleash for two centuries, that Rousseau was to fan into flames again, that Marx has kindled for our day. But Machiavelli was no Lenin—he had no carefully worked out program of unification. His passion was sentimental rather than rational. He appealed to Lorenzo in emotional tones, but without hope. The concluding chapter of the *Principe* is the exception, a peroration rounding off his advice on practical politics. But Machiavelli came to stand at the opposite pole from the rationalistic, legal-minded Grotius, who sought to control religious passions to construct a European community of nations. From Grotius stemmed later Liberalism; from Machiavelli came the sovereign state, which Rousseau showed the people could capture in the name of "democracy." Both men accepted and were prepared to work with the national territorial state in its independence. Gone was United Christendom, the "Monarchia" or "one world" of which Dante wrote.

III

A much more systematic thinker than the Italian diplomat, living in the midst of the French wars of religion and thoroughly committed to the party of the *Politiques,* the defenders of secular kingship, wrote a work in which he tried to bring Aristotle's *Politics* up to date, as a practical science founded on a comparative and historical method, adding to Greek experience Roman history and law, the Jewish tradition, and modern European history. He believed he was following a new method, combining philosophy with history. "Phi-

[5] *Discorsi,* Book III, ch. xli.

losophy dies of inanition in the midst of its precepts when it is not vivified by history." Machiavelli's omission of philosophy he held to be responsible for his lack of moral criteria. But he had no sympathy with Utopian schemes such as he found in Plato and Sir Thomas More. He thought in terms of an empirical subject-matter within the framework of general principles. But though he is responsible for some clear definitions, he is no more philosophical than Machiavelli in grounding them in general principles; and the mass of humanistic erudition in historical detail—his volume runs to 1222 pages —makes him seem more of an antiquarian than a philosopher. In Vico and Montesquieu he found worthy successors; in this sense Bodin is the modern founder of the historical study of political science that came into its own in the nineteenth century.

Jean Bodin (1530–96) came of a prosperous bourgeois family of Angers, joined the Carmelites, and was sent to Paris to be educated in their house. He was trained in the scholastic methods, but more attracted by the new humanistic learning of the Collège Royale, where Plato and languages took the place of Aristotle and dialectic. Dispensed from his vows, he studied law. Deeply interested in the variety of religions, he devoted his last book, *Heptaplomeres*,[6] to a dialogue between representatives of seven different religions. Devoid of religious prejudice himself, though not of religious feeling, his own faith was hard to discover—he was accused of being Catholic, Calvinist, Jew, Mohammedan, and atheist. His thought approaches Deism.

Bodin stayed ten years at Toulouse as student and teacher of law. In 1561 he returned to Paris at the bar. Here the legal teaching was to recover exactly the text of the *corpus iuris civilis*. Bodin was repelled; he was on fire with the desire to find a universal law, adapted to modern conditions, and became involved in the task of Catherine de' Medici's chancellor, Michel de L'Hôpital, to codify the divergent local laws of northern France, under universal principles, following the lead of the great medieval Italian civilists Bartolus and Baldus. This involved a universal religion, a continuing interest of Bodin. Universality, he was convinced, could be found only through the study of history. Following Hotman, the legal historian, he

[6] Unpublished. Partial version published, 1841; complete ed. by L. Noack, *Colloquium Heptaplomeres de abditis rerum sublimium arcanis* (1857).

published in 1566 his *Method for the Easy Comprehension of History*,[7] the first secular philosophy of history in modern times. Here he tries to understand the development of the best form of law.

In history the best part of universal law lies hidden; and what is of great importance for the appraisal of laws—the customs of peoples, and the beginnings, growth, conditions, changes and decline of all states—are obtained from it. The chief subject-matter of this *Method* consists of these facts, since nothing is more rewarding in the study of history than what is learnt about the government of states.

His interest in government aroused, in 1571 Bodin entered the household of the king's brother, the Duc d'Alençon, as councillor. He accompanied the Duke on his mission to Elizabeth, who, provoked at his view that women are unsuited to political life, called him "M. Badin." The Duke was official head of the party of *Politiques*, who were committed to a *de facto* recognition of religious differences in the kingdom—the policy of L'Hôpital, as stated in his speech to the Estates in 1560, that in the end triumphed with the Edict of Nantes. In 1562 the religious wars began. In 1576 Bodin published, as the fruit of his drive, his study, and his experience, *Six Books of the Commonwealth*.[8] This theory thus springs, like that of Hobbes, from a universalizing and centralizing secularist living in the midst of the anarchy of civil war. It upholds the absolute authority of the commonwealth, "to which, after immortal God, we owe all things."

In 1576 Bodin served as member of the Estates of Blois, which in 1579 presented the Ordinances of Blois. Bodin opposed reopening the war on the Huguenots, called for negotiation, defended the right of the third estate to dissent from the other two, and opposed raising money by alienating the royal domain. But the Catholic *Ligue* dominated the Estates, Henri III wanted to head it, and he lost the king's favor. He retired from court, became procurator of Laôn, and even in self-protection joined the *Ligue*. This precluded preferment when Henri IV triumphed in 1594. He wrote also on the universal system of nature (*Novum theatrum naturae*, 1594), rejecting Copernicus and embracing astrology, and a textbook on

[7] *Methodus ad facilem historiarum cognitionem. Oeuvres philosophiques*, ed. P. Mesnard, with Fr. tr. (1951); Eng. tr. B. Reynolds (1945).
[8] *Les six livres de la république;* Latin tr. (1586); Eng. tr. R. Knolles (1606). Abridged tr. by M. J. Tooley (1955).

sorcery (*La Démonomanie*, 1580); he was a zealous believer in witchcraft.

Bodin and the *Politiques* wanted to hold together the French national state despite religious differences, which on grounds of policy rather than of right it was expedient to allow. Order and political unity must prevail over religious diversity. Bodin's drive for unity and order has continued in French political life and theory, never so influential as in Rousseau, the Revolution, and Napoleon. It has not been an unmixed blessing. Bodin's greatest shortcoming is his total lack of the idea of federalism, upheld three years later, in 1579, in the *Vindiciae*, and developed in Althusius. Federal theory had to await the Americans to achieve popularity; it has never penetrated many French minds, to the confusion of French politics.

Bodin accepts without question the law of nature as the rules that distinguish right from wrong; he gives it no rational foundation. It is binding on the sovereign: he can dispense with the law of nations, but not with the law of nature. Bodin borrows the order of his book from Aristotle. He considers first the end of the commonwealth, then the family, as its unit, including its indefeasible right of private property, then the forming of the political association, the *respublica*. "A commonwealth is an aggregation of families and their common possessions, ruled by a sovereign power and by reason." [9] The basis of the commonwealth is the family; families have certain common interests; a supreme power is essential; and government has a moral end. As to the end, Bodin is not definite: the ends of Aristotle's *polis*, the moral excellence and well-being of the citizens, cannot be the end of a national state; to secure justice is a sufficient task. Yet the commonwealth has a soul, and higher ends than material prosperity and security. Bodin inclines towards Aristotle's end of fostering the life of *theoria*. But he gives no analysis of human nature and its needs or ends, even an inferior one like Machiavelli. Moral, rational, and intellectual satisfactions, however, seem to enter in.

The family is a natural community; Bodin conceives it under Roman and Hebraic ideas as ruled by a *paterfamilias* or patriarch. Like every association, it involves an infringement of the "natural

---

[9] Respublica est familiarum rerumque inter ipsas communium, summa potestate ac ratione moderata multitudo. (Lib. I, cap. i.)

liberty" nature has given individuals, to be under the control of no alien will. Under natural law only the *paterfamilias* is free and equal; outside the household he becomes the citizen. Society depends on a naturally implanted social instinct; but political association, the commonwealth, arises generally from force and conquest, though power alone does not entail an obligation to obey. Man's social instinct leads him to form many "civil" associations (*societates et sodalitia*) before government is forced. Political subjection and slavery came into existence together with conquest by a chief. Herodotus is wrong: the first monarchs were not freely chosen, they were military conquerors. The lesser forms of association are the family with its property, the *collegium*, the corporation or *corpus*, and the commune or *universitas*.[10] The Roman coloring given the family allows freedom of divorce. Slavery is neither natural nor useful. All the lesser associations are purely creatures of the sovereign power; as against the sovereign they have no rights. Bodin is trying to undercut the medieval arguments for limited sovereignty. Unlike the French Revolution, however, he does not want to abolish them all. All mankind is a series of associations; but only the most inclusive hold sovereign power over all the rest. Thus Bodin made Roman corporation law a part of political theory.

The citizen is the head of the family, which is the primary element in society, considered in his political relationship. A citizen is "a free man who is subject to the sovereign power of another." [11] "Free" excludes slaves but not women or those under parental authority. Citizens differ widely in rights and privileges: Bodin scorns the notion of equality. The nobility is an important institution; women are confined to the household; a man's occupation determines his rank and dignity, so that artisans and retailers are hardly citizens. But all are equally subjects. Subjection is the sole test of citizenship, as recognition of a common sovereign is the sole test of a commonwealth.

There are two kinds of state: one, the *civitas*, united in a com-

[10] A *collegium* is a lawful association (*consociatio*) of three or more persons of the same calling (*conditio*); a corporation (*corpus*) is a union (*coniunctio*) of a number of colleges; a commune (*universitas*) is the aggregation of all the families, colleges, and corporations of the same town (*oppidum*), united by a community of rights (*iuris communione*).

[11] Liber homo qui summae alterius potestatis obligatur. (Lib. I, cap. vi)

mon language, religion, and customs and laws; the other, the *respublica*, which need be united only in that its citizens are all subjects of the same sovereign power,

> even though they differ from one another in manners, laws, institutions and race (*infinita gentium varietate*). But if all the citizens have the same laws, there is not only a single commonwealth, but also a single *civitas*, even though the citizens live scattered about in many villages, towns, and urban communities.[12]

In his analysis, Bodin tries to build an impregnable foundation for the right of private property. By the law of nature property, *dominium*, belongs to the family, as an indefeasible right against the commonwealth, a "natural right," as in Locke. For Bodin, absolute sovereignty and absolute right of property are not opposed but complementary.

In his most famous definition, Bodin states sovereignty itself to be "supreme power over citizens and subjects, unrestrained by the laws." [13] This excludes social, ethical, and religious relationships from political theory. Practically, a common political bond can obtain together with differences in religion—the most revolutionary outcome of Bodin's view. *Maiestas* is perpetual, it is undelegated, it is *legibus soluta* because the sovereign is the source of all law, even customary law, which he sanctions by permitting it. Enactment can change even custom. The primary attribute of sovereignty or *maiestas* is the power to give laws, without the consent of anyone else. The power of war and peace, the power to commission magistrates, to judge as a court of last resort, to tax—these all follow from it.

Every "'well-ordered state" must have in it somewhere this indivisible legal source of authority. Just why, Bodin does not bother to tell; he is here prescriptive rather than philosophical. Hence there are only three forms of commonwealth, monarchy, aristocracy, and popular, though many complex forms of administration. There can be no mixed state, as Polybius wrongly held. The function of the Estates is advisory only. Bodin makes a clear-cut distinction between commonwealth, which is sovereign, and government, which may be delegated. Thus the Holy Roman Empire turns out to be an

---

[12] Lib. I, cap. vi.
[13] Maiestas est summa in cives ac subditos legibusque soluta potestas. (Lib. I, cap. viii)

aristocracy, not a monarchy. But England, France, and Spain are monarchies; the Tudor commonwealth he finds, despite the claims of Parliamentary lawyers, to depend on the ultimate authority of the Crown. These commonwealths are monarchies governed "democratically": that is, the king consults the estates and subjects from all classes are eligible to office. Hotman's contention that France was never an absolute monarchy he brushes aside.

There are three species of monarchy: the *dominatus*, or despotism, in which the monarch rules as *paterfamilias;* the chief instances are the Muscovites and the Turks. There is royal monarchy, in which as in France the subjects are secure in their rights of person and property, and the monarch respects the laws of God and of nature. Thirdly, there is tyranny, ruled by caprice. Passive obedience is owed even to a tyrant. The popular state seems more in conformity to nature (*magis consentanea naturae*); yet though Bodin admires the Swiss, popular commonwealths are notoriously fickle, venal, and inefficient. Aristocracy (the example is Genoa) has its own faults. Monarchy has difficulties over succession, and the corruption power brings the monarch; but it is on the whole the best form —here speaks the theorist of the Bourbons, and of Renaissance absolutism in general. The only question Bodin leaves unanswered— and in the sixteenth and seventeenth centuries no one asked the question—is why unified legal sovereignty is necessary.

Yet sovereignty, though "absolute," is not unlimited. It is bound by the laws of God and the law of nature: the sovereign is obligated to keep agreements, and to respect the family's right to private property. Property the sovereign cannot touch, by the law of nature, without the subject's consent. Hence, like the later Locke, Bodin insists that all taxation requires the assent of the Estates. He is left with two absolutes: the indefeasible rights of the family, and the unlimited legislative power of the sovereign. Of the two, the right of property is the more fundamental: he never argues it, as he does the other. That right is essential to the family, the family is essential to the commonwealth; the right to tax is the right to destroy; and the commonwealth cannot have the power to destroy its own members.

This right of property is one of several constitutional rights the sovereign must observe, what Bodin calls "*leges imperii,*" conditions of power. He cannot modify the succession: the Salic law is untouchable (it was Henri of Navarre's sole legal claim to the throne). Nor can he dispose of the royal domain: Bodin argued that point at the Estates of Blois. For he was both an absolutist and a defender of the historic constitution of the French monarchy, which did not permit the king to impose arbitrary taxation. The absolute sovereign operates within a fixed constitutional framework. American history and practice has had its own difficulties reconciling the same two absolutes. Bodin never decided between Hobbes's subordination of everything to sovereignty, or the alternative of Rousseau, of locating sovereignty elsewhere than in the prince. The fusion—or confusion—of prince and sovereign was due to the practical need of awakening loyalty to the personal head of the national state—as the Fronde was to make clear. But in the letter, Bodin's theory is one of constitutional monarchy.

The rest of Bodin's book, his examination of the well-ordered commonwealth, is largely a statement of the policy of the *Politiques*, carried out under the Bourbons. Bodin of course is proposing a program of reform, but he states it as a pronouncement of eternal truth. His idealism has more backbone than Machiavelli's, but he has not the Florentine's objectivity. He states his theory of sovereignty as a quality logically essential to every commonwealth; but it turns out there are few commonwealths or well-ordered states. The confusion of the necessary with the desirable springs ultimately from his combining history with philosophy.

I V

The first great defense of secular absolutism on a rational basis was stated by one who was himself committed, in the French religious wars, to the party of secular authority, the *Politiques*. It was this same religious dissension in France that provoked the first statement of the second major political theory of modern times, liberal or constitutional monarchy. This was the first enunciation of the principle of "liberalism," destined to triumph in England under the Whiggish policies of Locke and his eighteenth-century successors. By a theory of political "liberalism" is here meant a theory which against the power of the sovereign preserves certain rights to organized groups, and eventually to individual subjects, on the basis either of natural law or of some implicit or expressed voluntary engagement to obey the sovereign under stipulated conditions.

Such "liberalism" is to be sharply distinguished from the theory of "democracy"; in its French and English forms it was aristocratic, and appealed not to popular "rights" but to the ancient and traditional privileges or "liberties" of corporations and religious organizations. When a theory of "democracy" did make its appearance, in Spinoza and in Rousseau, it was fully committed to the great state, and displayed not the slightest trace of "liberalism." It was not until American experience that "liberalism" and "democracy" were combined, in a form Americans take for granted, but which is still puzzling to Continental tradition, including that of the "people's democracies." Such European "democracy" usually sees no need for the "liberalism," which it regards as a relic of economic *laissez faire*. On the other hand, the Whig tradition of England, in America embraced by conservative Republicans and southern Democrats, cannot understand the "democratic" component of the central American political tradition. For their part, those who wholeheartedly advocate the welfare state go back rather to the absolutism of Bodin and Hobbes—Justice Holmes was a convinced Austinian or Hobbist.

Such "liberal" constitutionalism, pressing for limited monarchy, appears in the religious wars as the defense of opposition religious parties. The classic document of the Huguenots, defending constitutionalism in systematic and generalized form, was the famous *Vindiciae contra Tyrannos, The Defense of Liberty against Tyrants*, or *The Grounds of Rights against Tyrants*.[14]

In the next generation an even more secular version of limited monarchy was upheld, in the light not only of the French situation, but of the relations between Spain and England, by the Spanish Jesuit writers, the historian Juan de Mariana, and the writer on jurisprudence and philosophy, Francisco Suarez. At this point, the Dutch jurists and political philosophers took up the case for liberal

---

[14] Published in Latin in 1579; French ed. in 1581, Eng. tr. in 1648. Ed. in Eng. by H. J. Laski in 1924. The book was issued under the pseudonym of "Stephen Junius Brutus," the name under which it was discussed at the time. Bayle's *Dictionary* attributes it to Hubert Languet, who was long taken as the author. After a paper by Max Lossen in 1887, it was assigned rather to Philippe du Plessis-Mornay. But Ernest Barker revived the claim of Languet in 1930, and at the moment he is the foremost contender, though J. W. Allen doubted both attributions. Grotius is emphatic that Languet wrote it.

constitutionalism, Althusius building on the *Vindiciae*, and Grotius both on it and on the Jesuit advocates of natural law. There is irony in the fact that it was Calvinists and Jesuits—whom the English under the Tudors and Stuarts normally linked together as subversive of the secular monarchy—who furnish the background and many of the ideas with which Locke and the Whigs later defended the rights of Englishmen. Being in opposition is a great stimulus to political philosophizing.

Both the Huguenots and the Jesuits, in opposing the new secular national state, drew upon medieval traditions and political concepts. The former made use of the arguments of antipapal writers, like William of Ockham and the Conciliarists, against an heretical pope. The latter bent to their ends the views of Thomas Aquinas and the papal theorists, restated in the light of the outcome of sixteenth-century experience by Robert Bellarmin,[15] greatest Catholic controversialist of the age. Bellarmin set the Jesuit pattern of abandoning all claims of the Papacy to direct authority in secular political matters. Still, as spiritual head of the Church, the pope has an "indirect power" over temporal affairs wherever they raise spiritual issues. Under certain circumstances he is justified in deposing an heretical ruler like Elizabeth. Bellarmin also emphasizes more strongly than St. Thomas the secular origin of royal power, to undermine the divine right of kings. Secular political power comes neither directly from God, nor from the pope, but arises from the community itself for the sake of its own secular ends. Among human rulers only the pope derives his authority directly from God. As human, secular authority cannot exact absolute obedience; and spiritual authority must direct and guide it for spiritual purposes.

Bellarmin's restatement of the Thomist position with modern revisions made Church and State two distinct societies. It satisfied neither the pope nor the Protestants nor the absolute Catholic monarchs: its abandonment of the claim to a direct authority in political affairs led Gregory XIII to put Bellarmin on the Index, while the others saw the revived claim to "spiritual authority" a license to interfere everywhere. James I coined the epigram, "Jesuits are nothing but Puritan-papists." In fact, both Jesuits and Calvinists were appeal-

[15] In the first volume of his *Disputationes* (1581): *De summo pontifice;* elaborated in his *De potestate summi pontificis* (1610), in answer to Sarpi's defense of Venetian privileges.

ing to medieval precedents in the vain effort to stave off the omnicompetent secular state. That precedent played so large a part in
all these arguments is not surprising. The debaters were all lawyers,
and the whole of political theory was couched in legal terms. Bentham's revolution, making social utility and policy, not juristic right,
fundamental, was still two centuries ahead.

St. Bartholomew's called forth indignant pamphlets from the Huguenots. In 1573 François Hotman published *Franco-Gallia,* an historical work claiming the French monarchy had never been absolute. Hereditary succession was a recent innovation, tacitly accepted;
the kingship had always been elective, and the king's power was always limited by the Estates-General. This was neither true historically, nor was it practical politics: the Estates-General last met in
1610, and was not called again until 1789. Hotman appealed to the
medieval theory lying back of the whole social contract position,
that the consent of the people to immemorial practices is the rightful basis of political power, and that the crown itself derives its authority from its legal position as the agent of the community, bound
together by a whole set of mutual but usually tacit obligations.

The *Vindiciae* of "Brutus" supplements this feudal background
of tacit consent to recognized obligations with the appeal to the Old
Testament Covenant between God and his people, and with the
theory embodied in Justinian's code, that all political authority
comes from the people, who by the famous *Lex regia* [16] voluntarily
assigned it to the *Princeps.* The *Vindiciae* tries to answer four contemporary issues: 1) Are subjects obliged to *obey* princes if they
command anything against the law of God? 2) Is it lawful to *resist*
(i.e., rebel against) a prince who desires to nullify the law of God
or who lays waste the *Church,* and if so, who has the right? 3) How
far is it lawful to resist a prince who is suppressing or destroying the
state? 4) Can neighboring princes, like Elizabeth, lawfully aid the
subjects of other princes, or are they obliged to, for the sake of true
religion or resistance to tyranny?

The negative answer to the first question is obvious on Christian

---

[16] The *Lex regia* of Roman law could be taken as justifying the fundamental
sovereignty of the people, who gave the emperor his powers, or equally the
omnipotence of the ruler, as being assigned them. Unfortunately the actual
text of the *Lex regia* is not itself given, it is only described: "Cum enim Lege
antiqua, quae regia nuncupabatur, omne jus omnisque potestas populi Romani
imperatori translata sunt." (C. I. 17. i.)

principles. The answer to the second question occasions the setting-forth of the twofold covenant or contract (*foedus*). First, on the model of the Old Testament Covenant, the king and people together contract with God to make the community a church, and to preserve true doctrine and worship. Secondly, the people as one party contract with the king as a second, in a purely political contract, whose details follow the form of civil law, to obey him so long as he rules well. The first contract imposes religious obligations, and guarantees the right to coerce an heretical king. In it the king's power comes from both God and the people, and to obey his lawful commands is a duty promised to God. The theory is still religious, not wholly secular. King and people are co-contractors to preserve sound religion. Each must watch over the other, for both are responsible. The people have gone surety for the king; if he defaults, they become themselves liable for the preservation of pure religion. In both contracts the powers are delegated to the king, in the first by God, in the second by the people.

The third question is answered by a secular theory of popular sovereignty. Kingship is an institution of convenience for the benefit of the people. A king never reigns in his own right; he is chosen by God and installed with the people's consent. The formal argument proves "*electionem regis tribui Deo, constitutionem populo.*" In the political contract, the form is the Roman *stipulatio:* the people is *stipulator*, setting down the conditions, the king accepts them; the people agree to obey him so long as he keeps his agreement. Thus the king contracts absolutely, the people conditionally.

In the first covenant or pact, piety comes under the bond; in the second, justice. In the one the king promises dutifully to obey God; in the second, justly to rule the people: in the one, to provide for the glory of God, in the other, to maintain the welfare of the people. In the first the condition is, if you observe my law; in the second, if you secure to each his own. Failure to fulfill the first pact is properly punishable by God; failure to fulfill the second, legitimately by the whole people, or by the magistrates of the realm who have undertaken to watch over the whole people.[17]

It is interesting to see how the *Vindiciae* turns to medieval modes of thinking to support the case for limited sovereignty against the

[17] *Vindiciae*, cited in W. A. Dunning, *History of Political Theories* (1905), II, 54.

"modern" position of the absolutists. The whole argument is a mixture of appeal to the network of feudal obligations and to ideas of commercial contracts.

Then therefore all kings are vassals of the King of kings, invested into their office by the sword, which is the cognizance of their royal authority, to the end that with the sword they maintain the law of God, defend the good, and punish evil.[18]

But behind the feudal and legal form, there is a strong utilitarian emphasis:

In the first place every one consents, that men by nature loving liberty, and hating servitude, born rather to command, than obey, have not willingly admitted to be governed by another, and renounced as it were the privilege of nature, by submitting themselves to the commands of others, but for some special and great profit that they expected from it. . . . Neither let us imagine, that kings were chosen to apply to their own proper use the goods that are gotten by the sweat of their subjects; for every man loves and cherishes his own.[19]

Taking Seneca's account of the state of nature as a golden age, the author ascribes the origin of kingship to the need for leadership occasioned by the recognition of private property. Monarchs were appointed to determine rights at home and lead armies abroad.

Cum igitur *Meum* illud et *Tuum* orbem invasissent ac de rerum dominio inter cives, mox vero de finibus inter finitimos, bella exorirentur . . . reges creati sunt ut domi ius dicerent, foris vero exercitum ducerent.[20]

The point of the contract theory is that the king may be held to account by the people for the legality and justice of his rule. A tyrannical king loses all right. But who has the authority to "resist" him? A usurper has no rights at all, and may be justly killed by anyone: this traditional doctrine, going back to John of Salisbury and approved by Thomas, caused shivers in Elizabeth and suspicions in William of Orange, whom Catholics regarded as not legitimate monarchs. But a lawful king who has become tyrannous—a "tyrant *exercitio*"—may be "resisted" only by the people as a corporate body; so far as individuals are concerned, the *Vindiciae* assert the duty of passive obedience as strongly as Calvin or Luther. The people must act through their natural leaders, the inferior magistrates and Estates

[18] *Vindiciae*, ed. Laski, pp. 7of.   [19] *Vindiciae*, ed. Laski, pp. 139f.
[20] Cited in Dunning, II, 53.

or assemblies expressing their corporate power. The multitude as a whole—"that monster with countless heads"—has no political rights. The Estates of the realm are assigned the maintenance of religion: the author draws on the arguments of the anti-papalists at the Councils of Constance and Basel.

The right of resistance belongs to corporate bodies, and not to individuals. The theory of representation implied assumes the representation of such corporations, towns, classes, etc. The *Vindiciae* is on the point of developing a theory of federalism; such a theory of the state as a federation of lesser corporate bodies was pushed by Althusius in Holland, where federalism was a political fact. The contrast with Bodin's unitary state is striking. The relation is not between "sovereign" and "subject," or isolated individual—the view later consecrated by the French Revolution—but between the responsible ruler and a complexly organized social community. The general council of the magistrates stands to the king like a coguardian (*contutor*), to see that he does not violate his obligations to his ward (*pupillus*), the people. "*Singulis neque a Deo neque a populo gladius concessus est.*" It is granted only to the council of corporate interests.

The fourth question, is it the right and duty of princes to intervene in behalf of neighboring peoples "who are oppressed on account of their adherence to the true religion, or by any manifest tyranny?" is answered in the affirmative. The ground is in the first case, the unity of the Christian Church; in the second, the unity of humanity: i.e., duty to God and to one's neighbor. This justifies Elizabeth and the German princes in aiding the Huguenots, on the basis of an enlightened view of international solidarity, like that institutionalized in our day in the United Nations.

In the same year the *Vindiciae* appeared, 1579, George Buchanan published his *De jure regni apud Scotos*, the classic revolutionary document of the Scottish Reformation. Buchanan was a humanist rather than a lawyer, and he draws more upon the Stoics: government originates in the social character of men, and is therefore natural. It springs from men's desire to get away from Polybius' bestial state of nature: "the time when men lived in tents and even in caves, without laws and without fixed abodes." [21]

[21] *De jure regni*, sec. 8.

The impulse to get together came partly from self-interest (which, however, can lead equally to the destruction of the community), but more fundamentally from the natural impulse to association. Justice is to society what health is to the individual. The function of the king is therefore to maintain justice. But experience teaches that justice is maintained better by laws than by kings. The maker of laws is the people, acting through a council representing all classes; and the interpreter of the laws should be, not the king, but a body of independent judges. The function of the king is to maintain morale by setting a high example of rational and virtuous living— a function not notably performed with success by Mary Queen of Scots. Buchanan sets forth the king's contract to conform to justice and law, much like the *Vindiciae*. But he goes farther with the right of resistance: even a legitimate ruler can become a tyrant, and the object of a just war of rebellion; and in such a war it is legitimate for individuals to slay the enemy. Only Buchanan and Mariana at this time justify the tyrannicide of a legal monarch. On the other hand, Buchanan has only a vague idea of legal resistance. The "whole people" may call the ruler to account; this means the majority, and if they will not act, the "good citizens." [22] Buchanan's book was written to instruct the young James VI. James's wholehearted Anglicanism was the result of having early learned both the theory and the practice of Presbyterianism.

V

The other *monarchomachi*, the Jesuits, were more influential, through Grotius, in developing the modernized theory of natural law that became the orthodox political theory on the Continent in the seventeenth and eighteenth centuries. This was partly due to the fact that the Jesuit support of limited secular monarchy was stated on a higher and more philosophical level than the Protestant. By conceding the fact that Europe had become a group of independent national states, the Jesuits hoped to save for the pope some leadership in spiritual matters. This attempt failed with nation-minded Catholics as with Protestants.

Juan de Mariana (1536–1624) was very Spanish and not typically

[22] "But even if the whole people (*tota plebs*) should dissent [from resisting], this has nothing to do with our discussion; for we are inquiring not what will happen, but what can justly happen." (Dunning, II, 61–62)

Jesuit. Primarily an historian, like Hotman in France he based himself on constitutional history. He especially admired the Estates of Aragon, who, in installing a king, proclaimed: "We, who are as good as you and are more powerful than you, choose you as king, etc." [23] The Estates are the guardians of the law, to which the king is bound, and for violating which he may be deposed. Civil society originates from a prior state of nature: Mariana elaborates on Polybius. Man's wants are greater than those of other animals, his means of protection less. So men grouped themselves under a leader, as a result of their timidity and weakness. The rule of one, unrestrained by law, came first. But the origin of private property called for some general system of law. The essence of government is personal rule under law. Democracy is plausible; but Mariana follows Pliny in pointing out, when power lies in a group of men, the less wise part will always prevail, "for the votes are not weighed but merely counted." [24] Monarchy restrained by law has fewer evils and greater efficiency than any other form. Its great danger is that the ruler will consider his own good rather than his people's: he will degenerate into a tyrant.

Sovereignty lies with the people. They grant the king his royal power. But in bestowing on him certain rights (*iura potestatis*), the people reserves the rights of taxation and legislation, and puts beyond the king's authority the established laws of succession, of revenue, and the form of religion. The people is above the monarch. The whole process of setting up law and of contracting with a king is a natural process, and Mariana is much more naturalistic in his account of secular government than the *Vindiciae*. He not only upholds the right of private individuals to kill a legal monarch who has become tyrannical; he openly defended the assassination of Henri III of France. This led the Parlement of Paris, as good Gallicans, to burn his book. But normally the organ of the popular will is the Estates of the realm—the bishops, nobles, and representatives (*procuratores*) of the cities. This assembly he calls the "*respublica*" and the "*populus*": its powers over the succession, the revenue, and religion are paramount. The prince must submit to divine and natural law, to the will of God, and even to public opinion (*populari etiam civium opinione*). Mariana mourns the decline in power of the Es-

[23] Dunning, II, 54n.   [24] *De rege*, Lib. I, cap. 2.

tates in Spain. He holds that war is inevitable, that standing armies are indispensable, and that they must be kept busy and supported by incessant war and pillaging abroad (III, ch. 5). Intentionally, Mariana lays little stress upon the spiritual power of the pope; and he offers, in a chapter on the *prudentia* of the king, a good deal of Machiavellian advice, in the spirit that came to be known as "Jesu-itical."

Mariana wrote his *De rege et regis institutione* in 1599. In the new century the great Jesuit political thinker was Suarez, the last major Thomist philosopher (though his Thomism has a strong strain of Scotism). The outstanding school of jurisprudence in Spain at this time included Vasquez, Soto, Victoria, Molina, and Ayala, as well as Suarez. The effect of their political theory, in which they tried to exalt the divine right of the pope by emphasizing the merely hu-man and secular and therefore limited power of the king, was to make their account of civil society as a purely natural phenomenon set politics off completely from theology. The law of nature became the independent foundation of civil government, and reached the form taken over by Grotius. A supreme and immutable natural law of justice, a further *ius gentium*, which introduced private property and slavery, a state of nature prior to the state of corruption—these were principles of all these writers on jurisprudence. They all started from the theory of justice, right, and law found in St. Thomas.

Francisco Suarez (1548–1617) states the scheme of this law in his *Tractatus de legibus ac Deo legislatore* (1612). All moral beings, endowed with reason and free will, are determined in all their rela-tions by law. Law is "a just and permanent precept, applying to a community and sufficiently promulgated." [25] Law must be both ra-tional and just, and willed. The law of nature (*lex naturalis* or *ius naturale*) is that law implanted in the human soul through which right is distinguished from wrong. Its source is God the Creator, its end the good of man. It is imperative as well as indicative: it is a true prescriptive law. Its most fundamental and general precepts, like the Golden Rule and the Decalogue, are present in every man's consciousness immediately. Others like the prohibition of fornica-

---

[25] *Tractatus de legibus*, Book I, ch. xii, sec. 2. Lex est commune praeceptum, iustum ac stabile, sufficienter promulgatum.

tion, of usury, and of unjust price, are derivative by reasoning from these general principles, but may never be known by the people (*ignari possunt invincibiliter, praesertim a plebe*).[26] The law of nature can be modified or dispensed from by no human power, even the pope, and by no human law, whether *ius civile* or *ius gentium*. It holds eternally, universally, inflexibly. But the subject-matter to which these precepts are applied may be "withdrawn" from their application, by God or by circumstance; so in practice dispensation is possible.

The *ius gentium*, men's actual practice, Suarez sets in sharp contrast to the *lex naturalis*. Thus by natural law community of goods and liberty are "natural." But the law of nations normally prescribes private property and slavery: it justifies the morally expedient,[27] and is of merely human origin. In it Suarez includes those rational principles that have arisen out of the inherent unity of mankind.[28] No state is so self-sufficing as to be free from the need of intercourse with other states; from this fact has arisen through custom (*usus*) the conditions on which an international law can be built.

Government Suarez discusses under positive human law, the power of man to prescribe laws to man. Men are born free (*omnes homines nascuntur liberi*). How then does one man come to have authority? Man is a social being, life in society is natural to him; but social life (*communitas*) necessarily implies a regulating power that must be exercised by men. Government was not introduced, as Augustine thought, because of sin: directive power is needed even among angels, if not coercive. Such power must be located in the whole community: a state is a socially organized body with a common political end, it is an organized moral unity. But this popular sovereignty, as the *Lex regia* showed, can be assigned to a monarch, by the consent of the people. This consent binds indefinitely, save in cases of injustice and tyranny, in which, by his indirect and spiritual power, the pope may intervene.

In setting forth the ultimate law-making authority (*potestas condendi leges civiles*), so far as concerns monarchies, Suarez approaches

---

[26] *Tractatus de legibus*, Book II, ch. viii, sec. 3.

[27] *Tractatus de legibus*, Book II, chs. xvii–xx.

[28] Humanum genus, quantumvis in varios populos et regna divisum, semper habet aliquam unitatem non solum specificam sed etiam quasi politicam et moralem. (Book II, ch. xix, sec. 5)

Bodin's conception of sovereignty. Only the supreme temporal authority can enact laws. But as in Bodin, this supreme power is limited, not only by the laws of God and of nature, but also by "fundamental laws" which in the transfer of power or contract with the monarch are either explicitly stated or implied in the custom of the country. Political sovereignty does not depend on the character of the prince; resistance is justified not because of the quality of the lawmaker, but because of the quality of his laws. A statute contravening natural justice is *ipso facto* void. The end of political action, as with Aristotle, is to make men good; it is not, as with Machiavelli, to augment the power of the state.

Suarez's position becomes clearer in his discussion of the practical issue of taxation. Spanish revenues were chaotic—reform was demanded. Taxes must be just, to be sure, by the law of nature. Is the consent of the subjects necessary to new proposals, as even Bodin had insisted? Spanish law required it, just as did the "fundamental law" of the French monarchy. No new tax might be imposed except with the previous summons and consent of the realm (*nisi prius convocato regno et illis consentientibus*). This might well be a law of Spain; Suarez refuses to admit it as a principle of the law of nature.

> This opinion . . . I find neither in common, canon, or civil law, nor in the ancient authors; and therefore I do not think such a condition necessary of natural right.[29]

A prince has the power to impose just taxes at his discretion. The general consent to his power covers the special authorization to raise revenue. Consulting the "realm" is only a benevolent concession, not a natural right.

The doctrine of the indirect and spiritual power of the pope over civil rulers might have been the attempt to salvage the right of interference on the ground, or pretext, that spiritual issues were involved. But its practical effect was to make the Church one independent community among many, whose relations to the others were to be regulated by international law, by treaties and concordats. Thus emerged the "modern" theory of the relations between Church and State. The pope is no longer the head of an international

---

[29] *Tractatus de legibus*, Book V, ch. xvii.

moral community; he is an independent sovereign, treating with other sovereigns. On this basis Grotius extended the Jesuit jurisprudence into a theory of international law.

VI

It was the Dutch form of limited or constitutional monarchy that by the early seventeenth century had triumphed. Henri IV sacrificed half his principles to win the French throne; William the Silent sacrificed only his life, to the Jesuit theory of tyrannicide. To the seventeenth century the Netherlands stood as the England of the Whig revolution did to the eighteenth, as a working model of free institutions, the triumph of the "liberal" theory for which the Huguenots had fought in vain, and which the Jesuits forgot when the settlement of 1648 gave them substantial power. The Dutch seemed to have solved the problem of combining liberty with the order demanded in the modern state. And they did it on the basis of federalism—a lesson the English did not learn until the American colonists revolted, and a lesson Rousseau and Revolutionary and Napoleonic France spurned.

Hence it is fitting that the States-General should have summed up all these theories of limited sovereignty and the right of resistance in deposing Philip of Habsburg in 1581. It remained for the Dutch to state the systematic principles on which their resistance had been carried on and justified. That was the work of two men, Johannes Althusius and Hugo Grotius. The two, especially Grotius, who carried on the Jesuit jurisprudence of natural law, transmitted the experience of the revolt of the United Netherlands to the English struggle of the Great Rebellion, and to those Continental jurists who were trying in the seventeenth century to make the society of warring sovereign states of Europe work.

Althusius' *Politica methodice digesta* (1603, 1610) is the statement in generalized philosophic form of the theory of all the *monarchomachi*, of the *Vindiciae* and of Mariana. It is the counterpart of the theory of the unitary absolute state of Bodin, the statement of the federal limited state of the liberals and constitutionalists. Both Bodin and Althusius show what a "science" and a "scientific treatment" of politics were like before Galileo and Descartes had captured the idea for social "physics."

Outside the Netherlands, Althusius was both too medieval, in seizing on the medieval notion of society as a *communitas communitatum*, and too far ahead of his time, in opposing his federalism to Bodin's unitary state, which he specifically criticizes and rejects, to have much immediate influence. Grotius entered much more fully into the main stream of European jurisprudence and political theory. Althusius' present reputation as the first scientific theorist of liberal constitutionalism is due to O. von Gierke's study of 1880, *Johannes Althusius und die Entwicklung der naturrechtlichen Staatstheorien.*[30]

Johannes Althusius was a German who served for thirty-four years (1604–1638) as chief magistrate of Emden in East Friesland, after being a professor at the University of Herborn. A convinced Calvinist, committed to a state church, a school system under its direction, and a far-reaching censorship of morals, he systematized the polemics of the *Vindiciae* in the light of the federalism of the Holy Roman Empire and of the experience of Dutch federalism. He tried to combine Bodin's legal theory of sovereignty—for him it was the States-General that was sovereign—with the theory of the popular origin of political power.

Althusius makes the social contract fundamental. But whereas the Protestants and the Jesuits made it a contract between "people" and king, Althusius makes it a genuinely *social* contract, the mutual agreement to live in an ordered association. Every species of associated life (*consociatio;* Althusius means something close to Aristotle's *koinōnia*) is founded on an agreement or contract among its members, involving a body of rules, and a relationship of command and obedience to administer them. Human society is made up of a series of more and more inclusive "associations," rising from the simplest, the family, to the most inclusive, the state.[31] The essence of the corporate life of each of these groups is the contract by which its

---

[30] The great jurist found Althusius congenial because he stated so clearly the theory of the *Genossenschaftsstaat*, as over against Bodin's theory of the *Herrschaftsverband*. Figgis held that the recognition of the reality of corporate communities, of the liberty and *Selbstständigkeit* of social organizations apart from the "state," is the next great step in the understanding of human societies. A pluralistic theory of sovereignty is certainly opposed to present-day totalitarianism and *étatisme*.

[31] *Vici, pagi, oppida*, and *civitates*—i.e., villages, parishes, towns, and cities—are lower forms of political organization. The five main forms are the family, the voluntary corporation (*collegium*), the local community, the province, and the state.

members are united to achieve the given end. The state (*politia, imperium, regnum, populus, respublica*) is defined as "a general public association, in which a number of cities and provinces, combining their possessions and their activities, contract to establish, maintain, and defend a sovereign power" (*ius regni*, identical with *ius maiestatis*).[32] The members of the state are not at all the individuals who live in it; they are the lesser corporations, cities, and provinces, which have united to form it. Sovereign power (*maiestas*) is the supreme and supereminent power of doing what the spiritual and bodily welfare of the members of the state demands. By the very nature of an association, sovereignty resides in the association, in the people as a corporate body, in the corporation itself, not in its individual members. It cannot be alienated or assigned to a monarch or an aristocracy. But the sovereign people can appoint agents to perform various functions, such as kings and magistrates, who remain subject to the people corporately organized, to the representative assembly. This follows not only from the nature of an association, but also from the nature of man himself: for all men being by nature free and equal, the exercise of authority over them can only be by their own consent.

The state has two classes of officials, "ephors" and the *summus magistratus*. The ephors include all the less inclusive associations and their agents; the chief magistrate is the king. If the ephors do not do their duty of watching over the state, the task falls on an assembly of the whole people. The king is the executive of the people, their agent (*mandatarius*). The people's contract with him, as in the *Vindiciae*, involves the people as *stipulator*, with a conditional obligation; the king's obligation is absolute.

The familiar right of resistance to tyranny follows: it resides in the ephors, private individuals being obligated to passive resistance. Althusius' federalism allows him to add the right of each member of the confederation, each province and city, to secede and join another political association—as the United Provinces had done.

The functions of the state being both religious and secular, it must supervise religion, prescribe and enforce rules of conduct, and promote the general welfare in positive ways. There can be only one form of state: the people remain sovereign. Government, however,

[32] *Politica*, ch. xi, sec. 1.

may be monarchic, oligarchic, or popular. Every government is normally a mixture of executive and council or assembly.

Althusius' theory was the clearest statement of popular sovereignty that had so far appeared. By making the organized people sovereign, and the king their agent, it avoids the confusions of Bodin between the sovereign and the limited monarch, and the confusions of Grotius as well. Yet the fundamental obligation to keep a contract is left unjustified. It is a principle of the natural law, which as a Calvinist Althusius identifies with the second table of the Decalogue.

VII

The Jesuits worked out a developed conception of the law of nature, and their notion of the indirect spiritual authority of the pope over secular monarchs recognized the existence of a group of independent and sovereign national states. But in northern Europe their jurisprudence was too closely bound up with the Catholic system, and unacceptable to Protestants; it was also stated in scholastic form, whereas the northerners wanted rather a humanist exposition, and were on the point of identifying the law of nature with the rational law of the emerging science. On all these scores Grotius was much more acceptable, and certainly far more influential in molding seventeenth-century jurisprudence. Contemporary with Galileo, he is the real founder of the science of man and society on the demonstrative model of the new science—the fountainhead of seventeenth- and eighteenth-century "rationalism" in political and moral affairs. He employed the modern and "geometrical" model, so soon to be illustrated formally by Hobbes and Spinoza, as well as Pufendorf and Leibniz. He freed the natural law from its theological basis and established it on the independent model of a science with axioms and demonstrations, like mathematics. Into its content went the fused traditions of Roman civil law, canon law, and the theories of theologians and philosophers.

Hugo de Groot (1583–1645) came of a patrician Dutch family. His father was Burgomaster of Leyden and curator of the University. A precocious genius, he carried off all the honors, became a leading light of the bar, and rose to be in 1613 the Pensionary (administrator) of the city of Rotterdam. He became an Arminian, joined the Remonstrants, and as a religious liberal supported the party of the liberal commercial aristocracy, headed by Oldenbarneveldt, against the popular party of strict Calvinists on whom the Stadtholder, Maurice of Nassau, leaned for support. After the defeat of Oldenbarneveldt's attempt to overthrow the House of Orange, as a republican leader he was condemned to life imprisonment. He escaped to France, and spent the rest of his life in exile. In France he wrote his *De jure belli ac pacis* (1625), and dedicated it to Louis XIII. Unable to get along with Richelieu, he was snapped up for the Swedish court by the astute Oxenstierna, and served for nine years as Swedish ambassador to France. This career helps explain Grotius' combination of theological liberalism and rationalism with a distaste for the popular and Calvinist party, and his distrust of popular rights. Grotius writes as a Humanist, in clear and forceful style, encumbered by masses of Humanistic erudition, in his day much admired.

His secular statement of natural law stems not from Aquinas, but from Cicero and the Stoics. Significantly, he writes not, like Suarez, of *lex naturalis*, with the Jesuit's strong emphasis on *Deus legislator*, but of *ius naturale*, as primarily a product of human reason—though he admits God wills it also. He treats as mutually exclusive "natural" right and "voluntary" right (*ius voluntarium*), the traditional "positive law"; the former is founded on reason, the latter on declared will.

The law of nature is a dictate of right reason, which points out that an act, according as it is or is not in conformity with rational nature, has in it a quality of moral necessity or moral baseness; and that, in consequence, such an act is either enjoined or forbidden by the author of nature, God.[33]

Such law is universal and absolutely immutable. God enjoins it, but it would be valid even if there were no God, or if he had no interest in human affairs.

Just as even God, then, cannot cause that two times two should not make four, so he cannot cause that which is intrinsically evil to be not evil.[34]

[33] *De jure belli ac pacis*, Book I, ch. i, sec. x. Tr. F. W. Kelsey (Oxford, 1925).
[34] *Ibid.*, Book I, ch. i, sec. x. See Prolegomena, sec. 11.

This law is founded on right reason, and reason belongs to every man by virtue of his humanity. The dictates of right reason are what human nature and the nature of things imply they must be. Will enters in, as one factor: man must will to follow right reason. But the law of nature is obligatory quite apart from the *sic volo, sic iubeo* of God or man. Grotius carefully distinguishes between the laws God proclaimed to his chosen people in the Old Testament, and the evidence Scripture shows of natural human relationships.

In his Prolegomena Grotius states the grounds of natural law in the form of a debate with Carneades, who staged a famous attack in Rome on the Stoic law of nature.[35] Carneades argued against eternal Justice, that all men's actions spring from self-interest, and that justice is a social convention generally useful and supported by prudence. Grotius refutes such utilitarianism by emphasizing, with Aristotle and the Stoics, man's social and rational nature. Rightness in human conduct is therefore conformity to social needs rationally discerned. The maintenance of society is a *social* utility, quite apart from any private interest; Grotius rejects egoism.

Man is, to be sure, an animal, but an animal of a superior kind, much farther removed from all other animals than the different kinds of animals are from one another. . . . But among the traits characteristic of man is an impelling desire for society, that is, for the social life—not of any and every sort, but peaceful, and organized according to the measure of his intelligence, with those who are of his own kind; this social trend the Stoics called "sociableness." (Prol., sec. 6)

Hence the preservation of a peaceful social order is an intrinsic good, and its conditions are morally binding on man.

The maintenance of the social order . . . is the source of law properly so called. To this sphere of law belong the abstaining from that which is another's, the restoration to another of anything of his which we may have, together with any gain which we may have received from it; the obligation to fulfill promises, the making good of a loss incurred through our fault, and the inflicting of penalties upon men according to their deserts. (Prol., sec. 8)

Certain conditions are necessary for orderly society: these make up the law of nature.

[35] The account in Cicero's *Republic* was preserved in Books V and VI of Lactantius' *Institutes*.

For the very nature of man, which even if we had no lack of anything would lead us into the mutual relations of society, is the mother of the law of nature. (Prol., sec. 16)

Derivatively, the law of nature gives rise to positive or "voluntary" law, the law of states, municipal law.

For those who had associated themselves with some group, or had subjected themselves to a man or to men, had either expressly promised, or from the nature of the transaction must be understood implicitly to have promised, that they would conform to that which should have been determined, in the one case by the majority, in the other by those upon whom authority had been conferred. (Prol., sec. 15)

Utility, Grotius admits, may be the *occasion* of a voluntary or positive law; but the *cause* is to be found, immediately, in the compact by which a state exists, ultimately, in the natural impulse to will the conditions of social existence. Just as it is the normal man who is possessed of senses that are veridical, so it is the "complete" (*perfectus*) and normal man who is immediately conscious of the propositions of natural law. Moreover, a harmony among the best minds also points to these propositions: Grotius cites fully the ancients. By adopting the traditional distinction between pure (*merum*) *ius naturale*, and that peculiar to certain circumstances (*praecepta quae pro certo statu sunt naturalia*), which belong to a developed society, Grotius is able to bring under natural law both the community of goods and private property, and similarly with other contradictory ideas.

As to the content of *ius naturale*, Grotius accepts the tradition. It is his method, not his conclusion, that is novel. By discarding all theological sanction, he has an appeal to reason and a precise conception of rationality on which pagans, infidels, and atheists, as well as Protestants and Catholics, can all agree. To the seventeenth century this seemed a rational and therefore "scientific" foundation for the knowledge of human affairs. And by his geometrical model, with its appeal to self-evident axioms and to conclusions demonstrated from them, he had a method that agreed perfectly with the demonstrative science of the new mathematical interpretation of nature. Grotius' repeated references to mathematics enabled men to take him as having reconstructed the traditional rationalism of the law of nature to fit the new rationalism of science.

Such a "scientific" basis of human affairs, on the model of the first of the great modern conceptions of science, as necessary demonstration of conclusions from self-evident axioms, captured all major minds down through Montesquieu. Even Newton and Locke took their own new conception of science—the second to emerge in modern times, "observationalism"—as a mere second-best in default of the possibility of obtaining the kind Grotius was following; Locke always held that ethics at least was thus "demonstrative" (see Book Four, chapter 8). There were two ambiguities present in the conception of natural law as both the rational statement of natural relations and as prescriptive. First, logical relations were identified with matters of fact. Secondly, the simple necessity of mathematics was identified with the hypothetical necessity of morals and law, in which certain conditions are necessary *for* achieving certain ends. These ambiguities were not clearly pointed out until David Hume (see Book Four, chapter 11), who forced a thorough reconsideration of the relation of means and ends, read out of philosophy by the new science, but necessary for any consideration of ends and "values."

Though Grotius' theory of the state and of sovereignty was subordinate to his treatment of the law of nature and the law of nations, it was hardly less influential. He combines the two theories of the origin of the state, that of the natural impulse to social life (Aristotelian and Stoic), and that of a contract motivated by self-interest (civil law and feudal). He probably held that *societas* is natural, while the *civitas* is founded on contract. The state of nature is prepolitical but not presocial. In it the pure or *merum ius civile* prevails: by nature every man has the right to enforce his own rights under it. But this was unsatisfactory.

Originally men, not by the command of God but of their own accord, after learning by experience that isolated families could not secure themselves against violence, united in civil society, out of which act sprang governmental power.[36]

Grotius' central idea of "public" war demands a clear definition of sovereignty. He builds on Bodin and Suarez, but modifies them. Sovereignty is supreme political power (*potestas civilis*), that "moral faculty of governing a state" vested in him whose acts are not sub-

[36] *De jure belli ac pacis*, Book I, ch. iv, sec. vii.

ject to the rights of any other, and cannot be rendered null by any other human will.[37] The common subject of sovereignty is the state itself (*civitas*); the special subject (*subiectum proprium*) is one or more persons with authority. Authority is a right (the *ius regendi* or *imperandi*) belonging to a person, like a private right. Such sovereignty is also exhibited in *dominium* over a piece of land: Grotius identifies public authority with patrimonial power over land, as in feudal theory. Such sovereignty may be possessed in full ownership, in usufruct, or for a term; as against Bodin, these are all equally sovereign power while they last. Sovereignty may also be held under promise to God or to subjects: the condition makes no difference. And sovereignty may be divided, between king and people, for instance. Tributary powers and vassals may even be sovereign in their own domains.

Grotius is not nearly so clear or precise as Bodin or Althusius. But he is concerned to define a public war, one conducted by a "sovereign," and hence anxious to be as inclusive as possible, to bring all conflicts under the rules of war. And he is also anxious to combat the doctrine of popular sovereignty. A people may choose any form of government it will. But having once assigned its powers, the decision is irrevocable (as in the *Lex regia*).[38] The transfer may be for reasons of extreme necessity, or acquired through a just war; popular sovereignty does not apply. Nor is the sole justifiable end of all government the good of the governed. The monarch may lawfully rule like a master over slaves, for his own good; or like a husband over his wife, for their joint good. The interest or judgment of the subjects is immaterial to the ruler's right. This absence of political liberty in no wise entails the absence of personal liberty. There is no right of resistance on the people's part, no recourse against a bad sovereign. A command in conflict with the law of God or nature must not be obeyed, but the subject must be prepared to take the consequences. The right of resistance even to usurpers is very doubtful and usually inexpedient.[39]

---

[37] Summa illa dicitur cuius actus alterius iuri non subsunt, ita ut alterius voluntatis humanae arbitrio irriti possint reddi. (Book I, ch. iii, sec. vii)

[38] Quidni ergo populo sui iuris liceat se unicuipiam aut pluribus ita addicere ut regendi sui ius in eum plane transcribat, nulla eius parte retenta? (Book I, ch. iii, sec. viii)

[39] Profecto gravissima cum sit deliberatio libertas an pax placeat. (Book I, ch. iv, sec. xix)

With Grotius the system of natural law became the foundation of political theory for the seventeenth century. What nearly all thinkers agreed upon was that to be genuinely binding an obligation must be freely assumed by the parties bound. Obligation rests on consent; the promise is the model, antedating the political contract, perhaps even the original social contract. Whether the agreement was taken to be historical, or a methodological fiction, the obligation was assumed to be self-imposed. Pufendorf stated this fundamental assumption, destined to flower in Kant's ethics:

> On the whole, to join a multitude, or many men, into one Compound Person, to which one general act may be ascribed, and to which certain rights belong, as 'tis opposed to particular members, and such rights as no particular member can claim separately from the rest; 'tis necessary, that they shall first have united their wills and powers by the intervention of covenants; without which, how a number of men, who are all naturally equal, should be linked together, is impossible to be understood.[40]

This unquestioned assumption led to theories of government by contract or consent. They seemed natural in a society that for centuries had taken as a matter of course the relation of a feudal lord to his vassals; they received support from the civil law of Rome. It soon, on analysis, became apparent that the ability of a people to contract with a ruler needed explanation. This led to the theory of the two contracts, one forming the community, the other the government, as in Althusius and Pufendorf.[41] Hobbes suppressed the second contract, Locke used both without distinguishing them clearly. Natural law never played so large a part in England as on the Continent, though Locke's early papers make it more fundamental to his thought than had been supposed. Hobbes and Spinoza use the contract theory to support an absolutism of the state; Althusius and Locke, to defend limited government. Most writers, like Grotius and Pufendorf, without justifying the right of resistance, emphasize moral limitations on rulers. Law and government are subject to ethical criticism.

The whole theory assumes that individuals are given, and that society needs accounting for. This is in marked contrast to the as-

---

[40] *De jure naturae et gentium* (1672); Eng. tr. Basil Kennett (London, 1710), Book VII, ch. ii, sec. 6.

[41] *De jure naturae*, Book VII, ch. ii, secs. 7–8.

sumption of the Greeks, Plato and Aristotle, that the organized community or *polis* is given, and that man's individual judgment and criticism needs explanation and justification. The assumption of the contract theory is a primary illustration of the individualistic emphasis that the revolutions of European society had produced by the seventeenth century. Here modern political theory differed markedly from both Greek and medieval. The primacy of the community was not rediscovered until the Romanticists of the second half of the eighteenth century, men like Rousseau, Herder, and Burke. Through Hegel and Marx this assumption has now become axiomatic once more for a large part of the world, perhaps less among the heirs of the British tradition than elsewhere. The problem then becomes, not how to account for or justify society, but how men can achieve individuality within a socialized industrial order. Only in the international field is the absence of a "community" still the major problem. Here sovereign national states, in great proliferation, still have to manage a *modus vivendi*—as for Grotius.

This was of course the major purpose of Grotius' book. The *ius gentium* or law of nations had had a long history; starting with the Romans as "the law common to all or many nations," it had become narrowed in late Roman times to "the law governing the intercourse between nations." Grotius made this meaning precise, freeing the *ius gentium* from the admixture with technical military topics it had acquired in the Italian writers. His chief predecessor was Alberico Gentili, an Italian Protestant teaching law at Oxford.

This "law of nations" is "voluntary," not natural law. Its content is what has been accepted as obligatory by the consent of all or many nations, as proved by constant usage or the testimony of the learned. It depends ultimately, not on mere self-interest, but on the natural impulse to social life.[42] Grotius tries, not too successfully, to distinguish between that law which is merely custom common to many peoples, and that which is essential to the bond of international society, and hence approaches *ius naturale* in binding force. The distinction is important, for grave violation of the latter, or of *ius naturale* itself, is a cause for just war, while violation of the former hardly is. Yet he cannot agree even with an authority like Gentili

[42] Certe et illa [societas] quae genus humanum aut populos complures inter se colligat, iure indiget. (Prol., sec. 23)

on where to draw the line. He condemns preventive wars, taking arms against a power which will become dangerous in the future, while Gentili emphatically endorses them.

War itself can be justly undertaken if it be started "solemnly," in defense of natural law or those conventions essential to international order. The one hope of order is that sovereigns keep their agreements; if they violate them, he urges the king of France to coerce them to keep the law. Throughout the Christian world he observes "a licentiousness in regard to war, a running to arms upon very frivolous occasions"; this spectacle of "monstrous barbarity brought many good men, among them our countryman Erasmus, to the view that Christians ought not to bear arms at all." (Prol., sec. 28) But, alas, this objection is impractical. The sole hope is to regularize the conduct of war, and ensure that it be undertaken only as a last resort. The only justification for war is to win peace. When peace has been established, rulers must observe it strictly, avoiding not only perfidiousness, but "whatever may exasperate the mind." "May the Almighty, who alone can do it," he concludes, "impress these maxims on the hearts of Christian princes." Grotius had defined a new law of nations, and laid a foundation for international law. But he accepted the framework of competing sovereign states, and its "uneasy Balance of Power."

BOOK TWO

The Coming of Humanism and Science

II: THE INTELLECTUAL REVOLUTION

THE RECONSTRUCTION OF THE INTELLECTUAL TRADITIONS

6

The Nature Enthusiasts: Nature as a Spectacle and as a System of Useful Forces

I

BOTH the humanistic Renaissance, in its eager exploration of other streams of ancient wisdom than those so well tamed and sluiced in the organized learning of the later Middle Ages, and the Reformation, in its appeal from the corruption of the medieval Church to Augustine, Paul, and the primitive Christian community, registered the recognition of a shift in values rather than a changed conception of the world. They were major events in the long career of human wisdom, but scarcely incidents in the slow acquisition of human science. Whether one considers the social experience western Europe had now generated for itself, with its altered balance of drives, ways of acting, and institutionalized ends and desires; or the lessons men learned when they turned once more to their familiar teachers, the ancients, for further light on how to organize that experience; or the transitory shifting compromises with which they emerged from that schooling to the past: one confronts new orientations to an intellectually familiar universe, but no real concern with the nature of that universe itself, and no suspicion that its very structure was destined to profound reconstruction. Both Renaissance and Reformation, in their characteristic philosophic expressions, were directed toward the problems of the chief end of human living in a changed social rather than a changed cosmic setting.

As contrasted with this shift in values, the intellectual revolution that brought prestige to a new kind of science and a new world-view came later and took longer to achieve. The change in social experience and in the orientation of human life had evidently to be assimilated first. Men needed a sense of new ends for living before they could feel the necessity of a new aim for knowledge, or work fruitfully upon a new method to serve that aim. By 1687, when Newton's *Principia* appeared, the first major stage in that intellectual revolution had been consummated; the next century was largely devoted to exploring its significance and further implications for human life, both theoretical and practical.

It is not hard to see a certain necessity in the successive steps by which this profound intellectual change was accomplished. Before our "modern science" could come into being or into wide popularity, a series of convictions had to be spread abroad. Slowly at first, and then with accelerating rapidity as the broad base was laid in economic activities and social feelings and desires, more and more men came to take attitudes toward their present experience and towards the past which naturally generated a new kind of intellectual interest, demanded a different set of intellectual materials and techniques, and set them in pursuit of an ideal of knowledge which they themselves felt to be novel and revolutionary. This very consciousness of fresh discovery and radical reorientation has of course obscured the countless bonds of continuity, in materials, methods, and even achievements, uniting this increasing band of men with their predecessors in the late Middle Ages. History has fallen into error in taking at its face value the estimate which the pioneer thinkers of the sixteenth and seventeenth century made of their own radical turning away from the heritage of the past; in present contrition the scholars who know are prone to withdraw all credit. Yet though it was no creation *ex nihilo*, the construction of seventeenth-century science was creation nonetheless; and the change in ideas from the first writing of Cusanus to the triumphant system of Newton is as clear a case—and an illustration—of an intellectual revolution as our record holds. Many were the eddies and the cross-currents; the great majority of those who spurned the fleshpots of medieval certainty never beheld the promised land. Yet each of the major movements of those two centuries played its part in the revolution; each found significant philosophic expression in those exuberant and emancipated times. What distinguishes all these figures and groups from the Humanists is the fact that they did not consciously seek wisdom and truth in ancient learning—though much of what they found they did discover by its help—but rather in the world about them and in man himself. And by the seventeenth century not the Humanists' authority of respected tradition but the appeal to experience and reason had been firmly established as the source of knowledge.

That science might come to its birth, it was first of all necessary to set over against the rather narrow and limited concentration of the Humanists upon man himself the sense and conviction of the value of the nature within which man is set. Such concern with nature was not at the expense of the dignity of man, but rather a natural extension of it; indeed, human life formed the bridge from God to nature, and without a sense of the worth of man nature would doubtless have remained the mere ladder to Deity. The vision of the universe as a graded hierarchy of levels, the great chain of Being set for the Middle Ages by the Neoplatonic thought of the Areopagite and Eriugena, and merely translated into the Aristotelian terms and distinctions by the Schoolmen of the thirteenth century, had remained as the general structure of nature for most of the Humanists, Padua Alexandrians and Florentine Platonists alike: it was man's status in that structure that concerned them. But beginning in the fifteenth century, and in swelling numbers thereafter, appeared men with a new vision, a new *theoria* of nature. At first for them too the vision was primarily aesthetic: the world presented a great spectacle to be enjoyed, especially to the Italians, those we call the "Nature Philosophers." But it was no longer the familiar hierarchy; it was rather a System, an Order, still a harmony, to be sure, but one exhibiting a fundamental unity and homogeneity rather than a series of graded classes. It remained for Copernicus to shatter the old conception as science, and for Bruno to pierce the limitless horizons of the new world; over a century before, however, Cusanus had caught something of the meaning of an infinite universe.

But the world was not only a system to be enjoyed as a spectacle; especially north of the Alps it seemed a system to be controlled for human ends, a system of powers and "forces" to be employed, and not merely understood—a system that could be used even though it remained an ultimate mystery. Dim traditions stretching back to the ancient world, always disreputable and suspect during the Middle Ages, now flowered, among the German alchemists, astrologers, and magicians, in that fantastic learning of which Faust is the symbol and Paracelsus the exemplar.

Intimately bound up with this vision of nature and her possibilities was the increasing sense of the value of a knowledge that would give power and control over nature. A minority amongst the Humanists emphasized the place of a natural science in human wisdom, but a natural science wholly unlike that Aristotelian variety that aimed at understanding divorced from power. The temper of the age found expression in a new humanistic aim for natural science, in Humanists like Vives, Bruno, and Bacon, as well as in scientists like Galileo and Descartes. Science should be directed not merely to understanding and vision, but to an understanding that should give power, action, and an improvement of the practical arts.

How could men find such a science? The most popular intellectual enterprise of the sixteenth century was the search for a fruitful method that would serve this new aim to which knowledge had been turned. Ironically enough, the method which finally emerged to fulfill these hopes proved to be the least novel of all the elements that went into the formation of the new science. After many blind alleys had been explored, men finally turned to one of the great medieval traditions, the mathematical interpretation of nature; not that method, but the practical aim, was the original note in the sixteenth and seventeenth centuries. In Leonardo the penetrating, in the Italian mathematicians and physicists of the sixteenth century, in Copernicus, Kepler, and Galileo, this method was elaborated into an instrument of surprising practical efficacy. With Descartes it became self-conscious as the sole and exclusive intellectual method, and ushered in the reign of mathematical physics as the unique truth about nature.

Such faith naturally gave birth to a new radical and intolerant cosmology, in which the mathematical world was finally freed from its earlier setting in the medieval Neoplatonic hierarchy, and from the teleology, the final causes, the functional structure of the Aristotelian physics. Such a cosmology, though implicit in Galileo, was first made explicit in Descartes, whose thought accordingly became the first "scientific" natural philosophy in modern times.

Finally, it remained for the seventeenth century to interpret the new science and the new cosmology, to generalize it, consolidate it, and adjust it to other ideas, in terms of each of the three great medieval philosophies of science, Augustinian Platonism, the realistic

Aristotelianism of Thomas and the Averroists, and the nominalistic Aristotelianism of the Ockhamites. The outcome of this enterprise was the great philosophic systems of the seventeenth century, those of Descartes, Spinoza, Leibniz, Hobbes, and Locke.

If we ask for the ultimate causes of this increased interest in nature, both as a spectacle and as a system of useful forces, they appear clear enough in general but infinitely obscure in detail. That devotion to the values which the men of the Renaissance so well expressed should sooner or later have led to the erection of such a science of nature, seems intelligible enough. It was almost inevitable that an expanding commercial society should seek a science that would give to those who found its pleasures sweet a new opportunity for enjoyment, and to those who shared its basic drive a further source of profit. What was not inevitable was that methods developed for quite different ends should have proved so astoundingly adapted to these.

We must be on our guard, however, lest we assume too facile and direct a connection between the commercial life of the Italian and German towns, and the various speculations that there appeared to provide the background against which the mathematical interpretation of nature was eventually developed. We must indeed beware lest we take those enthusiasts for a new vision of nature as in any sense sharing the scientific aims which triumphed with Galileo and Descartes. For the nature philosophers of the Renaissance, even the more hard-headed Italian empiricists, were not scientists themselves, but poets, artists, religious reformers and enthusiasts. And the current of scientific advance was indeed so self-contained; it developed so completely through the painstaking criticism and reconstruction of well-organized scientific traditions, by men themselves scientists, mathematicians, physicists, and astronomers, largely by profession, and till the time of Galileo working primarily upon specific problems, that we can easily overemphasize the influence upon their careful procedures of the undisciplined guessing that prevailed in their intellectual environment. Between the number mysticism of the devotees of the Cabbala and the mathematical thought of the creators of mechanics in sixteenth-century Italy there is indeed a wide gulf. Yet influence there undoubtedly was, though subtler than our crude conjectures would have it; if it furnished no determinate ideas to mathematicians, it at least led to the taking of mathematicians more seriously.

Two medieval traditions offered most inspiration to those seeking new insight into nature. Impatient of the Aristotelian universe, they turned naturally, like so many others, to the Platonists, and especially to that strain in Platonism which tended toward pantheism rather than toward transcendence, and found beauty, the divine ideas, and God shadowed forth on the face of nature. Such Platonism, strongly reinforced by direct contact with the ancients who had not fallen under the Christian influence, bade them seek the symbols of the divine not within the soul alone, as the Augustinians had it, but in the great book of nature. The thirteenth century had known that nature is a cipher, to which the answer is God. But now the cipher seemed as interesting as the solution, and the world itself awakened religious enthusiasm as more than a point of departure for higher things. With such this-worldly Platonism, already foreshadowed in the great founder of the Franciscans, there easily blended that strain we dub "Pythagorean," which came to the Renaissance largely through the Cabbala and Jewish number mysticism; the book of nature is writ in lines and figures, the world is not an uninteresting ladder of logical universals and genera, but a collection of fascinating mathematical mysteries and harmonies.

The other storehouse of ideas was the medical tradition, with its stronghold at Montpellier and Toulouse, always suspect of heresy, and at the definitely anticlerical Padua. At Padua it combined with Aristotelianism to produce a genuine science; elsewhere it lacked discipline and rational methodology. This tradition was Arabian and Jewish rather than Christian; it was allied with astrology and alchemy and the disreputable black arts generally. It stood for a crude kind of experimentalism, mixed with many a mystical idea and old wives' tales of ancient lineage. Its appeal lay in the fact that it stood not only for a medical art of human utility, but for a whole philosophy and conception of the world, quite irrelevant to ecclesiastical interests and to Christianity itself, though by no means antireligious. To it anyone tired of the dialectic of scholasticism would naturally turn; it was pored over by most of the Nature Enthusiasts, especially the Germans, with a delicious sense of revolt and daring. It does not enter into exact science until the time of Boyle, around 1660, though

Kepler exhibits a strong dose. For it nature is an interconnected system of divine forces, to be studied and controlled. On the edges of this medical tradition lurked Magic, the clearest example of a knowledge directed wholly to the control of nature. Magic shared the new aim; it lacked, however, the discipline of mathematics and of verification to become a genuine science. As Bacon put it, its ends were noble if its means were crude; and he thought so well of this "fantastic learning" that he called the fruit of a sound philosophy "natural magic."

Two main groups stand out in the sixteenth century as explorers of a new vision of nature, the Germans who like Paracelsus drew chiefly on the medical tradition and natural magic, and the Italians who followed either mathematics or the experience of uncommon sense. But before explaining their ideas, we must deal with the elusive figure of Cusanus, focus of all the streams of thought of the late Middle Ages, and original contributor to each of them, capable of tossing off idea after idea whose working out was to determine the history of the next two centuries.

II

Nicholas Krebs, born at Cusa on the Mosel in 1401, and dying in 1464 as Bishop and Cardinal of the newly militant church, lived in the center of the political and ecclesiastical movements of that turbulent time. Extraordinarily sensitive to all the currents of thought astir in the Germanies and Italy, and freed by their very multiplicity from bondage to any one, he was able to take ideas from all these sources and to explore their implications. Like so many others of the fifteenth century, he was encyclopedic and eclectic in his learning; but unlike the others he managed to reach startling conclusions and to move in an atmosphere of emancipated speculation that is his chief claim to the reputation for modernity his compatriots have conferred upon him. Learned in Greek and Hebrew, he stands as the father of German Humanism; devoted to the Church and the centralizing papacy, he was a leader in its last great attempt at a modernizing assimilation of the tendencies of the Renaissance, before the rigidity of the Catholic Reformation settled upon it; fully up to the minute in the latest developments in mathematics and Ockhamite physics, he bent them to the solution of the theological problems of the mystical Neoplatonic tradition, the first of the Renaissance Neoplatonists with a strong interest in nature. All his writings are concerned with the medieval problem of the relation of God to the world; yet the terms in which he dealt with it led him to formulate the very modern ideas of the relativity of human knowledge and the essential homogeneity of the universe, ideas which if taken seriously meant the crumbling of the medieval cosmos and the necessity of exploring nature anew. And the great Platonic tradition emerged from his hands transformed into what the world has since known as German transcendentalism.

The man whose suggestive ideas covered so wide a range enjoyed a very rich education. He studied first in Deventer, the great mystic center of the Brothers of the Common Life; and the tradition of the Areopagite and Eriugena, as transmitted through Eckhart and the other fourteenth-century mystics, remained the deepest strain in his thought. Then at Heidelberg he encountered the Ockhamite scholasticism of the terminists, and went on to Padua, in ferment with new ideas both scientific and humanistic. There he studied the mathematical discussions initiated in fourteenth-century Oxford and Paris, and pushed further at Padua itself; there he found the new dynamics of the Paris Ockhamites; there he learned Greek and absorbed both the spirit of the Humanists and the solid works of Greek Platonists and scientists. He emerged a thoroughgoing modernist with a passion for reconciling all groups and all ideas. Early plunged into practical affairs at the Council of Basel, he first gained prominence as an upholder of the conciliar party and representative government in the Church; but when the modernizing and centralizing pope came to an open break with that last protest of ecclesiastical feudalism, Cusanus, impelled both by ambition and experience, and with prophetic judgment, went over to the side of papal absolutism and thereafter was one of the chief instruments of its reforming modernism.

His earliest work, written at Basel, was *De concordantia catholica* (1433); and "universal reconciliation" was the aim of his life. Practically, in the Church, he sought to bring together council and papacy, the Eastern and the Western Church; more fundamentally, he sought to combine mystic supernaturalism and humanism, otherworldliness and modern culture. Intellectually also he aimed at the

reconciliation or *concordantia* of all opposites, each relatively justified in its own context, in a higher unity—of mystic theology and
natural science, of faith and reason, of mathematics and Aristotelian
metaphysics. This temper is strongly suggestive of the later German
figure of Leibniz, whom Cusanus also resembles in never working
out the system toward which he was groping, save in a sketch at the
beginning of his career. The two brief treatises *De docta ignorantia*
and *De conjecturis* (1440) state his basic problem, the relation of
the Absolute and the Relative, God and the world, and suggest some
of the conclusions to which he was driven; his many other writings
continue to grapple with the same difficulties, now in one terminology and now in another.

In the exceedingly subtle and never overclear thought of Cusanus
it is difficult to discern a single neat pattern. He can be viewed as
continuing the negative theology of the mystic tradition, which is
surely the thread on which his many interests are strung; or as the
propounder, impelled by his metaphysics and by his study of the
Ockhamite critics, of many an idea which later scientists were to
take up in more positivistic form; or as the first German to stand for
that universal religion which the Humanists were to popularize. It
was in the last two respects that he exerted his greatest influence
upon the new age; his metaphysical system stands rather as the culmination of the mystic Platonism of medieval thought, and found
only in Bruno a wholehearted disciple. Though Cusanus is an un-
mistakable link in the German tradition from Eckhart to Leibniz
and transcendental idealists like Schelling, his ideas seem to have
reached the latter indirectly.

If Cusanus be taken as rooted fundamentally in the Neoplatonic
tradition, his originality is clear: touched by the revival of Greek
learning, he went back behind the Christian Platonists, Dionysius,
Eriugena, and the later Augustinians, to the pagan Platonists, especially Proclus and Hermes Trismegistus. The Christian tradition
had firmly established the conception of the world as a graded hierarchy of levels, each upward step representing a different and higher
kind of reality; within this neatly ordered scheme each type of creature had its own appropriate station, and human thought, following
the Aristotelian logic, could mount easily from stage to stage. But
for the Greek Platonists the world presented not so much a chain of

different kinds of reality as the manifold image of the one supra-intelligible world. Each manifestation contains the whole of reality; only the fashion of the shadowing forth varies. The difference between these multiple expressions of the One Reality is therefore to be approached in terms of varieties of knowledge rather than of being. Hence the upward path to the Supreme One is not the advance from one type of being to another, but the clearer penetration into the single Truth of the universe. The goal of Cusanus' thought is thus a *visus intellectualis* beyond the ordinary human *ratio:* it is that vision above reason as well as above sense, that fuller vision of the world in which it is seen not *rationaliter* but *intellectualiter*, not by *dianoia* but by *Nous* itself.

This is the underlying motif of all Cusanus' many attempts. Hence his Platonism is distinguished from that of his medieval predecessors in two important ways. Since he is firmly impressed by the older Platonic conviction of the unity of all things in Supreme Being, he emphasizes the interconnectedness and relations of things, their nexus, as their intelligible aspect and hence the proper object of knowledge; it is these relations that are everywhere the sign or symbol of God, and not the logical essences of things. And in place of the medieval hierarchy he has returned to the fundamental Platonic dualism between the relative and transitory things of ordinary experience and the eternal and absolute Idea. The former constitute no ladder with many rungs leading gradually upward; what reality they possess they all derive equally through their participation in the Ideal and Absolute. Instead of a long chain of many links, there stand sharply contrasted the two worlds, the absolute and the relative. Though the latter clearly depends on the former, the precise relation of the two furnishes the chief problem of thought.

Cusanus approaches his problem in terms of knowledge rather than of being. All knowledge presupposes a comparison, and is, in fact, a kind of measurement. But all measurement demands a certain proportion, a certain homogeneity in its objects. And between the relative and the absolute, the finite and the infinite, there can be no proportion.

All investigators judge the uncertain by comparing its proportionality to some presupposed certainty. All inquiry is thus comparative, using the means of proportion. If the object examined can be compared to that

presupposed by a close proportional reduction, the judgment of apprehension is easy; if we need many intermediaries, there is difficulty and
trouble. This is clear in mathematics: the earlier propositions are easily
reduced to clear first principles, while the later ones, since they require
the earlier as intermediaries, are more difficult. All inquiry therefore
consists in a comparative proportion, easy or difficult; whence the Infinite, since as infinite it eludes all proportion, is unknown.[1]

In consequence of this radical disparity between the two realms,
there is no path by which thought can advance continuously from
the finite to the infinite; between the comparative and the superlative there yawns a gulf unbridgeable by reason. Yet without that
superlative, that "absolute maximum," there could be no comparison
at all.

In Cusanus' application of this traditional Platonic dilemma, the
familiar Aristotelian logic remains valid within the realm of the
finite; but it fails utterly to grasp the essence of the Infinite, of God.
The ladder of syllogisms carefully built up by the Schoolmen inevitably falls short of its final goal, the absolute maximum. And with
its limitation to the realm of the relative there crumbles the foundation of the medieval hierarchical cosmos, the whole "division of nature" so carefully traced by Eriugena. It is this essential relativity of
everything in nature in the light of Absolute Being that is the source
of Cusanus' most original insights. For the different types of determinate being, of the finite and concrete or *contractum*, as all alike
susceptible of more or less, no longer form a single scale of values;
each in its own way participates equally in absolute being.

Of this Maximum or infinite, therefore, the finite human reason
can have no knowledge.

Wherever is found anything which is more than some things and less
than others, we cannot arrive at the simple maximum; for that which is
more and less is finite, while the simple maximum is necessarily infinite
. . . It is clear we cannot find two or more objects sufficiently like and
equal that there cannot exist objects still more like in infinite number.
Let the measures and the objects measured be as equal as you will, there
will always remain differences. Hence our finite intelligence cannot by
means of likeness understand the truth of things. Indeed Truth is not
susceptible of more or less, but is of an indivisible nature, and whatever
is not itself the True is unable to measure it with precision . . . Hence

[1] Cusanus, *De docta ignorantia*, Book I, ch. 1. In *Philosophische Schriften*,
ed. A. Petzelt, Band I (1949); Eng. tr. G. Heron (1954).

the intellect, which is not Truth, can never grasp Truth with such precision that it cannot be grasped more precisely by the Infinite . . . Hence the quiddity of things, which is the truth of beings, cannot be attained in its purety; every philosopher has sought, but none has found it as it is; and the more profoundly we are learned in this ignorance, the more we approach the Truth itself. (I, 3)

Man can arrive therefore by reason only at a *docta ignorantia* even of finite things, to say nothing of the Absolute; an "ignorance" because, bound by the principle of contradiction, it is cut off from knowledge of the infinite and of the essences of finite things that exist through the infinite: but "learned," as knowledge critically aware of its limitations and of the necessity of that Absolute it can only approach as an ideal. But above *ratio* is *intellectus, Nous*, freed from the law of contradiction, and able with superrational insight to see the coincidence of contraries in the Infinite.

In such fashion Cusanus expresses the old Platonic distinction between the vision of the intellect, beholding the world as One, as a Unity of diversity, and the plodding work of reason lost amidst the Many—that distinction made by the Augustinians between *sapientia* and *scientia*, and destined to reappear in many forms down through the seventeenth century. This vision man can see, but he can give it rational expression only in the form of relative and comparative knowledge, of "conjectures": "We know the unity of unattainable truth in the otherness of conjecture." [2] As the means of achieving this vision, Cusanus rejects the Aristotelian logic of the finite; by its standard metaphysics and theology is non-rational.

The admission of the coincidence of opposites, considered heresy by the Aristotelian sect, is the beginning of the ascent into mystic theology.[3]

But more important than this rejection, shared by the Ockhamites and the mystics, and foreshadowing the wide revolt of the next century, is his equal rejection of blind faith or of mere ecstasy and contemplation. It is mathematics which alone can give even a limited and conjectural knowledge of the Infinite or God. It too as a rational science is bound by the law of contradiction:

[2] *De conjecturis*, Book I, cap. 2.
[3] *Apologia doctae ignorantiae, Opera* (Basel, 1565), p. 64; in Petzelt, pp. 277-78.

This is the root of all rational assertions, that the coincidence of opposites is unattainable . . . And to say much with brevity, nothing in mathematics can be known by any other root.[4]

Nevertheless mathematics can lead the intellect to the point where it can see beyond:

since all mathematical objects are finite, when we wish to make use of finite things in our ascent to the simple maximum, it is necessary first to consider the finite mathematical figures with their characters and reasons; secondly, to carry over the reasons themselves to the infinite figures which are like them, making a correspondence; and thirdly, to extend the reasons of the infinite figures more deeply, to the simple maximum, absolutely devoid of all figure; and at that moment our ignorance will learn in an incomprehensible manner the exact and true feeling we must have of the supreme profundity, we who labor in enigmas.[5]

Cusanus' favorite illustration is the polygon, whose sides, indefinitely increased in number, never reach a perfect circle, yet do approach it so that intellect can *see* the coincidence of chord and arc if the number could be made infinite.

There is no precise knowledge of any of the works of God save with him who made them; what knowledge we have of them we derive from the mirror of mathematics . . . If we then consider rightly, we have no certainty in our science except in our mathematics.[6]

And so Cusanus applied mathematics to the Platonic tradition, to make intelligible the superrational realm above dialectic, the Infinite and Absolute of the mystic's vision. Mathematical analogies point beyond the line between finite and infinite; in the mathematical infinite all opposites meet, the circle and the straight line, the triangle and the line—obvious symbols of the divine! Just so, in the infinite totality of God, all opposites are united; the distinctions in nature are obliterated, and God embraces good and evil, truth and error, God is and is not, for he is above all determinate being.

Into the details of this metaphysics there is no need to go; Cusanus explains how God is all things in a state of *complicatio,* while the world is all things as *explicatio;* the argument follows familiar Platonic lines except that the notion of emanation, with its scale of

[4] *De conjecturis,* Book II, cap. 1.   [5] *De docta ignorantia,* Book I, ch. 12.
[6] *De possest, Opera* (ed. 1565), p. 259.

value, is replaced by that of "exemplifying" or "signifying" in a unique and appropriate way. Just so the point contains "in complication" line, surface and solid, while the line is the "explication" of the point, and the surface of the line.

The mind contemplates the simple point before the composite line. For the point is the sign, and the line the thing signified.[7]

The line is the evolution of the point . . . If the point be removed, all magnitude is destroyed.[8]

Likewise rest is the unity which "embraces" movement, an ordered series of rest; and the present embraces time, identity complexity, simplicity distinctions. God is the maximum, than which nothing can be logically greater; he is also the minimum, just as unity belongs both to the totality of a series and to its generating element. Both God and the universe are each a maximum containing all the reality possible; but God is the absolute maximum, while the universe is the maximum existing in "contraction," that is, concretely and determinately in multiplicity. The totality of the universe exists *contracte* in each of its members. The universe is a unity made concrete (*contracta*) by plurality. The universe is the *alteritas*, the Otherness, of the absolute maximum.

In his later works Cusanus was still wrestling with the problem of conceiving the Infinite in terms of a name and a formula that would signify its relation to the world of the finite. God is the "not something else" (*De non aliud*, 1462); he is the unity of power and being, of *posse* and *esse* (*De possest*, 1460); he is the power to create, the *posse facere*, the ground of all *posse fieri* and *posse factum* (*De venatione sapientiae*, 1463). Finally, in *De apice theoriae* (1464) he arrived at bare *posse*, possibility or power, as that essence of which all that is is the manifestation. The highest *posse* is the *posse intelligere* which approaches most closely to *posse* itself. In all this long search Cusanus was gradually changing the Aristotelian conception of *posse* as potentiality or bare possibility into the notion of power, something already actualized, and preparing the path, eagerly fol-

---

[7] *De non-aliud*, Uebinger, *Die Gotteslehre des Cusanus* (1888), p. 192.
[8] *Idiota de sapientia*, Book III, cap. 9; in E. Cassirer, *Individuum und Kosmos*, as *Idiota de mente* (Book III of *Idiota*).

lowed in the sixteenth century, that led to the complete exclusion of the notion of potentiality from thought in the seventeenth.

But it is not this labored grappling with the medieval problem of determining the relation between a God and a world so defined as to have no mutual relations, that places Cusanus at the early springs of modern philosophy; it is the consequences of his viewing the world and man's knowledge of it as wholly relative that set him with those seeking a new vision of the world and of man. The universe is not the weakened image of the Deity; it is the Infinite itself existing in determinate or concrete form, a kind of "finite infinite" or "created God."

It is from that which is called the absolute maximum that it derives its universal unity of being; and hence it exists in contracted state as universe, with its unity contracted into plurality, without which it could not be at all. Although this maximum embraces all things in its universal unity, so that all that is derived from the absolute is in it and it is in all, yet could it not have subsistence outside that plurality in which it is, since it would not exist without such contraction, from which it cannot be freed.[9]

The universe thus derives all its being from the Absolute; and since the Absolute eludes human knowledge, so likewise is it impossible to know with precision its contracted form. At most we know that this contracted maximum imitates so far as possible the absolute maximum; yet our ignorance of how this created world is derived from the Absolute is a theme on which Cusanus never ceases to harp. His conception of the universe, and his calm brushing aside of a cosmology hallowed by tradition, come from this double source: on the one hand, the conviction of the relativity and lack of precision of human knowledge; on the other, that finite infinity of the universe itself. For the world is infinite, not in the sense that God is, but in the sense of having no determinate boundaries, no precisely fixed structure, of always admitting the more and less.

Although our world is not infinite, still it cannot be conceived as finite, since it has not limits within which it is inclosed. (II, 11)

Cusanus was the first to take the idea of an infinite universe seriously; he delighted in following out the implications of that novel

[9] *De docta ignorantia*, Book I, ch. 2.

idea, in a way that endeared him to the later Bruno. The upshot was to discard the essential features of the Ptolemaic and Aristotelian world. If no precise knowledge is possible of the heavens, if all motion is relative, the perfect motions of the celestial regions have disappeared.

If you turn to astronomy, you will see that its calculations lack precision . . . Even the disposition of the heavens, for him who is in any particular place, or of the rising and the setting of the stars, or of the elevation of the pole, or of anything connected with these subjects, is not knowable with precision. And since there are not two places which agree with precision in time or space, it is clear that the judgments of astronomy are far indeed from being precise. (II, 1)

The universe has therefore no fixed circumference or center.

The earth, which cannot be the center, cannot be deprived entirely of motion; it is even necessary that it should have a movement . . . The center of the world is no more within the earth than outside it. Nor has the earth nor any sphere a center; for since the center is a point equidistant from the circumference, and since it is impossible for a sphere or circle to exist so true that a truer one cannot be given, it is clear that no center can be given such that a truer and more precise one cannot be found. A precise equidistance to different points cannot be found outside God, since He alone is infinite equality. (II, 11)

It is already manifest that the earth truly moves, though it seems not to, for we grasp movement only by comparison with a fixed point. If one did not know that water flows, did not see the banks and found himself on a boat between them, how would he know that the boat was in motion? And for the same reason, if one is on the earth, on the sun, or some other star, it will always seem to him that he is in the motionless center and that all other things are in motion . . . Hence the world machine has so to say its center everywhere and its circumference nowhere. (II, 12)

If this relativity of motion be taken in conjunction with the relativity of value which follows the destruction of a fixed astronomical hierarchy, if it be fully realized that everything finite is relative in comparison with the Infinite, and that all parts of the universe have been created to be as like to God as possible, then it is seen that every creature is perfect in its own way, is equally divine and of equal value, and is at rest in its perfection without striving to be something else. The earth becomes itself a planet like the others.

The figure of the earth is mobile and spherical, and its motion circular, though it could be more perfect. And since the maximum in perfections, motions, and figures does not exist in the universe, it is not true that the earth is the vilest and basest of heavenly bodies.

Thus the earth is a noble star, which has a light and heat and influence other than and different from that of all the other stars.

Even in size it is not the smallest; the moon is smaller still, and also Mercury, and with all its enveloping spheres it may well be as large as the sun.

And it does not seem that there can be found a nature more noble and more perfect in being, than the intellectual nature which inhabits the earth as its proper region; and that even if on other stars there are inhabitants of another kind; indeed, man desires no other nature, but seeks to be perfect in his own. (II, 12)

Cusanus' whole argument from relativity is humanistic: the earth and its denizens are no longer at greatest remove from God in the distant empyrean, but are as near the divine as anything else in the universe; their value, in fact, comes from what they are and can do, not from their cosmic station. It is interesting to find Copernicus and Galileo, whose thought so powerfully reinforced this fundamental notion of relativity and homogeneity, using these same arguments for the earth as a "noble star" to the same humanistic end of the dignity of man.

As a further consequence, the fixed structure of the Aristotelian physics, with its nicely differentiated natural places, its absolute up and down, its processes passing from one distinct contrary to another, gives way to an Anaxagorean world in which "everything is in everything," the elements are mixed everywhere, in different proportions, and the heavenly bodies are homogeneous with the earth.

Were one in the sun, he would not see that brightness which we behold; for if we consider the body of the sun, we find it possesses a kind of central earth and a kind of fiery brightness at the circumference, and in the middle a watery cloud and a clearer air. The earth possesses the same elements. For were one beyond the region of fire, our earth would seem, in the circumference of its region, because of the fire, a luminous star, just as to us, who are at the circumference of the region of the sun, the sun appears most luminous. (II, 12)

Cusanus was well aware how these ideas reached from his general epistemological and metaphysical point of view fitted in with many of the critical suggestions of the Ockhamite physicists; he busied himself with astronomical and physical as well as mathematical problems, and in *De ludo globi* (1464) and elsewhere took over such hypotheses as the impetus theory and the rotation of the earth. It is clear, however, that he contributed little of originality to the details of physical science; most significant of all is that a man of his general Platonic and theological background should display such interests at all. He remained the philosopher of nature rather than the scientist.

The relativity which proved so revolutionary when applied to nature Cusanus did not hesitate to pursue into religious ideas as well. Men's knowledge of God is likewise a *docta ignorantia*. Just as God is related to the world, so is the single true religious spirit related to the various concrete religions. What is contained in complication in pure religion is made explicit in the multiplicity of worships: "one religion in a variety of rites." No one of them is an adequate symbol of the highest religious truth; every creed alike is a "conjecture," it can grasp Truth only as Otherness. But only in such individual and determinate way can the absolute thought be expressed by men. The diversity of cults is not the confusion of error, a mass of heterodoxies confronting orthodoxy; for Otherness, the *heteron*, is an inevitable part of all *doxa*. Only as thus differentiated and individualized can the Absolute appear on earth.

Though perchance this difference of rites will never be ended, and though it may not be fitting that it should, in order that diversity may be the increase of devotion, where every region carries on the work the more vigilantly with its own ceremonies as the more pleasing to Thee the king, still just as Thou art one, so let religion be one and one the practice of worshipping.[10]

In a certain sense all religions are true, for they all honor the Divine and Holy; none really grasps the Absolute, but all strive after it.

[10] *De pace fidei, Opera* (1565), cap. i.

Not by suppressing these differences, but by making the most of individual variations, and seeing them all as varying participations in the Divine, lies the way to reconciliation and peace. Such a universal religion, not merely tolerant of diversity but consciously devoted to including and embracing it, Cusanus sketched in *De pace fidei* (1454). For as the Apostle taught, men are saved not by their works, conceived in diversity, but by their faith, which aims at the One.

The soul of the just will inherit eternal life. If this be admitted, we shall not be disturbed by all those variations in rites, for they have been instituted and received as the sensible signs of the truth of faith; the signs suffer change, but not what they all signify. (xv)

All who have ever worshipped many Gods presupposed the existence of Divinity. For that same Divinity they adored in all the Gods as participators in it. Just as without the existence of whiteness there would be no white things: so without the existence of Divinity there would be no Gods. Thus the cult of many Gods is a confession of Divinity. (vi)

In such fashion Cusanus' relativity took him to the full spirit of the Renaissance, with its universal religion, its welcome of diversity, its cult of individuality. The religious solution to his problem of the relation of the world to God is likewise an expression of humanistic values. There must be a maximum of concretion or "contraction," a highest stage in the universe. This stage is man; as his intellect is the culmination of finite knowledge, so all beings in the world culminate in Humanity, the highest of all relative and finite existences. Human nature is a *media natura* between the concrete Many and the absolute One.

Human nature is that which is raised above all the works of God and but little less than the angels, combining the intellectual and the sensible nature and binding the universe within itself, as a microcosm or little world, as the ancients with reason called it.[11]

But Humanity demands a person in whom to find individual manifestation, and that Person, that intermediary between the finite and the infinite, is Christ. If God be the circle, and the universe be the totality of all possible polygons, Christ is that maximum of polygons in which the transition from polygon to circle, from relative to absolute, can be discerned. Not by a ladder, but by a single *natura*

[11] *De docta ignorantia*, III, ch. 3.

media, is the gap between the two worlds to be bridged. Humanity is that bridge, and Christ is the supreme manifestation of Humanity. And thus Cusanus finds the solution to his medieval problem of bringing the world and God together in the Renaissance glorifying of the dignity and worth of man, in a religious humanism and optimism.

> Everything that is rests in its own specific nature as in what is best as derived from the best.[12]

> For God created a nature to take part in his own goodness, the intellectual nature, which in its possession of free will is like the creator and is almost another God . . . That intellectual nature is capable of receiving God, for it is infinite in power: it can always know more and more . . . No other nature can become better of itself, but is what it is by the necessity which keeps it thus. The intellectual nature alone contains in itself principles by which it can become better and thus more like and more receptive of God.[13]

Despite his eager interest in scientific questions, Cusanus is clearly no scientist himself. He remained the mystic, the theologian, the Platonic metaphysician. But he transformed the Platonic tradition into a philosophy of nature, and by his very insistence on the relativity and finitude of man's powers and of the natural world in contrast with the Absolute and Perfect, he raised both the earth and man from the basest position in the cosmos to the highest; there could be no higher outside God himself. Cusanus is the first simon-pure German transcendentalist, the ancestor of Schelling's Absolute Identity, that night in which all cows are black which is at the same time the purest light. He confined the Platonic tradition within the relativities and limitations of human knowledge, where it has remained for the Germans ever since. It is little wonder that in Germany he is known as the first modern philosopher. He does in truth stand at the very turning point between medieval Neoplatonism and modern thought, its science, its humanism, and its romantic idealism.

III

In Cusanus the idea of the relativity of human knowledge led to the further conception of a homogeneous natural universe, equally

---

[12] *De dato patris luminum,* I, *Opera;* in Petzelt.
[13] *Excitationes,* Lib. V, f. 498.

divine in all its parts and to be understood throughout in terms of the same set of principles. This conviction of nature as a single unified Whole or Totality formed the core of the vision of all the nature enthusiasts of the next century, both the Italians with their primarily aesthetic interests and the Germans with their strong impulse to practicality and power. Among the latter it was reinforced by the Cabbalistic Neoplatonism which Reuchlin and his group took over from the Florentines, and by the elements of Stoic physics learned not only from Seneca and the great Romans, but also to be found in the natural philosophy of Plotinus, itself strongly Stoic in character. That Nature is a single great organism, with a soul of its own; that its operations are to be understood in terms of its animal forces and powers rather than of its logical structure; that man is an essential member of this organism, and that the powers of nature are manifested in the powers of man—all these Stoic ideas had filtered down through the Middle Ages to the sixteenth century, and now seemed to promise unlimited scope for an art of human control. "If we men but knew our own minds aright (*unser Gemüth*) there would be nothing impossible for us upon this earth," said Paracelsus.[14]

This vision of Nature as an interrelated system of powers and "hidden qualities" lay back of both astrology and alchemy; its fruition in a practical technique was most clearly expressed in the art of Magic. These men distinguished between "demonic magic," which attempted to operate by the secret power of symbols, words, and mysterious formulae, and the "natural magic" which depended upon the discovery of the regular and normal properties and forces inherent in things. They all insisted there was nothing supernatural about such a magic art; as Giambattista Porta summed it up,

The knowledge of the dependence of things in their succession is the foundation of every miraculous effect, and it is a mistake to believe that an event transcends and is contrary to nature which can occur only as a result of her powers and in accordance with them.[15]

It is too much to see such an attitude as the full realization of the idea of a system of uniform natural law; but like Pomponazzi's simi-

---

[14] *Liber de imaginibus*, cap. xii; *Werke* (Basel, 1589f.), IX, 389.
[15] Porta, *Magia naturalis* (1589).

lar notion of the natural laws of astrology it represents a groping toward that prerequisite of any natural science.

Both Platonists and Aristotelians regarded natural magic as the wisdom that follows upon a knowledge of nature's properties.

If Magic is the same as wisdom [said Pico] then deservedly is this practice of natural science, which presupposes an exact and absolute knowledge of all natural things, as the apex and summit of all philosophy, called by the peculiar and appropriate name of Magic, that is, of Wisdom, just as we call Rome the city, Vergil the poet, and Aristotle the philosopher.[16]

Pomponazzi too defended magic:

There is no doubt that natural magic is in itself a true productive science, depending on natural philosophy and astrology, like medicine and many other sciences; and in itself it is good, and a perfection of the intellect . . . and as such it does not make the man who possesses it a bad man.[17]

Campanella makes clear how a thoroughgoing empiricism did not find itself in opposition to Magic, but rather attempted to codify it; and in Bacon and the later work of the Royal Society experimentation served largely to confirm its techniques.

It was in Germany, however, that all these strains were gathered together by Paracelsus and his followers into a conception of nature directed toward a practical medical art. There Cornelius Agrippa of Nettesheim (1486–1535), drawing upon Reuchlin's Neoplatonic mysticism and magic, and initiated by Abbot Trithemius into the occult sciences, wrote as a young man *De occulta philosophia*, in sharp opposition to the academic Aristotelian physics and to mathematics as well, an opposition he later pushed into a complete scepticism as to secular learning. Within a Neoplatonic and Cabbalistic framework of three "worlds," intelligible, celestial, and elemental, in all of which man participates as microcosm and therefore all accessible to his knowledge, Agrippa emphasizes the unity of nature, bound together by a single *spiritus mundi;*

for it would be absurd if the heavens, the stars, and the elements, the source of life and animation for all things, should themselves lack them; if each plant and tree took part in a nobler determination than the stars and the elements which are their natural begetters . . . There is there-

[16] Pico della Mirandola, *Opera* (ed. 1573), *Apologia*, p. 170.
[17] Pomponazzi, *De causis admirandis*, Book I, ch. 5.

fore a World Soul, a single life filling and coursing through all things, holding together and binding all things within itself, so that the machine of the whole world is rendered a unity . . . Just as in the human body the movement of one member calls forth that of another, and as in a lute when one string is touched all the others vibrate with it, so each movement of one part of the world is reflected and imitated in all the others.[18]

In such an interconnected and unified universe, it is easy for man to discover the forces hidden in things and by the proper manipulations of "magic" to bend the higher powers to his service.

IV

The leader and exemplar of German nature philosophy was Philippus Aureolus Theophrastus Bombastus von Hohenheim, who in emulation of the renowned Roman physician assumed the name of Paracelsus (1493–1541). Born in Switzerland, educated as a physician in the universities of Germany, Italy, and France, early rejecting the Arabic tradition of Galen and Avicenna to return to the Hippocratic school, he spent his life wandering from one town to another in southern Germany and Switzerland, sometimes as respected surgeon and professor of medicine, more often in bitter conflict with his colleagues as the unconventional reformer of medicine, writing many a work in which wild, mystical, and theosophical ideas are combined with close observation. Dissatisfied with a tradition grown academic, he bade men consult nature, not the books of men; and so he consulted every wise woman, every quack doctor, in the hope that practical experience had revealed the secrets of nature to them.

Nature is the physician, not you; you must learn from her, not from yourself: she constructs, not you; look that you learn where her apothecaries are, where her virtues stand written . . . Therefore the physician must grow out of Nature with complete understanding. Complete understanding is when the hands grasp and the eyes see that which is intended in the hidden brainpan. For what is conceived as hidden gives only faith: it is works that give the outward and the complete: works are visible. Thus visible and invisible in one and not in two, the whole complete knowledge, in which lies blessedness, and from which all good work, teaching and instruction flow.[19]

[18] Agrippa, *De occulta philosophia*, Book II, chs. 56, 57, 60; *Opera* (1550 ed.), I, 294, 296, 303.
[19] Paracelsus, *Paragranum* (Leipzig, 1903), pp. 26, 41.

Mere tradition and speculation end in fantasy; knowledge must be such

that the eyes too comprehend the understanding; and that it sounds in the ears like the fall of the Rhine, and that the sound of philosophy lies as bright in the ears, as the rushing wind from the sea . . . Aside from knowledge such as this, everything attributed and given to Nature is empty of worth.[20]

But practice and experience alone make mere "experimentasters"; there must be "science" as well, the visible must be grasped in the invisible. Theory and observation must go hand in hand, the invisible must be seen directly in the visible. The physician must plan his experiments, he must analyze like the alchymist. There are two kinds of experience, the vulgar one opposed to reasoning, and the one that makes the fullest use of directing ideas. "The one is the ground and master of the physician, the other his error and seduction." The process of burning, which seems to destroy a substance, in reality reveals its essence and constitution to the true experience of the "medical eye." All that is observed must be tested by the "invisible."

The right experience of an astronomical and philosophical kind is to know all things in their invisibility.[21]

And Paracelsus counsels carefully planned experimentation:

Each experiment is like a weapon, which must be used in the fashion of its own power: as a spear for piercing, or a sword for hewing, so with experiments . . . Hence the chief thing is to know the powers of each experiment, and in what form it should be used. To use experiments takes a skilled man, who is certain of what they can do.[22]

Paracelsus sums up all his drive toward observation and experimentation in the notion of the "Light of Nature":

It is like a great blindness and a great straying to follow your own heads, which are not masters nor doctors: the Light of Nature is master, not our brain, and not our five senses.[23]

And yet at the same time the Light of Nature has its seat and source in ourselves, in the "Gemüth" of man.

In reality this wandering doctor groping toward the notion of a knowledge founded on experiment was giving philosophic expres-

[20] *Paragranum*, p. 25.   [21] *Paramirum, Werke* (1589 ed.), I, 72.
[22] *Chirurgische Bücher und Schriften* (1618), p. 300.
[23] *Vom Podagra*, Book I; *Werke*, IV, 263.

sion to the ideas of the medieval medical tradition and its world-view. Medicine is the highest science, but it must be firmly grounded on all the others, and especially on philosophy (or physics), astronomy, and theology. For the world is a unity, its forces form a great harmony, and God is in the world as living force, not as a logical system. Man is squarely a member of this world-organism: man is natural, and nature is like man human, and both are divine. Man as a microcosm is the replica and manifestation of the macrocosm: this common idea of the Renaissance Platonists Paracelsus develops in intense earnest.

Man is an image set into a mirror through the four elements.[24]

He belongs to three realms: he has an earthly and visible body composed of the elements, and controlled by the earth forces or "spirits," especially the creative force of Archeus; an invisible heavenly or "astral" body or *spiritus*, derived from the stars and under their control, in which all the arts and sciences have their seat; and a soul directly from God, endowed with an innate divine wisdom with its seat in the "soul of the soul," the *mens* or *Gemüth*. Hence the physician must study the science of nature or natural philosophy, and especially the practical science of the elements or alchemy; and the science of the stars, or astronomy, and especially the practical science of the stars or astrology, to understand man and to heal him. In Paracelsus it is clear how the very practical and humanistic interest of the physician in human nature could lead out to Man writ large in Nature. Man's salvation lies indeed in subordinating his earthly and astral bodies to his soul. But theology has nothing to do with reason and philosophy; it springs rather from the innate wisdom implanted in every man, not from experience and its interpretation, and the Aristotelian Schoolmen try in vain to reach God through human reason. In place of natural theology Paracelsus set a mystical theosophy which allied him with the universal theism of the Renaissance and entered deeply into the German tradition with Weigel and Boehme.

Nature like man is hence a mixture of elements. God created the world out of the divine abyss in which it existed invisibly, by his will first bringing forth a kind of primeval water or "Hyliaster," containing the three principles of Sulphur, Mercury, and Salt, which

[24] *Paragranum*, p. 27.

are not so much substances as living forces or "spirits." These principles are mixed in a balance in all things: out of them come the four common elements, through the creative and formative power of Archeus, the Life Spirit, which binds all Nature and man into one great organism, one great harmony of correspondences and sympathies. The task of the physician's art is to analyze things into their elements by fire, to cast horoscopes and read the signatures of heavenly things writ in their earthly counterparts, and thus incite the healing force of Archeus to re-establish the balance of the elements in man. Paracelsus worked long at this rationalization of the alchemical tradition, in the interests of his medical art. The details are bizarre enough: he had no conception of other than a qualitative knowledge, no appreciation of the power of mathematics. But he left a rich mass of ideas to German speculation, to the mystics and the nature philosophers alike.

His creative life principle of Archeus was developed further by the physician Johann Baptista van Helmont (1577–1644) into a dynamic and hylozoic physics. Franciscus Mercurius van Helmont (1618–1699), the latter's son, worked over the Paracelsus teaching into a comprehensive theory of monads with a marked resemblance to that of the younger Leibniz. Robert Fludd (1574–1637) carried these ideas of the German medical school, of Cusanus and Paracelsus, to England, and contentiously sought to adjust them to the new physics then abroad in many a polemic with Kepler and Mersenne. The whole school emphasized a naturalistic Neoplatonism allied to magic and occult wisdom. For them the world was a living organism, composed of elements and moved by elemental spirits, forces, or sylphs, and all bound together in a scheme of qualitative relations. God is the dominant Force or World Soul, man is the replica or microcosm of the world. Natural magic studies these forces or "spirits" and controls them for the good of mankind. Such ideas contributed powerfully to overthrowing the Aristotelian physics, and to the further development of biology, medicine, and chemistry; they cleared the ground for the mathematical and mechanical science of the more critical minds. And they implanted deep in the German tradition the conviction of the inner bond between man and nature which outlasted the domination of Newton and came to the fore once more with the Romanticists.

7

The Italian Nature Philosophers

I

DURING that same eager sixteenth century the thoughts of many an inquiring Italian were likewise turning toward the vision of a new truth to be found in nature. The Italians, however, were less mystical and romantic in their approach, less interested in plucking at once from some dubious medieval tradition any instrument that seemed to promise immediate power over natural forces: they were both more naturalistic and more concerned with a genuine understanding of the nature to which they turned. In one sense, to be sure, their ideas were just as speculative as those of the northern "magicians": in seeking escape from the constriction of the Aristotelian physics they often lost sight as well of the rigorous sense of method and demonstration which its best Italian representatives were at that very time deepening and extending. They also were too busy exploring the light that might be shed by the notions of "element" and "force" to bother to check up on their simplified hypotheses. But it is no mere accident that their most extravagant "mistakes" strike us as more "scientific" and critical than the fantastic learning of the followers of Paracelsus. For they had all grown up and been educated in an atmosphere in which a rigorous intellectual discipline had been directed toward genuinely scientific ends. They had studied in the universities of northern Italy, most of them at Padua itself. There for centuries Aristotelian science had been bent to the service, not of theology, but of medical training; there had been the stronghold of anticlericalism and freedom of thought. The controversies of the Averroists and the Alexandrists at the beginning of the century were, to be sure, over a humanistic rather than a scientific issue; but they had made it clear that Aristotle was even more of a scientist and less of a supernaturalist than had been supposed. And they had also loosened the body of complacent scientific dogma, and exposed the whole of the Aristotelian doctrine to critical re-examination. Italian Aristotelianism during the sixteenth century was in a living ferment; everywhere men were undertaking a reconstruction of its several parts. It was no mere body of dead academic dogma, but a vital scientific current. Many thought they could preserve its main outlines while revising its details, while even the most radical thinkers could hardly feel contempt for so vigorous an opponent. Despite themselves, they had to meet it with reasoned argument on its own naturalistic ground.

Accordingly, even those who departed furthest from the letter retained much of the Aristotelian critical spirit. They did not appeal to the dubious tradition of medieval alchemy, never so close an ally of medical learning in Italy as in Germany or France. Accustomed to studying Aristotle and the ancients as scientists, they turned rather to other relevant suggestions of the Greeks. They took up the hypotheses of the Ionian naturalists who had preceded Democritus: Empedocles was an especial favorite. They were too careful students of Aristotle to accept Democritean atomism itself. They were strongly influenced by the Stoic physics of tension or force: through Cicero and Seneca they gained the ideas of Poseidonius.

These nature philosophers fall into two main groups. First, there were those like Cardano, Scaliger, and Patrizzi who were impressed by the flourishing mathematical sciences, and themselves worked intensively in them. For them nature was ultimately a vision of mathematics. They were attracted by the mathematical Platonism of Cusanus, and by the more Pythagorean elements of the Platonic tradition revived by the humanists. Secondly, there were those who, like Fracastoro, Telesio, and Campanella, took seriously the Aristotelian insistence on observation and experience, so seriously that they turned it against Aristotle's own interpretation of experience. They would forget their books and really observe the world. And so they naturally went for help as to what to see to those various ancient thinkers who had likewise trusted observation above reason. Both groups found it necessary to develop justifying theories of knowledge against the reigning Aristotelian scientists. The first turned naturally to Platonism, the second worked out more original and distinctive philosophies of experience.

Through their considerable influence on both Francis Bacon and Gassendi, these empiricists left an imprint on one of the chief currents of modern thought. But like all the Renaissance thinkers who relied on experience and observation, they completely failed to create a genuine science themselves. The mathematicians on the other hand did make immediate contributions to the current that led to Galileo. They take their place with those who kept somewhat closer to the stream of critical reconstruction of the Aristotelian logic and physics, as pioneers of the mathematical science of nature. Indeed, between them and a man like Kepler only an arbitrary line can be drawn. They did not happen to hit like him upon ideas that were to be taken up into the body of scientific thought.

II

Earliest of these more independent nature philosophers, and closest to the Padua school of which they were all offshoots, was Girolamo Fracastoro (1483–1553), physician and teacher first in Padua and then in Verona. With the more radical Paduans he utilized Ockhamite ideas to break away from the orthodox Averroistic tradition of Aristotelian physics: his theory of knowledge is one of the first adaptations of the Ockhamite position to a world of bodies in motion. In his *De sympathia et antipathia rerum* (1545) he accepted the Aristotelian criticism of Democritean atomism; but since there can be no action without physical contact, all apparent action at a distance, like that of the magnet upon iron, demands that streams of invisible particles or corpuscles flow from the one into the pores of the other.

Since no action can take place except through contact, while these like things do not touch each other, nor are they moved by nature toward each other, it is necessary if they are to approach each other for something to pass from one to the other and touch it immediately, and thus be the principle of its approach. (This will be either a body, or some simple material or spiritual form) . . . If it be supposed then that imperceptible bodies stream out from things, we say that these corpuscles are transmitted reciprocally from one to the other; from them is formed a certain unified whole, heterogeneous in its parts.[1]

[1] *De sympathia et antipathia rerum* (1545), cap. 5.

This is the first of those corpuscular theories of early modern science, which lasted through the seventeenth century as the rivals of atomism: corpuscularism differed from atomism in denying both the indivisibility of its corpuscles and the existence of a vacuum.

In *Turrius sive de intellectione* (1555) by applying the same idea to knowledge Fracastoro pushed the terminist logic to a more mechanical conception of experience. He did not like Ockham deny the existence of sensible "species"; he made them corporeal *simulacra* or *spectra* of the object. Emitted by things, they touch and change the soul by physical contact, and there in the soul represent things without.

> At the outset we must agree, that all cognition takes place through the simulacra of things, which some have called "spectra": in our schools we call them the species of things . . . In knowing it is clear that the soul is altered by that which was there before it knew; but this alteration the thing itself cannot effect, since it is without and is usually called the object, inasmuch as *per se* and immediately it does not touch the soul. Nor does the soul alter itself. Therefore something must be sent off from the object, which will touch the soul immediately and alter it; this cannot be other than the simulacrum and species of the things without . . . Hence understanding seems clearly to be nothing else than the representation of the object, which is formed in the inward soul by the reception of the species of the object.[2]

In perception the soul is thus passive; to advance from perception to genuine knowledge the soul must perform a succession of operations upon these simulacra. First it analyzes them into their component parts, and orders and inspects these parts one after the other by a process called *subnotio*: Fracastoro is transforming the Aristotelian notion of actualization into the more mechanical one of analysis or resolution into elements and recombination or association in a new order.

> Now I call 'subnotion' that cognition, by which under a certain single apprehension many other things are presented at the same time in a certain confused order, at which the soul is in consequence moved to inspect them as it were one after the other. For it is evident that this motion takes place in the soul, a motion which is not that composition or ratiocination in which truth or falsity resides, but simply and solely the representation of one sensible thing after the other. Nor is this operation

[2] *Turrius*, Lib. I, in *Opera* (Venice, 1555), p. 166.

memory, though it be assimilated to memory, but in nature and time and reason it is prior to memory. . . . Wherefore we should diligently make investigation of it, since I know of nothing that has as yet been determined about it in proper fashion. Wherefore we have been forced to use a new word, since we have found no other name for this operation, whence we have called it 'subnotion.' . . . Sense does not cause this motion itself, but the inward soul, which is actualized at the same time as sense and has greater power. (I, 169, 170)

In this ordered material the soul distinguishes similarities and constructs its universal concepts.

Just as the universal 'whiteness' is formed from milk and snow, so universals and ideas are extracted from things that have been conjoined; by the same process the universal of place, and figure, and quantity and number is constructed. (I, 177)

Thereafter a single sensible simulacrum can stand for the whole class similar to it. These similarities or concepts are then combined into propositions by *compositio* or *ratiocination* in good Ockhamite fashion. Genus and species are merely second intentions: they are but conventional names useful in grammar. But the operations of the soul itself—understanding, abstraction, imagination, ratiocination, subnotion, etc.—are first intentions: they have objective reference to things; they are in the soul as though they were outside.

These operations of the soul should be said to be performed rather *by* the soul than *in* the soul, as we ordinarily distinguish being in the soul from being without the soul. For those things which are conceived according to the being which they have in the soul, possess a twofold being, the one without the soul, the other in the soul: but these operations of understanding and abstracting, etc., do not possess this twofold being, but are simply by the soul and in the soul. They are in the soul, as though they were without, which makes them first concepts, upon which second concepts can be constructed. (II, 192)

Though Fracastoro is making both sensible and rational experience more mechanical, it still remains for him logical as well: it generates meanings.

III

Bernardino Telesio (1509–1588) was a Neapolitan who studied philosophy, mathematics, and physics, first at Padua, under the Averroistic physicists, and then at Rome. Called to Naples as teacher, he helped found about 1560 the first of the definitely scientific academies, the Academia Telesiana or Consentina. He had read Aristotle in Greek at Padua, and listened to the scholars' debates; and he was amazed that these men seemed never to have looked at the world they were so confidently explaining. He resolved, therefore, to turn his attention to nature; and in the light of what he there observed, he found Aristotle contradicting both himself and sense. Telesio seems to have been one of the few men, at that time or any other, who actually discarded inherited doctrines to let themselves be guided by what they could see. Hence Francis Bacon, who likewise believed in sheer observation, called him the "first of the moderns," *primus novorum virorum*, but also launched a bitter attack upon him, because he saw the wrong things. To Bacon, he was "better at destroying than at building"; a judgment true of Bacon also, and of all those who relied on observation to the exclusion of reason and mathematics.

Telesio is the most empirical and naturalistic of the Italian nature philosophers, the one who seems to have broken most completely with the past—in his intention. There is irony, therefore, in the fact that his book, *De rerum natura juxta propria principia*, "Nature described in the light of her own principles" (first published in 1565, in expanded and augmented form in 1586), strikes the modern ear as much influenced by the Presocratics, by the Stoic physics and by Galen, as well as by contemporaries like Cardano and by the Averroistic philosophy of the heavens and their life-giving warmth. The truth is that when he set out to sketch the scheme of nature as a whole, he had no recourse but to supplement what he could see with what others had thought.

Forgetting books, and looking upon the world directly, what first impresses us is the sun and its warmth acting on the earth, which after sundown gives off cold. Everywhere what meets our eye is heat acting upon cold. There must therefore be two great principles, two active forces at work in nature, Heat and Cold, in continual struggle with each other over Body, *corporea moles*, which must exist in constant quantity. Exposed to these forces of expansion and contraction, of rarefaction and condensation, Body as taken on the individualized forms we can observe—the stars, the heavens, the earth, and all that is therein. All differences are due to the relative density or rarity of a qualitatively homogeneous matter. All change and all permanence—that *conservatio sui ipsius* shared by every existent thing—are due to the strife and balance of forces, not to forms. Telesio fought a great controversy with the Padua Aristotelians in defense of natural explanation through efficient rather than formal causes, through "forces" rather than intelligible principles: his contention was destined to alter the very face of science.

The Aristotelian *potentia* had meant equally "possibility" and "power." This potentiality had been always conceived by Aristotle himself as a specific and determinate power to perform certain definite operations; but in medieval thought, preoccupied with the "first matter" out of which God had created all things, potentiality had tended to be identified with the mere possibility of becoming anything whatsoever, the conception of a purely abstract and passive possibility. In the Padua tradition, however, more interested in the manipulation of nature than in creation, *potentia* had been early interpreted by John of Jandun as a real power tending towards its own operation. In the debates between Averroists and Alexandrists the question had been brought to the fore of the extent to which *potentia* was an effective force. Telesio and the other nature philosophers now elaborated this positive notion of *potentia* into the conception of a natural "force."

God, who created the universal world from nothing, can do whatsoever he wills; but he did not construct it in such a way that things should always need a new power of operating in order to bring forth their own proper operations. Instead, particulars being endowed by God himself with a proper nature and the power of effecting their proper operations, operate in accordance with that proper nature.[3]

Wherefore Aristotle is greatly to be wondered at, who declared that those things that are moved by nature are moved by something else separate and distinct from themselves, and that there is no motion in them, but comes from without; whence he was not afraid to say that all things are moved by something else. And therefore even the substances that are moved have no efficient principle of their motion and operation whatsoever in themselves, but are merely acted upon. He thus makes the proper natures and forms of things to lie idle and snore: for this is

[3] *De rerum natura*, Lib. IV, cap. 24.

what forms seem to be and are, if substances have no efficient principle of their motion and operation in themselves, but are merely acted upon. (Lib. IV, cap. 20)

Telesio not only worked over the Aristotelian conception of *potentia* into that of "force": he also elaborated the idea of "space." His physics demanded the notion of an empty "space" in which body could expand and contract under the influence of the cosmic forces. He attacked, therefore, the Aristotelian notion of relative and "natural" place: space exerts no force, has no power, and must be qualitatively identical throughout. Consequently neither explanations in terms of "natural motion" toward a localized "natural place," nor generalizations about nature abhorring a vacuum, have any validity: all action must be caused by particular and determinate forces working in bodies. Nor is time the mere measure of motion, though knowledge of it be so gained. Time would preserve its characteristic flow were all else annihilated. Through their adoption by Gassendi these ideas exerted much influence on Locke and Newton; though how they may be gained from the perception of bodies alone Telesio—like Newton—fails to make clear.

Therefore place (*locus*) must be made the container for all beings whatsoever; and when beings pass out of existence or are removed, place itself neither passes away nor is removed, but remains perpetually the same and most promptly receives the beings that succeed them; and is itself ever of the same magnitude as are the beings located in it. For without doubt it is ever equal to those things that are located in it, but is never identical with any one of them; rather is it completely different from them all. . . . Just because we never apprehend time apart from motion, or motion apart from time, but always both together, Aristotle was not justified in declaring time to be a certain condition or affection belonging to motion . . . Since time in no wise depends upon motion, but exists by itself, all the conditions it possesses it derives from itself, and not from motion. (Lib. I, caps. 25, 29)

Men like all else are exposed to the play of the cosmic forces: their knowledge is a genuine passion, a suffering, in which they give up a part of their own life to receive into themselves something of another. Every animal body is penetrated by a *spiritus*, a fine corporeal substance generated from the seed, with its central seat in the brain: this is the medium that binds the bodily parts together and is the instrument of sensation, motion, and desire. Sensation is an external force acting on this *spiritus* to contract or expand it, and not the reception of sensible forms. To be perceived, objects must establish physical contact with the soul; all forms of knowledge are but special kinds of such contact. Spirit alone of bodies has the power to preserve these motions produced in itself from without, and to call them up again at will. It can remember them, perceive them when their causes are no longer present, and recognize similarities between them. Knowing is a remembering together (*commemorari*) the other qualities of an object associated with the one you observe. Judgment (*existimatio*) too is a remembering, of the powers and conditions formerly found in the things similar to the one under observation. Like every intellectual process, it is a kind of sense (*sensus quidam*), a remembering of what is not immediately present. But naturally such perception of a mere copy of what was once directly perceived is far more imperfect than immediate sensing, and must be continually checked by observation. At its best it is a mere substitute for the only knowledge of things that is certain, an instrument and not an end.

Not only does the *spiritus* seem to be able to collect again the things perceived by sense and the motions by which they have moved it, even when they are absent and have ceased; and in a certain fashion to perceive them and to be acted upon and moved by absent things, and to discern the similarity in those passions and motions, whether present or absent, which it is suffering and by which it is moved. It is likewise able to discern the hidden conditions of those things of which but a single one is observed, in those cases in which that single one has already been observed in its total setting. This power is commonly called understanding (*intelligere*), but is rather to be named judgment (*existimari*) or better "remembering together" (*commemorari*) . . . Therefore the principle of every intellection is a similitude perceived by sense; while intellection itself is a kind of sense, doubtless imperfect and by a similarity made not by the thing itself which is understood, but by sense—a similarity which the *spiritus* perceives to be made from like things . . . Therefore this kind of knowledge is far inferior to sense. (Lib. VIII, cap. 3) [4]

[4] "For since the soul does not sense some things and understand others, but perceives and understands the same things; and intelligible things seem to differ from sensible only in that the latter are present and cause knowledge by their own action, while the former are remote and hidden and are known by a certain similarity; and everything that is understood would be sensed if it were present: what the soul senses is never to be reckoned unlike what it understands." (cap. 20)

Universals are only names for groups of similar individuals, thought to be the same because their differences are imperceptible. Even mathematics is empirical knowledge, dealing with sensible objects through signs; its definitions are descriptions of observed facts, its axioms are the relations inferred between them. All knowledge is thus ultimately the observation of things and their similarities; we can observe only operations and spatial relations. To be sure, man possesses, as a *forma superaddita*, an immortal soul created by God as form of both body and *spiritus*. For we can observe that men do not act always from the insistent drive for self-preservation, but can sacrifice themselves to the contemplation of divine things and to union with the supersensible world. But neither for the knowledge of nature nor for his ethics of self-preservation does Telesio make any use of this immortal soul.

I V

Contemporary with Telesio was Girolamo Cardano (1501–1576), born in Milan, educated at Padua, an influential physician and mathematician teaching mostly at Pavia. He was no empiricist, but a convinced follower of the mathematical Platonism of Cusanus, who shared his master's faith in mathematics as a direct vision of God in his world. Underneath the ceaseless transformation of things there must be a qualitatively indeterminate "first matter" filling the whole universe. Yet this matter cannot be wholly indeterminate, the mere possibility of things; it is rather an effective power.

It is manifest there is something lying hidden in nature beneath form, which neither comes into being nor passes away: and since this is something primary and underlies many forms, we are wont to call it "first matter," and regard it as without generation or perishing. It remains and is: for what remains is. Matter in act is such as we have described it; compared to forms, indeed, it is mere potentiality: it can receive them. But though matter, compared to form, is mere potentiality, in itself it is truly in act.[5]

For things to come into being and pass away there must be a world soul as principle of generation and movement in everything. Through this all-permeating soul are exerted the sympathies and antipathies of things; by its instrumentality the stars can act upon

[5] *De subtilitate*, in *Opera* (Leyden, 1663), III, 359.

man's destiny. It appears as warmth or light to constitute the heavens. Earthly things, generated by its action on first matter, are damp and cold; they arise from the three elements earth, water, and air. Fire is no substance, but a mere accident, as it has to be fed. The life force, warm and moist, generated first the form of worms, and from worms all animals have sprung. But man is no animal: he is the highest of created beings, for he has been made a microcosm to combine what is heavenly and earthly, to rule all that is earthly, and to know the divine. Besides his soul he has been given an immortal *mens* which never began nor changes. When this *mens* has learned enough of mathematics, it rises above its mortal conditions and merges in God. For mathematics is God's law and instrument in the world. Human science has the task of investigating and describing the immeasurable variety of things in the world (*De subtilitate,* 1552; *De varietate rerum,* 1556; *Arcana aeternitatis,* 1663).

V

The most imposing of the Italian nature philosophies was that of Francesco Patrizzi (1529–1597), who studied at Padua, came under the influence of Telesio, but found the Platonic tradition and its metaphysics of light more congenial, and expounded it for some twenty years at the brilliant court of Ferrara. In 1591 he published his comprehensive *Nova de universis philosophia,* "in which by the Aristotelian method we ascend to the first cause, though not through motion but through light; then by the method of Patrizzi himself the whole of divinity comes into contemplation; and finally by the Platonic method the whole universe is deduced from its creator God." This work he dedicated to the pope and recommended to the Jesuits as the best instrument for converting the Protestants: for in it he had completely reconciled science and religion in an imposing Neoplatonic scheme. It comprised four parts, Panaugia, Panarchia, Panpsychia, and Pancosmia: of which the first shows how everything is to be understood as the reflection of the Divine Light, the second, that it is rooted in a single primal principle, the third, that it is permeated by soul, and the fourth, that its universal order rests on these principles. But this scheme merely furnishes the framework within which Patrizzi may develop his system of nature, which like that of Cusanus, on whom he drew, rests on the application of mathematics to the traditional Neoplatonic metaphysics of light. First of all God created infinite and eternal space.

For what was it more fitting and necessary to produce first, than that which everything else required for its existence, and could not exist without, but which could itself exist without anything else and needed nothing for its own existence? For this must needs be before everything else; when it is present all other things can be, when absent, all others are destroyed. This is space itself.[6]

Next God made the divine light, which on condensing into heat became the principle of generation. Finally came a fluency (*fluor*) equally filling the infinity of space. From these four universal qualities have come all empirical things, *spatium, lumen, calor, fluor*. What is corporeal and earthly cannot exist by itself: it has no activity, but can only be acted upon. All its activity and movement it owes to something incorporeal and spiritual within it. Everything therefore must be filled with soul or *animus*, which, with light, forms the only intermediary between Spirit and earthly things. Soul is not unmoved like pure spirit, nor is it moved by other things like bodies: it is self-moving. The world has a rational soul of which every human soul is a part.

Patrizzi followed the Platonic views of knowledge: "All knowledge is occasioned by sense, but its origin is in the mind." He vigorously attacked the sensualism of Telesio. The soul, remembering its origin in the divine Truth, seeks to become one once more with the Logos of God. "*Cognitio*" is thus "*coitio cum suo cognobili.*"

Since it is an emanation from the Father, the Word feels itself to be such a self-emanation; it is the very wisdom of the Father . . . It perceives that it emanates from the First and that it comes into essence and life. This perception turns upon itself and is converted into ardent love for the Father. By this turning and conversion it recognizes itself and the Father and knows them . . . This knowledge is a kind of intuition of the Father . . . This conversion toward itself and its cause is the proper operation of intellect. And through its essence to see all other things.[7]

The revision of the Aristotelian notion of *potentia* and consequently of substance, and the primacy of space and the position it gives mathematics, are the most original parts of Patrizzi's system.

[6] *Nova philosophia* (1591), *Pancosmia: De spatio physico*, p. 61.
[7] *Nova philosophia, Panarchia*, Lib. XV, p. 31.

In what manner do things exist in seed? Surely in that manner which is appropriate to a seed. How is seed to be taken, as in act or in potentiality? the Peripatetic asks. We answer, in act. Nothing produces anything from itself unless both the producer and the product are in act. For nothing operates except what is in act . . . Let us then grant the *potentia* of the Peripatetic, which signifies nothing but a relation to a future thing. . . . Nothing acts unless it has the power to act. This power comes from act and essence. But the essence of anything is its existence in act, possessing powers and actions from those powers. And force comes from essence as it were persisting, and is in essence, and is a certain extension and inward preparation for the act, just as action is a putting forth of these powers without and a fulfilment of its own work.[8]

Therefore it is falsely said that matter is in its nature devoid of all form, that it has the potentiality for all forms, that it is nothing but pure potentiality. For that which is is in act. It always possesses first forms, and never loses them. For nothing is more absurd than that matter which in the dogma of the Peripatetic is well nigh nothing, is non-being, pure potentiality by nature without form: for all things that are have forms, are in act, and are most beautiful.[9]

And finally let that holy of holies be revealed, that secret of secrets, of which men ever speak without placing it before our eyes. What is Substance? I am asking for the thing, not the name: I want to know whether form constitutes substance in reality and not merely in name. I am at once answered, Substance is that which gives things their being. But I still ask, does form alone give being to the thing, or does matter also? Both, I am told, but matter gives only a potential being, while form gives actual being . . . Form is that which constitutes the essential in a thing, and that whence its characteristic activities spring . . . If the Aristotelians can solve all these difficulties, then we will gladly bow before the subtlety of their philosophy; but if they cannot, then let them confess the justice of our conclusion. Let them at last after so many centuries give us a general definition of substance, or let men cease to repeat in philosophy that monotonous old tale: Form is substance, because it constitutes the essential in the thing, because it bring forth activities characteristic of the thing, because it gives the thing its being, because it contains the "*to ti en einai*," the "what," the intelligible concept, the definition of the object.[10]

For all these operations can as easily be derived from the empirical qualities of things, which we may with equal propriety consider their true being.

[8] *Panarchia*, Lib. IV, p. 8.
[9] *Discussiones peripateticae* (Basel, 1581), Vol. IV, Lib. III, p. 396.
[10] *Discussiones peripateticae*, Vol. IV, Lib. III, p. 387.

Most interesting for the future is Patrizzi's treatment of space. Space eludes the traditional categories, yet it is the condition of the existence of everything else.

None of the categories embraces space; it is before them all, outside them all . . . Granted that the categories serve well for earthly things; space is not of earthly things, it is other than the world. It is the accident of no earthly things, whether body, or not body, whether substance or accident; it precedes them all . . . Therefore it must be treated differently from the categories. Space therefore is a hypostatic extension subsisting by itself and inhering in nothing else. It is not a quantity. If it be quantity, it is not that of the categories, but before it, and its source and origin. Nor can it be called an accident or the attribute of any substance. Is it then a substance? If that be substance which subsists through itself, space is the chief substance of all. It subsists through itself and is dependent for its being on nothing else; it requires nothing whereby it shall be sustained, but sustains all substances. If that be substance which exists through itself, space is the chief substance of all, because it exists through itself before all others. If that be substance which underlies other things, space is the chief substance of all, for it underlies all other things in nature . . . For these reasons it is most clear to all that space is the chief substance of all, but is not of the category of substance. For it is not an individual substance, since it is not composed of matter and form. Nor is it a genus, for it is predicated neither of species nor of particulars. But it is another kind of substance outside the table of categories. What then, is it, a corporeal or an incorporeal substance? Neither, but a mean between both . . . It is an incorporeal body and a corporeal non-body. And both subsisting through itself, existing through itself, and existing in itself.[11]

Here fully developed is the conception of absolute space, destined to have a great career in seventeenth-century science. Originating thus in the Platonic tradition, through Campanella it reached Gassendi, and through Gassendi and Henry More came to Newton's famous scholium. But the consequences Patrizzi develops are of even greater importance. Since space is the condition of all existence and the first-born of the Creator, geometry as the science of space must be the basic science. Extension, far from being abstracted from things, is presupposed by them: the mind perceives it first, and cuts individuals from it.

Our mind fixes its attention on those finite spaces, which are suited to be the spaces of earthly bodies. The mind does not separate them from

[11] *Nova philosophia, Pancosmia,* De spatio physico, p. 65.

those bodies by abstraction, as some maintain, since these spaces are not at first and in themselves in earthly bodies, but are in act before all bodies in first space. . . . But the mind by its own force cuts off those parts from that first space, which will be of future use to contemplation or action . . . And since space is the first of all natural things, it is obvious that the science of space, both of the continuous and the discrete, exists before all matter. From the same reason it follows, that mathematics is prior to physics. It is also a mean between the completely incorporeal and the completely corporeal, not for the reason the ancients held, that something incorporeal is formed by abstraction from natural things, but because indeed space is an incorporeal body and a corporeal non-body . . . Hence it is obvious that for the student of nature the science of space is to be studied and taught before natural science . . . Rightly therefore was there set forth at the door of the school of the divine Plato: Let no one ignorant of geometry enter here.[12]

The continuum must exist before it can be divided, measured, or counted: geometry is prior to arithmetic.

It is clear that the continuum is in its nature more ancient and prior to all division: by the force of human thought its division and cutting creates number. It is clear also that continuous quantity exists by nature, while for number there is need of the human mind. In earthly bodies divided from each other it exists also by nature. It is also clear that the continuum comes before the discrete, since discreteness could not be generated by any force unless the continuum preceded it.

In his further development of this conception Patrizzi followed Cusanus in denying the infinite divisibility of the continuum: it is made up of indivisible points or minima. For as there is an infinitely large, the "maximum" of space itself, so there must be an infinitely small: two opposites condition and necessitate each other.

VI

Both these two traditions of nature philosophy, the empiricism and sensationalism of Telesio and the Neoplatonism of Patrizzi, were merged in the thought of Tommaso Campanella (1568–1639). Campanella indeed summed up all the currents and all the contradictions of sixteenth-century Italy, and lived long enough to join the circle of Mersenne in Paris and to see the new science developing before his eyes. He was a Dominican monk from Calabria, and he remained faithful to the medieval vision of the Church. But he had a most

[12] *Ibid.*, De spatio mathematico, p. 68.

212 The Coming of Humanism and Science

un-Dominican eagerness to welcome every sort of new idea, religious, scientific, philosophical, and political, and fit them all into the framework of his faith. Accused of conspiracy against the Spanish government of Naples, he spent twenty-seven years in prison, and three more in the dungeons of the Inquisition at Rome; finally freed, he passed his last years in France, where he associated with Mersenne and met Gassendi. Like his fellow-countryman Telesio, for whom he had great admiration, he urged men to turn from the books of Aristotle to the book of nature, that second revelation of God. The world is the testament in which the Eternal Wisdom has written its thoughts, the living mirror in which we can behold God's countenance; the books of men are but dead copies of life, full of error and falsehood. And like Telesio he developed a thoroughgoing empiricism and philosophy of observation. But as befitted a Dominican who had studied Thomas, he put it in the framework of traditional metaphysics, embellished with all the Neoplatonic additions in which the age abounded.

Campanella accepted Telesio's vision of Nature as a struggle of Heat and Cold, and his fine corporeal *spiritus*. He accepted also his conception of force, and his basic construing of things in terms of their powers.

No being seems to exist except because it has the power to exist. . . . For that is termed power which is fitted to diffuse, to amplify, and to multiply itself in something else.[13]

If all the works of God are perfect, . . . we must confess that things are endowed by him with those powers which are needful to their conservation . . . Therefore it is to deny the proper nature and form of fire, if we assert that it is God himself who ascends upward with fire and shines in the sun . . . It follows that the human mind does not itself perceive or understand, but merely God operating in it; and that God himself desires and effects our operations, the evil as well as the good . . . These and other reasons show that things act by themselves . . . and that for particular actions particular causes are required as agents, so that heat truly makes warm, and not God in it, but with it . . . For God has clearly constructed the world and created things, and bestowed powers of self-preservation and mutual change through time; those powers

---

[13] *Universalis philosophiae seu metaphysicarum partes III* (1638), Part II, Lib. VI, cap. 5, art. 1; (Part II, p. 20).

remain as Nature, until the whole machine of things achieves its great end.[14]

Experience for Campanella must therefore be purely mechanical, a matter of motion and contact. Sensation is the source of all our knowledge: it is a perception of a passion, of a movement or change of state in the *spiritus*, accompanied by reasoning or judgment of the object sensed. Campanella agrees with Thomas, *cognoscere est fieri rem cognitam;* but it cannot be a becoming the *form* of the thing known, for then the object as well as the knower would lose its own essence; and the soul, filled with the form of one object, could not receive that of another to compare it with. No, *spiritus* must be determined by objects without changing its own essence: such *informatio* must be accompanied by an *immutatio* of the soul itself. It must become, not the forms, but the motions of things without: sensation is not like receiving a picture on a tablet, but like setting in motion waves in water. These motions generated in the *spiritus* remain and combine with each other without the need of any action of the soul.

Yet though Campanella thus transforms the Aristotelian theory of sensation by translating it into mechanical terms, experience remains for him a logical as well as a mechanical process. The spirit is active as well as passive; it knows its objects, and is not merely acted upon by them.

Sense does not seem to be the mode of any existence, but an essential thing and an active power. (Lib. I, cap. ii)

Sense is not merely a passion, but it takes place simultaneously with an act of discourse so swift that it is not perceptible. (Lib. I, cap. iv)

For neither sense nor intellect is a passion, nor is knowing a being acted upon: but rather a judging which is itself active on the basis of a passion, since it in some fashion comes into being through that passion.[15]

Indeed at times Campanella gives to the Telesian sensationalism a very Platonic interpretation.

We think that objects offer the occasion of knowing, not knowledge itself: the passive faculty (*potestativum*) receives motion from the ob-

---

[14] *De sensu rerum et magia* (1620), Lib. I, cap. vi; (p. 17).
[15] *Universalis philosophiae*, Part II, Lib. VI, cap. xii, art. 5; (Vol. II, p. 89).

ject, then the cognitive faculty judges on the basis of that passion as the occasion, but from itself as the real cause, what the object is . . . For it is not the stone as an object of sense and intellect that teaches us what a stone is, or causes us to know, or to know this particular thing; for the stone itself is senseless, and far more ignorant than we in knowledge of itself: but the stone offers the occasion for us to know this particular thing, though not for our knowing in general, for it does not move the mind to the exercise of its power (*actus*) but to the specification of that power.[16]

But if a judgment be concealed in every sensing, still all judging is like sense: and all the actions of the *spiritus* are forms of perception. Memory is the perception of motions remaining in the spirit, a weaker kind of sensing; *ratio* is a sensing of the common traits left from a group of individual motions. There are in things no universal natures, but only individuals; hence a knowledge of individuals is superior to the knowledge of the universals which represent no natural structure.

The only certain knowledge, the only proof, is sense observation. A single observation of fact will refute any amount of reasoning.

When all the sensations present and past of ourselves and others agree, we have certain science.[17]

Reasoning is uncertain knowledge, abstract, denuded, sketchy, a mere second best. We need deductive proof only when we have not the certainty of sense before our eyes; we get it only in terms of the common signs of a group of things, not of the concrete reality of any one. We want to know, not fever in general, but this kind, this particular case. For such knowledge we can only look at the world and observe facts.

Aristotle is deceived when he says that sense does not deliver the cause of the question as reason does, and hence makes sense more uncertain and ignorant than reason. For to deliver the cause, I say, is to explain whence comes something that is uncertain; but sense is certain and needs no proof, for it is its own proof. But reason is uncertain knowledge and needs proof; and even when proof is adduced from a cause, it is sought from some other certain sensation . . . Reason is a kind of imperfect sense, extraneous and not of things themselves but of like things. Never-

[16] *Universalis philosophiae*, Part I, Lib. I, cap. iv, art. 1; (Vol. I, p. 33); Part I, Lib. II, cap. v, art. 7; (Vol. I, p. 160).
[17] *Realis philosophiae epilogisticae partes IV* (1623), Part I, cap. 16, art. 2.

theless God has ordained that through it we are able to search out and know all things, though not perfectly . . . To understand is to sense confusedly and at a distance; to sense is to understand near by and close at hand.[18]

And yet, despite this sturdy devotion to observation, Campanella finds souls everywhere, mysterious forces, the sympathies and antipathies of the prevailing Platonism. Space abhors a vacuum and yearns to be filled; plants grieve when they wilt, and rejoice after a rain. How does he reconcile his uncompromising insistence on observation with the observation of such facts? By his theory of reasoning by analogy. For reasoning, though weak, though an imperfect sense, can yet go farther than sense itself. It operates by perceiving analogies between things. Like all reasoning, this is a sort of perception, a *sensus similis in simili*. We observe the majesty of God in the majesty of the pope, the tenuity of angels in the tenuity of the mind. Such reasoning by analogy can go as far as there are real resemblances in the world. Sensation alone is certain, but we can sense one thing in another because of the resemblances between them. The world resembles an animal: therefore we can *see* that it has a soul. But does the world really possess such resemblances? Here Campanella's Neoplatonic metaphysics steps in to supplement what his nominalism had excluded. The world was created to be the image and resemblance of God, and to shadow forth his divine perfection, his primalities of Power, Wisdom, and Love.

We easily reason to all objects since all are really like each other. They are all like, since they depend on the same most powerful and good Cause.[19]

This community of things corresponds to a single Idea of the divine mind, whence all community of things emanates in the degree of its own participation. To contemplate the Idea of the different degrees of participating in the First Idea, is the proper work of the mind with which God has endowed man; mind is excited to a knowledge of ideas by the similarities it finds in these ideas, which are generated in the spirit apprehending the communities of things.[20]

It is the structure of the universe as the semblance of God that makes reasoning by analogies possible.

---

[18] *De sensu rerum*, Lib. II, cap. 30 (pp. 174, 183); cap. 22 (p. 81).
[19] *De sensu rerum*, Lib. II, cap. 30.
[20] *Realis philosophiae*, Part I, Lib. I, Physiologica, cap. xvi, art. 8; (p. 186).

God's "primalities" of *Potentia*, *Prudentia*, and *Amor* are also made the basis of the political structure of the ideal commonwealth Campanella described in a work written while he was in the dungeons, the *Civitas Solis*, or *City of the Sun*, the only one of his writings to become well known, a utopia in the vein of the *New Atlantis* and Sir Thomas More's ideal state, sharing the former's emphasis on the fruits of technology, and the latter's on a government by reason and a rational religion. On many points Campanella follows the *Republic* closely, such as the community of women; he modifies the scheme Plato puts into Socrates's mouth in the light of his religious principles, emphasizing the monastic community as an ideal social organization, and the papal government as the ideal administration.

A Genoese sea-captain describes the City of the Sun, which he found terracing a high hill in a plain "immediately under the equator." [21] It is governed by a priest named Hoh, or Metaphysic. Three princes of equal power assist him, Pon, Sin, and Mor, or Power, Intelligence, and Love—the four always agree. Power is in charge of war and diplomacy, Intelligence rules over the sciences and arts and public works; Love has charge "of the race," including the breeding of children by matching suitable parents, and their education apart from their parents after they are weaned. There are two assemblies, the upper one consisting of priest-magistrates appointed by Hoh, the lower one including all the people. The latter's authority is limited to passing on questions of war and peace. Hoh is named for life by a college of priest-magistrates; his ministers Power, Intelligence, and Love together exercise all the functions of rational government. There is no private property, no domestic ties of loyalty to children or parents. Despite Aristotle's criticisms of Plato, the absence of domestic ties leads the citizens to "burn with so great a love for their fatherland, as I could scarcely have believed possible . . . All things are common with them, and their dispensation is by authority of the magistrates. Arts and honors and pleasures are common, and are held in such a manner that no one can appropriate anything to himself." (p. 225) The magistrates, who correspond to Plato's guardians, govern well; "no one wants either necessaries or

[21] *The City of the Sun*, in *Ideal Commonwealths*, ed. Henry Morley (Library of Universal Knowledge, London, Routledge).

luxuries." Not the "consideration of the dead signs of things," "the words of books," is esteemed the highest knowledge; but the sciences from mathematics down, and the useful arts. In Europe, "you consider that man the most learned who knows most of grammar, or logic, or of Aristotle." "They disbelieve in Aristotle, whom they consider a logician and not a philosopher," not agreeing that the world is uncreated. "Beyond all other things they venerate the sun, but they consider no created thing worthy of the adoration of worship." Of things below, "the Sun is the father, and the earth the mother." "They worship God in Trinity, saying God is the supreme Power, whence proceeds the highest Wisdom, which is the same with God, and from these comes Love, which is both Power and Wisdom; but they do not distinguish the persons by name, as in our Christian law, which has not been revealed to them. This religion, when its abuses have been removed, will be the future mistress of the world, as great theologians teach and hope. Therefore Spain found the New World." (p. 263)

Campanella follows Plato in providing for three classes; the middle class, however, serve the modern function of industry, in very Baconian terms, not the ancient function of military defense. The priest-magistrates are able to assign new citizens with perfect certainty to their proper class. Such was the vision of a perfect city that came to Campanella in his Neapolitan prison.

After his release in France, Campanella sketched a more universal if no less ideal social scheme in *De Monarchia Hispanica* (1640), in which Europe is organized into one commonwealth under Spain and the pope, on the same general principles as the City of the Sun. This is the outstanding utopia produced by the Counter Reformation.

In developing his metaphysics, Campanella begins with a thorough examination of the sceptical position, taken all the more seriously as he realizes the difficulties of a pure empiricism. How distinguish between the accidental and the essential motions that impinge upon us from bodies, how get out of the circle of our own sensations? Each man possesses his own picture of the world, as he has been affected in his particular way by the motions of things. The concepts man forms are empty and far from the richness of concrete individuals. Induction is a mere summing up of single observations, *experimen-*

torum multorum coacervatio; how can we hope that the axioms and principles so arrived at will not have overlooked the essential elements? And the very act of knowing itself is a kind of destruction of the mind, a becoming something else:

> to know is to be alienated, to be alienated is to become insane and to lose one's own being and acquire an alien one: therefore it is not to know things as they are, but to become things and suffer alienation. But alienation is madness and insanity, and hence a man becomes insane when he is changed to something else.[22]

Only through a closer examination of the two factors in knowledge, the object known and the knower, only through metaphysics and psychology, can these doubts be answered. For knower and known are not alien powers, but both the products of the same divine cause. In becoming what is a semblance of this cause, the mind does not really turn from its own nature, but rather toward the source of its own being. Knowing is a merging of the mind with the Divine Truth that created it: and Campanella finds certainty in the Augustinian vision of truth in God's Truth. On the other hand, if we examine ourselves rather than things, we find that doubt itself is a certainty:

> We may indeed think that this or that thing does not exist, but not that we ourselves do not exist, for how could we think without being?[23]

And to this Augustinian answer Campanella adds by identifying the soul with thinking itself: "the very being of the soul and of any thinking thing is its knowledge of itself."[24]

> Each thing understands itself by a hidden act of thought through its own essence: since to know external things is to be acted upon by them and to become them: intelligence becomes itself the intelligible thing. But that intellect may know itself, there is no need to be acted upon by itself, nor to become itself;—for it is. But what it is it does not become; hence it knows itself through its essence, and knowing and thinking is its essence.[25]

For all his openness to the rich world of ideas around him, Campanella had a poor opinion of mathematics, which he founded on his

[22] *Universalis philosophiae,* Part I, Lib. I, cap. i, art. 9; (Vol. I, p. 20).
[23] *Universalis philosophiae,* Part II, Lib. VI, cap. iii, art. 5; (Vol. II, p. 15).
[24] *Ibid.,* Part II, Lib. VI, cap. viii, art. 5; (Vol. II, p. 64).
[25] *Ibid.,* Part II, Lib. VI, cap. vi, art. 9; (Vol. II, p. 36).

empirical theory rather than on his Platonism, boasting that he had succeeded where Aristotle failed. Mathematics like logic fails to grasp the full reality of particular things: it is but the fragment of a science, a mere chain of empty identities between signs, fit only to be the handmaiden of physics. Its epicycles and rotations are mere ideal pictures which do not reach to the real processes and forces of nature. Yet mathematics has been empirically learned, not from things, but from the absolute space in which things exist.

Place is a first substance or seat or capacity, immovable and incorporeal, fitted to receive every body.[26]

I recognize space as the basis of all created being: it precedes everything else in origin and nature.[27]

Here in this absolute space are to be found the counterparts of all geometrical figures.

The intellect makes them in space, since it knows them in the ideal divine light: stimulated in a certain hidden manner by the likeness of sensible things . . . For the physical and mathematical world is founded on a prior mental one. Ideas are therefore as a sign in us . . . In this way do the things which are defined exist in mathematics: they can be assumed, because the idea is in us and space is in nature, in which they are represented.[28]

VII

If we attempt to sum up the core of the new vision of nature, shared by the German enthusiasts and the Italian nature philosophers alike, we may express it as the conviction that man and nature are similar, that man is through and through natural, and nature human. The new science was destined to sunder them sharply, to insist that nature is not human, but mathematical and mechanical, and that man lives as a kingdom within nature. Only against such a background can one understand, for example, Descartes's complete rejection of all action at a distance, his suspicion of all forces not strictly mechanical and kinetic. Such a clean break from the nature philosophy of the Renaissance was necessary for any manageable science. The reaction of the scientific thinkers of the seventeenth century against

[26] *Realis philosophiae*, Physiologica, cap. i, art. 2; (p. 4).
[27] *De sensu rerum*, Lib. I, cap. 12; (p. 40).
[28] *Universalis philosophiae*, Part III, Lib. XIII, cap. ii, art. 6; (Vol. III, p. 125).

the whole idea of man as a microcosm explains their purifying zeal and their mistrust of any appeal to observation unchecked by mathematical reasoning; it clarifies the turning to "rationalism" in theory on the part of men quite willing in practice to observe and experiment, but unwilling to traffic with the "experience" of this Renaissance tradition. The persisting influence of the nature philosophers thus had momentous consequences in the interpretation of the new science, and in driving it to an exclusive devotion to mathematics. It has proved a terrible job to get man back into nature again.

But at least two fundamental ideas of the nature philosophers were carried over into the new scientific world-view. Nature was already for them a single self-contained whole, a single total system. There were no other realms above or beyond it; God must appear in nature or not at all. The idea of the unity of the System of Nature was gained in the sixteenth century, and something at least was glimpsed of the notion of uniform natural law. And secondly, "force" came to the fore as the fundamental causal and explanatory concept, replacing that of "form." It was an easy step to taking forces as alone real, and to reading forms, species, ends, and entelechies completely out of nature. In the customary terminology, force and spirit were identical concepts. Thus Gilbert, writing in 1600 of the magnet, naturally attributed its behavior to the presence of a "soul" or "spirit"; and throughout the seventeenth century, whatever in nature was not clearly explicable as the effect of mechanical contact was readily assigned to "spirit" and dubbed "spiritual." Such terminology has caused untold confusion to simple-minded modernizing theologians to the present day!

8

The New Aim of Knowledge as Power

I

AS PART AND PARCEL of this eager interest in nature, and as a reflex of the growing dissatisfaction with the fruits of medieval knowledge, the suspicion took form that the Schools had been directing their inquiries to the wrong ends. Aristotelian science had originally come to the thirteenth-century Augustinians as a revolutionary discovery. Not only had it brought a body of independent knowledge of nature into an intellectual tradition which regarded nature as the mere symbol of higher things, and injected the world between the soul and God as a proper object of inquiry. Still more momentously, it had elevated human *scientia*, the sheer understanding and rational grasp of things, from a position of insignificant subordination to the divine *sapientia* into the most appropriate activity of the human intellect. To be sure, in the great compromisers of the thirteenth century such science still culminated in the vision of Truth that was God; but the whole drive of the "moderns" of the next hundred years was to destroy the ladder that led from scientific truths to the Divine Truth, and to relegate that ascent to faith alone. Under the influence of the logic of the "moderns," as practiced by both the Scotists and the Ockhamites, the university scholars drew finer and subtler distinctions in their inherited Aristotelian materials in the sheer intellectual delight of understanding their well classified subject-matter. The analytic mind can still admire the exact precision of this enterprise; but to the restless enthusiasm of the Renaissance it seemed but labor misdirected and wasted upon the empty forms of discourse, a net of subtility and "spinosity."

For the wit of man [complained Bacon] if it work upon matter, which is the contemplation of the creatures of God, worketh according to the stuff, and is limited thereby; but if it work upon itself, as the spider worketh his web, then it is endless, and brings forth indeed cobwebs of learning, admirable for the fineness of thread and work, but of no substance or profit.[1]

This mulling over of the same material by minds "shut up in the cells of a few authors," without further substantial additions, brought the whole aim of Aristotelian *scientia*, of sheer understanding and knowing, into disrepute, and sent men searching again for a wisdom beyond mere understanding that would be to their service and profit.

In this revulsion from Aristotelian "science," it was easiest, of course, to return to the traditional Augustinian "wisdom" directed toward beatitude and the soul's salvation; the fourteenth century saw many such an Augustinian attack on "science," not only from mystics like Eckhart, but even from learned doctors trained in the Ockhamite empiricism, like John Gerson, pupil of the scientifically minded Cardinal D'Ailly. This Augustinian scepticism of the works of human reason in the interests of a direct wisdom of God colored not only the thought of Luther and the whole German Reformation, until Melanchthon brought Aristotle back; it created a strong sceptic school in sixteenth-century France, contributed to the unique genius of Montaigne, and came to a final flower in Pascal.

But this same revulsion against scholasticism, this same turning to Augustinian "wisdom," produced an equal contempt for mere science or understanding in those more secular minds who found their inspiration in the literature of Rome and Greece. The practical-minded Latin writers could impart no interest in intelligibility; and the human wisdom of Cicero and the Stoics combined easily with the divine wisdom of Augustine in setting a concern with the chief end of man far above any mere understanding of nature. The typical humanist, indeed, like Erasmus, not only possessed no interest in natural science; he was apt to be actively opposed to it, and to regard even the mathematicians as devotees of a barren and futile learning. The main drive of the whole movement was not toward understanding but toward a knowledge that would further human action and practice.

[1] Bacon, *Advancement of Learning*, Book I, sec. 4, par. 5.

In such an intellectual atmosphere, and in a world vibrant with a new sense of human power, it is not surprising that the minority group fascinated by the secrets of nature should have felt that this knowledge too should be turned, not to the service of God, but to the utility of man. To the Augustinian mystics and sceptics who like Tauler counseled a "knowledge of the hidden truth of God, of the bondage of nature, of the deceitfulness of the world, and of the cunning of evil spirits," [2] and to the Humanists like Erasmus and Petrarch, who said, "Even if all these things were true, they help in no way toward a happy life." [3] Francis Bacon proclaimed:

I will give thee the greatest jewel I have. For I will impart unto thee, for the love of God and men, a relation of the true state of Salomon's House . . . The end of our foundation is the knowledge of causes and secret motions of things; and the enlarging of the bounds of human empire, to the effecting of all things possible.[4]

This new conception of knowledge, not as a divine wisdom in the soul, not as a human wisdom for the conduct of life, but as an effective power over nature through the investigation of the causes of things and the practice of "natural magic," we are apt to call "Baconian" because the great Elizabethan was the most eloquent of all its buccinators. But he only lent words to a sentiment already widespread in his day. As lawyer and orator he used his unsurpassed gift of language to immortalize the views of the small band among the humanists who had caught the vision of a practical science of nature. A few men, like Roger Bacon in the thirteenth century, had earlier proclaimed the same humanistic aim for natural knowledge; but only in Francis Bacon, Lord Verulam's generation was science turned definitely, not to the aesthetic *theoria* of the Greeks, not to the *visio Dei* of the Christians, but to human action and control.

That science should bear practical fruits, that any system of thought which does not flower in technology is in fact a mere idle speculation, is an idea so natural to us that we take it for granted, without realizing how sharply it sets off our own intellectual enterprise from the organized beliefs of other great civilizations. No other society, in fact, has aimed to make its systematic knowledge of

[2] *Johann Tauler's Sermons*, ed. H. R. Allinson, p. 354.
[3] Petrarch, *Opera* (1581 ed.), col. 1038.
[4] Bacon, *New Atlantis*, World's Classics ed., p. 265.

nature practically useful. Neither the imposing civilizations of ancient times nor the great cultures of the Orient have done so, though they have erected elaborate edifices of ideas, and though they have possessed as highly developed arts and technology, and as vigorous a commercial class, as sixteenth- and seventeenth-century Europe. The technological and economic growth of Western Europe is surely most important in generating this shift from a science of understanding to a science of power; but its unique consequences are intelligible only against the background of the Christian, and specifically the Augustinian tradition. For a thousand years the professed intellectual ideal of Europe had been not *scientia,* not understanding, but *sapientia,* the service of the chief end of man, salvation and beatitude. Understanding had been always in theory and generally in practice secondary to human utility, to the usefulness of knowledge for man's immortal soul.

The Aristotelian movement had indeed for a time made *scientia* or understanding primary; it had elevated reason above will and love, and set men to searching out the causes of things, with God as the ultimate reason why. The essential social function of this Aristotelian scholasticism was to provide an integrated intellectual life for a society seeking order; to control and organize men's knowledge and natural curiosity about the world in terms of their traditional values, of the Good; to explain everything obvious in nature and in man, and to carry that explanation up to the Supreme Reason Why, the Source of all Intelligibility. This was of course the same function as that performed by the Church herself in the thirteenth century, the intellectual expression of the Church's function. It was the function of an imaginative, aesthetic, and priestly religion: to rationalize a rich religious tradition, to express and consecrate and clarify natural curiosity and human values.

But after the brief interlude of the thirteenth century, European society no longer wanted order; it wanted freedom, escape from medieval organization, scope for its rapidly expanding activities. It sought the Chief Good through action, and a basis for action in the actual structure of things. In Scotism and Ockhamism alike, the two philosophies of the break-up of the Middle Ages, the will was primary, not the reason; and both combined this voluntarism with observation, with empiricism, and with an individualistic vision of the world. Men subordinated understanding to salvation again, but now to a salvation increasingly to be attained in this world. They turned away from Aristotle to the Augustinian tradition once more, the background of all later medieval thought, and of Humanism and the Reformation as well. It is significant that the practical science of the Middle Ages came from the Augustinians, like Roger Bacon, and not from the strict Aristotelians; from them too came the increasing criticism of the search for intelligibility and understanding as "useless." Renaissance and Reformation alike shared the distinctive modern trait of rejecting all understanding divorced from power. What they both wanted was rather a fruitful art of magic, an art useful for man's happiness—the Reformers, one still aimed at the salvation of man's immortal soul, though in it they consecrated this-worldly values: the Humanists one frankly this-worldly, bringing human goods here and now. For both, wisdom must be bent to the service of man. When an interest in nature and its possibilities was once roused, it had likewise to serve man. In its background the Baconian spirit can be best described as a kind of naturalistic Augustinianism, aiming at human salvation and beatitude in this world, through a natural wisdom controlling the forces of nature in the interests of human power.

In a society thus already committed to power and salvation as the ultimate aim of all knowledge, the developing technology, the increasingly elaborate forces of production, were able to give a strong impetus to the knowledge that would procure a power over nature. It is here that the stimulus of the many tools and instruments Europe had borrowed and improved belongs: the compass, gained in the eleventh century; the sextant, with its demand for accompanying astronomical tables for use in navigation; the introduction of gunpowder, the revolution in fortifications it brought, the need for a science of ballistics. Here falls the work of the great artist-engineers, Leonardo, Michelangelo, Raphael, Dürer, whose practical purposes drove them to explore anatomy, perspective, and mechanics. Both Stevinus and Descartes served as military engineers, and found great need of exact measurements and precise formulae. Medicine and surgery likewise had made strides in the fifteenth century. Out of all this activity there had developed a wealth of experience and facts and empirically tested formulae, quite independent of the Aristotelian natural philosophy; facts and formulae that seemed obviously useful and powerful, whatever their relevance to explanation.

II

This is the atmosphere in which were launched the many sixteenth-century attacks on the uselessness of the knowledge of the Schools. In his lawyer's indictment Bacon summed up the brief for the prosecution. He assailed three kinds of knowledge in particular, three "vanities in studies." Scholasticism is condemned on a double count: not only is it barren of all practical fruits, but in the Schools it has been turned into an instrument of power, not over nature, but over men—it has become primarily a "contentious learning." When rigorous it aims at demonstration, when looser, at persuasion, but in both cases at victory in debate. How true this had become in practice we learn from Peter Ramus:

Never amidst the clamors of the college where I passed so many days, months, years, did I ever hear a single word about the applications of logic. I had faith then (the scholar ought to have faith, according to Aristotle) that it was not necessary to trouble myself about what logic is and what its purpose is, but that it concerned itself solely with creating a motive for our clamors and our disputes. I therefore disputed and clamored with all my might. If I were defending in class a thesis according to the categories, I believed it my duty never to yield to my opponent, were he one hundred times right, but to seek some very subtle distinction, in order to obscure the whole issue. On the other hand, were I disputant, all my care and efforts tended not to enlighten my opponent, but to beat him by some argument, good or bad: even so had I been taught and directed. The categories of Aristotle were like a ball that we give children to play with, and that it was necessary to get back by our clamors when we had lost it. If, on the other hand, we should get it, we should not through any outcry allow it to be recovered. I was then persuaded that all dialectic reduced itself to disputing with loud and vigorous cries.[5]

Logic does not help us find new sciences. It is far too crude for the subtlety of nature. It commands assent to propositions, but it does not take hold of and master the thing. Its method is

upon every particular position or assertion to frame objections, and to those objections, solutions; which solutions are for the most part not

[5] Peter Ramus, *Studies in Dialectic*, Book IV, p. 151; cited in F. P. Graves, *Peter Ramus and the Educational Reformation of the Sixteenth Century* (1912), pp. 21–22.

confutations but distinctions . . . Were it not better for a man in a fair room to set up one great light, or branching candlestick of lights, than to go about with a small watch candle into every corner? And such is their method, that rests not so much upon evidence of truth proved by arguments, authorities, similitudes, examples, as upon particular confutations and solutions of every scruple, cavillation, and objection; breeding for the most part one question as fast as it solveth another; even as in the former resemblance, when you carry the light into one corner you darken the rest.[6]

Logic can disprove in detail, but it cannot discover. As Descartes put it,

In respect to logic, the syllogisms and the greater part of the other teaching served better in explaining to others those things that one knows (or, like the art of Lully, in enabling one to speak without judgment of those things of which one is ignorant) than learning what is new.[7]

This was the common complaint: Greek science did not investigate, it was not practical. The Greeks

assuredly have that which is characteristic of boys: they are prompt to prattle but cannot generate; for their wisdom abounds in words but is barren of works . . . From all these systems of the Greeks, and their ramifications through particular sciences, there can hardly after the lapse of so many years be adduced a single experiment which tends to relieve and benefit the condition of man, and which can with truth be referred to the speculations and theories of philosophy.[8]

They had the baneful conceit "that the dignity of the human mind is impaired with long and close intercourse with experiments and particulars, subject to sense and bound in matter." (Aphorism 83) Characteristically enough, Bacon like most of the Humanists includes mathematics in this condemnation of mere verbalism.

Consequently the recovery of the thought of the Greeks themselves—the humanist enthusiasm—is mere "delicate learning," a vain affectation conferring not power but ornament and decoration. It is ostentatious and luxurious, it leans "rather towards copie than weight," and is a study of other men's words rather than of things. Bacon was not, however, above making copious use of this "delicate learning" in his own writing.

[6] *Advancement of Learning*, Book I, sec. 4, par. 6.
[7] Descartes, *Discourse on Method*, in *Philosophical Works*, ed. Haldane and Ross, I, 91.
[8] Bacon, *Novum Organum*, Book I, Aphorisms 71, 73.

He has kinder words for the third sort of knowledge prevalent in his day, the "fantastical learning" of the nature philosophers and magicians. Its ends are noble, man's power over nature; unfortunately its means are crude and full of vanity. He regarded himself as seeking through observation and experiment to improve the methods of the nature philosophers; and in truth in his positive doctrine he belongs, not with the scientists—for he rejected mathematics and the new astronomy—but with these gropers after fantastic learning.

As against all three forms of knowledge, it is a practical philosophy for which Bacon calls:

Now the true and lawful goal of the sciences is none other than this: that human life be endowed with new discoveries and powers. (Aphorism 181)

We must study to "turn heaven and earth to the use and welfare of mankind." Nature to be commanded must be obeyed; not by the anticipation of nature in some magic dream, but by the study and interpretation of nature, will the kingdom of man arise. Such investigation is "laborious to search, ignoble to meditate, harsh to deliver, illiberal to practice, infinite in number, and minute in subtlety." (Aphorism 83) But it is the only instrument of power over nature. Nor did the real scientists disagree with Bacon in demanding power.

It is possible [said Descartes] to attain knowledge which is very useful in life, and instead of that speculative philosophy which is taught in the schools we may find a practical philosophy by means of which, knowing the force and the action of fire, water, air, the stars, heavens, and all other bodies that environ us, as distinctly as we know the different crafts of our artisans, we can in the same way employ them all in those uses to which they are adapted, and thus render ourselves the masters and possessors of nature.[9]

Power and possession, not understanding, above all, not the careful discrimination of the Good Life—such was henceforth to be the keynote of modern thought. Lost was the old Greek Wisdom, the tragedy of the modern age. And though that interpretation of nature, when it was found, turned out to be a natural development of what the Greeks had begun rather than its abandonment, and though

[9] Descartes, *Discourse on Method*, ed. Haldane and Ross, I, 119.

it was Aristotle's conception of science, and not Augustinian wisdom, Humanistic ethics, or natural magic, that came to new birth in the seventeenth century, it was to the effecting of all things possible, and not merely of those desirable, that it was bent.

The highest wisdom is that which gives power. It is not too much to see in Bacon, the prophet of the rich fruits of science who blindly opposed the scientific discoveries of his own day, who cherished in knowledge its power to effect all things possible, and fell for lack of common honesty, the epitome of the spirit in which the modern world has squandered the boundless gifts of nature's secrets. Science has indeed been a kind of magic, a natural magic, Bacon would have said—far too often a black magic, bringing death and destruction. We have learned the secrets of the atoms, and invent H-bombs and ICBMs; we have the power to turn the desert into a garden, and we make slums of our countryside. And yet—there remains the vision of those eighteenth-century prophets who were not content to confine science to a power over nature; who, building on Bacon's own vision, tried to extend the techniques of seventeenth-century natural science to the investigation of human nature and human society, in the conviction that only by an exact understanding of man's individual and social life can man hope to achieve power over himself and his own destiny, to the effecting, not of all things possible, but of those things which can contribute to the Good Life.

9

The Search for a Fruitful Method:
Humanistic Rhetoric and Experience

I

THE GREAT intellectual enterprise of the sixteenth century was the search for a method that would give men such a practical and useful science. This, we have seen, was just what the fantastic learning of the nature philosophers most sorely lacked. In both its traditional insights and its novel guesses the imagination needed the discipline of a critical method before there could be any significant observation of facts. It is hence not surprising that those whose intellectual energies were not absorbed by the theological disputes in terms of which the major battles of the sixteenth century were fought should have concentrated on this problem of method as the paramount scientific task of the day. For men profoundly dissatisfied with the results of existing science, yet with no other solid body of achievement to which to turn, there is no recourse but to some new method: our present predicament in the social sciences has evoked an equal concern. Without actual success, one needs to be all the more certain that he is on the right track. This is especially true of those consciously breaking with a well-recognized tradition; and when, as for these fifteenth- and sixteenth-century pioneers, that meant a break, not only with the academically respectable learning of the schools, but with the authority of the very ancients to whom the majority of radicals were appealing, the need for confidence in one's method was overwhelming. It was the humanistic movement that to effect its own break with the past had introduced intellectual authoritarianism; after the fourteenth century the medieval thinkers had become acquainted with so many *auctoritates* or authors that "natural reason" had to make the final decision, and authoritarianism had pretty completely broken down. The turbulent transitional period of the Renaissance and Reformation with its many warring programs saw a tightening of party lines and an appeal to sheer authority that Europe had not known for several centuries. Protestants now took their Bible literally, the Church crystallized its dogmas at Trent, and the Humanists attributed to the ancients an infallibility that even Aristotle had never earlier enjoyed. Amid this welter of conflicting authorities, the only alternatives for an independent mind were the scepticism to which the Wars of Religion drove the French, or faith in the infallibility of a certain method.

For all these reasons, clarity as to method seemed of transcendent moment. If only that problem could be solved, then the road would lie open. For intellectual powers were surely equal in all men, waiting but release from error and discovery of the proper instrument to behold the truth.

The cause and root of nearly all evils in the sciences is this, [Bacon said], that while we falsely extol and admire the powers of the human mind we neglect to seek for its true helps. Neither the naked hand nor the understanding left to itself can effect much. It is by instruments and helps that the work is done, which are as much wanted for the understanding as for the hand.[1]

Descartes went even farther in this confidence in the right method to overcome all obstacles:

The power of forming a good judgment and of distinguishing the true from the false—common sense or reason—is by nature equal in all men. The diversity of our opinions does not proceed from some men being more rational than others, but solely from the fact that our thoughts pass through diverse channels. For to be possessed of good mental powers is not sufficient; the principal matter is to apply them well.[2]

That men might differ in their intellectual endowments was not considered of serious moment, in fact, until the Romantic protest against the universal reason of the eighteenth century.

When the fruitful method was finally discovered and proved in practice, it turned out not to be new at all, but rather the orthodox

[1] *Novum Organum*, ed. Thomas Fowler (1878), Book I, Aphorism 2. Eng. tr. by R. Ellis and James Spedding in Vol. IV of *Works*, ed. Spedding, Ellis, and D. D. Heath (1857–59).
[2] *Discourse on Method*, Discourse I; in *Works*, ed. Haldane and Ross, I, 81–82.

tradition of the thirteenth- and fourteenth-century Franciscan
scholars, as carefully developed and expanded in anticlerical Padua.
The many Humanist seekers, revolting from the Aristotelian scholasticism of the Scotists, and the technical terminist logic—against
which the usual jibes were directed—seem to have displayed all the
customary ignorance and futility of intellectual revolutionaries, and
to have proposed methods distinguished chiefly by the novelty of
their ignorance. As might be expected, these servants of the word
for the most part sought a new method in language and in rhetoric,
and tried to erect a "natural dialectic" on the basis of Cicero and
Quintilian! Others were fascinated by the suggestions of Lully for a
universal language that might discover all truth. So eager were men
for such an instrument that Bruno, wandering from one university
to another, was able to support himself by lecturing to throngs on
just such a new method.

II

Since the time of Petrarch the chief criticism of the Humanists
against the Schoolmen had been of their unciceronian language.
Bruni complained that the incomplete state of Cicero's writings
made it impossible for moderns ever to perfect their philosophic
culture; and Ermolao Barbaro wrote to Pico that the Schoolmen,
because they had not known the value of good latinity, had never
really lived at all. At times, indeed, these critics of the scholastic
style in protesting against such neologisms as *entitas*, *quidditas*, or
haecceitas displayed true philosophic insight, for they seem to have
perceived that in turning all relations and activities into abstract
nouns the Schoolmen were expressing a characteristic and deep-
seated conception of nature and man, a quite different philosophy
from the Greek that Cicero had put into his Latin.

Lorenzo Valla (1407–1457), sceptical and ironic critic of tradition, was the first to attack the Aristotelian method formally in his
Dialecticae disputationes contra Aristotelicos. The scholastic logic
is mere sophistry, for the Schoolmen use such barbarous and complicated Latin. Logic must be made a rational science through a simplification of its language, until one can learn it in as many months as
it takes years to acquire rhetoric. Above all we must get rid of its
empty abstract terms and return to the concrete, to things. Since

thought is a practical activity leading to expression, the science of thought must be the science of language, a branch of the more inclusive rhetoric. Its conceptual analysis is a mere preparation for that art of persuasion which only the rhetorician and orator can wield; it is concerned with proof and refutation, which are parts of the "invention" in a completed rhetoric. It is in the persuasion of rhetoric that the gifted personality comes into actual contact with other living men:

> How much clearer, weightier, and more exalted are all the objects of the orator, than those treated by the confused, bloodless and dry dialecticians! [3]

Speech is the commander, philosophy the mere common soldier. Valla preferred Quintilian to Cicero: the latter was too much of a philosopher.

And yet Valla's historical criticism, whether he was pointing out the errors in the Vulgate or in Livy, or attacking the Donation of Constantine, breathes a new spirit of independence, a delight in the free play of the mind. Half believing, half ironic, he judges by "natural reason" even when, like Bayle, he finally accepts conclusions on authority. For reason is the best authority: "Is there a worse reason than the testimony of a man? . . . Or any better 'author' than reason?" [4] His worship of rhetoric is but an expression of this independence of the free personality; for how can a man better exercise his power than by the proper use of winged words?

Valla's path was followed by most of the Humanists. Rudolf Agricola (1442–1485), leader of the Humanistic circle at Heidelberg, drew on him to develop a rhetorical logic in his *De inventione dialectica*. Prudence and eloquence, right judgment and skillful expression, are the aim of knowledge; they can be learned only from the ancients. Aristotle, Cicero, and Seneca are supreme in practical wisdom, the Greeks in natural science. The goal of logic is *formare orationem* for statesmen; the *Topics* are to be rated most highly.

III

Most famous of all the humanistic reformers of logic was Petrus Ramus (Pierre de la Ramée, 1515–1572), who taught in the *Collège*

---

[3] Valla, *De voluptate*, I, cap. 10.   [4] Valla, *Opera* (Basel, 1543), p. 445.

Royale against the scholastic Sorbonne doctors, and turning Huguenot, was killed in the St. Bartholomew massacre at the instigation of an opponent. As the great Calvinist logician he enjoyed much influence for a century in Germany and Scotland. In his master's thesis, 1536, he announced, "Everything Aristotle has said is a lie"; but later, growing more temperate, wrote a *Defense of Aristotle* in which he proclaimed himself the only true Aristotelian, though he still maintained that the *Organon* was spurious. A perfect professor, he turned out edition after edition of his *Institutiones dialecticae* (1543; in French, 1555); Bacon called him the "father of textbooks," for his thought displays pedagogical clarity and simplicity rather than originality.

Aristotle tried to make two logics, one for science, in the *Analytics*, and the other for opinion, in the *Topics*. To this artificial complexity with its burden of useless rules Ramus opposed the single inborn "natural dialectic" of living discussion as practiced by the poets, orators, philosophers, and indeed by all excellent men.

The truth of the arts flourished in nature before any precepts were thought of . . . The true description of the art of logic should proceed from the observation of natural reason and usage. . . . The dialectic art is the image of natural dialectic; but in the commentaries of Aristotle there is nothing that points to nature: nothing, if you regard the truth of nature, that is not confused, muddied up, contaminated, and distorted.[5]

It was the Platonic dialogues that convinced Ramus of the unfruitfulness of the scholastic method; inspired by the idea of dialectic in the sixth book of the *Republic*, he too regarded it as the queen of the sciences, to be approached through grammar and rhetoric, arithmetic and geometry, music and astronomy. For actual content however he drew mostly on the rhetorical method of Cicero and Quintilian, and the *Topics*.

As its very name implies, dialectic is the art of disputation, *ars bene disserendi*. It culminates in speech and oratory, which to be convincing must be deductive, applying general arguments to particular cases. Natural dialectic starts with a problem to solve; it is frankly practical and useful. Arguments must be found which will settle the problem. The art of dialectic falls therefore into two parts,

[5] Ramus, *Aristotelicae animadversiones* (1543), p. 109.

Inventio, or the doctrine of thinking out and discovering arguments, and *Iudicium* or *Dispositio,* "the apt collocation of the things discovered, or the disposing of arguments for judging." Invention Ramus bases on Cicero and the *Topics;* disposition has two divisions, *axioma* or the "disposition of argument with argument by which it is judged that something is or is not"; and *dianoia,* "when something is deduced from something else." Dianoia has two parts, the syllogism and "method," which is "the arrangement of a variety of arguments so that the first in importance is placed first, the second next, the third in the third place, and so on in order." The liberal arts and sciences follow the "method of learning," from definitions and principles: such method always proceeds from universals to particulars. Poets, orators, and historians use the "method of sagacity," most important of all for Ramus, in which there are wide individual differences. Since dialectic is wholly an art of persuasion and not of discovery, invention has no relation to method or ordering; the arguments and premises are all found first, and then effectively put into order. Natural dialectic can be elevated into an art, however, only through repeated practice and careful exercise. Such natural thinking is to be fostered by close study of the ancients, by writing, and by speaking.

Despite this dominance of rhetoric, Ramus has much to say about mathematics as the model of dialectic. The scholastic logic was based on the categories, on grammar. But it is geometry which is even in the Aristotelian sense the only true science; and its rigor comes not from the syllogism, but from its definitions and postulates. Speech first shows us how the manifold of things can be expressed in thought. But we are then led on to the deeper insight of mathematics, which takes us from mere shadows to principles and causes. Arithmetic bestows not only rule over things, it brings to the mind a knowledge of its divine essence. And Ramus rises to a Platonic and Augustinian praise of mathematics:

In what other way do we arrive, in the midst of the illusion of mortal existence, at a deeper insight into the character and status of our immortal nature? Do we complain that man's vision is obscured by the darkness with which the body surrounds him? Mathematics brings him clarity and light, that he may distinguish the multiplicity of things according to number and property . . . How like heaven and how proper to the gods it is, when wandering blind in darkness, to number all things in the widest light! When held bound in a single place, to traverse all regions most quickly and freely! When exiled, to remain in the full light of your own land! When shaken, to remain steadfast! [6]

Ramus here indulges in rhetoric more than in mathematics, and not much of this fervor carries over into his actual practice; but the school of anti-Aristotelian logicians he left behind contributed greatly to increasing the prestige of mathematical studies.

What Ramus' method meant when applied to a subject matter becomes clearer in his criticism of the Aristotelian physics in *Scholarum physicarum libri VIII*, 1565, in which the same neat and systematic classification is used to force Aristotle's thought into a simple framework. There is sweeping criticism of Aristotle in general: he drew his material from logic rather than from nature, he has too many philosophic speculations.

If one should by means of his senses and reason investigate heaven and earth and all that is therein, as a physicist ought to do, and then compare his results with the Physica of Aristotle, he would find in that work no observation of anything in nature, but only sophisms, theoretical speculations, and unsupported assertions.[7]

The proper method is the contrary of Aristotle's: to avoid philosophic digressions, to search with sense through visible nature; the material needs only to be observed, tested, and methodically arranged for purposes of instruction. "The aim of a genuine natural science is to study first the heavens, then the meteors, then the minerals, vegetables, animals, and finally man." Ramus takes his facts from Aristotle, from Pliny's *Natural History*, and Virgil's *Georgics*, arranging them all in clear systematic order, under the heads fire, air, water, and earth. God and mind are the underlying principles of nature, but Ramus does not discuss them, and there is one brief chapter on motion. Astronomy, meteors, and agriculture form the bulk of the treatment, with some natural history. Rhetoric thus applied to the classics could not take one far in the study of nature.

IV

Marius Nizolius (1488–1567), a professor of classical studies who devoted his life to the interpretation of Cicero, is the last to criticize

[6] *Dialecticae institutiones* (1553), pp. 67ff.
[7] *Praefatio physica*, in *Collectan. praefat.* (1577), p. 69.

scholasticism in the interests of a rhetorical method. In his *Antibarbarus philosophicus* (1553) he advocates a turning from the authority of the ancients to a nominalistic empiricism. There is no sure classic guide to philosophy; Aristotle is fragmentary and partly spurious, Plato more poet than philosopher, and Cicero too sceptical. Freedom and independence of judgment is essential to sound thought. Rhetoric is the universal science, furnishing the forms and principles to all the others, especially to the sciences of facts, physics and politics; it judges them all for it determines the right use of words, and thus replaces both logic and metaphysics. The signification of words is the proper field of logic. Nizolius combines terminism with his rhetoric to construct a unique theory of universals. Universals have no real existence in things; that arbitrary assumption is useless for knowledge, and merely limits the free handling of facts. All that is needed is an expression with a universal signification. The traditional theory of the abstraction of universals from particulars, supposing an existent hierarchy of forms in nature, obscures the true function of universals. For it Nizolius substitutes the new process of *comprehensio:* "Universals, as they are made by nature without any abstraction, we say to be all the particulars of any one kind comprehended at once." [8] We do not abstract a common element or nature from things, we survey all our experiences of individual things at a glance and collect them in an abbreviated linguistic expression; universals are thus summary statements of particulars. This *comprehensio* is "a certain action or operation of the intellect, by which the mind of man comprehends all the particulars of a given genus at once." The relation of universal to particular thus gives way to that of whole to part. In the syllogism we reason from an aggregate to its members, in induction, from a few particulars to a group of many particulars. Deduction is a "division of many particulars into their separate parts." A universal thus signifies a mere aggregate or discrete whole. This notion of Nizolius, that the true method of thinking is to collect all the instances to get a general or summary statement, became, through the Italian empiricists, the core of Bacon's method, and persisted in the empirical tradition down to the Mills.

[8] Nizolio, *De veris principiis et vera ratione philosophandi contra pseudophilosophos* (1553); reprinted by Leibniz in 1671 as *Antibarbarus philosophicus.*

V

The empiricism Nizolius combined with his rhetoric received even stronger expression from the Spanish Humanist Luis Vives (1492–1540), friend and schoolmate of Erasmus, and like him a cosmopolitan figure who spent most of his life in the Low Countries, with visits to England. Intensely dissatisfied with his education —he wished to unlearn what others were so eager to acquire, and bewailed his own ignorant learning, including the Ockhamite science in his condemnation—he devoted himself to the reform of education. In a blast against the schools, *In pseudo-dialecticos* (1519), he sets purity of language as the test. Dialectic is the science of discourse, *scientia de sermone;* but what kind of discourse is scholastic logic? "A strange dialectic indeed, whose language, which claims to be Latin, Cicero would not understand could he rise from the grave." [9] Away with the subtleties of the schools, back to the natural language and forms of human thinking! As a science of symbols, dialectic is of value only as a tool and instrument for the knowledge of real things; why spend one's life polishing the instrument, instead of putting it to work?

It is in this drive toward real knowledge, toward experience, that Vives is most original. In theory, dialectic must forsake metaphysics and become a part of rhetoric; invention and judgment are its essential elements. But it is to experience that it must be applied. Observation cannot take place without some theory:

It is fitting, as Plato says in the Gorgias, that experience should beget art, and art rule experience. And as there is a certain power in the earth for producing herbs of all kinds, so by a certain power there are in our minds the seeds of all the arts and disciplines. [10]

But theory and reasoning apart from concrete materials of experience have no meaning. In Vives' great encyclopedia, therefore, *De disciplinis* (1531), it is the particular sciences that come first. Aristotle's chief error, shared with Plato, was to make dialectic a judge of matters of fact and truth. Logic is purely instrumental and formal; it is the sciences themselves which are their own guarantee of validity. Aristotle attempted to start with things as they exist abso-

[9] Luis Vives, *In Pseudo-dialecticos, Opera,* I, 54.
[10] Vives, *De tradendis disciplinis,* Lib. I; *Opera* (1545), I, 439.

lutely; had he followed the order of sense experience and human knowledge, he would have made primary not substance but *inhaerentia*, the related qualities and properties of things as we experience them.

Vives likewise objects strongly to Aristotle's foundation of first principles in the vision of the intellect. How can such psychological certainty constitute real proof? what will prevent its varying with different men? Natural reason is notoriously shifting and relative. And how could induction from a few instances give universal validity? Rigorous proof is in fact not to be found in most fields; men must be content with probability. In the natural sciences, in medicine and mathematics, nature must be investigated independently. Not by metaphysical reflection on what is observed, but by active search and experiment, is nature to be won. The true disciple of Aristotle will question nature himself, as the ancients did. He will seek the accidents and operations of things, not their essences and natures.

Vives was like Bacon keenest as critic and as analyst of the causes of the unsatisfactory state of the sciences (*De causis corruptarum artium*). He found no sure method, and made no startling discoveries; and like most of the Renaissance apostles of experience he observed a host of curious things. Perhaps his attempt at an empirical psychology (*De anima et vita*, 1539) is most interesting. Fresh observation should be directed, not to the essence of the soul, but to its properties and workings. In examining memory he arrived at a clear formulation of the law of association, and his analysis of the affects or passions anticipates the seventeenth-century theories.

VI

It is with these more empirically minded Humanists who sought to penetrate beyond words to direct contact with things themselves, that Francis Bacon belongs. Bacon is a man who has suffered greatly from his reputation. He has become a mythical figure, praised for achievements that were not his; and the Baconian myth has almost obscured his true significance. Since the days of the *Encyclopédie* he has been admired in France and England as the "father" of modern natural science and its inductive method; but neither the honor nor the responsibility is deserved.

Bacon was a critic of the past and a prophet of the future who had the misfortune to be honored as a constructive builder, to the confusion of his message and the misinterpretation of what he actually accomplished. According to the Baconian myth, he first broke with the Middle Ages, and founded modern science on the basis of observation and experiment; he taught the scientists the method and general outlook which they have since so fruitfully followed, and formulated the principles of scientific investigation and inductive logic at the basis of their subsequent triumphs. As a matter of fact, Bacon did none of these things. In his notions of the nature of science and its basic concepts, he remained essentially within the medieval framework. He was not the father of modern science, he had no part in its "founding," no influence on the scientists of his own day, or any other. The method he formulated bore no relevance to the methods the seventeenth-century pioneers employed. In the fields in which he has traditionally been praised he accomplished little or nothing; and that not for want of technical competence alone, but because he was definitely on the wrong track.

And yet—of all those restless minds of the Renaissance, Bacon managed to give the most consummate expression to what has become the very spirit of modern civilization. He was an inspired prophet of the basic intellectual tendencies of the modern age. He proclaimed the fundamental aim of human life which has dominated our world since the eighteenth century, and which for better or worse is the distinctive mark of our own culture: our faith in the power of science and technology to enhance the daily lot of man. Bacon was a humanist and a moralist, convinced of the human worth of a science that would give power over nature. It is ironical that his masterpiece, the *Novum Organum*, designed to be the new tool, the new instrument, the new means, is in reality the new goal, the new ideal—the greatest statement of the new vision which modern men have followed. He never discovered the new instrument, and remained blind to the work of those who had; he never found the way to the land of promise, to the Kingdom of Man. But he beheld that land and proclaimed that kingdom, and by faith he descried its features from afar.

Bacon's reputation is easy enough to undermine. The trick has been turned again and again of late, for it suits our temper. It is

more fruitful to try to explain it. Bacon's vogue as the philosopher
of science began with the observers and classifiers of the eighteenth
century. He achieved his doubtful paternity at the hands of Voltaire and Diderot, and was canonized in D'Alembert's *Discours préliminaire* to the *Encyclopédie*. Before then he had been valued
chiefly as a press-agent and publicity man for the scientific enterprise, as the great advocate who drew up the bill of indictment
against the Schools. His contemporaries, in Descartes's circle, thought
it a pity he had not followed up the attack constructively. The
Royal Society in the middle of the century did indeed point to the
Chancellor as their posthumous patron; but in their inspiration as in
their work they depended far more on the earlier Italian academies
than on the grandiose plans of Verulam. Newton mentions Bacon
but once, as author of the *History of Henry VII*. In the seventeenth
century only Boyle seemed to take Bacon seriously as a theorist
of science; and even his tribute lay in words rather than imitation.

It was not till a century and a quarter after his death that Bacon
became the father of natural science. The French *philosophes*, combatting Cartesian rationalism with English thought, then found in
his name a powerful weapon. This was just the time, also, when a
science of observation and classification was coming to the fore, and
needed a theory of descriptive empiricism and positivism. When
that theory achieved rounded form in Comte and Stuart Mill, Bacon's reputation was made. It is of some significance that all these
disciples of Bacon were themselves humanists rather than scientists,
and that those to whom his vision has especially appealed, down to
John Dewey, have been primarily interested in erecting a science
of man on the model of a successful natural science, not themselves
explorers of the secrets of nature.

This vogue of Bacon at the hands of the social scientists has drawn
vigorous protests from the natural scientists, beginning with Harvey
in Bacon's own day. Most famous of all the attacks, complicated, to
be sure, by German patriotism, is that of Liebig in 1863. And with
the more exact formulation of an experimental method, with the
more critical study of seventeenth-century science, and with the
knowledge of the medieval and Renaissance background of that
science, Bacon has lost his undeserved status as *the* philosopher of
science, which no informed scholar would today accord him. When

it is added that not only did he like all the observers of his time observe a host of traditional errors, that not only could he not have founded what was already a going concern, but that he opposed and rejected its real achievements and methods, the discoveries of Copernicus, Galileo, and the new astronomy, that he thought little of mathematics and mechanical explanations, as not observable, and that he dismissed the work of the most experimental of his contemporaries, Gilbert, as a waste of time and mere fables; we can understand why Harvey should have remarked, "He writes philosophy like a Lord Chancellor," [11] and why scientists have uniformly insisted that his method of "induction" is irrelevant to any scientific procedure and bound to lead to his errors.

In truth, of the several stages into which we have divided the rise of modern science, Bacon participated only in the first two: he remained with the nature philosophers, and the humanistic heralds of the power of knowledge. The *Novum Organum* contains two strains of very different value. On the one hand, it is the most eloquent statement of the new ideal, and the keenest summary of the current criticisms of the old ideal and method. On the other, it expresses Bacon's own peculiar conception and method of knowledge, which allies him, not with the seventeenth-century scientists, but with the sixteenth-century nature enthusiasts and magicians, and with the humanistic gropers after a new method.

VII

Bacon's eloquent criticism of the learning of his day we have already stated. It can be summed up as a complaint against complacent stagnation, against confident possession of a final truth which needs not to be discovered but only demonstrated and taught.

The logic now in use serves rather to fix and give stability to the errors which have their foundation in commonly received notions than to help the search after truth. So it does more harm than good.[12]

Truth is something to be searched after and discovered. To penetrate into the secrets of nature we need an active and elaborate technique of inquiry. We must overcome, not an adversary in argument, but nature in action. We must force the apparent facts into different

---

[11] Bacon, *Works*, III, 515; from Aubrey's *Lives*, II, 281.
[12] *Novum Organum*, Book I, Aphorism 12.

forms, we must make them tell the truth about themselves, as torture compels an unwilling witness. Nature is not an object of contemplation, but rather a mass of material to be overcome; Bacon approaches her, as has been well said, like a criminal prosecutor wringing his secret from the guilty culprit. For nature is infinitely complex:

The subtlety of nature is greater many times over than the subtlety of the senses and understanding; so that all those specious meditations, speculations, and glosses in which men indulge are quite from the purpose, only there is no one by to observe it. (I, 10)

There is indeed no natural correspondence, no harmony between the spirit of man and the spirit of nature; only by the most active efforts and by drawing on all possible helps can the understanding win its treasure.

There is a great difference between the idols of the human mind and the ideas of the divine. That is to say, between certain empty dogmas, and the true signatures and marks set upon the works of creation as they are found in nature. (I, 23)

It is a false assertion that the sense of man is the measure of things. On the contrary, all perceptions as well of the sense as of the mind are according to the measure of the individual and not according to the measure of the universe. And the human understanding is like a false mirror, which, receiving rays irregularly, distorts and discolors the nature of things by mingling its own nature with it. (I, 41)

Nature is no longer the intelligible counterpart of man's intelligence, as with Thomas; it is no longer the macrocosm of which man is the microcosm: it is not yet the rational harmony akin to human reason of the seventeenth century. Left to itself, the understanding arrives only at error and "idols" or illusions. There can therefore be for Bacon no question of a rational vision of nature, of a simple and comprehensive order; only with sharp weapons and tools can we win power over her bit by bit.

Hence the errors and shortcomings of knowledge have their foundation in human nature itself: man's reason is misleading and prey to dangerous bias unless corrected by a conscious critical method. Above all, the mind is prone to jump to conclusions. Contemplating nature as from a distant and lofty tower, it overlooks the manifold differences of things, and sees everything in a confused haze.

There are and can be only two ways of searching into and discovering truth. The one flies from the senses and particulars to the most general axioms, and from these principles, the truth of which it takes for settled and immoveable, proceeds to judgment and the discovery of middle axioms. And this way is now in fashion. The other derives axioms from the senses and particulars, rising by a gradual and unbroken ascent, so that it arrives at the most general axioms last of all. This is the true way, but as yet untried. The understanding left to itself takes the same course (namely, the former) which it takes in accordance with logical order. For the mind longs to spring up to positions of higher generality, that it may find rest there; and so after a little while wearies of experiment. But this evil is increased by logic, because of the order and solemnity of its disputations. Both ways set out from the senses and particulars, and rest in the highest generalities; but the difference between them is infinite. For the one just glances at experiment and particulars in passing, the other dwells duly and orderly among them. The one, again, begins at once by establishing certain abstract and useless generalities, the other rises by gradual steps to that which is prior and better known in nature. (I, 19, 20, 22)

These hastily generalized axioms are useless, because they cover only the few cases from which they are derived, and those but superficially; naturally they do not lead on to new particulars. Such is the barrenness of all rash and premature anticipations of nature. The whole purpose of method is to force the mind from its natural bent to dwell among the facts of experience and interpret them.

The understanding must not therefore be supplied with wings, but rather hung with leaden weights, to keep it from leaping and flying. (I, 104)

The first step toward the improvement of the mind's powers is hence to undertake a detailed pathology of human thinking, an analysis of the diseases and errors to which it is naturally disposed.

For the human mind, obscured and confused by the body, is so far from being like a plane, equal, and clear glass, which will truly receive and reflect the beams of things, that it is rather like an enchanted glass, full of superstitions and spectres.[13]

Reason by itself is like the spider spinning a cobweb for the unwary out of its own substance, a web of empty classifications, distinctions,

[13] *De augmentis scientiarum, Works,* Spedding, Ellis and Heath, Vol. I, Book V, cap. 4.

and abstractions. Like Aristotle it fashions the world out of the categories of speech. Traditional empiricism is little better than pure reason; like the ant, it scurries about to heap up a mass of raw material.

There is another class of philosophers who, having bestowed much diligent and careful labor on a few experiments, have thence made bold to educe and construct systems; wresting all other facts in a strange fashion to conformity therewith . . . The empirical school of philosophy gives birth to dogmas more deformed and monstrous than the sophistical or rational. For it has its foundations not in the light of common notions (which though it be a faint and superficial light, is yet in a manner universal, and has reference to many things) but in the narrowness and darkness of a few experiments.[14]

It is not to mere observation that Bacon is appealing: "the whole way from the first perceptions of the senses must be fortified by a sure reason," he holds. The true method is the middle course of the bee, which gathers its material, then by a power of its own digests and transforms it into pure honey.

There remains simple experience; which, if taken as it comes, is called accident; if sought for, experiment. But this kind of experience is no better than a broom without its band, as the saying is—a mere groping, as of men in the dark, that feel all round them for the chance of finding their way; when they had much better wait for daylight, or light a candle, and then go. But the true method of experience on the contrary first lights the candle, and then by means of the candle shows the way; commencing as it does with experience duly ordered and digested, not bungling or erratic, and from it educing axioms, and from established axioms again new experiments. (I, 82)

Thus there may be brought about a true and lawful marriage between the empirical and the rational faculty.

And so Bacon indulges in his most famous classification, that of the "idols" or illusions to which the mind is subject. In pregnant phrases he lists the Idols of the Tribe of mankind, the tendency to find more order, regularity and uniformity than the complexity of nature affords, to overlook exceptions, to jump to conclusions, to impose reason's own web on the pattern of things; the Idols of the Cave, springing from the peculiar constitution and education of different individuals, like those besetting Aristotle with his logic and

[14] *Novum Organum*, Book I, Aphorisms 62, 64.

Gilbert with his loadstone; the Idols of the Marketplace, of inter-course and language and taking words for things; and the Idols of the Theatre, of the systems of thought that are in fashion. True method must protect the mind against these its own natural tend-encies; it must teach it to undergo a patient apprenticeship to fact in its infinite variety and particularity; it must school it to obey nature in thought in order to command her in practice. It must sub-stitute the interpretation for the anticipation of nature. And since error is social and human in scope, so must its overcoming be a col-lective enterprise of research. Bacon's last work, the *New Atlantis*, puts into imaginative form the demand for the cooperative labors which the Italian academies had already established. Salomon's House is a kind of republic of researchers. With that love of classifi-cation which always obsessed Bacon's legal mind, he divided up the tasks between Merchants of Light who should seek strange facts abroad, Depredators who should pillage ancient books for them, Mystery-men who should go to the craftsmen, and Pioneers who should invent new experiments. Then Compilers should draw up these facts in tables, Benefactors extract tentative laws from them, Lamps devise experiments to verify them, Inoculators perform the experiments under their orders, and Interpreters of Nature raise their discoveries into axioms. Bizarre as is this neat division of labor, it rests on a sense of sustained and cooperative inquiry, which should make negligible all individual differences in ability: this is the king-dom, not of men, but of Man. Science is to be not an individual but a social possession.

For with his imaginative sweep and power Bacon combined a de-votion to methodical organization, a love of precise classifications and pigeon-holings, appropriate to the young legal reformer who had sought to codify the English law—a love which extended be-yond his great plans to his very conception of science itself. Early in life he sketched out a whole program for the reform of the sci-ences, his *Instauratio magna*, from which he did not depart for forty years. First should come a classification and codification of existent learning, with gaps indicated; then the new organon to replace Aristotle's should be worked out; then a great collection of facts, to be followed by generalizations from them, finally culminating in *scientia activa* or the exercise of human power. Aside from the

Novum Organum (1620), only the first of these sections was completed (*The Advancement of Learning*, 1605; *De augmentis scientiarum*, 1623).

VIII

But despite his vision and his critical insights, Bacon did not find the "new method." In his fear of speculation, of the free play of the mind when left to itself, he insisted that all the facts be gathered before interpretation should begin. In truth, the scientists of the seventeenth century "anticipated" nature in as wild an anticipation as any ever perpetrated. Bacon did not share their mathematical faith in a simple mechanical order. He clung to the main features of the Aristotelian world, and to its aim of a classificatory science. Hence the details of his method, and his very conception of the nature of science, were abortive of those practical results he so much desired. He remained a nature philosopher, not a scientist, closest to Nizolius and Telesio and their philosophy of observation. He played no part in the glorious science that led to Newton; he merely organized and codified the crude experimentalism of the Renaissance fantastic learning.

For Bacon, the aim of human power is on a given body to generate a new "nature" or observable physical property. The work and aim of human knowledge is therefore to discover the "form," that is, the formal cause, the essence or quiddity that constitutes that nature or property. In nature nothing really exists besides individual bodies performing pure individual acts; but these bodies are made up of a limited number of qualities or "natures." Gold, for example, is a troop or collection of such simple natures. It is yellow, heavy, malleable, etc. Bacon follows the familiar list of opposite qualities in the fourth book of Aristotle's *Meteors*, the hot and the cold, the heavy and the light, etc.; and like Aristotle he regards each "nature" as constituted and made what it is by its appropriate essence or form. Knowledge aims to discover what is the essence of qualities like hotness or heaviness, while power and operation, as with the alchemists, consist in producing them in a body which does not possess them. He who knows what these simple and general natures really are—who knows the forms of yellow, weight, and malleability—and the methods for generating them, will be able to join them together in a body, and transform it into gold. The School-men were mistaken, not in regarding nature as made up of individual substances with such properties, but in seeking at once the "compound forms" of such substances or "concrete natures" without having determined first the few "simple natures" of which they are combinations. They tried to arrive at the forms of the lion, eagle, rose, gold, and the like without knowing the alphabet out of which they are constructed. As substances are too perplexed to be inquired, naturally they reached only ill-defined and abstract forms and ideas. But if we can determine the forms of the more general qualities that are common to many different kinds of things, we shall not be limited to this verbal knowledge of concrete things; the power of man will be emancipated and freed from the common course of nature, and expanded and exalted to new modes of operation.

If a man be acquainted with the cause of any nature (as whiteness or heat) in certain subjects only, his knowledge is imperfect; and . . . his power is in like manner imperfect . . . But whoever is acquainted with Forms, embraces the unity of nature in substances the most unlike . . . From the discovery of Forms therefore results truth in speculation and freedom in operation. (II, 3)

The world is for Bacon thus a unity or hierarchy, but of natures or qualities rather than of substances. Some qualities are of wider generality than others. They appear in particular cases with limiting and specific differences.

He who seeks the form of lion, oak, or gold, and still more of water or air, works in vain; but to seek the form of the dense, the rare, the hot, the cold, the heavy, the light, the tangible, the pneumatic, the volatile, the fixed, is just what we are attempting.[15]

To find the "form" of any nature, therefore, means to find the general kind of quality of which that nature is an instance, together with the specific difference that sets it off from other kinds of instance. We must know just what it is that is present when these natures are present, and absent when they are absent.

This investigation of Forms constitutes Metaphysics, and bears practical fruits in Magic. Metaphysics thus aims to find the genus

[15] *De augmentis scientiarum*, Book III, cap. 4.

of which a particular quality or nature, like heat or color or sound, is a species. In Bacon's most extensive illustration, motion is the "nature" of which heat is a particular case; heat itself is motion and nothing else, but motion of a particular kind. The Form of heat is hence the "true definition" of its essence, in terms of genus and differentia. Metaphysics thus ends in a logical classification of the natural qualities or "natures" of which things are made up, in a "synopsis of all the natures in the universe," the statement of which Bacon calls "the summary law of nature." By a mere tabulation and exclusion of the instances of a nature, a "natural history of experiments," science achieves a scheme of the classification and definition of qualities. The difference between Bacon's conception and that of the contemporary scientists is clear. The latter were seeking the relations between properties, not their forms or essences; their laws of operation, not their definitions. They wanted to know how motion takes place, not what motion is. In contrast Bacon distinguishes nineteen different kinds of motion, each with its own principle, but gives no law describing motion.[16] This is not experimental science, it is not even "induction"; it is the scholastic abstraction of forms from observed facts in the interests of the definition of essences. Between it and Galileo's work there is all the difference between the logical classification of all cases and the keen analysis of a few, between the work of Linnaeus and the experimental biology of Darwin.

Natural philosophy has indeed another branch, physics, or the investigation of the transitive and relative material and efficient causes, the practical application of which is mechanics. But physics is of little importance, because what makes things happen, their latent configurations and processes, is unobservable. Efficient causes indeed are but slight and superficial, and contribute little if anything to true and active science; at best they are the mere vehicle of the form.

IX

And yet, though Bacon's conception of science as a search for forms and qualities remained scholastic, within its limitations he brought a new emphasis. His forms, bound together in the "unity of

[16] *Novum Organum*, Book II, Aphorism 48.

250 The Coming of Humanism and Science

nature," are not that whereby things *are* what they are, but that whereby they *act* as they do.

Matter rather than forms should be considered, its configurations and changes of configuration, and pure acts, and law of action or motion; for forms are figments of the human mind, unless you will call those laws of action forms. (I, 51)

Bacon has caught something of the dynamic sense of Aristotle himself.

It is strange how careless men are; for they study nature only by fits and at intervals, and when bodies are finished and completed, not while she is at work upon them. Yet if any one were desirous of examining and studying the contrivances and industry of an artificer, . . . he would wish to be present when the artificer was at his labors and carrying his work on. And a like course should be taken with the investigation of nature. (II, 41)

He who looks to works must inquire and examine into nature in motion. To contemplate and mark the quiet principles of things is enough for those who make speeches and carry on disputations. I call those principles "quiet" which teach how things are put together and constituted, and not by what force and manner they come into being.[17]

For a knowledge of forms must lead to action, to operation, to the power to produce new natures. It must look to the future, invade the unknown, use truth to gain further truth. It must aim at both certainty *and* "liberty," truth in speculation *and* freedom in operation. It must join contemplation and action. It must be real knowledge, and no easy pragmatism, but real knowledge of the kind that will give control. Hence though Bacon's method, like all those of the seventeenth century, appears as a reconstruction of Aristotle's theory of science: from facts to axioms by "induction," then back again to new facts by deduction; the emphasis is not on explaining and proving the facts by the axioms, but on suggesting new experiments. Bacon is committed, not to a logic of intelligibility, but to a logic of discovery.

And he comes close to the mechanistic view of the scientists, even if he does not clearly see its significance. Though he rejects atomism, like so many of them he is a corpuscularian—that is, he rejects

---

[17] *Cogitationes de natura rerum, Works*, III, 19.

the indivisibility of the ultimate particles, and refuses to grant a vacuum. The common simple natures at which he arrives turn out to be mechanical dispositions of matter; his method of induction eliminates all that is qualitative and peculiar to sense, to eventuate in what those natures are, not simply in relation to man's experience, but in relation to the universe. Yet as his attitude towards the astronomical discoveries shows, this mechanism is misleading. More significant than his rejection of Copernicus is his disapproval of mathematical procedure itself. A living science of the heavens would not rest with describing the motions of the stars, it would penetrate to the primary and universal axioms about their simple natures.

Let no one hope to decide the question whether it is the earth or heaven that really revolves in the diurnal motion, until he has first comprehended the nature of spontaneous rotation.[18]

This is a nature

by which bodies delighting in motion and favorably placed for it enjoy their own nature and follow themselves, not another body; and court (so to speak) their own embraces . . . Those which are favorably placed, if they delight in motion, move in a circle. (II, 48)

The astronomers are chiefly at fault for remaining with the measures and periods of the heavenly movements, and not seeking their true differences, which reside in the specific appetites and passions of the moving bodies.[19]

X

The chief concern of Bacon in his actual sketch of method is to prevent the mind from flying to the most general conclusions before all the facts are in. He compares the search for forms to the work of the alchemist in separating the pure matter from the dross with which it is mixed. Normally the form we are seeking is restrained and obstructed by other forms; our task is to separate it out. Induction is a process of elimination.

First of all we must prepare a *Natural and Experimental History*, sufficient and good; and this is the foundation of all; for we are not to imagine or suppose, but discover, what nature does or may be made to do . . . A nature being given, we must first have a muster or presenta-

---

[18] *Novum Organum*, Book II, Aphorism 5.   [19] *Works*, III, 21ff.

tion before the understanding of all known instances which agree in the same nature, though in substance the most unlike. And such collection must be made in the manner of a history, without premature speculation, or any great amount of subtlety.[20]

Which presentation having been made, Induction itself must be set at work; for the problem is, upon a review of the instances, all and each, to find such a nature as is always present or absent with the given nature, and always increases and decreases with it; and which is, as I have said, a particular case of a more general nature . . . We must make therefore a complete solution and separation of nature, not indeed by fire, but by the mind, which is a kind of divine fire. The first work therefore of true induction is the rejection or exclusion of the several natures which are not found in some instance where the given nature is present, or are found in some instance where the given nature is absent, or are found to increase in some instance when the given nature decreases, or to decrease when the given nature increases. Then indeed after the rejection and exclusion has been duly made, there will remain at the bottom, all light opinions vanishing into smoke, a Form affirmative, solid, and true and well defined. (II, 15, 16)

Not precision and care but inclusiveness and generality is the goal in the preliminary collection of facts. In practice indeed, in his great collection, the *Sylva sylvarum*, Bacon shows no concern with accurate observation at all, accepting his "facts" from any source, chance observation, the books of travelers, or mere hearsay. The tradition of a supposed observation is as good as experience itself. What is important is to have as large and varied a collection as possible; induction begins only after the facts are all in. Bacon has a picturesque scheme of helps in this multiplication of instances, and an elaborate set of tables in which to classify them. There must be a Table of Essence and Presence, of instances agreeing in the given nature, in the most unlike substances. There must be a Table of Absence in Proximity, in which the nature is missing in instances resembling those in which it is found. There must be a Table of Degrees or Comparison, in which the nature varies. Induction consists in inspecting these tables to separate out, almost automatically, the residue. Bacon sees clearly that what distinguishes his procedure from the "induction" of the Schoolmen, by simple enumeration, is his use of negative instances.

[20] *Novum Organum*, Book II, Aphorisms 10, 11.

The conclusions of the induction by simple enumeration are precarious, and exposed to peril from a contradictory instance . . . But the induction which is to be available for the discovery and demonstration of sciences and arts must analyse nature by proper rejections and exclusions; and then, after a sufficient number of negatives, come to a conclusion on the affirmative instances. (I, 105)

The logician's form of induction is utterly vicious and incompetent.

For to conclude upon an enumeration of particulars, without instance contradictory, is no conclusion, but a conjecture; for who can assure upon those particulars which appear of a side, that there are not other on the contrary side which appear not? [21]

Bacon did not wholly reject the use of hypothesis, and he condemns undirected investigation. But his elaborate table of twenty-seven kinds of "prerogative instances" or aids in drawing a first vintage has been of no practical use. He was, in fact, never able to distinguish between approaching experience with prejudice, and with a working hypothesis. He had an abiding fear of founding science on some idol rather than on facts. That would leave it dialectical in character, "floating in the air, a mere conceit and whimsy." It would lead to a dualism between the "world of science" and the "world of experience." It would, and did, and does: Bacon is here as so often a true prophet, of all the epistemological difficulties encountered down to Einstein, Jeans, Eddington, Bertrand Russell and A. J. Ayer. But his warning was of no avail, to Newton, or to present-day scientists. The unbridled play of hypothesis has been the source of an intellectual confusion, of a paradoxical divorce of man from nature, which Bacon's caution avoided. But it has been the source also of that very power over nature Bacon so ardently desired.

Bacon's scheme of collecting all the instances to get a general statement, a comprehension of all the facts at once, he seems to have derived from Nizolius through Telesio. It has proved unworkable in practice. His Tables indeed appear as a startling foreshadowing of Mill's canons of induction, of the methods of agreement, difference, and concomitant variation—until one realizes that Mill developed his own logic of science by reading Bacon rather than by understanding scientific procedure. Especially, Bacon condemned the mathematical hypothesis, that nature is a mathematical order of relations;

<hr />

[21] *Advancement of Learning*, Book II, sec. xiii, par. 3.

he persisted, like the other nature enthusiasts, in the search for an essentially qualitative science. Pure mathematics is a game like tennis. Mixed mathematics might indeed be used to formulate facts and give definiteness to natural philosophy, but not to give explanations; he agreed with Telesio it should be the handmaid, not the mistress. Measurements should be in the appendix to physics, not in the body. That was enough to deprive him of all influence in the seventeenth century.

At that time men needed above all a rational faith, an anticipation of nature: nature must be conceived as a simple mathematical order, if false observations were to be cleared away and exact relations discovered. Bacon's method seemed relevant in the eighteenth century, because men then needed to observe fresh material, to pile up facts, and to get rid of metaphysical assumptions. It ceased to be relevant in the nineteenth century, when there was need of generalization, of hypotheses deductively elaborated and experimentally tested. Bacon had counseled, observe nature first, without preoccupation; only then allow ideas to precipitate gradually. But experimental science starts with ideas, and uses observation to test and verify them. It operates with a mass of theories and assumptions, the deposit of previous science: of what to observe, of the precise method of observation, of the tests and standards of verification. And yet in the end it too finds its work primarily a process of elimination. But what is left is not the bare "form" of a nature, it is the best idea the wit of man has been able to devise.

Bacon was not the prophet of the method or spirit of our science, but of its value in human life.

Men have entered into a desire of learning and knowledge, sometimes upon a natural curiosity and inquisitive appetite; sometimes to entertain their minds with variety and delight; sometimes for ornament and reputation; and sometimes to enable them to victory of wit and contradiction; and most times for lucre and profession; and seldom sincerely to give a true account of their gift of reason, to the benefit and use of men: as if there were sought in knowledge a couch whereupon to rest a searching and restless spirit; or a terrace for a wandering and variable mind to walk up and down with a fair prospect; or a tower of state for a proud mind to raise itself upon; or a fort or commanding ground for strife and contention; or a shop for profit or sale; and not a rich storehouse for the glory of the Creator and the relief of man's estate . . . I do not mean, when I speak of use and action, that end beforementioned of the apply-ing of knowledge to lucre and profession . . . Neither is my meaning, as was spoken of Socrates, to call philosophy down from heaven to converse upon the earth; that is, to leave natural philosophy aside, and to apply knowledge only to manners and policy. But as both heaven and earth do conspire and contribute to the use and benefit of man; so the end ought to be, from both philosophies to separate and reject vain speculations, and whatsoever is empty and void, and to preserve and augment whatsoever is solid and fruitful: that knowledge may not be as a courtesan, for pleasure and vanity only, or as a bondwoman, to acquire and gain to her master's use; but as a spouse, for generation, fruit, and comfort.[22]

[22] *Advancement of Learning,* Book I, sec. v, par. 11.

The Medieval Roots of Galilean Science

I

THE HUMANISTS might seek the method of a new science in the rhetorician's art of persuasion; a Vives or a Bacon, recognizing no useful knowledge in the investigations of the mathematicians and astronomers of their day, might counsel experience and ever more experience. Their combined onslaught helped to shake the faith of men in the complacent academic traditionalism of the schools, already sorely disturbed by the new literary and theological interests; it hardly contributed much guidance to those already busily engaged upon scientific problems. The body of ideas which in Galileo and Descartes dared to arrogate to itself the name of "science," and which in Newton made good that proud claim, had other and far deeper roots, stretching back to the twelfth-century appropriation of ancient learning. The fact that the scientific pioneers of the seventeenth century, in revolt against the Humanists' appeal to the authority of the past, preferred to put their trust in natural reason alone, and hence cared nothing for historical continuity, has sadly misled our judgment as to the fashion in which their thought took form. Taking them at their own word, we have assumed that that cooperative criticism and reconstruction of a well-organized system of ideas, shaken from time to time by new insights which have had to be patiently worked into the logical structure, which has since the seventeenth century been so characteristic of the procedure of scientific advance, played no part in its earlier stages. One gathers, indeed, from our standard histories of the sciences, written mostly in the last generation, that the world lay steeped in the darkness and night of superstition, till one day Copernicus bravely cast aside the errors of his fellows, looked at the heavens and observed nature, the first man since the Greeks to do so, and discovered, as from some peak in Darien, the truth about the solar system. The next day, so to speak, Galileo climbed the leaning Tower of Pisa, dropped down his weights, and as they thudded to the ground, Aristotle was crushed to earth and the laws of falling bodies sprang into being. And thus was modern physics born full-grown from the head of Galileo, as Athene from the brow of Zeus.

This well-nigh universal belief, whether expressed this crudely or with the greater circumspection of our own generation, implies a conception of the nature and the function of science which is today very difficult to maintain. It implies that science is, and has been since the sixteenth century, a simple discovery of the facts of nature and the laws of her behavior; that scientists observe nature, and if they can but forget what has been told them, they will see the truth. Operating with this conception, historians of science have naturally set down a record of these successive discoveries: they have written chronicles rather than histories. These chronicles have two major faults: an untenable conception of the nature and procedure of science, and a very suspicious notion of the nature of the historical process—to say nothing of dubious facts and indubitable ignorance.

We have already explained how men have come to have a very different idea of the nature of history. They realize today that it involves a fundamental continuity of materials together with a novelty of experience, problems, and needs. That history is a reconstruction of traditions, not a creation *ex nihilo*, holds not only of economic and social materials, but of intellectual materials, the distinctions, concepts, and methods of science, as well. And in this generation much has been brought to light about the organized scientific traditions of the late Middle Ages in which the seventeenth-century pioneers did their work.

The nature of science also is becoming better understood today, even by scientists; for the recent fundamental revolution in physical concepts is making even those in the thick of it realize what philosophers have suspected since the time of Kant—though till the present generation they did not suspect the half of it. Science is not a simple intellectual vision of the structure of nature, nor is it the descriptive record of the observed course of events—the two theories that prevailed in the seventeenth and eighteenth centuries, in terms of which our chronicles are still written. Science is an active process of interpreting the world we live in, highly selective of the facts it chooses to interpret, and of the particular structural aspects of the world it is concerned to seize and express. Any system of science is thus the expression and formulation of certain natural relations in a definite language with a grammar of its own. Men cannot only change their language, when their interest in knowing shifts, as in the seventeenth century; that language has to extend its vocabulary and enlarge its grammar to express new facts and relations, as ever since. The history of our own science is the history of the continual criticism and modification of the basic assumptions in terms of which the structure of nature has been pieced together and rendered intelligible. Every recent analysis of the technique of scientific procedure has come to emphasize the importance of these assumptions and hypotheses: not only the concepts of science, but its tests of verification, even its facts themselves, remain hypothetical in character. If all science is thus founded on assumptions, its understanding demands a knowledge of why these assumptions were chosen rather than others. If scientific assumptions are continually changing, their history can throw light on that question. The great histories of scientific concepts written in this generation in German and French, have dealt, however, only with the assumptions within our own type of science. Its basic grammar, the mathematical interpretation of nature itself, they have left mysterious. They are far superior to the "peak in Darien" theory on which the chronicles are written; but they still offer as the foundation of this basic methodology only a "wild surmise"—men hit upon a wild surmise that happened to work, a colossal anticipation of nature. They do not explain, what is now abundantly clear, that it was a surmise with a long history behind it, and an anticipation that had been carefully and critically elaborated for generations.

We shall select frankly from the manifold currents of medieval intellectual life those that developed into "modern science"—specifically into what the Royal Society called "physico-mathematical experimental learning," the concepts, methods, and assumptions which Newton transmitted in organized form to the eighteenth century. For medieval thought contained various other types of science, with aims, problems, methods, and selections of facts and structures of their own, just as modern thought has by no means exhausted itself in mathematical physics but has produced other kinds, like the natural history of Linnaeus or Lyell, or the experimental biology of Pasteur or T. H. Morgan. In fact, each of the four great bodies of ideas inherited from the ancient world, Augustinian Platonism, Aristotle, the humanistic learning, and Alexandrian mathematical thought, generated its own characteristic and highly developed type of science, with its own organizing assumptions and principles. And in addition there gradually accumulated a great wealth of observed facts, and techniques discovered for the control of nature, recorded by recent chroniclers, ready to serve as the raw materials for a science—convincing evidence, if such be needed, that without assumptions and principles, without organizing ideas, no amount of mere observation or practical success will make science.

II

The basic idea of a mathematical and experimental science of nature appears as soon as Europeans began to explore the wisdom of the ancients. It developed within the general framework of the first body of materials to be assimilated, the Augustinian philosophy of reason—itself the platonized outcome of ancient thought. It drew specifically upon the Arabic versions of Alexandrian science, though direct contact with the whole of Hellenistic astronomy and mechanics was the last to be established; Archimedes was not known till the sixteenth century. But the idea of such a science, and much of its method and concepts, were in the possession of Europeans from the twelfth century on. Augustinian thought, with its strong Platonic emphasis on mathematics as the clearest example of the divine truth or wisdom, found very congenial the Arabian versions of Neoplatonism, which had directed their mathematical interests much more to the interpretation of nature. Under the double influence of mathematics and the Arabian developments of practical science, there existed from 1200 on a strong current of scientific Augustinism, side by side with the theological and mystical Augustinism of the twelfth-century schools, and often combined in the same man, as with Roger Bacon. This fusion of Arabian Platonism and genuine mathematical science with the Augustinian philosophy of reason, had its first great center at the School of Chartres around the middle of the twelfth century, the earliest of the philosophical and scientific schools, and one of the richest in the variety of its interests.

The twelfth century was the great period of assimilation of Arabian science. As early as 1060 Constantine the African was translating Hippocrates and Galen, and building up a medical school at Salerno near Naples. Scholars eagerly followed the Spanish armies in search of texts; after its capture by the Christians Toledo became a great center of study. Adelard of Bath traveled in Spain and in Sicily, translating mathematical and scientific works; Euclid was turned from the Arabic by 1100. Most prolific of all was Gerard of Cremona, who translated at Toledo some ninety-two Arabic works, including the *Almagest* of Ptolemy (1175) and the medical *Canon* of Avicenna. At Chartres this new material was used and taught by Thierry of Chartres (d. 1155), William of Conches (d. 1145), and many another. In Sicily direct contact was first established with the Greek texts; Euclid and Ptolemy were translated from the Greek in the 1160s. The Crusaders' conquest of Constantinople in 1204 sent a new flood of Greek manuscripts to the eager scholars of western Europe.

From Chartres, from Sicily, and from Toledo this Arabian science was carried to the Germanies and to England, where it was firmly established at Oxford by the conclusion of the twelfth century. The Arabic medical learning found its chief seat at Padua. There by the fourteenth century the systematic dissection of the human body was practiced. Measures were taken against infection as a source of disease, so that leprosy had largely disappeared. Mercury salve was being used against syphilis. Inhaled narcotics were employed as anaesthetics in surgery, and antiseptic methods, a so-called "pusless treatment" of wounds. Closer investigation of late medieval medicine has upset many traditional legends.

From the early twelfth century, therefore, there existed a continuous tradition of natural science, overshadowed during the brief period of Aristotelian domination, 1250–1300, and again by the literary grammarians and humanists in the fifteenth century—at least in our conventional perspectives—but living in the fifteenth and sixteenth centuries, and the direct background of the later developments. The idea of a mathematical physics was originally associated with the study of optics. Optics had been especially cultivated in the Arabian Neoplatonic tradition, which saw the divine emanation as quite literally light, and in consequence found all natural causation propagated to bodies as *Lumen*, which constituted their form. Hence all natural processes are subject to the laws of light or optics, which are wholly geometrical in character. This Neoplatonic metaphysics or dynamics of light, expressed in the *Perspective* of Alhazen, proved congenial to the Augustinians: it provided a mathematical physics as the welcome alternative to the qualitative physics of the Aristotelians. It was popularized especially from Jewish sources, notably Avencebrol's *Fons vitae*. Witelo, a Silesian teaching at Padua, wrote in 1270 a *Perspective* or optics largely based on Alhazen; Dietrich of Freiberg (1250–c.1310), though a Dominican, developed a very Neoplatonic metaphysics, which influenced Meister Eckhart; in his optical writings he gave the correct geometrical explanation of the rainbow. He also regarded experience as the final test of truth in physics. William of Moerbeke, best known for his translation of Aristotle from the Greek, also cultivated the Neoplatonic metaphysics of light.

The outstanding experimentalist of the twelfth century seems to have been Pierre de Maricourt, who wrote a work on the magnet in 1269. He believed that a mathematical science of nature must be corrected and extended by "the work of the hands"; he made many machines, and proceeded to experiment with magnetic phenomena. He was called by his pupil, Roger Bacon, "the master of experiments." Albert the Great, who shared Aristotle's biological interests, left a school of biological observers at Cologne. He amassed a wealth of firsthand observation of animals, plants, and stones. He had a real passion for natural history:

It is not enough to know in terms of universals, but we seek to know each object's own peculiar characteristics; for this is the best and perfect kind of science.[1]

III

In the thirteenth century the Augustinian tradition developed at Oxford a school of mathematical physicists, especially among the Franciscans, suspicious of the Dominican Thomas and his Aristotle.

[1] Albertus Magnus, *De causis et proprietatibus elementorum et planetarum;* cited in Lynn Thorndike, *History of Magic and Experimental Science,* II (1923), 535.

These men inherited their interest in mathematics, astronomy, and especially in optics, from the School of Chartres. The English were eager students of Arabian science. Alexander Neckham (d. 1217); Alfred the Englishman (c.1200), translator of Arabic physiology and natural history; Michael Scot (d. 1235), who traveled to Toledo, translated commentaries of Averroes, and works on alchemy and astronomy, the first defender of the mathematical astronomy of Ptolemy against Aristotle; Adam of the Marsh (d. 1258); John Peckham (d. 1292), Archbishop of Canterbury, and the great opponent of Thomas' modernism—all these men were Augustinians, suspicious of Aristotelianism, influenced by the metaphysics of light. All wrote on mathematics, optics, and astronomy.

Greatest of them was Robert Grosseteste, Bishop of Lincoln (1175–1253), a man of the widest learning, from Neoplatonic metaphysics to experimental science. He knew but rejected Aristotle's physics. For him nature was no hierarchy of logical forms, but the creation of light. *Lux* is a fine corporeal substance; a point of *lux* is a center of force, diffusing itself perpetually and instantaneously, and spreading out to form a finite spherical universe, most rarefied at the periphery, where it forms First Body or the firmament. It is then reflected back from the firmament as *lumen*, sensible light, which condenses to form the heavenly spheres and the earth. Light is thus the first form of body, corporeity; it is, like the later ether, the medium of all natural phenomena, from color to the generation of plants and animals, and the instrument by which the soul works on the body. Hence there is one universal science of nature, optics; and the mathematical principles of optics are the key to all knowledge of the world.

Every natural phenomena must be explained by geometrical lines, figures, and angles . . . Nature acts always in the mathematically shortest and best way possible.[2]

In many books the Bishop of Lincoln sought the simple mathematical relations of things. His words sound in the thirteenth century much

[2] Robert Grosseteste, *De lineis, angulis, et figuris*, in L. Baur, ed., *Die philosophischen Werke des Robert Grosseteste*, in Baeumker, *Beiträge zur Geschichte der Philosophie des Mittelalters*, IX (1912). Compare *De luce* in same volume; Eng. tr. by Clare C. Riedl (Milwaukee, Marquette University Press, 1942). See E. Gilson, *History of Christian Philosophy in the Middle Ages* (1955), pp. 263–64.

like those of the later Descartes: he was living in a similar geometrical world. He shows how the mathematical science of this Oxford school, in treating nature, not, like the Aristotelians, in its own terms, remaining close to sense experience, but in terms of the divine illumination, made a mathematical physics the Augustinian philosophy of nature.

Thus Roger Bacon (1214–1292), most famous of this group, is obviously neither a solitary nor a particularly original figure. He was a pupil of Grosseteste and Adam of the Marsh at Oxford, and of Pierre de Maricourt; his *Opus Majus* was produced when the pope asked him in 1266 to substantiate his boastful claims. He was temperamentally a prophet, like Francis Bacon; he suffered from a persecution complex, with little apparent basis. The only evidence that he was condemned and imprisoned by the general of his order in 1278 rests on one suspicious document. In fact, his ideas were widely popular, so popular that his works were pirated and he was revered in the fourteenth century as one of the lights of the order. He had an undue sense of his own originality, he was jealous, he slandered his fellow-scientists when he did not ignore them. He wrote in glittering generalities, and was surpassed by several of his contemporaries in actual scientific achievement. He was always complaining, calling names, finding excuses why he was not ready to make good his pretentious promises. He invented nothing formerly attributed to him, but wrote about inventions, like those of gunpowder, lenses, and the compass, already long known.

Fundamentally Bacon was an Augustinian scholastic. There is one real science, theology, to be served by philosophy and by law. It is a divine revelation, disclosed by God directly to Adam, and again to Solomon; science is complete in the Scriptures, if they be properly interpreted. Grammar is thus essential to natural science. The patriarchs lived to their great age in order to experiment and fill in the details. Truth is a revelation, Solomon had it, Aristotle rediscovered most of it, and now Bacon has it all: it is the one thing needful. The experimental science of which he writes is of two kinds: direct contact with nature, and direct contact with spiritual beings, the angels and God. The latter is by far the more important: and Bacon is a full-fledged mystic, with seven steps in the ascent to God. His whole aim, in fact, was not primarily natural science, but the reform of theology by the aid of physics, mathematics, and philology. He told the theologians they didn't know their business. Naturally he met with rebuffs, not because of his scientific interests—the Oxford Franciscans were enthusiastically for them—but for his tactless theological plans. He wanted the pope to turn over the revenues of the Church to him to reform theology and show up the theologians. And even when he insists the aim of all knowledge is its usefulness, he means its usefulness in promoting the salvation of the soul.

Yet amid these fantastic ideas are to be found many a prophetic insight: it is hard not to feel that he possessed a perception of the essential relation between mathematics and experience far superior to that of the later Elizabethan lawyer of the same name, though his applications are just as absurd. He urged men to abandon all authority—and go straight to the Bible; to burn all the Latin translations of Aristotle—and make accurate ones. There is no certain knowledge without mathematics, the "alphabet of all science." The book of nature is written in the language of geometry; without mathematics we can never hope to predict the future by astrology nor to interpret the Bible aright. "Experimental science" must come after we have worked out our optics and physics, to make their conclusions vivid and concrete and apply them. This is not the source of our knowledge, but a separate science; and Bacon has no hint of a clear experimental method. Experimental science has three prerogatives: It investigates the conclusions of other sciences, which derive their principles from experience, and their conclusions by demonstration from those principles. Experiment thus illustrates conclusions, it takes one beyond demonstration in nature, as mysticism does with spiritual beings: it enables us actually to see the results. We would never believe in magnets, for instance, unless we had actually seen them. And it helps us to decide which principles will apply in a given case—as Descartes later maintained. Its second prerogative is to deliver truths within other sciences not discoverable in any other way: it offers new facts to be deductively explained—also a Cartesian idea. And thirdly, it opens up an unexcelled knowledge of the past, present, and future, and can perform wonderful works, in applied science and machines. All this sounds at times close to Galileo or Descartes. But it is deceptive: for Bacon then goes on to give a mathematical interpretation of the dimensions of Noah's ark!

IV

The coming of Aristotle, of his logic, his theory of science and method, in the *Analytics*, gained during the first half of the twelfth century, and of his basic concepts and principles of natural science, in the *Physics*, in the second half, introduced a body of materials too impressive to be ignored. Thereafter the Aristotelian physical writings were taken as the starting point of all natural science, however far men might eventually depart from them; and the Aristotelian theory of science, however men might interpret it, remained dominant throughout the seventeenth century, to the time of Newton. From the beginning of the fourteenth century, however, there set in a persistent and searching criticism and reconstruction of the Aristotelian tradition, which when directed to the *Physics* led to the mechanical and mathematical problems and concepts of the Galilean age, and when directed to the *Logic* led to the formulation of the method and structure of science acclaimed by all the seventeenth-century physicists.

The Oxford school were the leaders in this intellectual revolt. In its headstrong youth, it was Oxford that broke up the medieval synthesis of Albert and Thomas. William of Ockham was the pioneer of this *Via moderna*. The thoroughgoing Aristotelian empiricism he elaborated had a double influence: in its critical and destructive use, it resulted in the complete annihilation of the thirteenth-century metaphysical systems, as devastating as the later eighteenth-century empiricists' demolition of the scientific rationalism of the seventeenth century; in its constructive employment, it began the building up of mathematical and experimental science. Once the logical structure of the Aristotelian universe was broken, the foundations were laid for the astronomy and dynamics which came into their own in the seventeenth century. By 1375, the Paris and Oxford Ockhamites had advanced as far as the scientists of 1575. A further rapid development was held back not only by the absence of mathematical and experimental techniques, but also by the shift in intellectual interest to the concerns of literary humanism, that is, by the necessity of assimilating a new set of values. But the essential ideas and concepts of mathematical physics were developed by the four-teenth-century Ockhamites two hundred years before technological and commercial experience had progressed far enough to support a steady growth.

The two main critical movements of the later Middle Ages, that of the Ockhamites, which began in Oxford in the thirteenth century, and found its stronghold during the next hundred years in the Faculty of Arts at Paris, and that of the Latin Averroists, which began in Paris in the thirteenth century and shifted to Padua in the fourteenth, both began by expressing a secular and anticlerical spirit, and undertaking a destructive criticism of Thomism and Scotism, the thirteenth-century syntheses of science and religion. But both soon advanced to the construction of natural science; they became the two great scientific schools of the later Middle Ages. The original work of the Ockhamites belongs to the fourteenth century, that of the Paduans, to the fifteenth and sixteenth centuries. The former was done in dynamics and the logic of mathematics, the latter, at first in methodology, and then in the further development of dynamics. Both turned from the religious synthesis to Aristotle himself, as a purely natural philosophy; and both developed primarily by a constructive criticism of the Aristotelian texts and doctrines. The Ockhamites were at first the more "progressive" and "modern"; they were interested in the free development of the Aristotelian physics, and their works take the form of questions and problems suggested by Aristotle's analysis. The Averroists, though much more secular and anticlerical, were more conservative in their attitude toward Aristotle and Averroes; their works are characteristically commentaries on the texts. From 1400 on, however, they knew and taught all the Ockhamite departures from Aristotelian doctrine: Paul of Venice (d. 1429) is remarkably up-to-date, and his *Summa naturalis* contains an exposition of all the ideas of the dynamics of the Paris Ockhamites and the Oxford logicians. The latter's works were printed in many editions so soon as the press reached Italy, all of them by 1490; and in the sixteenth century it was primarily the Italians who advanced by gradual stages to the formulations of Galileo.

V

Ockham himself was in his physics as in all else primarily a critic, reducing the distinctions in nature to distinctions in knowledge. For him the heavens and earth are composed of the same matter, and hence subject to the same principles. Motion itself is an empirical fact, given by the "intuitive knowledge" of the senses, needing no cause in general. It is not motion, but a change of motion that needs a cause. This basic conception, the foundation of the later law of inertia, was too radical for Ockham's immediate followers.[3] It was revived, however, around 1500 at Paris by Dullaert, and as an hypothesis given equal validity with the impetus theory adopted by Buridan: in the sixteenth-century discussions it is always considered carefully, and is hence no novel idea when it appears in Galileo. Again, for Ockham the magnet operates by attraction; therefore, action at a distance, since it is observed, is a fact, and mechanical contact is not, as Aristotle held, always necessary. In all these ways Ockham was breaking the sway of the letter of Aristotle. But he did not go on to elaborate a detailed alternative position.

VI

For over a generation students of medieval science have accepted, with increasing reservations, to be sure, the conclusions of the pioneer studies of Pierre Duhem, stated in the third volume of his *Études sur Léonard de Vinci* (1913), that a series of outstanding physicists in the Faculty of Arts at the University of Paris did go on to build up the principles of a constructive science of dynamics. Their terminology differed, of course, from that of the Galilean age; but their concern, Duhem brought to light, was with the problems of uniformly accelerated motion and gravitation, the concepts of weight and mass, the center of gravity and the rotation and revolution of the earth, and the laws of motion. In criticism of the very suspicious Aristotelian theory of the cause of the continuing

[3] They turned rather to the "impetus theory" of the ancient Greek commentator John Philoponus, characterized by the foremost present student of medieval science, Annaliese Maier, as "an independent and special intermediate stage between Aristotelianism and modern natural science, a stage which stands closer to the former than to the latter" (*An der Grenze von Scholastik und Naturwissenschaft*, Essen, 1943; 2d ed., Rome, 1952; p. 198).

motion of projectiles, they set about trying to discover the laws of ballistics, which they generalized to apply to the heavenly bodies.

Duhem arrived at his conclusions about the importance of the achievements in dynamics of the Ockhamite Masters in the Faculty of Arts at Paris in the middle of the fourteenth century through one of the classic detective investigations of scholarship. The successive volumes of his *Études sur Léonard de Vinci* (1906–13) tell the story of how he was forced back from his original assumption of a single great "précurseur" of genius of Leonardo, advanced in his *Origines de la statique* (1905–6), to the organized schools of fourteenth-century Paris and Oxford. His conclusion of 1913 runs:

> The science of mechanics, inaugurated by Galileo, by his rivals, by his disciples, is not a creation. The modern mind did not produce it at once and altogether as soon as the reading of Archimedes had revealed to it the art of applying geometry to natural effects. The mathematical skill acquired by acquaintance with the geometers of antiquity was used by Galileo and his contemporaries to develop and make exact a science of mechanics whose principles had been laid down and whose most essential propositions had been formulated by the Christian Middle Ages. This mechanics was taught by the physicists at the University of Paris in the fourteenth century . . . Galileo and his emulators were the heirs of this Parisian tradition. When we see the science of a Galileo triumph over peripateticism. . . . in our ignorance of the history of human thought, we believe that we are witnessing the victory of youthful modern science over medieval philosophy, obstinate and parrot-like. Actually we are watching the science which was born at Paris in the fourteenth century win out, after long preparation, over the doctrines of Aristotle and Averroes, which had been restored to honor by the Italian Renaissance.[4]

In the seventh volume of the *Système du monde,* first published forty years after his death, in 1956, Duhem states his own judgment about his historical discoveries:

> Those who in the sixteenth century were aware of this substitution of one science for another were seized by a strange delusion. They imagined that this substitution had been sudden and that it was their work. They proclaimed that peripatetic physics, the dark haunt of error, had just crumbled under their blows and that on the ruins of this physics they had constructed, as though by magic, the clear abode of truth. Of the sincere delusion or haughtily intentional error of these persons, the men

[4] *Études*, III, v–vi.

of the following centuries were the dupes or accomplices. The physicists of the sixteenth century were hailed as creators to whom the world owed the renaissance of the sciences; very often they were only continuators and somtimes plagiarists.[5]

Pierre Duhem was an inspired and imaginative historian of medieval science. The medieval discussions and suggestions to which he and those following his lead, in this country notably Ernest A. Moody and Marshall Clagett, have called attention, are of the first importance, and intensely interesting as the ideas of men who were undoubtedly "precursors" of Galileo. Duhem's own sober judgment runs, in the tenth and last volume of the *Système du monde*, published in 1959:

In order to make explicit all the wealth of ideas contained implicitly in the doctrines of Oresme, Buridan, and their contemporaries, first it was necessary to gain a more complete and more profound knowledge of mathematics than that with which these masters had to be content. Then experimental instruments and methods which permit bodies and their motions to be studied with greater precision had to be available. . . . First it was necessary that to the knowledge of Euclid's *Elements* should be added a mastery of the more advanced methods created by Archimedes; to revive them and recover their use was the task of the sixteenth century. Then the physicists had to acquire the art of making precise and delicate measurements with the aid of instruments. This art was revealed to them by Galileo's century. So long as these two progressive steps had not been taken, scholastic physics could not pass beyond the boundary to which the fourteenth-century Parisians had brought it.[6]

The historian on whose shoulders the mantle of Duhem has fallen, Annaliese Maier, though she has corrected many of Duhem's mistakes and has differed from him on a number of basic issues, is in fundamental agreement with this final estimate of the Masters of Paris, and the Oxford logicians. After examining the latter, she concludes:

Only one thing is missing from these attempts at a mathematical understanding of natural processes: the speculation is never accompanied by measurement. The idea of really testing the results of their calculations experientially does not occur to our philosophers. . . . The quasi-mathematical physics of the calculations always remained a purely deductive discipline limited to a priori computation, and in general did

[5] *Système du monde* (1913–1959), VII, 3–4.   [6] *Système du monde*, X, 45.

not carry deduction far enough to permit contact with and testing by experience.

Our philosophers failed to conceive the thought of applying the inductive method also to quantitative relations or, in other words, of basing inductive conclusions on precisely determined individual facts. This is the decisive defect in the later scholastic system of natural philosophy, and the point at which the great turn comes with Benedetti and Galileo.[7]

Duhem was a great historian. But his pioneer work has now been subjected to over a generation of penetrating criticism, which has clarified its limitations and its exaggerated claims. Duhem was a Frenchman, and he liked the University of Paris. He was also a faithful Catholic, and he admired the orthodox faith of his cherished Masters of Paris. He has been challenged on both scores. Ernest A. Moody and Marshall Clagett, after much painstaking investigation of the astounding school of logicians Thomas Bradwardine gathered about him at Merton College, Oxford, in the twenties and thirties of the fourteenth century, have pushed back a generation earlier to Oxford rather than to Paris the first appearance of many of the ideas which for Duhem seemed to originate at Paris with Buridan. These Oxford logicians and "calculators" hence seem to have been the real pioneers in suggesting non-Aristotelian principles: Heytesbury, Dumbleton, Swineshead. Moody and Clagett have found that Heytesbury had formulated between 1330 and 1335 the rule of the "intension and remission of forms," which Duhem calls the "law of uniformly accelerated motion," and attributes to Nicholas of Oresme; to the latter is merely due the rectangular coordinate diagram always used in reports and discussions thereafter. Since I myself suspected that Duhem's stalwart Catholicism had done less than justice to the anticlerical Italian writers on natural philosophy of the Quattrocento, I did some reading and found that all the presumably "novel" ideas associated with Leonardo before Duhem's discoveries, were known and taught in the fifteenth-century Italian universities—in Padua, Bologna, Pavia, and the rest. They all appear in the *Summa naturalis* of Paul of Venice (d. 1429) before 1420. Clagett has found that the Oxford logicians Heytesbury (Hentisberus, Tisberus) and Swineshead (Suisseth) were known at Padua and Bologna almost immedi-

[7] *Metaphysische Hintergründe der spätscholastischen Naturphilosophie* (1951), pp. 383-84, 397.

ately, shortly after 1350. All these ideas are expressed and discussed with great force and originality by Cajetan of Thiene (d. 1465) at Padua by the middle of the fifteenth century.

Moreover, a generation of research since Duhem has brought out more significant differences between the "impetus theory" of Buridan and the other Paris Masters, than Duhem himself was willing to recognize. The *Études galiléennes* (3 vols., 1939) of Alexandre Koyré have made this clear, as have above all the detailed and suggestive writings of Annaliese Maier. Edward Rosen has well summarized Maier's conclusions:

Impetus was considered an intrinsic tendency acting as a motive force within a moving body, and causing the continuation of a motion that had previously been initiated by some external agent. . . . The modern concept of inertia requires no inherent force for the continuation of motion, once it has begun. . . . In the inertial theory the application of a constant force such as the earth's gravitational pull, produces a uniform acceleration; "on the other hand, it is one of the most important principles of scholastic mechanics that from a constant force a constant velocity follows." [8] In the inertial theory, force is proportional to acceleration; in the impetus theory, force is proportional to velocity. [9]

Rosen's paper is the most drastic criticism of Duhem's "exaggerated claims" for his fourteenth-century physicists yet published. Rosen does not share the French and Catholic prejudices of Duhem. His own conclusion is to reinstate what is broadly the older view of Burckhardt, for instance, that Galilean science was a genuine "renaissance": that is, it sprang primarily from the re-establishment of direct contact with the mathematicians and physicists of the Greek Hellenistic Age, above all Archimedes. Rosen's arguments undoubtedly possess great cogency. Here as with other problems of the emergence of Galilean science, the situation prevails, that it is too early in the course of a rather recent research to judge the relative importance of the many different individual traditions whose convergence, in the century from Copernicus to Galileo, led to such momentous results. For one thing at least has now grown clear: that the "emergence of modern science" was a very complicated affair,

[8] Annaliese Maier, *Grenze*, p. 172.
[9] Edward Rosen, "Renaissance Science as seen by Burckhardt and his Successors," in *The Renaissance: a Reconsideration of the Theories and Interpretations of the Age,* ed. Tinsley Helton (1961), pp. 85–86.

and involved a great variety of factors. The central problem, however, is to appraise judiciously the relative importance of a number of different "necessary conditions"; and for such a wise balancing and weighing we seem as yet hardly ready.

Rosen agrees with Annaliese Maier's judgment about the impetus theory. Likewise, to him all the other novel and anti-Aristotelian ideas Duhem discovered and extolled are closer to the Aristotelian physics than to Galilean physics. He quotes Duhem's famous judgment (made so much of recently by Gilson):

One may say that the excommunications announced at Paris on March 7, 1277, by Bishop Étienne Tempier and by the doctors in theology [in which several hundred Averroistic theses, and thirty from Thomas Aquinas were condemned] were the birth certificate of modern physics.[10]

But he adds Duhem's acknowledgment in the next volume that what followed the condemnations of 1277 was

not a new physics, more accurately based on experience, but theology. Is not this fact perfectly clear to anyone who notices that most of the objections to Aristotle's dynamics were raised by professors of theology when their commentary on the *Sentences* led them to discuss the movement of the angels? [angels encounter no resistance of a medium, as physical bodies do] [11]

The Paris and Oxford discussions were carried on in an environment in which the central interest was undeniably rather in theology than in natural science. Even the fundamental rule for the "intension and remission of forms" discovered at Merton College around 1335, and provided with rectangular coordinates by Oresme—the diagram that figures in all the later discussions—can hardly be taken simply, as Duhem takes it, as the rule for "uniformly accelerated motion." Duhem himself held that in 1368 Albert of Saxony described the velocity of a freely falling body as uniformly accelerated, but that it was not until two hundred years later, in 1545, that Domingo de Soto applied this rule to the case of a freely falling body.[12] Clagett says de Soto's application was "casually suggested"; [13] it occurs in the middle of a theological discussion. It actually requires textual

---

[10] *Système du monde*, VII, 4.   [11] *Système du monde*, VIII, 119-20.
[12] *Études sur Léonard de Vinci*, III, 312, 398, 558.
[13] *The Science of Mechanics in the Middle Ages* (1959), pp. 255, 581.

emendation (p. 555); so does Albert's assertion of the uniform acceleration of a freely falling body, which he both asserted and denied.[14] Indeed, the whole discussion of the *intensio et remissio formarum* from Bradwardine on starts with the text in Peter Lombard that says: "In man, love increases and diminishes, and at different times it is more and less intense." [15] The discussion, and Oresme's rectangular coordinate, deal primarily with qualitative change or alteration. It is little wonder it took two centuries to realize it might apply also to local motion.

Rosen points to the central question as to the influence of these "precursors" of Leonardo and Galileo upon the sixteenth-century scientists:

The precise historical relation between the impetus theory and modern physics will be determined when it is learned to what extent Galileo, Descartes, and their contemporaries were familiar with fourteenth-century mechanics.[16]

My own tentative conclusion would not be so negative as Rosen's. He makes it clear that ideas developed in a theological interest were later given a relevance to natural philosophy and dynamics. This happened in fifteenth-century, anticlerical Italy, where the concern *was* with natural philosophy from the beginning, rather than with

[14] Maier, *Grenze*, p. 217; Clagett, *Mechanics*, pp. 565–66.
[15] Peter Lombard, *Book of Sentences*, I, 17, 7.
[16] Rosen, "Renaissance Science," in *The Renaissance: a Reconsideration*, p. 86. Rosen's own conclusion runs: "Did Galileo know about this thirteenth-century solution [of the problem of the force required to hold a weight in equilibrium on an inclined plane], or did he not? 'He may well have discovered this solution without help or suggestion from his medieval predecessor,' whose 'theorems and proofs involve numerous errors and frequent obscurities,' says Moody (Moody and Clagett, *The Medieval Science of Weights*, 1952, p. 169). . . . Galileo did not possess Duhem's enormous erudition. He was not an assiduous reader, preferring to consult what he liked to call the book of Nature. . . . Can we therefore accept Moody's assurance that 'the historical continuity of the development of modern mechanics, from the small beginnings found in Jordanus de Nemore through the fourteenth-century "impetus physics" and down to Galileo and his contemporaries, is discernible at each stage'? (p. 412). Can Moody, or any other follower of Duhem, really document 'each stage' in this allegedly continuous development? Until such proof is forthcoming, shall we not rather heed Koyré, who maintains that Galileo's mathematical-experimental physics was an intellectual mutation, noncontinuous with medieval physics, and Maier, who holds that the principle of inertia evolved, not out of, but in opposition to, the impetus theory?" (*Die Impetustheorie der Scholastik*, 1940, p. 167). Rosen, "Renaissance Science," pp. 87–88.

theology. And the reconstruction of these ideas of the fourteenth-century Ockhamites is primarily the work of the sixteenth-century predecessors of Benedetti and Galileo. To recognize, as recent criticism of Duhem's exaggerations has been doing, that the fourteenth-century Mertonians and Parisians were rather more "medieval" than Duhem claimed, merely magnifies the importance of what happened to these ideas in the Cinquecento, and emphasizes the Italian contribution to the emergence of Galilean science. For it is clear these ideas were thoroughly embodied in the academic teaching tradition of the Italian universities during the Quattrocento. And as far as Leonardo goes, Duhem's statement is still true: "In the mechanical work of Leonardo, there is no essential idea that does not come from the geometers of the Middle Ages" [17]—as taught at Bologna and Padua in the Quattrocento, we should add.

VII

After this critical digression, necessary because the most competent historians of medieval science are not yet in agreement, let us see what the fourteenth-century Ockhamites actually said. John Buridan (d. 1358) was the first of the Masters of Paris who tried to reconstruct Aristotle's mechanics. He exerted a tremendous influence, not only at Paris, but in the next century at Padua. He rejected Aristotle's theory of projectiles. Aristotle had held, somewhat incidentally, that a projectile when once propelled by violent motion is kept going by the push of the air behind it; since there can be no vacuum in nature, the air rent by the moving object reunites immediately behind it and propels it further. To this Buridan demurred, insisting that the air rather offers resistance to its progress. He suggested a variety of observations and experiments with canal-boats continuing to move against the wind, with windmills, mill-wheels, hoops and spears to prove the impossibility of the air acting as a motive force. In its place he took over and developed the idea of an "impetus," first suggested by the Greek commentator Philoponus, a certain force "impressed" on the moving body, proportional to the velocity of the propelling first body and to the "quantity of matter" of the body projected. The violent motion that is thus acquired would be perpetual if no resistance were offered by the

[17] *Origines de la statique,* I, 192.

air or other medium. This theory of impetus Buridan proceeded to apply to the heavenly bodies. At their creation God gave just such an "impetus" to the celestial spheres. Since they suffer no resistance, their motion is perpetual, and there is no need of "intelligences" or prime movers to keep them going. Such devices, adds Buridan, are not to be found in the Scriptures anyway. This seems to have been one of the earliest modern enunciations of the principle that the same dynamics apply to the earth and to the heavens. Rosen points out that the heavens receive their impetus supernaturally from God, while sublunar violent motion is initiated by natural forces. But of course even Newton in good Deistic fashion made the same distinction. And Duhem is entitled to say,

If we wished to separate the realm of ancient science from the domain of modern science by a precise line, we should have to draw that line, I believe, at the instant when . . . the heavenly bodies ceased to be regarded as moved by divine beings, when the celestial motions and the sublunar motions were recognized to be dependent on the same mechanics.[18]

Gravitation Buridan took to be uniformly accelerated motion. Aristotle had seemed to hold, again incidentally, that the velocity is proportional to the force ($\dot{\rho}o\pi\dot{\eta}$), and that in gravitation this force is weight, which increases as a body approaches its natural place. Buridan however attributed the acceleration of gravity to a uniformly increasing impetus, added to the weight and different from it, and, unlike the weight, an accident of body. This impetus of gravitation grows stronger in proportion to the time elapsed from the start of the fall: Buridan opposed the view of Simplicius and Thomas that the acceleration is proportional to the distance traversed from the starting-point. He also opposed attributing it to an "attraction" like that of the magnet, for it depends not on the nearness of the falling body to the earth but on the time since the start. In the case of projectiles or "violent motion," there are two separate impetuses involved, that of gravity bringing the body to the earth, and that of the initial force of propulsion.

Albert of Saxony (d. 1390) took over this theory of impetus, and

---

[18] *Études*, III, ix–x. Unfortunately for Duhem's hero, however, he was anticipated in this position by Robert Kilwardby at the end of the thirteenth century; see Gilson, *History of Christian Philosophy in the Middle Ages* (1955), pp. 357–59.

tried to formulate more precisely the laws of falling bodies. In his *Tractatus proportionum* he enumerates four simple relations as possible: the velocity is either directly proportional to the distance traversed, or to the time elapsed, or to the square of the distance, or to the square of the time. He follows the tradition in rejecting Buridan's solution, the second of these proportions. But it is very significant that both Galileo and Descartes started their own investigations of this problem with Albert's erroneous conclusion, that $v = d$, although since he also assumed that $d = t$, he gets close to the correct proportion in the first law of falling bodies.

Albert also gives a less tentative and more exact treatment of impetus than Buridan, with a greater concern for experimental proof: he adds a consideration of the momentum of a runner, the bouncing of balls, the inertia of a load of hay continuing to move against the wind; and he discusses what would result if a body were dropped down a hole through the center of the earth. He defines the essence of impetus as a quality of the second kind, a "certain aptitude or facility for motion"; and he is willing to consider seriously what motion would be like in a vacuum with no resistance offered. Albert also examines the arguments for the rotation of the earth, saying that one of his masters had defended that position, and for its revolution about the sun; although in the end he rejects the rotation on grounds of mechanics, especially because mere rotation would not explain the motions of the planets; and the revolution, because that would entail parallaxes of the stars—which were not in fact measured until 1838 by Bessel.

In statics Albert defined weight as the tendency for the center of gravity of a body, for which he suggested a method of determination, to coincide with the center of gravity of the earth, rather than to approach its natural place: the latter he redefined in terms of center of gravity. Albert carried this scientific Ockhamism to the University of Vienna, where he served as first rector on its foundation in 1365, and there built up a strong Ockhamite school. Marsilius of Inghen (d. 1396) established it at Heidelberg as first rector in 1386. Marsilius introduced a further distinction between the natural impetus of gravitation and the violent impetus of projectiles; on the whole, however, he tended to compromise with the *via antiqua* of the Scotists.

VIII

The Paris Master about whom Duhem grows most enthusiastic is Nicholas of Oresme (d. 1382). Even Annaliese Maier singles him out as "undoubtedly the greatest genius among the fourteenth-century philosophers of nature." [19] The first scientist to write in French, it is significant that he was also an economist, author of an important treatise on money, in which he challenged the power of the king to debase the coinage, and advocated stabilization in the interest of commerce. In natural science Duhem attributes to him three epoch-making ideas: the hitting on the root idea of analytic geometry, and the devising of coordinate systems in two and three dimensions for the equation of a line; better arguments than those of Copernicus for the rotation of the earth; and the formulation of the rule of uniformly accelerated motion. But Duhem's claims of "anticipation" of Descartes, Copernicus, and Galileo will hardly stand serious examination.

1. Duhem calls Oresme "the inventor of analytic geometry." But to his question, "Is it not proper to say that analytic geometry in two dimensions was created by Oresme?" [20] the historians of mathematics, led by Heinrich Wieleitner,[21] promptly answered, "No." Oresme did show how the changes in a variable could be represented on a graph of two intersecting straight lines. But his lack of geometrical knowledge and algebraic technique prevented him from pushing his graphs very far.[22] He did not systematically associate algebra with geometry, which is essential to analytic geometry; his own geometry remains Euclidean.

2. In his French commentary on the De Caelo of Aristotle, Le Livre du ciel et du monde (1377), Book II, chapter 25, Oresme has a long discussion of the possible rotation of the earth. He took this widely known hypothesis, which Franciscus Mayron had defended as the best as early as 1322, and offered better arguments in its support than Copernicus was to do. A plurality of worlds is quite pos-

[19] Grenze, p. 270. I find it difficult to concur in this judgment.
[20] Études, III, 375.
[21] Heinrich Wieleitner, "Der Tractatus de latitudinibus formarum des Oresme," Bibliotheca mathematica, XIII (1912–13), 115–45. See also Carl B. Boyer, History of Analytic Geometry (1956).
[22] Boyer, History of Analytic Geometry, p. 48.

sible, because weight is the tendency to approach the center of the earth, not of the universe; each world could have its own center. It is therefore possible that the earth is a planet revolving about the sun. Uniform principles of mechanics would then apply to all the heavenly spheres, for the earth too would have a natural circular motion. Since falling bodies would have two simple natural impetuses and motions, the rotation they would share with the earth, and that of gravity, bodies would fall straight down, and the chief objection to the rotation of the earth would thus be removed.

Duhem included extensive quotations from *Le Livre du ciel et du monde,* and claimed, "Oresme is a precursor of Copernicus; he actually maintained that to suppose the heavens motionless and the earth endowed with a daily motion of rotation was much more probable than to follow the contrary hypothesis." [23] When the text of *Le Livre* was published in full in 1943,[24] it was found that Oresme formally concluded against the rotation of the earth as "against natural reason" as well as Scripture. The arguments for rotation are "evidently not conclusive"; those against are "not evident." In the many discussions of the question in the fourteenth century, the "determination" is hardly important: it is the arguments that are of interest. Eventually men began to conclude for the opposite position they had been dialectically defending. But Oresme certainly does not "maintain" the rotation of the earth; and there is no evidence that Copernicus ever heard of Oresme.

3. Duhem seems on sounder ground in holding that Oresme formulated the law of uniformly accelerated motion, which he expounded with a rectangular graph, as everything measurable can be represented by a line. His statement of the rule Heytesbury first formulated at Merton in 1335 runs:

The distance traversed in a uniformly accelerated motion is that which would be traversed in a uniform motion in the same time, having the velocity attained by the first motion at its mean instant.[25]

Thus Oresme can indeed be called a "precursor" of Galileo. Oresme, however, did not apply his rule specifically to falling bodies, though

[23] *Système du monde,* VII, 534.
[24] Ed. A. D. Menut and A. J. Denomy (Toronto, 1943).
[25] Nicholas d'Oresme: *Tractatus de formarum latitudinibus* a venerabili doctore magistro Nicolao Horen editus . . . Paduae (1482) (a fragment from *De difformitate qualitatum*).

Albert of Saxony had already defined gravitation as uniformly accelerated motion. That is, Oresme worked out the logic and the mathematical formula of uniformly accelerated motion, with the well-known coordinate diagram: but Oresme's rule was not combined with Albert's definition and problem until Domingo de Soto at Paris in 1545—still sixty years before Galileo.

Oresme's formulation of the rule for uniformly accelerated motion and his coordinate methods proved immensely popular, however. They were used by both Albert and Marsilius, and also at Oxford. The logic of uniformly accelerated motion had in fact been developed first at Merton College. The group of Oxford logicians, Heytesbury (Tisberus), Dumbleton, Swineshead (Suisseth), was working at the same problems, investigating not only cinematics, but also the logic of the calculus and infinitesimals, and they discuss integration and the summation of a series. The motion they were concerned with was not merely local motion, but motion in its larger Aristotelian signification which included all types of change. They used coordinates to represent the intensity of qualities, thus introducing exact measurement and a mathematical treatment into the heart of the Aristotelian qualitative physics. This whole subject, which aroused interest pro and con, was called *intensio et remissio formarum.*

IX

This dynamics of the Masters of Paris was taught at the Sorbonne, with no very significant additions, until interest in it was revived once more at the very end of the fifteenth century. It was maintained at the many new German universities established under Ockhamite auspices. And the criticisms and discoveries of the Paris and Oxford Ockhamites were fully established at Padua and Bologna by about 1400. The issues involved in their conflict with a rigorous Aristotelianism were thereafter at the very center of attention in northern Italy; and the subsequent development of this critical activity is primarily the work of Italians. About 1400, therefore, the interest in the development of scientific ideas shifts from Ockhamite Paris to the Padua Averroists. From the time of Paul of Venice (d. 1429) to Cremonini (d. 1631) Aristotelian physics and a nascent Galilean physics were in definite and conscious opposition at Padua, and this critical opposition contributed greatly to the working out of the latter. Paul of Venice brought Oresme's rule and diagrams to Padua; thereafter it is accepted by the school, and appears in all their physical writings. He brought also the whole body of "modernist" Oxford logic, with all its subtlety of analysis. He had been sent by his order to Oxford in 1390, where he remained for three years; he then taught for two more in Paris at the time of the last great Ockhamite, Pierre d'Ailly. He thus knew all the Ockhamite developments at first hand, and explained them fully in his encyclopedic writings, though he was critical of the impetus theory.

His successor Cajetan of Thiene (d. 1465) was the most radical scientifically of the Padua Averroists, and the most sympathetic to the Paris dynamics; he not only follows the Oxford cinematics and Oresme's rule, he also adopts the views of Paris on projectiles and their impetus theory. He initiated a great controversy over the *Calculations* of Suisseth, in which all the arguments for a mathematical as against a qualitative physics are examined, so that the documents of this controversy, in many editions, were among the first works printed in Italy in the 1480s. Oresme's fundamental *De latitudinibus formarum* appeared at Padua in 1482, with a discussion by Blasius de Parma de Pelicanis; Albert of Saxony's *Tractatus de proportionibus*, arguing for a quantitative treatment of qualities (already reported in Paul of Venice's *Summa naturalis*) also appeared in the same year; in 1496 it was reprinted with the *De intensione et remissione formarum* of Walter Burleigh, a defense of the logic of qualitative change opposed to the spirit of Oresme, and with a full reply to Burleigh in behalf of quantitative analysis by the physician Jacopo da Forlì. Among the most interesting of all these documents, indicative of a lively concern with what was to become the fundamental scientific question, is the *Tractatus de proportionibus* of a Milanese physician, Johannes Marlianus (Pavia, 1482), which brings experimental proof to bear on the quantitative side, describes the rolling of balls down an inclined plane to measure their velocity and acceleration, and narrates experiments with pendulums.

X

At just this time, about 1500, there was a revived interest in the Ockhamite dynamics at Paris, where a group in the Collège de

Montaigu, Johannes Majoris, Coronel, and Dullaert, popularized the views of Buridan, Albert of Saxony, and Oresme. The latter's *Geometry* was published in 1486, and again in 1505; Lokert edited the writings of Buridan and Albert in 1516 and again in 1518. There is irony in the fact that Erasmus and Luis Vives, who were studying in the Collège de Montaigu at this time, satirized the "silly discussions" of uniformly accelerated motion, falling bodies, and infinitesimals, and bade men return to the Scriptures, Plato, and Aristotle— a fit measure of the scientific ignorance of the humanists. Though in the sixteenth century such interests were unpopular, the scholars of Paris persisted, until finally, in 1545, de Soto united Albert and Oresme, and arrived at the exact law of falling bodies. The ascent of a projectile is a uniformly retarded motion, its fall a uniformly accelerated motion; both proceed by the operation of a constant impetus to change their rate.

Meanwhile, in Italy Leonardo da Vinci was opposing all the essentials of a mathematical method and of dyamics to Aristotelian physics. It is now clear that he derived his mysterious insights, not by inspiration, out of thin air, but from reading the Masters of Paris: he cites the Lokert edition of 1516 in his notebooks, together with the works of the Padua teachers, especially Cajetan, and the Oresme treatise of 1482. Though the literary and artistic Renaissance, together with the discovery of the Greek Aristotle, brought to Padua a new respect for the authority of the latter as an ancient, so that the same Pomponazzi who taught the most radical views on the soul and human nature also vigorously opposed the Ockhamite departure from a qualitative physics, in his attack on Suisseth and Marlianus in *De intensione et remissione formarum;* there still remained in northern Italy a strong minority current of radical scientists, who turned the Ockhamite discussions of uniformly accelerated motion definitely to the problems of local motion, and developed their criticisms further, with much concern for ballistics and the theory of projectiles—by this time a very practical problem. Tartaglia in his *Nova Scientia* of 1537 still retains the Aristotelian view that a violent motion excludes all natural motion; but in his *Quaesiti et inventioni diverse* in 1546 he takes the trajectory of a projectile as the combination of an acquired *impeto* with the natural impetus of gravity. Niccolò Tartaglia (1499–1557) was the outstanding sixteenth-century Italian mathematician; he was not a university man but a self-taught practical geometer whose interest was in the application of mathematics to practical problems. Cardano's *De Subtilitate*, 1547, accepts the *impetus acquisitus*, and distinguishes three periods in violent motion: first, one of pure violence, then one of mixed violence and gravity, and finally one of pure gravity. Buridan's doctrine of impetus is fully accepted by Alessandro Piccolomini in 1547. Ten years later Julius Caesar Scaliger employed Buridan's views to criticize Cardano, ranking Ockham and Suisseth above Archimedes himself. Bernardino Baldi in 1582 followed Scaliger. Finally, in 1585 Giambattista Benedetti, accepting completely the Paris *impressio impetus*, and adding the notion of centrifugal motion, that all motion is naturally in a straight line, managed to formulate the main principles we know as Galileo's mechanics.

It is thus clear that the science of dynamics, as it reached Galileo, was the result of the careful reconstruction of the Aristotelian physics in the light of the idea of a mathematical interpretation of nature, following the suggestions and achievements consciously found in the Paris Ockhamites of the fourteenth century, as taught and discussed in the Italian universities, notably Bologna and Padua. Galileo himself knew this Italian version of the Ockhamite ideas, and cites Cajetan and others of the fifteenth century. Whether he had read the fourteenth-century Masters of Paris themselves is more doubtful. Duhem reported that Galileo twice cites in early writings Albert and Buridan in the 1516 Lokert edition.[26] But these writings are not by Galileo himself; they are merely works he had copied as a twenty-year-old student at the University of Pisa, probably by his teacher of natural philosophy, the learned and erudite Francesco Buonamici, to whose own opinions Galileo later offered the most vigorous objections.[27] Thus Galileo had heard of Albert, Buridan, Marsilius, and the Oxford logic of mathematics. Whether he had read and studied them is more dubious. But there is no question he was familiar with the contemporary university discussions of their ideas.

Galileo's first published formulation of the law of falling bodies

[26] *Études*, III, 582.
[27] A. Favaro, in *Opere di Galileo*, ed. Nazionale, I, 10. See Rosen, article cited, p. 87.

occurs in his letter of 1604 to Sarpi; [28] an earlier fragment *de motu* has been found, dating from 1590, giving a demonstration.[29] It reaches the correct conclusion, but starts from the wrong premise, because it begins with Albert of Saxony's error that $v = d$. Sometime between 1604 and 1630 Galileo arrived at Oresme's rule.

Galileo's originality lies in his addition of the mathematical methods of Archimedes to the ideas descended from the Masters of Paris. His formulation of dynamics derives, in fact, not from any experimental discovery; he tells us that he never resorted to experiment except to convince his Aristotelian opponents, who demanded the evidence of the senses. All his life he retained the very considerable error that g, the acceleration of gravity, is 15 feet per second (instead of the actual 32 feet). His formulation comes rather from the mathematical elaboration of the idea of taking t, d, and v as the three sides of a right triangle—an idea fully presented in the Parisians, and set forth with diagrams in the 1482 Padua edition of Oresme's treatise.

It is interesting to note that Descartes's first consideration of falling bodies, in 1619,[30] contains the same error as Albert. Descartes makes no mention of the Masters of Paris—he never mentioned the sources of his ideas, since they all came from God through reason alone—but he uses Oresme's figures and coordinates.

---

[28] *Opere*, ed. Nazionale, X, 115.   [29] *Opere*, ed. Nazionale, VIII, 373.
[30] Descartes, *Oeuvres*, ed. Adam et Tannery, I, 69.

The Padua Tradition of Method and the Revival of Greek Mathematics

I

IF THE CONCEPTS of a mathematical physics were arrived at by a long criticism of Aristotelian ideas, the "new method," the logic and methodology actually taken over by Galileo and destined to become the scientific method of the seventeenth-century physicists, as contrasted with the many noisy proposals of the sixteenth-century buccinators down to Francis Bacon, was even more clearly the result of a fruitful critical reconstruction of the Aristotelian logic, undertaken at Padua in particular, and fertilized by the methodological discussions of the commentators on the received medical writers. For three hundred years, after Pietro d'Abano brought the problem to the fore, the Padua medical teachers were driven by their texts, especially Galen, to a careful analysis of scientific procedure. The great commentators on Galen, Jacopo da Forlì (d. 1413), who incidentally wrote widely on the methods of the Paris physicists, especially Oresme, and Hugo of Siena (d. 1439), gradually built up a detailed theory of scientific method which the Aristotelian scholars, themselves holders of medical degrees, incorporated into their version of Aristotle. It is possible to trace step by step in rather beautiful fashion the gradual elaboration of the Aristotelian method, in the light of the medical tradition, from its first beginnings in Pietro d'Abano to its completed statement in the great

The substance of the first sixteen pages of this chapter, with considerable additional material, appeared as an article in the *Journal of the History of Ideas*, I (1940), 177–206. It was reprinted with the Latin texts in J. H. Randall, Jr., *The School of Padua and the Emergence of Modern Science* (Padua, 1961), in the series *Saggi e Testi* mentioned in the first note to Chapter 2 of this Book: pp. 15–68.

logical controversies of Zabarella, in which it reaches the form taken over by Galileo and familiar in the seventeenth-century scientists.

II

The whole question was raised by Pietro d'Abano in his *Conciliator differentiarum philosophorum, et praecipue medicorum* (1310). There are two kinds of science.

Science in the strictest sense is that through proximate and immediate causes, from which is inferred the conclusion . . . and this science is generated from demonstration *propter quid*, or what Galen called *doctrina compositiva*. . . . When from effects inhering in their causes we arrive by an opposite order at the cause we are seeking, we have science through demonstration *quia*, called also *doctrina resolutiva*.[1]

Here are the distinction and the terms to be elaborated for three centuries. Pietro treats it fully in Difference 8, dealing with the kinds of *doctrina* or teaching, and *order*, and the ways of demonstration. These terms are drawn from several sources. Galen's *Techne* or art of medicine commences with a prologue in which three doctrinae or ways of teaching medicine are distinguished, by *resolution*, by *composition*, and by *definition*. The first two are identified by the Arabic commentator on Galen, Hali, with the two Aristotelian kinds of demonstration, that which proceeds from causes to effects, or demonstration *propter quid*, and that which proceeds from effects to causes, demonstration *quia*. This division, however, was naturally confused with the threefold distinction made by Averroes in the Prohemium to the Physica of Aristotle, into demonstration *simpliciter*, or *of cause and being*, in which as in mathematics the causes are both first for us and for nature; demonstration *propter quid*, or *of cause*, in which, as in physics, we start with what is first in nature but not first for us; and demonstration *of being*, or *of sign*, in which we start with effects to arrive at causes. The distinction between the two procedures, that from effects to causes and that from causes to effects, is Aristotelian; Averroes set the procedure of mathematics off from the *a priori* procedure of demonstration in physics; from Galen, and also from

[1] Differentia 3.

the rhetorical method of Cicero and Boethius, came the terms *resolutive* and *compositive* to designate these two procedures.

For Pietro this distinction of *doctrina* was a distinction of two kinds of science, of which the first, or compositive, was alone science in the strict sense; the second or resolutive was science only because of the weakness of the human mind, which in natural science has to start from experienced effects to discover their causes or reasons why (*propter quid*). There are really only two kinds of demonstration; for the *a priori* method of mathematics and that of physics are two species of the one kind, demonstration *propter quid*.

III

The physician Jacopo da Forlì (d. 1413), who occupied in turn the chairs of medicine and of natural philosophy, followed Hali and Pietro in their distinction of the two ways of teaching, compositive and resolutive. He added, however, a further analysis of the method of resolution, bringing it closer to a procedure of investigation. Resolution is twofold, either real or logical. Real resolution is the actual separation of things into their component parts. Logical resolution is so called metaphorically.

When a logical resolution is made, a thing at first understood confusedly is understood distinctly, so that the parts and causes touching its essence are distinctly grasped, as with a feverish man you first have the concept of fever in general and confusedly, and then resolve the fever into its causes.[2]

Jacopo goes on to cite a number of medical examples of this resolution of effects into their causes.

Hugo of Siena (d. 1439), teacher of medicine at Padua, Ferrara, and Parma, is still more concerned with methodology. Starting with Galen, he defines *doctrina* as the setting forth of what is demonstrable (*manifestatio demonstrabilis*); it has two modes, resolution and composition, and in a complete science both are to be used,

because in the knowledge of causes we use demonstration *quia*, and in the scientific knowledge of effects we use demonstration *propter quid*. Both of these processes are necessary, as well as the explanation of many definitions.[3]

[2] Jacopo da Forli, *Super tegni galeni*, Text. 1.
[3] Hugo of Siena (Ugo Benzi), *Expositio tegni galeni*, Text. 1.

A proper scientific method will begin with effects, seek the cause, and then explain the effects from which it started by that cause.

In the discovery of the middle term, which is the cause, we proceed from effect to cause . . . such a mode of acquiring learning we call resolutive, because in that discovery we proceed from an effect which is commonly more composite to a cause which is simpler; and because by this discovery we certify the effect through the cause we say that demonstration *propter quid* and *of cause* guarantees resolutive learning. . . . I see in the discovery of a science of effects through their cause a double process, and likewise in the discovery of a science of causes through their effects: the one of the discovery of the middle term, the other its making known; and the process of discovery in demonstration through causes is resolutive, while that of making known is compositive, and the opposite in demonstration through effects.[4]

Thus Hugo refuses to distinguish sharply between the two processes; in any science, and in any demonstration, *inventio* and *notificatio* both enter as successive parts of the method to be employed. Discovery and proof are essential moments in all method.

IV

This notion of a "double process" in scientific method had already been set forth by Urban the Averroist in his large commentary on Aristotle's *Physics,* in 1334. Following Averroes, he distinguishes three modes of demonstration: the demonstration *simpliciter* of mathematics, in which the principles do not have to be sought after; demonstration *of sign,* proceeding from observed effects, by which the physicist learns the causes of natural things; and a third kind,

demonstrations which proceed from causes which though they are always prior and more known *quoad naturam,* are often posterior and less known to us. This occurs in physics, in which from those things prior to us whose modes are effects we investigate the causes which are posterior and less known to us. This is the mode of resolutive learning; but after the investigation of causes we demonstrate the effects through the causes, and this is the mode of compositive learning. Thus physical demonstrations follow mathematical demonstrations in certainty, because they are the most certain after those in mathematics.[5]

Paul of Venice examines still more closely this double process in physical demonstrations, defending it against the charge of being what Aristotle called a circle in proof.

[4] *Ibid.,* Text. 1.   [5] Book I, Text. 2.

Scientific knowledge of the cause depends on the knowledge of the effects, just as a scientific knowledge of the effects depends on a knowledge of the cause, since we know the cause through the effect before we know the effect through the cause. This is the principle of all investigation, that a scientific knowledge of natural effects demands a prior knowledge of their causes and principles.[6]

This is not a circle, however.

For in scientific method (*in processu naturali*) there are three knowledges: the first is of the effect without any reasoning, called *quia*, that it is. The second is of the cause through knowledge of that effect; it is likewise called *quia*. The third is of the effect through the cause; it is called *propter quid*. But the knowledge of why (*propter quid*) the effect is, is not the knowledge that (*quia*) it is an effect.[7]

Natural science begins both from the causes and from the things caused, but in different fashion. It begins from causes inclusively, that is, by knowing them; and from the things caused exclusively, that is, by knowing through them . . . A cause has a double knowledge, the one in the process *quia* and the other in the process *propter quid*. The second depends on the first, and the first is the cause of the second, so that the process *quia* is the cause of the process *propter quid*. In the same way the effect is said to have a double knowledge.[8]

V

During the sixteenth century attention was increasingly focused on this double process involved in scientific procedure. It came to be known by the Averroistic term of "regress"; the dependence of all strict demonstration on the prior investigation of principles was increasingly emphasized, and the details of that establishment were carefully examined. The fullest account of these problems is to be found in the commentary of Niphus on the *Physics* (1506).

After explaining the three kinds of demonstration in Averroes' prohemium, and assigning to natural philosophy the two procedures, "one from the effect to the discovery of the cause, the other from the cause discovered to the effect," [9] Niphus takes up at once the question of whether this is a circular proof, and cites Philoponus, Themistius, and Averroes in defense of such a *regressus*.

[6] *Summa naturalis*, Book I, cap. 9.   [7] *Summa naturalis*, Book I, cap. 9.
[8] *Super phys.*, Book I, Text. 2.
[9] *Expositio de physico auditu*, Book I, Text. 4.

Recent writers maintain that there are four kinds of knowledge (*notitia*): the first is of the effect by the senses, or observation; the second is the discovery of the cause through the effect, called demonstration of sign; the third is knowledge of the same cause by an examination (*negotiatio*) of the intellect, from which is first derived such knowledge of the cause as makes it fit to serve as the middle term of demonstration *simpliciter;* the fourth is a knowledge of the same effect *propter quid*, through that cause known so certainly as to be a middle term. (I, 4)

Since the second knowledge of the effect differs widely from its initial observation, this is no circle, but a regress. Niphus then asks, what is this *negotiatio* or examination of the intellect? It is not a demonstration, nor a definition, nor is it induction.

This *negotiatio* is composition and division. For when the cause itself has been discovered, the intellect composes and divides until it knows the cause as a middle term. For though cause and middle term be the same, they differ in their reason: a cause is so called in so far as the effect proceeds from it, whether it be better known than the effect or not. But it is called a middle term, in so far as it is a definition. From effect to cause is the procedure of discovering the cause; *negotiatio* leads to the cause as a middle term and a definition. But since the definition is not discovered except by composition and division, it is by them that the cause is discovered under the aspect of a middle term, from which we can then proceed to the effect. (I, 4)

In his *Recognitio,* added later, Niphus suggests another view of what he calls "demonstrative regress."

It is customary to treat at length the regress in physical demonstrations; I say physical, because there is no regress in mathematics. The younger men (*iuniores*) in this difficulty conceive three kinds of knowledge in demonstrative regress, of which the first is about the effect, that it is; that is, that the proposition signifying the effect is true; and this knowledge comes from the senses. That man has the capacity for science is known by sense. The second kind of knowledge is the reason why (*propter quid*) of that which is observed by sense. Thus we consider the reason why man has the capacity for science, and not the brute, and we say, because he has a rational soul. Therefore of the effect, or of the proposition signifying the effect, there are two kinds of knowledge, the one, that it is true, and this is clear to sense; the other, why it is, and this is known to us by the discovery of the cause. Of the cause, or of the propositions signifying the cause, there is one kind of knowledge, and this is discovery (*inventio*), which is nothing else than that it is the cause, or that the propositions are true which signify it to be the cause. They conceive therefore that by this knowledge which is the discovery of the cause, is secured the reason why of the effect, or the reason why the conclusion is true. Thus in the regress in physical demonstration there are three kinds of knowledge, of which two are of the effect, and the third is the discovery of the cause, which when related to the effect is its reason why, but which when related to the cause is the fact that it is cause; this discovery is acquired through the effect. (I, 4)

Niphus cites significantly examples from the *History of Animals,* the most empirical of the Aristotelian writings.

From this it is clear that there is no need of any *negotiatio,* to render greater our knowledge of the cause, as we formerly held, for the mere knowledge that it is a cause is the reason why of the effect. Yet when I more diligently considered the words of Aristotle, and the commentaries of Alexander and Themistius, of Philoponus and Simplicius, it seemed to me that in the regress in physical demonstrations the first procedure, by which the discovery of the cause is syllogized, is a mere conjectural (hypothetical) syllogism, since by it the discovery of the cause is syllogized merely in conjectural fashion; but the second, by which is syllogized the reason why of the effect through the discovery of the cause, is demonstration *propter quid,* not that it makes us know *simpliciter,* but on condition that that really is the cause, or that the propositions are true which represent it to be the cause, and nothing else can be the cause . . . Alexander asserts that the discovery of the cause is conjectural, while going from the discovery of the cause to the effect is demonstrative, not *simpliciter,* but on the condition that that is the cause, and that nothing else can be the cause. . . . But you object, that in that case the science of nature is not science at all. We must say that the science of nature is not science *simpliciter,* like the science of mathematics; yet it is science *propter quid,* because the discovery of the cause, gained by a conjectural syllogism, is the reason why of the effect . . . That something is a cause can never be so certain as the effect, whose existence is known to the senses. That it is a cause remains conjectural (hypothetical).[10]

VI

Here at the beginning of the sixteenth century is clearly expressed the structure of a science of hypothesis and demonstration, with the dependence of its first principles upon empirical investigation plainly set forth—the one element in the Aristotelian theory of science that had remained obscure. Each of the major logicians of the century added his bit to the rounding out of the conception. Achillini and Zimara (d. 1532) both sharpen the distinction between mathe-

[10] *Recognitio,* Book I, Text. 4.

matics, demonstrated *a priori*, and a science of nature, which is demonstrated *a posteriori*, even in the second part of its procedure, from causes to effects, or *propter quid*. Zimara makes a new distinction between *order*, concerned with the teaching and exposition of the subject-matter, and *method*, concerned with its discovery and demonstration. The order of exposition, Achillini holds, should follow the order of nature. Simon Porta, pupil of Pomponazzi and Achillini, though as a Hellenist he brushes aside the traditional long discussions on method, accepts the double method of natural science, following Alexander as the best interpreter. Natural things can be considered as they are made, or as they are; in the latter investigation we must proceed by dividing from effects. He admits the "regress" as the procedure to be followed in physics: first there is the way of discovery, by which alone principles are learned from the investigation of experience; then the way of science and judgment by which we explain that experience.

Pomponazzi's commentary on the *Physics* remains unpublished; in his available works his treatment of method is psychological rather than logical. His whole argument from the necessity of sense images in all knowing leads him to emphasize the intimate union of the particular and the universal, and the necessity of not only starting with the former but also of returning to it by a "*reditus.*" Like most of the later Paduans, he follows Alexander rather than Thomas and Averroes in maintaining that the intellect must know particulars directly, in order to abstract universals from them.

Since the human soul grasps the singular first through the cogitative power, and then the universal through the intellect, which it contemplates in the same singular that is known by sense image, it truly makes a return (*reditus*) and consequently a conversion, since from the singular known through a sense-image the same soul returns through the intellect to the same thing.[11]

The two operations of the intellect he takes to be composition and disjunction.

Bernardinus Tomitanus (d. 1576), holder of the chair in logic at Padua for years and teacher of Zabarella, carried the development a step further. He was almost wholly preoccupied with questions of method. In physics both discovery and demonstration proceed from

[11] *De immortalitate animae,* cap. XII, sec. 3.

sign, that is from particular effects; from universals to particulars is the way of explaining and stating what has been discovered the contrary way. He vigorously defends the regress as the method of natural science, the combination of demonstration *quia* and *propter quid*. And for the first time demonstration *quia* is formally identified with induction as the way of inquiry (*inquisitio*). Without the method of induction or the regress, there could be no science of nature at all for the peripatetic.

VII

With the same simplicity and lucidity with which he summed up the collective wisdom of the Padua school on all their other problems, Zabarella formulated the classic version of their teaching on method, in the terms and with the distinctions fruitfully employed and consciously expressed by Galileo. Out of this long and patient critique of the Aristotelian theory of science there developed the method that was to issue in fresh triumphs over nature. Logic Zabarella regards, following the Greeks, not as a science, but purely as an instrument.

The whole treatment of logic is about second notions; but these are our own work, and by our will can either be or not be. They are therefore not necessary things, but contingent, and hence do not fall under science, since science is only of necessary things.[12]

Logic is a tool, sought not for its own sake but for its utility in furthering science.

Logic is an instrumental intellectual state (*habitus*), or instrumental discipline, created by philosophers for the sake of philosophy, which constructs second notions in the concepts of things, and makes them into instruments by which in all things the true may be known and the false discerned.[13]

In this sense it is like the other instrumental discipline, grammar. But logic is double, "one applied to things, and already put to use; the other separate from things"; and the former is identical with science itself. For the sciences are "nothing else than logical methods put to use." [14]

---

[12] *De natura logicae*, Lib. I, cap. iii. Zabarella's logical writings are to be found in Jacobi Zabarellae Patavini *Opera Logica* (ed. 2d, Venice, 1586).
[13] *De natura logicae*, Lib. I, cap. 20.   [14] *De methodis*, Lib. I, cap. 1.

For Zabarella, therefore, logic and method are interchangeable terms; and he criticizes the logicians, who therefore ought to treat method carefully, for leaving it to the physicians, who in turn neglect Aristotle for their Galen. Method is "an intellectual instrument producing knowledge of the unknown from the known . . . Method has the force of inference (*vim illatricem*), and connects this with that." (III, 2, 1) Method is therefore the same as the syllogism: "the definition of method does not differ from the definition of the syllogism." The syllogism is, in fact, "the common genus of all methods and logical instruments." (III, 3) Since all necessary connection is causal in character, all method must be from cause to effect or from effect to cause. There are therefore only two possible methods, composition and resolution.

For all scientific progress from the known to the unknown is either from cause to effect, or from effect to cause; the former is the demonstrative method, the latter resolutive; there is no other procedure which generates a certain knowledge of things. For if we progress from something to something else, of which neither is the cause of the other, there cannot be between them any essential and necessary connexion, whence no certain knowledge can follow that progress. It is thus clear that there can be no scientific method except the demonstrative and the resolutive. (III, 17)

Demonstrative method is a syllogism generating science from propositions that are necessary, immediate, better known, and the causes of the conclusion . . . Resolutive method is a syllogism consisting of necessary propositions, which leads from posterior things and effects better known to the discovery of prior things and causes. (III, 18)

Zabarella makes the Averroistic distinction between the resolutive method suitable for natural science and the "analytic" method of mathematics. In the latter, both the principles and the consequences have the same certainty and are coordinate, so that whether we start with one or the other is merely a technical question. In natural science, however, we must start with effects observed by the senses.

Since because of our mental weakness the principles from which proof is to be derived are unknown to us, and since we cannot take our departure from the unknown, we must follow another way on which we are led by means of the resolutive method to the discovery of principles, so that after they are once found we can prove the natural phenomena and effects from them. (III, 18)

The resolutive method is thus the servant of the demonstrative.

The end of the demonstrative method is perfect science, which is knowledge of things through their causes; but the end of the resolutive method is discovery rather than science; since by resolution we seek causes from their effects so that we may afterwards know effects from their causes, not so that we may rest in a knowledge of the causes themselves. (III, 18)

There are two kinds of resolution or ways of discovery, "demonstration from effects, which in its proper function is most efficacious, and induction, which is much weaker than resolution." (III, 19) By induction we know only principles known according to nature; by resolution we can learn principles unknown according to nature. But Zabarella sometimes follows his teacher Tomitanus in identifying induction with resolution.

Induction does not prove a thing by another thing, but in a certain way reveals it through itself. The universal is not distinguished from the singular in the thing itself, but only by reason. And because the thing is better known as singular than as universal, since it is said to be sensible as singular and not as universal, induction is thus a process from the same to the same: from the same in that aspect in which it is more evident, to the knowledge of the same in that aspect in which it is more obscure and hidden. Therefore not only the principles of things, but also the principles of science, or the principles of knowing, which are said to be indemonstrable, are known by induction. (III, 19)

The originality of Zabarella, and of the whole development of which he is the culmination, is thus to set off scientific experience from mere ordinary observation, the accidental and planless collection of single cases. The weakness of the logic of the Schoolmen lay precisely in establishing first principles uncritically from such mere observation. Zabarella, and with him the whole new science, insisted that experience must be first carefully analyzed to discover the principle or cause of the observed effects. After this way of discovery has been followed, we can then deductively demonstrate how facts follow from this principle or cause: we can pursue the way of proof. Science proceeds, that is, from the rigorous analysis of a few selected instances to a general principle, and then from that principle to the systematized or ordered facts or science. Zabarella calls this the combination of the resolutive and compositive methods; and such was precisely the procedure and terms of Galileo.

The presupposition of this method, of course, is that there exists an intelligible structure in the subject-matter under examination; Zabarella makes this perfectly clear.

Demonstrative induction takes place in a necessary subject-matter and in things that have an essential connexion with each other. It therefore does not consider all the particulars, since after a few have been inspected our mind perceives at once the essential connexion and thus disregarding the remaining particulars at once collects the universal.[15]

No clearer statement could be made of the procedure of the seventeenth-century scientists.

This double method, and particularly the analysis of instances, Zabarella considers in his treatment *De regressu.*

The regress is between cause and effect, when they are reciprocal, and the effect is better known to us than the cause. For since we must always go from what is better known to us, we first demonstrate the unknown cause from the known effect, and then return (*regredimur*) from the cause so known to the effect to be demonstrated, that we may know the reason why it is. (cap. 1)

Zabarella does not bring in "nature," like Aristotle; for it is a logical and not a metaphysical question he is considering. "Both demonstrations are made by us and for ourselves, not for nature." (cap. 2) We are following the order of knowledge, not of things, in our way of discovery. Zabarella like Niphus finds four stages in the process of the regress. First we observe the single effect. Secondly, we resolve the complex fact into its component parts and conditions. Thirdly, we examine this supposed or hypothetical cause by a "mental examination" to clarify it and find its essential elements. Finally, we demonstrate the effect from that cause.

When the first process has been made, which is from effect to cause, before we return from the latter to the effect, there must intervene a certain third middle labor, by which we are led to the distinct knowledge of that cause, which so far is known only confusedly. Some men (Niphus) knowing this to be necessary have called it a *negotiatio* of the intellect; we can call it a "mental examination" of the cause itself, or a "mental consideration." For after we have discovered that cause, we begin to consider it that we may know also what it is. (cap. 5)

Zabarella then proceeds to a further analysis of this "mental examination."

---

[15] *De regressu*, cap. 4.

But what this mental consideration may be, and how it is accomplished, seems to have been explained by no one; for although some have said that this middle *negotiatio* of the intellect intervenes, still they have not shown how we are led by it to a distinct knowledge of the cause, and what is the force of this *negotiatio*. There are two things, as I judge, which aid us toward knowing the cause distinctly: one, the knowledge that it is, which prepares us to discover what it is; for when we form some hypothesis about the matter (*in re aliquid praenoscimus*) we are able to search out and discover something else in it; where we form no hypothesis at all, we never discover anything . . . When then we find that cause to be suggested, we are in a position to seek out and discover what it is. The other thing, without which this first would not suffice, is the comparison of the cause discovered with the effect, through which it was discovered, not indeed by knowing this to be the cause, and that the effect, but only comparing this thing with that. For thus it comes about that we are led gradually to the knowledge of the conditions of that thing, and when one condition has been discovered we are helped to the discovery of another, until we finally know this to be the cause of that effect. (cap. 5)

The regress thus consists necessarily of three parts: the first is a "demonstration *that*" (*quod*), by which we are led from a confused knowledge of the effect to a confused knowledge of the cause; the second is that mental consideration, by which from a confused knowledge of the cause we acquire a distinct knowledge of it; the third is demonstration itself, by which we are at length led from the cause distinctly known to the distinct knowledge of the effect. (cap. 5)

These three stages may be simultaneous; they are only logically distinct. "The end of the regress is a distinct science of the effect, which is called science *propter quid*."

The theory of science set forth in Aristotle's *Analytics* is a theory of proof, not of discovery. Here within the school of Padua Aristotelians there has been added what was so sorely needed, a logic of investigation and inquiry. No longer are the first principles of natural science taken as indemonstrable and self-evident: they have become hypotheses resting upon the facts they explain. If Zabarella did not follow up the suggestion of Niphus that all natural science therefore remains conjectural and hypothetical, it was because he believed that an examination of particular instances would reveal an intelligible structure there present; and that was precisely the faith of which modern science was born. Zabarella distinguishes between the principles of logic and the principles of physics.

Those are most properly called principles whose truth cannot be demonstrated in their science in any way, either *a priori* or *a posteriori;* for these are properly called *principia cognoscendi,* than which in that science nothing is more known. But *principia essendi* are not propositions but things, nor are they of necessity known beforehand, but often they are unknown, and can be demonstrated *a posteriori,* though not *a priori,* for if they had prior principles they would not themselves be principles.[16]

But these physical principles are no mere conveniences of knowledge; they belong to their subject-matter, and are a part of the intelligible structure of the world.

Propositions accepted in demonstrations from effects, if we consider things themselves, are not less necessary, less *per se,* nor less certain than propositions of strict demonstration; but if we consider our mind, they are not so known by us to be necessary, as the propositions of strict demonstration. Still we recognize some necessity in them; if not so much as is really there, at least so much as suffices for that syllogism to have the name and nature of demonstration.[17]

It is not surprising that Galileo should so often sound like Zabarella. For he arrived in Padua in 1592, while the echoes of the great controversies over method between Zabarella and Francesco Piccolomini and Bernardino Petrella in the 1580s were still resounding—controversies of which a witness has recorded:

The school of logic at Padua was divided into two sects, those who were partisans of Zabarella, and those who were partisans of Petrella, and a multitude seemed to stand on either side. After this most exalted and famous controversy, so useful and fruitful to all students of logic, both published commentaries on the Posterior Analytics; than which commentaries, though they are different, and contain divergent teaching, in the common judgment of learned men nothing can be found more exquisite and more clear.[18]

In these two controversies, the points at issue were relatively minor in comparison with the bulk of agreement on method. Piccolomini, an older man, holder of the first chair in natural philosophy since 1564, had come from Siena bringing a certain Platonism with his Aristotelianism; but though he defends some Platonic positions, he is as advanced on method as Zabarella, and as near the ideas of

---

[16] *De tribus praecognitis,* cap. 4.
[17] *De speciebus demonstrationis,* cap. 10.
[18] A. Riccoboni, *De gymnasio patavino,* Lib. IV, cap. 11.

the seventeenth-century scientists. He agrees on the importance of resolution as the way of discovery. But against his demand that metaphysics must furnish the starting-point and frame of reference in all science, and that such science must imitate the fixed structure of nature, Zabarella maintains the independence and self-sufficiency of natural science, and indeed of each particular subject-matter, making the end of knowledge and inquiry a human thing, and thus introducing pragmatic goals and aims into the sciences. He defends induction as giving knowledge perfect in its kind, the constitution of man being what it is, and not as a mere way of discovering something more perfect. And against Piccolomini's Platonic conception of a natural order of perfections which science must follow, he maintains a purely immanent conception of natural teleology: the perfect functioning of each kind of thing in the universe is its only end, and each subject-matter is to be understood in terms of its own principles. Indeed, in his criticism of Platonic views of teleology Zabarella went far along the path which his pupil Telesio was to follow.

Zabarella did not combat Aristotle, he tried to understand and interpret him; and where Aristotle seemed to him obscure or one-sided, he tried to carry on his thought in the direction that seemed needed.

Although I wish to be second to no mortal in admiration of the genius of Aristotle [he remarked], still I believe that he neither could have written everything nor known everything, nor did he so follow the truth in all that he did write that he was never able to err; for he was a man, and not God.[19]

The fruit of this cautious, critical, and independent discipleship was that Zabarella's version of the Aristotelian logic, though interpreted and colored in terms of the three great theories of knowledge inherited by the seventeenth century, and though receiving in practice a differing emphasis on its several parts, remained the method and ideal of all natural scientists until the fresh criticisms of Locke and Berkeley. For though the language varies, the whole great literature on method that fills the scientific writings of the seventeenth century is at bottom a series of footnotes to the *Organon* of Aristotle. Indeed today, when the functional concepts of the Aristotelian

[19] *De methodis*, IV, 22.

physics seem to be replacing the mechanical concepts of Newton, when the mechanistic emphasis of early modern science, from the Age of Newton to the late nineteenth century, is beginning to appear a transitory interlude in the development of scientific thought, a kind of adolescent stage, it is an appropriate time to revise our conventional notions of the so-called "origins" of modern natural science. The more fully the record of late medieval thought is studied, the clearer it becomes that the most daring departures from Aristotelian science were carried on within the Aristotelian framework, and by means of a critical reflection on the Aristotelian texts—however various the sources of the ideas that fertilized that criticism. The father of modern science, in fact, turns out to be none other than the master of them that know.

With Zabarella the Padua school had reached its culmination and done its work. His single successor, however, Cesare Cremonini (d. 1631), went still further in an appeal to experience. His *Tractatus de paedia* (1596) sounds like the warning of the great tradition of rational empiricism of the Aristotelians to the triumphant mathematicians.

Paedia [he says] is the faculty of judging rightly about the manner of teaching and learning, taking its rise from logic, with the opportune intervention of experience . . . It is its intrinsic function to understand, dispose, and constitute all teaching. As Paedia is the mother and nurse, so method is the daughter and child. I add, "with the intervention of experience," because, although one may be instructed by genius or logic, unless he be experienced in that about which he is to judge, he will not be able to form judgment. I say "opportune," or appropriate, because the same manner of experience is not found everywhere; but in mathematics for the confirming of principles it is sufficient to have observation with the help of induction of the materials whence mathematics is drawn; there the truth of principles is at once clear. But in natural science such observation is not so obvious for the gaining of principles, nor is the collection of principles by it so easy; there is indeed required a laborious attention with zealous application to comparison with things, through which the principles are received not without sharp thought. Moreover, this experience is necessary not only for natural science, for the acquiring of first principles: but it is requisite for almost all science: in morals in the same way, and even in divinity also, there is required a similar experience, since we do not ascend to those abstract causes without a manifold and laborious attention to the effects.[20]

[20] *Tractatus de Paedia*, ii.

And so he counseled ever closer attention to the way of discovery, to the method of resolution, within which he included as phases both induction and demonstration.

VIII

But one element was lacking in Zabarella's formulation of method: he did not insist that the principles of natural science be mathematical, and indeed drew his illustrations from Aristotle's biological subject-matter. Though he had studied mathematics under Catena and Barocius, and was accounted expert in optics and in astronomy, these subjects failed to leave any fundamental impress on his thought. The gradual emergence of mathematics into the dominant position it held in the seventeenth century is due to its cultivation by a small group of men working on the periphery of the main intellectual movements of the sixteenth century. Several practical considerations of technology combined to give support to their interest in a mathematical treatment of natural problems. The extended navigation of the preceding century had called for more exact tables of the stars; the measurement and calculation involved turned men to the mathematical astronomy of Ptolemy and finally drove out the Aristotelian non-quantitative teaching on the heavens. Astronomy became definitely a branch of mathematics. Secondly, the great artist-engineers, like Dürer and Leonardo, were driven to an eager search for whatever mathematical help they could find in perspective and construction. And the new problems of fortification and of artillery led to the demand for a practical science of mechanics. The theory of ballistics had been slowly built up in the Ockhamite tradition, as cultivated at Padua; when in his *New Science* in 1537 Tartaglia applied mathematical techniques to the study of trajectories, there was an immediate flood of works treating this all-important theme. The Oxford logic of quantity, so vigorously debated in the universities at the close of the fifteenth century, had prepared men to accept the mathematical and mechanical writings of the ancient Alexandrians; under the stimulus provided by Archimedes in particular, men hastened to work upon "practical geometries" and useful "new sciences." The quadrivium, with its arithmetic, geometry, and astronomy, had been long taught in the Arts faculties of the universities; now in the second half of the sixteenth century many of the Italian towns set up public lectures on Euclid in the vernacular for the benefit of the mass of artisans and craftsmen who, it began to appear, could find direct application for the truths formerly reserved for the scholar alone. Indeed, the painters and the architects, as the treatises on those arts reveal, had lost their earlier scientific interests; and it was left for the technicians to sustain an interest in mathematics, which in turning to practical problems naturally found itself more and more involved in questions hitherto treated in "natural philosophy." It was therefore most appropriate that Galileo should begin his *Two New Sciences* in the Arsenal of Venice.

There is a conventional view that this shift to mathematical interests was powerfully furthered by the Renaissance revival of Platonism and its number mysticism derived from Proclus, from the Pythagorean tradition, and from the Cabbala. In the Germanies this has some basis in fact, and Kepler may stand as its consummation. But it is difficult to find any support for the view that attributes the great achievements of the Italians in mathematics and mechanics to the influence of Neoplatonism. On the one hand the Italian Platonists had almost no scientific interest in mathematics, and their numbers led them at once to the mazes of theology and theosophy. And on the other, with rare exceptions the Italian mathematicians down through Galileo, when they possessed a philosophical interest at all, were not Platonists but Aristotelians in their view of mathematics, of its relation to physics, and of the proper method of natural knowledge. What they found in the ancients and what they worked upon themselves was no mathematical vision of the world, but rather effective techniques and practical problems of procedure and discovery. What they constructed as "new sciences" it remained for Descartes to interpret in the light of the tradition of Augustinian Platonism.

Indeed, the one contribution the Humanists can fairly claim to have made to the rise of modern science was in sending men to the study of the original ancient sources in mathematics. In re-establishing connection with the mathematics and mechanics of the Alexandrians, the appeal to the ancients introduced Archimedes and Hero, as well as Apollonius, Pappus and Diophantus. The mathematical methods of analysis and synthesis of Archimedes were the one element which neither the fourteenth-century Ockhamites nor the sixteenth-century Paduans possessed. From them the mathematicians took their start.

IX

The medieval quadrivium based its mathematical teaching upon the treatises on arithmetic, geometry, and music of Boethius. It also possessed Euclid and Ptolemy, and in the encyclopedic works of Leonardo Pisano, the *Liber abaci* (1202) and *Practica geometria*, it had a summary of Greek mathematics together with the additions of the Arabs in arithmetic and algebra. No other comprehensive mathematical treatise appeared until the *Summa de arithmetica, geometrica proportione, et proportionalitate* of Luca Pacioli in 1494 (reprinted 1523). But a translation of Euclid into Latin by Campano was printed in 1482 (1486, 1491), followed by one from the complete Greek text by Zamberti in 1505, and another by Pacioli. In his zeal for popularizing the Greeks, Tartaglia published the first Italian translation in 1543, which went into seven editions and lasted even after the better version of Commandino in 1575. Tartaglia also published the first Latin edition of Archimedes in 1543, superseded by that of Commandino in 1558; though Bessarion had had a Greek manuscript, and Regiomontanus brought one to Germany in 1461. Greatest of these editors of the Greeks was Federigo Commandino (1509–1575), who brought out Apollonius, Pappus, Aristarchus, and Hero, besides Euclid and Archimedes. And in 1572 Rafael Bombelli issued his *Algebra,* based on the rigorous Greek algebra of Diophantus, which he rediscovered in the Vatican.

The outstanding mathematician of the sixteenth century was Niccolò Tartaglia (1499–1557). Self-taught and with no formal education, he had to eke out a living in Verona and from 1534 to 1548 in Venice by teaching arithmetic to merchants and furnishing mathematical assistance to practical craftsmen, so that his writings breathe the accents of the Venetian workroom, shop, and arsenal. His first book, the *Nova Scientia* of 1537, was prompted by the questions of an artillerist about the trajectory of projectiles; his second, *Quesiti et inventioni diverse*, in 1546, treats a number of mathematical problems brought to him by all sorts of practical men. It opens with a conversation with the Duke of Urbino over his new science of ballistics, goes on to discuss statics with the Spanish ambassador, drawing on the *Tractatus de Ponderibus* of the thirteenth century Jordanus of Nemore, recently published in 1533, and concludes with the solution of cubic equations, over which he was involved in a tremendous controversy with Cardano. In 1556 he published his encyclopedic *General Trattato di numeri e misure*, which summed up all the discoveries made since Pacioli and set forth his algebraic teaching, in opposition to the *Ars Magna* (1545) of Cardano.

Tartaglia's interest in specific practical problems was carried on in a long line of "practical geometries" dealing with all kinds of measurement. His interest in the principles of machines was continued in the *Liber Mechanicorum* (1577) of Guid'Ubaldo, Galileo's patron, and Luca Valerio, professor at Rome. And his ballistics led the Aristotelians, in commenting upon the *Mechanical Questions* attributed to Aristotle, to carry still further the Ockhamite theory of projectiles: Alessandro Piccolomini in 1547, Scaliger in 1557, and Bernardino Baldi in 1582.

Tartaglia had a technical rather than a philosophical interest; he did not dream of challenging Aristotle except on specific mathematical points, and he followed the prevalent Padua theory of science and mathematics. Mathematics deals with continuous quantity abstracted from natural things.

> Thus the naturalist differs from the mathematician in that he considers things clothed, whereas the mathematician considers them as bare of any visible material . . . The purpose of the geometrical student is always to make things that he can construct in material to the best of his ability, so long as he never makes exact things.[21]

Since mathematics is thus derived from the world of physical objects, there is no question of its application; practical mathematics merely selects from experience those principles it needs, without bothering to abstract all those required for the pure mathematical disciplines of arithmetic and geometry.

This Aristotelian conception of mathematics is found in all these men. Giorgio Valla holds that "first principles are known through the intellect by means of sense"; [22] Girolamo Cataneo writes:

> The natural philosopher considers all things in the way in which they possess being or existence, in their own perceptible matter; but the geometrician . . . differentiates things which he considers by his intellect

---

[21] *Euclide Megarense*, First Lesson, sec. 5.   [22] *De geometria* (1501).

from perceptible material, from movement, and from any alteration; where the existence of quantity is indeed in natural bodies, nevertheless he considers it with his intellect without material, without perceptible accidents . . . And although the definitions and principles of geometry are intelligibles, and abstracted from the senses, nevertheless they still fit in with geometry, perspective, mechanics, and natural philosophy.[23]

And even Cardano, much under the influence of the mathematical vision of Cusanus, and giving free reign to a speculative and Neoplatonic philosophy of nature, regards mathematics in good Aristotelian fashion. By the analysis or resolution of natural bodies as we experience them, we can arrive at mathematical principles of great power for demonstrating them. The spirit of this whole mathematical movement is well expressed in Tartaglia's defense of his new science to Cardano:

Although the speaking of artillery and of the firing of it is not a thing very honorable in itself, yet, since it is a new matter and not barren of speculation, I thought well to say a little on it, and in connexion with that subject I am at present bringing out two sorts of instruments belonging to the art, a square to regulate the discharging of the said artillery, and also to level and to examine every elevation.[24]

X

The major motive, therefore, for insisting that natural problems be studied by mathematics was the practical utility and fruitfulness of mathematical analysis. Two men in the sixteenth century attempt a more philosophical explanation of the power of mathematics: they attribute it to its certainty. Leonardo da Vinci (1452–1519),[25] eager seeker after all that might penetrate nature's secrets, and the chief nonacademic reviver in Italy of the Ockhamite dynamics, was naturally attracted by the fertile and suggestive mind of Cusanus. Of the cardinal's many metaphysical speculations, however, it was the vision of mathematics that struck deepest. Leonardo became one of the earliest enthusiasts for the Greek mathematicians. Both in his teaching at Milan and in the manuscripts and notebooks circulated

---

[23] Dell' arte del misuare (1584), p. 4.　　　[24] Quesiti, p. 119.
[25] The material in Section X on Leonardo as working in the mathematical tradition was presented in expanded form and in another context in an article in the Journal of the History of Ideas, XIV (1953), "The Place of Leonardo da Vinci in the Emergence of Modern Science," pp. 191–202. It is reprinted, with the Italian texts, in J. H. Randall, Jr., The School of Padua and the Emergence of Modern Science (Padua, 1961), pp. 117–38.

after his death in 1519 he never tired of insisting that the only salvation from the magic and fantastic learning of the Quattrocento lay in seeking for certainty in science, and that to be certain all scientific method must be mathematical.

The truth, even if it treats of a little and inferior thing, surpasses uncertain opinions about the most sublime and lofty problems.[26]

Better a little certainty than a big lie.

There is no certitude where some one of the mathematical sciences can not be applied. (p. 86)

The man who blames the supreme certainty of mathematics feeds on confusion, and can never silence the contradictions of sophistical sciences which lead to eternal quackery. (p. 85)

No investigation can claim to be a true science if it does not proceed by mathematical demonstrations. (p. 83)

For every power of nature gives rise to effects of a definite kind, unfolding themselves in a definite order.

Necessity is the mistress and protectress of nature, necessity is the theme of nature and her discoverer, her eternal bond and rule. (p. 112)

For "nature is constrained by the reason of her law which lives infused in her." (p. 113) The essence of the powers of nature may lie beyond human investigation; but man can learn the invariable mathematical rule of their operation.

The definition of the quiddity of the elements is not in the power of man, but many of their effects are known. (p. 97)

Yet this does not mean for Leonardo any break with the Aristotelian conception of the relation between reason and experience, or with the method which the Paduans called the "regress." Experience completes itself in mathematics, because while experience is "known to us," it is mathematical principles that are "known to nature." And mathematics culminates in experience: "mechanics are the paradise of mathematical science, because here we come to the fruits of mathematics." (p. 86) Experience is the way by which nature reveals to us her mathematical constitution.

---

[26] *Frammenti letterari e filosofici di Leonardo da Vinci*, ed. and selected by Edmondo Solmi (Florence, 1900), p. 76. All citations are from this collection.

It is the interpreter between creative nature and the human race, the way in which Nature manifests her activities to us mortals; it shows us also that this operation, bound by necessity, can not take place otherwise than Reason her helmsman prescribes. (p. 86)

In a single experiment we can discover the mathematical order or "ragione" involved, and calculate therefrom many other effects which experience will then confirm. Experience is selective, for "Nature is full of infinite reasons which were never in experience." (p. 112)

The senses are earthly, reason stands outside them when it contemplates. (p. 93)

And this leads Leonardo to insist that there are mathematical relations everywhere.

Proportions are found not only in numbers and measures, but also in sounds, weights, times, places, and in every force. (p. 86)

And hence Leonardo is fascinated by the idea of the mechanical devices of nature, especially in living forms. Mechanics is the noblest and most useful of all sciences,

seeing that by means of this all animated bodies that have movement perform all their actions; and these movements are based on the center of gravity which is placed in the middle dividing unequal weights, and it has dearth and wealth of muscles and also lever and counter-lever. (p. 165)

The bird is a machine working through mathematical laws. Here speaks the painter and anatomist of the marvelous sketches and studies.

XI

At the very beginning of the sixteenth century Leonardo was thus suggesting the philosophy of science and scientific method destined to so glorious a career; at the end, Giambattista Benedetti, having advanced much further in the sure knowledge of the principles of dynamics, can write:

The name philosopher is more applicable to the mathematician than to any one else, for none of the others is so absolutely certain of what he affirms as the mathematician is . . . For the mathematician does not yield to sense, or presuppose anything which is not so true and so well known to the intellect that no power whatever can show it to be false.[27]

True and certain science is demonstration from mathematical principles; but those principles, and mathematical magnitude itself, are abstractions selected by the intellect from the sensible things of experience perceived in the imagination. Mathematics is demonstrative, but it is founded on selected properties of the world of physical objects.

With this mathematical emphasis added to the logical methodology of Zabarella, there stands completed the "new method" for which men had been so long seeking. By the mathematical analysis of a few simple instances we find the principle involved in them. From that principle we deduce further consequences, which we find illustrated and confirmed in experience. Science is a body of mathematical demonstrations, whose axioms are arrived at by the examination of instances in experience. This is the method called by Euclid and Archimedes a combination of "analysis" and "synthesis," and by the Paduans and Galileo, "resolution" and "composition." It is traditional and Aristotelian in regarding the structure of science as dialectical and deductive, and in seeing all verification and demonstration as inclusion within a logical system of ideas. But it has altered the scheme of the medieval Aristotelians in making both principles and demonstration mathematical in character, rather than syllogisms of logical genera; and to the scholastic empiricism it has added the insistence that the way of discovery is not mere observation and generalization, not mere abstraction from common experience, but a careful and precise mathematical analysis of a scientific experience—what the medical tradition of Padua called resolution, and what Archimedes called analysis. And to that experience demonstration must return, in a "regress," for confirmation, illustration, and the guarantee of the existence of deduced consequences. But the return to experience is not for proof: for throughout the seventeenth century no mere fact ever proved any truth.

[27] *Diversarum speculationum mathematicarum et physicarum libri* (1575), p. 298.

I 2

The New Cosmology: Copernicus, Kepler, and Bruno

I

WITH their practical and human aim for knowledge and their reconstructed method of mathematical analysis and demonstration, the scientists could now go forward in their eager exploration of nature's secrets; and go forward they did with such success that within a century they had revolutionized men's conception of the universe in which they live. This revolution in cosmology involved two fundamental changes, the one associated with the name of Copernicus, the other with that of Galileo. Copernicus and Galileo themselves were above all scientists, interested in the specific problems they were investigating; it remained for Kepler and Bruno to express the philosophical significance of what Copernicus had done, and for Descartes and still more Spinoza to carry out Galileo's suggested picture of the world in radical and thoroughgoing fashion. These philosophical cosmologists made a new religion out of the science they so deeply felt.

The first or Copernican revolution was primarily an affair of astronomy; its alteration was in the status of the earth and human life in the universe. It powerfully reinforced the faith in the mathematical simplicity of the solar system; though in Kepler the facts of Brahe's observations finally conquered the belief in too crude a simplicity. It was driven home by the telescopic observations of that pugnacious old fighter, Galileo; for not mathematics, but only the observations of sense, could convince the Aristotelian empiricists. Though mathematics was enough for Galileo himself, to conquer Aristotle it was necessary to look through the telescope, and actually see the mountains on the moon, the "blemishes" on the sun, and the satellites of Jupiter. What the heliocentric theory meant was not merely the position of the earth, but the more fundamental conception of the uniformity of nature. No longer was the world the medieval Aristotelian-Platonic hierarchy of perfections: it had come to be all of one piece, just as the ordered structure of feudalism had given way to the absolutism of the Renaissance, in which all subjects stood on the same level.

During the Middle Ages the earth had been indeed the center of the universe, but in that position it had held the lowest rank: whereas the heavens were perfect and unchanging, the sublunar sphere was manifestly variable and imperfect, and furthest from God in the empyrean. Now Copernicus had placed the terrestrial globe itself "in the heavens," and hence had elevated it to the perfection and divinity of those regions. We are accustomed to think of Copernicus as lowering the dignity of the earth and of man by removing them from the central position in the universe, as reducing man to a tiny speck on a third-rate planet revolving about a tenth-rate sun drifting in an endless cosmic ocean of nothingness. Far from it! Such an emotional reaction is the product of Romantic Weltschmerz and the fin-de-siècle wailings of the last generation; it has no counterpart in the seventeenth century. Then men thought the earth had been raised immeasurably in value, made equal to those noble stars, the planets, and rendered the proper sphere of science. As Galileo put it,

As to the earth, we seek to make it more noble and perfect, since we succeed in making it like the heavenly bodies, and in a certain fashion place it almost in Heaven, whence your philosophers have banished it.[1]

This was the real religious issue involved in the Copernican revolution, so soon as Galileo made it clear that it was no mere shift of mathematical hypotheses. The earth, and man, and the practical science of his environment and daily living, are as important as the contemplation of heavenly things, as theology. That is at bottom why the Reformers, convinced of human depravity, Luther and Melanchthon and Calvin, all rejected Copernicus instinctively. And that is why Kant was continuing a genuine Copernican revolution in increasing the importance of man in the structure of science itself. The whole impact, in fact, of the Copernican revolution was hu-

[1] Galileo, *Two Systems*, Dialogue I.

manistic, and pointed to a new glory of man in this world. Even Spinoza, who passes as the supreme critic of anthropomorphism, in calmly asserting, "The human mind has an adequate knowledge of the infinite and eternal essence of God or Nature," was led to express a supreme anthropocentrism. When the scientist claims that the science that builds our machines and drives our factories is final truth—as scientists did in the seventeenth century—he is elevating a human technique of control into ultimate cosmic truth; and no truly religious thinker has ever dared to attribute such cosmic importance to man's petty interests.

The Galilean or Cartesian revolution transformed not only astronomy but physics as well; it affected not only the status of man, but the fundamental character of the world in which he lives. It meant not merely the uniformity of nature, but the reign of immutable mechanical law. Descartes was the first to generalize this new science into a total cosmology, to claim that what it dealt with is alone real. He set forth the idea of an exclusively mechanistic world: Give me matter and motion, he boasted, and I will construct the universe. His cosmology was negative and intolerant, but purifying in its thoroughgoing zeal. Gone was the Neoplatonic hierarchy of forms; gone were all natural teleology, all final causes, all functional structure, all forms and species. Gone were "spirits" and action at a distance. In changing natural explanation from the "souls" of the Renaissance to the "force" of the seventeenth century, men gained a corporeal and mechanical conception of nature in place of a "spiritual" one. All causation is efficient, or mechanical; all is capable of geometrical formulation. As Kepler put it, the world is no longer to be seen as a living organism, it has become a clockwork. This Cartesian revolution left a single purpose in the universe, the will of God, whose decrees must be learned by patient investigation. For the first time the notion of a Creator God makes its appearance as an integral scientific conception. For the Schoolmen, the idea of a Creator, so alien to Aristotle, belonged not to science or physics, but to faith, to theology. Now it became a first principle of a physics all of whose principles had become efficient causes. And one alien substance was left in the universe, the human mind. That substantial mind remained till the eighteenth-century criticism of Hume and Kant removed it from philosophy, and the nineteenth-century Darwin removed it from science.

II

The man who finally managed to win acceptance for the rotation and revolution of the earth, so long discussed since the fourteenth century, Nicolaus Copernicus (1473–1543), was in the thick of the mathematical revival. At Cracow he had read the astronomical writings of the Nuremberg astronomers, Peurbach and Regiomontanus, who had given an exact mathematical elaboration to the Ptolemaic theory in the light of the new tables of observations; he then studied four years at Bologna and another three at Padua (1501–1503), not only mathematics and natural philosophy, but also law and medicine and the new humanistic learning. His heliocentric theory had taken form shortly after his return to Frauenburg; but he preferred to develop it for a small circle of friendly scholars: among them he circulated a *De hypothesibus motuum coelestium commentariolus*, written about 1530. A few papers on money and a Trigonometry published by his pupil Rheticus in 1542 appeared in his lifetime. Finally in his last year, 1543, he consented to publish his *De revolutionibus orbium coelestium*.

Though a man of the widest culture and learning, Copernicus approached his problem primarily as a mathematician and scientist, with little broader philosophical interest. It is true that he read widely, in Cusanus, in Ficino, and in the Pythagorean Greek astronomers; but their metaphysical background seems to have meant little to him. It is also true that his teacher and friend at Bologna, Dominicus Maria de Novara, not only criticized Ptolemy on observational grounds, but was attracted by the Florentine Neoplatonists and, calling himself a Pythagorean, preached a faith in the mathematical harmony of the world. Copernicus powerfully shared this faith in the mathematical simplicity of nature; and there are traces in his writing of that sun-worship which Kepler expressed.

For who could give the sun another and better place in this splendid temple of the universe than the center, whence it can illuminate the whole in its totality? Not without reason have some called it the candle of the world, others the mind, and others the director, Trimegistus the visible god, and the Electra of Sophocles the viewer of all. From its royal throne it rules the swarm of stars, as they circle about it, so that there is manifest to us in this order a wonderful symmetry of the world and a strong and harmonious connexion between the movement and size of the single heavenly spheres, such as is found nowhere else.[2]

But despite these evidences of aesthetic and perhaps religious feeling, Copernicus makes it clear that it is as a "practical mathematician" that he is proposing his theory, not as the proponent of a new cosmic philosophy.

When I noted these things, I often considered if perchance a more rational system of circles might be discovered, on which all the apparent diversity (of velocity) might depend, as the principle of absolute motion requires. Attacking a problem obviously difficult, and almost inexplicable, at length I hit upon a solution whereby this could be reached by fewer and much more convenient constructions than had been handed down of old, if certain assumptions, which are called axioms, be granted me. . . . Accorded then these premises, I shall attempt to show briefly how simply the uniformity of motion can be saved.[3]

And in his dedicatory letter to Pope Paul III, Copernicus explains the kind of problem he conceived himself to be working upon.

When therefore I had long considered this uncertainty of traditional mathematics, it began to weary me that no more definite explanation of the movement of the world-machine, established in our behalf by the best and most systematic builder of all, existed among the philosophers who had studied so exactly in other respects the minutest details in regard to the sphere. Wherefore I made every effort to read anew the books of all the philosophers I could obtain, in order to ascertain if there were not some one of them of the opinion that other motions of the heavenly bodies existed than are assumed by those who teach mathematical sciences in the schools. So I found first in Cicero that Hiketas of Syracuse believed the earth moved. Afterwards I found also in Plutarch that others were likewise of this opinion. . . . Starting thence I began to reflect on the mobility of the earth . . . and although the opinion seemed absurd, yet because I knew that liberty had been accorded to others before me of imagining whatsoever circles they pleased to explain the phenomena of the stars, I thought I also might readily be allowed to experiment whether, by supposing the earth to have some motion, stronger demonstrations than those of the others could be found as to the revolution of the celestial sphere. And thus, assuming the motions

[2] *De revolutionibus orbium coelestium,* Book I, ch. 10.
[3] *Commentariolus* (1878), Fol. 1a, 1b, 2a; in *Three Copernican Treatises,* tr. Edward Rosen (1939), pp. 57ff.

which in the following work I attribute to the earth, after long and careful investigation I have finally found that when the motions of the other planets are referred to the revolution of the earth and calculated for the revolution of that planet, not only the phenomena of the others followed from this, but the order and magnitude of the stars and all their orbs and the heaven itself are so connected that in no part can anything be transposed without confusion to the rest and to the whole universe.[4]

This does not mean that Copernicus himself agreed with the position cautiously taken by his editor, Osiander, that he was offering a mere mathematical hypothesis for calculation: he makes it clear that he believes he has discovered the actual constitution of the universe. Mathematical analysis, assumption, and demonstration could be trusted to reveal that constitution, despite all the evidence of the senses and common observation to the contrary. Such observation must be corrected by sounder reasoning; mathematical experience must take the place of the vulgar.

The stations of the planets, their retrogressions and progressions, seem to be motions, not of those planets, but of the earth. And the sun is thought to possess the center of the universe; all of which things we are taught by the order of succession in which those phenomena follow each other, and by the harmony of the whole world, if we will only, as they say, look at the matter with both eyes.[5]

Hence Copernicus insists that he is not addressing himself to those ignorant of mathematics:

Mathematics is written for mathematicians, to whom these my labors, if I am not mistaken, will appear to contribute something.[6]

And he took as his motto the Platonic "Let no one ignorant of geometry enter here." For the geometrician alone would understand the cogency of the reasoning, the mathematical superiority and "greater rationality" of a system which nevertheless demanded an incredible increase in the distance of the vault of the fixed stars to account for the absence of observed parallaxes, and suggested other mechanical difficulties that seemed almost insuperable.

What Copernicus meant by a "rational system," that is, what a mathematical hypothesis should aim at, he makes clear rather by his practice than by his precepts.

[4] *De revolutionibus*, Letter to Paul III.   [5] *De revolutionibus*, I, 9.
[6] Letter to Paul III.

We find then in this arrangement an admirable harmony of the world, and a dependable, harmonious interconnexion of the motion and the size of the paths, such as otherwise cannot be discovered. For here the penetrating observer can note why the forward and the retrograde motion of Jupiter appear greater than that of Saturn, and smaller than that of Mars, and again greater with Venus than with Mercury; and why such retrogression appears oftener with Saturn than with Jupiter, less often with Mars and Venus than with Mercury. Moreover, why Saturn, Jupiter, and Mars, when they rise in the evening, appear greater than when they disappear and reappear. . . . And all this results from the same cause, namely the motion of the earth.[7]

To find one cause for a multitude of phenomena, to relate mathematically what had before seemed distinct: this is what Copernicus means by "simplicity." The wisdom of nature, he says, attains her end elsewhere by the simplest ways, without circumlocutions, and by means of a harmonious interaction between all the elements involved. She seeks to bind many effects to one single cause, rather than to increase the number of causes. It must be so also with the stars: their motion must in reality be uniform.

This pioneer search for such simplicity of course led Copernicus astray. He still held that the universe was a finite sphere, with the fixed stars on its surface; though he greatly increased its diameter to fit the non-observation of parallaxes. He retained the notion that the orbits of the planets are circular, or composed of circular epicycles; though in a passage not printed he considers the possibility of their being elliptical. His reason was the good medieval Platonic one that any departure from uniform circular motion

must arise either from irregularity in the moving power, whether this be within the body or foreign to it, or from some inequality of the body in revolution . . . Both of which things the intellect shrinks from with horror, it being unworthy to hold such a view about bodies constituted in the most perfect order.[8]

He was therefore able only to reduce the seventy-nine Ptolemaic circles to thirty-four. And he still retained the Aristotelian notion that the stars were embedded in crystalline spheres—a view shaken by Tycho Brahe's observation of the new star in Cassiopeia in 1572, and by Kepler's powerful arguments on the occasion of a similar observation in 1604. But most important of all, his idea of the rela-

[7] *De revolutionibus*, I, 10.   [8] *Ibid*.

tivity of motion shattered the Aristotelian confidence in ordinary experience, and gave a powerful impetus to the conviction that only an experience analyzed and corrected by mathematical demonstration could be trusted.

III

The ideas bound up with Copernicus' theory and method received their first philosophic interpretation at the hands of two men thoroughly imbued with the naturalistic Neoplatonism of the Renaissance, Johannes Kepler and Giordano Bruno. Bruno was emotionally inspired by the relativity of motion and the new position of the earth; but he remained the typical though perhaps the most suggestive nature philosopher, with no sense of a fixed mechanical order. Kepler began with very much the same anthropomorphic conceptions; but at the most impressionable stage of his career he underwent a careful apprenticeship to the most careful astronomical observer since Hipparchus, Tycho Brahe. This rigorous discipline, combined with an exact mathematical training, made him a philosophic scientist rather than a metaphysician and the founder of a new humanistic religion. In Kepler there is abundant Platonism; but it is a Platonism disciplined by genuine mathematics and brought sharply face to face with facts. Kepler, indeed, is almost the sole example in that whole period of a Neoplatonic natural philosopher who managed to advance to a genuinely scientific point of view. In consequence, though his thought is set within the Platonic framework, at its core there was built up a natural science of observation, hypothesis, and mathematical demonstration. He not only made the many fertile scientific discoveries for which he is best known; he also worked out the first philosophic analysis of modern science, of its concepts and methods and implications, just as Bruno elaborated the first philosophic interpretation of the human significance of that science. That both Descartes and Newton pored over Kepler's writings was of great importance; for his analysis of scientific concepts had introduced a Platonic cast destined to be of lasting influence.

Kepler (1571–1630) studied at Tübingen under the mathematician Mästlin, an admirer of the harmony and order of the Copernican "hypothesis." In 1593 he defended the new astronomy in a dissertation. What he might have remained without Brahe is clear from his first work, *Mysterium cosmographicum* (1596), written while he was professor of mathematics at Graz. In 1600 he joined Brahe as assistant in the preparation of the Rudolphine Tables at Prague; when the latter died the next year, he continued the work as court mathematician and astrologer.

The *Mysterium cosmographicum* is a wholly Neoplatonic speculation, filled with a lyric worship of the simplicity and harmonious unity of the universe. The world is spherical in shape, as suits its divine perfection. In its center stands the sun, the image of God, whence stream all light, warmth, and life. The eternal and uncreated constitution of the world is the expression of the divine essence. The central sun is the Father, the surrounding sphere of stars the Son, and the geometrical relations between them and the orbits of the planets, with their reciprocal and pervasive harmony, form the Holy Spirit. Kepler's great discovery, the cosmic mystery unveiled, was that the five regular polyhedrons might be inscribed in succession in the spheres of the five planets, and that the dimensions of the universe thus depended on a basic geometrical harmony. The planets are moved either by separate intelligences, or by a moving *anima mundi*, a *facultas animalis*, exerted from the sun. Kepler's attitude at this time is revealed in a letter:

The intense pleasure I have received from this discovery can never be told in words. I regretted no more the time wasted; I tired of no labor; I shunned no toil of reckoning, days and nights spent in calculation, until I could see whether my hypothesis would agree with the orbits of Copernicus or whether my joy was to vanish into air.[9]

Even here the desire to verify his hypothesis in a mathematical structure actually to be found in the planets is apparent. Brahe stamped this necessity indelibly upon his mind. Tycho Brahe had gathered as accurate observations of the stars as was possible without a telescope; for twenty years he had constructed instruments and pursued the heavens in his castle of Uranienborg on an island near Copenhagen; the Kaiser provided him with an observatory and a staff in Prague in 1597. Kepler inherited all the Dane's data and tables, and in his inordinate desire to find new mathematical harmonies in the universe went to work upon them; in 1609 appeared

[9] Sir Oliver Lodge, *Pioneers of Science* (1928), ch. iii.

the result in *Astronomia nova, seu physica coelestis.* He had been working upon the orbit of Mars. One combination of circles had almost coincided with Brahe's observations, leaving an error of but 8'. But such was his respect for fact that he explains:

> Since the divine goodness has given to us in Tycho Brahe a most careful observer, from whose observations the error of 8' is shown in this calculation, . . . it is right that we should with gratitude recognize and make use of this gift of God . . . For if I could have treated 8' of longitude as negligible I should have already corrected sufficiently the hypothesis . . . But as they could not be neglected, these 8' alone have led the way toward the complete reformation of astronomy, and have been made the subject-matter of a great part of this work.[10]

A fact had conquered the too eager Platonic craving for simplicity.

Kepler now began with other figures than circles, trying at first to fit the data into an egg-shaped orbit. When he hit upon the simplest of all ovals, the ellipse, his success confirmed his faith in "the simplicity and ordered regularity of nature." He next tackled the problem that had vexed Copernicus as well, the varying speed of the planets in their orbits. To his immense joy, he found that though the rate varies, equal areas of the ellipse are swept out by the planet vector in equal times—and thus the uniformity of motion was saved. He was convinced that these two laws obtained for all the planets, since the harmony of nature demanded that all "have similar habits." This combination of faith in mathematical harmony and respect for experienced fact remains the key to all of Kepler's thought. The early "cosmographic mystery" had given way to a "celestial physics," but it still remained a "harmony of the world." All his other scientific achievements—his pursuit of continuity in mathematics, his work with infinitesimals and integration in his *Stereometria dolorum,* 1615, his *Optics,* 1604, and his *Dioptrics,* 1611, suggested by Brahe's work on refraction, which remained the standard treatise till Newton—sprang from the same double urge.

His basic conception of mathematical harmony Kepler examines most carefully in the work which also announced, incidentally, the third law of planetary motion, his *Harmonices mundi* (1619). Though he gives it a foundation in a Platonic theory of knowledge, he makes it clear that harmony is a matter, not of the substance of

[10] *Commentary on the Motions of Mars,* Part II, cap. 19.

the world being numbers or lines, but of the relations within the universe possessing a mathematical correspondence—a conception that leads beyond the mere traditional number mysticism to the demand for exact formulation. It is not that created things participate in the divine numbers: it is that they are related in a mathematical order. Harmony is not classification into numbered kinds, it is an exact quantitative relation. To be sure, Kepler still believes with the tradition that those relations must be grounded in the divine mind.

It is easy to understand that the nature of harmony is not to be defined through sensible things alone, as through a sound, or the ray of a star. For sound is one thing, and a certain order between different sounds is another . . . Further, because musical harmony is not sound, but an order of sounds, it follows that it falls under the category of relation. For the order of which we speak here is a relation, and things ordered are related to each other . . . But a relation without mind is nothing but the things related, for things are not said to be related unless some mind is supposed which relates the one to the other.[11]

Kepler follows Proclus in defending the reality of such ideas of relation against Aristotle's general criticism of the theory of ideas.

Of quantities . . . in so far as they are figures and in the fourth species of quality (where their material factor, quantity, and their formal factor, figure, are distinct) these criticisms very rarely make mention, and in so far as they are relations, plainly never. Aristotle never even dreams of the lengths of lines, which form proportion (that is, qualitative and figured relation).[12]

This fundamental concept of mathematical relation is, to be sure, embedded in the traditional Platonic view of knowledge.

What proportion may be without the action of mind can in no wise be understood.[13]

But this does not mean that order or relation is dependent on the human mind:

Someone may object here that the soul in comparing does not make but discovers an appropriate proportion . . . therefore the essence of harmony seems possible without any mind present. I answer, to discover an

[11] *Harmonices mundi*, Lib. IV, cap. 1, in *Opera omnia*, ed. Chr. Frisch, 8 vols. (1858–71), V, 214.
[12] *Ibid.*, V, 218.   [13] Book I; ed. Frisch, V, 81.

appropriate proportion in sensible things is to disclose and recognize and bring to light the similarity of that proportion in sensible things to some sure archetype of truest harmony which is within the soul . . . Thus the soul discovers order and proportion in sounds and in rays . . . But it is the soul itself that makes this proportion a harmony by comparing it with its archetype.[14]

In his *Optics* Kepler sought to develop this Platonic and Augustinian theory of perception to account for the mixture of sense and geometry in vision. The colors and forms of things are known by the reception of species from the object; but their relations and distance are an inference of the mind.

All location of the image is the work of the mind, or rather of the common sense.

For the eye does not see distance, but projects (*conjicit*) it, as the opticians say.[15]

It was this geometrical conception that aroused Berkeley's ire. Indeed, Kepler even played with the theory of reminiscence.

For Kepler, therefore, the geometrical constitution of the world is no mere useful discovery; it is a fundamental presupposition of all science. In 1596 he had written:

Although they flee to the inscrutable powers of the creative Wisdom, let them preserve this moderation in their flight . . . let them suffer us to render probable causes from quantities.[16]

In the second edition in 1621 he added the note:

See how firmly persuaded I was even then of the principle I have held for twenty-five years: that the causes of natural things are constituted by mathematics, (the dogma Aristotle rails at in so many places), because God the creator had mathematics as the archetype with him from eternity in most simple and divine abstraction from quantities materially considered.[17]

Perfect and certain knowledge is therefore always mathematical.

There are in fact not a few principles which are the special property of mathematics, such principles as are discovered by the light of nature, require no demonstration, and concern quantities primarily; then they

[14] *Harmonices mundi*, Lib. IV, cap. 1; *Opera*, V, 216ff.
[15] *Opera*, II, 55, 491.
[16] *Mysterium cosmographicum*, cap. 11; *Opera*, I, 135.
[17] *Opera*, I, 136.

are applied to other things, so far as the latter have something in common with quantities. Now there are more of these principles in mathematics than in the other theoretical sciences because of that very characteristic of the human understanding, which seems to be such from the law of creation, that nothing can be known completely except quantities or by quantities. And so it happens that the conclusions of mathematics are most certain and indubitable. (VIII, 148)

Just as the eye was made to see colors, and the ear to hear sounds, so the human mind was made to understand, not whatever you please, but quantity. (I, 31)

For the knowledge of quantities, innate in the soul, determines of what kind the eye must be: the structure of the eye follows the nature of the intellect, not vice versa. (V, 221)

It is this conviction about the mathematical character of the world and the necessarily mathematical character of human knowledge that makes Kepler break with the medieval tradition, stemming from Ptolemy, that astronomical hypotheses are merely convenient constructions for calculation. He first revealed Osiander's authorship of the preface to Copernicus' work; he insisted that astronomical hypotheses must be "real" and physical. The astronomer is no mere calculator: he belongs to the "community of natural philosophers."

First we must imitate the nature of things in our hypotheses, then on this foundation we erect a calculation, in which by deductive proof we construct the motions which follow from the assumed presuppositions. (I, 242)

Kepler was clearly aware of his break with Aristotle in this mathematical conviction. Quantity is the primary accident of substance, prior to the other categories. Aristotle explained nature in terms of qualitative and irreducible distinctions, and therefore left mathematics in an intermediate position; but Kepler had himself found quantitative proportions in all things, and therefore could elevate mathematics to the highest place.

Wherever there are qualities, there are likewise quantities, but not always vice versa. (VIII, 147)

The differences of things for Aristotle reside in their qualitative forms; but Kepler takes seriously matter as a principle of individuation:

To me differentiation in created things seems to come nowhere else than from matter or on the occasion of matter. But where there is matter, there is geometry. (I, 423)

Kepler is also very clear about what distinguishes him from the Pythagoreans. The latter saw mysterious numbers everywhere; for him the world is made, not of numbers, but of things embedded in a structure of geometrical relations.

All the nobility of numbers, especially admired by the Pythagorean theology and compared to divine things, comes originally from geometry . . . For the angles of a figure are not numerable because the concept of that number has preceded them, but the concept of the number follows because geometrical things have that multiplicity in themselves, existing themselves as a numbered number (*numerus numeratus*). (I, 134)

Geometrical relations exist in things; numbers are mere human concepts, which Kepler treats as a terminist:

About numbers I should not contend that Aristotle did not rightly refute the Pythagoreans; for they are only second intentions, nay, third and fourth.[18]

And Kepler is even more vigorous in setting himself off from the allegories and myths of his contemporary magicians and nature enthusiasts. They deal in mere analogies and symbols; for them there is no careful determination of fact, no precise mathematical analysis.

I too play with symbols [he wrote in a letter of 1608], and I have sketched a work that bears the title of *Geometrical Cabbala*, and is to treat of the ideas of things, so far as they are to be found in geometry. But I so play, that I never forget that it is mere play. For nothing is proven by symbols; no secret in natural philosophy is brought to light by geometrical symbols. They furnish only what was already known before, unless by certain evidence it is made clear that they are not only symbolic, but are the description of the modes and causes of the connection of both things.[19]

This disdain for fantastic learning is well expressed in his controversy with Robert Fludd, the English follower of Paracelsus, who had insisted that nature should be grasped in mystic immediacy, not through the abstractions of thought.

The commonplaces of the mathematicians [said Fludd] are concerned with quantitative shadows; the chymists and Hermeticists embrace the true marrow of natural bodies. (V, 18)

[18] *Harmonices mundi*, *Opera*, V, 221.   [19] *Opera*, I, 378.

Against this view Kepler vigorously defended the true aim of science as the expression of the real relations of things in abstract mathematical form. To seize the essences of things except by means of their relations and properties is quite impossible; without mathematics even the eye of the mystic is blind.

I seize, as you say, reality by the tail, but I hold it in my hand. You may continue to clutch at its head, if only you don't do it merely in dreams. I am satisfied with the effects, that is, with the motions of the planets. But if you can find in their causes themselves such transparent harmonious relations as I have found in their orbits, I wish you luck in this discovery and myself in its understanding, so soon as I am able to understand it. (V, 457–60)

And of Fludd he wrote:

He greatly delights in the dark riddles of things, while I try to bring into the light of the intellect things themselves involved in obscurity. The former is the familiar of chymists, Hermeticists, and Paracelsists; the latter is the possession of mathematicians. (V, 332)

It is obviously only by a great stretching of the term that Kepler himself is to be called a Pythagorean.

In the light of this clear perception of the aim of his science, Kepler was able to give lucid expression to the method of the new mathematical physics.

What occurs in all cognition, that beginning with those things which come to us through the senses we proceed by an activity of mind to higher things to be comprehended by no acuteness of sense, this same process takes place also in the affairs of astronomy. There we first note with the eyes the various positions of the planets at different times; following on these observations, reasoning leads the mind to the knowledge of the form of the world; the delineation of this form of the world thus concluded from observations later receives the name of Astronomical Hypothesis. (I, 242)

The fullest account of Kepler's views on scientific method is to be found in his *Epitome of Copernican astronomy* (1618).

The five principal parts of the astronomical function are Historical, concerned with observations; Optical, concerned with hypotheses; Physical, with the causes of hypotheses; Arithmetical, with tables and calculations; Mechanical, with instruments.[20]

[20] Ed. 1618, p. 2; *Opera*, VI, 136ff.

In the work of observation:

Tycho Brahe before all others had occupied himself with incredible diligence, leaving his own most copious and trustworthy observations of thirty-eight years. Observations of this kind should be artfully compared with each other, and arranged in certain classes, through certain periods of time, so that like may be joined to like. (p. 3)

Aristotle's History of Animals is the model. The optical part, dealing with hypotheses,

endeavors to penetrate to the causes which make species completely contrary to the truth appear before the eyes of men; . . . thus optics saves very many differences of appearances, and by itself effects some "form of movements" that is always the same, or some figure of bodies; . . . as a result, in the very nature of things, when such "forms of movements" are discovered, one becomes more like the other. Thus, in this difficult and blind search for causes, although those investigating nature may deviate from the truth in some part of their opinions, yet none the less by those opinions they save celestial appearances. It has become our use to give the name of Hypothesis to the opinion by which any of the more celebrated authors explains the causes of celestial appearances. (p. 4)

A "form of movements" is a geometrical relation which saves the appearances, that is, which demonstrates the orderly and rational mathematical connection of observations which do not at first seem to be related. United into a "form of hypothesis," these relations constitute a system of the heavens, like that of Ptolemy, Brahe, or Copernicus. Kepler is referring to what Mill called a "descriptive hypothesis," and Newton a *causa mathematica*. There could be no astronomy, insists Kepler, without such "laws or rules of the motions in which the stars are moved"; and he makes great sport of Ramus, who wanted an astronomy without hypotheses.

The third part of astronomical method is to seek the causes of hypotheses, that is, to establish them as part of the structure of the physical world. This was Kepler's great quarrel with preceding astronomers.

For astronomers should not be granted excessive license to devise anything they please, without reason: on the contrary, it is necessary to establish your hypotheses, which you recommend as the true causes of appearances. Hence you must first establish the principles of your astronomy in a higher science, namely physics or metaphysics; although you must not neglect those geometrical arguments, physical or metaphysical, which are supplied to you by the very separation of the disciplines proper, besides the things pertaining to those higher disciplines, provided you mingle no begging of the principle. As a result of this method, the astronomer (master of his proposition to the extent that he has devised causes of movements, causes which are in accord with reason, and are fit to effect everything in the history of observation) now may put into a single aspect what he had considered part by part before; and, with the greatest joy of philosophers, he may affect a higher end for the proposition (which was the demonstration of the phenomenon, and its utility in common life) the end of which previously had been concealed. To this end, he should refer all his own opinions, again by arguments both geometrical and physical; obviously, so that he may set before our eyes the genuine form and disposition, or adornment, of the entire universe. (p. 5)

Kepler's position is clear. As an hypothesis is true if it succeeds in uniting all the observations in its field into a single mathematical principle or law, so we have arrived at the "genuine form of the entire universe" if we have united all these hypotheses into one consistent system. Causation is mathematical harmony, in astronomy and in physics as a whole alike. What Kepler himself meant by this "simplicity" that united many facts "in a single bond" is clear in his discussion with his colleague Fabricius, who objected that Kepler left Mars with a varying orbit and velocity. Kepler replied that the simplicity lay not in the orbit but in the mathematical principle governing it.

This is genuine simplicity, considered in the principles themselves. If from so few principles so many things follow, the physical part of the equation, the optical, the distance, the elliptical orbit, will you then deny that the principles of these manifold events are simple? You forget the words of Plato: εἰς ἕν καὶ πολλά.[21]

Kepler has, in fact, arrived with clarity and precision at the conception of a scientific law.

That the motions of the planets are regular, that is, ordered and ascribed to a certain and immutable law, is beyond controversy. Were this not so, there would be no astronomy, nor could the heavenly motions be predicted. (VI, 370)

Kepler not only formulated clearly the notion of a science of mathematical relations, of laws rather than of logical kinds, with full

[21] *Opera*, III, 113.

awareness of his break with Aristotle and with the magicians; he made more precise the vague notion of force, which had been taken as synonymous with spirit or soul. His first work had shared this conception; as he explains in the note of 1621,

If for the word soul you substitute the word force (*vis*) you have the very principle on which the celestial physics in the Commentary on Mars is constituted. For formerly I believed the cause moving the planets to be absolutely a soul; I was imbued with the dogmas of Scaliger about the moving intelligences. But when I considered that this moving cause grows weaker with the distance from the sun, I thence concluded that this force was something corporeal, if not strictly, at least equivocally . . . Although the moving force is not strictly material, because it belongs to matter in conveying the body of the planet it is not free from geometrical laws, at least in this material action of conveying. (I, 176; III, 303)

Force is something measurable, soul is not.

Kepler's change was influenced by the work *On the Magnet* (1600) of William Gilbert, which interested Galileo also because of its "new art of philosophizing." In 1605 he wrote:

My scope here is to say that the machinery of the heavens is not like a divine animal, but like a clock (he who believes a clock has a soul attributes the glory of the workman to the work). Almost all the variety of its motions comes from one very simple bodily magnetic force, as in a clock all the motions come from a very simple weight. (II, 84)

Planetary motions are due to "a magnetic faculty, that is, a natural concourse (*consensus*) between the bodies of the planets and the sun." (III, 396)

Gilbert had considered the earth as a great magnet, and rejected the Aristotelian theory of natural place as the cause of gravitation—continuing a discussion begun in the fourteenth century Paris school. Kepler extended this magnetic force beyond the earth and made it an influence between the different heavenly bodies; thus he first attributed the tides to the moon's attraction. Moreover, he regarded it as a mutual force, resident in the relation between the two bodies, not in one alone; gravitation is a movement of the earth toward the moon as well as of the moon toward the earth.

If two stones were placed in any part of the universe near each other and beyond the sphere of the force of any third body, those stones like two magnetic bodies would come together in an intermediate place, the one approaching the other by a distance proportional to the mass of the other. (III, 511)

Kepler is characteristically led to seek to measure the relation involved, and to search for the geometrical law of this magnetic force. He actually suggested the Newtonian law, that the attraction is proportional to the masses and inversely proportional to the square of their distance apart; and though he rejects it, because he thought gravitation operated only on the plane of a planet's orbit, he placed the formula in the forefront of discussion. In this connection, he developed an idea of "mass" (*moles*) and "inertia":

Were there no inertia in the matter of the celestial globe, which is a kind of weight it possesses, there would be no need of any force to move the globe; and were there the slightest moving force, there would be no cause why the globe would not revolve in a single moment. But since the revolution of the globes takes place in a fixed time, longer in one planet than another, it is obvious that the inertia of matter is not to the moving force as nothing to something. (VI, 342)

And it was Kepler who first divorced the concept of "energy" from its connection with the Aristotelian entelechy, and identified it with force. In all these fundamental concepts of mechanics, he transformed inherited notions and problems which had been under discussion since the time of the Ockhamites in the light of his basic idea of measurable mathematical relation. If his astronomy is the disciplining of a mathematical Platonism by fact and experience, his dynamics is a similar disciplining of the ideas of the Italian heirs of the Aristotelian tradition.

IV

Giordano Bruno, the Dominican friar who fled the cloister to preach the gospel of the infinity of the universe and the plurality of its worlds in all the learned centers of Europe, was the first to bring the new astronomy to the support of the anticlerical and humanist religion of the Renaissance. He was accordingly the first to involve its cosmology in conflict with the Church. Though not prejudiced in favor of new scientific ideas, the Church had never opposed science; it is doubtful whether before the time of Trent it would have burned Bruno. Bruno died on the Campo dei Fiori in Rome in 1600, a martyr, not to Copernican astronomy, but to a heretical religious faith supposedly involved with that theory. He became the very symbol of anticlericalism; his statue may be found today in many an Italian town, erected there in the first enthusiasm of a newly united and liberated Italy, usually opposite the church of San Domenico, father of the Inquisition. And in truth his connection with science is largely symbolic; for though he praised Copernicus to the skies, and found in him support for several of his leading ideas, he seems never to have understood his reasoning, nor to have had any appreciation for the mathematical form which had made it acceptable. Like Kepler, he was a Neoplatonist and a poet; but unlike the German, he never managed to discipline his ideas with mathematics and exact observation. He remained the imaginative nature philosopher who beheld in poetic vision many of those truths which more plodding minds were to establish in detail; but he did not himself enter the promised land of science. He wrote from 1582 to 1591, before Kepler and Galileo had transformed the world into a mathematical machine; hence he was still able to give consummate expression to the anthropomorphic feeling of the Renaissance Neoplatonists, with an exuberance, an impatience of all restraint, a yearning after the infinite, that make him the most "Faustian" of all the nature philosophers. It was well enough to abandon the vows of St. Dominic; Bruno forswore also those of Euclid and Archimedes. His philosophy, therefore, has always been of interest chiefly to those for whom, like Schelling and the romantic nature philosophers, scientific precision is intolerable.

Bruno was born in Nola near Naples in 1548; he received a humanistic education before entering the Dominican order at the age of fifteen. There he read widely and not too wisely in the pre-Socratics and in the theological speculations of the Platonists. Accused of heresy because of doubts as to the Trinity, he renounced his frock in 1576 and began a fifteen-year pilgrimage to the various universities of Europe. Venice, Geneva, Lyons, Toulouse, Paris, London, Oxford, Marburg, Wittenberg, Prague, Helmstedt, Frankfurt—he appeared in them all to announce lectures on his art of memory and his great discovery of the new method of universal knowledge, elaborated from the *Ars Magna* of Raymond Lull. Having attracted large crowds eager for any new method, he would proceed to expound the Copernican theory and his new religion of the infinite universe pulsating with the divine life. For two years he was professor of philosophy at free-thinking Toulouse; at Paris the favor of the king won him a similar teaching post. He conducted a great but disappointing dispute at reactionary Oxford, and after another vigorous onslaught against the peripatetics he left Paris for Protestant Germany. Finally venturing back to Venice, he was denounced to the Inquisition, taken to Rome, and after nine years' incarceration burned at the stake in 1600.

Like all the Italian Platonists, Bruno drew on ideas from many sources without much discrimination, with a special love for those from Parmenides to his contemporary Patrizzi, in whom the impulse of dialectic led to metaphysical speculation.

For there is no single kind of philosophy, provided it be ordered by a sense of regularity, which does not contain some good peculiar to itself and not contained in others.[22]

It is evidence of an ambitious and presumptuous brain, full of vanity and envy, to wish to persuade others that there is but a single way of investigating and coming to the knowledge of nature; and of a fool and a man without judgment to believe that he possesses it.[23]

And therefore he could start in his first book with the remark,

We do not abolish the mysteries of the Pythagoreans. We do not make little of the faith of the Platonists, and insofar as they have a real foundation we do not despise the reasonings of the Peripatetics.[24]

Starting with this tolerant eclecticism, it is not surprising that the works which Bruno composed during the ten years from 1582 to 1591 should be full of a variety of often incompatible suggestions, nor that it should be impossible to trace a single consistent system in his fertile but undisciplined thought. Bruno felt profoundly the truth of certain imaginative insights: that the universe is really infinite; that it is one living and throbbing whole bound together in a dynamic and rhythmic life; that man is part and parcel of this divine universe, the manifestation of its striving forces; that knowledge must not remain with bare abstractions and empty words, but

[22] *De la causa, principio e uno,* in *Opere,* ed. Ad. Wagner (1830), I, 259.
[23] *De la causa,* I, 258.
[24] *De umbris idearum,* in *Scripta quae latine confecit,* ed. A. Fr. Gfrorer (1834), p. 299.

must grasp this universal power in its concreteness and immediacy. But he possessed neither the temper nor the ability to solve the intellectual problems such a naturalistic pantheism and mysticism presents. Like the Cusanus on whom he drew so heavily he wrestled with the mysteries of the relation of the all-embracing infinite unity of the world to its manifold "contracted" or concrete manifestations, of the penetrating insight of intellect to the particular existences that sense reveals; and like Cusanus he never satisfactorily or adequately expressed this relation in intelligible terms. For he did not arrive at the notion of a system of particulars, but remained caught in the Platonic vision of a single substance with inexplicable manifestations: unlike the Spinoza whom in religious feeling and piety he greatly resembles, he arrived at no conception of mathematical order. He could feel and express as a poet, but he could not render intelligible as a thinker.

His first work, *De umbris idearum*, written at Paris in 1582, is wholly in the Neoplatonic tradition. The series of Italian dialogues he dashed off in hot haste in London in 1584 and 1585 develop with originality the implications of his conception of infinity and the dynamic character of matter, and draw the consequences in an ethic of aspiration and yearning. The Latin poems produced in Germany attempt to justify his pantheistic faith to the learned world: they end, like Cusanus, in a theory of monads. They belong, indeed, with the other didactic poems of that century: the *Zodiacus vitae* (1531) of the Ferrarese Marcello Palingenio, who likewise taught the infinite power of God, the world soul, and the existence of other inhabited stars; the *De animorum immortalitate* of Aoni Paleario, like Bruno an anticlerical, and his predecessor at the stake in the Campo dei Fiori.

The *De umbris idearum* sets out to show that his Lullian art of combining concepts and images is modeled upon the order of nature itself. For

here is one and the same ladder, by which nature descends to the production of things and the intellect ascends to knowledge of them; and both proceed from unity to unity, passing through the multitude of means.[25]

---

[25] *De la causa*, Dialogo 4; Wagner, I, 285.

The intellect is the symbol and microcosm of the activity of the universe; its action is an imitation of that larger creation. God is the transcendent One of Plotinus, separated by an unbridgeable gulf from finite beings, to be described only in negatives. Matter and multiplicity are a descent into non-being; the knowledge that constructs concepts from sense-experience of this lowest scale of being is a mere shadow of the divine ideas.

Ideas are the cause of things before things themselves; the vestiges of ideas are things themselves or what is in things; the shadows of ideas come from things or are after things; they are said to possess as much less of reason than things themselves, which proceed from the bosom of nature, as those things possess than the divine mind, idea, and effective principle, supernatural, substance-creating, and superessential.[26]

But man can approach the divine ideas by striving after unity in his intellectual knowledge: that very striving is the image of the divine in his soul.

In the Italian dialogues appears much more of originality: for here Bruno is aflame with the idea of infinity, and with the Copernican notions of the complete relativity of sense-experience and the uniformity or *indifferenza* of nature. The *De la causa, principio e uno* starts with the exposition of the Copernican theory; but it soon shifts to the development of the Cusanian metaphysics. Bruno really believed in infinity; and with less reservation than Cusanus he insisted in *De l'infinito, universo e mondi* that the infinity of the world must follow from that of its "principle," God. If God be infinite substance, and infinite force, he must have infinite effects: there must be an infinity of worlds.

Why should or how can we suppose the divine potency to be idle? Why should we say that the divine goodness which is capable of communicating itself to an infinity of things and of pouring itself without limit, is niggardly? . . . Why should that center of deity which is able to expand itself into an infinite sphere (if we may so speak) remain barren, as if it were envious? Why should the infinite capacity be frustrated, the possibility of the existence of infinite worlds be cheated, the perfection of the divine image be impaired—that image which ought rather to be reflected back in a mirror as immeasurable as itself? . . . Why should we assert what is so full of absurdities and, while it in no wise

[26] *De imaginum compositione, Opera latine conscripta*, ed. Fiorentino, Tocco, etc. (1879–91), Vol. II, Part iii, p. 94.

promotes religion, faith, morals, or law, is destructive of so many principles of philosophy? [27]

These magnificent stars and luminous bodies, which are so many inhabited worlds, and great animals, and most excellent spirits, which seem
and are innumerable worlds, since they cannot have their being from
themselves, as they are composite and dissoluble, must necessarily know
a principle and cause: and consequently by the greatness of their being,
living, and operating they show and proclaim in an infinite space with
innumerable voices the infinite excellence and majesty of their first
principle and cause.[28]

In the later Latin rendering of the *De l'infinito*, *De immenso et
innumerabilibus* (1591), Bruno derives the infinity of the world
from certain *principia communia* universally admitted. The divine
essence is infinite; its *modus possendi* or power conforms to its
modus essendi, and to that in turn conforms its *modus operandi;*
if such infinite power exists, then an actual infinite is possible. But
it is axiomatic that in God "being, power, action, and volition . . .
are the same." Possibility and actuality must then be identical in the
universe as in God.

We insult the infinite cause when we say that it may be the cause of a
merely finite effect; to a finite effect it can have neither the name nor the
relation of an efficient cause.[29]

Hence matter cannot be finite, nor can there be empty space, mere
possibility of being, beyond the limits of our world. That such arguments are not only entirely extraneous to the Copernican astronomy,
but are the development of the premises of medieval Platonism, is
obvious: by consistently elaborating these theological axioms of the
medieval world Bruno destroyed the medieval cosmology.

But he reinforces these premises with the Copernican principles of
the relativity of motion and sense-knowledge, and the uniformity
of nature. Is the sun the center of an infinite universe? Where is the
center? As a candle-flame grows smaller as we draw away from it,
so do suns. Why may not all the stars be really suns, each appearing
the center of its own universe? Gone are the crystalline spheres:
there can be but one infinite region of ether, with infinite worlds,

[27] *De l'infinito, universo e mondi*, in *Opere*, ed. P. de Lagarde (1888), I, 314.
[28] *Opere*, ed. Lagarde, I, 229.
[29] *Opera latin.*, ed. Fiorentino, etc., Vol. I, Part i, p. 242.

all like ours, all inhabited like ours. Gone is all "natural place," all distinction between natural and violent motion. And what has become of man?

Man is no more than an ant in the presence of the infinite. And a star is no more than a man.[30]

Where is God? Perhaps he is at this moment redeeming the inhabitants of some other world. God is nowhere, or everywhere; "Nature is God in things." God is the world-soul, the immanent principle of the universe, its indwelling life-force, present everywhere in its rhythms, and filling the world as light fills finite regions, or a voice. And the cause of the universe, both efficient and final, is the universal intellect, the highest part of the world soul.

The universal intellect is the most intimate, real, and proper faculty and power of the soul of the world. It is the same intellect that fills all things. . . . illuminates the universe, and directs nature to produce her species as is fitting, and thus is related to the production of natural things as our intellect is related to the similar production of rational species.[31]

All things are thus participators in soul or spirit, united in bonds of sympathy and natural magic.

Not without a form of sense or consciousness, quite overlooked by superficial philosophers, do the water-drops take on spherical form, the best for their self-preservation.[32]

Throughout the infinite universe there beats the life of the great divine ordering force.

Beneath the fluctuating surface of things it is closer to all things than they are to themselves, the living principle of being, the source of all forms, mind, God, being, one, true, fate, word, order.[33]

Infinity is of course not an empirical idea: it is to be reached only by reason. Not the deceptive and relative senses, but intellect alone can arrive at fixed relations, at a unified substance of the world underlying its plurality. Bruno affords a striking illustration of the effect of Copernicus in driving men away from crude observation and

[30] In E. A. Singer, Jr., *Modern Thinkers and Present Problems* (1923), p. 26.
[31] *Opere*, ed. Lagarde, I, 231.
[32] *Opera latin.*, Vol. I, Part i, p. 103.
[33] *De immenso et innumerabilibus*, Book VIII, ch. 10; *Opera latin.*, Vol. I, Part ii, p. 320.

empiricism to a faith in the power of reason to see with more penetration, all the clearer in that his rationalism is not derived from any concern with mathematics. If the earth really moves, what sense observation can we then trust? The new cosmology went far beyond experience: it was based on a faith in reason and its implications. Hence it is not surprising that Bruno develops a Platonic theory of knowledge, close to the illumination theory of the Augustinians.

He who asks to know the infinite through the senses is like one who wants to behold substance and essence with the eyes; he who would deny all that is not perceptible to the senses would of necessity have to deny finally his own being and essence . . . Reason alone judges and decides all that is not given directly and immediately, but is distant from us in space and time. Truth comes in small part from the senses, as from a weak beginning; but it is not resident in the senses . . . It is in the sensible object as in a mirror, in reason in the form of argumentation and discourse, in the intellect in the form of principle or conclusion, and in the mind in proper and living form.[34]

What we see with the senses is there to be understood; what we do not see may be there in far more fundamental fashion. But intellect is both the light that illuminates and the eye that sees.

This light is more present, clear, and manifest to our intelligence than the light of the sun could be to our external eyes; for the latter rises and sets, nor is it present whenever we turn to it; but the former is no less present to us than we are to ourselves; it is so present to our mind, that it is that mind itself.[35]

True understanding is thus an "internal reading": *intellectio* is *interna lectio*. It is this intellectual intuition which Bruno throughout opposes to the empty concepts and abstract reasoning of the Schoolmen: it is the basis of his whole reform of mathematics and his monad theory.

Intellect receives and possesses with a certain simple intuition those things which reason (*ratio*) conceives through discussion and argument, and to speak properly through ratiocination and running over (*decurrendo*) . . . and it is called intellection as though it were internal lection, and as though it were a kind of living mirror, now seeing, now having visible things within itself.[36]

[34] De l'infinito, Opere, ed. Lagarde, I, 308.
[35] Opera latin., Vol. II, Part iii, p. 90.
[36] Opera latin., Vol. I, Part iv, p. 32.

Bruno was never able to achieve clarity on the precise relation between sense and intellect—a phase of his larger metaphysical difficulty of that between the particular and the universal whole. His metaphysical monism drove him at times to insist on the unity of all human powers of knowing, just as in nature there was a single universal intellect:

—thus the same power and principle of knowing receives different names from the differences of its functioning and means. . . . Whence we can demonstrate that if in sense there is a participation of intellect, sense will be intellect itself.[37]

But with the insistence on the principles of finite existence in his monadology, he likewise tended to justify each kind of knowledge within its own realm and function. The senses are not deceived, for they serve to indicate only the relations of objects to ourselves.

It is foolish to try to force on sensible things the same condition of knowledge in which rational and intelligible things are known. Sensible things are true, not by any common and universal measure, but by a measure which is, like them, particular, proper, mutable, and variable. Therefore to try to define sensibles as sensibles universally is the same as to try to define intelligibles by sense.[38]

Both sense and intellect have their own proper function. But Bruno never reached the clear conception of their union in a precise scientific method which his fellow-Platonist Kepler was able to attain.

Bruno not only developed the full consequences of the idea of the infinity of the universe: he made basic in his metaphysics the concept of power. Like all the nature philosophers, he departs from the Aristotelian identification of power with bare matter. There are two constant and eternal principles in nature, matter and form.

For it is necessary that there be a most substantial act, in which resides the active power of everything, and also a power (*potenza*) and a subject, in which there resides no less a passive power of everything; the former is the power (*potestà*) of making, the latter, the power of being made.[39]

Absolute potentiality and absolute actuality are identical; that whereby what is can be, is no different from that being. In absolute

[37] *Opera latin.*, Vol. II, Part ii, p. 175.
[38] *Opera latin.*, Vol. I, Part iii, pp. 191–94.
[39] *De la causa, Opere*, ed. Wagner, I, 251.

potentiality all opposites coincide. Finite things are each what they can be, but not all that they can be; they are ever striving to become more. But this matter or *potentia* is not the Schoolmen's mere power of receiving forms;

nothing can be conceived more barren than that first matter which was to Aristotle the principle of natural things.[40]

Matter is *potentia* in an active and dynamic sense: it does not receive forms from outside, but unfolds them from within itself; it is not form that molds matter, but matter that strives to clothe itself with form.

You must infer that matter is not that *prope nihil*, that pure potentiality, bare, without actuality, without virtue or perfection . . . It is, I say, deprived of forms and without them, not as ice is without heat, or darkness without light; but as the pregnant woman is without her offspring, who produces it from within herself . . . You must ask Aristotle, Why, prince of peripatetics, do you hold that matter is nothing since it has no actuality, rather than that it is everything since it possesses all actualities? [41]

We see that all natural forms proceed from matter, and return to matter; whence in reality nothing is constant, firm, eternal, and worthy of being considered a principle except matter, since forms have no being without matter, in which they are generated and corrupted, from whose bosom they issue, and into which they fall back. (I, 256)

It seems to me proper to say that matter possesses all things, as all are said to lie concealed in its bosom. (I, 276)

Matter is the very source of all actuality. (I, 278)

Matter is the world soul, the infinite Substance itself.

Matter, which remains ever the same and ever fertile, deserves the principal prerogative of being known as the sole substantial principle, as that which is and always remains. (I, 253)

It is in this dynamic conception that being is seen to be unified as a single whole, a single substance. One and the same are absolute possibility and absolute actuality, matter and form, cause and essence. It neither moves, nor changes; but only the things within it come into being and pass away. All multiplicity, all difference, are mere

---

[40] *Opera*, ed. Gfrorer, p. 44. [41] *De la causa*, Wagner, I, 229.

accidents of the infinite Substance, mere appearances to the senses; there are no separate and individual things, no individual substances, but only substance in "contraction," particularized in concrete modes.

Thus Bruno brings the old Eleatic dialectic to bear against the Aristotelian conception of a world of individual substances. Only the immutable and unchanging, the persistent and constant, possesses true being. As Telesio and the empiricists held fast to individual objects, and insisted that knowledge must therefore be likewise individual, so Bruno, faithful to the Platonic conception of a science only of the immutable and eternal, denied the existence of particulars and individuals. Reality can only be the whole of nature, for only nature as a whole can be grasped by intellect.

No natural body is in itself intelligible; the intelligible object of natural science can be nothing other than Nature herself, for that alone emerges from natural bodies as intelligible.[42]

Knowledge of particulars is mere history, not science; particulars are real and are known only as parts of the single all-embracing Whole. Here is the logical and metaphysical foundation which Bruno tried to give his emotional pantheism. Nature is an infinite substance, a unified system of force; it exists and is intelligible only as a unity; it is God himself, a divine life filling the interminable ranges of the ether, "that immense region in which the world lives and moves." [43]

This conception of a unified and single nature was destined to become central in modern thought. But in conceiving it as a single substance, rather than as a system of laws, in taking it to be a unifying life, rather than an all-embracing structure of mathematical and mechanical determination, Bruno was fighting for a lost cause. Only occasionally does he seem to escape from the relation of substance and accident to a clearer conception of system and order.

Nature is nothing but the power implanted in things and the law by which they complete their proper course.[44]

It remained for Spinoza to identify wholly the infinite substance with the mathematical order of nature.

[42] *Opera latin.*, Vol. I, Part i, p. 88.
[43] *De triplici minimo et mensura*, in *Opera latin.*, Vol. I, Part iii, p. 29.
[44] *De immenso*, *Opera latin.*, Vol. I, Part. ii, p. 310.

How the modes or parts of this Whole might be intellectually grasped remained the problem on which Bruno worked during his stay in Germany.

For surely it is this universal Nature or Substance which offers itself to scientific contemplation, . . . and not this world, not these stars, not any particular thing; such objects do not lend themselves to science, but only to sense and to opinion . . . What is in itself sensible cannot even by accident be intelligible; what is in itself particular and changing cannot even by accident be universal and unchanging.[45]

For reason to gain some particular foothold in things it must find the *minima*, the irreducible units out of which they are composed. And thus, in *De triplici minimo et mensura* (1591) and *De monade, numero et figura* (1591) he tried to work out a monadology, a theory of units, as Cusanus had done before him in the face of the same problem. Each particular field or problem demands its own intelligible *minimum*, to serve as the rational "measure" therein. The sensible world must be understood in terms of atoms borne in the ether, the principle of life and vehicle of all force and form. The mathematical realm demands a spatial minimum, the circle for the plane and the sphere for space. This general demand for logical units everywhere led Bruno to undertake a reform of geometry in the interests of his discrete theory: the continuum is really made up of irreducible spatial units, and only in concept is it infinitely divisible. Bruno's perverse attempt to deny irrationals and incommensurables differs from those of Hobbes and Berkeley in that it does not start with an empiricist reduction to indivisible sense impressions, but proceeds from wholly rationalistic motives: it is logical thought attacking mathematical thought. And he carefully distinguishes between the unit or minimum and a mathematical limit, which "are not in the same genus of quantity."[46]

But even here Bruno does not succeed. In the last analysis there are as many qualitatively different minima as there are individuals. And in the light of his criticism, the operations of mathematical thinking appear as a deceptive addition to nature.

There is one set of principles for Nature, and another for the conditions of our mind.[47]

[45] *Opera latin.*, Vol. I, Part i, pp. 84, 86.
[46] *De minimo*, Book I, ch. 13; *Opera latin.*, Vol. I, Part iii, p. 180.
[47] *De minimo*, Book II, ch. 8; *Opera latin.*, Vol. I, Part iii, p. 221.

Bruno is left with the unreconciled demands: on the one hand, reason craves continuity and unity; on the other, it must postulate irreducible *minima*, without which unitary elements no wholes are intelligible. And like all Platonists he was unable to solve the relation of the continuous and the discrete, of unity and individuality.

Only in living, in the striving of the individual after the infinite could Bruno find a way out. There, in the pursuit of the divine Beauty, in the Platonic Eros after infinite being, is found the real union of the finite and the infinite.

Just as true philosophy is at once music and poetry and painting, so is true painting at the same time music and philosophy, and true poetry an expression and image of the divine Wisdom.[48]

Degli Eroici Furori (1585) is Bruno's *Symposium*. Starting from the divine madness of the *Phaedrus,* it attacks the soberness and prudence of the Aristotelian golden mean, and extols the immoderate life of the passionate artist and hero. Burn with an infinite love for perfection, transcend all bounds. You will suffer, you will cry out with pain, but you will be living. Life is tragic, and you will go down to defeat: never can you attain your infinite goal. But if you are on fire with a yearning for the divine beauty, you will come as close to God as it is given to mortals to ascend.

Even if the longed-for goal be never reached, even though the violence of the striving consume the soul utterly, yet is it enough that it should have burned so nobly.[49]

So living, you find harmony at last in yourself, and between yourself and the world; you will be united with the creative process of the world itself; you will have found God, not in dreary mysteries,

—but in the inviolable and intemerable law of Nature, in the religion of a mind well directed toward that law, in the splendor of the sun, in the sight of the things produced from the womb of this our parent, in her true image made manifest in bodily fashion in the countenance of the innumerable living beings which shine in the immense web of a single heaven, which live, and feel, and understand, and praise that best and greatest One.[50]

[48] *Opera latin.,* Vol. II, Part iii, p. 198.
[49] *De gli eroici furori,* ed. G. Gentile, in *Opere italiane,* ed. Gentile e Spamponato (1907-9), Vol. II, Dialoghi morali.
[50] *Opera latin.,* Vol. I, Part ii, p. 316.

13

Galileo and the Pattern of the New Science

I

DESPITE his many startling insights, Kepler remained caught in the ideas of the Neoplatonic nature philosophers: the announcement of his third law of planetary motion occurs in the midst of the attempt to set down in musical notation the precise laws of the harmony of the spheres. In Galileo we seem to have emerged from that dawn into the full blaze of the seventeenth-century sun of Reason. In his work all the threads we have been examining are woven into the single fabric of the mathematical and mechanical interpretation of nature. The long critical tradition of the Ockhamites and the Padua physicists, so eagerly worked at by the sixteenth-century Italians; the carefully analyzed structure of scientific method, culminating in the formulation of Zabarella; the technical lore of the engineers and mechanics, so rapidly accumulating since the Renaissance; the new practical and human aim for a knowledge of nature, preached by the many critics of the theoretical science of the Schools; the restored mathematical techniques of Archimedes and Apollonius— all came together in the mind of a man able to make full use of them as materials, yet remarkably free from bondage to traditional ideas. Galileo was preeminently a scientist, rather than a philosopher: he had neither the speculative and systematic interest of the builders of the seventeenth century, like Descartes, nor the critical power of the analysts of the eighteenth. His greatest work is devoted to "two new sciences," not to "the mathematical principles of natural philosophy." And he was a consummate master of the rhetorical technique of the humanists, of that art of persuasion whereby ideas are most effectively presented in literary form. Yet what most distinguishes all his work from that of his predecessors, his conviction that he is at last upon the right track, that having found the proper procedure for investigating nature it is no longer a question of correcting Aristotle or of escaping from him, but of applying that procedure in fruitful inquiry, was profoundly stimulating to every philosophical mind. Galileo's procedure not only proved the inspiration of all natural scientists till it was taken up and embodied in Isaac Newton: it remained the starting point of all philosophic analyses of the new science and its relation to traditional human interests.

By early training and by temperament Galileo belonged to the long line of "practical geometers" of the sixteenth century, as heir of Tartaglia and of his interests in ballistics and hydraulics. He was, that is, a mathematician, but essentially an applied mathematician, not a pure mathematician like Descartes. He therefore never faced the problem that confronted Descartes, of how a mathematical system developed independently of its exemplification in nature could nevertheless hold true of natural relations; he felt no need for a metaphysical and epistemological guarantee of the validity of his discoveries, and his only argument against the protagonists of the older physics is that his propositions can be demonstrated mathematically and confirmed by experiment. He was under no temptation to turn, like the Frenchman, to a Platonic and Augustinian metaphysics; it is not so much that he rested in the common Aristotelianism of the Italian tradition as that, taking its fundamental position for granted, he felt no need whatever for engaging in metaphysical discussion. He was content to explore the intelligible structure of his chosen subject-matter, natural motions. His only quarrel with the peripatetics was that he had found some part of that natural structure, whereas they had not. What further philosophic and metaphysical suggestions he throws out in the heat of controversy are only to the effect that his subject-matter must present those conditions of which his mathematical procedure had been making practical use.

In saying, therefore, that Galileo's science is the culmination of the critical tradition of Italian Aristotelianism, it is not meant that he undertook any philosophical interpretation of it in Aristotelian terms, like Spinoza or Leibniz, for instance. He undertook no interpretation at all: he explored his subject-matter. Nor is the source of his quarrels with the peripatetics overlooked: he had learned from the mathematicians, above all from Archimedes, that certain of the aspects of nature can be expressed in mathematical discourse and dealt with by mathematical operations with remarkable power and fertility. Such power and fertility he did not find in the syllogism or in the nonquantitative principles on which the peripatetic physics depended. A verbal definition of the essence of a natural force like gravitation did not enable one to arrive at any new knowledge: a mathematical formulation of the measurable relations of falling bodies did. Therefore Galileo was convinced that mathematics did seize the natural structure of things, and that of the structure it grasped God himself could have no clearer knowledge. What is said in the discourse of mathematics is truly said, though much remains that is not expressed in that language.

It may be that every mathematician is at heart a Platonic metaphysician. In that case of course all modern exact science is a series of footnotes to Plato. There is then no difference between the philosophies of science of Galileo and Descartes; Leibniz and Clarke were in complete agreement in their controversy over space. But unless this be true, there is no evidence that Galileo was in any sense touched by Platonic metaphysics, or that he is any more of a Platonist than Aristotle himself. He certainly never showed any but a literary and humanistic interest in Plato's philosophy: this was, in fact, the great issue between himself and Kepler. On the fundamental issue in any philosophy of science, the relation of discourse to knowledge and to the subject-matter of knowledge, Galileo was one with the Italian and Padua tradition of realistic Aristotelianism. The subject-matter of knowledge is not an intelligible, "ideal" world dubiously related to the world of natural events: it is the intelligible structure of that world of events. And what the best human language expresses in intelligible terms is truly said, is genuine knowledge. Galileo's clear distinction, as every seventeenth-century scientist knew, was his startling illustration of the fact that the best human language is mathematics, and that the intelligible structure of things that knowledge when clearly formulated in discourse is able to grasp is mathematical in character. That structure is not what is presented immediately in sense, though without that presentation it must remain unknown. It is something arrived at by the intellect through the careful analysis of the instances of it we encounter in experience, as Aristotle had suggested and the Padua methodologists had more precisely stated.

II

This conception of science and its object, this combination of a vivid sense of fact with mathematical analysis and demonstration, grew for Galileo out of his actual practice and procedure in science. Of what that procedure was he became vividly conscious in the many battles of wits with the defenders of other methods and other languages. What it might be taken to imply about the world in which it could be carried on he did not critically analyze; nor was he interested in adjusting it to the procedures appropriate to other fields of interest. He does indeed throw out various suggestions, many of which were later elaborated by the systematic philosophers of the century; but those suggestions are for him always a matter of the conditions of his mathematical procedure, and not of the conciliation of that procedure with inherited ideas. Galileo therefore in his thought presents the pattern of the new science, the clear and conscious statement of what that science was and did. To others it was left to interpret that science philosophically, to try to assay what it meant. The great medieval traditions as to the meaning of science were brought to bear upon this new pattern in the philosophical systems of the seventeenth century. But until Newton significantly altered that pattern, it remained the science that was to be interpreted.

Galileo received his early training in the problems of the practical geometers. His father Vincenzio was a well-known writer on the theory of music; significantly, although he defended the Florentine school against the Venetians, he had no interest in the Pythagorean ideas on harmony that were then in fashion. Galileo himself at first studied medicine at Pisa; since no instruction was offered, he did not turn to mathematics until his twentieth year, when his father procured him lessons from Ostilio Ricci, teacher at the Academy of Art in Florence. Ricci taught just those branches excluded from the universities, the problems of practical and applied mathematics cultivated in the school of Tartaglia by the architects and technicians. Under his influence Galileo abandoned medicine to devote himself to the mechanical applications of mathematics in architecture and hydraulics. Ricci gave him a copy of Archimedes that opened a new world: he set to work on the problem of the density of bodies, and invented a *bilancetta* or hydrostatic scales which he described in a paper in 1586, praising especially its *esquisitezza* and *esattezza*. The same year he wrote a geometrical paper on determining the center of gravity of solids, which won him the patronage of the mathematician Guid'Ubaldo del Monte. The latter procured him the post of professor of mathematics at Pisa in 1589, at the age of twenty-five. Though his teaching was limited to Euclid and the Ptolemaic astronomy, he was busily engaged in mathematical researches on the theory of motion, and eagerly seeking suggestions, not only in the Italian writers on mechanics of his century like Scaliger and Benedetti, but also in the long Ockhamite tradition. About 1590 he set down the first of his treatments, *De Motu*, destined to a number of revisions before it finally appeared in 1638 as the *Two New Sciences*. In 1592, on the invitation of the Venetian Senate, he accepted the mathematics professorship at Padua; the eighteen years he spent in the free atmosphere of Padua, with its select body of students, were the happiest and most fruitful of his life. Here he discovered the parabolic form of trajectories, and laid the foundations for his dynamics; here he constructed his telescope, in 1609, after hearing reports of one made by a Dutch spectacle-maker. It is significant that it was this practical invention that led to his momentous discoveries of the satellites of Jupiter and the mountains on the moon, which, when announced in his *Sidereus nuncius* in 1610, initiated his long and tragic battle for the Copernican theory; just as it was a previous invention, of the geometric compass or proportional circle, described in his earliest published work in 1606, that involved him in the first of his many controversies. At Padua he had an elaborate workshop in his house; in addition to his university lectures he gave private instruction for the students in mechanics, dealing with practical and technical problems. All his writings of the Padua period, from the two essays on the art of fortification in 1592 on, deal with such problems, and are written in the Italian he there used. It is clear that like Tartaglia Galileo was the heir of the tradition of the mechanics of practice. His open publication of his Copernican views made his position as a teacher of Ptolemaic astronomy untenable;

in 1610 he left the protection of Venice to accept the post of court mathematician to the Grand Duke of Tuscany and professor of philosophy at Pisa, with freedom to pursue his own investigations.

It was as an astronomical observer that Galileo first won European reputation; and the acceptance of observed facts became the fundamental tenet of his fighting creed.

Our disputes are about the sensible world, and not one of paper.[1]

Experience is the true mistress of astronomy:

—the principal scope of astronomers is only to render reason for the appearances in the celestial bodies.[2]

In every hypothesis of reason, error may lurk unnoticed, but a discovery of sense cannot be at odds with the truth . . . How could it be otherwise? Nature did not make human brains first, and then construct things according to their capacity of understanding, but she first made things in her own fashion, and then so constructed the human understanding that it, though at the price of great exertion, might ferret out a few of her secrets.[3]

As to the "facts that," the subject-matter of all scientific explanation, Galileo is clear and consistent; the refusal to accept his observations with the telescope gave him an ingrained insistence on starting with the facts. To Kepler, who had come out in support of the *Sidereus nuncius*, he wrote in 1610:

I thank you for having accorded my assertions full belief, the first and almost the only man, after the first short glance, as was to be expected from the acuteness and freedom of your mind. But what will you say to the first philosophers of the university here [Padua], who despite a thousand requests in their iron stubbornness refuse to look at the planets or the moon or at my glass themselves, and who thus close their eyes forcibly against the light of truth? . . . These men believe that philosophy is a book like the *Aeneid* or the *Odyssey*, and that the truth is not in the world or in nature but (these are their own words!) to be sought in the comparison of texts. How you would laugh if you could hear the foremost philosopher of Pisa University wearing himself out to dispute away

---

[1] *Dialogue concerning the Two Great Systems of the World*, tr. Thomas Salusbury in his *Mathematical Collections and Translations*, I (London, 1661), 96.

[2] *Two Systems*, ed. Salusbury, I, 308.

[3] Letter, in *Opere*, ed. E. Alberi (Florence, 1842–56), VII, 341. See also *Two Systems*, in *Opere*, Alberi, I, 288.

and destroy the new planets by logical arguments, as though they were magic charms.[4]

Yet Galileo never falls into the easy accusation of the humanists and empiricists, and of pure experimenters like Gilbert, that these peripatetics are seeking to leave the rich concreteness of particular things for the dry and empty abstractions of thought. For not only is he too familiar with Aristotle himself to attribute any lack of respect for facts and experience to his principles: it is in "abstractions," that is, in universal and permanent elements isolated in the midst of the changing events and particulars, that he is convinced the proper objects of science are to be found. Indeed, the constant objection to his own procedure raised by the Schoolmen in letters and in his vigorous dialogues, is that while his reasoning may apply to "mathematical abstractions," it will not hold of "sensible and physical things." His universal laws and principles fail to take account of the diversity of phenomena and their different specific determinations. The physicist must patiently collect all these various kinds of fact to find his general principles; he must not sacrifice their particularity to a system of mathematical relations and abstractions. Thus it is Galileo, and not the Schoolmen, upon whom falls the accusation of empty abstraction. And what Galileo feels called upon to defend is not that sensible experience must furnish the subject-matter to be explained, but that explanation and intelligibility come from selecting the quantitative and measurable characters of that subject-matter for mathematical treatment.

It is impossible that sense experience should be in conflict with the truth. Yet we cannot stop with mere facts, which do not furnish their own explanation. Sense must be accompanied by *discorso*, by reason. For reason is the test of experience.

Against appearances, in which all agree, we make headway with reason, either to confirm the reality of that experience, or to discover its fallacy.[5]

And that *discorso* must be mathematical.

To be placed on the title-page of my collected works: here it will be perceived from innumerable examples what is the use of mathematics for judgment in the natural sciences, and how impossible it is to philoso-

[4] Letter to Kepler, cited in E. Cassirer, *Das Erkenntnisproblem*, ed. 3d (1922), I, 379.
[5] *Two Systems*, *Opere*, ed. Alberi, I, 270.

phize correctly without the guidance of geometry, as the wise maxim of Plato has it.[6]

Just what did the "guidance of geometry" mean for Galileo? In the answer to this question lies the secret of his method and the pattern of his science. But it is clear at the outset that it means no vague Pythagorean number mysticism.

Neither doth it suffice to know that falling bodies descend with accelerating velocity, but it is requisite to know *according to what proportion* such acceleration takes place; a problem that I believe was never hitherto understood by any philosopher or mathematician, although philosophers, and particularly the peripatetics, have writ great and entire volumes touching motion.[7]

In the early fragment *De Motu* of 1590 there is already a very clear realization of what distinguishes the mathematical method.

The method we shall employ in this treatise is always to make the things to be explained depend on explanations already given (*ut semper dicenda ex dictis pendeant*); nor if possible shall I ever assume that what is to be explained (*declaranda*) is true. This is the method my mathematicians have taught me: nor is it sufficiently used by certain philosophers, who in teaching the elements of physics too often assume what is handed down in the *De Anima*, the *De Coelo*, and the *Metaphysics;* nor is this all, for the teachers of logic itself continually have in their mouths what is contained in the later books of Aristotle. Thus while they are teaching their pupils the beginnings they assume that they know everything, and make their teaching (*doctrina*) depend not on what their pupils already know, but on what is unknown and unheard of.[8]

No more precise statement could be made of the demonstrative or compositive order of *doctrina* for which Zabarella had so doughtily fought.

It is in direct opposition to the peripatetic Simplicio, however, that he gives the most revealing examples. Simplicio is denying the "applicability" of geometry to concrete things, and drawing a distinction between its "abstract truth" and the truth of physical things.

Salviati: I do not think that Simplicio is one of these Peripateticks that dissuade their disciples from studying the mathematics, as sciences that vitiate the reason and render it less apt for contemplation.

[6] *Two New Sciences, Opere,* Edizione Nazionale, ed. A. Favaro (Florence, 1890–1909), VIII, 613.
[7] *Two Systems,* ed. Salusbury, p. 144.
[8] *De Motu, Opere,* ed. Favaro, I, 285.

Simplicio: I would not do so much wrong to Plato, but yet I may truly say with Aristotle that he too much lost himself in, and too much doted upon that his Geometry: for that in conclusion these mathematical subtilties, Salviati, are true in abstract, but applied to sensible and physical matter they hold not good. For the mathematicians will very well demonstrate for example that a sphere touches a plane in a point, a position like to that in dispute; but when one cometh to the matter, things succeed in quite another way. And so I may say of these angles of contact, and these proportions: which all evaporate into air, when they are applied to things material and sensible.

But Galileo does not understand mathematical "abstraction" in this fashion: for him there is no such Platonic dualism between a geometrical realm and the realm of experience.

Then whenever in concrete you do apply a material sphere to a material plane, you apply an imperfect sphere to an imperfect plane, and these you say do not touch in only one point. But I must tell you, that even an abstract and immaterial sphere, that is, not a perfect sphere, may touch an immaterial plane, that is, not a perfect plane, not in one point, but with part of its superficies so that hitherto that which falleth out in concrete doth in like manner hold true in abstract . . . So when the Geometrical Philosopher would observe in concrete the effects demonstrated in abstract, he must defalke the impediments of the matter, and if he know how to do that, I do assure you, the things shall jump no less exactly than arithmetical computations. The error therefore lyeth neither in abstract, nor in concrete, nor in geometry, nor in physics, but in the Calculator, that knoweth not how to adjust his accounts. Therefore if you had a perfect sphere and plane, though they were material, you need not doubt but that they would touch only in one point.[9]

The secret of the relation between geometrical structure and material things lies in "defalking the impediments of the matter," that is, in selecting those characters that can be mathematically formulated and defined and eliminating the properties that fall outside of such geometrical determination. If no perfect spheres and planes are to be found in nature, those that are found are just as geometrical as if they were more accurate. "Abstract" geometrical formulations have to be corrected for the individual variations of particular cases. But those variations are variations from a general geometrical rule, and corrections can in practice be made only in terms of that rule. That rule would never be achieved without putting aside these varying "impediments" of matter and assuming a simplicity and con-

[9] *Two Systems*, ed. Salusbury, pp. 181, 185.

stancy never exhibited in natural things. It is for the calculator to perform this task, to select the proper formalized geometrical structure, and to prescribe mathematical conditions to which natural events approximately conform. His mathematical demonstrations will hold of the latter in so far as they do conform to these conditions.

Salviati: I grant that conclusions proved in the abstract will be different when applied in the concrete, and will be fallacious to this extent, that neither will the horizontal motion be uniform, nor the natural acceleration be in the ratio assumed, nor the path of the projectile a parabola, etc. . . . When we wish to apply our proven conclusions to distances which, though finite, are very large, it is necessary for us to infer, on the basis of demonstrated truth, what correction is to be made for the fact that our distance from the center of the earth is not really infinite, but merely very great in comparison with the small dimensions of our apparatus.[10]

III

The scientist therefore begins with a "hypothetical assumption," a mathematical hypothesis which does not come immediately from the observation and measurement of facts, but rather analyses the mathematical relations that are involved in a given problem. Only after the mathematical relations involved in this initial hypothesis have been demonstrated does it possess such quantitative meaning and implication that it can be compared and measured with observations and experiments. The demonstration will be valid even if no natural object fulfills its conditions.

If experience shows that such properties as we have deduced find confirmation in the free fall of natural bodies, we can without danger of error assert that the concrete motion of falling is identical with that which we have defined and assumed; if this is not the case, our proofs still lose nothing of their power and conclusiveness, as they were intended to hold only for our assumptions—just as little as the propositions of Archimedes about spirals are affected by the fact that no body is to be found in nature that possesses a spiral motion.[11]

Demonstration or the "compositive" method thus precedes the rigorous examination or "resolution" of particular cases to determine how far they correspond with their assumed mathematical principle.

[10] *Two New Sciences*, ed. H. Crew and A. de Salvio (1914), pp. 251–52.
[11] Letter to Carcaville, 1637; *Opere*, ed. Alberi, VII, 156; ed. Favaro, XVII, 90.

And for Galileo's own practice this hypothetical and a priori procedure seems to have been typical: he once remarked that

ignorance had been the best teacher he ever had, since in order to be able to demonstrate to his opponents the truth of his conclusions, he had been forced to prove them by a variety of experiments, though to satisfy his own mind alone he had never felt it necessary to make any.[12]

Thus he writes Kepler:

Know then that about three months after Venus could be seen I began to observe it diligently with my glass, that what I held in my mind to be indubitable I might also grasp with the senses.[13]

Both in his own reflection on the laws of acceleration and in his exposition, he seems to have worked wholly as a mathematician in his geometrical analysis and demonstration before turning to any experimental confirmation. He proceeds by rational analysis:

Thus I conceive in my mind a movable object projected on a horizontal plane with all impediments removed; now it is certain that its motion will be equal and perpetual on that plane, if the plane be extended to infinity.[14]

Or again:

When, therefore, I observe a stone initially at rest falling from an elevated position and continually acquiring new increments of velocity, why should I not believe that such increase takes place in a manner which is exceedingly simple and rather obvious to every one? If now we examine the matter carefully we find no addition or increment more simple than that which repeats itself always in the same manner. This we readily understand when we consider the intimate relationship between time and motion; for just as uniformity of motion is defined and conceived through equal times and equal spaces (thus we call motion uniform when equal distances are traversed during equal time-intervals), so also we may, in a similar manner, through equal time-intervals, conceive additions of velocity as taking place without complication; thus we may picture to our mind a motion as uniformly and continuously accelerated when during any equal intervals of time whatever, equal increments of velocity are given it.[15]

[12] J. J. Fahie, *The Scientific Works of Galileo,* in C. Singer, *Studies in the History and Method of Science,* II (1921), 251.

[13] Letter to Kepler, in *Opere,* ed. Favaro, XI, 11; in Kepler, *Opera,* ed. C. Frisch (1858–71), II, 464.

[14] *Two New Sciences, Opere,* ed. Alberi, XIII, 221.

[15] *Two New Sciences,* Crew and de Salvio, p. 161.

And in connection with his defense of Copernicus Galileo had of course to deprecate common observation and extol mathematical demonstration.

I cannot sufficiently admire the eminence of those men's wits, that have received and held it to be true, and with the sprightliness of their judgments offered such violence to their own sense, as that they have been able to prefer that which their reason dictated to them, to that which sensible experiments represented most manifestly to the contrary . . . I cannot find any bounds for my admiration, how that reason was able in Aristarchus and Copernicus to commit such a rape on their senses, as in despite thereof to make herself mistress of their credulity.[16]

Yet Galileo is interested in the mathematical principles that are exemplified in nature: it is his subject-matter that holds him to facts.

And first of all it seems desirable to find and explain a definition best fitting natural phenomena. For anyone may invent an arbitrary type of motion, and discuss its properties; thus for instance some have imagined helices and conchoids, as described by certain motions which are not met with in nature, and have very commendably established the properties which those curves possess in virtue of their definitions; but we have decided to consider the phenomena of bodies falling with an acceleration such as actually occurs in nature and to make this definition of accelerated motion exhibit the *essential features* of observed accelerated motions. And this at last after repeated efforts we trust we have succeeded in doing. In this belief we are confirmed mainly by the consideration that experimental results are seen to agree with and exactly correspond with those properties which have been one after another demonstrated by us.[17]

For Galileo, therefore, the mathematical demonstration from an hypothesis comes first, after a preliminary analysis of the problem into its mathematical elements. Then succeeds the analysis of cases or illustrations of that hypothesis to discover how far it is really exemplified in them, and confirmed by them. The demonstration Galileo calls the *compositive method;* the term *resolutive method,* from its root meaning of analysis leading to causes and principles, he applies sometimes to the initial mathematical analysis of the problem, sometimes to the confirming analysis of the examples, and sometimes to the search for the still more fundamental principle on which that hypothesis depends.

[16] *Two Systems,* ed. Salusbury, p. 301.
[17] *Two New Sciences,* Crew and de Salvio, p. 160.

I do believe [the remarks of Aristotle] that he first procured, by the help of the senses, such experiments and observations as he could, to assure him as much as it was possible of the conclusion; and that he afterwards sought out the means how to demonstrate it; for this is the usual course in demonstrative sciences, and the reason thereof is, because when the conclusion is true, by the help of the resolutive method one may hit upon some proposition before demonstrated, or come to some principle known *per se;* but if the conclusion be false, a man may proceed *in infinitum,* and never meet with any truth already known.[18]

This mathematical analysis or resolution Galileo distinguishes carefully from the "induction" of the Schoolmen and the empiricists. Induction conceived as the mere heaping up of all the particulars is either impossible or unnecessary: impossible if the particulars be infinite, unnecessary and tautological if they be finite. The mere summary of particular cases can never lead to a universally applicable rule unless such a mathematical structure is actually present in those cases; and if it be so present, careful analysis of a single case will bring it to light. That is why the empirical facts of the artisans and engineers may furnish materials for scientific analysis, but never of themselves lead to certain principles.

The knowledge of a single fact acquired through the discovery of its causes prepares the mind to ascertain and understand other facts without need of recourse to experiments, precisely as in the present case, where by argumentation alone the author proves with certainty that the maximum range occurs when the elevation is $45°$. He thus demonstrates what has never been observed in experience.[19]

Confirmation through experiment is required only if the conclusion be one of whose rational and necessary basis we have no intuition. This theory of resolution is of course the Aristotelian analysis of the Paduans and Zabarella, applied specifically to the discovery of mathematical structure.

The mathematical principles of nature are thus arrived at by resolution of crucial cases. Their truth is immediately perceived.

I tell you that when a man does not know the truth immediately (*da per se*), it is impossible for others to make him know it; I can indeed teach you things which are neither true nor false, but the true, that is, the necessary things, that is, those which cannot possibly be otherwise, every

[18] *Two Systems,* ed. Salusbury, pp. 37–38.
[19] *Two New Sciences,* Crew and de Salvio, p. 276.

man of average reason either knows by himself (*da se*) or it is impossible for him ever to know them.[20]

This may have a Platonic ring, but if so it is but the Platonism of Aristotle himself, who like Galileo found the guarantee of first principles in such intellectual vision. And like a good Aristotelian Galileo insists that these principles must be seen in their particular exemplifications.

Simplicio: But as to whether this acceleration is that which one meets in nature in the case of falling bodies, I am still doubtful; and it seems to me, not only for my own sake but also for all those who think as I do, that this would be the proper moment to introduce one of those experiments—and there are many of them, I understand—which illustrate in several ways the conclusion reached.

Salviati: The request which you, as a man of science, make, is a very reasonable one; for this is the custom—and properly so—in those sciences where mathematical demonstrations are applied to natural phenomena, as is seen in the case of perspective, astronomy, mechanics, music, and others, where the principles, once established by well-chosen experiments, become the foundations of the entire super-structure.[21]

I V

This is the pattern of Galileo's mathematical procedure, and of the mechanical science he so brilliantly initiated. Naturally to a reflective mind this procedure, in which the invariant mathematical elements and relations of natural events are abstracted or isolated from their manifold accidental characters, may suggest many further questions about the nature of the world in which that procedure can be successfully carried on. On the whole Galileo raises far fewer of these questions about the status of the selected and restricted subject-matter of natural science than did the later seventeenth century physicists—fewer than Kepler, for example. When he does so proceed to a metaphysical inquiry, it is always in terms of what conditions that subject-matter must be assumed to possess if it is to be manipulated by mathematical operations. To go beyond such conditions to inquiries into its "real essence" may be interesting, but scarcely concerns the scientist.

Thus if bodies are to be dealt with geometrically, their matter must be taken to exhibit quantitative determinations.

[20] *Two Systems, Opere,* ed. Alberi, I, 175.
[21] *Two New Sciences,* Crew and de Salvio, p. 178.

Since I assume matter to be unchangeable, that is, always the same, it is clear that of it, as of an eternal and necessary property (*affezione*), we can construct demonstrations no less than in simple and pure mathematics.[22]

For exact knowledge can be had only of what is constant and unchanging:

This is as far as I can tell you in this matter, and as far perhaps as our knowledge can comprehend; which, mark you, cannot extend beyond those conclusions that are firm and constant . . . and depend on causes that are invariable, single, and eternal.[23]

The conclusions of natural philosophy cannot therefore be "for the most part," as Aristotle held: they must be as exact and rigorous as those of pure mathematics, unless mechanics be a mere chimera.

These reasons . . . do not connect and bind with that force which must be indubitably possessed by those that can be drawn from the conclusions of physics, necessary and eternal.[24]

And so Galileo is led to the further implication that to the "nature" of the natural scientist, in the strict and scientific sense of the term, there can belong only "true and necessary things, such as could not possibly be related otherwise."

But when the further question is raised whether this homogeneous, constant, and mathematically determinate matter is atomic in structure, Galileo does not press an issue he feels goes beyond the needs of exact science into metaphysical speculation. A corpuscular theory of matter, in which "infinitely small indivisible atoms" would possess only the mathematical properties of place, motion, figure, and size, would solve many physical problems of change of state, cohesion, and contraction, without the need of assuming empty space in solid bodies. But unlike the later Descartes, he spends little time on a hypothesis to which mathematical demonstration had not attained.

In his brilliant but mistaken polemic against Father Grassi's theory of comets, the *Saggiatore* (1623), Galileo goes so far as to defend the turning of the distinction between what is mathematically formulable and what is not into that between "real" primary qualities and

[22] *Two New Sciences, Opere,* ed. Alberi, XIII, 7.
[23] *Two Systems, Opere,* ed. Alberi, I, 497.
[24] *Two Systems, Opere,* ed. Alberi, I, 439.

merely "subjective" secondary qualities. The digression is not very germane to his argument, and is not pursued with a very critical sense: what is most interesting about it is the fashion in which he insists that to bodies themselves must be ascribed those mathematical determinations which are the necessary conditions of any science of nature. For Galileo it is a question of the delimitation of the field of physics, the selection of a subject-matter, of which the relativity of sense-experience furnishes only an illustration.

I say that I feel myself indeed impelled by the necessity, so soon as I conceive a bit of matter or corporeal substance, of at the same time conceiving that it is bounded and figured with such and such a figure, that in relation to others it is large or small, that it is in this or that place, in this or that time, that it is moving or at rest, that it touches or does not touch another body, that it is single, few, or many; nor can it by any imagining be separated from these conditions. But that it must be white or red, bitter or sweet, sounding or mute, of a pleasant or unpleasant odor—I do not find my mind forced to apprehend it as necessarily accompanied by such conditions; so that if the senses had not been our guide, perhaps reason or imagination would never have arrived at them by themselves. Therefore I am inclined to think that these tastes, odors, colors, etc., with regard to the subject in which they appear to reside, are nothing but mere names, and reside only in the sensitive body; so that if the latter were removed, all these qualities would be removed and annihilated; although we have imposed particular names upon them, different from those of the other and real accidents, and would fain persuade ourselves that they truly and in fact exist . . . But that external bodies, to excite in us these tastes, odors, and sounds, demand other than size, figure, number, and slow or rapid motion, I do not believe; and I judge that if the ears, the tongue, and the nostrils were taken away, the figure, the numbers, and the motions would indeed remain, but not the odors nor the tastes nor the sounds, which, without the living animal, I do not believe are anything else than names, just as tickling is precisely nothing but a name if the armpit and the nasal membrane be removed.[25]

Here even touch or weight has become a mere name: the necessary conditions of matter have been made purely mathematical. Galileo has been carried far by the inherent rationalism of his procedure along the path which later thinkers were to pursue, in converting a distinction in practice into one in ontology.

It is in the heat of this same polemic that Galileo borrows the common figure of the day.

[25] Il Saggiatore, Opere, ed. Alberi, IV, 333–36.

Philosophy is written in that great book which ever lies before our eyes —I mean the universe—but we cannot understand it if we do not first learn the language and grasp the characters in which it is written. This book is written in the mathematical language, and the characters are triangles, circles, and other geometrical figures, without whose help it is impossible to comprehend a single word of it, without which one wanders in vain through a dark labyrinth.[26]

This is of course a familiar Platonic figure; but it involves no commitment to a Platonic metaphysics, and its metaphor of language admirably suits Galileo's Aristotelian conception of the natural status of knowledge. Galileo indeed never mentions Plato except as one who recommended that we start with mathematics in studying natural philosophy.

Sagredo: What shall we say, Simplicio? Must we not confess that geometry is the most powerful of all instruments for sharpening the wit and training the mind to think correctly? Was not Plato perfectly right when he wished that his pupils should be first well-grounded in mathematics?[27]

And Simplicio is made to confess:

Believe me, if I were again beginning my studies, I should follow the advice of Plato and start with mathematics, a science which proceeds very cautiously and admits nothing as established until it has been rigidly demonstrated.[28]

Nowhere does Galileo set Plato and Aristotle in metaphysical opposition; indeed, the latter appears in the *Two New Sciences* as more interested in mechanical questions than Plato, and his principles are often accepted. The opposition Galileo sees is restricted solely to the use of mathematical procedure.

Judge, Sig. Rocco, which of the two ways of philosophizing is more to the point, your pure and simple "physical method," or mine, founded on some use of mathematics; and at the same time consider which discoursed the more judiciously, Plato in saying that without mathematics one could not learn philosophy, or Aristotle in chiding Plato for studying geometry too much.[29]

[26] *Il Saggiatore, Opere,* ed. Alberi, IV, 171; ed. Favaro, VI, 232. See also the letter to Liceti, 1641, *Opere,* ed. Favaro, XVIII, 295.
[27] *Two New Sciences,* Crew and de Salvio, p. 137.
[28] *Two New Sciences,* Crew and de Salvio, p. 90.
[29] *Esercitazioni filosofiche di Antonio Rocco,* in *Opere,* ed. Alberi, II, 329.

And to the contemporary Neoplatonism and Pythagoreanism Galileo is vigorously opposed. Simplicio is surprised at Salviati:

You that be a good mathematician, and believe many opinions in the Pythagorick philosophy, seem now to contemn their mysteries.

The reply is that the Pythagoreans thought highly of the *science* of numbers; but to suppose that what they concealed in their mysteries was "the follies that abound in the mouths and writings of the vulgar, I in no way credit." The mysteries were simply a means by which the Pythagoreans,

that admirable things might not be exposed to the contempt and scorn of the vulgar, censured as sacrilegious the publishing of the abstruse properties of numbers, and incommensurable and irrational quantities, by them investigated.[30]

Even in his friend Kepler Galileo objected to the appearance of this Neoplatonic strain: he would have no traffic with cosmic harmonies and perfections.

Profound considerations of this sort belong to a higher science than ours. We must be satisfied to belong to that class of less exalted workmen, who procure from the quarry the marble out of which later the gifted sculptor produces those masterpieces which lay hidden beneath its rough and shapeless exterior.[31]

And to Grassi he ironically objected that he had never studied the genealogy and descent of the geometrical figures, and did not know which held the older and higher rank. For building walls, however, cubes seem more perfect than spheres, just as for wheels circles are more perfect than triangles. To see everything with the Platonists as the result of the divine love of perfection explains nothing, because it could as easily explain anything else. God could with equal facility have made the sun move round the earth as not; therefore it is meaningless to seek the cause of astronomical motions in God's harmonious purposes. And Kepler's cosmic "magnetic attraction" of gravitation seemed to him likewise but a dangerous revival of the "occult qualities" of the Platonists: in his mechanistic zeal he developed his unhappy explanation of the tides in terms of the earth's motions alone. Of Kepler's attempt, he judged it better for men "to

[30] *Two Systems*, ed. Salusbury, p. 3.
[31] *Two Systems*, ed. Salusbury, p. 194.

pronounce that wise, ingenious, and modest sentence, 'I know it not,' rather than to suffer to escape from their mouths and pens all manner of extravagances." [32]

V

Indeed, it was just because he eschewed all such Platonic metaphysics that he was able to focus attention all the more on the mathematical laws of observed motions. To all questions of the real essences of things he had a single reply: unless we can express their mathematical structure, we are dealing in mere words.

Salviati: If he will but assure me what is the mover of one of these planets, I will undertake to be able to tell him what maketh the earth to move. Nay more: I will undertake to be able to do the same if he can but tell me what moveth the parts of the earth downwards.

Simplicio: The cause of this is most manifest, and everyone knows that it is gravity.

Salviati: You should say that everyone knows that it is *called* gravity; but I do not question you about the name, but about the essence of the thing . . . not as if we really understood any more, what principle or virtue that is, which moveth a stone downwards, than we know what moveth it upwards, when it is separated from the projicient, or what moveth the moon round, except only the name, which more particularly and properly we have assigned to all motions of descent, namely, gravity. [33]

This insistence that science must deal with mathematical relations, not with the nature of the terms related, is clearest in Galileo's letters about Father Scheiner and the newly discovered sunspots. The Jesuit mathematician denied that the spots could be on the sun itself, for as the most luminous of bodies the sun could not generate its opposite, darkness. As though things and essences existed for the sake of the name, not the names for the sake of the things, burst out Galileo.

Either we seek by speculation to penetrate into the true and inner essences of natural substances, or else we are satisfied with the knowledge of some of their empirical properties (*affezioni*). The first attempt I hold to be a task equally idle and vain with the nearest earthly substances and with those most distant in the heavens. We know as little the substance of the earth as of the moon, as little that of our earthly atmosphere

---

[32] *Two New Sciences, Opere,* ed. Alberi, XIII, 406.
[33] *Two Systems,* ed. Salusbury, p. 210.

as of the sunspots. For I do not see that we have any advantage in understanding nearby substances except the fulness of their individual determinations, which are all in their metaphysical essence unknown. If I ask about the substance of the clouds, I am answered, they consist of a damp mist; if I wish to know further what this mist is, so I am taught perchance that it is water rarefied through the force of warmth. If I remain in my doubt and wish to know what water really is, in all my investigations I will only learn in the end that it is that fluid which runs in streams and which we continually touch and taste: a knowledge which to be sure enriches our sense perception, but leads us no further into the interior of things than the notion I had of clouds to begin with. Thus I understand of the true and absolute essence of earth or of fire no more than of that of the moon or the sun: such a knowledge is rather reserved for the state of blessedness, in the immediate intellectual intuition of things. But if we are content to remain with an insight into the determinate properties of things, of them we need no more doubt in the most distant bodies than in the nearest; indeed the former we know more exactly than the latter. For do we not know the periods of the planets' revolutions better than the different tides of the sea? Have we not grasped the spherical form of the moon much sooner and more easily than that of the earth? . . . If it were therefore a vain beginning to inquire into the substance of sunspots, still it is not denied us to know their empirical properties, their position, their motion, their form and size, their transparency, their mutability, their genesis and their disappearance, all of which can again serve us as a means to a deeper insight into other more contentious questions of natural science.[34]

This fine mathematical positivism did not, to be sure, prevent Galileo from going on to explain the sunspots himself as black smoke given off by the ethereal pabulum of which the sun is continually devouring a constant supply to spread light and heat!

Causation Galileo treats in the same terms. "There can be but one true and primary cause of the effects that are of the same kind," some uniform, simple, and constant force whose operation can be treated mathematically, like gravitation. Secondary or immediate causes are always specific motions which produce changes in the operation of these primary forces.

That and no other is in the proper sense to be called cause, in the presence of which the effect always follows, and with the removal of which the effect ceases.[35]

[34] *Lettere intorno alle macchie solari,* in *Opere,* ed. Alberi, III, 462ff.
[35] *Il Saggiatore, Opere,* ed. Alberi, IV, 216.

How this positivism is consistent with his thoroughgoing mathematical realism Galileo tries to make clear by his distinction between
extensive and intensive knowledge.

It is well to recur to a philosophic distinction that knowing can be taken
in two ways, intensively or extensively; that is, with respect to the multitude of things to be known, which is infinite, the human understanding
is as nothing, for though it understand well a thousand propositions, a
thousand is to infinity as is zero; but taking knowing intensively, in so
far as that term means knowing perfectly any proposition, I say that
the human intellect understands some propositions as perfectly and has
of them as absolute certainty as nature herself: and such are the pure
mathematical sciences: of which the divine intellect knows indeed infinitely more propositions, since it knows them all; but of the few
understood by the human intellect I believe that our knowledge equals
the divine in objective certainty, because it succeeds in understanding
their necessity, beyond which it does not seem that there can be greater
certainty.[36]

What we know by mathematical demonstration is the very constitution and structure of things.

It was this conviction that Galileo transmitted to the seventeenth-
century scientists; it was this absolute confidence in mathematics as
the language by which the structure of the world can be grasped
that sustained him in his conflict with the Church. And it was this
scientific realism that, making him insist that the theory of Copernicus was true of nature just because it was mathematically demonstrable, led him to express the position on the relation between science and revelation which first initiated that conflict.

Methinks that in the discussion of natural problems, we ought not to
begin at the authority of places of Scripture, but at sensible experiments
and necessary demonstrations. For from the Divine Word, the sacred
Scriptures and Nature did both alike proceed . . . Nature, being in-
exorable and immutable, and never passing the bounds of the laws assigned her, as one that nothing careth, whether her abstruse reasons and
methods of operating be or be not exposed to the capacity of men; I
conceive that concerning natural effects, that which either sensible experience sets before our eyes, or necessary demonstrations do prove
unto us, ought not, upon any account, to be called into question, much
less condemned, upon the testimony of texts of Scripture, which may,
under their words, couch senses seemingly contrary thereto . . . Nor

[36] *Two Systems, Opere,* ed. Alberi, I, 116.

does God less admirably discover himself to us in Nature's actions, than in the Scripture's sacred dictions.[37]

This is the position the Church condemned in 1616, and in 1633; condemned mistakenly, for it is the position to which the Church has since returned. It is the position of Thomas Aquinas, founded on the Aristotelian faith in man's natural reason and science.

[37] *Letter to the Grand Duchess Christina*, 1615, *Opere*, ed. Alberi, Vol. II.

The Assimilation of Science

BOOK THREE

The Assimilation of Science

I

The Inherited Patterns of Interpretation

IN GALILEO the long tradition of the mathematical interpretation of nature, stretching back to the thirteenth-century Franciscans, and behind them to the mechanical science of the Alexandrians, finally joined hands with the critical and empirical developments of the Aristotelian physics and methodology. There in his *Two New Sciences* was the model finally achieved of a type of knowledge that would render man the master and possessor of nature; there was the intellectual instrument fully formed, the answer to more than a century of eager search after a fruitful and powerful method. But Galileo, for all his pugnacity, scarcely foresaw the shattering effect of his own discoveries. He was willing to fight with determined discretion for his new sciences; but even he had no realization that his battle was for science itself. It was the work of an entire century to consolidate and generalize the model and the instrument he had presented. Men had to explore the implications of this new type of knowledge, to fit it into the familiar pattern of their ideas and assimilate it to those categories through which they were accustomed to make their experience of the world intelligible. This was the task of the great philosophic systems, so tantalizing in their sublime disregard of paradoxes and problems in which later generations have floundered. For to understand and interpret the new science men naturally turned to the schemes of ideas they had inherited from the Middle Ages; and in their first confidence it seemed that "science" had furnished a definitive answer to all the medieval questions. Now at last men had discovered the very essence of nature and man and of God. They did not see that the ultimate consequence of the science they had formulated was to make all such questions meaningless; nor did they realize that the schemes of interpretation they fell back on to render that science intelligible, were destined themselves to grow unintelligible in the face of the materials to which they were applied. Those systems of the first age of science—Cartesianism, Spinoza, Leibniz, Hobbes, Newton, and Locke—stand consequently both as the highest development of the materials inherited from Greek thought, the final flowering of the classic tradition, and as the point of departure for that movement of intellectual criticism of the Greek tradition which in one form or another has dominated the philosopher's enterprise ever since.

It was this assimilation and interpretation of science, not its revolutionary application to human values and affairs, that was to furnish the chief stimulus to thought for the next hundred years. Not till the eighteenth century were men sufficiently acclimated to science to employ it to express their new social aspirations and struggles. Ironically enough, it was still in terms of the Reformation and Counter Reformation theologies, terms so soon to be pushed aside into irrelevance, that the seventeenth century fought the economic conflicts that were so basic in determining the future capitalistic structure of the world. Not only were those few scientific thinkers like Spinoza and Hobbes whose chief concern was man, without immediate influence on the course of events; the gospels of deliverance they preached in such clear-cut scientific terms were but rationalized renderings of medieval ways of salvation, and in their substance scarcely belong to the modern world. Men had to learn to handle science before they could use it as a new weapon in their fights.

To speed this handling, there were available three traditional interpretations of knowledge, three great philosophies of science inherited from the late Middle Ages. To one or another of them, or to some combination, the system-builders of the seventeenth century naturally and inevitably turned. On them they drew for the concepts of reason and experience, for the construings of the fact of knowledge, with which to make intelligible the new mathematical physics and the world it described. These three were the Platonic tradition, in its Hellenistic and Augustinian form; the realistic Aristotelianism of Thomas and Scotus, and of the Padua Averroists; and the nominalistic Aristotelianism of the Ockhamites and terminists.

The Augustinian theory of knowledge had been reinforced by

the Neoplatonists of the Renaissance; their holy Plato, as we have seen, they usually viewed through the familiar eyes of St. Augustine. It was rendered especially congenial by the actual mathematical character of the new science; and possessing a mathematical method but no physics of its own, it proved a seductive alternative to impatient rebels against the peripatetic philosophy of nature. For this great tradition, the proper object of science is a Logos, a rational structure or system of ideas, an intelligible realm the content of which is best illustrated by the truths of mathematics. The right method of science is the direct apprehension or intuition of these intelligible ideas and their relations or structure by *Nous* or Intellect. Experience is fragmentary and unimportant; at best it affords but a dim image or illustration of the ideas which intellect perceives in their purity. Indeed, the knowledge that experience does bring comes not from the action of sense from without, but from the internal action of reason itself when instigated by sense. In all its essential outlines, this is the theory of knowledge employed by Descartes, Malebranche, and the Cartesians; and so far as method is concerned, followed by Spinoza and Leibniz.

For the realistic Aristotelianism of the Thomists and the Paduans, the proper object of science is rather the reasons, the *archai* or principles, embedded in natural objects and in nature itself, explaining them and it; it is not a separate intelligible realm, but rather the intelligible structure of the world of ordinary experience. The right method is a rational interpretation of the materials furnished by sense-experience: for the Thomists, "abstraction" of the intelligible forms of things embedded in the phantasms of sense; for the Paduans, a critical analysis of sense facts taken as instances of intelligible structure. This was the interpretation followed by most of the scientists themselves, by Galileo, by the rational experimenters, and by Newton half the time. It was followed also, so far as the object and status of science are concerned, by Spinoza and Leibniz, in combination with Platonism as to method: their method is Platonic and mathematical, but its object is conceived in Aristotelian fashion, as the intelligible aspect or formal structure of the world. And since they held fast to the fundamental Aristotelian conviction, that ideas are the forms of substances, and the human soul the form of the body, they alone in the seventeenth century were able to make the new science intelligible. When this position was employed to interpret the new philosophy of nature, the intelligible aspect of the world was shorn of the teleology of the Aristotelian tradition and made purely formal or mathematical; and it was caught up in a unified mathematical system novel to the Aristotelian pluralism.

For the nominalistic Aristotelianism of the Ockhamites, the proper object of science is the precise definition and rigorous analysis of terms which signify or are the marks of individual things causally related; or, as we should say, a deductive postulate system that can serve as the interpretation of natural events. The right method is by sense or "intuitive knowledge" to observe things causing other things, and then so to define one's terms that the same consequences will follow logically from their analysis as are observed to follow in experience from the causes of which those terms are marks,—that is, to construct a rigorous postulate system that can "stand for" or "represent" the observed course of nature. This was the interpretation followed by Hobbes, by Locke, and by Newton the rest of the time; it furnished the presuppositions of British empiricism.

These were the three familiar construings of knowledge the scientific thinkers had inherited: their lineaments are clearly discernible in every philosophy of the century. Not for a hundred years was science conceived in fundamentally different terms. But they remained no mere external patterns of interpretation into which the new ideas could be fitted. In the very process of their employment they were themselves transformed. For they had been first worked out by the Greeks and then elaborated during the Middle Ages, not in isolation, but as integral parts of well-organized conceptions of the universe. They were not theories of any conceivable science: they were interpretations of science in a very definite kind of world. When that world had itself been transformed by Galileo and his colleagues, what had before seemed so simple and natural took on the aspect of a mystery. In the new world their renderings of knowledge appeared no longer as statements of a fact, but as posings of a problem. Fresh knowledge made knowledge itself seem impossible in the world it purported to describe.

In all three of these medieval philosophies of knowledge, man had existed as a rational animal in an intelligible world. The new science made the Logos, the intelligible structure of knowledge, a mathematical order; but it made the world itself and man's experience of it wholly mechanical, and robbed them of all intelligibility. Pouring mathematical physics into the Augustinian tradition transformed it into mathematical rationalism; it confronted men with a mathematical order directly open to mind, but it left unanswered the question of the relation of that order to the world itself. Pouring it into the Aristotelian tradition, created mechanistic empiricism; men had a mechanical system that must be derived from physical contact, but they had no notion how such contact could give rise to such a system. The rationalists emphasized the mathematical method of the new knowledge; with the Cartesians, the fact of systematic science grew all important, and the world itself vanished into the structure of science, becoming in Malebranche a mere system of mathematical propositions. The empiricists emphasized the outcome of that knowledge, the world of body in motion; with Hobbes and Locke, the fact of a mechanical world grew all important, and science vanished into a play of mechanical motions, or still more perplexingly, of ideas taken as the physical effects of mechanical motions. Such was the dilemma: either science but no world, or a world but no science. With the more critical generation of Leibniz and Locke the problem had grown more acute, and was launched for the eighteenth century as the basic "Problem of Knowledge." It was inevitable that a way out should be sought by the German physicists and Kant through combining the difficulties of both philosophies.

Thus to our sophisticated historical perspective, modern thought was far from starting out with a fresh clean slate, as its pioneers so fondly believed. Even in its most revolutionary thinkers, like Descartes and Hobbes, it was dominated by medieval traditions. These traditions were used, criticized, revised, reconstructed, and re-expressed, but their materials persisted. The major portion of the beliefs of the most radical of philosophers was as always old. New ideas, above all those of mathematical physics, were forcing their way in, but the old were left as the only means of understanding, till the discrepancies proved too great. All the great seventeenth-century systems, so proud in their independence, aimed essentially at conciliation; like Spinoza, they sought to bend the new physics to the support of old values. No wonder modern thought has presented so many well-nigh insoluble problems; it has from the beginning been a pouring of new wine into old bottles. Well may we in our ignorance exclaim, the happy Greeks! they had no problems of adjustment, they could interpret the world as they found it: they had no traditions. The moderns found so many worlds, so many traditions—the world of Aristotelian logic and metaphysics, and the world of mathematical physics; the world of medieval institutions, and the world of pushing commerce.

And thus in this fashion the central intellectual problem of modern thought became, how to adjust the classic conception of science as a system of implications to the Galileo-Cartesian conception of the world as a series of motions of independent particles of matter. How were men to understand both, and one in terms of the other? Men can easily believe and work with contradictions, but they cannot understand them. This emerged as the fundamental problem of modern philosophy, the "problem of knowledge," the problem of science itself. If men could not understand the fact of science, their chief tool and greatest glory, how could they hope to understand anything at all? All the other problems of modern culture, all the practical problems of liberation and adjustment and reconstruction, came ultimately to point toward this problem of knowledge; all programs of action came to be formulated in terms of some particular grappling with it. Just as all medieval problems received their ultimate expression in terms of the issues of logic, so modern problems have been voiced in terms of the issues of epistemology. We may ridicule the one, we may denounce the other; we cannot ignore the vast human significance each derived from its focusing of all the problems of conciliation and assimilation of new to old. Indeed, we may cherish more than a suspicion that few have really wanted to "solve" this problem of knowledge. Science worked too well, and was far too powerful an instrument, for the scientists to bother to make it intelligible in the old terms or to seek out new ones in its own processes. And for the practical fighters in the social struggles, the problem of knowledge proved more of an instrument than a difficulty. So easy a weapon was it for discrediting the beliefs and ideologies of their opponents that they had every motive to keep it alive.

In all this intellectual activity, the aim was given and rarely criticised. For the Greeks, the ultimate problem was that of the Good

Life: what is it? It was the problem of ends. The moderns have settled all that; or, rather, their own society has settled it for them: its drive is to make money and enjoy life, and gain the freedom to do so. Their problem has been, how? It is the problem of means; at its very best, how to get such freedom for all. This aim has been set by commerce and industry, by its wealth and power, by the "forces and relations of production," as the Marxians put it. When all institutions and beliefs favored the landholders, and hampered commerce, the problem was to alter them, and to get the intellectual basis for such an economic and class revolution. When medieval ideals and ecclesiastical and feudal institutions proved a hindrance, commerce brought new values and new social organizations in the Renaissance and the Reformation, and Puritanism came to express the individualistic commercialism, the rugged individualism of the seventeenth century. When medieval science proved useless and barren, commerce brought a science that is power over nature, and turned it equally into a new power over man. When the industrial revolution created two new classes out of the townsfolk, around 1850, those who got money and enjoyment, and those who didn't, it raised a dual problem: how to maintain these new ideas and institutions in the face of their consequences, or how to alter them again. And it led to a new religion and ethic of collectivistic hedonism, a new science of social control over industry and society.

These have been the practical motives back of modern thought and philosophy, as of all other manifestations of modern culture. They have commingled with the theoretical motives of how to incorporate what has been new into older traditions. Only with such a realization can we grasp why modern philosophy has been such a mixture of justification and understanding, and why there has been so much justification and so little understanding. Commerce injected the individual seeking his own self-interest into the nicely balanced institutional world of the Middle Ages, and created the basic problem of individualism versus collectivism, both economic and political: the problem of reconciling Liberty and Social Control. It injected the irresponsible national state seeking "national prosperity" into the body of unified Christendom, and created the problem of international relations, the problem of reconciling expansion and peace. Seventeenth-century science injected the content of mechanics into the Aristotelian deductive system of knowledge, a world of body and motion into the Greek tradition. It created the problem of reconciling the method of science with its outcome, the problem of knowledge. Eighteenth-century Newtonian science injected the Order of Nature into the Christian epic, and precipitated the conflict of science and theology. It injected man as a mechanism into a scheme of values based on man as a free moral agent, and generated the problem of the conflict of science with traditional morality, the problem of determinism. And philosophers have had to defend, criticize, adjust and understand all these elements; no single problem have they been able to consider in isolation. No wonder modern thought has been complicated and ingenious. And no wonder that it has been unstable and impermanent—thank God!

2

Descartes and the Cartesian Revolution

WITH DESCARTES a new factor enters into the stream of European thought, the fact of "modern science," as something to be defended, understood, adjusted, and used. It was not the first time that a modern science had insistently made its appearance, nor was it to be the last. Such an incursion had happened in the twelfth century, in the fourteenth, often in the fifteenth, and it was to happen again in the late seventeenth, in the nineteenth, and in our own century. Each time, to be sure, it was a different kind of science; but each time it was modern, each time it was the truth discovered at last, each time it was a turning away from futile metaphysics to what the world was really found to be. That is why the characteristic problem of modern philosophy has been the conflict of new knowledge with traditional thought, and the attempt to find some adjustment between them.

I

René Descartes (1596–1650) is the Frenchman who thus started modern philosophy. He was, of course, not the only man who performed this unique service. There was also an Englishman, a German, and a host of Italians who accomplished the same great end. But Descartes was unquestionably the major influence in seventeenth-century philosophical thought. The popularity of his ideas was for a generation like the later reign of Newton and Locke, or that of Kant, or of the idea of Evolution. His first work was published in 1637, and by his death in 1650 his philosophy of nature was established as supreme. There were on the important points few dissenters in the learned world, especially in France and Holland, which now took the intellectual leadership of Europe from the Italians. In the name of Descartes it was proclaimed that the Aristotelian world was dead, that the world was fundamentally mathematical and mechanical. There were, to be sure, divergences of interpretation; but they were largely within the stream of Cartesianism—it had no serious rivals. And though Newton in the next generation made certain modifications that seemed in his day fundamental, the main outlines of the Cartesian universe persisted for a hundred and fifty years, until a really different philosophic impulse set physics in a subordinate place. During this period every field of human interest was reconstructed on the basis of reason and mathematics. It was the task of the seventeenth century to make nature geometrical and mechanical, of the eighteenth century, to include man and society within the picture.

Descartes was the first to attempt to explore the further implications of mathematical physics—of the method of explaining natural events as the mechanical motions of bodies in simple mathematical relation. He was not content, like Galileo and his predecessors, to use this method to find out new facts about the world: he insisted on creating a new philosophy of nature that would answer all the questions. Galileo, he believed, had found the right method, "to examine physical matters by mathematics." He abandons the errors of the Schools. But he has built without a foundation, for he has not considered the first causes of nature. Men must have a complete, well-rounded philosophy in which all the traditional problems are solved, and a new picture of the world set in a metaphysical framework which both guarantees its validity and develops its implications. Hence Descartes became the symbol of the utter rejection, not only of the "errors of the Schools," of Aristotelian physics, but also of all the various abortive attempts of the Renaissance to interpret nature as essentially like man—to display man as natural and nature as human. Far from being macrocosm and microcosm, the two were henceforth to be sharply sundered.

But to defend, interpret, and develop the implications of mathematical physics, Descartes had no place to go for a theory of knowledge and metaphysical principles save those same despised Schools. He accordingly fell back on one of the great medieval philosophical traditions, Augustinian Neoplatonism; and he effected so complete a blend of the Augustinian philosophy and mathematical physics that Malebranche, the light of the Oratoire, found Descartes and St. Augustine in perfect accord, and *le grand siècle* closed in a blaze of Christian piety and Cartesian rationalism. It is ironical that the man who thought he was making a complete break with the past now appears as another stage in the tradition stretching back to Chartres and the Oxford Franciscans, and can be aptly called "the most profound of the followers of St. Augustine."

Descartes used Augustinian thought to interpret and understand the new science. This was momentous for science, for it gave an Augustinian, Platonic caste to its fundamental concepts, like space and time. It was also momentous for the Augustinian tradition, for that it transformed into mathematical rationalism, one of the two great philosophical currents of the modern era; and it raised the characteristic problems with which scientific Platonism has wrestled ever since. In the pages of Descartes is revealed what the Augustinian tradition became in a universe containing only matter in motion.

II

Descartes was at heart a mathematical physicist, not primarily a philosopher—though no one in the seventeenth century would have made such a sharp distinction between natural philosophy and first philosophy—a physicist who consummated a fundamental revolution in science because he was given to reflecting on the implications of the new concepts, and had a passion for generalizing and systematizing. He cared for little outside physics, and knew less; and he drew on a rather curious mixture of traditional metaphysical ideas as a support for his radical break with traditional physics. He is comparable today, not to Dewey, Morris Cohen, or Whitehead, but to men like Eddington and Jeans—i.e., he was a man of some scientific originality and great philosophic confusion.

His early years were spent in the full swing of the mathematical renaissance. He emerged from a good scholastic education at the Jesuit school of La Flèche, convinced that only analysis, or algebra, and geometry were sound knowledge. Like many another young man, he joined the army to see the world; but unlike most of them, he spent all his spare time poring over mathematical problems relating to falling bodies, water pressure, or music. He devoted himself to them until one memorable day, the tenth of November, 1619, when he was twenty-three years old, there came to him a dream, a kind of mystic vision, which left an indelible stamp upon his mind. The Angel of Truth visited him and the bade him trust his intuition that the world is fundamentally mathematical in structure, that the laws of mathematics are indeed the key to the mysteries of nature. Descartes never forgot this vision of a universal mathematics, a science of order and measurement applicable to any subject-matter, "a more powerful instrument of knowledge than any other." It seems to have been for him a genuine religious experience: he vowed and completed a pilgrimage to Loretto in gratitude. And it was undoubtedly the source of his "inexsuperable confidence" in the mathematical method, and his conviction that God himself guarantees the truth of the new science. Had not God sent one of His angels to tell him so? Descartes was, in fact, a pious physicist—than which there can be, as we have learned again of late, no more radical subverter of all sound theology. Inspired by this enthusiasm, he worked feverishly to combine analysis and geometry in treating spatial relations. He worked out analytic geometry; and he never got over this initial success. Ever after he saw the world as pure geometry, pure extension, and as such completely intelligible.

Descartes proceeded to sketch out the details of a mathematical physics. At first, he turned to specific problems: music, optics, the weight of the air, etc., without bothering to come to grips with the reigning Aristotelian explanations. Gradually he became aware it would be a battle to the death. The Aristotelian world of substances with objective qualities or "substantial forms" must be swept away, completely. He grew more and more radical, intolerant of everything not mathematical in character. He drew up a list of Aristotelian qualities: heat, levitation, gravitation, hardness, resolved to explain all of them, every quality of bodies, in terms of matter and motion alone.

About this time, in 1628, he withdrew from his friends to Holland, to think through this radical step and its implications; for he had come to realize that it was one thing, disregarding the established ideas of nature, to employ the mathematical method upon specific problems, and quite another to insist that only the results of that method are true, and all the established ideas are in error. He was seeking a foundation upon which he could erect a complete new philosophy of nature, and deny the truth of every other, especially of the Aristotelian. After nine months he was convinced that he had such a foundation; and upon it he proceeded to construct a systematic science of physics, in the *Traité du monde* (not published till 1664). Let us imagine, he bids us, how God might have created the world, using nothing but matter in motion. "We shall attribute to matter a nature in which there is nothing at all that anyone cannot know as perfectly as possible"—i.e., mathematically. On every page he insists: "there is nothing we cannot clearly conceive, nothing simpler or easier to understand, nothing which the dullest minds are not capable of conceiving." As to combustion, "another may imagine in the burning wood the form of fire, the quality of heat and the act which burns it, as three wholly different things; as for me, who am afraid of deceiving myself if I suppose anything more to be there than what I see must necessarily be present, I am content to conceive there only the movement of its parts." And he concludes, "Such a world must appear to its inhabitants just like ours." [1]

It is clear Descartes is offering not just a "new science," like Galileo, but a radical, intolerant, exclusive new philosophy of nature, in terms of nothing but matter and motion. It was so radical that when he heard in 1633 that Galileo had been condemned, he sent his treatise away, lest he be tempted to publish it. For he realized he must employ careful tactics: not merely to escape the Church, though he did wish to live untroubled by her inquisitors, not merely to win general acceptance—he must be absolutely certain, he must prove his views as demonstratively as Euclid. In 1637 he finally published three specimens of the fruits of the mathematical method, with a persuasive preface, not too shocking—the *Dioptrics, Meteors,* and *Geometry*, preceded by the *Discourse on Method*. In 1640 he prepared his *Meditations on First Philosophy*, to persuade men to accept the radical principles of his physics. They are a kind of combination of metaphysical arguments and spiritual exercises, to detach men from sense, from taking the world, like Aristotle, at its face value—quite literally meditations, culminating, not so much in the proof of the existence of material things, as in the proof that they consist of nothing but particles in motion. He sent copies to

[1] *Le Monde, ou Traité de la lumière*, chs. 6, 2, 15. In *Oeuvres*, ed. Victor Cousin, Tome IV; ed. Adam et Tannery, Tome XI; Eng. tr. in *Descartes Selections*, ed. Ralph M. Eaton (1927).

all the scientific men of his day, collected their objections, and carefully answered them all, altering not one jot or tittle of his own views. The ground thus cleared, he worked out in systematic form his *Principles of Philosophy*, which presented, in 1644, the main outlines of a new philosophy of nature, proved from absolutely certain axioms. This was the first of the great deductive systems of modern science, the ancestor of Newton's *Principia Mathematica*. It concludes: "There is no phenomenon in nature which has not been dealt with in this treatise"; and all the explanations, in terms of motion, magnitude, and figure alone, are derived in a continual series of demonstrations from the "first and most simple principles of human knowledge," and hence absolutely true.

III

The Cartesian physics has many aspects of fundamental importance both for his own and for subsequent philosophical thought. It was the first attempt to sketch the comprehensive plan by which the universe was made, and give an explanation of all phenomena in purely mechanical terms. Descartes believed the filling in of details would be, as it has been, the work of generations. It was the fundamental idea that most interested him: the thoroughgoing application of the method of reductive analysis, of explaining the whole in terms of the behavior of its separate parts, in sharp contrast to the Aristotelian method of functional analysis, of understanding the parts in terms of their operations in the whole.

Now Descartes's early scientific discoveries were the product of the application of mathematical technique to experience, and led to the formulation of natural laws in mathematical terms. In his actual practice he proceeded as mathematical experimentalists have always done: his basic optical discovery of the equality of the sines of the angles of incidence and of refraction was reached experimentally, in 1626, and only later fitted into the deductive proof given in the *Dioptrics*. It is in the analysis of light, in fact, that Descartes can be said to have succeeded measurably in erecting a mathematical science of nature. And as his correspondence reveals, he was always eager to work upon mathematical problems, like the laws of pendulums. But the striking thing about his systematic *Principia* is the absence of mathematical formulation, even of the attempt to arrive at mathematical explanations. Instead every phenomenon is dealt with by some assumed mechanism of particles of matter in motion. Open its pages, and in the many copper-plates with which they are provided you will find swarms of tiny billiard-balls producing all the features of the world we experience. It is somewhat puzzling that Descartes the inventor of analytic geometry should have made no use of it in his own physics, that he should have been content to give a purely mechanical interpretation of nature with no attempt at mathematical precision. For all his emphasis on the need of systematic deduction from rigorous principles, in his oversimplified mechanical constructions he lagged far behind the much less thoroughgoing Kepler or Galileo.

The secret lies in this very systematic and rigorous ideal itself. Descartes was not content with the mathematical formulation of the laws of phenomena in the gross. To be completely understood, the motion of each single particle of matter would have to be mathematically determined; and that was an impossible task. At bottom, of course, he did not possess the mathematical tool to deal precisely with motion; the calculus of Newton and Leibniz was needed to complete that task. Hence he could be strictly mathematical only where geometrical relations were sufficient, as with light rays. But Descartes was also convinced that the enormous complication of movements involved in the simplest phenomenon, the countless contacts of particles at each instant that would have to be calculated, precluded any hope of mathematical precision. No human mind could predict all the contacts to which a single body would be subject in our universe, nor its consequent velocity and direction. Such prediction is theoretically possible, *metaphysice loquendo;* but not *physice* or *moraliter loquendo.* It is certain that everything must be produced by mechanical contact; but the precise details must escape the wit of man. Even Descartes shrank before the task of constructing our universe in all its infinite variety out of its multitudinous parts. And thus the very magnitude of a completely deductive science drove Descartes, as it drove Newton, to another and more modest goal. Only God the perfect geometer could know the details of the pure space or extension out of which he created the world.

That he did so, that much we can know. What is material substance or body? Descartes asks. Take the example of wax, which can change all its "sensible species" without ceasing to be wax. The one thing that remains constant is its extension, its possession of dimensions. Material substance therefore consists of extension and nothing else. So runs Descartes's argument; but the reader suspects that back of it lies his epochal discovery of analytic geometry. If substance can be only that which can be mathematically conceived, and if mathematics can deal completely and adequately with extension alone, surely here is temptation enough to make the identification. Extended substance is one homogeneous matter, infinite both in compass and in divisibility; since it is itself pure space, there can be no vacuum, and nature is at all points completely occupied, a plenum. The particles of this extension differ in size, figure, and velocity; they possess the extra-geometrical property of impenetrability, necessary to make possible action by mechanical contact. This Cartesian view was known in the seventeenth century as the "corpuscular theory"; it was shared by many of the scientists, like Hobbes and Boyle. In contrast to it stood the opposing but equally mechanical "atomic theory" of Gassendi and Huygens, which gave to the elements of matter a physical indivisibility, admitted qualitative differences of kind among them, and located them in the traditional Democritean void. Descartes's mechanistic theory resembles the mathematical atomism of the Timaeus and the Platonic tradition, rather than the atomism of Democritus and the Epicureans.

Descartes in fact excluded everything from his world which his mathematical technique was unable to handle: as he himself would have put it, everything which he could not clearly and distinctly conceive. All the Aristotelian concepts for rendering nature intelligible which could not lend themselves to mathematical expression went by the board. The subsequent progress of physics can be viewed as the development of improved mathematical techniques to handle more and more of the experienced aspects of the world, until today most of the Aristotelian concepts have been brought back again, this time in precise mathematical form. There was for Descartes no concept of mass: it remained for Newton to define mass with precision. There was no notion of force, of gravitation, of attraction in the magnet. Force belonged to the nature enthusiasts, not the sober scientist, for whom kinetic energy, the energy of motion by contact, alone sufficed. The only admitted cause was mechanical contact; no action at a distance was conceivable. To orthodox Cartesians, Newton's "gravitation" seemed a surrender to the schools; force was an "occult power." This rigorous mechanism contrasts strangely with our own physics, in which no contact is presumed ever to occur.

IV

The peculiarities of Descartes's statement of the laws of motion had far-reaching ramifications. The quantity of matter and of motion remains constant in all change, assumptions which Descartes proves by the good Scotist doctrine of the constancy and immutability of God's will. Unfortunately the second constant is wrong. All motion is naturally in a straight line. There is no inner force, no inertia, in bodies; motion is an external quality, an accident added from outside (one recognizes the impetus theory of the Ockhamites). Hence there must necessarily be a source of motion, a first efficient cause, a Creator. Newton consecrated this mechanical theology, and the first cause lasted as a scientific concept until Hume and Kant. The quantity of motion and its direction are wholly unconnected; with no concept of mass, Descartes believed that the latter might be altered without changing the former. Hence the interaction of mind and body was no violation of his physics: the soul can change the direction of motion without altering its quantity.

Since matter is identified with extension or space, there is no empty space distinguished from matter or extended substance. There never had been, in fact, save in the discredited minor tradition of the Democritean void. The idea of a vacuum, of empty space, so closely identified with the scientific thought of the early modern period, belongs to Newtonian physics. It rose with it, and has fallen with it; and even there it had to be promptly filled with an "ether." The world for Descartes is a plenum: there is something doing something at every point. Today, Descartes is judged right, and Newton wrong. There is physical action everywhere, and space is not independent, but rather the structure of the cosmic field of energy. Descartes was wrong, not in making space a plenum, but in not making time one also, in assuming time to be an independent entity, measured by motion, instead of the measure or structure of motion. Like all the seventeenth-century physicists, except Leibniz, he turned from the Aristotelian to the Platonic doctrine of time— an idea natural to a geometer, for whom time is necessarily something external to his subject-matter. But Descartes held to the Aristotelian doctrine of place in its essentials: all motion is relative to an adjoining body or container. Since the earth is carried about the sun in its vortex, it does not move in relation to adjacent bodies; and thus Descartes was able to satisfy the Church in rejecting Copernicus.

These notions were all combined in the Cartesian vortex theory, the first attempt at a mechanical, contact theory on a cosmic scale. All motion in a plenum must be circular: something must move out of the way before anything else can move. The universe is consequently composed of a multitude of vortices or *tourbillons*, set in motion directly by the First Cause; they in turn cause all other phenomena. There are in these vortices three kinds of matter, which differ only in size and velocity. The slowest and largest particles are pushed by the more rapidly moving and finer ones to the center of the vortex, where they form the earth and the other heavenly bodies, just as logs cluster in the center of a whirlpool. The swiftest and subtlest particles form "first matter," which presses the rest toward the center. Gravitation is thus an affair of pressure, not attraction; light is due to centrifugal motion from the stars. Heat is the motion of particles. This First Matter was adopted and named "aether" by Hooke. It has been beloved by British physicists to recent times. Some such ether is necessary on any substantial, mechanical theory; it is needless if one thinks in functional terms. The most notable feature of this whole hypothesis is that it is a mechanical but not a mathematical theory; Descartes offers many a diagram and copper-plate, but never an equation. All the functions not amenable to geometrical treatment: momentum, inertia, acceleration, gravitation, etc., are performed for him by vortices of first matter, or fine billiard-balls. It is a magnificent and breath-taking theory; but it was an "hypothesis" that could not be verified, and was barren of all predictive value. It was consequently rejected by Newton, who framed no hypotheses, but deduced everything from phenomena.

The method Descartes actually followed in constructing this

cosmogony is clear. It was to devise some mechanism, in terms of his billiard-balls in constant mechanical contact, that would produce the effects which experience displays. "And in this the example of certain things made by human art was of no little assistance to me; for I recognize no difference between these machines and natural bodies," except in the scale of the tubes and springs employed.[2]

It must not be thought, however, that Descartes was no experimentalist; on the contrary, he had only scorn for those who explained the nature of the heavens without having observed their movements, who studied mechanics without reference to moving bodies, and sought to describe nature out of their own heads. Experience must indicate the precise character of the phenomena to be accounted for; the starting-point of every mechanical explanation must be a careful history in the style of Bacon, to whose rules for experimentation he had "nothing to add." The physicist can give no answer to the question, What is the magnet? but only to the question, "What must be inferred as to the nature of the magnet from that precise set of experiments which Gilbert asserts he has performed?"[3] And experience alone can indicate the particular effects that follow from the general principles of mechanics.

We are unable to determine by reason alone how great are the parts of this matter, how quickly they are moved, or what circles they describe; for these things could have been ordered by God in innumerable different ways, and which one he has chosen from the rest only experience can teach.[4]

It is experience that in good Aristotelian fashion establishes the "fact that"; reasoning adds the "reason why," which can only be a mechanism of bodies in motion.

Descartes applied his mechanical views to living organisms as well. He held to a thoroughly mechanistic biology and psychology. Life is a matter of motion and heat alone; there is no scholastic vegetative or sensitive soul, no vital principle. Animals are complete automata, mere complicated machines; and so are the bodies of men.

[2] *The Principles of Philosophy*, Part IV, Principle 203; *The Philosophical Works of Descartes*, tr. E. S. Haldane and G. R. T. Ross (1911), I, 299; ed. Adam et Tannery, VIII, 326.
[3] *Rules for the Direction of the Mind*, Rule 13; ed. Haldane and Ross, I, 49; Adam et Tannery, X, 431.
[4] *Principles*, Part III, Principle 46; ed. Cousin, III, 210-11; Adam et Tannery, VIII, 100-1.

Descartes's physiology is crude enough in detail; struck by Harvey's discovery of the circulation of the blood, he explained everything by the passage of particles of blood through the veins from the heart, which he took to be a furnace rather than a pump, to the various parts of the body where the heat performs the different bodily functions. It is the heat of the heart, "the great spring and principle of all bodily movements," which dilates the blood into that "very subtle air or wind" called the animal spirits, which circulates through the nerves.

Descartes's physiological interest was growing toward the end of his life, together with an increased concern for observation. To a visitor who asked to be shown his library, he pointed to a leg of mutton he was dissecting. How far this experimental interest might have taken him, had not the Queen of Sweden killed him by making him get up at 5 A.M. to give her lessons in science, there is no means of knowing. But it is significant that the greatest physiologists of the seventeenth century, especially the Dutchmen Leeuwenhoek and Boerhaave, were declared Cartesians and mechanists.

V

We have dwelt on Descartes's philosophy of nature, not merely because his vision of universal mathematics was his most important contribution to modern thought; but also because his first philosophy, so influential in formulating the problems with which the next two centuries were to wrestle, though his own solutions were soon rejected, is intelligible only as the thought of a man with such scientific interests and methods. It is not simply that Descartes worked out his physics, and then sought for a metaphysics to prove it: we know too much about the growth of his ideas to hold to any such simple relation between the two, even if it were not clear that in his final system, the *Principia*, they are indissolubly knit together. His first philosophy was rather the indispensable instrument for rounding out and generalizing his vision of method, and establishing it as the Truth by criticizing all other methods and physics.

It is not hard to realize Descartes's problem of defending and interpreting his radical new science. If mathematical physics is not only true, but is the only truth about nature, it surely needs a critical foundation. It is significant that Descartes raised the questions of the validity and certainty of his science only after he had for nine years practiced the mathematical interpretation as a method of discovery. Such questions must be answered if his method was to be raised to the level of a philosophy of nature. Cartesian rationalism is the first apologetic of the new science. It is an attempt to answer all the problems that occur to a modern reader, without the immense prestige of a successful mathematical physics to still such doubts. Descartes was no fool: he could see the difficulties as well as a modern student, and had he been blinded by his enthusiasm, his contemporaries would have opened his eyes. The objections and responses to his *Meditations* discuss all the questions which have ever been raised about the mathematical interpretation of nature. "Is the world nothing but a mathematical harmony? Do mathematical axioms apply exactly to all existence? Will the laws of physics always hold good of nature?" These questions are still fundamental in our own discussions of the philosophy of science.

Descartes never for a moment doubted that his own method, on its positive side, gave truth; though even he had difficulty in really believing its negative side, that the old Aristotelian world of common-sense was gone—in "detaching himself from sense," in refusing to find any truth in ordinary experience. He had had his vision, and retained the confidence it engendered. Suppose, he says, we have found the key to a cipher which gives us a rational and intelligible message. Surely we would have moral certainty that the cipher had been written with that key. But such moral certainty, however adequate for Descartes himself, was not enough to convince doubting theologians and humanists, and Aristotelian physicists, not enough even to establish his own faith in the sole sufficiency of mathematics and the absolute distrust of the qualitative world of sense. One gets in Descartes a vivid impression of how necessary it was, if modern science was to be born, to emancipate the mind completely from the views of the past. Had the seventeenth-century scientists not possessed their negative faith and their purifying zeal, they would all have succumbed to traditional old wives' tales, just as those did who lacked it. There was an historical necessity for wiping the slate clean, if the new science was to get under way at all: only that which was mathematically proved could be accepted.

VI

And so, in 1628, nine years after that youthful vision in the upper chamber, when his most original discoveries in physics and in mathematics had already been made, and the structure of his system of nature had been largely worked out, Descartes at last undertook to find a metaphysical foundation for his method that would purify the conception of the world of the results of other methods.

As we were born children, and have formed various judgments about sensible things before we possessed the whole use of our reason, we are led away from the knowledge of the truth by many precipitate judgments, from which we can in no wise be delivered unless once in our lifetime we undertake to doubt all those things in which we find the slightest suspicion of uncertainty.[5]

We must realize just what Descartes was doing as a scientist. He was making a colossal hypothesis, an immense "anticipation of nature"; and though it had been made before in one of the medieval traditions, it had appeared there always as a corollary of the imposing Neoplatonic-Augustinian metaphysical system. There was no achieved body of scientific results to silence doubts. In the second place, Descartes was employing a mathematical method: he was deducing the consequences of mathematical ideas, confident that what is true of those ideas holds also of things. In his actual way of discovery, to be sure, especially where he used his billiard-balls and not his mathematics, he proceeded like everyone else to investigate problems experimentally. But he remained the mathematician interested in chains of proof, devoted to the Aristotelian ideal of a science like geometry that would prove why things must be as they are; and his system of physics remains independent of experience, save for incidental illustration. Thirdly, he was boldly excluding from nature everything not "conceivable" in mathematical terms, in a world which still trusted in the uncriticized experience of common sense. He must establish conceivability as the sole test of knowledge, for he was staking everything upon it.

To combat the Aristotelian physics, and the empirical method upon which it was founded, which started with things, and ab-

[5] *Principles*, Part I, Principle 1; Haldane and Ross, I, 219; Adam et Tannery, VIII, 5.

stracted concepts and forms from them, he turned to the scholastic tradition that had always supported the mathematical method of starting with ideas and analyzing their implications in the intelligible realm, as the surest knowledge of things. He turned to the Augustinian philosophy. Descartes's interest in philosophy was always as the handmaiden of science. He read widely, but always in the hope of getting a convincing answer to all objections against the new mathematical physics. His primary concern was to justify a revolution in physics, not to create a new metaphysics. Hence his materials and his ideas are drawn rather eclectically from the several medieval traditions. He would have defeated his own purpose, had he not appealed to respectable positions widely accepted in his own day. Just so Jefferson, in drafting the Declaration of Independence, had to express what men believed rather than create a new political theory.

Now Aristotelian scholasticism, either Thomist or Scotist, was an unsatisfactory foundation: it peopled nature with substantial forms and real qualities, and it had an imposing physics of its own. It founded its validity upon the apprehension of intentional species in experience. A mathematical physics could never be founded on trust in common experience; there must be substituted an abiding faith in reason, despite the obvious appearances of nature. Aristotelian thought must be swept away, if nature was to be reduced to pure extension, completely intelligible in mathematical terms alone. There was need of another theory of knowledge and another first philosophy.

Descartes had been familiar with the scholastic writers since his college days. He read the theologians eagerly, to find support for his own views on nature. Hence he naturally turned to the Augustinian theory of knowledge and metaphysics, because its Platonic thought was not founded on the Aristotelian physics, or on any physics, and was hence compatible with his own; because it was founded on mathematics; and because it had for centuries been the support of a mathematical interpretation of nature. As secular statesmen had to support the divine right of kings against the Church, so Descartes had to defend the divine right of mathematics against Aristotle.

This turning to Platonism was a widespread movement among

sixteenth- and seventeenth-century Catholic theologians, beginning even in Suarez, the last great Thomist, whom Descartes had studied in college. Suarez had criticized Aristotle's theory of knowledge in terms of Augustinian innate ideas. It was flourishing among the thinkers of the Oratoire, Bérulle and Gibieuf, thoroughgoing Augustinian rationalists and the intimate associates of Descartes, the former even at one time his confessor. Silhon, in *Les deux vérités*, had in 1626 supported the ontological proof of God, founded on the *cogito ergo sum* argument. It was likewise upheld by his closest friend, Père Mersenne, who in his *Questiones celeberrimae in Genesim* in 1623 appealed to innate ideas and Anselm's argument.

Descartes, seeking in 1628 support for his physics, surrounded by Augustinian theologians, rethought the accepted theological position of the modernist Catholic thinkers of his day. He rethought it in the interest of the mathematical interpretation of nature. The result was that the first great metaphysical system used to interpret modern science was a form of Platonism, of medieval Augustinianism; and that the great Platonic tradition found itself, in the seventeenth century, reformulated and reorientated toward mathematical physics, and subtly transformed into Cartesian rationalism. In his theory of the soul, the freedom of the will, etc., Descartes was content to reproduce the commonplaces of contemporary thought; on the will he was following his Jesuit teachers in their favorite doctrine. All of this helps to explain why his ideas were so immediately popular.

VII

In mathematical physics, as the entire truth about the world, the whole structure depends upon the initial ideas. There is thus needed a criterion for the truth of those ideas. So Descartes seeks one by inquiring into what it is that makes an idea indubitable. His metaphysical doubt does not arise from any genuine scepticism on his part; probably there never lived a more self-confident mind than Descartes. If we have a basket of apples, he says, many of which are rotten, what do we do? We empty the entire basket, separate out the sound ones from the others, and put them back in the basket. The difficulty is to distinguish the sound apples. His aim is to take a typically indubitable idea, and by an examination of its character as beyond doubt, to derive therefrom a criterion of certainty. So he

turned to the time-honored and recognized example of an indubitable truth, the stock reply to the sceptic since St. Augustine, repeated in most of the Augustinian schoolmen, "Cogito, ergo sum."
Everyone recognizes that his own conscious existence is beyond all
question. Why is this so? What is the mark of its validity? Descartes
can find none save that the idea is clearly and distinctly conceived.
It is just seen to be true, by a kind of intellectual vision—by *Nous*,
the Greeks would have said. Descartes's "Cogito" is thus clearly an
example to be analyzed to find a general logical rule of evidence. It
is "a proof of the capacity of our soul to receive from God an intuitive knowledge," knowledge of a particular truth in itself.[6] It is
not the first premise of any argument, even though in another connection it is used to establish the self-sufficiency of the thinking
self; Descartes never makes the idealistic attempt to deduce God
and the world from the self. Descartes's thought, indeed, is not a
"single chain of reasoning." He recognizes, in fact, almost as many
indubitable and independent axioms as St. Thomas. "I may assume,"
he remarks, "as a general rule, that all things we conceive clearly and
distinctly are true";[7] and he did with a vengeance.

This general rule of self-evidence Descartes applies to two rather
different kinds of "ideas." It holds of "eternal truths" (*Principles*)
or "common notions" (*Rules*), which are propositions or elements
of knowledge; mathematical axioms are the stock example, but many
scholastic principles, like "Ex nihilo nihil fit," are also included
whenever the argument demands them. It holds also of what Descartes calls "essences" (*Principles*) or "simple natures" (*Rules*),
which are not propositions but the terms of propositions, and are in
fact very close to Aristotelian forms. It is in this sense that Descartes
defines an "idea" as "the thing thought of itself, in so far as it is
objectively in the understanding,"[8] and speaks of them as the in-

[6] *Lettre au Marquis de Newcastle*, March or April, 1648; Adam et Tannery,
V, 138.
[7] *Discourse on Method*, Part IV; Haldane and Ross, I, 102. The best critical
ed. of the *Discours* is ed. by Étienne Gilson (1930), p. 33.
[8] *Reply to First Set of Objections to the Meditations;* Haldane and Ross, II,
9. In seventeenth-century usage, in Descartes and Spinoza, e.g., to exist "objectively" in the understanding is contrasted with existing "formally" in itself.
It is primarily due to Kant that present usage has come to reverse the terms
of the distinction, so that today the contrast between "subjective" and "objective" existence corresponds to what Descartes understood as the contrast
between "objective" and "formal" existence.

telligible "images" of particular existences. It is in the last analysis this Aristotelian identification of the "formal existence" of things with their "objective existence" in the mind that kept Descartes's science a science of nature, a form of natural knowledge; it was this conception of "idea" which Arnauld opposed to Malebranche's Platonic usage. Such essences or simple natures fall into various classes. Some, like substance, duration, order, and number, range through all the kinds of real things; some, like perceptions and volitions, are the modes of thinking substance; some, like magnitude, depth, figure, movement, and situation, pertain exclusively to extended substance; and some, like the appetites, the emotions, and all the ordinary sensations, pertain to that union of thought and extension which is the complete man. Descartes's constant rule is that only the clear and distinct elements of an idea really belong to its formal existence; and when this negative insistence is applied to the ideas of natural bodies, the desired conclusion appears, that only their geometrical structure, their figure and magnitude, really pertain to their ideas.

This "clear and distinct conception," or intellectual intuition, is for Descartes thoroughly Augustinian in character:

Intuitive knowledge is an illumination of the soul, whereby it beholds in the light of God those things which it pleases him to reveal to us by a direct impression of divine clearness on our understanding, which in this is not considered as an agent, but only as receiving the rays of divinity.[9]

Descartes never managed to advance beyond it as an ultimate test. His physics remains a mathematical system based on self-evident axioms. Hobbes's objection is greatly to the point:

The term 'great mental illumination' is metaphorical, and consequently is not adapted to the purposes of argument. Moreover, anyone who is free from doubt claims to possess a similar illumination, and in his will there is the same inclination to believe that of which he does not doubt, as in that of one who truly knows. Hence while this illumination may be the cause that makes a man obstinately defend or hold some opinion, it is not the cause of his knowing it to be true.[10]

---

[9] *Lettre au Marquis de Newcastle*, March or April, 1648; Adam et Tannery, V, 136.
[10] *Third Set of Objections to Meditations*, Objection 13; Haldane and Ross, II, 75.

There is a certain irony in such an objection from Hobbes. But it remains true that any realistic, nonfunctional theory of knowledge, rational or empiricist, must be founded upon such an intuition. This is the "*nous*" or "*intellectus*" of the whole classic tradition. The only alternative is the verification of an idea by its functioning.

There can still remain doubts only if man's understanding is deceived by the devil. Even Descartes's demon has a respectable and ancient Ockhamite ancestry: he figures in John of Mirecourt around 1340. The existence of a perfect Creator must therefore be proved, who would not have created man capable of being so deceived. Descartes offers two major proofs. First, the idea of perfection man possesses can be caused only by a perfect being, for there must be at least as much of reality or perfection in the cause as in the effect. Therefore the perfect cause of the idea of perfection must exist. This is essentially the Thomistic proof of God as the necessary cause of a fact, nicely adapted to Thomistic readers, as Gilson points out, but in a world where the only facts are ideas. Secondly, Descartes adds an adaptation of Anselm's Augustinian ontological argument; the idea of a supremely perfect being must include existence as one of its perfections. He modifies the argument by adding infinite power as one of God's perfections, contained in the idea of God alone. Therefore God alone must necessarily exist, because the power to exist is included in his essence. God is thus the efficient cause of his own existence, as Gilson puts it.

God emerges from this reconstructed dialectic as the guarantee of the mathematical intelligibility of the world. Specifically, he guarantees that all axioms clearly and distinctly perceived will apply; that truths proved stay proved, since nature has a uniform and immutable order; and that that order is an order of real, material sense-objects. The last proposition is shown as follows. The existence of sensations in the soul must have a cause. By elimination, since that cause cannot be the soul itself, and since it cannot be God directly, for God would then deceive me into believing there are real things —Descartes refutes Berkeley in anticipation and the Ockhamite sceptics in retrospect—there must be real things. Descartes's proofs of the existence of God are really proofs of the fixed mathematical order of nature, which cannot be proved, as any proof has to assume it. The proofs of Descartes's epistemological God rely throughout on his test of clear and distinct axioms. In fact, as Descartes tells several correspondents, if the order of nature be substituted wherever he uses the term God, the demonstration will be equally valid. Spinoza was far wiser in making the truth of intuition an axiom: "The order and connexion of ideas is the same as the order and connexion of things."

Descartes is left, like every logical realist, with the problem of accounting for error; he has proved too much, and there seems no reason why men should ever be mistaken.

And no doubt respecting this matter could remain, if it were not that the consequence would seem to follow, that I can thus never be deceived; for if I hold all that I possess from God, and if he has not placed in me the capacity for error, it seems as though I could never fall into error. . . . Thus do I recognize that error, in so far as it is such, is not a real thing depending on God, but simply a defect; and therefore, in order to fall into it, that I have no need to possess a special faculty given to me by God for this very purpose, but that I fall into error from the fact that the power given me by God for the purpose of distinguishing truth from error is not infinite. . . . Whence then come my errors? They come from the sole fact that since the will is much wider in its range and compass than the understanding, I do not restrain it within the same bounds, but extend it also to things which I do not understand: and as the will is of itself indifferent to these, it easily falls into error and sin, and choses the evil for the good, or the false for the true.[11]

In judgment, the understanding perceives clear ideas, and the will affirms them. In error, the will affirms a confused idea. But Descartes was not really troubled by the problem of error, since he himself made no errors.

VIII

In this manner Descartes used the Platonic tradition to interpret and guarantee mathematical physics. But his reformation had unexpected consequences. What becomes of man in the Cartesian world? Descartes was hardly deeply concerned: he was too much fascinated by nature. Man's body is a beautiful machine, a complex assemblage of billiard-balls. But all the nonmathematical qualities taken out of nature had to go somewhere: they were located in the soul. Thus was the inevitable dualism of method between those things that could be mathematically treated and those that could not made

[11] *Meditations*, IV; Haldane and Ross, I, 172–73.

metaphysical and absolute. Soul and body are two distinct substances with nothing in common. Descartes's expressed reason is that each is clearly and distinctly conceived in itself; and he defined substance as "that which requires nothing but itself to exist and be conceived." Body is intelligible without reference to soul, soul without reference to body. There are thus three kinds of "substance" recognized by Descartes: corporeal substance or *res extensa*, created thinking substance or *res cogitans*, and uncreated thinking substance or God.

This "Cartesian dualism" is a natural methodological dualism in Cartesian science. The scientific method that could treat and explain certain selected aspects of nature, the geometrical and the mechanical, could obviously not treat and explain other aspects, including human experience and mind. Hence Descartes is left with a dualism between what his limited "scientific method" could handle, and what it clearly could not! This inevitable dualism of method was made metaphysical, ontological, and absolute, by Descartes's realism —by his conviction that his geometrical method gave him the truth and the only truth about nature. It is equally obvious, that such a dualism between "body" and "mind" is impossible in our own science. The case is the same with the analogous Kantian dualism between "facts" and "values." For our scientific enterprise has developed a much more adequate scientific method for dealing with all aspects of experienced nature, a method which no longer finds nature merely "material" or "mechanical," and has the power to deal equally with the subject-matters of physics, human experience, and "mental behavior." So in our day we are back once more where Aristotle stood, with a single intellectual method for dealing with all the aspects of the experienced world. It has become clear, in the light of these great historical experiments of modern philosophy, that any such "dualism"—like that of Descartes between "body" and "mind," or that of Kant between "facts" and "values," is always the sign of a methodological inadequacy, of the limitations of the intellectual method one is employing.

For Descartes, because of the terms in which it is set, the relation between "mind" and "body" ceases to be a fact to be described, and becomes a problem to be solved. In the Cartesian-Newtonian world, it was an insoluble problem. It was insoluble in terms of the new physics, because neither the soul nor its activities could be made intelligible in the only terms which in that world were thought to give intelligibility, the principles of mathematics and the mechanical principles of the new physics.

In his last work, the *Passions of the Soul* (1649), Descartes analyzes at some length the constitution of "thinking substance." Since "thinking," *"penser,"* forms the essence of the soul, all the phenomena of thinking: perceptions, images, emotions, volitions, are equally modes of "thought," *penser*. The traditional Aristotelian distinction between the "sensitive" and the "rational" soul—between sensing and imagination together as particular and material, in contrast to "thinking," which is of the universal and is immaterial—has disappeared. The functions of both Aristotle's sensitive and rational souls are included in Descartes's *"penser,"* in "thought." The familiar distinction has been replaced by that between the "active modes" of *penser*, known collectively as the "will," and the "passive modes," or "passions of the soul," which include "ideas" as well as perceptions and emotions, and are known collectively as the "understanding." Even in rational knowledge, the soul passively receives impressions of the world. But the "will" is active, and is free to assent or to refuse to assent to the ideas the "understanding" presents to it. It is in this power to give or withhold "assent," which Descartes calls "judgment," that the will's "freedom" lies. And such "freedom of judgment" is in the power of every man.

Descartes effected a revolution in psychological theory and classification of the first importance: it dominated all modern philosophizing down to the post-Darwinian coming of a biological psychology, and it is still a basic assumption for many present-day philosophical systems. The soul lost its function, and became a "ghost in the machine." The old contrast between particularity and universality, between sense and intellect, was transformed into the contrast between mechanical processes, or "body," and "mental" processes, or "mind," which Descartes called *penser*, the function of *l'âme* or *l'esprit*. Now, the objects of intellect or *nous* are common and shared; as universals they are not private and "subjective" in the post-Kantian sense. This fact has given rise to various theories of the "unity" of intellect in all men, or of "social intelligence." The objects of the sensitive soul share in privacy and inaccessibility from without. But they are not the objects of "mind," they are particular, extended, and bodily and material. Descartes changed all this. Sensations and images are no longer bodily, material, and physical, they are "mental," modes of "thinking." And "ideas" or universals are no longer common, social, and shared, they are private and inaccessible. Descartes's psychological revolution consisted in a profound "de-naturalizing" of mind. Even today those still concerned with the "mind-body problem" will take as the ultimate proof of the existence of distinctively "mental" processes—"ψ-processes," they have come to be called—the existence of private and personal pains and other internal feelings. This would have shocked the Aristotelian tradition, for which there is nothing whatever "mental" about pains: they are for it particular and individual bodily and material disturbances. The revolution involved in Cartesian dualism is not merely the sharp denaturalization of mind; it is the wholly new fashion in which "mind" as well as "body" were taken. The acceptance of Descartes's classification of processes far outlasted the acceptance of his "dualism"; to the present day it has created problems about knowledge and about proving the existence of "other minds" that are insoluble in terms of the assumptions that lead to them. Descartes can justly claim the dubious honor of having initiated "modern philosophy" and its "problem of knowledge."

In his treatment of the emotions or "passions" in the narrower sense, Descartes is in large part a physiological psychologist, close at times to the James-Lange theory. For the emotions caused by the body's actions on the soul have a natural utility, in leading the soul to will that for which they prepare the body, and in fortifying and strengthening ideas which are useful to the body. The emotions are by nature good; for from them comes all the sweetness and happiness of life, when they are properly subject to the will. By its power of giving attention to certain ideas and of so disposing the body as to change the emotions it produces, the will can exercise an indirect but unlimited mastery. The Cartesian ideal is *l'homme généreux*, whose intelligence reveals to the will the decision it must make, who is master of himself and his passions because his judgment has been fortified in the knowledge of the truth, and who knows himself and his own power of subordinating his will to the light of his understanding.

Soul and body form in man a single natural unity; body acts on soul through sensation and passions, soul acts on body through volition. This interaction takes place at a single point of contact, the pineal gland, chosen by Descartes as the only part of the brain not double and symmetrical, and as well suited to respond to the slightest motion of the heated "animal spirits" dilating the cavities of the brain. Here the soul is impressed by these streams of small and subtle billiard-balls coursing through the nerve tubes. Here in turn the soul changes the direction of the motion of these streams, just as the rider guides his steed by pulling on the reins. This is of course no satisfactory answer to the problem of interaction, especially for a good mechanist; and in his franker moments Descartes recognized the unintelligibility of the relation between soul and body. He hardly took seriously his own suggestion of the pineal gland.

That the mind, which is incorporeal, is capable of moving the body, neither general reasoning nor comparisons drawn from other things can teach us; yet none the less we cannot doubt it, since certain and evident experiences make it manifest to us every day of our lives.[12]

Heretofore in the Platonic tradition the soul had been at home in an intelligible universe; it was the body that had no real place or importance. But now the body had found a natural station in the mechanical world of billiard-balls, while the soul was left an incomprehensible alien. Descartes succeeded so well in rendering body intelligible without reference to soul, that the relation became an insoluble problem; and in the end Descartes gave it up. Malebranche, a more resolute if not more consistent Cartesian, reached the natural conclusion that we have no knowledge of the soul at all in terms comparable to our knowledge of the mathematical world, only a confused feeling, a "*sentiment confus*," for we can form of the soul no clear and distinct geometrical conception. On the other hand, the whole guarantee of the existence of bodies depended upon finding causes for the ideas in the soul, causes founded on the "analysis of thought"; and Descartes succeeded so well in making the "soul" as "thinking substance" intelligible without reference to body, that Malebranche was led to found the latter's very existence upon revelation in Scripture, and Berkeley to deny "body" entirely, as a use-

[12] *Lettre au R. P. Arnauld, Oeuvres,* ed. Cousin, X, 161; Adam et Tannery, V, 222.

less and meaningless concept. The mathematical system of nature thus collapses, and with it the whole metaphysics on which it is based. Thus the inevitable dualism of method inherent in the enterprise of the new science crystallized the seeds of dualism in the Platonic tradition. Men were confronted by the dilemma: either a world and no science, or science and no world.

The only consolation of the Platonists and Augustinians at this disaster was that the Ockhamite empirical tradition fared worse: it was left with neither world nor science. Only by holding fast to the Aristotelian position, that ideas are the forms of substances, and souls the forms of bodies, were men able to render the new science intelligible; and the only two interpretations of the seventeenth century that escape ultimate contradiction are those that clung to these essentials of the Aristotelian metaphysics, the systems of Spinoza and Leibniz.

3

The Triumph of Reason in France and Holland

I

DESCARTES'S *Discourse* and *Essays* were published in 1637; by the time of his death in 1650 his doctrines were taught and defended in the Dutch universities, and his disciples throughout Europe were "as numerous as the stars or the sands of the sea." Holland saw the first official teaching of Cartesianism; in France the new philosophy spread in the academies and in the smart set, not reaching university circles till the end of the century. In both countries it was the religious rationalism to which Descartes had appealed in defense of his revolution in physics that had the more immediate appeal. For the educated mind of the seventeenth century was still primarily occupied with religious questions; and for many the point had been reached at which rational argument seemed the way out of conflicting appeals to authority. The vision of a mathematical and mechanical universe was largely subordinated to a new and up-to-date defense of the essence of the Christian faith; for every physicist concerned to discover the secrets of nature there were a dozen theologians puzzling over vortices and infinite extension in the interests of humanizing and rationalizing the religious tradition. Thus the Cartesian philosophy became deeply involved even during Descartes's own lifetime in that long theological debate which lasted without cessation from the Reformation struggles of the sixteenth century to the indifference and secularism of the eighteenth. For a generation it seemed to those who prided themselves on being forward-looking that a common Christianity might be established on the firm foundation of reason. But reason led on to other experience, and it soon became clear that the Cartesian theology was as defenseless as the subtleties of the Schools before the weapons of the Enlightenment. The revolutionary *philosophes* were as ruthless to the plaster pilasters and porticos of the edifices of the *Roi Soleil* as to the barbarous Gothic piles of St. Louis.

The old ideas did not give way without a fight. Descartes's earliest Dutch disciples Réneri and Regius brought down upon themselves at Utrecht the onslaughts of the doughty reformed theologian Voetius, and involved Descartes himself in the unwelcome dispute. At Leyden Heereboord and de Raey precipitated such a tumult that it was forbidden to mention the new opinions, and only the intervention of the Prince of Orange made it possible for that University to become the center of scientific Cartesianism in the seventeenth century. At Catholic Louvain so alarming were the Cartesian inroads that official condemnation was pronounced in 1662; the next year Descartes' writings were placed upon the Roman index *donec corrigantur.*

In France Descartes early won adherents in all the great religious orders; even some of the watchful Jesuits favored their brilliant pupil. But his ideas soon came to grief amidst the complicated politics of the Jesuits, the Jansenists, and the Oratorians. Their popularity with the last two aroused the bitter enmity of the first, who occupied the seats of the mighty. When Descartes's remains were brought to France in 1667, no funeral oration was permitted, and no monument. In 1671 the king forbade Cartesian ideas in the Sorbonne; the provincial universities soon followed suit. The Sorbonne was even on the point of appealing to the *parlement* to renew its edict of 1624, prohibiting any philosophy but Aristotle's in France on pain of death; it took the ridicule of Boileau's burlesque edict banishing Reason *in toto* to laugh this proposal out of court. Most cruel of all, the Jesuits in 1678 forced the Oratorians to subscribe to substantial forms, real accidents, and a Thomistic soul. And there was a flood of polemical writing from the Jesuit camp, ranging from the witty satire of P. Daniel's *Voyage du monde de Descartes* (1690) to P. Valois's accusations of Calvinistic heresy (1680).

The net effect of this persecution and proscription, which abated rapidly after 1690—the empirical and sceptical attack of Bishop Huet in 1689 was the last serious shot from the conservative camp—was negligible: a certain circumspection in mentioning Descartes's name, and attempts to find his ideas in Aristotle. The banishment of Cartesianism from the universities contributed to their intellectual vacuity until the Revolution. Amusingly enough, by 1751, when the Abbé Prades tried to defend Lockean empiricism under the cloak of Aristotle, they had come around to support innate ideas.

The grounds of this opposition were varied and complicated; the reasons given ranged from general objections to the new science, the revolution of the earth and the infinity of the universe, to convinced support of Aristotelian physics. Unfortunately, Descartes, pushed by an overzealous Jesuit friend to explain the mystery of transubstantiation in terms of his billiard-balls, gave two conflicting accounts in private correspondence. As these were spread by enthusiastic Cartesians—the wiser of them protested in the name of Descartes himself—they gave just that theological leverage against his mathematical physics needed to convict him by the dogmas of Trent. It was in vain the Cartesians obtained a certificate from Queen Christina of Sweden, attributing to Descartes her conversion to Catholicism; the denial of real accidents became his chief crime, an assault upon the Holy Eucharist itself.

II

That Cartesianism nevertheless spread widely, and made its way even into the schools by the end of the century, is in large measure due to a successful text book, the *Art de penser* or Port-Royal Logic, first published by Arnauld and Nicole in 1662, and running into many editions in French, Latin, and English. An effective blend of Aristotelian logic and the Cartesian method, it formed a powerful defense of rationalism and "clear and distinct ideas" against authority; and it drove home its point by taking all its illustrations of fallacies from Aristotle, and its models from good Cartesians. By 1700 it had won over even the Sorbonne to its use. By its practical spirit, by its emphasis on method as well as reasoning, on discovery as well as proof and conviction, above all by its aim to cultivate the judgment, to form *bon sens*, to use the sciences as an instrument to perfect reason itself, it played a dominant role in fostering that passionate worship of "reason" which was for all good Frenchmen the chief legacy of Descartes's labors.

The Age of Louis XIV saw the triumph of this reason in every phase of life. How far the Cartesian philosophy was responsible is a question that can safely be left to those with simple convictions on cultural causation; certainly few philosophies have ever so admirably expressed the dominant currents of a period. From the rational, unsentimental, and Stoical conception of human nature, of which the *Passions de l'âme* is the exposition and the plays of Corneille the illustration, *l'homme généreux*, master of himself and his passions, the Don Rodrigue or Auguste, to that deification of clear ideas and reason which every French schoolboy absorbs from the pages of the *Discours*, Descartes formulated the intellectual ideal which French thought and expression, aside from a few heretics, was to set before itself for several generations. That there is a Divine Reason, single, universal, equal, identical for all, accessible to whomsoever will take the trouble to follow the right method and seek in order the clear ideas it embodies, became the unifying creed of that Augustan age. Not yet was this Reason completely identified with nature, for not yet were men fundamentally impressed by nature as its abode. Nature was, to be sure, a rational order, but in the last analysis it was not the Order of Nature but the Order of Reason itself which men saw in vision and in the intoxication of their discovery believed to be God. To this Divine Order nature was really irrelevant; hence the Cartesian philosophy was easily pushed to an Augustinian idealism from which the world had quite dropped away. Man's concern was with the God who is Reason and with his own soul, and Reason speaks to that soul directly. Paradoxically enough Cartesian rationalism, in sundering man from nature, centered his attention first on the source of the Reason to be found alike in himself and in all men, rather than on its natural object. Man rather than nature and man rather than men, than human society, was placed in sharpest focus. The typical nature poet of the *grand siècle* is La Fontaine.

The eighteenth-century Enlightenment, in so many ways the heir of this earlier rationalism, realized very clearly what it was that set its own Reason off from that of its fathers. The men of the seventeenth century all suffered from *l'esprit de système*. They were not critics of their institutions, but only of the inherited reasons for supporting them; they did not bring reason to bear against existing irrationalities, but sought a rational system that would persuade men to accept them. They did not try to build and construct a more rational social order, they found a rational order in what they possessed. Church and State, Catholic Christianity and the Bourbon monarchy, were for them seen as rational systems founded on clear ideas. They were Reason incarnate.

This faith in rational authority, in the Counter Reformation of the Jesuits and in the absolute monarchy, was the stage in the long series of shifting compromises between collectivism and individualism reached by seventeenth-century France. On the surface the unity and order imposed by authority seem a welcomed reaction against the strife and turmoil of Renaissance individualism, a clear direction as against the doubts and scepticisms of the sixteenth century. Under Richelieu and Mazarin the bourgeoisie were consolidating their position in preparation for the further attack. But it was an order increasingly founded on reason rather than custom, and accepted for the necessary discipline it brought. And the reason that was its support was a double-edged weapon. The very unity and order which made so brave a show of the Catholic monarchy enabled the third estate to wax in power and strength; and the *philosophes* of the Enlightenment drew their doughtiest weapons from the arsenals of the Cartesian defenders of Christian truth. The men of the seventeenth century did not build a new heaven or a new earth. But in appealing to the reason of the man of *bon sens*, in teaching him to look to his own mind for truth, and in carefully training him in the method of finding it, they prepared the instrument that was to bring their own heaven and their own earth tumbling to the ground. They wrote their literature about Man, about the power of his will when enlightened by clear understanding. The Man they created, Man the Thinker, began in the eighteenth century to think and act.

III

The most important function of Cartesianism, and the one in which Descartes himself would doubtless have had the greatest interest, was its service in fostering concern with and support for mathematics and experimental inquiry into nature. For a generation, until Newton became the great symbol of science in England and Leibniz in Germany, Cartesian physics and natural philosophy were well-nigh synonymous, in the minds of most men if not of physicists themselves. It is true that outside of Holland few scientists professed the Cartesian system in its entirety; those who did were rather teachers and professors than investigators. Not only the natural dislike of discipleship and of the dogmatism of the master kept original minds from surrendering their independence; most scientists shrank from that involvement in theological quarrels which the Cartesian banner brought. Yet without the army fighting against the old peripateticism, without the steady popularization of the idea of a mathematical and mechanical interpretation of nature, the more seminal minds of seventeenth-century science would have found their way much harder and their discoveries rejected. Huygens and Newton himself do not lend themselves to easy classification as Cartesians; yet the whole drive of their work makes them truer to the spirit of Descartes than many more faithful disciples. Pascal and Mariotte in France, Boyle in England, investigators in the *Académie des Sciences* and the Royal Society, worked eagerly at the details of the vision of a universal mathematics. Equally fertile was the mechanistic physiology which had occupied Descartes's last years. In the Dutch universities, especially in the great scientific center of Leyden, a series of physicians, Leeuwenhoek, Swammerdamm, and Boerhaave, more or less allied with Cartesian ideas, laid the foundation for the study of the functioning of the body.

In France Rohault was the outstanding physicist who professed the Cartesian faith; his *Traité de physique* (1671) became the classic textbook. Louis de la Forge, a physician, published in 1666 his *Traité de l'âme humaine*, primarily a physiological study. Sylvain Régis, after great success as a Cartesian missionary in the south, at Toulouse and Montpellier, became the encyclopedist of the school with his *Système de philosophie*, appearing in 1690, and his vigorous polemics against the attacks of Huet and the subtler reformulation of Malebranche.

In theory as well as practice these scientific Cartesians were led to supplement the rationalism of the master with an emphasis on experimental technique and even on a philosophical empiricism. Indeed, Regius, the earliest Dutch disciple, who was teaching medicine on Cartesian principles as early as 1638, soon developed a purely mechanistic and empirical view of the soul as a mode of corporeal substance, and attacked Descartes himself. Rohault and Pascal were both excellent experimentalists who followed Descartes the mature investigator rather than the early mathematical genius. And Régis, generally regarded as the most faithful of all the disciples in the later disputes with the Malebranchian idealists, insisted that all ideas, even those called innate, are the images of realities in the physical world, and derive their validity from their reference to these *causes exemplaires*. "Innate ideas" are those that are found in every experience: every experience, for example, involves the ideas of both extension and thought. All ideas alike come from the union of the soul with the body, that is, from the senses; body is as clearly known as thought itself. In refuting the empirical attack of Huet on the Cartesian physics, Régis went so far as to admit its hypothetical character; physics is problematic rather than demonstrative, and at most it conceives mechanical arrangements from which the observed effects can be deduced.

It was the Dutch scientists, Boerhaave and the physicists 'sGravesande and Musschenbroek,[1] who first developed the idea of a hypothetical-experimental science into a consistent theory, and traveled insensibly from Cartesianism to Newtonianism. From the time of the famous address of Boerhaave in 1715, *De comparando certo in physicis*, Dutch scientific literature abounds in treatments of experimental theory, and of the relation of mathematical deduction to observation. s'Gravesande raised the question of the foundation of induction, or "reasoning by analogy," which he justified partly by its practical necessity and partly by the divinely fixed laws of nature to which that necessity points. In his *Discours sur l'évidence*, in 1724, he distinguished carefully between mathematical evidence and the "moral evidence" alone attainable in physics, although the latter is not to be confused with mere vulgar probability, as the persuasion it induces is as absolute as that of mathematical evidence. Musschenbroek went even further in renouncing the mathematical certainty of Descartes. Dutch Cartesianism thus worked itself out, even as did English empiricism, to the new conception of science and its intellectual pattern which by the middle of the century had taken its place side by side with the deductive ideal.

---

[1] For a further account of 'sGravesande and Musschenbroek as Newtonian physicists, see Book Four, Chapter 14, section I.

I V

Curiously enough, those Cartesians whose chief interest was thinking and not extended substance arrived at a very similar positivism. The methodological device by which Descartes had rid the world of all those qualities not mathematical, locating them in a second and irrelevant substance, produced a dualism that could not rest in its unstable equilibrium. Inquiring Cartesians split on the question of the locus of the structure of science itself. If it were placed in nature, in extended substance, then nature became the natural home of body, and the human mind was left a homeless and inexplicable outcast in a universe to which it was irrelevant. Its only hope of naturalization lay in becoming itself a mode of body, in a return to empirical principles. On the other hand, were science located where it was discovered, in thought itself, its connection with a natural world became a problem, to be solved only through invoking God's will—that theological expression of empiricism. In either case the reason that is mathematical and directly accessible to man failed to attain the world that is mechanical. It took but a slight push to turn Cartesianism into a materialistic empiricism, or into an Augustinian idealism in which its mechanical physics was left as a kind of empirical appendix. That majority for whom Cartesianism was deeply involved in theological issues naturally chose the second course, and incidentally were led to a profound critique of scientific causation.

Descartes had made both soul and body absolutely passive. Motion, the only power left to body, was something foreign and external to it, an accident added by God from ouside and not of its essence. The soul Descartes likened to a piece of wax: the understanding corresponded to the impressions made on the wax, the will to the movements it underwent. The first cause tended, in Cartesian analyses, to absorb all force from extended substance, and finally from the soul as well. Force evaporated from science and took up its sole abode in theology, while in nature was left the mere constant succession of events. Secondary or scientific causation ceased to partake of the character of efficient causation, and became purely logical, reduced to the structure or formal cause of events. This process was hastened by the analysis of causation induced by that prime

Cartesian problem, the relation between a mind and a body so defined as to possess nothing in common. How could such disparate substances influence or affect each other? The relation was unintelligible, in terms, that is, of efficient causation. But was the transfer of motion between two billiard-balls in contact really any more intelligible? Was not all causation unintelligible, to be accepted as a brute fact—or, as the theological mind preferred to express it, as the will of God?

Descartes's unhappy suggestion that the soul was in contact with the body through the pineal gland, where it could alter the direction of the flow of corpuscular "animal spirits" without changing the constant quantity of their motion, was hardly taken as seriously by its proponent as by some of his followers.

Nothing can come from external objects to our soul through the agency of the senses save certain bodily movements; but neither these movements themselves nor the figures which come from them are conceived by us at all as they are present in the sense organs. . . . Whence it follows that even ideas of movement and of figures are "naturally" in us. And moreover the ideas of pains, of colors, of the senses, and of all such things must be "natural" to us, so that our soul, on the occasion of certain bodily movements with which they have no resemblance, can represent them to itself.[2]

Yet here yawns a still greater problem: if science is thus "innate" in the mind, has it any earthly connection with the world? No, relentlessly advanced Cartesian thought, its connection can only be divine, mediated by God himself.

All the Augustinian tendencies of the age, in concentrating upon God human knowledge and human action as well as the course of nature, helped to reinforce this way out of the Cartesian dilemma. The more naturalistic Platonism of the Renaissance was likewise drawn upon. The German Cartesian Johannes Clauberg (1622–1665) sought to fit Cartesianism into the Platonic tradition. No bodily motion can affect the soul, since the effect cannot be nobler than the cause. He takes the familiar Platonic position,

[2] *Notae in Programma quoddam,* sub finem Anni 1647 in Belgio editum, cum hoc Titulo: Explicatio Mentis humanae, sive Animae rationalis, ubi explicatur quid sit, et quid esse possit (1648), in Adam et Tannery, VIII, 358–59; French tr. in Cousin ed., X, 96. This was Descartes's comments on a work of Regius.

The movements of our body are only procatarctic causes which give occasion to the mind, as the principal cause, to draw from itself at that particular time certain of the ideas which it always possesses potentially.[3]

The union of such different things as body and soul cannot depend on their own nature, but only on the free cause of God himself. De la Forge also, in his treatise of 1666, had recourse to Augustine and Ficino to combat the objections of materialists and Cartesian physicists to the interaction of soul and body. The soul need not be corporeal for body to act upon it; for the clear idea of body itself contains no notion of motive force.

It is no more difficult and no easier to understand how a mind can act upon a body and move it than to conceive how one body can push another.[4]

The sole motive force is God. Bodies or minds can act on other bodies only "by determining and obliging the first cause to apply its force and motive power on those bodies to which it would not have been applied without them, . . . following the laws of motion." The same year de Cordemoy, lawyer and preceptor of the Dauphin, in his *Discernement de l'âme et du corps,* tried to reduce all motion to the bare facts of observation, denying any efficient activity even to the will of man, which de la Forge had been content to leave as the sole active cause outside God.

When we say that bodies move bodies, it is to be understood that being impenetrable, and thus not being able to be moved forever, at least with the same velocity, their contact is an occasion for the spirit which has moved the first to move the second. . . . A soul moves a body when because it wishes it happens that what was already moving the body comes to move it in the direction in which the soul wished it to be moved.[5]

There is no intrinsic relation between cause and effect; they might be connected in very different ways. One mind might well communicate its thought by the mere wishing. For de Cordemoy all intelligible relations have dropped out of the world, leaving a heap of atoms joined only by the arbitrary fiat of the Almighty; and even in

[3] Clauberg, *De corporis et animae in homine conjunctione,* ch. 16, in *Opera* (1691).
[4] De la Forge, *Traité de l'esprit de l'homme* (1666), p. 254.
[5] De Cordemoy, *Discernement de l'âme et du corps* (1666), 4. *Discours.*

his physics he replaced the Cartesian mathematical continuity with an atomistic view. Man can be sure only of himself and God; the very existence of a world of bodies rests on faith alone. "It is as impossible for our minds to have new ideas without God, as for a body to have new motions without him." [6] Cartesianism had been pushed to the Augustinian position implicit in its metaphysics. To God belong the power and the glory! But to observation and experience belongs the knowledge of God's world.

V

The Belgian Arnold Geulincx (1624–1669), professor originally at Louvain and then after his expulsion at Leyden, developed the Platonism of this position more fully, and was the first to work out a rounded theory of what came to be called "occasionalism." For him the soul and its immediate object, a science directly accessible to it, were primary; the character of the existing world is dubious and uncertain. But Geulincx was of those who pushed the Augustinian position in a sceptical direction, attacked the validity of human *scientia*, and emphasized man's knowledge of his own soul rather than of the Eternal Truth. In the last analysis mind can understand only what it produces consciously itself; of the world it knows only what mental operations read into it. What that world may be as God the supreme mind produces it, these human considerations through which we view it can only conceal and obscure. Fortunately we possess from God himself "ideas" radically distinct from human thoughts, which can serve as the rules and laws by which to judge them. And thus in the end Augustine's Platonism saves Geulincx from the fate of being a full-fledged *Vorkantianer*.

It is impossible that he should do a thing who is ignorant of how it is done.[7]

The only genuine action is that produced by a mind with full awareness of the manner. Hence not only can no body act of itself, nor act upon a mind: mind cannot act on body, since it knows not how to do so. The thinking self is but the spectator, not the actor; its body is but the instrument God employs to create in it the manifold

[6] *Ibid., Discours sur la parole.*
[7] Geulincx, *Ethica*, in *Opera Philosophica*, ed. J. P. N. Land (1891–93), III, 33.

diversity of thoughts. Bodies cannot cause sensations, volitions cannot cause effects; these are but the occasion for God's activity, the tools he uses. Mind and body are like two clocks created to keep the same time,

and that without any causality by which the one causes something in the other, but from the mere dependence, in which each was formed by the same art and a like industry.[8]

Or their relation is like that between money and the commodities it purchases, which is due not to the natural power of the metal but to human institution; just so corporeal motion corresponds to sensations and ideas not by its own power to produce them, but by divine institution.

I am therefore the bare spectator of this machine. In it I produce nothing, I reproduce nothing, nor do I build anything here, nor destroy anything. All that is the task of a certain other Being.

Even our vision of the world is due neither to us nor to the world, but to God alone.

The world cannot show itself to me for contemplation; only God can show me that spectacle, and that in a manner unspeakable and incomprehensible.[9]

We can see and know only in the infinite reason of God.

Geulincx' rational mysticism expressed itself most fully in the ethical consequences he drew from this vision of God's omnipotence. Man's only duty must be self-knowledge: γνῶθι σεαυτόν, *inspectio et despectio sui*, and knowledge and love of the right reason that insight discloses. Humility is the crown of virtue: *ubi nil vales, ibi nil velis*. Not in mere blind resignation to the will of God which must ever prevail, but in conscious and devoted love toward the Divine Reason, lies man's only salvation.

Equally productive of humility were the implications which Geulincx, in his attack upon the peripatetic realism, extracted from his principle that whatever the mind finds intelligible derives its intelligibility from the mind that has there introduced it. The world of bodies draws all its intelligible properties from the Divine Mind that so endowed it; we can gain knowledge of them only through those

[8] Geulincx, *Ethica*, in *Opera*, ed. Land, III, 205.
[9] *Ethica*, in *Opera*, ed. Land, III, 33.

divine ideas which are the rules and standards by which to judge our human thoughts. But the human mind has an ineradicable tendency to read into what it seeks to know, the modes of its own thinking: it finds in things the intelligibility it creates itself. Just as the sense qualities the mind ascribes to things and then takes as their real accidents, obscure the intelligible extension which the understanding finds to be their real essence; so the modes of our understanding serve as a screen to cut us off from things *ut sunt in se,* that is, in the mind of their Creator. We can correct the illusions of sense by means of thought; but what means have we to correct the illusions of thought itself? The Aristotelian philosophy canonized both types of error. Its concepts and categories, substance and accident, whole and part, unity, even being itself, are but modes of human thinking, human distinctions, no more independently real than right and left, or than the rules of grammar on which Aristotle founded them.

We call certain objects of our thought substances, accidents, relations, subjects, predicates, wholes, parts, etc., all of which, though they but express certain modes of our understanding, we are yet accustomed to consider as kinds of things, which are themselves colored by these intellectual images. . . . These modes belong to men themselves and not to the things which are objects of their thought.[10]

What things are really like we cannot know; we can know only that they are not as we conceive them, that all our human knowledge is conditioned by the limitations of the human mind.

We ought not to consider things in so far as they are sensible (that is, as they enter sense under a certain *species* or sensible form) nor as they are intelligible (that is, as they are known by us in a certain manner). But we are unable to consider them as they are in themselves; whence we see our great imperfection. This one thing then remains for us to do (which we are both able and obliged to perform), that whenever we understand anything by any mode of thinking (which we are always doing, and cannot do otherwise, so long as we are men), that we always keep firmly in mind, that the thing does not exist so in itself as it is understood by us.[11]

The highest human knowledge of the world, *Cognitio cum evidentia,* remains within the limits of man's categories and language. True *sapientia,* "that science which sets forth things bare and ab-

[10] *Metaphysica vera,* Intro., sec. 2; ed. Land, II, 204.
[11] *Annotata ad Met. Ver.,* ed. Land, II, 300ff.

stracted from all the modes and terms of human thinking," [12] can be only of what mind has itself produced. Man can have such *sapientia* of his own loves and hates, his affirmations and negations, and other mental acts; but the world only God who has created it can know as it truly is. Just as in Montaigne, the "wisdom" of this Augustinian tradition now finds itself directed, not toward the Truth of God, but toward human nature.

This Augustinian scepticism of human *scientia* Geulincx reaches, however, by a searching and penetrating criticism and analysis of its modes and categories. Being, unity, substance, are all operations of human thought.

Being . . . is nothing else but a mode of the subject, or such a mode of thinking by which we apprehend that about which we have resolved to affirm or say something . . . Just as a handful is *one* handful, because at one and the same time some things are grasped by the hand, even though many things go to make it up; so also what the mind brings together in its grasp at one and the same time, and collects into a sort of bundle, is from that very grasping and collecting called one.[13]

These categories are not attributes of things, but operations of the mind: we should speak rather of *unio* than of *unum*, of *totatio* than of *totum*. The Aristotelian substance is nothing but the grammatical subject, which we have singled out to talk about. The whole of the peripatetic philosophy, in fact, is a gigantic illusion of language. For like so many others before and since, Geulincx is convinced that language exists as an obstacle to thought rather than as its natural vehicle. In reality there are no individual substances or things; what we so single out are but modes of the one infinite extension or the one infinite mind.

We are but modes of mind; if you take away the mode, there remains God.[14]

On even this Cartesian dualism a doubt is cast:

For in that very way of speaking, in which we speak of things in themselves, as they are in themselves, we do not set them forth as they are in themselves, but give them the rationality (rationem) of the subject.[15]

---

[12] *Metaphysica vera*, Part III, sec. 6.
[13] *Metaphysica vera*, Part I, sec. 1; ed. Land, II, pp. 211, 227.
[14] *Metaphysica vera*, Part II, sec. 2.
[15] *Metaphysica vera*, Part I, sec. 1; ed. Land, II, 215.

VI

Thus far from Descartes's own sturdy scientific realism did his followers push the idealism latent in his methodological dualism. But what these ideas were to become at the hands of the two greatest Frenchmen who felt the strong impress of Cartesian currents, Pascal and Malebranche, demands some knowledge of the religious situation under Louis XIV and the basic issues in which Cartesianism came to perform a function more popular if not so important as its original one of scientific apologetic. Seventeenth-century France, having decided to remain Catholic—the Huguenots after their crushing defeat at La Rochelle in 1630 were a minor sect—found itself torn between two religious parties. The Jesuits stood for that comfortable and worldly political religion which to most Frenchmen was so welcome after the passions and bloodshed of the religious wars. Accommodating in their moral demands, and loyal to the Gallican Church so long as they could control it, they insisted on the theology of Trent and the Neo-Thomistic philosophy of their Spanish theologians. With their support the universities remained faithful to the peripatetic philosophies of the late Middle Ages. Opposed to them were those for whom religion was a personal way of life rather than a political and social institution. Foremost among these were those Catholic Puritans, the Jansenists, continuing the Catholic Reformation, and appealing to that patron saint of all Christian reform, St. Augustine. Like the Protestant reformers, they were religious moralists rather than humanists, emphasizing the moral life of the individual, his struggle and temptation, and his impotence to accomplish anything without divine aid. Like all religious moralists, they were pessimists as to man's ability to achieve the good without an external and supernatural power; what they saw as good was not human but divine, something infinitely perfect and yet compelling allegiance. The Jansenists were the ethical thinkers of France. The Cartesians at best had no really moral interests; they were optimists, believers in the possibility of human achievement, and inventors of the idea of progress. As such, they were the fathers of the eighteenth-century social reformers, whose thought, while directed to the amelioration of human living, was social rather than ethical, and lacked the underlying moral note of the individual's internal struggle to achieve what he clearly sees to be best.

In this, the Jansenists were one in spirit with the Calvinists; and the Catholic Church, if it was not willing to alter its fundamental policy of controlling the world through accommodating itself to it, was right in insisting on their heresy. Though their individualism and distrust of institutional control was destined to triumph, their protest against the secular and humanistic spirit of Jesuit complacency was a lost cause. But it was a noble protest; and in their defeat they brought their rivals down with them.

Between these two groups stood a third, the advocates of rational religion, represented by the liberal order of the Oratory, the modernists or Broad Churchmen of their day. They agreed with the Jansenists in their individualism; surely never did religious order allow its members greater freedom. They agreed too in their enthusiasm for St. Augustine and their contempt for the Schoolmen. But it was Augustine the Christian Platonist and rationalist, not Augustine the Manichaean anti-Pelagian, to whom they turned. They saw in the rational religion of the Platonic tradition the way to foster a purer and more unified religious life; and their Augustinism was closer to the humanistic Platonism of the Renaissance, fortified by the latest scientific rationalism, than to the tragic and rigoristic views of Calvin and Jansen. This humanism they shared in fact with the Jesuits; but it was a humanism from conviction rather than policy, and it culminated in a rational mysticism rather than in a clever worldliness. Their fate was that of all liberals, to receive the fire from both sides in their day, and to see their rational religion finally win out in a form they could not recognize.

The Jesuits would have no traffic with Cartesian ideas, although Descartes' own views on the great theological issue under debate, the nature of grace and the freedom of the will, were close to their own. The Oratorians, already Augustinian metaphysicians, found Descartes a glorious ally; and like all good religious liberals, they accepted his science in distorted form along with his theological support. The Jansenists believed profoundly that man's natural reason could never justify him before God and bring him salvation. But their pessimism and distrust of human nature was moral rather than intellectual; like Augustine himself they maintained that though sin had hopelessly corrupted man's will it had not prevented his reason from attaining truth. They combined, in fact, an intellectual with a moral earnestness which gave them a keen interest in the development of the natural and mathematical sciences. As Nicole said of geometry, "Its object has no connection with concupiscence." [16] Though they sharply sundered the realm of grace from the realm of nature, in the latter they were more hard-headedly and less mystically rationalistic than the Oratorians, who as good Augustinians were always eager to rise from the reason in nature to the Reason that is God. The Jansenists in fact were in their own way touched by the spirit of humanism: Arnauld might condemn with Augustine the virtues of the pagans as splendid vices, springing from ambition, vanity and self-love; but those vices served equally with Christian love to buttress an earthly state in accord with the justice whose law is innate in the human mind. As Nicole put it:

In those states where charity has no point of entrance because true religion is banished, men do not fail to live with as much of peace, of security, and of comfort as if they were in a republic of saints.[17]

The Port-Royalists were therefore among the earliest Cartesian enthusiasts. They had an additional reason for welcoming Descartes: he was a fellow-sufferer under the Jesuit persecution. And Port-Royal echoed equally with discussions of the automatism of animals and the necessity of grace.

[16] Cited by J. Laporte, *La doctrine de la grace chez Arnauld*, p. 111, n.74.
[17] Nicole, *Oeuvres philosophiques*, ed. Jourdain (1845), p. 181.

4

Augustinian Interpretations of the Cartesian Philosophy: Scepticism and Rationalism

BOTH Jansenists and Oratorians faced the fundamental problem of adjusting Cartesian philosophy to their Augustinian views. The former had a harder task, for Christian pessimism and Cartesian rationalism do not easily mix. Most, like Arnauld, were content to let them lie side by side. But the greatest of all the Port-Royalists, Pascal, was impelled by his equal devotion to mathematical physics and to the doctrine of human depravity to effect one of those imposing conciliations and adjustments to which religion has driven scientific minds, and to become the most serious of all critics of Cartesianism, the chief heretic from the true faith. It has recently been discovered that Pascal was criticizing Cartesianism from the position today likewise concerned with an exclusive "scientism's" limitations—the name such man-centered thinkers would apply to the enthusiasm for Cartesian science. Pascal was, we are told, an "existentialist" *malgré lui.*

The Oratorians had no such incompatibles to reconcile. It was possible for Malebranche to effect a subtle blend of Augustine and Descartes into one comprehensive Christian *sagesse,* and to draw together all those Platonic and idealistic threads which a generation of Cartesians had been spinning.

I

It is not hard to see in Pascal the continuing influence of that Augustinian scepticism most fully represented by Montaigne, whose views on the limitations of human science in certain moods he found so congenial. And though he never long forgot the relative validity of the Cartesian physics of which he was so distinguished a proponent, like Montaigne the wisdom which he set above science was essentially a human wisdom of the heart, even when its object was God, rather than the divine reason to which Malebranche's rational Augustinism led him. But Pascal is too unique a figure to fit neatly into any philosophical tradition; his philosophy is not a system to be adopted by others, but the intensely personal expression of a profound nature drawing like Augustine himself upon a wide variety of incompatible sources to give utterance to the many facets of a complex experience.

Pascal was a great man, where Descartes was only a great thinker. He alone, from within the scientific realm whence Cartesianism sprang, seriously questioned the great principle of Cartesianism, its absolute faith in reason. The rationalists of his time, and still more those of the next century, who no longer shared even his Christian ends, were a little afraid of him; like Voltaire, they hoped he was mad, and showed the zeal of a modern psychoanalyst in proving it. He stood in his day as the supreme example of temporal pride humbling itself before things eternal, as the pride of intellect laid low before the greatness of God. It was as though Huxley had become an evangelical preacher, or Bertrand Russell a barefoot friar. The genius of Pascal only began to be appreciated when in the nineteenth century men faced his problem seriously, and sought like him to reconcile the triumphs of human intelligence with the manifold irrational needs of human experience. His was an empiricism far deeper than that of the professed devotees of experience, an empiricism which like that of the Romanticists knew that experience stretches back into the mists of tradition. Hence his great unfinished apology for Christianity is the first of those modern defenses which forsake rational demonstration to appeal to human nature.

Pascal started as a precocious scientist and Cartesian. Brought up carefully by his father, on principles appropriate to a believer in innate ideas, and the opposite of those practiced by James Mill on his son—he was taught no book-learning, although he associated with his father's scientific friends—he reached the same early distinction. He was found working out Euclid for himself, and at sixteen he wrote a treatise on conics (1639) that made Descartes both suspicious and envious. One of the outstanding mathematicians in France, he profited by his early "dissipations" at the gaming table to develop the theory of probability and chance, and to show, in clear Cartesian fashion, how even that most chaotic realm could be reduced to order by applying the universal cipher of mathematics.

But he was more than a mathematician: he was an inspired experimentalist, with a marvelous gift for observation, for forming and testing hypotheses, and a keen appreciation of the distinction between a definition and a fact. He shocked Descartes by making the existence of a vacuum a question of experience rather than reasoning; and he further embittered the confident rationalist by the famous Puy-de-Dôme experiment proving the pressure of the air. In hydrostatics and aerostatics he ranks with the greatest of the seventeenth-century successors of Galileo.

Pascal never abandoned the mathematical billiard-ball world of Descartes. When most convinced of the futility of human science, he never seriously doubted the infinity of the universe, and its all-pervading mechanistic laws, extending even to the automata that were animals. Nor did he fail to recognize the Cartesian chasm dividing mind from body.

I can well conceive a man without hands, feet, or head (for it is only experience that teaches us that the head is more necessary than the feet). But I cannot conceive a man without thought: that would be a stone or a brute. It is thus thought which forms the essence of man, and he cannot be conceived without it.[1]

Man is visibly made to think; that is his whole dignity and his whole merit. (146)

The whole world of bodies, the firmament, the stars, the earth and its kingdoms, have not the worth of the least among minds; for that least knows them all, and himself, while bodies know nothing thereof. (792)

Man knows that he is miserable: he is therefore miserable, since he is; but he is very great, because he knows it. (416)

Man is but a reed, the feeblest thing in nature; but he is a thinking reed. The whole universe has no need to arm itself to crush him; a vapor, a

[1] Pensée 339, in Pascal, *Opuscules et Pensées*, Hachette ed. by Léon Brunschvicg (1897). Numbered *Pensées* hereafter refer to the Brunschvicg ed.

drop of water is enough to kill him. But should the universe crush him, man would still be nobler than that which killed him, because he knows that he is dying, and the advantage the universe has over him; the universe knows nothing thereof. (347)

And what finer expression of the Cartesian faith than:

Reason commands us much more imperiously than a master; for if we disobey the one we are unfortunate, but if we disobey the other we are fools. (345)

Nor even when humbling himself most before God did Pascal bow to human authority, or to that of God's church. To the Jesuits he proudly said:

It was in vain that you obtained against Galileo a decree from Rome condemning his opinion on the motion of the earth. That will never prove that it is at rest.[2]

And to the pope's condemnation of the antipodes he replied,

The king of Spain did well to believe Christopher Columbus who came from there rather than the judgment of the pope who had never been there.[3]

In his work on method, *De l'esprit géometrique* (1655), he developed in detail a purely rational and Cartesian ideal of science. Careful analysis of the rational structure of its subject-matter, rigid demonstration from precisely defined terms, and first principles known by the "natural light"—true knowledge must conform to the mathematical model. *"Ce qui passe la géometrie nous surpasse,"* for geometry is the very measure and standard of our intellect. What motion is, what truth is, such things the mind sees with no uncertainty.

Yet—this is the man who in another mood exclaimed,

We judge the whole of science is not worth an hour's trouble (Pensée 79)

To jest at philosophy is to philosophize truly; (4)

and even resolved:

To write against those who push science too far: Descartes. (76)

[2] *18th Provincial Letter, Oeuvres*, Ed. Les Grands Écrivains de la France, ed. Léon Brunschvicg, Pierre Boutroux, et Félix Gazier (1914), VII, 53–54.
[3] *Ibid.*, VII, 54.

The change of heart thus recorded in that repository of his later reflection, *Les Pensées,* is not unnaturally attributed to a conversion. Pascal's "conversion," however, was no psychological crisis, but rather a steadily growing conviction that science and reason is not enough, that it must be rooted in something far more profound to be worth anything. The exercise of reason is the purest of all earthly joys, but there be joys in heaven beside which all earthly joys pale into insignificance. This was no new belief for Pascal; he had always assented to it intellectually, and his family, especially his sister Jacqueline, had always drawn him to piety. It was intensified after a slip on the ice in 1646, but gave way again to worldly interests, and it was not till his second "conversion" after a carriage accident in 1654 that he resolved to throw his lot in definitely with the Jansenists of Port-Royal; almost at once he forged their greatest weapon against the Jesuits in the *Lettres Provinciales* (1656). Pascal suffered no "religious experience" in the Jamesian sense; rather there came to him a slowly increasing realization of what his Christian faith meant, a new appreciation rather than a new belief. He went to Port-Royal to find illumination and peace; but his was never the perfect abandon of the typical mystic. Always there was the persistent "perhaps—and yet—"

An inquiring, restless mind, infinitely subtle, but never satisfied, he loved to balance two extremes, and weigh them, and reach a state of precarious equilibrium; an ounce either way would tip the scales, and the deciding force came, not from the reason, but from the "heart"—God touching the heart, he believed. His well-known calculus of probabilities—one stands to gain more by betting on the truth of Christianity than on its falsity—is both typical and unfair to the temper of his spirit. Try religion, and you will discover how good it is to believe, for if you but turn your face to God, he will pour faith into your soul. There was something in Pascal of the long line of Augustinians, believing that they might understand, and something of the true pragmatist, the true will to believe, something of the subtle doubts of a John Henry Newman seeking a certainty that mere knowledge could never give.

And so he planned his great Apology for Christianity, an apology directed with a true instinct for the currents of his age toward the *libertins*, the free-thinkers, the scoffers and mockers, and even more toward the great mass of the worldly and indifferent. All the rational demonstration in the world would not convince them, for they had no interest in believing.

Metaphysical proofs of God are so remote from the ordinary reasoning of men, and so involved, that they carry little weight; and even should they serve for some, that would be only for the moment when they saw the demonstration, but an hour later they would fear they had been mistaken. (*Pensée* 543)

To say to persons destitute of faith and grace that they have only to look upon the slightest things about them and they will see God made manifest, and to furnish them, as the whole proof of this large and important subject, the course of the moon and the planets, and to claim to have finished the proof with such a discourse, is to give them reason to believe that the proofs of our religion are feeble indeed; and I know by reason and by experience that nothing is more apt to give them contempt for it. (242)

No, one must appeal to the heart, not the head; did not Descartes maintain that the will makes all the decisions for the understanding? One must indeed prove by reason to the reason that the heart has its reasons which the reason can never know.

It is the heart which feels God, and not the reason. For that is what faith is, God touching the heart, not the reason. (278)

One must abandon demonstration for rhetoric; one must develop an art of persuasion.

For every man alive is almost always led to believe not by proof but by making attractive (agrément). . . . It seems to follow that, whatever it is one wants to persuade another of, one must have regard to the person, whose mind and heart must be known, what principles he accepts, what things he loves; and one must then take notice, in the affair at issue, what relations it has with his avowed principles, or with the objects that attract him because of the charms attributed to them. Thus the art of persuasion consists just as much in that of making attractive as in that of convincing, so far are men governed by caprice rather than by reason.[4]

One must even reach the mind through the body.

Follow the manner in which the faithful began: it is by doing everything as if they believed, by taking holy water, by saying mass, etc. Naturally

[4] *De l'esprit géometrique, Opuscules,* ed. Brunschvicg, pp. 185–87.

that will make you believe and will mortify your reason.—But that is
what I fear.—And why? what have you to lose? (*Pensée* 233)

This enterprise thus involved for Pascal two stages: first, to show
the limits of human science and reason, how faith enters into the
very foundations of science, how religion and science are both
founded on acts of faith; and secondly, to show how the Christian
vision is rooted in human nature, how man needs the God of St.
Augustine with an infinite need, and how his life will remain incomplete and his soul restless without Him. There is much that is
Augustinian in the subtle critique of knowledge, and the God whom
Pascal finds as the answer to the troubled needs of the human soul
is the God of Augustine—the Augustine of the Fall and of Grace,
the Augustine of Jansen. But it is an Augustinism directed against
a confident rationalism, not against the tired scepticism which the
great Doctor encountered, and an Augustinism that consequently,
like Montaigne's, abases the intellect before God instead of lifting
it up to the certainty of the Divine Truth.

There is nothing so conformable to reason as the disavowal of reason in
those things which belong to faith. And nothing so contrary to reason
as the disavowal of reason in the things that do not belong to faith. There
are two excesses equally dangerous: to exclude reason, and to admit
reason alone.[5]

And the faith that brings salvation is a human faith that touches
the heart, not the Divine Faith of St. Augustine that illuminates
the mind. Pascal, in other words, is not a medieval spirit, but a
modern: his religion may be experienced, but it cannot be understood; it could be reconciled with what he knew to be true, but
it could not thereby be rendered intelligible. Faith was for him
not the ultimate completion of the intellect, it was a mystery beyond reason.

Pascal's critique of knowledge therefore reaches no Augustinian
unified *sapientia:* instead, it distinguishes and sets off the different
domains of knowledge and the methods appropriate to each. Each
type of problem is to be solved by a method nicely adjusted to its
particular demands. There is *l'esprit géometrique,* the familiar Cartesian method; but as Descartes's unhappy dogmatism and inflexi-

[5] *Pensées,* ed. Port-Royal (1670), sec. v; ed. Brunschvicg, *Pensées* 272, 253.

bility revealed, that spirit hardly suited even the mathematical physicist.

Two kinds of right sense (*sens droit*): some can draw consequences well from a few principles, and that is a rightness of sense. Others can draw consequences well in things in which there are many principles. For example, the first understand well the effects of water, in which there are few principles; but the consequences of those are so subtle, that only an extreme rightness can follow them. . . . There are then two kinds of spirit: the one, of tracing, quickly and profoundly the consequences of principles, and that is *l'esprit de justesse;* the other, of comprehending a great number of principles without confounding them, and that is *l'esprit de géometrie*. The one is force and rightness of mind, the other is amplitude of mind. (2)

And even this *esprit de justesse* hardly suffices to decide questions like the existence of a vacuum or the pressure of the air, which only experiment can determine. And how do any of these methods, each so well suited to its own subject-matter, compare with that worldly wisdom by which the man of intelligence so surely steers his course amidst human relations? His principles are "in common usage and before the eyes of everybody"; yet they are "felt rather than known," they are infinite in number, impossible of clear formulation or of explicit teaching. The man of intelligence knows, but "he does it tacitly, naturally, and without art." He possesses a method which Pascal contrasts sharply with all the methods of science, and especially with *l'esprit de géometrie:* he has *l'esprit de finesse*, he can "see the situation with a single glance, and not by progressive reasoning about it." (1) Pascal is here defending the quick intuition against methodical analysis, intelligence against "reason"; he is in the long line of those down to Poincaré and Bergson who have refused to cramp the life of the mind into syllogisms, who have refused to make men think by logic. And like so many of them, he at times hopes to think despite logic. To Descartes's universal method he opposes many methods for many ends; to Descartes's trust in *le bon sens* of the average man he opposes the skilled technique of the specialist; to Augustine's divine reason illuminating every mind he opposes a doctrine of intellectual election:

You understand nothing of the works of God if you do not take as principle that he has willed to blind some and to enlighten others.

There are consequently no universal principles: each is specific and limited in range.

We must say in general, that happens because of figure and motion, for that is true. But to say what motions, and to reconstruct the machine, that is ridiculous, for it is futile and uncertain and laborious. (79)

Yet principles are necessary; for though the perfection of geometrical, that is, of scientific method, would be to define all the terms and to prove all the propositions, that is absolutely impossible.

In pushing inquiry further and further, we arrive of necessity at primitive words which we can define no further, and at principles so clear that we can find no others which would serve better to prove them. Whence it appears that men are in a natural and ineradicable impossibility to treat any science whatever in an absolutely finished order.[6]

But though mathematics thus arrives at indefinable terms and indemonstrable propositions, it is not to be abandoned.

For it supposes only things clear and constant by the natural light, and that is why it is perfectly true, being supported by nature in default of discourse. . . . It does not define the things which are clear and understood by all men, but does define all the rest; it does not prove the things all men know, but does the rest.[7]

At times Pascal follows Montaigne in entertaining suspicions of the light of nature:

There is no principle, however natural, even though held from infancy, which cannot be made to pass for a false impression either of teaching or of sense. . . . What are our natural principles, but principles to which we are accustomed? (*Pensées* 82, 92)

And once he goes so far as to exclaim, "It is Pyrrhonism that is true!" (432) But though this holds for general and universal principles, it hardly applies to the principles which are relatively valid within restricted fields. Such principles, whose validity cannot be known by discursive reason, are known rather by what Pascal calls *le coeur*, "the heart."

We know truth not only by reason but also by the heart; it is by the latter that we know first principles, and it is in vain that reasoning, which has no part therein, tries to combat them. . . . Principles are felt, propo-

[6] *De l'esprit géometrique, Opuscules,* ed. Brunschvicg, p. 167.
[7] *De l'esprit géometrique,* ed. Brunschvicg, p. 168.

sitions are concluded; and both with certitude, although in different ways. (282)

It is *le coeur* which feels that space has three dimensions, that numbers are infinite. Pascal's "heart" is thus the heir of the traditional *nous* or *intellectus;* indeed, he uses at times *intelligence (intelligentia)* as a synonym. But he makes a genuine contribution to the traditional—and Cartesian—standard of self-evidence.

It is a malady native to man to believe that he possesses the truth directly; and hence he is always disposed to deny whatever is incomprehensible to him; whereas in fact he knows only falsehood immediately, and must take for true only those things the contrary of which seems false to him. And therefore, whenever a proposition is inconceivable, we must suspend judgment and not deny it because of its inconceivability, but examine the contrary; and if the latter is found to be manifestly false, the former can be boldly affirmed, no matter how incomprehensible it is.[8]

And this "heart" knows of human nature truth undreamed of by *intellectus.*

When I began the study of man, I saw that the abstract sciences are not proper to him, and that I was wandering further away from my condition in advancing in them than were the others in remaining ignorant of them. (*Pensée* 144)

Pascal therefore turned from the limited and relative validity of human knowledge or *scientia* to the study of man himself; like a good Augustinian he sought to find God through a knowledge of the soul. Man is a being of infinite contradictions: Epictetus has best of all depicted his strength and grandeur, Montaigne his weakness and folly.

The greatness and the misery of man are so visible, that true Religion must of necessity teach us that there is in him some great principle of greatness, and at the same time some great principle of misery. For true Religion must know the depths of our nature, it must know all that is great in it and all that is miserable, and the reason for both. It must explain the astonishing contradictions we find.[9]

Man is made to know the truth; he desires it ardently, he searches after it; and yet when he tries to seize it, he is dazzled and confused in such

[8] *De l'esprit géometrique, Opuscules,* p. 177.
[9] *Pensées,* ed. Port-Royal, sec. iii.

fashion that he has been denied its possession. That is the origin of the two sects of Pyrrhonists and Dogmatists. . . . All men desire to be happy, without exception. However different the ways they employ, they are all aiming at the same goal. . . . And still over so many years no one has ever arrived without faith at the point to which all are striving. All complain, princes, subjects, nobles, commoners, old, young, strong, weak, wise, ignorant, healthy, diseased; in all lands, in all times, in all ages, in all conditions. . . . We have an impotence to prove, invincible to all dogmatism. We have an idea of truth, invincible to all Pyrrhonism. We desire the truth and find in ourselves only incertitude. We seek happiness, and find only misery. We are incapable of not seeking truth and happiness and we are incapable of certainty and happiness.[10]

It is dangerous to make man see too clearly how much he is equal to the beasts, without showing him his greatness. It is also dangerous to make him see too clearly his greatness without his low degree. It is still more dangerous to leave him in ignorance of either. (sec. xxiii)

What a chimaera is man? What novelty, what chaos, what a subject of contradiction? Judge of all things, unthinking worm of the dust; depositary of truth, mass of uncertainty; glory and refuse of the universe. If he exalts himself, I shall abase him; if he abases himself, I shall exalt him, and ever contradict him, until he knows that he is an incomprehensible monster. (sec. xxi)

Religion must be grounded, as St. Augustine so well knew, in the nature of the human soul. Only the Christian faith, only the Divine Creation and the Fall, can explain the double nature man finds within himself.

For a religion to be true, it must have known our nature. For the true nature of man, his true good, true virtue and true religion are things the knowledge of which is inseparable. It must have known the greatness and the weakness of human nature. What other religion than the Christian has known all these things? . . . We are hateful; reason convinces us thereof. Now no other religion than the Christian tells us to hate ourselves. No other religion therefore can be received by those who know they are worthy only of hate. No other religion than the Christian has known that man is the most excellent of creatures. . . . It is in vain, O man, that you seek in yourself the remedy for your miseries. All your light can succeed only in knowing that it is not in yourself that you will find either truth or good. . . . Know then, proud being, what a paradox you are to yourself. Humble yourself, impotent reason; be silent, un-

---

[10] *Pensées,* ed. Port-Royal, sec. xxi.

thinking nature; learn that man infinitely surpasses man; and learn from your Master your true condition which you know not. (sec. iii)

Pascal has shifted the grounds of religion from the Divine Order of Reason to the weakness and needs of the human soul. For the rational religion of the Oratorians he has only contempt.

Should a man be persuaded that the proportions of numbers are immaterial truths, eternal and dependent on a first truth in which they subsist, and which is called God, I should not find him far advanced toward his salvation. The God of Christians does not consist in a God who is simply the author of geometrical truths and of the order of the elements; that is the view of pagans and Epicureans. He does not consist solely in a God who exercises his providence on the life and goods of men, to give years of happiness to those who adore him. That is the portion of the Jews. But the God of Abraham, the God of Isaac, the God of Jacob, the God of Christians, is a God of love and consolation, he is a God who makes them feel in their hearts their misery and his infinite mercy; who is united to them in the depths of their souls; who fills them with humility, joy, confidence, and love; who makes them incapable of any other end than himself.[11]

The doctrines of the Fall and of Original Sin may shock our reason and our sense of justice; without them we cannot understand our human estate.

Certainly nothing shocks us so rudely as this doctrine; and still, without this mystery, the most incomprehensible of all, we are incomprehensible to ourselves. The knot of our condition draws its windings and its coils from that abysm; so that man is more inconceivable without this mystery than this mystery is inconceivable to man. (Pensée 434)

Christianity may not explain the world, it may confer no additional intelligibility on human science; but it does explain man. Man is not to be understood until we have plumbed the depths of man's irrationality. And so Pascal's apology ends, not in an appeal to persuasion, but in a conviction of truth. Its fragments are read and reread, not to confirm the soul in faith, but to share their insight into human nature. Their influence has come, not from any new proof of Christianity, but from their vision into the sinuosities and caverns of the mind, from the natural portrait they depict of the human soul. The fate of Pascal's apology was like the fate of Butler's *Analogy*, and all such sceptical apologetics, to raise doubts rather than to still them. But Pascal remains the greatest of the *moralistes*,

[11] *Opuscules*; ed. Brunschvicg, *Pensée* 556.

the painters of men. His is no unfinished masterpiece, but rather like those sketches of a hand or an arm or a muscle that remain of Leonardo, where his more ambitious works were left incomplete or have perished.

II

Malebranche like Pascal devoted himself to the reconciling of the new science with religion; but as the foremost thinker of the forces of the liberal Oratory, it was not the nice adjustment between the realm of science and the realm of grace that occupied his attention, but rather the more popular blending of the two into one great whole, with natural emphasis on what they had in common, and a consequent minimizing in both of what would not lend itself to such a new synthesis. Gathering into his thought all the tradition of Augustinian Platonism to which as Oratorian he was heir, and all those tendencies in popular Cartesianism which a generation of religious discussion had driven toward Platonic idealism, he fitted them into his vision of Intelligible Order. That vision in its day expressed to the full the Religion of Reason in which the seventeenth century culminated; it played its part in fostering the more worldly Irreligion of Reason of the next age. But it stands primarily as the supreme imaginative embodiment of the new faith men had discovered, the consecration given to rational science by religious feeling. Like Pascal, Malebranche remains the poet; but he is a lyric rather than a tragic poet, the poet of man's soaring rational vision rather than of the depths of human experience. In his pages is the imaginative expression of the religion of the mathematician.

For Malebranche's vision the world of geometry is the real world. It is not the rational order of nature, but the order of reason all naked and alone, that he feels aesthetically and emotionally and religiously. There lies the realm of immutable truth, universal and common to every mind, infinite, unchanging, and necessary.

No one can feel my private pain: every man can see the Truth that I contemplate. It is because my pain is a modification of my own substance, while the Truth is a good common to every mind. And thus by means of Reason I have or can have some society with God, and with every intelligence that exists; for every mind possesses with me a common good, a single law, Reason.[12]

[12] Malebranche, *Traité de morale*, ed. Henri Joly (1882), p. 2.

This realm of truth does not depend on God, it is God himself, directly accessible without shadow of intermediary to our minds,

for only the universal and infinite Being can contain within himself a universal and infinite reason . . . But the reason we consult is not only universal and infinite; it is also necessary and independent, and we conceive it in a sense as more independent than God himself. For God can act only in accord with this reason; in a sense he is dependent upon it, he must consult it and follow it. But God consults only himself, he is dependent upon nothing. Hence this reason can not be a thing apart from him, it is coeternal and consubstantial with him . . . We are looking therefore upon the rule, the order, the reason of God; for what other wisdom than that of God could we be contemplating, since we are not afraid to say that God is obliged to follow it? [13]

This Truth that we know when we know anything is the Logos himself, the Word of God; it is the natural habitat, the "place" of minds, as space is the abode of bodies. It is the Wisdom of the Father himself, and to it Malebranche bends in prayer:

Speak, Eternal Word, Logos, Word of the Father, word that hath been forever proclaimed, is now, and ever shall be . . . He who knoweth thee knoweth thy Father, and he who knoweth thee and thy Father enjoyeth perfect bliss.[14]

To be sure, this was no unprecedented vision: it is the religious Platonism of the long Augustinian tradition, the direction of religious feeling to the one object man finds in himself higher than his own being, the realm of truth and reason in which the minds of all participate. It is the imaginative discovery of that same unchanging Truth which St. Bonaventura expressed in the thirteenth century in equally poetic terms, with equal identification of Truth and God; it is the Augustinian theory of divine illumination, so different in temper from the saint's harsh theory of grace, and so familiar in the Oratory, learnedly expounded just before Malebranche's entry into the order in P. André Martin's *S. Augustinus* (1653). But in the Oratorian's thought it blended with the mathematical vision of Descartes; and the two visions, so similar and yet so different in their motives and consequences, reacted upon each other, and produced a third, unique and distinctive.

[13] Malebranche, *De la Recherche de la vérité*, ed. Francisque Bouillier (1880), II, 373.
[14] Malebranche, *Méditations Chrétiennes*, in *Oeuvres*, ed. Jules Simon, II, v.

True to the spirit of rational religion, Malebranche's process of synthesis was not so much an enriching as a selection, the sloughing off of those elements in both Augustine and Descartes which were irrelevant to geometrical truth. Descartes' whole interest in mathematical physics and in the mastery of nature disappeared; Malebranche wished only to worship and adore. With it went the Cartesian problems of relating the realm of truth to nature: for Malebranche truth was sufficient in itself, and the very existence of a realm of bodies, being of "merely" pragmatic importance and irrelevant to truth, could safely be left to revelation.

It is in this world that we are and live, though the body we inhabit lives and moves in another. It is this world that we contemplate, that we admire, that we feel. But the world upon which we look or gaze when we turn our head from side to side, is but matter, in itself invisible, and has none of the beauty we admire and feel in beholding it.[15]

Geometry was not merely the model of all knowledge, it was become the only knowledge; nothing not extension or number can be truly known.

To demonstrate is to develop a clear idea and to deduce from it with certainty what that idea of necessity contains; and we have no ideas, it seems to me, clear enough to construct demonstrations except those of extension and number. Even the soul in no wise knows itself; it has only an internal feeling of itself and of its modifications.[16]

Applied thus to the soul, this rigid restriction of knowledge was Malebranche's greatest Cartesian heresy; but in removing intelligibility from physical action, from the relation of soul and body, it was merely pushing further the Platonic strain in Cartesian thought.

On the other hand, Cartesianism has altered the familiar outlines of the Augustinian theory of knowledge. Gone is the Neoplatonic and hierarchical conception which placed God as the sun of the intelligible world, making men see his reflection; there is but a single realm of truth, and God is the direct object of vision, not its transcendent cause. Knowledge is vision, not illumination: it is seeing things *in* God, not by God's light. Gone too are all traces of Platonic teleology: God's mind contains only mathematical truths, and those

---

[15] *Entretiens sur la métaphysique*, in *Oeuvres*, I, 12.
[16] *Correspondance avec Mairan*, in V. Cousin, *Fragments de philosophie cartésienne*, p. 345.

relations of perfection which Malebranche conceived as mathematically as possible. And gone is that hierarchy from sense to science to
wisdom: the divine truth is not the standard by which to judge the
lower truths of science and of sense, it is the only truth. Reason is
not only supreme, it reigns alone. No wonder this pure rationalism
frightened not only theologians like Arnauld and Bossuet, but even
physicists like Rohault.

What is it we know with such clairvoyant directness? God himself, who as the very structure of truth is inherent in all knowledge;
mathematical relations, those between the ideas of beings of the same
nature, which, as part of the intelligible order itself, are seen without
any intermediary; and the relations of perfection, those between
the ideas of beings of a different nature, which are the basis of the
demonstrative science of morals. In itself the sense-world, however,
is not intelligible: it contains an intelligible aspect concealed under a
mass of sense-qualities apprehended only *par conscience* or *par
sentiment intérieur*. Our only real knowledge of the world of
bodies must be a knowledge of this intelligible aspect, of the *étendue
intelligible* or intelligible space, which is "nothing but the very substance of God, in so far as it is representative of bodies, in which
they participate with the limitations or imperfections proper to
them." [17] In this intelligible or ideal space, which is not in itself actually extended, are "represented" the "ideas" or geometrical essences of all the particular sense-objects in the world. Such individual things can be known only through these "ideas," a term
Malebranche employs strictly in its Platonic sense of universal or
archetype. When we perceive an object, we know its mathematical
essence or "idea" as it is involved in the relations of intelligible or
geometrical space. In addition we have a "confused feeling" of its
sense-qualities, which individualize the mathematical universal for
us.

To see a sense object, the sun, a tree, a house, etc., there are necessary
two things, the modality of color, . . . and a pure idea, that is, the idea
of extension or intelligible space.[18]

[17] *Oeuvres*, I, 187.
[18] Malebranche, *Réponse a M. Arnauld*, in Arnauld, *Oeuvres*, ed. Jules Simon
(1843), p. 313.

For there are always both a pure idea and a confused feeling in our knowledge of the existence of objects, that of God and of our own soul alone excepted.[19]

An "idea" being for Malebranche always a clear universal, and never, as in Descartes, an image of a particular thing, there can be no such thing as the "confused ideas" of the Cartesians, nor can what mere *sentiment* gives us be knowledge at all. This theory of perception Malebranche calls "seeing things in God," or in their mathematically intelligible order. And finally, of our own selves, since we have no clear geometrical "idea" of the soul, we have a confused feeling alone; and of other minds there is but conjecture.

The soul does not know itself by an "idea" which it can contemplate, to discover the properties it possesses, as do the geometricians, who contemplate the "idea" which they have of extension, and discover its relations: it knows its own being only by the internal feeling which it has of itself. Nor can the soul know its own modifications: it can only feel them.[20]

Naturally this rigid mathematical Platonism aroused the more empirical Cartesians like Arnauld and Régis. Arnauld, already antagonized by Malebranche's unaugustinian views on grace, expressed in his *Traité de la nature et de la grâce* (1680), attacked him in *Des vraies et des fausses idées* (1683), identifying an idea with the particular perception of an object, and making it represent in the mind or correspond to the intelligible aspect of the object itself. In the long polemic against this semi-Aristotelian and Cartesian point of view, Malebranche made still clearer his thoroughly Platonic realism, citing the definition of Augustine:

Ideas are certain first models or stable and immutable archetypes of things, which have not been created, and which are consequently eternal and always the same in the eternal wisdom which contains them.

Ideas are in no sense themselves knowledge, they are the objects of knowledge; they are never particulars, but universal essences caught up in the relations of intelligible space. And against the charge that this intelligible space is the very essence of God, whom as infinite we are thus made to see directly, Malebranche replied, we do not see that essence of God which is infinitely infinite, but only that

[19] *Recherche*, ed. Bouillier, II, 385.
[20] Malebranche, *Réponse a M. Arnauld,* in Arnauld, *Oeuvres*, p. 315.

infinite essence which is not God in himself, but merely God in relation to his creatures:

He who says essence says absolute being, or being infinitely infinite, which can represent nothing that is finite, [while we see only the substance of God] taken as relative to his creatures or as they can participate in it.

Such a limitation of intelligibility to geometry alone naturally involved the adoption of that occasionalism implicit in the Cartesian developments. There being no idea of power or efficient causation in geometry, nor in the confused feeling we have of the soul, it is obvious that causation can reside only in the divine will. But that will acts always by fixed and immutable laws. Malebranche is no voluntarist: he rejected Descartes's "arbitrary decrees." God did not create eternal truths, God *is* Truth.

It has always been true that two and two are four, and it is impossible that it should ever become false. That is clear, without it being necessary that God, as sovereign legislator, should have ordained these truths, as M. Descartes maintains.[21]

In the simplest mechanical motion no force or power is observable, but there is a constant relation.

There are many reasons which prevent me from attributing to secondary or natural causes a force, a power, an efficacy to produce some effect. But the principal is that this opinion seems to me inconceivable. However great an effort I make to understand it, I can find in myself no idea which will represent to me what the force or power attributed to created things can be. . . . Those who maintain that created things have in themselves force or power are advancing something of which they have no clear conception. . . . Whatever effort of mind I make, I can find no force, efficacy, or power save in the will of the infinitely perfect Being. . . . When I see one ball strike another, my eyes tell me, or seem to tell me, that it is truly the cause of the motion it imparts; for the true cause which moves bodies does not appear to my eyes. But when I question my reason, I see clearly that bodies not being able to move themselves, and their moving force being only the will of God that preserves them successively in different positions, they cannot communicate a power which they do not possess, and that they could not even communicate it if it were at their disposal. For the mind will never conceive how a body, a substance purely passive, can transmit to another the power which moves it, even though it be true. (II, 437, 440)

[21] *Recherche*, ed. Bouillier, II, 379.

Natural or "occasional" causation is thus but the constant operation of God's creative force.

> God does not multiply his volitions without reason; he acts always in the simplest ways, and that is why he makes use of the contact of bodies to move them; not that their contact is absolutely necessary to their motion, as our senses tell us, but because such contact being the occasion of the communication of motion, there need be only a very small number of natural laws to produce all the admirable effects which we see. (II, 445)

What these unchanging laws are, only experience can reveal: they are not deducible, as Descartes thought, from any principle, like that of the conservation of motion. In that they follow constant laws, particular occurrences are not arbitrary; but, so far as human reason goes, those laws themselves are arbitrary.

> In such a case one can certainly discover the truth only by experience. For since we cannot compass the designs of the Creator, nor comprehend all the relations they have to his attributes, to preserve or not to preserve in the universe the same absolute quantity of motion, seems to depend on a purely arbitrary volition of God, of which in consequence we can learn only by a kind of revelation, such as experience gives. . . . As to the very existence of created things, . . . it is clear it can be discovered only by a kind of natural revelation; that is to say, by the sensations God gives us, in consequence of the general laws of the union of mind and body. (II, 188, 247)

Malebranche's keen and almost Humean analysis of the concept of causation in mechanics itself, combines the denial of any necessary or intelligible basis for the principles of physics with a strict determinism of immutable law. Mechanics is the scene of constant operations; but what those operations are we cannot demonstrate but only observe, and hence mechanics is not, in the strict seventeenth-century sense, a science.

The consequence of this view, that there can be no science of nature or of man, that science is a mathematics without application, meant of course that natural and moral philosophers must find a new conception of science, which they speedily did. Still more anticipatory of the thought of the Enlightenment were the theological consequences Malebranche drew. As God's mind contains only mathematical order, God acts always in universal and never in particular ways, and always in the simplest way possible. There can therefore be no particular providence, no miracles, no petitionary prayer. What seem to be miracles to us are really in accord with the universal laws of the Realm of Grace. Man is not justified, to be sure, without divine grace; but that grace is granted to him on the occasion of prayers and good works in accord with the fixed but inscrutable laws God has established. Nor can evil be attributed to God's laws, for they operate always with no concern for individuals, to the end of their own beauty and regularity. God's world exists, not for the avoidance of individual ill, but to manifest the glory of the unspeakable harmonies of geometry.

In such a world, man's duty is clear:

We are rational beings, and our virtue, our perfection, is to love Reason, or rather, to love Order.

Let us apply ourselves to knowing, loving, and following the relations of perfection enshrined in the Truth that is God. It is as clear that mind is superior to matter, or that man is above the beasts and the beasts above stones, as that two and two are four. No act is truly virtuous that is not inspired by the love of this divine order. The force of mind which will enable man to conform to this order, as God conforms to it, will come only with the constant practice of that liberty of the spirit which consists in retiring from the world to meditate on the inward vision of the divine order and in hearkening to that Word. Love of that order persists even in the most depraved: it is only the vision which is obscured. Through sin man has been subjected to the manifold errors induced by the imagination and the passions, and the consequent dependence of the soul on the body, a reversal of the divine order that prevailed before the Fall. It is for us to subdue the imagination to the understanding, the passions to those natural inclinations which are really directed toward reason. By study of these sources of error we can restore the rational vision of truth, which we cannot but love once we behold it. *La Recherche de la vérité* (1674), Malebranche's first and most extensive work, in the voluminous *Éclaircissements* to which are to be found his most penetrating insights, is thus both the greatest of those seventeenth-century negative aids to sound rational method, of which Bacon's doctrine of Idols is the prototype, and the guide to a moral achievement and salvation which can be found only as we attain a vision of truth.

Malebranche left a magnificent poem, perhaps best expressed in his *Entretiens sur la métaphysique* (1688), which vie with Berkeley's *Dialogues* in the competition for Platonic laurels. In it Cartesianism soared far above the problems of natural science to a vision of Truth eternal and unchanging. And yet:

Must we judge of the reality of ideas by the liveliness of the perceptions which they produce in us? If that is so, we must believe there is more of reality in the point of a pin which pricks us, in a coal which burns us, or in their ideas, than in the beauty and harmony of the Divine Order.[22]

This sudden descent to earth illustrates the pass to which religious Cartesianism had come. Best of all the Cartesians, Malebranche makes clear the ultimate inability of the great tradition of Augustinian Platonism to serve as the philosophy of natural science. Designed to raise men above worldly concerns to the vision of Eternal Truth, it performed only too well its immemorial service. With Malebranche Cartesianism forgot the world in beholding Order. It gazed on Reason, but Nature had been left far behind. Only by holding fast to the basic Aristotelian conviction that whatever order there be must be the order of Nature, that the natural abode of mind is the intelligible form or structure of the world, could Spinoza escape this self-immolation of reason. For in Malebranche, in the hour of its supreme triumph, reason abandoned all pretense of being the instrument of natural knowledge. *Deum et animam scire cupio. Nihilne plus? Nihil omnino!* As it was in the beginning, so was it in the end.

[22] *Entretiens sur la métaphysique*, in *Oeuvres*, ed. Simon, II, 325.

5

Spinoza: Rational Naturalist

I

BENEDICTUS DE SPINOZA (1632–1677) was the only man who really believed in the new science, believed that it answered all men's problems. He had no reservations about morals, like Descartes, no doubts about certainty, no problem of how to get knowledge into a world wholly innocent of knowledge, like Hobbes and Locke. He believed it because he understood it. He saw its implications as no contemporary did. He was hence able to generalize and complete what Kepler and Galileo had begun. After a hundred years, men like Hume and Kant began to see it too, though they interpreted it quite differently, and in opposed fashion. It was still another hundred years before it began to worry the average man.

The man who did this was a Portuguese Jew living in Holland. There is no real answer to the question why; though Veblen has suggested that, doubly uprooted, freed from the letter of the Jewish tradition and under no temptation to accommodate his views to Christian beliefs, he enjoyed a detachment that permitted him to follow out ideas to the bitter end. There is much in Spinoza's thought that is alien to the familiar channels through which the Jewish genius has expressed itself, perhaps most of all his disregard for the sharp gulf that has divided man from the Most High; but it is not hard to see therein the persistent impress of the core of the Hebraic tradition: the emphasis on one universal all-embracing cosmic Law. Christian thinkers were prevented by the hierarchical world of their Neoplatonic thought from thus reading the implications of the new science, so that one is tempted to say that only a Jew—only an excommunicated Jew—could have thought as Spinoza thought. Of course, for Jews this law was a moral order, while for the new science it was a mathematical and logical order; but the very essence of Spinoza's position is that the Logical Order of Nature is *ipso facto* a Moral Order.

Spinoza lived an uneventful life amidst the startling intellectual changes of the seventeenth century. Outwardly he was a poor lens-grinder, supporting himself by his labors and indulging much in study. It has been the fashion to indulge in sentimentality over the man whom Unamuno called the "tragic, sorrowful Jew of Amsterdam," cut off from his own people and leading a lonely and frustrated life. But Spinoza had risen above outward circumstance. When he was offered an academic post at Heidelberg, he refused, ostensibly because he was required to say nothing against the established Calvinism, but really because he had no desire to change his way of life. For under a rather drab exterior there burned the inward glory, the calm clear light of a mind that has looked upon the very face of God, and in the knowledge and the intellectual love of God found peace and blessedness.

His was an intensely religious and pious nature. He was deeply learned in Jewish scholastic theology, and in the mystic lore that had grown up through the ages. He was endowed with the passionate religious feeling that can sincerely maintain, "Though He slay me, yet will I worship Him." He was at the same time a thoroughgoing modernist, so intellectually honest that he had to answer all the inherited problems of religious thought in terms of the best "modern" knowledge. Spinoza's relation to Cartesianism has been the subject of much confusion, due to the tradition that persists in seeing in Descartes primarily a metaphysician; whereas, to his contemporaries, he was rather a philosophically-minded mathematical physicist, with a curious mixture of traditional metaphysical ideas. Spinoza, on the other hand, was in the great tradition of Aristotelian and Neoplatonic Jewish philosophy. Like all the outstanding seventeenth-century thinkers, he never considered Descartes's metaphysics important enough to honor it with formal refutation: he thought his pedagogical attempt to reduce it to geometrical consistency in *The Principles of Descartes's Philosophy* (1663) was answer enough. But, like most of his intelligent contemporaries, he regarded the Cartesian mathematical physics, its methods and its concepts, as very close to absolute and final truth about the world. He was dubious of the details, of course; but they hardly interested him.

Spinoza was, in fact, developing the problems of the later Jewish scholastics—like Crescas—largely the same as those of the Christian Schoolmen—in their own terminology, in an intellectual environment in which Cartesian science was the accepted truth about nature. He was working out the implications of Cartesian science—of its root idea—for the traditional Platonic and Aristotelian philosophy of the Middle Ages. As a result, to the old familiar terms: cause, God, substance, attribute, essence, power, freedom, and immortality, he gave a revolutionary new content; but he still felt profoundly the immemorial values for which those terms stood. In this he was the very antithesis of most of the leaders of the Renaissance and the Reformation, who poured new values into old and traditional intellectual symbols. Spinoza is thus the last major representative of the medieval way of life, of the medieval religious values, in the setting of the new science. He started with the deepest religious problems, and to them gave uncompromisingly "scientific" answers. One is tempted to say that his is the greatest religious philosophy of the Western tradition. Certainly it is far more religious than Aristotle's or Thomas's, though far less adequate as an interpretation of the whole of human experience. It is also "true," in so far as "science" is "true"; in so far, that is, as we can validly claim to possess science—and he never doubted the fact of science. Since he set out with the Aristotelian terms and distinctions, since he never wavered from the faith that the object of knowledge is the order of the world itself, he was able to make "science" intelligible; the only other serious "modern" attempt, that of Kant, was carried through at the cost of making the world unintelligible.

II

Spinoza's concern was not with the "problem of knowledge"— the existence of knowledge presented no "problem" to him—but with the implications of the fact of knowledge. His eye was set upon a rational vision: the vision of the fact of knowledge, of the power of the human mind to understand the world, and of a world that can be understood, that is through and through intelligible. If the mind can understand the universe—and of this he had no doubt—what must the universe be like, in which such understanding occurs? In what kind of a world can it be truly said, "The human mind has an adequate knowledge of the infinite and eternal essence of God or Nature"? What place is there in such a world for the mind that can understand it? These questions Spinoza sought to answer in his *Ethics*, long worked over, but published only after his death, in 1677.

Spinoza's vision of knowledge was a vision of the fact of science as it was in the seventeenth century—the fact of mathematics, of geometry. It was of that science in which "a knowledge of the effects depends on and involves a knowledge of the cause." It was of knowledge as a deductive system of implications, in which each idea is bound up with others in a logical order following from initial axioms. This alone is true knowledge; and it is the sure possession of mankind. All knowledge can with care and patience be so ordered. It was inevitable that Spinoza should write his book "*more geometrico*"; for it too was to be veritable knowledge. It was to be an illustration of that order whereof it spoke.

If knowledge is a system of ideas, a logical order, the world of which it must be the direct grasp must needs also be logically ordered. It must possess a logical structure the mind can grasp. The fact that the mind can understand the world implies that the world is understandable, is intelligible, is itself a natural and "rational" order. This fact of order or intelligible structure was for Spinoza something overwhelming, overpowering. He was convinced that every philosophy must begin with it. Everything else is to be understood only in terms of the Order of Nature, but the Order of Nature is not to be understood in terms of anything else. It is intelligible in itself, it "exists in itself and is conceived through itself." Every particular event is to be conceived as part of the system of nature. The one thing needing no further explanation is the system of nature itself: it is what Spinoza called "Substance," "*Causa Sui*."

In such a world, the problems that worried the Cartesians cease to be insoluble by definition. How is the presence of the human mind and its relation to the body to be explained? Such a fact is either unintelligible—the "miracle" or brute fact of the Occasionalists—or else it is a particular case of the universal presence of "mind" in the universe. The only intelligible "cause" or "origin" of the human mind is the logical structure of the universe itself, not a separate realm of reason whose connection with the natural universe must remain dubious. This universally present mind cannot be a particular entity that thinks, it cannot be an "intelligence," inhabiting a particular animal body; it can be only that mathematical and logical structure that makes it possible for human bodies to think, and be intelligent; just as the mechanical structure described in the laws of motion makes it possible for them to fall, and their chemical structure, to digest. In such a universe, the problem is not why the human body thinks, but why all bodies do not think; and to that question the answer is indeed a fact: "*Homo cogitat*." [1]

If matter and mind are intelligible, each in its own terms, and irreducible the one to the other—if the action of one body is intelligible only in terms of the system of bodies, and the thinking of one mind intelligible only in terms of the system of mind—then each must be a complete system, existing in itself and conceived through itself; each must be a *causa sui*, a "substance." There can be no further cause or explanation of the fact of the System of Nature or the fact of the System of Knowledge. Does this then mean that there are two systems, in Spinoza's language, two "substances"? No, for the system of knowledge is a system of "ideas," the ideas that are the intelligible aspects of bodies. It is a system of science, of knowledge of an intelligible universe. This is implied in the very fact that man thinks, that he possesses science. And thus both perceived systems are really the same system: they are two "attributes" of the one "substance" that is Nature, the same "Nature" "conceived under two attributes," each of which alike expresses the "essence" of the same Nature. That is, Nature and Science, the order of natural objects and the order of knowledge of them, are coextensive: "the order and connexion of ideas is the same as the order and connexion of things." (II, prop. 7) "An idea is one and the same thing with its object" (Scholium to II, prop. 7), for it is its intelligible expression or mathematical formula. And outside this order there is nothing else: the order of falling bodies, for example, and the laws of falling bodies, are identical.

---

[1] *Ethics*, Part II, Axiom 2. All citations without further indication, giving part and proposition numbers, are taken from the *Ethics*.

Spinoza is undoubtedly following the model of Cartesian analytic geometry. The relations between the two systems or orders, his two "attributes," he conceives as like the relation between geometry and algebra in that mathematical discipline. Analytic geometry maintains that the same mathematical order of relations can be expressed either geometrically or algebraically. The circle is thus either the idealized extended perfect figure suggested by the circle drawn; or it is the algebraic formula, $a^2 + b^2 = r^2$. The figure and the algebraic formula are both alike the circle: they are "one and the same thing" with the circle, "conceived under the attribute" of geometry or extension, and under the attribute of algebra or thought. This is the conception Spinoza is seeking to generalize in his doctrine of attributes.

Spinoza neither says nor means that the two attributes of substance that are the order of things and the order of ideas are "parallel." Psycho-physico-parallelism is a doctrine that belongs to nineteenth-century psychology, not to Spinoza's logic. Each attribute expresses the "essence" of Substance, each order is the one identical Order of Nature; and though Nature have infinite attributes, it has only one Order, which is completely intelligible in a single one. And thus, though man knows only two attributes, a fact that must be accepted as axiomatic, he knows everything, he has an adequate knowledge of the infinite and eternal essence of God. There is in the universe for Spinoza nothing unknowable.

"Whatever is, is in God, and without God, nothing can either be or be conceived." (I, prop. 15) All knowledge and all events are caught up and embraced in one great logical system. From this system, all things—laws, events, facts, knowledge, objects—flow forth of necessity, as from the nature of a triangle it follows that the sum of its angles is equal to two right angles. It is the cause of both the essence and the existence of things: things can exist and be intelligible only as elements in it, as members of the complete system. "Cause" for Spinoza means, not force, not mechanical or efficient cause, but that in terms of which a thing is intelligible—its logical ground, its *archē*, its principle of intelligibility. Though Spinoza characteristically refuses to define this basic concept, it is clear that to him "cause" is always to be identified with formal cause alone.

The system, or God, is eternal: once given, it could not be otherwise, any more than a triangle could have a different sum of its angles than two right angles. "Things could not have been brought into being by God in any manner or in any order different from that which has in fact obtained." (I, prop. 33) "God never can decree, nor ever could have decreed, anything but what is; God did not exist before his decrees, and would not exist without them" (Scholium to I, prop. 33)—for God is identical with his decrees, the order of nature itself. That order must be unchanging if there is to be science, and the existence of science is a fact. From this necessary uniformity of nature there follows a thoroughgoing logical determinism: the motive is always the demands of knowledge. "It is not in the nature of reason to regard things as contingent, but as necessary." (II, prop. 44) Everything is an event in a logically determined order, the actions of the human will like all else.

Does this mean that particular events can be deduced from the system, without reference to observed facts? Not at all! Universal causality can be, but every particular event is conditioned by some other particular event; and this particular conditioning, though in accordance with the system, and caught up in it—though a "finite modification of substance"—and intelligible only in the system, is in itself contingent. Spinoza makes this clear in Proposition 28 of Book I:

Every individual thing, or everything which is finite, and has conditioned existence, cannot exist or be conditioned to act, unless it be conditioned for existence and action by a cause other than itself, which also is finite and has a conditioned existence; and likewise this cause cannot in its turn exist, or be conditioned to act, unless it be conditioned for existence and action by another cause, which also is finite, and has a conditioned existence, and so on to infinity. . . .

That which is finite and has a conditioned existence cannot be produced by the absolute nature of any attribute of God; for whatsoever follows from the absolute nature of God is infinite and eternal. . . . But from God, or from any of his attributes, in so far as the latter is modified by an infinite and eternal modification, a conditioned thing cannot follow. Wherefore it must follow from, or be conditioned for, existence and action by God or one of his attributes, in so far as the latter are modified by some modification which is finite, and has a conditioned existence.

Particular events are to be discovered only by an appeal to facts, as Spinoza consistently maintains. In a deductive system, facts appear as fresh postulates. No particulars can be deduced from the first book of the *Ethics*, from God or the system. God remains the major premise throughout all five books; but the minor premises, the particular facts, appear as fresh axioms wherever necessary. Spinoza is not attempting the impossible task of deducing everything, all events and all modes, *a priori*. Only eternal laws, not finite modes or facts, can be so deduced. He specifically denies it in his letters to Tschirnhausen. Facts are not to be deduced beforehand; they are to be made intelligible *when given* as part of the order of nature. Spinoza is offering an interpretation of experience, not an *a priori* construction. There is a great deal in the universe besides God or the Order of Nature: there are all the events, the facts, the activities and happenings. They are all involved in the system, and intelligible only in its terms; but they are not deducible from the system alone. From the laws of digestion you can never infer any particular stomach-ache, except in conjunction with the particular fact of what you ate for dinner; from God you can never infer the fact that the human body thinks, though you can explain it, when it is given, and introduced into the system as an independent axiom in the second book, *"homo cogitat"* (II, Axiom 2), in terms of the logical structure of the universe or God.

Indeed, God or Substance or Nature is not the sum total of things, but their intelligible aspect, *the structure* or *the system of* the universe, not its totality. It is *"the Nature of"* the Universe, *"the Substance of"* things. Things exist in God, and are conceived through God; but Spinoza never says they *are* in themselves God. Spinoza is not in any strict sense a "pantheist." In fact, no facile category is applicable to his thought, which is truly unique. He cannot even be called a "Spinozist," when we remember what "Spinozists" have been. The Germans have invented a term for his position: they call him a "panentheist."

III

Spinoza does not hesitate to draw the full consequences of this vision of order. In Cartesianism, there had been left two substances outside the mathematical order of nature, God and the human soul. For Spinoza, God *is* the order itself, and the soul is in the system as an integral element. God is not to be anthropomorphically conceived; he is the logical order of Nature. He has no "intellect" or "will" in the human sense; for when those faculties are attributed to him, they are no more like the powers of the human mind than the dog, an animal that barks, is like the Dog, a star in the heavens. There are no purposes or teleology in nature. To find purposes and natural ends there makes the real cause, the structure of processes, an effect of what is in reality its consequence. Spinoza sketches a famous critique of natural teleology: natural ends are mere human ways of conceiving things. That is, under the spell of his mathematical vision, Spinoza is throwing out Aristotle's functional view. He is reducing all ends or "final causes" to purely formal causes, just as he transforms God from the ultimate end or final cause of the Aristotelian tradition to the supreme formal and mathematical cause of the universe—he transforms, we may say, "God" from an ideal to an equation. Because Spinoza recognizes that the ends achieved in natural processes are not efficient causes—they do not "make" the processes occur, as the medieval Platonizing theologians had perversely maintained—he denies that ends give any understanding, they are merely "human ways of conceiving." That is, Spinoza throws out the baby with the bath. He is consequently left without any place for potentiality: everything in his mathematical universe is "pure actuality." This seems the greatest inadequacy in Spinoza's metaphysics. There is no providence, save the *conatus sese conservandi* with which all things are endowed, and no miracles, which are imagined through human ignorance. But nevertheless God is divine and "perfect" or complete, the proper object of religious feeling. Spinoza would say he had at last found out what God really is.

Opinion as to the religious significance of Spinoza's views has vacillated between two extremes: there were those in his own day, who realized that his conception of God is miles removed from the traditional Jewish and Christian conceptions of God, and called him an atheist. This is also the view of the modern reader, with perhaps little enough sympathy for traditional religion, who asks, "Spinoza is indeed a supreme philosopher, but why on earth does he call his infinite Substance or Nature God?" Then there are those who, beginning with the German Romanticists, realizing his profoundly religious temperament and attitude, and having learned that religion is not merely a matter of conventional intellectual belief, but a way of life, have recognized in Spinoza a supreme expression of the religious temperament and way of life—of what Santayana calls "piety"—and have called him, with Novalis, the "God-intoxicated man"—which is true enough. This seems also to be the view of those modern Jews, who, with more cultural piety than perception of the essential core of the Hebrew religion, insist that Spinoza is the greatest Jewish religious teacher—which is probably true enough, especially if you insist on intellectual clarity in religious teaching—and hence claim him for the Jewish tradition—which is more questionable.

In truth, Spinoza is not a "Hebrew" in his religious thinking, or a "Christian," though doubtless he is as much so as many a reformed Jew or liberal Christian: but he is a profoundly religious man, more so than the great majority of them. He called the logical order of nature "God," not merely because it was his answer to the ultimate question of the scholastics, whose own answer they freely identified with the traditional Deity with equal justification, or lack of justification. After all, the "God" of Maimonides or of Thomas Aquinas is as far from Pascal's "God of Abraham, God of Isaac and God of Jacob," as Spinoza's "God": all three are "rational theologies." He called the Order of Nature "God" because he *felt* toward it precisely as the most pious theist feels toward God as he conceives him; because his "God" served as an adequate intellectual symbol for his religious experience. He found in the rational vision of that order, and of his relation to it, that peace and blessedness which the religious mystic finds in the *visio Dei*. He had at last beheld the very face of God.

And in sober fact Spinoza's "God" does possess certain of the essential values attributed to the "God" of the Hebrew-Christian tradition, and attributed to the rational God of the Schoolmen, worked out with complete clarity and consistency in the light of seventeenth-century science. Spinoza was willing to go to any length in sacrificing the details of the older tradition in order to save its substance.

Nature, as the object of knowledge, is capable of being the source of constant good and a rule of life, and thus has all the properties and the functions which the Jewish-Christian tradition attributed to God. He was hence entitled to confer upon it the title of *Natura sive Deus*. For Nature, as he conceived it, carried with it all the emotional associations and all the moral force and authority found in the older religious view of God. It provided an immutable End and Law for conduct, and it was the source, when rationally known, of perfect peace and unqualified security. Nature was naturally—that is, rationally—known, and knowledge of it was such a perfect good that when it takes possession of the human mind the lesser and otherwise disturbing objects of affection and passion are so included within it as to fall into their proper place of subordination: that is, of complete control. . . .

In Spinoza, more than in any other modern thinker, there are exhibited complete loyalty to the essential elements in the Hebraic tradition— ultimate and self-sufficing Being as the standard of all human thought and action—with perpetuation of the Greek theory of knowledge and its exaltation of reason over experience, together with enthusiastic adherence to the new scientific view of nature. Thus he sought to obtain from the very heart of the new science a conclusive demonstration of the perfection of Being through which the human soul can alone obtain absolute security and peace. A scientific comprehension was to give, in full reality, by rational means, that assurance and regulation of life that non-rational religions had pretended to give.[2]

IV

Where does man and man's mind fit into this scheme of things? No longer is it an alien outcaste; it is rather a natural consequence of the universe. The human mind is intelligible as an instance of the fact of Mind or logical order in the universe: it is the idea of the human body. All bodies have "ideas," are intelligible. Intelligibility means the fact of order present in bodies: in an intelligible universe, every body is involved in logical relationships. But only the human body is "intelligent," is conscious of itself and of the world. In saying that every body has an "idea," Spinoza does not mean that every body is conscious and thinks; Spinoza is not a pan-psychist, though since the romantic era his thought has often been so interpreted. An "idea" for him is an Aristotelian form made mathematical. Why is the human body, of all bodies in the world, intelligent as well as intelligible? The answer is to be sought in the nature of the human body: a knowledge of effects depends upon and involves a knowledge of the cause. The explanation, that is, is to be found in the facts of physiology. But Spinoza is not interested in physiological

---

[2] John Dewey, *The Quest for Certainty* (1929), pp. 56, 54.

inquiry; he accepts it as a fact that man thinks, and explains this thinking in terms of the system of the universe, not of the structure of the human body. Either system, that of idea or that of body, will give explanation: for the order of ideas and the order of bodies is ultimately one and the same order.

The idea that is the human mind is very complex, like the human body of which it is the intelligible expression, and which can reflect the action of the whole universe upon it. Our intellectual perception of objects is the idea of the effect produced by the object in our body, through the senses. Our idea of Peter is thus the idea of the effects caused by Peter in our body. It is not the idea of Peter's body that is Peter's mind, because not the whole of Peter's body is capable of affecting our body. Hence we have no adequate knowledge of our own body, or of any other body, whenever it is determined from without; for the whole of bodies never affects us, or modifies the whole of our body. Through the senses therefore we can derive only "confused" and "inadequate" knowledge. The source of error is hence the inability of our body to be influenced completely by other bodies through the sense-organs: it is a physiological limitation imposed upon us by our bodily nature. The only "adequate" knowledge we can possess of other bodies is of what, being common to all bodies, can therefore influence our bodies: it is the knowledge of matter and motion. The content of the knowledge of bodies which Spinoza accepts thus comes from the actual science of his day, mathematical physics. Through its laws we can get a sketch of the universal order of things, though not of its concrete filling of facts.

The difficulties involved in this conception of knowledge are not worked out; and they are very real difficulties. In the light of present-day science and philosophy, Spinoza of course presents a wholly inadequate interpretation of knowledge, far more inadequate than Aristotle. And the difficulties are not merely those of detail, for they go back ultimately to his fundamental assumption that the logical order of ideas is identical with the mathematical order of nature, that knowledge grasps the basic structure of the universe directly. It is hard to see how, if the logical order of ideas in reasoning merely reflects the mechanical order of the effects of other bodies upon our body, we could ever escape the dominion of inadequate and confused ideas. As Spinoza himself proves, "inadequate and confused ideas follow by the same necessity as adequate or clear and distinct ideas" (II, prop. 36), and consequently there seems to be no intelligible ground for believing that the mind can lift itself to a vision of truth under the form of eternity. That it can so know must be accepted as Spinoza accepts it, as a bare fact, as a basic assumption. Had he pushed his difficulties, he would have been driven either to Hobbes' reduction of all implication to the purely mechanical relations of bodies, and hence to all the paradoxes of the associationist psychology; or else to the rejection of Cartesian physics and a purely mechanical order of nature. Toward the close of his life he was actually moving in the latter direction. As a matter of fact, we are convinced today that however useful Cartesian physics may have been as a technique for dealing with the universe, it was not an adequate grasp of its structure, though it was clearly partial knowledge. Logical realism like Spinoza's offers no intelligible explanation of such a situation, which only a functional view of knowledge seems able to interpret. It is easy to be caught by Spinoza's vision and intoxicated by it, to be convinced that he has worked out a consistent system. It is easy to overlook the fact that he ultimately failed, and that however inspiring or true the last three books of the *Ethics* may appear, they are not adequately grounded in the first two.

These difficulties, which subsequent thought has rendered so insistent, Spinoza did not work out, because he was primarily concerned only with the fact of Order, the knowledge of the union that obtains between the mind and whole of Nature, and not with the full reading of the parts. That fact and that knowledge we get in the system of ideas and of bodies alike. Geometry is the only adequate knowledge of bodies, and the fact of geometry takes us to the realm of absolute reality—Cartesian analytic geometry.

V

The outstanding consequence for man's life of Spinoza's vision of order is the complete determinism that reigns in human actions. Man is not placed within nature as a kingdom within a kingdom, disturbing its laws. In reality, human actions and desires spring from determinate and fixed causes: and Spinoza is resolved to treat them as he would lines, planes, and solids. Man can indeed achieve the freedom that is the goal of all wisdom. Freedom consists in acting solely from the necessity of one's own nature. The stone is free when it is falling, as stones can and must; and man is free like that. But it must be remembered that it is the nature of a stone to fall, and the nature of the mind to think. The one is determined by mechanical principles, the other by the logical order of ideas. God determines the mind to know the truth, and the fullest and completest human determination is to know the whole truth, or God. Perfect knowledge is thus the completest expression of man's determinate nature, and hence is *ipso facto* perfect freedom. The ignorant man is determined from without, by particular causes, and hence has only confused and inadequate ideas, and lives a prey to his passions. The wise man is determined, not by the parts of nature, but by the whole rational order of nature, and acts always in the light of such complete knowledge, under the form of eternity. Ignorance and human bondage is thus partial determination, while the knowledge that is human freedom is complete determination, by the whole logical order of things. How is such perfect knowledge and freedom possible? *Homo cogitat*, man has an adequate knowledge of the infinite and eternal essence of nature. This is the supreme fact.

In the light of such a conception, what becomes of practical morality, of human responsibility? Only on such terms, Spinoza calmly insists, is a true ethics possible. It was Henry Oldenburg, the rather pedestrian secretary of the Royal Society, who asked Spinoza the questions which the common man has always propounded of such a rational determinism. In a series of letters Spinoza tried patiently to explain.

This inevitable necessity in things does away neither with divine nor human laws. The principles of morality, whether they receive from God himself the form of laws and institutions, or whether they do not, are still divine and salutary; whether we receive the good, which flows from virtue and the divine love, as from God in the capacity of a judge, or as from the necessity of the divine nature, it will in either case be equally desirable; on the other hand, the evils following from wicked actions and passions are not less to be feared because they are necessary consequences. Lastly, in our actions, whether they be necessary or contingent, we are led by hope and fear. Men are only without excuse before God, because they are in God's power, as clay is in the hands of the potter, who from the same lump makes vessels, some to honor, some to dishonor.[3]

This last observation excited Oldenburg to moralistic objection, and Spinoza had to be more explicit.

When I said in my former letter that we are without excuse, because we are in the power of God, like clay in the hands of the potter, I meant to be understood in the sense, that no one can bring a complaint against God for having given him a weak nature, or infirm spirit. A circle might as well complain to God of not being endowed with the properties of a sphere, or a child who is tortured, say, with stone, for not being given a healthy body, as a man of feeble spirit because God has denied to him fortitude, and the true knowledge and love of the Deity, or because he is endowed with so weak a nature, that he cannot check or moderate his desires. For the nature of each thing is competent to do only that which follows necessarily from its given cause. That every man cannot be brave, and that we can no more command for ourselves a healthy body, than a healthy mind, nobody can deny, without giving the lie to experience as well as to reason. "But," you urge, "if men sin by nature, they are excusable"; but you do not state the conclusion you draw, whether that God cannot be angry with them or that they are worthy of blessedness—that is, of the knowledge and love of God. If you say the former, I fully admit that God cannot be angry, and that all things are done in accordance with his will; but I deny that all men ought therefore to be blessed—men may be excusable, and nevertheless be without blessedness and afflicted in many ways. A horse is excusable, for being a horse and not a man; but nevertheless he must needs be a horse and not a man. He who goes mad from the bite of a dog is excusable, yet he is rightly suffocated. Lastly, he who cannot govern his desires and keep them in check with the fear of the laws, though his weakness may be excusable, yet he cannot enjoy with contentment the knowledge and love of God, but necessarily perishes. I do not think it necessary here to remind you, that Scripture, when it says that God is angry with sinners, and that he is a judge who takes cognizance of human actions, passes sentence upon them, and judges them, is speaking humanly, and in a way adapted to the received opinion of the masses, inasmuch as its purpose is not to teach philosophy, nor to render men wise, but to make them obedient.[4]

To another correspondent Spinoza replied, with less patience:

---

[3] Spinoza, *Letter 75; Spinoza Opera*, Heidelberg Academy ed., ed. Carl Gebhardt, IV, 312; *The Correspondence of Spinoza*, tr. A. Wolf (1928), p. 347.
[4] *Letter 78* to Oldenburg; ed. Gebhardt, IV, 326; ed. Wolf, pp. 357–58.

I cannot refrain from expressing my extreme astonishment, at your re-
marking, that if God does not punish wrongdoing (that is, as a judge
does, with a punishment not intrinsically connected with the offence,
for our whole difference lies in this), what reason prevents me from
rushing headlong into every kind of wickedness? Assuredly, he who is
kept from vice only by the fear of punishment, (which I do not think
of you), is in no wise acted on by love, and by no means embraces virtue.
For my own part, I avoid or endeavor to avoid vice, because it is at direct variance with my proper nature, and would lead me astray from
the knowledge and love of God.[5]

And commenting on such objections elsewhere, he says:

The creed of the multitude seems to be, that if they believed that minds
perished with the body, and that there is no prolongation of life for the
wretches exhausted with the burden of their piety, they would return
to their own inclinations, controlling everything in accordance with
their lusts, and desiring to obey fortune rather than themselves. Such a
course appears to me not less absurd, than if a man, because he does not
believe that he can by wholesome food sustain his body for all eternity,
should wish to cram himself with poisons and deadly fare; or if, because
he sees that the mind is not eternal or immortal, he should prefer to be
mad and live without the use of reason—absurdities so great that they
scarcely deserve to be repeated.[6]

In fact, a rational life can be led only when the necessity of human actions is recognized. Spinoza emphasizes the positive values
which a deterministic scheme offers. It gives a sense of man's participation in the divine order: the necessary service of God is in
itself blessedness and perfect freedom. It enforces a deep humility,
for all that man does is the act of God. Those who realize it cease
to fear God, and are consumed rather with a love for him. The
deepest religious feeling, indeed, has always insisted on determinism,
that all that takes place is the will of God. St. Augustine, Calvin,
Luther—all emphasized the important religious values which Spinoza derived from his rational necessity. Secondly, when we realize
that all things flow of necessity from the divine nature, we cease
from chafing and resentment, and can endure the smiles or frowns
of fortune with an equal mind. Determinism brings with it the peace
of resignation and acquiescence. Thirdly, it banishes hatred and
resentment toward our fellow men. We see why men have to be

[5] *Letter 21* to Blyenbergh; ed. Gebhardt, IV, 131; ed. Wolf, pp. 178–79.
[6] *Ethics*, Scholium to V, prop. 41; ed. Gebhardt, II, 307.

cruel, insulting, and persecuting; we understand what caused that sneer, that hot flash of anger. Understanding the utter necessity of all things, we can forgive all things. Determinism brings comprehension and tolerance. And finally, only by knowing the causes of human action can the commonwealth be truly served. Such causal knowledge teaches us how citizens should be governed and led, not so as to become slaves, but so that they may freely do whatsoever things are best. Determinism is necessary if we are to hope for a rational social control.

VI

These values take us very close to what Spinoza was seeking: a rational social life, resignation, tolerance, freedom, and peace. But not yet have we found the way to supreme, continuous, and never-ending blessedness. Spinoza started as a mystic seeking peace in God, through a scholastic rationalism surcharged with mystic feeling. He found both peace and God in science, in the vision of the rational order of nature. The last three books of the *Ethics* are its core: the first two serve primarily as an introduction, as the philosophical ground for a way of life. Why is the task so hard? Because man is a part of nature, caught in the web of circumstance. He acts and is acted upon in a vast causal network, he follows and obeys the general order of nature, from which there is no escape. He is forever a prey to his "passions," to the forces acting upon him from without. His life is a succession of emotions or "affects," confused bodily states and the corresponding inadequate ideas produced from without.

The fundamental impulse shared by the human mind with every other particular thing, is the endeavor to persist as it is, the *conatus sese conservandi*. In bodies, science calls this impulse inertia; in mind, it is will and appetite. The very essence of the mind is desire. As this desire is helped or hindered by external things, man feels pleasures or pains. Spinoza undertakes an elaborate analysis of the emotions or affects in these terms: he calls them significantly the "perturbations" of the mind.

On this basis he works out an ethics of conduct, the mental counterpart of mechanics. Men, being what they are, desire things. What they desire they judge to be good, what they hate, they judge to be bad. Nature acts always of necessity, with no ends in view; what men call "good" and "bad" are of no cosmic significance, they are mere things of human reason, relative to the desires of men, that is, to human nature. But human nature is part of the universal order of nature, and man's proper nature, as part of the wider whole, is to know—ultimately, to know the union which obtains between his mind and the whole of nature. Men's desires differ in kind; they are not all equally in accord with this their proper nature. All men have the fundamental desire or *conatus* to live, exercise their activities, and increase their power. What most completely satisfies that desire is in accord with their proper nature, is their true or highest good. But men are ignorant, and often deceived in their judgments: they do not know what will really satisfy their fundamental desire and procure the perfection of their nature. The miser desires gold, the lustful man sexual gratification; and all such fail to find their true good or blessedness. Only the wise man desires knowledge and the love of God. Virtue is power, the power to fulfill desire. Men, being men, strive for virtue or power, and are hence exposed to the storm of passions. Knowledge tells how to procure power; it is itself ultimately power. But who listens to reason? If men could, they would see that the good of all is bound up together, is essentially a social good. And so Spinoza sketches the principles of a utilitarian ethics, noble, generous, and exalted.

As reason makes no demands contrary to nature, it demands that every man should love himself, should seek that which is useful to him—I mean, that which is really useful to him—should desire everything which really brings man to greater perfection, and should, each for himself, endeavor as far as he can to preserve his own being. This is as necessarily true, as that a whole is greater than its part. Again, as virtue is nothing else than action in accordance with the laws of one's own nature, and as no one endeavors to preserve his own being, except in accordance with the laws of his own nature, it follows, first, that the foundation of virtue is the endeavor to preserve one's own being, and that happiness consists in the power of preserving his own being; secondly, that virtue is to be desired for its own sake, and that there is nothing more excellent or more useful to us, for the sake of which we should desire it; thirdly and lastly, that suicides are weak-minded, and are overcome by external causes, repugnant to their nature. Further, it follows . . . that we can never arrive at doing without all external things for the preservation of our being or living, so as to have no relations with things which are outside ourselves. Again, if we consider our mind, we see that our intellect would be more imperfect if mind were alone, and could understand nothing besides itself. There are, then, many things outside ourselves which are useful to us, and are therefore to be desired. Of such none can be discerned more excellent than those which are in entire agreement with our nature. For if, for example, two individuals of entirely the same nature are united, they form a combination twice as powerful as either of them singly. Therefore, to man there is nothing more useful than his fellowman—nothing, I repeat, more excellent for preserving their being can be wished by men, than that all should so in all points agree, that the minds and bodies of all should form, as it were, one single mind, and one single body, and that all should, with one consent, as far as they are able, endeavor to preserve their being, and all with one consent seek what is useful to them all. Hence men who are governed by reason— that is, who seek what is useful to them in accordance with reason— desire for themselves nothing, which they do not also desire for the rest of mankind, and consequently are just, faithful, and honorable in their conduct. Such are the dictates of reason, which I purposed thus briefly to indicate. I have taken this course in order, if possible, to gain the attention of those who believe, that the principle that every man is bound to seek what is useful for himself is the foundation of impiety, rather than of piety and virtue. (IV, prop. 18)

Is this, then, supreme blessedness? It is a sane, practical, even noble way of life; yet Spinoza includes it under the head "Of human bondage, or the strength of the passions." What does he mean? Men strive for the object of their desires. Perhaps they know what is their true good, perhaps they don't: it doesn't matter, for they are equally in bondage to their desires and emotions. The murderer, the saint, the libertine, the just man—all alike are caught up in the web of things. No blame and no praise can be rightfully given them, for each is doing what he must, what it is his nature to do. Who has more hopes and fears, more perturbations of the mind, than the earnest crusader for the Right? Whose reactions are more easily predictable, whose lives are more disturbed by passing events, than the editors of the *Nation* or the *New Republic?* They are slaves of desire, like drug addicts; they are not free! They are not at peace. Man cannot help struggling to be virtuous, yet that way lies no true peace and blessedness. Spinoza is uttering the old cry for deliverance—the cry of the Stoic, of the Christian monk, the troubled cry of generations of persecuted Jews.

Peace can come only through the stilling of all such emotions by a stronger emotion, the sheer delight in knowing for its own sake. If you understand your emotions, their causes, their objects, and yourself, and the great order in which they are all caught up, if you see the utter necessity of all things—why that man had to insult you, why you had to feel the hot flush of indignation—the perturbations will cease. The desires will persist, to be sure, but in their true perspective. You will do all that you can, realizing your limitations, your nature. You will fight all the better without, because you are at peace within. If you fail, you will not be cast down, but will try again.

Moreover, with the knowledge of the nature of the mind, and its union with the whole of nature, man gains power. He sees his own part in nature, and identifies himself with it—for the human mind can comprehend the universe. It knows that it is in God, and conceived through God. Such knowledge is the summit of human power and perfection, and the consciousness of this power is the highest pleasure. The eternal vision of the universe is the sheerest delight possible to man. But pleasure, accompanied by the idea of an external cause, is love; and delight in the vision of the order of nature, which reveals that order as itself the cause of the vision, is the love of the order of nature—what Spinoza calls the "intellectual love" of God. It is that passion of the knower that drives out all other passions; it is part of that very love of God whereby God loves himself, the delight of the universe, in man's mind, knowing itself.

Human salvation or freedom is thus the constant and eternal love toward the object of science, toward Truth. Through knowing the eternal order of nature, we become ourselves eternal: we realize we are part of it. Our mind is an eternal essence caught up in the eternal logical order. This does not mean that it will endure after the destruction of the body; its existence or exemplification is limited to the time the body exists. Spinoza has only scorn for the belief in personal survival. The essence of every body is likewise eternal; but the eternal idea of a stone, or a horse, does not know that it is eternal, while the idea of the human body that is the human mind, can feel and know its eternality. And thus Spinoza's vision culminates in the mystic immortality of the beholder of Truth.

I have thus completed all I wished to set forth touching the mind's power over the emotions and the mind's freedom. Whence it appears, how powerful is the wise man, and how much he surpasses the ignorant man, who is driven only by his lusts. For the ignorant man is not only distracted in various ways by external causes without ever gaining the true acquiescence of his spirit, but moreover lives, as it were, unwitting of himself, and of God, and of things, and as soon as he ceases to suffer, ceases also to be. Whereas the wise man, in so far as he is regarded as such, is scarcely at all disturbed in mind, but, being conscious of himself, and of God, and of things by a certain eternal necessity, never ceases to be, but always possesses true acquiescence of spirit. If the way which I have pointed out as leading to this result seems exceeding hard, it can nevertheless be discovered. Needs must it be hard, since it is so seldom found. How would it be possible, if salvation lay ready to our hand, and could without great labor be found, that it should be by almost all men neglected? But all things excellent are as difficult as they are rare. (Scholium to V, prop. 42)

VII

Spinoza's vision has risen above all the accidents of time; expressing far too clearly for his contemporaries the very essence of the rational faith of the seventeenth century, it nevertheless seems, even more than that of the Malebranche who retained the familiar Christian symbols, to belong to no single age or tradition. Yet, though Spinoza is the most eternal of philosophers, he did not remain indifferent to the men among whom his lot had cast him. For their political struggles, even for their religious faiths, he felt no contempt. He had found blessedness because he knew; others could find something of it without knowing, and find it best if the commonwealth were so ordered as to bring them peace and the freedom to learn. The one work of his own Spinoza published in his lifetime, the *Tractatus Theologico-Politicus* (1670), was directed to that widespread seventeenth-century ideal, the attainment of civil peace through agreement on the rational essentials of religion. It is a noble defense of his own course as well as a plea to his fellow-citizens for the liberty of philosophizing.

Spinoza believed that theological dissension would give place to peace if men recognized that religion is a nonrational means to a rational moral and social end. His argument rests on the fundamental distinction between the respective tasks of positive religion and of philosophy or science; and this denial of rational truth to religious faith was just what made his irenic effort the occasion of new polemic.

> Between faith or theology and philosophy there is no connection nor affinity . . . Philosophy has no end in view save truth: faith, no end save obedience and piety . . . We may take it for indisputable that theology is not bound to serve reason, nor reason theology, but that each has her own domain: Reason the realm of truth and wisdom, theology that of piety and obedience . . . Scripture does not teach philosophy, but merely obedience, and all it contains has been adapted to the understanding and established opinions of the multitude . . .
>
> the diverse and fickle Jewish multitude. It censures obstinacy, but not ignorance. The Law commands obedience, and obedience to God consists solely in love to our neighbor: this is our whole duty.
>
> Other speculative questions which have no direct bearing on this object, or are concerned with the knowledge of natural events, do not affect Scripture, and should be entirely separated from religion.[7]

The Bible contains no revelation of truth, but employs human images to reinforce its rules of conduct. Not to it are we to go to find true knowledge of the God whose laws are not particular but eternal. Had Moses seen things as they are, had he not been a prophet, endowed with unusually vivid imagination, but not with an unusually perfect mind, he would have perceived the Decalogue not as a command but as an eternal truth. But if under the persuasion of the Bible's images and myths men are led to practice the truth as God's command, they need not comprehend to be saved. How foolish, therefore, to persecute those whose religious beliefs differ! Thus is all civil peace destroyed, and the love and piety of true religion itself made impossible.

Men need only to believe such things about God as are essential to obeying his commands, such as are implied in the very act of obedience or loving one's neighbor. They all tend

> to this one doctrine, namely, that there exists a God, namely, a Supreme Being, who loves justice and charity, and who must be obeyed by whomsoever would be saved; that the worship of this Being consists in the practice of justice and love towards one's neighbor. (ch. 14)

[7] *Tractatus Theologico-Politicus* (1670), chs. 13, 14, 15.

The essential dogma is that God is just and merciful, the Exemplar of the true life.

But as to what God or the Exemplar of the true life may be, whether fire, or spirit, or light, or thought, or what not, this, I say, has nothing to do with faith. . . . Faith therefore allows the greatest latitude in philosophic speculation, allowing us without blame to think what we like about anything, and only condemning as heretics and schismatics those who teach opinions which tend to produce obstinacy, hatred, strife, and anger . . . I have become thoroughly convinced that the Bible leaves reason absolutely free. (ch. 14, Preface)

Seeing no truth in scriptural images, Spinoza went on to undertake a thorough examination of the literal text of Scripture, in the spirit of that historical criticism of which he was one of the first great practitioners.

He has no quarrel with those sectaries who have adapted the words of the Bible to their own opinions, if in so doing they can obey God in matters of justice and charity with a more full consent.

But we do accuse those who will not grant this freedom to their fellows, but who persecute all who differ from them as God's enemies, however honorable and virtuous be their lives; while on the other hand they cherish those who agree with them, however foolish they may be, as God's elect. Such conduct is as wicked and dangerous to the state as any that can be conceived . . . The safest way for a state is to lay down the rule that religion is comprised solely in the exercise of charity and justice, and that the rights of rulers in sacred, no less than in secular matters, should merely have to do with actions, but that every man should think what he likes and say what he thinks. (chs. 14, 20)

VIII

True religion is thus independent of particular beliefs or rites; toward the groups that maintain them the state should be impartial, taking as its supreme end the protection of the freedom of thought. Spinoza was a partisan of the liberal government of his friend Jan de Witt.[8] He bent the views of Machiavelli and of Hobbes, for whom he had the highest regard, to the service of Dutch constitutionalism. The ends of every political association are security and comfort.

[8] For an excellent recent account of Spinoza's relations to the various religious and political groups of the Holland of his time, see Lewis S. Feuer, *Spinoza and the Rise of Liberalism* (1958).

The formation of society serves not only for defensive purposes, but is also very useful, and indeed necessary, as rendering possible the division of labor. If men did not render mutual assistance to each other, no one would have either the skill or the time to provide for his own sustenance and preservation . . . We see that peoples living in uncivilized barbarism lead a wretched and almost animal life.[9]

Now every individual thing or mode in the universe has by nature as much right as it has power to exist and operate; for by "natural right" Spinoza means merely those natural laws whereby every thing is conditioned by nature to live and act in a fixed and determinate manner. Every thing has the right and power to do all that it can, since it acts as it is conditioned by nature, and cannot act otherwise; and in finite things this appears as the *conatus sese conservandi,* the endeavor to preserve itself as it is, without regard to anything else. Man like every other being strives thus to preserve his existence, for man is a part of nature, and what he does in thus following the necessity of his nature he does by natural right. But man is conditioned by nature to act by the power of his mind; and even in his fundamental *conatus* he is bound to his fellow man by ties of reason, for he can realize his natural rights or powers only in a union with other men. If two men come together and unite their strength, they have jointly more power, and consequently more right over nature than either of them separately, and the more there are that have so joined in alliance, the more right they all collectively will possess. If men were so constituted by nature that they desired nothing but what is designated by reason, society would have no need of human laws. But though men seek always their own interest, they do not do so in accordance with reason, but are guided by their instincts and emotions. No society, therefore, can exist without government and force and laws to restrain and repress men's desires and immoderate impulses. For man is but a speck in nature, and the laws of nature are not bounded by the laws of human reason which dictate man's true preservation.

A government, therefore, derives its power, and hence its right, only from those whose powers and rights its collective action secures. If each individual hands over the whole of his power to society, the latter will then possess sovereign natural right over all

[9] *Tractatus Theologico-Politicus,* ch. 5; tr. R. H. M. Elwes, p. 73. See also ch. 3; Elwes, p. 47.

things. Such a society, which wields all its power as a whole, is called a Democracy. Such a united power everyone is bound to obey in all things; for only through it can individuals realize their own rights and powers. The subject of such a state obeys the orders of the highest power, given for the common interest, wherein he is included. In a democracy it is almost impossible that the majority should agree in an irrational design.

Since reason teaches that only in the cooperative life of men united in such a state can individual powers be realized to the fullest, in so submitting subjects are most free; for he alone is free who lives with free consent under the entire guidance of reason. And that state is freest whose laws are founded on sound reason, so that every member of it may if he will so live and be free.

"I am altogether for calling a man so far free," Spinoza explains, "as he is led by reason; because so far he is determined for action by such causes as can be adequately understood through his nature alone." [10] Complete determination by reason is at once the completest power and the completest freedom. This Spinozistic conception of freedom as perfect obedience to perfect rational law, itself descended from the long tradition that stems from St. Augustine, was destined to have a momentous future in modern times: through Kant it became the classic conception of German philosophy, and from Rousseau on it has been back of every collectivistic social program that has opposed an individualistic liberalism. Freedom is not independence of governmental interference: that way lies only impotence, subjection, and brutality. Freedom consists rather in participation in a social order that is itself directed toward a rational good. Both Hegel and Marx have a high respect for Spinoza.

Spinoza admits in theory no limits to the power of the collective force of society. And on the chief political problem of the seventeenth century he is as Erastian as Hobbes himself. The supreme political authority has full right and power over things spiritual, and all outward forms of religion should be governed by it in accordance with the public peace and well-being. Sovereigns are no more likely to forsake reason and become wicked than ecclesiastics; and if they do, the state will plunge into ruin anyway, and all the

[10] *Tractatus Politicus*, ch. II, sec. 11.

faster if private citizens set up to champion the divine rights. But the power and right of the state is merely the collective powers and rights of the multitude of individuals who make it up, guided as it were by one mind; and like every other natural power, it is not absolute, but limited by the conditions determinately set by nature. Spinoza has a keen and realistic appreciation of the practical limits to political power. He who seeks to regulate everything by law is more likely to arouse vices than to reform them. There are many things political power is impotent to perform; there are many more to attempt which is to provoke rebellion. Thought is a power which no man can alienate to another if he would; nor, since not even the most experienced, to say nothing of the multitude, know how to keep silence, is speech. The attempt to control these uncontrollable things is contrary to reason, for it weakens the state itself. For just as that man who is led by reason is most powerful and independent, so that state will be most powerful and most independent that is founded on and directed by reason. A state that favors the natural inclinations of men to live together peaceably will wax in power, for in it will be united all the rational striving of its citizens for self-preservation, for peace and security. A state that destroys the rights of its members, hinders their powers, and excites hate between them, will be weak, and will naturally perish. And therefore it is a consequence of the natural conditions under which political power functions that the true aim of government is liberty: not to change men from rational beings into beasts or puppets, but to enable them to develop their minds and bodies in security, and to employ their reason unshackled.

Spinoza never finished his political theory begun in the *Tractatus Politicus;* it breaks off amid the details of the democratic government he so earnestly supported because of all forms he believed it the most natural and the most consonant with individual liberty. Though it utilizes the common materials of political thought, like everything Spinoza wrote it is suffused with the vision of rational order. Man has as much right as he has power; but both right and power in the end flow from reason alone and the harmony it brings.

6

Reason and British Experience

I

BRITISH THINKERS had contributed their full share to the different currents of medieval thought; indeed, the two great philosophical schools of the late Middle Ages, the Scotists and the Ockhamites, were both of British origin. The "new logic" of the terminists spread rapidly in both groups in the fourteenth century, and must have become deeply ingrained in the intellectual tradition; for after more than a hundred years of divers Humanistic and Puritan influences it was still strongly entrenched in the Schools, and through its enduring influence on the seventeenth-century pioneers who studied there it determined the nature of the "British empiricism" that then took form. Oxford remained under Tudors and Stuarts alike the impregnable stronghold of traditional Aristotelianism; Cambridge even then combined an essential traditionalism with an enthusiasm for new ideas. There the great Erasmus himself dwelt during the first two decades of the sixteenth century, and with his friend John Colet introduced that "philosophy of Christ" which continued to win a certain number of Cambridge men to the Humanistic religion down till the eighteenth century. There the Calvinistic Puritans soon established themselves, and in that learned air pushed behind Calvin to the Platonism of Augustine and his Greek masters. There Cartesianism won its first acceptance in England, and brought science to the defense of liberal and rational religion. And there taught Isaac Barrow and the great Newton, who shed the light of truth over all England even as Descartes had spread it in France.

England had little stomach for those far-ranging and self-confident speculations which make the sixteenth century in Italy and in France so tantalizing and so fascinating. Though distinguished continentals visited its shores to spread the new light—Vives from 1523 to 1528, Bruno in 1583–1585—Englishmen were too busy with their own affairs to receive it. Even when some British traveler brought back new ideas—Everard Digby (1550–1592) the cabbalistic Platonism of Reuchlin, Rober Fludd (1574–1637) the strange lore of Cusanus and Paracelsus' magic, Robert Greville, Lord Brooke (1608–1643) the Platonism of the Florentine academy, or Kenelm Digby (1603–1665) the scientific suggestions of Mersenne's circle and Descartes—his compatriots would not lend ears. The fight Hobbes had to make for Galileo's mechanics is historic. It was news from Geneva and Dort, not from Italy or Paris, that Englishmen wanted. For their intellectual energies were fully occupied by the struggle over the forms of Protestant polity, and it was not in terms of new philosophies or new sciences, but of the political principles of Church and State, that Englishmen fought their economic and social revolution. Not till the ecclesiastical and constitutional questions had been settled in 1689 could Locke and the Royal Society win their attention for science.

Amidst the turmoil of scriptural arguments there were a few voices that appealed to reason. The one great Renaissance intellectual impulse that reached England was the search for a law of reason in government and religion. Some of the humanists, like Thomas More, and some of those influenced by Dutch rationalism, like Lord Herbert of Cherbury, sought peace through rational agreement. At the very height of the Civil Wars a group at Cambridge found it in the "Antique Platonick" way, and like the learned Oratorians of France, though with more reservations, welcomed the new Cartesian science as an ally. Others, like Richard Hooker, hoped for a comprehensive Church of England; while, greatest of all, Thomas Hobbes proclaimed an uncompromisingly rational Erastianism as the only guarantee of peace and security. Meanwhile a small band of scientists, like Gilbert and Harvey, pursued their investigations, bothering little, in characteristic British fashion, with theory or philosophy. Become numerous enough to found the Royal Society under the Commonwealth, they produced in Boyle and Glanvill the pious yet determined defenders of their "physico-experimental mathematical learning." Joint heir of the Cartesian rational science of the Cambridge men and of the experimental techniques of the Royal Society, Newton transformed the mathematical vision of the world from an hypothesis into a law of nature, while Hobbes and Locke, both with an equal interest in a rational science of government, sketched out the interpretation of its meaning and significance which has persisted in Britain to this day.

Francis Bacon played little part in this movement toward a secular and scientific philosophy. His ideas belong to the Italy of the sixteenth century, his reputation to the France of the eighteenth, and his spirit to the whole of modern times. But his influence can hardly be discerned in the seventeenth. With the drive for rational religion he was wholly unsympathetic and unconcerned. Scientists like Harvey and mathematicians like Wallis were equally suspicious of the Lord Chancellor; even the Royal Society preferred his patronage to his precepts. And Hobbes, who had served as his secretary, preferred to forget whatever he had then learned.

The only real concern with the problem of a new method, so fascinating on the continent, was one of those familiar minor controversies between two Cambridge men, Everard Digby and William Temple, about 1580. George Buchanan and his pupil Andrew Melville had introduced the new logic of Ramus into Scotland; Ramus as a victim of St. Bartholomew's Day was much favored in the Calvinistic universities, for Aristotle was surely no Puritan. William Temple was an earnest advocate of Ramism, and indeed made Cambridge in the next century the chief seat of that Calvinistic logic. His master, Digby, however, was a confirmed Aristotelian, and against the Ramus doctrine of a single method, deduction from universals, he defended a double method in which the inductive advance from particulars to universals, as suited to our powers of knowledge if not to the nature of things, held equal importance. Added interest to this defense of "analysis" or induction comes from the fact that Digby was lecturing on logic while Bacon was an undergraduate.

II

It was Cartesianism, however, which finally drove Aristotle out of the British universities. This new radical philosophy of nature was enthusiastically received, especially at Cambridge, where John

Allsop had introduced it at Christ's. Henry More was teaching it during the 1640s, the *Discourse* was translated in 1649, the *Passions* the next year. There was no proscription in England, and the Royal Society welcomed Descartes as a great scientist. His metaphysics received little attention; the *Meditations* were not translated till 1680. The Franciscan missionary Antoine Le Grand taught Cartesianism as well as Catholicism; in 1671 he published an *Institutio Philosophiae secundum principia R. Des Cartes* which was much read at Cambridge. Rohault's textbook of physics appeared in England in 1682, and was so popular that Samuel Clarke chose to provide it with Newtonian notes in 1697. By 1681 Gilbert Burnet could write that Descartes was "easily the chief of all the philosophers who have flourished up to the present time." [1] Not till the 1690s did Newton and Locke supplant Descartes as texts at Cambridge. The Port-Royal logic appeared in English in 1685, Fontenelle's *Dialogues* in 1688, and even Malebranche's *Recherche* in 1694.

The influence of Cartesianism passed through three main stages. Until the 1660s there was enthusiastic welcome. Then began a period of much more critical appraisal. Finally, what was enduring in Descartes was embodied in the thought of Newton and Locke and passed on to the next century. Henry More wrote to and of Descartes at first in the greatest hyperboles, gladly furnishing the preface to the 1649 *Discourse*. Glanvill in 1661 set Descartes far above the peripatetics. Wallis and Boyle were approving though critical of details. Simon Patrick in 1662 followed More in praising the service of the "new philosophy" to liberal religion, and Cudworth in 1678 preferred Descartes's "Mosaical atomism" to the Democritism of Hobbes. But More was soon disillusioned, and the critical current set in. The method of doubt seemed precipitate and excessive to the more cautious English scientists. The identification of body with extension was never popular in England. Though the Cambridge Platonists approved innate ideas and Descartes's proof of God, most others preferred more empirical arguments and teleological proofs. The most widespread doctrine to be acclimated, the sharp dualism of mind and matter and the subjectivity of sense qualities, sprang not so much from Descartes as from the new science itself. And Descartes's radical mechanism was too strong for the less

[1] Gilbert Burnet, *Telluris theoria sacra* (1681), p. 184.

logically consistent Royal Society as well as for the religious rationalists. Boyle insisted on final causes—outside science—and Cudworth judged Aristotle sounder on that point.

In England Descartes had no really out-and-out disciples. Perhaps the nearest approach were Sir Kenelm Digby and his friend Thomas White, Catholics living in exile in Paris in close touch with the Mersenne circle, who had met the master in 1644. Digby's thought is a blend of Aristotelianism with atomistic and Cartesian ideas, which nevertheless manages to develop with marked originality a position not unlike that of Geulincx. His treatise *On the Nature of Bodies* (1644) propounds a new kind of corpuscular physics, in which substance is sharply distinguished from quantity; the one is absolute and permanent, the other relative to our knowledge. Corpuscles arise out of a combination of condensation, rarefaction, and weight; from their mixture come the four Aristotelian qualities. The treatise *On the Nature of Man's Soul* (1644) reveals the havoc introduced into the Aristotelian theory of knowledge by an atomistic conception of the world and the resulting Cartesian dualism. The soul is "a simple knowing act which is a pure substance." Perception is the mechanical action of corpuscles on the brain. Yet to be truly known perceived things must exist in the soul really and completely, though incorporeally. How mechanical corpuscles can be realized in Aristotelian fashion in a Cartesian soul is for Digby not unnaturally an insoluble mystery; but it must nevertheless be a fact. Perception is the presence in the soul of the objects themselves; but to advance beyond mere possession to genuine knowledge the soul must exercise upon them its active powers of "apprehension" to make them intelligible. Since truth is the conformity of the apprehending intellect with its objects, a conformity realized in the act of apprehension itself, analysis of that act will reveal at once the basic concepts of thought and the fundamental characteristics of things. And so not an examination of the incomprehensible process of perception but a Cartesian analysis of thought is the way to true knowledge. The Cartesian dualism makes it impossible for bodily action to contribute to knowledge at all.

The things of which these relations are expressed can be painted and sketched in their own colors; but how can the relations themselves be painted and what image can be formed of "half" or of "cause" and "effect"?

He who can think at all will not find it doubtful that concepts of this sort differ *toto coelo* from those which come through the senses . . . If we once understand the power of this proof, we shall see that the Aristotelian axiom, that nothing is in the intellect which was not before in the senses, is so little true in a strict sense, that it is rather the opposite which obtains: there is nothing in the intellect which was before in the senses.[2]

Digby goes on to develop acutely a position in which, as with Geulincx, all our basic categories, from the all-permeating "existence" to the various relations and distinctions, are human ways of apprehending what is not actually perceived in corpuscles at all, results of the comparing and combining power of the soul, which brings unity and order out of what in itself conveys no outline or form. Thus even the idea of "substance" is the product of an intellectual distinction:

substance, that is, a thing subsisting by itself and circumscribed by its own limits, furnishes the mind a convenient and solid foundation on which it can settle and in some wise fix itself.[3]

And thus out of undifferentiated "existence" thought traces and distinguishes an ordered world of "higher" reality. But Digby is enough of an Aristotelian to avoid Geulincx' distrust of the activity of intellect; apprehension does not distort, it actualizes and illuminates what is potentially in the world, but what sense leaves dark. His friend White (*De mundo*, 1646) developed Digby's position in more conventional language, emphasizing this fundamental Aristotelianism.

III

Yet though Cartesianism never became in England a religious faith and the expression of an entire culture, as in France, and though British science, both mathematical and experimental, managed until the days of Newton and Locke to get along very well without the philosophic support demanded on the continent, the seventeenth century did see emerging out of its theological controversies a religious and moral movement that sought to substitute a philosophy of reason for scriptural authority. So accustomed are

[2] Sir Kenelm Digby, *Demonstratio immortalitatis animae rationalis* (1664), p. 516.
[3] *Demonstratio immortalitatis*, p. 521.

we to view England as the great stronghold of the empirical philosophy that we forget that British empiricism has always been the critical weapon of a minority sharpened against a more widespread and usually more official view. Bacon, Hobbes, and Locke are so easily the outstanding British thinkers of the seventeenth century that we overlook their essential protest, not only against traditional authority and sectarian fanaticism, but also against a respectable current of rational idealism. From the sixteenth century on there has rarely been a period when that characteristic British impulse to compromise with tradition, to rationalize and liberalize the spirit of the past while preserving its forms, has not found congenial support in some form of intellectualism. This rationalistic and idealistic strain in British thought has usually borrowed heavily from foreign sources, and has seldom displayed the originality of the great empiricist thinkers; but to disregard it would not only falsify the picture of English intellectual life, it would make the empiricists themselves unintelligible through removing their great antagonists. The perplexing first book of Locke's *Essay*, his attack on a theory of "innate ideas" it seems difficult to imagine ever to have been seriously maintained, is quite meaningless unless seen against the background of the seventeenth-century group of liberal rationalists. And this rationalism in religion and ethics persisted during the whole succeeding century, strengthened by the popular interpretation of Newton, dominating religious thought among liberals and radicals alike, coloring social and political thought, and gaining new power from the currents of German idealism. It is hardly too much to say that the great current of humanitarian moralism that pervades the British tradition and has made its "liberalism" an ethical and religious ideal rather than a mere economic doctrine, owes far more to this strain of rational idealism than to its empirical opponents, and that where the latter have contributed to it, like Locke and the Mills, it has been the rationalistic elements in their "empiricism" that have been influential.

This liberal rationalism is in many respects the analogue of the work of the Oratorians in France, and like them it prepared the ground for the more radical rationalism of the eighteenth-century struggles. Cudworth is in temper and aim very close to the learned Père Thomassin, for example. British rationalism produced no individual as gifted in thought or in literary appeal as Malebranche, and it did not succeed in bringing the new science to its support, despite the efforts of Henry More to capture Descartes for his purposes. That happy alliance had to wait for Newton, and was consummated by men of the stamp of Samuel Clarke. In a deeper sense it is clear that the religious settlement and the adjustment of the position of economic classes it represented occurred earlier in France than in England, and not till Queen Anne could Englishmen consolidate their culture as the French had been able to under Cartesianism. But the secular humanitarianism which was to be the religious expression of the British nation in the eighteenth century had already been prepared by a long line of humanistic moralists.

In this slow movement of protest against theological and ecclesiastical religion, Hobbes plays a curious role. He was at once too radical and too conservative to be welcomed—too radical in failing to give the religious consecration that was demanded for secular moralism, too conservative in his acceptance and rationalization of the Calvinistic and Puritan contempt for human nature. For faith in man and man's natural powers, and in the benevolence of their Divine Source, were of the essence of this religious and pious humanism. Religious liberalism in England has a long history, from Colet and Thomas More to the Hibbert Journal; and its philosophic justification, from the Renaissance to T. H. Green, has always been some form of the Platonic tradition. The British liberal mind has kept up a running polemic against "atheism" and "materialism"; it has rarely been anticlerical and never irreligious. And it has never found any incompatibility between the religion of high-minded and sensible men and science, if only science be properly understood. Fortunately for this proper understanding, from Newton down most British scientists have themselves been religious liberals.

In the seventeenth century the small group of religious humanists drew for support on those bodies of ideas which had inspired their predecessors of the Renaissance, the Platonic philosophy and the Stoic notion of a law of reason. Already fused in Plotinus, and brought still closer together in Ficino and his Florentine circle, these notions presided equally over nascent English rationalism. Stoic legalism naturally appealed more strongly to those with an institutional sense and a demand for solidarity, whether in Church or State; Platonic ideas to those with a positive ideal of ethical religion rather than the mere negative aim of social peace and civic security. When John Colet returned from Italy in 1496 and began to lecture on the Epistles of Paul, he did not merely introduce into England the humanistic urge to get behind the medieval compendia to the ancient sources of Christianity. He brought with him the Christian Platonism of Ficino's *Theologia Platonica*, and he saw in Paul's doctrine of grace not a harsh theology but the moral truth of the mutual love of God and man: God turns to man in love, to kindle in man love for himself. The burden of his lectures was that knowledge of God is not granted to man here below, as the Schoolmen thought in their folly; what is demanded of man is rather love for God. Colet rejected not merely Thomas' pride of knowledge; with equal vigor he opposed Augustine's humbling of human powers before the omnipotence of God. He turned away, as so many Christian humanists have turned, from Augustine to Origen and the Greek fathers. Grace is nothing but the divine love; when we say that God has chosen some, we mean that they return the love God freely bestows on them. Election is the natural longing and the natural will of man developing in accordance with divine providence. Salvation is not the miraculous transformation of the human will; it is its education and discipline.

Colet's Christian humanism was shared by his friend Erasmus and by Thomas More. The latter sketches in his *Utopia* the undogmatic humanistic religion which is the purest and most complete worship of the Divine Being, a universal theism founded on reason. As the lawgiver of Utopia was not sure that God did not wish a manifold and various worship, hence giving to one man this form of devotion, to another that, he had ordained religious freedom. Only those who denied the universal truths of rational religion, the immortality of the soul, rewards and punishments in a future life, the existence of God and his providence, are forbidden public office, as creatures of a lower order than men. More passionately admired Pico, translated his life, and made his ideal of the religious hero his own.

Others outside this humanistic circle maintained the idea of religious tolerance and a liberal theology. Hooker and Hales, Taylor and Chillingworth, all stood for reconciliation and unity in the church as a practical measure for avoiding strife. It is contrary to the spirit of true religion, Chillingworth said, to force a particular belief. The Church should be a community of worship, not of creed. Hooker in particular relied upon the law of reason or nature, eternal and immutable, binding God and man alike, and needing neither revelation nor churchly authority to proclaim it. Even the Scriptures are to be judged by this law of reason; for they are in part erroneous and in part incomplete. Positive laws are relative and alterable; they depend on the implicit consent of men. It is the law of reason that men should have a government and a church; but what kind, is to be determined by the majority, and therefore the Church of England is rightly constituted by King and Parliament.

The first philosophic attempt to explore the foundations of such a rational religion was made by Lord Herbert of Cherbury. In his *De Veritate* (1624), he sought to defend the rational truths of religion against revelation and falsehood alike. The highest truth is the truth of intellect, whose principles dwell within the soul as something divine; they are so far from being the product of observation and experience that no experience is possible without them. Man's "natural instinct" reveals to him certain *"notitiae communes"*; the universal consent with which they are received is "the highest rule of natural instinct," and "the highest criterion of truth." [4] Only morals and mathematics are founded on such common notions alone, hence only in them is there full agreement. Even there they are not equally developed in all men, because of the obstacles to their perception, which Herbert examines in *De causis errorum* (1645); and most of them have to be completed by discursive reason. The five fundamental *notitiae communes* of rational religion, by which all positive religions are to be judged, are: 1) that there is some supreme Deity (numen); 2) that this Deity ought to be worshiped; 3) that a virtuous conformity of man's faculties has always been considered the chief part of divine worship; 4) that all vices and crimes should be expiated in repentance; 5) that there is reward or punishment after this life. Those who recognize these principles belong to the true catholic church; the further men depart from them, the more they fall into error, into uncertain opinions and dogmas. Revelation may add concrete images and expressions, but it can neither

[4] Lord Herbert of Cherbury, *De Veritate*, 3d ed. (1633), pp. 60, 39.

contradict nor establish these truths. In his *De religione Gentilium* (1663) Herbert went on to show how all human religions really contain them under the husks of superstition and distortion.

Herbert's rationalism is Stoic and Ciceronian rather than Platonic in its inspiration, and its "common notions" are Stoic "anticipations" of experience rather than Platonic ideas. Reason is to be found permeating nature, not divorced from it in a separate intelligible realm.

For natural instinct is the first, as discursive reason is the last of faculties. Thus in the elementary forms of life and even in the very embryo this faculty makes for self-preservation, and then gradually unfolding itself upon objects anticipates everywhere the notions of discursive reason . . . What you yourself bring to objects is the paternal dowry of nature and the knowledge imparted by natural instinct. Of this kind are the tokens by which in judging the outer world we distinguish true from false and in the inner good from evil. (pp. 60, 53)

The mind is like a closed book which can be opened only by the objects of the outer world, yet already contains a wealth of knowledge. We become aware of truths through experience, but we do not learn them from experience. The soul is provided with as many "faculties" or "rays of the soul" as there are different kinds of truth; these faculties are so in harmony with the world that on the proper stimulus they illuminate their objects.

Truth is a certain harmony between objects and their analogous faculties . . . Our whole doctrine of truth thus leads back to the right fixing and confirmation of these faculties, whose variety, corresponding to the differences in objects, each experiences in himself . . . What cannot be seen by these faculties as true, as adequate, as universal and necessary, can in no wise be proved. (pp. 68, 5, 38)

Herbert's doctrine of the light of nature and of self-evident truths was developed in comparative freedom from Platonic metaphysics; it was destined to vast popularity in the next century, even as his formulation of the nature and content of rational religion was to be widely shared by educated men.

Another isolated figure, Robert Greville, Lord Brooke, an ardent Puritan who died as a Parliamentary general, brought to England the elaborate Neoplatonism of Cusanus and Florence, which he expounded in *The Nature of Truth* (1641). The understanding, the soul, and truth are all one, the emanation of the Divine Light, in which every opposite is at one. All being is the refulgence of God; the diversities of things exist only in our apprehension. Space and time, the whole physical world, is mere appearance; no true causation is to be sought there, though when we see some things precede others we may call the one a cause, the other an effect. True philosophy and divinity are one; both enshrine the humanistic faith that knowledge is identical with love. "What good we know, we are; our act of understanding being a union." (*The Nature of Truth*)

IV

In the 1640s this persisting rational and Humanistic religion had a new birth among a group of Cambridge men, mostly students of Benjamin Whichcote, a tutor of Emmanuel College, and after 1644 Provost of King's. Emmanuel was of Protestant foundation, and strongly Puritan in its politics; together with Christ's, where Henry More taught, it was the intellectual center of Calvinism. Yet out of this background there came an unpartisan and rather unworldly appeal for a humane yet definitely Christian and spiritual Platonism which modestly but firmly maintained the rationality of true religion and the human goodness of God. Steering a precarious course between Puritan Calvinism and Royalist high churchmanship, which they regarded as equally antithetical to true Christianity and sound philosophy, these Humanists took no part in the bitter quarrels of their time, but serenely offered to men the alternative of the truth of reason and of God. This nonpartisanship earned for them the name of "men of latitude"; they are the lineal ancestors of the generations of Broad Churchmen who have relied on some form of rational idealism to support an attractive if often sentimental religious life.

It was the Platonic tradition to which they appealed against Calvinists and sacramentalists alike, and on which they relied in their long attack on atheism and materialism, as embodied in the dreadful Hobbes. They can hardly be said to have added much to the thought of the Plotinus and the Italian Neoplatonists they so zealously studied; but they stated well the Platonic case against the confident empiricists and mechanists of their day, and thus forced that rising tide of thought to more critical self-examination. Their originality would have been greater had they been able to assimilate the new science, like their brother Platonists of France; as it was, Henry More's dubious adventures in that field were very influential upon the Cambridge mathematicians and upon Newton himself. When their rational liberalism finally triumphed in the eighteenth century, it was in the form of a complacent worldliness and secularism far removed from their own pious and imaginative spirit. Theirs is the most elaborate expression of the appeal to reason in seventeenth-century England. But it is a rationalism that has not yet come to terms with British experience. Sharing their irenic purpose if not their piety, Locke was to implement it in a way more suited to sober British common sense.

Whichcote was the spiritual leader and inspiration of the group. His influence spread not through writings—his sermons did not appear till 1698—but through his personal teaching and preaching. For twenty years he delivered general University lectures on Sunday afternoons directed toward substituting a "moral divinity" for the "fanatic enthusiasm and senseless canting" then in vogue. The essence of his position is to be found in two of his aphorisms. "I oppose not rational to spiritual—for spiritual is most rational." "Nothing is more spiritual than that which is moral." [5] In his reply to his old teacher Tuckney, an earnest Puritan, who took him to task for devoting his time to the study of the heathen philosophers and the natural light, and being no better than an Arminian or Socinian, he quietly defended his rational convictions.

Truth remains truth, who ever may have expressed it. Every Christian must think and believe as he finds cause. If this liberty be not allowed to the university, wherefore do we study? A conviction so noble and excellent and blessed as that of the rationality of Christianity I can never give up. How could I express this conviction too strongly and too often? I oppose not rational to spiritual, for spiritual is most rational. But I contradistinguish rational to conceited, impotent, affected canting, as I may call it, when the ear receives words which offer no matter to the understanding, make no impression on the inward sense.[6]

To the demand for a uniform creed he opposed the freedom of reason.

[5] Whichcote, in E. T. Campagnac, The Cambridge Platonists (1901), p. 71.
[6] Correspondence of Whichcote and Tuckney, ed. S. Salter (1755), p. 108.

It is better for us that there should be difference of Judgment, if we keep charity; but it is unmanly to quarrel because we differ.[7]

Our fallibility and the shortness of our knowledge should make us peaceable and gentle: because I may be mistaken, I must not be dogmatical and confident, peremptory and imperious. I will not break the certain laws of charity for a doubtful doctrine or uncertain truth.[8]

This intellectual freedom he could insist upon with the better grace because he was convinced that in the end reason would unite men on fundamentals.

Those that differ upon reason may come together by reason. (p. 66) For reason teaches that religion is not a belief, but a temper and a way of living.

Religion is the introduction of the divine life into the soul of man.[9]

Natural religion was the very temper and complexion of man's soul, in the moment of his creation; it was his natural temper, and the very disposition of his mind; it was as connatural to his soul as health to any man's body; so that man forced himself, offered violence to himself, and his principles, and went against his very make and constitution, when he departed from God and consented to iniquity.[10]

Religion itself is always the same; but things about religion are not always the same. These have not in them the power or virtue of religion, they are not of a sanctifying nature; they do not purify our minds as the things of a moral nature do; so that religion may stand without them. (p. 67)

Religion in the subject is not a notion, but the frame and temper of our minds, and the rule of our lives. (p. 68)

Religion does not destroy nature; but is built upon it. (p. 68)

It is the chiefest of good things for a man to be himself. (p. 69)

Heaven is first a temper, and then a place. (p. 69)

Since religion is the completion of all man's faculties, it is above all the fulfillment of his highest, the power of reason.

---

[7] *Moral and Religious Aphorisms*, ed. S. Salter (1753), p. 509.
[8] Campagnac, *Cambridge Platonists*, p. 67.
[9] Cited in W. R. Sorley, *A History of English Philosophy*, p. 77.
[10] Campagnac, *Cambridge Platonists*, p. 24.

In the state of religion, spirituals and naturals join and mingle in their subjects; so that if a man be once in a true state of religion, he cannot distinguish between religion and the reason of his mind, and the reason of his mind is his religion. (p. 57)

That which is the height and excellency of human nature, viz., our reason, is not laid aside nor discharged, much less is it confounded, by any of the materials of religion; but awakened, excited, employed, directed, and improved by it: for the mind and understanding of man is that faculty, whereby man is made capable of God, and apprehensive of him, receptive from him, and able to make returns upon him, and acknowledgments to him. (p. 51)

To go against reason is to go against God: it is the selfsame thing, to do that which the reason of the case doth require; and that which God himself doth appoint: reason is the divine governor of man's life; it is the very voice of God. (p. 67)

But this rationalism was no empty intellectualism; it was the Platonic reason which is one with love to which appeal was made, the reason that is a moral principle of living.

The first act of religion is to know what is true of God; the second act is to express it in our lives. (p. 68)

Knowledge alone doth not amount to virtue; but certainly there is no virtue without knowledge. Knowledge is the first step to virtue and goodness: but goodness is not without delight and choice. (p. 65)

The moral part of religion never alters. Moral laws are laws of themselves, without sanction by will; and the necessity of them arises from the things themselves. All other things in religion are in order to these. The moral part of religion does sanctify the soul; and is final both to what is instrumental and instituted. (p. 68)

Nothing is desperate in the condition of good men; they will not live and die in any dangerous error.[11]

It was this humanistic, rational, and moral conception of religion which Whichcote taught his pupils, and which they endeavored to buttress by learned arguments and polemics. It was this conception which Cudworth tried to impress in his sermon delivered in 1647 to the House of Commons.

[11] *Sermons* (ed. 1751), II, 20.

Reason and British Experience

Christ came not into the world to fill our heads with mere speculations, . . . to possess our brains only with some cold opinions, that send down nothing but a freezing and benumbing influence upon our hearts. Christ was *vitae magister*, not *scholae:* and he is the best Christian, whose heart beats with the truest pulse toward heaven, not he whose head spinneth out the finest cobwebs.[12]

It was this conception which filled the attractive teaching of John Smith, and vivified his learned quotations.

Salvation is nothing else but a true participation of the divine nature. Heaven is not a thing without us, nor is happiness anything distinct from a true conjunction of the mind with God in a secret feeling of his goodness and reciprocation of affection to him.[13]

Divine truth is better understood as it unfolds itself in the purity of men's hearts and lives, than in all those subtil niceties into which curious wits may lay it forth. And therefore our Savior, who is the great master of it, would not, while he was here on earth, draw it up into any system or body, nor would his disciples after him; he would not lay it out to us in any canons or articles of belief, not being indeed so careful to stock and enrich the world with opinions and notions as with true piety, and a Godlike pattern of purity, as the best way to thrive in all spiritual understanding. (p. 86)

The true method of knowing is not so much by notions as by actions; as religion itself consists not so much in words as things. (p. 80)

Such a conception of human nature had of course to be defended on the one hand against the Calvinistic doctrine of total depravity, and on the other against the equally harsh materialism of Hobbes and the empiricists. Though the Cambridge Platonists were, like the Puritans, moralists, their humanism was revolted by the this-worldly asceticism and the external legalism of the Calvinists. It was the Puritan doctrine of election and predestination, as much as the necessity of the materialists, against which Cudworth compiled his great attack on "fatalism": "Democritic" and theistic fatalism were to him equally immoral. The moral law is to be sought in the reason of man; it must be liberated from any external decrees, whether of the Calvinistic God or the Hobbistic State.

---

[12] Cudworth, *A Sermon preached before the House of Commons March 31, 1647,* pp. 13–14.
[13] Campagnac, *Cambridge Platonists,* p. 196.

When I considered ethical matters more carefully, and clearly perceived that the natures of moral good and evil are immutable and do not depend on the will of God, . . . I could not ascribe to God those terrible decrees by which at his pleasure he inevitably condemned innocent men to guilt and sin incurring eternal torture.[14]

And Whichcote expressed the same humanistic determination to judge God by human standards of morality:

We do not limit God, nor do we do violence to his omnipotence, when we say that his actions also are bound within fixed limits and lie necessarily under these conditions. When for example God gives a promise he must keep it; when he creates an intelligent and free being, he must treat it as such. This is in accordance with reason and has its support in the Scriptures: there is something in God that stands higher than his power and his uncircumscribed might: his righteousness, his good will, his wisdom, his justice.[15]

In the last analysis this emphasis on the moral power of man lies back of the Platonists' rationalism and their opposition to empiricism. For it was not only reason that discovered God and moral good; it was reason that proclaimed the divinity of man himself, and of the whole creation. It was reason that led men to God, and reason that established the immortality of the soul. And they realized that such a reason could not exist side by side with a purely mechanical world; the universe must be either all corporeal, as Hobbes insisted, or else permeated through and through with spirit. Untouched by the Baconian spirit, and devoted to the contemplation of the beauty and harmony of nature rather than to its active manipulation and conquest, they had no comprehension of the problems of the scientists, and no sympathy for their desire to divide religion sharply from knowledge, that science might be free. When Bacon or Hobbes or Boyle set faith in another realm, they countered by proclaiming its identity with reason and knowledge. To their rational and moral spiritualism the empirical attempt at a natural history of mind seemed wholly disintegrating; to it they opposed the Platonic theory of innate ideas.

The truth of first inscription is connatural to man, it is the light of God's creation, and it flows from the principles of which man doth consist, in his very first make: this is the soul's complexion.[16]

---

[14] Cudworth, Letter to Limborch, 1688; in von Hertling, Locke und die Schule von Cambridge (1892), p. 164.

[15] Sermons (ed. 1751), II, 244.

[16] Campagnac, Cambridge Platonists, p. 4.

These men were not opposed to science, of course; liberal religion never is. John Smith was one of the first to popularize Descartes at Cambridge, and More's enthusiasm knew no bounds. Both More and Cudworth were members of the Royal Society; they were the intimates of Glanvill, its theorist, and admired Boyle. But their interest in natural science was not to discover the secrets of nature, it was to support their religious views. The inevitable result was distortion and misunderstanding. What they wanted was not a scientific philosophy, but a religious philosophy with a subordinate station in it for science.

V

Of Whichcote's pupils John Smith was truest both to the religious spirit of his teacher and to the Platonic tradition. His slender volume of *Discourses* (1660) moves wholly within the circle of Plotinus' thought, and is liberally sprinkled with quotations from the Greeks. His argument relies on careful analyses of the Platonic and Aristotelian theories of knowledge and the soul; he is the most authoritarian of the group, a true Hellenic humanist. The very nature of human knowledge reveals the utter disparateness between the mind, as "something within us that thinks, apprehends, reasons, and discourses," [17] and body or matter. Those that have gross material notions of their own souls are not ordinarily very free from atheism;

for indeed the chief natural way whereby we can climbe up to the understanding of the Deity is by a contemplation of our own souls. (p. 103)

The soul's incorporeal and immaterial nature is manifested by the fact that:

there is a higher principle of knowledge in man than mere sense, neither is that the sole original of all that science breaks forth in the minds of men. (p. 117)

For that which we call sensation is not the motion or impression which one body makes upon another, but a recognition of that motion; and therefore to attribute that to a body is to make a body privy to its own acts and passions, to act upon itself, and to have a true and proper self-feeling virtue. (p. 116)

If our senses were the only judges of things, this reflex knowledge whereby we know what it is to know would be as impossible as he makes

[17] Iohn Smith, in Campagnac, *Cambridge Platonists*, p. 136.

it for sense to have innate ideas of its own, antecedent to those stamps which the radiations of external objects imprint upon it. For this knowledge must be antecedent to all that judgment which we pass upon any sensatum, seeing except we first know what it is to know, we could not judge or determine aright upon the approach of any of these idola to our senses. (p. 117)

Yet cannot the power of sensation itself arise from (motions), no more than vision can rise out of a glass, whereby it should be able to perceive these idola that paint themselves upon it, though it were never so exactly polished and they much finer than they are or can be. Neither can those small corpuscula which in themselves have no power of sense, ever produce it by any kind of concourse or motion; for so a cause might in its production rise up above the height of its own nature and virtue. (p. 113)

There are some radical principles of knowledge that are so deeply sunk into the souls of men, as that the impression cannot easily be obliterated, though it may be much darkened. (p. 90)

Which we shall first consider in those *logoi mathematikoi* or mathematical notions which the soul contains in itself, and sends forth within itself . . . which every ingenuous son of that art cannot but acknowledge to be the true characters of some immaterial being, seeing they were never buried in matter, nor extracted out of it: and yet these are transcendently more certain and infallible principles of demonstration than any sensible thing can be. (p. 132)

It were no hard matter to prove that, as in this case Saint Austin did, when in his Book *De quantitate animae*, he would prove the immortality of the soul from these notions of quantity, which come not by any possible sense or experience which we can make of bodily being, and therefore concludes they must needs be engraven upon an immaterial soul. For though we could suppose our senses to be the school-dames that first taught us the alphabet of this learning; yet nothing else but a true mental essence could be capable of it. (p. 133)

These essences or ideas are beheld by the highest faculty of the soul,

—the naked intuition of eternal truth which is always the same, which never rises nor sets, but always stands still in its vertical, and fills the whole horizon of the soul with a mild and gentle light. (p. 135)

The soul through this intuition partakes

of time in its broken and particular conceptions and apprehensions, and of eternity in its comprehensive and stable contemplations. (p. 137)

Thus

the operations about truth . . . are the true badges of an eternal nature, and speak a *tautotes* and *stasis* (as Plato is wont to phrase it) in man's soul. Such are the archetypal ideas of justice, wisdom, goodness, truth, eternity, omnipotency, and all these either moral, physical, or metaphysical notions, which are either the first principles of science or the ultimate complement and final perfection of it. (p. 136)

And thus the analysis of human knowledge in the soul brings us to the goal of the Christian Platonist:

God is not better defined to us by our understandings than by our wills and affections: he is not only the eternal reason, that almighty mind and wisdom which our understandings converse with; but he is also that unstained beauty and supreme good which our wills are perpetually catching after: and wheresoever we find true beauty, love, and goodness, we may say, Here or there is God. (p. 173)

VI

Ralph Cudworth (1617–1688) is much closer to the Renaissance Platonism of Ficino, and to the curious learning that derived Plato's doctrines from Moses. But Cudworth was thoroughly familiar with what he called "the new philosophy" as well as with the old. He was a member of the Royal Society; in his library he had all the scientists, Harvey, Tycho Brahe, Copernicus, Galileo, Boyle, Newton; of philosophers, Bacon, Descartes, Hobbes, Gassendi, even Spinoza.[18] He disliked Bacon, but be was much taken, like Henry More, with Descartes, criticizing him only on specific points; he might even, like More at one time, be called a Cartesian, like him anxious to enlist the new science in the support of his liberal and rational religion. His chief dislike was the Calvinism of the Puritans; next to that came Hobbes, with which "atheistic politician" he kept up a running fight. Cudworth the scholar is one of the few English thinkers of the seventeenth century who was anxious to preserve continuity with Greek thought. He saw contemporary issues in terms of Greece: he was Plato to the Protagoras of Hobbes, he found an ally in Descartes, an enemy in Bacon.

He undertook an immense refutation of "fatalism," materialism,

[18] *Bibliotheca Cudworthiana*, a catalogue of the sale of books at Roll's Coffee-House (London, 1690); cited in J. A. Passmore, *Ralph Cudworth: an Interpretation* (1951).

and atheism, of which the first part, *The True Intellectual System of the Universe*, appeared in 1678. Its hostile reception—Cudworth was himself accused of heresy and even atheism—discouraged him from finishing it, and his *Treatise concerning Eternal and Immutable Morality* was not published till 1731. Cudworth in attacking fatalism found himself assailing both the theological determinism of the Puritans and the atheistic fatalism of the materialists, which he traced back to Democritus, and confronted in Hobbes, and, in lesser measure, in Descartes's physics. Not only the atomists, but also the "cosmoplastic" Stoics, who explained the world through one "plastic or methodical but senseless nature," and the "hylozoic Stratonists," who found in matter "a certain living and energetic nature, but devoid of all animality, sense, and consciousness," came in for attack. He himself held, however, to the theory of a plastic nature, conceived as an incorporeal substance employed by God as the instrument of his control of nature. This plastic nature expresses an unconscious teleology, operating fatally and sympathetically, vitally and magically, not mechanically.

For his refutations Cudworth relies principally upon a Platonic analysis of knowledge in the form of Augustine and Ficino.

The intelligible forms by which things are understood or known are not stamps or impressions passively printed upon the soul from without, but ideas vitally portended or actively exerted from within itself.[19]

The very root of all atheism is the notion that knowledge is produced by things rather than things by knowledge, that spirit is the creation of the universe rather than its creator.

It is an absurd thought that not only sense but also knowledge and understanding in man is nothing but a tumult which arises in him because of the contact of external bodily things. Were this true, then every thing that suffered an impression, as a mirror on which a beam of light falls, would possess sense and understanding. But it is clear that everything which comes from without consists in nothing but pressure and movement; neither is sense itself the mere passion of those motions, but the perception of their passions, in a way of phancy.[20]

Only intelligible natures and essences born within the soul itself can make even perception possible. It is the *rationes* of things the

[19] Cudworth, *A Treatise concerning Eternal and Immutable Morality* (1731).
[20] Cudworth, *True Intellectual System of the Universe* (ed. 1678), folio 731.

soul perceives, intelligible reasons which are the modes of its own substance. In natural objects "there is a complication of something noematical and something phantasmatical together." [21] But the innate ideas of such things as knowledge, duty, and truth, and of relations like order and cause, owe nothing to sense, though sense may be "the outward occasion by which they are excited." (Ibid.)

Wherefore the knowledge of this and the like truths is not derived from singulars, nor do we arrive to them in way of ascent from singulars to universals, but on the contrary having first found them in the universals, we afterwards descending apply them to singulars, so that our knowledge here is not after singular bodies, and secondarily or derivatively from them; but in order of nature before them, and proleptical to them.[22]

Self-evidence is the criterion: "whatever is clearly conceived is an entity and truth." [23] Such truths are modes of intellect and must exist in the divine mind.

The true meaning of these eternal essences is indeed no other than this, that knowledge is eternal; or that there is an eternal mind that comprehendeth the intelligible natures and ideas of all things, whether actually existing or possible only; their necessary relations to one another, and all the immutable verities belonging to them . . . These eternal essences themselves are nothing but objective entities of the mind, or noemata and ideas.[24]

Nathaniel Culverwell wrote a *Discourse of the Light of Nature* to elucidate that Candle of the Lord which Whichcote had made the most characteristic image of the whole school. He is more of a Stoic, like Herbert, in his rationalism than a Platonist; his grounding of rational religion is in terms of the law of nature rather than the divine ideas.

There are stamped and printed upon the being of man some clear and indelible principles, some first and alphabetical notions, by putting together of which it can spell out the law of nature.[25]

Experience furnishes the occasion to "look to that light of nature, that candle of the Lord, by which this law of nature is manifested

---

[21] *Eternal and Immutable Morality.*
[22] *True Intellectual System,* folio 732.
[23] *Eternal and Immutable Morality.*
[24] *True Intellectual System,* folio 835.
[25] Culverwell, *Discourse of the Light of Nature* (1669), ch. 7, in Campagnac, p. 255.

and discovered." (p. 262) His thought in consequence points forward rather than backward.

All the moral law is founded in natural and common light, in the light of reason; and there is nothing in the mysteries of the gospel contrary to the light of reason. (p. 221)

VII

By far the most interesting and influential of the group, however, not only for the vigor and literal-minded imagery of his style, but also for the untrammeled originality of his adventures among seventeenth-century ideas, is Henry More (1614–1687). More was a Calvinist converted to Platonism by the reading of Edmund Spenser, who became early acquainted with Descartes, and devoted his life first to the scientific defense of rational religion and then to the correction of that science the better to serve his religious interests. He is the ancestor of that long line of British liberal theologians who in defending a novel theology have done strange things to science, the founder of the Cambridge school of theological physicists.

"I look upon the Christian religion rightly understood to be the deepest and the choicest piece of philosophy that is," he remarks [26] and his enthusiasm for reason knew no bounds.

Take reason away, and all religions are equally true, just as when light is removed all things take on a single color.

"The perfecting of the human nature by participation of the divine" is the great mystery of Christianity.

Which cannot be understood so properly of this gross flesh and external senses, as of the inward humanity, viz., our intellect, reason, and fancy. But to exclude use of reason in search of divine truth is no dictate of spirit but of headstrong melancholy and blind enthusiasm. [27]

Those that talk so loud of that higher principle, the Spirit, betray their own ignorance; and while they would, by their wild rhetoric, dissuade men from the use of their rational faculties, under pretense of expectation of an higher and more glorious light, do as madly, in my mind, as if a company of men traveling by night with links, torches, and lanthorns, some furious orator amongst them should, by his wonderful strain of eloquence, so befool them into a misconceit of their present condition,

[26] More, *Divine Dialogues* (1668, 2d ed. used, 1713), p. 7.
[27] More, *Conjectura Cabbalistica*, Preface, p. 2.

comparing of it with the sweet and cheerful splendor of the day, as thereby to cause them, through impatience and indignation, to beat out their links and torches, and break apieces their lanthorns against the ground, and so choose rather to foot it in the dark, with hazard of knocking their noses against the next tree they meet, and tumbling into the next ditch, than to continue the use of those convenient lights, that they had in their sober temper prepared, for the safety of their journey.[28]

But More realized that all men might not view reason just as he did; and in this the modern reader may well agree.

I must ingenuously confess, that I have a natural touch of Enthusiasm in my complexion, but such as, I thank God, was ever governable enough, and I have found at length perfectly subduable.[29]

Above all he prides himself on an absence of superstition.

It is superstition where men have an overproportionate zeal for or against such things in religion as God puts little or no price upon either their performance or omission.[30]

After sinking himself deeply in Plotinus and his school, and publishing *A Platonical Song of the Soul* (1642), and other similar efforts (*Antipsychopannichia, Antimonopsychia*, etc.) he experienced an enthusiasm on discovering Descartes which he later found excessive. In 1648 he wrote a letter to Descartes informing him: "All great leaders of philosophy who have ever existed, or may exist, are mere dwarfs and pygmies in comparison with your transcendent genius." [31] In 1653 he writes:

And that Descartes may bear up in some likely equipage with the aforenamed noble and divine spirits; though the unskilfulness in men commonly acknowledged more of supernatural assistance in hot unsettled fancies and perplexed melancholy than in the calm and distinct use of reason; yet for mine own part (but not without submission to better judgment) I should look upon Descartes as a man more truly *inspired* in the knowledge of nature, than any that have professed themselves so these 1600 years; and being even ravished with admiration of his transcendent mechanical inventions for the salving the phenomena in the world, I should not stick to compare him with Bezaliel and Aholiab, those

[28] More, *A Collection of Philosophical Writings*, 4th ed. (1712), p. 38.
[29] More, *A Collection of Several Philosophical Writings*, 2d ed. (1662), Preface General, p. x.
[30] More, 1662 ed., p. xi.
[31] *Epistola prima ad Des-Cartes*, p. 61, in *Epistolae quatuor ad Renatum Des-Cartes*, included in *Philosophical Writings* (1662). In Descartes, *Oeuvres*, ed. Adam et Tannery, V, 235–46, Letter 531; ed. Cousin, X, 179.

skilful and cunning workers of the tabernacle, who, as Moses testifies, were filled with the Spirit of God, and they were of an excellent understanding, to find out all manner of curious works.[32]

More's letter was written "to clear Descartes from that giddy and groundless suspicion of atheism"[33] which many Cambridge men entertained.

That which enravishes me the most, is that we both setting out from the same lists, though taking several ways, the one traveling on the lower road of Democritism, amidst the thick dust of atoms and flying particles of matter, the other tracing it over the high and airy hills of Platonism, in that more thin and subtle region of immateriality, meet together notwithstanding at last at the same goal, namely, the entrance of the Holy Bible.[34]

Descartes in fact suggested to More a great idea. He had maintained that everything real in nature must be extended and geometrical. Why then can't spirit be extended too? What surer proof of the reality of God, the angels, and the soul? All substances are extended; extension is the criterion of reality, an essential property of *ens quatenus ens*. But some substances are still material and others spiritual, therefore something other than extension must be the distinguishing mark of body. More therefore agrees completely with Descartes, except in making body identical with extension.

You define matter or body in too general a manner. For God seems to be an extended thing, and an angel, and indeed anything that exists *per se*.[35]

Body is to be distinguished as being discerpible, impenetrable, and tangible; Spirit, on the contrary, is indiscerpible, penetrable, and intangible, though equally extended. It possesses the three ordinary dimensions as well as a fourth, spiritual spissitude or density, the "absolute power of self-contraction and dilation," together with the "relative faculties of penetrating, moving, and altering of the matter."[36] In thus attributing extension to spirit, More felt he had answered also Hobbes's inability to imagine an immaterial substance.

[32] *An Appendix to the Defence of the Philosophick Cabbala*, p. 104, in *Philosophical Writings* (1662).
[33] Preface General, *Philosophical Writings*, p. xi.
[34] Preface General, *Philosophical Writings*, p. xii.
[35] *Epistola prima ad Des-Cartes*, p. 62.
[36] *The Immortality of the Soul*, Book I, ch. 2; in *Philosophical Writings* (1662).

Although matter is not necessarily soft nor hard, nor hot, nor cold, still it is absolutely necessary that it be *sensible;* or, if you prefer, *tangible* . . . But if you do not want to define body by the relations it bears to our senses, let this *tangibility* be taken in a wider and more general sense, to signify the mutual contact and power of touching between any bodies whatsoever . . . This will suffice to demonstrate that it would have been much safer to have defined matter as tangible substance, or as impenetrable substance, than as extended being.[37]

And after expounding this brilliant suggestion, destined to be accepted by British science, More asks Descartes, don't you agree?

Descartes's reply, taking the eulogy for granted, shows not unnaturally a marked coolness to the young heretic, "You don't understand at all," is the general tenor. Shortly thereafter More's Cartesian enthusiasm commenced to wane, and he had to begin explaining away his eager advocacy.

This is the true and genuine meaning, [he announced in 1662], of my interweaving of Platonism and Cartesianism so frequently as I do in these writings. I make use of these hypotheses as invincible bulwarks against the most cunning and most mischievous efforts of Atheism.[38]

So far is it from true that I swallow whole all the crude Cartesian dishes, that I freely avowed to you that I observed in those writings many things which I could in no wise digest [he explained to a friend]. To three kinds of cause we can attribute whatever failings Descartes has had: to inadvertency, to too little penetration (he made animals automata;) and to a certain immense affectation of mathematical certainty and necessity in his particular conclusions.[39]

He felt there could be no certainty "if the divine counsels were mixed with the laws of matter and motion." (p. 111)

Why then do I profess to unfold the Cartesian philosophy with such zeal and pleasure? (p. 114)

First, because of the Cartesian attribution of all sense and sense qualities to motion alone; secondly, because the universal operation of the laws of motion depends on God, and not on independent substantial forms—More detected the Platonism of the Cartesian physics; secondary causes are explained better than in any other philosophy, though at times the exclusion of force, as in the foetus and the

[37] *Epistola prima,* pp. 62–63.
[38] Preface General, *Philosophical Writings* (1662), p. vi.
[39] *Epistola ad V.C.,* in *4 Epistolae,* pp. 109–10.

magnet, suggests the limits of mechanism; but above all Descartes is no atheist. He demonstrates the existence of God by an argument which is not only the best to which human reason can attain, but is indeed "an absolute and perfect demonstration." (p. 124)

It is the fate of all innovators to be dubbed atheists; suspicion was directed against Descartes because of his mechanism and his denial of final causes. But that sprang, not "from some atheistical disease, but only from a certain unbridled itch for drawing all his conclusions with a wholly mathematical certainty." (p. 123)

From the fact that the simple motion of matter can make plain certain phenomena, to trust that all can be explained in this way, seems to me a most abject kind of *hylolatry*, that is, a ridiculous and superstitious adoration and worship of blind matter, and not any legitimate rule of philosophizing. (p. 121)

More's dissatisfaction with the great hylolatrist grew rapidly. In 1659 he counseled that Descartes should be read in all public schools and universities,

that the students of philosophy may be thoroughly exercised in the just extent of the mechanical powers of matter, how far they will reach and where they fall short. Which will be the best assistance to religion that reason and the knowledge of nature can afford. For want of it we see how liable men are to be contemned and borne down by every bold, though weak, pretender to the mechanick philosophy.[40]

Three years later appears the further reservation,

not that there is any entire phenomenon consisting merely of mechanical causes, but because in every one almost there is that which, so far as it concerns its own nature, is merely mechanical.

Descartes is to be read,

so it be done with that faithfulness and care that his mechanick philosophy may be clearly and entirely understood. For they that so understand it will most undoubtedly be sensible of its notorious defects.

If read "with a lazy and stupid admiration," Descartes "will contribute more to atheism and the contempt of religion than to any solid knowledge of God or nature." (p. xvi) By 1668,

The truth is, that which makes Descartes his philosophy look so augustly on, 'tis in that he has interwoven into it that noble system of the

[40] *Immortality of the Soul*, in *Philosophical Writings* (1662), Preface, p. xiii.

world according to the tradition of Pythagoras and his followers, or, if you will, of the most ancient Cabbala of Moses. But the rest of his philosophy is rather pretty than great, and in that sense that he drives at, of pure mechanism, enormously and ridiculously false.[41]

Religion can suffer nothing by the lessening of the repute of Cartesianism, the notions that are peculiar thereto having so little tendency to that service. Indeed if Cartesius had so well demonstrated as affirmed that matter cannot think, he had directly deserved well of religion itself. But, however, Providence has so ordered things that in an oblique way his philosophy becomes serviceable to religion, whether he intended it or no, or rather, that of it that was most against his intention, namely, the flaws and defects so plainly discoverable in it. (p. xiii)

I am abundantly assured that there is no purely mechanical phenomenon in the whole universe. (p. viii)

And finally in 1671 his *Enchiridion metaphysicum* devotes long refutation to Descartes as a "nullubist" who denied the extension of spirit and granted it no place in the universe.

This increasing depreciation of Descartes went on side by side with More's growing spiritualism even in physics, and his devotion to Cabbalistic studies. Having turned to science to support religion, he proceeded to correct it wherever necessary and to introduce more and more theological speculations into his doctrine of nature. In this process, he brought into the stream of English physics itself certain conceptions with a definite Platonic background. In the first place, science was to be founded on a Platonistic conception of knowledge. Fundamental is

the belief and endeavor after a certain principle more noble and universal than reason itself, and without which reason will falter, or at least reach but to mean and frivolous things. I want a name for it, unless I should adventure to term it *Divine Sagacity*.

It is

a more inward, compendious, and comprehensive presentation of truth, even antecedaneous to that reason which in theories of greatest importance approves itself afterwards, upon the exactest examination, to be most solid and perfect every way.[42]

It is this Divine Sagacity that reveals to us innate ideas.

[41] *Divine Dialogues* (ed. 1713), Preface, p. ix.
[42] Preface General, *Philosophical Writings*, pp. vii–viii.

For there are unalterable and indelible ideas and notions in the mind of man, unto which when we are awakened, and apply to the known course and order of nature, we can no more forsake the use of them, than we can the use of our own eyes, nor misbelieve their dictates more, or so much, as we may those of our outward senses.[43]

Men question the existence of innate ideas only because they mistake the extrinsical occasion of thinking for its adequate or principal cause. External objects are rather the "reminders than the first begetters or implanters" of knowledge. Knowledge is really "a quick recollection, whereby some small business being hinted unto the soul, she runs out presently into a more clear and larger conception." [44] When outward objects jog the mind, "the soul sings out the whole song upon the first hint, as knowing it well before." [45]

More is contemptuous of the Cartesian theory of the relation of soul to body, which sees the great conflict of flesh and spirit waged over "the ridiculous noddings and joggings of a small glandulous button in the midst of the brain, encountered by animal spirits rudely flirting against it." [46]

It is plain, that this union of the soul with matter does not arise from any such gross mechanical way, as when two bodies stick one in another, by reason of any toughness and viscosity, or straight commissure of parts; but from a congruity of another nature, which I know not better how to term than *vital:* which *vital congruity* is chiefly in the soul itself, it being the noblest principle of life; but is also in the matter, and is there nothing but such modification thereof as fits the plastick part of the soul, and tempts out that faculty into act.[47]

Secondly, More became more and more convinced that nature is not a mere machine, but is permeated by a World Soul, a Spirit of Nature.

There is a principle in the world that does tug so stoutly and resolutely against the mechanick laws of nature, and that forcibly resists or nulls one common law of nature, for the more seasonable exercise of another.[48]

This Spirit of Nature is

[43] *Conjectura cabbalistica*, Preface, p. 4, in *Philosophical Writings* (1662).
[44] *Antidote against Atheism*, Book I, ch. v; in *Philosophical Writings* (1662).
[45] *Antidote against Atheism*, Book I, ch. vi.
[46] *Divine Dialogues* (ed. 1713), Preface, p. xii.
[47] *Immortality of the Soul*, p. 120, in *Philosophical Writings* (1662).
[48] *Antidote against Atheism*, p. 46.

a substance incorporeal but without sense and animadversion, pervading the whole matter of the universe, and exercising a plastical power therein, . . . raising such phenomena in the world by directing the parts of the matter and their motion, as cannot be resolved into mere mechanical powers.[49]

This Spirit is "the vicarious power of God upon matter"; [50] to it is assigned also "to lodge every soul according to her rank and merit whenever she leaves the body," (p. 223) and thus to serve as "the great quartermaster-general of divine providence." (p. 223) But chiefly the Spirit of Nature

remands down a stone toward the center of the earth, as well when the earth is in Aries as in Libra, keeps the waters from swilling out of the moon, curbs the matter of the sun into roundness of figure, which would otherwise be oblong, restrains the crusty parts of a star from flying a-pieces into the circumambient Aether, carries along those larger regions of lesser particles of the third element, together with the comets in their peregrinations from vortex to vortex, everywhere directs the magnetic atoms in their right road; besides all the plastick services it does both in plants and animals.[51]

This Spirit need not be perceptive itself, it being the natural transcript of that which is knowing or perceptive, and is the lowest substantial activity from the all-wise God, containing in it certain general modes and laws of nature, for the good of the universe. (p. xvi)

For the liveless spirit and the dead stone are alike easy to be taken hold upon, the Spirit of Nature penetrating them both alike; and body slipping up and down so easily in this Spirit of the World, as that it cannot be imagined that any mechanical power, but that only which is truly called sympathetical, must be the tye where any hold is taken. Which tye catches and lets go, for the direction and transmission of things to their proper places in the several parts of the world. (p. xvi)

It was thus that More turned to "plastick powers" where he felt the simple billiard balls of Descartes were inadequate. This world-soul became that concept beloved of English scientists, the "ether," and entered Newtonian thought as the vehicle of the force of attraction or gravitation. Made exact and constant, it is still with us

[49] *Immortality of the Soul*, Book I, chs. 11 and 12; Book III, ch. 12; in *Philosophical Writings* (1662).
[50] *Immortality of the Soul*, p. 44.
[51] Preface General, *Philosophical Writings*, p. xv.

as "the field." More was aware that it might be objected that before we have discovered what "mechanic powers" can really perform it is premature to introduce another type.

As for the Spirit of Nature, the greatest exceptions are, that I have introduced an obscure principle for ignorance and sloth to take sanctuary in, and so to enervate or foreslack the useful endeavors of curious wits, and hinder that expected progress that may be made, in the Mechanick Philosophy; and this, to aggravate the crime, before a competent search be made what the Mechanical Powers of Matter can do. To such I answer, that the principle we speak of is neither obscure nor unseasonable; nor so much introduced by me, as forced upon me by inevitable evidence of reason . . . If the introduction of this principle be not seasonable now, it will never be seasonable. For that admirable Master of Mechanicks, Des-Cartes, has improved this way to the highest, I dare say, the wit of man can reach to, in such phenomena as he has attempted to render causes of. . . . I have not only confuted their reasons, but also from mechanical principles granted on all sides, and confirmed by experience, demonstrated that the descent (suppose) of a Stone, or Bullet, or any such like heavy Body, is enormously contrary to the Laws of Mechanicks; and that according to them they would necessarily, if they lie loose, recede from the Earth, if some power more than mechanical did not curb that motion, and force them downwards towards the earth. So that it is plain we have not arbitrarily introduced a principle, but that it is forced upon us by the undeniable evidence of demonstration. From which to suspend our assent till future ages have improved this mechanical philosophy to greater height, is as ridiculous, as to doubt of the truth of any one plain and easy demonstration in the first Book of Euclide, till we have travelled through the whole field of that immense study of Mathematicks.[52]

More is an eternal figure: Canute stemming the tide of science to leave room for religion.

The most striking consequence of More's attribution of extension to Spirit is his conclusion that the absolute space and time within which the universe is contained is the extension of God himself. There is an immovable extension distinct from that of movable matter. This extension cannot be merely "imaginary."

It is so imaginary that it cannot possibly be dis-imagined by human understanding . . . Which methinks should be no small earnest that there is more than an imaginary Being there.[53]

[52] *Immortality of the Soul*, Preface, pp. xi–xii.
[53] *Divine Dialogues*, p. 54.

It is extended and measurable, "an extended substance far more subtile than body that pervades the whole matter of the universe." (p. 54)

I must confess I have always been prone to think this subtile extension (which a man cannot dis-imagine but must needs be) to be a more obscure shadow or adumbration, or to be a more general and confused apprehension of the Divine Amplitude. For this will be necessarily, though all matter were annihilated out of the world. Nay indeed this is antecedent to all matter, forasmuch as no matter nor any being else can be conceived to be but in this. In this are all things necessarily apprehended "to live and move and have their being." (p. 55)

Does not the Cabbala call God the immovable mover, receptacle and sustainer of all things? This extension is the ground of the existence of spirit: spirit is that in which matter moves.

This is the extension only which must imply the necessity of the existence of some real Being thereunto appertaining; which therefore must be coincident with the essence of God, and cannot but be a spirit, because it pervades the matter of the universe. (p. 56)

Therefore it is necessary that there be some real subject underlying this extension, since it is a real attribute. This argument is so strong, that none could be stronger. For were it shaken, we would at once be unable to conclude the existence of any real subject whatsoever in the universe.[54]

It is necessary to conceive it as existing in itself, since it is entirely independent of anything else. But that it depends on nothing else, is known by the most manifest sign, namely, that although we can conceive all other things as destroyed and expelled from nature, this infinite immobile extension cannot be expelled even from thought.[55]

More considers two main objections to his view of extension, the positions of Hobbes and of Aristotle. The Hobbist maintains that

extension being thus necessarily applicable as well to imaginary as to real, it is rather a logical notion than a physical, and consequently is applicable to all objects, as well metaphysical as physical.[56]

This is bound up with the identification of extension with the relation of distance.

[54] *Enchiridion metaphysicum*, Part I, ch. viii, sec. 6.
[55] *Enchiridion metaphysicum*, sec. 10.　　　　　[56] *Divine Dialogues*, p. 57.

Distance is no physical affection of anything, but only notional, because more or less of it may accrue to a thing, whereas yet there has been nothing at all done to that to which it does accrue.[57]

More's answer is that if space or distance be something real at all, even if only a relation, it must be grounded in an incorporeal substance.

Nor can the force of the argument be escaped by saying that distance is not the property of any physical thing, but is merely relational and notional. For let it be granted that at whatever distance two bodies are said to lie from each other, they are in this way related. Still the basis of this relation is something real, as in many other relations of physical things.[58]

More also takes up the Aristotelian objection that this extension is only the "capacity of matter, matter *in potentia*."

This imagination of Space is not the imagination of any real thing, but only of the large and immense capacity of the potentiality of the matter, which we cannot free our minds from, but must necessarily acknowledge, that there is indeed such a possibility of matter to be measured, upward, downward, every way *in infinitum*, whether this corporeal matter were there or no; and that, though this potentiality of matter or space be measured by furlongs, miles, or the like, that it implies no more any real essence or being, than when a man recounts so many orders or kinds of the possibilities of things, the compute or number of them will infer the reality of their existence.[59]

More's reply is that both matter and its potentiality are movable and discerpible, whereas this space is immovable and indiscerpible. And he proceeds to analyze certain "imaginary experiments." Shoot an arrow straight up into the air. Because of the motion of the earth it describes a curve; in what? Imagine a line drawn in a cylinder from the center of one end to the circumference of the other. Revolve the cylinder, and that line will describe a cone; in what?

If there were no matter, but the immensity of the Divine Essence only, occupying all by his ubiquity, the replication, as I may so speak, of his indivisible substance, whereby he presents himself entirely everywhere, would be the subject of that diffusion and mensurability. . . . Whence the idea of God being such as it is, it will both justly and necessarily cast this ruder notion of Space upon that infinite and eternal spirit which is God. (p. 163)

[57] *Appendix to Antidote against Atheism* (ed. 1662), ch. vii, p. 164.
[58] *Enchiridion metaphysicum*, Part I, ch. viii, sec. 5.
[59] *Appendix to Antidote against Atheism*, p. 164.

Now there is the same reason for Time (by Time I mean Duration) as for Space. For we cannot imagine but that there has been such a continued duration, as could have no beginning or interruption. And anyone will say, it is nonsense that there should be such a necessary duration, when there is no real Essence that must of itself be always, and forever so endure. What or who is it then that this eternal, uninterrupted, and never-fading duration must belong to? No philosopher can answer more appositely than the holy Psalmist, "From everlasting to everlasting, thou art God." Wherefore I say, that those unavoidable imaginations of the necessity of an infinite space, as they call it, and eternal duration, are no proofs of a self-existent matter, but rather obscure sub-indications of the necessary existence of God. (p. 164)

God and space, in fact, possess twenty identical attributes: each is

one, simple, immobile, eternal, perfect, independent, existing by itself, subsisting through itself, incorruptible, necessary, immense, uncreated, uncircumscribed, incomprehensible, omnipresent, incorporeal, permeating and embracing all things, essential being, actual being, pure actuality.[60]

More's original blend of Platonic and Cartesian views of extension and duration did not remain mere dubious religious apologetics. Through Isaac Barrow they were accepted by the Cambridge mathematicians, and appear bodily in the well-known scholia to Newton's *Principia* as the Absolute Time and Space which form the container of all mechanical action and are the divine presence in the world. Isaac Barrow was Newton's teacher, and a Cambridge rationalist. His is a world of absolute time and space and geometrical relations. Geometry is an existential science; it is the science of the relations in absolute space. The field of mathematics is identical with the field of physics and astronomy, and nature is thus a tissue of mathematical properties.

More's ethical teachings, contained in his poems and in his *Enchiridion Ethicum* (1666) resemble those of his fellow-Platonist Malebranche; they likewise culminate in the intellectual love of God, as the source and measure of all the different forms of human good. There are innate ideas of good and evil, ethical noemata or axioms, which serve to judge and order the passions. Derived from nature and through nature from God, the passions are good if directed by right reason. But just as the Divine Sagacity stands above

---

[60] *Enchiridion metaphysicum*, Part I, ch. viii, sec. 8.

discursive reason in things intellectual, so does a "boniform faculty" stand above right reason in morals. What is good is to be judged by right reason, but "its savor and sweetness are perceived by the boniform faculty of the soul; by it we relish or savor what is absolutely best and rejoice in it alone."

All moral good, properly so called, is intellectual and divine: intellectual in so far as its essence and truth are defined and known by intellect; divine, in so far as its sweetness is most pleasant and most effectually enjoyed in that divine faculty in which we cleave unto God—the most pure and absolute good.[61]

In the end Platonic *Nous* is one with Platonic love.

VIII

These Cambridge rationalists not only put their stamp upon the basic concepts of the mathematical scientists; their spirit and their method persisted in the religious and moral thought of the next generation, however much it may seem to be obscured by the new and fashionable terminology of Newton which replaced that of Plato. Whatever its pretenses of scientific foundation, liberal religion has rarely borrowed more than its language from the successive schemes of science it has so eagerly courted. Through Shaftesbury, who remained faithful even to the Platonic expression, More and Cudworth became one of the major sources of Enlightenment thought in Germany as well as in Britain. There were also a few Englishmen who even in the Newtonian age were unwilling to accommodate themselves to the new worship of experience; attracted by one or another of the more religiously minded Cartesians, they undertook an often acute but never popular criticism of the Locke who had succeeded Hobbes as the embodiment of irreligious empiricism. Of these lonely thinkers the ideas of Burthogge and Norris are the most suggestive, both in themselves and as foreshadowings of the direction which critical thought was to take in continental channels.

Richard Burthogge published in 1694 an *Essay upon reason and the nature of spirits*. He had already in 1678 formulated his views in his *Organum vetus et novum*, and hoped now to profit by the interest created by Locke, to whom he dedicated his essay. Burthogge had studied medicine in Leyden from 1658 to 1662, at the time

[61] *Enchiridion Ethicum*, Book I, ch. v, 1.

Geulincx was lecturing there; his ideas reveal not only the thorough assimilation of Geulincx's criticism of reason, but a further pushing as well. Building upon Locke's popular view of secondary qualities, he goes on to show that all human notions are equally "entities of reason conceived within the mind."

As the eye has no perceivance of things but under colors, that are not in them, so the understanding apprehends not things, or any habitudes or aspects of them, but under certain Notions, that neither have that being in objects, or that being of objects, that they seem to have; but are in all respects the very same to the mind or understanding that colors are to the eye and sound to the ear.

It is certain that things to us men are nothing but as they do stand in our analogy, that is, in plain terms, they are nothing to us but as they are known by us.

Thing, substance, accident, time, space, cause, effect, are all

entia cogitationis, all phenomena; appearances that do no more exist without our faculties in the things themselves than the images that are seen in water, or behind a glass, do really exist in those places where they seem to be . . . So that we apprehend not any things at all, just as they are, in their own realities, but only under the Top-knots and Dresses of Notions which our minds do put on them.[62]

Less bound than Geulincx by the sharp Cartesian dualism, Burthogge saw even the difference between mind and body as a notional distinction made by the mind itself within its experience. The qualities and accidents of appearances do seem to fall into two such groups; but as to what spirit or matter and motion may be in their own positive reality we can form only futile metaphysical hypotheses.

A philosophy that shall be solid and sound must have its groundwork and foundations firmly laid; which none can have, but that which is bottomed, raised and built upon *evidence;* I mean upon the certain testimony of our faculties. And therefore since our faculties do rather go upon Notions than upon realities, and do plainly distinguish between mind and matter, and do . . . contradistinguish them, I hold myself obliged to treat of these distinctly, but still in the real notional way . . . Thus it is in our refracted, inadequate, Real-Notional way of conceiving; and for an adequate and just one, as it is above our faculties. I do not find that Spinoza or Malebranche after all their ambitious researches in that

---

[62] Burthogge, *Essay upon Reason and the Nature of Spirits*, pp. 57ff.

higher way have edified the world thereby to any great degree. (pp. 106, 109)

Yet just as the eye perceives immediately only light and colors, and yet can serve as the basis for the notional distinction of relations, so the notions of the understanding can serve as the basis for something further.

So the understanding discerns infinite realities, infinite habitudes of things: not indeed immediately, but either under the sentiments of sense, or by means of its own, which I call notions. (p. 68)

Cause and effect cannot have merely an *"esse cognitivum or cognitum"*; else we should be shut up in a subjective scepticism. There must be a world of real things which furnish the occasion for our sensations and notions. And the only idea we can form of the nature of that Reality is of a single active spirit of nature; all things are the particular manifestations of the plastic faculty of God himself. And so Burthogge abandons the real notional way to end in the Platonic spiritualism of More.

John Norris (1657–1711), a man of greater repute and an active polemicist who drew a reply from Locke himself, but of lesser originality, was the outstanding English follower of Malebranche, whom he called the great Galileo of the intellectual world. His *Essay towards the Theory of the Ideal or Intelligible World* (1701, 1704) tries to lead Lockeans to the Platonic tradition of Augustine, More, and Malebranche.

'Tis generally allowed that the things without us are not perceived immediately, but by their ideas. The only question is, by what ideas, or what these ideas are.[63]

If as Locke admits truth is the agreement between ideas, then what must be the nature of that relation of agreement, and of the terms it relates? Norris's answer is the logical realism of the Platonic tradition.

Since by truth is meant only . . . certain habitudes or relations of union or agreement, disunion or disagreement between ideas, . . . to affirm that there are eternal truths imports as much as that there are such eternal habitudes and relations that never were made by any understanding or will, nor can ever be unmade by them, but have a certain stated and

[63] Norris, *Essay towards the Theory of the Ideal or Intelligible World*, II, 442.

unalterable order from everlasting to everlasting. . . . But these eternal habitudes and relations of things wherein consists the formal reason of eternal truths cannot exist without the reality of their respective correlates, those things or natures whose relations they are . . . I conclude therefore that these eternal relations of truth cannot exist by themselves, and if they do exist at all (as most certainly they do if they are necessary and eternal) the simple essences which they respect must exist too, . . . for can anything be more inconceivable than this, that there should be any relation of union, agreement, or connexion between things that are not? (I, 68 ff.)

The logical structure of truth the mind beholds and which is its science must have a real being; and where better can this being reside than "in God," as Malebranche put it? Sense gives no evidence of anything, not even of its own objects;

our senses are here dumb, as in all other questions, however clear the reports and narrations we may lend them; it is reason alone that speaks in us and to us . . . We should have to possess a very metaphysical "sense" indeed to perceive existence with it—and an understanding very little metaphysical to believe it possible. For to perceive that a thing exists is to perceive a judgment. We but feel ourselves continually determined and modified in many ways, so that we never possess a sensation of bodies, but only a bare sensation. (I, 198)

7

British Experimentalism before Newton

I

IT WAS NOT, however, from such men as the Cambridge Platonists, who took the metaphysical problems of Cartesianism and of Malebranche seriously, that the rationalism of eighteenth-century thought stemmed; it was not even from the great Platonic tradition in its Augustinian or Renaissance forms. It was rather from a reason that had been carefully accommodated to British experience in the suggestive but unstable syntheses of Newton and Locke. And though both these models and inspirations of the next generation were the heirs of the faith in reason and rational analysis of the continental Cartesians and of their English analogues, and though both were intimately acquainted with the Cambridge Platonists, and in their religious views regarded themselves rightly as carrying on the humanized rational religion of that group, both drew into their thought other strains in British intellectual life whose compatibility with its underlying rationalism could only be forced. The compromises of Newton and Locke, which the next century was to take as its point of departure, demand for their understanding some knowledge of the slowly developing tradition of British "experimental philosophy," as well as of the innovations introduced into the rather different medieval empirical tradition when it was employed as a principle of interpretation for seventeenth-century science.

If British religious and moral thought won independence of theological and ecclesiastical authority in terms of a rationalism as Platonic though less literally Augustinian than that on the continent, British "natural philosophy" endeavored rather to avoid so far as possible all speculative questions and metaphysical foundations. It advanced directly from the exuberant explorations of the Renaissance nature philosophy to the detailed investigation of particular problems, without feeling the necessity of a thoroughgoing mathematical rationalism to first clear the ground of inherited fancies and prejudices. As a consequence, traditional old wives' tales were treated seriously by British investigators far later than on the continent, where the rational faith of Cartesianism had made it clear they could not be true. The *Transactions* of the Royal Society are full of a hodgepodge of uncritically accepted ideas; the notions of magic and astrology, and indeed all kinds of traditional superstitions, are not only carefully investigated, but actually "experimentally" verified. The fashion set by Bacon's *Sylva Sylvarum* continued until the full influence of Newton's mathematical drive began to be felt. This fact makes clear how essential were the simplified mathematical faith and the purifying zeal for universal mechanism in enabling modern natural science to get under way; without those destructive instruments, mere open-minded observation had great difficulty in getting anywhere.

Yet at the same time it was just this cautious and reserved spirit which enabled British science to work out for itself in the next century a more positivistic and "empirical" or observational theory, untrammeled by the rationalistic dogmas which continental thinkers had to overcome in their turn. And the typical attitude of British scientists from Bacon down toward religious faith, reinforced this positivistic temper. Their very refusal to construct an imposing rational synthesis between faith and science, in which the principles of natural knowledge should be well integrated in a theological metaphysics, made it possible for them to avoid becoming involved in theological disputes. And their method of refraining from mixing theology and science was a powerful incentive in leading them to limit scientific knowledge to what could be "deduced from facts," and to distinguish its aims of "solving phenomena" and practical utility from that certainty which comes only from faith. The unquestioning religious piety of so many British scientists has played a large part in the positivistic empiricism of the British tradition in scientific theory.

In addition to the mathematical rationalism which allied itself to the Platonic and Cartesian tradition, especially at Cambridge, the "physico-experimental mathematical learning" of British science generated even in the seventeenth century a scientific theory of its own; and both these strains, the experimental as well as the rational, were caught up in the inconsistent thought of Newton and Locke. This nascent theory dominated the practice of the Royal Society. Its adherents called it "the experimental philosophy," and contrasted it sharply with the "notional way" of the rationalists. They thought of themselves as "scientific sceptics" or "seekers," employing "hypotheses" for the solution of particular phenomena. They found mathematical measurement and calculation an enormously useful tool in their investigations, and they had no doubts of the absolute certainty of mathematics itself. They looked with great favor on the "Cartesian hypothesis" of mechanism and on the "corpuscular philosophy," but they never forgot they were dealing with "hypotheses." Of this "experimental philosophy" of the Royal Society the best theoretical statement and the fullest exposition is to be found in Joseph Glanvill, while its greatest conscious practitioner before Newton is Robert Boyle.

II

Joseph Glanvill (1636–1680) was an Oxford man who wished he had been sent to Cambridge that he might have earlier learned the new philosophy of Descartes. He developed a great aversion both to the Puritan theological disputes and to the peripatetic philosophy, and a great passion for the new science and for the rational religion of the Cambridge Platonists. As a member of Henry More's circle and a latitudinarian he enjoyed patronage and preferment in the Church after the Restoration. For More himself he had the highest personal respect; and the speculations of that most excellent and ingenious man, though he could not quite accept them, seem to have kept him from unquestioning acquiescence in a thoroughgoing mechanism. His attack on Aristotle and the Schools and his enthusiasm for Descartes in *The Vanity of Dogmatizing* (1661) led to his election to the Royal Society in 1664; the next year he revised his book as *Scepsis Scientifica.*

Glanvill has nothing but eulogy for the character of the enterprise of the Royal Society.

You really are what former ages could contrive but in wish and romances; and Solomon's House in the *New Atlantis* was a prophetick scheam of the Royal Society.[1]

He especially praises

the credit which the mathematicks have with you, your experimental way of enquiry, and mechanical attempts for solving the phenomena; besides that some of you publicly own the Cartesian and atomical hypotheses. (p. liii)

The particular task of the Royal Society is to heap up in Baconian fashion an exact "natural history" or description of facts as the material of science.

From your promising and generous endeavors we may hopefully expect a considerable inlargement of the History of Nature, without which our hypotheses are but dreams and romances, and our science mere conjecture and opinion. For while we frame schemes of things without consulting the phenomena, we do but build in the air, and describe an imaginary world of our own making, that is but little akin to the real one that God made. And 'tis possible that all the hypotheses that yet have been contrived were built upon too narrow an inspection of things, and the phases of the universe. For the advancing day of experimental knowledge discloseth such appearances as will not lye even, in any model extant. (p. lxii)

As befits such a conception of science, Glanvill is one of the few seventeenth-century figures to speak enthusiastically of Bacon. He shares to the full the Baconian hope for the practical progress of mankind through the advancement of learning. His *Plus Ultra, or the progress and advancement of knowledge since the days of Aristotle* (1668), is a Baconian paean, and in his essay on *Antifanatick Theologie and Free Philosophy* he attempted a continuation of the *New Atlantis*. And his criticisms of the peripatetic philosophy he acknowledges have already been handsomely performed in the *Novum Organum*. But though Glanvill admires Bacon the critic of the Schools, Bacon the prophet of science, and Bacon the inspirer of the collection of natural histories, no more than any other Englishman of the day does he so much as mention Bacon's own theory of scientific method and induction.

Here the great leader is Descartes, the "Grand Secretary of Nature," (p. 182) "the master of mechanicks"; (p. 45) his is deservedly

[1] Joseph Glanvill, *Scepsis Scientifica*, ed. John Owen (1885), p. lxv.

entitled the "best philosophy." (p. 73) The glory and utility that can be urged for philosophy is "not so strictly verifiable for any that I know as the Cartesian." (p. 218)

The Cartesian philosophy in this regard hath shown the world the way to be happy . . . Should those heroes go on, as they have happily begun, they'll fill the world with wonders. And I doubt not but posterity will find many things that are now but rumors verified into practical realities . . . To them that come after us it may be as ordinary to buy a pair of wings to fly into remotest regions; as now a pair of boots to ride a journey. And to confer at the distance of the Indies by sympathetick conveyances may be as usual to future times as to us in a literary correspondence . . . Now those that judge by the narrowness of former principles and successes, will smile at these paradoxical expectations; . . . but notwithstanding this straightness of shallow observers, there are a set of enlarged souls that are most judiciously credulous; and those who are acquainted with the fecundity of Cartesian principles, and the diligent and ingenious endeavors of so many true philosophers will despair of nothing. (pp. 156–58)

What attracts Glanvill to Descartes besides this practical success in physics, is the method of doubt.

He that would rebuild a decayed structure must first pluck down the former ruins. (p. 63)

For the prepossessions of sense having so mingled themselves with our genuine truths, . . . we cannot gain a true assurance of any but by suspending our assent from all, till the deserts of each, discovered by a strict enquiry, claim it. Upon this account I think the method of the most excellent Des-Cartes not unworthy its author; and (since dogmatical ignorance will call it so) a Scepticism that's the only way to science. (p. 64)

But this Cartesian doubt is not for Glanvill nor his English colleagues the mere prelude to rational certainty.

Though the Grand Secretary of Nature, the miraculous Des-Cartes, hath here infinitely outdone all the philosophers that went before him, in giving a particular and analytical account of the universal fabric: yet he intends his principles but for Hypotheses, and never pretends that things are really or necessarily as he hath supposed them; but that they may be admitted pertinently to solve the phenomena, and are convenient supposals for the use of life. Nor can any further account be expected from humanity, but how things possibly may have been made consonantly to sensible nature: but infallibly to determine how they truly were effected, is proper to him only that saw them in the chaos, and fashioned them out of that confused mass. (p. 182)

Glanvill clearly formulates his conception of a probable and useful knowledge of nature.

The best Principles, excepting Divine, and Mathematical, are but Hypotheses, within the circles of which we may indeed conclude many things with security from error: but yet the greatest certainty advanced from supposal is still but Hypothetical. So that we may affirm that things are thus and thus, according to the Principles we have espoused: but we strangely forget ourselves, when we plead a necessity of their being so in nature, and an impossibility of their being otherwise. (p. 170)

Now I intend not anything here to invalidate the certainty of truths either mathematical or divine. (p. 179)

For mathematical sciences, he that doubts their certainty hath need of a dose of hellebore. (p. 180)

The indisputable mathematicks is the only Science heaven hath yet vouchsafed humanity. (p. 142)

Glanvill's conception of science is traditional enough. It is the rational deduction of conclusions from "congenite propositions." (p. 82)

In scientifical discoveries . . . there is no way to truth but by the most clear comprehension of simple notions, and as wary an accuracy in deductions. (p. 141)

But such strict "science" is possible only in mathematics (and Divinity):

and the knowledge we have of the mathematicks hath no reason to elate us; since by them we know but numbers and figures, creatures of our own, and are yet ignorant of our maker's. (p. 180)

A genuine science of nature is

the knowledge of things in their true, immediate, necessary causes; all knowledge of causes is deductive: for we know none by simple intuition; but through the mediation of their effects. So that we cannot conclude anything to be the cause of another, but from its continual accompanying it: for the causality itself is insensible. But now to argue from a concomitancy to a causality is not infallibly conclusive: yea in this way lies notorious delusion. (p. 166)

Moreover,

all things are mixed, and causes blended by mutual involutions. . . . To profound to the bottom of these diversities, to assign each cause its distinct effects, and to limit them by their just and true proportions, are necessary requisites of science; and he that hath compassed them may boast he hath outdone humanity. (p. 168)

Demonstrative knowledge of natural causes is impossible.

Can nothing be otherwise, which we conceive impossible to be so? Our demonstrations are levyed upon principles of our own, not universal nature. (p. 169)

The ultimate reason for this positivistic conception of natural knowledge is the fact that

we cannot conceive anything that comes not within the verge of our outward or inward senses; but either by like experiments which we have made, or at least by some remoter hints which we receive from them. (p. 21)

But now our senses being scant and limited, and Nature's operations subtil and various; they must needs transcend and outrun our faculties. They are only Nature's grosser ways of working which are sensible; her finer threads are out of reach of our dull percipient. (p. 59)

For Nature is set a going by the most subtil and hidden instruments; which it may be have nothing obvious which resembles them. (p. 155)

Since we cannot profound into the hidden things of nature, nor see the first springs and wheels that set the rest a going, we view but small pieces of the universal frame, and want phenomena to make intire and secure Hypotheses. (p. 15)

Even our own souls are "seen like other things in the mirror of their effects and attributes." (p. 16) At times Glanvill even despairs of the efficacy of sound method:

Most of our rarities have been found out by casual emergency; and have been the works of time and chance, rather than of philosophy. (p. 154)

The philosopher that proved motion by walking did in that action better define it [than Aristotle]. (p. 133)

Thus out of the very procedure of scientific investigation Glanvill developed many of those conceptions of the nature of science

which the empirical theory of Locke and his successors was later
to popularize. This was the positive content of his "scientific scepticism." It is true that he was versed in the arguments of Montaigne,
Charron, and even of "St. Austin," and uses them effectively against
the dogmatists in theology and metaphysics; but when he approaches natural philosophy it is more in the spirit of a Malebranche
recounting the sources of error to be guarded against than of a
Pascal turning men's minds to God. His scepticism even of the
senses is very moderate:

indeed sense itself detects its more palpable deceits by a counter-evidence;
and the more ordinary impostures seldom outlive the first experiments.
(p. 62)

At least the mathematicks must be privileged from the indictment. Neither
are we yet at so deplorable a loss in the other parts of what we call science;
but that we may meet with what will content ingenuity, at this distance
from perfection, though all things will not completely satisfy strict and
rigid inquiry. (p. 205)

Though I confess that in philosophy I'm a seeker; yet cannot believe that
a sceptic in philosophy must be one in Divinity. (p. 163)

Indeed, he confesses to having played with the dogmatist in a per-
sonated scepticism; and he affects the Socratic ignorance: "'tis a
good degree of science to be sensible that we want it." (p. 194) Let
lesser mortals be still, if the great and instructed spirits of the Royal
Society confess the narrowness of human attainments, and think
"we have not as yet phenomena enough to make as much as Hypotheses, much less, to fix certain laws and prescribe methods to
Nature in her actings." (p. 51) Glanvill's definition of "scientific
scepticism" is clearest in his spirited defense against Thomas White:

But the true philosophers are by others accounted scepticks, from their
way of enquiry: which is not to continue still poring upon the writings and
opinions of philosophers, but to seek truth in the great book of nature, and
in that search to proceed with wariness and circumspection, without too
much forwardness in establishing maxims and positive doctrines: to propose their opinions as hypotheses, that may probably be the true accounts,
without peremptorily affirming that they are. This among others hath
been the way of those great men, the Lord Bacon and Descartes, and is
now the method of the Royal Society of London, whose motto is *Nullius
in verba*. This is scepticism with some, and if it be so indeed, 'tis such

scepticism as is the only way to sure and grounded knowledge, to which confidence in uncertain opinions is the most fatal enemy. (p. xviii)

Most characteristic of Glanvill's distrust of dogmatism is his caution in denying that anything is impossible. Where Descartes employed his doubt in a sweepingly negative way, the English were willing to accord any notion the status of hypothesis till it had been convicted of falsity. Our understanding is forward to assent to slightly examined conclusions; hence we conclude many things impossibilities which are yet easy Feasibles, and within the sphere of action of nature. And the three instances of reputed impossibilities, which Glanvill sets out to defend, are telepathy, the ouija board, and sympathetic magic! His open-minded experimentalism, so rare in that confident age, has much of the spirit of a William James about it. And it is no accident that this scientific opponent of dogmatism thought it "a matter of astonishment that men, otherwise witty and ingenious, are fallen into the conceit that there's no such thing as a witch or apparition." [2] He was convinced that the testimony of all ages established the reality of witchcraft; and in his *Sadducismus Triumphatus, or Full and plain evidence concerning witches and apparitions* (1681) he exhibited hosts of plain facts and experiments proving it to be so. The undogmatic observation of the Royal Society tended to confirm traditional beliefs if not salted with the rational faith that such things could not be.

Characteristic also of the Royal Society was Glanvill's agnosticism as to the metaphysical problems of Cartesianism, the nature and origin of the soul, its union with the body, its operations, and the operations of the body itself, combined with an implicit acceptance of the Cartesian dualism and of the subjectivity of secondary qualities. That we are a compound of beings distant in extremes is clear as noon; but we know not how soul moves the body, or how the two are joined. In general Glanvill accepts the Cartesian psychology; the understanding perceives the changes which bodily motion produces in the brain: properly and formally heat is not in the fire, but is an expression of our sentiment, a name designating our passion.

[2] *Antifanatick Theologie, and Free Philosophy*, cited by W. R. Sorley, *A History of English Philosophy*, p. 102.

Now if this motive energy, the instrument of this active element (which produces the effect in us we call heat) must be called heat, let it be so, I contend not . . . I fight not with words. Only I would not that the idea of our passions be applied to anything without us, when it hath its subject nowhere but in ourselves.[3]

And characteristic also is the general acceptance of corpuscular mechanism as the best physical hypothesis, with no particular faith, however, in its universal validity. Glanvill has been influenced negatively if not positively by Henry More's theories. As to the bodily operations, "all the philosophy in the world cannot make them out to be purely mechanical." (p. 23) Can unguided matter keep itself in exact conformity to the species? It is likely that such conformity to kind is regulated by the immediate efficiency of some intelligent agent.

But what this hidden architect should be, and by what instruments and art this frame is erected; is as unknown to us as the thoughts of our cradles. The Plastick faculty is a fine word, and will do well in the mouth of a puzzled empirick; but what it is, how it works, and whose it is, we cannot learn; neither will the Platonick principles unriddle the doubt. (p. 38)

Glanvill halts before the enigmas of motion, magnetism, gravity, and the tides; he is especially struck by More's problem of the impossibility of accounting for the cohesion of bodies on purely atomistic principles. And to explain telepathy, "the Platonicall hypothesis of a mundane soul will handsomely relieve us. Or if any would rather have a mechanical account, I think it may probably be made out in some such way as follows" from Cartesian third matter. (p. 173) And Glanvill welcomes that "commentitious inanity," (p. 128) More's absolute space.

III

Robert Boyle (1627–1691), greatest of the seventeenth-century experimenters because he combined a strong mathematical sense with his experimentalism, was also less representative of the limitations and uncritical traditionalism of the Royal Society. With an insatiable curiosity and an indefatigable ingenuity in devising experiments, he combined a sobriety and restraint of interpretation.

[3] *Scepsis Scientifica*, p. 76.

He too had a strong religious interest, and the Boyle Lectures on natural religion which he founded became the Gifford Lectures of the next generation. It was primarily this piety that kept him from acquiescing in the radical metaphysics of the continental scientists, and led to his constant effort to limit science to secondary causes and to a positivistic conception based on human utility. To understand, a completely deductive system from first principles would be necessary; but such perfection is not needed for human control of natural forces. Probable knowledge is there enough.

There are two very distinct ends that men may propound to themselves in studying natural philosophy. For some men care only to know nature, others desire to command her; or, to express it otherwise, some there are, who desire but to please themselves by the discovery of the causes of the known phenomena; and others would be able to produce new ones, and bring nature to be serviceable to their particular ends, whether of health, or riches, or sensual delight. Now as I shall not deny, but that the atomical, the Cartesian, or some such principles, are likely to afford the most of satisfaction to those speculative wits, that aim but at the knowing of causes; so I think, that the other sort of men may very delightfully and successfully prosecute their ends, by collecting and making variety of experiments and observations; since thereby learning the qualities and properties of those particular bodies they desire to make use of, and observing the power that divers chymical operations, and other ways of handling matter, have of altering such bodies, and verifying their effects upon one another, they may, by the help of attention and industry, be able to do many things, some of them very strange, and more of them very useful in human life.[4]

Besides his experiments on *The Spring of the Air*, Boyle's scientific fame rests on his putting the problems of alchemy on an exact mechanical basis, and banishing both the "spirits" and the elementary qualities of Paracelsus in favor of a "corpuscular" analysis. He well saw his function of uniting the two scientific movements of his day.

Since the mechanical philosophers have brought so few experiments to verify their assertions, and the chymists are thought to have brought so many on behalf of theirs, that of those, that have quitted the unsatisfactory philosophy of the schools, the greater number . . . have embraced the doctrines of the latter, . . . for these reasons, I say, I hoped I might at least do no unseasonable piece of service to the corpuscular philosophers,

[4] *Some Considerations touching Experimental Essays in General,* in *Works,* ed. Thomas Birch (1744; 2d ed. used, 1772), I, 310.

by illustrating some of their notions with sensible experiments, and manifesting, that the things by me treated of, may be at least plausibly explicated without having recourse to inexplicable forms, real qualities, the four peripatetic elements, or so much as the three chymical principles.[5]

Boyle called himself the *Sceptical Chymist* (1661) in very much Glanvill's sense: the absolute elements of bodies may never be revealed to us, but if through experimental analysis we can discover certain constituent parts of bodies, such relative elements are all that is needful and fruitful for our knowledge. As a good experimentalist, therefore, Boyle sees clearly that the metaphysical differences between the two sects of mechanical philosophers are of little practical moment: the important point is that "both the Cartesians and the Atomists [like Gassendi] explicate phenomena by little bodies variously figured and moved"; whence "their hypotheses might by a person of a reconciling disposition be looked on as one philosophy. Which because it explicates things by corpuscles, or minute bodies, may (not very unfitly) be called *corpuscular*." [6]

Boyle's "corpuscular philosophy" is both mechanistic and mathematical: he accepted the Galilean dynamics and welcomed the Cartesian physics as an hypothesis. But it is an experimental mechanism and an applied mathematicism. It permits the application of pure mathematics to the production or the modification of the motions of bodies. For pure mathematics is most useful to human life, and to the experimental naturalist: it is not only the source of all the essential "mixed mathematics," it helps the naturalist to frame and judge hypotheses, it suggests divers new experiments, inferences, and applications. And Boyle shares the common notion that mathematical principles are "the alphabet in which God wrote the world."

That which I chiefly aim at, is to make it probable to you by experiments that almost all sorts of qualities, most of which have been by the schools either left unexplicated, or generally referred to I know not what incomprehensible substantial forms, may be produced mechanically. I mean by such corporeal agents, as do not appear either to work otherwise than by virtue of the motion, size, figure, and contrivance (which attributes I call the mechanical affections of matter, because to them men willingly refer the various operations of mechanical engines).[7]

[5] *Preface to Some Specimens of Chemical Experiments, Works*, I, 356.
[6] *Preface*, I, 355, 356.
[7] *The Origin of Forms and Qualities, Works*, III, 13.

I . . . allow that there is one catholick or universal matter common to all bodies, by which I mean a substance extended, divisible, and impenetrable . . . It will follow, that to discriminate the catholick matter into variety of natural bodies, it must have motion in some or all its designable parts, and that motion must have various tendencies.[8]

And there are some attributes, namely size, shape, motion, and rest, that are wont to be reckoned among qualities, which may more conveniently be esteemed the primary modes of the parts of matter, since from these simple attributes, or primordial affections, all the qualities are derived.[9]

These accidents may conveniently enough be called the moods or primary affections of bodies, to distinguish them from those less simple qualities (as colors, tastes, and odors) that belong to bodies upon their account.[10]

These "primary qualities" of bodies, bulk and shape—for motion is not included in their nature or essence—produce the sensible "secondary qualities"; Boyle originated the terms of the distinction.

Such secondary qualities, however, he is too good a naturalist to dismiss as "subjective," or as the arbitrary contributions of men's minds. The primary qualities are not more "real" than the secondary qualities; they are "absolute" and inherent in each body in itself, whereas the latter are relational and dependent upon the operations of bodies on other bodies.

If we should conceive that all the rest of the universe were annihilated, except any of these intire and undivided corpuscles, it is hard to say what could be attributed to it, besides matter, motion (or rest), bulk, and shape. Whence you may take notice that bulk, though usually taken in a comparative sense, is in our sense an *absolute* thing, since a body would have it, though there were no other in the world . . . But now we are to consider, that there are *de facto* in the world certain sensible and rational beings, that we call men; and the body of man having several external parts, as the eye, the ear, etc., each of a distinct and peculiar texture, whereby it is capable to receive impressions from the bodies about it, and upon that account it is called an organ of sense; we must consider, I say, that these sensories may be wrought upon, by the figure, shape, motion, and texture of bodies without them after several ways . . . And to these operations of the objects on the sensories the mind of man, which on account of its union with the body perceives them, giveth distinct names, calling the one light or color, the other sound, the other odor, etc. (III, 22, 23)

[8] *Origin of Forms and Qualities*, III, 15.
[9] *The History of Particular Qualities, Works*, III, 292.
[10] *Origin of Forms and Qualities, Works*, III, 16.

To be short, if we fancy any two of the bodies about us, as a stone, a metal, etc., to have nothing at all to do with any other body in the universe, it is not easy to conceive either how one can act upon the other, but by local motion, or how by motion it can do any more than put the parts of the other body into motion too, and thereby produce in them a change of situation and texture, or of some other of its mechanical affections; though this (passive) body being placed among other bodies in a world constituted as ours now is, and being brought to act upon the most curiously contrived sensories of animals, may upon both these accounts exhibit many differing sensible phenomena. (III, 26)

Boyle does not, in fact, allow the discovery of the mechanism of perception to destroy the essentially Aristotelian view that it is the actualization of something in bodies potentially.

I do not deny but that bodies may be said in a very favorable sense to have those qualities we call sensible, though there were no animals in the world: for a body may . . . have such a disposition of its constituent corpuscles, that in case it were duly applied to the sensory of an animal, it would produce such a sensible quality which a body of another texture would not: as though if there were no animals there would be no such thing as pain, yet a pin may, upon the account of its figure, be fitted to cause pain, in case it were moved against a man's finger . . . Thus snow, though if there were no lucid body nor organ of sight in the world, it would exhibit no color at all, yet it hath a greater disposition than a coal or soot to reflect store of light outwards, when the sun shines upon them all three . . . If there were no sensitive beings, those bodies that are now the objects of our senses would be but *dispositively*, if I may so speak, endowed with colors, tastes, and the like; and *actually*, but only with those more catholick affections of bodies, figure, motion, texture, etc. (III, 24)

What Boyle really objects to is the view

that there are in natural bodies store of real qualities and other real accidents, which not only are no moods of matter, but are real entities distinct from it, and . . . may exist separate from all matter whatsoever. (III, 16)

Boyle's most careful examination of this subject is in his *Origin of Forms and Qualities according to the Corpuscular Philosophy*, in 1666.

In accordance with these principles, Boyle found great help in Hooke's "aether" as the means of explaining the two great difficulties of the mechanical philosophy, the transmission of force through contact between moving bodies, and the workings of gravitation, magnetism, and cohesion—the functions for which

More had called upon the Spirit of Nature. Boyle followed Descartes, Gassendi, and Huyghens in elaborating a purely mechanical contact theory of gravitation, in contrast to the attempt of men like Gilbert, Kepler, and Galileo to attribute it to an occult force of attraction like magnetism.

In *A Free Inquiry into the Vulgarly Received Notion of Nature* (1686), Boyle undertook to explore the implications of his corpuscular philosophy. "Nature" had been loosely regarded as a force or power; is it really more than a human way of regarding the complexity of natural events? Is it not merely the expression for the manifold of rules and conditions that phenomena observe? Is it not but a system of motions? Boyle is here consciously trying to reduce the independence of "Nature" to a dependence on the divine power and creative energy: nature is merely a formal cause, God alone is efficient.

When it is said that nature does this or that, it is less proper to say, that it is done by nature, than that it is done according to nature: so that nature is not to be looked on as a distinct or separate agent, but as a rule, or rather the system of rules, according to which those agents, and the bodies they work on, are, by the great Author of things, determined to act and suffer.[11]

Here too Boyle's piety leads him to a positivistic conception.

Universal nature is the aggregate of the bodies that make up the world, framed as it is, considered as a principle, by virtue whereof they act and suffer, according to the laws of motion prescribed by the Author of things . . . I shall express what I called general nature by cosmical mechanism, that is, a comprisal of all the mechanical affections that belong to the matter of the great system of the universe. And to denote the nature of this or that particular body, I shall style it the private, the particular, or (if you please) the individual mechanism of that body, . . . that is . . . the comprisal of all its mechanical affections convened in the particular body, considered as it is determinately placed in a world so constituted as ours.[12]

In his general conception of the nature of science, Boyle was traditional enough, remaining true to the accepted theory.

Philosophy is a comprehension of all those truths or doctrines, which the natural reason of man, freed from prejudices and partiality, and assisted by

[11] *A Free Inquiry into the Vulgarly Received Notion of Nature, Works,* V, 219.
[12] *A Free Inquiry,* V, 177, 178.

learning, attention, exercise, experiments, etc., can manifestly make out, or by necessary consequence deduce from clear and certain principles.[13]

Experience is but an assistant to reason, since it doth indeed supply informations to the understanding; but the understanding remains still the judge, and has the power or right to examine and make use of the testimonies that are presented to it. The outward senses are but the instruments of the soul . . . The sensories may deceive us, if the requisites of sensation be wanting. . . . It is the part of reason, not sense, to judge whether none of the requisites of sensation be wanting, . . . and also it is the part of reason to judge what conclusions may, and what cannot be safely grounded on the information of the senses and the testimony of experience. So that when it is said, that experience corrects reason, it is somewhat an improper way of speaking; since it is reason itself, that upon the information of experience, corrects the judgments she had made before.[14]

Yet Boyle is led by the whole bent of his temper, as well as by his ingrained piety, to develop the conception of a genuinely experimental science and method. He is convinced of the dimness of our faculties, and the necessary imperfection of human nature; our knowledge is confined to "but a small share of the superficial part of a physical point." [15]

I see no necessity that intelligibility to a human understanding should be necessary to the truth or existence of a thing, any more than that visibility to a human eye should be necessary to the existence of an atom, or of a corpuscle of air, etc.[16]

The laws of motion may not hold in other worlds than ours; indeed,

I make great doubt, whether there be not some phenomena in nature, which the atomists cannot satisfactorily explain by any figuration, motion, or connexion of material particles whatsoever.[17]

Such are the operations of the rational soul in man, and why one motion from a bell, for example, produces in man sight, and another hearing. Hence it is ridiculous to project great systems.

It is not that I at all condemn the practice of those inquisitive wits, that take upon them to explicate to us even the abstrusest phenomena of nature . . . I admire them when their endeavors succeed, and applaud them

[13] *Considerations about the Reconcileableness of Reason and Religion, Works*, IV, 168.
[14] *The Christian Virtuoso, Works*, V, 539.
[15] *The Excellency of Theology, Works*, IV, 50.
[16] *Advices in Judging of Things said to Transcend Reason, Works*, IV, 450.
[17] *The Usefulness of Natural Philosophy, Works*, II, 47.

where they do but fairly attempt . . . But I have found . . . that what pleased me for a while, as fairly comporting with the observations on which such notions were grounded, was soon after disgraced by some further or new experiment, which at the time of the framing of those notions was unknown to me, or not consulted with.[18]

Boyle is fully aware of the importance of hypotheses in inquiry, provided they be such as can be experimentally verified.

For it is none of my design to engage myself with, or against, any one sect of naturalists, but barely to invite you to embrace or refuse opinions, as they are consonant to experiments, or clear reasons deduced thence, or at least analogous thereunto; without thinking it yet seasonable to contend very earnestly for those other opinions, which seem not yet determinable by such experiments or reasons.[19]

For the use of an hypothesis being to render an intelligible account of the causes of the effects or phenomena proposed, without crossing the laws of nature, or other phenomena; the more numerous and the more various the particles are, whereof some are explicable by the assigned hypothesis, and some are agreeable to it, or at least are not dissonant from it, the more valuable is the hypothesis, and the more likely to be true. For it is much more difficult to find an hypothesis that is not true, which will suit with many phenomena, especially if they be of various kinds, than but with a few.[20]

One of the considerablest services that men could do mankind, were to set themselves diligently and industriously to make experiments and collect observations, without being over-forward to establish principles and axioms, believing it uneasy to erect such theories, as are capable to explicate all the phenomena of nature, before they have been able to take notice of the tenth part of those phenomena that are to be explicated. Not that I at all disallow the use of reasoning upon experiments, or the endeavoring to discern as early as we can the confederations, and differences, and tendencies of things . . . For it has been truly observed by a great philosopher, that truth does more easily emerge out of error than confusion. That then, that I wish for, as to systems, is this, that men, in the first place, would forbear to establish any theory till they have consulted with (though not a fully competent number of experiments, such as may afford them all the phenomena to be explicated by that theory, yet) a considerable number of experiments, in proportion to the comprehensiveness of the theory to be erected on them. And in the next place, I would

[18] *Some Considerations Touching Experimental Essays in General, Works* I, 307.
[19] *Considerations Touching Experimental Essays, Works*, I, 311.
[20] *Experiments, Notes, etc. . . . about Qualities, Works*, IV, 234.

have such kind of superstructures looked upon only as temporary ones, which though they may be preferred before any others, as being the least imperfect, or, if you please, the best in their kind that we yet have, yet are they not entirely to be acquiesced in, as absolutely perfect, or uncapable of improving alterations.[21]

Hence qualitative explanations like the "force of gravity" will do in want of better: "for there are men," he observes, with unexpected recollection. Though mechanical explanations be the most satisfactory to the understanding,

yet are not these explications to be despised, wherein particular effects are deduced from the more obvious and particular qualities or states of bodies, such as heat, cold, weight, fluidity, hardness, fermentation, etc., though these themselves do probably depend on those three universal ones formerly named . . . He may be allowed to have rendered a reason of a thing proposed, that thus refers the phenomenon to that known affection of almost all bodies here below, which we call gravity, though he does not deduce the phenomenon from atoms, nor give us the cause of gravity; as indeed scarce any philosopher has yet given us a satisfactory account of.[22]

Thus, though teleological explanations have no place in physics, teleological relations are not, as Descartes thought, to be excluded from nature: they are indeed the chief basis of natural theology. Boyle can well be called the founder of that eighteenth-century rational theology which grounded the existence of God upon the "vastness, beauty, and regular motions of the heavenly bodies; the excellent structure of animals and plants, besides a multitude of other phenomena of nature, and the subserviency of most of these to man." [23] Such a world, so vast, beautiful, orderly, and admirable, must have been created by a supremely powerful, wise, and good Author; it can be sustained only by His "general concourse."

This most potent Author and Opificer of the world hath not abandoned a masterpiece so worthy of him, but does still maintain and preserve it, so regulating the stupendously swift motions of the great globes, and other vast masses of the mundane matter, that they do not, by any notable irregularity, disorder the grand system of the universe, and reduce it to a kind of chaos, or confused state of shuffled and depraved things. (V, 519)

[21] *Considerations Touching Experimental Essays, Works*, I, 302.
[22] *Considerations Touching Experimental Essays*, I, 308, 309.
[23] *The Christian Virtuoso, Works*, V, 515.

After the first formation of the universe, all things are brought to pass by the settled laws of nature . . . Yet I look upon a law as being indeed but a notional thing, according to which an intelligent and free agent is bound to regulate his actions. But inanimate bodies are utterly incapable of understanding what a law is . . . and therefore the actions of inanimate bodies, which cannot incite or moderate their own actions, are produced by real power, not by laws. (V, 520)

God might, indeed, at any time, "by withholding his concourse, or changing these laws of motion that depend entirely upon his will, . . . invalidate most, if not all, the axioms of natural philosophy."[24] Thus there is no impossibility of miracles or of a particular providence. And thus Boyle's positivism, induced by his piety, led him, as pure rationalism induced by a similar piety had led the later Cartesians, close to a position on causation that Hume was to formulate in nontheological terms.

Most of Boyle's suggestions, both scientific and theological, were accepted by Newton, and in some form by the dominant English philosophy of science. But this scientific scepticism of Glanvill, Boyle, and the Royal Society, with its hesitancies and its unresolved inconsistencies, needed the support of a thoroughgoing empirical philosophy to become a considered and effective critical instrument, that could take its place beside the imposing rationalisms of the day. Such an empiricism was developed when the medieval philosophy of experience was employed in its turn to interpret the new science. The consequences of that enterprise we shall now proceed to examine.

[24] *The Reconcileableness of Reason and Religion, Works,* IV, 161.

8

The Empirical Tradition

I

WE HAVE EXAMINED the various ways in which men in the seventeenth century endeavored to deal with the outstanding intellectual problem presented to them for solution: how to understand the new type of natural science they had invented and how to assimilate and adjust it to their inherited stock of ideas. We have so far confined ourselves to those efforts which relied on the great Platonic theory of the method and nature of science, the theory which had been so well embodied in the Augustinian tradition in the Middle Ages and had received various minor modifications through the more direct contact with its ancient representatives brought in by Renaissance thought. We have seen how natural it was, in that age of intense concern with method, for the mathematical procedure of the new science to appear its dominant feature; and we have observed how thoughtful men, seizing on that method and developing its implications, managed to transform the Platonic-Augustinian theory into a mathematical rationalism, the first great philosophical current inspired by the impact of modern natural science. It has been clear also how those features of the intrinsic methodology of the new science which made such an interpretation natural were powerfully reinforced by the practical uses to which the resulting philosophy was to be put. That reasonable and intellectualized religious life which the Platonic tradition, even in its Augustinian form, had always supported, had come to express the aspirations of an increasing number of men; and the mathematical rationalism that seemed implicit in the new science blended easily with the political and secular rationalism of the Stoic jurisprudence to which they turned in the escape from the religious authority of feudal social organization. The rational authority which seemed the way out from political and economic conflicts fought largely in terms of theological doctrine, found a buttress in the rational authority of scientific method; and the temporary compromises in which the seventeenth-century disputes eventuated seemed to triumph in the triumph of reason itself.

It is true that the Aristotelian *Analytics* continued to furnish the model and ideal of scientific structure: veritable science was like geometry a series of deductions from first principles intuitively perceived by intellect to be true. Even those who like the later Cartesians or like the English experimentalists had come to despair that a knowledge of nature could ever be made so "scientifical" and demonstrative, had no doubt that this was the type of science which physics ought to resemble; and the triumph of Newton did much to remove that premature despair. It is true also that the greatest of the scientists, Galileo himself, was the outcome of the Padua Aristotelian tradition, and that his theory of science if not of nature was definitely Aristotelian. The new science was what it was, in relative independence of all theory; its procedure and increasingly its very concepts were generated out of its own practice. It was not so much in what they were actually doing as in how they interpreted the significance of what they were doing to themselves and to others, that the thinkers of the seventeenth century were Platonic rationalists. And it is true finally that the two most consistent and successful attempts at making that science and that intellectual world intelligible, the systems of Spinoza and of Leibniz, owed their escape from the perplexing metaphysical problems which beset their fellow rationalists to their adherence to the basic principles of the Aristotelian metaphysics and their consequent freedom from entanglement in Platonic paradoxes. Yet the mathematical atmosphere in which they worked pulled even them far from the Aristotelian philosophy of experience in their theories of method and knowledge; and their very success in achieving intelligibility has stamped them as rationalists par excellence. It is equally significant that the most searching problems raised and explored in the second generation of scientific philosophers, problems which seem to point onward to the formulations of Hume or Kant, and appear first in the criticisms of a Malebranche or a Geulincx, or the searchings of a Pascal, came not from any professed empiricists but from the very heart of the new rationalism itself. Of all the figures treated only the "peripatetick" Kenelm Digby can be said to have started from a philosophy of experience.

It was the empirical interpretation, however, which was destined to triumph in the next century, and to press rationalism so far to the wall that only by admitting most of its opponents' fundamental contentions could it survive in Kantian form. It is true that the triumph of sensationalistic empiricism owed as much to external factors in the social situation as had the previous triumph of mathematical rationalism: it was in the name of experience and sense that the great critical battles of the cultural and social revolution of the eighteenth century were fought. So powerful, indeed, did empiricism prove as a critical weapon that it survived in England and in the Vienna Circle to the mid-twentieth century; were it not for its attested social function it is difficult to see how it could have persisted so long in the face of devastating criticism, both external and internal, and in an age of transformed science. For while rationalism soon confronted insuperable problems, and lost the world though it saved its soul with science, empiricism met an even worse fate: it found itself with neither world, soul, nor science. But it still had the middle class, and so it could not die.

Where the rationalists developed the implications of that reason which was the method and form of the new science, the empiricists turned rather to the content of that science, the purely mechanical world it described, and developed the implications of such a world for the experience man can have of it. The essential drive of any of the many philosophies of experience which have arisen in criticism of inherited and accepted beliefs, is the turning from what men have thought the world to be to what they can find it actually is. However refined and sophisticated it may eventually become, a philosophical empiricism starts as a physics, a theory of nature, before it is a psychology, a theory of human nature; and however subtle may be its attempt to analyze "pure" experience, that attempt inevitably is carried on in terms of the characters of the world in which men know experience is taking place. By focusing attention on man's experience of the world rather than on the world as experienced, it has indeed always been possible to bring to the fore certain natural traits previously overlooked; and the philosophy of experience, in whatever circumstances men have appealed to it and whatever forms it has revealed, has served always the critical function of confronting men's confident beliefs with fresh evidence and "facts" and forcing them to reconstruct those beliefs in more inclusive fashion. But men cannot forget what they know and approach experience as little children; when they try, they find only what little children find, the lessons others have already learned. There is nothing paradoxical in the fact that an analysis of human experience cannot be conducted in isolation from the experienced world. If what the Greeks first saw and so clearly expressed, and what our recent biologies and psychologies have reminded us of again, be indeed true, it is a natural consequence of the fact that experience is an interaction between man and his environment. How could the interaction between two characters be construed in disregard of either?

The medieval philosophy of experience had derived all man's knowledge from his contact with nature, not from his communings with the vision in his soul. But it was an intelligible nature with which experience brought man into contact, a nature whose basic characters and traits were suited to man's grasp and expression of them in discourse or *logos*. Experience was a *logical* process whereby these expressible or logical traits of nature were brought to embodiment and expression in the words of man. The Aristotelian analysis employed grammatical terms to render the anatomy of this process, for it was convinced that the grammar of nature and the grammar of thought are one and the same. Language it viewed as the vehicle and instrument of thought, not its betrayer; things truly are what they can be said to be. Not till the sophisticated fourteenth century did the relation between what man formulates as knowledge and that of which it is the formulation cease to be a fact and become a problem.

When for a variety of reasons men sought to analyze and measure nature with a view to modifying her actions, rather than merely to classify her and express her characteristics in words, they naturally disregarded and swept away those denotative and descriptive grammatical expressions which the Aristotelian language had made all too familiar. But in their impatience they forgot they were but substituting a new language and new expressions for the old. Their very practical success might have taught them that the analytic and measurable traits of natural things and events they were so admirably formulating in their new mathematical language were as much an intelligible and logical rendering of nature as had been the older classifiable and descriptive traits. Nature was as fully the abode of a natural intelligibility, and of natural relations adapted to logic or discourse, when that discourse spoke in mathematical terms as when it spoke in Greek. And human experience was equally the vehicle whereby the structure of the world was brought to intelligible expression whether that structure were viewed as comprising geometrical relations or intelligible species.

The philosophy of experience, that is, might have developed along Spinozistic lines, rectifying rather than forgetting Aristotle. It might have changed its conception of the intelligible structure or form in the world instead of denying it all existence. It might have continued to regard experience as the instrument whereby this structure was conveyed to the mind and given rational expression. So great, however, was the desire to escape from the constricting Aristotelian type of intelligibility that all intelligibility was thrown to the winds; and so clearly did the world seem to reveal itself as nothing but a great system of bodies in motion that it was easily overlooked that even a system of bodies in motion, if it were to be known, must be an intelligible system. The great tradition of medieval Aristotelianism, deriving all science from experience with the world, was perfectly consistent when that experience was conceived as taking place within the world it described; when applied to the interpretation of the mechanical world of seventeenth-century science, it was transformed into that sensationalistic empiricism which has become in modern times the very symbol of well-intentioned confusion and paradox.

II

Before Galileo and Descartes had succeeded in combining mathematics with mechanics, the chief refuge of hard-headed opponents of scholastic verbalism and Renaissance Platonism was the tradition of Greek atomism. The vision of Democritus and Lucretius had been one of the earliest ancient philosophies to be revived, by Valla, because of its worldly human wisdom; it remained one of the most persistent because of its simple anticlerical picture of nature. It appealed to thoughtful physicians, especially in France, where medicine had never been so closely bound up with Averroistic Aristotelianism as in Italy, and where the school of Paracelsus and natural magic had not become so entrenched as in Germany. It formed also the natural complement to scepticism among the worldly wits and *libertins* whom the religious wars had hatched, some of whom managed to survive even the popular Cartesian reconciliation with a rational and worldly church. Its chief representative during the period of Cartesian domination was Gassendi, who stands both as the climax of Epicurean atomism of the Renaissance in its accommodation to a mathematical science of nature, and as the first of the explorers of the implications of that science for the traditional empirical philosophy of knowledge. Gassendi is thus with Hobbes one of the fathers of "scientific" empiricism.

The earlier French atomists had been rather in the Renaissance tradition, mechanists quite innocent of the principles of dynamics. Sebastian Basso, a physician familiar with Bruno, in his *Philosophia naturalis* (1621) expounded against Aristotle an atomistic conception in which he left undecided whether the elementary parts of bodies are Democritean corpuscles or the geometrical surfaces of the Timaeus. These atoms exist in and are moved by a fine corporeal "ether" or "*spiritus*," which is what Democritus really meant by his void; this ether is the active mover in nature, and as the presence of the divine wisdom in the world is the power of God himself. Claude Bérigard (1578–1663), a French professor of medicine at Pisa and after 1640 at Padua, opposed to Aristotle what he regarded as the atomism of Anaxagoras. Things are made of tiny ball-shaped points, of qualitatively different kinds. Whether these corpuscles move in a void or not has not yet been experimentally determined; so long as a vacuum has not been so established, it is safer to assume that there is a plenum, and that motion occurs in a continuous ring or vortex of bodies. Jean Magnien, after 1646 professor of medicine at Pavia, in his *Democritus reviviscens* (1646) defended the existence of indivisible corpuscles which have an alterable structure of parts, so that the configuration of each indivisible atom can nevertheless change—a kind of molecular hypothesis. These atoms are not only in motion in the void; they have mutual sympathies which unite them to each other to produce definite and fixed forms of composite bodies.

III

Far more influential was Pierre Gassendi (1592–1655), exact contemporary of Descartes and equally devoted to a mechanical science of nature and an ultimate reconciliation with theology. Like Pascal, he was one of the few serious rebels against the reigning Cartesianism, a heretic from the dominant rationalism of the age of Louis XIV: but unlike Pascal his criticisms were not in the interests of religion and "the heart," but rather of an empirical theory of knowledge. His *Disquisitio metaphysica . . . adversus R. Cartesii metaphysicam* (1644), in which he replied to Descartes's answers to his objections to the *Meditations*, is the first great coming to grips of scientific empiricism with mathematical rationalism. And unlike Pascal, Gassendi was the head of a small but influential band of disciples, comprising not only the remaining *libertins,* but also such literary figures as Cyrano de Bergerac and Molière, who attended his private lectures. Gassendi's hypotheses were received on equal terms with Descartes's by the English scientists, and certain of his notions, like those of an absolute space and time, were of great influence on Locke and Newton. Gassendi indeed fancied himself the creator of the great rival scientific system to that of Descartes, the system founded on sound experience. History has reserved that distinction for Hobbes; yet it is probable that Gassendi contributed far more to the actual advance of scientific ideas than his more consistent and gifted British fellow-worker.

Gassendi was a priest, professor first of rhetoric and then of theology at Aix, canon of Dijon, and from 1645 through 1648 professor of mathematics at the Collège Royale. Into his thought there flowed most of the intellectual currents of his day. Provided with a good peripatetic education, he early felt the influence of the scepticism of Charron and of the demand of Ramus for a more fruitful dialectic than Aristotle's. He came into prominence through his ambitious *Exercitationes paradoxicae adversus Aristoteleos,* the first two books of which were published in 1624. This work aimed to attack in sceptical and Ramistic fashion the entire body of Aristotelian sciences, from dialectic to ethics. The storm aroused by the first onslaught, however, led in 1624 to the famous decree of parlement against all Aristotelian critcisms, and sent him back to his scientific studies again. But it also attracted the attention of the Mersenne circle, with whom he eagerly discussed his atomistic ideas. Urged on by Mersenne, but forbidden by the decree as well as by his character of priest to advocate atomism openly, he wrote rather in the form of historical studies of Epicurus, first in 1647 defending his life and personality, then issuing a translation and extensive commentary on the 10th book of Diogenes Laertius (1649), and finally drawing up a *Syntagma philosophiae Epicuri.* The systematic statement of his own philosophy, *Syntagma philosophicum,* appeared posthumously in 1658.

Gassendi's device of shielding himself under the name of Epicurus has caused him to be regarded unjustly as a mere humanistic reviver of ancient lore. But he was living in a different age from those earlier revivers, an age of vigorous scientific interest, and he entered eagerly into all the latest discoveries, conducting polemics against Robert Fludd and Lord Herbert as well as Aristotle and Descartes. He was familiar with the Italian empiricists, Telesio and Campanella; the latter he met in French exile at Aix. Above all he studied and wrote voluminously on the new astronomy of Kepler and Brahe, and followed the dynamics of Galileo with great enthusiasm. To the ancient as well as the Italian atomists he added an appreciation of the role of mathematics, without, however, managing to integrate it any more successfully than Descartes in the details of his natural explanations.

What distinguishes Gassendi's atomism is not so much any originality of formulation, or success of detailed application, as the fact that it had to defend itself against the mathematical rationalism of Descartes. Gassendi is therefore forced to consider its foundations much more critically than his predecessors, and to pay special attention to the derivation of its basic concepts from the experience its world describes. In this process he finds himself allied with rather than opposed to the Aristotelianism he had originally attacked so brashly. Although the Logic of his final *Syntagma* retains its Ramist emphasis on imagination and method as well as on judgment and deduction, it is much less sceptical, and aims to conciliate Aristotle with a mechanistic world.

Aristotle was right: the whole content of knowledge comes from the senses and rests on the *imaginatio*. Clarity and distinctness of sense-images is its first condition. But the only possible kind of experience a being can enjoy in a world of mechanically acting bodies is sheer physical contact with those bodies: sensation can be nothing other than the physical effect produced in the sense organs by the *idola* coming from objects. Aristotle was also right in maintaining that not the matter but only the form of objects is conveyed to sense. But that form, mechanically produced, can itself be conceived only as mechanical. Not that, as Epicurus held, these idola themselves enter the sense organ; but preserving as they do the pattern and configuration of the object whence they come, they excite in the sense organ a motion of similar pattern and configuration. Sensation is not the bodily entry of anything into sense, it is the conveying of a certain pattern of motion: it is mechanical but not material. Thus the "sensible species" received in the organ are really motions which can serve as the signs of the producing objects they resemble in structure.

Although it seems to be the opinion of Epicurus that the images or qualities of things proceed by means of the external sense organs into the sense or internal faculty and soul itself, . . . it is more probable that the corpuscles gliding into the external sense organs do not penetrate to the interior faculty residing in the brain, but there is merely generated a motion of the nerves and spirits; when this motion reaches the brain, the faculty residing therein is as it were excited and moved, and apprehends the very quality of the thing made known as the impression of the corpuscles . . . Now it is fair to think that Aristotle was considering this when he said, the sense receives sensible species without matter. For thus it seems is this to be understood: the faculty of sense, which is thought to reside in the heart, is therein so advised of the impression made in the external sense-organ, that the heart is actuated not by the reception of any taste, odor, or other quality which inheres in the sensible thing, and torn as it were therefrom has been transmitted into the heart; in which case it would be receiving the species or mark of the thing together with its matter; but is moved solely by the impression of the motion which begins in the external sense-organ and ends in the internal one; in which case it is understood to receive none of the matter which was in the sensible thing. Sometimes indeed he calls the species either the motion itself, or the mark impressed by the motion so that it may serve as a certain ectype of the sensible thing, by which we learn what is the character of the thing making the impression and existing as its type or protype.[1]

These passively received sensible species or motions are always true: they alone can assure us of the existence and qualities of objects without. They always point to a definite set of physical conditions that have produced them. The causes of error thus lie not in sense itself, but in the complexity of physical conditioning occurrences with which sense images are received—the distorting medium, the distance from the object, etc. What we perceive in sense is always as we perceive it; but we often mistake the result of such a complex set of conditions for the result of a single object, and judge falsely that what belongs to a motion received under particular conditions belongs "really" to its original producer. A tower is really perceived now as round, now as square; we err only if we attribute both figures to the tower itself rather than to the effects it produces at a distance.

Truth and falsity belong therefore not to sense, but to reason, and sense images have to be "reworked" by reason to give valid knowledge of their objects. We perceive the sun as small, but judge it to be large. Reason has to "correct" any particular sense image, which in itself is too particular to be trustworthy; but this correction can only be by comparing it with other sense-knowledge.

That we should perceive that vast idea of the sun by mind alone, does not show that it comes from any innate notion; but the idea which enters through sense, so far as experience proves and reason thereto conjoined confirms the fact that distant things appear smaller than those near at hand, is by the very force of mind itself so far enlarged as the sun is found to be distant from us, and made to equal in its diameter all those radii of the earth.[2]

Thus reason working on sense images, comparing them, putting them together, and altering their dimensions, constructs "ideas" which though founded wholly on experience are truer than any particular sense image.

We can distinguish a double criterion in us: the one, that by which we perceive the sign, namely, sense; the other, that by which we understand through thought the hidden thing itself, mind, intellect, or reason. For

[1] Gassendi, *Syntagma philosophicum*, Part II, sec. III, Membrum Posterius, Lib. VI, cap. 2.
[2] Gassendi, *Disquisitio metaphysica*, In Med. III, Dubium iii.

though it be admitted that sense is at times fallacious, and hence cannot be a safe sign: still reason, in that it is superior to sense, can so emend the perception of sense as to receive therefrom no sign until it be emended, and only then proceed to think and pass judgment about the thing.[3]

By such comparison and emendation of sense, rational experience generates what Gassendi, following Epicurus, calls "anticipations" or "prenotions," by which to interpret further sense experience.

An anticipation is the very notion and as it were definition of the thing, without which we could not inquire into anything, doubt it, opine, or even name it.[4]

Only if we already have the prenotion of "man" can we say that this object here is a man. If these prenotions be clear and distinct, we can apply them to objects in correct judgments. Demonstration from them as premises is the surest way of enlarging our immediate sense knowledge.

To the question of how these intelligible principles of interpretation are conveyed to the mind, Gassendi's only answer is to fall back on the Aristotelian view.

I understand that the notion or idea or form which is called an anticipation or prenotion, is generated in the mind by incursion, or, if you prefer, by incidence, when the thing directly and in itself comes or penetrates into the sense.[5]

Such an answer ill accords with his strictly mechanical conception of experience, in which only motions and not ideas are conveyed to sense, and with his atomistic view of the world, which has no place for such intelligible forms. Gassendi is here torn between the Aristotelian conception of experience as a logical process, and his mechanical contact theory. If the latter be really and exclusively true, then all such essential prenotions and concepts must be the product of the mind working on sense and not of sense itself: they must be creations rather than discoveries.

Nevertheless these prenotions and "reworkings" of sense are of fundamental importance in Gassendi's whole philosophy of nature; for he makes clear that the very concepts of mechanistic science

[3] *Syntagma philosophicum*, Institutio logica, cap. 1.
[4] *Syntagma philosophiae Epicuri*, sec. I, cap. 2, Canon ii.
[5] *Ibid.*, Canon i.

could not possibly be derived from mechanical contact alone. Its basic notions are anything but the immediate deliverance of sense. The whole scheme of mechanical atomism, for Gassendi as for Democritus, stands revealed as a rationalistic metaphysical assumption that could not be drawn solely from the experience it describes.

The very conception of an "atom" itself is of something never experienced. Bodies are sensed as continuous and divisible; that they are made up of indivisible and solid particles is a necessary "prenotion," a logical inference or hypothesis to explain their observed behavior. Since nothing can come out of nothing, or vanish into nothing, change is intelligible only as the changing relations of what does not change. But this *principium materiale*, this *prima materia*, existing in unalterable simple and qualityless particles as the substratum of all change, is not enough to explain natural occurrences. There must be a second principle of physics, the void, empty space; and there must be time. This independent space and time do not fall into any of the familiar Aristotelian categories. They are not substances, but rather the necessary conditions for the existence of any bodily substance. They are not accidents of body, for they would be there if all body were destroyed; they are not accidents of mind, modes of thought, or "subjective," for real things could not possibly exist without them. Nevertheless the absolute receptivity of space and the absolute flow of time are "true things and real entities." They form a second principle of nature besides the atoms, a kind of reality to which the distinction of substance and accident will not apply.

Because it seems that even were there no bodies, there would still be constant Space and flowing Time, Space and Time do not seem to us to depend on bodies, or to be corporeal accidents. Nor are they indeed incorporeal accidents, inhering in any incorporeal substance after the fashion of accidents, but they are something incorporeal of a different kind from those which are commonly called substances or accidents. Whence it is made clear, that Being in its widest acceptation is not adequately divided into substance and accident, but that Space and Time must be added as two further members to the division . . . Wherefore, since Space and Time must be considered true things or real entities, although they are not what is commonly considered either substance or accident, still they truly exist, nor do they depend upon the intellect like chimaeras, since whether the intellect be thinking or not, Space remains and Time flows onward.[6]

[6] *Syntagma philosophicum*, Part II, sec. I, Lib. II, cap. 1.

It is true that such an empty time and space are not given in sense experience: they could not well be, for they do not act or exert any influence, and are hence excluded from the possibility of all mechanical contact with sense. But we have the clear and distinct prenotion of time, space, and motion; and it is evident that if there is motion, there must be a void and time. Absolute time and space, as eternal, immovable, and infinite containers of all moving bodies, are the necessary assumptions of the mechanical world. These conceptions of Gassendi, first introduced by him into modern physics, were very influential on English thought; they fitted in well with More's suggestive conceptions. Both Locke and Newton, independently of each other, developed the same absolute time and space.

For Gassendi both atoms and the void were "prenotions," independent and absolute conditions of experienced motions, assumptions made to render the fact of motion intelligible, but not themselves the product of mechanical contact or immediate sense experience. Nor did he ever hesitate in his further physical concepts to make such inferences transcending sense. The existence of empty space makes it clear that atoms cannot be identified as by Descartes with extension alone. Besides size and shape they must possess solidity, or impenetrability, and weight. Weight is an "ungenerated, innate, native, and unlosable propension to motion and instrinsic propulsion and impetus." [7] These are all Newtonian as against Cartesian concepts, and over them Gassendi fought bitterly with his rival. He maintained that all atoms move with an equal velocity; when they bump, the direction but not the speed is altered. This view he combined with an atomistic view of time, space, and motion as composed of discrete points and instants: actual motion is a combination of atomic bits of motion and instants of rest, and different apparent velocities are due to different mixtures of motion and rest. In view of these details, it is not surprising to find Gassendi admitting that all such conclusions based on prenotions not immediately revealed in sense are probable rather than demonstrative, and maintaining against Lord Herbert that absolute knowledge of the essential natures of things is denied to man's inordinate curiosity.

But this sensationalism and materialism are not for Gassendi the whole story. Epicurus was wrong in believing the harmony and

[7] *Syntagma philosophicum*, Part II, Physica, sec. I, Lib. III.

order of the universe the result of a mere fortuitous concourse of atoms. Besides space, time, and atoms in motion, there must be an infinite spiritual substance, God, who created and ordered all things in their beauty and perfect adaptation. Nearly all men possess from experience a prenotion of God—though not an innate idea. His existence is proved by the teleological argument, though His nature is incomprehensible to human intellect, bound as it is to sense. And in man, besides the corporeal soul, the principle of motion, life, and sensation, "a certain most tenuous substance, like the flowering of matter," begotten in generation and perishing with the rest of the body, there is an immortal and incorporeal soul infused by God himself. The existence of this immaterial soul is proved by the reflective knowledge man has of himself—nothing bodily acts upon itself—by man's ability to think intellectually without images, and by his consciousness of moral ideals. It is this rational soul which is the source of human freedom. It possesses a *propensio* or *inclinatio* to the bodily soul, as the instrument and material for its own activity. That these Christian additions to his thoroughgoing atomism should have laid Gassendi open to the charge of mere accommodation to the doctrines of the Church is natural enough; certainly they show little originality or personal concern. Yet the combination of strong interest in mechanistic science with little critical modification of religious beliefs was common enough in that age, and is in this. That even more difficulties are created by dividing the soul itself into two substances, one corporeal and the other incorporeal, than by the Cartesian dualism between body and soul, is probably true. Yet it is not clear that Gassendi's dualism is ultimately more inconsistent, or even very different from Descartes's; and it must be remembered that the line between material and immaterial had traditionally been drawn as Gassendi drew it rather than as his rival disposed it. And in the last analysis the Thomistic tradition which Gassendi was transforming in the light of the new mechanical view of nature was equally a compromise, if more sincere and successful, between a naturalistic empiricism and a religious spiritualism.

Gassendi's empiricism emerges in the position that all knowledge is derived from experience, while experience can be only the mechanical effect of bodily motion upon the senses. His development makes it clear that if experience be indeed only mechanical contact, a science of mechanics cannot come from such experience alone, but only from experience interpreted and "corrected" by the scientist's "anticipations" or assumptions. That is, in Gassendi is clearly foreshadowed the essence of the Kantian view as the natural outcome of the empiricist interpretation of the new physics. The only alternative would be to abandon the "scientific" nature of mechanics itself. It remained for British thinkers to pursue this second course to an equally paradoxical outcome.

9

Thomas Hobbes: Rational Calvinist and Empiricist

I

AMIDST the many confident system-builders of the seventeenth century, Thomas Hobbes is the only worthy peer of Spinoza. And Hobbes too elaborated his system by developing the consequences of the new science. Like Spinoza, he was willing to go the full length, and like Spinoza he would brook no compromise with the prejudices of conventional ideas. All his life Hobbes was, as he confessed, a rather timorous soul, "a man of feminine courage." He was born in 1588, while the Great Armada was threatening the shores of England; his mother, he tells us, was brought to bed of twins, himself and fear. So fearful was he in the troublous times of the seventeenth century that he kept candles burning in every room at night. This fearful nature can be readily used to throw light on the overwhelming desire for security which inspires his political philosophy, and to which he was willing to sacrifice more than most others have been. Yet it remains a fact that he went on writing and publishing the most outrageous ideas, while Spinoza, less willing to violate the common decencies of thought, did not.

Both men, however, at bottom held the vulgar opinions of mankind in the same contempt, Spinoza with more of pity and understanding, Hobbes with more of impatience. Both took the same delight in the very idea of the necessity of things. Both held the conception of an all-embracing system, which should extend from the fundamental principles of the universe to their practical implications for ethics and politics. Both came to very similar political conclusions, that social life should aim primarily at securing harmony and peace between men; though they differed on the political mean for attaining it. And both maintained the same realistic and rather brutal view of human nature, having little forbearance for sentimental illusions.

At this point, however, the fundamental differences of temper and thought make their appearance. Hobbes was nothing if not British: to him everything intellectual was a plain matter, if we would but open our eyes and see. To Spinoza the true way of life was as difficult as it was rare. The delightful vigor of Hobbes's English abounds in acute and penetrating phrases; yet they are the happy hits of a poet rather than the subtleties of a thinker, for he had a fundamental dislike of intellectual refinement. He drives straight to the point without any beating around the bush: things are "nothing but" what his prejudice demands. He is the champion illustration among modern philosophers of the "nothing-butter." Spinoza was caught by the vision of the method of the new science, by the very fact of science itself, that things are bound up in a network of logical relations and implications; he worked out in detail what that mathematical method, that fact of a mathematical science, meant and implied. Hobbes drove impetuously straight to the world the new science purported to describe, to the results of that method; he worked out valiantly the implications of a world consisting of "nothing but" body in motion. In consequence the world of Spinoza is a geometrical world, that of Hobbes is a mechanical world: without, it must be noted, the mathematical exactness on which his master Galileo had insisted. Had Hobbes been seriously impressed by that condition of the new science, his all-embracing system would have been impossible. Spinoza, in a word, saw that man can *know* the universe: this fact suggested to his mind the question, What must the *universe* be like in which man *knows?* and the answer, It is caught up in that logical order of nature which is God. Hobbes saw rather that man knows the *universe* to be body in motion; this fact led to the question, What must *man* be like in such a universe? and to his vision of human nature.

II

Hobbes was a very vigorous personality, whose portrait will remain in the memory when the ideas he for the moment embodied and focused on his problems have been forgotten. Like Spinoza, he had been trained in the ideas of the Schoolmen; and that training remained with him for good or evil in his most "modern" moments. Aubrey, who has painted his lineaments in unforgettable fashion, tells us, "he did not much care for logick, yet he learned it, and thought himself a good disputant." The logic he learned in the Schools, and to which he never proved unfaithful, was, it is clear, the Ockhamite logic lingering on in the British universities. On leaving Oxford he took service with the Cavendishes as tutor to the young son, selected, we gather, more for his youth and spirits than his learning, a service destined to be lifelong. He entered into the social life and concern with the turmoil of public affairs which this connection made possible, learning much of human nature from primary sources. Nor did he neglect the histories and the poetry of the ancients. If he missed the true springs of human action, it was not for want of observation or record. For a time he was intimate enough with Francis Bacon to serve as amanuensis as the ex-Lord Chancellor walked about his estate at Gorhambury diligently collecting his thoughts. Despite, or perhaps because of this friendship, Hobbes never showed the slightest sympathy with experimentation or an experimental philosophy. It was not till he was forty that he discovered mathematics and the world of science it was opening up; geometry had not been highly thought of at Oxford, still wedded to Aristotle. In a gentleman's library he happened upon a copy of Euclid open at the 47th proposition of Book I, which he read. "By God," he exclaimed, "this is impossible." But that impossibility won his heart; his affection grew so ardent that he would lie in bed drawing diagrams on his thigh and on the sheets. The bent of his mind is revealed by his complaint that algebra was too much admired, and so hindered an appreciation of the power of lines. He undertook, in fact, the reform of geometry, in the interest of making it more like mechanics: all its concepts must come from constructions, for if we cause the figures ourselves we will then know their properties completely. He became involved in a long-drawn-out mathematical controversy with Wallis and other members of the Royal Society over the squaring of the circle, interminable because he obstinately refused to surrender his convictions.

From 1634 to 1637 he was traveling on the Continent, where he met and conversed with Galileo in his confinement, and also associated with Père Mersenne and the Cartesian circle in Paris, as well as with the more empirical Gassendi. After the Restoration he vigorously attacked Boyle and the Royal Society, which had refused him membership as no investigator: they were wasting their time with observation and experiments upon nature. They were in fact too Cartesian, and Descartes himself "relied too much on experiments." Mere experimentation, he was convinced, adds nothing to knowledge. This hostility is a clear illustration of the fact that "empiricism," of which Hobbes is generally regarded as the grandfather in its British form, has nothing to do with experimentalism: it is rather a dialectical elaboration of a mechanical conception of experience. Certainly in Hobbes's mind it is as deductive, as *a priori*, as rationalistic, as "rationalism" itself.

It was not till 1642, when he was already fifty-four years old, that he published his first philosophical work, *De Cive*. He thus appeared upon the stage of ideas as an opinionated old man; Descartes, it will be remembered, was a dogmatic young man. The year before in his objections to Descartes's *Meditations* he had indicated clearly his divergence from what was becoming the reigning intellectual system. Under the stimulus of Galileo and the Paris group he had already formulated his vision of a universe all of whose activities could be nothing but body in motion.

I was studying philosophy for my mind's sake, and I had gathered together its first elements in all kinds; and having digested them into three sections by degrees, I thought to have written them, so as in the first I would have treated of *body* and its general properties; in the second of *man* and his special faculties and affections; in the third, of *civil government*, and the duties of subjects. . . . Whilst I contrive, order, pensively and slowly compose these matters; (for I only do reason, I dispute not;) it so happened in the interim, that my country, some few years before the civil wars did rage, was boiling hot with questions concerning the rights of dominion and the obedience due from subjects, the true forerunners of an approaching war; and was the cause which, all those other matters deferred, ripened and plucked from me this third part. Therefore it happens, that what was last in order, is yet come forth first in time.[1]

And so what was to be the culmination of a great system of the philosophy of body, body natural, both lifeless and human, and

---

[1] *De Cive*, in *English Works of Thomas Hobbes*, ed. Sir William Molesworth (1839-45), II, xix-xx.

body artificial, or the state, was worked out under the pressure of circumstance before the foundation had been fully laid. Hobbes finished *The Elements of Law* in 1640, but fled to Paris without publishing it. The *De Cive* appeared there in 1642, the *Human Nature* and *De Corpore Politico*—selections from *The Elements of Law*—in 1650, and Hobbes's masterpiece, the *Leviathan*, in 1651. It was not till 1655 that the *De Corpore* was ready, and the *De Homine* not till 1658. This suggests what is in fact the case, that Hobbes's vision of human nature and of civil society owes much to his observation and experience of men and their passions, and little but its terminology to his philosophy of body. That philosophy came at middle age to the mind of a man with definite convictions about human nature and politics; he used it to round out and generalize, to rationalize his political conclusions. His philosophy of nature, his formal analysis of human nature, served, as such enterprises have ever served in the long stream of British empiricism, as the handmaidens of politics. They set upon his vision of man's estate, and what man must do to be saved, the stamp of a science destined soon to sweep away all those theological concepts and categories in which others were still fighting their battles. Hobbes is the first major thinker to apply the intellectual methods and concepts of the new science to human affairs: he did it to gain authority for his particular program. Yet so potent did that method and those concepts prove to be that they were adopted by men who bitterly opposed his program. And Hobbes's conception of science and his procedure of starting from an analysis of human nature entered into the main stream of British thought to become the great intellectual weapon for demolishing his own vision of the body politic, and to determine the subsequent course of British philosophizing. It became the intellectual method of the Liberal tradition.

III

Hobbes was enormously impressed by Galileo's mechanics. He swallowed it whole, as he counseled men to take their religion, without chewing. He never really understood it, nor the method by which it was supported; and his life was one long controversy, wrong-headed and perverse, with those who were defending and extending it in England. He contributed nothing to the new science himself; he would have been an obstacle had men been able to take his ideas seriously. Yet he got the main point very clearly: he saw its vision of a universe of bodies in motion. And when he came to interpret the nature of that science, he fell back on what he had learned in the Schools as his guide; and the theory he formulated, based as it was on the great medieval Ockhamite philosophy of science, laid down the main outlines and set the problems which the two luminaries of the next generation, Newton and Locke, so brilliantly developed. Hobbes is the first of that long line of British thinkers who explored what the Ockhamite theory of knowledge would become in a universe of bodies in motion. He transformed it into what the world has since known as "British empiricism."

Philosophy (or science) is "such knowledge of effects or appearances, as we acquire by true ratiocination from the knowledge we have first of their causes or generation: and again, of such causes or generations as may be from knowing first their effects." [2] This definition is carefully framed to exclude from science not only knowledge of particular facts by sense or memory, but especially theology: for God, being eternal, is not subject to generation, nor is revelation acquired by ratiocination. Science is thus very rigorously a knowledge of the "generations" of things, of the way they are produced and constructed. We can be said to know truly only when we have followed, either actually or in thought, the manner in which things are put together out of their component parts.

A cause is the sum or aggregate of all such accidents, both in the agents and in the patient, as concur to the producing of the effect propounded; all which existing together, it cannot be understood but that the effect existeth with them; or that it can possibly exist if any one of them be absent. [3]

When we know all these accidents or conditions, and see how they must inevitably give rise to the given effect, we can then demonstrate that effect from its generating causes. Wherever we can pick a phenomenon apart into its constituent elements and put it together again, there we can have science. In the strictest sense this is possible only with our own constructions:

Of those things only is science through *a priori* demonstration conceded to men, the generation of which depends on their own will. [4]

[2] *De Corpore, Eng. Works*, I, 3.

[3] *De Corpore, Eng. Works*, I, 77.

[4] *De Homine*, in *Latin Works* (*Thomae Hobbes Malmesburiensis Opera Philosophica quae Latine Scripsit*), ed. Molesworth (1839–45), II, 92.

This occurs in geometry:

For since the causes of the properties which the particular figures have lie in those lines which we have ourselves drawn; and the generations of those figures depend on our own will; no more is required to know any characteristic of a figure, than that we should consider whatever follows from the construction we ourselves have made in drawing the figure. Therefore from the very fact that we ourselves create the figures follows the existence of a geometry and its demonstrative nature. (II, 93)

And therefore Hobbes insisted that the definitions in geometry should be based on the manner of construction: they should give the generating causes.

On the other hand, because the causes of natural things are not in our power, but lie in the divine will, and because the greatest part of them, namely the ether, is invisible; we who cannot see them are unable to deduce their properties from their causes. Still it is granted us to proceed, by deducing the consequences of those properties which we do see, so far as to be able to demonstrate that their causes could have been such and such. This demonstration is said to be *a posteriori*, and the science itself, physics. And since we cannot proceed by thought even from effects to causes in the natural things which are produced by motion, without a knowledge of what follows from each kind of motion; nor to the consequences of motions without a knowledge of quantity, which is geometry; it cannot but be that some things even in physical demonstrations are demonstrable *a priori*. (II, 93)

Thus physics too must be a rigorous postulate system resting on constructions we ourselves make.

Science thus has two parts, the reduction of phenomena to their probable causal components and conditions, and the *a priori* reasoning from the presumed causes or modes of generation of things to the observed effects. Following Galileo, Hobbes calls these two aspects of method "resolutive" and "compositive," or analytical and synthetical. He has a very rigid conception of the process of reasoning itself: it must be based on strict identities, or what are now called "tautologies." It is essentially "computation," the addition and subtraction of names. Now a name is the "mark" of a "conception," a proposition is the "coupling of names," and truth is the "right coupling of names," in which the two names are both "marks" of the same thing. Scientific truth is thus a property of speech, not of things; science takes the form of long chains of identities. It must be a rigidly deductive system, standing as a whole as the "mark" of the order of nature because its first term is a "mark" of that which is the universal "cause" in that order, and because all subsequent terms are "marks" of the same cause. For this to be so, the "first terms" or principles must be names chosen to express the causes or manner of generation in the natural order: they must be causal definitions. If reasoning is to be a computation of causes, every "principle" employed must indicate a cause. Hence science is deduction from definitions which are the "marks" of natural causes. The object of science is thus to construct a rigorous postulate system that can "stand for" or serve as the "mark" of the observed causal order of events: its task is to throw that order into demonstrative form. Almost to the last detail this whole combination of a logical nominalism with a realistic empiricism as to perception is a version of the Ockhamite logic.

I V

What then *is* that cause of natural events from which proceed both the order of nature and the computation of reasoning? It is the motion of bodies.

The causes of universal things are manifest of themselves; or (as they say commonly) known to nature; so that they need no method at all; for they have all but one universal cause, which is motion.[5]

Had not the great Galileo himself said as much? And so Hobbes set out bravely to develop the implications of the view that all causation is efficient causation,—is the mechanical contact of bodies, and that every phenomenon that appears to experience is part of a system of mechanical motions. How could it be otherwise if reasoning is the construction of a chain of identities, and if the sole "cause" with which all its terms are identical must be motion? Like Spinoza, Hobbes refused to exclude man from his necessary system; he had the same philosophic and systematic rather than scientific and particular interest, the same goal of constructing a genuine science of human nature and conduct. What is the great world that confronts man's gaze? Body in motion. What is man himself? Body in motion. What is the human soul? Body in motion. What is desire?

[5] *De Corpore, Eng. Works*, I, 69.

Body in motion. And finally, what is knowledge itself? Body in motion. Psychology is a branch of mechanics, dealing with matter moving according to mechanical laws.

In terms of this mechanical system, knowledge must be a physical event, a "motion in the internal substance of the head." [6] It is to be explained in terms, not of the implications of ideas, not even of the "computation of names," as in Hobbes's theory of science, but of the purely mechanical relations between its elements. And its elements must be the physical effects of the mechanical contact of bodies with our body; they must be the products of "sense," and of that "decaying sense" that is "imagination":

The first beginnings of knowledge are the phantasms of sense and imagination. So that if the appearances be the principles by which we know all other things, we must needs acknowledge sense to be the principle by which we know those principles, and that all the knowledge we have is derived from it.[7]

Thus for Spinoza, knowledge is explained in terms of the implications between ideas, in terms of logic. For Hobbes, it is explained in terms of the mechanical contacts between bodies, in terms of mechanics. For Spinoza, a "cause" is logical, is always a formal cause, something intelligible in itself. For Hobbes, a "cause" is always a mechanical contact between bodies, is always an efficient cause; being thus given as brute fact, it is in itself unintelligible.

From this sturdy and fairly traditional Ockhamite empiricism Hobbes attempts to show how all the knowledge we have of the world is derived from the phantasms of sense. Since we cannot understand anything unless we have reduced it to its elements and constructed it out of them ourselves, let us undertake such a construction of our knowledge from sense, not as it actually grew, but as our analysis reveals it might have grown. Let us assume that all the world has been destroyed except a single man. There would still be left for him all the phantasms that had come from the objects he had seen. They would still appear as if they were external and had a being without him.

If therefore we remember or have a phantasm of anything that was in the world before the supposed annihilation of the same; and consider, not that

[6] *Human Nature*, in *Eng. Works*, IV, 4.
[7] *De Corpore, Eng. Works*, I, 389.

the thing was such and such, but only that it had a being without the mind, we have presently a conception of that we call *space:* an imaginary space indeed, because a mere phantasm, yet that very thing which all men call so . . . Space is the phantasm of a thing existing without the mind simply; that is to say, that phantasm, in which we consider no other accident but only that it appears without us.[8]

In analogous fashion we find by similar abstraction from the other qualities of bodies the phantasm of time, as that of movement in so far as we imagine in it only before and after; for a moved body leaves in the mind a phantasm of its motion. Unlike the various rationalists who turned to a Platonic conception of time, Hobbes remained true to the Aristotelianism of the Ockhamite tradition. The parts of space and time are divisible and enumerable by the intellect; "division is the work of the intellect, by the intellect we make parts . . . Therefore to make parts and to consider them are identical." [9] It is because we construct such series ourselves by a human process of construction that we can understand them.

When to these phantasms of space and time we add the notion of body, we find it contains nothing but the idea of a limited part of space existing independently of ourselves.

Having understood what imaginary space is, . . . let us now suppose some one of those things to be placed again in the world, or created anew. It is necessary, therefore, that this new-created or replaced thing do not only fill some part of the space above mentioned, or be coincident or co-extended with it, but also that it have no dependence upon our thought. And this is that which, for the extension of it, we commonly call *body;* and because it depends not upon our thought, we say is *a thing subsisting of itself;* as also *existing,* because without us; and lastly it is called the *subject,* because it is so placed in and subjected to imaginary space, that it may be understood by reason as well as perceived by sense. The definition, therefore, of *body* may be this, a body is that which having no dependence upon our thought, is coincident or coextended with some part of space.[10]

In the details of his physics Hobbes follows Galileo, making much of the idea of force or endeavor (*conatus*), defined as "the motion made through the length of a point and in an instant or point of time." (I, 206)

[8] *De Corpore, Eng. Works,* I, 93.
[9] *Examinatio et emendatio mathematicae hodiernae . . . Johannis Wallisii,* in *Latin Works,* IV, 56.
[10] *De Corpore, Eng. Works,* I, 101.

We have seen how knowledge can be constructed as a computation of marks, as a deductive postulate system; we have seen also how it can be constructed out of sense through a consideration of its simplest elements. But there remains a third way in which knowledge is to be understood, as it is actually generated by the impingement of the motions of the world upon our senses, through mechanical contact. And so Hobbes undertakes in good Ockhamite fashion to explain it through its physical origin and growth, having already determined what that origin and growth must be in a world where motion is the only cause. Knowledge takes its origin in sensation, which as the effect of mechanical contact must itself be mechanical, a motion. The senses are set in motion from without, that motion is transmitted first to the brain and then to the heart, and the heart commences a motion in reaction, the beginning of which (*conatus*) is the sensation proper. The growth of knowledge is to be understood as the mechanical succession of images or phantasms, themselves motions. Sensations are the images or representations of the qualities of the things that cause them from without. But the only qualities of things without are the mechanical powers to produce qualities in the brain; and qualities in the brain, ideas and conceptions, are really nothing but motions in the "internal substance of the head."

Hobbes's Aristotelian empiricism has run afoul of his Galilean conception of the world and of experience. For Aristotle sense was a vehicle of meaning, whereby the intelligible aspect of things is conveyed to the mind. But Hobbes's world possesses no forms, no sensible or intelligible species; that is mere "insignificant speech." A conception or phantasm is no longer the actualization of the intelligible aspect of something; it is the mechanical result of the motion of the object of the idea. The relation between knowledge and its objects is not the relation between a knowing mind and a knowable world, it is the relation between physical effect and mechanical cause, between two motions. Effects know their causes, motions know motions.

When we see an object, we do not see that object as it is, body in motion; we see colors in the head. When we see colors in the head, we don't really see colors, we contain the mechanical reaction of the "internal substance of the head" to motion from without. To be knowledge under these conditions, the phantasm or sensation must be an "image" or "representation" of its cause; but we know it is not. What we see, we cannot know, and what we know, we cannot see; yet what we see is the element and origin of all knowledge. Moreover, the relation between phantasms themselves is purely one of mechanical contact: they follow mechanically in the brain, in conformity with the laws of motion. Our science is a system of implications, a "computation of names"; that science is caused by mechanical contact with a world of bodies in motion. How is a system of implications to be extracted from mechanical contact? How is it to serve as the "mark" of motion? Here Hobbes is trying to develop the implications of the position that no implications exist. How are images which resemble objects to be derived from objects they don't resemble? In this application of Aristotelian empiricism to a world in which experience cannot be such as that empiricism assumed, and cannot satisfy the conditions of that empiricism, all the elements are present for a paradoxical "problem of knowledge." Mechanical science pictures a world in which the existence of a science of mechanics is unintelligible. The further that science is extended, the more pressing becomes the problem, how is any science possible?

At times Hobbes uses the language of a thoroughgoing phenomenalist:

If we do but observe diligently what it is we do when we consider and reason, we shall find, that though all things be still remaining in the world, yet we compute nothing but our own phantasms. (I, 92)

As for the causes of sense, we cannot begin our search of them from any other phenomenon but that of sense itself. But you will say, by what sense shall we take notice of sense? I answer, by sense itself, namely, by the memory which for some time remains in us of things sensible, though they themselves pass away. For he that perceives that he hath perceived, remembers. (I, 389)

But from his earliest writing Hobbes never abandoned his fundamental mechanism, and this suggested phenomenalism is never taken seriously.

Originally all conceptions proceed from the action of the thing itself, whereof it is the conception.[11]

[11] Human Nature, Eng. Works, IV, 3.

Hobbes is the first major illustration, abundantly confirmed by later "empiricists," that if experience be construed in terms that are exclusively mechanical, "empiricism" as a construing of knowledge becomes impossible and paradoxically self-contradictory. An "empirical" philosophy of science and knowledge has become possible for us again, only because our own science no longer conceives the world in exclusively mechanical terms. Hence there is no longer any reason to construe "experience" in the purely mechanical fashion that seemed demanded in Galilean and Newtonian science. We can take it also in biological and social terms, and hence in addition, like the Greeks, in logical terms. Kant, Hegel, Darwin, and Einstein —to say nothing of moderns like Dewey—have thus freed us from the epistemological dilemmas of Hobbes—and of Locke and Newton.

The problem of knowledge implicit in these joint assumptions Hobbes never himself set upon the stage. At the last moment he drew back, in the faith that the effect of a motion does know that motion: motion in the brain does "know" directly its external cause. He held fast to the Ockhamite realism as to sense-knowledge: whatever its mechanism, sensation is a genuine and "intuitive" knowledge. This realism was all the easier for him in that body and mind were not two alien and irrelevant substances; they were alike members of the same inclusive system of bodies.

The object is the thing received; and it is more accurately said that we see the sun, than that we see the light.[12]

That Hobbes never himself abandoned this realism for a subjectivism, even in those passages where his language seems clearly to point to later discussions, as in the "imaginary" character of space and time, is abundantly clear.

Actually, of course, despite Hobbes's saving insistence on this continuity between nature and mind, there yawns a gulf between his psychology and his mechanics, between phantasms and desires, and the motions of bodies. The psychology receives little support from the physics; to call the elements of human nature "nothing but motions" does not make them so, nor does it even make them appear to be so. Psychology must in fact use an introspective method.

[12] De Corpore, Eng. Works, I, p. 391.

Whosoever looketh into himself, and considereth what he doth, when he does think, opine, reason, hope, fear, etc., and upon what grounds; he shall thereby read and know what are the thoughts and passions of all other men upon the like occasions.[13]

And this method reveals "trains" of phantasms and desires which we may know must be motions in the internal substance of the head, but which we certainly do not observe to be. It is these trains of imagination which, psychologically considered, constitute reasoning. Sense persists by inertia, and the contact between different phantasms, in accordance with the laws of association or mental mechanics—since they are really motions—explains the following out of implications. Such trains, when "regulated," form intelligence: in them desire is in contact with the means of satisfying itself.

And so, as a result of its adventures in the world of bodies in motion, the Ockhamite theory of knowledge finds itself transformed in Hobbes's hands into modern sensationalism or "scientific" empiricism. Knowledge has now become a mechanical relation between images whose only connection with things is that of physical effects with their causes. Science is left as a system of implications of things that have no implications, but only contacts; and its origin lies in elements which are copies of things they don't resemble.

V

These paradoxical consequences, however, important as they were to become in shaping the intellectual problems of the succeeding age, were far from occupying the center of Hobbes's attention. It was no part of his ambitious program to become the grandfather of British empiricism, nor would the begetting of the intellectual method of the long tradition of liberalism and constitutionalism have struck him as other than a bastard spawning. His whole concern with physical science was in fact but instrumental, as a means of implementing his vision of human nature and what man must do to be saved. To Hobbes that vision had come as a veritable revelation of man's estate, and the way of salvation to him so clear he preached as a genuine gospel. For Hobbes was at bottom a profoundly religious nature, though like Spinoza his insight into man's great needs and what alone could satisfy them carried him far from

[13] *Leviathan, Eng. Works,* III, xi.

familiar creeds and churches of his day, so far that he too won the scornful epithets of atheist and blasphemer. And though like Spinoza he had the discernment to perceive the immense support the new science could bring to his prophetic vision, though like the Dutch Jew he is that rare figure, an utterly thoroughgoing and consequent modernist, willing to sacrifice all the familiar details of traditional faith the better to preserve its very essence, it was not science or the play of body upon body that held his heart. His insight was focused upon man: man's impotence and need, his bitter cry for salvation at any cost, and the true salvation that could come only through a realization of his utter and absolute dependence upon a power greater than himself.

For what was Hobbes's gospel of deliverance but in its own way a new reading of that very Augustinian and Calvinistic demand for authority and power above all things, for a visible grace that would make man whole, which in its familiar theological trappings he held in such scorn? What Hobbes had found was not so much a new religion as the true dwelling-place of God, the true Church and its sacraments. His life-long quarrel with the ministers, far deeper than his other ceaseless controversies, was not the intellectual opposition of an atheist. It was not even the political opposition of an Erastian. It was rather the religious opposition of the sectary who has discovered the true church polity to embody the common faith. Man can be saved only by unquestioning submission to that "mortal God," the great Leviathan, whose power transcendeth that of any man; and its stern decrees alone are the vehicle of saving grace. For in the midst of conflicting loyalties, of the claims of bishops and synods, priests and elders, Hobbes has found the ultimate spiritual power. He has discovered the real religion of modern times, that unshakable religion, founded on solid experience and confirmed by reason, the religion of the State. *Non est potestas super terram quae comparetur ei.*

Though Hobbes's enterprise was born of the conflicts of his own day, it was no particular set of party principles which he threw into rational form. It was not even a political theory expressive of those deeper and underlying class conflicts beneath the surface of party compromises that he formulated. Hobbes was no Locke, nor was his civil philosophy either so influential or so transitory as that of the Whig apologist. Hobbes rose above the defense of any particular form of state, whose destinies might for the moment be in the hands of this or that party or class. What he saw was rather the vision of the human Commonwealth itself as a spiritual power, of the political bonds that bind men together in society as the highest expression of the ordering might of God or Nature.

It is true indeed, that to man by nature, or as man, that is, as soon as he is born, solitude is an enemy; for infants have need of others to help them to live, and those of riper years to help them to live well. Wherefore I deny not that men (even nature compelling) desire to come together. . . . Although man were born in such a condition as to desire it, it follows not, that he therefore were born fit to enter into it. For it is one thing to desire, another to be in capacity fit for what we desire.[14]

Man needs his mortal God with an infinite need; yet only that God can bring man to him. In the words of the hard-headed Englishman we can almost catch the accents of Pascal, the cry of that Puritan generation for the mystery of grace.

Hence the religion that Hobbes seeks to blend with science is not that humanized and liberal faith of which the Cambridge Platonists spoke so persuasively; it is not that trust in man's rational moral powers, that confidence in the essential divinity of human nature, which suited so well the complacent worldliness of the succeeding Newtonian Age. The fact that Hobbes has succeeded in giving it completely rational expression, that it is in every fiber a wholly secularized faith, could not blind those serene rationalists or those comfortable humanitarians to its essential incompatibility with their own self-reliant and individualistic moralism. For a century, though they eagerly grasped his very weapons from his hand, and turned them toward the fight for his own secularism, they could not face a battle of their own without a preliminary skirmish against this religion of Hobbes as the very essence of irreligion. Their instinct was sounder than their reasons, usually Hobbistic to the core. Hobbes like Spinoza did indeed push the implications of natural science much further and much more plain-spokenly than any of the other compromisers of his day, or of a hundred years to come. But what divided him by a great gulf from the rational secularists of the Enlightenment was not that he had advanced further than

---

[14] *De Cive*, Eng. version entitled *Philosophical Rudiments Concerning Government and Society, Eng. Works*, II, 2n.

they along the intellectual road they too were traveling: it was that he had used his mastery of their own weapons to lend enduring form to that very conviction of human weakness, of an individual impotence which only submission to a miracle of power could transform, which they were most valiant to attack. The real crime of Hobbes, like that of Spinoza, was at bottom not that he had abandoned forms of religion which men still cherished, but that he defended the substance against which they were in full revolt. As Spinoza is the essence of medieval piety made wholly transparent and consistent, so is Hobbes the very spirit of the Reformation, of Calvin and the Puritans, brought down to earth and rendered in completely rational terms—total depravity and prevenient grace wholly naturalized in the world of bodies in motion. Such was his vision of man and man's deliverance; and after two centuries of liberalism, in religion and in politics, who is there today that can claim it is not still a living vision?

VI

Hobbes was not the first to strip the Augustinian insight of its theological verbiage. Machiavelli before him had shown equal power to express it in wholly secular and naturalistic terms. But those realists of the Renaissance who had not the imagination to fall into the snares of Platonic Humanism, did not advance to any science of politics; for them the political nature of man was the occasion of an intelligent art of social control rather than of a reasoned theory. This may have been wisdom as well as lack of demonstrative model; at least their thoughtful technique seems closer to modern needs than the social syllogisms of the eighteenth century. It remained for Hobbes to bend the new science definitely to political problems; his is the first serious attempt at working out a mechanical science of society, a social physics founded on a mechanistic rendering of human nature.

Hobbes's civil philosophy is usually viewed in the perspective of our own day rather than of his. He is taken as a reactionary defender of absolute government against the champions of popular liberties, a political theory in disrepute in the nineteenth century, though hardly without determined advocates in our own. His rational grounding of the "religion of the state" is certainly opposed to those liberal and constitutional theories that later borrowed his own methods; though whether it or they can pass as the more "modern" and "up-to-date" is still an open question. But to his contemporaries Hobbes's originality scarcely lay in the defense of a view of human nature and of the absolute sovereignty of a supreme controlling authority which all but a handful shared. What was novel to them and excited their wrath was his thoroughgoing and revolutionary secularism, his complete identification of this supreme authority, of all spiritual power, with the civil state. Not that human nature needed the yoke of organized control, and owed to it absolute obedience—Papists, Anglicans, and Puritans equally insisted on that —but that control should be concentrated wholly in and obedience owed exclusively to the secular Sovereign—that was his damning insistence. The aim of his whole great philosophy of body was to free morals and politics from subservience to theology—to make them branches of natural science, such as could be taught in the schools, he said. In his earliest statement, the *Elements of Law*, in 1640, he takes as his object the reduction of the doctrine of justice and policy in general to the rules and infallibility of reason after the fashion of mathematics, the one branch of learning "free from controversies and dispute." Hobbes's later adventures lend this praise of mathematics a touch of irony.

Hobbes wrote, not in favor of the Stuarts, which would have gained him the support of at least one party, but "against the ministers" of every party, which naturally won him the enmity of all. His fundamental opposition was to any sort of "spiritual" power, Catholic, Anglican, or Puritan; his fundamental aim, to vindicate the sovereignty of secular authority against any religious claims. Whether that secular authority was King or Parliament was a secondary matter.

Temporal and spiritual government are but two words brought into the world to make men see double and mistake their lawful sovereign.[15]

The claims of quarreling theologians to men's allegiance can lead only to anarchy. The dispute "between the spiritual and civil power has of late, more than any other thing in the world, been the cause of civil wars in all places of Christendom." The only alternative is that

[15] *Leviathan, Eng. Works*, III, 460.

all church government depend on the state and authority of the kingdom, without which there can be no unity in the church. . . . There is hardly a dogma touching the service of God, or the human sciences, from which is not born first dissensions, then quarrels, outrages, and little by little wars; which happens not at all because of the falsity of the dogmas, but because such is the nature of men that flattering themselves their opinions are of some wisdom, they desire all others to hold them in the same esteem.[16]

Religion must remain wholly in the control of the secular Sovereign, not only because otherwise it is a perpetual menace to civil peace; by its very nature religion is a civil matter. Religion is essentially law, a means of governing men; it is not an intellectual affair, a matter of knowledge and belief, at all. It is an instrument of social control and social cohesion, not of truth. Theology is not a science; we can know rationally nothing of God. The attributes we ascribe to him signify only our desire to honor him; "all that will consider, may know that God is, though not what he is." [17] Above all there must be no arguing. "For it is with the mysteries of our religion, as with wholesome pills for the sick, which swallowed whole, have the virtue to cure; but chewed, are for the most part cast up again without effect." [18] Hobbes belonged, in fact, like most sensible Englishmen in that age of uncontrolled chewing, to that school of Anglicans which regards the Church of England as a branch of the Civil Service, and the Archbishop of Canterbury as the Secretary of State for Divine Affairs. In this he was not only a prophet of what the Church of England was to become—with Parliament deciding for her what true religion is, and what God is, as by law established; he points to that whole modern conception of religion, which makes the Church the best instrument for maintaining morale in times of foreign war and domestic dissension. That is, in the midst of the theologically minded seventeenth century, he was a singularly modern Christian. And like many such today, as Aubrey relates, "he would have the worship of God performed with musique."

A Church is a company of men professing the Christian religion, united in the person of one Sovereign, at whose command they ought to assemble, and without whose authority they ought not to assemble. (III, 459)

[16] Cited without source in W. R. Sorley, A History of English Philosophy (1920), pp. 53-54.
[17] Human Nature, Eng. Works, IV, 60.
[18] Leviathan, Eng. Works, III, 360.

The Sovereign is the supreme Pastor; bishops derive their powers, not *Dei gratia*, but *regis gratia*. Reason would even dictate that the sovereign should impose his own creed and worship on all his subjects:

for I do not see at all why he should permit things to be taught and done from which he judges eternal damnation will follow.

To be sure, general toleration is usually the wisest policy, so long as it does not lead to discord and disturbance of the peace; but there can be no "right" to freedom of worship. The doctrines "that every private man is judge of good and evil actions," and "that whatsoever a man does against his conscience is a sin," (III, 310, 311) are utterly seditious and repugnant to civil society. By the very fact of living in a commonwealth a man surrenders his "conscience" to the law. There is no argument by which a man can be convinced that God has spoken immediately to some other man, "who, being a man, may err, and, which is more, may lie." (III, 362)

To be sure, the law commanded and revealed by God is the highest of all authorities. But only the Sovereign can decide what *is* the divine law. He alone can determine what books are canonical, and what is their authorized interpretation; else there would be open anarchy. Even the Decalogue and the Gospels owe their authority to the sovereign. The former were the civil laws of Moses as Sovereign of the Jews, and hence have only the authority of civil laws; the latter are not laws at all, but only appeals to faith. Moreover, a law such as, Thou shalt not steal, has no meaning until the Sovereign has determined what is property. Only the Sovereign has the authority to interpret, "Thou shalt not kill," to mean, "Thou shalt kill, if the scale be large enough." Sin, justice, and injustice alike receive a definite content only from the civil law. The Christian, indeed, owes perfect obedience to the laws even of an infidel Sovereign. His faith is internal and invisible; if he resists the command of his Sovereign to practice an infidel worship, he ought to expect his reward, not on earth, but in heaven, and should rejoice in his just martyrdom.

From the same motives of social peace and cohesion, Hobbes opposed the other chief claim to a divided sovereignty raised in his day. He defended Parliament against the judges, like Coke, who protested at its acts in the name of the Common Law. Law cannot be custom, tradition, or prescription; else would it be something irrational and anarchic. It must be a statute consciously commanded, or the equity of a rationalizing chancellor with Sovereign authority.

Law is the word of him who by right hath command over others.[19]

Custom can be law only on the principle that what the Sovereign permits he commands. It is this side of Hobbes's doctrine of sovereignty which was adopted in the early nineteenth century by Austin and the Utilitarian Radicals, and used by them in support of the authority of reforming Parliaments against tradition-bound judges. It was in the name of this Austinian revival of Hobbesian principles that Justice Holmes defended the right of Congress to pass social legislation in defiance of a presumed "spirit of the common law" and the corporation lawyers; and it has entered deeply into the American debates over the Supreme Court.

Hobbes's aim, in all this harsh defense of a unified sovereignty, was to establish a strong central government, able to enforce peace, that men might enjoy their individual goods unmolested. He had no special interest in whom or what this power should be; though he thought monarchy was strongest, he never felt its superiority to rule by an assembly could be "demonstrated" rigorously like the rest of his theory. He had no love for Charles; and when rebuffed by the Anglican clerics at his court in Paris, and frightened at the uproar his Erastian views had caused amongst the French ecclesiastics, he easily transferred his allegiance to Cromwell. This return to England in 1651 makes clear that he was inspired, not by any sentimental loyalty to the Stuart cause, but by devotion to a strong government that would give law and order. His view was, any old Sovereign will do if he be but strong enough, and no Sovereign is of much value who lets theologians dictate to him, or allows his subjects to beat him in battle, like Charles. Peace is the indispensable means to securing the end of the commonwealth, men's common enjoyment of their several goods: the one common good is peace, and the power of the Sovereign is the indispensable means to peace. No matter how arbitrary it may prove, that power is better than the anarchy that must reign when private judgments as to the common good are allowed free sway. To prevent such dis-

[19] III, 147; see also *A Dialogue of the Common Law*, VI, 26.

cord, the Sovereign should have complete power over all expression of opinion; he should have unrestricted control over all property—Hobbes allows no right of private property save on sufferance—he should rule the courts, the magistrates, the resources for war. The "liberty of subjects" is only that which the Sovereign deems it wise to permit, or which he cannot alienate. Since men submit to this power to preserve their lives, a subject can "justly" oppose the attempt of the Sovereign to destroy him. He may, in fact, "justly" refuse to serve in the army. But if he so assert his natural and inalienable right of self-preservation, the Sovereign has an equal natural right to kill him for disobedience, if he can apprehend him. There is no injustice on either side, but only power against power; men are then back in the state of nature.

For the admirer of strong government, man is "by nature" an anarchist. Like all such, Hobbes insists on sovereignty from without, because in his view of human nature he is an individualist. Man acts always from self-interest, from desire, from "motion toward or fromward"; his existence is one perpetual striving of power after power. This is Hobbes's secularized version of the Calvinistic doctrine of "original sin," a view familiar enough today. Such a view of man is the very antithesis of that entertained by nineteenth-century liberalism. For that rosy doctrine, men can be trusted to be social, to act justly and rationally toward each other; therefore government should keep its hands off, except to guarantee individual freedom. For liberalism, man is by nature social, therefore he should strive for individuality as an end. For Hobbes, men can always be trusted to seek their own private interests; therefore government must force them to cooperate for their own good. "Individuality" and conflict is the essence of human nature; for that very reason conflicts need to be harmonized by social control, by a social power from outside.

In terms of our own more complexly organized society, Hobbes's vision of human nature and its needs is that held by those "realistic" enough to be aware of the many power struggles between groups and classes, not to say nations, a truly Hobbesian *bellum omnium contra omnes*. It is the vision shared by the late Nazi government of Germany and by the present Marxian government of Russia in forcing cooperation for their respective versions of Hobbes's social peace and common good. Marxian political theory merely replaces Hobbes's individuals by economic classes; and the Communists are perfect Hobbesians in giving the Communist Party unrestricted power to end economic conflict and to establish the "classless society"—Hobbes's social "peace."

VII

For Hobbes, this vision of human nature drawn from shrewd observation and reflection coincided with his vision of nature learnt from Galileo. It was essential to his aim of freeing morals and politics from theology and making them branches of natural science, to fit them into his deductive system of bodies in motion. So moral and civil philosophy must have the same mechanical principles as natual philosophy: bodies artificial must resemble bodies natural. The life of men is really a play of body on body; there is no order in motion, whether in nature or in society, save as it is imposed from without. Men are bodies in motion, to be restrained only by force; their "desire" or "endeavor" is but the universal *conatus* or "inertia" shared by all bodies. As bodies have no logical relations of implication, but only sheer contacts, actions and reactions; just so men have no natural social relations, but only sheer bumpings.

Hence the method of establishing this vision rationally must be that of mechanics: "composition" from the "simple motions" of human nature. Just as our reason can fully grasp a phenomenon only when we can put it together out of the elements and "simple motions" which combine to generate it, so too we can understand the commonwealth only as the "compounded effect" of the "natural motions" of its parts, when we can construct it rationally out of the actions and desires of men taken in isolation.

Geometry is demonstrable, for the lines and figures from which we reason are drawn and described by ourselves; and civil philosophy is demonstrable, because we make the commonwealth ourselves.[20]

Politics and ethics, that is the sciences of what is just and unjust, equitable and iniquitable, can be demonstrated *a priori;* because we ourselves make the principles by which we know what justice and equity, and their op-

---

[20] *Six Lessons to the Professors of the Mathematics,* Epistle Dedicatory, *Eng. Works,* VII, 184.

posites injustice and iniquity, are, that is, the causes of justice; laws and compacts.[21]

What, then, are the "simple motions" of human nature? what are the desires and endeavors of man? What would man be like in a "state of nature"? And what "compounding" of these desires or motions, what agreement of wills, is necessary, if there is to be a commonwealth? What "social contract" must men observe if they are to live together in peace for their common good? The nature of that commonwealth can be understood only in terms of its elements and its manner of generation out of them.

There is no question here of historical genesis, but only of rational construction; Hobbes is concerned, not with the past, but with what the commonwealth must be. The "social contract" never took place as an historical event, it is always taking place; for without it men could not possibly live. The state of nature is "natural" only in the sense that the "natural motion" of a cannon-ball is in a straight line: it is what human life would be like if man's natural impulses were allowed free sway, without the necessary restraint of authority. The social contract is a rational postulate, a "definition" containing the "cause and generation" of society, not a brute event. What man would be like could he live without a sovereign, what the "natural motions" of men would be were they not in fact always compounded, we can only infer from how they act even in a compounded state.

When taking a journey man arms himself and seeks to go well accompanied; when going to sleep he locks his doors; when even in his house he locks his chests; consider what opinion he has of his fellow subjects, when he rides armed; of his fellow citizens, when he locks his doors; and of his children and servants, when he locks his chests.[22]

Observe what happens in times of civil war; observe the normal relations between sovereign states with no superior, "having their weapons pointing and their eyes fixed on one another." (III, 115)

From such evidence we can infer that *homo homini lupus*, that left to themselves men would be in a state of perpetual war, *bellum omnium contra omnes*, in which every man is enemy to every man. Hobbes gives an unforgettable description. There would be no difference between right and wrong, for "force and fraud are in war

[21] *De Homine, Latin Works*, II, 94.   [22] *Leviathan, Eng. Works*, III, 114.

the two cardinal virtues." (III, 115) There would not even be the right of might, for the weakest has strength enough to kill the strongest. The only right men would possess, the sole "natural" right or *ius naturale*, is "the liberty each man hath to use his own power, as he will himself, for the preservation of his own nature, that is to say of his own life"; (III, 116) and to that end "every man has a right to everything, even to one another's body." (III, 117) Little good it would do him, for every other man would have the same right; there would be only "continual fear and danger of violent death; and the life of man solitary, poor, nasty, brutish, and short." (III, 113)

Reason points to the conditions that must be established if civil peace is to prevent this open war. It makes clear that for their own self-preservation men must seek peace and follow it, and the conditions necessary for peace, and that to secure it a man must lay down his right to all things if others are also willing to do so. If men are to live in peace they must keep their promises; they must return good for good, and not ingratitude; they must practice mercy, and refrain from vengeance, cruelty, outrages, and pride; they must display moderation and justice; they must submit their differences to impartial judges. These things they must do if they are to live together at all. Taken together, they constitute the "law of nature," *lex naturalis,*

a precept or general rule, found out by reason, by which a man is forbidden to do that which is destructive of his life, or taketh away the means of preserving the same, and to omit that by which he thinketh it may be best preserved. (III, 116)

This law of nature lays down the conditions without which society and human life would be impossible: it supplies the postulates from which alone civil peace and self-preservation can be deduced; it prescribes what men must do to be saved.

But while these conditions, this law of nature, is binding *in foro interno*, and man cannot but desire they should prevail, they do not of themselves obtain *in foro externo*; it is not safe for one man to practice them alone, man cannot save himself.

For he that should be modest and tractable, and perform all he promises, in such time and place where no man else should do so, should but make himself a prey to others, and procure his own certain ruin, contrary to the ground of all laws of nature, which tend to nature's preservation. (III, 145)

Reason dictates that to attain peace all men must agree to abide by its conditions; but no man will or can, unless he is sure the rest will keep their agreement. The only motive that can insure the keeping of this "contract" is the guarantee that a sufficient power will enforce it.

Covenants of mutual trust where there is a fear of not performance on either part are invalid. (III, 131)

Without such an adequate power of enforcement, without the willingness to abide by that power, social existence is inconceivable.

A commonwealth is said to be instituted when a multitude of men do agree and covenant, every one with every one, that to whatsoever man or assembly of men shall be given by the major part the right to present the person of them all, that is to say, to be their representative, every one, as well he that voted for it, as he that voted against it, shall authorize all the actions and judgments of that man or assembly of men, in the same manner, as if they were his own, to the end, to live peaceably amongst themselves, and be protected against other men. (III, 159)

To appreciate the cogency and plausibility of Hobbes's argument, we have only to consider our own "state of nature," present international relations. Reason makes clear that giving up the H-bomb and other nuclear weapons is necessary to maintain peace. But no nation judges that it can do this alone, without the guarantee that the others will do so also. And as yet there is no international Sovereign with power and authority to enforce such an agreement.

In Hobbes's version of the "social contract," each individual pledges himself to every other,

I authorize and give up my right of governing myself, to this man, or this assembly of men, on this condition, that thou give up thy right to him, and authorize all his actions in like manner. (III, 158)

Since peace and defense is the end of his contract, obedience to the Sovereign must be rendered until he proves powerless to enforce them, when the contract is dissolved until a new power is accepted. The Sovereign himself, being no party to this contract, cannot be held any account; Hobbes is careful to leave no loophole for sedition. Only on such terms can the power to enforce social peace be obtained.

Hobbes is still operating with the traditional concepts of political theory—the state of nature, natural rights, the laws of nature, the social contract, implied consent. He interprets them throughout with an eye to the analogies of mechanics, in terms of inertia, contact, action and reaction. But though his concepts are legal in form, like those of all political theory till Bentham, and though he gives them a mechanical twist to ground them in his philosophy of body, their real content is utilitarian. Given human nature, an absolute sovereign power is necessary to make human existence possible.

All actions and habits are to be esteemed good or evil by their causes and usefulness in reference to the Commonwealth.[23]

And though the Sovereign is author of all civil law, the sole interpreter of the law of nature and the law of God; though "justice" and "injustice," "right" and "wrong," are his to define and command: "good" and "evil" are not, nor are the conditions of their attainment. Good and evil are no arbitrary fiats, they are independent and objective, inherent in the natural relations of things to man. The moral laws built on the basis of the "laws of nature" or of self-preservation are the rational means of attaining these natural goods. The indispensable rational condition of finding it safe to observe these moral laws is the presence of a power compelling others to be rational also; for rational action is not an individual but a social matter. The conditions of rationality in conduct are inherently social. Man cannot act rationally toward his fellows without the social power of enforcing rational action on all men hanging over all. In the last analysis, the "arbitrary commands" of the Sovereign are not wholly arbitrary: unless they regard the conditions of civil peace, his power will crumble. As the instruments of that power, they have a moral sanction rooted in the nature of things, for they are the indispensable means of attaining man's natural good. Fear is the only binding force, the only motive that can subdue man's desires to the service of his own rational good. The presence of the policeman is a rational necessity for human morality. No mere future damnation, but swift and certain earthly punishment, must be the lot of the transgressor.

Thus Hobbes works out the notion of a science of human nature

[23] *Behemoth, Eng. Works,* VI, 220.

operating through an art of social control for the common good. His psychology may be inadequate: of that there can be no doubt. His vision of human nature may be one-sided and distorted: of that there is more question, for it is a recurrent vision. Least of all should it shock the heirs of Paul and Augustine and Calvin; nor should good Christians complain that morality is built around the need for personal salvation, and buttressed by the threats of wrath to come.

But in the very process of lending a rational structure to man's ancient lack of faith in himself, Hobbes forged the rational tool whereby his successors were to triumph in their overweening confidence and self-esteem. For Hobbes's method can be easily turned against his vision: is absolute power necessary to social peace? is human nature a sheer bumping? And the liberals of the next age, Locke and Bentham and the rest, owed far more to the method of Hobbes than to that of his theological and legal opponents.

The Order of Nature

BOOK FOUR

The Order of Nature

I

The Newtonian Age

HOBBES was the first to erect a science of man and of society on the model and with the principles of the new mechanical physics. His was the first thoroughgoing attempt to explain the acts of man and society through knowledge of their causes and generations rather than of their purposes and ends—in terms, that is, of the springs of action rather than the ends of conduct. But the only immediate effect of Hobbes's pioneer enterprise was to engender a swarm of horrified refutations; and the elaboration of his scientific vision, the erection of a structure that could pass as a social physics, belongs to the eighteenth rather than the seventeenth century. Hence when it came the working out of the science of man was directed, not to Hobbes's social peace and the "common good," but to that freedom from interference by a meddling government which made it the "ideology" of the middle class: it became the great intellectual weapon and achievement of the Enlightenment.

I

The term "enlightenment," which is used in various languages—*Aufklärung, éclaircissement, illuminazione*—to denote the widely shared intellectual currents distinctive of the eighteenth century, expresses the judgment of its inventors upon their own attainments. It suggests an independence of the past, a self-reliance and a valuation of new intellectual methods which the term "renaissance" does not emphasize; though to our own sophisticated eyes the difference between a period of "renaissance" and one of "enlightenment" is not great, and the "Heavenly City of the eighteenth-century philosophers" now seems to us to illustrate a type of mentality not essentially alien to that of the thirteenth-century Schoolmen. Indeed, the thirteenth and the eighteenth centuries are the two great "Ages of Reason" in Western culture. It is our generation, of course, that has made the real break with the past, and is for the first time genuinely on its own—so runs our prejudice.

Viewed with what objectivity we can summon up, the Enlightenment strikes us as the first thoroughgoing attempt to reconstruct the traditional ideas and institutions of Western society in the light of the demands of the triumphant business spirit, by means of the intellectual method presumed to have led to the triumphs of Newtonian science. The middle class at last possessed a powerful, well-organized instrument for criticism, and an adequate intellectual basis on which to erect a new type of social organization. The major social changes, the fundamental shift of economic power from landlords to business men, had already been largely completed, at least in Holland and England and France. The new scientific spirit to consolidate and extend these changes was now ready at hand. The intellectual leverage to alter the lagging political and legal "superstructure," as the Marxians have it, and to adapt it to the existing economic realities, was ready for the elaboration.

So the Enlightenment really meant the rapid spread of the aims and ideals of business enterprise and of the intellectual tests and method and model of Newtonian mechanics. It meant the emergence of a rounded middle-class culture, an ideology capable of satisfying most of the intellectual needs of those it served. This alliance of the middle-class mind with the ideas discerned in the new science was of incalculable significance. It meant that a definite and intellectually imposing expression was given to middle-class ideals, which gained all the prestige accruing from the success of mathematical physics. It meant that the creation of a social science, which then as today seemed to promise so much for the human spirit, if only it could—or can—be achieved, was carried through with a pretty single-minded attention to the interests of the middle class. The first body of ideas which in modern times could claim to be a science of man and society became quite naturally the creed of the merchant and the business man, and was bent to the service of private gain and commercial prosperity. We can understand the momentous consequences of this alliance of the middle-class mind with the ideas of the new science of man and society, by considering what might have happened had the achievement of a social science been delayed a century, and then worked out under the conditions of the early industrial revolution and the emergence of an industrial proletariat.

The set of ideas which constituted the Enlightenment represented a far greater break with the past than the compromises of the Renaissance and the Reformation. The intellectual foundations of the world in which we are still lingering were laid in the eighteenth century. Even today in America only a few, and those mostly in academic circles and hence unimportant, have ever got beyond them in their thinking. Men still consider their world in terms of Newtonian science; they are still living, as Whitehead has put it, upon the accumulated capital of ideas laid up by the scientific pioneers of the seventeenth century. They still feel bewildered and afraid when it begins to dawn upon them that it is no longer possible to live by the political and economic theory worked out for the business men and proprietors of the Age of Reason—and free competition. The method and aim of Newtonian science have been transformed by the scientists; that earlier commercial individualism has in fact been rapidly giving way to newer forms of corporate industrial organization and welfare politics. Yet the most widely accepted social theory and ideals, in America rather more than in Europe, still bear the impress of Newtonian science, with its rigid, deductive, and inflexible concepts, and of the private self-interest, the irresponsible competition, the "rugged individualism" of that earlier commercial age. Under those eighteenth-century ideas business triumphed; they are still good enough for the practical business man.

On the other hand, under the Enlightenment there were worked out the highest ideals of cooperative human living our Western world has ever achieved: the ideals of freedom, of the equal worth of all men, of toleration, of cosmopolitanism, of peace. These eighteenth-century moral ideals men fell away from in the nineteenth century, under the influence of Romantic non-rationalism; and they have been actively challenged by great organized social programs in the twentieth century. But in the midst of our present ideological conflicts, we have been driven to realize that despite their difficulties in adapting themselves to the demands of an industrial civilization, the moral foundations of our own world were also laid in the eighteenth century.

Two major intellectual enterprises color the thought of the Enlightenment, and set its philosophic problems. First, the mathematical physics of the seventeenth-century scientists was erected into a dominating system of "natural philosophy," which profoundly affected all other ideas of the world and tended to push into the background everything that could not be comprehended in its rather narrow and precise terms. Secondly, human nature was subjected to a detailed causal analysis in terms modeled as closely as possible upon the successful mechanics; this generated a "mental and moral philosophy" which its creators hoped could stand side by side with natural philosophy and determine the principles of all social science. Isaac Newton was the preeminent exemplar of the first enterprise, John Locke of the second. In England and in France, and to a considerably lesser extent in Germany, they stood as the twin gods of the Age of Reason, the twin symbols of science in the emerging middle-class culture.

Both Newton and Locke were not so much pioneering minds exploring on the frontiers of human knowledge as systematizers of traditions that had already acquired considerable momentum—Newton, of the conflicting intellectual methods, the ideal and world-view of seventeenth-century science; Locke, of the political and religious struggles of the middle class for constitutional government and secularism and humanism in religion. Hence their ideas could become immediately popular and influential. Neither was a really original mind, as some of their contemporaries were original: both were rather a single jump ahead of their informed co-workers. To be sure, both were much more original than what they were taken to stand for. But both offered successful compromises; and, like all compromisers, they raised far more problems than they settled, and became the starting-point for further inquiry.

Newton became in his own lifetime the symbol of both a method and an idea. The method for which he came to stand was usually called in the eighteenth century the "geometric spirit." It meant the endeavor to find a deductive system of science, depending on initial axioms themselves discovered by "analysis." Inspired by his example, men set to work confidently to become the Newtons in every field, especially in the various branches of the science of man and of society—in business life, in politics, in religion, art, and morality. They undertook an initial analysis of their complex subject-matter to find the axioms involved—an analysis which not unnaturally usually confirmed their previous insights and prejudices—and then arrived at their conclusions by a dialectical development of the consequences of these principles. Newton's success in Natural Philosophy stamped this "geometrical" or "analytic" method as the one scientific method to be applied universally. Locke for his part showed, as Voltaire put it, that it was possible to share fully this geometrical spirit "without undergoing the hard labor of learning mathematics."

Newton stood also as the symbol of an idea, the idea of nature as a rational and harmonious order, to be found by this method in any subject-matter—an order in striking contrast to the confusion and irrationality introduced by previous men into their traditional ideas and institutions. The goal of thinking was the search for this rational order. What was rational was *ipso facto* natural, and what was natural was what appealed as reasonable to the enlightened common-sense of the progressive thinker—especially, for the middle-class business man, what led to prosperity and wealth. The history of eighteenth-century thought is therefore largely the story of the search for the rational order of nature, expressing itself in natural laws, natural rights, a natural religion and a natural morality.

This method and this idea were what Newtonian science meant to the intelligent and educated men of the Age of Reason. For them, science was essentially a great liberating idea, an idea that could free men from the past they so much wanted to leave behind. In the nineteenth century science became what it so largely is today, primarily a marvelous technique bearing miraculous practical fruits. But in the eighteenth century science meant rather a secular explanation of life, a rational alternative to tradition, a revolutionary substitute for a theology of whose controversies men had grown tired, and for an antiquated set of social institutions from which they desired release. In the eighteenth century, the word "scientist" conjured up the image of the astronomer in his observatory scanning the heavens with his telescope and reflecting upon the marvelous mechanism of creation: today it most often suggests the inventor in his laboratory smock, holding up a test-tube in which he has himself created a startling improvement in No-u-dont Toothpaste. We have advanced from mathematical calculation and mathematical order to their more important fruits in television, electronic computers, and Sputniks. Consequently our own science is both far more deeply rooted in the technical processes of our society, and far less appealing as a philosophy of life, that can set men free from their prejudices and prepossessions.

It was of such a scientific rationalism that Newton served as the eighteenth-century symbol. This rationalism was the constructive intellectual force of the Age of Reason, relied upon for building the new ideas and social organizations. John Locke served rather as the symbol of sensationalism and empiricism, of the critical force capable of destroying the old superstitions and institutions. Empiricism, because it contained the seeds of scepticism—seeds which acute minds speedily coaxed into bloom—because it made every "reason" for anything ultimately unintelligible, was the great weapon of the radical critics, the best leverage for getting rid of old beliefs and institutions. But empiricism was inadequate by itself to suggest any substitute for what it had destroyed; and when pushed to the bitter end, as by Hume, it destroyed all rational faith in anything new as well, even in science itself. Such sceptical empiricism ends always as a conservative apologetic: in default of the reason that is no more, man has only the wisdom of experience to trust. Thus end the Humes, the Burkes, and the A. J. Balfours.

Rationalism, on the other hand, though it can show how everything has its reason, and has to be so, and hence easily becomes the weapon of conservatives and apologists, a leverage for supporting that which is, as in the Thomists and Scotists before, and in the right-wing Hegelians afterwards; can also be easily pushed into the rational proof that something better is possible than that which happens to exist. It is the great constructive radical philosophy; and today the most confirmed of "rationalists" are the Marxians—in both the social functions of rationalism.

Neither rationalism nor empiricism, in fact, is inherently conservative or radical. Both when pushed to the limit, develop conservative implications; and when fused, checking and aiding each other, they form together an admirable critical instrument. The philosophy of the eighteenth century, consequently, taken as a whole, can be best described as a rationalistic empiricism. Though the two types of thought certainly constituted different strains, and could easily be pushed into opposition if the full implications of either were worked out, an opposition that justifies the traditional contrast; in fact, and certainly in their social function during the Age of Reason, they were fused into a powerful if inconsistent body of ideas. Both followed essentially the same method, analytical and dialectical; both made many of the same ultimate assumptions. Under the aegis of nineteenth-century science, both were constructively combined into an "experimentalism" whose intellectual power still impresses us. But the problems of the eighteenth century were essentially critical; so at that time they were combined in a double-edged critical weapon, a weapon double-edged in every sense. For empiricism, destroying older ideas, soon got out of bounds, turned against its ally, and attacked any rational science itself. Behind this intellectual attack is the fact that in reality science soon went too far for the middle class, as it shows signs of doing again today; and the Enlightenment ended in a return to non-rationalism and faith, in the Romantic reaction. Ostensibly stabbed in the back by its ally, empiricism, science in fact was too successful for the middle class: it had to be discarded when it began to prove dangerous, and they had secured what they wanted from it, emancipation. The philosophers were called in once more to set limits to its activity. It was as technology that science became popular once more in the mid-nineteenth century.

The philosophic record of the eighteenth century shows consequently a double growth of ideas: the development of Newtonian science into the idea of a universal rational order, and the development of empiricism into a universal negation. The two movements went on hand in hand, indeed, especially if one considers those who used ideas as weapons rather than as toys, in the same man. Voltaire admirably illustrates their perfect fusion. Newton and Locke, in fact, though taken as symbols of two different things, were actually, as Locke would have been the first to insist, in pretty complete philosophic agreement. They shared the same method, they made the same assumptions, they were led to face the same problems, and to emerge, quite unintentionally in both cases, at the same conclusions. Both were typically eighteenth-century blendings of the empirical and rationalistic tendencies of the day.

II

Isaac Newton (1642–1727) won his reputation and influence as a symbol because he actually succeeded in realizing the ideal of the seventeenth-century scientists: he was really able to formulate a mathematical interpretation of nature, and unlike Descartes, to do it in genuinely mathematical terms. Like Galileo and Descartes, he too regarded nature as a tissue of properties, precisely ordered, the connections of which can be expressed in terms of mathematics. Like them, he aimed "to subject the phenomena of Nature to the laws of mathematics"; [1] but unlike them he had succeeded. He had found the mathematical principles and techniques to fit the various observations of the astronomers, like Kepler's three laws of planetary motion, and the "two new sciences" of Galileo, into a single mathematical system. He had done what had been predicted: he had furnished the mathematical proof that the universe is a perpetual motion machine. And so he reaped the glory of a century of patient work. No wonder Pope exclaimed,

> Nature and Nature's laws lay hid in night;
> God said, Let Newton be, and all was light.[2]

God had let others be also; but Newton reaped the harvest. Newton's name became synonymous with Science. The eulogies ranged from Addison's sober prose, "the greatest mathematician and philosopher that ever lived," [3] to more imaginative ranges of fancy:

> 'Twas thence great Newton, mighty genius, soar'd
> And all creation's wondrous range explored.
> Far as th'Almighty stretched his upmost line,
> He pierced, and thought, and viewed the vast design.[4]

> From Heav'n's unbounded depth, she cried, I stole
> Angelic fire and form'd a Newton's soul.

[1] *Principia Mathematica*, Andrew Motte tr., Preface (ed. 1803), p. ix.
[2] Pope, *Intended Epitaph for Sir Isaac Newton, Works,* Cambridge ed., p. 135.
[3] Addison, in *The Tatler,* Aug. 30, 1710.
[4] William Melmoth, *Of Active and Retired Life.*

Taught him the secret walks of God to tread;
And twixt the starry worlds his spirit led . . .
Yet when the suns he lighted up shall fade,
And all the worlds he found are first decay'd,
Then void and waste Eternity shall lie,
And Time and Newton's name together die.[5]

Halley in his *Eulogy* went even further:

Newton, that *reach'd* th'inseparable line,
The nice barrier twixt human and divine! [6]

By 1789 eighteen editions had been published of the *Principia*. Newton himself was rather hard to read, and more fitting to repose on the shelves of a gentleman's library than to be found in his hand. So a flood of popularizations in the vernaculars began to flow steadily to satisfy the popular demand to know what it was all about. By 1789, there had appeared forty in English, seventeen in French, eleven in Latin (for the German and continental trade), three in German, and one each in Italian and in Portuguese. Perhaps the most popular of all was Count Alogrotti's *Newtonianism for Ladies*.

Newton was able to enjoy his triumph in part at least because a multitude of scientific workers had prepared the ground. Since the days of Galileo there had been a detailed working out of the mathematical interpretation of nature in a number of specific fields, accompanied by an experimental application and checking of many of its principles. These men had early banded together to pool their ideas and discoveries in societies called "academies" and modeled on the academies of the Humanists, whose primary purpose was to purify the various vernacular tongues. In the seventeenth century, scientists, outside Holland at least, were rarely connected with a university: it was not till the very end of the period that the newer German universities and Cambridge opened their doors to the new science. The earliest of these scientific societies, after that of Telesio, was the Accademia dei Lincei, which flourished at Rome from 1600 to 1630; perhaps the most fruitful was the Accademia del Cimento, which published between 1657 and 1667 the records of the investigations of Galileo's associates and pupils, of whom Torricelli was

[5] Aaron Hill, *Tears of the Muses, Epitaph.*
[6] Edmund Halley, *Eulogy of Newton.*

preeminent. The Royal Society, first organized in 1645, received its charter in 1662, the Académie des Sciences was established in 1666, and Berlin followed in 1700 with Leibniz at the head of its Prussian Academy. Thus was gained a certain modicum of that official support for science of which Bacon had dreamed in his Salomon's House.

The most fruitful work was done with fluids and gases. Torricelli and Pascal laid the foundations of an exact hydrostatics; Guericke, Mariotte, and Boyle developed the principles of aerostatics. In optics, Huygens had carried further the earliest triumphs of the mathematical interpretation of nature of Kepler and Descartes himself.

Newton was also greatly assisted by the fact that the advance of mathematical thought enabled him at last to formulate the mathematical instrument for reducing motion to mathematical law, the lack of which had held back Descartes, Hobbes, and others. He developed the "method of fluxions," a form of the calculus. The calculus was invented independently by Leibniz, and had been closely approached by several other mathematicians; that generation was ready for this indispensable instrument. Newton did not formulate his method of fluxions very well or very logically, and the acute Berkeley was able to shoot logical holes in it. But it was adequate for his purposes, for dealing in precise manner with the direction and growth of a curve; and since any regular motion can be represented as a curve, it was able to subject all motions to the laws of mathematics.

Newton effected one other specific scientific discovery of major importance: in optics he succeeded in applying the method of mathematical analysis to color, which emerged not as the simple quality it had been in Aristotelian physics, but as a complex relational thing. Newton's analysis made more plausible than ever the exclusion of such qualities from the "real world" of matter in motion. Newton always insisted that "the science of colors becomes a speculation as truly mathematical as any other part of optics." [7]

Newton himself was not technically a "philosopher." He was at once something less, and something more,—one of those men, like Darwin, Planck, Einstein, Boas, or Freud, who succeed in formulating ideas that make philosophers necessary, and to whom philoso-

[7] *Opticks* (ed. 1721), p. 218.

phers should look with a mixture of extreme annoyance and deep gratitude. It is safe to say that had Newton—or someone else—not published his *Principia Mathematica* in 1687, there is hardly a single subsequent thinker whose thought would not have been profoundly different. It might perhaps have been more sterile, perhaps less confused and more consistent; but at least it would have been different. The ideas formulated by Newton have been ever since an intellectual fact to be reckoned with, and his philosophy of nature has been the starting-point of all attempts to understand nature, whether men have accepted it as ultimate, or have attempted to get behind it to something more ultimate and real. Not till this century have the facts amassed by inquiry seriously shaken its main outlines. This body of Newtonian ideas can be viewed objectively today, for it has disappeared from our own rapidly shifting natural philosophy. The great Newtonian system of thought—as contrasted with his specific scientific discoveries—which for two centuries passed as the truth about our world, has crumbled before our eyes. It is now dead, we are told—so dead that most of our philosophical works discuss it interminably, and vie in pointing out just where Newton made the wrong assumptions. A strange kind of mortality, to be sure! Newton may be dead, but he is certainly not buried; and his ghost seems as healthy as ever, and busily engaged in haunting us.

Newton's own thought turns out on examination to be rather different from Newton the symbol, both in method and idea. We shall consider his method, in which he worked out a quite different conception of the nature and goal of science than that for which he came to stand in the popular mind, a conception elaborated by Locke, and developed in detail by Berkeley and Hume into the main stream of the British tradition, the conception here called "observationalism." At the same time he both suggested and made inevitable a second interpretation of science and its goal, an interpretation destined to come down through the nineteenth century as the great rival philosophy of science to that of the British thinkers: the Kantian critical philosophy. We shall then examine Newton's idea of what he called "the real world." His notions, especially his ideas of mass, space, and time, created puzzling problems for scientists, theologians, and philosophers. They not only raised insuperable difficulties for Locke, Berkeley, and Hume, and for subsequent

British empiricists to this day. In the hands of Euler and the German physicists they led straight to Kant. Together with his conception of God as a principle of mechanics, they determined the course of Protestant rational theology. They form the background of nineteenth-century philosophic idealism, and they remain, one suspects, partly responsible for the recent outburst of speculative theology on the part of contemporary British and American mathematical physicists.

To understand the double aspect of Newton's method, as well as the concepts in terms of which he suggested his thought about the "real world," it is necessary to remember something of the background these ideas had in the British scientific mind of the previous generation. We have already touched on the two main strains in British science, the one predominantly mathematical and allied with the Platonic tradition in its metaphysical presuppositions and its basic physical concepts, the other primarily experimental and not nearly so hostile to Aristotelian ideas. The former was much influenced by the speculations of Henry More and his fellow Platonists, and received scientific statement in the words of Isaac Barrow, Cambridge mathematician and Newton's own teacher. The latter was associated more closely with the "physico-mathematical experimental learning" of the Royal Society; we have seen it illustrated in Joseph Glanvill, and most brilliantly represented in the outstanding English scientist before Newton, Robert Boyle. Newton himself was very consciously the heir of both these scientific traditions, the mathematical and the experimental; the characteristic ideas of both flowed together in his own inconsistent thought.

2

Newton's Philosophy of Nature:
Its Problems and Consequences

I

IN HIS METHOD Newton was closer to Galileo than to any of the
other seventeenth-century variations upon the method of the *Posterior Analytics,* and to those more experimentally minded Frenchmen who kept a critical attitude toward Descartes: to Roberval,
Gassendi, and Pascal. He had not seen Descartes's vision of a universal mathematics, and while he hoped that all phenomena might
be mathematically explicable as forms of motion, he was not certain: he lacked what More called Descartes's "inexsuperable confidence." He was delighted to have reduced the palette of color to a
mathematical pattern: he always insisted that "the science of colors
becomes a speculation as truly mathematical as any other part of
optics." [1] But he carefully distinguished between mathematical and
physical propositions. He thought it possible that some physical
propositions might not be expressible in mathematical terms. On
the other hand, while he was sympathetic to confirmed experimentalists like Boyle, and quite willing to lend the prestige of his name
to the rather aimless fooling around with things that consumed the

This chapter has already appeared, in different form, with additions from
Chapter 1, in *Philosophical Essays in Honor of Edgar Arthur Singer, Jr.,* ed.
F. P. Clarke and Milton C. Nahm (Philadelphia, 1942), pp. 335–57.
   The attempt is being made here to distinguish sharply between Newton's
science, which, following his own usage, is called his "natural philosophy,"
philosophia naturalis, the eighteenth-century term for "physics," and his more
general philosophical interpretation of that science, here called his "philosophy
of nature." It is somewhat doubtful whether Newton himself felt the need
of making this distinction as clear-cut as seems necessary to positivistically inclined thinkers today.
   [1] *Opticks* (1721 ed.), p. 218.

time of many of the members of the Royal Society, he insisted strongly that nothing could be called really scientific knowledge that was not mathematically demonstrable. He tried, indeed, to keep a proper balance between an unlimited confidence in mathematics unchecked by experience, and mere experimenting unaccompanied by mathematical analysis and demonstration. He was the harmonizer of the two main methodological currents that had come down to him, the compromiser rather than the extremist.

Hence the general statements of his method which he permitted himself to set down sound much like Galileo, or any other seventeenth-century physicist: "From the phenomena of motions to investigate the forces of nature, and then from these forces to demonstrate the other phenomena." [2] Again: "To derive two or three general principles of motion from phenomena, and afterwards to tell us how the properties and actions of all corporeal things follow from those manifest principles." [3] But he gave this method an experimental coloring, more even than Galileo had done, who after establishing the laws of motion felt no need of checking by observation on any of the consequences mathematically deduced from them. Newton did feel the need for such a check. The logical inclusion of a proposition within a deductive system was not enough to provide full verification: there might always be exceptions! Hence on the one hand he agreed with all the seventeenth-century scientists that mathematical deduction from first principles alone gives intelligibility and understanding, alone shows why phenomena are as they are, gives the *causa mathematica*. But he did not agree that it supplies in itself a sufficient logic of proof to establish a fact. With Newton, the experimental analysis of instances in nature, direct observation, forms a part not only of the method of discovery, as it did for all his contemporaries, but enters also into the logic of proof. It guarantees the *physical reality* of what has been mathematically demonstrated. In the language of Locke, whose problems of knowledge reflect much more closely than is usually supposed the problems of Newton's own thought, it transforms "certain" knowledge into "real" knowledge.

[2] *Principia Mathematica* (Motte tr., 1803); Preface, I, p. x.
[3] *Opticks*, p. 377.

This experimental emphasis Newton signalized in his Fourth Rule of Reasoning in Philosophy:

In experimental philosophy we are to look upon propositions collected by general induction from phenomena as accurately or very nearly true, notwithstanding any contrary hypotheses that may be imagined, till such time as other phenomena occur, by which they may either be made more accurate, or liable to exceptions.[4]

Mathematical principles, that is, are always open to experimental revision in the light of freshly observed facts. He feels, indeed, that experimental proof is needed even of the basic principle of the uniformity of nature laid down in the Second and Third Rules:

That it should be so [that the theorem of the uniform proportion of the sines applies to all rays of light] is very reasonable, nature being ever conformable to herself; but an experimental proof is desired.[5]

He distinguished carefully between the certainty attainable in mathematical demonstration and the certainty attainable in physical science, even when mathematics is employed:

I should take notice of a casual expression which intimates a greater certainty in these things than I ever promised, viz., *the certainty of mathematical demonstrations*. I said, indeed, that the science of colors was mathematical, and as certain as any other part of optics; but who knows not that optics, and many other mathematical sciences, depend as well on physical sciences, as on mathematical demonstrations? And the absolute certainty of a science cannot exceed the certainty of its principles. Now the evidence, by which I asserted the propositions of colors, is in the next words expressed to be from experiments, and so but *physical;* whence the propositions themselves can be esteemed no more than *physical principles* of a science. And if those principles be such, that on them a mathematician may determine all the phenomena of colors, . . . I suppose the science of colors will be granted mathematical.[6]

The best statement of what may be called Newton's mathematical experimentalism is to be found at the conclusion of the *Opticks:*

As in mathematics, so in natural philosophy, the investigation of difficult things by the method of analysis, ought ever to precede the method of composition. This analysis consists in making experiments and observations, and in drawing several conclusions from them by induction, and

---

[4] *Principia Mathematica*, Book III; Motte tr., II, 162.   [5] *Opticks*, p. 66.
[6] *Opera*, Horsley ed., IV, 342.

admitting of no objections against the conclusions, but such as are taken from experiments, or other certain truths. For hypotheses are not to be regarded in experimental philosophy. And although the arguing from experiments and observations by induction be no demonstration of general conclusions; yet it is the best way of arguing which the nature of things admits of, and may be looked upon as so much the stronger, by how much the induction is more general. And if no exception occur from phenomena, the conclusion may be pronounced generally. But if at any time afterwards any exception shall occur from experiments, it may then begin to be pronounced with such exceptions as occur. By this way of analysis we may proceed from compounds to ingredients, and from motions to the forces producing them; and in general, from effects to their causes, and from particular causes to more general ones, till the argument end in the most general. This is the method of analysis: and the synthesis consists in assuming the causes discovered, and established as principles, and by them explaining the phenomena proceeding from them, and proving the explanations.[7]

II

Newton's procedure may therefore be said to consist of three stages: 1) Analyze the observed facts, to discover the principles therein involved. This process Newton called "deducing principles from phenomena" to emphasize the rigorous sense in which they are to be found involved in the data of observation, and not added by thought as an explanation of what is observed—in which, as Aristotle would have put it, they are seen to be there by *Nous*. 2) Then make all the relevant phenomena of the field under investigation intelligible by fitting them into a mathematical system depending on these principles, as he had himself done with Kepler's laws. This is the process Galileo called "composition," and Descartes "synthesis." 3) Finally, verify the physical reality of these conclusions by experiment.

When this has been accomplished, we have a mathematical system or order of phenomena, resting on experiment: a system of mathematical laws experimentally verified. But we have not yet discovered the physical or mechanical *cause* of these laws. It remains to find the *mechanism* involved. For instance, when we have proved that bodies tend to approach each other with a force directly proportional to the product of their masses and inversely

[7] *Opticks*, p. 380.

proportional to the square of their distance apart, we can still ask, Why do they act that way? What makes them do it? From these phenomena of motions we must still investigate the "forces of nature."

At just this point, on the *causes* of mathematical laws, Newton's thought divides. He was convinced that he *did* know the cause of the laws of motion: it is the *vis inertiae* resident in all mass. He was equally convinced that he did *not* know the cause of the law of gravitation, or the force involved. So his confidence in having found the force lying back of the laws of motion led his incipient experimentalism back to the orthodox conception of seventeenth-century science, as demonstrative knowledge from causes; while his ignorance of the force involved in the law of gravitation led it on to a novel conception of the nature of science, from which the concept of causality ultimately vanishes. This is a fundamental methodological dualism in Newton's thought which has been reflected in Locke's difficulties and in most subsequent philosophy.

On the question of the causes of the laws of nature, Newton was extremely cautious. He distrusted the unverified mechanical hypotheses such as Descartes and many of his successors had reveled in, like the mechanical explanation of gravitation in the Cartesian vortex theory, in Gassendi, Huygens, Hooke, and Boyle. He was much interested in such explanatory hypotheses suggesting possible mechanisms for the operations of nature; he himself advanced several different versions of a plausible mechanism for gravitation, and worked upon the idea all his life. But he rigidly excluded from "experimental philosophy" or science such "propositions assumed or supposed without any experimental proof."

I frame no hypotheses; for whatever is not deduced from the phenomena is to be called an hypothesis; and hypotheses, whether metaphysical or physical, whether of occult qualities or mechanical, have no place in experimental philosophy.[8]

What Newton meant precisely by "hypotheses" in this pronouncement is clear from a letter to Cotes:

As in Geometry the word Hypothesis is not taken in so large a sense as to include the Axioms and Postulates, so in experimental Philosophy it is not to be taken in so large a sense as to include the first Principles or

[8] *Principia Mathematica*, General Scholium to Book III; Motte tr., II, 314.

Axioms which I call the laws of motion . . . And the word Hypothesis is here used by me to signify only such a proposition as is not a Phenomenon, nor deduced from any Phenomenon, but assumed or supposed without any experimental proof.[9]

Generalizations ordering and describing observed phenomena, or "mathematical causes," are not called hypotheses but axioms or first principles. In other words, Newton is excluding what J. S. Mill called physical explanations or *causal* hypotheses, not *descriptive* or coordinating hypotheses. The engraver well understood this distinction who expressed his admiration for Newton, on a picture in which he appears as "a star of the first magnitude," in the lines:

> See the great Newton, he who first surveyed
> The plan by which the universe was made;
> Saw Nature's simple yet stupendous laws,
> And proved the effects, though not explained the cause.

He would have been still more accurate had he said, "not yet explained the cause"; for that there was a mechanical cause of gravitation to be found Newton never doubted.

Hence Newton recognized two kinds of cause or force in nature: the force of inertia, a real power inherent in matter, and deduced from phenomena; and the force of gravitation. What the latter might be, he never committed himself upon; experimental philosophy had proved the "cause" of motion to be the force of inertia, but as yet had found only the law, not the "cause" of gravitation.

We must universally allow that all bodies whatsoever are endowed with a principle of mutual gravitation . . . Not that I affirm gravity to be essential to bodies: by their inherent force (*vis insita*) I mean nothing but their *vis inertiae*. This is immutable. Their gravity is diminished as they recede from the earth.[10]

I use the words attraction, impulse, or propensity of any sort toward a center, promiscuously and indifferently, one for another; considering those forces not physically but mathematically: wherefore, the reader is not to imagine, that by those words I anywhere take upon me to define the kind, or the manner of any action, the causes or the physical reason thereof, or that I attribute forces, in a true and physical sense, to certain centers (which are only mathematical points); when at any time I happen to speak of centers as attracting, or as endued with attractive powers.[11]

[9] March 28, 1713; cited in Rosenberger, *Isaac Newton*, p. 372.
[10] *Principia Mathematica*, Book III, 3d Rule of Reasoning; Motte tr., II, 162.
[11] *Principia Mathematica*, Book I, Def. 8; Motte tr., I, 6.

I use the word attraction in general for any endeavor, of what kind soever, made by bodies to approach to each other; whether that endeavor arise from the action of the bodies themselves, as tending mutually to or agitating each other by spirits emitted; or whether it arises from the action of the aether or of the air, or of any medium whatsoever, whether corporeal or incorporeal, any how impelling bodies placed therein towards each other. In the same general sense I use the word impulse, not defining in this treatise the species or physical qualities of forces, but investigating the quantities and mathematical proportions of them.[12]

And yet, despite this habitual caution, Newton allowed Roger Cotes to write the preface to the second edition of the *Principia*, making "attraction," a force acting at a distance, the real cause of gravitation, a power in bodies attracting other bodies. To be sure, as late as 1717, in the second edition of his *Opticks*, he wrote:

To show that I do not take gravity for an essential property of bodies, I have added one question concerning its cause, choosing to propose it by way of a question, because I am not yet satisfied about it for want of experiments.[13]

Yet this lapse from caution outraged every mechanistic conscience, called down the wrath of Huygens as "absurd," and provoked Leibniz to dub it a relapse into the barbarism of the occult qualities of the Schoolmen, the negation of all science. Nevertheless it became the orthodox interpretation; and a new kind of physical cause, "attraction," entered the body of science alongside of the contact of billiard-balls.

Hence it is clear how Newton could have two distinct types of influence on ideas of the nature and method of science. The first was orthodox, conservative, realistic, continuing the seventeenth-century versions of the Aristotelian doctrine of science: science is a demonstrative system explaining facts by mathematical deduction from their causes. The second was radical, novel, and "positivistic": science is a description of the experimentally observed relations between phenomena, expressed in mathematical language. The one sprang from Newton's conviction that inertia is the real cause of motion, and fitted a new cause, attraction, into the traditional scheme. The other sprang from his realization that he did not know the physical cause of gravitation, and assimilated the laws of

[12] *Principia Mathematica*, Book I, Prop. 69; Motte tr., I, 174.
[13] *Opticks*, Advertisement II.

motion to the law of gravitation as mathematical statements of the observed mathematical relations between phenomena, without seeking the causes of those relations. The first view, that science is a deductive system of causes, when combined with Newton's insistence that it must be a system deduced wholly from phenomena, led in the more penetrating Newtonians, Keill, Freind, Euler, and the other German physicists, directly to Kant. The second view, that science is a description of the observed course of nature, led in Berkeley, Hume, Maupertuis, Condillac, and Diderot to the empiricism of Mill and the British tradition, and to the positivism of Comte and the French. Hence while the popular mind, following Newton's supposed example rather than his precepts, took Newton as the triumph of the rationalistic, deductive method, and his ideal of science as realistic, the discovery of "the plan by which the universe was made," those who bothered to read and study him made him the father either of the Kantianism of the continental tradition, or of the observationalism of the British empiricists. Kantianism took its rise in the confident possession of an exact science of nature, whose validity could not be experimentally established yet ought to be; empiricism, in the confession of an ignorance only too apparent.

III

Just because Newton was so cautious, so convinced that all the ideas he admitted to his experimental philosophy were "deduced from phenomena," he made a number of uncriticized assumptions that have persisted in the structure of physical science and in the general philosophy of nature until this generation. It is well to be suspicious of all men who proclaim that they are making no assumptions, that their ideas are forced upon them by the obvious facts. In large part, to be sure, Newton's assumptions were those implicit in the whole method of seventeenth-century science, in the mathematical interpretation of nature itself; and hence Newton can be said to have crystallized rather than originated them, though his own determination of the concepts of mass and inertia added further details, and his vacillation as to method created new presuppositions. Certain of the more famous of Newton's assumptions—like those of absolute time and absolute space, which awakened vigorous criticism in his own generation—were made more plausible by the theological background of his natural philosophy; but in general it seems fairly clear that Newton's theological ideas were determined by his scientific concepts rather than *vice versa*. Theology, indeed, rarely distorts science; but science, in the hands of modernists, is always corrupting sound theology.

Indeed, Newton was surprisingly conservative in his view of the nature of "the real world." He had played a major part in making the concept of "force" and the ideas of the calculus an essential part of scientific thought, and it might have been expected that he would make these notions fundamental in his interpretation of the structure of nature. But he quite failed to develop the implications of his own discoveries; he assumed without serious question the main outlines of the geometrical world as they had been laid down by Galileo and Descartes, and his own novel concepts made little difference. This is especially striking if Newton's natural philosophy be compared with that of his contemporary Leibniz. Leibniz, operating with similar concepts of force and the calculus, did make them basic in his thought; and in consequence he gives today an impression of much greater insight and profundity. The German seems really to have thought in terms of the calculus, not in terms of the more traditional geometry and matter in motion.

The two great contemporaries in fact illustrated a difference in mentality that has persisted through the many adventures that have since befallen the two traditions on which each left so profound an impress. English thought has been dominated by the conception of knowledge as a matter of sense-images; German, by the view that it is an affair of equations. The English thinker has been unhappy when he could not picture a world of substances; the German has been quite content with a world of functional relations. The English scientist has been unwilling to rest content until he has pictured a world he could imagine; the German has sought rather for a system he could conceive. Like Kelvin, British scientists have had to invent a mechanical model before they have felt they really understood, and they have frequently been held back by their refusal to admit the unimaginable. The empirical tradition, in which the elements of knowledge are invariably sensations or images, has proved ineradicable in British thought; the rationalistic tradition, with its emphasis on relations, concepts, and systems of laws, has been as characteristically German. It goes without saying that in the present state of physical science this British preference for the substantial and concrete is having a hard time of it. Image and substance seem to have disappeared from contemporary physical theory. No mechanical model has yet proved possible for the systems of radiation we now handle mathematically with such assurance; our physicists offer us a world that is certainly unimaginable, and, one sometimes suspects, may in the end prove inconceivable as well! Leibniz seems to have the upper hand over Newton; Einstein has vanquished Oliver Lodge, and Heisenberg, Bohr.

Newton's method we have characterized as a mathematical experimentalism; and in his actual procedure he certainly introduced as many mathematical postulates as he found necessary to build up a rational system of mechanics or optics—postulates which it remained for the eighteenth-century physicists to disentangle and state precisely, in the manner which Kant elevated into a philosophy. But, like so many other Englishmen of the seventeenth century, and later, his own theory of the logic of science was neither rational nor experimental, but "empirical." That is, he was convinced that the ultimate subject-matter of science—what empiricists call the "data of science"—can consist only of what is directly given in sensation, that the origin and justification of science, and of all scientific concepts, of all the properties of matter figuring in his experimental philosophy, must be sought in ideas received through the senses. This insistence that the ultimate validity of science lies in its foundations in sense is as cardinal an assumption for Newton as for Locke, an assumption which makes inevitable the "problem of knowledge" that has created so many technical difficulties for subsequent philosophical thought, and is the tragic guilt initiating the long drama of epistemology.

In Newton as in Hobbes or Locke, this empiricism may well be due ultimately to the strong persistence in English thought of the Ockhamite logic, coming down through the Schools from the late Middle Ages. In Newton's case it was certainly reinforced by the desire to defend himself against the charge of having reintroduced the occult qualities of the Schoolmen, especially the traditional scholastic "gravitation." He always insisted with great touchiness that the objects to which his calculations applied were not abstractions of thought, but were given directly in sense: that all the scientific concepts he employed were "deduced from phenomena." His *Hypotheses non fingo* states this empiricism negatively; it is put positively in the Third Rule of Reasoning:

> The qualities of bodies which admit neither intension nor remission of degrees, and which are found to belong to all bodies within the reach of our experiments, are to be esteemed the universal qualities of all bodies whatsoever. . . .
>
> We no other way know the extension of bodies than by our senses, nor do these reach it in all bodies; but because we perceive extension in all that are sensible, therefore we ascribe it universally to all others also. That abundance of bodies are hard, we learn by experience; and because the hardness of the whole arises from the hardness of the parts, we therefore justly infer the hardness of the undivided particles not only of the bodies we feel but of all others. That all bodies are impenetrable we gather not from reason, but from sensation. . . . The extension, hardness, impenetrability, mobility, and *vis inertiae* of the whole result from the extension, hardness, impenetrability, mobility, and *vires inertiae* of the parts; and thence we conclude the least particles of all bodies to be also all extended, and hard, and impenetrable, and movable, and endowed with their proper *vires inertiae*. And this is the foundation of all philosophy.[14]

Newton was obviously not unacquainted with what Locke called "simple ideas."

Now Newton's actual mathematical procedure made it necessary for him to assume much that his empiricism could not justify; and in his ideas of "the real world" his scientific procedure and his empirical theory collide violently. What his procedure led him to assume as mathematical postulates his empiricism made him treat as real physical existents, at least potentially observable. So he was led to describe the real world as consisting of entities with properties which by definition ought to be observable, yet in fact were not; at the same time that he insisted that sense observation alone furnishes the data and the validation of the science of the relations of these entities.

Newton's real world is therefore made up of absolute masses endowed with an absolute force of inertia, and perhaps with a force of "gravitation," in absolute motion in absolute space and time; while sense experience supplies no evidence for any of these concepts. They could of course all be justified as logical assumptions,

---

[14] *Principia Mathematica*, Book III; Motte tr., II, 160, 161.

as mathematical principles employed to make intelligible what is directly experienced, as the later Newtonians and Kant did justify them. But when it is insisted, as Newton did, that science is a system of the relations of physical existents which are potentially perceptible, which ought to be perceived, and yet which cannot be, there are obviously at hand all the makings for a perplexing "problem of knowledge."

Nature consists, then, of unobservable particles of matter, provided with those properties universally present in every object we do perceive.

It seems probable to me, that God in the beginning formed matter in solid, massy, hard, impenetrable, movable particles, of such sizes and figures, . . . as most conduced to the end for which he formed them.[15]

In this world as it came from the hands of the Creator were no sounds, no colors, no warmth, no odors. It is the Cartesian world of extended particles, to which have been added, however, the solidity, mass, hardness, and impenetrability which distinguish bodies from space: a world of masses endowed with the force of inertia and the other tangible qualities of experience. To these elementary masses moving in empty space are added, in the case of man, souls on the Cartesian model, joined to the human body in what Newton calls the "sensorium." Only by the sense of touch can we know the qualities of bodies as they really are, for mechanical contact is the only relation they can really have to us; but we see only images produced in the sensorium, hear only sounds, perceive only odors there generated, not the real things which produce these sensations in the sensorium.

What the real substance of anything is we know not. In bodies, we see only their figures and colors, we hear only the sounds, we touch only their outward surfaces, we smell only the smells, and taste the savors; but their inward substances are not to be known, either by our senses, or by any reflex act of our minds.[16]

Newton still insists that he is being strictly empirical; for his non-sensible ultimate particles have no qualities save those found by experience to belong to all bodies of which we do have sensible experience. Yet the very existence of such particles is of course a dialectical necessity of thought, not an empirical fact; for they can-

[15] *Opticks*, p. 375.
[16] *Principia Mathematica*, Book III, General Scholium; Motte tr., II, 312.

not possibly be observed. There is no conceivable way of reaching these ultimate masses by the only method which Newton recognized, the analysis of what is given in sense, "deduction from phenomena." They can have no empirical standing, and must remain dialectical postulates. Hence the "real essences" of the bodies we do observe remain unknown, especially the crucial force of gravitation. Yet science is of the relations of these essences. Locke had merely to elaborate Newton's assumptions to generate his characteristic problems. These particles or tiny billiard-balls are not even necessary for the formulation of Newton's mathematical laws of motion. The whole *Principia* could equally well stand if taken as applying to geometrical points endowed with mass, as Berkeley showed.

Why then did Newton desert his professed empiricism, which Berkeley later carried out consistently as an interpretation of mechanics, for dialectic? Because his mathematical procedure made him assume certain concepts, like inertia, which his very empiricism made him regard as physical existents and therefore potentially observable. Mathematical causes, principles of intelligibility, must be for him physical forces, real causes, lodged in real substances. The real cause of motion must be a physical force, inertia; just as for Euler it was another physical property of the particles, impenetrability. And these ultimate bearers of force must be permanent substances.

While the particles continue entire, they may compose bodies of one and the same nature and texture in all ages; but should they wear away, or break in pieces, the nature of things depending upon them would be changed . . . And therefore that Nature may be lasting, the changes of corporeal things are to be placed only in the various separations and new associations and motions of these permanent particles.[17]

"That Nature may be lasting" Newton assumes a plurality of fixed, unchanging, discrete substances, under the spell of the old Eleatic dialectic. Newton has surely gone a long way from his insistence that all the concepts of physics must be given directly in sense! Starting with a subject-matter directly experienced, he was led to seek by dialectic its necessary conditions. He found them in a realm which his own method of verification, the direct appeal to sense, could not possibly reach. His absolute fixed masses or in-

[17] *Opticks*, p. 376.

trinsically immutable particles can be deduced from phenomena as perceived only as the logical presuppositions of experience, making it possible and intelligible. They cannot be perceived in sensation, yet they must be real and objective; and to be real and objective they must be somehow involved in sensation. Thus the whole Kantian position is clearly implicit in Newton's combination of the procedure of making mathematical postulates with the empirical logic that they must be immediately involved in sense observation.

Nor is this all. These fixed masses must have fixed essences, that is, unchangeable properties, the permanent sensible qualities of solidity, mass, impenetrability, motion, and inertia. All change must be accidental and external, must affect only the relations of these masses, not their fixed qualities or essences. Scientific procedure thus deals with the mathematical relations between masses. Yet science is defined as demonstration from causes, and the causes of phenomena are the non-relational powers and properties of these masses, their "real essences," which are inaccessible to scientific procedure. It would seem obvious that a science that deals primarily with relations must define its concepts relationally. Yet Newton was led to conceive the real world as a world of masses with non-relational powers and properties, unknowable in terms of his science. The "causes," then, of the mathematical relations between bodies are to be sought in their real essences, and their real essences are by definition unknowable. Thus the whole Lockean position is clearly implicit in Newton.

Moreover, by making like Boyle half the qualities of bodies relational, dependent, that is, on the interaction of bodies, and hence observable—the so-called "secondary qualities"; while the other half, the "primary qualities"—likewise all relational in present-day physical theory—were left as self-contained and absolutely inherent in absolute masses, Newton established a gulf between objects experienced and the objects of science, between the world men live in and what empirical theory still calls "the physical world." Unlike Boyle, he assumed the latter to be alone real, the former to be present only in the sensorium. Science is thus left with the task of demonstrating the relations between unknowable elements in terms of unknowable causes. No wonder Locke, reflecting on this state of affairs, was led to comment, "We can have a useful and experimental, but not a scientific philosophy of natural bodies." Newton's procedure implied that the concern of science was with mathematical relations in the experienced world. Yet his empirical logic drove him to assume that the terms of those relations are not in the experienced world at all, and yet are the only reality. The absolute masses of classical mechanics, instead of being taken as mathematical abstractions or isolates, were regarded as the sole components of nature. Here is a cardinal illustration of what Whitehead has called the "fallacy of misplaced concreteness."

IV

Still further, the assumption that the mathematical constants involved in his system were physical existents led Newton frankly to abandon even his professed empirical method with regard to motion, space, and time. He had perfectly satisfactory notions of motion, space, and time, as relative to the observer's frame of measurement, and only this measurable, "relative" motion, space, and time are actually employed in the *Principia*, in the application of the laws of motion to astronomy, for example. Yet the definition of motion, space, and time from the relation they bear to sense is a vulgar prejudice. So he is constrained to assume the physical existence of an "absolute" motion, space, and time. Absolute space is a fixed container, "in its own nature, without regard to anything external, always similar and immovable." Absolute time is also a physical existent, "of itself and from its own nature always flowing equably without regard to anything external." [18] This space and time provide a fixed frame within which masses have an absolute and intrinsic motion and rest of their own, independent of any relation to any other body or observer. This is the true nature of absolute motion, space, and time—though we can never observe them, but can measure and use only relative motion, space, and time.

It is a standing question why Newton brought in these absolutes at all; and many are the answers that have been given. In the light of the totality of his thought, it seems clear that they are implied in his mathematical procedure. His very statement of the first law of motion is in terms of absolute motion: "Every body perseveres in its state of rest or uniform motion in a straight line, unless it is com-

[18] *Principia Mathematica*, Book I, Scholium to Definitions; Motte tr., I, 6.

pelled to change that state by forces impressed thereon." Such absolute velocity and acceleration demand absolute positions and dates —i.e., these absolutes are the logical presuppositions of the laws of motion of fixed, independent masses. They are principles in terms of which the observed motions of bodies are made mathematically intelligible. This was pointed out by Maclaurin, the most penetrating of the British Newtonians: "This perseverance of a body in a state of rest or uniform motion, can only take place with relation to absolute space, and can only be intelligible by admitting it." [19] The same position was developed at some length by Leonhard Euler, the greatest and most original of the second generation of Newtonians. Absolute space and time are mathematical postulates, "ideas of reflection," and not physical existents. Yet they are objectively true, and not merely "ideal" or "imaginary"—Euler was a Newtonian compelled to defend himself against a scientific opinion in which Leibnizians predominated—because they are necessary to make the experience which is adequately described in the laws of motion intelligible.[20]

But Newton did not himself follow this line of thought, which points so clearly to Kant. As usual he was forced by his empiricism to assume that mathematical postulates must be at least potentially observable, must be physical existents. In this case he actually tried to obtain experimental proof of the existence of absolute rotary motion, of an absolute acceleration wherein absolute space and time would be directly implied, and as it were almost visible. He twirled a pail half-full of water, and in the resulting concave surface thought he beheld the immediate effect of absolute motion. To imagine that mathematical postulates must be given immediately in sense is a confusion typical of the whole empirical philosophy of science down to our own day.[21]

It is also true that such physical absolutes were necessary if New-

[19] Colin Maclaurin, *An Account of Sir Isaac Newton's Philosophical Discoveries*, 1748; Book II, ch. I, sec. 9.

[20] *Vid.* L. Euler, *Réflexions sur l'Espace et le Temps*, 1748.

[21] This empiricist assumption is beautifully illustrated in the early Whitehead: "The whole investigation is based on the principle that scientific concepts of space and time are the first outcome of the simplest generalizations from [perceptual] experience, and that they are not to be looked for at the tail end of a welter of differential equations." *Principles of Natural Knowledge* (Cambridge, 1919), p. vi. This is Locke's "idea of solidity" in modern dress (*Essay*, II, 4).

ton's absolute massy particles were to remain unchanged. Without a fixed container of absolute space, any interaction between substances would of necessity result in internal changes—and nature would not be lasting. Thus Leibniz, assuming a purely relative time and space, was forced to posit the absence of any interaction; and Whitehead today, assuming both relativism and interaction, is logically compelled to make his elements or events parts of a system of internal relations, continually modifying each other *ad infinitum*. In other words, if the masses which serve as terms in Newton's equations are to be absolute physical constants, so must the rest of the concepts of the *Principia*. As Euler put it, whatever is necessary to validate the mathematical laws of motion is *ipso facto* a real element in the experienced world, even though it never be found directly in observation.

V

Thus Newton's philosophy of nature ultimately purported to describe a world, every element in which was inaccessible to observation, yet was also potentially observable to a perfect mind, ought to be observed, and cried aloud for such a mind to observe it. Hence it is not surprising that he should have given all his absolutes a home in the mind of God. Absolute time and space are God's sensorium: by existing God constitutes them, as the container wherein all motions take place. This Divine Sensorium or Mind sustains the entire field of physics, just as the Divine Will, or ether, the vehicle of force, holds the system of moving masses together. This theological foundation of Newton's philosophy of nature thus needs no extraneous religious reasons to account for its presence, though such reasons were undoubtedly influential in his background, and his pronouncements are strikingly reminiscent of Henry More. It is there primarily because such a world needed a supreme observer to constitute it and hold it together. The consequences of the necessity of such a constitutive mind have been momentous for the subsequent philosophy of physical science. In Kant's version, "pure reason," a generalized form of the human mind, has replaced the mind of God; but the divine mind returned with the idealists, and throughout the nineteenth century down to our present-day gropings, the world of physics—the so-called "physical world"—when conceived in Newtonian terms as existing in sharp contrast to the world of human experience, has always craved a Supreme Mind to lend it structure and permanence. Despite all the drive towards positivism, such a mind, whether taken as God or Reason, has persisted in some form as an ultimate physical concept. Where such a constitutive mind has been wholly lacking, as in the empirical tradition, natural science has had little structure or permanence; and empiricists have been always committed to trying to persuade physicists that their science ought to be a far different kind of thing, and ought to have a far different kind of structure, from what it in fact is and has.

VI

The consequences for rational theology have been equally momentous. Newton, like most of his British predecessors, turned the assumptions of mechanics into religious principles. Mechanics and theology were fused into one, and became the basis of the rational theology of the eighteenth century. In this Enlightenment attempt to harmonize religion and science by reducing religion to the compass of the foundations of mechanics, religion inevitably vanished. Newton himself was quite orthodox, for his day: he thought he believed in the religious tradition. But he was a modernist: he poured the content of mechanics into it. It is little wonder that Berkeley was alarmed! Newton had, to be sure, certain Arian doubts concerning the Trinity; for such a Platonic concept, however significant in its own terms, is quite meaningless in Newton's mechanical world.

It must be remembered that in that world there is no place for any real change, any of the growth and development that has since become a commonplace of thought. All its processes are cyclical, and return to their starting point in the perpetual motion machine. Hence a first efficient cause, a creator, for all this intricate machinery was a necessary scientific concept. Newton was right: either his cosmic machine had sprung from the hands of a Creator, or else its existence must remain unintelligible, the negation of all science. All intelligibility, all understanding, it must be remembered, was still for Newton in terms of origins and efficient causes. God figures, therefore, in Newton's thought first as the Creator, as the origin of order in the universe. Why are not the planets like the comets, fly-ing off and never returning? he asks. Their orderly behavior must be "the effect of counsel." Mechanics alone can hardly explain why there is a universe at all, any more than it can explain why there is a particular clock. A machine is obviously designed by man for a purpose; how could a machine-universe be otherwise? If one asked Newton and his contemporaries what was the great purpose for which God had created the structure whose harmonious rationality, so recently discovered, still intoxicated them, there could be but one answer: it was to establish the great Order of Nature. God's aim could not be other than to establish law and order in his domains. And thus the whole long painful struggle of the middle class to win law and order for themselves took on cosmic significance, and re-ceived a divine sanction.

This did not end God's function for Newton himself. God is not only the Creator—he is also the great Conserver. He is exercising ceaseless vigilance to maintain his Law and Order against the sub-versive forces in the universe. He keeps the stars from bumping to-gether, and gathering in an inert cluster in the center of space, as they otherwise would through the operation of universal gravita-tion. He also corrects the irregularities which Newton's equations had been unable to banish from the cosmic machine; he repairs and winds up the clock from time to time, and adjusts its operations. Force is needed for this work, and is supplied through the ether that is the vehicle of God's will. This notion awakened Leibniz's scorn: Newton's God could not even create a machine that would run by itself without continual adjustment! And with the perfecting of the system of celestial mechanics during the century, these ir-regularities were themselves reduced to cyclical law, until Laplace was able to tell Napoleon he had no need of the hypothesis of a Creator in his system.

The religious result of this impingement of the new mechanics, in the hands of devout physicists, upon traditional theology, was to establish God as first and foremost the First Efficient Cause, the Creator of the world in time. Such a God, such an original Power, even if it be an intelligent Power, soon proved to have no religious value whatever. It possessed no rationally discoverable moral quali-ties at all, it was not divine: in a mood of disillusionment, like Voltaire's after the disaster of Lisbon, it might well seem rather the Devil himself. And the concept of a mechanical Creator of course was quite defenseless against the more satisfying scientific explanation of a world that had gradually grown and developed into its present form. There is no essential conflict between the concept of cosmic evolution and Aristotelian theology. There has been an irrepressible conflict between evolution and the ideas of eighteenth-century rational theology, of God as a mechanical Creator. It is little wonder that the Newtonian Creator God was murdered in the nineteenth century. Such a deity really deserved his fate.

3

John Locke: The Original, Certainty, and Extent of Knowledge

I

LOCKE's *Essay* stands with Newton's *Principia* as the fountainhead of British and French thought in the eighteenth century, as a classic illustration of the application of the Newtonian "geometrical" or "analytical" method to human nature. It stands also as the classic document of British empiricism, a philosophical movement of the first importance. Not only has this body of ideas been one of the three great interpretations of science in modern times, an interpretation which down to the present continues to control the problems and the assumptions of most British philosophers, even of those who have rebelled against certain of its tenets, like the idealists of the last century and the realists of the first generation of this. Not only did it enter, through the strong impress it made upon Kant, into the main stream of continental thought, where to this day it exerts a curious distorting influence on the other elements there present. It was the set of ideas and the intellectual method in terms of which the middle class of the eighteenth century fought its struggles against the landed interests in the political, economic, and cultural revolutions of the Age of Reason. It was the "ideology of the bourgeois revolution"; comparable, that is, to the philosophy in terms of which the revolutions of the mid-twentieth century are being fought, Marxism. And like Marxism, it is a philosophy which in spite of its importance in practice is of somewhat dubious theoretical consistency and validity.

In terms of its antecedents, British empiricism was the outcome of the employment of the third great medieval philosophy of science, the Ockhamite logic, to interpret the new physics of the seventeenth century. It was what the Ockhamite position became as the result of its adventures in the world of bodies in motion. It is the essence of an empirical philosophy to bring all traditional beliefs to the test of experience; British empiricism is what eventuated when this traditional way of regarding knowledge was brought to the test of the only kind of experience conceivable in the Newtonian world.

In terms of its intentions, British empiricism was the application of the best scientific method known to the investigation of human affairs. It was concerned, not with vision, but with method: with a method of criticizing the confident visions of others, especially those visions which, institutionalized and embodied in the cherished beliefs and habits of men, seem left behind by a changing human experience, and grown out of touch with altered human needs. It was a philosophy of social criticism; what it was attempting is obviously of fundamental importance, and the efforts to effect it, however suspicious we may be of the method of criticism and the conception of experience, possess an undying fascination of their own.

It was a method worked out by men with a keen appreciation of Man the Doer as well as Man the Knower, by men themselves, with one exception, doers. Its major figures—Hobbes, Locke, Berkeley, Bentham, J. Mill, J. S. Mill—were all familiar with affairs, all concerned with liberating the energies of men for action by ridding them of the incubus of outworn beliefs. They were all primarily moralists, all anxious to apply the successful methods of the natural sciences to the field of human affairs, to render the conduct of men more enlightened, intelligent, and humane. Even Hume, the one outstanding representative not primarily a doer, did himself contribute mightily to this end. It was a method of patient analysis and careful criticism rather than imaginative sweep and speculation. It emphasized human experience in its soberer phases: observation and trying out, reflection on what has been observed and tried out; and the necessity of bringing to the test of experience that stock of ideas by which men were trying to lead their lives, curbing unguarded flights of fancy, criticizing traditional assumptions, bringing the mind back to solid foundations. Its spirit has been well expressed by an outstanding contemporary empiricist:

What passes for knowledge in ordinary life suffers from three defects: it is cock-sure, vague, and self-contradictory. The first step towards philosophy consists in becoming aware of these defects, not in order to rest content with a lazy skepticism, but in order to substitute an amended kind of knowledge which shall be tentative, precise, and self-consistent.[1]

Surely such a philosophy and such a method, elaborated by able minds thoroughly conversant with human affairs, striving with moral fervor for the practical and tangible good of mankind, must have contributed a useful and potent instrument for the clarification of human thought and the guidance of human action. Even if in calling philosophy down from the clouds of idle speculation to the service of human living it seems rather unappreciative of the poet's imagination, the mystic's vision, or the prophet's crusading zeal, it must have borne fruits in more enlightened and intelligent conduct and clearer thinking. It would be folly to underestimate the power and the influence of British empiricism, the hold it has gained on British thinkers, and their genuine intellectual achievements when they have applied this philosophy to the criticism of religion, morals, and social institutions and thought. But—as to the clarification of thought, in any ultimate sense; as to any real understanding of the fact of science and its implications; as to the formulation of a consistent and intelligible philosophy—it is one of the ironies of intellectual history that the appeal to the "obvious facts of experience" has given rise to more empty dialectic, the drive to make thought "practical" has resulted in more abstract and unnecessary reasoning, than any other philosophy in modern times. It has developed a philosophy of science peculiarly unsuited to interpret the scientific procedure and concepts of the present day, with their elaborate theoretical constructions; and the effort to do so is involved in a host of unnecessary dialectical problems whose solution demands a tremendous superstructure of theory. In general, the effort to rid men of the incubus of traditional beliefs, in the interests of tentativity, precision, and self-consistency, has resulted in a philosophy founded on traditional assumptions, and involved in vagueness, confusion, and ultimate self-contradiction. Perhaps there is something to be said for the Knowers after all.

[1] Bertrand Russell, *Outline of Philosophy* (published in U.S.A. as *Philosophy*, 1927), p. 1.

II

John Locke (1632–1704) wrote a book, tantalizing, perverse, yet fascinating. Like the two other major classics of empiricism, Hume's *Treatise* and Mill's *Logic*, it is a masterpiece—of confusion, contradiction, and ultimate inexplicabilities. Yet like them it is worthy of continued study and repeated analysis; and like them immensely stimulating: for in it Locke is working out a new conception of science. The major empiricists are in fact always starting with the assumptions involved in one conception of science, while their procedure always leads them to emerge with another. Locke began with the rationalistic conception of Descartes, and emerged with "observationalism"; just as Mill started with observationalism and emerged with experimentalism.

Locke himself was a good, honest, plainspoken Englishman. He was a physician who had studied in Holland, tutor and confidential adviser to the first Earl of Shaftesbury, much mixed up in politics and, we now know, in conspiracy on the Whig side, the official apologist for the Whig revolution of 1688/89. He was eminently respectable, and gifted with much common sense; but he was not clever. In many respects he was the typical Shavian Englishman, neither acute nor subtle, and hence the easy butt of ridicule; but honest and solid—so honest that he frankly exposed all his own difficulties, and so solid that he managed nonetheless to muddle through to sure ground. And it was sure ground, though he himself had no clear idea why: it took the combined efforts of an Irishman and a Scotsman to explain that.

As Locke himself records his book's history, he became involved with a group of friends in a discussion; James Tyrrell notes it was at Exeter House in 1671, and was about "the principles of morality and revealed religion." Locke went home resolved to "examine our own abilities, and see what objects our understandings were, or were not, fitted to deal with." He set out to use the "historical, plain method." [2] There were to be no frills, no metaphysics; that belongs in the Schools, and Locke had already had enough of it at Oxford. The statement was to be put down on a single sheet of paper. But the at-

[2] Locke, *An Essay concerning Human Understanding*, ed. A. C. Fraser (1894), I, 9, 27. Further references in this chapter are to this edition.

tempt grew and grew, the difficulties increased, and the problems appeared well-nigh insoluble. For Locke had unsuspectingly opened the door and discovered the skeleton in the closet of the new science. He started, naturally enough, with a profound faith in Cartesian physics, in the laudable desire to make morality and religion "scientific" also. He arrived at the conclusion that it was doubtful whether man could ever have any strict "science" of physics. Locke was far too honest to conceal his surprise, although more and more things turned out to be "plainly facts, but incomprehensible." For he had shown the fundamental incompatibility between knowledge conceived as a system of meanings, and knowledge conceived as the succession of physical contacts. The natural science the seventeenth century did possess led irresistibly to the denial of the possibility of a demonstrative natural science! The Newtonian world, in a word, was unintelligible! It might be practically known and dealt with, but logically it could not be reduced to a consistent body of ideas.

Locke had been from his student days an intelligent follower of Cartesian science. To the end he could never really doubt it. His was, however, an essentially unmathematical mind. When the *Principia* appeared, he consulted his mathematical friends as to whether Newton's figuring could be trusted. Assured that it could, he tried to puzzle out the conclusions. This must be the truth.

The commonwealth of learning is not at this time without master-builders, whose mighty designs, in advancing the sciences, will leave lasting monuments to the admiration of posterity: but every one must not hope to be a Boyle or a Sydenham; and in an age that produces such masters as the great Huygenius and the incomparable Mr. Newton, with some others of that strain, it is ambition enough to be employed as an under-labourer in clearing the ground a little, and removing some of the rubbish that lies in the way of knowledge. (I, 14)

But Locke was led by his close contact with political movements to a great interest also in the practical questions of morality and religion, at that time so exercising the body politic. He hoped, indeed, to make the consideration of these fields as "scientific" as mechanics, by following the same intellectual model. He was trying to extend the certainty of the new science to human conduct, like the Cambridge Platonists before him, and like Samuel Clarke and the eighteenth-century advocates of a rational religion and morality after him. He hated the quarreling sects which had for so long dominated English life; he wanted certain knowledge agreed upon, and the mere speculations of the fighting Puritans, the authoritarian Anglicans, and the troublesome Papists put in their proper place, so that Englishmen could get down to their rightful business. Himself a convinced mercantilist, he was the spokesman of the secular and commercial spirit of the age, of the middle class.

In religion, his sympathies lay with the liberal or Latitudinarian party, which wanted the Church to agree on fundamentals, and for the rest tolerate the diverse speculations of different groups on non-essentials. In his *Reasonableness of Christianity* (1695) he attempted to set forth what was essential, the belief in God and in Christ as the Messiah. In his *Letter concerning Toleration* (1689) he made one of the first pleas for union of different theologies within the Church, leaving only atheists and Papists beyond the pale. To effect this end, his friends, rationalists like the Cambridge Platonists, had appealed to "Reason," the "Light of Nature," Platonic "innate ideas," as furnishing sure ground amidst the warring faiths. This had been the immemorial Catholic wisdom in the search for unity of belief. But this did not satisfy Locke: to him it seemed one speculation the more, and to rest ultimately on what Bentham later called "mere ipse-dixitism." Hence Locke, agreeing with the end of these irenic religious rationalists, proposed a new means. In experience, in ideas tested by this firmest of foundations, lay the only way out, the only way to show up the "enthusiasm" of the Quakers and the authoritarianism of the bigoted conservatives.

III

But there were difficulties even with experience: her voice came with a different tone to different men. So Locke embarked upon his attempt to inquire into "the original, certainty, and extent of human knowledge." Much is implied, to be sure, in this essay. To examine into the "origin" of knowledge before you are sure whether you have it or not, presents difficulties of its own. It is hard not to assume it all in the first place. Indeed, the most that can be hoped for from such inquiry is to render your beliefs consistent; and, alas, the inconsistency of those with which Locke started stood revealed. Moreover, much lurks behind the basic notion that the "extent and certainty" of knowledge can be tested by its "origins." It is not immediately apparent that the way men get beliefs will determine their validity.

In point of fact, Locke assumed to begin with and without question the whole of Newtonian science, both its verdict on the nature of science and on the nature of the world. He assumed that science is "the perception of the agreement or disagreement of ideas" (II, 167); that is, it is a deductive system of the implications of ideas, implications taken as natural relations. Science is a system of universal and necessary truths; all else is mere "experimental" or historical knowledge. And these implications are perfectly real and objective. In the second place, he assumed that the real world consists of solid, hard, massy particles, of substances connected by mechanical causation—a world in which there are no ideas and no implications, but only mechanical contact. Thirdly, there are minds, which contain ideas, much as a room contains furniture; ideas and knowledge are quite literally "inside" the mind. Fourthly, ideas are "objects of the understanding when a man thinks." (I, 32) They are the objects, the materials of knowledge, *what* we know, not knowledge itself. Knowledge is concerned with the relations between these materials, and its validity and certainty must come from a logical analysis of these relations. Finally, ideas for Locke are also the *knowledge* of objects, and to be "real" knowledge, must "conform with" their objects. But since the only relation between physical objects and the mind is one of mechanical causation—a physical object can produce an idea "in the mind"—this relation cannot be logical at all, and the validity of ideas taken as knowledge can come only from a mechanical analysis of the causes of knowledge. Knowledge is to be tested by its physical origins, "how ideas come into the mind"—a typical Newtonian causal explanation.

It is obvious that these last two assumptions are contradictory. The former, the view that ideas are to be taken as *objects of knowledge*, is of course the classic tradition coming down from Greek thought. Where so found—in Plato, in Aristotle, in Spinoza—an idea has always a natural status in the world to be known. An idea can be the proper object of knowledge in any intelligible sense only if ideas have their locus in intimate relation with the world to be known, if they are "in" things, the intelligible aspect of things and their relations. If

they are means to the knowledge of nature, they must be discoverable elements in nature, caught up in its structure. On the other
hand, if ideas are conceived, not as the objects of knowledge, but as
themselves *knowledge of objects*, then to be knowledge at all they
must bear the logical relation of "meaning" or signification to the
objects of which they are the knowledge. Thus, in the Aristotelian
tradition, the idea which is the form or intelligible aspect of the
thing is identical with the idea which is actualized in the human
mind.

But Locke, living in the Newtonian world, combines and confuses these two conceptions of "idea." Ideas are "in" the mind, and
not in things; hence things are not the objects of knowledge, nor are
their relations. On the other hand, ideas are not in the mind as bits of
knowledge of nature, but as themselves objects to be known—not as
logical meanings, but as the mechanical effects produced by natural
objects upon the mind. They are the *effects* of objects, but not
knowledge of those objects. In other words, things in nature are not
objects of knowledge, and ideas are not a knowledge of objects.
Knowledge is only of the contents of the mind, not of the world at
all. Ideas and their relations are known, but they are only dubiously
"real." This was Locke's "new way of ideas."

Why did Locke adopt these inconsistent assumptions, so fraught
with difficulties and paradoxes? It can only be because he took Newtonian science at its face value. The world contains only tiny particles of matter in motion; it has no place for forms or meanings.
These particles can serve only as the mechanical causes of knowledge. Physical contact is the only relation these particles can have
to mind, as to each other. What we know is therefore the incomprehensible effect of something we can never know, of an "X," an
"I know not what." Ideas have no status in nature, and the only
knowable objects are mental. As Berkeley so clearly saw, the inevitable result of Locke's assumptions, when carried out with rigor
to the disregard of common sense, is scepticism. We know only the
contents of our own minds; there is no place on such a view for any
knowledge of an extra-mental world at all. Locke's long essay is in
large part the effort of a sober mind to escape this conclusion, so unsatisfactory to one who always tempered the dialectic of his position
with common sense.

IV

The second book of the *Essay*, by far the most influential on the critical method of eighteenth-century thought, analyzes the "origin" of human knowledge on these assumptions. It undertakes to show how the mind comes to be furnished with ideas, as a criterion of what ideas are valid. It is an attempt to apply to the materials of knowledge the kind of "analysis" which the seventeenth-century scientists had made popular. It is not a psychological account of the data of knowledge, which must include meanings; it is not an introspective description of anything that can actually be observed in mental processes; it is not a genetic account in physiological terms— all these things Locke specifically eschews. It is rather an application of the Cartesian method of analyzing knowledge into "simple ideas" or analyzable elements. It is at bottom not a psychological analysis at all, but a logical analysis of knowledge into indefinable concepts, which *ex hypothesi* must be identified with what a mechanical analysis suggests can result from the impact of Newtonian corpuscles upon the sense-organs. Of course, Locke has great difficulty in making these two radically different types of analysis reach the same conclusions. Concepts which are clearly reached by Locke himself as the result of a complicated train of reasoning upon many observations are asserted to have come from "sense" alone. Just how, Locke finds incomprehensible. Thus, in his chapter upon the idea of solidity —so fundamental in the Newtonian scheme of things—after a long discussion in which a satisfactory definition is finally arrived at, Locke concludes, "If any one asks me, What this solidity is, I send him to his senses to inform him. Let him put a flint or a football between his hands, and then endeavor to join them, and he will know." (I, 156) These ultimate ideas must come from sense, they must be the pure effects of natural objects upon a wholly passive mind, or else they will be affected by an arbitrariness that will impugn the certainty of knowledge.

In fact, the "simple ideas" which furnish the ultimate materials of all knowledge turn out to be, aside from the various sense qualities, the fundamental categories of Newtonian mechanics, like space, time, motion, and mass. They are "simple," not because they can be psychologically reduced to a single sensation; they are gained in fact through several senses at once. They are simple because they are ultimate concepts, logically irreducible, not because any simplicity can be shown in their origin. If they are "real," that is, if they are to "conform to" aspects of the real world, they must be the immediate effect of bodies. Even ideas obviously not produced by bodies in nature, like perception and volition, must come from an "inner sense" which is reflection.

Complex ideas, on the other hand, are the result of the work of the mind upon these simple materials. They hence involve an element of arbitrariness: the mind has put together in some fashion the materials with which sense has provided it. How does this process of unification take place? Locke is here torn between the mechanical method of "compounding," in which simple ideas are merely juxtaposed, by contact and addition, and the logical methods of comparing and abstracting—that is, of deducing the implications of simple ideas. For the first method ideas can have no relations save those of contact or contiguity; for the second and third, they must have logical relations whose structure can be isolated and traced. The later association psychologists like Condillac and James Mill followed out consistently the mechanical method of compounding, and hence naturally found no place for logical relations in knowledge, no system and no laws. Knowledge became a heap of marbles, a kaleidoscope of different elements. The relations which it is so difficult to exclude entirely from knowledge must come from outside: from what Hume called a "habit of mind," and what Kant called the "categories of the understanding."

Locke's Cartesian conception of knowledge as a system of implications was far too strong for him to take this course. So he soon abandons the method of compounding, and turns to the comparing and abstracting which can reveal a logical structure obtaining between ideas. A general idea is a concrete image with which is associated a meaning. Locke's analysis of complex ideas is in fact logical throughout, not genetic; his classification into substances, modes, and relations, is metaphysical and not psychological at all.

It is in the analysis of the complex idea of substance, especially bodily substance, that Locke reaches the heart of his problem and the root of his difficulties. Substance or "mass" is the basic category of Newtonian mechanics. Nature is made up of independent and absolute masses, each with its own inner constitution or essence, and each endowed in itself with certain qualities or "powers," quite apart from any other substance. We are clearly in the presence of Newton's fixed masses in this discussion of substance. This essence, the "real essence" of substances, which makes them what they are, consists of "those qualities utterly inseparable from a body in what state soever it be; such as it constantly keeps." (I, 169) As would be expected of a man in touch with the new science of the day, this real essence is not the traditional "form" of a body, stoniness, iron-ness, or the like; such forms are merely "nominal essences," abstract ideas useful for classifying. It is rather "the constitution of the in-sensible parts of a body, upon which its powers depend" (II, 57)— its atomic structure. The qualities of bodies are thus the properties of the unobservable particles of which it is composed, intrinsic and internal. Since knowledge is of the relations between what can be observed, it is not surprising that substance cannot be "known" at all. Yet the existence of such substance is a necessary implication of thought; we must assume an "unknown X," an "I know not what." (I, 230, 392) These "real essences" are ultimately unknowable: the essence of body, cohesion and motion by contact, is incompre-hensible, and the essence of mind is equally incomprehensible. Locke even suggests, in a passage which gave great comfort to Voltaire and the French materialists, that quite possibly body might be endowed with the power of thinking, and mind might be no separate sub-stance of its own.

Following both Boyle and Newton, Locke makes a fundamental distinction between the intrinsic and essential properties inherent in a body taken by itself, and the extrinsic and relational properties which belong to bodies by virtue of their existence in a world of other bodies, their "powers" to produce changes in those other bodies—between the primary qualities of bodies, and their sec-ondary and tertiary qualities, which characterize bodies in con-nection with other bodies, and exist only when bodies are found acting on and being acted upon in relation to other bodies.

We are wont to consider the substances we meet with, each of them, as an entire thing by itself, and independent of other things. Put a piece of gold anywhere by itself, separate from the reach and influence of all other bodies, it will immediately lose all its color and weight, and perhaps malleableness; which, for aught I know, would be changed into a perfect friability. Water, in which to us fluidity is an essential quality, left to itself would cease to be fluid. (II, 260)

Primary qualities form the real constitution of bodies, and consist of "their bulk, figure, number, situation, and motion of their solid parts. Those are in them, whether we perceive them or not, and when they are of that size that we can discover them, we have by these an idea of the thing as it is in itself." (I, 178) It is these primary qualities that form the real essence of bodies. "By this real essence I mean the real constitution of anything, which is the foundation of all those properties which are combined in and are found constantly to coexist in it; that particular constitution which everything has within itself, without any relation to anything without it." (II, 61) Locke frequently refers to these primary qualities as "the texture of its insensible parts upon which its powers depend." It is to be noted that these qualities, all relational in modern physics, are for Locke intrinsic and absolute. They constitute what bodies really are, for Newton and science said so. Our ideas of these primary qualities "resemble" them, "by general agreement." (I, 175)

Secondary qualities are the source of all other simple ideas of bodies. They are "the power that is in any body, by reason of its insensible primary qualities, to operate after a peculiar manner on any of our senses, and thereby produce in us the different ideas of several colors, sounds, smells, tastes, etc." (I, 178) For Locke, these qualities are "real," as the powers of bodies, springing from their internal, atomic constitution; they are not "subjective," but *relational*, depending on the complex relations of bodies to each other and to minds. Our ideas of these secondary qualities, however, are not copies or images of the atomic constitution which produces them; they serve rather as "distinguishing marks." Yet the ideas of primary qualities are "copies." It is easy to ask, why did not Locke make all ideas distinguishing marks, and treat all knowledge as functional, as a matter of meaning?

Our simple ideas are all real, all agree to the reality of things: not that they are all of them the images or representations of what does exist; the contrary whereof, in all but the primary qualities of bodies, hath been already shown. But though whiteness and coldness are no more in snow than pain is; yet those ideas of whiteness and coldness, pain, etc., being in us the effects of powers of things without us, ordained by our Maker to produce in us such sensations; they are real ideas in us, whereby we distinguish the qualities that are really in things themselves. For these several appearances being designed to be the mark whereby we are to know and distinguish things which we have to do with, our ideas do as well serve us to that purpose, and are as real distinguishing characters, whether they be only constant effects, or else exact resemblances of something in the things themselves: the reality lying in that steady correspondence they have with the distinct constitutions of real beings. But whether they answer to those constitutions, as to causes or patterns, it matters not; it suffices that they are constantly produced by them. (I, 498)

The real basis of this distinction, in Locke as in the science upon which he drew, that primary qualities lend themselves to mathematical treatment, while secondary qualities do not, is pragmatic and relative; yet Locke follows Newton in making it metaphysical and absolute.

Tertiary qualities are "the power that is in any body, by reason of the particular constitution of its primary qualities, to make such a change in the bulk, figure, texture, and motion of another body, as to make it operate on our senses differently from what it did before. Thus the sun has a power to make wax white, and fire to make lead fluid." (I, 179) Like secondary qualities, they are "powers" to produce certain observable effects in other bodies. These qualities are obviously most important of all, so far as a science of bodies is concerned. It is to be noted that Locke identifies the idea of "cause" with a "*power*" in bodies capable of "producing" certain effects. These "powers" of Locke are the equivalent of Newton's "forces": just as Locke identifies "cause" with a power inherent in bodies to produce effects on other bodies or on minds, so Newton defined "cause" as the "force" in a mass to alter its velocity, or that of another mass. Locke like Newton takes "cause" as an inherent, nonrelational "power" or "force" to produce certain effects that are observable. Causation is not defined as a relation; and hence, since only relations are knowable, "causes," "powers," or "forces" must remain incomprehensible, though they are a necessary implication of motion. There must be causal connections between bodies, but we can never know them, because we cannot discover the real essence of substances and their powers.

The outcome of Locke's analysis of substance is the sharp distinction between the intrinsic, essential properties inherent in a body taken by itself, and the external and relational properties which are powers to produce changes in other substances—between the primary qualities or real essences of bodies, and their secondary and tertiary qualities. The properties of bodies are consequently left half relational and observable, and half absolute or not observable; but the relational properties, though observable, since they depend on the absolute ones, are not intelligible: their causes remain unknown.

V

The inquiry into the extent and certainty of knowledge, which fills the fourth book of the *Essay*, is the problem in which Locke's most significant achievement appears: he is here driven to the elaboration of a new theory of science, which Berkeley developed with such insight and consistency that it has lasted to this day as one of the major philosophies of science. This enterprise of Locke is to be understood only against the background of Newton's thought; partly because Locke's problems, though worked out in relative independence—they are already clear in the first drafts of the *Essay*, dating from 1671—are the problems implicit in Newton's assumptions, which Locke also shared; and partly because Locke's examination of the extent and certainty of knowledge is very definitely of the extent and certainty of knowledge possible in the world of Newtonian mass-particles.

Newton had defined science as a deductive system of relations between bodies, mathematically demonstrated from first principles or causes; and he had defined causes as the powers, forces, and properties of bodies deduced from phenomena. Science is a system of the necessary connections of bodies having properties disclosed to the senses. He also assumed that the ultimate elements of bodies, the particles of which they were composed, though they possessed such powers, were not themselves accessible to sense. Now there are clearly two alternative ways of developing these assumptions. If you hold firmly to the conviction that the science of bodies is such a demonstrative system, then that system must be implied in phenomena, even if it be not directly observed there. Since for them science was demonstrative, this Kantian position was the one naturally developed by the physicists. On the other hand, if you analyze sense to see what properties of bodies are actually disclosed there, you find it difficult to discover "powers" and "properties" in sense which can be made the basis of a system of necessary connections, especially powers of particles inaccessible to sense—as Newton himself found with that power or force which must be the cause of gravitation. Science then becomes the pure statement of the observed relations of phenomena whose "causes" or "powers" are unknown.

Locke, setting out to test beliefs in terms of their origins in experience, that is, in sense, naturally followed the second alternative. He found himself confronted by two separate problems. The first is that of the *certainty* of knowledge. If science is such a demonstrative system of necessary connections, of what subject-matters can we hope to have science? In particular, is our knowledge of bodies thus "certain," and hence truly science? The second problem is that of the *reality* of knowledge. If science is a system of the relations of what is disclosed in sense, does it "conform with the real world," with the order of necessary connections there obtaining? Do the relations of what is observed in sense conform with the order of relations of the unobservable Newtonian particles? The difficulties of the first problem, of the "certainty" of knowledge, were what impressed Locke himself; he was forced to a negative answer so far as a science of bodies was concerned. Knowledge of natural bodies is not "certain," and so cannot be "scientifical"; and hence he was led to work out another conception of what the knowledge of bodies is, a new theory of science. This theory at which Locke rather unexpectedly arrived became the second great philosophy of science in modern times, a philosophy which can in general be called "observationalism," or "positivism." Observationalism, we may note, does not in itself constitute modern "empiricism," in which there is added another cardinal assumption. The second problem, of the "reality" of knowledge, however, seemed more fundamental and more perplexing to Locke's successors, though it did not really disturb Locke himself. To it he gave an affirmative answer: science is "real" knowledge, and does conform to the order of the real world. These two problems are often confused; it is in fact the essence of modern empiricism to confuse them, and to shift easily from one problem to the other.

Locke's difficulties with the certainty of knowledge sprang from his unquestioning acceptance of the orthodox and traditional definition of science of the seventeenth-century physicists.

Knowledge is the perception of the connexion of and agreement, or disagreement and repugnancy of any of our ideas. . . . In this alone it consists. For . . . when we possess ourselves with the utmost security of the demonstration that the three angles of a triangle are equal to two right ones, what do we more, but perceive, that equality to two right ones does necessarily agree to and is inseparable from the three angles of a triangle? (II, 167, 168)

Knowledge is a perception of necessary relations, of the logical implications of ideas. It is a deductive system, of necessary and "general" truths. Geometry is the model, intuition and demonstration is the method. Ideas Locke defines in the most general terms.

I must here in the entrance beg pardon of my reader for the frequent use of the word idea in the following treatise. It being that term which, I think, serves best to stand for whatsoever is the object of the understanding when a man thinks, I have used it to express whatever is meant by phantasm, notion, species, or whatever it is which the mind can be employed about in thinking. (I, 32)

It is past doubt that men have in their minds several ideas, such as those expressed by the words whiteness, hardness, sweetness, thinking, motion, man, elephant, army, drunkenness, and others. (I, 121)

An idea is any object of the mind, anything that can be observed and known, any subject-matter of knowledge, any intelligible aspect or relation or quality of things. Locke's usage conforms closely to Newton's employment of "phenomenon," and both terms are at the outset similarly free from any trace of subjectivity: the emphasis in both is on accessibility to mind. Knowledge is of the connections of these ideas or "forms" or "species" or "phenomena," of their logical relations.

Locke's conception of knowledge is Cartesian in its details. Knowledge is either intuitive, a direct perception of a logical relation, of the "2 plus 1 equals 3" type; or else demonstrative, defined, as by Descartes, as a chain of successive intuitions:

Certainty depends so wholly on this intuition, that in demonstrations this intuition is necessary in all the connexions of the intermediate ideas, without which we cannot attain knowledge and certainty. (II, 178)

Now in every step reason makes in demonstrative knowledge there is an intuitive knowledge of that agreement or disagreement it seeks with the next intermediate idea it uses as proof. . . . By which it is plain that every step in reasoning that produces knowledge has intuitive certainty. (II, 180)

And Locke adds, in good Cartesian fashion,

These two, viz., intuition and demonstration, are the degrees of our *knowledge;* whatever comes short of one of these, with what assurance soever embraced, is but faith or opinion, but not *knowledge,* at least in all general truths. (II, 185)

Such demonstrative, certain knowledge—"scientifical philosophy" —is of course possible in mathematics, where quantitative relations are concerned; and Locke makes an earnest plea that it is possible in ethics also, that ethics can be a real science (see Book Four, Chapter 8). But he runs into difficulties when he comes to the powers and properties of bodies. He has defined science as a perception of relations, in accordance with the procedure of the science of the day: mathematically demonstrated relations between bodies. But he also embraced Newton's carrying over of the older notion that bodies are independent substances with absolute powers and properties. Knowledge is of relations, but bodies possess attributes, certain powers and qualities which cause those relations, but are themselves by definition unknowable.

Locke might have retained the Aristotelian conception that substances have observable attributes, that knowledge is of these attributes, and been consistent. Or he might have developed a consistent relational theory, that bodies are fundamentally related, and that knowledge is of these relations. On such a view causation would be, not a power, but a relation; all properties would be relational, as they were for Berkeley. But his definition of knowledge as a perception of relations collided with his notion of bodies as having inherent powers and properties; and so he reached the curious conclusion that a knowledge of bodies is of the relations of their powers and properties to each other, of the *coexistence* of those powers in the same body, "in which consists the greatest and most material part of our knowledge concerning substances." (II, 199)

Hence the science of bodies is of the relations between their properties, their properties are powers of their insensible parts, and we cannot observe either these invisible parts or their powers. We can know the real "essences" of substances only through their powers, and their powers only through their observable effects. Since we cannot penetrate to the "inner constitution" or atomic structure of bodies, we cannot perceive the agreement or necessary connection of any of these powers with each other, or with the effects they produce. All we can perceive is the effects; but we can perceive no necessary connection between bodies and their effects, why certain powers coexist in bodies, why bodies have the effects on other bodies that they do—why, as in Newton's problem, bodies gravitate toward each other. The only certain knowledge of substances would be of the "internal constitution of their parts," and the mechanical reasons why they exhibit the powers they do. From such science we are shut off because of the limitations of our means of observation, our sense organs. Such necessary connections of the properties of a body in its real essence are there and are known to angels, though not to men.

Had we senses acute enough to discern the minute particles of bodies, and the real constitution on which their sensible properties depend, I doubt not but they would produce quite different ideas in us; and that which is now the yellow color of gold would then disappear, and instead of it we should see an admirable texture of parts, of a certain size and figure. This microscopes plainly discover to us, for what to our naked eyes produces a certain color is by thus augmenting the acuteness of our senses discovered to be quite a different thing. (I, 401)

Not knowing the root they spring from, not knowing what size, figure, and texture of parts they are, on which depend and from which result those qualities which make our complex idea of gold, it is impossible we should know what other qualities result from or are incompatible with, the same constitution of the insensible parts of gold; and so consequently must always coexist with that complex idea we have of it. (II, 201) As to the powers of substances to change the sensible qualities of other bodies, . . . I doubt as to these whether our knowledge reaches much further than our experience. . . . Because the active and passive powers of bodies and their ways of operating consisting in a texture and motion of parts which we cannot by any means come to discover, it is but in very few cases we can be able to perceive their dependence on, or repugnance to, any of those ideas which make our complex one of that sort of things. (II, 205) Not knowing, therefore, what number of particles, nor what motion of them, is fit to produce any precise degree of whiteness, we cannot demonstrate the certain equality of any two degrees of whiteness; because we have no certain standard to measure them by, nor means to distinguish every the least real difference. (II, 185)

If we could observe this texture of parts, we could then have a demonstrative science of bodies.

I doubt not but if we could discover the figure, size, texture, and motion of the minute constituent parts of any two bodies, we should know *without trial* several of their operations one upon another; as we do now the properties of a square or a triangle. . . . We should be able to tell *beforehand* that rhubarb will purge, hemlock kill, and opium make a man sleep. . . . But whilst we are destitute of senses acute enough we must be content to be ignorant of their properties and ways of operation. (II, 216) Had we such ideas of substances as to know what real constitutions they possess, we could, by the specific ideas of their real essences in our own minds, more certainly find out their properties than we can now by our senses; and to know the properties of gold it would be no more necessary that gold should exist, and that we should make experiments upon it, than it is necessary for the knowing the properties of a triangle, that a triangle should exist in any matter. . . . Then the truth of this proposition, all gold is malleable, would be as certain as of this, that the three angles, etc. (II, 260)

The result of this state of affairs is that while we can have "intuitive" knowledge of the existence of ourselves, and "demonstrative" knowledge of that of God, of bodily substances and their real relations we can hope to possess only "sensitive" knowledge, mere observation, and not demonstration or science.

Therefore I am apt to doubt that how far soever human industry may advance useful and experimental philosophy in physical things, scientifical will still be out of our reach: because we want perfect and adequate observation of those very bodies which are nearest to us, and most under our command. . . . Certainty and demonstration are things we must not, in these matters, pretend to. . . . Thus having no ideas of the particular mechanical affections of the minute parts of bodies that are within our view and reach, we are ignorant of their constitutions, powers, and operations. . . . As to a perfect science of natural bodies, we are, I think, so far from being capable of any such thing, that I conclude it lost labor to seek after it. (II, 217, 223)

It is well to note that Locke attributes the lack of certainty and demonstrative science in physics to the inadequacy of our means of observation. This signifies that it can be remedied by improved means, that is, by instruments. Locke consequently leaves the way open that has actually been followed since; and with most of Locke's examples, improved instruments have revealed the relations involved, and made a "scientific" knowledge possible. Locke has thus reduced the question of the certainty of knowledge to a practical problem; his discussion is an instance of empirical analysis at its best. But, in default of such means, Locke is forced to admit, we must be content with another kind of knowledge, of the experimentally observed relations between the properties we can observe. Here we can reach no deductive system, no general and necessary truths, no reasons why. We can observe "a constant and regular connection in the ordinary course of things," (II, 221) between the effects of the unknown powers of bodies.

Possibly inquisitive and observing men may, by strength of judgment, penetrate further, and on probabilities taken from wary observation, and hints well laid together, often guess right at what experience has not yet discovered to them. But this is but guessing still. . . . We must appeal to trial in particular subjects, which can reach but a little way. . . . Experience here must teach me what reason cannot; and it is by trying alone that I can certainly know what qualities coexist. . . . This way of getting and improving our knowledge in substances only by experience and history, which is all that the weakness of our faculties . . . can attain to, makes me suspect that natural philosophy is not capable of being made a science. (II, 263, 265, 348, 350)

Physics may not be a science, but it is nevertheless sufficient for our purposes.

Herein, therefore, is founded the reality of our knowledge concerning substances—that all our complex ideas of them must be such, and such only, as are made up of such simple ones as have been discovered to co-exist in nature. And our ideas being thus true, though not perhaps very exact copies, are yet the subjects of real (as far as we have any) knowledge of them. Which (as has been already shown) will not be found to reach very far: but so far as it does, it will still be real knowledge. Whatever ideas we have, the agreement we find they have with others will still be knowledge. (II, 237)

We shall not have much reason to complain of the narrowness of our minds if we will but employ them about what may be of use to us; for of that they are very capable. And it will be an unpardonable as well as childish peevishness, if we undervalue the advantages of our knowledge, and neglect to improve it to the ends for which it was given us, because there are some things that are set out of the reach of it. It will be no excuse to an idle and untoward servant, who would not attend his business by candle light, to plead that he had not broad sunshine. The candle that is set up in us shines bright enough for all our purposes. The discoveries we can make with this ought to satisfy us; and we shall then use our understandings right, when we entertain all objects in that way and proportion that they are suited to our faculties, and upon those grounds they are capable of being proposed to us; and not peremptorily or intemperately require demonstration, and demand certainty, where probability only is to be had, and which is sufficient to govern all our concernments. If we will disbelieve everything, because we cannot certainly know all things, we shall do muchwhat as wisely as he who would not use his legs, but sit still and perish, because he had no wings to fly. Our business here is not to know all things, but those which concern our conduct. If we can find out those measures, whereby a rational creature, put in that state in which man is in this world, may and ought to govern his opinions, and actions depending thereon, we need not be troubled that some other things escape our knowledge. (I, 29–31)

Locke, it is clear, is really working out a new conception of science, what we have called the "observational" theory. He has been driven to it, like Newton, by the realization of his ignorance of the "powers" of the unobservable particles. He is convinced, like Newton, that this is a provisional ignorance, a "not yet." But the mathematical and scholastic ideal of the nature of science is too much for him; "science" must be what it was for Descartes and Newton, the demonstration of necessary relations from causes or powers. Therefore instead of a consistent conception of science, and a metaphysics based on the actual procedure of the scientists, seeking knowable relations in nature, Locke remained caught in a dualism between the method and the ideal of science, inherent in Newtonian thought. Science is a system of logical relations, the world is a collection of unobservable, independent substances, with inaccessible powers and properties. The only knowledge possible of such a world is not "scientific," but merely the record of the constant and regular connection of the observed effects of unknown powers. It remained for Berkeley to develop this conception of the nature of science in consistent form.

V I

Locke's second difficulty, that of the "reality" of knowledge, is a much more paradoxical problem. It springs from his further assumption that what is disclosed in sense is "in us," that ideas are not the observable aspects of bodies, the "phenomena" of Newton, as they are throughout the problem of certainty, but are the effects produced "in us" by the contact of the particles of the real world.

I cannot conceive how bodies without us can anyway affect our senses, but by the immediate contact of the sensible bodies themselves, as in tasting and feeling, or the impulse of some sensible particles coming from them, as in seeing, hearing, and smelling; by the different impulses of which parts, caused by their different size, figure, and motion, the variety of sensations is produced in us. (II, 184)

We are struck upon the eyes by tiny billiard-balls, and we see, not billiard-balls, but stars. How then can we ever perceive the agreement between ideas and the things that cause them? How can we ever know whether the effects that the world produces "in us" resemble their causes? Is not science shut up "inside the mind"? If the Newtonian world is never directly observable, but only its effects upon the mind, if science is of the relations of what is observed, how can we ever know the relations in the Newtonian world? How, indeed, can we know there really is such a world of nature, of masses in motion? Is not knowledge inevitably caught in *subjectivism?* This conclusion is the second basic assumption in the position of "empiricism."

If our knowledge of our ideas terminate in them and reach no further, where there is something further intended, our most serious thoughts will be of little more use than the reveries of a crazy brain; and the truths built thereon of no more weight than the discourses of a man who sees things clearly in a dream, and with great assurance utters them. (II, 227, 228) It is evident that the mind knows not things immediately, but only by the intervention of the ideas it has of them. Our knowledge therefore is real only so far as there is a conformity between our ideas and the reality of things. But what shall be here the criterion? How shall the mind, when it perceives nothing but its own ideas, know that they agree with things themselves? This seems not to want difficulty. (II, 228)

This is obviously a problem to be solved, not by improved instruments, but by changed assumptions. It is not a practical, but a "dialectical" difficulty, generated by contradictory assumptions. There are many ways of altering the set-up which generates it. Locke himself fell back on a functional theory of knowledge: the ideas of the secondary qualities or powers of bodies conform to those powers, not by resembling or agreeing with them, but as "distinguishing marks." The perceived *relations* of the effects of the powers of bodies do "conform to" and "have a steady correspondence with" the relations of the powers themselves, and the system of knowledge does conform to the order of real bodies and powers. Yet even here Locke falls into confusion, for he leaves the ideas of primary qualities as resemblances or copies. The ideas of secondary qualities are signs by which we learn the relations of bodies; the ideas of primary qualities are themselves a direct intuition of bodies, of their real essences, which have no relations.

Once again, the division of the properties of bodies into those relational and knowable, and those inherent, absolute, and hence unknowable if knowledge is of relations, enters in to cause confusion. An unknowable real world is the cause of what is known; what is known gives no knowledge of its cause, yet is the only evidence of its existence. This gulf, so clear in both Newton and Locke, between unknowable essences and powers, and knowable relations, was broken down by Berkeley, who made all the properties of bodies and the concepts of science relational, and knowledge wholly functional. "The connection of ideas does not imply the relation of cause and effect [that is, of power and production] but only of a mark or sign with the thing signified." [3] Berkeley was hence able to give a consistent answer to both Locke's problems. Knowledge is not "certain," but it is completely "real." And yet British empiricists down to Bertrand Russell and A. J. Ayer have kept up the confusion of the two problems: we know the world only by experience, not by reasoning; yet what we know is not the world, but only experience. We must defer to facts, but there are no facts, only ideas. [4]

[3] Berkeley, *Principles of Human Knowledge*, Part I, par. 65; Fraser, I, 294; Jessop ed., II, 69.
[4] For Locke's political philosophy, see Book Four, chapter 6; for his religious rationalism, see chapter 7; for his moral theories, see chapter 8, section IV.

4

George Berkeley: Realist and Objective Relativist

SHORTLY AFTER Locke had been laid in his grave at Highe Laver, and while the incomparable Mr. Newton was still enjoying the height of his adulation, a young Irish student of Trinity College was reading at Dublin all the latest philosophers—Descartes, Malebranche, Newton, Boyle, and Locke—and, like many another young student since, not reading the great philosophers of the past. Though George Berkeley (1685–1753) was greatly interested in the mathematics which then stood as the summit of human wisdom, like so many of his fellow-countrymen he smelled out inconsistency in what seemed to Englishmen sober common sense. To him, in the first flush of his youthful intellectual enthusiasm, the Newtonian world view, the whole mathematical interpretation of nature, seemed unintelligible. Its system of solid massy particles which cause in some incomprehensible way effects in us, a system of nature that cannot be known in itself, but only through the dubious medium of its mysterious effects, can lead to but one end, scepticism. To proclaim that we have no knowledge of the real world seemed to this young Irishman merely absurd. So with the courage of youth, and of his Celtic heritage, he calmly brushed it aside. He had never, however, studied the history of philosophy, and so he knew of no more satisfactory alternative. He had to invent one for himself, and naturally it sounded rather funny; though when one penetrates below its new-fangled terminology it proves to be not nearly so funny nor so novel as it sounds.

Berkeley insisted that we do know the real world. Common sense, and indeed the whole philosophical tradition, maintains that the real world is what we know, not the unknowable cause of what we do know. In his student commonplace book he set down, "I side in all things with the mob." [1] In the pursuit of this laudable resolution he succeeded in developing the philosophy of present-day physics, as practiced upon British soil.

Berkeley started with Locke's second problem. In its terms he was an uncompromising realist, affirming the reality and validity of human knowledge. The system of nature is what we know directly, it is the object of the mind when a man thinks. The world is knowable; only the new-fangled mathematicians have thought of denying it. Do they tell us that "ideas" are what we know, the immediate objects of the mind? Then "ideas" must be the real things of which the choir of heaven and the furniture of earth is composed; ideas must be "any sensible or imaginable thing." [2] They are not copies of things they do not resemble, they are not the effects in the mind of the contacts of our body with other bodies: they are real things.

I do not pretend to be a setter-up of new notions. My endeavors tend only to unite, and place in a clearer light, that truth which was before shared between the vulgar and the philosophers:—the former being of opinion, that those things they immediately perceive are the real things; and the latter, that the things immediately perceived are ideas, which exist only in the mind. Which two notions put together do, in effect, constitute the substance of what I advance.[3]

We see the house itself, the church itself; it being an idea and nothing more. The house itself, the church itself, is an idea, i.e., an object—immediate object—of thought.[4]

Berkeley employed this novel terminology, drawn from the latest philosophers, to express an ancient conviction. The notion of vague substances, of "real essences," of an absolute time and space—all notions indeed of things that can never be perceived—seemed to him useless and silly. The only substances are the things we do perceive

[1] Berkeley, *Philosophical Commentaries*, Notebook A, note 405, in *Works*, A. A. Luce and T. E. Jessop ed. (1948), I, 51; in ed. A. C. Fraser (1901), I, 7.
[2] *Philosophical Commentaries*, Notebook A, n. 775, Luce ed., I, 93; Fraser ed., I, 47.
[3] *Third Dialogue between Hylas and Philonous*, Jessop ed., II, 262; Fraser ed., I, 484.
[4] *Philosophical Commentaries*, Notebook A, n. 427, Luce ed., I, 53; Fraser ed., I, 9.

and know. The perceived world is the only real world, for it is the only one actually experienced.

> The supposition that things are distinct from ideas takes away all real truth, and consequently brings in a universal scepticism; since all our knowledge and contemplation is confined barely to our own ideas.[5]

> We have been led into very dangerous errors, by supposing a twofold existence of sense—the one intelligible or in the mind, the other real and without the mind . . . So long as men thought that real things subsisted without the mind, and that their knowledge was only so far forth real as it was conformable to real things, it follows that they could not be certain that they had any real knowledge at all. For how can it be known that the things that are perceived are conformable to those which are not perceived, or exist without the mind? Color, figure, motion, extension, and the like, considered only as so many sensations in the mind, are perfectly known; there being nothing in them which is not perceived. But if they are looked on as notes or images referred to things or archetypes existing without the mind, then are we involved all in scepticism . . . What may be the extension, figure, or motion of anything really and absolutely, or in itself, it is impossible for us to know, but only the proportion or relation they bear to our senses.[6]

Now the science of optics was one of the strongholds of the mathematical interpretation of nature. It maintained that we "see by geometry,"[7] that we "see external space and bodies actually existing in it, some nearer, others farther off";[8] that we see the primary qualities of bodies, their true position in space. Berkeley resolved to bring this theory to the test of experience, to examine vision to see what could actually be deduced from phenomena, "to consider how it is that we perceive distance, and things placed at a distance, by sight."[9] He concluded that vision is a matter of signs, not of geometrical relations at all.

> Distance or outness is neither immediately perceived by sight, nor yet apprehended or judged of by lines and angles, or anything that hath a necessary connexion with it; but it is only suggested to our thoughts by certain visible ideas and sensations attending vision, which in their own nature have no manner of similitude or relation either with distance or

[5] *Philosophical Commentaries*, Notebook A, n. 606, Luce ed., I, 75; Fraser ed., I, 30.
[6] *Principles of Human Knowledge*, par. 86; Jessop ed., II, 78; Fraser ed., I, 305.
[7] *A New Theory of Vision*, par. 53; Luce ed., I, 191; Fraser ed., I, 152.
[8] *Principles*, par. 43; Jessop ed., II, 58; Fraser ed., I, 279.   [9] *Ibid.*

with things placed at a distance; but, by a connexion taught us by experience, they come to signify and suggest them to us, after the same manner that words of any language suggest the ideas they are made to stand for . . . So that in strict truth the ideas of sight, when we apprehend by them distance, and things placed at a distance, do not suggest or mark out to us things actually existing at a distance, but only admonish us what ideas of touch will be imprinted in our minds at such and such distances of time, and in consequence of such and such actions.[10]

Visible ideas serve as signs of certain tangible ideas. But Berkeley does not mean that when we think we are seeing distance, we are really feeling it. Under other conditions—in the dark, for instance —tangible ideas serve as signs of what we would see if it were light. Tangible ideas are no more real than visible ideas: along that path lurks Newton. In all our perception we are really sharing in a system of universal symbolism. Perceiving one idea, we can predict what other ideas it has in our experience been the sign of.

The connexion of ideas does not imply the relation of cause and effect, but only of a mark or sign with the thing signified. The fire which I see is not the cause of the pain which I suffer upon my approaching it, but the mark that forewarns me of it. In like manner the noise that I hear is not the effect of this or that motion or collision of the ambient bodies, but the sign thereof.[11]

In the New Theory of Vision (1709) Berkeley maintained that through experience our visible ideas and tangible ideas become symbols for one another. In The Principles of Human Knowledge (1710) he extends this notion of signification to all our ideas. Knowledge is a universal system of mutual symbols based on the perceived order of ideas or things; and all these symbols or ideas are derived from perception.

The principle that Esse est percipi, which serves as Berkeley's philosophical tag in the marts of thought, thus means that perception is the criterion of reality. It is opposed to the Newtonian and Lockean principle that Esse est causare perceptiones. "Idea" is the term for whatever is perceived; therefore every real thing is an idea. That such ideas "exist in the mind" means for Berkeley that they are knowable, are phenomena, not that they are "inside the head"; for with Berkeley, unlike Hobbes or Locke, neither ideas

[10] Principles, Jessop ed., II, 58; Fraser ed., I, 280.
[11] Principles, par. 65; Jessop ed., II, 69; Fraser ed., I, 294.

nor heads exist in an independent Newtonian space. For an idea to be "in the mind" means that it is in relation to a perceiving mind.

But *Esse est percipi* is also a principle to be opposed to *Esse est intelligi*, the principle of the Greek tradition, of the rationalists, of Spinoza. What can be known directly is sense objects, sensible or imaginable things, not axioms, concepts, forms, relations. It is this insistence that is the new and startling aspect of Berkeley's thought. The image is the element of knowledge, not the concept, the universal, the meaning. How did he arrive at this novel position? Apart from the fact that Berkeley, like so many British thinkers, seems to have been what psychologists call a visualist, and thought in terms of images rather than of words, such a conclusion was natural enough to one so wholly immersed in contemporary currents of thought. He took over the identification of idea with sensation, though he rejected the reason for that identification in Locke and his followers, belief in the sole reality of the Newtonian world. For them, contact of bodily particles upon the sense organs could produce only sensations. Though for Berkeley ideas are not so produced, he still develops with rigid consistency the implications of that position. Images are particular things; as such they can have no relations save coexistence and succession. The only logical relations possible between such pure particulars, that of being signs of each other, is purely arbitrary, founded on their observed coexistence and succession, and not upon any relation of implication.

Berkeley is in this youthful work a consistent imagist. He uses his position to criticize all necessary connections between things. He retains real substances, as perceived, outside the mind, and not part of the mind; but there are no causal connections, no necessary relations between them. Only particular, concrete things exist and are known. Thus he is led to deny all wholes, all unities, and universals. There is room only for aggregates and series, for bundles of particulars. There can be no such thing as a general or abstract idea. As he calmly sets down in his notebook, "What becomes of the Eternal Truths? They vanish." [12] Here was a radical, critical weapon indeed!

Hence Berkeley offers a world of real, knowable objects, called

[12] *Philosophical Commentaries*, Notebook A, n. 735; Luce ed., I, 90; Fraser ed., I, 44.

in the latest fashion "ideas." These objects, Berkeley was quite willing to recognize, were "external in origin, without the mind, and distinct from it," [13] though he insisted they were not independent of it and hence unknowable. They have no relations to each other save those of coexistence and succession. They are wholly passive, and cannot "cause" other objects or "ideas." The Newtonian powers of bodies have disappeared. There is no idea of causation as a productive power; what we call causation is the mere observed succession of ideas. Knowing is a wholly passive process; things do not cause knowledge. The relation between things and the mind is logical, not mechanical. In knowledge the mind too is wholly passive; it is a pure spectator, a great Eye. This passivity of the mind in all knowing, the identification in the last analysis of knowing with perceiving, has remained basic for subsequent empiricism down to Whitehead. Berkeley has thus stated consistently the new conception of science hinted at in Newton and suggested by Locke: science is knowledge of the succession of nature, the "course of nature," not of a logical order or system of nature. It describes phenomena and predicts their occurrence, it does not attempt to explain or prove them.

But besides natural objects or "ideas" there is mind also. Mind is not always passive; it rearranges ideas, it wills. Mind is not an idea or thing at all, it is absolutely different from the ideas that constitute the course of nature. It is an active cause, a productive power, Spirit. Spirit is known directly by experience in ourselves, as a real cause or power. Now things do not cause each other, nor are they caused by the minds that perceive them. Certainly I do not create the world! But they must be caused by Something, by a substance with real power. The only such power known to us is Spirit. Hence we must infer a Spiritual Power or Force back of things or ideas and causing them and their constant succession. For Berkeley shared with Newton the demand for a cause of the observed relations of things. But he lodged it, not in the unknowable powers of inertia and gravitation with which God has endowed bodies, but in the unknowable power of God himself. Newton's unknowable intermediaries are useless; observable things are enough. In both cases

[13] *Principles*, par. 90; Jessop ed., II, 80; Fraser ed., I, 308. *Philosophical Commentaries*, Notebook A; Luce ed., I, 102; Fraser ed., I, 56.

the world is contained and supported by an infinite omnipresent Force, which both, with equal justification, or lack of justification, call God.

To me it is evident that sensible things cannot exist otherwise than in a mind or spirit. Whence I conclude, not that they have no real existence, but that, seeing they depend not on my thought, and have an existence distinct from being perceived by me, there must be some other mind wherein they exist. As sure, therefore, as the sensible world really exists, so sure is there an infinite omnipresent spirit who contains and supports it.[14]

The outcome of Berkeley's resolve to side with the mob against the mathematicians is to provide a real field for science, to destroy scepticism as to the existence of a world of objects, and to relieve common experience of the burden of being "merely subjective." There is no Lockean subjectivism in Berkeley's thought. We know things directly by observation. The world is knowable, as the expression of Force, defined in terms of its observable manifestations. But Berkeley has changed the conception of the nature of science. He has worked out observationalism, the theory of a purely descriptive science. He has transformed all Newton's intrinsic powers and properties into observed relations, and made science and its concepts wholly and consistently relational.

This translation of Newtonian mechanics into relational terms is most clearly and elaborately carried out in the little essay *De Motu*, written for a prize competition in 1721. Whether because of the occasion, or because he was reaching maturity, Berkeley here adopts the accepted vulgar terminology. The task of science is to observe and describe the constant and uniform succession of phenomena. The laws of nature are descriptive, in mathematical language, of the observed course of nature. But they express no necessary logical connections, deducible without observation. There is no observable causality in nature. Nature has no productive powers, no forces, no gravitation. No causal power is ever observed; we see and measure only motions and their effects. Science is limited to the perceptible relations between bodies (the language of ideas has been discarded). Preceding events are not causes of subsequent

[14] *Second Dialogue between Hylas and Philonous,* Jessop ed., II, 212; Fraser ed., I, 424.

events; they are merely signs of what is to come, sufficient for prediction. Berkeley undertakes a keen critique of the Newtonian absolute motion, space, and time. All motion is relative, and is measured ultimately with reference to the fixed stars; Berkeley brushes aside Newton's pail as irrelevant. Both time and space are relative to the observer, schemes for measuring relations. The system of nature is really the language of nature, revealing her constant and uniform working. The ultimate cause of the laws of nature is not any necessary connections between things, but is arbitrary and inscrutable: it is the expression of the free will of Spiritual Force, given as signs for practical purposes.

Berkeley's world is thus not silly or paradoxical, but the commonplace of present-day physics: which, like Berkeley, sees nature as the expression of force or energy, in phenomena observed always by measurements relative to the observer. The world of unintelligible absolute massy particles has disappeared. Berkeley, in a word, gives a perfectly consistent interpretation of the world of modern physics; and he has been appealed to by physicists like Whitehead and Eddington who, being in the British tradition, find his assumptions congenial, as the inspired critic of the Newtonian absolutes from the standpoint of a relational theory. Berkeley made Newtonian science consistent, though not as a necessary deductive system, by abolishing the gulf between the absolute and the relational properties of bodies, and thus eliminating scepticism and subjectivism. On only one point did he fail to be consequent, in making the cause of natural relations unknowable: he retained the conception of causation as power, though he specifically banished it from science. Why did he not make causation a relation, and hence observable? Why did he not identify it with the orderly seriality of events? In part, the hold of the Newtonian notion was too strong; in part, he acted from religious motives, which account, not so much for his carrying the criticism of the Newtonian world as far as he did, but for his not carrying it further, to a completely positivistic view. Incidentally, the common dismissal of Berkeley's views as appropriate to a bishop is hardly accurate: for the works perpetrated as a young man delayed his preferment for many years. He seemed far too erratic to be even an Irish bishop.

Grown older, he studied the Greeks, and brought his views more into line with the classic tradition. It is clear that his earlier startling terminology was the result of pure ignorance. By 1734, when the second edition of the *Principles* appeared, he had come to realize that there is much in knowledge that is not mere "idea" or image. He introduced at this time the term "notion" for a knowledge, not only of spirits, but of relations. All knowledge of particular things or "ideas" is perceptual, is an image; but other knowledge, especially of intelligible relations, is gained by "notions." This is Berkeley's grudging recognition of a non-perceptual type of knowledge.

We know and have a notion of relations between things or ideas; which relations are distinct from the ideas or things related, inasmuch as the latter may be perceived by us without our perceiving the former. To me it seems that ideas, spirits, and relations are all in their respective kinds the object of human knowledge and subject of discourse; and that the term idea would be improperly extended to signify everything we know or have any notion of.[15]

In *Siris or Tar Water*, published in 1744, he added to his observational, relational science a Platonic metaphysics, without, however, modifying the theory of science. Science still gives no ultimate explanations; it discovers the laws of nature, not their causes, laws which are mathematical hypotheses. Scientific causation, which he now admits, is limited to the rules of the modes of operation of nature. Knowledge of these rules enables us to predict the constant and uniform succession of "phenomena" (not "ideas"). He treats of science in terms of the metaphor of language, which he enjoyed elaborating. The relation of sign to thing signified, developed into a universal system of mutual symbols founded on the observed course of nature, is the language in which God speaks to us. Science is a rational discourse between God and man. God's language has an orderly structure or grammar, a set of rules or laws which it follows. Science is the study of God's grammar. Knowing the grammar of science, we can understand what God is telling us for the conduct of our practical life. We can read this language of God writ in nature, and predict the ideas we shall perceive on perceiving others. The laws of motion are important rules of God's grammar, knowing which we can share correctly in the system of mutual

[15] *Principles*, par. 89; Jessop ed., II, 80; Fraser ed., I, 307. This important passage was not added until the second ed. (1734).

symbols which is the rational discourse between God and man.

But mere sense images, the perception of phenomena, are now deprecated; they reveal only the course of nature. To find its cause, we must rise to Reason, to the intelligible realm of Platonic Ideas with a capital I, of which the "ideas" or phenomena God uses in his discourse to man, the human experience of the course of nature, are but faint shadows. Perception gives mere phenomena; the criterion of reality is conception, reason. The *Siris* is chiefly concerned, not with a science of nature founded on perception, but with the real knowledge God has of His Ideas, and of their eternal and necessary relations. God speaks to us by means of the ideas we perceive, and in science we study the grammar of His tongue. But we have real knowledge when to the perception of his syllables we add, by reason, an understanding of His discourse—when we comprehend, not merely God's grammar, but the significance of His message. God's message is something appropriate, not to scientists, but to saints and bishops. But, alas, even bishops fall short of perfect comprehension, and, like other mortals, must realize we can parse God's sentences but we cannot understand God's discourse. This is unfortunate for us, as pious worshipers; but as scientists it makes no difference. For God's message has no relevance for natural science; and could we comprehend it completely, it would still remain necessary for the conduct of our life to predict the succession of our ideas which is the course of nature. And so Berkeley's early radicalism is rightly remembered by an impious posterity, not his mature Platonism.

As a religious apologist Berkeley must be said to have failed. His conclusion, that God is not Time and Space, but Force, has no more religious value than the view it combatted. It is, in fact, the same Newtonian scientific modernism, the same identification of theology with mechanics. As a critic of Newtonian science, he made the world knowable if not intelligible. His translation was rejected in his own day, for scientists were not yet prepared to view the laws of nature as mere descriptions of a constant succession. All, save the radical Newtonians, demanded a necessary system of mathematical demonstrations. But his ideas fell into the hands of a clever and malicious Scotsman, David Hume, who forged them into the keenest weapon ever raised against bishops, and incidentally removed from the Newtonian theory of science the last trace of the Newtonian powers and necessary connections. Berkeley answered Locke's two problems just as Locke had answered them: our knowledge of natural bodies is real, but not certain. Yet he succeeded in transforming the notion of the world in which science has a setting so as to exhibit, as Locke had not, why science is real knowledge; and in transforming the notion of science so as to make clear, what for Locke was due to human ignorance, why it is lost labor to seek for the kind of knowledge of nature Locke had set out to find.

5

David Hume: Radical Empiricist
and Pragmatist

I

IT WAS David Hume (1711–1776) who completed the criticism of the presuppositions of Newtonian science. And it was Hume who first worked out the full implications of the empiricist interpretation of that science, and in so doing transformed empiricism into something else—into what William James called "radical empiricism," and John Dewey, "experimental naturalism." The procedure he employed in carrying out his criticism led him to the further position which both James and Dewey called "pragmatism," and which Kant might well have recognized as an at least incipient "critical philosophy."

Recent careful examination of Hume's complex thought has concluded that his dialectical elaboration of the assumptions of British empiricism, and his reconstruction of those assumptions into a less limited and more consistent philosophy of science, was rather incidental to his main philosophical purpose, and not central to his own intentions. Since Kant made epistemology the controlling philosophical problem, and especially since Hegel and the historians of philosophy who followed him came to see Kant as a "synthesis" between the "thesis" of Continental rationalism and the "antithesis" of British empiricism, it has been conventional to view Hume as the successor of Locke and Berkeley, and the provoker of Kant's enterprise of synthesis. But the best recent critical literature [1] has made

This chapter has already appeared in *Freedom and Experience: Essays presented to Horace M. Kallen*, edited by Sidney Hook and Milton R. Konvitz (Ithaca, New York, 1947), pp. 289-312.

[1] John Laird, in his *Hume's Philosophy of Human Nature* (1932), and Richard H. Popkin in several articles, have brought out the background in

it clear that Hume's immediate intellectual background is not Berkeley but Hutcheson, and that while Locke looms large for him, as for Hutcheson himself, the French observationalists Malebranche and Pierre Bayle are equally important; while Cicero's account of the ideas of the ancient sceptics, especially Carneades, is as influential for his "great philosophical discovery" as either Locke or the French.

II

Hume stands for all time as the antithesis of Spinoza in his thought. Spinoza was profoundly moved by his vision of the fact of knowledge, of the power of the human mind to understand the universe, and of a universe that is through and through intelligible. He summed up his vision: "The human mind has an adequate knowledge of the infinite and eternal essence of God or Nature." Hume, bringing this confidence to the test of experience, reached the conclusion that the world is not "intelligible" at all. Whatever is, may not be; and the nature of that evidence which assures us of any real existence and matter of fact beyond the present testimony of our senses, is such as to throw doubt on all our beliefs, a doubt stilled only by the need for action.

Hume stands as the antithesis of Spinoza in personality as well. Spinoza found supreme, continuous, and never-ending blessedness in that knowledge of the union which obtains between the human mind and God, that union that is the intellectual love of God; and for it he gladly gave up all the usual surroundings of social life, riches, fame, and the pleasures of the senses—the last because they are followed by melancholy, riches because they create an insatiable craving, and fame because it compels its votaries to order their lives

Malebranche and Bayle of Hume's thinking. Popkin has pointed out that it is doubtful whether Hume ever read Berkeley at first hand, though he had a general sense of his position and mentions him at least twice. Norman Kemp Smith in *The Philosophy of David Hume* (1941), and J. A. Passmore, in *Hume's Intentions* (1952), both agree that it is moral philosophy that is basic in Hume's thinking, and that he began with its problems, following the lead of Hutcheson, and only later became involved in the "logic" of Book I of the *Treatise*. This general orientation of Hume's intellectual drive, and his early division of the "moral sciences," will be considered in chapter 11, "Hume's System of Ethics." The present chapter will treat Hume's theory of knowledge or "logic," which, whatever his "intentions," has proved extremely influential on both the British and the German traditions ever since.

according to the opinions of their fellow-men, shunning what they usually shun, and seeking what they usually seek. Hume, who doubted there was a God, and certainly did not love him, set as his goal precisely those usual surroundings of social life, the pleasures of the senses, riches, and fame. He was never melancholy, but "of an open, social, and cheerful humor"; he was satisfied when he had made a competence; and he delighted all his life in setting forth opinions diametrically opposite to those of his fellow-men.

If we may trust his own account in his brief autobiography, Hume wrote for two purposes: to make money, and to gain a literary reputation. He acknowledged, "My ruling passion is the love of literary fame." [2] As a youth he studied Locke, Malebranche, and Bayle, and Cicero and the ancient Academic sceptics; in their thought he saw the chance to reach startling conclusions and become a shocking success. Berkeley had attacked Newtonian science for serious reasons; he was a crusader, interested in a sound and consistent science. Hume subtly criticized it primarily to attract attention to the Scotsman David Hume. He hated Newton and Locke as Englishmen, besides; for next to priests, Englishmen were his most cordial hatred. In 1768 he wrote, "O! how I long to see America and the East Indies revolted, totally and finally—the revenue reduced to half—public credit fully discredited by bankruptcy— the third of London in ruins, and the rascally mob subdued! I think I am not too old to despair of being witness to all these blessings." [3] It would be easy to interpret Hume's life as the expression of an inferiority complex, as a writer and a Scotsman. He was always complaining of the lack of recognition, of prejudices, of his failure to create a stir; he was always extremely touchy about everything Scottish. A profound dissatisfaction runs through his letters, full of doubts and misgivings; which in his autobiography, when he knew he had succeeded despite Englishmen, has turned into a complacent discontent.

He was early seized with a passion for literature. After unhappy experiences in business in Bristol, he resolved "to regard every object as contemptible, except the improvement of my talents in

[2] "My Own Life," in *Essays*, ed. Green and Grose (London, 1875), I, 8.
[3] Letter to Sir Gilbert Elliot, 1768; in J. H. Burton, *Life and Correspondence of David Hume* (Edinburgh, 1846), II, 417.

literature." [4] At twenty-three he went into retreat at La Flèche in France, the very birthplace of Cartesian rationalism. There he set down his *Treatise of Human Nature*, which saw the light in 1739 (volume III came out the next year), and waited. "Never literary attempt was more unfortunate than my Treatise of Human Nature. It fell *dead-born from the press*, without reaching such distinction, as even to excite a murmur among the zealots." [5] Since he couldn't shock men by a new theory of science, he would try politics; his *Essays* appeared in 1741–1742. "The work was favourably received, and soon made me entirely forget my former disappointment." (I, 2) In 1748 came *Of Miracles* and *Of Providence and a Future State*. Replies were written by theologians; Hume was happy, for he dearly loved to shock the reverend doctors. Resolved to make Englishmen recognize him in spite of themselves, he rewrote the first part of his *Treatise* as *The Enquiry concerning Human Understanding*, leaving out all the hard parts. "But this piece was at first little more successful than the Treatise." (I, 3) He spent some time in the country.

Meanwhile my bookseller informed me that my former publications (all but the unfortunate Treatise) were beginning to be the subject of conversation; that the sale of them was gradually increasing, and that new editions were demanded. Answers by Reverends, and Right Reverends, came out two or three in a year; and I found, by Dr. Warburton's railing, that the books were beginning to be esteemed in good company. . . . In 1751 was published at London, my Enquiry concerning the Principles of Morals; which, in my opinion (who ought not to judge on that subject), is of all my writings, historical, philosophical, or literary, incomparably the best. It came unnoticed and unobserved into the world. (I, 4)

Philosophy was after all a rather narrow field; so he turned to history, and wrote a good Tory history of the Stuarts because the Whigs were in power. "I scarcely, indeed, heard of one man in the three kingdoms, considerable for rank or letters, that could endure the book. I must only except the primate of England, Dr. Herring, and the primate of Ireland, Dr. Stone, which seem two odd exceptions. These dignified prelates separately sent me messages not to be discouraged." (I, 5) But he was discouraged, and had not war

---

[4] *Essays*, "My Own Life," I, 2.
[5] *Ibid.*, I, 2. In 1740 Hume printed an *Abstract* of the *Treatise*, explaining his central contentions (ed. Keynes and Sraffa, 1938).

broken out, would have retired to some provincial town in France and changed his name. By 1761, however, his History was beginning to meet with "a tolerable, and but tolerable success." (I, 6)

But, notwithstanding this variety of winds and seasons, to which my writings had been exposed, they had still been making such advances, that the copy-money given me by the book-sellers, much exceeded any thing formerly known in England; I was become not only independent, but opulent. (I, 6)

At this time Hume took a post in the Embassy at Paris.

Those who have not seen the strange effects of modes, will never imagine the reception I met with at Paris, from men and women of all ranks and stations. The more I recoiled from their excessive civilities, the more I was loaded with them. There is, however, a real satisfaction in living at Paris, from the great number of sensible, knowing, and polite company with which that city abounds above all places in the universe. I thought once of settling there for life. (I, 6)

But what was the good of the French lionizing him?

The taste for literature is neither decayed nor depraved here, as with the barbarians who inhabit the banks of the Thames. . . . I do not believe there is one Englishman in fifty, who, if he heard I had broke my neck to-night, would be sorry. . . . The rage and prejudice of parties frighten me; and above all, this rage against the Scots, which is so dishonourable, and indeed so infamous to the English nation.[6]

Clearly the praise of the whole world was hollow in his ears if he could not excite the English.

Actually he had won fame and riches; and he retired to Edinburgh, "to pass all the rest of my life in a philosophical manner." He devoted himself to his friends and to the science of cookery, preparing *soupe à la reine* and sheep-head broth. He finally realized he was suffering from an incurable disease; yet he contemplated death with equanimity, with good spirits and even gaiety. Reckoning upon a speedy dissolution, he set down the brief record "Of my Own Life."

I consider that a man of sixty-five, by dying, cuts off only a few years of infirmities; and though I see many symptoms of my literary reputation's breaking out at last with additional lustre, I knew that I could have but few years to enjoy it.[7]

[6] Burton, *Correspondence*, II, 196, 238, 265.
[7] *Essays*, "My Own Life," I, 7.

He awaited the end cheerfully, reading Lucian and jesting with his friends. Even in his death he was successful: for several bishops wrote pamphlets attacking the manner of it. He was buried on Calton Hill, under a neat but pretentious Roman temple, set up in accordance with his will; and upon it was placed, by his order, the two words, "David Hume," as a sign that he had won literary fame at last, and the inscription would be self-explanatory.

And yet—David Hume is beyond all question the ablest British philosopher; though his interest in philosophy was largely to startle Englishmen into recognizing the Scottish writer David Hume, and he remained a good sound Tory at heart. His mother is reported to have said of him as a bairn, "Davy is a well-meanin' critter, but uncommon weak-minded." She should have waited for experience on matters of facts; for she turned out to be wrong on both counts. He was extremely acute, and malicious throughout. Just because he had no real interest in either science or religion, no deep feeling for the values involved, he was able to be utterly consistent in the pricking of metaphysical bubbles, both scientific and theological. Like F. H. Bradley, another thinker curiously remote from the values of his time, he was able, just because of his detachment, to exhibit so completely the implications of a philosophical tradition, that he transformed it into something else.

This intellectual personality of Hume's makes clear why his thought is so elusive, why it is so difficult to emerge from his subtle dialectic with definite conclusions. He was wholly uninterested in building up a consistent position of his own, either a new theory of science or a new natural theology. Though the former is certainly implied in his thought, he was always ready to sacrifice it to the literary display of his dialectical skill. And though a negative answer to the problems of rational theology is certainly the outcome of his theological discussions, and though he dearly loved to discomfit the "priests" by puncturing their arguments, it is by no means clear that he was not sincere in stating, "Our most holy religion is founded on faith," and historians are still arguing over whether he "believed" in God or not—whatever "belief" might mean for a mind like Hume's! He was interested, not in establishing a method and conclusions of his own, but in commenting on the methods and conclusions of others. He delighted to follow out the implications of accepted positions, and to show with consummate skill that their dialectic forced one to unacceptable conclusions that could not be refuted without altering the assumptions. He called this result "scepticism." Those arguments are "sceptical" which "admit of no answer and produce no conviction. Their only effect is to cause that momentary amazement and irresolution and confusion, which is the result of scepticism. . . . So that nothing can be more sceptical, or more full of doubt and hesitation, than scepticism itself." [8] Hume's whole attitude is: I don't for a minute believe it, any more than you do. But refute it if you can; I won't.

Hume employs this scepticism, not as a position to be defended, but as a literary device. He ends both his volumes with a statement of the academical or sceptical philosophy, not as the conclusion of his argument but as a literary climax; and then at once dissents—not only in the *Treatise*, where his dialectical interest in playing with ideas is allowed to run wild, but also in the *Enquiry*, where it appears as a kind of dramatic appendix to the straightforward development of his "great philosophical discovery."

III

In so far as Hume can be said to have had a serious interest at all, it lay in his desire to limit "the narrow capacity of human understanding" to its "proper subjects of science and inquiry," to "undermine the foundations of an abstruse philosophy, which seems to have hitherto served only as a shelter to superstition, and a cover to absurdity and error." [9] Hume's practical scepticism, as distinguished from his literary scepticism, is a religious scepticism. It was prepared by reading Cicero and the ancient religious sceptics, the Academics, and also the religious doubts of Montaigne and Bayle. Whatever his intentions, its outcome was to sweep away all metaphysics and theology based on causal inferences from observed facts to unobservable beings and conditions, to the Cause of the world as a whole, to Providence, to a future life. There are no necessities of thought, the world is as we find it, there are no reasons why; there is no rational basis for a First Cause, for miracles, for im-

---

[8] *Enquiry concerning Human Understanding*, in *Essays*, ed. Green and Grose, II, 127, 129.

[9] *Enquiry*, in *Essays*, II, 133, 13.

mortality. Hume pulverized the scientific or rational theology of Aristotle, of the Schoolmen, of the Newtonians; it has never recovered from his thrusts. This was the practical, revolutionary outcome of British empiricism. It was an outcome accepted by Kant and German philosophy. Hume's posthumous *Dialogues on Natural Religion* are his masterpiece; they are quite free from the intentional confusions of the *Treatise* and the *Enquiry*.

These latter analyses contain two separate positions, distinguishable, yet never quite distinguished by Hume. The first is the working out of the new conception of science found in Malebranche and in Berkeley, "the attempt to introduce the experimental method of reasoning into moral subjects." Science gives the descriptive laws of the observed relations between objects, as a basis for prediction; it is not a demonstrative system. Physics is a "moral subject," i.e., it offers only "moral certainty" or probability, not mathematical certainty. This position we shall here call "observationalism." It became the theory of nineteenth-century science in England and in France. But Hume was himself far more interested in criticizing contemporary science than in elaborating a new theory. Such knowledge, he holds, is not science, for everybody says science is a system of rational demonstration.

The second position in Hume is the working out of Locke's notion that the only objects of knowledge are our ideas, and the relations between such mental images; hence all knowledge is of the contents of our own minds, and is in our minds. Hume had no religious interest, like Berkeley, so for him there are no "notions" of "spiritual" power, either in ourselves or God, but only the relations between images. Hence the object of knowledge is not the world, but is rather "experience." Such knowledge cannot be science, for everybody says science is a knowledge of the real world. This second position Hume called accurately the "double existence hypothesis"; it is usually known as "subjectivism."

The empiricist analysis of knowledge, as it has persisted in the British tradition, is the combination of these two positions: of Berkeley's "perception is the criterion of reality" with Locke's "ideas, not real things, are the object of knowledge"—the combination of observationalism with subjectivism. Now obviously it is very difficult to believe at the same time that perception is the criterion of reality, and that we do not perceive real things. Hume was quite aware of this discrepancy, and hence there is much evidence that he never took subjectivism seriously: in practice he certainly disregards it. Yet throughout the *Treatise*, and to a much lesser extent in the conclusion of the *Enquiry*, he confuses observationalism with subjectivism. Observationalism is the position that the *relations* between objects are known *only by means of experience* or observation, as opposed to reasoning. Subjectivism is the position that the *objects of knowledge*, what we know, *are* elements of our own "*experience*," as opposed to being elements of the real world. For observationalism, "experience" is taken as a *method* of knowing; for subjectivism, it is taken as the *subject-matter* of knowledge. For the first, experience is *how* we know; for the second, it is *what* we know. As a result of Hume's intentional confusion of the two assumptions, empiricists have since kept up the confusion: we must defer to facts, though the only facts are our own ideas.

Why did Hume combine these contradictory positions? Had he been genuinely interested in working out a consistent theory of science, he would not have toyed with subjectivism. He would have followed Berkeley's thoroughgoing realism,[10] and not the subjectivistic side of Locke, which he never took very seriously anyway. Perhaps Hume's chief reason was that subjectivism is immensely shocking, and the combination of subjectivism with observationalism is still more productive of a literary scepticism—it has great publicity value. But there is also another reason more deeply rooted in Hume's thought. His procedure in establishing observationalism is subjectivistic throughout; and this characteristic procedure is exceedingly difficult to handle without giving at least the appearance of accepting subjectivism. That Hume himself knew better is clear; for the way he employs his procedure leaves little doubt that he is interested in establishing observationalism rather than subjectivism.

The observationalism of Hume is of great importance; for it came to be recognized in British and French thought as the only theory of science, and the seventeenth-century Aristotelian theory was there damned as "metaphysics." It is the culmination of the theory

[10] Cf. F. J. E. Woodbridge, "Berkeley's Realism," in *Studies in the History of Ideas*, ed. Dept. of Philosophy, Columbia University, Vol. I (New York, 1918).

suggested by Newton and Locke because they realized their ignorance of the "real powers and connexions" of bodies, and elaborated by Berkeley as a statement of the nature of human knowledge
rather than as a provisional second-best. It is now seized upon by
Hume with a full awareness of its negative implications, and
sharpened into a keen critical weapon. Hence we shall first state
Hume's observationalism as a formulated position, and then examine
the procedure by which he attempts to establish it, in which he becomes entangled with subjectivism and other sceptical conclusions.

Hume's position runs in his own words somewhat as follows. "Experience is our only guide in reasoning concerning matters of
fact." [11] We discover the world, we do not demonstrate it. "All
reasonings concerning matter of fact seem to be founded on the
relation of *Cause and Effect*." (II, 24) "Causes and effects are discoverable, not by reason, but by experience." (II, 25) And they
are discoverable: "none but a fool or madman will ever pretend to
dispute the authority of experience." (II, 32) We discover individual
things and their relations. What kinds of things and relations do
we discover? Concrete, particular things, in juxtaposition and succession. Perception is the test, as for Berkeley. Hume calls things
"perceptions" or "objects" indifferently, without any subjective
connotation: he means that they are observed, that they are what
Newton called "phenomena." "Everything in nature is individual." [12]
"Every perception is a substance," [13] if by "substance" we mean
something which may exist by itself, that is, as an individual and
independent existence, a *causa sui*, known in and through itself. The
world is a collection and succession of independent particulars, disposed in a certain manner, and succeeding each other in a certain
manner or order. It is not a mathematical system of logically related
things, a tissue of properties, precisely ordered, the relations of
which can be expressed in terms of mathematics. There is no reason
for the world being as it is found to be, in contrast with the view
that it had to be that way, and we can prove it. "The contrary of
every matter of fact is still possible"; [14] "whatever *is* may *not be*"; [15]
"nothing we imagine is absolutely impossible." [16] Why does the
magnet attract iron? It just does, and that ends the matter; there

[11] *Enquiry*, in *Essays*, II, 89.
[12] *A Treatise of Human Nature*, ed. Selby-Bigge (Oxford, 1896), p. 19.
[13] *Treatise*, p. 244.   [14] *Enquiry*, in *Essays*, II, 23.
[15] *Enquiry*, in *Essays*, II, 134.   [16] *Treatise*, p. 32.

is no reason that can be demonstrated from first principles. "All events seem entirely loose and separate. One event follows another; but we never can observe any tye between them. They seem *conjoined*, but never *connected*." [17] There are no real, intelligible connections between events, but merely discovered relations, which might have been entirely different.

For such a view, the relation of cause and effect means "observed succession," "experienced union," not logical necessity, intelligible implication. It means, in Hume's habitual terms, "constant conjunction," not "necessary connexion." There is no "power" in a cause to produce its effect. Until we have observed the relations that do in fact obtain, "Any thing may produce any thing." [18] Before they have been observed, the effects of given causes are wholly unpredictable; no one could predict that the loadstone would attract iron, or that gunpowder would explode. Hume is fundamentally denying that causation involves logical necessity, that every event flows forth from the nature of God with the same necessity by which it follows from the nature of a triangle that the sum of its interior angles is equal to two right angles. As against seventeenth-century science, which maintained that the laws of nature form a logical system that has to be as it is, Hume insists that they are arbitrary, bare facts with no reason for their being so.

Yet Hume is a consistent determinist. Nature does follow constant laws, and man shows as much constant conjunction of cause and effect in his actions as anything else. Hume's whole attack on miracles is based on such a determinism. The fact that man feels no compulsion in his conduct, but just acts in that uniform way, is not surprising: there is no compulsion or power in any cause. But it is meaningless to say that the uniformities which do obtain had to be, or that any particular law had to have the form it does, and could not have been otherwise. In fact, bodies tend to approach each other with a force directly proportional to the product of their masses and inversely proportional to the square of their distance apart. But things might easily have been so ordered that they would tend to approach each other with a force inversely proportional to the product of their masses and directly as the square of their distance apart.

Hume draws all the negative consequences of this position. There

[17] *Enquiry*, in *Essays*, II, 61.   [18] *Treatise*, p. 173.

are no necessities of thought concerning matters of fact and existence. We can infer no causal relation save where we can actually observe a relation between events. There are only those causal relations we can observe, and there is no justifiable inference to any unobserved First Cause, Creator, or Intelligible Source of order. The world needs neither to be caused nor sustained or held together; and rational theology collapses. Hume is, in fact, a "radical empiricist": we observe, by experience, things and events in a natural order. His is a consistent theory; whether it be adequate or not is another matter—certainly there are alternative theories of science.[19]

IV

The procedure by which Hume establishes this observational position and destroys other theories is fascinating, curious, and suspicious, and has many further implications which Hume himself does not explicitly draw. It is this procedure which provides the dialectical fireworks, the exciting parts of his thought. He is not content to say, with Newton, that knowledge is "deduced from phenomena"; or with Locke, that "experience and reflexion are the twin sources of all our knowledge." He asks rather, "What is the *foundation* of all conclusions from experience?"[20] He is concerned, not with knowledge, but with the beliefs men actually entertain, and with the nature of the *evidence* for those beliefs. He shares with Locke the fundamental assumption of empiricism, that the "extent and certainty" of knowledge are to be determined by examining its "original," the data from which that knowledge is derived. In good empiricist fashion, he seeks the evidence for beliefs in sense, in "impressions which arise in the soul originally, from unknown causes."[21] His procedure is to analyze a belief into the component ideas constituting it, and then to ask, from what impression is each idea derived? He lays down the proposition, "All our simple

---

[19] In this statement of Hume's radical empiricism, I am indebted for suggestions to S. P. Lamprecht, "Empiricism and Epistemology in David Hume," in *Studies in the History of Ideas,* ed. by Dept. of Philosophy, Columbia University, Vol. II (New York, 1925). What I have called "observationalism," Lamprecht calls "empiricism"; what I call "subjectivism," he calls "epistemology." For a criticism of the inadequacies of Hume's observationalism, see Randall, *Nature and Historical Experience* (New York, 1958), pp. 173–76, and 185–86.

[20] *Enquiry,* in *Essays,* II, 28.   [21] *Treatise,* p. 7.

ideas in their first appearance are derived from simple impressions, which are correspondent to them, and which they exactly represent." (p. 4) The difference between impressions and ideas lies only in the "force and liveliness" of the former; ideas are simply impressions without their "first vivacity."

Hume thus asks, why do we hold certain beliefs? He answers, the causes that induce us to believe, are thus and so; and he finds those causes uniformly in certain impressions, either of sensation, or reflection—the latter are impressions of other impressions or ideas. He asks for "the evidence that assures us" of a belief; but he answers in terms of the impression that causes it. This procedure seems rather strange. All beliefs have causes, and all these causes are on the same plane and have the same status: they are all impressions. Then how could the discovery of the causes of beliefs have any bearing on the evidence for one belief as against another? The evidence for all beliefs is of equal value. If all beliefs are thus similar in their origin, how can their origin in impressions, in "experience," possibly be the test of their validity? Yet it is the fundamental principle of empiricism that the original of knowledge is the test of its extent and certainty!

Still stranger, Hume finds the causes for the major beliefs of man's intellectual life in impressions of certain operations of human nature, certain "natural processes of the imagination," by which ideas are united or associated by a gentle force, in accordance with three universal principles of the imagination, Resemblance, Contiguity, and Cause and Effect. Our basic beliefs are thus founded on the way the mind actually operates. But the "effort of thought" by which we discover the mechanism that causes belief "disturbs the operation of our sentiments, on which the belief depends," (p. 185) so that when we have found the cause of any belief, and consequently by definition the evidence that assures us of it, we find that we no longer believe it! Every belief for which we find the evidence in terms of the original impression that causes it, disappears forthwith. Thus if origin in experience is evidence of truth, all beliefs ought to be true; yet the examination of every belief leads us to doubt it. Surely this is a rather amazing procedure—that is, a procedure that leads us to be sceptical of it!

It is fruitful to compare Hume's procedure in the crucial instance of belief in cause and effect with that in the case of belief in the existence of body, that is, in the continued existence of objects distinct from the mind and perception. In the latter case he starts out, "We may well ask, *What causes induce us to believe in the existence of body?* but 'tis in vain to ask, *Whether there be body or not?* That is a point, which we must take for granted in all our reasonings." (p. 187) He then completes a very acute analysis of the three impressions that cause us to believe in body, and concludes:

I begun this subject with premising, that we ought to have an implicit faith in our senses, and that this would be the conclusion, I should draw from the whole of my reasoning. But to be ingenuous, I feel myself *at present* of a quite contrary sentiment, and am more inclined to repose no faith at all in my senses, or rather imagination, than to place in it such an implicit confidence. I cannot conceive how such trivial qualities of the fancy, conducted by such false suppositions, can ever lead to any solid and rational system. (p. 217)

Had Hume followed this procedure with the belief in cause and effect, he would have concluded, "The examination of the causes of the belief in causation has caused me not to believe in causation." But it is illuminating that he did not. Instead, the examination of the causes of the belief in causation caused him to believe that causation is not necessary connection (the discovery of that belief destroyed it) but is constant conjunction.

This twofold use of his procedure has important implications. It suggests first that Hume did not take the question of whether there be bodies or not very seriously. He did take seriously the question of whether the idea of causation should include that of necessary connection, or merely that of constant conjunction. His subjectivism was not serious, but merely "sceptical"; his observationalism was serious, his "great philosophical discovery." The second and perhaps more important implication is that something more is needed than the origin of a belief in an impression to reach a "solid and rational system." The cause of the belief in body is enough to cause that belief, but not enough to afford evidence to assure us of it. Both the belief in constant conjunction and that in necessary connection are caused, and in the same way; but one is a solid system, the other is not. Of the one belief we are assured, of the other we are not. The one belief is justified, the other is held not justified.

Hence it is clear that Hume's procedure led him to distinguish the validity of beliefs in other terms than those of their origin in impressions. It thus revealed the futility of the basic principle of empiricism, that beliefs are to be tested by their origins in experience. All beliefs have an origin in experience; this origin is the cause of all beliefs, but it is not enough to justify any one of them. And the empiricist principle, that the validity of beliefs can be determined by their origins, collapses. Many other analyses than Hume's can be made of the origins of beliefs. But Hume's procedure does reveal that all of them would be equally irrelevant to the justification or the validity of beliefs. And this seems to be a solid conclusion. It means that all attempts to determine the validity of any set of ideas —of natural science, for example—by an analysis of their origins, or to discredit them by the same method—as in the case of theological beliefs—are not worth the paper they are written upon. It means that all the analyses of the "data" of science, in which the British tradition in particular abounds, are worthless. "Commit them then to the flames, for they can contain nothing but sophistry and illusion."

What then did justify a belief for Hume? The answer is clear, not only in what he says, but in his procedure itself. It is not its origin in experience, but its consequences in experience. All beliefs have the same kind of origin, but not all have the same kind of logical consequences. The denial of certain beliefs would make all experience useless, and all inference impossible: these beliefs are justified. The denial of other beliefs would not have such serious logical consequences: we could still be guided by experience and draw inferences and conclusions. Hume felt he could afford to be sceptical about such beliefs; they made no real difference. Such a test, in terms, not of origins, but of consequences, Hume does not explicitly elaborate. He is interested, not in establishing beliefs, but in reducing them to a necessary minimum. To be at all adequate, such a test demands further development, and it did lead straight to Kant and to pragmatism. But Hume clearly illustrates this test in his procedure, with reference to each of the major beliefs he examines.

V

The Belief in Bodies. By ringing the changes on the dialectic of the "vulgar hypothesis of the continued and distinct existence of the bodies experienced," and of the Lockean hypothesis of the "double existence of bodies and ideas," Hume throws doubt on both. The cause of the belief in the existence of bodies he finds to be an impression of coherence derived from the constancy of our perceptions, and from the tendency of the mind to feign uniformity where frequent conjunction has been observed. " 'Tis a gross illusion to suppose, that our resembling perceptions are numerically the same; and 'tis this illusion, which leads us into the opinion, that these perceptions are uninterrupted, and are still existent, even when they are not present to the senses." (p. 217) While "philosophers deny our resembling perceptions to be identically the same, and uninterrupted; yet they have so great a propensity to believe them such, that they arbitrarily invent a new set of perceptions, to which they attribute these qualities." (p. 218)

Hume's conclusion is sceptical, for neither belief has important consequences:

As to those *impressions*, which arise from the *senses*, their ultimate cause is, in my opinion, perfectly inexplicable by human reason, and 'twill always be impossible to decide with certainty, whether they arise immediately from the object [the view of Newton and Locke], or are produced by the creative power of the mind [that of the Cambridge Platonists], or are derived from the author of our being [Berkeley]. Nor is such a question any way material to our present purpose. We may draw inferences from the coherence of our perceptions, whether they be true or false; whether they represent nature justly, or be mere illusions of the senses. (p. 84)

Subjectivism, in other words, can never be judged either true or false, for belief or disbelief in it has no pragmatic meaning. The constant conjunction of perceptions, however, is a "solid system," a justified belief, for its denial would be serious. It is the essential idea in the belief in bodies.

Belief in Personal Identity. Hume notoriously denied there is any immediate impression of the Self. The only immediate impression we obtain when we look into ourselves is of "a bundle or collection of different perceptions, which succeed each other with an inconceivable rapidity, and are in a perpetual flux and movement." (p. 252) There is no impression of a spiritual power, of a simple substance, the cause of thinking and willing. Yet men believe in a simple, identical, permanent Self. How much of this idea is justified? What is the cause of this belief? The mind has the idea of an object that remains invariable and uninterrupted, and also, the idea of a succession of related objects. The actions of the imagination, by which the two ideas are considered, are almost the same to feeling, so the mind usually confounds them. It thinks it perceives identity, where there is really only a succession of related objects. To cover up this confusion, the mind runs to a new principle, connects the objects, and feigns a Self. The cause of the belief in the Self as simple and identical is thus the propensity of the mind to feign; and an analysis of the cause of this belief causes the belief in the simplicity and identity of the Self to vanish.

But there is a justified belief in the Self. "The true idea of the human mind, is to consider it as a system of different perceptions or different existences, which are linked together by the relation of cause and effect, and mutually produce, destroy, influence, and modify each other. . . . We add a *sympathy* of parts to their *common end*, and suppose that they bear to each other, the reciprocal relation of cause and effect in all their actions and operations." (pp. 261, 257) The Self is a kind of republic or commonwealth. "And as the same individual republic may not only change its members, but also its laws and constitutions; in like manner the same person may vary his character and disposition, as well as his impressions and ideas, without losing his identity. Whatever changes he endures, his several parts are still connected by the relation of causation." (p. 261) "In this view, memory does not so much *produce* as *discover* personal identity, by shewing us the relation of cause and effect among our different perceptions." (p. 262)

The unjustified belief in the Self and personal identity is belief in a simple permanent substance. The justified belief in the Self and personal identity is belief in an organic system of constantly conjoined perceptions. Both beliefs have their origins in perceptions, neither in an immediate impression, which is only of a bundle of different perceptions. What is the difference between these two beliefs? The simple substance can be denied without serious logical consequences, the organic system of constantly conjoined perceptions cannot.

In explaining the operations of the mind, of what he usually calls "natural imagination" or "custom," Hume finds three principles of human nature regularly at work, three laws of custom or habit by which the imagination unites or associates ideas: Resemblance, Contiguity, and Causation. Causation reduces to Contiguity or conjunction, so Hume is left with Contiguity and Resemblance. He attempts to carry through a pure contact theory, in which all association is by contiguity, and ideas recur in the same order as impressions have been received. Where then is the tracing of implications, of logical thought? Hume admits it in mathematics, where ideas are "similar," and in purposive thinking—in what he calls "relations between ideas" or dialectic. Ideas do have logical, nonexistential relations; they fall into resembling instances or classes, in all inferences from experience. Yet the finding of resemblances is inexplicable, "a kind of magical faculty in the soul." (p. 24) In truth, Hume is no more a consistent associationist than Locke. He is forced to bring in relations of implication as well as of mental contact, and he is forced largely by mathematics, with which he had much difficulty. Perceptions or substances do have mathematical relations; but these relations remain dialectical and nonexistential.

Belief in Causation. The analysis of the idea of Causation is Hume's basic analysis. Involved in that idea are the three ideas of contiguity, succession, and constant conjunction. Two events are observed to be constantly conjoined, like fire and burning wood. From that impression of constant conjunction comes the idea of cause and effect. But men believe also in a necessary connection between the two. From what impression comes this idea of necessary connection? It comes not from the objects themselves, but from a multiplicity of resembling instances. This multiplicity can never produce any new quality in the objects concerned; the millionth fire burning can be no different from the first. But the observation of the resemblance produces a new impression in the mind, which is the source of the idea of "power" or "necessary connection." For after a certain number of instances we feel a determination of the mind to pass from one object to its usual attendant. This propensity to infer the effect when we perceive the cause is the source of the idea of necessary connection, which is thus founded on an impression of reflection, of the way the imagination operates in inferring.

Hence the "necessity" of the relation is something that exists only in the mind, not in objects. In them there is only constant conjunction. We believe that fire has to burn, and water drown. In reality, we find that they always do, and recurrent observation generates the belief that they have to:

> That the operations of nature are independent of our thought and reasoning, I allow it; . . . like objects may be observed in several instances to have like relations; and all this is independent of, and antecedent to the operations of the understanding. But if we go any farther, and ascribe a power or necessary connexion to these objects; this is what we can never observe in them, but must draw the idea of it from what we feel internally in contemplating them. (p. 168)

We observe a constant conjunction; we hence infer by custom or habit that like will be followed by like. This inference itself causes the idea of necessary connection: because "the mind has a great propensity to spread itself on external objects, and to conjoin with them any internal impressions, which they occasion, and which always make their appearance at the same time that these objects discover themselves to the senses," (p. 167) we confuse the internal impression of necessary connection with the constant conjunction observed between the objects themselves.

This seems a simple distinction. The justified belief in causation as constant conjunction comes from our observation of the experienced union of objects; the unjustified addition of necessary connection comes from confusing a habit of the mind with the relations between objects. But it is not so simple as it seems. For Hume goes on to point out, in the *Enquiry*, that what we really observe is not constant conjunction but frequent conjunction. The idea that objects are constantly conjoined has in fact the same cause as the idea that they are necessarily connected: "we have no argument to convince us, that objects, which have, in our experience, been frequently conjoined, will likewise, in other instances, be conjoined in the same manner; nothing leads us to this inference but custom or a certain instinct of our nature." [22] Both beliefs, that in constant con-

[22] *Enquiry*, in *Essays*, II, 130–31.

junction, and that in necessary connection, have ultimately the same cause and origin in the same internal impression; yet one is justified and accepted, and the other is unjustified and rejected! It is obvious that the origin of these beliefs has nothing whatever to do with their justification; and Hume in fact seeks that justification in a quite different quarter. "Every part of mixed mathematics [or natural science] proceeds upon the supposition, that certain laws are established by nature in her operations." (II, 28) "All inferences from experience suppose, as their foundation, that the future will resemble the past, and that similar powers will be conjoined with similar sensible qualities. If there be any suspicion, that the course of nature may change, and that the past may be no rule for the future, all experience becomes useless, and can give rise to no inference or conclusion. It is impossible, therefore, that any arguments from experience can prove this resemblance of the past to the future; since all these arguments are founded on the supposition of that resemblance." (II, 33) Hume here saw much more clearly than Mill. The ground has been shifted from what causes belief to the foundations of belief, from psychology to logic; and the answer is in terms of the logical consequences in experience, not in terms of the causes of beliefs in experience. The belief in necessary connection can be denied without serious logical consequences; the belief in constant conjunction cannot.

Kant's so-called "answer" to Hume thus turns out to be in reality an agreement with Hume, even to the confusion, which dogs Kant no less than Hume, of the way the mind operates with the logical postulates implied in its operations, the confusion of psychology with logic. Hume not only developed the implications of the assumptions of empiricism. He revealed clearly the futility of its basic assumption, that beliefs can be tested by their origin in experience, that the original of knowledge can serve as the adequate test of its extent and certainty. He transformed that principle into a test in terms of the logical consequences in experience; he stated explicitly the main outlines of what Kant called the "transcendental deduction of the categories." And incidentally he forged a powerful weapon for destroying any belief upon which it might be brought to bear—which is the primary reason why British thinkers, despite Hume's clear demonstration of the insufficiency of the principles of empiricism, have never been willing to abandon those principles.[23]

VI

To Hume's relentless pushing of the implications of the empiricists' assumptions, however, there rose the united cry, this will never do! The opposition sprang not merely from those who saw religious beliefs deprived of all rational basis, and no proofs left even of the existence of God; while the whole spirit of the eighteenth century was to make religion rational and "scientific," to prove its "truth." Observationalism raised very genuine problems for the scientist himself. If the "laws of nature" are just arbitrary and given, how can we count upon their permanence? What guarantee is there that the operations of nature will continue uniform? In the eighteenth century the scientist felt there must be some such guarantee. Hume held that all "experimental reasoning" must presuppose the uniformity of nature; yet he left the question, is it more than an unverified assumption, a "habit of mind"? He freely admitted it was a logical assumption necessary for any science, and that its presupposition is a natural presumption of human nature. But to the scientist that seemed hardly enough.

Secondly, science was thoroughly mathematical, a systematic deduction from first principles. If mathematical relations are non-existential, as Hume insisted, and not to be found in experienced nature, why does mathematics apply so beautifully to our experience of nature? Where does the mathematical and systematic aspect of natural science come from, if it is not to be found in experience? Hume had no answer.

Thirdly, science does generalize from crucial instances, and does it "beforehand," "*a priori*." It does infer from its principles further consequences that have not yet been observed, and then proceeds to observe them. It makes discoveries of fact that have been mathematically predicted. It calculates exactly where Neptune will

[23] This analysis of Hume's abandonment of any genetic test of the validity of beliefs, and of his actual turning to a functional or pragmatic test, was worked out first in connection with the brilliant thesis of Dr. Francis Chilton Bayley, *The Causes and Evidence of Beliefs: An Examination of Hume's Procedure* (Mount Hermon, Mass., 1936). I owe much to the analytical skill of Dr. Bayley. And I refer those interested to Dr. Bayley's thesis for a more detailed elaboration of the essential contentions here set forth.

be found, turns its telescope upon the heavens, and discovers Neptune there. It confidently declares just which of the elements in the periodic table have not yet been "discovered," and where they will be found to fall, and then goes on to isolate them. It does not have to wait for experience for knowledge of all matters of fact.

Fourthly, science does furnish "reasons" for causal relations being what they are. It can derive them from more general formulations. Could fire fail to burn wood? Does it not follow from the properties of the elements chemical analysis reveals wood to be composed of, and from the nature of the process of combustion or oxidation? Does not Hume's observationalism, in fact, deny the whole value of prediction based upon analysis, with all its triumphs?

Hume was no scientist, and to these questions he had no real answer. Kant saw these problems, and the failure of "empiricism" to supply adequate answers pushed him to the critical philosophy, which did at least attempt to furnish answers. Many scientists in England and America to this day accept Hume's construing of their enterprise: science, they agree, is "descriptive," not demonstrative. But it is doubtful whether a single scientist has ever allowed this agreement to interfere with his practice of inquiry. And it is not easy to understand the sense in which present-day physical theory can be said to be "descriptive," and derived from "impressions" of sense alone. Philosophers have always been able to persuade scientists to admit their views; the latter have been willing enough to do so in order to get rid of their critics. The British empiricists in particular have always been committed to the difficult position of trying to convince scientists that science ought to be different from what it actually is. They have been forced, by their dubious philosophical principles, to make desperate efforts, down to Whitehead, to show that science really is what their assumptions would indicate it ought to be, even when they have not been engaged in this futile effort to reform scientists. For a hard-boiled description and analysis of what science at any epoch actually has been and is, we must turn, not to the British empirists, but to the Kantians.[24]

[24] For Hume's criticism of rational religion, see chapter 7; for his moral and political philosophy, see chapter 11.

6

Locke's Empirical Theory of
Constitutional Liberalism

LOCKE'S *Essay on Human Understanding*, his *Two Treatises of Government*, and his *First Letter concerning Toleration* were all "published" the same year, 1690; they all actually came out in 1689, between October and December. The *Essay* bore his name, and speedily won him an enormous reputation. The *Treatises* and the *Letter* were issued anonymously; he did not acknowledge them until he wrote a codicil to his will a few days before his death in 1704, and jealously preserved until then the secret of his authorship of the *Treatises*, quarreling with his best friend, James Tyrrell, for suspecting it. He had been meditating and working on all three books for over twenty-five years.[1]

Locke had thus been thinking and writing both on his theory of knowledge and his political theory for a long time. Yet he wanted to be known by the first, and refused to acknowledge the second—though he did think well of it, recommending it twice along with Aristotle's *Politics* and Hooker's *Ecclesiastical Polity*. These two sides of his thought he clearly wanted to keep separate. The very anonymity of the political philosophy makes it all the better a statement of what it really is, the accepted social and political theory of the party that came to power in 1688-89, and was to dominate what can be called the English Enlightenment. It sets forth the

[1] Locke's views on toleration are already formulated in a letter to Henry Stubbe of 1659; in 1667 he wrote *An Essay concerning Toleration* (Fox Bourne, 174-94). In 1689 Limborch published the Latin original of the *First Letter* at Gouda, *Epistola de Tolerantia*. We have two early versions of the *Essay*, both written in 1671 (A, ed. R. I. Aaron and Jocelyn Gibb, 1936; B, ed. Benjamin Rand, 1931). The version of 1690 was finished Dec. 31, 1686, in Holland. The *Second Treatise* was largely finished, it is now known, in 1679, the *First* on Filmer, during the next year or two.

philosophical foundations of the now triumphant middle-class culture in the form that was to prevail in England for a century. And it very definitely expresses the views, not of Locke the philosophical empiricist in the technical sense, but of that other Locke who had been led almost inadvertently into his "empiricism," Locke the empirical thinker, the man content with the probabilities that are sufficient for our purposes, the Locke who could open the *Essay* by saying:

> We shall not have much reason to complain of the narrowness of our minds, if we will but employ them about what may be of use to us; for of that they are very capable. . . . The Candle that is set up in us shines bright enough for all our purposes. . . . Our business here is not to know all things, but those which concern our conduct. If we can find out those measures, whereby a rational creature, put in that state in which man is in this world, may and ought to govern his opinions, and actions depending thereon, we need not be troubled that some other things escape our knowledge.[2]

This is the practical, sober, judicious, common-sense Locke, the Locke familiar enough with affairs to recognize that often we must look at things from different points of view that cannot be logically reconciled within a neat system, that we must say things that contradict what we have just said, without being able to harmonize them. This is the Locke for whom experience is not a process by which ideas are generated mechanically by Newtonian billiard-balls, in accordance with a neat theory; it is the Locke for whom experience means what it meant for Justice Holmes when he said "The life of the law is not logic but experience." This is Locke the medical "empirick," not the epistemological "empiricist." Indeed he himself puts it, in his Journal for June 26, 1681:

> [The truths of mathematics are certain.] But whether this course in public or private affairs will succeed well, whether rhubarb will purge or quinquina cure an ague, is only known by experience, and there is but probability grounded on experience, or analogical reasoning, but no certain knowledge or demonstration.[3]

[2] *Essay concerning Human Understanding*, Introduction, secs. 5–6; ed. A. C. Fraser (1894), I, 29–31.
[3] R. I. Aaron and J. Gibb, *An Early Draft of Locke's Essay* (1936), pp. 117–18. Peter Laslett comments: "Empirical medicine, rather than philosophy, seems to be the model for the man who sets out to comment on political matters. Locke the doctor rather than Locke the epistemologist is the man w

We should not forget that Aristotle also was a physician, nowhere more so than in the practical and architectonic science of politics.

It is rather surprising that although the fundamental approach and temper are the same, the ideas in the *Essay* and in the *Treatises* have almost no connection with each other. Locke is the very antithesis of those rationalists of the earlier seventeenth century who feel they must proceed from the first principles of the universe demonstratively to the human situation and what man must do to be saved, individually and collectively. Locke is at the opposite pole from both Spinoza and Hobbes. Although he grounds his political thinking on the "law of nature," he rarely attempts to make clear what it is or how we may find it out; and when he does raise the question, he never succeeds in answering it. "The original, extent, and certainty of knowledge" may be his central concern in the *Essay*, which he was working on at the same time. But he scarcely bothers about such questions in the *Government.* The most we can say is very general: Locke could state of his political theory what he concludes reluctantly about physics: "We can have a useful and experimental philosophy, but not a scientifical philosophy, of natural bodies." Perhaps we could add: just as he tries to construct knowledge out of atomistically conceived and disconnected sensations, so he tries to construct political society out of atomistically conceived individuals. But we have seen how the former attempt soon breaks down, and it is just as true that the latter one—if that atomism was really his assumption—soon breaks down also. Locke may have wanted to be an "individualist" in this sense, had he been able to understand what the term might mean. But careful reading makes clear that he is actually "individualistic" neither in his starting-point nor in his conclusions.

Not only does Locke nowhere try to define the fundamental terms of his political theory, save political power and property: freedom, consent, law, reason, will, even government, are all left vague, their meaning assumed. It is equally striking that writing in a century whose constitutional battles had been fought in terms of historic rights and traditional precedents, Locke nowhere appeals to history, either English, or like Machiavelli and the later French

should have in mind when we read his work on *Government*." *Two Treatises of Government*, ed. Peter Laslett (1960), p. 85.

theorists, Greek and Roman. There is no attempt, as in the *Essay*, to furnish a "plain historical account." At most, it can be said that while the *Essay* endeavors to treat the original, extent, and certainty of human knowledge, the *Second Treatise* is entitled *An Essay concerning the True Original, Extent, and End of Civil-Government.* But here the major emphasis is not upon the "original," but upon the "end." It is not without significance that in the 1690s he often gave the advice he wrote the Countess of Peterborough in 1697: "A young man should begin with Aristotle and then read the moderns if he please." (Laslett, p. 89)

Locke is as inconsistent in the *Treatises* as in the *Essay* because he is bound by no rigid system. He lays down a general principle, but he loves facts better: he is genuinely empirical. This taste for what is, binds Locke far more closely to Machiavelli and the statesmen-writers than to Hobbes, or the later French theorists, even Montesquieu. And all these qualities together—the autonomy of political theory, the absence of definition, the vagueness and ambiguity of his key concepts, the lack of appeal to concrete English history (when he does refer to it, he usually calls England "certain governments")—which so exasperate the lover of precision and consistency, are the very traits which made Locke's doctrine so influential for so many men in such different later situations, in the American colonies, in pre-Revolutionary France, in the Italy of the Risorgimento. Originally written to unite men of different faiths behind the constitutional party in its struggle against incipient absolutism under Charles II, it could be reinterpreted and adapted to later struggles and other adversaries. Discussing the medieval theorists, Locke wrote: "Notwithstanding these learned disputants these all knowing doctors, it was to the unscholastic statesmen that the governments of the world owed their peace, defence, and liberties." (*Essay*, III, x, 9; Fraser, II, 128) In his political theory Locke was proud to write as an "unscholastic statesman." He was uninterested in a political science, either the popular Enlightenment idea of a social physics, or Montesquieu's natural history of laws. That is one reason why it is appropriate to consider him here rather than in the chapter on the science of society.[4]

[4] Laslett concludes: "Locke's influence as a political writer probably arose because of his philosophical fame. Nevertheless it is of importance to see in

On the one hand, Locke summed up the ideas that had been worked out in the seventeenth-century constitutional struggles in England, and formulated them into a system that somewhat by accident could serve as the official Whig apology for the English Revolution of 1688–89. On the other, they became the starting-point for later eighteenth-century theorizing, and received in America and in France an elaboration that would have much surprised and perturbed Locke himself, extending far beyond the limits of British middle-class culture.

Locke wrote as apologist for the Whigs while they were still planning their revolution. Now an apologist is bound by definite limitations. He can hardly propound a novel and original political theory, or his whole argument will fail of the universal acceptance he desires. He must operate with familiar concepts and ideas. He can push them further in certain directions, but he must not reach propositions which have not been long before his audience. Hence neither Locke's justification of the Whig program in the 1680s and 1690s, nor the Americans' justification of their revolution, could be in any but an indirect sense novel and original. They were rather systematic reworkings of notions already emotionally accepted, to persuade to certain definite contentions. Only in France, where there had been little seventeenth-century political support for constitutionalism and natural rights, did political theory assume startling new forms.

Hence we find Locke discussing the law of nature, the rights men enjoy in the state of nature, the reasons for instituting government, and the right of "appealing to Heaven"—the right of revolution. These concepts had come down from an almost immemorial antiquity, and had furnished the terms in which the controversies of the late medieval and early modern political conflicts had in theory been fought out. Thus Locke assumes without question "the law of nature," and appeals to the authority most likely to persuade the court Tory party, Richard Hooker's (1553–1600) *Laws of Ecclesiastical Polity* (Books i–v, 1594–97; Books vi–viii, 1648), an original adaptation of the Thomistic position to the service of the

Locke, the recognized point of departure for liberalism, the liberal dilemma already present, the dilemma of maintaining a political faith without subscribing to a total, holistic view of the world." *Two Treatises,* p. 89.

Anglican Church. The quotations from Hooker were apparently the last thing to be added to the *Treatises*, in 1681, before the final revision after the Revolution itself.

Two more original ideas came into the argument, the first accidentally. In 1687, two years before the appearance of the book in October, 1689, Newton had published his *Principia Mathematica*. Hence no reader encountering the adjective "natural" could help thinking of the harmonious and rational divinely ordained "laws of nature" which Newton there popularized. Newton had brought the authority and support of science to the ancient Stoic "natural law," transmitted through St. Augustine, St. Thomas, and Hooker to seventeenth-century England. The other influential original idea in Locke was his rejection of the traditional biblical primitive communism of property, and his insistence that private property prevailed in the state of nature itself, even before the establishment of political society through the setting up of government. Private property thus became at Locke's hands a "natural right," antedating all positive law. And Locke went on to justify its unlimited extent in political society. This doctrine is the primary reason why Locke has been held to be not only the apologist for the Whig revolution of 1688–89, but also the spokesman of the middle class and "the spirit of capitalism" (Max Weber), and the "emancipation of acquisitiveness" (Leo Strauss), distinctions not only dubious in themselves but also dubiously deserved.

Locke also follows, or rather serves to establish, the pattern of rationalistic thinking, as exemplified in Newton. First, we start with an analysis of human nature as it presumably would be without civil government, and thus try to determine the "natural" needs of man that led to the institution of government, and prescribed the form it must take if it is to answer those needs. In other words, Locke is trying to follow the accepted scientific methods of analysis and synthesis. For him, it must be the Cartesian rather than the Newtonian pattern, since he began in the 1670s, long before 1687. He starts with axioms that seem "natural" and rational to him, that is what seems to him to be reasonable, and socially useful to the middle class. Such axioms are necessarily written into God's system of natural laws for the universe. Thus, Locke appeared to be enlisting the Creator of the world behind the particular political demand

shared by him with the Whigs. Not until Bentham and the Utilitarians do we find men who are willing to acknowledge that what
is socially useful can stand on its own feet, without the additional
support of roots in the "natural" and "divine" order.

II

Locke had started his career in 1658 as medical Student (or Fellow) of Christ Church, Oxford, though he never took the M.D.
degree. He came of a Puritan family; his grandfather had made a
fortune as a cloth contractor, and purchased an estate; his father
was a Calvinist attorney, and had served as captain in the parliamentary armies. At Oxford Locke's interests were political; he wrote
on the *Civil Magistrate*, and as Censor of Moral Philosophy in 1664
lectured on Natural Law; between 1660 and 1664 he wrote in Latin
eight *Essays on the Law of Nature.*[5] He had already drifted away
from the Calvinism of his family and patrons. The Broad Church
Anglicans like Tillotson and Barrow attracted him more; he admired Richard Hooker and, when it came out in 1660, Samuel Pufendorf's *Elementa Jurisprudentiae Universalis.* His attitude toward
politics in these early Oxford—and Restoration—days was traditional
and authoritarian. Each individual grants his whole liberty to the
supreme legislative power; its decisions bind all consciences, and in
case of conflict the only remedy is passive obedience. Despite this
Hobbistic ring, it is doubtful whether he ever read Hobbes at first
hand; but he was already familiar with Filmer.

In the fourth *Essay on the Law of Nature*, in answer to the question, Can reason attain to the knowledge of natural law through
things derived from the senses?, Locke gives his fullest account of
how the law of nature may be known. In the *Essay on Human
Understanding* he merely says it is "knowable by the light of nature," explaining that he means "without the help of revelation":
it is "something that we, being ignorant of, may attain to the knowledge of, by the use and due application of our natural faculties."
(*Essay*, I, ii, 13) The second Latin Essay of 1664 distinguishes
three sources of knowledge, *inscriptio*, or innate knowledge, *traditio*,
and *sensus*. If the law of nature were innate, it should be universally
acknowledged, which it is not; and tradition would not explain how

[5] Published in 1954 by W. von Leyden.

the first author learned it. Only sense is left: the "light of nature" is a combination of sense and reason. Sense furnishes reason with ideas of particular sensible things; reason directs sensation, arranges images derived from sense, and forms new images from them. It is this collaboration of the senses and reason that leads to knowledge of the existence of an omnipotent and wise First Cause who created the world, and the natural law that is his will.

Locke went as secretary to a diplomatic mission in 1665 to Cleves, capital of Brandenburg, and was offered a like post in Madrid. But he preferred the life of an Oxford don. In July, 1666, however, Lord Ashley met him in Oxford; within a year Locke was installed in Ashley's Exeter House in London as his physician and confidential secretary. He cured his patron of a liver abscess; but it was his political advice that above all drew the two together. Locke had passed into the *haute bourgeoisie;* he became involved in all Ashley's investments, and political schemes. It was this intimate association with Anthony Ashley Cooper, first Earl of Shaftesbury, that gave Locke his direct experience of political things. It lasted fifteen years, till Shaftesbury's death in exile in 1682.

It is now clear from Locke's papers that he was much more deeply involved in Shaftesbury's various plots and conspiracies than he ever admitted, and than had been supposed. Locke was summoned back from France in 1679, where he had gone expecting to die of tuberculosis, to help with the fight for the Exclusion bill, to keep the Catholic Duke of York from the succession to his brother. The bill was defeated by the king; Locke took part in the meetings at which armed resistance was planned if it were lost again, the so-called Insurrection plot, in 1682. Even after Shaftesbury's exile and death, in 1683 Locke took part in the consultations of the Assassination or Rye House plot. When this was exposed, Locke fled to Holland the same year; the king ordered his removal as Student of Christ Church in 1684.

This is significant, for it has now been established that the *Two Treatises* were not written, as had been recently supposed, after the Revolution of 1688–89, as an apologetic for the winning government. They were written rather between 1679 and 1681, to support the Protestant plot against Charles II. They were indeed an apologetic and a tract for the times, but not a Revolution pamphlet; they were rather an Exclusion Tract. That is, at that date they were a seditious and inflammatory document.[6]

After the *Essay* came out in December, 1689, Locke was turned into a national institution and an international influence. Everything else he wrote was important because of the *Essay*. Thus the *Treatises* provoked no reply until 1705, when Locke's authorship had been made known. Locke himself became the confidential adviser to Lord Somers, the chief figure in the government of William III until 1700, and played the elder statesman in his residence at Otes with Lady Masham (the daughter of Henry More) and her husband, whither he had retired in 1691. Locke himself may have had pretensions to gentility, and may have distrusted commercial men like those who set up the Bank of England. But the rising middle class certainly accepted him as their spokesman.

The study of Locke's papers from the Lovelace collection seems to suggest the following view about the actual writing of the *Two Treatises*. The book was written as a whole, a Discourse on Government. It started with the second treatise, begun in 1679; the quotations from Hooker were added in June, 1681, when Locke purchased a copy. In the middle of 1679, Filmer's tracts of 1648, 1652, and 1653 were collected and printed; in January the *Patriarcha* was issued for the first time. Locke bought both and at once began extracting them, as was his wont. Locke first resolved to write against Filmer, and began the second treatise. The *Patriarcha* proved enormously popular, and Locke during 1680 decided to refute it point by point in the first treatise. At the same time Locke's closest friend, James Tyrrell, resolved to undertake a similar refutation, in his *Patriarcha non Monarcha*, prefacing it to what he had already written. Thus the second treatise was written in the winter of 1679–80; early in 1680 the first treatise was added to it. The Hooker references were added in the summer of 1681. From February to August, 1689, on Locke's return from exile, the preface, the title pages, and some twenty-five new paragraphs were added: these alone belong to the year of the Revolution.[7]

[6] It was Sir Leslie and Sir James Fitzjames Stephen, T. H. Green, and above all Sir Frederick Pollock, who are responsible for the assumption that Locke wrote the *Treatises* after the victorious Revolution. Pollock seems also mainly responsible for the view that Locke was writing chiefly against Hobbes.

[7] See Laslett, pp. 45–67. Laslett adds the conjecture that the mss., which Locke did not take with him to Holland, is referred to in his letters as *De*

Moreover, it has also been established that Locke wrote both his two treatises to refute Filmer. As Laslett puts it: "Locke did not write with Thomas Hobbes in mind, either to refute him as we all so recently supposed, or to adopt his doctrine without confessing it, as some authorities now claim." [8] Laslett says elsewhere: "There would have been no point whatsoever for the intellectual champion of the Whig exclusionists to produce one more criticism of Hobbes, the most rejected, and politically the least important of all the absolutist writers. Filmer, on the other hand, was the man of the moment, a formidable and growing force with those whose political opinions mattered, and representing in himself the *ipsissima verba* of the established order." [9] Filmer's doctrine was in fact the recognized and almost official creed of the Court Tory party. Its publication in 1679–80 provoked a wave of popularity the Whigs had to answer. Even as late as 1689, when Locke came to publish, Filmer was still very influential; his works were reprinted in 1696.

Filmer clearly determined the structure of the *Second Treatise* as well as the *First*. Thus Locke had shown no sign of interest in a theory of property until he had to reply to Filmer's version of primitive communism. Locke's writing is intellectually and historically important because it is directed against Filmer, not in spite of the fact.

III

Just as in the case of Newton, we have to distinguish with Locke's political doctrine between what he was taken as maintaining, what views he came to symbolize in the popular mind, and the much subtler and more qualified, not to say conflicting variety of views, to be found in what he actually wrote. The former, Locke the political symbol, came to stand for many of the shifting currents of constitutional liberal theory in the later eighteenth century. He was identified with the doctrine of absolute natural rights, espe-

Morbo Gallico (tyranny). Locke gave his copy to his agent Edward Clarke, with orders to destroy it if necessary. This was done, leaving only the half copy Locke had left with his landlady. This accounts for the first treatise breaking off in the middle.

[8] *Two Treatises*, p. x. The reference is to Leo Strauss, *Natural Right and History* (Chicago, 1953), pp. 202–51. To him might be added Richard H. Cox. *Locke on War and Peace* (Oxford, 1960), especially section I.

[9] *Ibid.*, p. 67. See also Peter Laslett, *Patriarcha and other Political Works of Sir Robert Filmer* (Oxford, 1949).

cially the natural right of private property, and with the view that government exists solely to guarantee these natural rights. Thus Blackstone could conclude:

The principal aim of society is to protect individuals in the enjoyment of those absolute rights which are vested in them by the immutable laws of nature; . . . the first and primary end of human laws is to maintain and regulate these absolute rights of individuals.[10]

Locke was identified also with the labor theory of value. So Adam Smith writes:

The property which every man has in his own labor, as it is the original foundation of all other property, so it is the most sacred and inviolable.[11]

Locke stood also for the sovereignty of the people, for government by consent, for the separation of powers. Usually these doctrines were interpreted as meaning, "as practiced under the present constitution of Great Britain," which would doubtless have satisfied Locke himself. But it was easy to push these same vague ideas into either an extreme individualism and laissez faire, or into the majority rule collectivism of a Rousseau. Passages in Locke could be cited in support of both extremes, which he had put there just because his own thought was so extremely moderate. Sabine comments on the complexity of Locke's theory: "Locke saw with great clarity a multitude of issues involved in the politics of the seventeenth century and tried conscientiously to combine them all. But his theory had no logical structure elaborate enough to contain so complicated a subject-matter. Though circumstances made him the defender of a revolution, he was by no means a radical, and in intellectual temperament he was the least doctrinaire of philosophers." [12] Locke's method of writing, one begins to suspect in reading him carefully, was to include what a later logic would have called both thesis and antithesis, leaving the synthesis up to the reader and his particular situation. This method has much to recommend it in a political writer. Locke is at least a refreshing alternative to the rigid but equally imprecise social syllogisms of the later practitioners of "social physics."

[10] *Commentaries*, Book I, ch. i.
[11] *Wealth of Nations*, Book I, ch. x, Part 2.
[12] George H. Sabine, *A History of Political Theory* (1937), p. 537.

Locke's new Preface in 1689 makes clear that he wants to support the policies of the Whig Revolution:

Reader, thou hast here the beginning and the end of a discourse concerning government; . . . [The papers] which remain, I hope are sufficient to establish the throne of our great restorer, our present King William; to make good his title, in the consent of the people, which being the only one of all lawful governments, he has more fully and clearly than any prince in Christendom: and to justify to the world, the people of England, whose love of their just and natural rights, with their resolution to preserve them, saved the nation when it was on the very brink of slavery and ruin.[13]

The *Second Treatise* opens with one of Locke's few definitions, that of political power:

Political power then I take to be a right of making laws with the penalty of death, and consequently all less penalties, for the regulating and preserving of property, and of employing the force of the community, in the execution of such laws, and in the defense of the commonwealth from foreign injury, and all this only for the public good. (par. 3; Laslett, p. 286)

The "end of civil government" is thus defined as regulating and preserving property, and national defense, for the sake of the public good. "Property" is defined in the *Epistola de Tolerantia* (1689) as civil interests (*bona civilia*), that is, "life, liberty, health and indolency of body, and the possession of outward things, such as lands, money, houses, furniture and the like." (Laslett, p. 286n.)

In chapter ii, "Of the State of Nature," with which Locke presumably originally began the *Treatise*, Locke starts:

To understand political power right, and derive it from its original, we must consider what state all men are naturally in, and that is, a state of perfect freedom to order their actions, within the bounds of the law of nature, without asking leave, or depending upon the will of any other man.

A state also of equality, wherein all the power and jurisdiction is reciprocal, no one having more than another. (par. 4; Laslett, p. 287)

In this state of nature, men are governed by a law of nature: moral principles are prior to political power, so that all persons and all institutions are subject to moral judgment.

But though this be a state of liberty, yet it is not a state of licence, though man in that state have an uncontrollable liberty, to dispose of his person

[13] *Two Treatises*, ed. Laslett, p. 155.

or possessions, yet he has not liberty to destroy himself, or so much as any creature in his possession, but where some nobler use, than its bare preservation calls for it. The state of nature has a law of nature to govern it, which obliges every one: and reason, which is that law, teaches all mankind, who will but consult it, that being all equal and independent, no one ought to harm another in his life, health, liberty, or possessions. (par. 6; Laslett, pp. 288–89)

How is the law of nature enforced? In the state of nature, every man has the "executive right" to enforce it:

And that all men may be restrained from invading others' rights, and from doing hurt to one another, and the law of nature be observed, which willeth the peace and preservation of all mankind, the execution of the law of nature is in that state, put into every man's hands, whereby every one has a right to punish the transgressors of that law to such a degree, as may hinder its violation. (par. 7; Laslett, p. 289)

Every man hath a right to punish the offender, and be executioner of the law of nature. (par. 8; Laslett, p. 290)

This may seem a "strange doctrine," says Locke. But on what other grounds has a State the right to condemn an alien? In a state of nature, every one has the executive power of the law of nature. This situation has its "inconveniences, which must certainly be great, where men may be judges in their own case." But Locke asks, how does this differ from the case of the absolute monarch, who also has the liberty to be judge in his own case?

When were men ever in such a "state of nature"? Well, "all princes and rulers of independent governments all through the world" are in a state of nature. Locke, who read indefatigably the reports of foreign travelers, cites also "the promises and bargains for truck, etc., between the two men in the desert island" cited by Garcilasso de la Vega in his *History of Peru;* "or between a Swiss and an Indian, in the woods of America." Locke seems to think that "the state of nature" may have been historical, unlike most of the political philosophers who employed it. He did not romance about it, like Rousseau; but neither did he make clear that he regarded it as a theoretical historical construct, like Pufendorf, for example.

Locke never attempts to list the laws of nature or to relate one to another. "The first and fundamental natural law . . . is the preservation of the society, and (as far as will consist with the public good) of every person in it." (par. 134; Laslett, pp. 373–74) "Natural reason tells us, that men, being once born, have a right to their preservation, and consequently to meat and drink, and such other things as nature affords for their subsistence." (par. 25; Laslett, p. 103) There is a "fundamental, sacred, and unalterable law of self-preservation"; (par. 149; Laslett, p. 385) "Nature willeth the preservation of all mankind as much as possible." (par. 182; Laslett, p. 407) "Every one as he is bound to preserve himself, and not to quit his station wilfully; so by the like reason when his own preservation comes not in competition, ought he, as much as he can, to preserve the rest of mankind, and may not unless it be to do justice on an offender, take away, or impair the life, or what tends to the preservation of the life, the liberty, health, limb or goods of another." (par. 6; Laslett, p. 289)

Moreover, the law of nature enjoins the keeping of promises and agreements: "For truth and keeping of faith belongs to men, as men, and not as members of society." (par. 14; Laslett, p. 295)

This I am sure, [princes] owe subjection to the laws of God and nature. No body, no power can exempt them from the obligations of that eternal law. Those are so great, and so strong, in the case of promises, that Omnipotency itself can be tied by them. Grants, promises and oaths are bonds that hold the Almighty. (par. 195; Laslett, pp. 413–14)

Adam and Eve, and after them all parents were, by the law of nature, under an obligation to preserve, nourish, and educate the children, they had begotten. (par. 56; Laslett, p. 323)

In return, though on attaining majority a child comes to be free from the will and command of his father, "yet this freedom exempts not a son from that honor which he ought, by the law of God and nature, to pay his parents." (par. 66; Laslett, p. 329) Children, brought into the world

by a natural birth, that produced them ignorant and without the use of reason, were not presently under that law: for nobody can be under a law, which is not promulgated to him; and this law being promulgated or made known by reason only, he that is not come to the use of his reason, cannot be said to be under this law. (par. 57; Laslett, p. 323)

Surprisingly, "captives taken in a just war" are the slaves of their captors, and "by the right of nature subjected to the absolute dominion and arbitrary power of their masters." (par. 85; Laslett, p. 341) But "he that conquerors in an unjust war, can thereby have no title to the subjection and obedience of the conquered." The latter may "appeal, as Jephtha did, to Heaven, and repeat their appeal, till they have recovered the native right of their ancestors, which was to have such a legislative over them, as the majority should approve, and freely acquiesce in." (par. 176; Laslett, p. 404) The people also have the natural right "to judge whether they have just cause to make their appeal to Heaven," "by a law antecedent and paramount to all positive laws." (par. 168; Laslett, p. 398) And finally, the law of nature, as we shall see, gives some remarkably precise directions in the sphere of property rights.

From all these rights and obligations entailed by the law of nature, it is clear that Locke thinks of the state of nature as social in character. Though Locke agrees with Hobbes in giving each man his own individual rights, as though he were an atomic entity all by himself, he also insists on the fundamentally social nature of mankind, even in the state of nature. The state of nature is pre-political, but it is not pre-social. In this Locke disagrees with Hobbes's notion, and follows rather the earlier tradition of natural law, as represented by Hooker and Pufendorf. Hooker held, in a passage cited by Locke:

The laws which have been hitherto mentioned [the laws of nature] do bind men absolutely even as they are men, although they have never any settled fellowship, never any solemn agreement amongst themselves what to do or not to do. But forasmuch as we are not by ourselves sufficient to furnish ourselves with competent store of things needful for such a life as our nature doth desire, life fit for the dignity of man; therefore to supply those defects and imperfections which are in us living single and solely by ourselves, we are naturally induced to seek communion and fellowship with others. . . . Two foundations there are which bear up public societies: the one, a natural inclination, whereby all men desire sociable life and fellowship; the other, an order expressly or secretly agreed upon touching the manner of their union in living together.[14]

And Pufendorf, in *De jure naturae et gentium* (1672), holds that the state of nature is characterized not by indiscriminate war but by

[14] Richard Hooker, *Of the Laws of Ecclesiastical Polity* (Everyman ed., ed. Ronald Bayne), Book I, sec. x, par. 1; I, 187–88; in Locke, par. 15; Laslett, pp. 295–96).

general peace. Men are rational beings from their creation and the dictates of reason guide them before as well as after the formation of the commonwealth. The law of nature prevails in the state of nature; it makes men refrain from reciprocal injury, respect one another's property, and keep their promises and contracts.

For Locke, then, there is no need of any contract to make men social; they are social by nature. Indeed, contracts could hardly be made unless men were social before entering into agreements with each other—unless the law of nature itself enjoined the keeping of promises.

God made man such a creature that, in his own judgment, it was not good for him to be alone, put him under strong obligations of necessity, convenience, and inclination to drive him into society, as well as fitted him with understanding and language to continue and enjoy it. (par. 77; Laslett, p. 336)

By the law of nature, which is common to all men, a man "and all the rest of mankind are one community, make up one society distinct from all other creatures. And were it not for the corruption, and viciousness of degenerate men, there would be no need of any other; no necessity that men should separate from this great and natural community, and by positive agreements combine into smaller and divided associations." (par. 128; Laslett, p. 370)

Thus Locke is led to contrast the state of nature sharply with what he calls "the state of war."

And here we have the plain difference between the state of nature, and the state of war, which however some men have confounded, are as far distant, as a state of peace, good will, mutual assistance, and preservation, and a state of enmity, malice, violence, and mutual destruction are one from another. (par. 19; Laslett, p. 298)

The "some men" are clearly the Hobbists; and this is often taken as the chief difference in theory between Locke and Hobbes.[15] Actually, when Locke has gotten through depicting the "inconveniences" of the state of nature, his picture is not so different from that

[15] In the fifth *Essay on the Law of Nature*, Locke holds it possible that "as is maintained by some (quod aliqui volunt), there is in the state of nature a general war and a perpetual and deadly hatred among men." (Von Leyden, 162–63) But in the eighth, he comes out against the Hobbists: "Men are, as they say, by the law of nature in a state of war; thus all society is abolished and all trust, which is the bond of society" (tollitur omnis societas et societatis vinculum fides). (pp. 212–13)

of Hobbes,[16] and he has even been called a crypto-Hobbist. Locke would have presented his own view more accurately had he contrasted the state of peace with the state of war, and included them both within the state of nature: in the former, the law of nature was obeyed, in the latter it was violated. His common sense certainly told him Hobbes's account—ultimately, his judgment of human nature and its great diversity of impulses and motives—was overdrawn and directed to establishing his own program of security through setting up absolute power. But Locke was no Rousseau. In his *Thoughts concerning Education* he held that children love dominion, "the first original of most vicious habits." (sec. 103) In the *Treatises* he recognizes the inordinate envy and ambition in men's make-up: the "pravity" of mankind renders the state of nature unendurable.

Locke as usual avoided extremes. Having no rancor against the priests and leaders of organized religion, he did not share the superficial optimism of the Deists, who idealized the natural goodness of all men. On the other hand, since he did not build his ethics on the striving of power after power, he did not have to assert with Hobbes the utter selfishness of all men unless restrained by superior force. His political views were founded on the rationalistic strain in his ethical thought, in which the spring of action is the rational consideration of various goods rather than a scramble for private pleasure.[17] The state of nature is for him neither a golden age nor a war of all against all.

I V

The only natural right Locke examines at any length is that of property: this had a profound effect on his whole social philosophy, to say nothing of his influence in the ensuing commercial age. He passes easily back and forth between using the term to include all natural rights—his customary phrase when he enumerates them more fully is "life, liberty, and estate"—and using it in the more restricted sense to mean material possessions. He never said, and certainly did not believe, that there was no natural right except property: but he constantly assumes that this is the type to which

[16] See Leo Strauss, *Natural Right and History*, pp. 224–26.
[17] See the treatment of Locke's ethics in Chapter 8 of Book Four.

all natural rights are analogous, and it was inevitable that it should stand out as the most important and controlling. He conceived all natural rights in the same way as property, that is, as belonging inherently to the individual person and born with him, and hence as presenting indefeasible claims upon both society and government. Such rights can be regulated only to the extent that is necessary to give them effective protection. The right of property is thus prior even to the state of nature itself. Property is "without any express compact of all the commoners." (par. 25; Laslett, p. 304)

Though the things of nature are given in common, yet man (by being master of himself, and proprietor of his own person, and the actions or labor of it) had still in himself the great foundation of property. (par. 44; Laslett, p. 316)

This was a sharp break with previous theory. The medieval tradition of natural law regarded common ownership as a more "natural" state than private ownership, which is due to the effects of sin on human nature. Roman law held that private property begins with the appropriation of things which before had a common use though no communal ownership. Locke states his novel view, in what is probably his best known and most influential passage:

Though the earth, and all inferior creatures be common to all men, yet every man has a property in his own person. This nobody has any right to but himself. The labor of his body, and the work of his hands, we may say, are properly his. Whatsoever then he removes out of the state that nature hath provided, and left it in, he hath mixed his labor with, and joined to it something that is his own, and thereby makes it his property. . . . For this labor being the unquestionable property of the laborer, no man but he can have a right to what that is once joined to, at least where there is enough, and as good left in common for others. (par. 27; Laslett, pp. 305-6)

By labor a man extends his own personality into the objects produced. By expending his energy upon them he makes them a part of himself.

The refutation of Filmer by Locke's friend James Tyrrell, *Patriarcha non Monarcha* (1681), sets forth much the same argument; and Richard Baxter, the Puritan divine, key figure in Weber's "spirit of capitalism," *The Second Part of the Nonconformist's Plea for Peace* (1680, but "written many years past"), states it in vaguer but similar terms. Locke himself was probably generalizing from the example of colonists in a new land like America. He seems also to have been influenced by his strong sense of the greater productivity of private agriculture as compared with the more primitive communal tillage system: the enclosure of common land in England, just beginning, did greatly increase the yield.

We see in commons, which remain so by compact, that 'tis the taking any part of what is common, and removing it out of the state nature leaves it in, which begins the property; without which the common is of no use. . . . Thus the grass my horse has bit; the turfs my servant has cut; and the ore I have digged in any place where I have a right to them in common with others, become my property, without the assignation or assent of anybody. The labor that was mine, removing them out of that common state they were in, hath fixed my property in them. (par. 28; Laslett, pp. 306–7)

The conditions of human life, which requires labor and materials to work on, necessarily introduces private possessions. (par. 35; Laslett, p. 310)

This appropriation from a common does not depend on the express consent of all the commoners.

So long as there was abundance of land and resources—when "all the world was America"—this appropriation worked well. But finally a limit had to be set by the law of nature. A man is entitled by that law to own only so much of the earth's goods as he can use; no one is justified in wasting or destroying what other men need.

The same law of nature, that does by this means [by the exercise of labor] give us property, does also bound that property too. "God has given us all things richly" is the voice of reason confirmed by inspiration. But how far has he given it us? "To enjoy." As much as any one can make use of to any advantage of life before it spoils; so much he may by his labor fix a property in. Whatever is beyond this, is more than his share, and belongs to others. Nothing was made by God for man to spoil or destroy. (par. 31; Laslett, p. 308)

Locke proceeds to extend his theory of the origin of property rights through labor to land also.

But the chief matter of property being now not the fruits of the earth, and the beasts that subsist on it, but the earth itself. . . . I think it is plain, that property in that too is acquired as the former. As much land as a man tills, plants, improves, cultivates, and can use the product of, so much is his property. He by his labor does, as it were, inclose it from the common. (par. 32; Laslett, p. 308)

God gave the world to men in common . . . but it cannot be supposed he meant it always should remain common and uncultivated. He gave it to the use of the industrious and rational, (and labor was to be his title to it;) not to the fancy or covetousness of the quarrelsome and contentious. (par. 34; Laslett, p. 309)

The rule of property, that every man should have as much as he could make use of, would still hold "without straitening anybody," since there is land enough in the world to suffice double the inhabitants, had not the invention of money revolutionized the situation, introducing by consent both large possessions and the right to them. (par. 36; Laslett, p. 311) Money is "some lasting thing that men might keep without spoiling, and that by mutual consent men would take in exchange for the truly useful, but perishable supports of life." (par. 47; Laslett, pp. 318–19) Since money does not spoil, there is no limit set to the amount a man can accumulate. If a man traded the products of his labor for these "lasting things," he could keep those by him all his life. "He invaded not the right of others, he might heap up as much of these durable things as he pleased; the exceeding of the bounds of his just property not lying in the largeness of his possession, but the perishing of anything uselessly in it." (par. 46; Laslett, p. 318)

"It is plain," Locke admits—or perhaps proudly follows his logic —"that men have agreed to disproportionate and unequal possession of the earth, they having by a tacit and voluntary consent found out a way, how a man may fairly possess more land than he himself can use the product of." This is "without injury to anyone." It took place "out of the bounds of society, and without compact," simply by putting a value on gold and silver and tacitly agreeing in the use of money. But unlimited acquisition is now no longer possible: "For in governments the laws regulate the right of property, and the possession of land is determined by positive constitutions." (par. 50; Laslett, p. 320)

In political society, then, property is held on conditions regulated by positive law. But the right of property is still sacred: such society does not create it, but is itself created in order to protect it. "The prince or senate, however it may have the power to make laws for the regulating of property between the subjects one amongst another, yet can never have the power to take to themselves the whole or any part of the subjects' property, without their own consent. For this would be in effect to leave them no property at all." (par. 139; Laslett, p. 379) It is fitting that every man who enjoys the protection of government should pay his due share of the expense. "But still it must be with his own consent, i.e., the consent of the majority, giving it either by themselves, or their representatives chosen by them. For if any one shall claim a power to lay and levy taxes on the people, by his own authority, and without such consent of the people, he thereby invades the fundamental law of property, and subverts the end of government." (par. 140; Laslett, p. 380)

No wonder Locke was popular in the American colonies. He here clearly lays down the principle, "No taxation without representation." To the Americans this meant the not unpopular principle of "no taxation"; Locke would doubtless have argued for a more effective representation in Parliament. Englishmen in the eighteenth century greatly preferred indirect to direct taxation, on the ground that the purchaser of taxed articles thus taxed himself "by his own consent." Pitt's income tax of 1799 was opposed because it sacrificed "optionality," which was the "very essence of taxation in a free country." [18]

Locke's doctrine of property is the most characteristic part of his political teaching, even as the insistence on the consent of Parliament to all revenue measures was the central core of English constitutionalism. He was defending that constitutionalism, just as he accepted the economic arrangements of his day. He was no advocate of laissez faire, but a mercantilist who believed in regulating trade. He played a great part in the creation of the old colonial system. He stated clearly the labor theory of value, already anticipated in Hobbes and in Sir William Petty: it is labor that "puts the difference of value on everything"; "labor makes the far greatest part of the value of things we enjoy in the world"; (par. 42; Laslett, p. 315) " 'Tis labor which puts the greatest part of value

[18] See P. Larkin, *Property in the 18th Century, with Special Reference to England and Locke* (Cork, 1930), pp. 115–18.

upon land." (par. 43; Laslett, p. 316) But he saw no implication in this view for a revolutionary economics, either of the classical or the socialist type. In civil society, labor no longer creates a sufficient title to property, as it did in the state of nature. But in justifying the "emancipation of acquisitiveness" in his own day, in setting forth what became the classic doctrine of the "spirit of capitalism," Locke still felt he had to prove that the unlimited acquisition of wealth is not unjust or morally wrong. In the medieval tradition property was subject to detailed moral regulation. Locke does not try to justify morally the abandonment of all those restraints by appealing to an absolute right of property enshrined in the law of nature of a now bygone age, or in a new version of that law, like the Physiocrats. He turns to the utilitarian strain in his moral theory: he shows that unlimited acquisition is conducive to the common good, to public happiness and the temporal prosperity of society.

In saying, "The great and chief end . . . of men's uniting into commonwealths and putting themselves under government is the preservation of their property," (par. 124; Laslett, p. 368) in so far as this means property in the narrower sense, Locke does not mean the preservation of those "narrow bounds of each man's small property" within which their desires were confined "by the simple poor way of living," (par. 107; Laslett, p. 357) "in the beginning of things" or in the state of nature. Men set up political society to enlarge their possessions. As Madison put it:

The protection of these faculties (the diversity in the faculties of men from which the rights of property originate) is the first object of government. From the protection of different and unequal faculties of *acquiring* property, the possession of different degrees and kinds of property immediately results.[19]

In this sense we can speak of Locke's doctrine of property having a revolutionary character. Man and not nature, the work of man and not the gift of nature, is the origin of almost everything of value: in the bread we eat, "nature and the earth furnished only the almost worthless materials, as in themselves." (par. 43; Laslett, p. 316) Man owes almost everything of value to his own efforts: the forms he supplies himself. Just so, there are no natural principles

[19] *The Federalist Papers* (Everyman ed., Ed. W. J. Ashley), p. 42.

of understanding: all knowledge is *acquired* from "the given," sensation, all knowledge depends on labor and is labor. Abstract ideas are "the inventions and creatures of the understanding, made by it for its own use." And this invention is made possible in economic life by the original of all human conventions, money.

V

The state of nature differs from civil society on one major point: in the former there is not, and in the latter there is, a common organ for interpreting and executing the law of nature.

It is easy to discern who are, and who are not, in political society together. Those who are united into one body, and have a common established law and judicature to appeal to, with authority to decide controversies between them, and punish offenders, are in civil society one with another; but those who have no such common appeal, I mean on earth, are still in the state of nature, each being, where there is no other, judge for himself, and executioner; which is the perfect state of nature. (par. 87; Laslett, p. 342)

Wherever therefore any number of men are so united into one society, as to quit everyone his executive power of the law of nature, and to resign it to the public, there and there only is a political, or civil society. (par. 89; Laslett, p. 343)

It follows that absolute monarchy is inconsistent with civil society, for there is no one to whom the absolute prince and those under his dominion can appeal to as an impartial authority to decide their disputes.

Hence men agree to set up such an impartial authority.

Men being by nature, all free, equal and independent, no one can be put out of this estate, and subjected to the political power of another, without his own consent. The only way whereby anyone divests himself of his natural liberty, and puts on the bonds of civil society, is by agreeing with other men to join and unite into a community, for their comfortable, safe, and peaceable living one amongst another, in a secure enjoyment of their properties, and a greater security against any that are not of it. (par. 95; Laslett, pp. 348–49)

This social agreement—Locke avoids the term contract—involves the submission of the individual's right to protect his "properties" or rights to the determination of the majority. This single right he gives up completely, the better to secure the others. Locke tries to justify the principle of majority rule:

When any number of men have, by the consent of every individual, made a community, they have thereby made that community one body, with a power to act as one body, which is only by the will and determination of the majority. For that which acts any community, being only the consent of the individuals of it, and it being necessary to that which is one body to move one way; it is necessary the body should move that way whither the greater force carries it, which is the consent of the majority. (par. 96; Laslett, pp. 349–50)

Every individual agrees that it should act as one body; by a curious mechanical analogy, Locke tries to show it would be impossible for it to act as one body unless it acted by the majority; "and so everyone is bound by that consent to be concluded by the majority." The body politic has thus been "incorporated," says Locke the man of affairs.

Locke considers the objection that there are no instances to be found in "story" of a company of independent men thus setting up "a government." Of course, records begin only after the institution of civil society. Besides, consider the beginnings of Rome and of Venice, which all agree were thus formed. And it happens every day in America, in Florida and Brazil, where "troops of men" choose captains in war and peace. Locke argues that this agreement was an historical event that often actually takes place. He seems to have in mind just such contracts founding some of the English colonies in America; he and Shaftesbury had collaborated in drafting such a document, published in 1675, *The Fundamental Constitutions of Carolina*, which he probably wrote himself. He was secretary of the Proprietors. So far as the individual is concerned, by his mere remaining in a community or holding property there, Locke maintains, he gives a tacit consent to the terms of the agreement. Curiously, he holds this does not take place till a man has become twenty-one.

Like all the eighteenth-century theorists, Locke cared little about how governments had actually been instituted, but was intensely interested in the question whether there was any justification of their being what they were. Such justification he believed his theory offered. But it defined carefully the functions of all governmental authority, and provided a test whereby to judge when that government had departed from its proper purpose.

Why does man give up the freedom he enjoys under the state of nature?

'Tis not without reason, that he seeks out, and is willing to join in society with others who are already united, or have a mind to unite for the mutual preservation of their lives, liberties, and estates, which I call by the name, property.

The great and chief end therefore, of men's uniting into commonwealths and putting themselves under government, is the preservation of their property. To which in the state of nature there are many things wanting.[20]

First, there wants an established, settled, known law, received and allowed by common consent to be the standard of right and wrong, and the common measure to decide all controversies between them. . . .

Secondly, in the state of nature there wants a known and indifferent judge, with authority to determine all differences according to the established law. . . .

Thirdly, in the state of nature there often wants power to back and support the sentence when right, and to give it due execution. (pars. 123–26; Laslett, pp. 368–69)

A man has two powers in the state of nature. The first is the power to do whatever he thinks fit for the preservation of himself and others within the law of nature. The second is the power to punish crimes committed against that law. The first power he gives up to be regulated by the positive laws of the society. The second he gives up wholly, and agrees to contribute his force to carry out the decisions of the political authority to which he consents to submit.

But this agreement sets definite limits on what government can rightfully do. "For no rational creature can be supposed to change his condition with an intention to be worse." Civil authority can rightly extend no further than the securing of men's natural rights.

The power of the society, or legislative [21] constituted by them, can never be supposed to extend farther than the common good; but is obliged to

---

[20] Locke had earlier said, "Government has no other end but the preservation of property." (par. 94; Laslett, p. 347)

[21] Locke seems to make a careful distinction, as reflected in the corrections to his copy, between the "legislature," which is a body of men, and the "legislative," which is a function of government.

secure everyone's property by providing against those three defects above-mentioned, that made the state of nature so unsafe and uneasy. And so whoever has the legislative or supreme power of any commonwealth, is bound to govern by established standing laws, promulgated and known to the people, and not by extemporary decrees; by indifferent and upright judges, who are to decide controversies by those laws; and to employ the force of the community at home, only in the execution of such laws, or abroad to prevent or redress foreign injuries, and secure the community from inroads and invasion. And all this to be directed to no other end, but the peace, safety, and public good of the people. (par. 131; Laslett, p. 371)

The difficulty with Locke's theory is that he nowhere answers the question, Just what is set up by the "original compact"? Is it society itself, the "community" he talks of, or only the government, or both? Paragraph 100 speaks of instances of in this way setting up "a government." Generally he uses the term "community"; and perhaps most precisely, "commonwealth"—the latter term is the only one he tries to define.

By commonwealth, I must be understood all along to mean, not a democracy, or any form of government, but any independent community which the Latins signified by the word *civitas*, to which the word which best answers in our language, is commonwealth, and most properly expresses such a society of men, which community or city in English does not, for there may be subordinate communities in a government. (par. 133; Laslett, p. 373)

Locke emphatically asserts that society and government are different in paragraph 211 (Laslett, p. 424), where he argues that a political revolution which dissolves the government does not as a rule dissolve the community which that government rules.

Althusius and Pufendorf had tried to solve this problem by introducing two contracts, one between individuals creating a community, and then a second contract between the community and its government. Pufendorf, trying to reconcile Grotius and Hobbes, makes explicit what Grotius implies, that the social instinct is responsible for the formation of society; it may be satisfied by the "primary" societies, family, religious bodies, commercial organizations, etc. But a deliberate act of will through contract is necessary to explain the origin of the state: "*Ex adpetitu* [sic] *societatis non statim sequitur adpetitus civitatis.*" [22] A twofold contract is nec-

[22] Pufendorf, *De jure naturae et gentium* (1672), VII, i, 3.

essary: both Hobbes's social contract and the governmental contract of the antimonarchist theories are essential. The process runs: first each individual contracts with each to form a lasting *civitas* (the "commonwealth" of Locke?), and to determine by majority vote what arrangements shall be made for the common safety and welfare. Then a vote is taken as to what form of government is to be adopted, and those who have joined the society conditionally on the adoption of a particular form are at liberty to withdraw if their preference is not carried out. Finally, a second contract is made between the designated bearers of governmental power on the one hand, and the rest of the community on the other, the former promising to promote the common welfare, and the latter to obey faithfully.

The older theory, which Locke got from Hooker, started by assuming the existence of a community under the law of nature, which is ultimately the law of God: this community can hold its magistrates morally responsible, and in various versions may or may not actually set them up. Locke follows this traditional notion in defending the Revolution.[23] He follows the newer view, that to begin with there are only individuals and their private interests, in holding both the commonwealth and government to be agents for protecting "life, liberty, and estate." Locke never brought these two views, Hooker and Hobbes, together, and he never mentions explicitly a twofold contract. But he often writes as though he were following Pufendorf on this point, and he certainly distinguishes between the existence of the commonwealth (the "body politic") and the actual government its people might choose. Thus he says explicitly: "The constitution of the legislative is the first and fundamental act of society, whereby provision is made for the continuation of their union, under the direction of persons, and bonds of

---

[23] Hooker, however, had not used the social contract to justify revolution, and constitutionalism. He insisted that the contract, once made, was permanent and could not be abrogated or undone. Hence the logical conclusion was royal absolutism. "And to be commanded we do consent, when that society whereof we are part hath at any time before consented, without revoking the same by the like universal agreement. Wherefore as any man's deed past is good as long as himself continueth; so the act of a public society of men done five hundred years sithence standeth as theirs who presently are of the same societies, because corporations are immortal; we were then alive in our predecessors, and they in their successors do live still." (*Ecclesiastical Polity*, Book I, x, 8; Everyman ed., I, 194–95)

laws made by persons authorized thereunto, by the consent and appointment of the people, without which no one man, or number of men, amongst them, can have authority of making laws, that shall be binding to the rest." (par. 212; Laslett, pp. 425–26) And he seems to be following Pufendorf's argument that the fiction of a social contract must be supplemented by the further fiction of unanimous consent. Apart from English constitutional procedure, it is also hard to find Locke's argument for submission to majority rule convincing. Why should an individual with indefeasible rights submit to a majority? Or if there is really a "community," why cannot the "prevailing part" be weighted for quality as well as quantity? These were the problems Rousseau was wrestling with when he rediscovered the community and its "general will."

In any event, Locke treats the relation of the government to the community, commonwealth, or people who set it up, on the model of a legal trust: government is a political "trustee" or a "fiduciary power." The people erect a legislative to have supreme power over them, while the executive (who may, like the king of England, also have a share in the legislative power), "is visibly subordinate and accountable to it, and may be at pleasure changed and displaced." (par. 152; Laslett, p. 386) The legislative, while supreme over the other branches of government, cannot be absolutely arbitrary; "their power in the utmost bounds of it, is limited to the public good of the society." "The obligations of the law of nature, cease not in society, but only in many cases are drawn closer. . . . Thus the law of nature stands as an eternal rule to all men, legislators as well as others." (par. 135; Laslett, p. 375) "The community put the legislative power into such hands, as they think fit, with this trust, that they shall be governed by declared laws." (par. 136; Laslett, p. 377) Government is "entrusted with this condition, and for this end, that men might have and secure their properties." (par. 139; Laslett, p. 379) Locke states his theory of political trusteeship most fully:

The legislative being only a fiduciary power to act for certain ends, there remains still in the people a supreme power to remove or alter the legislative, when they find the legislative act contrary to the trust reposed in them. For all power given with trust for the attaining an end, being limited by that end, whenever that end is manifestly neglected, or opposed, the trust must necessarily be forfeited, and the power devolve into the hands of those that gave it, who may place it anew where they shall think best for their safety and security. (par. 149; Laslett, p. 385)

VI

Originally written in 1679–80 to foment a subversive Whig insurrection, and published in 1690 to defend a successful Revolution, the *Treatise on Government* reaches its climax in Locke's thesis, that under certain conditions when government has failed to fulfill its trust and has violated the rights it was set up to protect, the people is rationally and morally justified in resorting to revolution —in the end, in "appealing to Heaven." In the first place, neither an absolute monarch nor a usurper has any moral or legal right to rule—the *de facto* possession of power confers no such right. Locke's rationalism as well as his moderation comes out in the limitations he sets to the right of revolution. The people are under both legal and moral obligation to fulfill their side of the contract they have freely entered into, in setting up a commonwealth. They must observe the legal clauses of their contract with their rulers; they are not justified in overturning the government whenever they can thereby serve their own interests. A minority are never warranted in rebelling; only a majority can abrogate its contract.

Yet within these narrow legal limits, the right of revolution is indefeasible:

The community perpetually retains a supreme power of saving themselves from the attempts and designs of anybody, even of their legislators, whenever they shall be so foolish, or so wicked, as to lay and carry on designs against the liberties and properties of the subject. (par. 149; Laslett, p. 385)

Wherever law ends, tyranny begins, if the law be transgressed to another's harm. And whosoever in authority exceeds the power given him by the law, and makes use of the force he has under his command, to compass that upon the subject, which the law allows not, ceases in that to be a magistrate, and acting without authority, may be opposed, as any other man, who by force invades the right of another. (par. 202; Laslett, pp. 418–19)

The last chapter, "Of the Dissolution of Government," is Locke's Declaration of Independence, listing the crimes of the Stuarts. He starts by distinguishing sharply between the dissolution of the society and the dissolution of the government. That which makes the community, and brings men into a body politic, is the agreement to incorporate. Almost the only way by which this may be dissolved is by foreign conquest. The government is much more easily subverted. One point at least is clear—it is the last one Locke makes.

The power that every individual gave the society, when he entered into it, can never revert to the individuals again, as long as the society lasts, but will always remain in the community; because without this, there can be no community, no commonwealth, which is contrary to the original agreement: so also when the society hath placed the legislative in any assembly of men, to continue in them and their successors, with direction and authority for providing such successors, the legislative can never revert to the people whilst that government lasts. (par. 243; Laslett, pp. 445–46)

Locke's most ringing declaration is in his longest section, Par. 222.

Whensoever therefore the legislative shall transgress this fundamental rule of society; and either by ambition, fear, folly or corruption, endeavor to grasp themselves, or put into the hands of any other an absolute power over the lives, liberties, and estates of the people; by this breach of trust they forfeit the power, the people had put into their hands, for quite contrary ends, and it devolves to the people, who have a right to resume their original liberty, and, by the establishment of a new legislative (such as they shall think fit) provide for their own safety and security, which is the end for which they are in society. (par. 222; Laslett, pp. 430–31)

But Locke's attack on legislatives unfaithful to their trust is only the beginning. He goes after his chief game, James II:

What I have said here, concerning the legislative, in general, holds true also concerning the supreme executor, who having a double trust put in him, both to have a part in the legislative, and the supreme execution of the law, acts against both, when he goes about to set up his own arbitrary will, as the law of society. He acts also contrary to his trust, when he either employs the force, treasure, and offices of the society, to corrupt the representatives, and gain them to his purposes; or openly pre-engages the electors, and prescribes to their choice, such, whom he has by solicitations, threats, promises, or otherwise won to his designs; and employs them to bring in such, who have promised beforehand, what to vote, and what to enact. (par. 222; Laslett, p. 431)

Locke goes on to enumerate the crimes of James.

Locke asks, will not this "hypothesis" provoke frequent rebellion?

No. People rebel because of grievances, not because of writings. Moreover, such revolutions happen not upon every little mismanagement in public affairs, but only after a long train of abuses. Thirdly, the threat of revolution "is the best fence against rebellion," and the probablest means to hinder it. "The properest way to prevent the evil, is to show them the danger and injustice of it, who are under the greatest temptation to run into it." (par. 226; Laslett, p. 434)

The last question is, "Who shall be judge whether the prince or legislative act contrary to their trust? . . . To this I reply, the people shall be judge; for who shall be judge whether his trustee or deputy acts well, and according to the trust reposed in him, but he who deputes him, and must, by having deputed him still have a power to discard him, when he fails in his trust?" (par. 240; Laslett, pp. 444-45) There is a higher judge: "But farther, this question [Who shall be judge?] cannot mean, that there is no judge at all. For where there is no judicature on earth, to decide controversies amongst men, God in Heaven is judge: he alone, 'tis true, is judge of the right. But every man is judge for himself, as in all other cases, so in this, whether another hath put himself into a state of war with him, and whether he should appeal to the supreme judge, as Jephtha did." (par. 241; Laslett, p. 445)

Locke is not too explicit upon the way in which this dissolving of a tyrannical government is to take place. He is far more concerned with supporting the Whig rebellion, and with justifying the Whig Revolution of 1688-89, than with paving the way for new revolutions against the economic and political domination of the propertied classes with which he so fully sympathized. He can only say that the people possess ultimately the right of "appealing to Heaven." He seems confident that they will exercise this right against any proper English government only under extreme provocation.

It is clear that Locke, like all the eighteenth-century theorists of government, is concerned primarily with setting limits to the power of any government over men's lives, religious beliefs, and property: government is under obligation to observe the natural laws guaranteeing freedom, especially religious freedom, and security, especially security of property. In this he is rationalizing and stating the outcome of the long struggle of the English people, led by the middle class, against the Stuarts. He differs from the rational absolutists in France, like the Physiocrats, not in his view of the aim and function of government, but in fearing the infringements of the monarch more than those of the poorer classes. Hence all his arguments for the English constitution emphasize the checks it puts upon governmental and royal power rather than the authority an enlightened monarch of good will might possess to institute reforms. This well illustrates the differing needs of the middle class in England and on the Continent—traditional governmental regulation and ecclesiastical privilege had lasted longer there, and needed a strong opposition.

Locke insists on the advantage of separating the legislative power, which must inhere in the representatives of "the people," from the executive. If the latter also make the laws, "they may exempt themselves from obedience to the laws they make and suit the law, both in its making and execution, to their own private advantage, and thereby come to have a distinct interest from the rest of the community." (par. 143; Laslett, p. 382) Hence the legislative and the executive power (the latter includes also the "foederative" power, dealing with treaties and foreign relations) are kept distinct in "all moderated monarchies, and well-framed governments." (par. 159; Laslett, p. 392) To achieve the same ends, the Continental absolutists counseled rather keeping the monarch and the judicial power separate. Locke does not distinguish a separate "judicial" power, but he seems to take "indifferent judges" for granted.

7

Rational Religion—Supernatural and Deistic

WITH Locke's "natural history of the mind," the critical weapon of Enlightenment thought was forged, though it was sharpened to its keenest on the whetstone of Hume. With Newton, perhaps still more with his popularizers, the age received its constructive tool, the positive ideal and method or, as we say today, the model, of "science." In the light of what the subtle thought of these two towering figures came to mean in the far from subtle mind of the educated classes, we can understand the terms in which was carried on the great intellectual enterprise of the century, making every branch of human activity "scientific." Never was "science" so respected and idolized. From 1859 to 1914—symbolic dates, of course —science might superficially seem to have enjoyed an even greater reverence in Western culture; and this period it has become the fashion to call "a generation of scientism." For the United States the symbolic terminus would be 1929; for Russia, the end is not yet.

But this later reign of the "scientific" model is far more complex than its predecessor in the Enlightenment. Science itself had grown much more complicated, and it was far more difficult to know what one really meant by "being scientific" and using "scientific methods." The Enlightenment thinkers had no doubts on this score. To be scientific meant to follow reason, like Newton the mathematician; or else it meant to consult nothing but experience with regard to matters of fact, like the empiricists who culminated in Hume. Indeed, the men of the eighteenth century were more likely to appeal to "reason" or to "experience"—or to both—than to "science." But after 1859, what did "science" mean? Did it mean a mechanistic determinism, the iron laws governing what one was investigating?

Did it mean evolution and the genetic method, the explanation of everything human in terms of its origin in that new state of nature before man and human society emerged from the great apes? Did it mean the inductive sciences, and the employment of Mill's canons of inductive generalization? Did it mean the sheer positivistic description of facts, and their analysis by the principles of statistics? Did it mean the experimental method, with its hypotheses, its theory construction, its probabilities and its disconfirmations? Did it mean the historical method with its laws of development, its dialectics, and its assorted historicisms? Did it mean relativism, historical and cultural? Did it mean a psychological method, associational, introspective, muscle-twitch or depth? And whose depth? It was now all very confusing and perplexing to those trying to extend science and scientific methods to human affairs and human activities.

Equally important, when science regained intellectual respectability after 1859 among the educated classes, this ideal had now become what the twentieth century in its sophistication has come to call "scientism." That is, the scientific ideal was no longer opposed, as during the simplicity of the Age of Reason, only by the obscurantism, superstition, and error of irrational tradition. The Romantic revolt from the Newtonian ideal and model had made prominent and reputable a number of other ways of looking at the world; and science was now, for all its practical importance, intellectually but one "ism" amidst many others. These assorted voluntarisms and antirationalisms were growing rapidly in number and in strength during the very era of the supposed dominance of "scientism," and after 1914 they burst out in Europe, with the depression in America, leaving the scientific ideal as a useful tool of technology and power, but as really irrelevant to any philosophic understanding of the world or human life. Science may produce much that is good, and much—very much, as we know to our discomfort and peril—that is evil. The one thing, it often seems to the unregenerate left over from the age of Bertrand Russell and John Dewey, no serious up-to-date and contemporary philosopher would expect science to produce, is understanding and philosophic truth. So the eighteenth century can probably still hold its edge on the claim to be the great age of science in Western culture.

There is much irony in the fact that just when philosophy was actually becoming most abstract and technical, as it proceeded from the plain historical account of how ideas come into the mind in Locke to the transcendental analysis of the conditions of experience in Kant, it was most vitally bound up with living problems. Locke's pages, so dull and stodgy to the modern reader, were actually burning firebrands to Voltaire and his disciples. The eighteenth-century philosophers managed to create a "science" of human nature and a "science" of society which are shot through and through with the values men felt and sought passionately. We have all been taught, since Hume and Kant, that this is something no self-respecting science can possibly tolerate. So today we are doubtful how "scientific" these eighteenth-century human "sciences" really were, and we now tend to label them all the work of philosophers rather than scientists. Be that as it may, they were surely achievements of the human mind. And if we can admit the use of ideas as weapons and as tools to the practice of the philosophic enterprise, we shall have to recognize them as significant products of human thought and passion and vision.

In creating these sciences of man, the eighteenth-century pioneers followed for the most part the more conservative scientific method inherited from the seventeenth century, the deductive elaboration of premises derived from analysis—the rationalistic rather than the observational side of Newton, the traditional conception of a demonstrative rather than the newer conception of an observational and positivistic science. The empiricist analysis was employed wholly in the destructive work of clearing the ground; then, in good Newtonian fashion, men sought the rational order of nature in human affairs. Voltaire, as we have seen, was typical: for critical purposes he is an empiricist and Lockean, for constructive purposes in formulating his own beliefs he is a thoroughgoing rationalist.

Two complete and utter failures, however, confronted Enlightenment thought when it attempted to apply its ideal and model to the various ideal enterprises of man. And these failures led directly to the overthrow of the rule—should we say the tyranny?—of the Newtonian scientific ideal. These failures occurred when Newtonian thought was applied to religion and to art.

The fortunes of that ideal when applied to the religious tradition are both interesting and instructive. For the story is a complete episode, with a beginning, a middle, and an end, as any proper tragedy—or comedy—should display. The rise and fall of rational or scientific religion in the seventeenth and eighteenth centuries is one of the great historic dramas of ideas. It is the kind of story that appealed to the eighteenth-century mind: two of that age's greatest intellects chose just such a theme for their masterpieces, Montesquieu, *Observations on the Grandeur of the Romans and their Fall*, and Gibbon, *The Decline and Fall of the Roman Empire*. The search for the tragic guilt lying behind the fall of rational religion was the occasion for the three great intellectual reconstructions of the religious tradition of the West that marked the early nineteenth century. Reflective Westerners ever since, when they have engaged in philosophical examination of the role of religion in human life, however their analyses have been deepened and their horizons extended, have been guided by the light of these Romantic reconstructions.

The drama of rational religion was enacted in each of the great European cultures. The course it ran, earliest of all, in the British Enlightenment, will be treated here. It took a new turn in the French *éclaircissement;* the drama exhibits a rather different structure in the German *Aufklärung.*

The rational or scientific religion of the seventeenth and eighteenth centuries is the outcome of the second great attempt of Western culture to adapt its religious tradition to the forces of contemporary life. The first of these attempts, usually taken as ushering in the "modern world" or the "modern period," played a central role in the Renaissance and the Reformation. As we have seen, these great movements meant intellectually primarily the assimilation of new values: individualism, commercialism, this-worldliness and secularism, in many of the meanings we give those terms. This first adaptation was highly successful: the religious tradition managed to assimilate all these modern values. But intellectually the Renaissance proved too radical; it provoked a reaction and a return to the ideas of the earlier medieval and even the pre-medieval Hellenistic eras, against the too rapidly modernizing papacy. This theological reaction left the Puritans of both the Protestant and the Catholic Reformations intellectually in the world of St. Augustine, minus its Platonic philosophy, while in their values they were living with the commerce, the profit-seeking, and the business enterprise that were coming to characterize the new day.

The second attempt at adapting the religious tradition to the modern world made the intellectual assimilation of Newtonian science central, though the social values of the Enlightenment were an important phase of it also, especially the lessening of the emphasis on a this-world asceticism, in response to the rapidly increasing material prosperity. So long as the Newtonian world endured, this intellectual adjustment seemed to be highly successful: rational religion was pretty universally popular in educated circles between 1689 and 1750. "Religion," to be sure, lost pretty much all its traditional values except that of furnishing the ultimate categories for a "scientific" system. But it seemed at least to be "scientific" in the sense the great Newton himself understood the term. But then, rational religion collapsed completely before the critique the empiricists directed against those concepts that had been taken as the basic categories of the "scientific system." The very success of Protestantism in particular in becoming individualistic and rationalistic turned into a liability in the nineteenth century.

II

From Lord Herbert of Cherbury in 1624 to William Paley in 1798, men turned to emphasizing science and reason in religion as a way out from theological controversy. This was the primary motive of the irenic Locke in his specific contribution to the cooling of religious passions, *The Reasonableness of Christianity* (1695). Approaching the religious tradition in this spirit, such men proposed two new tests for what was important and reasonable in religion. The first was practical utility. What *earthly* use is religion? What in it will make a man the better citizen? The whole spirit of such an ideal, and its disintegrating effect upon the traditional beliefs, is well illustrated by a remark of one of the characters in an early work of Diderot, *Le Promenade du sceptique*. To a speaker who is maintaining the importance of keeping the people in bondage to certain prejudices, he retorts:

What prejudices? If a man once admits the existence of a God, the reality of moral good and evil, the immortality of the soul, future rewards and punishments, what need has he of prejudices? Supposing him initiated in all the mysteries of transubstantiation, consubstantiation, the Trinity, hypostatical union, predestination, incarnation, and the rest, *will he be any the better citizen?* [1]

Such is the test—good citizenship, social utility. All that can pass this test is the religion of reason; all that cannot is relegated to the other field of revealed or supernatural religion.

The second test of the tradition was its scientific reasonableness. What in religion gives a scientifically true explanation of things? Such a test naturally made religion into a set of scientific propositions offering an incentive to the social virtues of an individualistic society. Out of all the wealth of aspiration, feeling, emotion, expression, symbolism and poetry of the great Christian tradition, the men of the age of reason looked for the two things it had never pretended to give, scientific truth and the pattern of commercial prosperity.

This is really quite extraordinary; the popular mind has hardly even today gotten over the effects of judging religion by such standards. Indeed, the emerging American religion sociologists are beginning to distinguish in the United States is the lineal descendant of this eighteenth-century religion of reason. Men still think the "Jewish-Christian tradition" must somehow give a "scientific explanation" of the world; and when they realize that it does not, they are tempted to judge it of no value. Or they still imagine the Jewish-Christian ethics will solve the moral problems of an industrial world, and hardly dare contemplate the possibility that it will not. Any freshman will still say, we must believe in God to explain how the world, or how life, got started. And when it is pointed out that the hypothesis of a creator, whatever its very real value as a symbol in the religious life, cannot possibly "explain" the "origin" of anything; that every intelligent theologian, from Aristotle, Maimonides, and Thomas down, has realized this, and hence has used "God" to explain other things than origins, he will imagine you are taking away all "reason" for religion. Such are the continuing results of Newtonian science in turning men away from sound theology.

Though foreshadowed by the Polish Brethren of Socinians, a group emphasizing the cardinal humanistic principle of the dignity of human nature, and by the much more traditional Arminians of

[1] Diderot, *Oeuvres*, ed. Assézat et Tourneux, I, 182.

Holland, whose break with strict Calvinism represented the same humanistic and scientific tendencies at work, it was in England that the religion of reason was first consistently worked out. Because Reformed Calvinism insisted more on a rational interpretation of the Scriptures, because in it new sects multiplied most rapidly, and because Calvinism in itself was the most medieval of all the Protestant theological systems, carrying on the tradition of the Scotism dominant in the late medieval Church, religious rationalism first gained a foothold in the Calvinistic ranks, in seventeenth-century Holland and in Puritan England. The English constitutional struggles, fought largely under a theological ideology, terminating in the Toleration Act of 1689, which made all dissent from the Thirty-nine Articles legal save Catholicism and Unitarianism; and the very fact that the Anglican national church was the result of a compromise holding together men of a great variety of opinions, transferred the seat of the new religion of reason to that country, whence it spread in turn throughout the next century in great streams to France and the Germanies.

Already, in *De Veritate* (1624), Lord Herbert of Cherbury had sought certain universal Christian principles that could be agreed upon by all men regardless of their specific theological differences. He based these principles on a view of knowledge and truth that made "natural instinct, or the common reason of God's providence," the highest mental faculty. It is the abode of the "common notions" that underlie experience, whose mark is both logical—independence, certainty, and necessity—and psychological—priority in time and universality. He makes the last mark, "universal consent," "the highest rule of natural instinct," and "the highest criterion of truth." [2]

This largely Stoic view Lord Herbert applied to the first principles of morality and science, but examined in detail only the common notions of religion. These are: 1) there is a supreme Deity (*esse deum summum*, or, *esse supremum aliquod numen*); 2) this Deity ought to be worshiped; 3) virtue combined with piety is the chief part of divine worship; 4) men should repent of their sins and turn from them (*dolendum esse ob peccata, ab iisque resipiscendum*);

[2] Lord Herbert of Cherbury, *De Veritate, prout distinguitur a Revelatione, a Verisimili, a Possibili, et a Falso* (1624; 3d ed. used), pp. 70, 60, 39.

5) reward and punishment follow from the goodness and justice of God, both in this life and after it.[3] These five articles contain the whole doctrine of the true catholic church, and of the religion of reason. They also formed primitive religion before the people "gave ear to the covetous and crafty sacerdotal order." What is contrary to the five points is contrary to reason and false; what is beyond reason but not contrary to it may be revealed. But the record of a revelation is not itself revelation but tradition; and the truth of a tradition depends on the narrator, and can never be more than probable.

Herbert sought to verify his common notions in a work that tried to make a systematic study of comparative religion, *De religione Gentilium* (not published till 1663). He had no sense of historical development, and looked on all actual religions, in so far as they went beyond his five articles, as simply corruptions of the pure and primitive rational worship.

The whole pattern of rational religion is to be found in Herbert, and he is conventionally taken as the first Deist. We have seen how the Cambridge Platonists tried to secure the same rational agreement on a Platonic rather than a Stoic view of knowledge, and how Locke's appeal to experience had the same irenic end. As controversy went on such attempts proved increasingly popular. By the end of the century, most intelligent religious leaders fell into one of two parties. Both agreed that the core of religion is a set of doctrines that can be established by unaided natural reason: both orthodox and radicals accepted as fundamental what could pass the two tests of rational or natural religion. The orthodox insisted also on the importance of revelation besides: they were *supernatural rationalists*, who distinguished sharply between what could and what could not be rationally established, but accepted both elements of the tradition. These men were in fundamental agreement with the Thomistic position: they accepted both rational and revealed religion. The radicals, who came to be called "Deists," differed from them in rejecting revelation completely, and in insisting on the sufficiency of natural and rational religion.

Herbert's five articles were usually simplified into three tenets:

[3] In G. V. Lechler, *Geschichte des Englischen Deismus* (1841), p. 42; also in *De religione Gentilium, errorum apud eos causis* (1st ed., 1645; complete ed. 1663; tr. as *The Ancient Religion of the Gentiles* (1705), pp. 3–4.

There is a Supreme Being,[4] he holds men morally responsible, and will reward and punish them in a future life. These were accepted as the "essence of religion" by the overwhelming body of educated Englishmen in the post-Revolutionary world. There followed two great controversies. For a generation the polemics were waged between the rational supernaturalists and the Deists, over the issue of whether revelation was or was not necessary in addition to natural religion. Then more thoroughgoing critics came to question the premises of natural religion or theology itself, and the second controversy broke out, between those who did and those who did not accept rational theology. The latter group were usually called sceptics, and included both the fideists who founded religion on faith rather than reason, and the atheists who rejected theology entirely. Social conditions made the development of a strict atheism largely a matter of the French Enlightenment, which had started as Deistical: Voltaire remained a Deist all his life, and Rousseau popularized a sentimental version of the same faith. In Britain, the sceptics usually maintained in public, like Hume, that "our most holy religion is founded upon faith."

III

The three outstanding leaders of the more traditional rational supernaturalists were, aside from Newton himself, John Tillotson, Archbishop of Canterbury, Locke, and Samuel Clarke, foremost theologian and after Locke's death the most famous philosopher in England. These men were all convinced Newtonians, believing in Newton's method of scientific rationalism and in the order of nature. They all agreed that religion is neither a form of feeling, nor a form of action, nor an instinctive need and activity of the human soul; it is a system of rational propositions given from without and to be tested as any other propositions are tested, by the evidence of human reason operating upon self-evident axioms. Its only method of arriving at the truths that must be believed is the same kind of reason one employs in accepting a law of physics: religion is a science on the model of rational mechanics. Its value and purpose is likewise very definite: it is solely to provide a divine sanction for

[4] The American political tradition is officially committed to rational religion. Thus for his claim to be legally valid, a conscientious objector must be at least a Deist.

a satisfactory human morality, to insure that rewards and punishments in the life to come will provide a powerful motive for doing good and avoiding evil. All that is irrelevant to this specific purpose is unimportant. Rational religion provides such a sanction and motive. Man, employing his reason, will see the advantages of living a righteous life, and will rationally order his own life in such a way as to attain a reward in heaven.

This simple creed remained throughout the century the content of rational religion. Kant summed it up as God, freedom, and immortality—it was primarily Rousseau who had defined moral responsibility in terms of freedom. William Paley, writing at the end of the century, went so far as to define virtue as: "the doing good to mankind in obedience to the will of God and for the sake of future rewards." [5] This creed was accepted, by orthodox and radicals alike, as the essential content of the religious tradition of Christianity. It seemed to them so obviously true that until confronted by more thoroughgoing critics they hardly bothered to try to prove its validity, concentrating their energies rather on debating whether it alone was a sufficient incentive to morality. The orthodox said no, the Deists yes.

On rational religion itself there was singular unanimity: from Herbert in 1624 to Paley in 1798, its purpose and its content remained unaltered. Conservative Locke wrote:

In all things of this kind, there is little need or use of revelation, God having furnished us with natural and surer means to arrive at a knowledge of them. For whatsoever truth we come to the clear discovery of from the knowledge and contemplation of our own ideas, will always be certainer to us than those which are conveyed to us by *traditional revelation*. [6]

In such a spirit Locke examined the New Testament, and there found set forth only two conditions of salvation: to believe that Jesus is the Messiah, and to live righteously:

These two, faith and repentance, that is, believing Jesus to be the Messiah, and a good life, are the indispensable conditions of the new covenant to be performed by all those who would obtain eternal life. [7]

[5] *Moral and Political Philosophy*, Book I, ch. 7.
[6] Locke, *Essay*, Book IV, ch. 18, sec. 4.
[7] *The Reasonableness of Christianity as Delivered in the Scriptures* (1695; 1696 ed. used), p. 202.

Matthew Tindal, in *Christianity as Old as the Creation, or, The Gospel a Republication of the Religion of Nature* (1730), which remained the best statement of the radical position and earned the title of "the Deists' Bible," expresses precisely the same idea of natural religion. True religion consists

in a constant disposition of mind to do all the good we can, and thereby render ourselves acceptable to God in answering the end of his creation.[8]

The only difference between morality and religion is that the former is "acting according to the reason of things considered in themselves," while the latter is "acting according to the same reason of things considered as the will of God."[9]

The rational supernaturalists added to this natural religion revelation. Revelation is a supplement; it is directed to the same end, it teaches the same truths, what every man could arrive at through his own reason, merely adding a few additional truths and a few extra duties. Locke lays down the principles on which revelation is to be accepted. There are three classes of religious truths.

By what has been before said of reason, we may be able to make some guess at the distinction of things into those that are according to, above and contrary to reason. 1. *According to reason* are such propositions whose truth we can discover by examining and tracing those ideas we have from sensation and reflection; and by natural deduction find to be true or probable. 2. *Above reason* are such propositions whose truth or probability we cannot by reason derive from those principles. 3. *Contrary to reason* are such propositions as are inconsistent with, or irreconcilable to our clear and distinct ideas. Thus the existence of one God is according to reason; the existence of more than one God contrary to reason; the resurrection of the dead above reason.[10]

The first group constitute natural religion; the second, superstition; the third, revelation. Locke's disciple John Toland, in his *Christianity not Mysterious* (1696), further pointed out that the first and last groups of propositions really form a single class: reasonable truths may be discovered by us for ourselves, or they may be made known to us by the testimony of others, and this testimony may

[8] Matthew Tindal, *Christianity as Old as the Creation: or, The Gospel a Republication of the Religion of Nature* (1730; 2d ed. 1732 used), p. 18.
[9] *Christianity as Old as the Creation*, p. 272.
[10] Locke, *Essay*, Book IV, ch. 17, sec. 23.

be given by revelation. But all that contradicts what experience teaches must be discarded.

The rational supernaturalists had to prove two things in order to support revelation: first, that it was not inconsistent with rational religion—that is, that it was both rational in itself and in accordance with natural morality; and secondly, that there were positive grounds for believing in the specific Christian revelation, which amounted to pointing to two kinds of evidence, prophecy and miracles.

Tillotson's arguments are typical. Natural religion is not sufficient; men need a stronger motive to make them act morally. Revelation does not alter natural religion, it merely makes it clearer and more effective. "Natural religion is the foundation of all revealed religion, and revelation is designed simply to establish its duties." [11] Revelation does not impart any new faculty of truth or any new test; it gives an additional motive for acting on what we already know to be true. Why do we accept it? First, because it is in complete harmony with natural religion and with human nature; secondly, because it was foretold in the Old Testament by prophecies, and confirmed in the New by miracles. Both are visible signs to prove the divine mission of the prophet or worker of miracles, a sort of stamp of genuineness, like "sterling" or "twenty-four carat."

Now there are two things must concur to give the mind of man full satisfaction that any religion is from God. First, if the person that declares this religion gives testimony of his divine authority, that is, that he is sent and commissioned by God for that purpose. And secondly, if the religion which he declares contain nothing in it that is plainly repugnant to the nature of God. . . . For though a doctrine be never so reasonable in itself, this is no certain argument that it is from God if no testimony from heaven be given to it; because it may be the result and issue of human reason and discourse; and though a doctrine be attested by miracles, yet the matter of it may be so unreasonable and absurd, so unworthy of God, and so contrary to the natural notions which man has of him, that no miracles can be sufficient to give confirmation to it; and therefore in some cases the Scripture forbids men to hearken to a prophet though he work a miracle.[12]

Locke's position is identical.

[11] John Tillotson, *Works* (ed. 1857), II, 333.
[12] John Tillotson, *The Miracles Wrought in Confirmation of Christianity*, *Works*, III, 493.

For since no evidence of our faculties by which we receive such revelations can exceed, if equal, the certainty of our intuitive knowledge, we can never receive for a truth anything that is directly contrary to our clear and distinct knowledge. . . . There can be no evidence that any traditional religion is of divine origin. . . . so clear and so certain as that of the principles of reason.[13]

Divine revelation receives testimony from no other miracles but such as are wrought to witness his mission from God who delivers the revelation. All other miracles that are done in the world, how many or great soever, revelation is not concerned in.[14]

In his *Reasonableness of Christianity as delivered in the Scriptures* (1695), Locke contended that the Christian revelation passes such tests—that is, in its Anglican form.

Revelation was necessary because, in spite of the fact that reason alone could have sufficed to lead them to it, men had widely lost the knowledge of natural religion. As Samuel Clarke puts it succinctly:

There was plainly wanting a divine revelation to recover mankind out of their universal corruption and degeneracy, and without such a revelation it was not possible that the world should ever be effectually reformed. For if the gross and stupid ignorance, the innumerable prejudices and vain opinions, . . . which the generality of mankind continually labor under, make it undeniably too difficult a work for men of all capacities to discover every one for himself, by the bare light of reason, all the particular branches of their duty, . . . there was plainly a necessity of some particular revelation, to discover in what manner, and with what kind of external service, God might acceptably be worshipped. . . . There was a necessity of some particular revelation, to give men full assurance of the truth of those great motives of religion, the rewards and punishments of a future state, which, notwithstanding the strongest arguments of reason, men could not yet forbear doubting of.[15]

To such a pass had Newtonian reason brought the great Christian tradition, with all its passionate feeling and yearning for God. It had become merely a philosophical system appealing to the cool and deliberate reason of the man of common sense. The inner ex-

[13] Locke, *Essay*, Book IV, ch. 18, secs. 5, 10.
[14] Locke, *Discourse of Miracles* (posthumous); *Works of John Locke*, collected ed. (London, Thomas Tegg, etc., 1823), IX, 257.
[15] Samuel Clarke, *Boyle Lectures* (1705), *A Discourse Concerning the Unchangeable Obligations of Natural Religion, and the Truth and Certainty of the Christian Revelation*, II, Proposition VII (10th ed. used, 1766), 153–54.

perience of the presence of the Divine, the immediate vision of the living reality of God, was condemned as unwholesome "enthusiasm" —the unforgivable sin during the Age of Reason. It is little wonder that soon mystics began to hear the voice of God again within the heart, and that the same century saw the great revivals of medieval faith that in Germany became Pietism, and in England Wesleyan Evangelicalism. But such rude things were not for the man of reason, or for the middle class; they spread among the lower classes first.

IV

With revelation appealing to such arguments, it is not at all hard to understand that many not obligated to maintain their own position as priests or bishops should see little reason for maintaining it. On every hand there sprang up Deists [16] who clung only to what Arthur Bury in 1690 called *The Naked Gospel*. In attacking revelation, the Deists used three main arguments. The first is an appeal to universality. A particular revelation is not "reasonable": the God who created the Newtonian order of nature and always rules by universal laws could not possibly give a single, exclusive revelation. Herbert of Cherbury maintained that God's perfection demands a way of salvation open to all men. Particular revelations are necessarily partial and preferential, and the universal God possesses no such character. What is necessary for man's salvation must have been implanted by him in man's natural reason, and must be equally accessible to all ages and places. Matthew Tindal's *Christianity as Old as Creation* gives this argument most elaborately. Natural religion has always existed as a perfect thing, and therefore revelation can add nothing to it. God asks only the good of man, human perfection and happiness, secured by universal benevolence.

[16] *The Shorter Oxford English Dictionary* defines "Deism": "usually, belief in the existence of a God, with rejection of revelation; 'natural religion.'" It defines "Deist": "One who acknowledges the existence of a God upon the testimony of reason, but rejects revealed religion. (The term was originally opposed to *atheist*, and was interchangeable with *theist* even in the end of the 17th century.)" "Deist" occurs first in 1621, "Deism" in 1682, when Bentley wrote: "Deism being the same with old Philosophical Paganism."

"Deist" was taken over from the French "déiste"; *Petit Larousse* says: "Système de ceux qui, rejetant toute révélation, croient seulement a l'existence de Dieu et a la religion naturelle: *Jean-Jacques Rousseau a defendu le déisme*. (Le déisme se distingue du *théisme*, qui, se fondant sur une revelation, reconnait en outre une Providence et admet parfois un culte.)"

To imagine God can command anything inconsistent with this universal benevolence is highly to dishonor him; 'tis to destroy his impartial goodness, and make his power and wisdom degenerate into cruelty and craft.[17]

Duties neither need nor can receive any stronger proof than what they have already from the evidence of right reason.[18]

Miracles and prophecy, and all particular religious rites and beliefs, are mere superstition.

The second Deistic argument against revelation is that the content of revelation—i.e., the Christian revelation in particular—is irrational, and of no use in fostering virtue. The Deists waged a vigorous attack on all that distinguished Christianity from natural religion—an attack fairly calm and moderate in England and in the Germanies, but exceedingly bitter and impassioned in the France of corrupt Catholic prelates, of Cardinals Dubois and d'Orleans and du Rohan, of Voltaire's "l'infâme." Tindal and Thomas Morgan, a physician (*The Moral Philosopher: In a Dialogue between Philalethes a Christian Deist and Theophanes a Christian Jew*, 1737), delighted in pointing out the irrational absurdities and the cruel inhumanities and futilities of much of historical Christianity; Thomas Chubb, an obscure tradesman of Salisbury, with no pretensions to scholarship or education (*The True Gospel of Jesus Christ*, 1739), declared that Jesus was a Deist, and in typical humanist fashion opposed the "religion of Jesus" to Christianity. The French of course went much further in attacking the irrationality of Christianity.

The third argument of the Deists against revelation was their contention that all the positive, "external" evidence for revelation breaks down at the slightest touch of critical analysis. Prophecy and miracles were criticized in a fashion that has become classical in the philosophical tradition ever since. Anthony Collins, friend and disciple of the great Locke, who had already written a *Discourse of Free-Thinking* (1713), in *The Scheme of Literal Prophecy Considered* (1727), maintained both that the only proof of the divine origin of the Christian revelation is the prophecy in the Old Testament, and that a careful examination of this prophecy, taken in a literal and not in a highly figurative sense, makes it quite impossible to believe that Jesus ever fulfilled a single prophecy. The last stand

[17] Tindal, *Christianity as Old as the Creation*, p. 63.
[18] *Christianity as Old as the Creation*, p. 342.

of the rational supernaturalists was hence made upon miracles. But Thomas Woolston, fellow of Sidney College, Cambridge (*The Old Apology for the Truth of the Christian Religion . . . Revived*, 1705), and above all the great philosopher Hume, so demolished the value of the accounts of miracles as evidence for anything, that ever since Christian apologists have encountered their greatest difficulties, not in proving the truth of Christianity, from the "evidence" supposed to be furnished by the record of miracles, but rather in explaining how such impossible delusions ever crept into the record at all. Woolston, scurrilous in language but acute in criticism, claimed that the miracles recorded in the New Testament were in most cases foolish, trivial, contradictory, absurd, unworthy of a divinely commissioned teacher, and characteristic only of a sorcerer and wizard. Even if historically true, they offer not a jot of evidence as to the moral and spiritual value of the teachings of Jesus. Since miracles have most often been performed under diabolical influence, they have in themselves absolutely no value in establishing the Divine mission of him who worked them.

It remained for Hume to administer the *coup de grâce*. In his famous essay *Of Miracles* of 1748, one of the classic philosophical instances of an irrefutable argument permanently accepted as valid, he proved so conclusively that intelligent men have rarely questioned it since, that a miracle, in the sense of a supernatural event given as a sign of the divinity of its worker, cannot possibly be established. Even could it be shown that the events recorded did actually take place, the fact that they were "supernatural," and that they suffice to prove the truth of a religion, it is impossible to demonstrate.

No testimony is sufficient to establish a miracle, unless the testimony be of such a kind, that its falsehood would be more miraculous, than the fact, which it endeavors to establish.

The fallibility of the witness, through ignorance, gullibility, or malice, would have to be absolutely excluded; which is contrary to our experience of human nature.

A miracle can never be proved, so as to be the foundation of a system of religion. . . . Suppose all the historians who treat of England should agree [that Queen Elizabeth died, and after being buried a month returned to her throne and governed England again]. I should not doubt of her pretended death, and of those other public circumstances that followed it: I should only assert it to have been pretended, and that it neither was, nor possibly could be real. . . . I would still reply, that the knavery and folly of men are such common phenomena, that I should rather believe the most extraordinary events to arise from their occurrence, than admit of so signal a violation of the laws of nature. But should this miracle be ascribed to any new system of religion; men, in all ages, have been so much imposed on by ridiculous stories of that kind, that this very circumstance would be a full proof of a cheat, and sufficient, with all men of sense, not only to make them reject the fact, but even reject it without farther examination. . . . As the violations of truth are more common in the testimony concerning religious miracles, than in that concerning any other matter of fact; . . . this must make us form a general resolution, never to lend any attention to it, with whatever specious pretence it may be covered.[19]

In other words, for one who accepts the Newtonian vision of an order of nature, unless he assumes that he has so complete a knowledge of the workings of that order as to be able to exclude every possible natural cause—a thing obviously impossible—it is impossible to prove that any event was "supernaturally" produced. Thus, Hume holds, whatever its cause, it is far easier to believe, and far more "logical," that it is effected by some natural factor. Hume's argument has never been conclusively refuted, and since it was fully understood, no man has ever attempted to establish the truth of "revelation" upon any such purely external grounds as satisfied the rational supernaturalists.

The core of Hume's argument is that, in trying to establish a miracle as evidence, we are opposing one single experience against the uniform experience we have of natural law.

A miracle is a violation of the laws of nature; and as a firm and unalterable experience has established these laws, the proof against a miracle, from the very nature of the fact, is as entire as any argument from experience can possibly be imagined. . . . It is a miracle that a dead man should come to life; because that has never been observed in any age or country. There must, therefore, be a uniform experience against every miraculous event, otherwise the event would not merit that appellation. And as a uniform experience amounts to a proof, there is here a direct and full *proof*, from the nature of the fact, against the existence of any

[19] David Hume, *Enquiry concerning Human Understanding*, sec. 10; *Essays, Moral, Political, and Literary*, ed. Green and Grose, II, 94, 105-7.

miracle; nor can such a proof be destroyed, or the miracle rendered credible, but by an opposite proof, which is superior.[20]

Hume adds in a note: "A miracle may be accurately defined, 'a transgression of a law of nature by a particular volition of the Deity, or by the interposition of some invisible agent.'"

Hume's critique is thus based upon the principle of the uniformity of nature. That is, the faith in miracles was destroyed, not by "empiricism," in any distinctive sense, but by the rational faith in the order of nature. Miracles had actually been shown to be untenable by Spinoza and Malebranche, almost a hundred years earlier. It is logically inconsistent to believe both in the principles of science and in the occurrence of miracles.

V

By such arguments the Deists refuted the contention of the supernatural rationalists, that revelation was necessary and true, in addition to rational theology or natural religion. But before the Deists had well concluded their attack upon revelation, a more thoroughgoing philosophical criticism had launched its sharp arrows against natural religion itself. The second stage of the debate over rational religion in the eighteenth century was thus no longer over whether a reasonable man should accept revelation in addition to natural theology. It was whether such a man was justified in accepting rational religion itself. What was involved was the question, was God, conceived as a creator of the world-machine, a necessary ultimate category of Newtonian science itself?

The negative answer to this question was the outcome of the empiricist analysis of causation. This was the practical consequence of the searching criticism of Hume. Even Holbach and Diderot, who stood in France for the destruction of rational theology, and who would hardly be considered "empiricists," employed in their demolition empirical arguments. And Kant in Germany accepted completely the empiricist contention that it is illegitimate to infer any causal relation other than what can be observed in experience, any "cause" for the whole of the experienced world.

The arguments in support of eighteenth-century rational the-

[20] Hume, *Enquiry concerning Human Understanding*, sec. 10; Green and Grose, II, 93.

ology were developed in the Newtonian setting, and could be taken for valid scientific thinking and concepts only in that setting. They were three in number: the necessity of a "first cause," the necessity of an intelligent creator to explain the apparent "design" in the world, and the necessity of a moral order—the so-called cosmological, teleological, and moral arguments. The traditional ontological argument was hardly appealed to in England, though it still found support in Germany and demanded Kant's criticism. British rationalism was not an *a priori* rationalism, but an empirical rationalism, which, like Newton, "deduced" principles and axioms "from phenomena." All these arguments were of course traditional, and go back to the thirteenth century and even to ancient times. But in the Age of Reason they were given a Newtonian stamp: "First Cause" meant in England and France always a First Efficient Cause, a Creator. In Germany the older scholastic notions of First Formal Cause and Ultimate Final Cause were still alive.

The rational theologians had more trouble with their two other tenets of a future life and of a moral order in the world. The Newtonian world gave no support to the doctrine of a personal future life. The most men could say was that since the world was rationally ordered, it must be so ordered as to meet the needs of reasonable beings. Even Kant could say no more in his hypothetical rational theology. With the question of the moral governance of the world, the age-old theological problem of evil, the advocates of natural religion could do no better than their predecessors; they could only have faith that a rational order must be a moral order. Some, like Leibniz, took pages to prove that this is the best of all possible worlds. This belief is conventionally styled "optimism." But it is pertinent to quote the remark of Santayana: "Leibniz's optimism holds that this is the best of all possible worlds, and that everything in it is a necessary evil." Pope's ringing "Whatever is, is right," sounded even to eighteenth-century ears suspiciously like whistling to keep one's courage up. Others, like Voltaire, were too keenly aware of the evils that nature and man do to man not to be revolted by such "positive thinking." Voltaire's most famous tale, *Candide*, is one long mockery of the Leibnizian position.

It was inevitable that when God was coming more and more to be identified either with the mathematical order of nature itself, or with its Creator, once the consequences of such views were consistently worked out he should lose any moral quality whatsoever. Spinoza had arrived at the same conclusion a century before: nature has nothing to do with human standards of right and wrong. It was probably just because the Deists realized their logic pointed to such a conclusion that they hated and shunned Spinoza. It took a man with a very different conception of religion, Herder, to make Spinoza a living force in the ensuing period. For the most part, the Deists closed their eyes to such disagreeable logic, and tried their best to worship harmony and order as supremely good.

When the attack had once shifted to a questioning of this reasoning offered in support of natural religion, it was not too difficult to sweep it away by the same methods the Deists had employed against revelation. Two groups undertook this task, the convinced "sceptics" and materialists, and the traditionalists who fancied that by showing the obvious inconsistencies of natural religion, they could convince men that it rested on as shaky a foundation as revelation. This was easy to accomplish. But the fideists did not find that men proceeded to adopt their corollary, that therefore both revelation and natural religion must be accepted "on faith."

In England, two men in particular tried to defend Christianity by such a "sceptical" questioning of natural religion, William Law and Bishop Joseph Butler. Law wrote *The Case of Reason, or Natural Religion fairly stated* (1732), as an answer to the "Deists' Bible" of Tindal. Law was a famous mystic, and he declared that religion need not submit itself to any test of reason or of morality. Its sole "proof" was derived from prophecy and miracles.

It seems, therefore, to be too great and needless a concession which some learned divines make in this matter, when they grant that we must first examine the doctrines revealed by miracles, and see whether they contain in them anything absurd or unworthy of God, before we can receive the miracles as divine.

Law clearly has Tillotson in mind.

Miracles in such a state as this are the last resort; they determine for themselves and cannot be tried by anything further.[21]

---

[21] William Law, *The Case of Reason, or Natural Religion, fairly and fully Stated* (1732), p. 109.

A course of plain undeniable miracles attesting the truth of a revelation is the highest and utmost evidence of its coming from God, and not to be tried by our judgments about the reasonableness or necessity of its doctrines.[22]

This is of course a complete denial that reason can establish any religious truth whatsoever. For those adopting such a position, the choice was clear: decide between abandoning religion or abandoning reason. Law the mystic took the latter course; the eighteenth-century rationalists naturally chose rather to abandon religion. The same choice had already been offered by the scholarly "sceptic" Pierre Bayle. But in fact, while bishops might prefer to abandon reason, more and more men chose rather the other horn of the dilemma.

The other great apology for religion which really led men to choose "scepticism" was Bishop Joseph Butler's famous *Analogy of Religion, Natural and Revealed, to the Constitution and Course of Nature* (1736). Butler claimed that the much-heralded natural religion was really just as irrational as the specific Christian revelation, and just as much a matter of faith. In other words, the religious tradition was really all of one piece, and had to be accepted or rejected as a whole; no halfway compromise was tenable. Butler pointed out in particular that the actual course of nature, the handiwork of God and his divinely established moral order, is much more incomprehensible to human reason than the so-called injustices taught in Scripture.

Upon supposition that God exercises a moral government over the world, the analogy of His natural government suggests and makes it credible that His moral government must be a scheme quite beyond our comprehension, and this affords a general answer against all objections against the justice and goodness of it.[23]

Never, probably, was such a double-edged sword employed to defend the Christian faith. It seems not to have occurred to the good bishop that if, rationally considered, natural religion were on no firmer a foundation than revelation, there might be men bold enough to reject them both. Nevertheless, Butler's analogy was

[22] Law, *The Case of Reason*, p. 110.
[23] Joseph Butler, *The Analogy of Religion, Natural and Revealed, to the Constitution and Course of Nature* (1736), Part I, ch. 7.

used in colleges as a text in Christian apologetics well toward the end of the nineteenth century.

In 1742 Henry Dodwell published a work called *Christianity not Founded on Argument* (the title sounds reasonable enough). This was the first turning of such reasoning to a definitely "sceptical" purpose. But the three great and conclusive summaries of all that could be said against natural religion, books which made it quite impossible for an intelligent mind any longer to attempt the apology for even rational religion by the customary arguments of the century, were written by Hume, by the Frenchman Holbach, and by the German Kant. In religious matters at least Hume was a typical "sceptic": he refused to draw any positive conclusions from his destructive critique of rational theology. Holbach was a convinced materialist and a good deal of a pantheist; while Kant, summing up the attack of the rationalistic empiricists on rational theology, also laid the foundations for the various attempts made in the early nineteenth-century Romantic movement to establish religion upon feeling and intuition and some special religious sense—attempts which, however successful in themselves, have at least avoided the keen edge of the rationalistic sword.

We have already seen Hume's powerful criticism of the argument from miracles in support of revelation. His equally telling attack on natural religion is to be found in his essay *Of Providence and a Future State*, first published in 1748, and in his *Dialogues concerning Natural Religion*, written as early as 1751, but not published till after his death, in 1779. Hume, it will be remembered, was the most consistent of the empiricists; that is, he eschewed all rationalistic argument from self-evident axiomatic principles, and brought to bear upon every belief the test of its origin in experience. His method in natural theology was to ask, how much of traditional religious beliefs could be actually derived from facts observable in the experienced world? And his verdict was, very little. He pointed out that there is no justification for first observing that the present world is imperfect, and then from that imperfect world trying to argue to the existence of a perfect Creator who will yet some day be able to produce a perfect world. Likewise, we have no valid reason for concluding from a human life in which rewards and punishments do not accord with human deserts, that there is another life in which they do.

That the divinity may *possibly* be endowed with attributes which we have never seen exerted; may be governed by principles of action, which we cannot discover to be satisfied: all this will freely be allowed. But still this is mere *possibility* and hypothesis. We never can have reason to infer any attributes, or any principles of action in him, but so far as we know them to have been exerted and satisfied. *Are there any marks of a distributive justice in the world?* If you answer in the affirmative, I conclude that, since justice here exerts itself, it is satisfied. If you reply in the negative, I conclude, that you have then no reason to ascribe justice, in our sense of it, to the gods. If you hold a medium between affirmation and negation, by saying, that the justice of the gods, at present, exerts itself in part, but not in its full extent: I answer, that you have no reason to give it any particular extent, but only so far as you see it, *at present,* exert itself.[24]

Having thus disposed of the rational basis for any faith in the moral governance of the world, Hume went on, in his *Dialogues,* to show that there could not even be any argument for the existence of an all-wise and all-good Creator. There is no necessity of the universe having had a "first cause," in the temporal sense assumed in the empiricists' view of causation. It is just as easy to conceive of the world as self-existent and eternal, as to assume an external "cause" with those qualities. Moreover, there is no valid analogy between an object in the world, like a watch, and the entire universe; we have seen watches made, but we have never seen a world made. Order may be as "natural" as chaos, and hence harmony and universal law need no further reason for their existence in our world, other than that we find them in fact to obtain. From a finite world as effect we could at most validly assume only a finite cause. If the universe did indeed have an author, he may well have been an incompetent workman, or he may have long since passed away after completing his work, or he may have been a male or a female god, or indeed a great number of gods. He may have been entirely good, or entirely evil, or both, or neither—the last is the more probable guess.

Thus the argument from design permits us to infer a "cause" only as intelligent as the facts observed can justify. It does not entitle us to

[24] Hume, *Of a Particular Providence and of a Future State,* sec. 11 in *Enquiry concerning Human Understanding* (1748); ed. Green and Grose, in *Essays,* II, 116-17.

conclude to any new facts about the universe. The argument from analogy—that the world is an unfinished piece of work—breaks down over the fact that we have no other experience of God than what he has already created. The argument of a First Cause at best can prove only a finite, imperfect, and very possibly a plural God or gods. The problem of evil either robs God of all moral character, or else must be left as rationally insoluble. We are left rationally free to adopt atheism, or fideism. Hume himself concludes, formally at least, "Our most holy religion is founded on faith." And he may well have meant it—though just what "faith" could mean for a mind so subtle and so "sceptical" as Hume's is another question not too easy to determine. His most recent editor, studying the changes he made in the manuscript he kept by him for twenty-five years, was convinced that Hume's doubts became more and more searching.[25]

Hume suggested doubts; he questioned the tenets of natural religion. Holbach categorically denied God, freedom, and immortality —though he was glad, as we shall see, to worship and pray to Mother Nature. Kant attempted to prove conclusively that reason and science are valid only within a certain field, and that outside this field, faith—Kant called it "practical reason"—could still establish the tenets of natural religion, God, freedom, and immortality, not as proved, but as permissible and irrefutable hypotheses. Kant's arguments seemed epoch-making. More than any other single intellectual factor they saved the day for religious belief, and made possible an intellectual justification for the great religious revivals of the early

[25] Norman Kemp Smith, *Hume's Dialogues concerning Natural Religion* (1935). Hume's manuscript of the *Dialogues*, with his revisions over the years, is in The Royal Society of Edinburgh, and was printed by Kemp Smith; 2d ed., 1947. The *Dialogues* existed in substantial form in 1751. For ten years Hume circulated and revised them. In 1776, ten days before his death, Hume writes Adam Smith he is revising them again, "which I have not done these fifteen years." So he left them untouched from 1761 to 1776, before undertaking a final revision.

Kemp Smith points out, "The additions referable to 1776 (notably in part XII, which concludes the discussion) are, as we find, among the most definitely negative utterances in the *Dialogues*. This has a very important bearing on the issues that arise when we seek to determine how far, and in what precise respects, the spokesmen in the *Dialogues* express Hume's personal views." Evidence from Hume's letters and other writings at the time "corroborates the conclusion to which the clues in the manuscript would appear to point, namely, that the teaching of the *Dialogues* is much more sheerly negative than has generally been held. . . . He is consciously, and deliberately, attacking 'the religious hypothesis,' and through it religion as such." (Preface, pp. vi–vii)

nineteenth century. Here it is only to be noted that Kant, in "destroying reason to make room for faith," seemed to have disproved forever the possibility of a purely rational religion. It was not until Hegel offered a wholly reconstructed conception of "reason" itself that men could dare to think once more of working out a new "rational religion."

While Deism and natural religion lingered on after Hume and Holbach and Kant in some minds—Paley wrote in England in 1798, Robespierre remained a convinced Rousseauian Deist during the Revolution, and German rational theologians taught well into the nineteenth century—to the majority of intelligent minds interested in religion it seemed that the primary task, in view of the apparent demonstration that no rational basis could be established for the religious life, was to effect a reconstruction of religion itself on some nonrational or superrational principle.

The net result of the eighteenth-century critiques of rational religion was to make it appear impossible to harmonize the religious tradition and science by identifying religious with scientific beliefs. The working out of the principles of nature and reason, the cardinal ideals of the age that worshiped Newton and tried to reconstruct religion on the model of his mechanics, when applied to the great Christian tradition seemed wholly destructive. The attempt to build a new scientific religion upon those Newtonian ideals had failed completely. Multitudes, of course, were quite untouched by this drama of ideas, just as they were quite impervious to the new scientific knowledge itself. But the thinking middle class, to whom the immediate future belonged, on the whole accepted them unreservedly. When the reconstruction of the Christian tradition and its adaptation to the new intellectual world was undertaken once again, it was with the clear understanding that the eighteenth century had made the foundation of religion upon the principles of Newtonian reason—Hegel called it "abstract reason," *Verstand*—henceforth impossible.

To model religious upon scientific beliefs resulted first, in the loss of nearly all religious values, and then, in the loss of all supposed scientific values as well. Many were tempted to try the alternative: make science itself religious, found it on a religious world-view. And thus were born the many systems of Romantic idealism.

The question might well be raised, when "God" as a Creator was shown not to be a scientific category, why did not men abandon religion? In that Revolutionary age, particularly in France, there were indeed many who confidently looked forward to such an eventuality. After two centuries of philosophical reconstruction of the Christian tradition, and after almost as long a period of the scientific study of religion itself, a present-day responsible thinker would answer: men did not abandon religion, because religion is clearly a much deeper part of human experience and life than any particular idea of God, or indeed than all "belief" in God. It is one thing to destroy the "presumed" evidence for the existence of God; it is quite another to destroy "religion." Even the Christian tradition was not destroyed, though it has been so profoundly reconstructed that it might well be plausibly argued that it confronted a fate worse than death. But religion is a continuing activity of human life, that no more requires "evidence" to sustain it than does music.

The failure of the eighteenth-century attempt to harmonize religion and science was clearly due to the fact that men, intoxicated by the newly discovered order of nature, tried to make religion like science. This meant throwing overboard the whole world of values embedded in the religious tradition. The Romantic movement, in the broad sense in which Americans have come to use the designation, was really a reaction, not against Hume and Holbach. Their criticism Kant could admit easily if sadly. It was a reaction against Newton and Locke, and a "reasonable Christianity" as "old as creation" and "not mysterious." It was a reaction against the disintegrating effects, not of atheism and scepticism, which in comfortable eighteenth-century England found only a bare handful of supporters, but of scientific liberalism and modernism in religion. The eighteenth-century rational religion, for all its generous toleration and benevolence, seems to be a perfect example of how not to reconcile religion and science. It forms, we have said, a complete episode. And every thoughtful religious leader facing the changed problems presented by such a reconciliation today might well ponder it carefully.

8

English Rational Morality:
From Natural Law to Newtonian Reason

IT IS A conventional view, springing from the central role played by the theory of knowledge in Kant's critical philosophy, that the great achievement of British thinkers in the eighteenth century lay in their elaborating the analysis of sense perception, on which they erected an observational construing of knowledge and a philosophical phenomenalism in general. This observationalism they then brought to bear on English rational religion and Deism: their analyses culminated in the penetrating critique of all "religion of reason" by David Hume. This latter achievement, as we shall see, greatly impressed the later French Enlightenment; and they also adopted, in Diderot and Condillac, and their Idéologues successors, the sensationalism and phenomenalism on which it was based. Then, the conventional story goes, Kant took over the empirical theory of sense of the great British thinkers, and combined it with the rationalism of the Continental thinkers, Descartes, Spinoza, Leibniz, and Wolff, in his own critical "epistemology"—the term was one of Wolff's inventions. This is the organization of the central epistemological thread of "modern philosophy" perpetuated in the great nineteenth-century histories of philosophy that began with the generation after Kant.

But it is probable that the most enduring achievement of eighteenth-century British philosophizing lay rather in the analysis of the moral life in those we call the "British moralists." Viewed from this perspective, the thought of the British Enlightenment—or rather, Enlightenments, for there were two, one English, the other Scottish, and the latter was somewhat the more important—takes on a different set of contours. In the English Enlightenment there were two quite different traditions, set respectively by the Cambridge Platonists and by the greatest English philosopher of the seventeenth century, Thomas Hobbes. To escape warring faiths, irenic Englishmen in the seventeenth century used Platonic rationalism to erect a rational science of morals, in Henry More and in Cudworth's *True Intellectual System of the Universe* (1678), and *Treatise Concerning Eternal and Immutable Morality* (1731). This enterprise was carried on by Locke, who though he came to an observational and probable rather than a "scientifical philosophy of nature," never ceased to hold that the science of morals at least could be "demonstrative." The fullest expression of such a science is to be found in Samuel Clarke. This rational morality of Platonic provenance was for a century directed against Hobbes's Erastian views: his contention that it is for the Sovereign to determine what is right and wrong. But the Sovereign needs his own standards of good and evil, and here Hobbes introduces an incipient utilitarianism. This was seized upon by John Gay, in his preface to King's book on the problem of evil, which is usually taken as the first explicit statement of a utilitarian ethics. Developed by Hartley, this tendency culminated in the Utilitarianism of William Paley and Jeremy Bentham. Bentham, however, came after and was much influenced by the utilitarianism of the French hedonist Helvétius (*De l'esprit*, 1758), who must be drawn into the picture at this point.

But the outstanding English moralists of the first half of the eighteenth century, as the tradition of rational morality was dying out, and before the utilitarian view had received full development, were the Earl of Shaftesbury, whose *Characteristics* came out in 1711, and Bishop Joseph Butler, whose *Sermons* appeared in 1726. Shaftesbury is usually taken as the last of the Cambridge Platonists. But his Platonism shares Plato's own intimate relation between the Good and the Beautiful. He tries to carry through a parallel between the moral sense and the sense of beauty, and makes the former a disinterested sentiment of approbation for what is good. His is definitely an ethic of the detached observer, not an ethic of commitment.

Shaftesbury was very influential. He was instrumental to Butler's adding of a benevolent impulse to Hobbes's analysis of the self-regarding impulse in human nature, which thus tended to bring together the two strains in the English moral tradition, Platonic rationalism and Hobbes's *conatus sese conservandi*. The only real defender of Hobbes's ethics of self-interest as leading to a social good during this period was Mandeville in his *Fable of the Bees* (1714), a forerunner of Adam Smith's faith in the "unseen hand."

Shaftesbury was influential also in the Germanies, where through his congenial Platonic views he did much to introduce other English thinkers to the German *Aufklärung*. And Shaftesbury was influential on the Scottish Enlightenment.

Scotland during the eighteenth century can be said to have enjoyed an "Enlightenment" analogous to that of France or Germany in a more exact sense than England. For if all these "Enlightenments" be taken as a passing beyond the rational defense of tradition and the existing order, which was the social function of seventeenth-century rationalism, to a rational and empirical critique of that tradition and order, England had already advanced to social and religious criticism after the Civil Wars and during the age of Queen Anne. For England, the later eighteenth century came more as an age of compromise, of steady expansion of tendencies already existing, than an outburst of "Enlightenment."

But eighteenth-century Scotland was making the first serious break with her traditional Calvinistic orthodoxy, as well as enjoying her first great wave of real commercial prosperity—the two facts are not without a connection. And Scotland had long had much closer ties to France than to England, so that she was much more receptive to the intellectual currents of the French Enlightenment than her southern neighbor. There came into existence intellectual societies in both Glasgow and Edinburgh more cosmopolitan than anything eighteenth-century London had to offer, which remained more insular and self-contained. It was no accident that at the very end of the century Scotland was the first to begin to feel the powerful new currents emanating from the Germanies, and that Kant and Hegel first entered Great Britain by way of Scotland.

The Scottish Enlightenment was not unfamiliar with English thought, especially with the classic figures of Newton and Locke. But it was equally familiar with the classic figures of the Age of Louis Quatorze—with Malebranche, with Fontenelle and Bayle. David Hume, the culmination of the Scottish Enlightenment, is often taken as the third of the succession of great "British" empiricists—the man who carried farthest the criticisms Berkeley had begun to make of Newton and Locke. But this is to misconceive Hume's intellectual background—just as it is to misconceive Kant's to see him as the "successor" to Hume in his turn, rather than as coming out of his own background of German analytic empiricism and Newtonian thought. Actually, though Hume mentions his views in two places, it is doubtful whether Hume ever read Berkeley at first hand. And he is fully as indebted to the tradition of French scepticism—to the operationalism of Malebranche, and the humanistic scepticism of Bayle—as he is to the "empiricism" of Locke. After all, Hume wrote the *Treatise* in La Flèche, not in Dublin or London. Above all, he was familiar with the Academic philosophy of ancient scepticism, which he found in Cicero, and followed up in Sextus Empiricus and Pierre Bayle.

In his moral philosophy Hume belongs definitely with the moralists of the Scottish philosophy. He is in the tradition of the older Francis Hutcheson and the younger Adam Smith. It is their problems he is concerned with, their approaches he is exploring.[1] Hutcheson gives form to Shaftesbury's theory of the moral sentiments, making it more precise and modifying it in detail. Hume adds in 1751 searching questions, in which he penetrates to the foundation of the psychological feelings of praise and blame—their bases in human nature, he would have said. Adam Smith, Hume's younger friend, in his *Theory of the Moral Sentiments* (1759), sums up the conclusions of this Scottish tradition of psychological analysis, and then goes on to apply them to political economy.

The next great movement in Scottish philosophy attempted to defend "common sense" against Hume's observationalism and phenomenalism. In this sense it was an attempt to "answer" Hume's analysis, and is comparable to Kant's "answer" to Hume—though of course if we emphasize certain strands in Hume's thought, Kant's "answer" to Hume turns out to be rather an agreement with his ultimate radical empiricism and experimentalism.

But taken in the sense in which it "needed" an answer, it is sig-

[1] Norman Kemp Smith, *The Philosophy of David Hume: A Critical Study of its Origins and Central Doctrines* (1941), esp. Part I. See also E. C. Mossner, *The Life of David Hume* (1954).

nificant that Hume's phenomenalism is answered by the next generation of Scottish "realistic" philosophers in his own terms, through a
more careful if not always a more subtle analysis of the powers of
the human mind or "imagination." It does not bring in the elaborate
transcendental apparatus of Kant's analysis of knowledge, which was
needed in his own German tradition to establish his formulation of
German analytic and critical empiricism, but which was not needed
and would scarcely have been understood in the tradition of Scottish empiricism. To the movements of twentieth-century "realism,"
like those initiated at Cambridge by G. E. Moore and Bertrand
Russell in 1902, or by the New Realists in America about the same
time, the answer to the earlier Scottish phenomenalists given by the
later generation of Scottish realists from 1780 to 1810 appeared
much more suggestive and sound than that of Kant. There has been
a twentieth-century revival of the reputations of Thomas Reid,
Thomas Brown, and Dugald Stewart, in England and America; and
though with the death of G. E. Moore English philosophers seem to
have abandoned realism once more, there still persists a strong current in America.

This Scottish realistic philosophy of common sense not only dominated Scotland for some two generations, till about 1840; it was
adopted in America after 1815, as the first major academic philosophy to be taught in American colleges and seminaries, and lasted
there until in 1885 Royce introduced Kant and Hegel; they had
been familiar nonprofessionally through W. T. Harris and others.
German philosophy had been brought into Scottish philosophy a
generation before, by Sir William Hamilton. It was introduced into
English philosophy about 1870, to combat the strong current of
utilitarianism that had dominated English thought during the first
two generations of the century, by T. H. Green and a few predecessors—though of course Coleridge had much earlier tried to acclima-
tize it. But influential as was Coleridge's thought in religious circles,
it was not academic or professional.

The reasons why Kant's "answer" to Hume ultimately superseded Reid's in Scottish and American philosophical circles are complex, and doubtless had much to do with the power of German
thought, and its appeal to a Romantic century. But perhaps the
root reason is that the central problem had shifted. It was no longer

Hume's phenomenalism, but his critique of any rational defense of religion, that needed answering—no longer the *Treatise*, but the *Dialogues on Natural Religion*. And the great German reconstructions of the religious tradition, the philosophies of religion worked out first by Kant and then by the post-Kantian generation of Hegel and Schleiermacher, were far better answers to Hume's *Dialogues* than that of the Scottish realists. The Germans accepted Hume's critique of rational theology, and went on from there to new reinterpretations of the nature and function of religion, whereas the Scottish realists either defended the rationality of the tradition, or sympathized with Hume.

II

A guide has been here attempted through the complex currents of some century and a half of the two British Enlightenments, the English and the Scottish—through a hundred and fifty years of British moral philosophizing. In the English Enlightenment there are to be found two major traditions, one stemming from the Cambridge Platonists, and culminating in the rational and demonstrative science of morals of Locke and Clarke. The other tradition, stemming rather from Hobbes, includes Mandeville, John Gay, Hartley, Paley, and, with a detour through Helvétius, Bentham, leading on into the nineteenth-century Utilitarianism of James and John Stuart Mill. The Scottish Enlightenment likewise includes two major traditions, though successive rather than simultaneous, the earlier, the moralists Hutcheson, Hume, and Adam Smith, the later one, the common-sense realists Thomas Reid, Thomas Brown, and Dugald Stewart.

Here we shall deal in order with Cudworth, Locke, Clarke, Cumberland, Wollaston, and Price, the rational moralists; with the more isolated figures of Shaftesbury, Mandeville, and Butler, the moralists of the natural passions; and with the Scottish moralists of the sentiments, Hutcheson, Hume, and Adam Smith. The development of English Utilitarianism through Bentham and beyond, and the Scottish realists, is appropriate to a later time. For though the thought of both the Utilitarians and the Scottish realists is rooted in the British Enlightenment, their main work was done in the Revolutionary and post-Revolutionary eras, and their main influence, in

England, Scotland, and America, belongs to that later period of pre-Darwinian nineteenth-century thought.

III

Ralph Cudworth (1617–1688), master of Christ's College, Cambridge—the college of Milton—has already appeared as one of the Cambridge Platonists, the most learned and erudite of all the upholders of the Platonic theory of knowledge and the ontological primacy of mind. In his moral writing, the *Eternal and Immutable Morality*, not published till forty-three years after his death, in 1731, when his strong intellectualism had already become outmoded, his central interest is in the source of moral knowledge: not in the human faculty of acquiring it, which he takes for granted is reason, but in the objective natures and essences of things themselves, which are eternal and immutable. He is opposed equally to any relativistic conception of moral truth, which he met in the "Protagorean philosophy," and to any form of voluntarism, whether it makes moral truths the commands of some human will, like Hobbes, or of the Divine Will, like the Calvinistic Puritans and "the ingenious philosopher Renatus Des Cartes."

Now the demonstrative strength of our cause lying plainly in this, that it is not possible that anything should be without a nature, and the natures or essences of all things being immutable, therefore upon supposition that there is anything really just or unjust, due or unlawful, there must of necessity be something so both naturally and immutably, which no law, decree, will, nor custom can alter.[2]

Cudworth starts his argument with the incontestable truth:

In the first place, it is a thing which we shall very easily demonstrate, that moral good and evil, just and unjust, honest and dishonest . . . cannot possibly be arbitrary things, made by will without nature; because it is universally true, that things are what they are, not by will but by nature.[3]

Things are white by whiteness, triangular by triangularity; and Omnipotence itself cannot change these natures.

[2] Cudworth, *A Treatise concerning Eternal and Immutable Morality* (1731), Book II, ch. 1. In *British Moralists*, ed. L. A. Selby-Bigge (1897), par. 830.
[3] *Treatise*, Book I, ch. 2; ed. Selby-Bigge, par. 813.

For though the will of God be the supreme efficient cause of all things, and can produce into being or existence or reduce into nothing what it pleaseth, yet it is not the formal cause of anything besides itself, as the Schoolmen have determined in these words, *Deum ipsum non posse supplere locum causae formalis*, that God himself cannot supply the place of a formal cause; and therefore it cannot supply the formal cause, or nature of justice or injustice, honesty or dishonesty.[4]

Everything is thus immutably determined by its own nature: theological voluntarism is impossible. So is the dependence of morality on the commands of the sovereign. The right or authority of the commander is founded in natural justice and equity, which are not made by laws, but presupposed by all positive laws. Thus to keep faith and perform covenants is what natural justice obliges to absolutely. No positive commands can make anything morally good or evil, which nature had not made such before. Cudworth places morality and mathematics on the same footing, like a good Platonist.

Now it is certain that if the natures and essences of all things, as to their being such or such, do depend upon a will of God that is essentially arbitrary, there can be no such thing as science or demonstration, nor the truth of any mathematical or metaphysical proposition be known any otherwise, than by some revelation of the will of God concerning it, and by a certain enthusiastic or fanatic faith and persuasion thereupon, that God would have such a thing to be true or false at such a time, or for so long.

We have now abundantly confuted the Protagorean philosophy, which, that it might be sure to destroy the immutable natures of just and unjust, would destroy all science or knowledge, and make it relative or phantastical.[5]

Cudworth goes on to confute Hobbes's "phantasticism," "that the soul is . . . a mere *rasa tabula*, a naked and passive thing, which has no innate furniture or activity of its own" (Cudworth was of course writing before Locke). Plato, to show that ethics, politics, and morality are as real and substantial things as, and as truly natural as matter, holds that they "have an independent and self-subsistent being, which in the order of nature, is before all matter, all particular created minds being but derivative participations of one infinite Eternal Mind, which is antecedent to all corporeal things." In refuting Descartes Cudworth rejects theological voluntarism:

[4] *Treatise*, Book I, ch. 2; ed. Selby-Bigge, par. 813.
[5] *Treatise*, Book I, ch. 3; Book IV, ch. 6; ed. Selby-Bigge, pars. 827, 831.

There is an eternal and immutable wisdom in the mind of God, . . . Now the wisdom of God is as much God as the will of God: and whether of these two things in God, that is, will or wisdom, should depend upon the other, will be best determined from the several natures of them. For wisdom in itself hath the nature of a rule and measure, it being a most determinate and inflexible thing; but will being not only a blind and dark thing, as considered in itself, but also indefinite and indeterminate, hath therefor the nature of a thing regulable and measurable. Wherefore it is the perfection of will, as such, to be guided and determined by wisdom and truth; but to make wisdom, knowledge and truth, to be arbitrarily determined by will, and to be regulated by such a plumbean and flexible rule as that is, is quite to destroy the nature of it.[6]

It was in fact the Calvinism of the Puritans that Cudworth first attacked. He points out that his B.D. thesis *Dantur boni et mali rationes aeternae et indispensabiles* was defended in 1644, seven years before the *Leviathan* appeared.[7]

IV

Despite the long Aristotelian tradition that ethics is a practical and not a demonstrative science, the seventeenth century was inspired by its faith in reason and its desire for certainty in moral knowledge to seek to formalize ethics. Spinoza is the best known instance; there was also Geulincx's *Ethica* (1675). John Locke had set out, a young Cartesian, to find principles of morality and religion that would be as certain as the new physics. So it was natural for him to hope that ethics might be thrown into demonstrative form. For him, only demonstrative and intuitive knowledge were certain; all else was mere "sensitive knowledge" or probabilities. His first notion of ethics, that appears in the 1671 Draft A of the *Essay*, runs:

The rectitude of actions . . . is nothing but the relation or conformity of the actions of men to some rule, and this is that which we call moral goodness and badness, and the judgment about this is nothing but the comparing the action with the rule.[8]

But in the Journal of Locke for June 26, 1681, appears a very different conception:

[6] *Treatise*, Book IV, ch. 6; Book I, ch. 3; ed. Selby-Bigge, pars. 835, 838, 828.
[7] In Graf von Hertling, *John Locke und die Schule von Cambridge* (1892). Cited in J. A. Passmore, *Ralph Cudworth: an Interpretation* (1951), p. 11n.
[8] R. I. Aaron and Jocelyn Gibb, *An Early Draft of Locke's Essay* (1936), p. 11.

He that has a true idea of God, of himself, as his creature or the relation he stands in to God and his fellow-creatures, and of justice, goodness, law, happiness, etc., is capable of knowing moral things, or having
a demonstrative certainty in them. . . . I cannot but think morality as
well as mathematics capable of demonstration if men would employ their
understanding to think more about it and not give themselves up to the
lazy traditional way of talking one after another.[9]

This hope for a demonstrative science of morality may well have
been the result of the impact of Cudworth on Locke, and of additional influences from Cumberland, who was the chief inspiration
of Samuel Clarke: Richard Cumberland (1632–1718), Bishop of
Peterborough, had published in 1672 a *De legibus naturae disquisitio philosophica*.[10] John Wilkins, Bishop of Chester, who in 1678
brought out *On the Principles and Duties of Natural Religion*, may
have also helped. Cudworth certainly influenced Locke's moral psychology and conception of the will.

But in any event, Locke's views on morality are extraordinarily
complex. He never worked them out in detail: he would have had
great difficulty adjusting his several rationalistic theories to his
hedonistic view. There seem to be at least four different conceptions
of the nature of ethics to be found in Locke: this is typical of his
extreme moderation and his desire to do justice to all views. Strongest is the rationalistic conception which makes him a link between
Cudworth and Clarke. The most familiar passage is where, discussing relations between abstracted ideas, he remarks:

I doubt not but from self-evident propositions, by necessary consequences, as incontestible as those in mathematics, the measures of right
and wrong might be made out, to any one that will apply himself with
the same indifference and attention to the one as he does to the other of
these sciences. . . . The idea of a supreme Being . . . and the idea of
ourselves, as understanding, rational creatures, . . . would . . . afford
such foundations of our duty and rules of action as might place *morality*
amongst the sciences capable of demonstration. . . . The *relations* of
other *modes* may certainly be perceived, as well as those of number and
extension; and I cannot see why they might not also be capable of
demonstration.[11]

[9] Aaron and Gibb, pp. 116–17.
[10] See Passmore, pp. 91–95; Graham P. Conroy, "George Berkeley on Moral
Demonstration," *JHI*, vol. 22 (1961), pp. 206–8.
[11] *Essay*, Book IV, ch. 3, sec. 18; ed. A. C. Fraser, II, 208.

Locke gives two examples: " 'Where there is no property there is no injustice,' is a proposition as certain as any demonstration in Euclid. . . . Again: 'No government allows absolute liberty.' " [12] Locke's argument runs: Morality is concerned with those abstract ideas which are mixed modes, which in turn are those ideas the mind can construct by compounding simple ideas into one complex whole. They are not attempts to copy external objects. "In framing these ideas the mind searches not its patterns in nature, nor refers the ideas it makes to the real existence of things, but puts such together as may best serve its own purposes, without tying itself to a precise imitation of anything that really exists." Moral ideas are "the creatures of the understanding rather than the works of nature." Yet that does not make them "fantastic," for they are "real essences": in the case of substances, both spiritual and bodily, the nominal and the real essences are quite different, but mixed modes are known in their real being, and in them nominal and real essences coincide.[13]

Unfortunately, as Berkeley was quick to note, Locke's theory and examples made all the propositions of morality into "trifling propositions":

To demonstrate morality it seems one need only make a dictionary of words, and see which included which. At least, this is the greatest part and bulk of the work. Locke's instances of demonstration in morality are, according to his own rule, trifling propositions.[14]

Secondly, the system of morality built on Locke's "mixed modes" could give no account of the fact of moral obligation. It was indeed this defect of the theorists who made knowledge and reason the determining factor in the moral life that led to the reaction in Shaftesbury and Hutcheson, who emphasized "feeling" and emotion, the "affections," as the motive in moral living, and stamped this concern with motives on the whole later tradition of British moralists. The central question became, "Why do men act morally?" The more important question was almost forgotten, What are the moral ways in which to act? The former is a psychological question

[12] *Essay*, Book IV, ch. 3, sec. 18; ed. Fraser, II, 208.
[13] *Essay*, Book III, ch. 5, sec. 6; Book III, ch. 5, sec. 12; Book III, ch. 3, secs. 16, 18; ed. Fraser, II, pp. 46, 51, 27, 29.
[14] Berkeley, *Philosophical Commentaries*, in *Works*, ed. A. A. Luce (1948), I, 84; *Commonplace Book*, in *Works*, ed. A. C. Fraser (1901), I, 39.

which clearly demands experimental investigation; it cannot be decided by brilliant essays written with literary distinction. The latter is a philosophical question—*pace* Kant and Ritschl, not to mention their epigone, Wittgenstein—and as such has to be faced in the moral life. The limitation of the British moralists lies in their consistent refusal to ask, even to raise, the central questions of ethics.

This mathematical demonstrative science of ethics was only one of the views Locke entertained of a possible rationalistic science of morality. When he looked upon ideas, not as "the objects of the mind when it thinks," but as instruments by which the mind gains knowledge of objects which lie beyond it, as he did about half the time, morality becomes, not the relations of "abstract ideas," but of experienced realities themselves. This is true of his use of the traditional "law of nature" both in the *Essays* of 1661–64 and in the *Treatises of Government.* For Locke, of course, the law of nature is the law of reason, and is not innate. His realistic ethical thought is worked out most clearly where he is least concerned with the theory of knowledge and the "origin" of ideas. Reason alone can rule man's stormy passions and establish "the eternal, immutable standard of right." The law of reason is prior to human reason; man does not create it, but discovers it. It is knowable only because the nature of things and the reason of man come from the same Creator. It holds in the prepolitical "state of nature."

There is a third rationalistic strain in Locke's ethical theory, in which he founds ethics on the idea of God. The existence of God is "so fundamental a truth, and of that consequence, that all religion and genuine morality depend thereon." [15] A moral theory without God is impossible.

He also that hath the idea of an intelligent, but frail and weak being, made by and depending on another, who is eternal, omnipotent, perfectly wise and good, will as certainly know that man is to honor, fear, and obey God, as that the sun shines when he sees it. For if he hath but the ideas of two such beings in his mind, and will turn his thoughts that way, and consider them, he will as certainly find that the inferior, finite, and dependent, is under an obligation to obey the supreme and infinite, as he is certain to find that three, four, and seven are less than fifteen, if he will consider and compute those numbers: nor can he be surer in a

[15] *Essay,* Book IV, ch. 10, sec. 7; ed. Fraser, II, 311–12.

clear morning that the sun is risen; if he will but open his eyes, and turn them that way.[16]

Locke is as emphatic as Cudworth in rejecting the voluntarism of the Calvinists. The moral part of the law of Moses is "of eternal obligation"; God would not be "an holy, just, and righteous God" if he changed one jot of the moral law. He cannot overturn "the measures of right and wrong" so long as the nature of things remains unchanged; if he tried to, he would "be introducing and authorizing irregularity, confusion, and disorder in the world." [17]

Side by side with this strong strain of rationalism, there is also in Locke's remarks about morality a hedonistic strain, derived partly from Hobbes, and more from the Deists. Good is what produces pleasure:

Now, because pleasure and pain are produced in us by the operation of certain objects, either on our minds or on our bodies, and in different degrees, therefore, what has an aptness to produce pleasure in us is that we call good, and what is apt to produce pain in us we call evil; for no other reason but for its aptness to produce pleasure and pain in us, wherein consists our happiness and misery.[18]

Locke of course does not state his hedonism, like Hobbes, in materialistic terms. Pleasure and pain are states of mind which "join themselves to almost all our ideas."

By pleasure and pain, delight and uneasiness, I must all along be understood . . . to mean not only bodily pain and pleasure, but whatsoever delight or uneasiness is felt by us, whether arising from any grateful or unacceptable sensation or reflection.[19]

Locke distinguishes between natural good and evil, and moral good and evil; the latter are the rewards and punishments attached to a law ordained by some law-maker. The law of God is such a law. Reason of course has still to calculate future rewards and punishments in this theological hedonism.

Locke notoriously got out of his depth in examining the question of man's freedom, in his chapter on Power. He set forth one view,

[16] *Essay*, Book IV, ch. 13, sec. 4; ed. Fraser, II, 359.
[17] *The Reasonableness of Christianity, Works,* 11th ed. (London, 1810), VII, 3, 11-12.
[18] *Essay*, Book II, ch. 21, sec. 43; ed. Fraser, I, 340.
[19] *Essay*, Book II, ch. 20, sec. 15; ed. Fraser, I, 306.

was dissatisfied, worked out another, and merely added it, so that both are now present in that chapter. His first view is that liberty consists "in our being able to act or not to act, according as we shall choose or will." Liberty is possessed by a person, not by the will—a view Locke seems to have got from Cudworth. "Freedom consists in the dependence of the existence, or not existence of any *action*, upon our *volition* of it; and not in the dependence of any action, or its contrary, on our *preference*." [20] But this seemed far too close to Hobbes to satisfy Locke; in the second edition of the *Essay* he added another quite different view. Liberty he regarded as quite indispensable to morality; there could be no obligation if either matter or God controls man by an external power. He saw no way to reconcile divine omnipotence with human freedom, yet he insisted on remaining "as fully persuaded of both, as of any truths I most firmly assent to." [21]

Locke turned from the freedom of the person—he never upheld the freedom of the "will"—to the freedom of reason. Liberty is now "a power to act, or not to act, according as the mind directs." It is "a power to suspend the execution and satisfaction of any of [the mind's] desires, and so all, one after another." It is "a power to direct the operative faculties to motion or rest in particular instances." [22] Liberty is not merely freedom from external constraint, as Hobbes [23] had held; it is the subjection of the passions to the control of reason. It gives a chance for reason to prevail.

Locke never tried to work out in detail any of his versions of ethics; he never even tried to harmonize the seemingly inconsistent strains. Is virtue primary, and pleasure its accompaniment? Or is pleasure the end, and virtue a means to it? Does the moral law depend on God's will, or does God will to enforce the moral law? Locke seems to take both alternatives on such questions; what his position was, is an unanswerable question. The nearest approach to a systematic statement in Locke is the brief paper, *Of Ethics in General*. In it he distrusts the ability of unaided reason to establish a theory of ethics.

[20] *Essay*, Book II, ch. 21, sec. 27; ed. Fraser, I, 329.
[21] *Works*, ed. 1810, IX, 305; Letter to Molyneux.
[22] *Essay*, Book II, ch. 21, secs. 73, 48; ed. Fraser, I, 367, 345.
[23] In his *Treatise of Liberty and Necessity; Works*, ed. Molesworth (1840) Vol. IV.

Whoever treats of morality so as to give us only the definitions of justice and temperance, theft and incontinency, and tells us which are virtues, which are vices, does only settle certain complex ideas of modes with their names to them . . . but whilst they discourse ever so acutely of temperance or justice, but show no law of a superior that prescribes temperance, to the observation or breach of which law there are rewards and punishments annexed, the force of morality is lost, and evaporates only into words, disputes, and niceties. . . . Without showing a law that commands or forbids them, moral goodness will be but an empty sound.[24]

The later British moralists found themselves deeply involved in the psychological question of the springs of action in human conduct.[25] Does reason or do pleasure and pain control man's action? The question goes back to Aristotle, though he stated it in terms of reason and "desire," *orexis*, rather than reason and pleasure; and concluded, both: "reason (*nous*) does not seem to be a mover without desire"; the spring of action is reason in the service of desire. Locke considers this question carefully. Naturally, to each of his theories of ethics there corresponds a different view of the springs of action.

To his rationalistic theory answers the view expressed in the short essay on the *Conduct of the Understanding*, written in 1697. "The will itself, how absolute and uncontrollable soever it may be thought, never fails in its obedience to the dictates of the understanding." A man is governed by ideas and knowledge. "The understanding, with such light as it has, well or ill informed, constantly leads; and by that light, true or false, all his operative faculties are directed." The springs of action are "the ideas and images in men's minds." [26]

To the hedonistic theory of ethics of the first edition of the *Essay* corresponds a pleasure-pain psychology of action. "The preferring the doing of anything to the not doing of it . . . is nothing but the being pleased more with the one than the other." "Pleasure and pain, and that which causes them, good and evil, are the hinges on which our passions turn." [27] But Locke was dissatisfied with this

[24] *Of Ethics in General*, in Lord Peter King, *Life and Letters of John Locke* (London, 1858), pp. 309–13.

[25] See Brand Blanshard's Gifford Lectures, *Reason and Goodness* (1961), ch. iv, "The Dialectic of Reason and Feeling in British Ethics."

[26] *Conduct of the Understanding*, ed. Thomas Fowler (1901), par. 1; *Works*, 12th ed. (London, 1823), III, 205.

[27] *Essay*, 1st ed. (1690), Book II, ch. 21, sec. 28; Book II, ch. 20, sec. 3; ed. Fraser, I, 375, 303.

pleasure-pain spring of action: it seemed to him to make all moral education impossible. After some thought, he changed his view in the second edition of the *Essay* (1692).

This later, mature view recognized that man can remain indifferent to the object of pleasure. Only a present pain of body or mind immediately gives rise to activity seeking to escape it. So the spring of action is "uneasiness," which is the same thing as pain, torment, anguish, misery, or desire. A future pleasure may be the end of conduct, but it is not the spring of action, unless it arouses uneasiness.

"Uneasiness" is Locke's term for desire: he has come the full circle back to Aristotle once more. "The uneasiness a man finds in himself upon the absence of anything whose present enjoyment carries the idea of delight with it, is what we call *desire*." [28] "What is it that determines the will in regard to our actions? And that . . . I am apt to imagine is not, as is generally supposed, the greater good in view; but some (and for the most part the most pressing) uneasiness a man is at present under." [29] " 'It is better to marry than to burn,' says St. Paul, where we may see what it is that chiefly drives men into the enjoyments of conjugal life. A little burning felt pushes us more powerfully than greater pleasures in prospect draw or allure." [30]

There is no *summum bonum*, for though all men desire happiness, the "variety of pursuits shows, that everyone does not place his happiness in the same thing, or choose the same way to it. . . . Hence it was, I think, that the philosophers of old in vain did inquire, whether *summum bonum* consisted in riches, or bodily delights, or virtue, or contemplation: and they might as reasonably have disputed, whether the best relish were to be found in apples, plums, or nuts, and have divided themselves into sects upon it." [31] But if there is no *summum bonum*, there is a *summum malum*. It is pain. "Desire is always moved by evil, to fly it: because a total freedom from pain always makes a necessary part of our happiness." [32] Thus pain is the cause of all man's reason and action, all human

---

[28] *Essay*, Book II, ch. 20, sec. 20; ed. Fraser, I, 304.
[29] *Essay*, Book II, ch. 21, sec. 31; ed. Fraser, I, 332.
[30] *Essay*, Book II, ch. 21, sec. 34; ed. Fraser, I, 334.
[31] *Essay*, Book II, ch. 21, secs. 55, 56; ed. Fraser, I, 350–51.
[32] *Essay*, Book II, ch. 21, sec. 73; ed. Fraser, I, 367.

achievement. "The chief, if not only spur to human industry and action is uneasiness." [33] The pain which removes pain is labor. As Leo Strauss, acute and perceptive student of the history of political philosophy, puts it: "Hobbes identified the rational life with the life dominated by the fear of fear, by the fear which relieves us from fear. Moved by the same spirit, Locke identifies the rational life with the life dominated by the pain which relieves pain." [34]

In Locke's "second thoughts," the spring of action is desire, the desire to relieve present distress. His position can be called hedonism only in the sense in which that of Epicurus can be so called. It is a very negative hedonism. It is much more negative than Aristotle's view of the springs of action. And happiness is not for Locke an activity; it is not even an enjoyment of anything. "For, as pleasant tastes depend not on the things themselves, but on their agreeableness to this or that particular palate, wherein there is great variety; so the greatest happiness consists in the having those things which produce the greatest pleasure, and in the absence of those which cause any disturbance, any pain." [35] Happiness lies in "having things," in possession, in what Locke would call "property."

In these terms, Locke set forth his *Thoughts concerning Education* (1693), the most consistent of all his writings touching on moral theory. In this first major English writing on the philosophy of education, he emphasizes the natural aptitudes of the child, his native propensities. He counsels the use of the natural pleasures and pains as motives, as well as rewards and punishments; esteem and disgrace are especially important. And since the law of God depends on wholly future rewards and punishments, he urges the development of the power of self-direction in children as soon as possible. "The principle of all virtue and excellency lies in a power of denying ourselves the satisfaction of our own desires, where reason does not authorize them." Children like to be "treated as rational creatures"; of almost any boy, "the sooner you treat him as a man, the sooner he will begin to be one." [36]

[33] *Essay*, Book II, ch. 20, sec. 6; ed. Fraser, I, 304.
[34] Leo Strauss, *Natural Right and History* (1953), p. 250.
[35] *Essay*, Book II, ch. 21, sec. 56; ed. Fraser, I, 351.
[36] *Thoughts concerning Education*, ed. R. H. Quick (1913), pars. 38, 81, 95. *Works*, 12th ed. (1823), IX, 32, 69, 88.

V

Samuel Clarke (1675–1729) studied mathematics and natural philosophy before devoting himself to the Church. In 1697 he published an annotated Latin translation of the Cartesian Rohault's *Traité de physique*, to prepare the way for the introduction of Newton's books as texts at Cambridge; for he was the great supporter and popularizer of Newton in English academic life, the most distinguished English theologian, and after Locke's death in 1704 England's most famous philosopher. He wrote the actual replies of Newton to Leibniz's inquiries, in the famous controversy over time and space, from November, 1715, to October, 1716.[37] He also translated Newton's *Opticks*. In 1704 and 1705 he delivered two courses of Boyle Lectures, entitled *A Demonstration of the Being and Attributes of God*, and *A Discourse concerning the Unchangeable Obligations of Natural Religion, and the Truth and Certainty of the Christian Revelation*. Clarke was a rational supernaturalist who argued with the Deists.

With Clarke morality is an affair just like mathematics. He sought in the Order of Nature the eternal fitness of things.

The same necessary and eternal different Relations, that different Things bear to one another, and the same consequent Fitness or Unfitness of the Application of different things or different Relations one to another, with regard to which, the Will of God always and necessarily does determine itself, to choose to act only what is agreeable to Justice, Equity, Goodness, and Truth, in order to the Welfare of the whole Universe, ought likewise constantly to determine the Wills of all subordinate rational Beings. . . . These eternal and necessary differences of things make it fit and reasonable for Creatures so to act; they cause it to be their Duty so to Do, even separate from the consideration of these Rules being the positive Will of God, and also antecedent to any respect of any particular private and personal Advantage or Disadvantage, Reward or Punishment, either present or future, annexed either by natural consequence or by positive appointment to the practising or neglecting of those Rules. . . . He that refuses to deal with all men equitably, is guilty of the very same unreasonableness and contradiction in one Case, as he that in another Case should affirm one Number or Quantity to be equal to another, and yet That other at the same time not to be equal to the first. . . . In a word; All

---

[37] *The Leibniz-Clarke Correspondence*, ed. H. G. Alexander (1956).

wilful wickedness and perversion of Right, is the very same Insolence and Absurdity in Moral Matters, as it would be in Natural Things for a man to pretend to alter the certain Proportions of Numbers, to take away the Demonstrable Relations and Properties of Mathematical Figures.[38]

Clarke's position is that judgments of right and wrong are purely the expression of reason: reason has an insight into, a rational cognition of, moral truths that are logically self-evident, just like the axioms of Euclid.

That there is a Fitness or Suitableness of certain Circumstances to certain Persons, and an Unsuitableness of others, founded in the Nature of Things and the Qualifications of Persons, antecedent to all positive Appointment whatsoever: also, that from the different Relations of different Persons one to another, there necessarily arises a Fitness or Unfitness of certain Manners of Behavior of some Persons toward others: is as manifest, as that the Properties which flow from the Essences of different mathematical Figures, have different Congruities or Incongruities between themselves; or that, in Mechanics, certain Weights or Powers have very different Forces, and different Effects one upon Another, according to their different Distances, or different Positions and Situations in respect to each other.[39]

Clarke lays down three such axiomatic eternal rules of rightness or "fitness":

First, in respect of God, that we keep up constantly in our Minds, the highest possible Honor, Esteem, and Veneration for him. . . . Secondly, in respect to our Fellow-Creatures, that in particular we so deal with every man, as in like circumstances we could reasonably expect he should deal with Us, and that in general we endeavor, by an universal Benevolence, to promote the welfare and happiness of all Men. The former Branch of this Rule is Equity, the latter is Love. . . . Thirdly, with respect to ourselves, that every Man preserve his own Being, as long as he is able, and take care to keep himself at all times in such temper and disposition both of Body and Mind, as may best fit and enable him to perform his Duty in all other Instances.[40]

Clarke himself says he learned to compare moral with mathematical relations from Cumberland.[41] He quotes Cumberland:

[38] Samuel Clarke, *Boyle Lectures on Natural Religion*, 10th ed. (1766), pp. 5, 41, 42; *British Moralists*, ed. Selby-Bigge, pars. 482, 491.
[39] *Natural Religion*, pp. 29–30; ed. Selby-Bigge, par. 483.
[40] *Natural Religion*, pp. 51, 53, 60–61; Selby-Bigge, pars. 499, 500, 504.
[41] Cumberland, *De legibus naturae*, p. 23. Clarke, *Natural Religion*, p. 97; Selby-Bigge, par. 524. See J. A. Passmore, *Ralph Cudworth*, p. 103n.

Pari sane ratione (*ac in Arithmeticis operationibus*) Doctrinae Moralis veritas fundatur in immutabili cohaerentia inter Felicitatem summam quam Hominum vires assequi valent, et Actus Benevolentiae universalis.

Indeed, in his running battle with Hobbes, Cumberland is almost the only modern he quotes frequently, along with Cicero, Seneca, and Plato; Cudworth is cited once. Of course, the comparison of morals with mathematics was a familiar practice among the Augustinians; thus it is central in Malebranche's *Traité de morale* (1683).

Clarke admits the rather important distinction:

The only difference is, that assent to a plain speculative Truth (like 2 plus 2 equals 4), is not in a Man's Power to withhold, but to Act according to the plain right and reason of things, this he may, by the natural Liberty of his Will, forbear. But the One he ought to do, and 'tis as much his plain and indispensable Duty, as the other he cannot but do, and 'tis the Necessity of his Nature to do it.[42]

Clarke is unable to fit consequences into his mathematical notion of a rational ethics. He did point out that many of our duties would remain duties, even though there was nothing to choose between the foreseeable consequences of doing or not doing them. But in considering the Stoics, he admits that consequences must be considered:

That Virtue is truly worthy to be chosen, even merely for its own Sake, without any Respect to any Recompense or Reward, must indeed necessarily be acknowledged. . . . But 'tis very plain that the general Practice of Virtue in the World can never be supported upon this Foot, it being indeed neither possible, nor truly reasonable, that Men, by adhering to Virtue, should Part with their Lives, if thereby they eternally deprived themselves of all Possibility of receiving any Advantage from that Adherence . . . Men never will generally, and indeed it is not very reasonably to be expected that they should, part with all the Comforts of Life, and even Life itself, without Expectation of any future Recompense.[43]

Clarke is really setting up two quite different kinds of reasonableness, one of which lies in doing the duty prescribed by abstract reason, and the other in ordering one's actions in the light of their consequences. He never managed to harmonize them.

[42] *Natural Religion*, p. 40; ed. Selby-Bigge, par. 491.
[43] *Natural Religion*, pp. 108-9, 75; Selby-Bigge, par. 510.

VI

Richard Cumberland (1632–1718), Bishop of Peterborough, has already figured as one of the thinkers who influenced the rationalistic ethics of John Locke, through his *De legibus naturae disquisitio philosophica* (1672). An able and original thinker, though very prolix and discursive, Cumberland teaches a doctrine of morality based on the traditional notion of the law of nature, and keeps up a running polemic with Hobbes. This law of nature can be inferred from observation of physical and mental phenomena, themselves produced by the will of God. But like Locke, Cumberland transforms the law of nature into something that seems to be an incipient utilitarianism. It indicates "that possible action of a rational agent which will chiefly promote the common good of all." Cumberland seems to have been the first to use the latter phrase, "the common good of all"; it is the supreme end and standard, to which all other rules and virtues are to be subordinated. The supreme law of nature he states: "The greatest possible benevolence of every rational agent towards all the rest constitutes the happiest state of each and all, so far as depends on their own power, and is necessarily required for their happiness; accordingly Common Good will be the Supreme Law." He explains that he means by this, "*effective* benevolence, not a languid and lifeless principle that fails to take effect in outward acts." He defines "good" as "that which preserves, or enlarges and perfects, the faculties of any one thing or of several"; but he also uses the term as equivalent to "happiness."

The "rules of life," Cumberland holds, are as plain as the "art of numbering": here he anticipates Locke and Clarke. These propositions are necessarily true: 1) "that the good of all rational beings is greater than the like good of any part of that aggregate body, that is, that it is truly the greatest good"; 2) "that in promoting the good of this whole aggregate, the good of individuals is contained and promoted"; and 3) "that the good of every particular part requires the introducing and settling of distinct property in such things, and such services of rational agents, as contribute to the common happiness" (here he also anticipates Locke). That this common good is the expression of the divine will, Cumberland, "not being so fortunate as to possess innate ideas," tries to demonstrate by a long inductive examination of the essentially social nature of man, as exhibited in man's physical and mental constitution. He emphasizes both the internal and the external rewards of virtue and punishments of vice; and explains that moral obligation lies primarily in the force these sanctions exert on the will. While this self-regarding motive is indispensable, and is the normal spring of action in the earlier stages of man's obedience to the moral law, yet rational beings tend to rise above this to the higher motives of love to God, regard for his honor, and disinterested affection for the common good. It is obvious that Cumberland furnished ideas to many better-known moral philosophers: he raised most of the problems discussed for over a century by all the differing strands of the British moralists. His insistence on the standard of the common good of all, as the supreme principle of morality, and on the essentially social nature of man, was accepted in one form or another by nearly all of them.

VII

In taking Cudworth, Clarke, and the later Richard Price as examples of what he calls "dianoetic ethics," and what has here been called intellectualism or rationalism in morals—i.e., the theory, that "we approve the Right, because it is *true*"—James Martineau perceptively contrasts Cudworth and Clarke. "In Cudworth the disposition to intellectualize morals was not inconsistent with a large survival of Puritan enthusiasm and devout fervor. . . . The theory, at its next stage, loses much of its earthly glow, and, in the person of Dr. Samuel Clarke, assumes some of the harder features of what is called Rationalism." [44]

The "Rationalism" has grown still "harder" in William Wollaston (1659–1724). His *Religion of Nature Delineated* (1722) is chiefly famous for carrying Clarke's intellectualistic argument to its logical conclusion. What Clarke had called "fitness" Wollaston held to be an actually existent relation or quality. His argument runs:

II. Those propositions are true, which express things as they are: or, truth is the conformity of those words or signs, by which things are expressed, to the things themselves.

III. A true proposition may be denied, or things may be denied to be

[44] James Martineau, *Types of Ethical Theory*, 3d ed. (1891), II, 459.

what they are, by deeds, as well as by express words or another proposition. It is certain there is a meaning in many acts and gestures. Everybody understands weeping, laughing, shrugs, frowns, etc., these are a sort of universal language. . . .

If a body of soldiers, seeing another body approach, should fire upon them, would not this action declare that they were enemies; and if they were not enemies, would not this military language declare what was false? . . .

I lay this down then as a fundamental maxim, That whoever acts as if things were so, or not so doth by his acts declare, that they are so, or not so; as plainly as he could by words, and with more reality. And if the things are otherwise, his acts contradict those propositions, which assert them to be as they are.

IV. No act (whether word or deed) of any being, to whom moral good and evil are imputable, that interferes with any true proposition, or denies anything to be as it is, can be right. For, if that proposition, which is false, be wrong, that act which implies such a proposition, or is founded in it, cannot be right: because it is the very proposition itself in practice. . . .

Lastly, to deny things to be as they are is a transgression of the great law of our nature, the law of reason. For truth cannot be opposed, but reason must be violated.[45]

Moral wrong is intellectual error, a simple mistake. A wrong act is simply the assertion in conduct of a false proposition. Wollaston illustrates:

If a man steals a horse, and rides away upon him, he may be said indeed by riding him to use him as a horse, but not as the horse of another man, who gave him no license to do this. He does not therefore consider him as being what he is, unless he takes in the respect he bears to his true owner.[46]

Wollaston can even see active benevolence as affirming a true proposition:

[45] Wollaston, *The Religion of Nature Delineated* (1726 ed.), pp. 8, 13, 15; excerpts in *British Moralists*, ed. L. A. Selby-Bigge (1897), Vol. II, pars. 1025, 1026, 1028, 1029, 1034.

[46] *Religion of Nature*, p. 18; ed. Selby-Bigge, par. 1038. Jeremy Bentham made sport of this argument: "We have one philosopher, who says, there is no harm in any thing in the world but in telling a lie: and that if, for example, you were to murder your own father, this would only be a particular way of saying, he was not your father. Of course, when this philosopher sees anything that he does not like, he says, it is a particular way of telling a lie. It is saying, that the act ought to be done, or may be done, when, *in truth*, it ought not to be done." Bentham, *Principles of Morals and Legislation* (ed. Oxford, 1907), p. 18. See the discussion in David Baumgardt, *Bentham and the Ethics of Today* (1952), pp. 204–7.

Should I . . . find a man grievously hurt by some accident, fallen down, alone, and without present help likely to perish; or see his house on fire, nobody being near to help, or call out: in this extremity if I do not give him my assistance immediately, I do not do it at all: and by this refusing to do it according to my ability, I deny his case to be what it is; human nature to be what it is; and even those desires and expectations, which I am conscious to myself I should have under the like misfortune, to be what they are.[47]

Wollaston states his general principle:

If the formal ratio of moral good and evil be made to consist in a conformity of men's act to the truth of the case or the contrary, . . . the distinction seems to be settled in a manner undeniable, intelligible, practicable. . . . So it will be easy for anyone, so far as he knows any [true] propositions and facts, to compare not only words, but also actions with them.[48]

Wollaston tries to separate "moral good" from "natural good" or happiness. "Those pleasures are true, and to be reckoned into our happiness, against which there lies no reason. . . . Happiness is some quantity of true pleasure: and that pleasure, which I call true, may be considered by itself, and so will be justly desirable. . . . Happiness must not be denied to be what it is: and it is by the practice of truth that we aim at that happiness, which is true." [49] Wollaston goes on to work out a "moral arithmetic," thus anticipating Bentham's "felicific calculus."

For nine degrees of pleasure, less by nine degrees of pain, are equal to nothing; but nine degrees of one, less by three degrees of the other, give six of the former net and true . . . the excess gives the true quantity of pleasure or pain. . . . Ultimate happiness is the sum of happiness, or true pleasure, at the foot of the account.[50]

Wollaston is the most extreme of the rigidly rationalistic theorists of ethics, stemming from the Cambridge Platonists, but owing allegiance in the eighteenth century rather to Newtonian ideals. It is interesting that Herder, usually taken as Romantic of the Romantics, counted him among the great moralists of the century.[51] It is less surprising that Kant, himself fully aware of the power of reason,

[47] *Religion of Nature*, p. 18; ed. Selby-Bigge, par. 1037.
[48] *Religion of Nature*, p. 25; ed. Selby-Bigge, par. 1052.
[49] *Religion of Nature*, pp. 40, 38, 31; ed. Selby-Bigge, pars. 1070, 1066, 1061.
[50] *Religion of Nature*, pp. 36, 38; ed. Selby-Bigge, pars. 1063, 1065.
[51] Herder, "Adrastea," Band II, *Werke*, ed. Suphan (1885), Band 23, p. 147.

especially in ethics, should present an extremely refined version of Wollaston's faith in that power. It is also significant that a sophisticated modern historian of ethics can point to one of the most respected of contemporary philosophers as virtually a follower of Wollaston's intellectualism.[52]

VIII

The last of the major rationalistic moral philosophers in England in the eighteenth century, and the classic prototype of contemporary moral intuitionism, was Richard Price (1723–1791). Price was a Unitarian minister, who wrote freely on a wide variety of themes, as is the Unitarian wont. His place in history was won when, on November 4, 1789, he delivered an address to a group celebrating the Revolution of 1689, entitled *A Discourse on the Love of our Country*. He closed with the words: "After sharing in the benefits of one Revolution, I have been spared to be a witness to two other Revolutions, both glorious." Edmund Burke took poor Price as the point of departure for his polemical skill in *Reflections on the Revolution in France*. But the intellectual position of Price depends rather on the book he published in 1757 as a young man, *A Review of the Principal Questions in Morals*.

The *Review* is an excellent statement of the position British moral discussion had reached by mid-century, before the rising tide of utilitarianism had made itself felt, and two years before Adam Smith's treatise. Price approved Clarke; and he had read Cudworth's *Eternal and Immutable Morality*, published twenty-six years before, which Clarke had never seen. He was writing for a new generation, which had read Shaftesbury and Hutcheson, and Butler, and was talking about a moral sense, beauty of character, and disinterested feeling. He did not like connecting man's capacity for duty with sense, a faculty man shares with the animals. Above all, his generation had been reading Hume; Price's running polemic is no longer with Hobbes, but with Locke and Hume. Like Cudworth and Clarke, he resolved to defend man's intellectual powers against domination by the sensitive and the aesthetic. But the empiricists he is attacking dominate his problems, if not his conclusions. Hume sets the questions. What is the *origin* of our ideas of right and wrong?

[52] David Baumgardt, *Bentham*, p. 206.

What is the *origin* of our desires and affections, of the springs of action? How far do ideas of beauty and deformity of actions need to be considered?—here Shaftesbury and Hutcheson are the antagonists. To answer these questions of a new day, Price goes to Cudworth's arguments. His theory of knowledge is all Cudworth; on ethical issues he stands much closer to Clarke. Indeed, on the side of positive theory, he comes close to anticipating Kant. The merit of an action depends entirely on the "formal rightness" or intention of the agent's act. Writing after the demonstration by Shaftesbury and Butler of the existence of disinterested impulses in human nature, he can insist that right actions are to be chosen by virtuous agents because they are right: we are not acting morally unless we are acting out of regard for rectitude. Indeed, an act loses its moral worth in proportion as it is done from natural inclination.

Price early flings the gage at Locke and Hume:

I do not at all care what follows from Mr. Hume's assertion, that all our ideas are either impressions, or copies of impressions; or from Mr. Locke's assertion that they are all deducible from sensation and reflexion.—The first of these assertions is, I think, destitute of all proof; supposes, when applied in this as well as in many other cases, the point in question; and when pursued to its consequences, ends in the destruction of all truth and the subversion of our intellectual faculties.—The other wants much explication to render it consistent with any tolerable account of the original of our moral ideas: Nor does there seem to be anything necessary to convince a person, that all our ideas are not deducible from sensation and reflexion, except taken in a very large and comprehensive sense, besides considering how Mr. Locke derives from them our moral ideas. He places them among our ideas of relations, and represents rectitude as signifying the conformity of actions to some rules or laws; which rules or laws, he says, are either the will of God, the decrees of the magistrate, or the fashion of the country: From whence it follows, that it is an absurdity to apply rectitude to rules and laws themselves, to suppose the divine will to be directed by it; or to consider it as itself a rule or law.[53]

Price announces his inquiry as concerned with "the foundation of morals"; he defines "the foundation of" as meaning, "an account or origin of." (p. 13n.) Though he is challenging the answer of Locke and Hume, he accepts the "new way of ideas," and its basic assumption, that the original of knowledge is the criterion of its

[53] Price, *A Review of the Principal Questions in Morals*, ch. I, sec. iii; 3d ed. (1787), pp. 61–62. There is a new edition by D. Daiches Raphael (1948).

extent and certainty. He proceeds to state *the question* concerning the foundation of morals:

> Some actions we all feel ourselves irresistibly determined to approve, and others to disapprove. Some actions we cannot but think *right*, and others *wrong*, and of all actions we are led to form some opinion, as either *fit* to be performed or *unfit*. . . . What the power within us is, which thus determines, is the question to be considered. (p. 8)

Thus, though Price is challenging the answer of Shaftesbury and the moral sense school, he is accepting their basic assumption, that *the question* of the foundation of morals is the origin of the feelings of approval and disapproval of a *disinterested spectator* of the human scene. The question is not, as with the Greeks, what is justice, or what is the good? It is not, as with Kant, what is the source of the moral law we must *ourselves* obey? It is not, as with the utilitarians and their progeny, how, facing a problem of moral choice, can we make a decision most rationally or intelligently? It is rather, what makes us approve one action or character rather than another kind? It is a question on the model of the question, what makes us like one painting, and dislike another, or prefer one quartet to another? Such a question naturally leads to the morality of the observing critic, not the morality of commitment.

This was the question the British moralists, the schools of Shaftesbury and Locke—Locke's own moral theory, we have seen, is much more complicated and engaged—were led to explore. Their answers to this question grew increasingly complex and subtle; but the question itself remained simple and narrow. Men like Butler, Hume, and Adam Smith went about as far as literary psychology, without any experimental evidence, could take an analytic and critical mind, in considering this psychological question. It is traditional to call this theory worked out in analysis of the observer of life's drama, "psychological ethics." It is the "phenomenological" analysis of a pre-scientific psychology. Is it any wonder that in the nineteenth century men turned to the two types of ethical theory worked out to guide the actor on the scene, utilitarianism, and the analysis of Kant and the post-Kantian Germans? And have the recent subtle British analyses of the meaning of ethical language and of ethical terms, though they have added a further dimension, really altered the basic assumptions?

In his rearguard action, Price proceeds to engage the prevalent answer to the question, what is it makes us pass moral judgments?

A late very distinguished writer, Dr. Hutcheson, deduces our moral ideas from a *moral sense;* meaning by this sense, a power within us, different from reason, which renders certain actions pleasing and others displeasing to us. . . . He has indeed well shown, that we have a faculty determining us *immediately* to approve or disapprove actions, abstracted from all views of private advantage. . . . Our ideas of morality, if this account is right, have the same origin with our ideas of the sensible qualities of bodies, the harmony of sounds, or the beauties of painting or sculpture. . . . Virtue is an affair of taste. Moral right and wrong, signify *nothing in the objects themselves* to which they are applied, any more than agreeable and harsh; sweet and bitter; pleasant and painful; but only *certain effects in us.* Our perception of right, or moral good, in actions, is that agreeable emotion, or feeling, which certain actions produce in us; and of wrong, or moral evil, the contrary. (pp. 8–11)

The question then is, is this a true account of virtue? Does virtue have a "foundation" in the nature of its object? Are right and wrong "real characters of actions," or only "qualities of our minds," sensations depending on our frame? This is "the only question about the foundation of morals, which can rationally and properly be made a subject of debate." Moreover, "the power of perceiving moral right and wrong must be, either that power whose object is truth, or some implanted power or sense." What is the power that gives us "perceptions of moral right and wrong"? "My answer is: the *understanding.*" (pp. 12–15)

Price treats of the origin of our ideas in general before that of our ideas of right and wrong in particular. This gives him a chance to criticize Locke, as Cudworth and Cumberland had had no opportunity to do, and as Clarke and Wollaston had chosen not to do. Locke is wrong: some of our most important ideas do not come from sense. "The power that understands . . . is a spring of new ideas: I mean here . . . simple ideas, or original and uncompounded perceptions of the mind." Among these are solidity—shades of Locke!—necessity, substance, entity, possibility, actual existence, indeed, all our abstract ideas. To Cudworth Price adds Newton's *vis inertiae* and of gravity. Price states the Platonic principle: "As bodily sight discovers to us *visible* objects; so does the understanding (the eye of the mind, and infinitely more penetrating) discover to us *intelligible* objects." Nor are these only "in the mind": "Every perception being the perception of something, it must imply some kind of reality distinct from and independent of itself; nothing being more grossly absurd, than to suppose the perception, or apprehension of a thing, to be the same with the thing itself." This source of new simple ideas is not to be confused with the power of *reasoning;* it is *nous* or *intellectus,* the historian would say. Price admits freely the contention of Malebranche, to whom he adds Hume's *Enquiry:* "What we observe by our external senses, is properly no more than that one thing *follows* another, or the *constant conjunction* of certain events." But "the necessity of a cause of whatever events arise is an essential principle, a primary perception of the understanding." (pp. 15–16, 22–26, 37, 51, 44, 56, 29–30)

It is not difficult to predict how Price applies his general theory of the origin of our ideas to the origin of our ideas of moral right and wrong. His conception of "right" and "wrong" as simple ideas incapable of analysis or definition, saves him from the difficulties of Clarke and Wollaston in identifying moral and mathematical truth.

'Tis a very necessary previous observation, that our ideas of *right* and *wrong* are simple ideas, and must therefore be ascribed to some power of *immediate* perception in the human mind. He that doubts this, need only try to give definitions of them, which shall amount to more than synonymous expressions. (pp. 57–58)

Some actions must be ultimately approved, and some ends ultimately desired, for which no rational justification can be given; else there would be an infinite regress.

This power of immediate perception is the understanding. "It is undeniable that many of our ideas are derived from our *intuition* of truth, or the discernment of the natures of things by the understanding. . . . Right and wrong may denote what we understand and know concerning certain objects, in like manner with proportion and disproportion, connexion and repugnancy, contingency and necessity, etc." Hutcheson has offered nothing to prove the contrary.

As there are some propositions, which, when attended to, necessarily determine all minds to believe them: and as there are some ends, whose natures are such, that, when perceived, all things immediately and necessarily desire them; so it is very credible, that, in like manner, there are some actions whose natures are such, that, when observed, all rational beings immediately and necessarily approve them. (pp. 59–60)

It follows that morality is immutable and eternal; and no will, even that of Omnipotence, can render anything good and obligatory, which was not so from eternity.

But Price is willing to concede to the "Protagorean" philosophers that feeling also plays a part in moral approbation. "We are plainly conscious of more than the bare discernment of right and wrong, or the cool judgment of reason concerning the natures of actions." From those natures, there must result certain emotions and affections.

I cannot perceive an action to be right, without approving it; or approve it, without being conscious of some degree of satisfaction and complacency. I cannot perceive an action to be wrong, without disapproving it; or disapprove it, without being displeased with it.

But these accompanying feelings are subjective ideas, varying from man to man according to his particular frame: they are relative. They are given to man because of the weakness and "infancy" of his intellectual faculties.

In men it is necessary that the rational principle, or the intellectual discernment of right and wrong, should be aided by these instinctive determinations. . . . In short, the truth seems to be that, in contemplating the actions of moral agents, we have both a *perception of the understanding*, and a *feeling of the heart;* and that the latter, or the effects in us accompanying our moral perceptions, depend on two causes. Partly, on the positive constitution of our natures: but principally on the essential congruity or incongruity between moral ideas and our intellectual faculties. (pp. 87, 89, 91–92, 95–96)

Price seems to foreshadow Kant in his account of our ideas of "the beauty and deformity of actions."

Price foreshadows Kant also in holding that the presence of natural inclinations detracts from the moral worth of an action. He has just argued that "Instincts . . . are not necessary to the choice of ends. The intellectual nature is its own law. . . . Rectitude is itself an end, an ultimate end. . . . To act from affection to it, is to act with light. . . . But acting from instinct is so far acting in the dark. . . . Instinct drives and precipitates; but reason commands. The impulses of instinct we may resist, without doing any violence to ourselves. . . . The dictates of reason we can, in no instance, contradict, without a sense of shame." (p. 317) He continues:

It being therefore apparent that the determination of our minds concerning the nature of actions as morally good or bad, suggests a motive to do or avoid them; it being also plain that this determination or judgment, though often not the prevailing, yet is always the first, the proper, and most natural and intimate spring and guide of the actions of reasonable beings: let us now enquire, whether it be not further the *only* spring of action in a reasonable being, as far as he can be deemed morally good and worthy; whether it be not the *only* principle from which all actions flow which engage our esteem of the agents; or, in other words, whether virtue be not itself the end of a virtuous agent as such. (p. 318)

The answer is, it is the only one: "he cannot be properly said to practise virtue who does not *design* to practise it, to whom it is no object of regard, or who has it not at all in his view." Is not Benevolence a virtuous principle?

Rational benevolence entirely coincides with rectitude, and the actions proceeding from it, with the actions proceeding from a regard to rectitude. . . . But *instinctive benevolence* is no principle of virtue, nor are any actions flowing merely from it virtuous. As far as this influences, so far something else than reason and goodness influence, and so much I think is to be subtracted from the moral worth of any action or character.

This agrees with the common sentiments of mankind. Such natural instincts may make us love a person, as we love the lower animals; but they will not lead us to call him virtuous.

The tenderness of parents for their offspring, a fond mother's exposing her life to save her child, and all actions proceeding from the nearer attachments of nature appear to have as much less moral value, as they are derived more from natural instinct. (pp. 323–24)

On other issues, it is against Butler that Price tries to defend his rationalism. Thus, examining the origin of our desires and affections—the springs of action—he agrees that man is moved both by self-love, the desire for private happiness, and by benevolence, the desire for public happiness. But where Butler had taken these to be "instincts," which might well have been different, Price insists they spring rather from "the nature of happiness," from "the natures of things and of beings." A purely rational being, without sense (the medieval thinkers would have said, an angel), would perceive the nature of virtue, and would love it. He would see the truth of the proposition, "Happiness is better than misery," for he would understand what both *are*—their "natures." He would see that pain could not possibly be desired, and that happiness could not possibly be regarded with aversion. "Better than" is a simple idea, like "greater than." Neither is definable. "Both denote simple ideas, and both truth."

It is interesting, in the light of present concerns in moral philosophy, that Price should devote a chapter of fifty pages to "the various forms of expression, which have been used by different writers in explaining morality," and should have set out to analyze "the meaning of several terms and phrases, which are commonly used in speaking on this subject." (p. 168) Price seems to have shared all the predilections and prejudices of a present-day Oxford don. It is also interesting that he argues powerfully against the necessity of a theological foundation for morals. (p. 168)

Price is the last defender of the morality of reason in England. Thereafter, the defenders of "a feeling of the heart" had it all their own way. What is the source of this wave of feeling in moral theory that engulfed the embattled rationalists? The answer is Shaftesbury.

9

The Morality of the Natural Passions
and Affections

IN CONSIDERING Price's Review of the situation in 1757, it was seen
that at that time the British discussion of moral theory was dominated
by two major assumptions. The first was that the primary question
about moral ideas, which included feelings, sentiments, and affections, as well as cognitive notions, is their origin. The second assumption was that the moral philosopher is concerned with asking
why we make moral judgments, and why we make the kind we do,
considering the matter in the same light as the question, why do
we make judgments of beauty? The first of these assumptions came
from Locke's "new way of ideas"; it had been strongly reinforced
by Hume's habit of asking of every belief, from what impression is
it derived? The second assumption, which finally forced even so
rigid a rationalist as Price to recognize the importance of "the feelings of the heart," came from Shaftesbury.

I

Anthony Ashley Cooper, third Earl of Shaftesbury (1671–1713),
was the grandson of the first Earl, the politician who had been
Locke's friend and patron, and had himself been educated under
Locke's supervision. After three unhappy years at Winchester, he
spent three more in travels with a tutor through Holland, France,
Germany, and chiefly Italy. Though he became M.P. in 1695, and
served from then on, he was debarred by delicate health from an
active political career, and devoted himself chiefly to intellectual
interests, study, writing, and art collecting. He loved the classics,
Plato, Aristotle, Epictetus and Marcus Aurelius, and Plotinus; he
was devoted to liberty in politics and thought, to beauty in art, a

philosopher, a virtuoso, a well-bred gentleman. He spent 1703–4 in Holland recuperating from political life. In 1711, gravely ill, he went to Italy, where he died in Naples two years later.

Shaftesbury's writings are based on a personal aesthetic view of life. He sees in the universe an artistic harmony of life—he was something of a pantheist, more of a Platonist; and in his own life he sought to realize the formation of a harmonious and creative personality. In his writing Shaftesbury worked for an informal and literary elegance; he hated pedantry and technicalities, and modeled his masterpiece, *The Moralists, a Philosophical Rhapsody* (1709), on the Platonic dialogues. What he actually achieved was a style overpolished and often artificial: Lamb called it too "genteel." And his gentlemanly aversion to technicalities makes it at the crucial points vague and imprecise, to say nothing of Shaftesbury's lack of concern with any consistency, so that it is almost impossible to define his position exactly on any point. His penalty for employing a free and popular way of writing was the same incurred by William James, misunderstanding and continued argument over just what he meant. Thus he was accounted a Deist in his day, though he remained Broad Churchman to the end; but it is extremely difficult to decide whether he thought of God as transcendent, immanent, or Anglican. His writings were published in three small volumes, entitled *Characteristicks of Men, Manners, Opinions, Times,* in 1711; a revised and enlarged edition came out after his death, in 1714.

It is clear to modern scholarship [1] that Shaftesbury derived all his leading ideas from the Cambridge Platonists. His first publication, as a young man of twenty-seven, was a preface to the first edition of Benjamin Whichcote's *Select Sermons* (1698), in which he states what was to be one of his central ideas, attributing it to the Platonists: that there is in man a "principle of good nature," in opposition to the view of Hobbes. Indeed, Shaftesbury was fundamentally a Cambridge Platonist. As Cassirer puts it, that Cambridge Platonism did not remain locked up in the scholar's study of Cudworth, but rejoined the intellectual life of the world—this it owes to "the one great writer who took sides with it and defended its central con-

[1] See Ernst Cassirer, *The Platonic Renaissance in England* (Eng. tr., 1953, of *Die platonische Renaissance in England und die Schule von Cambridge,* 1932, ch. 6); and J. A. Passmore, *Ralph Cudworth* (1951), pp. 96–100.

victions with all the splendor of his poetic and rhetorical diction. It is principally Shaftesbury who saves the Cambridge School from the fate of a learned curiosity and makes it a philosophic force in the century to come."[2] For the ethics of the Cambridge School was humanistic, like Shaftesbury's; and like his ethics of good breeding, it was aristocratic and intellectualistic, for all its formulation within a Christian framework. And the intellectualism of men like Cudworth and John Smith did not lead them to reject passion as ethically undesirable. Their rationalism has a place for what Shaftesbury emphasized, the emotional impulses that prompt to social duties; and he is not an opponent of the Platonists, but their disciple, in both religion and ethics. What Shaftesbury is opposed to is not the warm intellectualism of the Cambridge men, with its Platonic Eros, but the cold hard Newtonian rationalism of Clarke and Wollaston, which built on the other strain in the Cambridge teaching. Thus both the two schools of British moralists of the next hundred years, the rationalists who derived from Cudworth, and the "moral sense" school derived from Shaftesbury, were rooted in the Platonism of Cambridge. One can say that the first identified the Good with the True, while the second identified it with the Beautiful. The Platonists made a trinity of all three. It was the third and later school, that triumphed with Bentham after 1780, that found its intellectual ancestor in Hobbes.

In discussing the similarity between the "virtuoso, or refined wit of the age," and the philosopher, Shaftesbury states his philosophic ideal. Philosophy he defines as "mastership in life and manners."

To philosophise . . . is but to carry good breeding a step higher. For the accomplishment of breeding is, to learn whatever is decent in company, or beautiful in arts; and the sum of philosophy is, to learn what is just in society, and beautiful in nature, and the order of the world. It is not wit merely, but a temper, which must form the well-bred man. In the same manner, it is not a head merely, but a heart and resolution, which must complete the real philosopher. Both characters aim at what is excellent, aspire to a just taste, and carry in view the model of what is beautiful and becoming. Accordingly, the respective conduct and distinct manners of each party are regulated; the one according to the perfectest ease, and good entertainment of company; the other according to the strictest interest of mankind and society: the one ac-

[2] Cassirer, *Platonic Renaissance*, pp. 159–60.

cording to a man's rank and quality in his private nation; the other according to his rank and dignity in nature.[3]

It is clear that such a man as Shaftesbury would not conceive moral judgments on the model of mathematics. He chose instead that of aesthetics. Not to judgments of necessity, but to judgments of beauty, must the moralist look for clues. Now, judgments of beauty are most like moral judgments of character and dispositions or habitual "affections," as distinguished from judgments of obligation, for instance, or of proper punishment, or of decision-making. So it is on moral character, on virtue and vice, that Shaftesbury concentrates his attention, rather than on more perplexing problems of the moral life. What kind of dispositions and affections do men display? What is it about these that leads us to call some men virtuous, and others not, some good and others bad? What is it about certain acts that leads the observer to call them beautiful, and about others that leads him to call them ugly? Why was it beautiful of Sir Philip Sidney to pass the cup to the wounded soldier, and why was it ugly of Iago to deceive Othello? Note, we do not say that Sidney's act itself was beautiful, we say that it revealed something *about him* that was so, just as we do not say that Iago's acts were themselves ugly, but that they pointed to an inner ugliness *in him*.

When we call a character or disposition good, what are we attributing to it? Is it simply beauty? Shaftesbury often writes as if that were the case. But he really means, it is some quality *like* beauty; it is the same sort of quality, and it arouses in the spectator similar feelings. In the case of beauty, in which Shaftesbury was so keenly interested—he was the first major writer in English on what since Baumgarten we have called "aesthetics"—this quality in a painting consists in the harmony and proportion of its elements (Shaftesbury has inherited the Neoplatonic conception). In the case of goodness or virtue of character as a whole, it lies similarly in the harmony and proportion of the "affections." And the harmony that is beauty produces in the observer a disinterested pleasure (this was taken up by German aesthetics, developed by Mendelssohn, and systematically propounded by Kant); just so the harmony of the affections that is moral virtue produces in the spectator a disinterested appro-

---

[3] *Miscellaneous Reflections*, Miscellany III, ch. 1, in *Characteristics* (ed. 1758), III, 109, 111–13.

bation, apart from all personal advantage or disadvantage to himself. It is to be noted that the moral judgment as to virtue of character is, like the aesthetic judgment of beauty, the judgment of the *disinterested onlooker*. Goodness or virtue is thus a quality belonging, not to outward behavior, and not to any consequences of that behavior, but to the attitude of will and feeling it springs from. As Hutcheson, following Shaftesbury, was later to put it: "We have a distinct perception of beauty, or excellence in the kind of affections of rational agents." [4]

What power or process is it by which we grasp this quality? Hardly reason, for it is neither reasoning nor the traditional *nous* or intellect of Wollaston. It is more like sympathy. How, then, do we perceive beauty? The beauty is a quality of the arrangements of the sounds; our experience of it is not active, like thinking, but passive, as in sensing. We may well call it a process of "sensing," but distinguish it from the other senses as the "aesthetic sense." Very similar is the perception of goodness, a quality attaching to the harmony and balance of the affections. It is a kind of "moral sense"; and it is so laden with feeling that Shaftesbury does not hesitate to call it itself a kind of feeling. To perceive the goodness of an action is to approve it; to approve it is to feel approbation for it or to appreciate it; and appreciation is feeling. In comparison with Clarke and Wollaston, the Newtonian rationalists, what is approved in moral conduct is not a "fitness" apprehended by reason, but a "quality" belonging to the organization of the actor's feelings, a quality whose apprehension is itself essentially a matter of feeling. This is all involved when Shaftesbury says, "It is not a head merely, but a *heart*, which must complete the real philosopher."

This is the revolution in moral theory Shaftesbury accomplished. In the generation after the appearance of the *Characteristics*, though Wollaston and Price bravely kept the faith with reason, for most moralists the consideration of abstract rational principles, whether in the form of the older natural law, or the newer Newtonian law, fell into the background; its place was taken by an empirical study of the human mind, observation of the actual play of its various impulses and sentiments. Of course, the "passions" had been discussed

[4] Hutcheson, *Inquiry into the Original of our Ideas of Beauty and Virtue* (ed. 1726), Treatise II, sec. i, p. 118.

since Descartes and Hobbes, and Locke had made his elaborate analysis of the origin of ideas and sentiments. But Shaftesbury is the first, certainly the most influential, moralist to base his ethics squarely on psychological experience. The substance of his views was adopted by Butler, with major reconstructions; and they furnished the starting-point of the great Scottish moralists, Hutcheson, Hume, and Adam Smith. And Shaftesbury's moral optimism impelled Mandeville to revive and continue the tradition of Hobbism, which led into the later Utilitarians.

In this revolution, Shaftesbury's influence flowed together with that of Locke's new way of ideas, the central emphasis on the origin of ideas, beliefs, sentiments, and passions. Indeed, Shaftesbury had absorbed much of this "new way" himself; though, ironically enough, Locke had not been able to convert to the central parts of his theory his most intimate pupil. Locke's rational ethics and Shaftesbury's aesthetic ethics were in fact carrying on different strains of the teachings of the Cambridge Platonists. Shaftesbury indulges in no polemics against his old tutor; instead, like Cudworth, he keeps up a running fire against Hobbes through all his writings, always harping on the same theme. Bacon had sought a method for the subjugation of nature; Hobbes's civil philosophy would teach a method for the subjugation of men. For Shaftesbury, the aim is not to conquer nature, but to contemplate it; so likewise, not to conquer men, but to contemplate the human world, to enjoy the intuitive knowledge of the bond which holds it, also, together.

This social bond cannot be founded on contracts alone. What would give them their sanction, unless prior to any contract there were in force original standards regarding right and wrong? Shaftesbury reveals the circle in which Hobbes is caught, when he bases all obligation on consent alone, and yet has to make consent itself absolutely obligatory.

'Tis ridiculous to say, there is any Obligation on Man to act sociably, or honestly, in a form'd Government; and not in that which is commonly called the State of Nature. . . . Now the Promise itself was made in the State of Nature: and that which could make a promise obligatory in the State of Nature, must make all other Acts of Humanity as much our real Duty, and natural Part. Thus Faith, Justice, Honesty, and Virtue, must have been as early as the State of Nature, or they could never have been at all. The Civil Union, or Confederacy, could never make Right or Wrong; if they subsisted not before. He who was free to any Villainy before his Contract, will, and ought to make as free with his Contract, when he thinks fit. . . . A man is obliged to keep his Word. Why? Because he has given his Word to keep it—Is not this a notable Account of the Original of moral Justice, and the Rise of Civil Government and Allegiance! [5]

To escape Hobbes's *petitio principii*, we must assume some form of "natural sympathy" as a basis for conventional, social, and juridical order. Without some kind of natural human fellow-feeling, we can understand neither the natural nor the human world. To know nature, we must be and remain one with nature; the same is true of the social world. It is therefore necessary to exhibit the naturalness of man's social affections. This Shaftesbury set out to accomplish in his *Inquiry concerning Virtue or Merit*. This was first printed in 1699 from an early draft, without the author's knowledge, by Locke's friend, the Deist John Toland, for whom Shaftesbury had served as patron. Shaftesbury's pointing to the significance of the "social affections" became a permanent deposit with later British moralists. Butler, Hutcheson, Hume, and Adam Smith all made it central.

Cudworth had made his long attack on Hobbes because he refused to admit eternal moral truths. Shaftesbury disagrees rather with his conception of human nature.

Thus the wisdom of what rules, and is first and chief in nature, has made it to be according to the private interest and good of every one, to work toward the general good; which if a creature ceases to promote, he is actually so far wanting to himself, and ceases to promote his own happiness and welfare. . . . Virtue, . . . that single quality, thus beneficial to all society, and to mankind in general, is found equally a happiness and good to each creature in particular. . . . To be well affected both towards the public interest and one's own, is not only consistent, but inseparable: and moral rectitude, or virtue, must accordingly be the advantage, and vice the injury and disadvantage of every creature.[6]

Virtue Shaftesbury defines as the harmony between a man's affections or passions and the good of the system to which he belongs: concretely, it is for the love of humanity to rule the other passions.

---

[5] *Sensus Communis; an Essay on the Freedom of Wit and Humour*, Part III, sec. i; *Characteristics* (ed. 1758), I, 84.

[6] *An Inquiry concerning Virtue*, Book II, Conclusion; Book II, Part I, sec. I; *Characteristics*, II, 131, 59.

To be a "friend to anyone in particular, it is necessary to be first a friend to mankind." [7]

To deserve the name of good or virtuous, a creature must have all his inclinations and affections, his dispositions of mind and temper, suitable, and agreeing with the good of his kind, or of that system in which he is included, and of which he continues a part.[8]

This harmony between the individual and his "system" is an instance of the larger vision of the world Shaftesbury insists on. Each creature is a part of a "system," his species; all species of animals are parts of a "system of all animals; an animal order or economy, according to which the animal affairs are regulated and disposed." Animals, vegetables, and all things on earth are part of the "system of the globe"; the earth belongs to the solar system. "There is in like manner a system of all things, and a universal nature; there can be no particular being or system, which is not either good or ill in that general one of the universe." [9]

In the whole of things, (or in the universe), all is according to a good order, and the most agreeable to a general interest. . . . If every thing which exists be according to a good order, and for the best, then of necessity there is no such thing as real ill in the universe, nothing ill with respect to the whole. . . . To believe that every thing is governed, ordered, or regulated for the best, by a designing principle or mind, necessarily good and permanent, is to be a perfect Theist. . . . Whatever the order of the world produces, is in the main both just and good. . . . It is impossible that such a divine order should be contemplated without ecstasy and rapture. . . . And thus the perfection and height of virtue must be owing to the belief of a God.[10]

In *The Moralists*, Theocles, Shaftesbury's spokesman, bursts into a "rhapsody to Nature":

O mighty Nature! wise substitute of providence! impowered Creatress! Or thou, impowering Deity, supreme creator! thee I invoke, and thee alone adore . . . whilst thus inspired with harmony of thought, though unconfined by words, and in loose numbers, I sing of Nature's order in created beings, and celebrate the beauties which resolve in thee, the source and principle of all beauty and perfection. . . . Thus powerfully

[7] *The Moralists*, Part ii, sec. 2; *Characteristics*, II, 184.

[8] *Virtue*, Book II, Part 1, sec. 1; *Characteristics*, II, 56.

[9] *Virtue*, Book I, Part 2, sec. 1; *Characteristics*, II, 11–12.

[10] *Virtue*, Book I, Part 1, sec. 2; Book I, Part 3, sec. 3; *Characteristics*, II, 3–5, 53, 55.

are the systems held entire, and kept from fatally interfering. . . . How narrow must this globe appear, compared with the capacious system of its own sun? And how narrow, or as nothing, in respect of those innumerable systems of other apparent suns? . . . Even so canst thou convert these jarring motions of intelligent beings, and in due time and manner cause them to find their rest; making them contribute to the good and perfection of the Universe, thy all-good and perfect work.[11]

Thus for Shaftesbury, the harmony of man with his "system," all mankind, is an instance and a part of the increasing set of systems that culminate in the system of nature as a whole. This metaphysical scheme, at once Platonic and Newtonian, is an essential part of his thought. Yet the whole argument of Book I of his *Inquiry* is devoted to proving that morality does not follow from and depend upon theism, but rather, a sound theism is the culmination of morality.

For whoever thinks there is a God, and pretends formally to believe that he is just and good, must suppose, that there is independently such a thing as justice and injustice, truth and falsehood, right and wrong, according to which he pronounces that God is just, righteous, and true.[12]

Shaftesbury's theology, his "theism," is the attempt to banish the supernatural while retaining the divine element in religion. He scorns the notion of God's providence, of any supernatural interference in the cosmic harmony. And he scorns the resort to future rewards and punishments as the sanction for morality.

If . . . through hope merely of reward, or fear of punishment, the creature is incited to do the good he hates, or restrained from doing the ill to which he is not otherwise the least degree averse; there is . . . in this case no virtue or good whatsoever. The creature, notwithstanding his good conduct, is intrinsically of as little worth, as if he acted in his natural way, when under no dread or terror of any sort.[13]

Shaftesbury's "theism" has been called both Deism and pantheism. He had himself no interest in making the theological distinction; he certainly believed that God is an immanent, all-pervading force in nature. It has also, with greater justice, been called "optimism." If Shaftesbury got all his ideas from the Cambridge Platonists, Pope got his inspiration for the *Essay on Man* from Shaftesbury: the

---

[11] *The Moralists*, Part iii, sec. 1; *Characteristics*, II, 259, 279–80.
[12] *Virtue*, Book I, Part 3, sec. 2; *Characteristics*, II, 34–35.
[13] *Virtue*, Book I, Part 3, sec. 3; *Characteristics*, II, 39.

First Epistle is the most famous summary of a philosophical position ever written:

> "No," 'tis replied, "the first Almighty Cause
> Acts not by partial but by general laws;
>
> . . . .
>
> The gen'ral order, since the whole began,
> Is kept in Nature, and is kept in Man,
>
> . . . .
>
> All are but parts of one stupendous Whole,
> Whose body Nature is, and God the soul;
>
> . . . .
>
> All Nature is but Art unknown to thee;
> All chance direction, which thou canst not see;
> All discord, harmony not understood;
> All partial evil, universal good:
> And spite of Pride, in erring Reason's spite,
> One truth is clear, Whatever is, is right.

As to "partial evil," the *Inquiry* opens by showing there can be no real ill in the universe. The weakness of infants is the cause of parental affection; all philanthropic impulses are founded on the wants of man. "What," Shaftesbury asks, "can be happier than such a deficiency as is the occasion of so much good?" The examples are from Whichcote.

In his first officially published writing, *A Letter concerning Enthusiasm* (1708, occasioned by the appearance of some French religious fanatics in London), Shaftesbury took care to discard all the supposed supernatural elements in religion as "enthusiasm." The distinction is not too easy to make. "For inspiration is a real feeling of the divine presence, and enthusiasm a false one. But the passion they raise is much alike." [14] He kept aloof from the noisy dispute between the Deists and the supernatural rationalists, looking upon both parties with the supercilious contempt of a disinterested spectator. In *Sensus Communis: an Essay on the Freedom of Wit and Humor* (1709) he recommends ridicule as the proper remedy for religious fanaticism and superstition, or "enthusiasm." Ridicule is the test of truth, "For truth . . . may bear all lights, and one of those principal lights . . . is Ridicule itself, or that manner of proof

---

[14] *A Letter concerning Enthusiasm*, sec. 7, in *Characteristics*, I, 40.

by which we discern whatever is liable to just raillery in any subject." Ridicule is the natural retort to tyranny. " 'Tis the persecuting spirit that has raised the bantering one." But it should be "good-humored," not scoffing. "Good humor is not only the best security against enthusiasm, but the best foundation of piety and true religion. . . . Ours is in the main a witty and good-humored religion." [15] Shaftesbury's good humor deserts him only when he encounters the enthusiasm of the ancient Hebrews—and their Puritan admirers.

The two doctrines of Shaftesbury most influential on his moralist successors are those of the moral sense and of the social passions. The term "moral sense," which he invented, and Hutcheson took over, indicates the natural tendency to virtue, denied by the "enthusiastic" doctrine of human corruption. It is a divine or natural instinct which leads us to tell right from wrong.

There is in reality no rational creature whatsoever, who knows not, that when he voluntarily offends, or does harm to any one, he cannot fail to create an apprehension and fear of like harm, and consequently a resentment and animosity in every creature who observes him. So that the offender must needs be conscious of being liable to such treatment from every one as if he had in some degree offended all. Thus offense and injury are always known as punishable by every one. . . . Of this even the wickedest creature living must have a sense. . . . Sense of right and wrong, therefore, is as natural to us as natural affection itself, and is a first principle in our constitution and make.[16]

The moral sense is merely a particular application of the faculty by which we apprehend the universal harmony. The harmony, as revealed to our imagination, produces the sense of the beautiful; as partially understood by reason, it generates philosophy; as shown in the workings of human nature, it gives rise to the moral sense. The aesthetic and the moral perceptions are really the same; they differ only in their objects. He says in *The Moralists*, "Beauty and good with you, Theocles, I perceive, are still one and the same." [17] In the *Miscellanies* he puts it, "what is beautiful is harmonious and proportionable; what is harmonious and proportionable is true; and

---

[15] *Sensus Communis: An Essay on the Freedom of Wit and Humor*, Part I, secs. 1, 4, *Enthusiasm*, sec. 3; *Characteristics*, I, 46, 55, 16; *Miscellany* II, ch. 3; *Characteristics*, III, 69.

[16] *Virtue*, Book I, Part 3, sec. 1; *Characteristics*, II, 29–30.

[17] *Moralists*, Part iii, sec. 2; *Characteristics*, II, 300.

what is at once both beautiful and true is of consequence agreeable and good." [18] He draws the parallel:

The case is the same in the mental or moral subjects, as in the ordinary bodies, or common subjects of sense. The shapes, motions, colors, and proportions of these latter being presented to our eye, there necessarily results a beauty or deformity, according to the different measure, arrangement, and disposition of their several parts. So in behavior and actions, when presented to our understanding, there must be found, of necessity, an apparent difference, according to the regularity or irregularity of the subjects. [19]

Thus in his aesthetic theory of morals, Shaftesbury finds a moral criterion, not in moral rules but in the canons of aesthetic criticism.

By making morality an affair, not of abstract rules the sceptic may challenge, but of the workings of human nature, Shaftesbury thinks he has escaped the dilemmas of scepticism, in Pyrrhonic or Lockean form:

For let us carry scepticism ever so far, let us doubt, if we can, of every thing about us; we cannot doubt of what passes within ourselves. Our passions and affections are known to us. They are certain, whatever the objects may be on which they are employed . . . whether we wake or dream. For ill dreams will be equally disturbing. And a good dream (if life be nothing else) will be easily and happily passed. [20]

The affections or passions are the springs of action in conduct; they alone are the subject of moral judgment.

A sensible creature . . . then only is supposed good, when the good or ill of the system to which he has relation, is the immediate object of some passion or affection moving him. Since it is therefore by affection merely that a creature is esteemed good or ill, natural or unnatural, our business will be, to examine which are the good and natural, and which the ill and unnatural affections. [21]

Shaftesbury distinguishes three kinds of these springs of action:

1. The *natural affections*, which lead to the good of the public.
2. Or the *self-affections*, which lead only to the good of the private.
3. Or such as are neither of these, nor tending to any of the public or the private, but contrariwise; and which may therefore be justly styled *unnatural affections.*

[18] *Miscellany* III, ch. 2; *Characteristics*, III, 127.
[19] *Virtue*, Book I, Part 2, sec. 3; *Characteristics*, II, 18–19.
[20] *Virtue*, Book II, Conclusion; *Characteristics*, II, 129.
[21] *Virtue*, Book I, Part 2, sec. 2; *Characteristics*, II, 13.

The latter sort of these affections, it is evident are wholly vicious. The two former may be vicious or virtuous, according to their degree.[22]

In some cases, public affection may be too high, and private affection may be too weak, though it is usually the reverse. "Too strong" and "too weak" mean, "with respect to a certain constitution or economy of a particular creature or species." It is the same with affections as with the strings of a musical instrument: the affections must be properly tuned. In general, Shaftesbury demonstrates:

1. That to have the natural, kindly, or generous affections strong and powerful toward the good of the public, is to have the chief means and power of self-enjoyment, and that to want them, is certain misery and ill.

2. That to have the private or self-affections too strong, or beyond their degree of subordinacy to the kindly and natural, is also miserable.

3. That to have the unnatural affections is to be miserable in the highest degree.[23]

Pleasures or satisfactions, "from whence happiness is generally computed," are either of the body or of the mind. Most people agree the latter are the greatest. Shaftesbury argues that both depend on natural affection: that both are social—even the pleasures of the body are enjoyed in companionship and society.

Shaftesbury spends by far the most time on the "natural" or social affections; he is arguing against the egoism of Hobbes and Locke, though it is significant he takes the existence of such social drives for granted, and never considers the position taken by the generous Helvétius, for example, that our most social actions are ultimately motivated by self-interest. By temperament and by Platonic philosophy, Shaftesbury could not take a thoroughgoing individualism seriously in analyzing human nature. Occasionally he calls his "natural affections" "social love."

To eliminate the unnatural affections, and to establish a just harmony between the natural and the self-affections, is the problem of the practical moralist. He will judge of the harmonious development of a man as a critic would judge of the harmony of a pictorial or a musical composition. It is again significant that Shaftesbury shows no interest in the practical question: he is throughout the aesthetic onlooker. He is content to have shown that virtue, in the

[22] *Virtue*, Book II, Part 1, sec. 3; *Characteristics*, II, 63–64.
[23] *Virtue*, Book II, Part 1, sec. 3; *Characteristics*, II, 72.

sense of love for mankind, is the best means to private happiness.

It was Shaftesbury's emphasis on the social impulses in man, and his doctrine of the moral sense, that most impressed his immediate successors in the eighteenth-century debate over morals. But one man was filled with disgust at his polished optimism, Mandeville. He pugnaciously returned to the low estimate of Hobbes and of the Calvinists.

II

Bernard de Mandeville (1670–1733) was a Dutch physician in London. In 1705 he published a pamphlet of some four hundred lines of doggerel, called *The Grumbling Hive, or Knaves turn'd Honest*. He republished this as a volume in 1714, together with *An Enquiry into the Origin of Moral Virtue*, and extensive *Remarks* on the verses, and with further additions in 1723 and again in 1729, the whole entitled *The Fable of the Bees; or, Private Vices Public Benefits*. The volume was presented as a nuisance in 1723 by the Grand Jury of Middlesex. For a generation Mandeville replaced Hobbes as the foil against whom to develop a juster view of human nature and morals. Hutcheson wrote three letters in the *Dublin Journal* criticizing him in 1723; when republishing them as *Remarks upon the Fable of the Bees* the same year, he described them on the title page as a defense of Shaftesbury against Mandeville. William Law wrote a penetrating and brilliant pamphlet, *Remarks upon a Late Book, entitled The Fable of the Bees* (1723). Berkeley included a reply, the second dialogue, in *Alciphron* (1732); Lysicles represents Mandeville; the latter answered the same year in *A Letter to Dion*, complaining that Berkeley could not have read the book itself. Warburton and John Brown also wrote against Mandeville, the latter attacking him in the second of three essays (in *Essay on the Characteristics*, 1751) with a utilitarian argument.

Mandeville combined a coarse humor with a shrewd realism. He is reported to have been in the habit of entertaining his patrons in the public house with ribald conversation. He has a contempt for humbugs, and extends it to all men, including himself. There is something of Swift about him, but he ends with a horse-laugh. There is more of a middle-class contempt for Shaftesbury, with his fine aristocratic airs and his own prejudices against trade. There is something of an eighteenth-century Reinhold Niebuhr, with an exalted ideal of virtue and perfection joined to the realism that recognizes the sinfulness of human nature. But it is Niebuhr in reverse: it is man that is immoral and society that, by the working of the unseen hand of God, reaps the moral fruits. His ideas are not original in themselves, but he constructed an original and startling pattern by putting together familiar materials. He took something from Hobbes and the libertines, something from the ideal of Christianity and its doctrine of original sin, and something from the eighteenth-century optimistic belief that there is a natural identity of interest between self-love and social, so that each man by following his own private interests is in fact promoting those of the whole. Remove his Hobbist view of human nature, and there is left the laissez-faire individualism developed by Bentham and the Utilitarian economists. Remove his realistic acceptance of life amongst the Yahoos, and he is an austere Christian moralist.

The original Hudibrastic verse tells of a bee-hive that is prosperous so long as every kind of vice flourishes in it. One day Jove "rid the bawling Hive of fraud." Trade and the professions languished, unemployment and depopulation set in, and the few surviving bees left their hive for a hollow tree, where, "Blest with Content and Honesty," they made their home. The poem concludes:

> Then leave complaints: Fools only strive
> To make a Great an Honest Hive.
> T'njoy the World's Conveniencies,
> Be famed in War, yet live in Ease,
> Without great Vices, is a vain
> Eutopia seated in the Brain.
>
> Bare Virtue can't make nations live
> In splendor.[24]

What is the moral? The simple life to which Shaftesbury paid lipservice? The recognition that what had been "vices" in the Christian, agricultural past were no longer vices in a commercial age, where all depends on profit, as the Utilitarians were to maintain? Mandeville himself seems rather to accept the wave of the future while scoffing at it. This is the coming way of the world; but since it is to vice, fraud, and the rest that we owe all our public benefits, let

[24] *Fable of the Bees* (ed. 1723), p. 23.

us be honest and realistic enough to recognize that it is really vice. Let us not be hypocrites, and pretend we are really acting the way we know we ought to be. Let us recognize ourselves for the sinners we are—happy, laughing sinners, without a contrite heart, but with honest self-acceptance. With Machiavelli, Mandeville knows "most men are bad"; with him, he judges more is to be learned from looking at what men actually are than by indulging in empty talk about what they ought to be. In modern terms, Mandeville was outraged by the moral "perfectionism" of the moralists like the polished Shaftesbury. For him, there lived more faith in honest vice than in half the moral creeds. Mandeville was a "realist" in the modern temper.

Mandeville uses a perfectionist moral ideal: his notion of virtue is as rigorous as that of Butler, Price, or Kant. Virtue is "every Performance, by which Man, contrary to the impulse of Nature, should endeavor the Benefit of others, or the Conquest of his own Passions, out of a Rational Ambition of being good." [25] Self-control, altruism, rational conduct—Mandeville is for all the proprieties. He then proceeds to show that men never do and never have behaved with self-control, altruistically, or rationally. And it is good they do not. For "What we call evil in this world, moral as well as natural, is the grand principle that makes us sociable creatures, the solid basis, the light and support of all trades without exception." [26] In his formal defense, Mandeville explains this as irony; what he really meant was, that

every want was an evil; that on the multiplicity of those wants depended all those mutual services which the individual members of society pay to each other; and that, consequently, the greater variety there was of want, the greater the number of individuals who might find their private interest in laboring for the good of others; and, united together, compose one body.[27]

Mandeville is arguing from the economic principle that consumption, instead of saving, keeps the economy going. He anticipates the later economists who taught that the accumulation of wealth affords the essential material base for all the virtues of civilization,

[25] Enquiry into the Origin of Moral Virtue, in Fable of the Bees (ed. 1723), p. 34. There is a two-volume critical ed. of the Fable by F. B. Kaye (1924).
[26] A Search into the Nature of Society, in Fable, p. 428.
[27] Fable (ed. 1729), p. 251.

and the still later ones who teach that the waste-makers are necessary to a really affluent society:

It is the sensual courtier that sets no limit to his luxury; the fickle strumpet that invents new fashions every week; the haughty duchess, that in equipage, entertainment, and all her behavior, would imitate a princess; the profuse rake and lavish heir, that scatter about their money without wit or judgment, buy everything they see, and either destroy or give it away the next day; the covetous and perjured villain that squeezed an immense treasure from the tears of widows and orphans, and left the prodigals the money to spend. . . .

these societies need to set laborers to work, and

to procure an honest livelihood to the vast numbers of working poor that are required to make a large society.

He pronounces the Reformation to have been hardly more efficacious in promoting prosperity than "the silly and capricious invention of hoop'd and quilted petticoats." "Religion is one thing and trade is another. He that gives most trouble to thousands of his neighbors, and invents the most operose manufactures, is, right or wrong, the greatest friend to society." It is useful even to destroy capital. "The fire of London was a great calamity, but if the carpenters, bricklayers, smiths," and others furnished work, "were to vote against those who lost by the fire, the rejoicings would equal, if not exceed, the complaints." [28] All this has a strangely familiar ring to a post-Keynesian ear.

These emerging economic doctrines of the new commercial age Mandeville translates into the old moral terms, with startling effect. Contempt for the world and for wealth, and for the natural passions, would reduce men to a set of naked savages. The ethics of commerce and even more of industry are fundamentally opposed to those of the older agricultural and religious tradition. Mandeville admits with the latter that the pursuit of wealth is intrinsically vicious, and argues with the former that it is essential to civilization. If virtue consists in renouncing luxury, then the ascetic monk is the highest conceivable type; but the ideal of the Trappist is incompatible with an affluent society.

The new utilitarians asked, how can any conduct which benefits society be called a "vice"? Mandeville sticks to his rigorous principle

[28] *A Search into the Nature of Society,* in *Fable* (ed. 1723), pp. 410–11, 415.

—that of the moralists from Cudworth to Price and Kant—that virtue is to be judged, not by the consequences of actions, but by their motives, and that human motives are almost invariably impure. They asked, how can private "vices" or self-interest work together for public good? Mandeville answers with what Adam Smith was to secularize as "the unseen hand":

Nothing can render the unsearchable depth of the Divine Wisdom more conspicuous, than that Man, whom Providence had designed for Society, should not only by his own Frailties and Imperfections be led into the Road to Temporal Happiness, but likewise receive, from a seeming Necessity of Natural Causes, a Tincture of that Knowledge, in which he was afterwards to be made perfect by the True Religion, to his Eternal Welfare.[29]

A Search into the Nature of Society, added in the 1723 edition, is a direct answer to Shaftesbury's optimistic view of man's social nature.

The Generality of Moralists and Philosophers have hitherto agreed that there could be no Virtue without Self-denial, but a late Author who is now much read by Men of Sense is of a contrary Opinion, and imagines that Men without any trouble or violence upon themselves may be Naturally Virtuous. This Noble Writer (for it is the Lord Shaftsbury I mean in his Characteristicks) Fancies, that as Man is made for Society, so he ought to be born with a kind Affection to the whole, of which he is a part, and a propensity to seek the Welfare of it. . . .

Two Systems cannot be more opposite than his Lordship's and mine. His Notions I confess are generous and refined: they are a High Compliment to Human-Kind, and capable by the help of a little Enthusiasm of Inspiring us with the most Noble Sentiments concerning the Dignity of our exalted Nature. What a pity it is that they are not true! . . . The Solidity of them is inconsistent with our Daily Experience.[30]

Mandeville opposes moral relativism to Shaftesbury's supposed absolutism. "He looks upon Virtue and Vice as permanent Realities that must ever be the same in all Countries and all Ages. . . . The *pulchrum et honestum*, excellency, and real worth of things are most commonly precarious and alterable as Modes and Customs vary." (pp. 372, 394–95)

On Shaftesbury's problem, Mandeville concludes: "The hunting after this *pulchrum et honestum* is not much better than a wild-

---

[29] *Enquiry*, in *Fable*, p. 44.   [30] *Search*, in *Fable*, pp. 371–72.

goose chase." (p. 380) Again, "That boasted middle way, and the calm Virtues recommended in the Characteristicks are good for nothing but to breed Drones. . . . Man's natural Love of Ease and Idleness and Proneness to indulge his sensual Pleasure, are not to be cured by Precept: His strong Habits and Inclinations can only be subdued by Passions of greater Violence." Mandeville turns Shaftesbury's argument from man's natural sociability against him. "Another Argument to prove the kind Disposition and real Affection we naturally have for our Species, is our Love of Company and the Aversion, Men that are in their Senses generally have to Solitude beyond other Creatures." He is reminded of shoals of herring; he recalls men's aversion for disagreeable company; he shows that men of the greatest parts can bear to be alone longest. Above all, "does not Man love Company as he does everything else for his own sake," for the satisfaction it gives *him?* "Our Love of Company and Aversion to Solitude . . . all center in Self-Love." (pp. 382, 386, 390, 392, 395)

His blackest picture of human nature Mandeville gives in *An Enquiry into the Origin of Moral Virtue.*

Most Writers are always teaching Men what they should be, and hardly ever trouble their heads with telling them what they really are. As for my part . . . I believe Man to be a Compound of various Passions, that all of them, as they are provoked and come uppermost, govern him by turns, whether he will or no. . . . I have thought fit to enquire, how Man no better qualify'd, might yet by his own Imperfections be taught to distinguish between Virtue and Vice: and . . . when I say Men, I mean neither Jews nor Christians; but mere Man, in the State of Nature and Ignorance of the true Deity.[31]

"Being an extraordinarily selfish and headstrong, as well as cunning Animal, . . . it is impossible by force alone to make [Man] tractable." The chief thing therefore that the lawgivers who set up society aimed at, "has been to make the People they were to govern, believe, that it was more beneficial for every body to conquer than indulge his Appetites, and much better to mind the Publick than what seemed his private Interest." They did this by *flattery,* which must be the most powerful argument that could be used to human creatures, since they observed that "none were either so savage as not to be charmed with Praise, or so despicable as patiently to bear

[31] *Enquiry,* Introduction, in *Fable,* pp. 25–26.

Contempt." They appealed to man's passion of *pride;* they extolled the excellency of our nature, setting forth with unbounded praise the wonders of our sagacity and the vastness of our understanding, the rationality of our souls. They instructed men in notions of honor and shame; they emphasized how glorious it was to control the passions. To introduce an emulation, they divided men into two classes, the abject and low-minded who always followed their appetites, and the lofty high-spirited ones, free from sordid selfishness, who aimed to improve their minds, despised whatever they had in common with irrational creatures, and "aimed at no less than the Publick Welfare and the Conquest of their own Passions."

The finest animals have the greatest pride; "so in Man . . . it is inseparable from his very Essence." Thus "the skilful Managements of wary Politicians" by appealing to the pride of the élite with flattery, persuaded them to practice virtue, to be social and self-controlled. The élite took pride in their fortitude and self-conquest; with the authority of the government on their side they enforced the esteem that was due them from the lower class, as well as their superiority to it.

This was (or at least might have been) the manner after which Savage Man was broke; from whence it is evident, that the first Rudiments of Morality, broached by skilful Politicians, to render Men useful to each other as well as tractable, were chiefly contrived that the Ambitious might reap the more Benefit from, and govern vast Numbers of them with the greater Ease and Security.

It may be objected that the notions of good and evil, and the distinction between virtue and vice, were never the contrivance of politicians, but the pure effect of religion. No, in the state of nature, ignorant of the true Deity, superstition had no force to excite men to virtue. And in all considerable societies that have achieved riches and power, "Human Nature has ever exerted itself in all its branches, and there is no Earthly Wisdom or Moral Virtue, but at one time or another Men have excelled in it in all Monarchies and Commonwealths." Everywhere, men have been taught morality by politicians who flattered their pride. Thus, "the Moral Virtues are the Political Offspring which Flattery begot upon Pride." (pp. 28–37)

It may have happened this way; we cannot be sure Mandeville is not scoffing at the theorists of the state of nature. In any event, this fable makes clear why "Sagacious Moralists draw Men like Angels, in hopes that the Pride at least of some will put 'em upon copying after the beautiful Originals which they are represented to be." (p. 38)

Mandeville goes on to insist that self-love and pride ultimately motivate the most disinterested actions. Even pity, "the most amiable of all our weaknesses," is as much a frailty of our nature as anger, pride, or fear. "It has helped to destroy the Honor of Virgins, and corrupted the Integrity of Judges."

There is no Merit in saving an Innocent Babe ready to drop into the Fire; the Action is neither good nor bad, and what Benefit soever the Infant received, we only obliged ourselves; for to have seen it fall, and not strove to hinder it, would have caused a Pain, which Self-preservation compelled us to prevent.

In general, "it is impossible to judge of a Man's Performance, unless we are thoroughly acquainted with the Principle and Motive from which he acts." There are some men, indeed, who from no other motive but their love to goodness perform a worthy action in silence.

Yet even in these we may discover no small Symptoms of Pride, and the humblest Man alive must confess, that the Reward of a Virtuous Action, which is the Satisfaction that ensues upon it, consists in a certain Pleasure he procures to himself by Contemplating on his own Worth: which Pleasure, together with the Occasion of it, are as certain Signs of Pride, as looking Pale and Trembling at any imminent Danger, are the Symptoms of Fear. (pp. 42–43)

Thus Mandeville serves as a link between Hobbes's egoism and Helvétius' universality of the motive of self-interest, the view Butler and the school of Shaftesbury so vigorously opposed.

It remains only to remark that Mandeville attacks vigorously also Shaftesbury's doctrine of the universal harmony of nature. Nature remains for him an inscrutable secret, revealing no design or order; it is full of waste of life, cruelty, voracity, and lust. In his *Free Thoughts on Religion* (1720), he calls Manichaeanism the theory most consonant to reason (p. 105). Man is no angel, but nature acts like the Devil.

III

When Samuel Clarke's Boyle Lectures were printed, he received a series of criticisms from an anonymous correspondent in Gloucester. They were so acutely argued that Clarke printed them with his answers in the next edition. It transpired the penetrating critic was a twenty-one-year-old student in Mr. Jones's academy at Tewkesbury, who had had a friend post them in nearby Gloucester. The writer of the letters later became Bishop Joseph Butler; his friend grew up to be Archbishop Secker of Canterbury. Not many years later Clarke got his young friend appointed to the Rolls Chapel, where Butler preached his classic *Sermons on Human Nature*, the ablest discussion of moral theory in eighteenth-century England before Hume.

Joseph Butler (1692–1752) was a thoroughly unworldly man whom the world treated very well. Son of a retired linen-draper in Wantage, Berkshire, he was intended for the Presbyterian ministry, and was sent to dissenting academies, first at Gloucester and then at Tewkesbury, where he stayed on as assistant. His good sense led him into the more reasonable Anglican Church. He persuaded his father to send him to Oriel College, Oxford. After taking his degree in 1718, through Samuel Clarke he secured appointment as preacher. He soon advanced through various livings to become Clerk of the Closet to Queen Caroline, a very intellectual lady, in 1736; she died the next year after recommending Butler to the Archbishop of Canterbury. But Walpole offered him only the bishopric of Bristol, one of the poorest English sees, over which he presided from 1738 to 1750. In 1747 he was offered and declined the See of Canterbury, but in 1750 he accepted the rich bishopric of Durham. Broken in health, he retired and died in 1752.

Butler published two books, the *Fifteen Sermons* delivered in the Rolls Chapel but issued only after he had left, in 1726. The first three, on human nature, contain his moral analysis. In 1736 came out his *Analogy of Religion, Natural and Revealed, to the Constitution and Course of Nature*. Appended to it was a brief dissertation *Of the Nature of Virtue*.

Butler stands closer to Shaftesbury than to any other predecessor; he adopts Shaftesbury's approach to the problems of moral theory, and takes over some of his central ideas, while criticizing him on specific points. There is an air of definitiveness and finality in the way he rounds out Shaftesbury's insight. Human nature is what the moralist should study; and it is a system or constitution embracing a variety of internal "principles" or passions—what Shaftes-

bury usually called "affections." This constitution is presided over
by a guiding principle of reflection, the conscience. The particular
passions seek each its particular object, not pleasure or happiness.
The general desire for one's own happiness is the "principle of reflection" that is self-love; it involves a rational organization of the
passions, directed toward their fulfillment. Benevolence is the rational organization of the social passions; when both organizations
are fully developed, they are completely consistent and merge. Su-
perintending both is the conscience that guides their proper fulfillment, the highest authority in human nature, which imposes moral
obligation. The various passions, their different rational organizations, the authority that is conscience, and "the whole nature of
man," all have determinate natural capacities directed toward their
natural ends. Everything in the "frame of man" is adapted toward
its role in his system or constitution; and the constitution as a whole
is adapted toward virtue.

Butler, in the full Newtonian age, is not thinking mechanically,
like the Hobbes he censures. He is not even thinking in terms of
Newtonian law, like Clarke and Wollaston. He is thinking teleologi-
cally and functionally; not so much in terms of Shaftesbury's systems of aesthetic harmony—beauty does not come in for mention at
all—but more like Cicero and the Stoics. The world for him is not
a *cosmos*, beautiful for its aesthetic harmony, as it was for the Greeks
and for Shaftesbury. It is a *mundus*, with a moral government, as it
was for Cicero and the Romans. And like the world, man as a whole,
and each particular man or "economy of human nature," has his
own moral government. "Moral government must consist in rendering [human creatures] happy and unhappy, in rewarding and pun-
ishing them, as they follow, neglect, or depart from, the moral rule
of action interwoven in their nature, or suggested and enforced by
this moral faculty." [32]

Butler can accept as his own the Stoic principle of "following
nature." It means for him, as for the Stoic, following human nature;
and that in turn means for him, following the law of man's own
nature, given by his ruling principle of reflection. Butler insists as
strongly as Kant that the principle of the moral life is autonomy.

[32] *Dissertation of the Nature of Virtue*, in *Analogy of Religion; British
Moralists*, ed. Selby-Bigge, Vol. I, par. 249.

But whereas Kant makes autonomy obedience to a self-imposed law of reason, Butler makes it the functioning of the powers of human nature as revealed by rational analysis; not obedience to rational commands, but the releasing of natural powers and capacities. Butler's is a natural morality—the morality of human nature.

> Nothing can be more evident, than that, exclusive of revelation, man cannot be considered as a creature left by his Maker to act at random, and live at large up to the extent of his natural power, as passion, humor, wilfulness, happen to carry him; which is the condition brute creatures are in: but that from his make, constitution, or nature, he is in the strictest and most proper sense a law to himself. He hath the rule of right within: what is wanting is only that he honestly attends to it.[33]

Such is Butler's vision of human nature. With it his ethics stop short. He makes no attempt to explain the relation of conscience to reason, he does not introduce the idea of will at all; he is not concerned to derive from conscience in any systematic way the content of morality. For, important as is the idea of system in his moral theory, he himself worked out no system, like those of Clarke or Hutcheson. He distrusted such systems of philosophy, and was resigned to accept, not aesthetic taste, like Shaftesbury, but probability, like Locke, as the guide to life. Like Locke he was empirical, not like Hume, empiricist.

In the Preface to the *Sermons* added in the second edition in 1729, Butler states the principle followed by Shaftesbury and all his successors:

> There are two ways in which the subject of morals may be treated. One begins from inquiring into the abstract relations of things: the other from a matter of fact, namely, what the particular nature of man is, its several parts, their economy or constitution; from whence it proceeds to determine what course of life it is, which is correspondent to this whole nature. In the former method the conclusion is expressed thus, that vice is contrary to the nature and reason of things: in the latter, that it is a violation or breaking in upon our own nature.[34]

The first three Sermons, on Human Nature, proceed wholly by the latter method. They explain what is meant by the nature of man,

---

[33] Sermon III, in Selby-Bigge, Vol. I, par. 222. The text for this Sermon is, For when the Gentiles, which have not the law, do by nature the things contained in the law, these, having not the law, are a law unto themselves. Rom. 2:14.

[34] Preface to *Fifteen Sermons;* Selby-Bigge, Vol. I, par. 188.

when virtue is said to lie in following it, and thus show that the view is true. In contrast, for Wollaston "following nature" means "but acting as any of the several parts, without distinction, of a man's nature happened most to incline him." (par. 189)

Mankind has various instincts, some leading most directly to the good of the community, and some most directly to private good. Man has several the brutes lack: "particularly reflection or conscience, an approbation of some principles or actions, and disapprobation of others." (par. 192) Conscience or reflection "plainly bears upon it marks of authority over all the rest, and claims the absolute direction of them all." (par. 194) "Neither can any human creature be said to act conformably to his constitution or nature, unless he allows to that superior principle the absolute authority which is due it." (par. 194)

The practical reason of insisting so much on this natural authority of the principle of reflection or conscience is, that it seems in great measure overlooked by many, who are by no means the worse sort of men. It is thought sufficient to abstain from gross wickedness, and to be humane and kind to such as happen to come in their way. Whereas in reality the very constitution of our nature requires, that we bring our whole conduct before this superior faculty; wait its determination; enforce upon ourselves its authority, and make it the business of our lives, as it is absolutely the whole business of a moral agent, to conform ourselves to it. This is the true meaning of that ancient precept, Reverence thyself. (par. 195)

Butler criticizes Shaftesbury for not recognizing this authority of the principle of reflection; if a man does not see that virtue is his natural interest, his mistaken choice would be "without remedy," he says. In reality "the natural authority of the principle of reflection is an obligation the most near and intimate, the most certain and known. . . . Though a man should doubt of everything else, yet, he will still remain under the nearest and most certain obligation to the practice of virtue." (pars. 195–96)

At one point Butler speaks rather casually of "our nature, i.e., the voice of God within us." [35] Although Butler makes a fairly successful attempt at a thoroughly naturalistic theory of morality, that is, one derived from an examination of human nature without reference to its Maker, it is clear that ultimately the authority of con-

[35] Sermon VI; Bohn ed. (1871), p. 439.

science has for him a theological foundation in its divine source. He would put it the other way around: the adaptation of human nature to its conditions is the best illustration of that design from which we infer the existence of a Creator.[36] Hence the sovereign ruler demanded by the moral government of man's constitution derives its authority from the Author of its being, and rules the passions by divine right.

Not all action springs from self-love. Epicurus and Hobbes are mistaken: their confusion consists in calling actions "interested" which contradict the most manifest known interest, merely to gratify a present passion. We must sharply distinguish between "the idea of self-love in general," and the mere appetites toward particular external things.

When this is done, if the words 'selfish' and 'interested' cannot be parted with, but must be applied to everything; yet, to avoid such total confusion of all language, . . . the first may be called cool or settled selfishness, and the other passionate or sensual selfishness. But the most natural way of speaking plainly is, to call the first only, self-love, and the actions proceeding from it, interested: and to say of the latter that they are not love to ourselves, but movements towards somewhat external: honor, power, the harm or good of another.[37]

There is a sense, innocuous enough, in which all action is "interested": for all action springs from desire, and "no one can act but from a desire, or choice, or preference of his own." (par. 198) In this sense, benevolence is no more disinterested than any of the other particular passions. It follows, that benevolence, virtue and interest are not to be opposed, but only to be distinguished from each other: "everything is what it is, and not something else." The goodness or badness of actions will then be irrelevant to whether they are interested or disinterested. "We may judge and determine, that an action is morally good or evil, before we so much as consider, whether it be interested or disinterested." (par. 200)

There is no reason to wish self-love weaker than it is. "The thing to be lamented is, not that men have so great regard to their own good or interest in the present world, for they have not enough;

---

[36] "The several passions and affections in the heart of man" afford "as certain instances of final causes as any whatever, which are more commonly alleged for such."

[37] Selby-Bigge, Vol. I, par. 198.

but that they have so little to the good of others." Self-love—or "enlightened self-interest," as it came to be called—is a far better motive than mere appetite, will, and pleasure. (par. 201)

Applying to human nature as well as to society the "body and its members" text, Sermon I considers "the whole nature of man, and all the variety of internal principles which belong to it." It emphasizes against Hobbes the social drives in man.

There are as real and the same kind of indications in human nature, that we were made for society and to do good to our fellow-creatures; as that we were intended to take care of our own life and health and private good: and the same objections lie against one of these assertions, as against the other. (par. 203)

There is a natural principle of benevolence in man; Hobbes was wrong on the question of fact. There is such a thing in some degree as real good-will in man towards man; there is a disposition to friendship, compassion, paternal and filial affection. In fact, benevolence and self-love are perfectly coincident: they are both natural. (par. 204) The several particular passions, appetites, and affections are quite different from self-love as well as from benevolence. A man would feel pain even if he hated himself; "one man rushes upon certain ruin for the gratification of a present desire." All the passions tend toward public good; some, like hunger, are private appetites; others, like the desire for esteem, the love of society, are "public passions."

All have a tendency to promote both public and private good: . . . but some of them seem most immediately to tend to public good; others . . . tend to private good: as the former are not benevolence, so the latter are not self-love. (par. 205)

"We were made for society, and to promote the happiness of it; as we were intended to take care of our own life, and health, and private good." (par. 207)

In addition, there is a principle of reflection in men, by which they distinguish between, approve and disapprove of their own actions. This is conscience, which restrains men from harming each other, and leads them to do good. "It cannot possibly be denied, that there is this principle of reflection or conscience in human nature." (par. 206)

Has not man a tendency to do evil? Butler raises the old question of original sin. He asks, has not man an equal tendency to do evil to himself? The answer to both questions is the same:

Mankind have ungoverned passions which they will gratify at any rate, as well to the injury of others, as in contradiction to known private interest: but as there is no such thing as self-hatred, so neither is there any such thing as ill-will in one man towards another, emulation and resentment being away; whereas there is plainly benevolence or good-will: there is no such thing as love of injustice, oppression, treachery, ingratitude; but only eager desires after such and such external goods. (par. 208)

Butler and his age had not read Freud; nor did they have an excessive tragic sense of life.

In gratifying all these passions, is not the middle way obvious? Happiness consists in pursuing them only to a certain degree. Beyond that, only inconvenience and misery is brought to a man's self.

The nature of man . . . is adapted and leads him to attain the greatest happiness he can for himself in the present world. [It] . . . leads him to a right behavior in society, to that course of life which we call virtue. Men follow or obey their nature in both these capacities to a certain degree, but not entirely; their actions do not come up to the whole of what their nature leads them to . . . ; and they often violate their nature in both. (par. 210)

"It is manifest that nothing can be of consequence to mankind or any creature, but happiness." (par. 241)

Happiness consists in the gratification of certain affections, appetites, passions, with objects which are by nature adapted to them. Self-love [the general desire for happiness] may indeed set us on work to gratify these: but happiness or enjoyment has no immediate connection with self-love, but arises from such gratification alone. Love of our neighbor is one of those affections. (par. 236)

It is clear, Butler's psychology is not hedonistic, but Aristotelian.

In Sermons II and III Butler goes into further detail about the "principle of reflection" and its authority and obligation. He distinguishes the senses of "following nature": "If by following nature were meant only acting as we please, it would indeed be ridiculous to speak of nature as any guide in morals: nay the very mention of deviating from nature would be absurd. . . . Language itself should teach people another sense to the word 'following nature,' than barely acting as we please." Every man is naturally a law to himself.

"Every one may find within himself the rule of right, and obligations to follow it," as the Apostle says. (par. 214)

There is a superior principle of reflection or conscience in every man, which distinguishes between the internal principles of his heart, as well as his external actions: which passes judgment upon himself and them; pronounces determinately some actions to be in themselves just, right, good: others to be in themselves evil, wrong, unjust: which, without being consulted, without being advised with, magisterially exerts itself, and approves or condemns him the doer of them accordingly. . . . It is by this faculty, natural to man, that he is a moral agent, that he is a law to himself. (par. 216)

Conscience is often violated; it is not always stronger than the other passions. But it is "manifestly superior and chief, without regard to strength." It is not mere power; indeed, even when it lacks the power to control and direct the passions, its moral authority is still recognized by every man. Without it there would be no moral judgment. (pars. 218–19)

Human nature consists "in the several passions being naturally subordinate to the one superior principle of reflection or conscience." For Butler takes human nature to be essentially, not what is given at birth, with the Darwinians, nor any or all its impulses and drives taken by themselves. It is a certain *organization* of impulses: "It is the inward frame of man considered as a system or constitution." (pars. 221, 222n.) It is not man in a primitive "state of nature," it is, in modern terms, an integrated personality. The moral constitution of man is like a tree, an organism, kept in delicate balance by its ruling principle of reflection. "Your obligation to obey this law [of conscience] is its being the law of your nature. . . . Conscience carries its own authority with it, that it is our natural guide." (par. 223) Obligation comes from moral autonomy. General rules and principles of morality are useful, but they are unnecessary. Conscience speaks in particular cases. And conscience and self-love, if we understand our true happiness, always lead us the same way.

Sermons XI and XII develop this harmony further; they deal with the love of our neighbors, the relation of benevolence to self-love, of private to public interest. Self-love is the general desire of one's own happiness. Happiness or satisfaction consists only in the enjoyment of those objects which are by nature suited to our several particular appetites and passions. So if we aim only at happiness,

we achieve no enjoyment; for happiness presupposes having particular desires to be fulfilled. These desires are not for the "pleasure"
that arises from securing our external objects, but for the objects
themselves; hedonism is a false psychology. To be sure, every passion or drive is one's own; this has led some to assert that no creature
can possibly act but merely from self-love. But this is a language
mistake: "this is not the language of mankind: or if it were we
should want words to express the difference, between the principle
of an action, proceeding from cool consideration that it will be to
my own advantage; and an action, suppose of revenge, or of friendship, by which a man runs upon certain ruin, to do evil or good to
another." (par. 229) Epicurus and Hobbes were wrong; they failed
to make a necessary distinction in language. "The cool principle
of self-love" is a motive of rational self-interest, it is not to be identified with "the particular affections."

There is no inconsistency between self-love, as a truly enlightened
self-interest, and benevolence, another rational motive. Strictly, self-
love is "interested," while particular desires are not. Such self-interest is no more in conflict with benevolence than with any other
particular drive. "Does the benevolent man appear less easy with
himself, from his love to his neighbor?" "There have been persons
in all ages who have professed that they found satisfaction in the
exercise of charity, in the love of their neighbor." "Being in good
humor, which is benevolence, . . . is itself the temper of satisfaction and enjoyment." (par. 235)

Butler acutely remarks that the mistaken assumption that there
is a conflict between doing good to others and our own self-interest
seems "to arise from our notions of *property;* and to be carried on
by this property's being supposed to be itself our happiness or good.
People are so very much taken up with this one subject, that they
seem from it to have formed a general way of thinking, which they
apply to other things that they have nothing to do with." (par.
238) They confusedly think that the more interest in a property
you have, the less I have: the more I promote your happiness, the
less happiness I have myself. Butler rises above Locke and his middle-
class "general way of thinking" in terms of property.

Does the precept, to love our neighbor as ourselves, include in it
all the virtues, as the Apostle says in Romans, 13:9? Butler in-

creasingly doubts the universalizing of benevolence. Such universal benevolence cannot be a blind propension, it must be "directed by reason," which will consider "distant consequences." And he distrusts the confidence of the utilitarians that they can make the necessary calculations.

As there are numberless cases in which, notwithstanding appearances, we are not competent judges, whether a particular action will upon the whole do good or harm; reason . . . will teach us to be cautious how we act in these cases of uncertainty.

For instance: as we are not competent judges, what is upon the whole for the good of the world, there may be other immediate ends appointed us to pursue, beside that one of doing good, or producing happiness. Though the good of the creation be the only end of the Author of it, yet he may have laid us under particular obligations, which we may discern and feel ourselves under, quite distinct from a perception, that the observance or violation of them is for the happiness or misery of our fellow-creatures. And this is in fact the case. (pars. 240, 242n)

There are certain dispositions of mind and certain actions that men immediately approve or condemn, quite apart from their consequences, like treachery, indecencies, meanness of mind. As C. D. Broad remarks, God, who foresees all consequences, can be a utilitarian consistently; man, confronting the incalculable complexity of the moral life, with a candle of reason that casts a dim light, can scarcely afford to be without stronger means of condemning certain things as wrong and recognizing others as right, even though he cannot see what they will in fact lead to.

In the *Dissertation on Virtue*, Butler puts this mistrust of the utilitarian principle still more strongly. Since he is not preaching on the text, And if there be any other commandment, it is briefly comprehended in this saying, Thou shalt love thy neighbor as thyself, he can afford to assert much more strongly than before, "benevolence, and the want of it, singly considered, are in no sort the whole of virtue and vice." (par. 249) We do not disapprove injustice and falsehood merely because of their consequences to human unhappiness.

Some [authors: Shaftesbury] of great and distinguished merit have, I think, expressed themselves in a manner, which may occasion some danger, to careless readers, of imagining the whole of virtue to consist in singly aiming, according to the best of their judgment, at promoting the happiness of mankind in the present state; and the whole of vice, in doing what they foresee, or might foresee, is likely to produce an overbalance of unhappiness in it; than which mistakes none can be conceived more terrible. (par. 250)

Crimes and injustices often do not add to the world's miseries, yet are clearly vicious. "The happiness of the world is the concern of him who is the lord and proprietor of it; nor do we know what we are about, when we endeavor to promote the good of mankind in any ways but those which he has directed; that is, indeed, in all ways not contrary to veracity and justice." Twentieth-century experience has exhibited many instances of what happens when men seek to improve the lot of their fellows at the expense of "veracity and justice." And Butler adds, with prescience: "The truth seems to be, that such supposed endeavors proceed, almost always, from ambition, the spirit of party, or some indirect principle, concealed perhaps in great measure from persons themselves." (par. 250) Butler's position is in line with the best religious morality of our own time, that justice and love are independent of each other and both essential ideals.

Butler ends with his usual caution:

And though it is our business and our duty to endeavor, within the bounds of veracity and justice, to contribute to the ease, convenience, and even cheerfulness and diversion of our fellow creatures; yet from our short views, it is greatly uncertain, whether this endeavor will, in particular instances, produce an overbalance of happiness upon the whole; since so many and distant things come into the account. And that which makes it our duty is, that there is some appearance that it will, and no positive appearance sufficient to balance this, on the contrary side. (par. 250)

Do good to mankind with caution, with justice, and balance the probabilities.

The *Dissertation* is the clearest of all Butler's statements, especially of the positive content of the moral life. Men are capable of moral government because they have a moral nature, and moral faculties of perception and of action. We have a capacity of reflecting on actions and characters, and of passing moral judgment. In reality there is "an universally acknowledged standard" of virtue and vice: "namely, justice, veracity, and regard to common good." "Great part of common language, and of common behavior over the world, is formed upon supposition of such a moral faculty." It does not matter how we analyze it, whether we call it "conscience, moral reason, moral sense, or divine reason; whether [we] consider it as a sentiment of the understanding, or as a perception of the heart; or, which seems the truth, as including both." (par. 244) The theory of it does not matter: Butler is empirical, not empiricist. Its objects are actions, and their practical principles, which, "when fixed and habitual in any person, we call his character." (par. 245)

It is hard to judge merit or desert, because, "concerning our perception of good and of ill desert, the former is very weak with respect to common instances of virtue. One reason of which may be, that it does not appear to a spectator"—here Butler is definitely in the Shaftesbury tradition—"how far such instances of virtue proceed from a virtuous principle . . . : since a very weak regard to virtue may be sufficient to make men act well in many common instances. And . . . our perception of ill desert in vicious actions lessens in proportion to the temptations men are thought to have had to such vices." (par. 246)

Butler is the very entelechy of the eighteenth-century British moralists who started from the psychology of the moral life. So British is he, in fact, that Whewell tells us that in the mid-nineteenth century Butler's writings were accepted as the official moral philosophy of the University of Cambridge; and Matthew Arnold [38] recounts how at Oxford Butler's *Sermons* and Aristotle's *Ethics* shared equal honors. And C. D. Broad [39] could conclude his discussion of Butler in his *Five Types of Ethical Theory* (1930): "Though his system is incomplete, it does seem to contain the prolegomena to any system of ethics that can claim to do justice to the facts of moral experience." How the Germans, and the pragmatists, judged him, will appear in due course.

[38] Arnold, "Bishop Butler and the Zeitgeist," in *Last Essays on Church and Religion* (ed. 1883), p. 235.
[39] C. D. Broad, *Five Types of Ethical Theory* (1930), p. 83.

The Morality of the Sentiments and
the Scottish Enlightenment

WHILE BUTLER inherited from Shaftesbury the approach to the questions of moral theory of the spectator observing human conduct, rather than the approach of the actor who must make moral choices and decisions himself, he developed that side of Shaftesbury's thought that emphasized the springs of action—what Shaftesbury called "affections" and passions, and what he himself called "principles of action" in human nature. He also emphasized what linked the Englishman with the objective attitude of the ancient moralists, with Plato and the Stoics and Cicero: his general rule of "following nature" is Stoic, and his view of human nature as an ordered polity of impulses with a moral government, like Shaftesbury's idea of it as a system harmoniously balanced, is distinctly Platonic.

With Hutcheson we find ourselves in a somewhat different atmosphere. He is conventionally taken as the systematizer of Shaftesbury's rather loosely developed thought, and he follows him in many ideas: in identifying virtue with benevolence, and in playing up the regulating and controlling function of the moral sense. He follows Butler too in sharply separating "calm self-love," to which he adds a "calm benevolence," from the turbulent passions. But the objective attitude of Butler has gone. No longer does the "principle of reflection" concern itself with actions, intentions, and tendencies to act. It is centered on the "affections," now taken as mere passive feelings or sentiments. There is a new subjectivistic attitude, a considering all moral problems in terms of the feelings and "sentiments"; the moral life has retreated from the objective world of conduct, action, and decision, to an abode which, if not exclusively in the heart, is at least inside the mind. Locke, or, if you will, Cartesian dualism, has conquered. Morality has been reduced to the moral sentiments of the ghost in the machine, even when the machine itself has vanished. This new attitude is still stronger and more insistent in the world of impressions and sentiments of Hume and Adam Smith. Throughout all three, central is the attitude of the observer who *apprehends* qualities of actions, affections, passions.

I

Francis Hutcheson (1694–1746) was grandson of Alexander Hutcheson, who had come from Monkswood in Ayrshire to serve as minister in the Presbyterian Church in Ulster. His son John was also a Presbyterian minister in Armagh, where Francis was born in 1694. Destined himself for the ministry, he was first sent to be educated to his grandfather Alexander, and then in 1711 he entered the University of Glasgow. He took his degree in 1717, returned to Ulster, was ordained, and soon went to Dublin to set up in 1721 an academy for the education of Presbyterian youth. Such dissenting education was first made legal in Ireland by the Toleration Act of 1719. After his letters against Mandeville in the *Dublin Journal* in 1723, he published in 1725 his *Inquiry into the Original of our Ideas of Beauty and Virtue*, consisting of two *Treatises, Concerning Beauty, Order, Harmony, and Design*, and *Concerning Moral Good and Evil*. In 1728 he brought out his *Essay on the Nature and Conduct of the Passions and Affections, with Illustrations on the Moral Sense*, dealing with the springs of action rather than with the moral sense. His teaching was so successful that in 1729 he was called to the chair of Moral Philosophy at Glasgow, the first major British philosopher to serve as a professor since the days of Duns Scotus and Ockham. At Glasgow almost single-handed he initiated the Scottish Enlightenment, and introduced the new English ideas of Locke and Shaftesbury into the still traditional philosophical teaching of Psychologia Rationalis. He published nothing further until 1742, when he issued *Philosophiae moralis institutio compendaria . . . Ethices et jurisprudentiae naturalis . . .* (Eng. tr. 1747); and the same year a *Metaphysicae synopsis*. After his death in 1746 his son edited his lectures in two quartos as *A System of Moral Philosophy*, published in 1755, and a compendium of logic the next year. It is the *Inquiry* by which Hutcheson was known; in it he is dominated by Shaftesbury and Cicero, and tries to assimilate ethics to aesthetics. In his *An Essay on the Passions* he begins to exhibit the influence of Butler; in his posthumous *System*, as well as in the revision in his fourth edition of the *Inquiry*, he shows a strong admixture of Aristotle. Adam Smith was a student under Hutcheson, and succeeded to his chair in 1752.

Hutcheson starts very close to Shaftesbury, whom he praises. In his rather complacent Deism he shares the easy-going optimism of his master. He attributes a slightly more distinct personality to the Creator: it is not "Nature," but the "Universal Parent," he refers to. But he passes easily from Shaftesbury's aesthetic appreciation of the universal harmony to the benevolence that makes for the happiness of all men. Likewise, where Butler considers each man as a little constitution, in which conscience rules by divine right, Hutcheson has abandoned the divine right of conscience to justify the rule of the moral sense as leading to the welfare of the subject. Hutcheson thus represents the transition from the intuitionists like Shaftesbury and Butler to the utilitarians like Hume and Bentham. The most striking difference with Shaftesbury is that where he had used the term moral sense, quite incidentally, Hutcheson has crystallized it into the keystone of a system that grew increasingly elaborate. In the *System of Moral Philosophy* he undertakes one of the most complex analyses of the "literary psychology" of the moral life ever worked out.

As a young man of thirty, introduced to the ideas of the English philosophers by the Dublin circle of intellectuals that included several enthusiasts for Shaftesbury, Lord Molesworth, a wealthy merchant, and James Arbuckle, a young literary poet and son of the minister of Usher's Quay Congregation, Hutcheson set out to combine Locke and Shaftesbury, in his two treatises on "the original of our ideas of Beauty and Virtue." In the Preface he explains, "There is no part of Philosophy of more importance, than a just Knowledge of Human Nature and its various Powers and Dispositions." [1] Recent inquiries have explored the understanding and the several methods of obtaining truth. There is room for an inquiry into the non-cognitive ideas of beauty, happiness, and pleasure, and into which

---

[1] *An Inquiry into the Original of Our Ideas of Beauty and Virtue*, 2d ed. (1726), p. ix.

are the most lasting pleasures. Perceptions of pleasure and of pain do not depend on the will, but on the very frame of our nature. The mind is determined to be pleased with many forms of beauty, order, harmony, and design. "These Determinations to be pleased with any Forms, or Ideas which occur to our Observation the Author chooses to call 'Senses'; distinguishing them from the Powers which commonly go by that Name, by calling our Power of perceiving the Beauty of Regularity, Order, Harmony an 'Internal Sense'; and that Determination to be pleased with the Contemplation of those Affections, Actions, or Characters of rational Agents, which we call virtuous, he marks by the name of a 'Moral Sense.'" (pp. xiii, xiv) Human nature was not left indifferent in the affair of virtue, to be guided by rational advantage.

The Author of Nature has much better furnished us for a virtuous Conduct, than our Moralists seem to imagine. . . . He has made Virtue a lovely Form, to excite our pursuit of it; and has given us strong affections to be the spring of each virtuous action. (p. xv)

This "moral sense of beauty" in Shaftesbury offended the rationalists accustomed to attribute approbation to "rational views of intellect," who have "such a horror of innate ideas, which they imagine this borders upon. But this moral sense has no relation to innate ideas." (pp. xv, xvi)

To recommend the Lord Shaftesbury's Writings to the World, is a very needless attempt. They will be esteemed while any Reflection remains among Men. It is indeed to be wished, that he had abstained from mixing with such Noble Performances, some Prejudices he had received against Christianity. (p. xxi)

Hutcheson sets out by defining moral goodness. "The Word Moral Goodness, in this Treatise, denotes our Idea of some Quality apprehended in Actions, which procures Approbation, and Love toward the Actor, from those who receive no Advantage by the Action." [2] He raises the Lockean question, "Whence arise these different Ideas of Actions?" Pleasure gives us our first idea of natural good, or happiness; all objects which excite it we call good, all which procure such objects we call advantageous, and pursue both from interest, or self-love. Thus the sense of pleasure is the founda-

---

[2] *Inquiry concerning Moral Good and Evil*, in *British Moralists*, ed. Selby-Bigge, Vol. I, par. 68.

tion of interest. (par. 69) Most moralists take virtue as obedience to the law of a superior, by motives of self-interest, hope of reward and fear of punishment. But Shaftesbury supposes "an immediate natural Good in the Actions called Virtuous; that is, that we are determined to perceive some Beauty in the Actions of others, and to love the Agents, even without reflecting upon any Advantage which can any way redound to us from the Action." Hutcheson proposes to prove,

I. "That some Actions have to Men an immediate Goodness; or, that by a Superior Sense, which I call a Moral one, we perceive Pleasure in the Contemplation of such Actions in others, and are determined to love the Agent, (and much more do we perceive Pleasure in being conscious of having done such Actions ourselves) without any View of further natural Advantage from them."

II. It may perhaps also appear, "That what excites us to these Actions which we call Virtuous, is not an Intention to obtain even this sensible Pleasure; much less the future Rewards from Sanctions of Laws, or any other natural Good, which may be the Consequence of the virtuous Action; but an entirely different Principle of Action from Interest or Self-Love." (pars. 69, 71, 72)

These are Hutcheson's two problems: what is the source of moral insight, and what is the spring of moral action? The answer to both he calls that "internal sense" that is the moral sense, which is at one and the same time a feeling of approbation for actions and dispositions that conduce to the public good, and a passion or drive impelling us toward such benevolence. Like every sense, the moral sense is also a power—a more recent psychology would say, the internal senses, like the external ones, are stimuli to action and not purely passive.[3] He also speaks of "the delightful consciousness which arises from the moral sense." [4]

Later in the *Inquiry*, when his utilitarian emphasis has grown stronger, Hutcheson states his aim, "Now the principal Business

[3] Cf.: "This moral sense from its very nature appears to be designed for regulating and controlling all our powers. This dignity and commanding nature we are immediately conscious of, as we are conscious of the *power* itself. Nor can such matters of immediate feeling be otherwise proved but by appeals to our hearts." (*System of Moral Philosophy*, 1st ed., 1755, Book I, sec. vi; Selby-Bigge, par. 472) See also: "To each of our powers we seem to have a corresponding taste or sense commending the proper use of it to the agent, and making him relish or value the like exercise of it by another." (*System*, I, 66)

[4] *Inquiry*, ed. Selby-Bigge, par. 174.

of the Moral Philosopher is to show, from solid Reasons, 'That universal Benevolence tends to the Happiness of the Benevolent.' " (par. 168) And in discussing particular problems he becomes a pure utilitarian.

Hutcheson begins the *Inquiry* proper by distinguishing between moral and natural good, or advantage. "We are all conscious of the Difference between that Love and Esteem, or Perception of moral Excellence, which Benevolence excites toward the Person in whom we observe it, and that Opinion of natural Goodness, which only raises Desire of Possession toward the good Object." The distinction would be meaningless if goodness were merely natural advantage. Actually, we can often perceive moral goodness in actions that are against our interest, as in the liberators of Holland from Spain who raised it up to be a dangerous trade rival to Britain.

We must then certainly have other Perceptions of moral Actions than those of Advantage; and that Power of receiving these Perceptions may be called a "Moral Sense," since the Definition agrees to it, viz., a Determination of the Mind, to receive any Idea from the Presence of an Object which occurs to us, independent on our Will. . . . As the Author of Nature has determined us to receive, by our external Senses, pleasant or disagreeable Ideas of Objects, according as they are useful or hurtful to our Bodies; and to receive from uniform Objects the Pleasures of Beauty and Harmony, to excite us to the Pursuit of Knowledge, and to reward us for it: . . . in the same Manner he has given us a "Moral Sense," to direct our Actions, and to give us still nobler Pleasures; so that while we are only intending the Good of others, we "undesignedly promote our own greatest private good." (pars. 74, 87)

Some moralists of self-love hold, that whatever profits one part profits the whole. It is rather the other way round: what profits the whole profits the part. Nor again is the belief in future rewards and punishments at all correlated with virtuous action.

Turning toward the springs of action that motivate virtuous deeds, Hutcheson remarks: "Every Action, which we apprehend as either morally good or evil, is always supposed to flow from some Affection toward rational Agents; and whatever we call Virtue or Vice, is either some such Affection, or some Action consequent upon it." (par. 89) None of these affections springs from self-love. Love of complacence, esteem, or good-liking, clearly does not. Nor does love of benevolence. As all men have self-love as well as benevolence, these two principles may jointly excite a man to the same action; the observer can never be sure which is stronger. The self-love, however, does not produce the esteem, but the other ingredient. Benevolence is rooted in the "very frame of our nature," as an instinct to study the good of others. Hutcheson gives various types, like parental love. On patriotism, which he does not take individualistically as "the last refuge of scoundrels," he says:

Here we may transiently remark the Foundation of what we call national Love, or Love of one's native Country. Whatever Place we have lived in for any considerable Time, there we have most distinctly remarked the various Affections of human Nature; we have known many lovely Characters; we remember the Associations, Friendships, Families, natural Affections, and other human Sentiments; our moral Sense determines us to approve these lovely Dispositions where we have most distinctly observed them; and our Benevolence concerns us in the Interests of the Persons possessed of them. When we come to observe the like as distinctly in another country, we begin to acquire a national Love toward it also; nor has our own Country any other Preference in our Idea, unless it be by an Association of the pleasant Ideas of our youth, with the Buildings, Fields, and Woods where we received them. (par. 109)

Hutcheson, with none of Butler's reservation, holds that "the sense of virtue, and the various opinion about it, are reducible to one general foundation. . . . They always appear as benevolent, or flowing from love of others, and a study of their happiness." (sec. III, heading; par. 110) In all sects and parties, "this is still allowed to be the way of deciding the Controversy about any disputed Practice, viz., to enquire whether this Conduct, or the contrary, will most effectually promote the public good." "There is a universal Determination to Benevolence in Mankind, even toward the most distant parts of the Species. But we are not to imagine that this Benevolence is equal, or in the same degree toward all." (par. 145) There is no universal determination to evil, "when it is conceived no way useful to our Interests." "The ordinary Springs of Vice among men, must be a mistaken Self-Love, made so violent as to overcome Benevolence." (pars. 114–15) Hutcheson has clearly rejected the Calvinism of his youth and of the ministers he was combatting. He has adopted Shaftesbury's view, that "every moral agent justly considers himself as a Part of this rational System, which may be useful to the Whole; so that he may be, in part, an Object of his own Benevolence." (par. 117)

In the full swing of his utilitarianism, Hutcheson goes on to state the Principle of Utility itself:

The Virtue is as the Quantity of the Happiness, or natural Good. . . . In the same Manner, the moral Evil or Vice is as the Degree of Misery, and Number of Sufferers; so that, that Action is Best, which procures *the greatest Happiness for the greatest Numbers;* and that, worst, which, in like manner occasions Misery. (par. 121)

Bentham tells [5] that he first thought of the principle on reading Joseph Priestley's *Treatise on Government.* But Hutcheson can clearly claim the right of priority. He goes on to develop an elaborate mathematical calculus of Benevolence, Self-Love, and "abilities," to figure the public and private good. After pages of this, he remarks, "The applying a mathematical calculation to moral Subjects, will appear perhaps at first extravagant and wild," [6] and then continues with the corollaries. This moral calculation seems to him an excellent illustration of the role of reason and the passions in virtue, in which Hume followed him:

I know not for what Reason some will not allow that to be Virtue, which flows from Instincts, or Passions; but how do they help themselves? They say, "Virtue arises from Reason." What is Reason but that Sagacity we have in prosecuting any End? The ultimate End proposed by the common Moralists is the Happiness of the Agent himself, and this certainly he is determined to pursue from Instinct. Now may not another Instinct toward the Publick, or the Good of others, be as proper a Principle of Virtue, as the Instinct toward private Happiness? And is there not the same Occasion for the Exercise of our Reason in pursuing the former, as the latter? [7]

Hutcheson later goes so far as to reduce natural law to the utilitarian principle. A precept of the Law of Nature is "no more than a conclusion from observation of what sort of conduct is ordinarily useful to society." [8]

Hutcheson frankly confronts "the vast Diversity of moral Principles, in various Nations, and Ages; which is indeed a good Argument against innate Ideas, but will not evidence Mankind to be void

[5] *Works*, ed. Bowring, X, 79–80.   [6] *Inquiry*, ed. Selby-Bigge, par. 132.
[7] *Inquiry*, ed. Selby-Bigge, par. 130.
[8] *System of Moral Philosophy*, I, 273.

of a moral Sense to perceive Virtue or Vice in Actions." He attributes this variation to different opinions of happiness and of the most effectual means to advance it. Even the most revolting reports of customs point to action taken "under some Appearance of Benevolence." There is secondly the diversity of systems to which men from foolish opinions confine their benevolence. There are also the false opinions of the will or laws of the Deity. In general, the variety is "not owing to any irregularity in the moral sense, but to a wrong judgment or opinion." [9]

Hutcheson tries to deduce the ideas of obligation and right from the moral sense, as against those claiming their origin in the law of a superior. He distinguishes the senses of the word "obligation."

If by Obligation we understand a Determination, without regard to our own Interest, to approve Actions, and to perform them; which Determination shall also make us displeased with ourselves, and uneasy upon having acted contrary to it; in this meaning of the word "obligation," there is naturally an Obligation upon all Men to Benevolence. . . . But if by Obligation, we understand a Motive from Self-Interest, sufficient to determine all those who duly consider it, and pursue their own Advantage wisely, to a certain Course of Actions; we may have a Sense of such an Obligation, by reflecting on this Determination of our Nature to approve Virtue, to be pleased and happy when we reflect upon our having done virtuous Actions, and to be uneasy when we are conscious of having acted otherwise; and also by considering how much superior we esteem the Happiness of Virtue to any other Enjoyment. (pars. 166, 167)

Even the laws of God are just and holy and good, not because they are his commands—"that must be an insignificant Tautology, amounting to no more than this, 'that God wills what he wills' "— but because there is something in his actions which is absolutely good, and is so apprehended by the moral sense.

The Deity is called good, in a moral sense, when we apprehend that his whole Providence tends to the universal Happiness of his Creatures; whence we conclude his Benevolence, and Delight in their Happiness. (par. 173)

Even God has a moral sense, judges Hutcheson. "Why may not the Deity have something of a superior Kind, analogous to our moral Sense, essential to him?" [10]

[9] *Inquiry*, ed. Selby-Bigge, pars. 136, 137, 139, 142.
[10] *Illustrations upon the Moral Sense*, ed. Selby-Bigge, par. 459.

Hutcheson goes on to deduce the complex moral idea of "rights" from the moral sense. "Whenever it appears to us, that a Faculty of doing, demanding, or possessing any thing, universally allowed in certain Circumstances, would in the Whole tend to the general Good, we say that any Person in such Circumstances, has a Right to do, possess, or demand that Thing." "The Rights called perfect, are of such Necessity to the public Good, that the universal Violation of them would make human Life intolerable . . . Imperfect Rights are such as, when universally violated, would not necessarily make men miserable." (pars. 175, 176) Inalienable rights are those it is not in our power to transfer, like "the Right of private Judgment, or of our inward Sentiments," or, "our Right of serving God, in the manner which we think acceptable." (par. 179)

Hutcheson founds the right of private property on the social good. "A necessity arises, . . . that such a Tenor of Conduct be observed, as shall most effectually promote Industry. . . . The depriving any Person, of the Fruits of his own innocent Labor, takes away all Motives to Industry from Self-love, or the nearer Ties: . . . nay, it exposes the Industrious as a constant Prey to the Slothful, and sets Self-love against Industry. This is the Ground of our Right of Dominion and Property in the fruits of our Labors, without which Right, we could scarce hope for any Industry, or any thing beyond the Product of uncultivated Nature." (par. 180) Hutcheson's ideas on economics were very influential in molding the approach of his pupil Adam Smith.

His *An Essay on the Passions* (1728) continues the theory of the *Inquiry*, but overlays it with ideas borrowed from Butler. It attempts to classify and order the springs of action, and clarifies ideas left vague in the *Inquiry*. It starts by pointing to our "Multitudes of Perceptions which have no relation to any external Sensation," and which are simple and immediate. Locke should not have reduced his "ideas of Reflection" merely to "reflex Acts upon external Sensations"; speaking of "internal Sensation," he should have just "as carefully examined into the several kinds of internal Perceptions," as he did into the external sensations.[11]

There are then five classes of "senses," defined as

---

[11] *An Essay on the Nature and Conduct of the Passions and Affections* (1728), in Selby-Bigge, par. 431.

determinations of our Minds to receive Ideas independently of our Will, and to have Perceptions of Pleasure and Pain: the External Senses, universally known; secondly, the pleasant Perceptions arising from regular, harmonious, uniform Objects; as also from Grandeur and Novelty. These we may call, after Mr. Addison, the Pleasures of the Imagination; or we may call the Power of receiving them, an Internal Sense. Whoever dislikes this Name may substitute another. Thirdly, the next class of Perceptions we may call a Publick Sense, viz., 'our Determination to be pleased with the Happiness of others, and to be uneasy at their Misery.' This . . . was sometimes called *Sensus Communis* by some of the Ancients. . . . [It is] an inward Pain of Compassion. . . . The fourth Class we may call the Moral Sense, by which 'we perceive Virtue or Vice, in ourselves, or others.' This is plainly distinct from the former Class of Perceptions, since many are strongly affected with the Fortunes of others, who seldom reflect upon Virtue or Vice, in themselves or others, as an Object: as we may find in natural Affection, Compassion, Friendship, or even general Benevolence to Mankind, which connect our Happiness or Pleasure with that of others, even when we are not reflecting upon our own Temper, nor delighted with the Perception of our own Virtue. The fifth Class is a Sense of Honor, which makes the Approbation, or Gratitude of others, for any good Actions we have done, the necessary occasion of pleasure; and their Dislike, Condemnation, or Resentment of Injuries done by us, the occasion of that uneasy Sensation called Shame, even when we fear no further Evil from them. (par. 433)

There are other perceptions in human nature; there are also desires, which "arise in the Frame of our Nature, upon Apprehension of Good or Evil in Objects, Actions, or Events." These are divided into "original Desires," which fall into five Classes; and "secondary Desires," of everything that can gratify the original desires. It is argued, that "no Desire of any event is excited by any view of removing the uneasy Sensation attending the Desire itself." The uneasy sensations will raise a desire of what will remove them; the desire is for that thing, not the removal. Likewise, there is a sensation of joy that attends the gratification of any desire. But "Desire does never arise from a view of obtaining that Sensation of Joy, connected with the Success or Gratification of Desire." It is for the object whose attainment will bring joy. Hutcheson is restating Butler's psychology of determinate desires. (pars. 435, 437) Thus benevolence is a desire for the happiness of others, not for the pleasure that happiness will give us. Hedonism is a false psychology: desires are specific and disinterested.

The Occasion of the imagined Difficulty in conceiving disinterested Desires has probably been from the attempting to define this simple idea, Desire. It is called an uneasy Sensation in the absence of good [Locke]. Whereas Desire is as distinct from any Sensation, as the Will is from the Understanding or Senses. This everyone must acknowledge, who speaks of desiring to remove Uneasiness or Pain. (par. 441)

Hutcheson follows Butler in distinguishing between

the calm Desire of Good, and Aversion to Evil, either selfish or publick, as they appear to our Reason or Reflection; and the particular Passions towards Objects immediately presented to some Sense. (par. 442)

He identifies the former with the Scholastic *Appetitus rationalis,* or *boulēsis,* and the latter with the *Appetitus sensitivus. Appetitus rationalis* is found only in men, and is a " 'constant natural Disposition of Soul to desire what the Understanding, or these sublimer Sensations, represent as Good, and to shun what they represent as Evil, and this either when it respects ourselves or others.' This many call the Will as distinct from the Passions." (par. 442n.)

In the companion treatise, *Illustrations upon the Moral Sense,* Hutcheson distinguishes between "election" or decision, and approbation. "The Qualities moving to Election, or exciting to Action, are different from those moving to Approbation." [12] He asks, what do we mean by saying, a moral decision or a moral judgment is "agreeable to reason"? Reasonableness, whether a motive to election, or the quality determining approbation, is a very common but very confused expression. It cannot here mean "conformity to true propositions." And not reason, but passion, is always the motive:

As to exciting Reasons, in every calm rational Action some end is desired or intended; no end can be intended or desired previously to some one of these Classes of Affections, Self-Love, Self-Hatred, or desire of private Misery (if this be possible), Benevolence toward others, or Malice: all Affections are included under these: no end can be previous to them all; there can therefore be no exciting Reason previous to Affection. (par. 449)

To the common objection, no act is good not excited by reason, he replies: "As if indeed Reason, or the Knowledge of the Relations of things, could excite to Action when we proposed no End, or as if Ends could be intended without Desire or Affection." (par. 449)

[12] *Illustrations upon the Moral Sense* (1728), in Selby-Bigge, par. 447.

Hutcheson is consciously following the Schoolmen and Aristotle in the conclusion he transmitted to Hume. There are four faculties of the soul, Reason, Will or *Appetitus rationalis*, *Sensus*, and *Appetitus sensitivus*.

Aristotle long ago answered, 'that there are ultimate Ends desired without a view to anything else, and subordinate Ends or Objects desired with a view to something else.' To subordinate Ends those reasons or Truths excite, which show them to be conducive to the ultimate End, and show one Object to be more effectual than another: thus subordinate Ends may be called reasonable. But as to the ultimate Ends, to suppose exciting Reasons for them, would infer, that there is no ultimate End, but that we desire one thing for another in an infinite Series. (par. 451)

There is in fact, Hutcheson insists, in his emphasis on specific and determinate desires, no infinite Good, no greatest possible aggregate of Happiness, no one great ultimate End of human action, no "system of rationals." Even the desire for the greatest quantity of happiness for mankind cannot be an "exciting reason" or motive; it presupposes public affections. By anticipation, Comte was wrong.

Secondly, with the approbation of actions, with moral judgments rather than motives, what does it mean to be reasonable? In what sense are "justifying reasons" "conformable to reason"? Again, being reasonable here cannot mean being conformable to a true proposition. "The justifying Reasons then must be about the Ends themselves, especially the ultimate Ends. . . . For example, we approve pursuing the publick Good. For what Reason? Or what is the Truth for Conformity to which we call it a reasonable End? I fancy we can find none in these Cases, more than we could give for our liking any pleasant Fruit." (par. 454)

Reason deals with means, not with ends.

We may transiently observe what has occasioned the Use of the Word reasonable as an epithet of only virtuous Actions, though we have Instincts determining us to desire Ends, without supposing any previous Reasoning; yet it is by Use of our Reason that we find out the Means of obtaining our Ends. When we do not use our Reason, we often are disappointed of our End. We therefore call those Actions which are effectual to their Ends, in one Sense reasonable of that word. . . . We are convinced by our Reason, that it is by publickly useful Actions alone that we can promote all our Ends. (par. 456)

True, we judge all our senses by reason, and correct them. "Just so a compassionate Temper may rashly imagine the Correction of a Child, or the Execution of a Criminal, to be cruel and inhuman: but by reasoning may discover the superior Good arising from them in the whole; and then the same moral Sense may determine the Observer to approve them." (par. 458) Thus like any other sense the moral sense is subject to correction and modification by reason. Again, there is often a conflict between passion and reason when our particular desires, grown violent and passionate, make us incapable of considering calmly the whole tendency of our actions.

This indeed may give some ground for distinguishing between passionate Actions and those from calm Desire or Affection which employs our Reason freely: but can never set rational Actions in Opposition to those from Instinct, Desire or Affection. (par. 461)

How do we know that our affections are right when they are kind? What does the word "right" mean? Does it mean what we approve? This we know by consciousness of our sense. How do we know that our sense is right, or that we approve our approbation? This can only be answered by another question, How do we know we are pleased when we are pleased? Or does it mean, "how do we know that we shall always approve what we now approve?" We must first know that the same constitution of our moral sense shall always remain. Of its continuance we are as sure as of the continuance of gravitation, or any other law of nature. And finally, may not the moral sense become diseased? To be sure. But "we do not denominate Objects from our Perceptions during the Disorder, but according to our ordinary Perceptions, or those of others in good Health." (par. 465) But this moral sense is not a rule. No, the understanding has to construct rules by reflecting upon it. "But what Rule of Actions can be formed, without Relation to some End proposed? Or what End can be proposed, without presupposing Instincts, Desires, Affections, or a moral Sense, it will not be easy to explain." (par. 467) Hutcheson concludes his discussion of the relation of reason to the passions, "Thus there seems no part of that Reasoning which was ever used by Moralists, to be superseded by supposing a moral Sense." (par. 464)

From Hutcheson's letters we gather the *System of Moral Philoso-*

phy was completed in 1737; the next year he issued the extensively revised fourth edition of the *Inquiry*. During his Glasgow period he was subjected to much criticism both from the egoists, whom he was prepared to combat, and the rational moralists, whom he was not. They satirized his moral sense as a mere instinct. In the third stage of his thinking he tried to defend himself by turning to the Greeks, who were having a revival at Glasgow under Dunlop; he himself began to lecture on ancient philosophy, and came under the strong influence of Aristotle, as well as the Roman Stoics. The moral sense becomes the "moral faculty," and calm self-love becomes "the will." There is an inconsistent development of the passivity of the mind in "reflection"—the Lockean element—and the perfected activity of its powers, their *energeia kat' aretēn*—the Aristotelian element. In his elaborate analysis of human nature he employs both the spectator or observer conception for the internal senses, and the Aristotelian functionalism for the affections and desires. Excellence of function replaces "the good" as the end of action, the ideal of individual perfection becomes an alternative for the highest self-love or desire for happiness. It can hardly be said that this complex texture of themes is satisfactorily woven together, and the *System* played little role in the rising tide of utilitarian ethics.

Hutcheson's Aristotelianism comes out:

> The *proairesis* which is necessary to virtuous actions is *orexis bouleutikē*; and virtue needs not only the *logon alēthē* but the *orexin orthēn*. These very authors who deny any motions or affections of the will to be the proper springs of sublime Virtue, yet, inconsistently with themselves, must allow in men of sublime virtue, and even in the Deity too, a settled disposition of Will.[13]

> The calm self-love, or the determination of each individual toward his own happiness, is a motion of the will without any uneasy sensation attending it. But the several selfish desires, terminating on particular objects, are generally attended with some uneasy turbulent sensations in very different degrees: yet these sensations are different from the act of the will to which they are conjoined; and different too from the motives of desire. The motive is some good, apprehended in an object or event, toward which good the desire tends; and in consequence of desire, some uneasiness arises till the good is obtained. . . . It would be absurd to say that this joy in the success was the motive to the desire. . . . 'Tis trifling therefore to say

---

[13] *Inquiry*, 4th ed. (1738), p. 195n.

that all desires are selfish, because by gratifying them we obtain the joy of success, and free ourselves from the uneasy feelings of desire.[14]

This is very close to Aristotle's analysis of *orexis* or desire, and of the soul as mover.

Hutcheson now has reservations about the utilitarian criterion.

The *righteousness* or *goodness* of actions is not indeed the same notion with *their tendency to universal happiness*, or flowing from the desire of it. This latter is the highest species of the former. Our *moral sense* has also other immediate objects of approbation, many narrower affections, which we must immediately approve without thinking of their tendency to the interest of a system. (par. 480)

Still, he undertakes an elaborate examination and classification of the varieties of pleasure. Their respective dignity and worth depend upon their "intenseness" and duration. He also examines the difference in men's tastes for enjoyment. Pleasures differ in quality, in dignity, and in importance. The superior orders in this world probably experience all the sensations of the lower orders, and can judge of them. But the inferior do not experience the enjoyment of the superior: "Of mankind these certainly are the best judges who have full experience, with their tastes or senses and appetites in a natural vigorous state." (par. 478) Hutcheson has passed from his hedonistic calculus to qualitative differences in pleasure; he has traveled from Bentham to J. S. Mill.

The disposition which is most excellent, and naturally gains the highest moral approbation, is the calm, stable, universal good-will to all, or the most extensive benevolence. And this seems the most distinct notion we can form of the moral excellency of the Deity. (par. 474)

Starting from the moral intuitionism of Shaftesbury, Hutcheson was driven further and further to utilitarianism. In his earlier works, dating from his Dublin stay, he uses two standards—the approval of the moral sense, and the public good; he uses them indifferently, because he is convinced of their absolute identity. In the light of criticism, during his Glasgow teaching he tried to reconstruct and combine them both in terms of a third standard, the Aristotelian perfected functioning of man's natural powers.

[14] *A System of Moral Philosophy* (1755); Selby-Bigge, par. 471.

II

If Hume's moral theory be really very simple, especially in the *Enquiry*, after he had ceased to follow the false scent of his elaborate mechanism of association—even if not so blunt and uncompromising as that of Hobbes—the moral philosophy of the last great Scottish moralist of the sentiments, before common sense conquered Scotland and utilitarianism England, Adam Smith (1723–1790), is intricate and complicated. He is fascinated to observe the working of the mechanism of human nature, an elaborate machine designed by nature to produce human happiness, and to trace the interactions of its passions. Starting with an analysis of the particular qualities of the various moral sentiments, a task Hume had failed to undertake, Smith finds no need to assume a specific moral sense, like his teacher, Hutcheson; with his friend Hume, he thinks sympathy will carry a man beyond self-regarding impulses. Where Butler had made "conscience" the final arbitrator of the passions, and Hutcheson the moral sense, Smith finds that "impartial spectator" of our own actions, that ideal observer with whom by sympathy we can identify one of our two selves, the one the judge of the actions of the other, the agent. This impartial spectator started for Smith as largely a projection of the moral "imagination," a mythical judge. But as he revised his ideas this ideal judge became an inner reality, the very essence of what Butler had called "conscience," a genuine personal possession though a product of sympathy. With such an arbiter of one's own merit, Smith passed from his initial morality of propriety, prudence, and especially benevolence, to an ethic of "self-command." Starting with Hutcheson and Butler, he ended with a psychological and socialized version of the Stoic ethics. Self-command and freedom meant for him, in ethics and jurisprudence, self-reliance, "let us act for ourselves, a better general maxim than, Guard us, help us, ye mighty." They meant, in other words, laissez-faire, which he made the basis of his philosophical study of the natural laws of prudence, and of a social art of self-command, in his *Wealth of Nations*.[15]

[15] For a perceptive and suggestive statement of the development of Smith's thought from Hutcheson, his teacher, to the Stoicism of his final ethic of self-command and self-reliance, see *Adam Smith's Moral and Political Philosophy*, ed. Herbert W. Schneider (1948), Introduction. Schneider's account is being largely followed here.

Adam Smith was born at Kirkcaldy, near Edinburgh. He attended the University of Glasgow at fourteen, and studied under Hutcheson, in preparation for the ministry. In 1740 he was sent to prepare for orders at Oxford, but seems to have studied instead rhetoric and *belles-lettres* for six years. He returned to Edinburgh, and from 1747 to 1749 gave public lectures "On Taste, Composition, and the History of Philosophy." In 1751 he was elected to the chair of Logic in his university of Glasgow; the next year he became Professor of Moral Philosophy, taking over Hutcheson's old chair. In 1759, his *The Theory of the Moral Sentiments* (1759) made him overnight one of the leaders of the now flourishing Scottish Enlightenment. In it he tried to exhibit his literary skill as a student of rhetoric; to its rhetorical quality it owed its immediate popularity. In 1764 he resigned his professorship to accompany the young Duke of Buccleuch to France, where they traveled, like Hume, for over two years. He was there received into the society of the Physiocrats; he had already lectured on political economy at Glasgow as part of his duties as teacher of jurisprudence, a branch of moral philosophy. He was enthusiastic about the Physiocrats' objection to mercantilism and their approval of commercial freedom; he did not share their notion that agriculture is the sole source of wealth, and their consequent advocacy of a single tax on land. At Toulouse he started his book on "objective prudence," *The Wealth of Nations;* only Quesnay's death prevented a dedication to him. Smith finished the book at home with his mother at Kirkcaldy, issuing it in 1776. In 1778 he moved to Edinburgh as commissioner of customs, and lived there in the philosophical and literary circle till his death in 1790.

At Glasgow Smith followed the curriculum in moral philosophy set up by Hutcheson, which became standard in the Scottish universities for several generations. It had four parts: Natural Theology, Ethics, Jurisprudence, and Political Economy. We have nothing of his lectures on Natural Theology; he burned his notes before his death, to avoid theological polemic. Smith was an optimistic Deist like his teacher, with a faith in natural law and natural religion. He refused to heed his friend Hume's request to publish the *Dialogues concerning Natural Religion* after the author's death. There is evidence that he tried to give a rational interpretation of the Calvinistic doctrines, like the atonement. His whole ethics and political economy rest on the Deistic faith in "the unseen hand." Smith's *Lectures on Justice, Police* (policy), *Revenue, and Arms,*[16] that is, on Jurisprudence, have been preserved in students' notes. Jurisprudence for Smith is the objective analysis of "the natural laws or principles of private and public social order." It deals legally and institutionally with what ethics deals with in terms of psychology and inner sentiment, just as political economy is the objective analysis of prudence. The psychological analysis of propriety, benevolence, justice, and prudence, is treated in *The Theory of Moral Sentiments;* for the "natural law" of these virtues, we must resort to jurisprudence and political economy. The two approaches are complementary. *The Wealth of Nations* is thus not founded on the psychological motive of self-interest, or on a theory of "natural wants." Smith rested his case for self-command in production on man's "constant effort to better his own condition," and on his "tendency to barter," both expressions of self-reliance. Competition he took to be not a type of struggle, but a positive interest in "improvement." *The Wealth of Nations* was a treatise, not on the national welfare, nor on the greatest public happiness, but on "public opulence." [17]

The Theory of Moral Sentiments (1759) is Adam Smith's contribution to the psychological analysis that is "ethics strictly so called." In the last year of his life he issued an extensively revised version, the sixth edition of 1790, in which he added a long historical account of previous systems of ethics and related his own to them (Part VII), and the whole of Part VI, culminating in the section on "self-command." [18] The historical survey starts:

In treating of the principles of morals, there are two questions to be considered. First, wherein does virtue consist, or what is the tone of temper and tenor of conduct which constitutes the excellent and praiseworthy character? And, secondly, by what power or faculty in the mind is it that this character, whatever it is, is recommended to us?

[16] Critical edition, by Edwin Cannan (1896).

[17] *A Treatise on Public Opulence,* an early draft of the *Wealth of Nations,* dating from early 1764, before Smith went to France, was first published by W. R. Scott in his *Adam Smith as Student and Professor* (1937).

[18] Walther Eckstein's German tr. of the *Moral Sentiments* (2 vols., 1926) gives the best account of the changes in the successive revisions.

These are the two questions of the *nature* of the *disposition* that is morally approved, and of the *basis* of *moral judgments*. As to the first question, excellence of character has been identified with propriety, with prudence, and with disinterested benevolence. "1. According to some, the virtuous temper of mind does not consist in any one species of affections, but in the proper government and direction of all our affections. . . . Virtue consists in propriety. 2. According to others, virtue consists in the judicious pursuit of our own private interest and happiness. . . . Virtue consists in prudence. 3. Another set of authors make virtue consist in those affections only which aim at the happiness of others. . . . Disinterested benevolence is the only motive" that can make an action virtuous. The three possibilities are, the adjustment of all the affections; or the selfish, or the benevolent affections, the two major classes.

"According to Plato, to Aristotle, and to Zeno, virtue consists in the propriety of conduct, or in the suitableness of the affection from which we act to the object which excites it." Smith devotes over twice the space to discussing the Stoics as to Plato and Aristotle combined. What attracts him to Stoicism is the fact that "The Stoical wise man endeavored to enter into the views of the great Superintendent of the universe and to see things in the same light in which that divine Being beheld them." The Stoic faith in the benevolence of Nature suits his Deistic optimism. But he concludes,

The plan and system which nature has sketched out for our conduct seems to be altogether different from that of the Stoical philosophy. . . . Nature has not prescribed to us this sublime contemplation as the great business and occupation of our lives. She only points it out to us as the consolation of our misfortunes. The Stoical philosophy prescribes it as the great business and occupation of our lives.

Among moderns, Dr. Clarke, Mr. Wollaston, and my Lord Shaftesbury all held that virtue consists in propriety, in the suitableness of the affection from which we act. But none gives any "precise or distinct measure" by which propriety of affection can be ascertained or judged.[19]

The philosophy that puts virtue in prudence, or the pursuit of private interest and happiness, is Epicurus' (Cicero's *De Finibus* and

[19] *Adam Smith*, ed. Schneider, pp. 8–9, 22, 25, 27.

Diogenes Laertios are followed here, as with the previous ancients). Epicurus unduly simplified matters through indulging a propensity ingenious philosophers are prone to: "the propensity to account for all appearances from as few principles as possible."

The philosophy that identifies virtue with benevolence includes the later Platonists, and the Cambridge Platonists Cudworth, Henry More, and John Smith: "But of all the patrons of this system, ancient or modern, the late Dr. Hutcheson was undoubtedly, beyond all comparison, the most acute, the most distinct, the most philosophical, and, what is of the greatest consequence of all, the soberest and most judicious." Smith concludes:

Benevolence may, perhaps, be the sole principle of action in the Deity. . . . It is not easy to conceive what other motive an independent and all-perfect Being, who stands in need of nothing external and whose happiness is complete in himself, can act from. But whatever may be the case with the Deity, so imperfect a creature as man, the support of whose existence requires so many things external to him, must often act from many other motives.

Besides these three systems for distinguishing virtue from vice, there are also "licentious systems" which fail to make the distinction. The great example is Mandeville, clearly Smith's *bête noire*. Smith was in lifelong revolt against the Calvinists' conception of the corruption of human nature, which Mandeville was trying to put on a rational basis. "It is the great fallacy of Dr. Mandeville's book to represent every passion as wholly vicious, which is so in any degree and any direction." [20]

As to the second main question, there are also three classes of views on the issue of the basis of moral judgments of approbation: those who hit on self-love, or the tendency to our own happiness, those who uphold reason, by which we distinguish truth and falsehood, and those who choose immediate sentiment and feeling. "I must observe that the determination of this second question, though of the greatest importance in speculation, is of none in practice."

Hobbes rather confusedly supports self-love as the source of moral approbation, but "sympathy cannot in any sense be regarded as a selfish principle." Hobbes's views are not only peculiarly offensive to all theologians because of his Erastianism; they are likewise "of-

[20] *Sentiments*, ed. Schneider, pp. 33, 35, 39–40, 48.

fensive to all sound moralists, as [they] supposed that there was no natural distinction between right and wrong, but these were mutable and changeable, and depended upon the mere arbitrary will of the civil magistrate." Cudworth is the great proponent of reason as the organ of moral judgment. "Dr. Hutcheson had the merit of being the first who distinguished with any degree of precision in what respect all moral distinctions may be said to arise from reason, and in what respect they are founded on immediate sense and feeling." Further dispute can come only from inattention to his analysis, or from "a superstitious attachment to certain forms of expression."

Those systems which make sentiment the principle of approbation are of two sorts: 1) those which found it upon a sentiment of a peculiar nature, upon a particular power of perceiving, the moral sense; and 2) those which find "no occasion for supposing any new power of perception which had never been heard of before. . . . Sympathy, a power which has always been taken notice of, . . . is . . . sufficient to account for all the effects ascribed to this peculiar faculty." Here Smith disagrees with his revered teacher. He states his own "system":

When we approve of any character or action, the sentiments which we feel are . . . derived from four sources which are in some respects different from one another. First, we sympathize with the motives of the agent; secondly, we enter into the gratitude of those who receive the benefit of his actions; thirdly, we observe that his conduct has been agreeable to the general rules by which those two sympathies generally act; and, last of all, when we consider such actions as making a part of a system of behavior which tends to promote the happiness either of the individual or of the society, they appear to derive a beauty from this utility not unlike that which we ascribe to any well-contrived machine.

There is another system from Smith's, which likewise derives the moral sentiments from sympathy. "It places virtue in utility, and accounts for the pleasure with which the spectator surveys the utility of any quality from sympathy with the happiness of those who are affected by it. . . . This sympathy is different both from that by which we enter into the motives of the agent, and from that by which we go along with the gratitude of the persons who are benefited by his actions. . . . But no machine can be the object of either of those two last mentioned sympathies." (pp. 51, 53, 55, 57–58, 64–65)

Sympathy is thus the basis of the sense of propriety. In it, we conceive what we ourselves should feel in the like situation. By imagination, based upon the impressions given by our own senses of the situation of the other, we place ourselves in his situation. It is not the other's feelings, but his situation that excites those feelings, that gives rise to sympathy. Thus we can sympathise with the dead, who have no feelings themselves. Thus the way in which we judge of the propriety of the affections of other men, Smith states:

When the original passions of the person principally concerned are in perfect concord with the sympathetic emotions of the spectator, they necessarily appear to this last just and proper, and suitable to their objects; and, on the contrary, when on bringing the case home to himself, he finds that they do not coincide with what he feels, they necessarily appear to him unjust and improper, and unsuitable to the causes which excite them. To approve of the passions of another, therefore, as suitable to their objects, is the same thing as to observe that we entirely sympathize with them.

In the same way, "to approve of another man's opinions is to adopt those opinions, and to adopt them is to approve of them." (pp. 78–79)

Thus there is built up through sympathy the ability to take each other's place, to see ourselves as others see us (Burns too was a Scot):

In order to produce this concord, as nature teaches the spectators to assume the circumstances of the person principally concerned, so she teaches this last in some measure to assume those of the spectators. As they are continually placing themselves in his situation, and thence conceiving emotions similar to what he feels, so he is as constantly placing himself in theirs, and thence conceiving some degree of that coolness about his own fortune with which he is sensible that they will view it. As they themselves are constantly considering what they themselves would feel if they actually were the sufferers, so he is constantly led to imagine in what manner he would be affected if he was only one of the spectators of his own situation. (p. 85)

It is on this basis that Smith works out his theory of justice as the point of view of the "impartial spectator" developed through self-judgment in every social being—"the man within the breast" that judges oneself and the justice of others.

There is another set of qualities ascribed to actions, distinct from their propriety or impropriety; these are merit and demerit, the qualities of deserving reward and of deserving punishment. In addition to sympathy with the sentiments of the agent, they involve also sympathy with the *gratitude* felt by the person benefited. But "we do not thoroughly and heartily sympathize with the gratitude of one man towards another, merely because this other has been the cause of his good fortune, unless he has been the cause of it from *motives* which we entirely go along with." When, however, to the gratitude of the recipient is joined "the propriety of the affections from which it proceeds," then "the love which we conceive for him upon his own account enhances and enlivens our fellow-feeling with the *gratitude* of those who owe their prosperity to his good conduct." Likewise, we cannot sympathize with the resentment of one who has been injured, unless the injurer acted from motives which we cannot enter into. Our sense of the *propriety* of an action comes from a "direct sympathy" with the motives of the agent. Our sense of its *merit* comes from an "indirect sympathy" with the gratitude of the recipient.

So, upon this account, the sense of merit seems to be a "compounded sentiment," and to be made up of two distinct emotions: a direct sympathy with the sentiments of the agent, and an indirect sympathy with the gratitude of those who receive the benefit of his action. (pp. 109–10)

With both propriety and merit, Smith has considered the origin and foundation of our judgments concerning the sentiments and conduct of others. In Part III, "Of the Foundation of our Judgments concerning our own Sentiments and Conduct, and of the Sense of Duty," he considers those of ourselves. Smith holds that our approbation or disapprobation of our own conduct and feelings is socially derived: we transfer the judgments we first pass upon others, by sympathy, to judgments upon ourselves. The principle of judging is "altogether the same."

We either approve or disapprove of our own conduct according as we feel that, when we place ourselves in the situation of another man and view it, as it were, with his eyes and from his station, we either can or cannot entirely enter into and sympathize with the sentiments and motives which influenced it.

We can never view our sentiments and motives unless we remove ourselves, as it were, from our own natural station, and endeavor to view them as at a certain distance from us. But we can do this in no other way than by endeavoring to view them with the eyes of other people, or as other people are likely to view them.

Could a man be brought up in complete solitariness, he could no more think of the moral qualities of his acts than he could of the beauty of his face; he would be provided with no mirror to bring either into view. "Bring him into society, and he is immediately provided with the mirror which he wanted before." "Our first moral criticisms are exercised upon the characters and conduct of other people; and we are all very forward to observe how each of these affects us."

But we soon learn that other people are equally frank with regard to our own. We become anxious to know how far we deserve their censure or applause, and whether to them we must necessarily appear those agreeable or disagreeable creatures which they represent us. We begin, upon this account, to examine our own passions and conduct, and to consider how these must appear to them, by considering how they would appear to us if in their situation. We suppose ourselves the spectators of our own behavior, and endeavor to imagine what effect it would, in this light, produce upon us. This is the only looking-glass by which we can, in some measure, with the eyes of other people, scrutinize our own conduct. If in this view it pleases us, we are tolerably satisfied.

Smith pushes his analysis of the social generation of self-awareness.

When I endeavor to examine my own conduct, when I endeavor to pass sentence upon it, and either to approve or condemn it, it is evident that, in all such cases, *I divide myself*, as it were, *into two persons;* and that I, the examiner and judge, represent a different character from that other I, the person whose conduct is examined into and judged of. The first is the spectator whose sentiments with regard to my own conduct I endeavor to enter into, by placing myself in his situation and by considering how it would appear to me when seen from that particular point of view. The second is the agent, the person whom I properly call myself, and of whose conduct, under the character of a spectator, I was endeavoring to form some opinion. The first is the judge; the second the person judged of. But that the judge should, in every respect, be the same with the person judged of, is as impossible as that the cause should, in every respect, be the same with the effect. (pp. 137-40)

Man not only loves praise, he loves to be praiseworthy; and he not only dreads blame, he dreads to be blameworthy. Smith traces the effects. "Nature, when she formed man for society, endowed him with an original desire to please, and an original aversion to offend his brethren."

But this desire of the approbation, and this aversion to the disapprobation of his brethren, would not alone have rendered him fit for that society for which he was made. Nature, accordingly, has endowed him not only with a desire of being approved of, but a desire of being what ought to be approved of, or of being what he himself approves of in other men. The first desire could only have made him wish to appear to be fit for society. The second was necessary in order to render him anxious to be really fit. The first could only have prompted him to the affectation of virtue, and to the concealment of vice. The second was necessary in order to inspire him with the real love of virtue, and with the real abhorrence of vice. (p. 144)

So far, for Smith virtue consists in agreeing with public opinion, in sympathizing with what the public's feelings approve.

The all-wise Author of nature has . . . taught man to respect the sentiments and judgments of his brethren, to be more or less pleased when they approve of his conduct, and to be more or less hurt when they disapprove of it. He has made man, if I may say so, the immediate judge of mankind; and has in this respect, as in many others, created him after his own image, and appointed him his vice-gerent upon earth to superintend the behavior of his brethren.

But public opinion is not the ultimate judge, it is only the court of first instance; there is a higher tribunal.

But though man has, in this manner, been rendered the immediate judge of mankind, he has been rendered so only in the first instance; and an appeal lies from his sentence to a much higher tribunal, to the tribunal of their own consciences, to that of the supposed impartial and well-informed spectator, to that of the man within the breast, the great judge and arbiter of their conduct.

These two tribunals are founded upon principles which are really different and distinct.

The jurisdiction of the man without is founded altogether in the desire of actual praise and in the aversion to actual blame. The jurisdiction of the man within is founded altogether in the desire of praiseworthiness and in the aversion to blameworthiness, in the desire of possessing those qualities and performing those actions which we love and admire in other people, and in the dread of those we hate and despise. But even "this demi-god within the breast" is partly of mortal though partly of immortal extraction. His judgment is perverted by the clamor of the man without. "We scarce dare to absolve ourselves when all our brethren appear loudly to condemn us." In such cases, the only consolation of humbled and afflicted man "lies in an appeal to a still higher tribunal, to that of the all-seeing Judge of the world, whose eye can never be deceived and whose judgments can never be perverted." "That there is a world to come where exact justice will be done to every man," is "a hope and expectation deeply rooted in human nature," which can alone support man under "the weakness and despondence of his own mind, under the perturbation and astonish-ment of the man within the breast whom nature has set up as, in this life, the great guardian not only of his innocence but of his tranquillity." Our happiness in this life is thus dependent on "a firm confidence in the rectitude of this great tribunal, before which his innocence is in due time to be declared." (pp. 156–58) But un-fortunately, this Supreme Court takes jurisdiction only in the other world, and it issues no declaratory judgments: Smith makes no reference to any revelation of what is Right.

Man has no ultimate standard of right and wrong. General rules are merely formulations of the manner in which sympathy habitually acts; they are convenient standards of reference, but not the ulti-mate foundations of morality. Utility is of strictly subordinate value. It is not the foundation of our sentiments, as Hume thought; for we praise a man for other reasons than those which lead us to praise "a chest of drawers," and the usefulness of a disposition is not the "first ground of approbation."

In the new section added only in 1790, the culmination of the moral life has become "self-command."

The man who acts according to the rules of perfect prudence, of strict justice, and of proper benevolence, may be said to be perfectly virtuous. But the most perfect knowledge of those rules will not alone enable him to act in this manner; his own passions are very apt to mislead him, some-times to drive him, and sometimes to seduce him, to violate all the rules which he himself, in all his sober and cool hours, approves of. The most perfect knowledge, if it is not supported by the most perfect self-com-mand, will not always enable him to do his duty. . . . Self-command is not only itself a great virtue, but from it all the other virtues seem to derive their principal lustre. . . .

But though the virtues of prudence, justice, and beneficence may, upon different occasions, be recommended to us almost equally by two different principles [concern for our own happiness, and concern for that of other people], those of self-command are, upon most occasions, principally and almost entirely recommended to us by one—by the sense of propriety, by regard to the sentiments of the supposed impartial spectator. (pp. 251, 255, 275)

For a man living in an "age of atomic individualism," Adam Smith has managed to work out a very socialized conception of the "origin" of moral judgment, obligation, and conscience. For some today, his "impartial spectator, the man within the breast," will suggest the biological version of a similar conception in George Herbert Mead. For others, it will be a reminder of Talcott Parson's "taking the role of the other." Still others will think of Hegel and the "divided consciousness." And some, surely, will exclaim, "Ah! the Super-Ego, of course." But all such comparisons, of course, leave out the fact that "the man within" can *criticize* public opinion: the mores are not always right. Perhaps the "impartial spectator," after all, was still a denizen of Scotland, and still closely related to the Presbyterian conscience of those lands, though now, at the hands of the brilliant Professor Smith, soon to voyage in France with the Duke of Buccleuch, become a man of the world—of the Scottish Enlightenment.

I I

Hume's System of Ethics

IN TURNING TO the greatest of the Scottish moralists, and indeed of all eighteenth-century British philosophers, David Hume, we encounter a thinker who, like Hutcheson, came out with the Aristotelian conclusion, "reason is, and ought only to be the slave of the passions." Hume arrived at Aristotle in his morals, like Hutcheson, on the basis of the Lockean view of human nature, though he was much more consistent in his moral philosophy than Locke himself ever managed to be. His peculiar problems, his conclusions, his very language, owe more to Hutcheson[1] than to any other predecessor—save possibly Carneades, whose views he found in Cicero.

[1] N. Kemp Smith concludes: "Book III of the *Treatise* is a masterly restatement, with a clarity and self-consistency beyond anything possible to Hutcheson, of Hutcheson's own main theses." Chief of these is that reason enters into the moral life only to calculate the means to ends determined by the passions. Hume like Hutcheson uses "passion" to cover all types of feeling, which Hume is apt to call "tastes or sentiments."

Kemp Smith also argues that Hume's "new scene of thought," which Hume describes in the letter to his physician of March or April, 1734, a few months prior to his settling in France to complete his *Treatise*, as having been "opened up to him" when he was about eighteen (1729), was occasioned by his reading of Hutcheson's *Illustrations* and *An Essay on the Passions*, which came out in 1728. If the fundamental judgments of morals rest on feeling, not on reason, may it not be so also in the field of knowledge? May not our judgments of matters of fact be also acts of belief rather than knowledge? Belief, for Hutcheson, is a passion, and like all passions determined by the "frame of our nature." Smith suggests this line of reasoning as the one Hume *may* have taken. It is the positive teaching of Book I of the *Treatise*. Negatively, if, as Hutcheson held, moral judgments express only a passion or sentiment of approval or disapproval, does not this hold also as to judgments of matters of fact from experience? Do not judgments of causal connection express also belief or "passions," resting only on the apprehension of mere succession, coupled with a feeling or sentiment of the mind?

Kemp Smith's reconstruction of Hume's intellectual development is cogent if not conclusive. In any event, it is clear Hume wrote the *Treatise* as a Hutchesonian, and did not advance far beyond him in moral philosophy. N. Kemp Smith, *The Philosophy of David Hume* (1941), p. 43.

I

In the first and second editions of the *Enquiry concerning Human Understanding* (1748 and 1751; thereafter removed, and not reprinted in Selby-Bigge's edition of the *Enquiries*), Hume wrote:

That Faculty, by which we discern Truth and Falsehood, and that by which we perceive Vice and Virtue had long been confounded with each other, and all Morality was supposed to be built on eternal and immutable Relations, which, to every intelligent Mind, were equally invariable as any Proposition concerning Quantity or Number. But a late Philosopher [2] has taught us, by the most convincing Arguments, that Morality is nothing in the abstract Nature of Things, but is entirely relative to the Sentiment or mental Taste of each particular Being; in the same Manner as the Distinctions of sweet and bitter, hot and cold, arise from the particular feeling of each Sense or Organ. Moral Perceptions therefore, ought not to be classed with the Operations of the Understanding, but with the Tastes or Sentiments.[3]

It is clear that Hume began as a moral philosopher as a follower of Hutcheson. In a note to a passage in the Introduction to his *Treatise*, in which he specifies, as some "late philosophers in England," "Mr. Locke, my Lord Shaftesbury, Dr. Mandeville, Mr. Hutchinson [*sic*], Dr. Butler, etc.," "who have begun to put the science of man on a new footing, and have engaged the attention, and excited the curiosity of the public," [4] Hume makes it clear that it was moral philosophy that from the beginning occupied the center of his interest. The *Treatise* is described as "an attempt to introduce the experimental method of reasoning into moral subjects." The science of man is the foundation of all the sciences, including mathematics and the physical sciences of natural philosophy and natural religion: "since they lie under the cognizance of men and are judged of by their powers and faculties." But "we ourselves are not only the beings, that reason, but also one of the objects, concerning which we reason." The "moral sciences" in the narrower sense are logic, morals, criticism, and politics.

The sole end of logic is to explain the principles and operations of our reasoning faculty, and the nature of our ideas; morals and criticism regard

[2] Mr. Hutcheson (Hume's footnote).
[3] *An Enquiry concerning Human Understanding* (1st and 2d ed., 1748 and 1751); ed. Green and Grose, *Essays*, II, 10n.
[4] *Treatise*, ed. Selby-Bigge, p. xxi; ed. Green and Grose, I, 308.

our tastes and sentiments: and politics consider men as united in society, and dependent on each other. In these four sciences of *Logic, Morals, Criticism, and Politics,* is comprehended almost everything, which it can any way import us to be acquainted with, or which can tend either to the improvement or ornament of the human mind. [We may first] extend our conquests over all those sciences, which more intimately concern human life, and may afterwards proceed at leisure to discover more fully those, which are the objects of our curiosity [mathematics and natural philosophy]. There is no question of importance, whose decision is not comprised in the science of man; and there is none, which can be decided with any certainty, before we become acquainted with that science. In pretending therefore to explain the principles of human nature, we in effect propose a complete system of the sciences, built on a foundation almost entirely new, and the only one upon which they can stand with any security.[5]

The four moral sciences were thus Hume's principle concern from the very beginning. In turning to politics and history he was not abandoning his chosen domain of "the science of man," but extending some of its branches. Hume was the child of his age. The theme of the very representative *Essay on Man* is:

> And all our knowledge is, *ourselves to know.*

. . . .

> Know then thyself, presume not God to scan,
> The proper study of mankind is Man;

and Newton is duly put in his place:

> Could he, whose rules the rapid comet bind,
> Describe or fix one movement of his mind? [6]

Malebranche and Bayle, on whom Hume drew so heavily, agree with Pope.

Into these moral sciences of man, Hume wanted to introduce the "experimental method of reasoning," so successful in Newton. He meant by this the exclusion of hypotheses, the search for general laws "deduced from phenomena."

> For to me it seems evident, that the essence of the mind being equally unknown to us with that of external bodies, it must be equally impossible to form any notion of its powers and qualities otherwise than from careful

---

[5] *Treatise,* Introduction, ed. Selby-Bigge, pp. xix–xx; ed. Green and Grose, I, 306–7.

[6] *Essay on Man,* Epistle IV, l. 398; Epistle II, ll. 1–2; ll. 35–36.

and exact experiments, and the observation of those particular effects, which result from its different circumstances and situations. And though we must endeavor to render all our principles as universal as possible, by tracing up our experiments to the utmost, and explaining all effects from the simplest and fewest causes, 'tis still certain we cannot go beyond experience; and any hypothesis, that pretends to discover the ultimate original qualities of human nature, ought at first to be rejected as presumptuous and chimerical.[7]

The conclusion of the *Enquiry concerning Human Understanding* spells out Hume's aim in greater detail than the Introduction to the *Treatise*.

It is only experience, which teaches us the nature and bounds of cause and effect, and enables us to infer the existence of one object from that of another. Such is the foundation of *moral reasoning*, which forms the greater part of human knowledge, and is the source of all human action and behavior.

Moral reasonings are either concerning particular or general facts. All deliberations in life regard the former; as also all disquisitions in *history*, *chronology*, *geography*, and *astronomy*. [Emphasis supplied.]

The sciences, which treat of general facts, are *politics*, *natural philosophy*, *physic*, *chemistry*, etc., where the qualities, causes and effects of a whole species of objects are enquired into. . . .

Morals and criticism are not so properly objects of the understanding as of taste and sentiment. Beauty, whether moral or natural, is felt, more properly than perceived. Or if we reason concerning it, and endeavor to fix its standard, we regard a new fact, to wit, the general tastes of mankind, or some such fact, which may be the object of reasoning and enquiry.[8]

Hume explains what he means by "moral reasonings" in Section IV, Part ii, of the *Enquiry*. "All reasonings may be divided into two kinds, namely, demonstrative reasoning, or that concerning relations of ideas [in mathematics], and moral [or *probable*] reasoning, or that concerning matter of fact and existence." [9] Hume appeals in his *Abstract of the Treatise*, a statement trying to emphasize his main themes and central contentions, to Leibniz. "The celebrated

[7] *Treatise*, Introduction, ed. Selby-Bigge, pp. xx–xxi; ed. Green and Grose, I, 307–8.
[8] *Enquiry concerning Human Understanding* (1748), ed. Selby-Bigge, par. 132; ed. Green and Grose, II, 135.
[9] The words "or probable" appear in the editions of 1748 and 1751. They were thereafter withdrawn, and do not appear in the Selby-Bigge ed. See Green and Grose ed., II, 311n.

Monsieur Leibniz has observed it to be a defect in the common systems of logic that they are very copious when they explain the operations of the understanding in the forming of demonstrations, but are too concise when they treat of probabilities, and those other measures of evidence on which life and action entirely depend, and which are our guides even in most of our philosophical speculation." [10] Hume makes it clear, he considers he has remedied this defect in our knowledge.

Of his scheme of moral sciences, Hume claims in Book I of the *Treatise* to have dealt with the Logic of the Moral Sciences. "The author has finished what regards logic, and has laid the foundation of the other parts in his account of the passions." [11] Book I is thus what Hume calls "logic."

It is to be noted, that both in the Introduction to the *Treatise* and in the *Enquiry* Hume relegates "morals" proper to the "tastes and sentiments," and excludes them from even "moral or probable reasoning." Hume is still the faithful disciple of Hutcheson, even in the later *Enquiry concerning the Principles of Morals* of 1751.[12]

II

Hume wrote four volumes on moral philosophy. Book II of the *Treatise*, *Of the Passions*, came out with Book I in 1739; Book III, *Of Morals*, appeared in 1740. This latter book was reworked in

[10] *An Abstract of a Treatise of Human Nature* (1740), in *Hume: Theory of Knowledge*, ed. D. C. Yalden-Thomson (1951), pp. 248-49. This *Abstract* was first edited by J. M. Keynes and P. Sraffa in 1938.

[11] *Abstract*, ed. Yalden-Thomson, p. 248.

[12] Mr. Passmore calls the aim of Hume, the attempt to work out a "methodology of the social sciences." He states Hume's "intention" as: "Hume's main object, then, in Book I of the *Treatise* is to show that the moral sciences can be established on a secure footing. This involves the formulation of a general theory of probable inference, which must leave room for the employment of taste and sentiment, while at the same time excluding, as unscientific, the arguments of the metaphysician and the fancies of the enthusiast. Hume's positivism arises out of his attempt to develop a nonmetaphysical, nondeclamatory moral science; his phenomenalism serves to buttress the doctrine that the science of man is primarily and pre-eminently secure; his scepticism is intended as a rebuke to physicists and metaphysicians." J. A. Passmore, *Hume's Intentions* (1952), p. 15.

It is significant that both Mr. Passmore, in this small but penetrating volume, and Norman Kemp Smith, in *The Philosophy of David Hume* (1941), argue convincingly that it is moral philosophy that is basic in Hume's thought, and determines even his theoretical position in the "logic" dealt with in Book I of the *Treatise*.

1751 into *An Enquiry concerning the Principles of Morals*. Book II
was reworked into *A Dissertation on the Passions*, and issued in
1757 as one of *Four Dissertations*. This reworking was not successful: "by general consent it is the least satisfactory of all his
writings," remarks Kemp Smith.[13] It consists largely of verbatim
extracts from Book II of the *Treatise*, with some trifling verbal alterations; the philosophically interesting discussion of liberty and necessity had already been taken out and put where it really belongs,
after the chapter on necessary connection in the *Enquiry concerning Human Understanding* of 1748. This left largely the elaborate
mechanism of association for "originating" the passions; but Hume
had become disillusioned with his principle of association, and he
shortened the account so greatly that the argument is left barely
intelligible. Hence the *Dissertation* needs no further consideration.

Book II, *Of the Passions*, is Hume's version of Hutcheson's *Essay
on the Passions*, which had originally opened up for him his "new
scene of thought." He calls it "a solid system" of the passions, in
which he tries to work out an elaborate machinery of association
to account for their "origin." In the *Treatise* Hume is very optimistic
about the explanatory possibilities of the principles of association.

Here is a kind of *attraction*, which in the mental world will be found to
have as extraordinary effects as in the natural, and to show itself in as
many and as various forms. Its effects are everywhere conspicuous; but
as to its causes, they are mostly unknown, and must be resolved into
original qualities of human nature, which I pretend not to explain. Nothing
is more requisite for a true philosopher, than to restrain the intemperate
desire of searching into causes, and having established any doctrine upon
a sufficient number of experiments, rest contented with that, when he
sees a farther examination would lead him into obscure and uncertain
speculations. In that case his enquiry would be much better employed in
examining the effects than the causes of his principle.[14]

It is clear Hume at this time fancied himself as the Newton of the
"mental world," even to his exemplary caution in framing no causal
hypotheses. Hume was still enthusiastic when he wrote the *Abstract:*

Through this whole book there are great pretensions to new discoveries
in philosophy; but if anything can entitle the author to so glorious a name
as that of an *inventor*, it is the use he makes of the principle of the as-

[13] N. K. Smith, *Philosophy of David Hume*, p. 535.
[14] *Treatise*, Selby-Bigge, pp. 12-13; Green and Grose, I, 321.

sociation of ideas, which enters into most of his philosophy. . . . It will be easy to conceive of what vast consequence these principles must be in the science of human nature, if we consider that, so far as regards the mind, these are the only links that bind the parts of the universe together, or connect us with any person or object exterior to ourselves. . . . They are really to us the cement of the universe, and all the operations of the mind must, in a great measure, depend upon them.[15]

But by the time of writing the first *Enquiry*, Hume's enthusiasm had markedly waned. Sympathy he no longer tries to explain by a double association; it is now an ultimate propensity of the mind. Hume's good sense foresaw the inanities of the future association psychology. It was left to David Hartley to become the "Newton of the mental world," in 1749, and for James Mill to become its Samuel Clarke.

Hume begins his "solid system of the passions" with definitions.

As all the perceptions of the mind may be divided into *impressions* and *ideas*, so the impressions admit of another division into *original* and *secondary*. This division of the impressions is the same with that which I formerly made use of [in *Treatise*, Book I, Part I, sec. 2] when I distinguished them into impressions of *sensation* and *reflexion* [Locke's distinction]. Original impressions or impressions of sensation are such as without any antecedent perception arise in the soul, from the constitution of the body, from the animal spirits, or from the application of objects to the external organs. *Secondary*, or *reflective* impressions are such as proceed from some of these original ones, either immediately or by the interposition of its idea. Of the first kind are all the impressions of the senses, and all bodily pains and pleasures; of the second are the passions, and other emotions resembling them.[16]

Passions are thus, in the first place, "impressions": they are the passive effects of something acting on the mind. (Of course, Hume's analysis of causation as "constant union" or "succession" makes the distinction between "action" and "passion" meaningless.) Secondly, passions are "secondary impressions"; that is, they proceed from the primary or original impressions, they are "meta-sensations," a present-day thinker might say. Hume adds, "There must be some impressions, which without any introduction make their appearance in the soul. As these depend upon natural or physical causes, the examination of them would lead me too far from my present

[15] *Abstract*, in Yalden-Thomson, pp. 264–65.
[16] *Treatise*, Selby-Bigge, p. 275; Green and Grose, II, 75–76.

subject into the sciences of anatomy and natural philosophy." [17]
Hume continues:

> The reflective impressions may be divided into two kinds, *viz.*, the *calm* and the *violent*. Of the first kind is the sense of beauty and deformity in action [Hutcheson's "sense of beauty"], composition, and external objects. Of the second are the passions of love and hatred, grief and joy, pride and humility. This division is far from being exact.[18]

The passions are violent reflective impressions. They are themselves divided into *direct* and *indirect*.

> By direct passions I understand such as arise immediately from good or evil, from pain or pleasure. By indirect such as proceed from the same principles, but by the conjunction of other qualities. This distinction I cannot at present justify or explain any farther. I can only observe in general, that under the indirect passions I comprehend pride, humility, ambition, vanity, love, hatred, envy, pity, malice, generosity, with their dependants. And under the direct passions, desire, aversion, grief, joy, hope, fear, despair and security. I begin with the former.[19]

Pride and Humility occupy the first of the three Parts on the *Passions*. Being simple and uniform impressions, like all simple impressions, they can never be defined; we can only describe them, "by an enumeration of such circumstances as attend them."

> By *pride* I understand that agreeable impression, which arises in the mind, when the view either of our virtue, beauty, riches or power makes us satisfied with ourselves: and by *humility* I mean the opposite impression.[20]

Pride and humility are not motives to action; they are "pure emotions in the soul, unattended with any desire, and not immediately exciting us to action." [21] The *cause* of a passion is different from its *object:* the object of both pride and humility is the same, the self, "or that succession of related ideas and impressions, of which we have an intimate memory and consciousness." The causes are complex and different; here Hume brings in his mechanism of the "like association of impressions." "All agreeable objects, related to ourselves, by an association of ideas and of impressions, produce pride, and disagreeable ones, humility." [22]

[17] *Treatise*, Selby-Bigge, pp. 275–76; Green and Grose, II, 76.
[18] *Treatise*, Selby-Bigge, p. 276; Green and Grose, II, 76.
[19] *Treatise*, Selby-Bigge, pp. 276–77; Green and Grose, II, 76–77.
[20] *Treatise*, Selby-Bigge, p. 297; Green and Grose, II, 94–95.
[21] *Treatise*, Selby-Bigge, p. 367; Green and Grose, II, 153.
[22] *Treatise*, Selby-Bigge, p. 290; Green and Grose, II, p. 88.

As to vice and virtue, Hume does not in the *Passions* take sides upon "the controversy, which of late years has so much excited the curiosity of the public, whether these moral distinctions be founded on natural and original principles, or arise from interest and education." Hume here endeavors to show, "that my system maintains its ground upon either of these hypotheses; which will be a strong proof of its solidity." In either case, "vice and virtue produce in us a real pain and pleasure. . . . The very essence of virtue . . . is to produce pleasure, and that of vice to give pain." This is clear in the utilitarians; it is equally clear in the advocates of "moral sense," "who maintain that morality is something real, essential, and founded on nature." "The most probable hypothesis," Hume continues, speaking of Hutcheson, "which has been advanced to explain the distinction betwixt vice and virtue, and the origin of moral rights and obligations, is that from a primary constitution of nature certain characters and passions, by the very view and contemplation, produce a pain, and others in like manner excite a pleasure. The uneasiness and satisfaction are not only inseparable from vice and virtue, but constitute their very nature and essence. To approve of a character is to feel an original delight upon its appearance." [23]

On *beauty* and *deformity* Hume also follows Hutcheson: "Beauty of all kinds gives us a peculiar delight and satisfaction." "But the relation . . . which of all others produces most properly the passion of pride, is that of *property*." Property Hume defines as "such a relation betwixt a person and an object as permits him, but forbids any other, the free use and possession of it, without violating the laws of justice and moral equity." [24]

In discussing the love of fame as a "secondary cause" of pride, Hume introduces the principle of *sympathy*.

No quality of human nature is more remarkable, both in itself and in its consequences, than that propensity we have to sympathize with others, and to receive by communication their inclinations and sentiments, however different from, or even contrary to our own. . . . To this principle we ought to ascribe the great uniformity we may observe in the humors and turn of thinking of those of the same nation; and 'tis much more probable, that this resemblance arises from sympathy, than from any

[23] *Treatise*, Selby-Bigge, pp. 295–96; Green and Grose, II, 92–93.
[24] *Treatise*, Selby-Bigge, pp. 309–10; Green and Grose, II, 105.

influence of the soil and climate, which, though they continue invariably the same, are not able to preserve the character of a nation the same for a century together.[25]

Hume refutes Montesquieu nine years before the *Esprit des Lois*. He attempts an elaborate analysis of the "first principles" of sympathy through association. He takes sympathy as "a communication of sentiments."

The Second Part of the *Passions* deals with Love and Hatred, also unanalysable "simple impressions."

As the immediate *object* of pride and humility is self, . . . so the *object* of love and hatred is some other person, of whose thoughts, actions, and sensations we are not conscious. Our love and hatred are always directed to some sensible being external to us; and when we talk of *self-love*, 'tis not in a proper sense, nor has the sensation it produces any thing in common with that tender emotion, which is excited by a friend or mistress.[26]

The other person, the *object* of love, is not the same as its *cause;* here Hume proposes a complex association. He then proceeds to confirm his "observations" by trying "to make some new experiments upon all these passions." This is concretely what he means by "the experimental method of reasoning" he is trying to introduce. It has little to do with Newton: it means finding *illustrations* and perplexing cases—as moralists have always done. It suggests the "ideal experiments" of Henry More. Thus,

the *satisfaction* we take in the riches of others, and the *esteem* we have for the possessors may be ascribed to three different causes. First, to the objects they possess; such as houses, gardens, equipages; which, being agreeable in themselves, necessarily produce a sentiment of pleasure in every one, that either considers or surveys them. Secondly, to the expectation of advantage from the rich and powerful by our sharing their possessions. Thirdly, to sympathy, which makes us partake of the satisfaction of every one, that approaches us. All these principles may concur in producing the present phenomenon. The question is, to which of them we ought principally to ascribe it.

By "experiments" or instances, Hume resolves the first and second cause into the third, sympathy.

The first principle, *viz.* the agreeable idea of those objects, which riches afford the enjoyment of, resolves itself in a great measure into the *third*, and becomes a *sympathy* with the person we esteem or love.

[25] *Treatise*, Selby-Bigge, pp. 316–17; Green and Grose, II, 111.
[26] *Treatise*, Selby-Bigge, p. 329; Green and Grose, II, 121.

Expectation of advantage also is resolved into friendship and good-will in the owner. Thus

> Upon the whole, there remains nothing, which can give us an esteem for power and riches, and a contempt for meanness and poverty, except the principle of *sympathy*, by which we enter into the sentiments of the rich and poor, and partake of their pleasures and uneasiness.[27]

With benevolence and anger, Hume confesses a methodological difficulty:

> There is always some phenomenon, which is more stubborn, and will not so easily bend to our purpose. We need not be surprised, that this should happen in natural philosophy. The essence and composition of external bodies are so obscure, that we must necessarily, in our reasonings, or rather conjectures concerning them, involve ourselves in contradictions and absurdities. But as the perceptions of the mind are perfectly known [!], and I have used all imaginable caution in forming conclusions concerning them, I have always hoped to keep clear of those contradictions which have attended every other system. Accordingly, the difficulty . . . is no-wise contrary to my system; but only departs a little from that simplicity; which has been hitherto its principal force and beauty.[28]

Where pride and humility are "pure emotions of the soul, unattended with any desire, and not immediately exciting us to action," love and hatred are always followed by benevolence and anger. They are not "completed within themselves." "Love is always followed by a desire of the happiness of the person beloved, . . . as hatred produces a desire of the misery . . . of the person hated." Love and hatred have not only a *cause* which excites them, pleasure and pain; and an *object*, the *person*. They have also an *end*, the happiness or misery of the person. But these three may be related in a hundred ways; they are only united by the "original constitution of the mind," which rationally considered, is arbitrary. Benevolence and anger are passions different from love and hatred, and only arbitrarily conjoined in human nature.

III

In the Part III, Hume turns from the indirect to the direct passions, "which arise immediately from good or evil, from pain or

---

[27] *Treatise*, Selby-Bigge, pp. 357–58, 360, 362; Green and Grose, II, 145–46, 148, 149–50.
[28] *Treatise*, Selby-Bigge, pp. 366–67; Green and Grose, II, 153.

pleasure." Such are desire and aversion, grief and joy, hope and fear, and volition.

Of the immediate effects of pain and pleasure, there is none more remarkable than the *will*. . . . By the *will*, I mean nothing but the internal impression we feel and are conscious of, when we knowingly give rise to any new motion of our body, or new perception of our mind.

The emphasis is on will as an *impression*, not on the "knowingly." Hume at once proceeds to "that long disputed question concerning *liberty* and *necessity*," and, by a careful examination of his terms, comes out strongly for necessity. These two sections were presumably written before the searching examination of the idea of cause and effect in Book I; but in transferring them to the *Enquiry concerning Human Understanding*, Hume only made brief additions without substantially modifying his position.

Men agree, the operations of external bodies are "necessary," with no trace of "indifference" or liberty; they are instances of necessary actions, "determined by an absolute fate." But we can never discover the "ultimate connection" of any two objects, since we cannot penetrate into the "essence and construction of bodies, to perceive the principle on which their mutual influence depends" (this was Locke's difficulty, and Newton's). It is the "constant union alone, with which we are acquainted; and 'tis from the constant union the necessity arises," from the "uniform and regular conjunction" of bodies. The necessity is "nothing but a determination of the mind to pass from one object to its usual attendant."

Here then are two particulars, which we are to consider as essential to necessity; *viz.* the constant *union* and the *inference* of the mind; and wherever we discover these we must acknowledge a necessity. As the actions of matter have no necessity, but what is derived from these circumstances, and it is not by any insight into the essence of bodies we discover their connection, the absence of this insight, while the union and inference remain, will never, in any case, remove the necessity. 'Tis the observation of the union which produces the inference. . . . I shall first prove from experience that our actions have a constant union with our motives, tempers, and circumstances. . . . A . . . general view of the common course of human affairs will be sufficient . . . the same uniformity and regular operation of natural principles are apparent. Like causes still produce like effects. . . .

I define necessity in two ways, conformable to the two definitions of *cause* of which it makes an essential part. I place it either in the constant union and conjunction of the objects, or in the inference of the mind from the one to the other.[29]

Hume points to the many types of "uniformity of human actions." "As the *union* betwixt motives and actions has the same constancy, as that in any natural operations, so its influence on the understanding is also the same, in *determining* us to infer the existence of one from that of another."

> There is no philosopher, whose judgment is so riveted to this fantastical system of liberty, as not to acknowledge the force of *moral evidence*, and both in speculation and practice proceed upon it, as upon a reasonable foundation. Now moral evidence is nothing but a conclusion concerning the actions of men, derived from the consideration of their motives, temper, and situation. . . . Whoever reasons after this manner, does *ipso facto* believe the actions of the will to arise from necessity, and he knows not what he means when he denies it. . . .
> The necessary connection is not discovered by a conclusion of the understanding, but is merely a perception of the mind. Wherever we observe the same union, . . . we have the idea of cause and necessity. . . . 'Tis impossible for the mind to penetrate farther. From this constant union it *forms* the idea of cause and effect, and by its influence *feels* the necessity. . . .
> Natural and moral evidence cement together; . . . they are of the same nature, and derived from the same principles. . . . The same experienced union has the same effect on the mind, whether the united objects be motives, volitions, and actions; or figure and motion.

And Hume concludes his argument for naturalizing the mind and will in nature, as thoroughly as ever Spinoza had done, by wholeheartedly embracing the idea of necessary connection in both man and nature:

> According to my definitions, necessity makes an essential part of causation; and consequently liberty, by removing necessity, removes also causes, and is the very same thing with chance.[30]

There is no middle ground between necessity and pure chance.

Why then do men support the "doctrine of liberty"? First, in our acts we are not sensible of any force or constraint. "Few are capable of distinguishing betwixt the liberty of *spontaneity*, as it is called in the schools, and the liberty of *indifference;* betwixt that which is opposed to violence, and that which means a negation of

---

[29] *Treatise*, Selby-Bigge, pp. 399–401, 409; Green and Grose, II, 181–83, 190.
[30] *Treatise*, Selby-Bigge, pp. 404–7; Green and Grose, II, 186–88.

necessity and causes. The first is even the most common sense of the word . . . and 'tis only that species of liberty, which it concerns us to preserve." Secondly, there is a "false sensation or experience [changed in the *Enquiry* version to "*seeming* experience"] even of the liberty of indifference." The necessity of any action "is not properly a quality in the agent, but in any thinking or intelligent being who may *consider* the action," in the observer. Liberty or chance is nothing but the want of determination to infer causal connection. "Though in reflecting on human actions we seldom feel such a looseness or indifference, yet it very commonly happens, that in performing the actions themselves we are sensible of something like it: and . . . this has been employed as a demonstrative or even an intuitive proof of human liberty. . . . We may imagine we feel a liberty within ourselves; but a *spectator* can commonly infer our actions from our motives and character." [31]

Thirdly, men fear the dangerous consequences of necessity to religion and morality. But, as Hume contends, in the schools, the pulpit, and common life, men actually do employ the notion of necessity in the two senses he has defined. Men may not call it "necessity"; but why quarrel over words? "I do not ascribe to the will that unintelligible necessity, which is supposed to lie in matter. But I ascribe to matter that intelligible quality, call it necessity or not, which the most rigorous orthodoxy does or must allow to belong to the will. I change nothing in the received systems with regard to the will, but only with regard to material objects."

Nay I shall go farther, and assert, that this kind of necessity is so essential to religion and morality, that without it there must ensue an absolute subversion of both, and that every other supposition is entirely destructive of all laws both *divine* and *human*.

For it alone holds men responsible for their actions.

Here then I turn to my adversary, and desire him to free his own system from these odious consequences before he charges them upon others. [32]

Hume concludes:

'Tis only upon the principles of necessity, that a person acquires any merit or demerit from his actions, however the common opinion may incline to the contrary. [33]

[31] *Treatise*, Selby-Bigge, pp. 407–8; Green and Grose, II, 188–89.
[32] *Treatise*, Selby-Bigge, pp. 410, 412; Green and Grose, II, 190–92.
[33] *Treatise*, Selby-Bigge, p. 411; Green and Grose, II, 192.

It is obvious, Hume did not come from a long line of Calvinists for nothing.

In the *Enquiry concerning Human Understanding* version of this discussion, Hume adds one further objection to the doctrine of necessity which he alone allows to have real force—the doctrine of theological determinism.

I pretend not to have obviated or removed all objections to this theory. . . . It may be said, . . . there is a continued chain of necessary causes, pre-ordained and pre-determined, reaching from the original cause of all to every single volition of every human creature. No contingency anywhere in the universe; no indifference; no liberty. . . . The ultimate Author of all our volitions is the Creator of the world . . . whence every subsequent event, by an inevitable necessity, must result. Human actions, therefore, either can have no moral turpitude at all, . . . or . . . they must involve our Creator in the same guilt, while he is acknowledged to be their ultimate cause and author.

This theological determinism goes back at least to Scotists like Bradwardine. Hume's favored answer seems to be, "An absurd consequence, if necessary, proves the original doctrine to be absurd." The objection has two parts. If all events be the will of God, then none can be criminal. "The answer to the first objection seems obvious and convincing." Hume points to the Stoic view of the Universal harmony, revived by Shaftesbury and Pope. The Whole is ordered with perfect benevolence. "But though this topic be specious and sublime, it was soon found in practice weak and ineffectual. . . . These enlarged views may, for a moment, please the imagination of a speculative man, who is placed in ease and security. . . . Are such remote and uncertain speculations able to counterbalance the sentiments which arise from the natural and immediate view of the objects?" The mind of man is so formed by nature that it judges by "an economy, more suitable to the infirmity of human minds," and approves such characters "as contribute to the peace and security of human society." Secondly, it is objected that universal necessity makes God the author of sin and moral turpitude.

The second objection admits not of so easy and satisfactory an answer. . . . These are mysteries, which mere natural and unassisted reason is very unfit to handle; and whatever system she embraces, she must find herself involved in inextricable difficulties, and even contradictions. . . . To reconcile the indifference and contingency of human actions with prescience; or to defend absolute decrees, and yet free the Deity from being the author of sin, has been found hitherto to exceed all the power of philosophy. Happy, if she . . . . return, with suitable modesty, to her true and proper province, the examination of common life, where she will find difficulties enough to employ her enquiries.[34]

The Hume speaking here against the Calvinistic ministers is clearly *le bon David*, who dearly loved to bait the reverend doctors, and followed up this passage with the sections *On Miracles* and *Of a Particular Providence and of a Future State*.

The other major change in the *Enquiry* is the treatment in Section VII of the will. In Book II of the *Treatise*, the will is classed with direct passions, like desire and aversion; there is one sentence on it, "The *will* exerts itself, when either the good [pleasure] or the absence of the evil [pain] may be attained by any action of the mind or body." [35] Here voluntary actions are treated like any other impression or perception, as items in a causal sequence, as either effects or causes in relation to their antecedents or consequents. They are "impressions" the spectator or internal observer feels and is conscious of. As simple, a volition is "original" and ultimate, not further analyzable, but only seen in its place in the succession of perceptions. In the section on the idea of necessary connection in the *Enquiry*, Hume is much closer to common experience, and has pushed into the background his artificial mechanism of association.

We are every moment conscious of internal power; while we feel, that, by the simple command of our will, we can move the organs of our body, or direct the faculties of our mind. An *act of volition* produces motion in our limbs, or raises a new idea in our imagination. This influence of the will we know by consciousness. Hence we acquire the idea of power or energy; and are certain, that we ourselves and all other intelligent beings are possessed of power. This idea, then, is an idea of reflection, since it arises from reflecting on the operations of our own mind, and on the command which is exercised by will, both over the organs of the body and faculties of the soul.

But Hume continues (in the first and second editions, 1748 and 1751):

We shall proceed to examine this Pretension; and shall endeavor to avoid, as far as we are able, all Jargon and Confusion. . . . I assert, then,

[34] *Enquiry concerning Human Understanding*, ed. Selby-Bigge, pars. 78–81; ed. Green and Grose, II, 81–84.

[35] *Treatise*, Selby-Bigge, pp. 438–39; Green and Grose, II, 214–15.

in the first Place, that the Influence of Volition over the Organs of the Body, is a Fact, which, like all other natural events, can be known only by experience. . . . The motion of our body follows upon the command of our will. Of this we are every moment conscious. But the means, by which this is effected; the energy, by which the will performs so extraordinary an operation; of this we are so far from being immediately conscious, that it must forever escape our most diligent enquiry.

Is there any principle in all nature more mysterious than the union of soul with body? "If by consciousness we perceived any power or energy in the will," we would know this power and its connection with its effects. Nor can we move all our organs; why does will move tongue and finger, and not heart or liver? Thirdly, we learn from anatomy that the will moves immediately, not the organs, but certain muscles, and nerves and animal spirits; this whole operation is "to the last degree, mysterious and unintelligible." We may conclude, that "our idea of power is not copied from any sentiment or consciousness of power within ourselves, when we give rise to animal motion." That the motion of our limbs follows the command of the will is a matter of common experience, like other natural events: but the "power or energy" by which this is effected, like that in other natural events, is unknown and inconceivable. And the same holds true of any "power or energy" in our own minds. "Volition is surely an *act* of the mind." But we know only the frequent conjunction of perceptions, as of objects.

Malebranche, from whom Hume learned much of this argument, lodged all causal "power" in the particular volitions of God. But this hypothesis is "too bold ever to carry conviction." "We are got into fairy land, long ere we have reached the last steps of our theory." Moreover, the argument has no force, for "we are equally ignorant of the manner or force by which a divine mind could operate." And Hume appeals to Newton's *vis inertiae*. This marks observed facts, without any idea of the power itself. Newton framed his hypothesis of an "ether" to explain the facts of gravitational movement, but he did not trust it "without more experiments." Let us be cautious and modest, like Newton. That the will acts, we know by experience; but we observe only the frequent conjunction of perceptions.[36]

---

[36] *Enquiry concerning Human Understanding*, Sec. VII, Part i.

I V

In Section III of Book II of the *Treatise, Of the Passions*, Hume restates Hutcheson's favorite teaching, the Aristotelian doctrine that reason alone is never a motive determining the will. In the Platonic and the Stoic traditions, reason is supposed to be preeminent above passion; men are virtuous only as they conform themselves to the dictates of reason. "In order to show the fallacy of all this philosophy, I shall endeavor to prove *first*, that reason alone can never be a motive to any action of the will; and *secondly*, that it can never oppose passion in the direction of the will." [37] Hume's classic discussion can stand with that of Aristotle in *De Anima* III, chs. 9, 10, and *Nicomachean Ethics* VI.

The understanding exerts itself after two different ways, as it judges from demonstration or probability; as it regards the abstract relations of our ideas, or those relations of objects, of which experience only gives us information.

The first, mathematics and mechanics, are very useful, but " 'tis not of themselves they have any influence." They serve our other ends or purposes. When we have the prospect of pain or pleasure from any object, we feel an "emotion of aversion or propensity."

This emotion, . . . making us cast our view on every side, comprehends whatever objects are connected with the original one by the relation of cause and effect. Here then reasoning takes place to discover this relation; and according as our reasoning varies, our actions receive a subsequent variation. But 'tis evident in this case, that impulse *arises* not from reason, but is only *directed* by it [emphasis added]. 'Tis from the prospect of pain or pleasure that the aversion or propensity *arises* towards any object. . . .

Since reason alone can never *produce* any action, or give rise to volition, I infer, that the same faculty is as incapable of preventing volition, or of disputing the preference with any passion or emotion. This consequence is necessary. 'Tis impossible reason could have the latter effect of preventing volition, but by giving an impulse in a contrary direction to our passion; and that impulse, had it operated alone, would have been able to produce volition. Nothing can oppose or retard the impulse of passion, but a contrary impulse.

"The principle, which opposes our passion, cannot be the same with reason, and is only called so in an improper sense. We speak

[37] *Treatise*, Selby-Bigge, p. 413; Green and Grose, II, 193.

not strictly and philosophically when we talk of the combat of passion and of reason. Reason is, and ought only to be the slave of the passions, and can never pretend to any other office than to serve and obey them." [38]

Note that Hume does not deny the importance of reason in influencing and modifying the direction of a passion. Reason can and does direct and guide passion by enlarging its "view." But Hume's central concern here was not to glorify reason or to exhort men to let it direct their passions; it was to analyze the operation of motives.

Moreover, "a passion is an original existence," it is not a copy or representation of any other existence.

'Tis impossible, therefore, that this passion can be opposed by, or be contradictory to truth and reason; since this contradiction consists in the disagreement of ideas, considered as copies, with those objects, which they represent.

Hume here follows Locke's representative or copy theory of ideas.

Passions can be contrary to reason only so far as they are accompanied with some judgment or opinion . . . 'tis only in two senses, that any affection can be called unreasonable. First, when a passion . . . is founded on the supposition of the existence of objects, which really do not exist. Secondly, when in exerting any passion in action, we choose means insufficient for the designed end, and deceive ourselves in our judgments of causes and effects.

In any other sense, reason can neither justify nor condemn a passion. " 'Tis not contrary to reason to prefer the destruction of the whole world to the scratching of my finger. 'Tis not contrary to reason for me to choose my total ruin, to prevent the least uneasiness of an *Indian* or person wholly unknown to me."

A passion must be accompanied with some false judgment, in order to its being unreasonable; and even then 'tis not the passion, properly speaking, which is unreasonable, but the judgment. . . .

'Tis impossible, that reason and passion can ever oppose each other, or dispute for the government of the will or actions. The moment we perceive the falsehood of any supposition, or the insufficiency of any means, our passions yield to our reason without any opposition. . . . I may will the performance of certain actions as means of obtaining any desired good; but as my willing of these actions is only secondary, and

[38] *Treatise*, Selby-Bigge, pp. 413-15; Green and Grose, II, 193-95.

founded on the supposition, that they are causes of the proposed effect; as soon as I discover the falsehood of that supposition, they must become indifferent to me.[39]

It is the *light* of reason rather than its *force* that gives it power.

Why then do men fall into confusion, and think "reason" can directly oppose passion? Now, reason exerts itself without producing any sensible emotion. "Hence every action of the mind, which operates with the same calmness and tranquillity, is confounded with reason." There are "certain calm desires and tendencies, which though they be real passions, produce little emotion in the mind." These are of two kinds: "either certain instincts originally implanted in our natures, such as benevolence and resentment, the love of life, and kindness to children; or the general appetite to good, and aversion to evil. . . . When any of these passions are calm, and cause no disorder in the soul, they are very readily taken for the determinations of reason, . . . because their sensations are not evidently different." There are also "violent emotions of the same kind," like violent resentment, or fear. These make "men often act knowingly against their interest. For which reason the view of the greatest possible good does not always influence them." [40]

Hume goes on to consider *custom*, so important for the knowledge of cause and effect. Custom bestows "a *facility* in the performance of any action or the conception of any object; and afterwards a *tendency or inclination* towards it; from these we may account for all its other effects." [41] Imagination has the power to confer "a new vivacity" on our ideas of good and evil.

The direct, as contrasted with the indirect passions, are desire and aversion, grief and joy, hope and fear, along with the volition already examined. Like the indirect, they are "founded on pain and pleasure," occasioned by the view of some good or evil. "Desire arises from good considered simply, and aversion is derived from evil." But "beside good and evil, or in other words, pain and pleasure, the direct passions frequently arise from a natural impulse or instinct, which is perfectly unaccountable. Of this kind is the desire of punishment to our enemies, and of happiness to our friends; hunger, lust, and a few other bodily appetites. These passions, prop-

[39] *Treatise*, Selby-Bigge, pp. 415–17; Green and Grose, II, 195–96.
[40] *Treatise*, Selby-Bigge, pp. 417–18; Green and Grose, II, 196–97.
[41] *Treatise*, Selby-Bigge, p. 422; Green and Grose, II, 201.

erly speaking, produce good and evil, and proceed not from them, like the other affections." [42] With these "natural impulses," even so important a one as the desire for the happiness of others, hedonism breaks down.

Aristotle began the *Metaphysics* with the desire to know. Hume ends his *Passions* with curiosity, or the desire for truth. "The first and most considerable circumstance requisite to render truth agreeable, is the genius and capacity, which is employed in its invention and discovery." In addition, "the truth we discover must also be of some importance," though many most passionate in discovering truths they esteemed important and useful to the world have shown no particular concern in the interests of mankind. Here a "remote sympathy" seems to operate. But while "the pleasure of study consists chiefly in the action of the mind," "the importance of the truth is requisite to complete the pleasure," in order "to fix our attention." The passion most nearly resembling that for philosophy is hunting, where likewise the pleasure is in the process, but a useful end is requisite to define the process. Winning at the gaming table is also similar. "Human life is so tiresome a scene, and men generally of such indolent dispositions, that whatever amuses them, though by a passion mixed with pain, does in the main give them a sensible pleasure." Hume, we know, was addicted to backgammon.

But besides the love of knowledge, there is a certain curiosity implanted in human nature, which is a passion derived from a quite different principle. "Some people have an insatiable desire of knowing the actions and circumstances of their neighbors." [43]

V

Hume's "system of ethics" is quite simple. It maintains two main theses: 1) the motive or spring of action in moral conduct is *not reason* but some *passion* or combination of passions; 2) the basis of moral judgment is not reason alone, but reason enlightening the moral sentiments of feeling. The emphasis in his two writings on morals is rather different. The first, Book III of the *Treatise*, is very close to Hutcheson, and presses the latter's favorite doctrines. It is directed against the rational moralists, Clarke and Wollaston:

[42] *Treatise*, Selby-Bigge, p. 439; Green and Grose, II, 215.
[43] *Treatise*, Selby-Bigge, pp. 448–53; Green and Grose, II, 223–27.

the latter is criticized by name. It shares Hutcheson's interest in an elaborate psychology of the passions; following Hume's own "system," in which association played a large part, it leaves the question of the springs of action to Book II, concentrates on moral judgment, and sets forth a utilitarian criterion. The *Enquiry concerning the Principles of Morals*, eleven years later, has forgotten Clarke and Wollaston: it has lost interest in the "system of the passions," especially the machinery of association; it is less utilitarian, definitely not hedonistic, and emphasizes the sentiments. It is less polemical: the attacks on reason in morals, and on self-love and egoism, are relegated to appendices. Above all, in the complete rewriting, Hume improved both the literary style and the structure of his arguments. He "polished and burnished" it, so that he can judge, it is "of all my writings, historical, philosophical, or literary, incomparably the best." [44]

Part I of Book III of the *Treatise* includes two sections: "Moral Distinctions not derived from Reason," and "Moral Distinctions derived from a Moral Sense." It starts: "Nothing is ever present to the mind but its perceptions; and all the actions of seeing, hearing, judging, loving, hating, and thinking fall under this denomination." Every action of the mind is a "perception": so also will be "those judgments, by which we distinguish moral good and evil. . . . To approve of one character, to condemn another, are only so many different perceptions."

Perceptions are either impressions or ideas. The question of moral philosophy is, "Whether 'tis by means of our *ideas* or *impressions* we distinguish betwixt vice and virtue, and pronounce an action blamable or praise-worthy?" This defines Hume's central problem, as that of moral judgment, not moral deliberation, or the springs of action; it puts him squarely in the school of Shaftesbury and Hutcheson. He proceeds to attack the rational moralists.

Since morals have an influence on the actions and affections, it follows, that they cannot be derived from reason; and that because reason alone, as we have already proved, can never have any such influence. Morals excite passions, and produce or prevent actions. Reason of itself is utterly impotent in this particular. The rules of morality, therefore, are not conclusions of our reason.

[44] "My Own Life," in Green and Grose, *Essays*, I, 4.

Reason, however, does have an influence on morals:

> Reason, in a strict and philosophical sense [which Hume limits to reasoning] can have an influence on our conduct only after two ways: either when it excites a passion by informing us of the existence of something which is a proper object of it; or when it discovers the connections of causes and effects, so as to afford us means of exerting any passion.[45]

Reasoning can deal only with means, with the relations between ideas, or between real existences. It cannot make a mistake about what is *right;* for that "supposes a real right and wrong; that is, a real distinction in morals, independent of those judgments." It can make mistakes of *fact;* but our actions never cause any factual judgments in ourselves, but only in other observers of our actions. Hume is arguing against Wollaston's view that wrong action is telling a lie; in that case, if it be concealed, it no longer deceives anyone, and so is not wrong. "Reason and judgment may, indeed, be the mediate cause of an action, by prompting, or by directing a passion."

Against Clarke's "eternal immutable fitnesses and unfitnesses of things," Hume points out that they must lie either in some relations of objects or in some matter of fact. If the former, there is nothing distinctively *moral* about them: in *relation* alone, a sapling that overshadows and kills its mother tree is no different from an Orestes; nor is incest in animals in *relation* different from incest in man. If the fitness lies in some matter of fact, produce the impression, of the *quality* of vice in murder, for instance. "The vice entirely escapes you, as long as you consider the object. You never can find it, till you turn your reflection into your own breast, and find a sentiment of disapprobation, which arises in you, towards this action. Here is a matter of fact; but 'tis the object of feeling, not of reason. It lies in yourself, not in the object." Vice and virtue are like secondary qualities, not located in objects, but perceptions in the mind.

Hume concludes his polemic against the rationalists with the classic statement of the distinction that Kant was to make central. In every system of morality, the author proceeds in the ordinary way of reasoning about human affairs.

> When of a sudden I am surprised to find, that instead of the usual copulations of propositions, *is,* and *is not,* I meet with no proposition that is

[45] *Treatise,* Selby-Bigge, pp. 456–57, 459; Green and Grose, II, 234–37.

not connected with an *ought*, or an *ought not*. This change is imperceptible, but is, however, of the last consequence. For as this *ought*, or *ought not*, expresses some new relation or affirmation, 'tis necessary that it should be observed and explained; and at the same time that a reason should be given, for what seems altogether inconceivable, how this new relation can be a deduction from others, which are entirely different from it.[46]

"Thus . . . since vice and virtue are not discoverable merely by reason, or the comparison of ideas, it must be by means of some impression or sentiment they occasion, that we are able to mark the difference betwixt them. Morality, therefore, is more properly felt than judged of; though this feeling or sentiment is commonly so soft and gentle, that we are apt to confound it with an idea." Of what nature are these impressions? "We must pronounce the impression arising from virtue, to be agreeable, and that proceeding from vice to be uneasy. . . . There is no spectacle so fair and beautiful as a noble and generous action." This agreeableness and uneasiness "are nothing but particular pains or pleasures."

In giving a reason, therefore, for the pleasure or uneasiness, we sufficiently explain the vice or virtue. To have the sense of virtue, is nothing but to *feel* a satisfaction of a particular kind from the contemplation of a character. The very feeling constitutes our praise or admiration. . . . We do not infer a character to be virtuous, because it pleases: but in feeling that it pleases after such a particular manner, we in effect feel that it is virtuous. The case is the same as in our judgments concerning all kinds of beauty, and tastes, and sensations. Our approbation is implied in the immediate pleasure they convey to us.[47]

The young Hume could hardly go farther in the direction of Hutcheson and Shaftesbury.

This moral sentiment is a peculiar and distinctive kind of pleasure, different from all other pleasures. Now, virtue and vice must necessarily be placed either in ourselves or others, and must excite either pleasure or uneasiness, and therefore must give rise to one of the four "indirect" passions, pride, humility, love, or hatred. This is the distinctive character of moral pleasure and pain.

[46] *Treatise*, Selby-Bigge, pp. 460–63, 468–69; Green and Grose, II, 238–41, 245–46.
  The role of reason in moral judgment has recently been defended, and Hume's arguments searchingly scrutinized, by C. D. Broad, in *Five Types of Ethical Theory* (1930), ch. IV, and, rather more perceptively and acutely, by Brand Blanshard, in *Reason and Goodness* (1961), pp. 81–90.
[47] *Treatise*, Selby-Bigge, pp. 470–71; Green and Grose, II, 246–47.

From what principles is it derived, and whence does it arise in the human mind? It is absurd to imagine that in each particular instance there is a distinctive mechanism, "an original quality and primary constitution." " 'Tis necessary, therefore, to abridge these primary impulses, and find some more general principles, upon which all our notions of morals are founded." Hume is trying to unify Hutcheson's long and miscellaneous list of the moral qualities approved by the moral sense. Ought we to search for these principles in *nature?* He distinguishes three main senses of the term "nature": "nature" is opposed to miracles, in which case every virtue and vice is "natural"; "nature" is opposed to the rare and unusual, in which case "perhaps virtue will be found to be the most 'unnatural' "; "nature" is opposed to artifice, in which case "our sense of some virtues is artificial and that of others natural." Thus benevolence turns out to be "natural," while justice and the political virtues are "artificial." " 'Tis certain that both vice and virtue are equally artificial, and out of nature," that is, performed with "a certain design and intention." Nothing can be more unphilosophical than those systems which identify virtue with "the natural." " 'Tis impossible that the character of natural and unnatural can ever, in any sense, mark the boundaries of vice and virtue." [48] Hume is disagreeing at once with Clarke and Wollaston, the Stoics, and with Shaftesbury and one strain in Hutcheson.

The introductory Section I of an *Enquiry concerning the Principles of Morals*, entitled *Of the General Principles of Morals*, is much briefer and more elegant. The argument with the Rationalists has been pushed into Appendix I. Hume starts with "a controversy started of late . . . concerning the general foundation of Morals; whether they be derived from Reason, or from Sentiment." The ancients, though they all state that virtue is conformity to reason, yet "seem to consider morals as deriving their existence from taste and sentiment." Our modern enquirers have commonly tried to account for virtue and vice "by metaphysical reasonings, and by deductions from the most abstract principles of the understanding." "The most elegant Lord Shaftesbury" in general agreed with the Ancients, but he is not entirely free from confusion. Both sides have "specious arguments." The arguments are so plausible, "I an

[48] *Treatise*, Selby-Bigge, pp. 473-75; Green and Grose, II, 249-51.

apt to suspect," they may both be "solid and satisfactory, and that *reason* and *sentiment* concur in almost all moral determinations and conclusions."

The final sentence, it is probable, which pronounces characters and actions amiable or odious, praise-worthy or blameable; that which stamps on them the mark of honor or infamy, approbation or censure; that which renders morality an active principle and constitutes virtue our happiness and vice our misery: it is probable, I say, that this final sentence depends on some internal sense or feeling, which nature has made universal in the whole species. . . . But in order to pave the way for such a sentiment, and giver a proper discernment of its object, it is often necessary, we find, that much reasoning should precede, that nice distinctions be made, just conclusions drawn, distant comparisons formed, complicated relations examined, and general facts fixed and ascertained.

The same holds of taste, the sense of beauty.

In many orders of beauty, particularly those of the fine arts, it is requisite to employ much reasoning, in order to feel the proper sentiment.

Hume closes Section I with remarks on method.

We shall endeavor to follow a very simple method: we shall analyze that complication of mental qualities, which form . . . Personal Merit: . . . . We can only expect success, by following the experimental method, and deducing general maxims from a comparison of particular instances. The [deductive method] may be more perfect in itself, but it suits less the imperfection of human nature.[49]

In the light of present-day philosophical concerns, Hume's remarks on language are of interest. He is proposing to analyze that "complication of mental qualities which form what, in common life, we call Personal Merit":

The very nature of language guides us almost infallibly in forming a judgment of this nature; and as every tongue possesses one set of words which are taken in a good sense, and another in the opposite, the least acquaintance with the idiom suffices, without any reasoning, to direct us in collecting and arranging the estimable or blameable qualities of men.[50]

The polemic against the rationalists has been put into Appendix I, *Concerning Moral Sentiment*. The arguments have been set in better order, and strengthened with new ones. The more the em-

[49] *Enquiry concerning Morals*, Selby-Bigge, pars. 134, 137–38; Green and Grose, II, 170, 173.
[50] *Enquiry*, Selby-Bigge, par. 138; Green and Grose, II, 173.

phasis on utility, the more place there is for reason to judge it. So this time Hume begins with the need for reason:

One principal foundation of moral praise being supposed to lie in the usefulness of any quality or action, it is evident that *reason* must enter for a considerable share in all decisions of this kind; since nothing but that faculty can instruct us in the tendency of qualities and actions, and point out their beneficial consequences to society and to their possessor.[51]

Some single instances of justice may be pernicious, and escape the general rule; but even here, "a very accurate *reason* or *judgment* is often requisite" to adjust opposite utilities. In fact, reason and sentiment are not opposed, they are both necessary conditions of the moral judgment in which they are now seen to cooperate. Reason "is not alone sufficient. . . . It is requisite a *sentiment* should here display itself, in order to give a preference to the useful above the pernicious tendencies. This sentiment can be no other than a feeling for the happiness of mankind, and a resentment of their misery; since these are the different ends which virtue and vice have a tendency to promote. Here therefore *reason* instructs us in the several tendencies of actions, and *humanity* makes a distinction in favor of those which are useful and beneficial." Where in the *Treatise* reason had a subordinate use, here Hume asserts the "partition between understanding and sentiment in all moral decision." Hume has ceased to be the partisan of Shaftesbury and of Hutcheson.

He still opposes the one-sidedness of Clarke and Wollaston. Reason alone can still not prove ingratitude a moral crime. The crime is neither any particular individual fact which reason could judge— it arises from a complication of circumstances; nor is it a relation, like contrariety. It is not even a relation to a rule of right; for that rule would have to be generalized from particular instances known to be right. "Is not this fine reasoning?" Hume states his hypothesis: "It defines virtue to be whatever mental action or quality gives to a spectator the pleasing sentiment of approbation."

Secondly, moral deliberation is not like solving a geometrical problem, though both involve complex relations. In the latter, we proceed from known to unknown relations, in inquiry. But for Hume

---

[51] Quotations on the following pages are from the *Enquiry concerning the Principles of Morals*, Appendix I, *Concerning Moral Sentiment*. Selby-Bigge, pp. 285–94; Green and Grose, II, 258–66.

moral deliberation is not an inquiry. It is the *decision* that comes after inquiry is finished.

In moral deliberation we must be acquainted beforehand with all the objects and all their relations to each other; and from a comparison of the whole, fix our choice or approbation. No new fact to be ascertained; no new relation to be discovered. . . . After every circumstance, every relation is known, the understanding has no further room to operate, nor any object on which it could employ itself. The approbation or blame which then ensues, cannot be the work of the judgment, but of the heart.

For Hume, then, reason *reasons*, but reason cannot reach *decisions;* this is a crucial point on which twentieth-century "intelligence" differs from eighteenth-century Newtonian "reason." It is obvious Hume's problem would be clarified by some more precise definitions, as well as by a subtler psychology, based on a factual study of decision-making.

Thirdly, moral beauty resembles natural beauty, in that the beauty of an action, like that of a circle, is not in the action or the circle taken by itself. "The beauty is not a quality of the circle. . . . It is only the effect which that figure produces upon the mind." It is, in other words, a Lockean "idea," the effect of some impingement from without on the mind, and in the mind. Hume did not here push his emerging "radical empiricism" and "objective relativism" far enough. He remains caught in what he calls the Lockean "double existence hypothesis," in Locke's assumption of *subjectivism.*

Fourthly, the matricides of the sapling and Nero are brought in: the relation itself has no moral quality. And fifthly,

The ultimate ends of human actions can never, in any case, be accounted for by *reason,* but recommend themselves entirely to the sentiments and affections of mankind, without any dependance on the intellectual faculties.

Ask a man why he does this and avoids that; push him, and he will reply, this gives me pleasure, that causes pain. Ask him why he chooses the pain and avoids the pleasure, and he will have no answer.

Something must be desirable on its own account, and because of its immediate accord or agreement with human sentiment and affection.

As is the case with his view of theoretical knowledge, Hume's position with regard to moral judgments is clear and consistent.

But just as with the former, it can be asked, as Kant did, whether Hume's observational theory is adequate to the facts of scientific experience, so it can be asked, as many have since, including Kant, whether his theory of moral judgment is adequate to the facts of moral experience. It has, as Broad has pointed out, the curious consequence, not that disputes on moral questions are resolved into matters of taste, and we end with a *de gustibus*.[52] The logical consequence is that every dispute on questions of right and wrong is capable of being settled completely by the simple method of collecting statistics, and tabulating the answers to the poll question, "Do you feel an emotion of approval on contemplating X?"

Approved by whom? Basil Willey adds a further pertinent comment.

"This is good" means "This is approved," but—approved by whom? The fact that Hume does not feel called upon to raise and answer this question indicates how complete was his acceptance of current values. . . . For his purpose it is sufficient to make a catalogue of the qualities approved and condemned by his own age and social group. The moral judgments of this group, he evidently feels, are sufficiently representative to be taken as those of average humanity. . . . This assumption, I think, indicates what may be called the social and cultural solidarity of the "republic of letters" in the pre-revolutionary eighteenth century.[53]

It was not till the Romanticist thinkers that there was developed an appreciation of the fact of individual differences amongst any but barbarians.

Part II of Book III of the *Treatise* deals with the "artificial" virtue of justice; only with Part III, on the natural virtues, does Hume get to benevolence. In contrast, the second section of the *Enquiry* at once treats Benevolence, before Justice in Section III. Hume's other great dispute was with the egoists, the partisans of self-love. On the issue of reason and sentiment, Hume grew more aware of the complexity of the factors involved in moral judgment; on self-love, he grew more insistent on the passion of benevolence or "humanity" in human nature.

Hume comes to terms with the egoists in Appendix II to the *Enquiry, Of Self-Love*.[54] There are two sorts. The first maintain a

---

[52] C. D. Broad, *Five Types of Ethical Theory*, pp. 114-15.
[53] Basil Willey, *The Eighteenth Century Background* (1940), p. 122.
[54] The quotations from this appendix are taken from Appendix II to the *Enquiry*, Selby-Bigge, pars. 247-54; Green and Grose, II, 266-72.

principle "utterly incompatible with all virtue or moral sentiment."
They hold that "all *benevolence* is mere hypocrisy, friendship a
cheat, public spirit a farce, fidelity a snare to produce trust and confidence; and . . . that all of us, at bottom, pursue only our private
interest." Such views come, if not from a "corrupted heart," at
least from "the most careless and precipitate examination." The second group is quite different. There is another principle, much insisted on by philosophers, that "no passion is, or can be disinterested"; the most generous friendship is a modification of self-love.
"Even unknown to ourselves, we seek only our own gratification,
while we appear the most deeply engaged in schemes for the liberty
and happiness of mankind." This view is quite compatible in practice
with benevolence and genuine virtue. "Probity and honor were
no strangers to Epicurus and his sect." Horace had a generous and
friendly disposition. "And among the moderns, Hobbes and Locke,
who maintained the selfish system of morals, lived irreproachable
lives." They readily allow a friendship without hypocrisy. For
they can still distinguish between virtue and vice.

I esteem the man whose self-love, by whatever means, is so directed as
to give him a concern for others, and render him serviceable to society:
as I hate or despise him, who has no regard to anything beyond his own
gratifications and enjoyments. . . .

But though the question concerning the universal or partial selfishness
of man be not so material as is usually imagined, to morality and practice,
it is certainly of consequence in the speculative science of human nature,
and is a proper object of curiosity and enquiry.

Universal self-love is "contrary to common feeling." "To the
most careless observer there appear to be such dispositions as benevolence and generosity; such affections as love, friendship, compassion, gratitude." There is both a *general* and a *particular* benevolence. "Both these sentiments must be allowed real in human nature.
. . . General benevolence, or humanity, or sympathy . . . I assume
as real, from general experience, without any other proof." Hume
relies on an interesting methodological principle. Fontenelle suggested that in natural philosophy, when a phenomenon can be produced in several ways, "there is a general presumption for its arising from the causes which are the least obvious and familiar. But
the presumption always lies on the other side, in all inquiries concerning the origin of our passions, and of the internal operations of

the human mind. The simplest and most obvious cause which can there be assigned for any phenomenon, is probably the true one." Hume might not have been able to convince Freud or Jung of this principle of method. Hume's best argument against egoistic hedonism is the view he took from Butler and Hutcheson, that passions are determinate, and directed toward their objects, not pleasure.

Book III, which finally arrives at benevolence in section 3 of Part III, treats it rather incidentally, in offering a psychological account of its origin. Benevolence is one of the natural virtues; they all have "no dependance on the artifice and contrivance of men." Moral distinctions depend entirely on certain peculiar sentiments of pain and pleasure. "If any action be either virtuous or vicious, 'tis only as a *sign* of some quality or character" in the actor. If they proceed from no constant principle, they have no influence on the indirect passions, love or hatred, pride or humility. Mere actions "consequently are never considered in morality." Hume's is definitely a morality of motives, not of consequences.

"The chief spring . . . of the human mind is pleasure or pain." Sympathy enables us to share the pleasures and pains of others. We are sensible of the causes and effects of another's passion, from *them* infer the passion itself; and "consequently *these* give rise to our sympathy." As is the case with the sense of beauty, so with our sentiments of morals:

Now justice is a moral virtue, merely because it has that tendency to the good of mankind; and indeed is nothing but an artificial invention to that purpose. The same may be said of allegiance, of the laws of nations, of modesty, and of good-manners. All these are mere human contrivances for the interest of society. It follows that sympathy is the source of the esteem, which we pay to all the artificial virtues. . . . Sympathy is a very powerful principle in human nature.

Indeed, many of the natural virtues have this same tendency to the good of society.

Natural generosity is very limited. "Being thus acquainted with the nature of man, we expect not any impossibilities from him." Any passion tends to work to the advantage or disadvantage of the circle it influences. Though this be often remote from ourselves, at times it is near, and "interests us strongly by sympathy." Thus we may account for the merit ascribed to generosity, humanity, compassion, gratitude, friendship, fidelity, zeal, disinterestedness, liberality, which form the character of "good" and "benevolent." These virtues, like love, are *"immediately agreeable* to the person, who is actuated by [them], and hatred *immediately disagreeable."* Hence the peculiar merit of benevolence in all its shapes and appearances. "Even its weaknesses are virtuous and amiable; and a person, whose grief upon the loss of a friend were excessive, would be esteemed upon that account." [55]

In contrast with the very sober treatment of Benevolence in the *Treatise,* Section II of the *Enquiry, On Benevolence,* opens with several pages of panegyrics: it is estimable. Then Hume recalls that his object is "more the speculative, than the practical part of morals." In praising any beneficent man, observers always insist on "the happiness and satisfaction, derived to society from his intercourse and good offices." This suggests that "the utility, resulting from the social virtues, forms, at least, a *part* of their merit."

Upon the whole, then, it seems undeniable, that nothing can bestow more merit upon any human creature than the sentiment of benevolence in an eminent degree; and that a *part,* at least, of its merit arises from its tendency to promote the interests of our species, and bestow happiness on human society. . . . In all determinations of morality, this circumstance of public utility is ever principally in view.[56]

We approve what is useful for the public good. The question remains, why does such utility please us? "We need be at no loss to account for the influence of utility, and to deduce it from principles, the most known and avowed in human nature." It has been held that being so useful to society, all moral distinctions arise from education, and were invented by politicians (like Mandeville's law-givers). But this is wrong; had nature made no such distinctions, politicians could never have built on anything.

The social virtues must be allowed to have a natural beauty and amiableness. It follows that the end, which they have a tendency to promote, must be some way agreeable to us, and take hold of some natural affection. It must please either from considerations of self-interest, or from more generous motives and regards.

[55] *Treatise,* Selby-Bigge, pp. 574–75, 577, 602–5; Green and Grose, II, 334–35, 337, 358–61.
[56] *Enquiry,* Selby-Bigge, pars. 140–41, 143–44; Green and Grose, II, 174–76, 178–79.

Judicious moralists, like Polybius, have tried to deduce all morals from self-love. But "the voice of nature and experience seems plainly to oppose the selfish theory." We approve virtue even in our enemies, though it injure us. Hume states his own position:

Usefulness is agreeable, and engages our approbation. . . . But, *useful?* For what? For somebody's interests, surely. Whose interest then? Not our own only: for our approbation frequently extends farther. It must, therefore, be the interests of those, who are served by the character or action approved of; and these we may conclude, however remote, are not totally indifferent to us.

Universal self-love is untenable, in the light of observation.

We must adopt a more public affection, and allow, that the interests of society are not . . . entirely indifferent to us. . . . Everything, which contributes to the happiness of society, recommends itself directly to our approbation and good-will. . . .

It is needless to push our researches so far as to ask, why we have humanity or a fellow-feeling with others. It is sufficient, that this is experienced to be a principle in human nature. . . . No man is absolutely indifferent to the happiness and misery of others. The first has a natural tendency to give pleasure; the second, pain. This everyone may find in himself. It is not probable, that these principles can be resolved into principles more simple and universal, whatever attempts may have been made to that purpose.

Hume has abandoned the effort to give a psychological explanation of "origins." "What sympathy then touches every human heart! . . . If any man from a cold insensibility, or narrow selfishness of temper, is unaffected with the images of human happiness or misery, he must be equally indifferent to the images of vice and virtue." It is well that most resulting benevolence is particular rather than general, "otherwise our affections and actions would be dissipated and lost, for want of a proper limited object."

Hume states again his fundamental morality of motives:

The tendencies of actions and characters, not their real accidental consequences, are alone regarded in our moral determinations or general judgments. . . . Why is this peach-tree said to be better than that other; but because it produces more or better fruit? And would not the same praise be given it, though snails or vermin had destroyed the peaches, before they came to full maturity? In morals too, is not *the tree known by the fruit?* [57]

[57] *Enquiry*, Selby-Bigge, pars. 172–74, 177, 178n., 183, 185n.; Green and Grose, II, 203–4, 206–8, 212, 214–15.

VI

Hume has two treatments of justice, allegiance to government, the law of nations, chastity and good manners. In the central Part II of Book III of the *Treatise,* he finds them related as "artificial virtues," set up by human contrivance and "convention," in contrast to the "natural virtues" of greatness of mind and benevolence. Sections III and IV of the *Enquiry* still group these virtues, but the notion of "artificial" is played down, as is their derivation from self-interest. This is part of Hume's reversion away from his early enthusiasm for the mechanism of association back to a position closer to Hutcheson's. The treatment of political society is also much briefer in the *Enquiry;* much of it had been worked up into the Essays of 1742 *Of the Origin of Government* and *Of the Original Contract.*

In Book III of the *Treatise,* Hume explains that when he denies justice to be a natural virtue, he uses "natural" only as opposed to "artificial." "In another sense of the word; as no principle of the human mind is more natural than a sense of virtue; so no virtue is more natural than justice. Mankind is an inventive species; and where an invention is obvious and absolutely necessary, it may as properly be said to be natural as any thing that proceeds immediately from original principles, without the intervention of thought or reflection. Though the rules of justice be *artificial,* they are not *arbitrary.*" [58]

The artificial virtues "produce pleasure and approbation by means of an artifice or contrivance, which arises from the circumstances and necessity of mankind." Now, in praising actions, we regard only the motives of the agent; the external performance has no merit. Hence the first virtuous motive can never be a regard to the virtue of that action, but must be some other natural motive or principle. Thus, if I ask, what motive have I to restore money lent me? I cannot answer, before man has been educated in a civilized state, the reason is justice. The reason for being honest can be said to be, "the regard to public interest." But public interest is not naturally attached to observing the rules of justice. It is only connected with it "after an artificial convention for the establishment of these

[58] *Treatise,* Selby-Bigge, p. 484; Green and Grose, II, 258.

rules." And experience proves that in being honest "men look not so far as the public interest; . . . That is a motive too remote." Nor is the motive private benevolence to the creditor. Suppose him an enemy? Now men are very selfish; "yet 'tis rare to meet with one, in whom all the kind affections, taken together, do not over-balance all the selfish." In the inconvenience of the natural state, men seek a remedy.

This can be done after no other manner, than by a convention entered into by all the members of the society to bestow stability on the possession of those external goods, and leave every one in the peaceable enjoyment of what he may acquire by his fortune and industry. By this means, every one knows what he may safely possess; and the passions are restrained. . . . Instead of departing from our own interest, or from that of our nearest friends, by abstaining from the possessions of others, we cannot better consult both these interests than by such a convention.

Hence it is from self-interest that the institution of justice arises.

'Tis only from the selfishness and confined generosity of men, along with the scanty provision nature has made for his wants, that justice derives its origin. . . . This convention is not of the nature of a *promise:* for even promises themselves . . . arise from human conventions. It is only a general sense of common interest.[59]

Two men who pull the oars of a boat, do it by an agreement or convention, though they have never given promises to each other.

This is what Hume makes out of the "social contract" of the tradition, of Hobbes and Locke. He thinks the resulting social system of justice is as yet pre-political, but not pre-social; its status he takes to be that of the Law of Nations, which is likewise observed out of self-interest, with no further sanction.

Philosophers may, if they please, extend their reasoning to the supposed *state of nature;* provided they allow it to be a mere philosophical fiction, which never had, and never could have any reality. . . . The *state of nature* is to be regarded as a mere fiction not unlike that of the golden age, which poets have invented; only with this difference, that the former is described as full of war, violence and injustice; whereas the latter is painted out to us, as the most charming and most peaceable condition, that can possibly be imagined.[60]

[59] *Treatise,* Selby-Bigge, pp. 477, 480–81; 487, 489–90; Green and Grose, II, 252, 255, 260, 262–63.
[60] *Treatise,* Selby-Bigge, pp. 490, 493; Green and Grose, II, 263, 265–66.

Hume points out, in the state of nature violation of property rights cannot be said to have been allowed, as there were no property rights.

Why, then, do we annex the idea of virtue to justice, and of vice to injustice? What is its moral obligation and sanction? "However single acts of justice may be contrary, either to public or private interest, 'tis certain, that the whole plan or scheme is highly conducive, or indeed absolutely requisite, both to the support of society, and the well-being of every individual. 'Tis impossible to separate the good from the ill. Property must be stable, and must be fixed by general rules."

The three fundamental laws of nature [are], that of the stability of possession, of its transference by consent, and of the performance of promises. 'Tis on the strict observance of these three laws, that the peace and security of human society entirely depend; nor is there any possibility of establishing a good correspondence among men, where these are neglected. Society is absolutely necessary for the well-being of men; and these are as necessary to the support of society.

Hume finds sympathy enters into the process by which we approve justice.

Thus self-interest is the original motive to the *establishment* of justice; but a *sympathy* with public interest is the source of the *moral approbation* which attends that virtue.[61]

Even more than for the moderate liberal Locke, for the Tory Hume justice means the system of property arrangements. He well typifies the spirit of the British Enlightenment, boldness in speculation coupled with conservatism in practice, complacent acceptance of the eighteenth-century Establishment. The stability of possession is not only useful, but absolutely necessary to human society. But it needs specification, general rules regulating it, which in particular cases may even conflict with public utility. After society is established, by the convention setting up justice or the system of property rights, property may be acquired by occupation, by prescription, by accession, or by succession. Property by accession includes the fruits of the garden, the offspring of our cattle, and the work of our slaves. Promises or the rights of contract entail

[61] *Treatise*, Selby-Bigge, pp. 497, 526, 499; Green and Grose, II, 269, 293, 271.

obligations because of the artifice or convention setting the scheme up.

Allegiance to government, like justice, is founded on interest. In general, Hume follows Locke, except with the right of revolution, which he abhors.

Men are not able radically to cure, either in themselves or others, that narrowness of soul, which makes them prefer the present to the remote. They cannot change their natures. All they can do is to change their situation, and render the observance of justice the immediate interest of some particular persons, and its violation their more remote. These persons, then, are not only induced to observe those rules in their own conduct, but also to constrain others to a like regularity, and enforce the dictates of equity through the whole society. . . .

But this execution of justice, though the principal, is not the only advantage of government. . . . The same persons, who execute the laws of justice will also decide all controversies concerning them; and being indifferent to the greatest part of the society, will decide them more equitably than every one would in his own case.[62]

Hume follows Locke as to the aim of government.

By means of these two advantages, in the execution and decision of justice men acquire a security against each other's weakness and passion, as well as against their own, and under the shelter of their governors, begin to taste at ease the sweets of society and mutual assistance. . . .

There arises a new set of duties among [independent] states, suitable to the nature of that commerce which they carry on with each other. . . . The three fundamental rules of justice . . . are duties of princes as well as of subjects. . . . The advantages of peace, commerce, and mutual succor make us extend to different kingdoms the same notions of justice, which take place among individuals. . .

But though the morality of princes has the same *extent*, yet it has not the same *force* as that of private persons, and may lawfully be transgressed from a more trivial motive. . . .

Though the intercourse of different states be advantageous, and even sometimes necessary, yet it is not so necessary or advantageous as that among individuals, without which 'tis utterly impossible for human nature ever to subsist. Since, therefore, the natural obligation to justice, among different states, is not so strong as among individuals, the moral obligation, which arises from it, must partake of its weakness.[63]

The *Enquiry* deals with the material of Part II of Book III of the *Treatise* in two sections, *Of Justice*, and *Of Political Society;*

---

[62] *Treatise*, Selby-Bigge, pp. 537–38; Green and Grose, II, 303.
[63] *Treatise*, Selby-Bigge, pp. 538, 567–69; Green and Grose, II, 303, 328–30.

property is treated in Part II of the former. The section on Justice wastes no time with the "artificial virtues"; it starts out, "That Justice is useful to society, and consequently that *part* of its merit, at least, must arise from that consideration," needs no proof. "That public utility is the *sole* origin of justice, and that reflections on the beneficial consequences of this virtue are the *sole* foundation of its merit," is what Hume sets out to demonstrate. Were there no scarcity of goods, "the cautious, jealous virtue of justice" would never have been dreamed of. Were human benevolence universal, justice would never be needed. Such benevolence prevails in families and between married couples. Or if no goods were available, justice would be suspended, as in cities under siege.

The use and tendency of [justice] is to procure happiness and security, by preserving order in society. . . . The rules of equity or justice depend entirely on the particular state and condition in which men are placed. . . . Hence the ideas of property become necessary in all civil society: hence justice derives its usefulness to the public: and hence alone arises its merit and moral obligation.[64]

"The philosophical fiction of the *state of nature*" is depicted in Hobbes as a war of all; but Hobbes was not the first to set this low estimate on human nature. Plato presents it in Thrasymachus' speech; it is taken for granted by Cicero (*Pro Sexto*). Hume comments: "Whether such a condition of human nature could ever exist, or if it did, could continue so long as to merit the appellation of a 'state,' may justly be doubted. Men are necessarily born in a family-society, at least; and are trained up by their parents to some rule of conduct and behavior."

Were men associated with a race of rational beings so weak that their resentment need not be feared, we should be bound to treat them humanely, but we should "not lie under any restraint of justice with regard to them." Such is the way Europeans treat the Indians; and thus have women been treated in many societies. Or were an individual completely self-contained, he would be incapable of justice. Actually, the family has its rules, these are extended into a society, with its own rules; the societies form an international community. "History, experience, reason sufficiently instruct us in this

[64] *Enquiry*, Selby-Bigge, pars. 145-47, 149; Green and Grose, II, 179-80, 182-83.

natural progress of human sentiments, and in the gradual enlarge-
ment of our regards to justice in proportion as we become acquainted
with the extensive utility of that virtue." [65] Hume has burst the
bonds of the traditional legal conception of the origin of social
organization and its authority and arrived at the notion of a gradual
process of social development.

He goes still farther in his *Essays* of 1742. In *Of the Origin of
Government*, he begins:

Man, born in a family, is compelled to maintain society, from necessity,
from natural inclination, and from habit. The same creature, in his farther
progress, is engaged to establish political society, in order to administer
justice.

Thus Hume distinguishes two stages: the "convention" by which
the system of justice is set up, and the establishment of government,
by which it is administered. He is following Pufendorf's position,
and also Locke's, if that be Locke's considered view. "We are to
look upon all the vast apparatus of our government, as having ultimately no other object or purpose but the distribution of justice, or,
in other words, the support of the twelve judges." "All men are sensible of the necessity of justice to maintain peace and order; and all
men are sensible of the necessity of peace and order for the maintenance of society."

Hume thinks government originated in military leadership: "the
first ascendant of one man over multitudes begun during a state of
war." The leader was necessary, he satisfied interest, and he was
soon obeyed through habit. "In all governments, there is a perpetual
intestine struggle, open or secret, between authority and liberty;
and neither of them can ever absolutely prevail in the contest."
Every government requires "a great sacrifice of liberty"; while the
authority can never become "quite entire and uncontrollable." "The
sultan is master of the life and fortune of any individual; but will
not be permitted to impose new taxes on his subjects: a French
monarch can impose taxes at pleasure, but would find it dangerous
to attempt the lives and fortunes of individuals. Religion also, in most
countries, is commonly found to be a very intractable principle."
The government acknowledged to be free admits a "partition of
power"; and "it must be owned, that liberty is the perfection of

[65] *Enquiry*, Selby-Bigge, pars. 151–53; Green and Grose, II, 185–87.

civil society"—that is, action by general and equal laws known to all.[66]

In *Of the Original Contract*, Hume demolishes the social contract theory as it appears in most influential form in Locke. That theory is a Whig "system," opposed to the Tory "divine right of kings"; its essence is to assert the power of resisting the sovereign. Both principles are just, though both are asserted in fictional form. Hume accepts the idea of an original contract:

> The people, if we trace government to its first origin in the woods and deserts, are the source of all power and jurisdiction, and voluntarily, for the sake of peace and order, abandoned their native liberty, and received laws from their equal and companion.

The conditions were so clear it seemed superfluous to express them. "If this, then, be meant by the original contract, it cannot be denied, that all government is, at first, founded on a contract." This is Hume's concession to the established view; it is his "original convention" establishing a system of justice. But "no compact or agreement, it is evident, was expressly formed for general submission."

But philosophers (*lege* Locke) have used this fact to found political allegiance on a *promise*, which they take to be conditional on good behavior. This promise is the "foundation of authority in every government; and of the right of resistance possessed by every subject." But if these reasoners should look abroad into the world, they would find nothing to correspond with their ideas. Hume points out, that no actual government was ever founded in this fashion. Rather, usurpation, or conquest have prevailed. In his "more philosophical" refutation, he asserts: All moral duties spring from either natural instinct, or from reflection upon utility. Allegiance to government comes from the latter. "It is thus *justice* or a regard to the property of others, *fidelity* or the observance of promises, become obligatory, and acquire an authority over mankind." The same holds of the political or civil duty of allegiance.

> Our primary instincts lead us, either to indulge ourselves in unlimited freedom, or to seek dominion over others: and it is reflection only, which engages us to sacrifice such strong passions to the interests of peace and public order. . . . Allegiance and fidelity . . . are both submitted to by mankind, on account of the apparent interests and necessities of human society.

[66] *Essays*, ed. Green and Grose, I, 113, 115–16.

With any royal family, "its first authority was derived from usurpation and violence." There is no property in land, "but must, in some period, have been founded on fraud and injustice." Here, to the question, Who is our lawful sovereign?, we can appeal only to public opinion. Hume states his basic principle, which he shares with Protagoras, and which today would probably be called "democratic":

Though an appeal to general opinion may justly, in the speculative sciences of metaphysics, natural philosophy, or astronomy, be deemed unfair and inconclusive, yet in all questions with regard to morals, as well as criticism, there is really no other standard, by which any controversy can ever be decided.[67]

Locke's social contract theory leads to "paradoxes, repugnant to the common sentiments of mankind, and to the practice and opinion of all nations and all ages." It led Locke to hold, absolute monarchy is no form of civil government at all, and that the government cannot tax men without their consent. Berkeley, attacking Newton and Locke, "resolved to side in all things with the mob." In morals, Hume makes the same claim. Both claims have been doubted—as was the view of Protagoras in ancient Greece.

Two other of Hume's political essays are of philosophical moment. Essay III argues *That Politics may be reduced to a Science*. It is not true that the character of the administrator is the only difference between governments; human affairs admit of greater stability than that, though it is one of the inconveniences of absolute government that there it is more nearly true.

So great is the force of laws, and of particular forms of government, and so little dependence have they on the humors and tempers of men, that consequences almost as general and certain may be deduced from them, as any which the mathematical sciences afford us. . . . Politics admit of general truths, which are invariable by the humor or education either of subject or sovereign.

Hume's examples of the principles of this science are:

It is an universal axiom in politics, That an hereditary prince, a nobility without vassals [like the Venetian], and a people voting by their representatives, form the best *monarchy, aristocracy,* and *democracy*.

Though free governments have been commonly the most happy for

[67] *Essays,* ed. Green and Grose, I, 445, 454–56, 460.

those who partake of their freedom; yet are they the most ruinous and oppressive to the provinces [witness the Roman Republic].

The ancient Persians had no nobility; European princes allow such a class to remain in a conquered territory.

In the former species of government, after a conquest, it is impossible ever to shake off the yoke; whereas, in the latter, the least misfortune, or discord among the victors, will encourage the vanquished to take arms, who have leaders ready.

Hume leads up to the axiom, that in parliamentary government, those who either attack or defend a minister like Robert Walpole always exaggerate his merit or demerit with the public.

Somewhat surprisingly for a defender of experience against reason, in Essay VII, *Whether the British Government inclines more toward Absolute Monarchy, or to a Republic,* Hume takes the first side. In the classic spirit he remarks,

It is well known, that every government must come to a period, and that death is unavoidable to the political as well as to the animal body. . . . Here I would frankly declare that, though liberty be preferable to slavery, in almost every case, I should rather wish to see an absolute monarch than a republic in this island. For, let us consider, what kind of republic we have reason to expect. . . . Absolute monarchy, therefore, is the easiest death, the true Euthanasia, of the British constitution.[68]

In the *Enquiry,* Hume complacently justifies existing property arrangements on grounds of social utility. He has no patience for those "sublime theorists" who would advocate changes, especially in the direction of equality. Rationally, it is most obvious "to assign the largest possessions to the most extensive virtue," and thus proportion the power to the inclination to do good. There were religious fanatics in England during the civil wars, who supposed "that dominion is founded on grace, and that saints alone inherit the earth." "Perhaps the levellers, who claimed an equal distribution of property, were a kind of political fanatics." Sparta made it work.

But historians, and even common sense, may inform us, that, however specious these ideas of perfect equality may seem, they are really, at bottom, *impracticable,* and were they not so, would be extremely *pernicious* to human society. Render possessions ever so equal, men's different degrees of art, care, and industry will immediately break that equality. Or if you check these virtues, you reduce society to the most extreme

[68] *Essays,* ed. Green and Grose, I, 99, 101, 104, 126.

indigence; and instead of preventing want and beggary in a few, render it unavoidable to the whole community.

We may conclude, therefore, that in order to establish laws for the regulation of property, we must be acquainted with the nature and situation of man.

"Who sees not . . . that whatever is produced or improved by a man's art or industry ought, for ever, to be secured to him, in order to give encouragement to such *useful* habits and accomplishments? That the property ought also to descend to children and relations, for the same *useful* purpose?"

Even the writers on the law of nature "assign, as the ultimate reason for every rule which they establish, the convenience and necessities of mankind." The actual rule of property will vary with circumstance: Hume has approving words for the one French social theorist who shared his temper, "a late author of genius, as well as learning," Montesquieu, though he thinks the Frenchman went wrong in founding morality on *relations*, a view which in "Cudworth, Clarke, and others," he traces to "Father Malebranche," the Augustinian (*Traité de morale*, 1684).

The question remains, "As justice evidently tends to promote public utility and to support civil society, the sentiment of justice is either derived from our reflecting on that tendency, or . . . arises from a simple original instinct in the human breast . . . and is not ascertained by any argument or reflection." But who ever heard of such an instinct? The details of both property and the administration of government are too intricate to attribute to an instinct. "Have we original innate ideas of praetors and chancellors and juries? Who sees not, that all these institutions arise merely from the necessities of human society?" Birds make nests by instinct, but men build houses from reason and custom. The former are always the same, the latter vary infinitely. Such is the difference between the instinct of generation and the institution of property.

The necessity of justice to the support of society is the *sole* foundation of that virtue. . . . Usefulness has, in general, the strongest energy and most entire command over our sentiments. . . . We ascribe it a like energy in all similar instances. This indeed is Newton's chief rule of philosophizing.[69]

[69] *Enquiry*, Selby-Bigge, pars. 154–56, 158, 160–61, 163; Green and Grose, II, 187–89, 190–91, 194–96.

Hume ends on the note of Newton's method. It is pertinent to point out that the basic principle of method Hume employs, throughout both his analysis of "speculative" and of moral ideas, is the same: show me the impression whence the idea is derived, show me the passion whence the sentiment arises. Hume's thought is indeed the thorough working out of Newton's notion that all causation is efficient causation, as developed by Locke, into the principle, the original is the test of the extent and certainty of knowledge.

12

The Dawn of the French Enlightenment

WE HAVE ALREADY SEEN how Isaac Newton, as the spokesman of a highly successful mathematical science of nature, became in the eighteenth century the symbol of an intellectual method and of a great idea: of the "geometric" or "analytic" method, and of the idea, the imaginative vision, of nature as a rational and harmonious order. We have also seen how the empirical philosophy, bringing all beliefs to the test of their origins in a sensationalistic experience, developed, at the hands of British thinkers, into a powerful critical weapon capable of destroying any belief upon which it might be turned. In the eighteenth century these two methods and philosophies worked hand in hand, and were often employed by the same man, the sensationalism and empiricism serving him as the critical weapon for destroying the old, the method and model of natural science serving as the constructive tool for laying the foundations of the new. The eighteenth century had need of both weapon and tool. And in fact scientific rationalism and sensationalistic empiricism were two complementary aspects of the same intellectual temper. For they were two different outcomes of applying the same "geometrical analysis" to experience. And neither expressed the experimental attitude or formulated the experimental method that were to dominate thinking during the next century. The first consistent philosophical expression of that careful reconstruction of these two eighteenth-century philosophies into an experimental philosophy of science is to be found in the critical philosophy of Immanuel Kant. Its major forerunners were the Dutch Newtonians.

This temper, this joint employment of rationalism and empiricism, is the philosophic expression of the Enlightenment. That intellectual movement we have tried to define as the first thoroughgoing attempt to reconstruct the traditional beliefs, values, and institutions of European society in the light of the demands of the triumphant business spirit, and by means of the methods of Newtonian science. Thus the Enlightenment is essentially the use of the ideas whose working out we have been tracing, to influence a social situation, and to reconstruct an entire culture. If one prefers, it can be called the use of these ideas to provide intellectual justification for the practical efforts of practical men. Hence the incidence and the course of Enlightenment thinking proved to be quite different in the different major European cultures, England, France, and Germany. We have seen how the chief outcome of Enlightenment ideas in England was the creation of a middle-class culture. There is a sense, indeed, in which Englishmen had no real need of being "enlightened" to devote themselves wholeheartedly to business enterprise. The only movement in Britain that can be accurately called an "Enlightenment" took place in Scotland, where clericalism was still a living force, as it was not south of the Tweed.

The reconstruction of traditional ideas was most thoroughgoing and radical in France, as a result of the peculiar problems of French culture: the ideas of British origin that were now grafted on to the native trunk of Cartesian rationalism were carried furthest by writers who, if not French, were at least like Holbach and Rousseau writing in France for Frenchmen. And France was the scene of the most dramatic practical revolution, whose effect was to provoke both England and Germany to a reaction against Enlightenment thought. Ironically enough, France failed to feel deeply throughout the nineteenth century the most revolutionary social force of the time, the transforming power of industrial technology. Hence France remained down through World War I closer to these eighteenth-century ideas than any other European culture, and is probably still the most conservative of the major cultures of the West.

As we shall see, it can be argued with great plausibility that Enlightenment ideas had a more profound and lasting effect upon Germans than even upon Frenchmen, bringing as they did in very brief span a series of intellectual revolutions that the cultures west of the Rhine had been assimilating for some three hundred years. The

German *Aufklärung* shook men's souls. The effect was to make Germany for a century the source of major new ideas in Western culture. But it was also to make it almost impossible down to this day for German thinkers to take seriously those eighteenth-century ideals which French, Americans, and even British accept as a matter of course.

I

It is both difficult and easy to treat French thought in the eighteenth century, an age when every man of letters was a "philosopher," and when there was no systematic nor, by common agreement, any "profound" philosophy. That the philosophy of the Enlightenment was not "profound" may be true. But it is not too clear just what this rather facile judgment means. Certainly there was nothing comparable to classic German metaphysics. There were no imposing philosophical systems like the tours-de-force of the seventeenth century. There was in France no criticism of Newtonian science so acute as Berkeley's, or so diabolically clever as Hume's, or so patient and thoroughgoing as Kant's. It is true that the greatest philosophic constructions, in modern times at least, have sprung from the attempt to hold together in one body of ideas both traditional beliefs and values and novel concepts and aims. In the eighteenth century French thinkers were too prone to abandon tradition to undertake such a task. Their reputations paid the penalty in the nineteenth century when the intellectual temper had significantly altered.

Was it, therefore, a shallow and superficial century? The answer is far from clear. The foundations of most of the modern sciences were laid at that time. There was a rapidly increasing army of investigators in all fields; no longer do we encounter a single name here and there. The scientific academies were flourishing at their height. It was a time of intellectual ferment. "Enlightenment" meant at least a rapid increase in the number of those who possessed the knowledge available. A new social class was eagerly learning and coming to the fore. The philosophers no longer sprang from the nobility or the clergy, but were mainly bourgeois men of letters. The science of man and human nature, and the sciences of society, were being vigorously worked out.

And these *philosophes* possessed a vision: the Heavenly City of the eighteenth-century philosophers is surely as inspiring as any City of God—or any City of Moscow. It has, to be sure, grown somewhat worn and tawdry, because during the nineteenth century it gradually and insensibly merged into the City of Mammon, and ideas that in the eighteenth century had served as flaming standards of revolt came to furnish convenient excuses for not facing resolutely an entirely different situation and a set of new needs. That eighteenth-century City of Reason cannot be ours. Yet few of us can escape a pang of regret, when we are told, what is perfectly true, that those eighteenth-century ideals of humanity, toleration, peace, progress, cosmopolitanism, freedom, and democracy were expressions of a bourgeois ideology, and, what seems a more dubious fact, that they can have little place in our industrialized and nationalistic world.

Eighteenth-century French thought is difficult to delineate, because there are few figures that stand out head and shoulders above the rest, like Descartes or Malebranche or Pascal in *le grand siècle*. And those that are outstanding are distinguished primarily as personalities, as centers of intellectual influence and activity, rather than as deeply original thinkers. But eighteenth-century French thought is also easy to analyze, for the thinking is unified by certain great social problems. All men are in some fashion caught up in *"la lutte philosophique,"* all thinkers are united in the desire to overcome the Old Regime. It is remarkable that until the Revolution was well under way, the system found no intellectual defender. This philosophizing may not have been profound, but it was at least a vital, living force, an instrument of radical criticism. Philosophy can be either a bulwark of the existing order, as in seventeenth-century France, or in Germany and Oxford in the nineteenth century. Or it can be a patient and persistent seeking of new truth, of something better, a searching for the highest and the best, undismayed by the fact that existence may not correspond to its demands. In eighteenth-century France it was the second.

What was the situation confronting critical thinkers? Here was a social and religious system handed down from the remote past, a system originally developed in feudal times to meet the needs of the experience of feudal society—a system not at its inception bad, and once adequate enough, but now clearly outgrown. It embraced a huge and conglomerate mass of old and time-honored customs and institutions and beliefs that had largely lost their meaning, and had become obstacles in the way of a realistic adaptation to the needs of a very different kind of social experience. And such systems readily lend themselves to a host of abuses, as vermin find shelter in the crannies of ramshackle buildings.

The rich flood of new life springing from Descartes and the science of the seventeenth century, to say nothing of the rapid growth of trade and the professions, could no longer be confined within the limits of the Cartesian compromise. There was an unstable social equilibrium: the monarchy and the Church were decaying, the new knowledge and attitudes and the new class of commercial and professional men were rapidly growing.

The problem confronting thinkers was how to get rid of the old, and, intellectually, how to provide a leverage for criticism. Incidentally, there was a need to find something to take the place of the old, and to work out a method for the new order and its justification. But this latter was not the immediately pressing problem; it could be worked out, or at least worked upon, later. And it was this constructive problem that was left as a legacy to the nineteenth century, as the men from 1815 to 1848 realized.

Hence the net result of eighteenth-century thought in France was destructive and subversive, not because no positive solutions were offered, but because they proved to be premature. Nevertheless, we must not forget the constructive side of Enlightenment thinking, which emerged as the old rubbish was cleared away. The seventeenth century had laid the foundations of modern natural science. The eighteenth century not only toiled valiantly at this enterprise. It also laid the foundations of the science of man, and proclaimed the discovery of natural laws of human nature and human society that should be as universally true as the laws of physics. It laid the foundations of a science of human behavior, in its psychology; of man in society, or sociology; of man in agriculture, commerce and industry, in political economy; and of man in the commonwealth, in its science of government. And the French Revolution carried all these ideas far and wide, even to those, like the Germans and the English, who rejected its immediate fruits.

The aim of Voltaire, and of the eighteenth-century French thinkers in general, was "*écraser l'infâme*," to smash the System. It was put rather melodramatically, "to throttle the last king in the bowels of the last Jesuit." Such statements at least make clear that reason had not suppressed all passion in the *éclaircissement*. Was such heat justified? We can call as witness the normally sober John Morley:

In estimating an innovator's method, all depends on the time and the enemy; and it may sometimes happen that the time is so out of joint and the enemy so strong, so unscrupulous, so imminently pernicious, as to leave no alternative between finally succumbing, and waging a war of deliverance for which coming generations have to bear the burdens in feuds and bitterness. . . . For let us not forget that what Catholicism was accomplishing in France in the first half of the eighteenth century, was really not anything less momentous than the slow strangling of French civilization. Though Voltaire's spirit may be little edifying to us, who after all partake of the freedom which he did so much to win, yet it is only just to remember what was the spirit of his foe . . . Let the scientific spirit move people to speak as it lists about Voltaire's want of respect for things held sacred, for the good deeds of holy men, for the sentiment and faith of thousands of the most worthy among his fellows. Still there are times when it may be very questionable whether, in the region of belief, one with power and with fervid honesty ought to spare the abominable city of the plain, just because it happens to shelter five righteous. . . . Voltaire had no calm breadth of wisdom. It may be so. There are moments which need not this calm breadth of wisdom, but a two-edged sword, and when the deliverers of mankind are they who "come to send fire on the earth." [1]

We must remember two facts. First, in attacking religion the French *philosophes* were attacking the Catholic Church of eighteenth-century France, the Church that burned Protestant pastors for performing their ministry, that broke Calas on the wheel, that hounded Sirven, that killed eighteen-year-old La Barre for singing an unseemly song; the Church whose Jesuits were intriguing, bringing about wars in which peasants' homes were devastated, which set the country groaning under taxation; the Church which officially opposed science and enlightenment, and served as the bulwark of the whole iniquitous and rotten social system; the Church whose high officials denied God in private, and burnt men for making jests, who gave themselves up to a riotous life of luxury at Versailles while extorting greater and greater sums from the peasants.

[1] John Morley, *Voltaire* (London, 1872), pp. 29-31.

This was "the Infamous." And it was in the name of justice and mercy and humanity, and of a benevolent God, of a religion that may not stir our souls today, but assuredly represented something better than the regnant intolerance and bigotry and corruption, that the eighteenth-century *philosophes* shot their poisoned darts. And they shot them, not at Malebranche or Bossuet, but at Cardinal de Rohan, and all he stood for.

Secondly, if we can now appreciate the abiding value of the traditional Christian system, it is only because Voltaire and his followers destroyed the moral authority of that body which called itself the Catholic Church in the eighteenth century. A Renan or a Santayana, even a Châteaubriand, can only come after a Voltaire and a Holbach. The striking renascence of Christianity and of Catholicism in nineteenth-century France was possible only because the *philosophes* forced the Church to put its own house in order. A religious organization must in the end reform itself by heeding its own prophets; but again and again it has been external criticism that has forced a church to listen to them. Just as Luther was responsible for the Catholic Reformation of the sixteenth century, so was Voltaire responsible for the Catholic Revival of the nineteenth.

II

How could eighteenth-century France develop out of *le grand siècle*, a sceptical, anticlerical, atheistic, critical and destructive age out of so imposing a blending of reason and art as the French Catholic monarchy of the arge of Louis XIV? Three continuing and transitional strains of thinking help to explain the new temper: 1) There is the scepticism of the *libertin* or free-thinking group in high society, which had taken form as early as Gassendi. 2) There is the scientific rationalism that represented the working out of Cartesian ideas themselves; though reluctant to admit it, the rationalism of the French Enlightenment owed as much, if not more, to Descartes as to Newtonian thought from across the Channel. Fontenelle, born in 1657, continued to popularize Cartesian rationalism until 1752. 3) The historical criticism of existing institutions and beliefs, of which the *Dictionary* of Pierre Bayle was the outstanding achievement, was really the application of Cartesian doubt to human affairs.

The two men who typify the last two tendencies are always coupled together, though their personalities and their achievements are wholly different. Fontenelle (1657–1757) was the brilliant popularizer of Cartesian science. Others had popularized Descartes's theology and his metaphysics; Fontenelle rejected the metaphysics, and by emphasizing the science had much to do with changing the character of French culture from literary, oratorical, and poetic to scientific. In the process he changed the method and scope of science itself: it ceased to be a rigorously systematic method, and became instead a method of analysis that could be applied to any question of interest.

What is true is simple and clear; and when our way of arriving at the truth is intricate and confused, we may say the way leads to the truth, but it is nevertheless not the true way.[2]

Since men were interested in human and social affairs, scientific method was to be applied everywhere, to morals, politics, criticism, and eloquence. And since the method of science was still mathematical, that application must be made in the geometrical spirit: simplify, abstract, analyze, generalize, and deduce.

The geometrical spirit is not so bound up with geometry that it cannot be abstracted and carried into other sciences. A work of morals, of politics, of criticism, perhaps even of eloquence, will be all the better, other things being equal, if it is created by the hand of a geometrician.[3]

This is really the key to eighteenth-century French thinking. Without being rigorously mathematical, it tries to make a thoroughgoing application of certain of the main ideas of mathematics: order, law, universality, independence of observation and experiment, to everything in the universe, and especially to the various pursuits of man and his social life. In the nonhistorical spirit of mathematics, it meant an appraisal of existing institutions and ideas in terms of their present value. What are they really worth today?

Fontenelle's distinctive literary method is beautifully illustrated in the engraving that serves as frontispiece to the second volume of his collected *Oeuvres* of 1766, an elegant little tooled leather duodecimo. Madame is seated at her dressing table in her baroque chamber.

---

[2] L. Lévy-Bruhl, *History of Modern Philosophy in France* (1899), p. 126.
[3] Fontenelle, *Oeuvres* (1818), I, 34.

One hand is performing her toilette, the other is measuring a globe with a pair of compasses. The legend runs:

> De l'Esprit et des appas   Wit and allurement
> L'eventail et le compas   The fan and the compasses

Fontenelle was a provincial wit who came to Paris to make a name. He tried his hand at writing about nearly all subjects. In 1686 he wrote *Entretiens sur la pluralité des mondes*, an admirable piece of popular science, a true wedding in the eighteenth-century spirit of literature and science. It was also one of the very earliest really popular statements of the Copernican system, set forth in the elegant conversation of ladies and gentlemen. "All the play of nature consists in the figures and movements of bodies," he explains in true Cartesian fashion. Yet Fontenelle never changed his ideas, and as late as 1752, when Newton had won the day, he was still defending Cartesian physics against the confused Newtonian notion of gravitation.

He also opposed strongly the anthropocentrism of Bossuet.

Our folly is to believe that all of nature, without exception, is destined for our uses. And when we ask our philosophers, of what use is the prodigious number of fixed stars, of which a small part would do what they all do, they answer coldly that they serve to make a pleasing spectacle . . . I am very grateful to Copernicus for having lowered the vanity of men, who had set themselves in the finest place in the universe; and I am pleased to see the earth at present amidst the throng of planets.[4]

Yet like Voltaire he held that such knowledge is only for the élite.

In 1687 Fontenelle published *L'Histoire des oracles*, one of the earliest attacks on religion. Its spirit is suggested by another engraving, in which a man in the cellar is uttering the oracular pronouncements. Were ancient oracles given by demons, who ceased their deviltry after Christ? No, the orthodox answer is wrong. Oracles stopped because of the decline of superstition as a result of the advance of science. Fontenelle is writing a history of superstition; and where he mentioned "oracles" his readers rightly read "miracles." He has a rather modern view of the origin of myths, attributing them to the process now called "projection."

Fontenelle took a prominent part in the quarrel between the An-

[4] *Entretiens, Premier soir, Oeuvres,* II, 12, 15.

cients and the Moderns, supporting strongly the idea of progress. All men are of the same stuff: we moderns are just like Homer or Plato, except that we have learned much more. This view is typical both of Cartesian and of Enlightenment thinking. Yet Fontenelle also displays traces of scepticism: might there not be a sixth sense inaccessible to us?

Fontenelle painted the world as a huge watch, entirely subservient to mechanical laws. In it was to be found a God, the watch-maker; and also a being, Man (not men) who was as invariable in his behavior as were the drops of water. Such a science of man, a social physics, was the outcome of the full application of Cartesian ideas.

Pierre Bayle (1647–1706) is a man of a very different stamp, not the brilliant and elegant popularizer, but the learned scholar and critic, who grubbed in the past and turned up disquieting opinions and annoying facts. He loved to show the excellent arguments that could be put forward for refuted and forgotten theories. Above all, he delighted to show up men's superstitious beliefs.

Bayle was a Calvinist who had been converted briefly by a Jesuit, and then recanted. He was at first a teacher in the Protestant Academy at Sedan, where he came to dislike the reformed orthodoxy of Jurieu; after his recantation he had to leave France and settle in Rotterdam as a publicist and scholar. What was his own position? What did he actually believe? Was he a "Cartesian," or was he a "sceptic"? The answer is far from clear. For he was not, like Fontenelle, interested in science, perhaps not even in truth, but in men's beliefs and theories and opinions. They were all so different! And the refuted errors do seem so reasonable! How infinitely blessed are we to have divine revelation to protect us from such plausible errors! Such was Bayle.

From 1684 to 1687 Bayle edited one of the first European literary journals, *Nouvelles de la république des lettres*. In 1681 he had made a name for himself with his *Pensées diverses sur la comète* of the preceding year, a study of superstition and "prejudice," in which all his characteristic themes are suggested. In 1692 he began work on a vast *Dictionnaire historique et critique*, which came out in 1697; it had a second enlarged edition in 1702, and many reprintings. It is an erudite and scholarly work devoting ten times as much space to footnotes as to text, embodying much curious lore.

The net impression Bayle leaves is clear: revelation is not reasonable. Do not try to defend it, or you will be open to attack. The axiom of identity is abrogated in transubstantiation. Such doctrines are mysteries: believe them, but do not try to rationalize them. He addresses the philosophers:

Do not try to understand mysteries; if you could understand them they would be mysteries no longer. Do not even try to lessen their apparent absurdity. Your reason here is utterly powerless; and who knows but that absurdity may be an essential ingredient of mystery. Believe as Christians; but as philosophers abstain.

And to the theologians he says:

You are quite right in demanding that we should believe; but make this demand in the name of authority only, and do not be so imprudent as to try to justify your belief in the eyes of reason. God has willed it so, God has done so; therefore it is good and true, wisely done and wisely permitted. Do not venture any further. If you enter into detailed reasons for all this you will never see the end of it, and, after a thousand disputes, you will be compelled to fall back upon your original reason, authority. In this matter, the best use to make of reason is not to reason. Moreover, if you consent to discuss the point, you will be beaten.[5]

Humanly and logically speaking, Manichaeism, the belief that there is a principle of good in continual strife with a principle of evil, and that neither is able to triumph over the other, is the only rational conclusion of experience.

Revelation is the only storehouse from which arguments can be produced against such people; by it alone can we refute the alleged eternity of the evil principle. (p. 117)

Leibniz's *Théodicée* was the attempt of reason to answer Bayle; in *Candide* and the *Poème sur le désastre de Lisbonne* Voltaire brings experience to the support of Bayle.

Bayle is likewise insistent on the Protestant principle that the moral conscience must be the criterion for the interpretation of revelation.

If anybody presumes to assert that God has revealed to us a moral maxim in direct opposition to the first principles of all morals, we must deny the assertion, and maintain that such a person is misinterpreting the text, and that one ought rather to reject the testimony of one's criticism and grammar than that of one's reason. (p. 119)

[5] Lévy-Bruhl, pp. 114-15.

Bayle vigorously defends tolerance against both Catholics and Protestants like Jurieu. He did so before Locke had published his famous letter, and he argues more in the spirit of Montaigne than of the eighteenth century. No heretic can be justly punished for honest ignorance. "All that an enlightened conscience permits us to do for the advancement of truth, a mistaken conscience permits us to do for what we believe to be the truth."

Perhaps Bayle's basic principle is the independence of morals from any theological or religious sanction. This Cartesian principle was of course reinforced by his Protestant orientation. He points out how often religious men are bad, and irreligious men good. A major question he left to the eighteenth century was, "Could there be a society consisting wholly of just atheists?"

Bayle clearly stated the alternative: be a Christian, and an upholder of the old order, or follow reason—you cannot do both at the same time. In a sense it is Pascal's alternative also. But the Enlightenment was not prepared to give Pascal's answer. And from Voltaire down, its thinkers drew on Bayle's *Dictionary* as an inexhaustible arsenal of weapons against Christianity.

III

We can well take Voltaire as the symbol of the problems faced by the French Enlightenment and of the materials it drew upon to meet them. Voltaire (1694–1778) represents almost single-handed in his writings of the 1730s the first generation of Enlightenment thinkers. The second generation, beginning about 1745, had already passed beyond him: it went on to push his ideas to their more radical implications. The third generation was more specifically interested in social and political problems, and in erecting a suitable science of man.

Voltaire is an excellent example of the intellectual middleman. He did not himself originate any of his ideas: he is no original thinker. But he took ideas from the unread books of others, and gave them life. He forged them into weapons that cut sharp and true. He gave them a slight twist or change that transformed them from interesting speculation to deadly rapiers. To anyone interested in the adaptation of ideas, Voltaire's virtuosity is fascinating. He displays a marvelous technique and artistry.

Voltaire the man is a rather unattractive, not to say quite despicable character—shallow, superficial, mean-spirited, prone to petty quarrels, cringing before Frederick, narrow in mind and soul, inordinately vain, cowardly, afraid to acknowledge his scurrilous attacks. This was the Voltaire who rebuilt Ferney church, preached in it, confessed and went to mass, and had a notary make a record of the events—the Voltaire who accepted the post of temporal father of the Capucins. His bedroom at Sans Souci has appropriately large gaudily painted wooden parrots inserted in each panel.

But Voltaire was also something more. A man with such qualities alone would never have become the intellectual master of Europe, swaying enlightened kings from his seat at Ferney. He hated falsehood, and he hated injustice: he waged a lifelong battle against their united power. He never gave up; each new outrage only inflamed his heart the more. He never tired in defending the persecuted—Calas, Sirven, La Barre, even the Jesuits in disgrace in 1764.

Voltaire embodied the temper of his age, and indeed his century, in rejecting the old seventeenth-century system, which in France, as worked out by the later Cartesians, had meant reestablishing on the basis of reason most of the traditional religious and social beliefs, in new and rationalized form. To him, "metaphysical" and "systematic" were terms of reproach.

Metaphysics contains two things: the first, all that men of sound sense know anyway; the second, what they will never be able to know.[6]

Metaphysics is more amusing than geometry; it is often the romance of the mind. In geometry, on the contrary, we must calculate and measure. It is a continual work, and many minds like sweet dreams better than tiring themselves.[7]

"Metaphysics" is synonymous with l'esprit des systèmes. The trouble with Descartes is that he suffered from "the systematic spirit"; in fact, only Bacon, Newton, and Locke are wholly free from it. This meant positively that reason was to be applied to the analysis of any subject matter directly, preferably in a little dialogue.

Secondly, Voltaire is specifically anti-Cartesian in not only rejecting Descartes's metaphysics, but also in destroying it by dis-

---

[6] Letter to Frederick, August 17, 1737.
[7] Philosophical Dictionary, article "Métaphysique."

crediting the physics on which it was founded. He turned to the English thought of Newton for an alternative.

A Frenchman who arrives in London finds things much changed in [natural] philosophy as in everything else. He has left the world full, he finds it empty. At Paris we see the world composed of vortices of subtle matter; in London we see nothing of the sort. At home it is the pressure of the moon that causes the tides of the sea; with the English it is the sea which gravitates toward the moon.[8]

"Our Descartes," says Voltaire, "was born to discover the errors of antiquity, but to substitute for them his own." "Descartes was a dreamer, Newton a sage."

[Descartes] made a philosophy as we make a good novel; everything seemed probable, and nothing was true. He imagined elements, vortices which seemed to give a plausible reason for all the mysteries of nature; but in philosophy we must mistrust what we think we understand too easily just as well as the things we do not understand. Descartes was more dangerous than Aristotle, because he had the air of being more reasonable. M. Conduit, nephew of Sir Isaac Newton, has assured me that his uncle had read Descartes at the age of twenty, that he pencilled the margins of the first pages, and that he set down there only a single note, often repeated, consisting of the word, error; but that, tired of writing error everywhere, he threw the book aside and never reread it. . . .

Geometry was a guide which he had himself in some fashion formed, and which would have conducted him safely in his physics; and yet he abandoned this guide in the end, and delivered himself over to the systematic spirit. Then his philosophy was no more than an ingenious romance, and all the more plausible for the ignorant philosophers of the time. He was mistaken on the nature of the soul, on the laws of motion, on the nature of light. He admits innate ideas, he invents new elements, he creates a world, he made man in his fashion; and it is rightly said that the man of Descartes is only in fact the man of Descartes, far away from true man. . . . If he invented new chimaeras in physics, at least he destroyed the ancient ones; he taught the men of his time to reason and to use his own weapons against himself. If he did not pay in good money, it is much to have denounced the false.

I do not think that we can in truth dare compare his philosophy in anything with that of Newton; the first is a sketch, the second a masterpiece; but he who has set us on the road to truth is perhaps worth as much as he who has since come to the end of that path.[9]

[8] *Lettres philosophiques*, Lettre XIV, "Sur Descartes et Newton"; ed. G. Lanson, II, 1.

[9] *Lettres philosophiques*, Lettres XV, XIV; Lanson, II, pp. 16, 6, 7.

Thirdly, Voltaire rejected the gorgeous rationalization of Christianity developed by Bossuet and the other churchmen under Louis XIV. He rejected it, of course, because he was opposed to the Church as a social, political, and economic institution; all French thinking on religion during the Enlightenment is basically anticlerical.

Nevertheless, in spite of his professed hostility to Cartesianism, Voltaire with his age retained a great deal of the Cartesian spirit. The eighteenth century followed Voltaire in crediting most of its ideas to English sources. But it is doubtful whether there was real need for it, or for us, to look outside the French seventeenth-century intellectual tradition for its characteristic attitudes and assumptions. In the first place, the method of analysis and deductive reasoning— what it followed Fontenelle in calling "the geometrical spirit"—was Cartesian. This was now applied in entirely new fields, and without mathematical rigor. "Locke," Voltaire claimed, "showed how one might possess the geometrical spirit without going through the hard work of studying geometry." When directed to the critical appraisal of existing institutions and ideas taken at their face value, it asked, are they reasonable? are they such as to appeal to developed common sense? what are they worth today? This is the essence of what is called the antihistorical spirit of the eighteenth century, which reaches its climax in Rousseau.

Secondly, with Descartes Voltaire relied on that good sense found in every man, that universal reason given as a weapon to all who were educated. There is no special intellectual authority save reason, no experts to be deferred to. Thirdly, this reason was to be applied especially to the development of a natural science of man, in the confidence it could discover laws of human nature as universally valid as the laws of physics. It was to be applied to the soul of man, to his ideas and his prejudices and their manner of acquisition, as well as to his body. This went far beyond Descartes, but it was an extension of the Cartesian method. And finally, Voltaire shared the Cartesian faith in reason and progress, the optimism born of rational confidence. This was not shaken seriously even by the Lisbon earthquake or the mood of *Candide*, which was directed against Leibniz's formulation of optimism as faith in providence, but not against optimism as to man's powers of advancing through the use of human reason.

To this turning of the Cartesian spirit against the Cartesian system must be added the typical eighteenth-century lightness and even frivolity of spirit—the mocking laugh of wit, the shafts of ironical satire. This has at times been judged in Voltaire superficial, cynical, and heartless. But it is in truth the sardonic grin that hides an aching heart. Voltaire could well say with Byron:

> And if I laugh at any mortal thing,
> 'Tis that I may not weep.

D'Alembert, concluding an account of the execution of La Barre, proclaimed that he meant only to mock at whatever might happen. But Voltaire wrote back:

What, would you be content to laugh? We ought rather to resolve to seek vengeance, or at any rate to leave a country where day after day such horrors are committed. . . . No, once more, I cannot bear that you should finish your letter by saying, I mean to laugh. Ah, my friend, is it a time for laughing? Did men laugh when they saw Phalaris's bull being made red-hot? [10]

Finally, Voltaire typified his century in his intense passion for England and English thought, without any very exact understanding of either, especially without any appreciation of the way English thought was rooted in English institutions. His enforced visit to England in 1726–28 had a profound influence on Voltaire, and through him, on three score years of French thinking. Previously he had been a vain and ambitious member of the *libertin* set, a cynical scoffer. Now he was the apostle of Justice. Condorcet puts it in his *Vie de Voltaire:*

The example of England showed him that truth is not made to remain a secret in the hands of a few philosophers, and a limited number of men of the world, instructed, or rather indoctrinated, by the philosophers; smiling with them at the errors of which the people are the victims, but at the same time making themselves the champions of these very errors when their rank or position gives them a real or chimerical interest in them, and quite ready to permit the proscription, or even persecution, of their teachers, if they venture to say what in secret they themselves actually think. From the moment of his return, Voltaire felt himself called

[10] Corr., July 16, 1766. *Oeuvres,* ed. Baudouin (1826), LXXV, p. 359.

to destroy the prejudices of every kind, of which his country was the slave.[11]

In England Voltaire discovered the land of Queen Anne and the Augustan Age, the literary and scientific center of Europe. He there got enough suggestions to last the rest of his life. Characteristically, he never thought of going back to England again. He used these half-understood ideas as weapons in the good fight. English thought furnished Voltaire and the Encyclopedists with the raw materials they turned to good account. The process was no slavish copying, but a new synthesis, a genuine creation.

The England of Queen Anne and George I exerted a profound influence on eighteenth-century French thinking. In 1725 the Club de l'Entresol was founded to propagate English ideas; the same year Boissy brought out his *Le Français à Londres*. In 1733 appeared P. Catrou's *Histoire des trembleurs;* the next year, the fruit of Voltaire's experience, the *English Letters*. In 1733 A. Prevost started *Pour et Contre*, a journal of English affairs. The communication was aided by English travelers, like Bolingbroke, as well as by the Protestant refugees who went to England.

During the two generations which elapsed between the death of Lewis XIV and the outbreak of the Revolution, there was hardly a Frenchman of eminence who did not either visit England or learn English; while many of them did both.[12]

Among those who actually went to England were Buffon, Brissot, Helvétius, Gournay, Jussieu, Lafayette, Montesquieu, Maupertuis, Morellet, Mirabeau, Roland and Mme. Roland, Rousseau.

Voltaire and his successors took over and used four main bodies of English ideas. First, there was Newtonian science, which was developed in France into a thoroughgoing materialism. Secondly, there was natural religion, or Deism, which the French pushed to atheism. Thirdly, there was Locke and British empiricism, which became theoretically a thoroughgoing sensationalism, and practically the omnipotence of the environment. Finally, there were British political institutions, as interpreted by Locke, the apologist for 1688, which became the basis of the political theories of the Revolution.

[11] Condorcet, *Vie de Voltaire, Oeuvres*, IV, 20.
[12] Buckle, *History of Civilization* (1857), I, 657.

These French developments, however, were the work of a later generation; none of them is to be found in Voltaire himself, who was no materialist, no atheist, no sensationalist, and no revolutionary. For Voltaire, Newton meant merely that Descartes was wrong, that the Cartesian metaphysics and physics were dead. The main idea he found in Newton, the order of natural law, is of course equally central in Descartes.

Voltaire seized on the natural religion of Newton and Locke, and the Deism of Bolingbroke and Shaftesbury, as a weapon against Christianity. In England Deism, the belief in the sole sufficiency of natural religion, was a rather sober intellectual speculation: it was hard to get really excited against the Christian tradition, for in the eighteenth century the Anglican Church had been thoroughly tamed, domesticated, made a branch of the Civil Service, and a scheme of outdoor relief for the upper classes. Voltaire made Deism a terrible anticlerical weapon against the Catholic Church, a warfare forever associated with his name. He aimed it especially at intolerance: all religions are true in so far as they contain natural religion, and false when they make special pretensions to truth.

Voltaire expressed his Deism in his *English Letters* in 1734; he persisted in it until his death in 1778. In 1734 he takes the existence of a wise creator as reasonable and probable.

Faith consists in believing what seems false. To believe in a wise Creator, eternal and supreme, is not faith, it is reason. . . .
It seems to me that we can make only sophisms and say absurdities when we try to force ourselves to deny the necessity of a being existing by itself, or when we try to maintain that matter is that being. But when it comes to discussing and establishing the attributes of this being, whose existence is demonstrated, it is a wholly different matter. . . . In the opinion that there is a God there are found difficulties; but in the contrary opinion there are absurdities.[13]

Later, as atheism emerged in French thought, Voltaire grew more and more convinced of the necessity of belief in God for moral and social reasons. But as to his attributes he remained agnostic: omnipotence is not one, however. Voltaire's arguments are those for a necessary first cause, and from design: he finds the watch analogy convincing.

Voltaire believes in the natural moral law of benevolence and

[13] *Traité de métaphysique*, chap. ii.

humanity. On the third tenet of natural religion, future rewards and punishments, he vacillates. Immortality is probable:

> Without wanting to deceive men, it can be said that we have as much reason to believe in as to deny the immortality of the being that thinks . . . I advance no further in this darkness; I stop where the light of my candle fails me: it is enough for me that I see how far I can go. I by no means claim I have any demonstrations against the spirituality and immortality of the soul; but all the probabilities are against it, and it is equally unjust and unreasonable to want a demonstration in an inquiry which is susceptible only of conjectures.
>
> Only we must anticipate those who would believe the mortality of the soul contrary to the good of society, and remind them that the ancient Jews, whose laws they admire, believed the soul material and mortal, without counting the great sects of philosophers who were worth as much as the Jews and who were very good people.[14]

On the whole, Voltaire takes over the familiar positive arguments for natural religion, and adds nothing of his own. He was all the more powerless against the rising tide of criticism directed against them by the sceptics and atheists.

But Voltaire adds a passion and an intensity of his own to the familiar Deistic attacks on revealed religion and Christianity. He could well agree with Diderot:

> The Christian religion is to my mind the most absurd and atrocious in its dogmas; the most unintelligible, the most metaphysical, the most intertwisted and obscure, and consequently the most subject to divisions, sects, schisms, heresies; the most mischievous for the public tranquillity, the most dangerous to sovereigns by its hierarchic order, its persecutions, its discipline; the most flat, the most dreary, the most Gothic, and the most gloomy in its ceremonies; the most puerile and unsociable in its morality, considered not in what is common to it with universal morality, but in what is peculiarly its own, and constitutes its evangelical, apostolical, and Christian morality, which is the most intolerant of all. Lutheranism, freed from some absurdities, is preferable to Catholicism; Protestantism to Lutheranism, Socinianism to Protestantism, Deism, with temples and ceremonies, to Socinianism. Since it is necessary that man, being superstitious by nature, should have a fetish, the simplest and most harmless will be the best fetish.[15]

Eighteenth-century French Deism was preeminently anticlerical in motive, just as eighteenth-century theology was primarily clerical:

[14] Traité de métaphysique, chap. vi.
[15] Diderot, To Damilaville, 1766, Oeuvres, ed. Assézat et Tourneux, XIX, 477.

neither was particularly religious. Rousseau could well remark, "I am the only man in France who really believes in God."

The grounds for the criticism of revelation are, first, that its metaphysics is purely speculative and irrational. Voltaire rings the changes on the distinctions and subtleties of theology. On all such questions he remains agnostic. Secondly, revelation is immoral: consider the Bible stories. The doctrines of original sin and the vicarious atonement reveal no worthy conception of human nature, no sense of the glory of man. It is cursed with asceticism. And above all it is incurably intolerant. As to Jesus himself, as the Christ of the Church he is of no earthly use; as an historical character, he was far too noble to be a Christian. Voltaire identifies the "religion of Jesus" with natural religion, following Chubb and the English Deists, and sets it in sharp contrast to Christianity.

The third set of English ideas, Locke and the British tradition of empiricism, were imported into France by Voltaire for their critical use. For the whole of eighteenth-century French thought, Locke was "the Philosopher." His empiricism appealed because of its destructive implications for traditional theology, ethics, politics, and education. D'Alembert defined: "Philosophy is the application of reason to the different objects upon which it should be exercised; metaphysics is the science of the origin and generation of our ideas." Condillac followed D'Alembert in this new identification of metaphysics in a legitimate sense with the theme of the second book of Locke's *Essay;* he in turn was followed by the Idéologues in this theoretical analysis, and by Helvétius in drawing the practical consequences for the science of human nature.

The great predecessor of Locke, and the father of the appeal to experience and experimental philosophy, came to be Francis Bacon, who as the foil to Descartes began to enjoy a great vogue around 1750. Diderot boasts "I have taught more people to esteem and read Bacon than ever did so before." Diderot himself started with a very Baconian philosophy of science, in his *Thoughts on the Interpretation of Nature* (1754)—the title itself comes from Bacon. The *Advancement of Learning* was the conscious model for *La Grande Encyclopédie*. D'Alembert's *Discours préliminaire* contains high eulogy.

At the head of these illustrious personages must be placed the immortal chancellor of England, Francis Bacon, whose works, so justly esteemed, and yet more esteemed than known, are still more worthy of our reading than of our eulogy. To consider the sane and broad views of this great man, the multitude of objects with which his mind was occupied, the boldness of his style, which everywhere unites the most sublime images with the most rigorous precision, one would be tempted to regard him as the greatest, the most universal, and the most eloquent of philosophers. . . . His other writings are formed on the same plan: everything, down to their titles, announces the man of genius, the mind which has broad views.[16]

The thirteenth of Voltaire's *Lettres philosophiques*, following the one that praises Bacon, is *Sur M. Loke*, preceding those on Newton. For, Voltaire tells us, "Locke created metaphysics as Newton created physics." He was prudent and modest, and certainly no genius.

Perhaps there was never a mind wiser or more methodical, a logician more exact than Locke; nevertheless he was not a great mathematician. He had never been able to submit to the toil of calculations nor to the dryness of mathematical truths, which at first present nothing sensible to the mind; and no one has proved better than he that one could have the geometrical spirit without the help of geometry.[17]

Locke applied this spirit to new fields, to the analysis of the mind. Diderot points out:

The chemists, the physicists, the naturalists, and all those devoted to the experimental art . . . say: Of what use are all these profound theories of the celestial bodies, all these enormous calculations of rational astronomy, if they do not make it unnecessary for Bradley or LeMonnier to observe the heavens? [18]

and Diderot also says, "What is useful in geometry can be learned in six months; the rest is pure curiosity." D'Alembert, the mathematician, had other ideas on this score.

Of "M. Loke" Voltaire writes:

So many reasoners having written the romance of the soul, a wise man has come who has modestly written its history. Locke has unfolded human reason to man, as an excellent anatomist explains the springs of the human body. He is helped everywhere by the torch of physics; he dares sometimes to speak affirmatively, but he also dares to doubt. Instead of defining all at once what we do not know, he examines by degrees

[16] D'Alembert, *Discours préliminaire*, ed. F. Picavet (1899), pp. 92–93.
[17] *Lettres philosophiques*, Lettre XIII; Lanson, I, 166.
[18] *Pensées sur l'interprétation de la Nature*, Pensée 3.

what we are trying to know. He takes a child at the moment of birth, he follows step by step the progress of his understanding; he sees what he has in common with the beasts, and what he has that is above them; he consults especially his proper evidence, the awareness of his thought.[19]

Voltaire, like his successors in France, took Locke's gospel to be that all our ideas come from our senses, and are hence to be tested by an appeal to sense: what Locke meant was the appeal to the test of verification by the senses. Indeed, from what Voltaire seems to have remembered of the *Essay*, one gets the impression that the chief thing in Locke for Voltaire was the rather incidental suggestion, that perhaps matter can think.

The wanderings of all those who have tried to plumb what is impenetrable for us should teach us not to try to exceed the limits of our nature. True philosophy is to know how to stop where we must, and never to advance except with a sure guide. There remains enough ground to cover without traveling in imaginary spaces. Let us then be content to know by experience, supported by reasoning, the only source of our knowledge, that our senses are the doors by which all our ideas enter into our understanding.[20]

It remained for Condillac to work this sensationalism out in theoretical detail, with an eye to its critical and destructive side; and for Helvétius to use it to establish the omnipotence of the environment, and hence of the dictum that all men are born equal.

The fourth body of English ideas, destined to so influential a career in France, those embodied in British political institutions and thought, were not nearly so central in Voltaire's own thinking as the anticlerical implications of British Deism.

I do not enter at all into politics. . . . Politics is not my business. I have always limited myself to making my little efforts to render men less foolish and more honest.

British political arrangements always meant to Voltaire their fruits in civil liberty, freedom of opinion, and toleration. He never understood the British constitution; he forever marveled that so clumsy an instrument as Parliament could have such admirable results. Like nearly all Frenchmen until Rousseau, he thought a benevolent and enlightened despot would be much more efficient at securing them. His idea was natural rights secured by the rational expert.

[19] *Lettres philosophiques*, Lettre XIII; Lanson, I, 168–69.
[20] *Traité de métaphysique*, chap. iii.

Voltaire was lost in admiration of English freedom of opinion, but he never understood it. The scene was stormy, but somehow the outcome was liberty.

If there were only one religion in England, its despotism would be fearful; if there were only two, they would cut each other's throats; but there are thirty, and they live in peace and happiness. . . .
There is an essential difference between Rome and England, which puts all the advantage on the side of the latter: the fruit of the civil wars in Rome was slavery, and that of the troubles in England, liberty. The English nation is the only one on earth that has succeeded in regulating the power of its kings by resisting them, and which by successive efforts has finally established that wise government where the prince, all-powerful to do good, has his hands tied from doing evil; where the lords are great without insolence and without vassals, and where the people takes part in government without confusion.[21]

Voltaire clearly has no conception of the basis of English liberties in a long historical growth, or in the development of habits of self-government. Morley passes the definitive judgment of British political experience on Enlightenment "reason":

The great Frenchmen, who have been most characteristically French, while valuing all and envying many of the best products of our liberty, may be said generally to have failed entirely to detect that the salt of English character, in days when it had more robustness than we can see just now, sprang from the double circumstance of every man being at liberty to have, and being inclined to take the trouble to have, an opinion about the method and doings of his government; and of so many men being called upon in high capacity or low, in an important function or an obscure one, to take an independent and free share in controlling or initiating the doings of their government. Montesquieu. . . . saw no deeper into the spirit of our institutions than to fix on the constitutional balance of powers as the great secret of our freedom and order. And Montesquieu, in spite of this, was wiser than most of his contemporaries, for he at least saw the worth of constitutional freedom, if he failed to see other ingredients of still more importance. French statesmen and publicists have been systematically blind to the great truth that there is no royal road to national well-being, and that nations will deliberately put away happiness from themselves, unless such happiness comes to them in a given way. The Physiocrats, who were with all their shortcomings the most nearly scientific social thinkers France possessed, could rise to no higher conception of a national life than the supreme authority of a wise and benevolent monarch, giving good gifts to his subjects.

[21] *Lettres philosophiques*, Lettres VI, VIII; Lanson, I, 74, 89.

Turgot, with all the breadth and sagacity of his genius, when five and forty years after our present date he came into power, austerely clung to the same disastrous idea of passing reasoned laws, in the shape of the beneficial edicts of an absolute power. Voltaire, in the same way, never rose above the simple political conception of an eastern tale, a good-tempered despot with a sage vizier. In politics, then, he failed to carry away from England the very essence and principle of our institutions, with which it was so much more important that his countrymen should be familiarized than that they should follow inoculation.[22]

In his political theory Voltaire is actually a monarchist. A republic, ancient history convinced him, causes factions. It can be only of limited extent; and anyway, self-government is strictly impossible. Representative government he opposed, since all the Parliaments he knew were, like the British, opponents of reform. Voltaire's ideal was of a benevolent, enlightened despotism: he thought of Marcus Aurelius, Frederick the Great, Catherine the Great. The English monarchy, he was convinced, had nothing to offer France. These conclusions, as Morley points out, were shared by all the Enlightenment *philosophes* down to Rousseau the Genevan: their best political thought came to rest in the *Roi-Philosophe*.

This benevolent despot would secure to men their natural rights. These for Voltaire included the liberty of the person, of thought and the press, of conscience in religion, and equality before the law. Such equal freedom does not apply to any supposed freedom of material goods, or of social conditions: there is no equality of talents for Voltaire. Diderot makes it equally plain that in any representative assembly it is property that is to be represented. "It is property that makes the citizen." [23] Perhaps to this brief summary of Voltaire's political theory ought to be added his consuming faith in education, so touching a confidence in human rationality during the Enlightenment. Those who have lived under universal education are naturally less sentimental about it.

Voltaire had no illusions, however, about the common man.

Philosophize among yourselves as much as you please. I fancy I hear the dilettanti giving for their own pleasure a refined music; but take good care not to perform the concert before the ignorant, the brutal, and the vulgar; they might break your instruments over your heads. Let a philos-

[22] John Morley, *Voltaire*, 4th ed. (1882), pp. 58-59.
[23] *Encyclopédie*, article "Représentants."

opher be a disciple of Spinoza if he likes, but let the statesman be a theist.

The whole Enlightenment idea of an intellectual aristocracy or élite is well expressed in the conclusion of Voltaire's chapter *Sur M. Loke:*

We need never fear that any philosophic sentiment can destroy the religion of a country. It is in vain that our mysteries are contrary to our demonstrations, they are not the less revered by our Christian philosophers, who know that the objects of reason and of faith are of a different nature. Philosophers will never form a religious sect. Why? Because they do not write for the people, and because they are without enthusiasm. Divide the human race into twenty parts, there will be nineteen made up of those who work with their hands, and who will never know whether there has been a M. Locke in the world. In the twentieth part that remains how few men do we find who read? And among those who read, there are twenty who read novels for one who studies philosophy. The number of those who think is excessively small, and they do not think about troubling the world.

It is not Montaigne, or Locke, or Bayle, or Spinoza, or Hobbes, or Lord Shaftesbury, or Mr. Collins, or Mr. Toland, or Fludd, or Becker, or the Comte de Boulainvilliers, etc., who have carried the torch of discord in their country. It is for the most part the theologians, who having first had the ambition to become the heads of sects, have soon had that of being heads of parties. What am I saying? All the books of the modern philosophers put together will never make even as much noise in the world as was made in the past by the dispute of the Capuchins about the form of their sleeves and their hoods.[24]

This is the spirit of the Enlightenment, of *les philosophes.* One can understand how Rousseau could come like a breath of vivifying air into such an atmosphere.

---

[24] *Lettres philosophiques*, Lettre XIII; ed. Lanson, I, 175–76.

I 3

The Age of the Grande Encyclopédie

I

IT WAS THE YOUNGER generation, in the very middle of the century, that really opened the *lutte philosophique* against the *Ancien Régime* and *l'infâme*. In 1748 Montesquieu published his *Spirit of the Laws;* in 1749 Buffon's *Natural History* came out; in 1750 appeared Rousseau's prize essay on the arts and sciences; in 1751 were issued the first two volumes of *La Grande Encyclopédie*, and the affair of the Abbé de Prades opened the eyes of the conservatives to their danger. The battle was on.

But before turning to the cooperative enterprise that gave the name of "Encyclopedists" to the whole second generation of French Enlightenment thinkers, and before examining the two great men, Diderot and D'Alembert, who directed its fortunes, we must glance at the coming of Newtonian science to France, and the development of a scientific method sharply distinguished from that of Cartesian rationalism. This new method borrowed from Newton the name of "the experimental philosophy," and in certain of its exponents it could well claim to be the forerunner of the experimental philosophy of science that came to the fore in the nineteenth century. But for the most part the desire to escape from the rigidities of Cartesian physics led French thinkers to work out their own version of the observational theory we have seen as one of the strands in Newton's own thought, a view of science elaborated in various ways in Britain by Locke, Berkeley, and Hume. The scientist who introduced Newtonian physics to France, Maupertuis, is the pioneer name here; Diderot and D'Alembert, inspired by Bacon as well as by Newton, combined the observational theory with a thoroughgoing sensationalism and a rather narrow pragmatism into a logic of science that foreshadows the later positivism of Comte.

In the background of French Newtonianism stands the experimental philosophy of the Dutch Newtonians. Holland had been the cradle of Cartesian physics, the one land whose universities welcomed the new science shortly after Descartes's death. Appropriately, it was the first continental land whose academic tradition accepted Newtonian thought. Huygens had early taken his stand with the more experimental Cartesians. The great Dutch physiologists, Leeuwenhoek, Nieuwentyt, and Boerhaave, applying Cartesian mechanism to biology, grew more and more experimental, and predisposed the Dutch universities to welcome Newton. In 1715 'sGravesande, in London on a diplomatic mission, became acquainted with Newton himself. The same year Boerhaave, in an address at Leyden, *Oratio de comparando certo in physicis*, laid down the program of the experimental method. We can know nothing of the reality that lies behind change and appearances. Atoms, monads, extension, gravitation are names for observed effects, not principles of explanation. "Attraction" is only a prudent name given to an unknown cause.

Attraction in fact signifies nothing other than an unknown cause, which creates a movement in some fashion natural, in virtue of which certain bodies have a tendency to meet; but it does not explain the nature of that cause and does not make clear in what intelligible way it produces that movement.[1]

Motion itself is an unclear notion, whose first cause is unknown; so likewise is life. Positively, we must seek to know of things only what experience reveals. We can generalize the results of experience by geometry; but experience must be our point of departure. In physics we must rely on experience, and affirm only those things known by experience.

'sGravesande, installed at Leyden as professor of mathematics in 1717, came out for Newton's experimental philosophy, which, rejecting the method of ontological hypotheses, admitted only what could be mathematically demonstrated to follow from phenomena. Musschenbroek was at the time working in London under Newton's direction; he soon had a chair at Utrecht. In 1720 'sGravesande pub-

[1] *Oratio*, etc., *Opuscula Omnia* (Leyden, 1738), p. 30.

lished his course under the title, *Physices elementa mathematica experimentis confirmata sive introductio ad philosophiam Newtonianam*. In 1723 Musschenbroek, called to Utrecht, spoke *De certa methodo philosophiae experimentalis*. In 1724 'sGravesande delivered an influential address *On Evidence*. Distinguishing the moral evidence in physics from the mathematical evidence that is the perceived comparison of ideas, he finds the former persuasive rather than compelling. It takes three forms, the senses, testimony, and analogy. Analogy is based on the assumption that the universe is governed by constant laws. This is a necessary condition of all reasoning by analogy, that is, by induction, which thus rests on an hypothesis. In raising the question of the foundation of the principle of induction, 'sGravesande himself suggests a theological answer, like Descartes.

In an address of 1730 *De methodo instituendi experimenta physica*, Musschenbroek takes up the rules of experimentation. The English are the true followers of Galileo in carefully observing experimental conditions, in uniting mathematics with physics; and tribute is paid to the Accademia del Cimento of Torricelli. Analogy or induction is uncertain, not because of doubts as to the constancy of natural laws, but because recurring situations are complex and never exactly the same. 'sGravesande's fullest discussion of method is in his *Introductio ad philosophiam* of 1736. Where Musschenbroek, following Newton's fourth Rule, takes the results of physics as having merely a high probability, 'sGravesande holds that the persuasion that follows moral evidence is absolute, as compelling as mathematical evidence. But

It often happens, when we examine a subject, that we find no route that will lead us directly to certainty. In this case we must search for a probability; even at this we can often not arrive without having recourse to hypotheses, which lead us at time to a probability, which we can confuse with certainty.[2]

We must examine the hypothesis, deduce its consequences, so as to discover new phenomena, and then observe whether these phenomena really take place. 'sGravesande is stating the method of a genuinely experimental science here, and using "hypothesis" in the modern rather than in the Newtonian sense.

[2] *Introductio ad philosophiam* (Leyden, 1736), p. cxxxv.

I do not deny that sometimes hypotheses lead to truth; but when what was formerly hypothetical is found to be true, there is no longer any hypothesis.[3]

We must not, in other words, ever stop with a hypothesis as a definitive principle of explanation, especially for the mere reason we can think of no other.

II

If the Dutch Newtonians worked Newton's precepts out into an experimental conception of science, the great French Newtonian Maupertuis came rather to a form of positivism. Maupertuis' *Discours sur la figure des astres* in 1732 was the first work by a Newtonian published in France.

It was not a great glory to be presenting to one's compatriots a discovery made by others fifty years before. So I can say that I am the first to dare in France to propose attraction, at least as a principle to be examined. It was in the *Discours sur la figure des astres*. One can see there with what circumspection I presented the principle, the timidity with which I hardly dared to compare it with compulsion, the fear I was in in presenting the reasons which had led the English to abandon Cartesianism. All this was futile, and if this *discours* had some fortune in foreign lands, it made me personal enemies in my own country.[4]

In 1734 Voltaire came out for Newton and attraction in his *Lettres philosophiques*, and J. Bernoulli was half convinced. The dikes had broken.

The figure of the earth was the experimental difference between Descartes and Newton. On Cartesian principles, the earth should be a spheroid slightly elongated at the poles; on Newtonian ones, it should be an oblate or flattened spheroid. An expedition sent to Peru had seemed to verify the former. Maupertuis led in 1736 a great royal expedition to Lapland to measure a meridian; and lo! after innumerable adventures, it turned out, Newton was right. Maupertuis enjoyed immense acclaim as "the Flattener of the Earth." In 1740 he was called by Frederick II to Berlin, where in 1746 he was made president of the Prussian Academy, and thereafter becomes an important figure in the German Enlightenment, and one of the outstanding German physicists who in his philosophy of sci-

[3] *Éléments de physique*, 3d ed., trad. Joncourt, I, xxvii.
[4] *Lettre XII, Oeuvres* (Lyon, 1768), II, 284.

ence was working out the main structure of the Kantian analysis.

Maupertuis takes the position which in its British versions we have been calling "observationalism."

> I believe that after so many centuries have passed and after the efforts of so many great men, if we must not despair of finding the cause of gravitation, it is always more reasonable to endeavor to know its effects; for knowing well what are its effects on one occasion, we can determine what effects it will have on another; we can even, by means of experience, discover the laws in accordance with which it acts, and that, it seems to me, is all that is to be desired in physics; it is at least, in my opinion, all that is to be hoped for. . . .
>
> Galileo, without knowing the cause of the gravitation of bodies toward the earth, was not kept from giving us a very fine and very certain theory about this gravitation, and from explaining the phenomena that depend on it.[5]

The test case is Newton's "attraction," for which Maupertuis was fighting against the Cartesian vortex "hypothesis."

> If bodies still gravitate toward each other, why would it not be thus permitted to seek for the effects of that gravitation, without getting at the cause? Everything would thus be reduced to examining whether bodies have this tendency toward each other: and if it is found that they in fact have it, we can be satisfied to deduce from it the explanation of the phenomena of nature, leaving to more sublime philosophers the inquiry into the cause of this force. This decision would seem to me to be the wiser, in that I do not think it is permitted to us to ascend to first causes, or to understand how bodies act on each other.[6]

Such questions are all matters of experience. Maupertuis constantly affirms:

> We must seek out by experience everything that could furnish some light . . . All we can do now is to accumulate as may experiences as we can. . . . Were they made at random, they could throw light on this Physics. . . .
>
> This science is wholly founded on experience. Without experience, the reasoning, always liable to go wrong, is lost in systems which experience denies.[7]

Maupertuis is led to an observational view of causality.

Some do not want to admit causality between what is called motion, force, action, effect of bodies. They base themselves on the fact that we do not

[5] *Discours sur la figure des astres*, in *Oeuvres*, I, 93.   [6] *Oeuvres*, I, 93.
[7] *Oeuvres*, IV, 215; II, 424; III, 289.

at all conceive clearly how bodies act on each other. But they do act, either as immediate causes, or as occasional causes; and they act always with a certain uniformity, and in accordance with certain laws: and if we lack something to explain the manner in which they act, we have no less right to call *effect* what always follows a phenomenon and *cause* what always precedes it. If those philosophers want to try, in any other way whatever, to give a more perfect idea of what everybody calls cause and effect, they will perhaps find themselves so embarrassed that they will no longer dispute our usage in a matter where perhaps their relation is less obscure than any other.[8]

Maupertuis has a characteristic comment on Hume:

While the words causes and effects are thus abused and placed everywhere, some other philosophers deny all causality: the arguments used to do so by one of the greatest men of England (M. Hume) are assuredly most ingenious and most subtle. However, it seems to me that between finding causes everywhere and finding them nowhere there is a just mean where truth is found.[9]

On the foundation of induction, the uniformity of nature, Maupertuis says:

Never has a general and rigorous demonstration been given of these principles; but never will anyone accustomed to judge in the sciences, who knows the force of induction, doubt their truth. When we have seen that on a thousand occasions Nature acts in a certain manner, there is no man of sound sense who believes that on the thousand and first it will follow other laws.[10]

To this observationalism Maupertuis adds a thoroughgoing phenomenalism and subjectivism.

If we believe that in this pretended essence of bodies, in extension, there is more of reality belonging to the bodies themselves than in the odor, the sound, the taste, the hardness, that is an illusion. Extension like the rest is only a perception of my soul carried to an external object, without there being in the object anything which could resemble what my soul perceives. . . . Hence reflecting on the fact that there is no resemblance, no relation between our perceptions and external objects, it will be agreed that all objects are only simple phenomena: extension, which we have

---

[8] *Avant-propos de l'Essai de Cosmologie, Oeuvres*, I, xv.

[9] *Examen philosophique de la preuve de l'existence de Dieu employée dans l'Essai de Cosmologie*, sec. XXIV, in *Mémoires de l'Académie de Berlin* (1756), p. 406.

[10] *Loi du repos, Oeuvres*, IV, 46.

taken for the basis of all those objects, for what concerns their essence, extension itself will be no more than a phenomenon.[11]

Maupertuis emphasizes his agreement with Berkeley, referring to the *Dialogues between Hylas and Philonous*, whose aim is

to deprive bodies of that reality independent of our perceptions which the vulgar attribute to them, and of which our negligence and our prejudices have put them in possession.[12]

Maupertuis concludes:

We live in a world in which nothing that we perceive resembles what we perceive. Unknown beings excite in our soul all the feelings, all the perceptions it encounters; and without resembling any of the things that we perceive represent them all. . . . I admit there is a cause on which all our perceptions depend, because nothing is as it is without reason. But what is that cause? I cannot penetrate it, since nothing I have resembles it. On that let us confine ourselves to the limits prescribed to our intelligence.[13]

Maupertuis does not, however, hold a pure sensationalism.

All our ideas coming to us from the senses, we can say that in their origin they are all only sensations: it is only after our mind has reflected on them, combined them, so to say worked over them, that we have left to some the name of sensations, and given to others the name of ideas. It is thus that from the most local and confused sensations we have arrived at the most abstract and clearest ideas, which owe the least to sense.[14]

Maupertuis has pushed his phenomenalism and observationalism to a point where it is very close to the Kantian analysis. He takes his place with Leonhard Euler among the German physicists who were preparing the main outlines of the critical philosophy.

III

Maupertuis' positivism is that of the Newtonian physicist reacting against Cartesian speculation. Diderot's is that of the Baconian with a practical interest in technology, the Diderot who included in his *Encyclopédie* eleven volumes of plates of the arts and crafts and industrial processes. For him experimental science is the great thing; he cavalierly brushes mathematics aside as completed.

[11] *Lettre IV, Oeuvres*, II, 232, 233.   [12] *Oeuvres*, I, 298.
[13] *Oeuvres*, II, 234; I, 283.
[14] *Examen philosophique*, etc., sec. XIV, in *Mémoires de l'Académie de Berlin* (1756), 394.

We are at the moment of a great revolution in the sciences. From the inclination which the intelligent seem to me to have for morals, belles-lettres, natural history and experimental physics, I should almost dare to be certain that within a hundred years there will not be counted three great geometricians in Europe; this science will stop short where it has been left by the Bernoullis, the Eulers, the Maupertuis, the Clairauts, the Fontaines and the d'Alemberts. They will have erected the pillars of Hercules; men will not go beyond them; their works will remain in the centuries to come like those pyramids of Egypt, whose masses, charged with hieroglyphics, awake in us a terrifying idea of the power and resources of the men who erected them.[15]

Diderot brought out his ostensibly Baconian *Thoughts on the Interpretation of Nature* in 1754, when he was at the height of his powers, and had already issued four volumes of the *Encyclopédie*. They contain the meditations of a humanist on the human aspects, especially on the human values, of a technological scientific enterprise. His strain of naturalistic experimentalism is well expressed:

We have three principal means: the observation of nature, reflection, and experience. Observation gathers the facts, reflection combines them, experience verifies the result of the combination. The observation of nature must be assiduous, reflection must be profound, and experience must be exact. These means are rarely seen united. Hence creative geniuses are not common.[16]

Diderot is far from Cartesian mathematicism: the seventeenth century has gone, and mathematics must not be overemphasized.

One of the truths that has been announced in our days with the most courage and force [by the natural historian Buffon], which a good physicist will never lose sight of, and which will certainly have the most advantageous results, is that the religion of the mathematicians is an intellectual world where what are taken as rigorous truths lose that advantage absolutely when they are brought down to our earth. From this men have concluded that it was for experimental philosophy to correct the calculations of geometry, and this consequence has been admitted even by the geometers. But what is the use of correcting geometrical calculation by experience? Is it not shorter to hold to the results of the latter? Whence we see that mathematics, transcendent above all, lead us to nothing precise without experience: that they are a kind of general metaphysics, in which bodies are deprived of their individual qualities, and that it would remain

---

[15] *Pensées sur l'interprétation de la nature*, pensée IV.
[16] *Interprétation de la nature*, pensée XV.

at least to write a great work which we could call *The Application of Experience to Geometry*, or *Treatise on the Aberration of Measurements*.[17]

But these Baconian relegations of mathematics to the appendix must not be taken too seriously: side by side with them must be put other acknowledgments, like that in the *Letter on the Blind* of 1749:

What are we to think of the results of the calculation? First, that it is sometimes extremely difficult to obtain them, and that it would be to little purpose that a man of science could form the most plausible hypotheses, were he not able to verify them by geometry; accordingly, the greatest physicists, Galileo, Descartes, and Newton, were great geometers.[18]

The core of Diderot's rather simple and untechnical experimentalism comes out in a passage like the following; the example, significantly enough, comes from Newton. The contrast with Diderot's own practice of scientific speculation is striking.

We have distinguished two kinds of philosophy, experimental and rational. The one has its eyes bandaged, gropes always as it walks, seizes everything that falls into its hands, and in the end encounters precious things, and tries to make out of them a torch; but this supposed torch has up to the present been of less service to it than groping to its rival, and that ought to be the case. Experience multiplies its motions to infinity; it is ceaselessly in action; it uses to look for phenomena all the time that reason employs in looking for analogies. Experimental philosophy does not know what will come or what will not come from its work, but it labors without respite. On the contrary, rational philosophy weighs the possibilities, makes its pronouncement and stops short. It says boldly, "Light can not be analysed." Experimental philosophy listens and remains silent before her for whole centuries; then all at once it displays the prism and says, "Light is analysed." [19]

It is not surprising that when Auguste Comte drew up his list of one hundred and fifty books to which the Positivist's library should be limited, he placed Diderot's *Interpretation of Nature* on one side of the *Discourse on Method*, and the *Novum Organum* on the other. It is the less surprising as Diderot shared with Comte the notion, to us so perplexing, but in the seventeenth and eighteenth

[17] *Interprétation de la nature*, pensée II.
[18] *Letter on the Blind, Early Philosophical Works*, ed. M. Jourdain (1916), p. 102. Actually, Diderot was working on a synthesis between his professed "experimentalism" and his underlying rationalism.
[19] *Interprétation de la nature*, pensée XXIII.

centuries so natural to rationalists and experimentalists alike, that scientific inquiry would soon complete its work.

It is utility that circumscribes all. It will be utility that in a few centuries will set bounds to experimental physics, as it is on the eve of setting bounds to geometry. I grant centuries to this study, because the sphere of its utility is infinitely more extensive than that of any abstract science, and it is without contradiction the base of our real knowledge. . . .

Since reason cannot understand everything, imagination foresee everything, sense observe everything, nor memory retain everything; since great men are born at such remote intervals, and the progress of science is so interrupted by revolution, that whole ages of study are passed in recovering the knowledge of the centuries that are gone—to observe everything in nature without distinction is to fail in duty to the human race. Men who are beyond the common run in their talents ought to respect themselves and posterity in the employment of their time. What would posterity think of us if we had nothing to transmit to it save a complete insectology, an immense history of microscopic animals? No—to the great geniuses great objects, little objects to the little geniuses.[20]

This narrow pragmatism of Diderot recommended itself not only to the aberrations of Comte in the nineteenth century; in the twentieth it had much to do with his great popularity as a forerunner of Dialectical Materialism, and the exigencies of Communist research during the Stalin era.

In fairness to Diderot, it must be said that he concludes his *Interpretation of Nature* by insisting that the chief value of science is the scientific spirit and the scientific imagination, which are able to make predictions in novel circumstances. The scientific spirit he defines as:

a facility of supposing or perceiving oppositions or analogies, which has its source in a practical knowledge of the physical qualities of beings considered in isolation, or of their reciprocal effects, when they are considered in combination.[21]

IV

The great organ for the propagation of the new ideas was the *Encyclopédie*. This originated as a publisher's enterprise. In 1727

---

[20] *Interprétation de la nature*, pensées VI, LIV.

[21] *Interprétation de la nature*, pensée XXXI. Actually, Diderot's own gift was for sweeping imaginative hypotheses, and his panvitalism outdid anything in Descartes. The two strains in the *Interpretation of Nature* are in a certain tension, just as that whole methodological work is in tension with his biological speculations. See A. Vartanian, *Diderot and Descartes* (1953).

Chambers Cyclopedia, or Universal Dictionary of the Arts and Sciences, had appeared in England. In 1742 an Englishman and a German approached a Paris printer, Le Breton, with a French translation. He obtained a privilege, but quarreled with the translators, sought a new editor, and in 1745 came to Diderot with the project Diderot saw the chance to spread Enlightenment ideas, fired the printer with enthusiasm for a much more ambitious enterprise— *Chambers Cyclopedia* was only two folios—and a fresh privilege was obtained in 1746. D'Alembert wrote the *Discours préliminaire,* which came out in 1750. The next year volume one was issued, and in 1752 the second volume.

This famous cooperative work has two significant aspects. The first, often forgotten, is that it was a potent instrument of enlightenment and education. Everyone, it maintained, ought to know something at least about everything, and to enjoy the latest and most up-to-date knowledge. The *Encyclopédie* is the epitome of this typically eighteenth-century point of view. Voltaire has left a picture of a party of Louis XV's at the Trianon, where the question of the composition of black powder was raised. Sending for the *Encyclopédie,* they found the answer. They also found the difference between Spanish and French rouge, how stockings were made by loom, what the rights of the crown were. "Sire," said the Count de C——:

how happy you are that under your reign men should be found capable of understanding all the arts and transmitting them to posterity. Everything is here, from the way to make a pin down to the art of casting and pointing your guns; from the infinitely little up to the infinitely great.[22]

D'Alembert states the aim of the work:

The work of which we today offer the first volume has two objects: as an Encyclopedia it aims to set forth as far as possible the order and connections of the branches of human knowledge; as a reasoned Dictionary of the Sciences, the Arts and the Crafts, it aims to contain on each science and on each art, either liberal or mechanical, the general principles which are its basis, and the most essential details which make up its body and substance.[23]

[22] Voltaire, *Facéties;* in John Morley, *Diderot* (1886), I, 173.
[23] *Discours préliminaire,* ed. Picavet (1899), p. 12. The object of setting forth "the order and connection of the branches of human knowledge" is modeled on the scheme of Bacon's *Advancement of Learning.* D'Alembert puts it

The second significant point about the *Grande Encyclopédie* is that from the outset it became a weapon in the *lutte philosophique* for nature, reason, and humanity against the "Infamous." Even here it was, however, not the open and direct assault on the enemy's position it is often supposed to have been. There was much actual dissembling. Says D'Alembert:

neatly: "The objects with which our soul occupies itself are either spiritual or material, and our soul occupies itself with these objects either by direct ideas or by ideas of reflection. The system of direct knowledge can consist only in the collection, purely passive and in a sense mechanical, of this knowledge; this is what we call memory. Reflection is of two kinds, we have already observed: either it reasons about the objects of direct ideas, or it imitates them. Thus memory, reason properly so-called, and imagination are the three different ways in which our soul operates on the object of its thoughts." D'Alembert, in Picavet, p. 63.

Diderot continues: "Physical beings act on the senses. The impressions of these beings excite perceptions in the understanding. The understanding occupies itself with these perceptions in only three ways, in accordance with the three principal faculties, memory, reason, imagination. Either the understanding makes a catalogue pure and simple of its perceptions by memory; or it examines, compares, and digests them by reason; or it is pleased to imitate and counterfeit them by imagination. Whence results a general distribution of human knowledge, which seems sufficiently well founded, into *history* which relates to *memory*, into *philosophy* which comes from *reason*, and into *poetry* which comes from *imagination*. . . .

"History is of *facts;* and these facts are either about *God*, or about *man*, or about *nature*. The facts which are about God belong to *sacred history*. The facts which are about man belong to *civil history;* and the facts which are about nature are related to *natural history*. . . .

"Philosophy, or the portion of human knowledge which must be related to reason, is very extensive. . . . Its chief objects are *God*, to the knowledge of whom man is raised by reflection on natural history and on sacred history; *man*, who is sure of his existence by consciousness or inner sense; *nature*, of which man has learned the history by using the external senses. *God, man* and *nature*, will thus furnish us a general distribution of *philosophy* or of *Science* (for these words are synonymous); and *philosophy* or *Science*, will be *Science of God, Science of man*, and *Science of nature*. . . .

"The distribution of the Science of man is given us by that of the faculties. The principal faculties of man are the *understanding* and the *will;* the *understanding*, which must be directed toward *truth;* the *will*, which must be bent to *virtue*. The one is the goal of *logic*, the other is that of *morality*. . . .

"Morality, which we have made the second part of the *Science of man*, is either *general* or *particular*. The latter is distributed into *natural, economic*, and *political jurisprudence*. *Natural jurisprudence* is the Science of the duties of the individual man; *economic*, the Science of the duties of man as member of the family; *political*, that of the duties of man in society. But morality would be incomplete, if these treatises were not preceded by that of the *reality of moral good and evil; of the necessity of fulfilling one's duties*, of being good, just, virtuous, etc., which is the object of general morality." Diderot, in Picavet, pp. 163, 166–67, 169.

No doubt we have bad articles in theology and metaphysics, but with theologians for censors, and a privilege, I defy you to make them any better. There are other articles that are less exposed to the daylight, and in them all is repaired. Time will enable people to distinguish what we have thought from what we have said.[24]

In the *Encyclopédie* itself Diderot sets forth the method:

In all cases where a national prejudice would seem to deserve respect, the particular article ought to set it respectfully forth, with its whole procession of attractions and probabilities. But the edifice of mud ought to be overthrown and an unprofitable heap of dust scattered to the wind, by references to articles in which solid principles serve as a base for the opposite truths. This way of undeceiving men operates promptly on minds of the right stamp, and it operates infallibly and without any troublesome consequences, secretly and without disturbance, on minds of every description.[25]

D'Alembert could boast to Voltaire:

Our fanatics feel the blows, though they are sorely puzzled to tell from which side they come.[26]

Perhaps the greatest influence of the work came from its new emphasis on the power of man and of man's reason. Here the eleven volumes of copper-plates illustrating the different processes of the mechanical arts and crafts were most impressive. Diderot's Baconian mind was fascinated with technology, and he did much of this investigating himself.

The religous and theological articles were written by fairly orthodox abbés, though as it turned out, in D'Alembert's words, "The first theologian was excommunicated, the second expatriated, the third died, and the fourth is l'Abbé Morellet." Yvon retired upon his excommunication; the second, l'Abbé de Prades, went into exile in Prussia after the famous affair of his thesis at the Sorbonne, where he was found to have maintained Locke's theory of the origin of knowledge; the third was Mallet, known as "Enfer" Mallet; and the last, Morellet, was finally Bastilled for his *Vision de Palissot*. His articles, on such subjects as *Fils de Dieu*, *Foi*, and *Gomaristes*, are quite objective. Polier, a Calvinist, wrote on *Liturgy*, and naturally had a hard time making it seem "Christian."

[24] D'Alembert, letter of July 21, 1757. [25] Article "Encyclopédie."
[26] To Voltaire, Feb. 15, 1757.

The persecution endured during the course of publication was petty rather than serious: the chief controller of printing, or censor, Malesherbes, was himself favorably inclined to the Encyclopedists. Its fortunes varied with the power and standing of the Jesuits at court. Volume II came out in January, 1752; then the affair of the Abbé de Prades caused a stopping. As the Jesuits could not carry on the work, Mme. de Chateauroux, the king's mistress, had the ban lifted. From 1753 to 1757 volumes III to VII were delivered. In 1758 Helvétius's *De l'esprit* caused an uproar, and it was found that in his article "Génève" D'Alembert had praised the Socinians. The Parlement of Paris in 1759 condemned the work, and to forestall the lawyers Malesherbes withdrew the privilege. For his part, the printer Le Breton undertook a private censorship, simply omitting dangerous passages. In 1763 Mme. de Pompadour had the privilege renewed, and taking no more chances, Diderot brought out the last ten volumes together in 1765, printed ostensibly at "Neufchatel." The eleven volumes of plates were delivered in 1772, and in 1777 five supplementary volumes, printed at "Amsterdam." The set cost a thousand livres (some $600); there were at first two thousand subscribers, the number finally going up to ten thousand.

Contributors included all the famous eighteenth-century thinkers, from Montesquieu (*Goût*) to Condorcet in the Supplement. Voltaire wrote on literary items, Buffon on *Nature*, Holbach translated German pieces on physical science, Rousseau wrote on *Musique* and *Économie Politique*, Quesnay on *Fermiers* and *Grains*, Turgot on *Étymologie, Existence, Foires* and *Fondations*. D'Alembert wrote on mathematics, on Cartesianism and on Locke; Diderot himself handled ancient philosophy, and all the mechanical arts.

V

Denis Diderot (1713–1784) was a man of boundless energy, ever overflowing with ideas, brilliant. He was one of those men who are sure to write a masterpiece someday, and who go through life always just about to do something really great. He just missed it. Was his life wasted on the editing of the *Encyclopédie?* No, he was just the man for that task. He possessed encyclopedic knowledge, in science, in the history of philosophy, in the arts and industries. He was an art critic, playwright, novelist, poet, always dashing off short pieces in the intervals of his more serious work. Like his greatly admired master, Francis Bacon, he took all knowledge for his province. He had brilliant insights into every field, which he never had the time to follow up. Thus he suggested a theory of biological evolution, for instance: the idea was in the air. In his personal character he was generous and kindhearted in the extreme, always supporting a huge crowd of often ungrateful literary hacks. He was easily imposed upon, yet always trustful of human nature. The one great event in his life was his trip to St. Petersburg in 1773, to talk with Catherine the Great. He stayed five months, and they had many an informal conversation—Diderot was a marvelous talker. He was greatly impressed by the Empress' mind, she not so much so by his political acumen, finding Grimm much more tactful and shrewd. Diderot was known as "*le Philosophe*" of eighteenth-century France.

It is impossible to do more than indicate two or three of the lines of thought of this extraordinarily versatile man. His strain of Baconian positivism in science has already been examined. Coupled with this were some of his brilliant suggestions in biology. The idea of evolution fascinated him all his life. In the *Letter on the Blind* (1749) he has the blind mathematician Saunderson adopt approvingly the speculations as to the survival of the fittest that are found in Empedocles and Lucretius.[27] In his *Thoughts on the Interpretation of Nature* (1754) Diderot asks:

Just as in the animal and vegetable kingdoms an individual begins, so to speak, grows, endures, perishes and passes away; would it not be the same with whole species? . . . Could not the philosopher abandoned to his conjectures suspect that animality had from all eternity its particular elements, scattered and confused in the mass of matter; that these elements happened to unite, because that was possible; that the embryo formed by these elements passed through an infinity of organizations and developments; that it had in succession motion, sensation, ideas, thought, reflection, consciousness, feelings, passions, signs, gestures, sounds, articulated sounds, a language, laws, sciences, arts; that millions of year elapsed between each of these developments; that perhaps there are still other developments to come, and other growths to take, unknown to us? [28]

In his *Rêve de D'Alembert* (1769) he says, "Organs produce needs, and reciprocally needs produce organs."

[27] *Early Philosophical Works*, ed. M. Jourdain, p. 111.
[28] *Interprétation de la nature*, pensée LVIII, Question 2.

The origin of life was another question that fascinated Diderot. He worked out a panvitalism, in which all matter is in some sense alive and sentient, and takes on new forms through the operation of mechanical laws, thus preserving an essential continuity and even homogeneity through the appearance of living organisms and the variety of species. The first statement of this all-embracing hypothesis is put the mouth of the blind Saunderson in 1749. The questions at the end of the *Interpretation of Nature* (1754) emphasize the essential homogeneity of material substance. Buffon had distinguished between "living matter" and "dead matter." Seeming to accept Buffon's distinction, Diderot asks:

It is evident that matter in general is divided into dead matter and living matter. But how can it be that matter is not one, all living, or all dead? Is living matter always living? And is dead matter always and really dead? Does not living matter ever die? Does not dead matter ever begin to live?

Is there any assignable difference between dead matter and living matter, other than its organization and the real or apparent spontaneity of motion? Is not what we call living matter merely a matter that moves by itself? And what we call dead matter, something that is moved by another material object? . . . .

Does living matter combine with living matter? How does this combination take place? I ask the same about dead matter.[29]

In 1769, after he had been defending his panvitalism against D'Alembert, he wrote down the *Entretien entre D'Alembert et Diderot*, and then imagined a *Rêve de D'Alembert*, in which the sleeping man gives voice as in a kind of delirium to Diderot's speculations—perhaps thinking of Descartes's dream of a universal mathematics. In these two writings Diderot sets forth most fully his great hypothesis and the questions it raises. All matter is living, and all matter possesses sensibility; at times these properties are purely potential, as in what we call dead matter; at times, with the proper organization, the same matter will display itself as alive. The questions such a view raises are those of:

universal sensibility, the formation of the sentient being, its unity, the origin of animals, and all the questions to which these views lead.[30]

[29] *Interprétation de la nature*, pensée LVIII, Questions 3–5, 14.
[30] *Rêve de D'Alembert*, in *Ouvrages Inédits* (1834), IV, 150.

These matters are of basic importance for deciding between a religious and a nonreligious view of the cosmos.

Do you think you can take a position about a supreme intelligence, without knowing what to hold about the eternity of matter and its properties, the distinction between the two substances, the nature of man and the production of animals? (IV, 150)

If man is an aggregate of animalcules, how is the unity of consciousness and personality to be explained? This is Diderot's central problem.

As a drop of mercury melts into another drop of mercury, a sensible and living molecule melts into a sensible and living molecule. . . . First there were two drops, after the contact there is but one. . . . Before the assimilation there were two molecules, after the assimilation there is only one. Sensibility becomes common to the common mass. . . . Indeed, why not?

Diderot suggests the analogy of a swarm of bees, of organs united in a sympathy, a unity, a general identity, of a spider at the center of his web, to try to account for the unity of consciousness.

Without doubt the fact is clear, but the reason for the fact is not at all, especially on the hypothesis of those who admit only one substance and who explain the formation of man and animals in general by the successive opposition of several sensible molecules. Each sensible molecule had its own self before the application; but how has it lost that self, and how from these losses does there result the consciousness of a whole?

Then there is the question of the persistence of personal identity, if all the molecules in a body change and are renewed. Diderot finds the answer in memory. It is like a monastery, in which the monastic spirit is preserved because whenever a new monk enters he finds a hundred others who train him to think and feel like them. (IV, 133–34, 136, 158, 188–90)

Diderot includes the notion of a universal evolution.

What is our life in comparison with the eternity of time? Less than the drop I have taken up with the point of a needle, in comparison with the limitless space that surrounds me. An indefinite series of animalcules in the atom that ferments, the same indefinite series of animalcules in the other atom we call the earth. Who knows the races of animals that have preceded us? Who knows the races of animals that will succeed to ours?

Everything changes, everything passes, only the whole remains. The world begins and finishes without end; it is at each instant at its beginning and at its end; it has never had another, and it will never have another. (IV, 145)

The only God conceivable would be the soul of the whole: Diderot ends in a naturalistic pantheism.

This was the outcome of the progression of Diderot's religious sentiments as well. He started in the 1740s with the common Deism of the time, then became more and more sceptical, and ended up with a pantheistic naturalism close to Holbach. In the preface to his first work, an adaptation of Shaftesbury's *Essai sur le merite et la vertu* (1745), he begins:

Yes, my brother, religion well understood and practiced with an enlightened zeal cannot fail to elevate the moral virtues. . . . The goal of this work is to show that virtue is almost indivisibly attached to the knowledge of God, and that the temporal happiness of man is inseparable from virtue. No virtue, without believing in God; no happiness, without virtue: these are the two propositions of the illustrious philosopher whose ideas I am going to set forth. Atheists who pride themselves on their probity, and men without probity who boast of their happiness: these are my adversaries.[31]

Diderot puts the arguments for Deism in a supplement to his *Pensées philosophiques* (1747):

Natural religion is the work of God or of men. Of men you cannot say, since it is the foundation of revealed religion. If it is the work of God, I ask to what end God has given it. The end of a religion which comes from God can only be the knowledge of essential truths, and the practice of important duties. A religion would be unworthy of God and of man if it proposed another end.

Hence, either God has not given to men a religion which satisfied the end God proposed to himself, which would be absurd, for that would suppose in him lack of power or evil will; or man has obtained from him what he needed. Hence he needs no other knowledge than that received from nature.

As to the means of satisfying duties, it would be ridiculous that he should have refused them; for, of these three things, the knowledge of teachings, the practice of duties, and the force necessary to act and to believe, the lack of one renders the others futile. It is in vain that I am instructed in teachings if I do not know my duties. It is in vain that I know my duties, if I fall into error or into ignorance of the essential truths. It

[31] *Essai sur le merite et la vertu, Oeuvres,* ed. Naigeon (1821), I, 5, 11.

is in vain that the knowledge of truths and duties is given me, if the grace to believe and to practice is refused me.

Hence I have always had all these advantages; hence natural religion left to revelation nothing essential or necessary to add to it; hence, that religion was not insufficient. . . .

Could we not say that all the religions of the world are only sects of natural religion, and that the Jews, the Christians, the Mussulmen, the pagans are only heretical and schismatic naturalists? [32]

The *Pensées philosophiques* (1746) express this Deism. But in the *Lettre sur les Aveugles* (1749) Diderot goes further. This piece takes its place with the popular literature dealing with the difference the absence of one sense would make in knowledge, if all knowledge comes from the senses. Condillac's *Essai sur l'origine des connaissances humaines* had popularized sensationalism in 1746; Diderot drew the consequences, in a sceptical relativism. In morality, for instance, the blind would abhor theft, but would show little sense of modesty, and not much pity. Diderot confronts the blind mathematician Saunderson with a clergyman: the blind man is not at all impressed by the beautiful spectacle of the world, or the argument from design. "Let me touch God," he asks. The doubts raised are not about revelation, but about natural religion itself. They express effectively the sceptical doubts of the *Promenade d'un sceptique* of 1747 about the argument from design.[33]

Diderot looms as a large figure, and an attractive personality, brilliant, energetic, at times reaching lyrical heights. He just missed real greatness as a thinker, yet his work lives in the *Encyclopédie*. He is the most pragmatic of pragmatists, the best baker amongst the *philosophes*, not the lonely thinker, but the brave, doughty, if hard-pressed leader of the hosts of the Enlightenment. He is the great rebel, with a marked resemblance to William James in his chosen task, the brilliant if rather desultory attack on the old, and above all in his kindly, warm-hearted and hospitable personality.

VI

Jean Le Rond D'Alembert (1717–1783) is forever linked with Diderot in the editing of the *Encyclopédie*. He is, however, a man

[32] *De la suffisance de la religion naturelle* (1747), parts i, xxv. (*Oeuvres*, I, 259, 275).

[33] *Promenade d'un sceptique, Ouvrages Inédits*, IV, 330–31.

of a very different stamp, and for that very reason all the more useful to the enterprise. He was a prudent, reserved, highly esteemed scientist and mathematician. A foundling who never left his foster-mother's roof—he derived his name from the church on whose steps he had been abandoned as an infant—he was tempted neither by Frederick II, who in 1754 wanted him to be the successor to Maupertuis, nor by Catherine II. D'Alembert had two great passions: for mathematics, and against the priests. At the age of twenty-four he became a member of the Académie des Sciences; in 1772 he was made Secretary of the Académie Française. He was a scientist and a geometrician, a positivist in his philosophy of science and of mathematics, in a sense official and "safe." This was the reason why he seemed just the scholar to present in 1750 the *Discours préliminaire* of the *Encyclopédie*. He had already published in 1743 a highly esteemed *Traité de la dynamique*.

In 1759 D'Alembert went in for popular science with an *Éléments de la philosophie,* an eighteenth-century "outline of science." He shows a keen sense of living in the midst of an intellectual revolution:

However little we consider with attentive eyes the middle of the century in which we are living, the events that occupy us, or at least excite us, our ways, our works, and even our conversations, we easily perceive that there has taken place in many respects a quite remarkable change in our ideas—a change which by its rapidity seems to promise us a still greater one to come. The time has come to fix its object, the nature and the limits of this revolution, of which posterity will know better than we the drawbacks and the advantages.[34]

The whole face of natural science is changing:

In a word, from the earth to Saturn, from the history of the heavens to that of the insects, the face of physics has changed. With it almost all the other sciences have taken on a new form, and in fact they should. . . .

Thus from the principles of the profane sciences to the foundations of revelation, from metaphysics to matters of taste, from music to morality, from the scholastic disputes of the theologians to the objects of commerce, from the rights of princes to those of peoples, from the natural law to the arbitrary laws of nations, in a word from the questions which touch us most to those which interest us most slightly, everything has been discussed, analysed, at least agitated. (II, 10–11)

As D'Alembert saw it, the *Encyclopédie* contains man's knowledge, his opinions, his disputes and his manifold errors. His own

[34] *Essai sur les éléments de la philosophie, Oeuvres* (1805), II, 8–9.

book will include, "not what has been thought, but what truths have been found out." Philosophy is the application of reason to the different objects about which it can be exercised. Only revealed religion is excluded. Faith, D'Alembert suggests, is a kind of sixth sense.

Revealed religion is absolutely foreign to the human sciences in its object, in its character, even in the kind of conviction it produces in us. Made rather, as Pascal remarks, for the heart than for the mind, it spreads the living light which is proper to it only in the soul already prepared for the divine illumination; faith is a kind of sixth sense which the Creator grants or refuses at his pleasure; and far as the sublime truths of religion are elevated above the arid and speculative truths of human science, just so far is the internal and supernatural sense by which chosen men grasp these first truths elevated above the gross and vulgar sense by which every man perceives the second. (II, 24)

But reason must examine the grounds of belief. The historical evidences of religion must be criticized by the critical rules of evidence. Revelation is supported by prophecies, miracles, and martyrs. Here reason must guide us.

D'Alembert is an empiricist, even in mathematics, like Mill. The first truths of the sciences are not their axioms, which are barren and sterile, but facts.

What then in each science are the true principles from which we must take our departure? The simple and recognized facts, which call for no other presuppositions, and which in consequence can be neither explained nor disputed. In physics, the everyday phenomena which observation reveals to every eye; in geometry, the sensible properties of extension; in mechanics, the impenetrability of bodies, source of their mutual action; in metaphysics, the result of our sensations; in morals, the first feelings common to all men. . . . Philosophy is the science of facts, or those of chimaeras. (II, 30)

Perhaps these facts are only the corollaries of further principles. Science deals not with the nature of things, but with things as we conceive them.

D'Alembert's plan assigns eight pages to logic, thirty to metaphysics, sixty to morals, nine to grammar, sixty-eight to mathematics, and seventy-two to physics. Reasoning is to perceive the agreement or disagreement of our ideas. Metaphysics is the science of the generation of our ideas: everything else in it is either insoluble or frivolous. The fact of our knowledge of the external world is assumed; the question is, how do we come by such knowledge? What is our idea of matter? We have none; we have no idea of the essence of matter; our senses satisfy our needs, but not our curiosity. Whatever matter may be, we know it cannot desire or think. On the soul and its relations to the body D'Alembert is agnostic.

In religion D'Alembert is a Deist. He wrote Frederick, November 30, 1770:

Christianity was in its origin a pure Deism; Jesus Christ, a kind of philosopher. . . . enemy of persecution and of the priests, preaching to men, doing good and justice, reducing the law to love of one's neighbor and worshiping God in spirit and in truth. St. Paul, the Fathers, the councils changed this religion. We should render a great service to the human race if we made it forget dogmas and limited it to preaching a God of rewards and punishments who reproves superstition, who detests intolerance, and who asks for no other worship on the part of men than that of loving each other and supporting each other.[35]

But like all the Encyclopedists D'Alembert grew more sceptical and positivistic.

In faith and on my oath [he wrote Voltaire on August 29, 1769], I find in all the metaphysical shadows no reasonable position but scepticism. . . . [To Frederick, August 2, 1770] The device of Montaigne, *Que sais-je?* seems to me the answer we must make to almost all the questions of this sort. . . . Those who deny the existence of a supreme intelligence [he said of the *Système de la nature* of Holbach] go much farther than they can prove. . . . The author seems to me too firm and too dogmatic, and in this matter I can see only scepticism as reasonable.[36]

In morals D'Alembert's views form part of the general Utilitarianism of the day, best exemplified in Helvétius. His position is naturalistic, founded on the incontestable fact of the mutual need of men, and the duties this need establishes. The test of all good government is its ability to establish equality, security, and tranquillity.

D'Alembert was a scientist and mathematician who looked beyond his own field to the whole sweep of knowledge, deeply interested in the suffering of mankind, warm-hearted and passionately intolerant of injustice and wrong. He was a typical eighteenth-century French *savant*, and a real man.

[35] *Discours préliminaire*, ed. Picavet, p. xv.
[36] *Discours préliminaire*, p. xvi.

14

The Materialistic Alternative

I

THE THOUGHT of Diderot's generation, the "Encyclopedists" in the narrower sense, the men who came to intellectual maturity during the 1740s, normally started with the rational religion of the English Deists. But like Diderot himself most of them went on to a more complete scepticism of the entire religious world-view. In France this was not the effect of Hume's careful pointing out that that world-view could not be rationally established, but it was equally the destructive effect of the empiricists' criticism of all religious metaphysics. This was a challenge to work out a positive alternative, and to develop a consistent materialism. It was inevitable that the Encyclopedists should have undertaken this task, for in it converged their strongest faith, in Newtonian science, and their controlling passion, anticlericalism. Two thousand years earlier Epicurus had turned to the atomistic materialism of Democritus for the same reasons; every French schoolboy knew his ideas through Lucretius. Now the *philosophes* had a motive for believing him.

The notion that the Newtonian world is self-sufficient, a perpetual motion machine that needs no external supplement, came from the rationalistic strain in Enlightenment thought, not from empiricism. Indeed, the sensationalistic psychology that traced the origins of all men's ideas to the physical senses entered into the thought of the system-makers of materialism only to add a confusing note. The mechanical contact theory of knowledge proved in fact to be the skeleton in the closet of materialism. An ultimate scepticism of the existence of the "external world" was always lurking in the background, and materialists were always falling into a phenomenalism indistinguishable from subjective idealism, before the coming of a more adequate biological psychology in the nineteenth century altered the set-up completely.

The genesis of materialism, as it was elaborated in the later nineteenth century, dates from the Encyclopedists. A hundred years earlier Gassendi and Hobbes had worked out fairly thoroughgoing materialist systems, but Gassendi was a churchman, and Hobbes was an Anglican, if not a Christian: they lacked the anticlerical motive. Now in the eighteenth century the main positions of materialistic metaphysics were worked out, and the chief problems formulated, discussed, and dealt with. The next century added more scientific facts, though it also created many more difficulties; but the essential structure of the argument endured, till it was transformed by the evolutionary ideas of the 1860s and by our recent revolution in physical theory. Holbach's *Système de la nature* remains the most consistent and profound materialism of the pre-evolutionary age; he in fact went far to push materialism into a genuine naturalistic metaphysics.

The motives for this materialism were primarily anticlerical, for it was a French movement, and was directed against the Church as a social and economic institution of the *ancien régime*. In the Western tradition from Epicurus to Marx materialism has always been a moral and anticlerical philosophy. The conviction that "matter" is enough has never been central in a purely scientific philosophy. Such philosophies have always tended to emphasize mind, reason, structure, order, as in Aristotle, Spinoza, Kant, down to present-day logical positivism. One additional motive dominated the medical materialism as well: the opportunity opened to control mental disease by reducing mind to the behavior of body.

There are three distinguishable strands in the fabric of Enlightenment materialism. First is that of medical materialism, elaborated by physicians in the interests of therapy. It was La Mettrie's *Histoire naturelle de l'âme* (1745) and *L'Homme machine* (1748) that initiated the whole movement. It was with Pinel's *Traité médical et philosophique sur l'aliénation mentale* (1800) and Cabanis' *Rapports du physique et du morale de l'homme* (1802) that the movement was brought to an end, unless we want to include Lamarck's *Philosophie zoologique* of 1809.

Secondly, there is what we may call the biological materialism of the natural historians. We have already encountered it in Diderot himself. It is found also in Buffon, in Maupertuis' biological writings, in Robinet, and in Lamarck. This was concerned with a materialistic interpretation of life, and was usually associated with evolutionary ideas.

Thirdly, there is the mechanical materialism which generalized the inorganic science of Newton himself. Here the systematic work is Holbach's *Système de la nature* (1770); the self-sufficiency of the Newtonian world was finally established in Laplace's *Traité de mécanique céleste* (1799). French naturalistic thought passed beyond materialism with Auguste Comte, whose *Cours de philosophie positive* came out between 1830 and 1842.

II

Julien Offray de la Mettrie (1709–1751) after a good Jansenist education decided he could make more from a prescription than from an absolution, and studied medicine in Leyden under Boerhaave. He was an earnest physician who assailed quacks, a man of fashion, and for a while a regimental doctor. The inspiration of his thought came to him during an illness at the siege of Freiburg, which convinced him of the dependence of the mind on the body. In 1745 he published the *Histoire naturelle de l'âme*, fled from France to Leyden, and there in 1748 published *L'Homme machine*. This time he fled to the court of Frederick II, where he became a favorite, a kind of gay-sad jester. He died, the story went, from overeating, and Frederick delivered a respectful eulogy. Voltaire and Diderot, and of course Rousseau, despised him, or affected to. La Mettrie was the first materialist in point of time in the French Enlightenment, and remained in many ways the most extreme. He gave all the arguments from a physician's point of view, thus initiating the medical materialism that culminated in Cabanis. He also expounded a naturalistic ethic of pleasure, which many took as an ethic of lust; above all, men believed he had died from eating too large a truffle patty.

The *Natural History of the Soul* is relatively cautious, and uses the older vocabulary. The soul is the principle of motion, that which feels and thinks, and conscience, the source of moral light.

La Mettrie takes the Aristotelian view that the soul is the form of the body, a harmony resulting from a particular organization of matter. Above all, there must be no dualism, no ghost in the machine. Matter of itself needs no "soul" or "principle of motion" to set it going; rather, motion is a natural property of all matter, and all motion comes from moving matter. Descartes's sharp gulf between men and animals has no basis. Comparative anatomy makes it clear that men are like animals; if so, animals like men can feel. Both are clearly mechanical. Can matter, which all philosophers before Descartes affirmed can feel, also think, as Locke and Voltaire had suggested? Why not? We do not even know what motion is, let alone the powers of matter.

We know in bodies only matter, and we observe the faculty of feeling only in bodies: on what foundation then can we erect an ideal being, disowned by all our knowledge? However, we must admit, with the same frankness, that we are ignorant whether matter has in itself the faculty of feeling, or only the power of acquiring it by those modifications or forms to which matter is susceptible: for it is true that this faculty of feeling appears only in organic bodies.[1]

This became the central problem of biological materialism.

Man a Machine was written in Leyden, not in France; it is the boldest statement of materialism until Holbach's in 1770. It is an impassioned torrent of words, which seeks to persuade rather than to prove. It professes to rely entirely on experience and observation. Where are they to be found?

Experience and observation should therefore be our only guides here. Both are to be found throughout the records of the physicians who were philosophers, and not in the works of the philosophers who were not physicians . . . Thus only the physicians have the right to speak on this subject. What could the others, especially the theologians, have to say? [2]

Man is a machine, capable of winding his own springs. The Cartesians were right, but they did not go far enough. The soul is completely dependent on the body, as is shown by disease, sleep, food, drugs, climate, etc.

Raw meat makes animals fierce, and it would have the same effect on man. This is so true that the English who eat meat red and bloody, and not as

[1] *Histoire naturelle de l'âme*, ch. vi; in La Mettrie, *Man a Machine*, ed. G. C. Bussey (Chicago, 1912), p. 160.

[2] *L'Homme machine*, Bussey ed., p. 88; A. Vartanian ed. (1960), p. 151.

well done as ours, seem to share more or less in the savagery due to this kind of food, and to other causes which can be rendered ineffective by education only. This savagery creates in the soul, pride, hatred, scorn of other nations, indocility and other sentiments which degrade the character.[3]

Man is like the other animals; the sole difference between them is man's possession of speech. Teach a monkey to talk, and he will be the equal of Louis XV. It is his inherited organism plus his acquired education that makes the man. But is not man distinguished by possessing morality as well? Even other animals recognize the natural law: consider how repentant dogs can be, consider the lion of Androcles. It is true that they do not recognize it all the time; but then neither do men. And La Mettrie sets forth a list of heinous crimes that raise a doubt about the universality of the moral law.

Now, I believe and admit that these wretches do not for the most part feel at the time the enormity of their actions. . . . Doubtless it is much to be wished that excellent physicians might be the only judges. They alone could tell the innocent criminal from the guilty. If reason is the slave of a depraved or mad desire, how can it control the desire? . . .

Nature has created us all solely to be happy—yes, all of us from the crawling worm to the eagle lost in the clouds. For this cause she has given all animals some share of the natural law, a share greater or less according to the needs of each animal's organs when in a normal condition. Now how shall we define natural law? It is a feeling that teaches us what we should not do, because we would not wish it to be done to us. Should I dare add to this common idea, that this feeling seems to me but a kind of fear or dread, a salutary to the race as to the individual; for may it not be true that we respect the purse and life of others only to save our own possessions, our honor, and ourselves? [4]

On metaphysics and theology, La Mettrie is a sceptic.

I do not mean to call in question the existence of a supreme being: on the contrary it seems to me that the greatest degree of probability is in favor of this belief. But since the existence of this being goes no further than that of any other toward proving the need of worship, it is a theoretic truth with very little practical value. Therefore, since we may say, after such long experience, that religion does not imply exact honesty, we are authorized by the same reasons to think that atheism does not exclude it. . . . Besides it does not matter for our peace of mind, whether matter be eternal or have been created, whether there be or be not a God. How

[3] L'Homme machine, Bussey ed., p. 94; Vartanian ed., p. 155.
[4] L'Homme machine, Bussey ed., pp. 119, 121; Vartanian ed., pp. 173, 175.

foolish to torment ourselves so much about things which we cannot know, and which would not make us any happier even were we to gain knowledge about them! [5]

La Mettrie ends in a paean on the blessings of atheism.

"The universe will never be happy, unless it is atheistic." . . . If atheism were generally accepted, all the forms of religion would then be destroyed and cut off at the roots. No more theological wars, no more soldiers of religion—such terrible soldiers! . . . Deaf to all other voices, tranquil mortals would follow only the spontaneous dictates of their own being, the only commands which can never be despised with impunity and which alone can lead us to happiness through the pleasant paths of virtue. . . . Let us then conclude boldly that man is a machine, and that in the whole universe there is but a single substance differently modified.[6]

La Mettrie sets forth a naturalistic ethics. His *Art de jouir* horrified the world, yet is an excellent exposition of hedonism; it is the foundation of Helvétius's theory of utilitarianism, and thus indirectly of Jeremy Bentham's. It is a law of nature that man is to seek his own happiness: pleasure and the avoidance of pain are the aim of man. We are bodies, hence the most spiritual pleasures have their physical basis. The pleasures of the senses are the most intense, but they are short. Happiness consists in a harmonious organization of such pleasures. Reflection heightens sense pleasures, but reflective pleasure is impossible alone. Such reflective or "higher" pleasure is really "higher," but thought generally destroys pleasure by creating longing and unattained desires. Think of the happy life of the oyster! He has no worries, no unfulfilled desires, no unrequited passions. An opium dream is worth more than all your philosophic discussions.

But education can change, and reason organize pleasures, following nature. The good is not absolute but relative: actions are only good or bad in relation to society. Good men will do what is socially useful from motives of honor and sympathy. Remorse is useless; it does no good and destroys happiness. If you have done wrong, you could not have helped it. The criminal is really a sick man; do not punish him, but try to heal him. And La Mettrie advocates humane reforms.

[5] *L'Homme machine*, Bussey ed., p. 122; Vartanian ed., pp. 175–76.
[6] *L'Homme machine*, Bussey ed., pp. 127, 147–48; Vartanian ed., pp. 179, 196–97.

III

La Mettrie opened the whole debate by stating the case for materialism of the medical variety in extreme terms. With Maupertuis' *Vénus physique* (1745) and *Système de la nature* (1751) and Buffon's *Histoire naturelle* (1749) the problems of biological materialism were brought to the fore. Whence come life, consciousness, and thought? How are they to be accounted for on the purely mechanical principles of Newtonian science? Two main issues are here involved. First, how explain the genesis of living organisms and their bewildering variety of forms? Secondly, how explain the functioning of living and intelligent organisms in terms of the principles of mechanics? To the first question Buffon answered with a theory of the evolution of species, or "transformism" as it was called, which was speedily taken over by Diderot and Robinet, and reached something like precision with Lamarck. But in the early nineteenth century this transformism was largely abandoned for the special creation hypothesis of Cuvier, because no adequate mechanism for the process of evolution could be developed.

On the second issue, the functioning of living organisms, two main views were held. The first is the explanation through mechanistic analysis: we can call it the brick method. Find the elements out of which organisms are composed, and then put them together out of those elements. But, like the small boy who takes apart father's watch, we then find that something is left out: the way the elements are put together. Does organization then produce something new? Surely the beauty of the house does not reside in the heap of bricks alone: it appears when the bricks are put together "in a certain way." Matter organized "in a certain way" can act differently from unorganized matter, and follow different laws. This was the answer of a good mechanist like Holbach. But how does it occur? There is the rub. Men felt a marked dislike of the appearance of something new: such novelty sheerly accepted seemed the denial of explanation. The virtues of "creativity" had to await the Romantic publicity agents. And even today careful thinkers have no love for such "creative" or "emergent" evolution: it seems the negation of analysis.

So, much more popular, and followed by nearly all the natural historians, was the life-stuff and mind-stuff theory we have already encountered in Diderot. Set forth by Maupertuis, and adopted by Buffon and Robinet, it read back the new function into the element itself. "Life" and "mind" must be properties of all matter, as inexplicable and ultimate as motion itself. All matter is potentially alive and potentially conscious, just as the brick is potentially a contributor to the beauty of the house. The trouble with this recourse, which was actually a revival of the pre-Cartesian ideas of the alchemists, is that while it undoubtedly states a fact, it furnishes no explanation. Life-stuff and mind-stuff throw no light on the actual functioning of the living, intelligent organism. The "life" or the "feeling" a molecule can be said to exhibit remain qualitatively different from the processes of living and thinking.

The real problem, in other words, is not one of substance at all, but of behavior: how account for living, intelligent behavior? Molar masses and organisms exhibit different patterns of functioning. How are we to understand the relations between the two kinds of pattern? How can we "derive" the pattern of the living organism from the pattern of mechanics? How can a "purely" mechanical nervous system react to "meanings," to the nonmechanical logical structure of truth? If all his actions are "mechanically" determined, how can man discover truth rather than error? That he can is a fact essential to science; and for it materialism of the Enlightenment variety offers no explanation: of the "freedom of reason" to know. This was the central problem of Kant and the idealists: to explain rational freedom as not inconsistent with mechanical determination. This involved for them the unquestioned acceptance of Newtonian mechanical determinism. They tried to get beyond it, but they were afraid to criticize it in its own field.

IV

Pierre Louis Moreau de Maupertuis (1698–1759) showed a penchant for biological speculation. In his *Vénus physique* he raised the question, does not instinct belong to all parts of matter as well as to organized bodies? Is not a living body rather a republic than an absolute monarchy? These were the two questions the biological materialists could never answer satisfactorily. In his *Système de la nature,* published in 1751 in Latin under the *nom de plume* of Dr. Baumann, he undertakes to push the issues. The subtitle is, "Essay on the Formation of Organic Bodies." Matter and motion alone are insufficient to explain all phenomena. Even with Newton's addition of impenetrability, mobility, inertia, and attraction, the properties of matter are still not enough to satisfy chemistry and biology. To add an immaterial soul would be of no avail: such a soul could work on matter only by a miracle. And special creation is "rather to recount a miracle than to give a physical explanation." The problem of materialism is, whence comes consciousness? Is it due wholly to the organization of matter, or is it potentially there all along?

A mere uniform force of attraction could not account for the simplest organism. We must have recourse to some "principle of intelligence," something like what we call desire, aversion, and memory. And if we admit some principle of intelligence in complex organisms, what is the harm in attributing it to the smallest particles of matter? If we say that organization alone makes the difference, can we conceive that the arrangement of parts could ever give birth to a thought? The two Cartesian substances, each with a single property, might be a single subject, whose essence is unknown, but with both properties. Does this make matter too complex? But no explanation is too complex if it is necessary to account for the facts. Existence is always a miracle.

If God has endowed each of the smallest parts of matter, each element, with some property like what we call in ourselves desire, aversion, memory; the formation of the first individuals having been miraculous, those that have succeeded them are only the effects of these properties.[7]

Maupertuis is here taking the Deist position: creation is a miracle, but thereafter everything follows immutable laws.

How account then for the unity of consciousness? Maupertuis uses the figure of the swarm of bees and the army that Diderot takes over. His answer is to appeal to the gathering of all the partial perceptions in man into a single unity of perception, one sensation. Here as in so much else he anticipates Kant's problems, and

[7] *Système de la nature,* par. XXXI; Maupertuis, *Oeuvres* (Lyon, 1768), II, 157-58.

sketches Kant's solution. But is this matter endowed with intelligence, this mind-stuff, like human thinking? This is the major objection to Maupertuis' hypothesis.

All the systems of the formation of organic bodies thus reduce to three; it does not seem they can be extended to a greater number:

1. That in which brute elements without intelligence by their chance encounters alone are supposed to have formed the universe.

2. That in which the Supreme Being, or beings subordinate to him, distinct from matter, are supposed to have employed the elements, as the architect employs stones in constructing edifices.

3. Finally that in which the elements themselves, endowed with intelligence, arrange themselves and unite to fulfill the views of the Creator.[8]

Here in Maupertuis' thesis of 1751 were set forth ideas that were to dominate the biological materialism of a generation.

V

Georges-Louis Leclerc de Buffon (1707–1788), great scientist and writer, a typical eighteenth-century "natural historian," Director of the Jardin du Roi, now the Jardin des Plantes, had already in 1749 begun to issue his large *Histoire naturelle*. A respected scientist who stood aloof from the polemics of the Encyclopedists, Buffon wrote the *De rerum natura* of the Enlightenment. Like the *Story of Mankind* of H. G. Wells, it is a great epic poem, in rolling prose, starting with the beginnings of the earth and extending to the summit of Nature in man. The emphasis throughout is on the glory of mankind, and man's gradual ascent with no sharp breaks from the bosom of Nature. The account is thoroughly naturalistic: there is no recourse to any supernatural intervention, once the Creator has established the sun—for Buffon still needs a Deistic commencement. The method is patient "observation," and experimentation: here is a naturalism without mathematics.

What is Nature? Not a thing, not a being, but "the system of laws established by the Creator for the existence of things and the succession of beings." Nature is alive, an eternal process; "time, space, and matter are its means, the universe its object, motion and life its goal." Buffon sees two different kinds of matter, dead and living. Dead matter obeys the laws of attraction alone, living matter obeys also the laws of attraction and expansion; the latter are

[8] *Système de la nature,* par. LXVII; *Oeuvres,* II, 183–84.

by reaction the effect of attraction. The living and the animate is thus a physical property of matter. Life appears on earth as an accident. Vegetables have the force of expansion: they are able to organize matter. Animals are unities, individuals; they can feel, think, and will. Men have emotions, ideas, plans, reflection, choice; they can control Nature to their social purposes.

In 1779 Buffon completed his *Histoire naturelle* with the *Époques de la nature*. Through seven epochs he traces the development of the earth from its original fire. The earth broke off from the sun and began to cool gradually. After thirty-five million years, animals and plants appeared; orthodoxy still held the world was created 4004 B.C. After twenty-five million years more, man made his appearance.

Buffon is the first propounder of a theory of evolution that can be called modern. The idea was in the air, and was speedily taken up by the more imaginative minds, like Diderot. Species are not fixed types, but rather a human classification; Buffon himself was a convert from Linnaeus' careful classification of plants. The changes in species are caused by the environment, and Buffon tries to trace a theory of the way it works, emphasizing temperature, climate, and food supply. The environment operates both negatively, through permitting only the fittest to survive, and positively, in the way developed by Lamarck; the changes are then inherited. Buffon, in fact, seems to have seen and asked all the questions of fundamental importance that have been answered and that remain unanswered today. And he was much interested in experimental breeding of plants, a kind of eighteenth-century Luther Burbank.

Man is the goal and the lord of the evolutionary process of Nature. With Turgot and Condorcet, Buffon is one of the great prophets of the idea of progress and of human perfectibility. Man is the great revolutionary, changing the very face of the earth. Man uniting with his fellows to subdue nature is the magnificent climax to the long story of the slow development of Nature.

Man has not known till lately the extent of his power, and he does not yet know it enough; it depends entirely on the exercise of his intelligence; thus the more he observes, the more he cultivates nature, the more means he will have to subject her to himself, and the more facilities for drawing from her bosom new riches, without diminishing the treasures of her inexhaustible fecundity.

And what could he not do with himself, I mean with his own species, if his will was always directed by his intelligence! Who knows to what point man could perfect his nature, either mental or physical? Is there a single nation that can boast of having arrived at the best possible government, which would be to make all men not equally happy but less unequally unhappy, in watching over their preservation, and sparing their sweat and blood through peace, through the abundance of food, through the amenities of life and the aids to its propagation? This is the moral goal of every society which would improve itself. And as to the physical side, medicine and the other arts whose object is to preserve us, are they as advanced and as well known as the destructive arts born of war? It seems that at all times man has reflected less on good than sought after evil: all society is a mixture of both; and just as of all the feelings that affect the multitude, fear is the most powerful, the grand talents in the art of doing evil have been the first to strike the mind of man; then those which have amused it have occupied his heart; and it is only after a too long employment of these two means of false honor and sterile pleasure, that at last man has recognized that his true glory is science, and that peace is his true happiness.[9]

Buffon was the spiritual father of modern biological science, as Lamarck was of zoology, and Bichat of histology.

V I

Another who pushed Maupertuis' hylozoism or panpsychism—his mind-stuff view—was Jean Baptiste Robinet (1735–1820), an ex-Jesuit and hack writer in Holland, and after 1778 royal censor in Paris. In 1761 he issued *De la nature*, in which he held that all beings are reducible to a single element, matter endowed with the property of life, that is, the power to assimilate, to grow, and to reproduce. In *Considérations philosophiques sur la gradation naturelle des formes de l'être* (1768) he set forth a "scale of beings" in accordance with the law of continuity. Nature's problem was to perform the three functions of living matter with the greatest perfection possible; man is the most elegant and complicated answer to the problem. The advance toward man consists in a sort of progressive liberation of activity which makes use of matter. In the mineral, activity is completely subjected to matter; in living things, activity begins to lift itself above matter; in man matter is only the

---

[9] *Époques de la nature*, end of Seventh Epoch, ed. P. Bonnefon, *Pages choisies des grands écrivains* (1903), pp. 321–22.

tool of activity; and beyond man there will be an activity that needs no material organs, dematerialized pure intelligence.

But the laws of this development are mechanical throughout. All thought and volition are merely the subjective side of the brain processes. And Robinet tries to locate the precise fibres which are the basis of the moral sense. Freedom for him means the power to do what we will, not the power to will what we wish. Robinet at times expresses a complete epiphenomenalism, based on a neural mythology; but it is hard to find all his ideas consistent.

VII

French materialism began with La Mettrie, a medical materialist. In a sense it reached its most careful thought fifty years later with the two great medical materialists, Pinel and Cabanis. For these physicians the motive was the hope of controlling disease through physical treatment, especially mental disease. They did not want to have to deal with any elusive or unpredictable "mental substance," but with a deranged human organism. It is not surprising that with Pinel such views were associated with the first scientific treatment of insanity as a physical disease, not a crime. Pinel was the great authority called upon in 1789 to treat the demented King George III. Thus a materialistic view of human nature was closely associated with the humanitarian movement, of which Beccaria with his medical view of crime is the best known representative.

Philippe Pinel (1745–1826) brought out a *Nosographie philosophique* in 1798, and his major work, *Traité médical et philosophique sur l'aliénation mentale*, in 1800. He was the real founder of abnormal psychology. And he was passionately devoted to spreading the realization that the insane are not criminals, or possessed of a devil, but are sick men. They should be treated with kindness and pity, and not with the customary brutality. Nor are all insane men alike; many are curable with proper treatment. Pinel's interest in the reform of barbarous treatment of the insane and his medical materialism are completely fused.

Pierre Jean Georges Cabanis (1757–1808) is also a physician, but his interest is rather in physiological psychology. Left in Paris at the age of fourteen to fend for himself, he studied letters and the sciences, and chose medicine as a profession. He became a member of the circle of Mme. Helvétius, and met Franklin, Condillac, Garat, Volney, and Condorcet, to whom he furnished the poison for his suicide. His career was under the Republic and the Empire. In 1795 he was made Professor of Hygiene, and in 1796 read to the Institute the lectures that were published in 1802 as *Rapports du physique et du moral de l'homme.* Cabanis makes his motives and his method clear.

Medicine is at the foundation of all sound rational philosophy, for it lays bare the physical man, of which the moral man is but a part or another aspect. It furnishes a solid foundation to the philosophy that seeks the source of man's ideas and passions. It should be the guiding force in every good system of education, and find in the eternal laws of nature the foundation of the rights and the duties of man, trace the art of guiding and perfecting the understanding, and the art of happiness. Moreover, it is eminently fitted to dispel the phantoms that fascinate and torment men's imaginations, and to destroy all superstitious beliefs.[10]

Cabanis was associated with the Ideologists: that is, he was in the tradition of Locke, Condillac, and Helvétius, the French sensationalists. But his importance does not come from this epistemology, or, as they would have put it, "metaphysics" of sense experience. Ideology, it was said, is the algebra of the soul, whereas Cabanis was trying to work out "the natural history of the soul." Locke, Condillac, and the rest, have analyzed men's thought into the sensations from which it is derived. But whence come the sensations? Let us get rid of metaphysics and theories, and examine the facts impartially and scientifically, as though we were dealing with physics.

A study of man's physical and mental processes leads to the conclusion that physiology, the analysis of ideas, and morals are but three branches of one single science, the science of man.[11]

If we start from physiology, we arrive at sensations; if we start from the analysis of ideas, we likewise arrive at sensations.

Physical sensibility, is the last term at which we arrive in the study of the phenomena of life, and the methodical inquiry into their true connection. It is also the last result, or, following the common fashion of speech, the most general principle furnished by the analysis of the intel-

---

[10] *Degré de certitude de la médecine* (1798), in F. Picavet, *Les Idéologues* (1891), p. 211.

[11] *Rapports du physique et du moral de l'homme,* 2d ed. (1805), I, 7.

lectual faculties and of the affections of the soul. Therefore, the physical and the moral are one at their source; or, better, the moral is only the physical considered under certain more particular points of view. (I, 39)

The relation between mind and body is not a mystery to be accepted on faith, not even the incomprehensible problem of how two different substances are united, as the Cartesians held, but rather a physiological fact to be described. It is the relation between two different sets of physical activities.

In his second mémoire, *The Physiological History of Sensations,* Cabanis takes sensationalism as established beyond question. All our ideas come from sensations, and all our actions result from sense-stimuli.

We are doubtless not still required to prove that physical sensibility is the source of all the ideas and of all the habits which constitute the moral existence of man: Locke, Bonnet, Condillac, Helvétius have carried this truth to the last degree of demonstration. Among informed persons who also make some use of their reason, there is now none who can raise the least doubt in this regard. On the other hand, the physiologists have proved that all the vital movements are the product of impressions received by the sensible parts: and these two fundamental results, brought together in a reflective examination, form a single and identical truth. (I, 85)

But do all man's acts spring from ideas or conscious choice? No, Condillac was wrong—Cabanis is reacting against such excessive intellectualism. Impressions come from without and from within; the latter are unconscious, and are called instinct. Sensation is caused by the nerves: when the nerves act on the muscles, they effect movement; when they act on themselves, they produce sensations.

The most famous passage in Cabanis attempts to deal with thinking:

To gain a just idea of the operations from which thought results, we must consider the brain as a particular organ, especially destined to produce it; just as the stomach and the intestines are destined to produce digestion, the liver to filter the bile, the parotids and the maxillary and sublingual glands to prepare the salivary juices. The impressions, arriving at the brain, set it in activity; as foods falling into the stomach excite it to secrete more abundantly the gastric juice, and to movements which favor their own dissolution. The proper function of the one is to perceive each particular impression, to attach signs to it, to combine the different impressions, to compare them with each other, to draw judgments and determinations from them; as the function of the other is to act on the nutritive substances, whose presence stimulates it, to dissolve them, and to assimilate the juices to our nature.

Will it be said that the organic movements by which the functions of the brain are carried out are unknown to us? But the action by which the nerves of the stomach determine the different operations that constitute digestion, the manner by which they impregnate the gastric juice with the most active dissolving power, are no less concealed from our inquiry. We see the food fall into the viscera, with the qualities proper to it; we see it emerge with new qualities: and we conclude it has truly caused this alteration. We see equally the impressions arrive at the brain, by means of the nerves; they are then isolated and without coherence. The brain enters into action; it acts on them: and soon it returns them changed into ideas, which the language of physiognomy and gesture, or the signs of word and of writing, manifest externally. We conclude, with the same certitude, that the brain in some manner digests the impressions; that it makes organically the secretion of thought. (I, 153–54)

The analysis of both processes is hardly carried very far. But it is clear that what Cabanis is presenting is not the crude identification of thought with a secretion, but rather a behaviorism, a method for analyzing human processes.

The bulk of the work is a careful and detailed study of the influence of various physical factors on mental life: age, sex, temperament, disease, diet, climate, etc., all of which suggests a pretty complete dependence of mental life on bodily conditions. These factors all operate physically on the nervous system. The treatment of sex is not the most successful, but it will suggest the method. It is the great physical difference between the bodies of man and woman that leads to the chasm between their minds. Cabanis enumerates the physiological differences, finding that a woman's brain is much softer than a man's; the greatest difference lies in the glands.

Man must be strong, brave, enterprising; woman must be feeble, timid, dissimulating. Such is the law of nature. . . .

While man acts on nature and on other animate beings by the force of his organs, or by the ascendancy of his intelligence, woman must act on man, by the seduction of her manners and by the continual observation of everything that can flatter his heart or captivate his imagination. For this, she must know how to bend to his tastes, give way without constraint even to the caprices of the moment, and seize the intervals when some observations thrown out as by chance can take effect. . . .

Now, the happiness of women will always depend on the impression they make on men: and I do not think that those who truly love them could take great pleasure in seeing them carrying the musket and marching to the charge, or ruling from a throne, still less from the tribune where the interests of a nation are discussed. (I, 354, 358, 371)

In order to win back to materialism a still larger group than the half of mankind this may have alienated, let us consider the effect of wine:

By the habit of the happy impressions it occasions; by a sweet excitation of the brain; by a strong sentiment of increase in the muscular forces, the use of wine nourishes and renews gaiety, maintains the mind in an easy and constant activity, causes to be born and develop benevolent attitudes, confidence, cordiality. In the land of vineyards, men are in general gayer, wittier, more sociable; they have more open and more prepossessing manners. Their quarrels are characterized by a ready violence: but their resentments have no depth, their revenge nothing of black perfidy. (II, 97)

We may doubt whether this is the law of nature or the French tradition. But the latter would be no refutation of Cabanis' position. For nothing is more incontestable than the influence of mind upon matter, as in the case of fear on digestion, etc. For Cabanis, this is merely the influence of one bodily process on another.

Hence we can no longer be embarrassed to determine the true sense of the expression, Influence of the moral on the physical: we see clearly that it designates the influence of the cerebral system, as the organ of thought and will, on the other organs which its sympathetic action is capable of exciting, to suspend and even to alter the nature of all their functions. That is what it is; it can be nothing more. (II, 522)

In Cabanis we no longer have a dogmatic or metaphysical materialism, but something close to a true positivism, an observational theory of human behavior. In this sense Cabanis is the precursor of Comte.

The inscription on one of the ancient temples, where wisdom seemed to have taken refuge, before charlatanism had there raised its throne, has the first cause of the universe speak in a truly great and philosophical manner: I am what is, and what has been, and what will be; and no one has known my nature. Another inscription said: Know thyself.

The first is the confession of an inevitable ignorance. The second is the formal and precise indication of the goal which rational philosophy and moral philosophy should follow: it is, in a sense, the summary of all the lessons of wisdom about the two great subjects of our meditation. (I, 160)

Cabinis' materialism was an observational method applied to human processes.

The last great figure in the movement of the materialism of the Enlightenment, before Auguste Comte appeared to give a new direction to "scientific" and anticlerical thinking in France, was Lamarck. He is himself a biological materialist, successor to Buffon; but in a sense he also completes the analysis of Cabanis, and may stand as the transition to the Darwinian ideas of the nineteenth century.

VIII

Jean Baptiste Pierre Antoine de Monet, Chevalier de Lamarck (1744–1829), was a physician and a naturalist, as a young man the friend of Buffon. He wrote a *Flore française*, describing two thousand species. In 1794 he was appointed in charge of invertebrates in the Jardin des Plantes; from 1815 to 1822 he brought out a large *History of Invertebrates*. In 1809 appeared his major theoretical work, the *Philosophie zoologique*. He points out that life cannot be identified with sensation. Life is an organic phenomenon, the result of the relations existing between portions of the body, the various fluids they contain, and the exciting cause of the changes and movements there operative. Life is really a state of chemical tension. Sensation is found only with a nervous system. Lamarck emphasizes comparative biology—he was an expert on invertebrates —and he insists strongly on instinct.

His theory of the "degradation" or transformation and evolution of species is his best known idea. Science, he holds, studies secondary causes. Nature is uniform. And Nature has an urge to create and develop higher types of life. It does this indirectly, by means of the operation of the environment! Animals change their form through the use and disuse of various organs under different environmental conditions. These acquired characteristics are then inherited—the Lamarckian thesis modern biology has rejected since Weismann, and more particularly since the acceptance of Mendelian genetics. Lamarck puts his position:

But great changes in environment bring about changes in the habits of animals. Changes in their wants necessarily bring about parallel changes in their habits. If new wants become constant or very lasting, they form new habits, the new habits involve the use of new parts, or a different use of old parts, which result finally in the production of new organs and the modification of old ones.[12]

Lamarck states his four laws of evolution:

First Law: Life by its own forces tends continually to increase the volume of every body that possesses it, as well as to increase the size of its parts, up to a limit which it itself sets.

Second Law: The production of a new organ in an animal body results from a new need that has appeared and continues to be felt, and from the new movement which this need initiates and causes to continue.

Third Law: The development of organs and their force of action are always in direct relation to the employment of these organs.

Fourth Law: All that has been acquired or altered in the organizations of individuals during their life is preserved by generation, and transmitted to new individuals which proceed from those which have undergone these changes.[13]

Lamarck stands with Darwin as one of the greatest apostles of the idea of evolution, even though his own description of the mechanism of the process is no longer accepted as warranted.

IX

It is the great representative of mechanical materialism, Baron d'Holbach, who produced the most searching and profound statement of the whole position in his *Système de la nature* of 1770. Holbach (1723–1789) was the "Maecenas of the *philosophes*," their "*maître d'hôtel*." He was an attractive man, upright and benevolent; even Rousseau admired him, and used him as the model for Wolmar, Julie's husband, in *La nouvelle Éloise*. He hated the tyranny not only of the Church, but also of the King, which was a new thing, and not appreciated by Frederick II. A man with scientific training, especially in chemistry and physics, he was imaginatively inspired by the new world of law unfolded by Newton; he carried out all its implications, making no compromise with Deism, and hence produced a really great world-view, consistent throughout. His philosophy of Nature bore all the emotional aura of a

[12] *Philosophie zoologique;* cited in Henry Fairfield Osborn, *From the Greeks to Darwin: an Outline of the Development of the Evolution Idea* (1894), p. 168.

[13] Osborn, French text cited, p. 167; from introduction to *Histoire naturelle* (1815).

religion; it could easily pass into Hébert's "worship of Reason" in Notre Dame. Above all, Holbach was sincere and outspoken, save in never publishing under his own name: he had no desire to leave Paris.

Paul Heinrich Dietrich, Baron von Holbach, was born in 1723, the son of a rich parvenu of the Pfalz on the Rhine. He came to Paris at twelve, was educated there, and in Leyden, and became a typical eighteenth-century cosmopolitan. He knew French, German, English, Italian, and Latin fluently, and had studied all the sciences; he translated German scientific articles for the *Encyclopédie*. He had a rich art collection, and a well-stocked natural history cabinet. In 1749 he settled in Paris as a young man of the world. His dinners on Sunday and Thursday were famous. They lasted from two to eight, and everybody came. Diderot was his best friend; so intimate were they that long passages appear that are identical in the writings of both. Rousseau finally broke with him over a curé who was mocked for reading a religious tragedy of his composition. He died the year of the Revolution.

Holbach published an immense number of pamphlets and translations, generally under some other name. In 1752 he issued a translation on the art of glass-blowing, which Diderot snapped up for the *Encyclopédie:* after 1760 he brought out a number of anti-religious and Deistic translations from the English. In 1766 he published *Antiquity Unveiled* (by M. Boulanger), a curious work on the influence of the environment on ancient history and civilization. Its thesis is that man failed in his struggle with the elements, and became religious because of his practical defeat. In 1767 there came out *Christianity Unveiled, an examination of the principles and the effects of the Christian religion* (also by M. Boulanger). Voltaire exploded, and Grimm called it "the boldest and most terrible book that has ever appeared anywhere in the world." It holds: 1) Neither Christianity nor any other religion is necessary to preserve law and order in a just society; 2) Christianity is absurd and irrational; 3) Christian-morality, in so far as it is valuable, is common to all nations; what is particular is only for "enthusiasts," not for good citizens; 4) Christianity has had sinister and terrible political results; it is responsible for most of the ills of society.

In 1768 Holbach published a *Natural History of Superstition;* in

1769 *Intolerance Convicted of Crime and Madness, and Hell De-stroyed, an examination of the dogma of eternal punishment;* in 1770 a *Critical History of Jesus Christ*, and a *View of the Saints.* The last holds: "Men are measured by their utility which results to the species. The saints thought they were deserving heaven through rendering themselves perfectly useless on earth." In the same year came out an *Essay on Prejudices, or the influence of opinions on the morals and happiness of men.*

In 1770 appeared Holbach's serious masterpiece, the *Système de la nature:* in 1772, *Le bon-sens,* an abridgment that proved im-mensely popular. D'Alembert called the latter "much more terrible than the *System of Nature.*" In 1773 came the *Système social.* These are Holbach's three best works. Finally, in 1776 came the *Elements of Universal Morality*, a textbook in moral instruction.

The *Système de la nature, ou des lois du monde physique et du monde moral,* purported to have been written by M. Mirabaud, a deceased Secretary of the French Academy. It was burnt by the hangman in 1770, with three other books of Holbach. Thirteen volumes in all were written in direct reply: the chief were those by Voltaire and by Frederick II, who complained that in Holbach kings were treated no better than God. Voltaire wrote Frederick: "Thus God has for him the two least superstitious men in Europe, which ought to please him greatly."

The work is divided into two parts, on Nature and Man, and on God. Part I sets forth a thoroughgoing naturalism. There is one great system of law from whose dominion nothing is excluded, Nature, consisting of matter in motion. There is nothing else. But man seeks another realm, and so allows tyrants and priests to en-slave him. Learn this system of Nature and be happy and free. The Lucretian motive is strong in Holbach.

Man is an essential part of this great whole, as much a part of it as anything else. He is the work of nature, he exists in Nature, he is submitted to her laws. There is no distinction between the physical and the moral man; man is a being purely physical. The physical organization that makes man a moral being is itself the work of Nature. Holbach is here making two cardinal assumptions. First, the methods and concepts of mechanics are being universal-ized, and held to be exclusively valid. Since it is obviously impossible to prove this thesis, it is clearly an assumption being read into Nature. Kant's step in making it a necessary assumption of reason is now easy to take. Secondly, all knowledge comes from sense contact. Nothing else is knowable: there is no *ignotum per ignotius*. There can be no explanation of observed facts by unobserved entities.

Those beings which cannot act on any of our organs, either immediately, and by themselves, or mediately, by the intervention of other bodies, do not exist for us; since they can neither move us, nor consequently furnish us with ideas; they can neither be known to us, nor of course be judged by us. To know an object, is to have felt it; to feel it, it is requisite to have been moved by it.[14]

The universe presents only matter and motion, an uninterrupted succession of cause and effects. Matter and motion have existed from all eternity. They are ultimate facts, needing no cause or explanation. Holbach criticizes the argument for a First Cause.

We cannot go beyond this aphorism, Matter acts because it exists, and exists to act. If it be inquired how or why matter exists, we answer, we know not: but reasoning by analogy of what we do not know to what we do, we should be of the opinion, it exists necessarily, or contains within itself a sufficient reason for its existence. In supposing it to be created or produced by a being distinguished from it, or less known than itself, which it may be for anything we know to the contrary, we must still admit that this being is necessary, and includes a sufficient reason for its own existence. We have not then removed any of the difficulty, we have not thrown a clearer light on the subject, we have not advanced a single step; we have simply laid aside a being, of which we know some few of the properties, but of which we are still extremely ignorant, to have recourse to a power of which it is utterly impossible we can as long as we are men, form any distinct idea; of which, notwithstanding it may be a truth, we cannot by any means we possess, demonstrate the existence. . . .

Is it not more natural and more intelligible to derive everything which exists from the bosom of matter, whose existence is demonstrated by every one of our senses, whose effects we each instant experience, which we see acting, moving, communicating motion and generating ceaselessly, than to attribute the formation of things to an unknown force, to a spiritual being which cannot develop from its nature what it is not itself, and which, by the spiritual essence attributed to it, is incapable of doing anything and of setting anything in motion?[15]

[14] *Système de la nature*, Part I, ch. 2; ed. "Londres" (1771), I, 14; Eng. tr., London (1840), p. 10.
[15] *Système de la nature*, Part I, ch. 4; I, 59–60n; Eng. tr., p. 35; *Le Bon-Sens*, sec. 22, "Londres" (1772).

On the problem of the biological materialists, Holbach is clear: living matter is composed of the same elements as inorganic matter: the entire difference lies in the arrangement and organization. And there is one great chain of cause and effect, no slightest element of chance. In a great whirlwind, there is not a mote of dust that has not a sufficient cause for moving just as it does; in a revolution, "there is not a single action, a single word, a single thought, a single will, a single passion, that is not the necessary result of the causes operating." Here too the step to Kant is short.

There is no intelligent designer, no Newtonian or Deistic Creator God. For the distinction between "order" and "confusion," so important for the eighteenth-century argument from design, is man-made, and not "real." A simple series of phenomena that recurs, man calls order; when such a series is affected by other more complex laws, man in his ignorance calls it confusion. Order is what is conformable to man's mode of being; confusion, what is opposed. Man finds much order in nature and concludes, it was made for him, when in reality he was made for it and came out of it. Why should we assume that Nature should "naturally" be chaos rather than order? that the latter needs an explanation, while the former does not? Nature is just what it is found to be! There is no more explanation called for of the order of the universe than of its existence. Nature is all of one piece: human distinctions are gone. The order in it is not anthropocentric: there is no special providence directed toward man. Yet there is order and system: it is a rational universe intelligible to the *philosophe*. Is it also intelligent? No, an intelligent being is one that acts like man, has faculties proper to his self-preservation, and acts to encompass ends. Man reads this into Nature: Nature acts to accomplish some of his ends, and hence he assumes Nature is like himself intelligent. Just as wine makes me witty and happy without being itself happy, so Nature produces intelligent beings, without herself being intelligent.

And yet—the fundamental motive of theism is to find something in the universe like man, some friend behind phenomena to foster and sustain his ideals and interests. Holbach's "naturalism," by making man part and parcel of Nature, Nature acting in human form, does make Nature in sophisticated form "anthropomorphic." If Nature is mechanical, and man too is a machine, then Nature is like man, and man is made in Nature's image, man is a microcosm. Are not theistic interests and religious values really saved? Whether it be God the Father or Mother Nature, both construings are opposed to the alien world view in which man is quite alone, and in which there is a sharp dualism between man and Nature.

In a thoroughgoing naturalism such as Holbach's, man is once more at home in his world. Man and his interests are natural products. Such a view can well serve as the basis for religious piety and confidence. And Holbach ends as a pantheist with deep religious feeling: Nature is really divine! He forgets all his keen arguments against the existence of God based on the manifold ills of life, and justifies the ways of Nature to man. Indeed, he prays to Nature; and the only difference is that he uses the feminine rather than the masculine pronoun.

Holbach ends on an I-Thou conversation between Nature and man:

"O thou!" cries Nature to man, "who, following the impulse I have given thee, during thy whole existence, incessantly tend towards happiness, do not strive to resist my sovereign law. Labor to thine own felicity; partake without fear of the banquet which is spread before thee, with the most hearty welcome; thou wilt find the means legibly written on thine own heart." . . .

O Nature, sovereign of all beings! and ye, her adorable daughters, Virtue, Reason, and Truth! Remain forever our revered protectors; it is to you that belong the praises of the human race, to you appertains the homage of the earth. Show us then, O Nature! that which man ought to do, in order to obtain the happiness which thou makest him desire. Virtue! animate him with thy beneficent fire. Reason! conduct his uncertain steps through the paths of life. Truth! let thy torch illumine his intellect, dissipate the darkness of his road. Unite, O assisting deities! your powers, in order to submit the hearts of mankind to your dominion.[16]

In Part I, man is treated as a part of nature, an organization of matter and motion, submitted to the same laws of necessity as the other parts. Man is an extremely complicated machine: "soul" is but the name for our ignorance of the operations of the human machine. Primitive man perhaps differed more from present man than the quadruped from the insect. It is as impossible to know what the

[16] *Système de la nature*, Part II, ch. 14; "Londres," II, 442, 453; Eng. tr., pp. 511, 519.

human species will change into, as what it has changed out of. Anyway, present man is pretty insignificant, hardly the lord of creation. His intellectual faculties are a determinate manner of acting resulting from the peculiar organization of his body: that is, they are a form of behavior, all springing from feeling. Sensation is the shock given to the organs, perception is the shock in the brain, idea is the image of the object that caused the shock. Matter can think, for man thinks. Do we ask how? How does one body attract another? Do we understand any better by assuming an immaterial soul? There is of course no freedom of the will. Man chooses what he believes offers the greatest advantage. Thinking is neither voluntary nor free. And this offers promise for education: we can hope to control men's actions for good by presenting the proper motives to them. The immortality of the soul is a chimaera. Death is a profound sleep. We live in the memory of our friends. And immortality has no social utility at all, anyway.

Part II, of the Divinity, is a remorseless attack upon Deism and theism as well as on Christianity. Holbach pulverized the eighteenth-century notions of God the watchmaker, and the rest. Natural religion was destroyed. Proofs of God's existence since the eighteenth century have had to depend on far different considerations. Man created God in his own image because of his failure, impotence, want, and evil. Ignorance and want are the fathers of the gods. First man invented an animistic mythology, then refined it into a theology. God was given contradictory attributes, as the negations of man's limitations. Above all is the conflict between God's all-power and his all-goodness: it makes God worse than any man, and creates the problem of evil in its acutest form. Holbach quotes the dilemma of Epicurus: God is either wicked or not omnipotent, and comments:

For more than two thousand years the candid have been waiting for a reasonable solution of these difficulties, and our learned doctors teach us that they will not be removed until the future life.[17]

Yet Holbach has a physiodicy, if not a theodicy: evil is necessary for thinking, for an intelligent being to develop and function. He dwells also on the pernicious effects of a theological basis for mo-

[17] *Le Bon-Sens*, sec. 57.

rality, which introduces extraneous material and contradictory attributes. Morality must be founded on man, not on some imagined deity.

To discover the true principles of morality, men have need neither of theology nor revelation nor gods: they have need only of good sense; they have only to enter into themselves; to reflect on their own nature; to consider their sensible interests; to consider the end of society and of each of the members that compose it; and they will easily recognize that virtue is of advantage, and that vice harms beings of their species.[18]

Here is the beginning of the French tradition of a wholly secular ethics, which was made central in the schools of the Third Republic by Jules Simon. Holbach himself left a textbook for such moral instruction. Experience in France and elsewhere has shown that to make morality dependent on politics shares some of the dangers of making it dependent on theology. Holbach himself worked out in his *Système social* a thoroughgoing utilitarianism, not sufficiently original to set forth in detail here.

Holbach ranks as one of the great critics of rational theology, who in France, like Kant in Germany and Hume in Britain, put an end to what the eighteenth century called "natural religion." And unlike Hume or Kant, he did it without regret or sadness; for it seemed to him a great work of the emancipation of the human spirit.

Cease then, O Mortal! to let thyself be disturbed with chimaeras, to let thy mind be troubled with phantoms, which thine own imagination has created, or to which arch imposture has given birth. . . .
If man must have his chimaeras, let him at last learn to permit others to form theirs after their own fashion; since nothing can be more immaterial than the manner of men's thinking on subjects not accessible to reason, provided those thoughts be not suffered to embody themselves into actions injurious to others; above all, let him be fully persuaded that it is of the utmost importance to the inhabitants of this world to be *just*, *kind*, and *peaceable*.
Far from injuring the cause of virtue, an impartial examination of the principles of this work will show that its object is to restore truth to its proper temple. . . . whose homage shall open to the world a new era; by rendering general the belief that happiness, the true end of man's existence, can never be attained but by promoting that of his fellow creature.[19]

[18] *Le Bon-Sens*, Preface, p. xi.
[19] *Système de la nature*, Part I, Conclusion, Preface; I, 396–97, end of Preface; Eng. tr., pp. 242, vii.

X

We have closed the examination of medical materialism with an outstanding physician and physiologist, Cabanis, and that of biological materialism with an eminent biologist, Lamarck. It is appropriate to show how Holbach's mechanical materialism was crowned by the most distinguished physicist and astronomer of the second half of the century, Pierre Simon, Marquis de Laplace (1749–1827). Laplace in a sense completed Newton's work on its mathematical side: he gave the scientific proof that the universe is really a perpetual motion machine, and that all its motions are cyclical. He also consummated the banishment of teleology from physics and astronomy. In 1796 he published a gem of scientific popularizing, *Exposition du système du monde*. In 1799 he published his magnum opus, *Traité de Mécanique céleste*. This had two major aims, one of which pointed to the past, the other to the future. The first was to complete the solution of the mathematical problems of the mechanics of the solar system. His goal was "to get rid of all empirical equations," a goal that would have delighted Descartes's drive for formalization. The second goal was to explain the origin of the solar system, an aim that puts Laplace at the outset of the intellectual revolution that culminated in Darwin. Is the universe like a watch made by a watchmaker? Descartes held that God started the vortices and kept them in motion. Newton held that God made the universe and its laws, as a machine, but a machine made for a purpose, and a machine that needed to be periodically adjusted. Buffon held that a comet fell on the sun, and started a swirl of fiery matter—a form of the planetesimal hypothesis. Laplace, convinced that final causes are only an expression of our own ignorance, proposed a nebular hypothesis. Starting with a nebula with a kernel, Laplace suggested that cooling caused condensation into concentric rings, which themselves condensed into new nebulae, and finally into the planets. After explaining his theory to Napoleon, the famous anecdote goes, in response to the Emperor's query about the place of God in the theory, Laplace drew himself up and replied, "Sire, I have no need of that hypothesis."

This probably apocryphal anecdote can serve as the symbol for the whole materialistic movement during the French Enlightenment. All these passionate fighters for human emancipation from superstition and freedom, from intellectual authoritarianism, arrived at hypotheses that had no need for the hypothesis of God. Whether their own suggestions went very far to furnish an alternative intellectual explanation is more dubious.

The Science of Human Nature:
The Associationist Psychology

I

THE WORKING OUT of a science of human nature was the great constructive achievement of eighteenth-century thought, as the erection of a science of physical nature had been the work of the seventeenth century. Both Hobbes and Spinoza had gained the idea of a human and social science; each in his own way had beheld the vision of man and society as part of the great new intoxicating order of nature. But such sciences were actually built up a hundred years later, and when they were built, it was upon the model of Newtonian mechanics.

Two motives dominated this intellectual enterprise. The first was the middle-class demand for a new social order, as a standard for criticizing the Old Regime, now outgrown and inadequate, and as a framework for its own activities. The second was the intellectual demand to make men's views of society "scientific," that is, to find a natural order of society that would be as valid and certain as Newtonian mechanics. In thus creating a "social physics," men would not only understand at last the actions of men in groups. They would also have a greater leverage for change than the mind of man had ever possessed before: they could now appeal to the authority, not of religion, but of science itself. Hence the method and model to which men turned was throughout that of the science of the day, Newtonian mechanics as popularly taken. First find the axioms governing human actions through an analysis of human nature itself; then from these psychological axioms develop deductively a science of society.

This enterprise was not disinterested, but apologetic: the actual conclusions arrived at were what was "reasonable" to middle-class businessmen, the concrete demands of the eighteenth-century commercial interest. Such desired conclusions determined the psychological analysis given to human nature, and, though they were ostensibly the result of scientific analysis, the axioms that supported them. The consequence was that men found that "human nature" demanded natural rights, constitutionalism, popular sovereignty, democracy, economic liberalism and laissez-faire. All these social programs were read into the natural order of unchangeable "laws of nature," like the laws of mechanics. This furnished the strongest possible leverage for tearing down the Old Regime, politically, legally, and economically. But at the same time it crystallized and hardened the demands of eighteenth-century commerce into universal principles. And what started as a radical philosophy of social criticism became, in the nineteenth century, the intellectual bulwark of economic conservatism. Thus "political economy," which at first promised the "wealth of nations," became the "dismal science," proving that the new factory owner had to make profits without interference, no matter what the social cost. For men had succeeded in stamping the rigidity and inflexibility of mechanics on popular "social science," a rigidity that has hardly been lost even today.

A prime example of the consequences of employing the Newtonian method and concepts to express and justify eighteenth-century commercial demands, is the new science of human nature, or psychology. Methodologically, this represented a consistent carrying through of the contact theory of mental life, resulting in a psychology that was mechanistic, though not materialistic. "Mind" was still taken as a distinct substance; it was analyzed into its elements, "sensations" coming entirely from without. This was the assumption of Hobbes and Locke, that the elements of mind are the passive effects of the actions of bodies upon it—the doctrine of *sensationalism*. These elements in the mind are then combined and united in accordance with the mental counterparts of the mechanical laws of motion, the principles of association—the doctrine of *associationism*. This view was first clearly articulated by David Hartley, in his *Observations on Man* (1749). It was most fully developed by Condillac in a long series of writings. Its practical consequences for the

The Science of Human Nature

science of society were developed by Helvétius in France and Jeremy Bentham in England. The associationist psychology was most fully formulated in England in James Mill's *Analysis of the Human Mind* (1829).

For this associationist psychology, mind has become entirely passive, purged of all active powers. Locke's activity of "reflection" has been reduced to pure sensation. Mind does nothing: it is the pure scene of the mechanical jostling of ideas. The only active elements are the ideas of pleasure and pain, which pull or push in action. Sensationalism holds that all knowledge and all action come from sensations, that is, from without, from the environment. Associationism holds that all complex beliefs and habits are built up by associating sensations contiguous in origin.

The motives for this analysis are in part the model of Newtonian mechanics. They are also in part the basic motive of all enlightenment empiricism: the analysts were social radicals and reformers. They made the environment omnipotent in producing human nature. Hence, by changing the environment, it seemed possible to change human nature itself. Sensationalism implies that all men are equal at birth, since they are all blank tablets to be written upon. All observed differences between men are due to a faulty environment. Education and legislation thus appeared to be the means to an unlimited progress. This is an admirable psychology for the liberal social reformer, offering a tremendous incentive to changing institutions. The psychology of innate powers and abilities, unchanging I.Q.'s, has always proved a conservative factor, assuring men that "you can't change human nature," and present inequalities. Associationism was the "scientific" basis for the demands of the middle class for social, political, and economic equality. It was written into all the eighteenth-century constitutions: "All men are created equal."

This analysis of human nature maintained a third doctrine, an intellectualistic hedonism. The sole spring of action in man is the rational foreseeing of pleasures and pains, the only human motive is rational self-interest, the conscious calculating and choosing of the more pleasant course. This principle sprang also from the model of Newtonian science: human nature must be rational, like the universe; and from a strong reformer's motive: you can calculate, predict, and control the action of such men, by legislation providing the proper pleasures and pains, rewards and punishment. It is much harder to legislate for a bundle of irrational impulses. The legislator is always tempted to think that no man ever acts save on his lawyer's advice. Moreover, so far as human conduct is rational, it is part of the universal order and harmony, and you can trust an enlightened rational self-interest. Such an analysis of conduct implies freedom from governmental interference, laissez-faire.

Such sensationalism, associationism, hedonism, and intellectualism were ostensibly the outcome of a mechanical analysis of human nature. Actually, they were dictated by the demands of the middle class for social change. They became the philosophic justification of nineteenth-century British Liberalism, its method of criticizing traditional institutions, by their consequences in individual pleasures and pains. They provided a "rational" basis for a society of laissez-faire and free competition, the trust in the reason of the common man.

II

David Hartley (1705–1757), in his *Observations on Man: His Frame, His Duty, and His Expectations* (1749), made a systematic attempt at a physiological psychology, in the course of which he developed the theory of the association of ideas in a fashion which had far more influence on the later school of associationist psychologists stemming from James Mill than did Hume, with whom the Mills had a very slender acquaintance. Hartley himself attributed his interest in making association the basic principle of psychology to a certain John Gay, fellow of Sidney Sussex College, Cambridge, who had written *A Preliminary Dissertation* printed in William Law's English translation of Archbishop William King's *Origin of Evil* (1731). "About eighteen years ago I was informed that the Rev. Mr. Gay, then living, asserted the possibility of deducing all our intellectual pleasures and pains from association. This put me upon considering the power of association." [1] Gay used the principle to explain the connection of morality with private happiness.

Hartley had been a fellow of Jesus College, Cambridge, and then

[1] David Hartley, *Observations on Man* (1749; ed. 1791 used), Vol. I, Preface, p. iii.

became a physician. Starting out to apply to the mind "the method of analysis and synthesis followed by Newton," he tried to describe "the influence of association over our opinions and affections, and its use in explaining those things in an accurate and precise way, which are commonly referred to the power of habit and custom, in a general and indeterminate one." [2] He believed his principle of association would do for human nature as much as Newton's law of gravitation had done for astronomy. He still employs the geometrical method, in a series of propositions:

The proper method of philosophizing seems to be, to discover and establish the general laws of action, affecting the subject under consideration, from certain select, well-defined, and well-attested phenomena, and then to explain and predict the other phenomena by these laws. This is the method of analysis and synthesis recommended and followed by Sir Isaac Newton. [3]

Hartley seized on certain suggestions in Newton's *Opticks* that external objects acting on the sensory nerves excite "vibrations in the aether residing in the pores of these nerves": these vibrations enter the brain, are "propagated freely every way over the whole medullary substance," and result in perceived sensations. They leave traces behind them, and this is the origin of ideas, which depend on minute vibrations or "virbratiuncles." The association of ideas has for its basis and cause the association in the brain of the vibratiuncles, which preserve a tendency to reproduce themselves in the same order in which they were originally produced by sense. Hartley thus offered a physiological explanation (with of course no experimental basis) of the law of association itself, and applied it to the details of mental life. But in the form in which Hartley's associationism was popularized, in Joseph Priestley's *Theory of the Human Mind* (1775), it was purged of its materialism, and became purely subjective and mental, though it remained mechanistic.

Sensations, by being often repeated, leave certain vestiges, types, or images, of themselves, which may be called, Simple Ideas of Sensation. [4]

Sensory vibrations, by being often repeated, beget, in the medullary substance of the brain, a disposition to diminutive vibrations. [5]

[2] *Observations on Man*, Vol. I, ch. I, p. 5.
[3] *Observations on Man*, Vol. I, ch. I, p. 6.
[4] *Observations on Man*, I, ch. I, sec. ii, proposition VIII, p. 56.
[5] *Observations on Man*, I, ch. I, sec. ii, proposition IX, p. 58.

Any sensations, A, B, C, etc., by being associated with one another a sufficient number of times, get such a power over the corresponding ideas, a, b, c, etc., that any one of the sensations A, when impressed alone, shall be able to excite in the mind b, c, etc., the ideas of the rest. . . . Simple ideas will run into complex ones, by means of association.[6]

Hartley makes quite clear the implications of his analysis of mental life for morals and politics.

It is of the utmost consequence to morality and religion, that the affections should be analyzed into their simple compounding parts, by reversing the steps of the associations which concur to form them. For thus we learn how to cherish and improve good ones, check and root out such as are mischievous and immoral, and how to suit our manner of life, in some tolerable measure, to our intellectual and religious wants. And as this holds, in respect of persons of all ages, so it is particularly true, and worthy of consideration, in respect of children and youth. If beings of the same nature, but whose affections and passions are, at present, in different proportions to each other, be exposed for an indefinite time to the same impressions and associations, all their particular differences will, at last, be overruled, and they will become perfectly similar, or even equal. They may also be made perfectly similar in a finite time, by a proper adjustment of the impressions and associations.[7]

III

Étienne Bonnot de Condillac (1715–1780) was an eighteenth-century French abbé who moved in the circle of the *philosophes* in Paris. He was the first Frenchman to undertake a serious study of Locke, and to work out a thoroughgoing sensationalism on the basis of the second book of the *Essay;* he had no concern with the fourth. He became really interested in Locke's theory of the origin of all knowledge in sense experience; he reduced it to a pure sensationalism by omitting reflection as one of Locke's twin sources of ideas, and thus made a genuine contribution to the new science of human nature. Condillac was the only technical and professional philosopher in eighteenth-century France, outside the traditionalists of the universities. He introduced "modern philosophy" to the country, and founded a school, which later became the "ideologists" and influenced the academic tradition.

[6] *Observations on Man*, I, ch. I, sec. ii, propositions X, XII, pp. 65, 73.
[7] *Observations on Man*, I, ch. I, sec. ii, proposition XIV, corollaries 5 and 6, pp. 81, 82.

Condillac was an important figure. All the *philosophes* knew his sensationalism as "philosophy" in the narrow sense; and it was very, very narrow. It was called "the analysis of ideas," conceived on the model of physical analysis. Voltaire said of Condillac: "He is one of the first men in Europe. He would have written the *Human Understanding* if Locke hadn't done it, and thank God, he would have made it shorter." Condillac's writings are dull and uninteresting today; he almost spoiled the French tradition of close connection between philosophy and life. Yet he preserved a vital relation with science and thought, and was never wholly academic.

In 1746 Condillac published an *Essai sur l'origine des connaissances humaines;* in 1749, a *Traité des systèmes.* In 1754 came his *Traité des sensations,* following Diderot's *Lettre sur les aveugles* of 1749, and Buffon's *Natural History* of 1749. He got into a dispute over his example of the statue, and in 1755 wrote a *Traité des animaux* against Buffon. In 1758 he was suddenly named preceptor of the Prince of Parma, grandson of Louis XV, and stayed in Parma till 1767. The prince was seven years old, and Condillac went off to teach him Lockean epistemology by new methods of education. But D'Alembert wrote Voltaire in 1769: "I learn that the prince passes his days running after monks, and that his wife, an Austrian, is the real ruler." In 1773 Condillac published the *Cours d'études* he had written for the prince, in thirteen volumes. In 1779, he wrote a *Logique* for Poland.

Condillac's great emphasis is on the method of analysis. In his *Logique* he puts it: "Analysis is the only method for acquiring knowledge." He imagines a chateau at which we have arrived at night. When the sun rises, the window is thrown open for a moment, then closed again. In that instant we have seen the whole landscape, but we know nothing about it.

To have a knowledge of that landscape, it is not enough to see it all at once; we must see each part one after the other; and instead of embracing everything with a glance, we must rest our eyes successively on object after object. This is what nature teaches all of us. If she has given us the faculty of seeing a multitude of things at once, she has also given us the faculty of looking at only one, that is, of directing our eyes toward a single one; and it is to that faculty, which is a consequence of our organization, that we owe all the knowledge we acquire through sight.[8]

[8] Condillac, *La Logique, Oeuvres,* ed. Houel (1798), XXII, 17.

We thus commence with the principal objects: we observe them successively, and we compare them, to judge the relations in which they stand. When by this means we have their respective situations, we observe successively all those objects which fill the intervals, we compare each with the nearest principal object, and we determine their position.

We then distinguish all the objects whose form and situation we have grasped, and we embrace them in a single glance. The order between them in our mind is no longer successive; it is simultaneous. It is the same as that in which they exist, and we see them all at once in a distinct manner. (XXII, 19–20)

We make this analysis only because for us a single instant is not enough time to study all these objects. But we analyse only to synthesize; and when the knowledge has been acquired the things, instead of being successive, have in the mind the same simultaneous order they have without. It is in this simultaneous order that the knowledge we have of them consists: for if we could not put them together again, we could never judge the relations in which they stand to each other, and we should be knowing them badly.

Analysis is thus no different from observing in a successive order the qualities of an object, in order to give them in the mind the simultaneous order in which they exist. This is what nature makes all of us do. Analysis, which we think is known only to philosophers, is thus known to everybody, and I have taught the reader nothing; I have only made him attend to what he is doing continually. (XX, 22)

This method of analysis, Condillac held, should be followed in every subject-matter. It proved immensely fruitful in natural science: Lavoisier consciously applied it to chemistry, others to anatomy, Cabanis to psychosomatic relations. When applied to knowledge itself, it produced a new science which Condillac called "the analysis of ideas," and was later named "ideology." Here, unfortunately, it proved not fruitful but barren. It took mental life to be composed of isolated atoms or chunks; the relations, above all what James called the stream of consciousness, were lost sight of. The result was a kind of mental chemistry, with only association holding ideas together. The whole enterprise strikes us today as immensely artificial. It was no wonder that men came to feel there must be some "supersensible ego" to hold the discrete marbles together. Such were the consequences of applying to "mind" a reductive analysis modeled on physical analysis.

In his first work, the *Essay on the origin of human knowledge*, Condillac offered a free paraphrase of Locke's *Essay:* he accepted

Locke's two sources of ideas, the "inner sense" of reflection as well as outer sense. But in his *Treatise on Sensations*, having been freed, he tells us, of his prejudices by his friend Mlle. Ferrand, he holds that Locke's "reflection" is only the residue Locke had been unable to reduce to sensation. And Locke had accepted all our mental powers and faculties as innate; but the faculties of the soul themselves originate in sensation. "Locke thought we naturally make use of our senses by a sort of instinct." But we must learn to use them.

If he could have undertaken to begin his book over again, there is reason to conjecture that he would have developed much better the springs of the human understanding. Since he did not do it, he has passed too lightly over the origin of our knowledge, and that is the part he has least explored. He supposes, for example, that as soon as the soul receives ideas through the senses, it can at pleasure repeat them, compound them, unite them together with an infinite variety, and out of them make all kinds of complex notions. But it is certain that in infancy we have experienced sensations long before we know how to derive ideas from them. Thus, the soul not having at its first instant the exercise of all its operations, it was essential, to develop better the origin of our knowledge, to show how it acquires this exercise, and what is its progress. It does not appear that Locke has thought of that, nor that anyone has made him the reproach, or tried to supplement this part of his work.[9]

The mental faculties must be shown to be themselves "transformed sensations." Condillac thus announces his program:

Descartes did not know either the origin or the generation of our ideas (I refer to his third Meditation. Nothing seems to me less philosophical than what he says on this subject). It is to this we must attribute the insufficiency of his method; for we shall never discover a sure manner of conducting our thoughts, so long as we do not know how they are formed. (I, 4)

It seemed to me one could reason in metaphysics and in morals with as much exactitude as in geometry; construct accurate ideas as well as geometers; like them, determine the sense of expressions in a precise and invariable manner; finally, prescribe to oneself, perhaps better than they have done, an order simple and easy enough to arrive at self-evidence. (I, 2)

Condillac begins his *Treatise on Sensations:*

The principal object of this work is to show how all our knowledge and all our mental faculties come from the senses, or, to speak more exactly,

[9] Condillac, *Essai sur l'origine des connaissances humaines, Oeuvres,* I, 14, 15.

from sensations: for in truth the senses are but the occasional cause. They do not sense, it is the mind alone which senses, on the occasion of the sense organs; and it is sensations which modify it, from which it draws all its knowledge and all its faculties.[10]

The last sentence makes clear that though Condillac is a sensationalist and a mechanist, he is by no means a materialist, like Hartley. It seems to him impossible that matter should feel or think; for matter is an extended and divisible aggregate, while feeling and thinking presuppose the unity of their substratum. He accepts without question an immaterial mental substance. The self, however, is merely the totality of its sensations:

The self of every man is only the collection of the sensations which he is experiencing and of those which memory recalls to him, it is at once the consciousness of what he is and the memory of what he has been. (III, 119)

Condillac distinguishes between those senses which do not of themselves judge external objects—smell, taste, hearing, and sight—and touch. He assumes we are shut up in our private consciousness: sensations are a part of ourselves. Through touch alone do we discover any outside reality: touch is "the only sense which of itself judges external objects," through the resistance they offer. The sensation of touch is both a sensation, and an idea of something else; the other senses are then interpreted in the same fashion by analogy.

In a purely artificial construction, which suited the temper of the time and won him his great reputation, Condillac takes the example of a marble statue, which he proceeds to endow first with the sense of smell alone, then with the others in succession.

We have imagined a statue organized like ourselves within, and animated by a mind deprived of any kind of ideas. We have supposed also that its exterior, all of marble, does not permit the use of any of its senses, and we have reserved the liberty of opening them at our choice to the different impressions of which they are susceptible.

We have thought we should commence with smell, because of all the senses it is the one which seems to contribute the least to the knowledge of the human mind. The others have then been the object of our investigation, and after having considered them separately and together we have seen the statue become an animal capable of watching over its own preservation. (III, 49–50)

[10] Condillac, *Traité des sensations, Oeuvres*, III, 3.

Condillac goes on to show how with the sense of smell alone his statue would develop all the mental faculties possessed by those beings enjoying five. The comparison of smells, the perception of resemblances, and differences, or judgment, reflection, imagination: all would come from smell alone; and the understanding is the whole of the faculties thus generated. His basic principle is that any sense is equivalent to any other, or any number, in producing the "transformed sensations" that are the mental faculties. One striking or strong sensation is attention; one strong past sensation is memory. Two furnish comparison; the perception of their difference, judgment. Each sensation has pleasure or pain attached, which is will. Habits are formed; when reflection has been forgotten, these become instincts. All animals got their instincts through first reflecting, then forgetting. In all this process, the mind is completely passive.

I V

Claude-Adrien Helvétius (1715–1771) was not interested in the analysis of ideas or in Locke for their own sake, but for their implications for ethics and politics. His social message shows how the empirical theory of knowledge could be bent to social ends. Helvétius was one of the kindly and charming *philosophes*. His father was physician to the Queen; he thus grew up in the medical tradition. As a gay, young handsome fellow he plunged into dissipation; at twenty-three he was a farmer-general. Even then, however, he delighted in helping literary young men. He suddenly resigned his position, married, and retired to Voré, after purchasing the position of maître d'hôtel to the Queen, and devoted himself to poetry and mathematics.

In 1748 Montesquieu brought out his *Esprit des lois*. Helvétius resolved he would write a big book too; what should it be upon? Why not just *De l'esprit*? After nine years he had finished it, and in 1758 the censor passed it and there was published his *Traité de l'esprit*. It excited a furor of admiration, though Voltaire, Frederick, Diderot, and Turgot criticized it. Then came persecution: the volume was burnt, and Helvétius, as a martyr, was taken up all the more. His book went through fifty editions. In 1764 he made a triumphant journey to England, being received by the king himself; the next year he visited Frederick in Potsdam. *De l'homme*, a defense of *De l'esprit*, more angry and outspoken, was published only after his death, in 1772.

Helvétius had two main interests. Education was for him the all-important thing in life: you can do anything with man by giving him the right education. And legislative reform is omnipotent: you can make men happier by beneficent legislation. "The vices of a people are rooted in its laws; there one must dig if one would unearth the roots of its vices." " 'Tis the good law-maker who makes the good citizen; 'tis only by good laws that you can make virtuous men." Together these two interests make up a true social science, founded on a naturalistic analysis of human nature, and a practical social program. Helvétius was a utilitarian in his interests, in fact the inspiration of Jeremy Bentham. James Mill said: "Helvétius alone is an entire army. Bentham himself was but a disciple of Helvétius." Helvétius is the best representative of one of the three intellectual currents that flowed together in the Revolution.

You can get at man from the outside, and pass laws to make him good. Man himself is a *tabula rasa* on which the reformer can engrave what he will. Rousseau likewise urged men to abandon the old methods of legislation and education. But he held that man will then *ipso facto* be good: it is all in man already. It is easy to see why Helvétius should appeal to Locke and Condillac and empiricism for his science of man, and why such an appeal should have been so popular in that hopeful age.

Like Condillac, Helvétius maintained an absolute sensationalism. All our ideas come from the experience of the senses; like Condillac, Helvétius abandons Locke's inner sense of reflection. Even judgment is the perception of the resemblances or differences between our ideas; that is, it is a physical sensation.

On this supposition, what art should the poet or the orator employ to make us more vividly perceive that justice, preferable in a king to kindness, preserves more citizens for the state?

The orator will present three pictures to the imagination of the same man: in one he will paint the just king who condemns and has executed a criminal; in the second, the kind king who opens the cell of the same criminal and strikes off his irons; in a third, he will represent the same criminal who, arming himself with a dagger on leaving his cell, rushes to massacre fifty citizens. Now, what man, at the sight of these three pictures, will not feel that justice, which by the death of a single individual prevents the death of fifty men, is in a king preferable to kindness? Nevertheless, this judgment is really only a sensation. For if, by that habit of uniting certain ideas to certain words, we can, as experience proves, in striking the ear with certain sounds excite in us almost the same sensations we would feel in the presence of the objects themselves, it is evident that, when these three pictures are shown, to *judge* that in a king justice is preferable to kindness, is to *feel* and see that in the first picture we sacrifice only one citizen, and that in the third we massacre fifty: whence I conclude that all *judgment* is only *sensation*.[11]

We can grant Helvétius his case. But we then still have to discover the difference between the sensation we call "sensation" and the sensation we call "judgment"; the distinction is still there. But it is easy to see why Helvétius minimized it. Reflection or judgment is something much more inaccessible from without by education or law.

Secondly, from this sensationalism there follows the equality of all men, and the importance of wise education. If all knowledge comes from outside, if the mind is truly at birth a blank tablet, then of course all men are *at birth* equal; their present differences are due to a faulty education and environment. This is the whole logic of Lockean thought, of empiricism, the "scientific" basis for the demands of the middle class for social, political, and economic equality with the nobility. This view of human nature was fused in the American Declaration of Independence with Rousseau's moral equality of men: "All men are *created* equal," and in the French Declaration of the Rights of Man and the Citizen: "All men are *born* free and equal."

Helvétius' genetic equality is a protest against existing inequalities. More important, it promises a golden opportunity.

Quintilian, Locke, and I myself say, The inequality of minds is the effect of a known cause, and this cause is the difference of education.[12]

If I could demonstrate that man is indeed but the product of his education, I should undoubtedly have revealed a great truth to the nations. They would then know that they hold within their own hands the instrument of their greatness and their happiness, and that to be happy and powerful is only a matter of perfecting the science of education.[13]

The general conclusion of this discourse is that genius is common,

[11] Helvétius, *De l'esprit*, in *Oeuvres* (Liege, 1774), Vol. I, Discours I, ch. 1, pp. 13-14.
[12] Helvétius, *De l'homme*, *Oeuvres*, Vol. III, sec. II, ch. 1, pp. 113-14.
[13] *De l'homme*, *Oeuvres*, Vol. III, Introduction, ch. 2, p. 4.

and the circumstances proper to its development very rare. If we can compare the profane with the sacred, we can say that in this matter many are called and few are chosen. . . .

The man of genius is only the product of the circumstances in which he has found himself. Also, all the art of education consists in placing young people in a concourse of circumstances proper to develop in them the germ of mind and virtue. Love of paradox has not led me to this conclusion, but only the desire for the happiness of men. I have felt both what a good education would spread of illumination, of virtues, and consequently of happiness in society; and how much the persuasion we are in that genius and virtue are pure gifts of nature is opposed to the progress of the science of education, and favors in this respect laziness and negligence. It is in this view that examining what nature and education could do for us, I have perceived that education was making us what we are. Consequently I have thought that it was the duty of a citizen to proclaim a truth proper to draw attention to the means of perfecting that education itself.[14]

Here is the faith in education, progress, and the perfectibility of human nature. Helvétius points forward to Fourier's dream of a nation of thirty-seven million Humes and Newtons.

Thirdly, Helvétius is committed to two propositions of a utilitarian ethics. All men always act from motives of self-interest; and the good is that which is most useful to the greatest number: those actions and opinions are to be sought and followed which possess the greatest utility. On the first proposition, Helvétius says: "It is as impossible to love the good for the sake of the good, as to love evil for the sake of evil." Self-sacrifice springs from "an enlightened pride, in obedience to the law of personal interest."

There are men to whom a happy disposition, a lively desire for glory and esteem, inspire the same love for justice and virtue as men commonly have for greatness and riches. The actions that are personally useful to these virtuous men are just actions, conforming to the general interest, or at least not contrary to it. . . .

From this point of view, I say that probity is only the stronger or weaker habit of actions particularly useful to this small society. It is not that certain virtuous societies do not often seem to divest themselves of their self-interest, to pass on the actions of men judgments in conformity with the public interest; but they are then only satisfying the passion which an enlightened pride gives them for virtue, and consequently obeying, like every other society, the law of self-interest. What other motive could determine a man to generous actions? It is as im-

[14] *De l'esprit, Oeuvres*, Vol. I, Discours III, ch. 30, pp. 618–20.

possible for him to love the good for the sake of the good, as to love evil for the sake of evil.[15]

Here again, we must still distinguish between "selfish" self-interest and "unselfish" self-interest: Helvétius puts it, between self-interest that is socially useful, and self-interest that is not. Ultimately, Helvétius insists on the universality of the motive of self-interest because such a motive is much easier for the legislator to deal with, and is determinable from without the individual.

The second proposition, maintaining that social utility is the criterion of virtuous action, meets the demand for a standard to get away from a moral relativism, and for a leverage for criticism. The eighteenth century was much disturbed by the goings on of newly discovered barbarians.

If they had wished to form for themselves an idea of virtue purely abstract and independent of practice, they would have recognized that by the word "virtue" can be understood only the desire for the general happiness; that consequently the public good is the object of virtue, and that the actions it commands are the means it employs to accomplish that object; that thus the idea of virtue is not at all arbitrary; that in different ages and countries all men, at least those living in societies, have had to form the same idea of it; and finally, if different peoples represent it to themselves under different forms, it is because they take for virtue itself the different means it employs to accomplish its object.[16]

Now, when the interests of a state have changed, and the laws which were useful at its foundation have become harmful to it, those very laws, by the respect men still preserve for them, must necessarily lead the state to its ruin.[17]

Helvétius' utilitarianism is the moral theory for the reformer, the statesman.

The whole study of the moralist consists in the use to be made of rewards and punishments, and the help that can be derived from them for uniting personal interest to the general interest. This union is the masterpiece at which morality must aim. If citizens could not gain their private happiness without serving the public good, the only wicked men would then be the madmen. All men would be necessitated to virtue; and the felicity of nations would be the outcome of morality.[18]

[15] De l'esprit, Oeuvres, Vol. I, Discours II, ch. 2, p. 67; ch. 5, p. 96.
[16] De l'esprit, Oeuvres, Vol. I, Discours II, ch. 13, p. 173.
[17] De l'esprit, Oeuvres, Vol. I, Discours II, ch. 17, p. 220.
[18] De l'esprit, Oeuvres, Vol. I, Discours II, ch. 22, p. 289.

V

Condillac had been the one major technical and professional "philosopher" among the *philosophes*. The science of human nature he started was carried on in France during the Revolution and the Empire, and persisted well into the Restoration, where it finally diverged into the two groups of the positivists and the spiritualists, the latter embracing such figures as Maine de Biran, Laromiguière, Royer-Collard, and Victor Cousin. The earlier movement stemming from Condillac is known as that of the "idéologues," who took their name from Destutt de Tracy's *Éléments d'idéologie,* published as a text book in 1801. This French ideology, together with the associationist psychology of James Mill, launched the eighteenth-century analysis of the human mind upon the stormy waters of nineteenth-century psychology.

The ideologists had their stronghold in two institutions set up by the Convention in 1795, the École Normale and the Institut. At the former, J. D. Garat taught "the analysis of the understanding," Bernardin de Saint-Pierre morals, Volney history, La Harpe literature, Berthollet chemistry, and Laplace and Lagrange mathematics. The Institut National was set up in 1795, and held its first session in April of the next year. Its second class was the Académie des Sciences Morales et Politiques, which embraced sections "on the analysis of sensations and ideas," on morals, on law, on political economy, on history, and on geography. The section on the analysis of sensations and ideas included Volney, Garat, Cabanis, and as associates Destutt de Tracy and Laromiguière, and later Maine de Biran. Many of the most important philosophical writings of the time, like Maine de Biran's *Mémoire sur l'habitude* of 1802, were read to the Institut.

Most of the ideologists had been partisans of Napoleon at the 18 brumaire; but they soon went into the opposition, and awakened his ire. In 1803 he suppressed the Academy of Moral Sciences; in 1812 he accused the party of being responsible for the conspiracy of Mallet: "It is to ideology, to that gloomy metaphysics which, in seeking with subtlety first causes, wants to found on their basis the legislation of peoples, instead of drawing laws from the knowledge of the human heart and the lessons of history, that we must attribute all the evils our *belle France* is experiencing." [19] The ideologists were especially opposed to Napoleon's re-establishment of religion. Destutt de Tracy put it:

Theology is the philosophy of the world's childhood; it is time that it gave place to that of its age of reason; it is the work of the imagination, like the bad physics and bad metaphysics that were born with it in the times of ignorance, and serve as its support, while the other philosophy is founded on observation and experience.[20]

The two major figures in the group are de Tracy and Cabanis. Destutt de Tracy (1754–1836) was descended from a Scottish Walter Stutt who had established the family in France in the fifteenth century. He was sent to the Constituent Assembly in 1789 as a liberal follower of Lafayette in the estate of the Nobles. Thrown into prison, he there read Locke and Condillac. He was a member of the Senate after the 18 brumaire, and Cabanis got him elected to the *Institut*. For the new *écoles centrales* the ideologists were organizing, he wrote a series of works on the *Éléments d'idéologie*, including the *Idéologie* (1801), the *Grammaire générale* (1803), the *Logique* (1805), and the *Traité de la volonté* (1815).

Ideology (de Tracy invented the term to replace "the analysis of sensations and ideas") is the science of the phenomena of thought and their laws. It is a branch of zoology, and is allied to physiology and to grammar, the study of signs and discourse. The *Treatise on the Will* includes morals and economics. The object of ideology is "to study what takes place in us when we think, speak, or reason," as the basis of all the moral and social sciences and legislation.

De Tracy is opposed to Condillac's reductive analysis in the *Treatise on Sensations*, with its resulting complete passivity of the mind. He has no interest in the question of the origin of the mental faculties out of sensation: he is no "genealogist." Condillac was wrong to separate the will from attention, which is only its effect; and to separate judgment from comparison; imagination and reflection are not separate faculties. Throughout de Tracy opposes the concrete and immediate observation of introspection to the arbitrary

---

[19] Quoted in E. Bréhier, *Histoire de la philosophie*, II, *La Philosophie moderne* (1932), 600.
[20] Destutt de Tracy, *Analyse* of Dupuis, *L'Origine de tous les cultes*, quoted in Gilbert Chinard, *Jefferson et les idéologues* (1925), p. 239.

results of Condillac's reductive analysis. He recognizes four irreducible modes of sensibility: willing, judging, feeling, and remembering. To feel is to feel a sensation; to remember is to feel a memory; to judge is to feel a relation; to will is to feel a desire. In general, to think is to feel; *penser* should be abolished.

De Tracy also disagrees with Condillac in emphasizing our activity as the basis of all knowledge of an external world. None of the five senses is sufficient; they are all passive, even touch, on which Condillac had relied.

As long as we are motionless, as we do not act ourselves, as we only receive passively the impressions that come to us, those that affect our touch enlighten us no more than the others. Even passive touch must be recognized to be as incapable as the other senses of making us suspect the existence of bodies.[21]

Without motion on its part, Condillac's statue could never know anything. Our voluntary or willed action meets resistance; thus arises the contrast between our activity and resistance, and from this comes all knowledge and judgment. De Tracy is introducing the activity of mind and will which Maine de Biran carried much further.

That is why to have knowledge of something else than my feeling, than myself, it was necessary for me to have the faculty of making movements; and why the first manner in which beings appeared to me, is by the property they have of resisting the movements I make. This fundamental property of bodies, which we call the force of *inertia*, is thus necessarily the first by which we perceive them: it is the basis of all those we know about them, and join to it to form the complete idea of each of those beings. Without it we should not have known bodies foreign to us or even our own; we should not even have perceived our own movements; for it is the resistance of the matter of our members to movement which occasions our sensation of movement; thus, if matter had been without resistance, we should never have known anything but ourselves, and we should have known of ourselves only our feelings.[22]

It is interesting that almost the only connection between Thomas Jefferson and the more technical philosophers of his time was with the French ideologists. He was the friend of several of them, especially de Tracy, with whom he kept up a correspondence for twenty years, from 1806 to 1826. He translated and published de Tracy's commentary on the *Esprit des lois*, bringing it out in 1811; it did not appear in France till 1819. He revised and corrected de Tracy's *Treatise on Political Economy* (1818). For this edition he wrote: "Mr. Tracy is the author of a treatise on the Elements of Ideology, justly considered as a production of the first order in the science of our thinking faculty, or of the understanding." He wrote de Tracy in 1818: "I hope this book [*Éléments d'idéologie*] will become the manual of our students, of our statesmen, and will produce with us progress towards a science in which we have committed many errors." [23]

The contribution of Cabanis (1757–1808) to ideology was to supply the relation between the mental faculties and their organic basis which the ideologues, especially Condillac and Helvétius, in their complete ignorance of physiology, had neglected. He emphasized also the multiplicity of internal sensations—of which as a valetudinarian he was keenly aware—which so powerfully influence the functioning of the mental faculties. And he pointed also to the vast realm of "sensations" that never come to the attention of the conscious self, but determine the regular functioning of the organs. This led to the distinction between organic irritability, and sensibility in the narrower sense.

[23] *The Complete Jefferson*, ed. Saul K. Padover (1943), p. 369; Chinard, *Jefferson et les idéologues*, p. 184.

16

The Science of Society: Montesquieu, Vico, the Physiocrats, and Rousseau

I

WE HAVE DEFINED the Enlightenment as the coming together of the ideal of Newtonian science and the demands of the rapidly expanding business enterprise. The latter demand pointed to a reconstruction of economic institutions: to a liberation from the older economic regulations and restrictions which, originating in the medieval guild system, had been taken over by the new national governments under the régime we call mercantilistic. It also pointed to a reconstruction of political institutions, to insure that the government at the very least should not interfere with the freedom of business enterprise, and at the best should actively foster it. The intellectual ideal and method of Newtonian science demanded that these reconstructions be undertaken on a "scientific" basis: that is, they must be made in the light of a discoverable natural order in human societies and their productive processes. The stage was hence set for the working out in the eighteenth century of a science of society, or rather, of two sciences of society: a science of political economy, and a science of politics and government.

Hobbes was the first to propose a science of human affairs on the model of the new Galilean science: he was the first to propose a "social physics." Before him both Machiavelli and Bodin had suggested a secular art of human control and government—something close to what Aristotle meant by the "practical science" of politics. The two traditions thus inherited by the eighteenth century were the older Aristotelian conception of a practical science or art of government, and the newer conception of a theoretical science of human affairs on the model of physics. The fullest development of the idea of a theoretical science of society is to be found in the Physiocrats. Their political ideal of the benevolent despot, the enlightened expert, though approached by a number of eighteenth-century monarchs—Frederick II, Joseph II, Charles III of Spain—received little further theoretical elaboration until it was taken up in the ideal of the Prussian *Beamtenschaft* or bureaucracy in the nineteenth century. But their ideal of a natural science of political economy, based on the natural laws of wealth, though it started with them in the interest of applying business methods to agriculture, was taken over by Adam Smith and J. B. Say in application to commerce and industrial production, and, consecrated by Ricardo, was destined to a long history in the nineteenth century. The fullest development of the older conception of government inherited by the eighteenth century, the idea of a practical science or art of government, is to be found in Jeremy Bentham and the Utilitarians; starting from an initial analysis of human nature and its needs for social organization, it endeavors to work out a viable scheme of social control for best satisfying these needs.

These two conceptions gave rise to the two intellectual methods of nineteenth-century conservatism and liberalism, respectively: government by the scientific expert, and government that should leave a large area for individual initiative. This analysis also makes clear how the new science of wealth, or political economy, usually identified with the "liberal" tradition in the nineteenth century, originally took form with the Physiocrats in conjunction with the ideal of benevolent despotism in government. Hence Napoleon could easily incorporate its laissez-faire in economics into his authoritarian scheme of government, and Metternich's régime, politically authoritarian, could at the same time pursue a policy of economic "liberalism." And later in the century, when other economic ideals had come to the fore—the technocracy of the Saint-Simonians in France, the state socialism of the Bismarckian empire—Napoleon III could go in for a more collectivistic approach to the problems of industrializing society, and Bismarck could put through his program of the welfare state.

But this classification, made primarily on a methodological basis, fails to include the two most influential political theories of the century, the constitutional natural rights liberalism of John Locke, and the democracy of majority rule of Rousseau, which easily passed into a national socialism in Mably and Morelly. Both constitutional liberalism and democracy had already appeared with certain minor groups during the English Civil Wars. Harrington had set forth a liberal republicanism, and all during the eighteenth century there were in England a line of "commonwealth men" who advocated a liberal and constitutional republic. These included Robert Molesworth until his death in 1727, Francis Hutcheson and Isaac Watts in the second generation, and Joseph Priestley in the third; their successors were the Philosophical Radicals in the early nineteenth century.

John Locke was not, in intention at least, primarily an epistemologist. He was interested in political affairs, he was the intellectual apologist for the Whigs. He made himself the defender of the Glorious Revolution of 1688–89; he served as the brain trust of Lord Somers under William and Mary. His *Two Treatises on Government*, printed in 1690, though largely written in 1679–80, aimed to set forth the principles on which the Revolution had been planned and carried through. This book proved in England, France, and America by far the most influential exposition of liberal constitutionalism, as the Whigs understood it. Too radical for the comfortable eighteenth-century Whig tradition of Walpole and the Pitts, the second *Treatise*, in simplified and distorted form, was adopted as a bible in the American colonies; it is best embodied in Jefferson's Declaration of Independence and the American Bill of Rights. Side by side with it must be placed his *Epistle on Toleration* (1690), in which he advocated complete toleration for all religious dissenters. Only Catholics and atheists remain beyond the pale, the first because they owe allegiance to a foreign sovereign and are hence subversive, not merely heretics but also conspirators—Locke had lived under Charles II and James II—the second because their oaths are not binding. This suggests that Locke's natural rights liberalism has not only an economic basis, like that of the Physiocrats, but also reflects the long struggle for religious freedom in the seventeenth century. Anglo-American constitutional liberalism owes much of its strength to this religious strand; where that is lacking, as on the Continent, liberalism has been weak and anaemic, and has never long endured.

There are two sports in eighteenth-century political philosophy who fail to fit neatly into the classification, Montesquieu and Vico. Montesquieu, too, had the idea of a theoretical science of society. But unlike the Physiocrats, this did not mean for him the approximation to a natural order everywhere and eternally valid. It meant a comparative study of different forms of government, their respective "principles," or what made them tick, and the conditions under which each form made its appearance. Montesquieu emphasized climate heavily, but this meant for him the natural conditions in general. In his *Spirit of the Laws* (1748) he misinterpreted the British constitution almost as badly as had Voltaire in his *English Letters* of 1734: he found in it a calculated system of checks and balances, which in fact parliamentary and cabinet government was in the process of transforming. But Montesquieu's interpretation was as influential on the body of the American Constitution as Locke was on the Declaration of Independence and the Bill of Rights.

Vico, the isolated figure in Naples, an original genius and a polymath, a man if ever there was one born ahead of his time, likewise sought to work out a "new science" of society, based on the "laws and habits of the human spirit." But unlike Montesquieu, it was not to comparative study that he turned to escape the limitations of the "geometrical" method of Descartes and Newton applied to human affairs. In the first quarter of the eighteenth century he attempted to work out a historical method based on his wide learning of the past and his deep historical sense and historical intuition. Vico's historical sociology linked him to earlier thinkers like Machiavelli and Bodin, those historically minded humanists who had lived too soon to be seduced by the appeal of "social physics." Like them it carried him close to the spirit of the pioneering Aristotle himself. On the other hand, it seems to place him at the beginning of that line of development of Romantic thinking, which, starting with Herder, culminated in Hegel in a similar deterministic law of the development of human institutions, and makes Vico appear a man of the nineteenth century rather than of the early eighteenth. Though he left a school of "Vichiani" at Naples, who supported the Parthenopean Republic and Murat's Kingdom of Naples, and only died out under the Bourbon restoration, Vico received little attention in his own day. It was Michelet who in 1827 published selections from his works[1] in French and introduced his organic and comprehensive interpretation of history to French, German, and Italian scholars. Vico's insistence that history is a form of man's knowledge of himself led in our own day to Croce's revival and championing of his fellow-Neapolitan's philosophy.[2]

With Jean-Jacques Rousseau's *Social Contract* (1762) there appears for the first time a major social thinker who sets forth democratic political theory based on majority rule. Among moderns, Spinoza is Rousseau's only real predecessor, aside from the extremists of the English civil wars. Rousseau's conception of liberty as self-imposed law was extremely influential in forming Kant's conception, and through him the whole classic German tradition through Hegel and Marx. But Rousseau, though a "democrat," has not the slightest trace of "liberalism": there are no limits set by natural rights or social utilities to the scope of majority rule. And the ideal goal—the "general will"—need not be consciously willed by the majority. Robespierre could easily bend Rousseau into an apologetic for the Terror, which "forced men to be free"; and the whole line of nineteenth-century liberals, from de Tocqueville and John Stuart Mill down, could easily be provoked by Rousseau into an immense fear of the tyranny of the majority. Mably and Morelly could push Rousseau into forms of national socialism; the Bonapartes could justify their plebiscite Caesarism in his pages; and it can be plausibly argued that Hitler's National Socialism was the end product of Rousseau's "democracy without liberalism."

It remained for American experience in the early nineteenth century to combine liberalism with democracy, under the Jacksonians, and erect that novelty in the Western tradition, a *liberal* constitutional democracy. Nowhere in eighteenth-century political theorizing had this been done. The excesses of the French Revolution can plausibly be attributed intellectually to the failure of these two great eighteenth-century traditions of political thinking to come together.

In the absence of that combination, it is little wonder that most Continental political theorists, from Voltaire on to the Physiocrats,

---

[1] Michelet, ed., *Oeuvres choisies de Vico* (1827; 2d ed. 1835). See *Opere*, ed. Ferrari, 6 vols. (1836); and ed. Nicolini, 8 vols. (1914–42).

[2] Benedetto Croce, *Giambattista Vico*. See also Vico, G. B., *The Autobiography of*, tr. M. H. Fisch and T. G. Bergin (1944).

while they appreciated the liberties enjoyed by Englishmen, felt that the British parliamentary set-up, the old unreformed Parliament with its aristocratic representation, its small commercial minority, its chicanery and open bribery, its factions and its politics in the worst sense, was a very inefficient means of gaining what they wanted, emancipation from the constriction of outworn institutions, and guarantee of individual rights. The enlightened expert, the benevolent despot, was clearly the most efficient instrument of needed reform. The future seemed obviously to lie with him, not with the bumbling British parliamentary anachronism. Just so, even today, to those lands without political experience, an energetic Communist Party leadership seems by far the best way to bring an economy up to date, not the cumbersome and slow machinery of representative government. So enlightened despotism, the uncontrolled rule of the expert, had an immense appeal on the Continent in the eighteenth century, the more where it was honored in the breach, as in Bourbon France. Even the astute Diderot admired Catherine II, whose despotism history emphasizes more heavily than her enlightenment. It was not until Joseph II's efforts at drastic reform from on top began to provoke insuperable opposition at home in Austria, and open rebellion in the Austrian Netherlands, that doubts began to arise as to the "efficiency" of enlightened despotism.

It remained for Jeremy Bentham to provide a new and frankly utilitarian method for criticizing the limitations both of the appeal to natural rights—"nonsense, nonsense on stilts," he called it—and of the unlimited rule of the majority of Rousseau. He thus ushered in the political theory of the nineteenth century, the Age of Liberalism.

II

We thus have, as the major political theories of the Enlightenment, John Locke, Montesquieu, the Physiocrats, and Rousseau. Locke's constitutionalism has already been treated. It is the French thinkers who are to be considered. In the eighteenth century all French thought was essentially colored by political and social considerations. If the thinkers were antireligious, it was because of the social role of the Church. If they were sensationalistic and "Lockean," it was because of the social consequences. Naturally, their thinking about society was most of all influenced by their views on this great issue.

The thought of all of them followed a set form. Politics is a science, a part of the great new Science of Man. Its method is naturally the approved scientific method of the day, the method of mathematics and physics: the "geometric method." It is deductive: "Man is thus and so; hence society should be thus and so." Observations are brought in to back up these conclusions. But it is clear that the results desired—the social program of the middle class—determined the reasoning. Three main types of thinking prevailed: they differed not on the end desired, but on the means to achieve it. First, there were the *constitutionalists*, like Montesquieu, the lawyers of the *parlements*, and the practical leaders, like Mirabeau. Secondly, there were the advocates of *enlightened despotism*, which included most of the Encyclopedists, the Physiocrat economists, and in the flesh, Napoleon, who was the nearest the French ever came to embodying that great eighteenth-century ideal. Thirdly, there were the advocates of *democracy*: Rousseau, and the more radical democrats, de Mably and Morellet; during the Revolution, these views were upheld by the Girondists and Robespierre. All these political thinkers agreed on the outcome they desired. Negatively, they were all united in the fight against the Church, in their hatred of war—they were all cosmopolitans—and in their criticisms of the financial policy of the Monarchy. Positively, they were all in support of religious toleration, and of civil liberties, especially the freedom of speech and of the press: and of economic "freedom," laissez-faire. Of these views, enlightened despotism was by far the most popular in France, in the middle of the century: it was the great philosophy of reform.

Of all these political thinkers, there were two outstanding men: Montesquieu, and Rousseau. Just before the Revolution, Rousseau seems to have been the more influential. But Montesquieu seems to have been the more helpful: when the call came to assemble at Versailles, in 1789, men turned first to Rousseau, but then to Montesquieu, as a practical textbook and manual for dealing with the issues to be raised in the National Assembly.

III

Charles de Secondat, baron de Montesquieu (1689–1755), had the idea of a unified science of society. But unlike all the other pioneer social scientists of the eighteenth century, he did not conceive it as a social physics on the Newtonian model. Rather, such a science should be a natural history of human societies, based not on the geometric method but on the method of naturalists like Buffon or Linnaeus: the patient investigation of facts, the careful classification of types of society, the exact study of their careers and their relations to their environment, bringing to light general principles. He loved variety and differences, and he voyaged up and down Europe gathering new specimens. He delighted in adding Hungary, the perfect specimen of the feudal, agricultural type. He voyaged in his library also, studying the record of the past. He was fascinated by Rome, a wonderful specimen of a completed and finished career; surely you could derive a law from it. And so he collected and classified for twenty years.

Montesquieu was a Bordelais from Bordeaux, like Montaigne, and like him a very complex figure, of many different aspects. In him were many different men united together. Like Montaigne he was a moderate, who felt the pull of a great variety of opinions, and tried to hold the balance between them. Like him, he had a great fear; but for Montesquieu it was not so much the fear of anarchy as the fear of despotism.

Montesquieu came of the *noblesse de la robe*, of an old family with Protestant traditions making for tolerance. His uncle was president of the *parlement* of Bordeaux. At the age of eleven, in 1700, he was sent to school with the Oratorians, those liberal classical scholars. He studied law, of course, from 1709 to 1713 in Paris. In 1714 he became councillor at the Bordeaux *parlement;* in 1716 his uncle left him the presidency. Montesquieu always defended the venality of judicial positions, as guaranteeing independence of the crown.

Montesquieu was a man of the time, the Regency, the break-up of the seventeenth-century structure of society. He was witty, sparkling, clever, cynical. He belonged to Bordeaux society, and took his place in the world of literature and science. In 1712 he was elected to the Bordeaux Academy. He dabbled in microscopic investigation, and in politics. In 1721 he published his *Persian Letters*, a satirical romance in the spirit of the age, Voltairean in tone, and not religious enough to be atheistical. This mood remains; but in the *Letters* there appears also another Montesquieu, the detached observer of customs, of politics, of institutions.

What I say of this prince should not astonish you: there is another magician stronger than he, who is not less master of his own mind than he is of the minds of others. This magician is called the Pope. At times he makes it believe that three are only one, that the bread we eat is not bread, or that the wine we drink is not wine, and a thousand other things of that sort.[3]

The work had a great success. In 1726 Montesquieu sold his judicial charge, and prepared to devote his life to a great work on society. His experience as a lawyer in Bordeaux had made him realize the need of a comparative and objective treatment; Bordeaux courts had to apply Roman law, eight kinds of local custom, royal decrees, and canon law. So he set out to travel; he visited Germany, Vienna, Hungary, Italy, the republic of Venice in 1729; Switzerland, the Rhine, staying in England until 1731. The English visit made a great impression on him. He says: "Germany is made to travel in, Italy to spend a vacation in, England to think in, France to live in." His attitude was that of the naturalist hunting new specimens: he took immense delight in adding to his collection. He loved differences, and hated uniformity—rank heresy in eighteenth-century France.

He also undertook voyages in his library, exploring history, especially that of Rome. The epic of the rise and fall of that great people fascinated him, by its grandeur. Rome was a wonderful specimen, because it exhibited a perfected and finished career. He felt deeply the religion of republican Rome, not the free and spontaneous art and thought of Greece, to be sure, but the simplicity, austerity, and frugality of the Roman, conscious of his destiny and his duty. Montesquieu had much to do with stamping Roman republicanism on the French Revolution. In 1734 he published his *Considerations on the Cause of the Grandeur of the Romans and their Fall*. To be scientific, he had to examine the causes.

Finally, feeling he was growing old, he made a selection from his great mass of material and published it as *L'esprit des lois*, in 1748. This is not a system, but a mine of facts, with intelligent comment, in six hundred chapters. It expresses a point of view, a method of inquiry, a critical standard applied to the whole field of man in society and the infinite diversity of human institutions. Montesquieu

[3] Montesquieu, *Lettres Persanes* (1721), Lettre 24; ed. Ch. Gaudier (Bibliothèque Larousse), p. 62.

is essentially a critic of social man, always sympathetic, always aiming to understand differences and interpret why they are and how they work. Hence he needed a standard, and tended to develop one.

I have first examined men, and I have thought that in the infinite diversity of laws and customs, they were not led solely by their fancies.

I have set up principles, and I have seen the particular cases submit as of themselves; the histories of all nations are but their consequence, and each particular law is linked with another law, or depends upon another more general.[4]

Underlying all positive laws, Montesquieu sought their "spirit," their reason, the universal laws of nature guiding all human institutions. What makes men here desire one thing, and there another; here develop one institution, there another? He sought the answer in an objective study of the natural conditions of men's well-being, their needs, in the particular situation in which they are placed. Here is the same desire to get an objective standard, to escape relativism, as in the utilitarianism of Helvétius. But where the utilitarian starts with man's desires, Montesquieu tries to ascertain what would really satisfy his needs; the one accepts what men want, the other seeks what is best for them. Montesquieu's attitude comes out clearly in his definition of liberty:

Political liberty does not consist in doing what we want. In a State, that is, in a society where there are laws, liberty can only consist in being able to do what we ought to will and in not being constrained to do what we ought not to will.[5]

Here "what we ought to will" is defined as objectively determined by reason: this is the classic tradition of the freedom of reason. The reconciliation between the two conceptions is precisely the problem of Rousseau: how can the will of all, what we actually want, be harmonized with the general will, what is best for us, what we ought to will? Rousseau finds the answer in autonomy, obedience to a self-imposed rational law—the solution Kant took over.

What is law? Montesquieu attempts an inclusive definition:

Laws, in their most general signification, are the necessary relations deriving from the nature of things: and in this sense, all beings have their laws: the divinity has its laws, the material world has its laws, the in-

[4] Montesquieu, *L'esprit des lois* (1748), Préface.
[5] *L'esprit des lois*, Livre XI, ch. 3.

telligences superior to man have their laws, the beasts have their laws, man has his laws. . . . There is, then, a first reason; and laws are the relations found between it and the different beings, and the relations of these different beings among themselves. . . . Particular intelligent beings can have laws of their own making: but they also have some they never made. Before there were intelligent beings, they were possible: they had therefore possible relations, and consquently possible laws. Before laws were made, there were possible relations of justice. To say that there is nothing just or unjust except what positive laws ordain or prohibit, is to say that before we have drawn a circle all its radii were not equal.

We must therefore acknowledge relations of equity antecedent to the positive law that establishes them: as, for example, supposing that human societies existed, it would be just to obey their laws; or, if there were intelligent beings who had received some benefit from another being, they ought to show their gratitude; or, if an intelligent being had created an intelligent being, the latter ought to remain in the dependence he derived from his origin; an intelligent being who has done ill to another intelligent being deserves to receive the same ill; and so on.[6]

"Justice is eternal, and does not depend on human conventions. . . . If it did, that would be a terrible truth that man would have to conceal from himself. . . . If there is a God, it is necessary that he be just. . . . It is impossible for God ever to commit an injustice. . . . If we suppose that he sees justice, he must follow it." [7]

Montesquieu holds that man in a state of nature would be impotent and weak, with excessive fears and apprehensions. Every man would feel inferior. "There would therefore be no danger of their attacking one another; peace would be the first law of nature." [8]

"As soon as man enters into a state of society he loses the sense of his weakness; equality ceases, and then commences the state of war." (I, 3) Montesquieu disagrees with Hobbes: in a state of nature man is not aggressive, that comes only with social motives for hostile attacks and self-defense, generated only in civilized society.

In general, law is human reason in so far as it governs all the peoples of the earth; and the political and civil laws of each nation ought to be only the particular cases in which human reason is applied. (I, 3)

There are three kinds of positive law: international law, political law, which is that between the governed and the governor, and civil law, which is between fellow-men.

[6] *L'esprit des lois*, Livre I, ch. 1.
[7] Cited in Émile Faguet, *Dix-Huitième siècle*, p. 152.
[8] *L'esprit des lois*, Livre I, ch. 2.

They should be adapted in such a manner to the people for whom they are framed that it is a very great chance if those of one nation suit another.

They should be related to the nature and principle of the government that is established, or that we want to establish, whether they form it, like political laws, or maintain it, like civil laws.

They should be related to the physical features of the country, to the frozen, broiling, or temperate climate; to the quality of its soil, to its situation, to its size, to the manner of life of the people, laborers, hunters, or herdsmen: they should be related to the degree of liberty the constitution can suffer; to the religion of the inhabitants, to their inclinations, their riches, their number, their commerce, their customs, their manners. Finally, they have relations to each other, to their origin, to the object of the legislator, to the order of things over which they are established. They ought to be considered in the light of all these things.

This is what I am undertaking to do in the present work. I shall examine all these relations: all of them together form what I am calling "the spirit of laws." (I, 3)

This is Montesquieu's framework. Within it there operates both a patient and sympathetic critic of human institutions, and a reformer gradually building up his own ideal.

As a scientist, Montesquieu combines a vivid historical imagination, gleaning lessons from the past, and the patient observer of present conditions. The value of his enterprise lies neither in the originality of his analysis, nor of his observation; both are rather crude and traditional. It lies rather in his temper of mind and attitude, in the idea itself rather than in its carrying out.

There are three different types of government: republican, which can be either an aristocracy or a democracy, monarchical, and despotism. Each has a nature, which makes it what it is, and also a principle, which makes it act; the one is the structure, the other, the human passions and motives. For a republic, Montesquieu goes to antiquity, to Rome. Its principle is virtue, the love of country, equality, frugality, political virtue. The best examples of Roman civic responsibility are Cato and Brutus. For monarchy he looks at France. Its principle is honor: the honors a sovereign bestows, the enjoyment of royal favor, posts and positions at court. Despotism is his great fear: the Oriental, effeminate, willful ruler, who has a vizier, a favorite, but no law whatsoever. The example is Louis XV and Mme de Pompadour. The principle of despotism is fear.

The causes of these differences are to be sought in large measure in physical conditions, in the environment, especially in climate, already emphasized by La Mettrie. Men are vigorous in a cold climate, lazy in a warm one. The answer is far too narrow, but Montesquieu has a keen sense of the interrelation of all institutions, of the social context in which each functions. Hence does he propose a rigorous determinism? Not at all. "A region is monarchist, not a man; a zone is republican, not a man." The wise law-givers will seek to correct by legislation the bad tendencies of their people, and of their environment and climate. "Bad law-givers are those who favor the vices of their climate, and good ones are those who oppose them." But the law-giver must determine the limits of his corrections, the particular needs of his people that must be somehow satisfied. He must oppose "moral causes" to physical causes.

Here Montesquieu passes beyond the scientist to become the law-giver himself, like Solon or Lycurgus of old, or like the Jeremy Bentham to come—and the various constituent assemblies of modern times. There is no fixed system or scheme advocated in the *Spirit of Laws*, but it is not hard to pick out his own standard, by which he judges all other systems. He was gradually building up his own ideal. He was a moderate, by birth, training, and temperament; he hated violence and brutality, particularly what he saw about him, the violence and brutality of the closing years of Louis XV, with their ignorance in ruled and ruler alike. He wanted law and order, not personal caprice and whim. His great fear was arbitrary rule. He mistrusted democracy as the slippery path to despotism: he had of course ancient democracies in mind. In a famous prophecy, he predicted the rise of a Napoleon:

Democracy has, therefore, two excesses to avoid: the spirit of inequality, which leads to aristocracy or to the government of a single man; and the spirit of extreme equality, which leads to the despotism of one individual, just as the despotism of one individual finishes with conquest. (VIII, 2)

Equality and a master means despotism; inequality is the root of liberty.

Montesquieu's aim is to find a method of preserving men from despotism—to keep away from the depotism of the monarch, the mob, and the demagogue alike. Maintain a balance, a mean: create "a masterpiece, requiring much intelligence." We need a delicate combination, a "system of checks and balances," to keep the government from doing too much—that typical eighteenth-century ideal. He admired aristocracy, with its principle of moderation and virtue: he was himself an aristocrat, he wanted a Platonic governing class, hereditary and well-educated. "It must be hereditary, but that is the very source of its corruption." A governing class is needed for its intelligence, but such a class is never devoted to the common good. How can the faults of aristocracy be overcome? By monarchy, but not by despotism, by a ruler who rules by law, not by caprice. Honor is more powerful as a motive than patriotism: there was as yet little nationalism, and no wide reading public to appeal to.

Montesquieu greatly admired the English constitution of the eighteenth century, which he knew partly from Locke and partly from his personal observation. He liked its "mixed government," with monarchy represented in the king, democracy in the House of Commons, and an intermediary buffer of aristocracy in the House of Lords. Combined with this mixture of the three traditional forms of government was the principle of the separation of the legislative, the executive, and the judicial functions. The peculiar merit, he thought, of the English constitution was its happy fusion of these two principles. The separation of powers made arbitrary government impossible, while the combination of the forms of government preserved what was best in each. The essence of the English constitution lay in putting the executive power in the hands of the monarch, giving the judicial and part of the legislative power to the aristocracy, and the rest of the legislative power to democracy. If any one of the three powers is combined with another, liberty will be destroyed.

There would be an end of everything, were the same man or the same body, whether of the nobles or of the people, to exercise those three powers, that of enacting laws, that of executing the public resolutions, and of trying the causes of individuals. (XI, 6)

Montesquieu opens his chapter by insisting on a sharp separation of the three powers, in a famous passage that was taken up by Blackstone and the Founding Fathers of the American Constitution, who seem not to have gotten beyond it. Montesquieu himself goes on to give the executive a veto over the legislative; he approves the

English arrangement by which the judicial power is exercised by "the part of the legislative body that is composed of nobles"—the House of Lords as the supreme court of appeal. The House of Lords also rightly tries peers, and is the court in cases of impeachment.

Locke had distinguished the legislative, the executive, and the federative functions, combining the last two in the same man. Montesquieu's terms are different, but his distinction is about the same.

> In each State there are three kinds of power: the legislative power, the executive in respect to things dependent on the law of nations; and the executive in regard to matters that depend on the civil law.
>
> By virtue of the first, the prince or magistrate enacts temporary or perpetual laws, and amends or abrogates those that have been already enacted. By the second, he makes peace or war, sends or receives embassies, establishes the public security, and provides against invasions. By the third he punishes the crimes or determines the disputes that arise between individuals. The latter we shall call the judicial power, and the other simply the executive power of the State. (XI, 6)

Thus Locke and Montesquieu make the same distinctions, but Montesquieu calls Locke's "federative power" the executive, and Locke's "executive power" the judicial. Both fail to distinguish executive from judicial, as is familiar in Blackstone and in the American Constitution. The chief difference between Montesquieu and Locke is that Locke emphasizes the supremacy of the legislative, while Montesquieu regards the three as equal—none is sovereign.

Neither Locke nor Montesquieu, of course, originated the general principle of the separation of the powers of government. That had grown out of the British constitutional struggles of the seventeenth century, and had by the days of Locke and Montesquieu become a commonplace of current English political theory. The long clash between king and parliament made central the difference between the executive and the legislature; while the independence of the judiciary from royal influence had been a part of the contest, won only in the Act of Settlement of 1701, by which judges held office during good behavior, not at the pleasure of the king. Where Montesquieu went wrong was in not foreseeing the rise of cabinet government, which was soon to unite the executive and the legislative power, and to issue in what Dicey called the sovereignty of Parliament, in which checks and balances are done away with.

But great as was Montesquieu's admiration for the English constitution as he saw it in his day and understood it, he did not want
France to copy the British government. For France, his model was
the ancient French monarchy: he favored an intelligent development of the ancient "gothic government," an enlightened feudalism. This was the true principle of France; it suited well her special
needs. Montesquieu has indeed been called a Frondeur.

There is infinitely more in Montesquieu. The practical importance of his book lies in its recommendations for specific reforms:
the abolition of Negro slavery, the humanizing of punishment, religious tolerance, peace, tax reform, etc. It was a monumental work.
Everybody read it; they were then carried away by Rousseau, but
they came back to it for their facts and their specific reforms. Montesquieu stood for a philosophy, a temper of mind, an attitude, the
idea of a comprehensive science of society, the method of patient
investigation, comparison, going to observation and history for principles. Of all the social theorists of the eighteenth century he and
Vico strike the reader today as the sanest, the most solid, the most
fully acquainted with history and with a wide range of human societies. These two are the ones who have aged the least, a real land-
mark in social thinking.

I V

Giambattista Vico (1668–1744) was a poor, sickly, and largely
self-educated boy from the slums of Naples, with an omnivorous
intellectual interest that embraced history, medieval as well as Greek
and Roman, the poets, especially Homer and Dante, the ancient
mythologies, and law and jurisprudence—in fact the entire gamut
of the humanistic learning of the times. In 1699 sheer merit won
him election to the chair of Rhetoric (or literature) at the University of Naples, still center of a flourishing school of jurisprudence. In 1735 he became Historiographer Royal. His son succeeded to his chair in 1741.

Vico early attacked the limitations of the Cartesian theory of
knowledge. The proper study of mankind is man, and man can
know himself and his products, human institutions and laws, human languages and mythologies and the history, which is the story
of human motives and their effects, in which all these institutions are

inextricably involved, far more profoundly and clearly than even Newton can know the laws of matter; the nonhuman world remains ultimately opaque, the human world can be known minutely. There is need therefore of a "new science," a *scienza nuova*, of the laws of the human spirit, which are laws of history and of social development. This new science can be called either a historical sociology or a secular philosophy of history. It is a "universal history, certain and reasoned" (*storia universale, certa e ragionata*), which arrives at the cyclical law of development of human institutions through which God makes manifest his providence by working through the mind of fallen man. Hence Vico elaborates one of those imposing theories of the cyclical and recurrent stages through which all things human must pass, familiar in our own day in Oswald Spengler and Arnold Toynbee. God's providence operates deterministically through the laws of man's nature: Vico foreshadows Hegel and Marx, who were acquainted with his scheme. Vico's theory of the recurrent cycles of history is set in a larger metaphysical framework in which all the phenomena of humanity are in the last analysis reducible to the three categories of knowledge, will, and power (*nosse, velle, et posse*).

Most of his ideas on the historical science of society Vico set forth in his *De uno universi juris principio et fine uno* in 1720; here is the fullest exposition of the repeated pattern of the forms of government. But he brought all his varied interests and ideas together in his *Scienza Nuova*, finished in 1724, published after a financial struggle in 1725, rewritten and expanded in 1730; third edition, uncompleted, in 1744. It received one short and unfavorable review in a German periodical, and was otherwise ignored. The work, written in a vigorous Italian and not in academic Latin, is entitled *Principi di scienza nuova d'intorno alla commune natura delle nazioni*. In the dedication to Cardinal Corsini, Vico states that many learned men have speculated on the natural law of nations (*Diritto natural delle genti*), but they have all been *ultramontani*, foreigners. Now for the first time an Italian writing in Italian, and in conformity with the orthodox teachings of the Church, is sketching a new science in accordance with the "nature of nations."

What sets Vico off from the reigning natural law theorists of his day is that their ideal is an eternally just system of laws; his is a historically developing set of institutions. The former must be good for all times and places; for Vico there is no perfect and unchanging reason save God's, and in all human affairs, law, rights, and authority must vary according to the stage of human enlightenment reached. He admires Grotius, but he mocks his attempt to ascribe validity for all ages and places to the rational interpretation of the law of nature which actually belongs only to his own age. Hence Vico refuses to follow Grotius, Hobbes, and Pufendorf in explaining the origin of law through a rational contract. Primitive man was quite incapable of such a feat. Elaborate legal codes are a slow growth: they develop gradually out of primitive custom. Justice arose not from personal and rational planning but from the "instinctive wisdom" of custom. Vico sounds like the nineteenth century admonishing the abstract reason of the seventeenth and eighteenth.

In the first book of his *New Science* Vico starts with the Fall of Man, the consequence of his excessive curiosity. Thereafter the Jews alone through revelation retained direct contact with God; the rest of the human race, which interests Vico the humanist far more than the exceptional Jews, was thenceforth on its own, guided only by the immanent law of God's providence embodied in human nature and its instincts. Even after the Fall the Gentile nations retained a certain "common wisdom" (*sapienza volgare*),[9] springing from two great principles, that Divine Providence governs men's affairs, and that man enjoys free will. From the second principle it follows that men desire to live according to justice.

By thus confining revelation to the history of the Jews, Vico gains a free hand to treat Gentile history objectively and rationally. Hence he could break the scriptural framework that still confined even Hobbes and Spinoza. Vico no longer has to interpret history in terms of revealed religion; he has escaped the conventional limitations of his day while still preserving his orthodoxy. The fallen Gentile world has followed its own instincts and achieved civilization: in the course of history man has made himself. Even after the Fall man remains attached to God through instinct. Men still retain a dim knowledge of the Divine purpose by a "common wisdom," which the challenge of the environment brings out. All nations

[9] See *De antiquissima italorum sapientia* (1710).

possess three instincts: the belief in Providence, the recognition of parenthood, and the instinct to bury their dead. Religion, marriage, and burial are universal institutions. Civilization is based on these instincts, on them is built the whole structure of the arts and sciences.

Just how did Gentile civilization emerge from primitive times? No one has yet considered the problem of the way in which nations are perfected. This occurs when on the firm basis of primitive custom, "recondite wisdom" (*sapienza riposta dei filosofi*, the stored-up wisdom of the philosophers) is joined to "common wisdom." The Stoics and Epicureans ignored this common wisdom; only Plato respected it. But even he fell into the "learned error" of thinking that laws were devised by philosophers. The actual process is very hard to recover:

> Because of which harsh uncertainties and almost desperate difficulties involved in such a project, where we know nothing either of these first men or, in consequence, of those original places in the world from which the Gentile nations began to emerge, we, following in our thought the animal wanderings of such people, have as the heading of this work, put forward this first book of ours, the substance of which can be summed up briefly in these words: . . . *Ignari hominumque locorumque erramus,* "we wander ignorant of the men and the places." [10]

The second book applies these principles to the science of history. After the Deluge the human race became divided into two kinds, men of normal stature, and idolatrous and bestial giants, living in the marshes left by the flood. From these giants, who gradually reverted to human size, the Gentile nations descended. Fear of thunder and lightning first civilized the giants: it caused them to feel shame. They dragged their mates into caves, and set up the family and family life. From this first act of "violent authority" comes the "natural docility" of women and the "natural nobility" of men (II, 13). By examining the Old Testament and Greek legends of giants, Vico elucidates this first stage of human history, "The Age of the Gods," in which men devised the pagan deities. There followed the Heroic Age, in which the fathers of families became an aristocracy of virtue and ability. Two types of men appeared, "one noble because intelligent, the other common because stupid" (II, 16). The

[10] *Scienza Nuova*, Book I, ch. 13.

former attained the full stature of human nature, and took the latter for their "clients." After the Heroic Age these plebeians asserted themselves. The Heroic élite was responsible for the progress of the arts, agriculture, industry, colonization, and morals. The Roman Republic was the apex and highest achievement of humanity (Vico has been reading Machiavelli's *Discorsi*). The third stage of history is the Human Age of the Roman Empire, displaying civilized rationality, majority participation in government, a comprehensive system of laws, and alphabetic writing. But like all things human it cannot endure; men become overcivilized and decadent; luxury and class conflicts provoke dictatorship. In the end they bring conquest by more virile peoples, "since he who cannot govern himself must be governed by another." Vico admired the brutality of the early Romans and the severity of their laws: he was an admirer of force.

This cycle of Roman history has been repeated since the fall of the Empire. The Dark Ages correspond once more to the original Age of the Gods, the Heroic Age of antiquity finds its counterpart in the Middle Ages; while the Renaissance begins the sophisticated period of the later Roman Empire. Thus history must always proceed, by cyclical recurrences, *"corsi e ricorsi."*

In the third book Vico utilizes the study of language, of mythology and poetry, to throw light on the mind of primitive man. During the Age of Gods language was vague and poetical; in the Heroic Age it remained symbolic. Homer dates from the close of the Heroic Age. After careful examination Vico concludes that "Homer" was a number of poets writing over several generations. Dante, too, is a poet of the heroic virtues: both he and Homer are superior to the sophisticated and civilized Vergil, despite his refined technical skill.

The fourth book is brief; the fifth overflows with ideas. The second chapter, comparing Greek and Roman history, maintains that all nations pass through the same inevitable stages of development. Chapter four attributes all social development to the three punishments inflicted on fallen man, the sense of shame, curiosity, and the need to work. The earlier kingdoms of the East are examined: they passed through the first two stages of the historical cycle. Greek mythology is thoroughly analyzed, the hero myths in particular. The book concludes:

This was the idea of the work, at the very beginning of which we quoted the words, "With Jove my lay begins" (Vergil, Ec. III, l. 60); and now we close with the other half of the line, "the world is full of Jove." . . . For without a providential God there would not be in the world any condition but that of error, bestiality, brutality, violence, savage pride, corruption and blood; and it may well be perhaps and we need not say "perhaps," the great wilderness of the world would be ugly and dumb, without a human race. (V, 11)

Aside from his controlling idea of an "evolution" of social institutions, the most suggestive part of Vico's historical science of society is his account of the sequence of the forms of government. The three forms—like Hegel, Vico is wedded to triads—are theocracy, aristocracy, and the "free state," which includes both republics and monarchies. In theocracy, the direct authority of God revealed through oracles is the source of all political power. In aristocracy, the organization of power lies with the independent heads of families; this can persist even when a king has come to stand at the head, *primus inter pares*. In the free republic, the whole mass of the population has come to share in political power with the ancient aristocracy. In free monarchy, authority has been taken over by an individual, to be exercised on behalf of the people—the benevolent despot idea. The so-called mixed forms of government, like the Senate in the Roman Republic, or the representative character of the monarch in the Principate, are merely transitional phases between two forms. Vico derives his scheme from Roman history, but applies it universally, especially to the Europe of the Teutonic invasions. The aristocracy of the second stage, still lingering on, is bound to give way to the free commonwealth and the free monarchy. He goes on to analyze the characteristic institutions of each of these three stages of governmental form. There are three corresponding forms of "nature," of *moeurs* or national character, of language and alphabet, of jurisprudence, of authority, of reason, and of judicial procedure. Much of his detail, on national character and on the influence of the environment, is strongly suggestive of Montesquieu, whose thought is not so unprecedented as he himself imagines. Perhaps Montesquieu alone in the eighteenth century would have appreciated Vico. The post-Hegelian and post-Darwinian social scientists have done so to the full.

Enlightened despotism, with no nonsense about asking the consent of the governed, is the natural creed of the reformer, as every college dean knows; the great revolutionary movements of our own day would suffice to make its appeal clear. Voltaire and the Encyclopedists maintained it in the Enlightenment, Helvétius on utilitarian grounds. Holbach is the chief political theorist of this group. In 1773 he published his *Système social* and his *Politique naturelle*, or *Discours sur les vrais principes du gouvernement*, and in 1776 his *Éthocratie*, or *Le Gouvernement fondé sur la morale*.

These confident reformers all admired the fruits of the English constitution, civil liberty, jury trial, toleration, freedom of speech and of the press. Above all they liked commercial liberty or laissez-faire, and the absolute right of private property, with its freedom from any arbitrary confiscation. But from Voltaire down they hardly understood how these desirable rights depended on the political structure of the English constitution itself. They all hated despotism, religious authority, military government—this was their rallying cry. But they were not democrats; they had no idea of political liberty as involving universal suffrage, or of political equality. Holbach puts it:

Liberty is the power of taking the measures necessary to procure our well-being. This liberty is limited by reason or by the interest in our own self-preservation, even when we are alone. In the state of society the limits of the liberty of the citizen are fixed either by the natural equity which keeps him from harming others or by positive laws aimed to make him observe his duties towards others.

Liberty, therefore, does not consist, as some people imagine, in a supposed equality between fellow-citizens: that chimaera, adored in democratic states, is totally incompatible with our nature, which makes us unequal in our faculties of body and mind. That equality would still be unjust, and moreover incompatible with the good of society, which asks that the citizens most useful for the public good should be the most honored, the best rewarded, without for that reason being freed from the general law, which prescribes uniform rules for every one. True liberty consists in obeying the laws which rectify the natural inequality of men, that is, which protect equally the rich and the poor, the great and the little, sovereigns and subjects. Whence we see that liberty is equally advantageous to all members of society.[11]

[11] Holbach, *Système Social* (1773), Partie II, ch. iii.

What these men wanted was a philosopher-king, who would reform society in the light of reason—an ideal they thought measurably incarnated in a Frederick the Great or a Catherine II.

Politics ought to be the art of regulating the passions of men, of directing them to the welfare of society, of diverting them into a genial current of happiness, of making them flow gently to the general benefit of all.[12]

Helvétius also wants reform from on top:

These principles, adopted by an enlightened and benevolent Prince, could become the germ of a new legislation, and more conformable to the happiness of mankind.[13]

VI

The Physiocrats, who founded the science of political economy in the practical interest of relieving economic distress, were the major group and party who popularized the ideal of benevolent despotism in France. They believed in a "legal despotism," an absolute monarch governing in accordance with the natural laws of society—in "the rule of nature" or physiocracy. Gournay (1712–1759), the theorist of laissez-faire, and Dr. Quesnay (1694–1774), physician to Louis XV, who added the theory of the soil as the only producer of wealth, were the two leaders of the school. Quesnay wrote the article on *Fermiers* for the *Encyclopédie* in 1756, and the one on *Grains* the next year; in 1758 he brought together his *Maximes générales du gouvernement économique* and his *Tableau économique*; in 1765 appeared his *Droit naturel*. The Marquis de Mirabeau issued *Philosophie rurale* in 1763; Turgot, who had written on *Foires et marchés* and on *Fondations* for the *Encyclopédie*, brought out in 1766 his *Formation et distribution des richesses*; Mercier de la Rivière, *L'Ordre naturel et essentiel des sociétés politiques* in 1767. Dupont de Nemours, who gave the name to the school and popularized its teachings, wrote *Origine et progrès d'une science nouvelle* in 1768, and in 1773 the widely read *Abrégé des principes*.

The Physiocrats believed in the absolute hereditary monarchy of the eighteenth century, like Bossuet; but they founded it on the theory of the natural rights of man: they were the real popularizers

[12] Holbach, *Système de la Nature* (1770), Partie I, ch. ix.
[13] Helvétius, *De l'homme* (1772), sec. VIII, ch. xxvi.

in France of the doctrine of natural rights. The laws of society are natural, they never change. Man is born free, he is still free; by natural right he is master of his person and of his labor and the fruits thereof. He gives up no rights in society. There are two natural rights, liberty and property—especially property. The aim of society is to guarantee these rights; to do so, it must be strong, and power is gained only by the unity of the legislative and executive power in one man (Rousseau also believed monarchy the strongest form of government). This must not be despotism, for there must be an independent magistracy applying the law in particular cases (this is Rousseau's "executive"). Whence come the laws? There are natural social laws, immutable, eternal, inevitable natural laws of society. Judges must judge all positive laws by them. Hence the need of education in political science, so that public opinion will support the judges.

The judges must be trained in the natural science of political economy, or of the production of wealth.

All social facts are linked together in the bonds of eternal, immutable, ineluctable, inevitable laws, which individuals and governments would obey if they were once made known to them.

The task of government is to find these laws and to conform to them. Turgot did accomplish this, in his province of Limoges, with great success. They comprised the liberty of conscience, of commerce, of work, of instruction, and of property.

Laws are rules of justice, of morality, of conduct, useful to each and all. Neither men nor their governments *make* them, nor can they *make* them. They recognize them as conforming to the supreme reason that governs the universe; they declare them: they *bring* them to society; they present them to the obedience of men of good will, and to the conscience even of the wicked.—That is why we say bringer of law, legis*lator*, and call a collection of laws brought, legis*lation*, and why we have never dared to say, maker of laws, legis*factor* or legis*faction*.

Laws are irrevocable, they pertain to the essence of men and things; they are the expression of the will of God; and the more we reflect upon them the more we revere them.[14]

Sovereign authority is not instituted to *make laws*; for *laws are all made* by the hand of him who creates rights and duties.

[14] Dupont de Nemours, *Maximes du Docteur Quesnay; in Les Écrivains politiques du XVIIIe siècle,* ed. A. Bayet et F. Albert (1917), p. 332.

Social laws, established by the Supreme Being, prescribe only the preservation of the *right of property*, and of the *liberty* which is inseparable from it.

The ordinances of sovereigns called *positive laws* should only be *acts declarative of the laws essential to the social order*.

If the ordinances of sovereigns were contradictory to the *laws of the social order*, if they prohibited respect for property, if they commanded burning the harvest, if they prescribed the sacrifice of little children, they would not be *laws*, they would be senseless acts which would not be obligatory on anyone.[15]

VII

Jean-Jacques Rousseau (1712–1778) is a strange figure, certainly a striking contrast to Montesquieu. Uneducated, he wrote the most influential book ever written on education. Almost incapable of fulfilling any social duties whatsoever, he wrote the most powerful book ever written on the supreme duty of political obligation. Hating society and the company of men, he captured their imagination as few others ever have, and became the vogue in society. Distrusting progress and advance through the application of reason, he contributed more than any other individual in his century to the progress of society.

It is easy enough to make fun of Rousseau. The sport has been especially popular since 1914; since then we have reacted away from Rousseau's "democracy," from his Romanticism, from his individualism in education and social matters. No man ever gave greater opportunity for satirical treatment. The contrast is so great between his ideals and his conduct, his preaching and his despicable, pathological, "neurotic" character. Above all, he has the unforgivable sin of taking himself too seriously, of overweening pride and self-esteem.

Yet—there is something there, something sterling at the bottom of his character, something that attracted many friends, and gained him patient indulgence for all his foibles from competent observers. In a real sense he rang true. Into that eighteenth-century atmosphere of unreality and artificiality, of cynicism and insincerity, of intellectual abstractions, he brought something new, something needed, something powerful and strong. And the old

[15] Dupont de Nemours, *Origine et Progrès d'une Science Nouvelle* (1768); in Bayet and Albert, pp. 334–35.

structure of thought and of society crumbled away. Voltaire demonstrated the idea of the existence of God—was it for his servants? Rousseau proclaimed that God is! There is a sturdy simplicity and republican virtue in his very self-pride. He put himself into all his works, without reserve.

Rousseau cared nothing about facts. All his works, his life itself, in his *Confessions*, turned into a romance. "Nature" is the great word in his thinking; yet in no possible sense can he be called a naturalist. He never saw things as they are, in any ordinary sense. Nevertheless, he perceived very, very clearly certain great truths, certain problems and principles to which the rest of the eighteenth-century thinkers were blind, and which his contemporaries recognized when he proclaimed them. He took the common stock of eighteenth-century political and social ideas, disregarded the science of man from which they had been carefully demonstrated, and proposed to put them into effect. Where others had expressed the thought of the day, Rousseau gave form to its feelings. Relying on his own pathologically sensitive and emotional temperament, he overemphasized just what the Age of Reason had systematically underplayed.

There is a sense in which Rousseau is not French, is in fact alien to the French genius, however that be conceived. Catalogue the traits of French culture, and then look at Rousseau. No wonder the classicist is disgusted. Rousseau is neither the Voltairean nor the Pascalian. Yet he has been passionately admired by Frenchmen to this day. He is a Protestant, an individualist, with no corporate sense. In that age of ecclesiastical passions, he is neither clerical nor anticlerical. He found God, and all truth, neither in a great tradition, nor in the naturalistic, objective observation of life, but in his own heart. He is a Romanticist—and the citizen of Geneva.

Rousseau never had an education. He grew up on sentimental romances; till he was forty, he never knew anything about society. At sixteen he set out on a life of vagabondage, of thievery and roguery, of amours and affairs. Having by accident gained a reputation as a social thinker, through a paradoxical work denying the possibility of moral progress, in 1749, he was suddenly taken up and lionized by society. He did not fit in, naturally, he was repelled and choked by it, and he returned to his "natural life" of the countryside, in his haughty pride. Resolved to justify his accidentally won reputation, he set about the serious study of social theory. After ten years of hard work, he had changed his views completely, and published his reversal of opinion in two books in 1762, *Émile* and *The Social Contract*.

Rousseau's central problem is simple. Man is born good—he felt it in his heart, he knew he was himself good. Yet men are bad, society is evil—his pride and failure told him that. How? Why? What can be done about it? Here Rousseau had his big idea and his simple message. Men are really fundamentally good at heart, they are born good, they might have been good, they are still potentially good, they can still become far better than they are. Why did they become bad? Their education is all wrong, their society is all wrong. Give them a new education and a new society, and their goodness will flower out naturally, they will realize their inborn capacity for goodness. Men must be made by art what they are naturally in germ; let intelligence seize upon these native tendencies and develop them, let the arts of education and government lead them to realize their true potentialities.

Whence did Rousseau derive this idea? In part it was in the air; from Voltaire and Diderot on the reformers had emphasized the power of education and institutional change. In part it came from Rousseau's own experience: he had been born good, until society got in its evil work upon him. There is a double optimism in Rousseau. The Encyclopedists like Helvétius held that human nature is a blank tablet, it can be made good as well as bad. Rousseau holds that man was born good, he has fallen from grace, but he can be raised up and restored to his original goodness. It was not for nothing that Rousseau grew up in Calvinistic Geneva, and could interpret the Fall in social terms.

In 1749 the Academy of Dijon proposed the question, "Has the restoration of the arts and sciences had a purifying effect upon morals?" In his essay which won the prize in 1750, *A Discourse on the Moral Effects of the Arts and Sciences*, Rousseau answered paradoxically in the negative. He denounced all society, contrasting with it man in the state of nature with his natural liberty. He is usually taken as the symbol of this idea set forth in his first discourse. In reality, having won popularity and reputation by his paradox, he began to consider it seriously, and came to feel he had a real idea that needed only some small reinterpretation. It took only a little reflection to bring him to the diametrically opposite point of view from that maintained in the work that first gained him notoriety. He set forth his reconstructed position in a second *Discourse on the Origin and Foundation of the Inequality of Mankind,* in 1755.

Man is potentially capable of much better things than he has realized as yet. What are his capacities? What is the "original nature" of man *now?*

How can man distinguish what is fundamental in his nature from the changes and additions which his circumstances and the advances he has made have introduced to modify his primitive condition? . . .

It is by no means a light undertaking to distinguish properly between what is original and what is artificial in the actual nature of man, or to form a true idea of a state which no longer exists, perhaps never did exist, and probably never will exist; and of which it is, nevertheless, necessary to have true ideas, in order to form a proper judgment of our present state. It requires, indeed, more philosophy than can be imagined to enable any one to determine exactly what precautions he ought to take, in order to make solid observations on this subject; and it appears to me that a good solution of the following problem would be not unworthy of the Aristotles and Plinys of the present age. *What experiments would have to be made, to discover the natural man? And how are those experiments to be made, in a state of society?* [16]

This knowledge is the indispensable prerequisite to any social science:

It is this ignorance of the nature of man, which casts so much uncertainty and obscurity on the true definition of natural right: for the idea of right, says Burlamaqui, and more particularly that of natural right, are ideas manifestly relative to the nature of man. It is then from this very nature itself, he goes on, from the constitution and state of man, that we must deduce the first principles of this science. (*OI,* p. 170)

Utilitarianism demands just such an investigation:

Modern writers begin by inquiring what rules it would be expedient for men to agree on for their common interest, and then give the name of natural law to a collection of these rules, without any other proof than the good that would result from their being universally practised. This

[16] *Discours sur l'origine de l'inégalité parmi les hommes* (1755); Eng. tr. by G. D. H. Cole in *The Social Contract and Discourses* (Everyman ed.), pp. 168–69. Indicated by *OI.*

is undoubtedly a simple way of making definitions, and of explaining the nature of things by almost arbitrary conveniences.

But as long as we are ignorant of the natural man, it is in vain for us to attempt to determine either the law originally prescribed to him, or that which is best adapted to his constitution. (*OI*, p. 171)

Rousseau goes on to make his own analysis of human nature:

Throwing aside, therefore, all those scientific books, which teach us only to see men such as they have made themselves, and contemplating the first and most simple operations of the human soul, I think I can perceive in it two principles prior to reason, one of them deeply interesting us in our own welfare and preservation, and the other exciting a natural repugnance at seeing any other sensible being, and particularly any of our own species, suffer pain or death. It is from the agreement and combination which the understanding is in a position to establish between these two principles, without its being necessary to introduce that of sociability, that all the rules of natural right appear to me to be derived—rules which our reason is afterwards obliged to establish on other foundations, when by its successive developments it has been led to suppress nature itself. (*OI*, pp. 171–72)

Rousseau makes it clear that he is proposing a psychological, not an historical investigation:

Let us begin then by laying facts aside, as they do not affect the question. The investigations we may enter into, in treating this subject, must not be considered as historical truths, but only as mere conditional and hypothetical reasonings, rather calculated to explain the nature of things, than to ascertain their actual origins; just like the hypotheses which our physicists daily form respecting the formation of the world. (*OI*, p. 175)

So he undertakes his "hypothetical history of government," which he describes at length; inevitably, being Rousseau, he tends to romance about it.

Let us conclude then that man in a state of nature, wandering up and down the forests, without industry, without speech, and without home, an equal stranger to war and to all ties, neither standing in need of his fellow-creatures nor having any desire to hurt them, and perhaps even not distinguishing them from one another; let us conclude that, being self-sufficient and subject to so few passions, he could have no feelings or knowledge but such as befitted his situation; that he felt only his actual necessities, and disregarded everything he did not think himself immediately concerned to notice, and that his understanding made no greater progress than his vanity. If by accident he made any discovery, he was the less able to communicate it to others, as he did not know even his own children. Every art would necessarily perish with its inventor, where there was no kind of education among men, and generations succeeded generations without the least advance; when, all setting out from the same point, centuries must have elapsed in the barbarism of the first ages; when the race was already old, and man remained a child. (*OI*, p. 203)

Man by nature thus possesses the two instincts of self-preservation and compassion. Society multiplies our interests and our wants; and they conflict with each other; man comes to gain by serving his fellows, but he comes to gain more by injuring them. This seems to be true: the greater the number of interrelations between men in a complex society, the greater the opportunity for maladjustments and twisted human relations. But also, the greater becomes the opportunity for a richly developed life, for what Spinoza considered to be social freedom. And Rousseau came to realize it:

What, then, is to be done? Must societies be totally abolished? Must *meum* and *tuum* be annihilated, and must we return again to the forests to live among bears? This is a deduction in the manner of my adversaries, which I would as soon anticipate as let them have the shame of drawing. . . . As for men like me, whose passions have destroyed their original simplicity, who can no longer subsist on plants or acorns, or live without laws or magistrates; . . . they will respect the sacred bonds of their respective communities; they will love their fellow-citizens, and serve them with all their might: they will scrupulously obey the laws, and all those who make or administer them. . . . But they will not therefore have less contempt for a constitution that cannot support itself without the aid of so many splendid characters, much oftener wished for than found; and from which, notwithstanding all their pains and solicitude, there always arise more real calamities than even apparent advantages. (*OI*, pp. 245-46)

Rousseau is urging, by 1755, no "return to nature," to savagery and barbarism, but a rational and intelligent development of man's native traits, "the artificial cultivation of the natural." He is advocating that man's instincts should be controlled and guided through reason.

God makes all things good; man meddles with them and they become evil. . . . Yet things would be worse without this education, and mankind can not be made by halves. Under existing conditions a man left to himself from birth would be more of a monster than the rest. Prejudice, authority, necessity, example, all the social conditions into which we are plunged, would stifle nature in him and put nothing in her place. She would be like a sapling chance sown in the midst of the highway, bent hither and thither and soon crushed by the passers-by. . . .

Good social institutions are those best fitted to make a man unnatural, to exchange his independence for dependence, to merge the unit in the group, so that he no longer regards himself as one, but as a part of the whole, and is only conscious of the common life.[17]

But human nature does not go backwards, and we never return to the times of innocence and equality, when we have once departed from them; this is one of the principles on which he [Rousseau] insisted most strongly. Therefore his object could not be to recall numerous people, or large States, to their first simplicity, but only to stop, if it were possible, the progress of those whose smallness and situation have preserved them from a somewhat rapid march toward the perfection of society, and towards the deterioration of the species. These distinctions deserve to be made and have not been. Men have persisted in accusing him of wanting to destroy the sciences, the arts, theatres, academies, and plunge the universe back into its first barbarism; and he has always insisted, on the contrary, on the preservation of existing institutions, maintaining that their destruction would only remove palliatives while leaving the vices, and substitute brigandage for corruption; he had worked for his own native country and for the small States constituted like it.[18]

We can thus distinguish three stages of growth in Rousseau's concept of "nature." First, in the *Discourse on the Arts and Sciences*, the state of nature is the chronologically original state of man. Secondly, with the *Discourse on Inequality*, "nature" has become what is native in man, his original endowment—what man would be if he could be taken out of society, a conception clearly the product of analysis, not of history. This "state of nature" "never did exist and never will exist"; yet a knowledge of human nature is necessary for any wise law or education. Such a "human nature" is a hypothesis calculated to explain man as he is, not an historical account of anything. Thirdly, "human nature" has become the fullest development of human capacities, the product of an intelligent education and a properly ordered society. Thus when Rousseau comes to write the *Social Contract*, and *Émile*, far from deploring the influence of "society" he praises it as the means for saving man from being "a stupid and unimaginative animal," for making him "an in-

[17] *Émile* (1762), Book I; Eng. tr. B. Foxley (Everyman ed.), pp. 5, 7.
[18] *Rousseau juge de Jean-Jacques*, Dialogue III; in Bayet et Albert, pp. 243–44.

telligent being and a man." He now advocates no return to an impossible savagery and barbarism, but rather a rational and intelligent development of man's instincts and capacities.

At the same time, there was taking place a parallel growth in Rousseau's conception of freedom. At first, freedom meant for him simply the lack of all restraint. But he soon saw that the "freedom" of the state of nature was worth nothing, even if it were possible, which it is not. "Freedom is diametrically opposed to unbridled license." (*OI*, p. 159) He ended by speaking of the State by law "forcing men to be free," even when it condemns them to prison for violating rational law. Liberty is now obedience to the law of reason, not to individual desire or caprice. Rousseau has been reading Montesquieu. Yet he still feels that liberty should take account of men's actual desires: so he is led to his famous definition: liberty is autonomy, obedience to a *self-imposed* law of reason. Man is free in obeying the law of gravitation, or even the laws of thought; for these are all laws of his own being.

There are two kinds of dependence: dependence on things, which is the work of nature; and dependence on men, which is the work of society. Dependence on things, being non-moral, does no injury to liberty and begets no vices; dependence on men, being out of order, gives rise to every kind of vice, and through this master and slave become mutually depraved. If there is any cure for this social evil, it is to be found in the substitution of law for the individual; in arming the general will with a real strength beyond the power of any individual will. If the laws of nations, like the laws of nature, could never be broken by any human power, dependence on men would become dependence on things; all the advantages of a state of nature would be combined with all the advantages of social life in the commonwealth. The liberty which preserves a man from vice would be united with the morality which raises him to virtue.[19]

Rousseau's final position is stated in the famous passages in the *Social Contract:*

In order, then, that the social compact may not be an empty formula, it tacitly includes the undertaking, which alone can give force to the rest, that whoever refuses to obey the general will shall be compelled to do so by the whole body. This means nothing less than that he will be forced to be free; for this is the condition which, by giving each citizen to his country, secures him against all personal dependence. In this lies the key to the working of the political machine; this alone legitimises

[19] *Émile*, Everyman ed., p. 49.

civil undertakings, which, without it, would be absurd, tyrannical, and liable to the most frightful abuses. . . .

We might, over and above all this, add, to what man acquires in the civil state, moral liberty, which alone makes him truly master of himself; for the mere impulse of appetite is slavery, while obedience to a law which we prescribe to ourselves is liberty.[20]

This is the source of Kant's conception of liberty as autonomy, obedience to a law we prescribe to ourselves; its occurrence in Rousseau is one of the reasons why Kant kept the *Social Contract* on his desk and read it through every year. In Rousseau himself, it is related to Calvin's notion of liberty as obedience to the sovereign will of God, combined with the idea of freedom as obedience to rational law. Through Hegel, it came to have a tremendous influence on German philosophy and on those who were inspired by it, like Bosanquet—to say nothing of Marx.

Rousseau saw two means of attaining this kind of freedom: individually, through a proper education; and collectively, through a proper ordering of society. In the *Émile*, he describes most elaborately a very artificial process of developing the natural potentialities of the child, devices for making him want to do what is best for him, for making him want to obey a self-imposed rational law. *Émile* is a kind of romance of education, a highly artificial education to be natural. That is, in *Émile* Rousseau gives the "natural" a very positive content. What is bad in it is the negative side: the child should be brought up apart from all society, not sharing even that of his parents. He must be preserved from any "dependence" on "the will of others." On the positive side, Rousseau insists that education should be indirect: it should come from things, not from books. This is of course a reflection of the general empiricism of the day, the "materialisme du sage." Don't tell the child about anything, make him find out for himself. The aim of Rousseau's program of education was to produce men like Rousseau: that is, good men, neither scholarly bookworms nor inhumanistic scientists. Education should make men, not mere citizens.

The real value of Rousseau's educational philosophy is its rejection of the traditional ideal. Education is not to be taken as pouring in "knowledge" with a funnel. It is rather the "drawing out" of what

[20] *Le Contrat Social* (1762), Everyman ed., pp. 18–19. Indicated by *SC*. Book I, chs. vii, viii.

is in the child. It should seize on what is native to the child, all his possibilities, and foster and guide them in accordance with reason. Rousseau was one of the great inspirations of "progressive" education in the United States during the last generation. But his actual views have been misinterpreted and misused as much as those of John Dewey.

Rousseau's conception of freedom determines also the basic problem of the *Social Contract:* In what form of association will men actually impose upon themselves a law that is rational, that makes for the common good? Only in one in which they at least tacitly consent to be bound by measures making for the common good. This is the principle Rousseau calls the "social contract."

VIII

The *Social Contract* is the most influential book on political philosophy ever written, too influential to be very original, yet certainly a great book. G. D. H. Cole could call it: "By far the best textbook of Political Philosophy." Why? Because it is philosophy, not history or sociology. It deals with what ought to be done, with what is right: it is frankly ethical. It starts out by stating its normative aim:

I mean to inquire if, in the civil order, there can be any sure and legitimate rule of administration, men being taken as they are and laws as they might be. . . . Man is born free, and everywhere he is in chains. One thinks himself the master of others, and still remains a greater slave than they. How did this change come about? I do not know. What can make it legitimate? That question I think I can answer. (*SC,* p. 5; Book I, ch. i)

What is the basis of political obligation? Not *why* do men obey government; that is a question of fact, of psychology. But why *ought* they to obey government? Why is it *right* to do so? This is not a fact at all.

The strongest is never strong enough to be always the master, unless he transforms strength into right, and obedience into duty. Hence the right of the strongest, which, though to all seeming meant ironically, is really laid down as a fundamental principle. But are we never to have an explanation of this phrase? Force is a physical power, and I fail to see what moral effect it can have. To yield to force is an act of necessity, not of will—at the most, an act of prudence. In what sense can it be a duty? . . .

Let us then admit that force does not create right, and that we are obliged to obey only legitimate powers. In that case, my original question recurs.

Since no man has a natural authority over his fellow, and force creates no right, we must conclude that conventions form the basis of all legitimate authority among men. (*SC*, pp. 8, 9; Book I, chs. iii, iv)

Under what conditions will a government have a moral right to obedience, will obedience be a duty? In the fifth book of *Émile* Rousseau distinguishes his question sharply from Montesquieu's. "Montesquieu did not intend to treat of the principles of political right; he was content to treat of the positive right (or law) of established governments; and no two studies could be more different than these."

"The problem is to find a form of association which will defend and protect with the whole common force the person and goods of each associate, and in which each, while uniting himself with all, may still obey himself alone, and remain as free as before." This is the fundamental problem of which the *Social Contract* provides the solution. . . .

Indeed, if there were no prior convention, where, unless the election were unanimous, would be the obligation on the minority to submit to the choice of the majority? How have a hundred men who wish for a master the right to vote on behalf of ten who do not? The law of majority voting is itself something established by convention, and presupposes unanimity, on one occasion at least. (*SC*, pp. 14, 13; Book I, chs. vi, v)

The social contract is therefore not an event, but a principle. When a candidate is elected by a narrow margin, why do not his rival's supporters organize and force him out? Because they believe in majority rule, and they want majority rule more than they want their particular candidate in office. When did they agree to it? Can we explain it on other grounds? Can we justify it? How is majority rule to be justified? Is it simply that counting heads is better than breaking them? Why do we condemn dictatorships by a minority with an intelligent program? Rousseau makes clear that the political problem is to effect some kind of harmony between well-being and liberty, between getting what will be good for us and getting what we actually want. How can they be combined?

Each of us puts his person and all his power under the supreme direction of the *general will*, and, in our corporate capacity, we receive each member as an indivisible part of the whole. (*SC*, p. 15; Book I, ch. vi)

At once, in place of the individual personality of each contracting party, this act of association creates a moral and collective body, composed of as many members as the assembly contains votes, and receiving from this act its unity, its common identity, its life and its will. This public person, so formed by the union of all other persons, formerly took the name of *city* (houses make a town, but citizens a city), and now takes that of *Republic* or *body politic;* it is called by its members *State* when passive, *Sovereign* when active, and *Power* when compared with others like itself. Those who are associated in it take collectively the name of *people,* and severally are called *citizens,* as sharing in the soverign power, and *subjects,* as being under the laws of the State. (*SC,* pp. 15, 16; Book I, ch. vi)

What does Rousseau mean by the "general will," which gives the majority the right to force the minority to be free, in so far as the majority coincides with it? The general will is that which wills the common good; it "comes from all, and applies to all." All men in society really and at bottom want and will what is rationally best for every citizen; but they do not always know what is best for all, and often actually desire something else. Rousseau is assuming that there is a common good, and that all citizens share the eighteenth-century ideas as to the functions of government. The general will is not an expressed will at all, but is defined as an ideal, as that which *by definition* wills the common good. If it does not will the common good, it is not the general will. Hence *by definition* the general will is infallible. The notion of general will is stated most fully and perhaps least unclearly in the article on *Économie politique* in the *Encyclopédie* (1755): "The body politic is a moral being possessed of a will; this general will tends always to the welfare of the whole, is the source of the laws, and constitutes the rule of what is just and unjust." (*SC,* p. 253)

The Sovereign, being formed wholly of the individuals who compose it, neither has nor can have any interest contrary to theirs; and consequently the sovereign power need give no guarantee to its subjects, because it is impossible for the body to wish to hurt all its members. We shall also see later on that it cannot hurt any in particular. The Sovereign, merely by virtue of what it is, is always what it should be. (*SC,* p. 17; Book I, ch. vii)

The general will is to be sharply distinguished from "the will of all," what men think they want, and actually desire; this is decided by a majority vote, it is a fact, not an ideal. But the general will is not merely an ideal; it is also something which under certain conditions can be actual. What men "really" want is realized in a successful republican election, which thus coincides with the general will.

> When in the popular assembly a law is proposed, what the people is asked is not exactly whether it approves or rejects the proposal, but whether it is in conformity with the general will, which is their will. Each man, in giving his vote, states his opinion on that point; and the general will is found by counting votes. When therefore the opinion that is contrary to my own prevails, this proves neither more nor less than that I was mistaken, and that what I thought to be the general will was not so. If my particular opinion had carried the day, I should have achieved the opposite of what was my will; and it is in that case that I should not have been free.
> This presupposes, indeed, that all the qualities of the general will still reside in the majority: when they cease to do so, whatever side a man may take, liberty is no longer possible. (SC, pp. 93–94; Book IV, ch. ii)

The problem of government is hence to bring about conditions under which the general will and the will of all will coincide, in which the majority will actually want that which is best for all, in which autonomy and well-being will both be achieved. What will unite them? When will this occur? How can we be sure that the majority will know what is best? Only when the citizens are educated and wise, and the fundamental problem of government is thus to secure an informed and intelligent citizenry. Men will be free only when as a body of voters they are wise enough to know what is good for them. The great problem for Rousseau's democracy is thus education.

Rousseau judges this union of well-being and freedom is possible only under certain very definite conditions: in a city-state of intelligent voters, like Geneva. It will occur only in a small state, with simple problems, with a general equality of rank and fortune, with no moneyed or privileged class.

> How many conditions that are difficult to unite does such a goverment presuppose! First, a very small State, where the people can readily be got together and where each citizen can with ease know all the rest; secondly, great simplicity of manners, to prevent business from multiplying and raising thorny problems; next, a large measure of equality in

rank and fortune, without which equality of rights and authority cannot long subsist; lastly, little or no luxury. . . .

Were there a people of gods, their government would be democratic. So perfect a government is not for men. (*SC*, pp. 58–59; Book III, ch. iv)

The conclusion is, majority rule is only right, and justified on grounds other than force, when the citizens are wise.

How can a blind multitude, which often does not know what it wills, because it rarely knows what is good for it, carry out for itself so great and difficult an enterprise as a system of legislation? Of itself the people wills always the good, but of itself it by no means always sees it. The general will is always in the right, but the judgment which guides it is not always enlightened. It must be got to see objects as they are, and sometimes as they ought to appear to it; it must be shown the good road it is in search of, secured from the seductive influences of individual wills, taught to see times and spaces as a series, and made to weigh the attractions of present and sensible advantages against the danger of distant and hidden evils. The individuals see the good they reject; the public wills the good it does not see. All stand equally in need of guidance. The former must be compelled to bring their wills into conformity with their reason; the latter must be taught to know what it wills. If that is done, public enlightenment leads to the union of understanding and will in the social body: the parts are made to work exactly together, and the whole is raised to its highest power. (*SC*, p. 34; Book II, ch. vi)

The problem is indeed acute. When the majority is not wise enough to know what is for the common good, "liberty is no longer possible." There is no need to dilate on the frequency with which this has happened among Rousseau's followers, or on the danger that any majority—or any individual, like Robespierre or Napoleon —will convince itself or himself that it represents the general will. The net effect of Rousseau's analysis has been in practice to give supreme power to a popular majority to do what it wishes, and thus force minorities to be "free." Men have no rights against the common good—if it be really good.

The Sovereign is the general will when it is active, a "public person," inalienable, indivisible: the Sovereign cannot be represented. It is all-powerful: since it is directed toward the good of all, why should there be guarantees of individual rights against it?

Each man alienates, I admit, by the social compact, only such part of his powers, goods and liberty as it is important for the community to control; but it must also be granted that the Sovereign is the sole judge of what is important. (*SC*, p. 27; Book II, ch. iv)

Where then is freedom? I am free in so far as I accept the general will. Law is a decree by the whole people for the whole people; it comes from all and applies to all. Hence law cannot be unjust. A republic is a State governed by law: there are not many. Government is an intermediate body, set up to execute the laws; Rousseau carefully excludes any legislative power from government, which is the executive, the prince. The mandate of government is revocable: it is not set up, as in Hobbes, by the social contract. Democracy is where all the citizens govern, but "real democracy" is only an ideal. Rousseau judges an elective aristocracy, that is, representative government, is best.

Finally, Rousseau advocates a civil religion:

There is therefore a purely civil profession of faith of which the Sovereign should fix the articles, not exactly as religious dogmas, but as social sentiments without which a man cannot be a good citizen or a faithful subject. While it can compel no one to believe them, it can banish from the State whoever does not believe them—it can banish him, not for impiety, but as an anti-social being, incapable of truly loving the laws and justice, and of sacrificing, at need, his life to his duty. If any one, after publicly recognizing these dogmas, behaves as if he does not believe them, let him be punished by death: he has committed the worst of all crimes, that of lying before the law. (*SC*, p. 121; Book IV, ch. viii)

This has indeed a very modern sound. Our religions of nationalism are following Rousseau to the letter.

Rousseau the individualist sets up the omnicompetent state, the tyranny of the crowd. He justifies collectivism; for the State is master of everything, even all property. To be sure, the State gives back possessions as property to its citizens; but there is no natural right of property. The seeds of socialism in Rousseau's doctrine were speedily developed by the radical Rousseauians Mably and Morelly: socialism for the sake of individual well-being.

Rousseau consecrated and made republican the *Étatisme* that had developed under the Bourbon monarchy, the administrative centralization that made France a prey to whoever could get hold of the top and center, and has endured down to the present day, that makes it so difficult for Frenchmen to understand federalism and decentralization. He not only raised many of the fundamental problems of democratic government. He justified the modern collectivistic state, and provided it with intellectual weapons against laissez-faire and natural rights. He made it very difficult for a tradition of anything like British liberalism to develop in France.

Why was he so popular? To his age, he sounded a clarion call of rebellion against the Old Régime. Who possesses sovereign power? The people. Who can alone make laws? Who can alone set up a just government? In whose interest does the general will function? In case of abuse, who has the right to depose the government and set up a new one? The people.

> The institution of government is not a contract, but a law; the depositaries of the executive power are not the people's masters, but its officers; it can set them up and pull them down when it likes; for them there is no question of contract, but of obedience; and in taking charge of the functions the State imposes on them they are doing no more than fulfilling their duty as citizens, without having the remotest right to argue about conditions.
>
> When therefore the people sets up an hereditary government, whether it be monarchical and confined to one family, or aristocratic and confined to a class, what it enters into is not an undertaking; the administration is given a provisional form, until the people chooses to order it otherwise. (*SC*, p. 88; Book III, ch. xviii)

The Enlightenment began by developing weapons against the System; it ended with the resolute demand that the System depart.

IX

The Physiocrats might be expressing the central drive of the Third Estate in their great emphasis on the natural right of private property. A few thinkers of the Enlightenment, more democratically inclined, discovered that nature has rather decreed a communism of possessions. Morelly, in his *Code de la nature* of 1755, sketches a form of utopian socialism that foreshadows the later Charles Fourier. And Mably pushed Rousseau's principles in a socialistic direction. Morelly argues that the code of nature is completely communistic. Avarice is the worst moral evil; in an ideal communistic society it would be "impossible to de depraved." No private property would be permitted; everyone would be fed by the State and working for it. Morelly goes into the detailed regulation of men's lives much in the spirit of the utopian socialism of the men of 1848.

Gabriel Bonnot de Mably (1709–1785), the brother of Condillac, starts rather from a Rousseauian passion for equality. Trained as a priest, he became secretary to the Minister of Foreign Affairs, and as that incompetent cardinal could hardly manage his own, Mably ran the ministry and received a practical training in diplomacy. When the cardinal annulled a marriage between a Catholic and a Protestant, Mably retired to devote himself to study. In 1776 he published *De la législation ou principes des lois;* in 1781, *Du Gouvernement de Pologne;* in 1783, *De l'étude de l'histoire;* in 1784, *Observations sur le gouvernement et les États-Unis d'Amérique.* Mably was read widely, and his writings were very popular. His ideas were more closely followed in the Revolutionary councils than those of any other thinker: he seemed to combine Rousseau's democratic principles with sound common sense.

Inequality, he is convinced, is the source of all political ills, particularly economic inequality; it is the source of all men's artificial needs. The equality of a community of farmers is the only healthy society. Natural inequalities between men exist, to be sure; but they are nothing like as great as social inequalities—Mably is following Rousseau.

It is proved that the Spartans lived for six hundred years in the greatest equality; and you could not deny that institutions that have subsisted for six centuries did not belong to a fashion, to an enthusiasm, to a passing fanaticism, and could consequently be preserved for a million years. What was the secret of Lycurgus to produce such a prodigy? He felt the force of your objection [an English lord had held that if equality were introduced, the inequality of rich and poor would speedily be reestablished], and not being content to divide the land equally and to produce only a passing and very brief good, he took from his fellow-citizens the ownership of their lands. They belonged to the Republic, which distributed to each father of a family a portion, to enjoy in the quality of simple usufruct. If different abuses crept in with the Spartans, if they were finally masters of disposing at their pleasure of their lands, and if that deadly revolution destroyed without resource the Republic and the laws of Lycurgus, it seems to me that we can draw from this fact the most useful instruction on the nature of property; it seems to me we must conclude that we can find happiness only in the community of goods.[21]

[21] *De la législation* (1776), Book I, chap. ii; in Bayet et Albert, p. 308.

Moreover, Mably opposes legal monarchy, the theory of the king ruling in accordance with natural law: he punctured the ideal of benevolent despotism. In practice, he pointed out, despots were not generally benevolent:

> Let us have no illusion, monsieur, the past ought to teach us about the future; and since despotism and ignorance have always hitherto been associated, let us be certain that they will still be so in the centuries to come: the same causes will always produce the same effects. But let us suppose for a moment that this alliance should cease and that social truths should be generally spread throughout a people subjected to despotism, is it not evident that public happiness will not thereby ensue? History will teach you that the simplest and clearest truths have been imprudently despised by princes whom the excess of their power has intoxicated. Why, you ask me, are truths subject to this sad destiny? Because they speak only to our cold reason, while passions agitate our heart, and our heart makes us act. Must we say once more what we have already said a hundred times, that the mind is the dupe of the heart? [This is pure Rousseau.]
>
> You thus see that legal despotism is only and can only be a word devoid of meaning.[22]

Mably urges the separation of powers: there should be a legislature and a king—the executive is the eternal enemy of the legislature. But the king must be a figurehead, to preserve order and harmony —Mably is thinking of Poland. He criticizes severely the English constitution: the king has far too much power—he has in mind George III and Lord North.

Sovereignty belongs to the whole people, to all rational beings; but representative government is necessary to obviate the ignorance and the passions of the populace. Mably is recommending a government of the type of the National Convention: a powerful single chamber with a weak executive.

And Mably upholds the right and duty of rebellion.

> Must I then humble my common sense, to the point of submitting it blindly to the decrees of an assembly which is only a crowd? Is it not permitted to me as to Lycurgus to conspire against laws which are inflicting evil on my country? If it pleases the Athenians to decree the penalty of death against any one who proposes to use for the expenses of war the funds intended to put on comedies, will Phocion respect that

[22] *Doutes sur l'ordre naturel et essentiel des sociétés politiques* (1768); in Bayet et Albert, pp. 312–13.

ridiculous law? Should Demosthenes obey it? And must I, without being either of these two great men, go gaily to the spectacle, while Philip is advancing toward our gates? . . .

Nay, nay; Cicero was right: we are agreed, as an incontestable truth, that a citizen must obey the magistrate, and the magistrate the laws; and you may be sure that in a republic where that order is observed the injustice of the laws will never give rise to pernicious quarrels. But since those happy republics are rare in this world, since men, always borne along toward tyranny or toward slavery by their passions, are evil or foolish enough to make unjust or absurd laws, what other remedy can we apply to this evil than disobedience? From it will rise some troubles; but why be frightened of that? The trouble is itself a proof that we love order and that we want to restore it. Blind obedience is on the contrary a proof that the doltish citizen is indifferent to good and to evil; and then, what will you hope for? The man who thinks works to strengthen the empire of reason; the man who obeys without thinking throws himself into slavery, because he favors the power of the passions.[23]

There will be no attempt to draw together here the many strands of eighteenth-century thought. The currents of the later Enlightenment in France were indeed brought to a brief focus in 1789 by history itself; the English and the Scottish Enlightenments came to no such unifying perspective. Rather, as always in the Western tradition, there is exhibited a plurality of different attempts to make sense out of man's rapidly changing experience. The eighteenth century is often thought of as an "age of synthesis." But it is doubtful whether the expansive nineteenth century displays a wider range of intellectual diversity. Even at its most novel, eighteenth-century philosophy is rooted in the past, and that past in all its variety lives mightily in it, in the many intellectual traditions in which men were still working. And the various reconstructions they effected were big with the equally divided thought of the future. The ideas of Hume or of Rousseau were greater forces in the thinking of the nineteenth century, to say nothing of our day, than in their own.

But amid this normal diversity of answers, the central problems remained. They were not solved by the confident thinkers of the eighteenth century; they have not been solved yet. How was the enterprise of science to be understood? What were its implications for everything else that men were doing and thinking? How were

[23] *Des droits et des devoirs du citoyen* (published after his death in 1785), IV; in Bayet et Albert, pp. 327–29.

men's inherited social arrangements to be reconstructed to furnish a more satisfying life? These central problems of modern Western culture were not solved in the Age of Reason, because even as men were working upon them and proposing preliminary answers, their very conditions were changing at an accelerating rate. A genuinely experimental science was emerging, destined to burst the neat Newtonian framework. A technological society was on the point of transforming the whole of men's life and experience.

The need to understand an ever-growing science, the demand to reconstruct once again an ever-expanding society, have been the persisting impulses driving thinkers to pursue in their several ways the career of Western philosophizing in modern times. At any one stage the answers have always remained many and divergent, and they have always stood in need of further reconstruction. What the thinkers of the eighteenth century made out of the ideas they had inherited, through employing them to work upon the forms the persisting problems took in their day, has remained an indispensable stock of tools and building materials for all who have come later.

Index